BCIS
Independent cost information
for the built environment

CW00361992

ALTERATIONS & REFURBISHMENT PRICE BOOK

18th Edition 2013

MAINTENANCE & OPERATING COSTS

BCIS is the Building Cost Information Service of **RICS** | the mark of property professionalism worldwide

BCIS
Independent cost information
for the built environment

Comprehensive Building Price Book 2013
Major and Minor Works dataset

The Major Works dataset focuses predominantly on large 'new build' projects reflecting the economies of scale found in these forms of construction. The Minor Works Estimating Dataset focuses on small to medium sized 'new build' projects reflecting the increase in costs brought about the reduced output, less discounts, increased carriage and supervision, to the similar items in the Major Works dataset. The dataset is presented in trade order. Revised and reworked items in underpinning composites; flue linings and rainwater goods.

Item code: 19215   **Price: £165.99**

SMM7 Estimating Price Book 2013

The SMM7 Estimating dataset focuses predominantly on large 'new build' projects reflecting the economies of scale found in these forms of construction. The dataset is presented in SMM7 grouping and order in accordance with the Common Arrangement of Work Sections. It is compiled using the latest independent costing information from manufacturers, material and plant suppliers, legislation effects and working rule agreements. Revised and reworked items in underpinning composites; flue linings and rainwater goods.

Item code: 19216   **Price: £139.99**

Alterations and Refurbishment Price Book 2013

The Alterations & Refurbishment dataset focuses on small to medium sized projects, generally working within an existing building and reflecting the increase in costs brought about the reduction in output, smaller discounts, increased carriage, increased supervision, and less productivity brought about by smaller economies of scale, increased production costs, more difficult access and the possibility of working in occupied premises. The dataset is presented in trade order. Revised and reworked items in underpinning composites; flue linings and rainwater goods.

Item code: 19217   **Price £109.99**

BCIS Guide to Estimating for Small Works 2012

The BCIS Guide to Estimating for Small Works 2012 is a unique dataset which shows the true power of resource based estimating. A set of composite built-up measured items are used to build up priced estimates for a large number of common specification extensions. The intention is to show estimating techniques in use and allow users to build up accurate estimates for their own projects, simply and easily, with up-to-date and independent cost information.

Item code: 19064   **Price: £59.99**

BCIS Painting and Decorating Price Book 2012

The BCIS Painting and Decorating dataset is the most handy pricing tool available to the painting and decorating sector of the industry, suitable for all projects needing more than a 'guess-timate'. Using this dataset a more accurate calculation based quotation or variation can be prepared. From these calculations an assessment of labour, plant and material content can be produced. This in turn enables the contractor to negotiate discounts on known material requirements and the effect of this workload on the availability of labour.

Item code: 19065   **Price: £39.99**

For more information call **0870 333 1600** email
contact@bcis.co.uk or visit **www.bcis.co.uk**

BCIS is the Building Cost Information Service of **RICS** the mark of property professionalism worldwide

Preface

BCIS ALTERATIONS AND REFURBISHMENT ESTIMATING PRICE BOOK 18TH EDITION

Preface to the 18th edition

This important addition to the BCIS range of building price books has been compiled in recognition of the importance of the building refurbishment market.

The last 20 years has seen a substantial increase in the volume of building alteration and refurbishment activity in the United Kingdom. This has been encouraged by an increased awareness of the value and importance of historic buildings and the built environment. More recently, the depressed state of the economy has led to building owners and users amending plans to build and move into new buildings and consider, instead, improvements to their existing premises.

In compiling this revised price book, BCIS has drawn upon the vast resources of its Building Database to provide in a single volume the most comprehensive selection possible of prices for alteration and refurbishment work, including the addition of helpful information on the Landfill Tax.

As with all BCIS price books, each section is presented in an easy-to-understand layout, giving the labour time, together with a detailed cost analysis for every item of work split into labour, plant and material content. These are totalled to show a competitive and realistic total unit price requiring only the addition of the user's own profit and overheads. The format and breakdown of the unit rates allows users to make adjustments to suit local conditions with ease.

The data contained in this book is intended for use on projects consisting entirely or substantially of alterations and improvements to existing buildings, from simply taking out a door and blocking up the opening, to projects up to £150,000 in value.

MATERIAL PRICES
Material prices used in this book are based on national average best trade prices. The base date used for these materials costs is 1st July 2012.

LABOUR RATES
The Alterations and Refurbishment Estimating Price Book is based on the Building and Allied Trades Joint Industrial Council wage agreement.

The wage rates agreed by the Joint Industry Board for Plumbing and Mechanical Engineering Services in England and Wales have been used where applicable.

PLUS RATES
In order to reflect the more costly nature of alterations and refurbishment work a plus rate of 10 pence per hour has been incorporated into the hourly cost calculation.

We would recommend that users study the introduction, Section A, to familiarise themselves with the basis for pricing this year.

PARTNERING FOR EXCELLENCE

BCIS and EC Harris share many beliefs and ideals in the provision of quality information and service to all our clients and we are proud of our partnership.

EC Harris LLP

EC Harris is a leading global built asset consultancy. As an ARCADIS company, we have access to approximately 21,000 professionals worldwide operating in over 70 countries, 300 offices and generating in excess of €2.4 billion in revenue. Working across a wide range of market sectors, we help our clients make the most from the money they spend on their built assets. For more information visit http://www.echarris.com/.

In this Edition EC Harris has assisted BCIS with items on Asbestos in Buildings (see Section 9 page 1). The partnership will bring extended valuable information in future publications.

N.P. Barnett BSc (Hons)
Information Services & Cost Resource Manager
BCIS

BCIS ALTERATIONS AND REFURBISHMENT ESTIMATING PRICE BOOK 2013

BCIS
Suite 1, Ground Floor, 376 Ringwood Road, Poole, Dorset BH12 3LT

Tel: +44 (0)870 333 1600
Fax: +44 (0)20 7695 1501

Web Site: www.bcis.co.uk
E-Mail: contact@bcis.co.uk

August 2012

ACKNOWLEDGEMENTS
BCIS ALTERATIONS AND REFURBISHMENT ESTIMATING PRICE BOOK 2013

18th Edition

BCIS would like to thank our members of staff and all those who assisted in the preparation and production of the database from which this book is compiled. We also wish to acknowledge the invaluable assistance given by the following individuals, organisations, manufacturers, suppliers, contractors and Associations, including those who have given their kind permission for the reproduction and publication of copyright material.

Technical Editor

N P Barnett BSc (Hons)

Editorial staff and contributors to original material:

A J Hobbs DMS, FRICS, FBIM
C J Horsey BA
C F Isgar FRICS
L J Turnock FRICS, MCIOB
C A Rowe MRICS

Mrs M Damon-De Waele
Mrs R Read
Mrs C Barnett

Associations and Organisations:

Building and Allied Trades Joint Industrial Council
Building Cost Information Service
Building Employers Confederation
Construction Industry Training Board - Levy Department
E C Harris, Built Asset Consultancy
H M Revenue & Customs
Joint Industry Board for Plumbing and Mechanical Engineering Services in England and Wales
Royal Institution of Chartered Surveyors

Suppliers and Services:

A & C Dunkley (Boscombe) Ltd
4/10 Kemp Road
Winton
Bournemouth
BH9 2PW

☎: 01202 526206
🖷: 01202 526209
✉: showroom@dunkleytiles.co.uk
🖳: www.dunkleytiles.co.uk

A Andrews & Sons (Marble & Tiles) Ltd
324-330 Meanwood Road
Leeds
LS7 2JE

☎: 0113 262 4751
🖷: 0113 262 3337
✉: contracts@andrews-tiles.co.uk
🖳: www.andrews-tiles.co.uk

Aggregate Industries UK Ltd
Bradstone Structural
North End Farm Works
Ashton Keynes
Wiltshire
SN6 6QX

☎: 01285 646884
🖷: 01285 646891
✉: bradstone.structural@aggregate.com
🖳: www.bradstone-structural.com

Alumasc Exterior Building Products Limited
White House Works
Bold Road
Sutton
St Helens
Merseyside
WA9 4JG

☎: 01744 648400
🖷: 01744 648401
✉: info@alumasc-exteriors.co.uk
🖳: www.alumasc-exteriors.co.uk

Anderton Concrete
Anderton Wharf
Soot Hill
Anderton
Northwich
Cheshire
CW9 6AA

☎: 01606 79436
🖷: 01606 871590
✉: sales@andertonconcrete.co.uk
🖳: www.andertonconcrete.co.uk

Aspect Roofing
The Old Mill
East Harling
Norwich
Norfolk
NR16 2QW

☎: 01953 717777
🖷: 01953 717164
✉: enquiries@aspectroofing.co.uk
🖳: www.aspectroofing.co.uk

Bells Plastics Ltd t/a Safetytread
Unit 2, 450 Blandford Road
Poole
Dorset
BH16 5BN

☎: 01202 625596
🖷: 01202 625597
✉: safetytread@bellplastics.co.uk
🖳: www.safety-tread.co.uk

Blucher UK Limited
Station Road Industrial Estate
Tadcaster
North Yorkshire
LS24 9SG

☎: 01937 838000
🖷: 01937 832454
✉: mail@blucher.co.uk
🖳: www.blucher.co.uk

Burlington Slate Limited
Cavendish House
Kirkby-in-Furness
Cumbria
LA17 7UN

☎: 01229 889661
🖷: 01229 889466
✉: sales@burlingtonstone.co.uk
🕸: www.burlingtonstone.co.uk

C & W Berry Ltd
262 Goldenhill Lane
Leyland
Lancashire
PR25 2YH

☎: 01772 431216
🖷: 01772 622314
✉: enquiries@cwberry.com
🕸: www.cwberry.com

CEMEX
Cemex House
Coldharbour Lane
Thorpe
Egham
Surrey
TW20 8TD

☎: 01932 568833
🕸: www.cemex.co.uk

CPM Group Ltd
Mells Road
Mells
Nr Frome
Somerset
BA11 3PD

☎: 01179 812791
🖷: 01179 814511
✉: sales@cpm-group.com
🕸: www.cpm-group.com

Caparo Merchant Bar Plc
Caparo House
PO Box 15
Scunthorpe
North Lincolnshire
DN16 1XL

☎: 01724 853333
🖷: 01724 403044
✉: sales@cmbplc.co.uk
🕸: www.cmbplc.co.uk

Catnic
Pontypandy Industrial Estate
Caerphilly
Mid Glamorgan
CF83 3GL

☎: 029 2033 7900
🖷: 0870 024 1809
✉: catnic.technical@tatasteel.com
🕸: www.catnic.com

Cavity Trays Limited
Boundry Avenue
Lufton Trading Estate
Yeovil, Somerset
BA22 8HU

☎: 01935 474769
🖷: 01935 428223
✉: enquiries@cavitytrays.co.uk
🕸: www.cavitytrays.co.uk

Cementatation Skanska Ltd
Maple Cross House
Denham Way
Maple Cross
Rickmansworth
Hertfordshire
WD3 9SW

☎: 01923 423100
🖷: 01923 722702
✉: skanska@skanska.co.uk
🕸: www.skanska.co.uk

Charcon Hard Landscaping
Aggregate Industries UK Limited
Hulland Ward
Smith Hall Lane
Ashbourne
Derbyshire
DE6 3ET

☎: 01335 372222
🖷: 01335 370074
✉: sales.charcon@aggregate.com
🕸: www.charcon.com

Coppard Plant Hire Ltd
Wraysbury
Crowborough Hill
Crowborough
East Sussex
TN6 2JE

☎: 01892 662777
🖷: 01892 667094
✉: info@coppard.co.uk
🕸: www.coppard.co.uk

Cordek Ltd
Spring Copse Business Park
Slinfold
West Sussex
RH13 0SZ

☎: 01403 799600
🖷: 01403 791718
✉: info@cordek.com
🕸: www.cordek.com

Crittall Windows Limited
Francis House
Freebournes Road
Witham
Essex
CM8 3UN

☎: 01376 530800
🖷: 01376 530801
✉: hq@crittall-windows.co.uk
🕸: www.crittall-windows.co.uk

Croft Preservation Ltd
Unit 1
14 Broom Road
Poole
Dorset
BH12 4NL

☎: 01202 737739
🖷: 01202 737735
✉: enquiries@croftpreservation.co.uk
🕸: www.croftpreservation.com

Cumberland Reinforcements Ltd
St. Georges Avenue
Parkstone
Poole
BH12 4ND

☎: 01202 743311
🖷: 01202 715336
✉: cumberlandreinforcements@btconnect.com
🕸: www.cumberlandreinforcements.co.uk

Dorset Joinery Ltd
Unit 3, Slader Business Park
Witney Road
Poole
Dorset
BH17 0GP

☎: 01202 241089
🖷: 01202 676593
✉: sales@dorsetjoineryltd.co.uk
🖱: www.dorsetjoineryltd.co.uk

Everbuild Building Products Ltd
Site 41
Knowsthorpe Way
Cross Green Industrial Estate
Leeds
LS9 0SW

☎: 0113 240 2424
🖷: 0113 240 0024
✉: sales@everbuild.co.uk
🖱: www.everbuild.co.uk

Expamet Building Products - Hyrib
UK Sales and Distribution Centre
Greatham Street
Longhill Industrial Estate (North)
Hartlepool
TS25 1PU

☎: 01429 866688
🖷: 01429 866633
✉: sales@expamet.net
🖱: www.expamet.co.uk

Farmington Natural Stone Ltd
Farmington Quarry
Northleach
Cheltenham
Gloucestershire
GL54 3NZ

☎: 01451 860280
🖷: 01451 860115
✉: info@farmington.co.uk
🖱: www.farmington.co.uk

Fillcrete Limited
Maple House
5 Over Minnis
New Ash Green
Longfield
Kent
DA3 8JA

☎: 01474 872444
🖷: 01474 872426
✉: sales@fillcrete.com
🖱: www.fillcrete.com

Formerton Ltd
Forton Works
First Avenue
Millbrook Trading Estate
Southampton
SO15 0LG

☎: 023 8036 5555
🖷: 023 8070 1197
🖱: www.formertonroofing.co.uk

Garage Door Superstore
Unit 8, Phoenix Business Park
Spur Road
Quarry Lane Industrial Estate
Chichester, West Sussex
PO19 8PN

☎: 0845 450 7330
🖷: 01243 776555
✉: info@garagedoorsuperstore.co.uk
🖱: www.garagedoorsuperstore.co.uk

Gawler Tapes & Plastics Ltd
7 Easter Court
24 Woodward Avenue
Westerleigh Business Park
Yate
Bristol
BS37 5YS

☎: 01454 324265
🖷: 01454 315158
✉: enquiries@gawlertapes.co.uk
🖱: www.gawlertapes.co.uk

Glulam Timber Engineering LLP
2A Severnside Industrial Estate
St Andrews Road
Avonmouth
Bristol
BS11 9YQ

☎: 01179 828181
🖷: 01179 828182
✉: sales@glulamte.co.uk
🖱: www. glulamte.co.uk

Grace Construction Products Ltd
580/581 Ipswich Road
Slough
SL1 4EQ

☎: 01753 490000
🖷: 01753 490011
✉: uksales@grace.com
🖱: www.graceconstruction.com

Grass Concrete Limited
Duncan House
142 Thornes Lane
Thornes
Wakefield
West Yorkshire
WF2 7RE

☎: 01924 379443
🖷: 01924 290289
✉: info@grasscrete.com
🖱: www.grasscrete.com

Hambleside Danelaw Limited
Long March
Daventry
Northants
NN11 4NR

☎: 01327 701900
🖷: 01327 701909
✉: marketing@hambleside-danelaw.co.uk
🖱: www.hambleside-danelaw.co.uk

Hanson Aggregates
The Ridge
Chipping Sodbury
Nr Bristol
BS37 6AY

☎: 0845 120 6310
🖱: www.hanson.co.uk

Hanson Building Products
Stewartby
Bedford
MK43 9LZ

☎: 08705 258258
🖷: 01234 762042
✉: marketing@hansonbp.com
🖱: www.hanson.co.uk

Hanson Building Products
(Aggregate Blocks)
222 Peterborough Road
Whittlesey
Peterborough
Cambs
PE7 1PD

☎: 0330 123 1015
🖨: 01733 206170
✉: aggregateblock.sales@hanson.biz
🕸: www.hanson.co.uk

Hanson Building Products
Wilden Road
Pattinson South Ind. Estate
District 8
Washington
Tyne & Wear
NE38 8QB

☎: 0191 417 0066
🖨: 0191 417 0131
✉: omniasales@hansonbp.com
🕸: www.omnidec.co.uk

Heatrae Sadia
Hurricane Way
Norwich
Norfolk
NR6 6EA

☎: 01603 420100
✉: sales@heatraesadia.co.uk
🕸: www.heatraesadia.co.uk

Hilti (GB) Limited
1 Trafford Wharf Road
Trafford Park
Manchester
M17 1BY

☎: 0800 886 100
🖨: 0800 886 200
✉: gbsales@hilti.com
🕸: www.hilti.co.uk

ICI Paints AkzoNobel
Wexham Road
Slough
Berkshire
SL2 5DS

☎: 01753 550 000
🕸: www.icipaints.co.uk

IKO PLC
Appley Lane North
Appley Bridge
Wigan
Lancashire
WN6 9AB

☎: 0844 873 1065
🖨: 0844 873 1067
✉: sales@ikogroup.co.uk
🕸: www.ikogroup.co.uk

Icopal Ltd
Barton Dock Road
Stretford
Manchester
M32 0YL

☎: 0161 865 4444
🖨: 0161 864 2616
✉: info.uk@icopal.com
🕸: www.icopal.co.uk

J & J Asphalt
47 Kingsfield Drive
Enfield
Middlesex
EN3 6UA

☎: 01992 638 824
🖨: 01992 638 825
🕸: www.jandjasphalt.co.uk

J Suttles Transport Ltd
Swanworth Quarry
Worth Matravers
Swanage
Dorset
BH19 3LE

☎: 01929 439444
🖨: 01929 439446
✉: sales@suttles .co.uk
🕸: www.suttles.co.uk

James Latham
Unit 3, Swallow Park
Finway Road
Hemel Hempstead
HP2 7QU

☎: 01442 849100
🖨: 01442 267241
✉: marketing@lathams .co.uk
🕸: www.lathamtimber.co.uk

Jaymart Rubber & Plastics Ltd
Woodlands Trading Estate
Eden Vale Road
Westbury
Wiltshire
BA13 3QS

☎: 01373 864926
🖨: 01373 858454
✉: sales@jaymart.co.uk
🕸: www.jaymart.net

John Newton & Co Ltd
12 Verney Road
London
SE16 3DH

☎: 020 7237 1217
🖨: 020 7252 2769
✉: general@newtonmembranes.co.uk
🕸: www.newton-membranes.co.uk

Johnson Tiles Ltd
Harewood Street
Tunstall
Stoke-on-Trent
ST6 5JZ

☎: 01782 575575
🖨: 01782 577377
✉: info@johnson-tiles.com
🕸: www.johnson-tiles.com

Kingspan Insulation Ltd
Pembridge
Leominster
Herefordshire
HR6 9LA

☎: 01554 388601
🖨: 01554 388888
✉: info@kingspaninsulation.co.uk
🕸: www.kingspaninsulation.co.uk

Lignacite Ltd
Norfolk House
High Street
Brandon
Suffolk
IP27 0AX

☎: 01842 810678
🖷: 01842 814602
🕸: www.lignacite.co.uk

Long Rake Spar Co Ltd
Youlgrave
Nr Bakewell
Derbyshire
DE45 1LW

☎: 01629 636210
🖷: 01629 636247
✉: info@longrakespar.co.uk
🕸: www.longrakespar.co.uk

MEA UK Ltd
Rectors Lane
Pentre
Deeside
CH5 2DH

☎: 01244 534455
🖷: 01244 534477
✉: uk.technical@mea.de
🕸: www.mea.uk.com

Magnet Limited
Royd Ings Avenue
Keighley
West Yorkshire
BD21 4BY

☎: 01535 661133
🖷: 01535 610363
✉: info@magnet.co.uk
🕸: www.magnet.co.uk

Manhole Covers Limited
Airfield Industrial Estate
Cheddington Lane
Long Marston
Bucks
HP23 4QR

☎: 01296 668850
🖷: 01296 668080
✉: sales@manholecovers.co.uk
🕸: www.manholecovers.co.uk

Marley Eternit Ltd
Lichfield Road
Branston
Burton on Trent
Staffordshire
DE14 3HD

☎: 01283 722588
🖷: 01283 722219
✉: roofinginfo@marleyeternit.co.uk
🕸: www.marleyeternit.co.uk

Marshalls
Landscape House
Premier Way
Lowfields Business Park
Elland
West Yorkshire
HX5 9HT

☎: 01422 312000
✉: contractsales@marshalls.co.uk
🕸: www.marshalls.co.uk

Mayweld Engineering Co. Ltd
Banners Lane
Halesowen
West Midlands
B63 2SD

☎: 01384 560285
🖷: 01384 411456
✉: sales@mayweld.co.uk
🕸: www.mayweld.co.uk

Metsec Plc
Lattice Division
Broadwell Road
Oldbury
Warley
West Midlands
B69 4HF

☎: 0121 601 6000
🖷: 0121 601 6109
🕸: www.metsec.com

Minsterstone Ltd
Pondhayes Farm
Dinnington
Hinton St George
Crewkerne
Somerset
TA17 8SU

☎: 01460 52277
🖷: 01460 57865
✉: varyl@minsterstone.ltd.uk
🕸: www.minsterstone.ltd.uk

Muraspec Ltd
74-78 Wood Lane End
Hemel Hempstead
Hertfordshire
HP2 4RF

☎: 08705 117118
🖷: 01442 215430
✉: customerservices@muraspec.com
🕸: www.muraspec.com

Newark Copper Cylinders Co. Ltd
Brunel Drive
Northern Road Industrial Estate
Newark
Nottinghamshire
UK
NG24 2EG

☎: 01636 678437
🖷: 01636 678964
✉: sales@newarkcoppercylinder.co.uk
🕸: www.newarkcoppercylinder.co.uk

OutoKumpu Stainless Ltd
PO Box 161
Europa Link
Sheffield
UK
S9 1TZ

☎: 0114 2616112
✉: sales.rebar@outokumpu.com
🕸: www.outokumpu.com

Pegler Yorkshire Group
St Catherines Avenue
Doncaster
South Yorkshire
DN4 8DF

☎: 0844 243 4400
🖷: 0844 243 9870
✉: uksales@pegleryorkshire.co.uk
🕸: www.yorkshirefittings.co.uk

Pipe Center (Wolseley UK)
The Wolseley Center
Harrison Way
Spa Park
Royal Leamington Spa
Warwickshire
CV31 3HH

☎: 01926 705000
🕸: www.pipecenter.co.uk

Plumb Center
855 Ringwood Road
West Howe
Bournemouth
Dorset
BH11 8NE

☎: 01202 874996
🖷: 01202 580901
🕸: www.plumbcenter.co.uk

Polypipe Plc
Broomhouse Lane
Edlington
Doncaster
DN12 1ES

☎: 01709 770000
🖷: 01709 770001
✉: sales@polypipe.com
🕸: www.polypipe.com

Premdor
Birthwaite Business Park
Huddersfield Road
Darton
Barnsley
South Yorkshire
S75 5JS

☎: 0844 2090008
🖷: 01226 388808
✉: ukmarketing@premdor.co.uk
🕸: www.premdor.co.uk

R C Cutting & Co. Limited
10-12 Arcadia Avenue
Finchley Central
London
N3 2JU

☎: 020 8371 0001
🖷: 020 8371 0003
✉: info@rccutting.co.uk
🕸: www.rccutting.co.uk

R.M.Smith Fencing Limited
Duck Island Lane
Ringwood
Hampshire
BH24 3AA

☎: 01425 476617
🖷: 01425 476610
✉: enquiries@smith-fencing.co.uk
🕸: www.smith-fencing.co.uk

RIW Limited
ARC House
Terrace Road South
Binfield
Bracknell
Berkshire
RG42 4PZ

☎: 01344 397777
🖷: 01344 862010
✉: enquiries@riw.co.uk
🕸: www.riw.co.uk

Rawlplug Ltd
Unit 3, The Courtyard
Whitewick Business Park
Stenson Road
Coalville, Leicester
LE67 4JP

☎: 0141 638 2255
✉: rawlinfo@rawlplug.co.uk
🕸: www.rawlplug.co.uk

Redland Head Office
Monier Redland Ltd
Sussex Manor Business Park
Gatwick Road
Crawley
West Sussex
RH10 9NZ

☎: 01293 618418
🖷: 01293 614548
✉: sales.redland@monier.com
🕸: www.redland.co.uk

Richard Lees Steel Decking Ltd
Moor Farm Road West
The Airfield
Ashbourne
Derbyshire
DE6 1HD

☎: 01335 300999
🖷: 01335 300888
✉: rlsd.decks@skanska.co.uk
🕸: www.rlsd.com

SBA Ltd
National Distribution Centre
Freemans Common Road
Leicester
LE2 7SQ

☎: 0116 257 6595
🖷: 0116 247 0072
✉: sales@sba.co.uk
🕸: www.sba.co.uk

Saint-Gobain Pipelines
Lows Lane
Stanton by Dale
Ilkeston
Derbyshire
DE7 4QU

☎: 0115 930 5000
🖷: 0115 932 9513
🕸: www.saint-gobain-pam.co.uk

Sandtoft Roof Tiles Limited
Belton Road
Sandtoft
Doncaster
DN8 5SY

☎: 0870 145 2020
✉: support@sandtoft.co.uk
🕸: www.sandtoft.co.uk

Schiedel Chimney Systems Ltd
14 Haviland Road
Ferndown Industrial Estate
Wimborne
Dorset
BH21 7RF

☎: 01202 861 650
🖷: 01202 861 632
✉: sales@isokern.co.uk
🕸: www.isokern.co.uk

Siesta Cork Tile Co.
Unit 21, Tait Road
Gloucester Road
Croydon
Surrey
CR0 2DP

☎: 0208 683 4055
🖨: 0208 683 4480
✉: siestacork@aol.com
🕮: www.siestacorktile.com

Sydenhams Ltd
Hamworthy Wharf
Poole
Dorset
BH15 4BA

☎: 01202 673646
🖨: 01202 665605
🕮: www.sydenhams.co.uk

Tarkett Limited
Dickley Lane
Lenham
Maidstone
ME17 2QX

☎: 01622 854040
🖨: 01622 854520
✉: marketing@tarkett.com
🕮: www.tarkett.co.uk

Tarmac CMS Pozament
Swains Park Ind. Estate
Overseal
Swadlincote
Derbyshire
DE12 6JT

☎: 01283 554800
🖨: 01283 550486
✉: enquiries@tarmac.co.uk
🕮: www.cmspozament.co.uk

Tarmac National Contracting South West
Stancombe Quarry
Stancombe Lane
Flax Bourton
Bristol
BS48 3QD

☎: 01275 464441
✉: info@tarmac-contracting.co.uk
🕮: www.tarmac.co.uk

Wavin UK (Hepworth Building Products Ltd)
Hazelhead
Crowedge
Sheffield
S36 4HG

☎: 01226 763561
🖨: 01226 764827
✉: info@hepworth.co.uk
🕮: www.hepworth.wavin.com

Wavin UK (Hepworth Building Products Ltd)
Edlington Lane
Edlington
Doncaster
DN12 1BY

☎: 01709 856 300
🖨: 01709 856 301
✉: info@hepworth.co.uk
🕮: www.hepworth.wavin.com

Wavin Plastics Ltd
Parsonage Way
Chippenham
Wiltshire
SN15 5PN

☎: 01249 766600
🖨: 01249 443286
✉: info@wavin.co.uk
🕮: www.wavin.co.uk

William T Eden
5-7 Queensway
Stem Lane Industrial Estate
New Milton
Hampshire
BH25 5NN

☎: 01425 632000
🖨: 01425 616991
✉: sales.newmilton@edens.co.uk
🕮: www.edens.co.uk

Diploma in Adjudication in the Construction Industry

Comprised of four units, this qualification is designed for those **seeking to become an adjudicator**, and provides a pathway towards potential entry onto the **RICS Panel of Adjudicators**.

With a focus on contract and tort law and how they apply to adjudication, this course is designed to prepare you to progress to practice as an adjudicator. This course is suitable for those with experience in dispute resolution procedures with an understanding of the general principles of construction adjudication. The course content will focus on the format and content of an enforceable decision.

Learning Outcomes:

- Knowledge and understanding of the nature of law and its' place in society
- How the law of contract is applied to the practice of adjudication
- How the law of tort is applied to the practice of adjudication
- The practical application in the production of an enforceable decision.

Attainment of the learning outcomes will be assessed by a case study, whereby candidates will be required to produce an enforceable reasoned decision, based on material supplied in the case study.

Contents

BCIS
Independent cost information
for the built environment

CONSTRUCTION

LESS DESK TIME
MORE FREE TIME

THE REVOLUTION OF THE PRICE BOOK IS HERE
BCIS ONLINE RATES DATABASE

What the service can do for you:

Accuracy: You can benchmark against 18500 separate Supply Prices of which there are over 9,000 material costs and over 8000 specialist prices collected from independent suppliers. It will ensure that your information is accurate and reliable, reducing the margin of error.

Futureproof: You can adjust the prices using industry standard BCIS Tender Price Index and Location Factor adjustments so you can forecast your figures for projects up to two years ahead, putting you a step ahead of your competitors. It makes your project cost predictions more robust.

Value for money: It provides an expert opinion at your fingertips to give you the confidence that you are not over or underestimating quotes and costs. It could mean the difference between winning or losing a tender or being over charged for your works.

Saves time: The easy navigation system helps you find what you are looking for quickly and effortlessly. Add the information you want to a list for download to Excel.

Flexible: With a subscription to suit your job, you can access a variety of new and historical price data. This allows you to build up your own prices from individual elements so you can make your own decisions about how you cost your projects.

Customise: Adjust your data to your location and time frame and it will do the calculations for you. You can download the results, keep track of your adjustments and reduce your margin of error.

Portable: This service can be accessed on your computer and just as easily on your iPad or netbook on site.

Comprehensive: Everything you need is in one place; you have a full library of information at your disposal.

Offering immediate online access to independent BCIS resource rates data, quantity surveyors and others in the construction industry can have all the information needed to compile and check estimates on their desktops. You won't need to worry about being able to lay your hands on the office copy of the latest price books, all of the information is now easily accessible online.

For a **FREE TRIAL** of BCIS online rates database register at
www.bcis.co.uk/ordbdemo

BCIS is the Building Cost Information Service of **RICS** | the mark of property professionalism worldwide

Alterations and Refurbishment
Contents

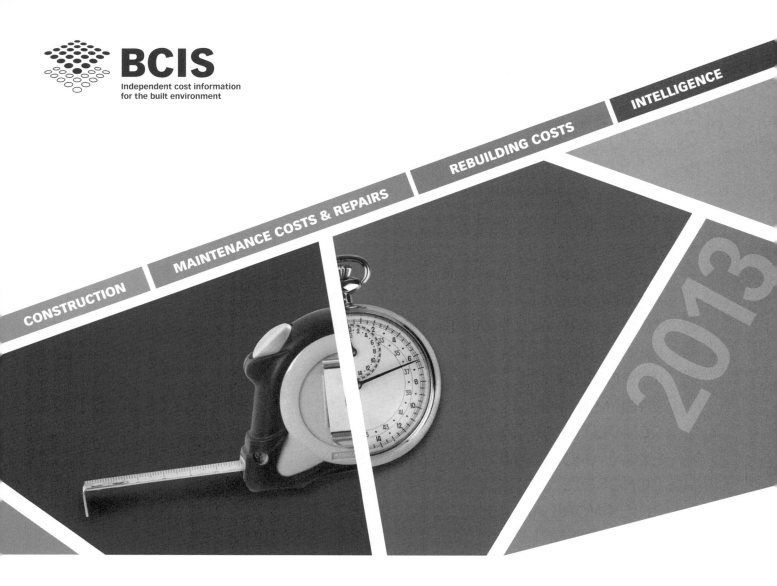 

Index

Independent cost information
for the built environment

Comprehensive Building Price Book 2013
Major and Minor Works dataset

The Major Works dataset focuses predominantly on large 'new build' projects reflecting the economies of scale found in these forms of construction. The Minor Works Estimating Dataset focuses on small to medium sized 'new build' projects reflecting the increase in costs brought about the reduced output, less discounts, increased carriage and supervision, to the similar items in the Major Works dataset. The dataset is presented in trade order. Revised and reworked items in underpinning composites; flue linings and rainwater goods.

Item code: 19215   **Price: £165.99**

SMM7 Estimating Price Book 2013

The SMM7 Estimating dataset focuses predominantly on large 'new build' projects reflecting the economies of scale found in these forms of construction. The dataset is presented in SMM7 grouping and order in accordance with the Common Arrangement of Work Sections. It is compiled using the latest independent costing information from manufacturers, material and plant suppliers, legislation effects and working rule agreements. Revised and reworked items in underpinning composites; flue linings and rainwater goods.

Item code: 19216   **Price: £139.99**

Alterations and Refurbishment Price Book 2013

The Alterations & Refurbishment dataset focuses on small to medium sized projects, generally working within an existing building and reflecting the increase in costs brought about the reduction in output, smaller discounts, increased carriage, increased supervision, and less productivity brought about by smaller economies of scale, increased production costs, more difficult access and the possibility of working in occupied premises. The dataset is presented in trade order. Revised and reworked items in underpinning composites; flue linings and rainwater goods.

Item code: 19217   **Price £109.99**

BCIS Guide to Estimating for Small Works 2012

The BCIS Guide to Estimating for Small Works 2012 is a unique dataset which shows the true power of resource based estimating. A set of composite built-up measured items are used to build up priced estimates for a large number of common specification extensions. The intention is to show estimating techniques in use and allow users to build up accurate estimates for their own projects, simply and easily, with up-to-date and independent cost information.

Item code: 19064   **Price: £59.99**

BCIS Painting and Decorating Price Book 2012

The BCIS Painting and Decorating dataset is the most handy pricing tool available to the painting and decorating sector of the industry, suitable for all projects needing more than a 'guess-timate'. Using this dataset a more accurate calculation based quotation or variation can be prepared. From these calculations an assessment of labour, plant and material content can be produced. This in turn enables the contractor to negotiate discounts on known material requirements and the effect of this workload on the availability of labour.

Item code: 19065   **Price: £39.99**

For more information call **0870 333 1600** email
contact@bcis.co.uk or visit **www.bcis.co.uk**

BCIS is the Building Cost Information Service of  **RICS** the mark of property professionalism worldwide

(Bold italic numbers refer to section numbers, plain numbers are page numbers)

-M-

Wrought softwood, *18*-13
    sawn softwood, *18*-12
    staircases, *18*-34
    standard mouldings, *18*-19

-Y-

Yard gullies
    vitrified clay, *26*-14

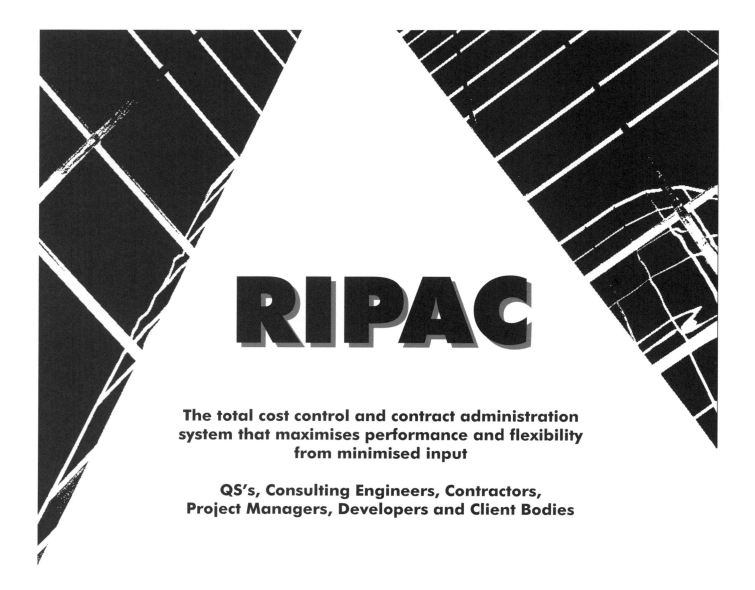

RIPAC

The total cost control and contract administration system that maximises performance and flexibility from minimised input

QS's, Consulting Engineers, Contractors, Project Managers, Developers and Client Bodies

- Budget estimates
- Cost planning
- Bills of quantities
- Measurement from CAD
- Tender pricing and appraisal
- E-tendering
- Resource analysis
- Programme planning links
- Post contract administration
- Payments
- Cash flow
- Whole life costing

Integrated cost control through all project stages.
Easy manipulation of data.
Outputs in user defined formats.
Speedy revisions and updates.
Previous projects available for re-use, analysis and benchmarking.

Various standard libraries of descriptions and price data bases including :

BCIS Price Books

General Information

GENERAL INFORMATION

The publishers include here some general information on listed buildings, as alteration and refurbishment work may well be required to be carried out on buildings of special architectural or historic interest.

Buildings which may be protected by law

The five categories of listed buildings are:

All buildings built before 1700 which survive in anything like their original condition.

Most buildings of 1700 to 1840.

Buildings of between 1840 and 1914 which are of definite quality and character.

Selected buildings of high quality constructed between 1914 and 1939.

A few selected buildings erected after 1939.

The statutory lists for England may be inspected at:

The National Monuments Record
23 Saville Row
London
W1S 2ET

OR

The National Monuments Record Centre
Kemble Drive
Swindon
SN2 2GZ

or at the office of the relevant County or District Council (in London, at the office of the appropriate London Borough Council).

Listed Building Consent

Anyone who wishes to demolish a listed building, or to alter or extend one **in any way** that affects its character, must obtain a 'listed building consent' from the local planning authority (the District or London Borough Council), or in some circumstances the Secretary of State.

It is an offence to demolish, alter or extend a listed building without listed building consent.

If you are granted listed building consent to demolish a building or part of a building, English Heritage must first be given the opportunity to record this fact. In this case, you should obtain a form from your Local Authority to give notice to the relevant English Heritage regional office.

Alterations to Listed Buildings

Useful guidelines on alterations to listed buildings are contained in Appendix IV of the Department of the Environment Circular 8/87 dated 25 March 1987. This gives advice on the restoration, repair and replacement of various features of listed buildings, so that any items will be in keeping with the general character and style of construction. In addition, it may be helpful to consult DETR Circular 1.2001.

Local Authority Grants

Local authorities may make grants for a building of architectural or historic interest and are not restricted to outstanding or listed buildings. Enquiries should be addressed to the appropriate local authority.

Further Information

For more details regarding proposed alterations to, or refurbishment of, listed buildings, contact the local authority concerned, or the Department of the Environment (See Section 5 for addresses).

Comprehensive Building Price Book 2013
Major and Minor Works dataset

The Major Works dataset focuses predominantly on large 'new build' projects reflecting the economies of scale found in these forms of construction. The Minor Works Estimating Dataset focuses on small to medium sized 'new build' projects reflecting the increase in costs brought about the reduced output, less discounts, increased carriage and supervision, to the similar items in the Major Works dataset. The dataset is presented in trade order. Revised and reworked items in underpinning composites; flue linings and rainwater goods.

Item code: 19215   **Price: £165.99**

SMM7 Estimating Price Book 2013

The SMM7 Estimating dataset focuses predominantly on large 'new build' projects reflecting the economies of scale found in these forms of construction. The dataset is presented in SMM7 grouping and order in accordance with the Common Arrangement of Work Sections. It is compiled using the latest independent costing information from manufacturers, material and plant suppliers, legislation effects and working rule agreements. Revised and reworked items in underpinning composites; flue linings and rainwater goods.

Item code: 19216   **Price: £139.99**

Alterations and Refurbishment Price Book 2013

The Alterations & Refurbishment dataset focuses on small to medium sized projects, generally working within an existing building and reflecting the increase in costs brought about the reduction in output, smaller discounts, increased carriage, increased supervision, and less productivity brought about by smaller economies of scale, increased production costs, more difficult access and the possibility of working in occupied premises. The dataset is presented in trade order. Revised and reworked items in underpinning composites; flue linings and rainwater goods.

Item code: 19217   **Price £109.99**

BCIS Guide to Estimating for Small Works 2012

The BCIS Guide to Estimating for Small Works 2012 is a unique dataset which shows the true power of resource based estimating. A set of composite built-up measured items are used to build up priced estimates for a large number of common specification extensions. The intention is to show estimating techniques in use and allow users to build up accurate estimates for their own projects, simply and easily, with up-to-date and independent cost information.

Item code: 19064   **Price: £59.99**

BCIS Painting and Decorating Price Book 2012

The BCIS Painting and Decorating dataset is the most handy pricing tool available to the painting and decorating sector of the industry, suitable for all projects needing more than a 'guess-timate'. Using this dataset a more accurate calculation based quotation or variation can be prepared. From these calculations an assessment of labour, plant and material content can be produced. This in turn enables the contractor to negotiate discounts on known material requirements and the effect of this workload on the availability of labour.

Item code: 19065   **Price: £39.99**

For more information call **0870 333 1600** email
contact@bcis.co.uk or visit **www.bcis.co.uk**

BCIS is the Building Cost Information Service of  **RICS** | the mark of property professionalism worldwide

Memorandum

HOW LONG? HOW MUCH?

THE FASTEST, MOST UP-TO-DATE ANSWERS ARE AVAILABLE NOW

Cost information underpins every aspect of the built environment, from construction and rebuilding to maintenance and operation publications.

BCIS, the RICS' Building Cost Information Service, is the leading provider of cost information to the construction industry and anyone else who needs comprehensive, accurate and independent data.

For the past 50 years, BCIS has been collecting, collating, analysing, modelling and interpreting cost information.Today, BCIS make that information easily accessible through online applications, data licensing and publications.

For more information call **0870 333 1600** email **contact@bcis.co.uk** or visit **www.bcis.co.uk**

BCIS is the Building Cost Information Service of

MEMORANDA

METRIC CONVERSION FACTORS

		Metric	= Imperial	Imperial	= Metric
LENGTH		1 mm	= 0.0394 inches	1 inch	= 25.4 (exact) mm
		1 m	= 3.2808 feet	1 foot	= 0.3048 m
		1 m	= 1.0936 yards	1 yard	= 0.9144 m
		1 km	= 0.6214 miles	1 mile	= 1.6093 km
AREA		1 mm2	= 0.0016 square inches	1 square inch	= 645.1600 mm2
		1 m2	= 10.7639 square feet	1 square foot	= 0.0929 m2
		1 m2	= 1.1960 square yards	1 square yard	= 0.8361 m2
		1 km2	= 0.3861 square mile	1 square mile	= 2.5900 km2
		1 ha	= 2.4711 acres	1 acre	= 0.4047 ha
VOLUME		1 m3	= 35.3147 cubic feet	1 cubic foot	= 0.0283 m3
		1 m3	= 1.3080 cubic yards	1 cubic yard	= 0.7646 m3
		1 litre	= 1.7598 pints	1 pint	= 0.5683 litres
		1 litre	= 0.2200 gallons (UK)	1 gallon (UK)	= 4.5461 litres
	Note:	1 litre	= 1000 cm3		
		1 m3	= 1000 litres		
WEIGHT		1 kg	= 2.2046 pounds	1 pound	= 0.4536 kg
		1 kg	= 0.0197 hundredweight	1 hundredweight	= 50.8024 kg
		1 tonne	= 0.9842 ton	1 ton	= 1.0161 tonnes
FORCE		1 N	= 0.2248 pdf	1 pdf	= 4.4482 N
		1 N	= 7.2330 pdl	1 pdl	= 0.1383 N
		1 kN	= 0.1004 tonf	1 tonf	= 9.9640 kN
	Note:	Standard gravity (gn)	= 9.80665 m/s2 (exactly)		
PRESSURE		1 kpa	= 0.1450 lbf/square inch	1 lbf/square inch	= 6.8948 kpa
	Note:	1 kpa	= 1 kN/m2	= 0.001 N/mm2	
ENERGY (work and heat)		1 kJ	= 0.9478 Btu	1 Btu	= 1.0551 kJ
POWER		1 W	= 3.4121 Btu/Hr	1 Btu	= 0.2931 W
		1 kW	= 1.3410 hp	1 hp	= 0.7457 kW

METRIC CONVERSION TABLE
Inches and fractions of inches to millimetres

millimetres

Inches	0	1	2	3	4	5	6	7	8	9	10	11
		25.400	50.800	76.200	101.600	127.000	152.400	177.800	203.200	228.600	254.000	279.400
1/32	0.794	26.194	51.594	76.994	102.394	127.794	153.194	178.594	203.994	229.394	254.794	280.194
1/16	1.588	26.998	52.388	77.788	103.188	128.588	153.988	179.388	204.788	230.188	255.588	280.988
3/32	2.381	27.781	53.181	78.581	103.981	129.381	154.781	180.181	205.581	230.981	256.381	281.781
1/8	3.175	28.575	53.975	79.375	104.775	130.175	155.575	180.975	206.375	231.775	257.175	282.575
5/32	3.969	29.369	54.769	80.169	105.569	130.969	156.369	181.769	207.169	232.569	257.969	283.369
3/16	4.762	30.162	55.562	80.962	106.362	131.762	157.162	182.562	207.962	233.362	258.762	284.162
7/32	5.556	30.956	56.356	81.756	107.156	132.556	157.956	183.356	208.756	234.156	259.556	284.956
1/4	6.350	31.750	57.150	82.550	107.950	133.350	158.750	184.150	209.550	234.950	260.350	285.750
9/32	7.144	32.544	57.944	83.344	108.744	134.144	159.544	184.944	210.344	235.744	261.144	286.544
5/16	7.983	33.338	58.738	84.138	109.538	134.938	160.338	185.738	211.138	236.538	261.938	287.338
11/32	8.731	34.131	59.531	84.931	110.331	135.731	161.131	186.531	211.931	237.331	262.731	288.131
3/8	9.525	34.925	60.325	85.725	111.125	136.525	161.925	187.325	212.725	238.125	263.525	228.925
13/32	10.319	35.719	61.119	86.519	111.919	137.319	162.719	188.119	213.519	238.919	264.319	289.719
7/16	11.112	36.512	61.912	87.312	112.712	138.112	163.512	188.912	214.312	239.712	265.112	290.512
15/32	11.906	37.306	62.706	88.106	113.906	138.906	164.306	189.706	215.106	240.506	265.906	291.306
1/2	12.700	38.100	63.500	88.900	114.300	139.700	165.100	190.500	215.900	241.300	266.700	292.100
17/32	13.494	38.894	64.294	89.694	115.094	140.494	165.894	191.294	216.694	242.494	267.494	292.894
9/16	14.288	39.688	65.088	90.488	115.888	141.288	166.688	192.088	217.488	242.888	268.288	293.688
19/32	15.081	40.481	65.881	91.281	116.681	142.081	167.481	192.881	218.281	243.681	269.081	294.481
5/8	15.875	41.275	66.675	92.075	117.475	142.875	168.275	193.675	219.075	244.475	269.875	295.275
21/32	16.669	42.069	67.469	92.869	118.269	143.669	169.069	194.469	219.869	245.269	270.669	296.069
11/16	17.462	42.862	68.262	93.662	119.062	144.462	169.862	195.262	220.662	246.062	271.462	296.862
23/32	18.256	43.656	69.056	94.456	119.856	145.256	170.656	196.056	221.456	246.856	272.256	297.656
3/4	19.050	44.450	69.850	95.250	120.650	146.050	171.450	196.850	222.250	247.650	273.050	298.450
25/32	19.844	45.244	70.644	96.044	121.444	146.844	172.244	197.644	223.044	248.444	273.844	299.244
13/16	20.638	46.038	71.438	96.838	122.238	147.638	173.038	198.438	223.838	249.238	274.638	300.038
27/32	21.431	46.831	72.231	97.631	123.031	148.431	173.831	199.231	224.631	250.031	275.431	300.831
7/8	22.225	47.625	73.025	98.425	123.825	149.225	174.625	200.025	225.425	250.825	276.225	301.625
29/32	23.019	48.419	73.819	99.219	124.619	150.019	175.419	200.819	226.219	251.619	277.019	302.419
15/16	23.812	49.212	74.612	100.012	125.412	150.812	176.212	201.612	227.012	252.412	277.812	303.212
31/32	24.606	50.006	75.406	100.806	126.206	151.606	177.006	202.406	227.806	253.206	278.606	304.006

THICKNESS OF SHEETING ETC.

12 inches	=	304.800 mm
1000 gauge	=	250 mµ
1200 gauge	=	300 mµ

MEASUREMENT FORMULAE

Perimeters or circumferences of planes
Circle: 3.14159 x Diameter

Ellipse:
$$3.14159 \frac{(\text{major axis} + \text{minor axis})}{2}$$

Sector:
$$\frac{\text{Radius x Degrees in Arc}}{57.3}$$

Surface areas of planes and solids
Circle: 3.14159 x Radius Sq

Sphere: 3.14159 x Diameter Sq

Ellipse: 0.7854 (major axis x minor axis)

Cylinder: (circumference x length) + (2 x area of end)

Cone:
$$\frac{\text{Area of base} + (\text{circumference x slant height})}{2}$$

Frustum of cone: 3.14159 x slant height (radius at top + radius at bottom) + area of top + area of bottom

Pyramid:
$$\frac{(\text{sum of base perimeters}) \text{ slant height} + \text{area of base}}{2}$$

Sector of circle:
$$\frac{3.14159 \times \text{Degrees in Arc} \times \text{Radius Sq}}{360}$$

Segment of circle: Area of sector LESS area of triangle

Segment of arc:
$$\frac{2(\text{chord} \times \text{rise})}{3} + \frac{\text{rise}3}{2 \times \text{chord}}$$

Bellmouth at road junction: Area 'A' = $\frac{3 \times \text{Radius Sq}}{14}$

Volumes of solids

Sphere : 4.1888 x Radius cubed

Cone : $\frac{\text{height (area of base)}}{3}$

Frustum of cone: $\frac{\text{height} (3.14159 \times R\ Sq + r\ Sq + Rr)}{2}$ where R and r are radius of base and top

Pyramid: $\frac{\text{height (area of base)}}{3}$

Frustum of pyramid: $\frac{\text{height} (A + B + \text{square root} (AB))}{3}$ where A and B are areas of base and top

Lengths of rafters

To calculate the lengths of rafters:
Multiply the lengths on plan (from centre line of ridge to extreme horizontal projection of rafter) by the secant of the angle.

Pitch in degrees	Natural Secant	Pitch in degrees	Natural Secant	Pitch in degrees	Natural Secant
5.0	1.0038	25.0	1.1034	45.0	1.4142
7.5	1.0086	27.5	1.1274	50.0	1.5557
10.0	1.0154	30.0	1.1547	55.0	1.7435
12.5	1.0243	32.5	1.1857	60.0	2.0000
15.0	1.0353	35.0	1.2208	65.0	2.3662
17.5	1.0485	37.5	1.2605	70.0	2.9238
20.0	1.0642	40.0	1.3054	75.0	3.8637
22.5	1.0824	42.5	1.3563		

EXCAVATION AND EARTHWORK

Bearing capacities of soils

Nature of soil:	Approximate bearing capacity; kN/m2
Peat and bog	0 - 20
Clay, marl, loam	330 - 750
Solid chalk	110 - 450
Solid rock (unweathered)	220 - 2000
Gravel, coarse	660 - 900
Gravel, fine	450 - 660
Sand	220 - 550

Bulkage of soils after excavation

Nature of soil:	Approximate bulkage of 1 m3 after excavation:
Vegetable soil and loam	1.25 - 1.30 m3
Soft clay, marl	1.30 - 1.40 m3
Sand	1.10 - 1.15 m3
Gravel	1.20 - 1.25 m3
Chalk	1.40 - 1.50 m3
Stiff clay	1.40 - 1.50 m3
Rock, weathered	1.30 - 1.40 m3
Rock, unweathered	1.50 - 1.60 m3

CONCRETE WORK

Note: The following quantities allow for the increase in bulk of moist sand and moist all-in aggregate.

Quantities of materials per 1 m3 of hardened concrete				Quantities of materials per 50 kg bag of cement			
Nominal mix by volume	Cement tonnes	Moist sand m3	Gravel m3	Nominal mix by volume	Cement 50 kg bag	Moist sand kg	Gravel kg
1:3:6	0.215	0.55	0.88	1:3:6	1	130	205
1:2:4	0.304	0.53	0.84	1:2:4	1	85	140
1:1.5:3	0.389	0.50	0.80	1:1.5:3	1	65	105
		Moist all-in aggregate (m3)				Moist all-in aggregate (kg):	
1:6	0.304	1.45		1:6	1	240	
1:9	0.214	1.52		1:9	1	355	
1:12	0.167	1.55		1:12	1	465	
Nominal mix by weight	Cement tonnes	Moist sand tonnes	Gravel tonnes	Nominal mix by weight	Cement 50 kg bag	Moist sand kg	Gravel kg
1:3:6	0.216	0.81	1.31	1:3:6	1	190	305
1:2:4	0.312	0.81	1.24	1:2:4	1	130	200
1:1.5:3	0.391	0.74	1.17	1:1.5:3	1	95	150
	Cement tonnes	Moist all-in aggregate (tonnes)				Moist all-in aggregate kg	
1:6	0.312	2.15		1:6	1	345	
1:9	0.217	2.26		1:9	1	520	
1:12	0.172	2.38		1:12	1	690	

Weights of steel bar reinforcement

Diameter	kg/m	m/tonne	Cross-sectional area mm2
6 mm	0.222	4505	28.3
8 mm	0.395	2532	50.3
10 mm	0.616	1624	78.5
12 mm	0.888	1126	113.1
16 mm	1.579	634	201.1
20 mm	2.466	406	314.2
25 mm	3.854	260	490.9
32 mm	6.313	158	804.2
40 mm	9.864	101	1256.6
50 mm	15.413	65	1963.3

Weights of steel bar reinforcement in various percentages of 1 m3 of concrete

Percentage of reinforcement	0.5	0.75	1.00	1.25	1.50	1.75	2.00	2.50	3.00	3.50	4.00	4.50	5.00
Weights kg per m3	39	59	79	98	118	137	157	196	236	275	314	353	393

Weights of stainless steel bar reinforcement

Diameter	kg/m	m/tonne	Cross-sectional area mm2
10 mm	0.667	1499	78.5
12 mm	0.938	1066	113.1
16 mm	1.628	614	201.1
20 mm	2.530	395	314.2
25 mm	4.000	250	490.9
32 mm	6.470	155	804.2

Weights of steel fabric reinforcement
Fabric reinforcement to BS 4483:

SQUARE MESH FABRIC	Mesh size: Main	Mesh size: Cross	Wire size: Main	Wire size: Cross	Weight per m2
BS reference	mm	mm	mm	mm	kg
A 393	200	200	10	10	6.16
A 252	200	200	8	8	3.95
A 193	200	200	7	7	3.02
A 142	200	200	6	6	2.22
A 98	200	200	5	5	1.54
STRUCTURAL MESH FABRIC					
B1131	100	200	12	8	10.90
B 785	100	200	10	8	8.14
B 503	100	200	8	8	5.93
B 385	100	200	7	7	4.53
B 283	100	200	6	7	3.73
B 196	100	200	5	7	3.05

Fabric reinforcement to BS 4483:

LONG MESH FABRIC					
C 785	100	400	10	6	6.72
C 503	100	400	8	5	4.34
C 385	100	400	7	5	3.41
C 283	100	400	6	5	2.61
WRAPPING FABRIC					
D 98	200	200	5	5	1.54
D 49	100	100	2.5	2.5	0.770
CARRIAGE WAY FABRIC					
C 636	80-130	400	8-10	6	5.55

BRICKWORK AND BLOCKWORK

Bricks and mortar required per m2
Bricks 215 x 102.5 x 65 mm with 10 mm joints:

Wall thickness	Number of bricks (no waste allowance)	Mortar (m3) no frogs	Mortar (m3) one frog	Mortar (m3) two frogs
102.5 mm (half brick)	59.25	0.017	0.024	0.031
215 mm (one brick)	118.50	0.045	0.059	0.073
327.5 mm (one and a half brick)	177.75	0.072	0.093	0.114
440 mm (two brick)	237.00	0.101	0.128	0.155

Length of pointing to one face per m2:

Extra common brickwork for facing and pointing one side in:	Number of bricks (no waste allowance)	Horizontal joints	Vertical joints	Combined
English bond	89.0	13.3 m	5.8 m	19.1 m
Flemish bond	79.0	13.3 m	5.1 m	18.4 m
English garden wall bond	74.0	13.3 m	4.8 m	18.1 m
Flemish garden wall bond	68.0	13.3 m	4.4 m	17.7m

Blocks and mortar required per m2
Blocks 440 x 215 mm on face with 10 mm joints require 9.88 blocks per m2 (exclusive of waste)

Wall thickness (mm)	50	60	70	75	90	100	115	125
Mortar (m3/m2)	0.003	0.004	0.005	0.005	0.006	0.007	0.008	0.008
Wall thickness (mm)	140	150	190	215	220	250	255	305
Mortar (m3/m2)	0.009	0.010	0.013	0.014	0.015	0.017	0.017	0.020

Analysis of mortar mixes per m3				Analysis of mortar mixes per 50 kg bag of Cement			
Nominal mix by volume	Cement tonnes	Lime tonnes	Sand (moist) m3	Nominal mix by volume	Cement 50 kg bag	Lime 25 kg bag	Sand (moist m3) kg
1:3	0.52	-	1.36	1:3	1	-	168
1:4	0.43	-	1.50	1:4	1	-	224
1:1:6	0.27	0.13	1.38	1:1:6	1	1	327
1:2:9	0.19	0.19	1.44	1:2:9	1	2	486

ROOFING

Quantities of slates, tiles etc. per m2

Note: The quantities in the table below are net with no allowance for waste.

Type:	Size (mm)	Lap (mm)	Gauge (mm)	Number (Nr)	Battens (m/m2)	Slate or tile nails (Nr)		Batten nails (Nr)
Natural slates - uniform sizes:	610 x 305	75	268	12.26	3.75	25		10
	455 x 255	75	189	20.64	5.30	42		12
	405 x 255	75	165	23.75	6.10	48		14
	355 x 205	75	140	34.84	7.15	86		16
	305 x 205	75	115	42.42	8.70	85		20
Natural slates - uniform length Random widths:	560 long	75	243	14.73	4.12	29		10
	510 long	75	218	18.18	4.60	36		11
	405 long	75	165	29.93	6.10	60		14
	355 long	75	140	40.24	7.15	81		16
	305 long	75	115	57.02	8.70	114		20
Natural slates - random length, random widths; length:	1220 - 760	75	455	4.55	2.20	9		5
	760 - 560	75	294	10.36	3.40	21		8
	610 - 305	75	192	22.59	5.20	45		12
	510 - 305	75	165	26.35	6.10	52		14
	455 - 230	75	135	38.98	7.40	78		17
	355 - 255	75	115	58.00	8.70	116		20
						Hooks (Nr)		
Eternit slates - hook fixing:	600 x 300	110	245	13.50	4.08	14		7
		90	255	13.00	3.92	13		7
	500 x 250	110	195	20.50	5.13	21		9
		90	205	19.50	4.88	20		8
	400 x 270	110	145	25.50	6.90	26		12
		90	155	23.90	6.45	24		11
	400 x 200	110	145	34.50	6.90	35		12
		90	155	32.30	6.45	32		11
						Slate fixing nails (Nr)	**Slate fixing discs (Nr)**	
Eternit slates - nail and disc rivet fixing:	600 x 300	70	265	12.50	3.77	25	13	6
		76	262	12.60	3.82	25	13	6
		90	255	13.10	3.92	26	13	7
		100	250	13.30	4.00	26	13	7
		110	245	13.60	4.08	27	-	-
	500 x 250	70	215	18.60	4.65	37	19	8
		76	212	18.90	4.72	38	19	8
		90	205	19.50	4.88	39	20	8
	400 x 270	70	165	22.50	6.06	45	23	10
		76	162	22.80	6.17	46	23	10
		90	155	23.80	6.45	48	24	11
	400 x 200	70	165	30.00	6.06	60	30	10
		76	162	30.70	6.17	61	31	10
		90	155	31.90	6.45	64	32	11
Bradstone slates - Cotswold pattern	380 x 330 (average)	75	150	20.21	6.67	42		15
Moordale pattern	480 x 375 (average)	75	200	13.35	5.00	26		12
Cedar shingles - uniform lengths random widths:	400 long	210	95	1.77	10.53	84		18
		146	127	2.39	7.87	64		13
		120	140	2.63	7.14	58		12
		100	150	2.86	6.67	54		11
		70	165	3.10	6.06	48		10
		44	178	3.34	5.62	46		10
Vertical cladding shadow coursing (double thickness)		146 (av.)	175 & 178	2.39	7.87	64		13
		70	165	1.60	6.06	48		11
		44	178	1.70	5.62	45		10
				Number (Nr)				
Marley concrete tiles	413 x 330	75	338	***10.20	2.96	10		5
		100	313	**11.00	3.20	11		5
	419 x 330	75	344	9.70	2.91	10		5
		100	319	10.50	3.14	11		5
	380 x 230	75	305	16.10	3.28	16		6
		100	280	17.50	3.57	18		6
Redland concrete tiles	430 x 380	75	355	8.21	2.82	8		6
	417 x 332	75	342	9.75	2.92	10		7
		100	317	10.52	3.16	11		7
	417 x 330	75	342	9.75	2.92	10		7
	381 x 229	75	306	*15.94	3.27	16		7

Type:	Size (mm)	Lap (mm)	Gauge (mm)	Number (Nr)	Battens (m/m2)	Slate fixing nails (Nr)	Slate fixing discs (Nr)	Batten nails (Nr)
*** Yeoman 9.96								
** Yeoman 10.76								
* Redland 49 16.34								
						Tile fixing nails (Nr)		
Sandtoft Goxhill	470 x 285	100	370	11.50	2.70	12		6
clay tiles	342 x 266	75	267	17.80	3.75	18		8
	342 x 241**	75	267	18.50	3.75	19		8
	342 x 241*	75	267	18.80	3.75	19		8
** Old English								
* Gaelic								
Plain tiles	265 x 165	65	100	60	10.00	24*		23
		75	95	64	10.53	26*		24
		85	90	68	11.11	28*		25
	(Vertical)	37	114	54	8.77	108		20
* Nailing 5th Courses								

Thicknesses of sheet metal

Lead BS 1178: BS Code	lbs/ft2	Thickness (mm)	kg/m2	Colour code
3	2.91	1.25	14.18	Green
4	4.19	1.80	20.41	Blue
5	5.21	2.24	25.40	Red
6	5.82	2.50	28.36	Black
7	7.33	3.15	35.72	White
8	8.26	3.55	40.26	Orange

Copper BS 2870: Thickness (mm)	Bay width Roll (mm)	Bay width Seam (mm)	Standard width to form bay	Length of each sheet (m)
0.45	500	525	600	1.80
0.60	500	525	600	1.80
0.70	650	675	750	1.80

Zinc BS 849: Zinc Gauge Nr	Thickness mm	Weight kg/m2	Weight Oz/ft2
10	0.48	3.2	11.39
11	0.56	3.8	13.18
12	0.64	4.3	14.98
13	0.71	4.8	16.78
14	0.79	5.3	18.58
15	0.91	6.2	21.57
16	1.04	7.0	24.57

Approximate numbers of copper nails per kg

	Length (mm) x Shank (mm)	Number per kg
Round lost head nails	65 x 3.75	178
	50 x 3.35	292
	40 x 2.65	474
Clout nails	65 x 3.75	170
	50 x 3.35	241
	45 x 3.35	308
	40 x 3.35	335
	30 x 3.35	448
	25 x 2.65	740
	20 x 2.65	920
Cut clout nails	50 x 3.00	275
	45 x 2.65	330
	40 x 2.65	440
	30 x 2.36	627
	25 x 2.00	1298
Extra large head felt nails	25 x 3.35	440
	20 x 3.35	544
	15 x 3.00	691
	13 x 3.00	880

Approximate number of aluminium nails per kg

	Length (mm) x Shank (mm)	Number per kg		Length (mm) x Shank (mm)	Number per kg
Plain roundhead nails	115 x 5.00	159	Clout, slate and tile nails	65 x 3.75	504
	100 x 5.00	184		60 x 3.75	550
	90 x 4.50	246		50 x 3.75	644
	75 x 4.00	338		45 x 3.35	924
	65 x 3.75	490		40 x 3.35	980
	60 x 3.35	714		30 x 3.00	1512
	50 x 3.35	812		25 x 3.35	1540
	45 x 2.65	1428		20 x 3.00	2300
	40 x 2.65	1610			
	30 x 2.00	3276	Tile pegs	40 x 5.00	450
	25 x 2.00	4004		30 x 5.00	545
	20 x 1.60	7588		30 x 4.50	600
Round lost head nails	75 x 3.75	448	Extra large head felt nails	25 x 3.35	1296
	65 x 3.35	672		20 x 3.35	1848
	60 x 3.35	756		15 x 3.35	1840
	50 x 3.35	860			
	40 x 2.64	1390			

WOODWORK

Approximate numbers of steel wire nails per kg

	Length (mm) x Shank (mm)	Number per kg		Length (mm) x Shank (mm)	Number per kg		Length (mm) x Shank (mm)	Number per kg
Round wire nails with plain heads	200 x 8.00	13	Cut floor brads	75 x 3.35	100	Oval brad head and oval lost head nails	150 x 7.10 x 5.00	31
	180 x 6.70	22		65 x 3.35	154		125 x 6.70 x 4.50	44
	150 x 6.00	29		60 x 3.00	198		100 x 6.00 x 4.00	64
	125 x 5.60	42		50 x 2.65	264		90 x 5.60 x 3.75	90
	115 x 5.00	57		45 x 2.36	330		75 x 5.00 x 3.35	125
	100 x 5.00	66		40 x 2.36	396		65 x 4.00 x 2.65	230
	90 x 4.50	88					60 x 3.75 x 2.36	340
	75 x 4.00	121	Cut clasp nails	200 x 6.00	11		50 x 3.35 x 2.00	470
	65 x 3.75	175		175 x 5.60	13		45 x 3.35 x 2.00	655
	60 x 3.35	255		150 x 5.60	19		40 x 2.65 x 1.60	940
	50 x 3.35	290		125 x 5.00	30		30 x 2.65 x 1.60	1480
	45 x 2.65	510		100 x 4.00	48		25 x 2.00 x 1.25	2530
	40 x 2.65	575		90 x 3.75	66		20 x 2.00 x 1.25	4500
	30 x 2.36	840		75 x 3.35	103			
	25 x 2.00	1430		65 x 3.00	171	Round lost head nails	100 x 4.50	75
	20 x 1.60	2710		60 x 2.65	202		90 x 4.50	85
				50 x 2.65	286		75 x 3.75	150
Round lost head nails	75 x 3.75	160		40 x 2.00	616		65 x 3.75	180
	65 x 3.35	240		30 x 1.80	858		50 x 3.75	230
	60 x 3.35	270		25 x 1.60	1384		45 x 3.35	330
	50 x 3.00	360					40 x 3.35	350
	40 x 2.36	760					30 x 3.00	540
	30 x 2.00	1190					25 x 2.65	815
	25 x 1.00	6100					20 x 2.65	1035
	20 x 1.00	8030					15 x 2.36	1540
	15 x 1.00	9400						

Lengths of timber per m3

mm	m/m3	mm	m/m3	mm	m/m3	mm	m/m3
16 x 16	3906	19 x 19	2770	22 x 22	2066	25 x 25	1600
19	3289	22	2392	25	1818	32	1250
22	2841	25	2105	32	1420	38	1053
25	2500	32	1645	38	1196	44	909
32	1953	38	1385	44	1033	50	800
38	1645	44	1196	50	909	63	635
44	1420	50	1053	63	722	75	533
50	1250	63	835	75	606	100	400
63	992	75	702	100	455	125	320
75	833	100	526	125	364	150	267
100	625	125	421	150	303		
125	500	150	351				
150	417						
25 x 175	229	32 x 32	977	38 x 38	693	44 x 44	517
200	200	38	822	44	598	50	455
225	178	44	710	50	526	63	361
250	160	50	625	63	418	75	303
300	133	63	496	75	351	100	227
		75	417	100	263	125	182
		100	313	125	211	150	152
		125	250	150	175	175	130
		150	208	175	150	200	114
		175	179	200	132	225	101
50 x 50	400	200	156	225	117	250	91
63	317	225	139	250	105	300	76
75	267	250	125	300	88		
100	200	300	104				
125	160						

continued over...

mm	m/m3	mm	m/m3	mm	m/m3	mm	m/m3
150	133	63 x 63	252	75 x 75	178	100 x 100	100
175	114	75	212	100	133	150	67
200	100	100	159	125	107	200	50
225	89	125	127	150	89	250	40
250	80	150	106	175	76	300	33
300	67	175	91	200	67		
		200	79	225	59	200	33
200 x 200	25	225	71	250	53	250	27
250 x 250	16	250	63	300	44	300	22
300 x 300	11	300	53				

Standard lengths of timber

1.8 m
2.1 m, 2.4 m, 2.7 m,
3.0 m, 3.3 m, 3.6 m, 3.9 m,
4.2 m, 4.5 m, 4.8 m,
5.1 m, 5.4 m, 5.7 m,
6.0 m,+ 6.3 m,+ 6.6 m,+ 6.9 m,+
7.2 m,+
+ These lengths may only be available from North American sources

Ends, angles, mitres, intersections and the like

SMM6 Clause N1.10 requires ends, angles, mitres, intersections and the like to be enumerated where the cross-sectional area of wrought timber exceeds 0.002 m2.
Where the cross-sectional area is less than 0.002 m2 then ends, angles, mitres, intersections and the like are 'deemed to be included'.
The following scantlings DO NOT exceed 0.002 m3 and ends etc. are 'deemed to be included'

13 mm x 13 mm	16 mm x 16 mm	22 mm x 22 mm	25 mm x 25 mm	32 mm x 32 mm	38 mm x 38 mm	44 mm x 44 mm
16 mm	19 mm	25 mm	32 mm	38 mm	44 mm	
19 mm	22 mm	32 mm	38 mm	44 mm	50 mm	
22 mm	25 mm	38 mm	44 mm	50 mm		
25 mm	32 mm	44 mm	50 mm	63 mm		
32 mm	38 mm	50 mm	63 mm			
38 mm	44 mm	63 mm	75 mm			
44 mm	50 mm	75 mm				
50 mm	63 mm					
63 mm	75 mm					
75 mm	100 mm					
100 mm	125 mm					
125 mm						
150 mm						

STRUCTURAL STEELWORK

Dimensions and weights of structural steel sections

Universal beams		Universal beams		Universal columns	
Size (mm) x kg/m		Size (mm) x kg/m		Size (mm) x kg/m	
914 x 419	388	457 x 152	82	356 x 406	634
	343		74		551
914 x 305	289		67		467
	253		60		393
	224		52		340
	201	406 x 178	74		287
838 x 292	226		67		235
	194		60	356 x 368	202
	176		54		177
762 x 267	197	406 x 140	46		153
	173		39		129
	147	356 x 171	67	305 x 305	283
686 x 254	170		57		240
	152		51		198
	140		45		158
	125	356 x 127	39		137
610 x 305	238		33		118
	179	305 x 165	54		97
	149		46	254 x 254	167
610 x 229	140	305 x 127	48		132
	125		42		107
	113		37		89
	101	305 x 102	33		73
553 x 210	122		28	203 x 203	86
	109		25		71
	101	254 x 146	43		60
	92		37	203 x 203	52
	82		31		46
457 x 191	98	254 x 102	28	152 x 152	37
	89		25		30
	82		22		23
	74	203 x 133	30		
	67		25		

Joists	
Size (mm)	x kg/m
254 x 203	81.85
254 x 114	37.20
203 x 152	52.09
203 x 102	25.33
178 x 102	21.54
152 x 127	37.20
152 x 89	17.09
152 x 76	17.86
127 x 114	29.76
127 x 114	26.79
127 x 76	16.37
127 x 76	13.36
114 x 114	26.79
102 x 102	23.07
102 x 64	9.65
102 x 44	7.44
89 x 89	19.35
76 x 76	14.67
76 x 76	12.65

Channels	
Size (mm)	x kg/m
432 x 102	65.54
381 x 102	55.10
305 x 102	46.18
305 x 89	41.69
254 x 89	35.74
254 x 76	28.29
229 x 89	32.76
229 x 76	26.06
203 x 89	29.78
203 x 76	23.82
178 x 89	26.81
178 x 76	20.84
152 x 89	23.84
152 x 76	17.88
127 x 64	14.90
102 x 51	10.42
76 x 38	6.70

Equal angles (Imperial sizes)

Size and	thickness (mm)	x kg/m
203 x 203	25	76.00
	24	71.51
	22	67.05
	21	62.56
	19	57.95
	17	53.30
	16	48.68
152 x 152	22	49.32
	21	46.03
	19	42.75
	17	39.32
	16	36.07
	14	32.62
	13	29.07
	11	25.60
	9	22.02
127 x 127	19	35.16
	17	32.47
	16	29.66
	14	26.80
	13	23.99
	11	21.14
	10	18.30
102 x 102	19	27.57
	17	25.48
	16	23.37
	14	21.17
	13	18.91
	11	16.69
	9	14.44
	8	12.06
89 x 89	16	20.10
	14	18.31
	13	16.38
	11	14.44
	9	12.50
	8	10.58
	6	8.49

Size and	thickness (mm)	x kg/m
76 x 76	14	15.50
	13	13.85
	11	12.20
	9	10.57
	8	8.93
	6	7.16
64 x 64	12	11.31
	11	10.12
	9	8.78
	8	7.45
	6	5.96
57 x 57	9	7.74
	8	6.55
	6	5.35
	5	4.01
51 x 51	9	6.85
	8	5.80
	6	4.77
	5	3.58
44 x 44	8	5.06
	6	4.02
	5	3.13
38 x 38	8	4.24
	6	3.50
	5	2.68
32 x 32	6	2.83
	5	2.16
	3	1.49
26 x 26	6	2.23
	5	1.72
	3	1.19

Unequal angles (Imperial sizes)

Size and	thickness (mm)	x kg/m	Size and	thickness (mm)	x kg/m	Size and	thickness (mm)	x kg/m
229 x 102	22	53.77	203 x 102	19	42.75	152 x 89	16	27.99
	21	50.21		17	39.32		14	25.46
	19	46.45		16	36.07		13	22.77
	17	42.87		14	32.62		11	20.12
	16	39.20		13	29.07		9	17.26
	14	35.43					8	14.44
	13	31.56	179 x 89	16	31.30			
				14	28.28	152 x 76	16	26.52
203 x 152	22	58.09		13	25.31		14	23.99
	21	54.22		11	22.36		13	21.45
	19	50.32		9	19.22		11	18.92
	17	46.30					9	16.39
	16	42.32	152 x 102	19	35.16		8	13.69
	14	38.29		17	32.47			
	13	34.10		16	29.66	127 x 89	16	24.86
				14	26.80		14	22.64
				13	23.99		13	20.26

Unequal angles (Imperial sizes) – Contd.

Size and	thickness (mm)	x kg/m	Size and	thickness (mm)	x kg/m	Size and	thickness (mm)	x kg/m
			152 x 102	11	21.14	127 x 89	11	17.89
				9	18.30		9	15.35
							8	12.94
127 x 76	14	21.17	102 x 64	11	13.40	76 x 64	8	8.19
	13	18.91		9	11.61		6	6.65
	11	16.69		8	9.69			
	9	14.44		6	7.69	76 x 51	11	10.12
	8	12.06					9	8.78
			89 x 76	14	16.83		8	7.45
102 x 89	16	21.75		13	15.20		6	5.96
	14	19.67		11	13.40		5	4.62
	13	17.72		9	11.61			
	11	15.62		8	9.69	64 x 51	9	7.74
	9	13.55		6	7.89		8	6.55
	8	11.31					6	5.35
			89 x 64	11	12.20		5	4.01
102 x 76	14	18.31		9	10.57			
	13	16.38		8	8.93	64 x 38	8	5.80
	11	14.44		6	7.16		6	4.77
	9	12.50					5	3.58
	8	10.58	76 x 64	11	11.17			
				9	9.68	51 x 38	8	5.06
							6	4.02
							5	3.13

Unequal angles (metric type)

Size and	thickness (mm)	x kg/m	Size and	thickness (mm)	x kg/m
200 x 150	12	32.00	100 x 65	7	8.77
	15	39.60		8	9.94
	18	47.10		10	12.30
200 x 100	10	23.00	80 x 60	6	6.37
	12	27.30		7	7.36
	15	33.70		8	8.34
150 x 90	10	18.20	75 x 50	6	5.65
	12	21.60		8	7.39
	15	26.60			
150 x 75	10	17.00	65 x 50	5	4.35
	12	20.20		6	5.16
	15	24.80		8	6.75
125 x 75	8	12.20	60 x 30	5	3.37
	10	15.00		6	3.99
	12	17.80			
100 x 75	8	10.60	40 x 25	4	1.93
	10	13.00			
	12	15.40			

Equal angles (metric sizes)

Size and	thickness (mm)	x kg/m	Size and	thickness (mm)	x kg/m	Size and	thickness (mm)	x kg/m
250 x 250	25	93.60	100 x 100	15	21.90	50 x 50	5	3.77
	28	104.00	90 x 90	6	8.30		6	4.47
	32	118.00		7	9.61		8	5.82
	35	128.00		8	10.90	45 x 45	3	2.09
200 x 200	16	48.50		10	13.40		4	2.74
	18	54.20		12	15.90		5	3.38
	20	59.90	80 x 80	6	7.34		6	4.00
	24	71.10		8	9.63	40 x 40	3	1.84
150 x 150	10	23.00		10	11.90		4	2.42
	12	27.30	70 x 70	6	6.38		5	2.97
	15	33.80		8	8.36		6	3.52
	18	40.10		10	10.30	30 x 30	3	1.36
120 x 120	8	14.70	60 x 60	5	4.57		4	1.78
	10	18.20		6	5.42		5	2.18
	12	21.60		8	7.09	25 x 25	3	1.11
	15	26.60		10	8.69		4	1.45
100 x 100	8	12.20	50 x 50	3	2.33		5	1.77
	12	17.80		4	3.06			

Circular Hollow Sections (CHS)

Outside diameter (mm)	Thickness (mm)	Weight (kg/m)	Outside diameter (mm)	Thickness (mm)	Weight (kg/m)	Outside diameter (mm)	Thickness (mm)	Weight (kg/m)
457.0	10.0	110.0	323.9	8.0	62.3	219.1	6.3	33.1
	12.5	137.0		10.0	77.4		8.0	41.6
	16.0	174.0		12.5	96.0		10.0	51.6
	20.0	216.0		16.0	121.0		12.5	63.7
	25.0	266.0		20.0	150.0		16.0	80.1
	32.0	335.0		25.0	184.0		20.0	98.2
	40.0	411.0	273.0	6.3	41.4	193.7	5.4	25.1
406.4	10.0	97.8		8.0	52.3		6.3	29.1
	12.5	121.0		10.0	64.9		8.0	36.6
	16.0	154.0		12.5	80.3		10.0	45.3
	20.0	191.0		16.0	101.0		12.5	55.9
	25.0	235.0		20.0	125.0		16.0	70.1
	32.0	295.0		25.0	153.0	168.3	5.0	20.1
355.6	8.0	68.6	244.5	6.3	37.0		6.3	25.2
	10.0	85.2		8.0	46.7		8.0	31.6
	12.5	106.0		10.0	57.8		10.0	39.0
	16.0	154.0		12.5	71.5			
	20.0	166.0		16.0	90.2	42.4	2.6	2.55
	25.0	204.0		20.0	111.0		3.2	3.09
							4.0	3.79
139.7	5.0	16.6	76.1	3.2	5.75	33.7	2.6	1.99
	6.3	20.7		4.0	7.11		3.2	2.41
	8.0	26.0		5.0	8.77		4.0	2.93
	10.0	32.0	60.3	3.2	4.51			
114.3	3.6	9.83		4.0	5.55	26.9	3.2	1.87
	5.0	13.50		5.0	6.82			
	6.3	16.80				21.3	3.2	1.43
88.9	3.2	6.76	48.3	3.2	3.56			
	4.0	8.38		4.0	4.37			
	5.0	10.30		5.0	5.34			

Square Hollow Sections (SHS)

Outside dimensions (mm)	Thickness (mm)	Weight (kg/m)	Outside dimensions (mm)	Thickness (mm)	Weight (kg/m)	Outside dimensions (mm)	Thickness (mm)	Weight (kg/m)
400 x 400	10.0	122.0	150 x 150	5.0	22.7	70 x 70	3.6	7.46
	12.5	152.0		6.3	28.3		5.0	10.10
350 x 350	10.0	106.0		8.0	35.4	60 x 60	3.2	5.67
	12.5	132.0		10.0	43.6		4.0	6.97
	16.0	167.0		12.5	53.4		5.0	8.54
300 x 300	10.0	90.7		16.0	66.4	50 x 50	3.2	4.66
	12.5	112.0	120 x 120	5.0	18.0		4.0	5.72
	16.0	142.0		6.3	22.3		5.0	6.97
250 x 250	6.3	48.1		8.0	27.9	40 x 40	2.6	3.03
	8.0	60.5		10.0	34.2		3.2	3.66
	10.0	75.0	100 x 100	4.0	12.0		4.0	4.46
	12.5	92.6		5.0	14.8	30 x 30	2.6	2.21
	16.0	117.0		6.3	18.4		3.2	2.65
200 x 200	6.3	38.2		8.0	22.9	20 x 20	2.0	1.12
	8.0	48.0		10.0	27.9		2.6	1.39
	10.0	59.3	90 x 90	3.6	9.72			
	12.5	73.0		5.0	13.30			
	16.0	91.5		6.3	16.40			
180 x 180	6.3	34.2	80 x 80	3.6	8.59			
	8.0	43.0		5.0	11.70			
	10.0	53.0		6.3	14.40			
	12.5	65.2						
	16.0	81.4						

Rectangular Hollow Sections (RHS)

Outside dimensions (mm)	Thickness (mm)	Weight (kg/m)	Outside dimensions (mm)	Thickness (mm)	Weight (kg/m)	Outside dimensions (mm)	Thickness (mm)	Weight (kg/m)
450 x 250	10.0	106.0	250 x 150	6.3	38.2	160 x 80	5.0	18.0
	12.5	132.0		8.0	48.0		6.3	22.3
	16.0	167.0		10.0	59.3		8.0	27.9
400 x 200	10.0	90.7		12.5	73.0		10.0	34.2
	12.5	112.0		16.0	91.5			
	16.0	142.0	200 x 100	5.0	22.7	150 x 100	5.0	18.7
300 x 200	6.3	48.1		6.3	28.3		6.3	23.3
	8.0	60.5		8.0	35.4		8.0	29.1
	10.0	75.0		10.0	43.6		10.0	35.7
	12.5	92.6		12.5	53.4	120 x 80	5.0	14.8
	16.0	117.0		16.0	66.4		6.3	18.4
120 x 60	3.6	9.72	90 x 50	3.6	7.46		8.0	22.9
	5.0	13.30		5.0	10.10		10.0	27.9
	6.3	16.40	80 x 40	3.2	5.67			
100 x 60	3.6	8.59		4.0	6.97			
	5.0	11.70	60 x 40	3.2	4.66			
	6.3	14.40		4.0	5.72			
100 x 50	3.2	7.18	50 x 30	2.6	3.03			
	4.0	8.86		3.2	3.66			
	5.0	10.90						

FLOOR WALL AND CEILING FINISHINGS

Average coverage of Gypsum plasters

Finishing plasters	Thickness (mm)	Coverage (m2/tonne)	Undercoat plasters	Thickness (mm)	Coverage (m2/tonne)
Thistle multi finish	2	350 - 450	Thistle browning	11	140 - 240
Thistle board finish	5	160 - 170	Thistle bonding coat	11	100 - 115
Thistle universal one coat	5	225 - 235	Thistle hardwood	11	115 - 130
	10	105 - 115	Thistle tough coat	11	135 - 150
	13	85 - 95			
Thistle projection one coat	5	140 - 160			
	10	70 - 80			
	13	60 - 70			

PAINTING AND DECORATING

Average coverages of paint per coat

The following table is reproduced by permission of: The Paint and Painting Industries' Liaison Committee - Constituent bodies: - British Decorators Association, National Federation of Painting and Decorating Contractors, Paintmakers Association of Great Britain and Scottish Decorators Federation.

The schedule of average coverage figures in respect of painting work is the 1974 revision (with amendments as at April 2000) of the schedule compiled and approved for the guidance of commercial organisations and professional bodies when assessing the values of materials in painting work

In this revision a range of spreading capacities is given. Figures are in square metres per litre, except for oil-bound water paint and cement-based paint which are given in square metres per kilogram.

For comparative purposes figures are given for a single coat, but users are *advised* to follow manufacturers' recommendations as to when to use single or multicoat systems.

It is emphasised that the figures quoted in the schedule are practical figures for brush application, achieved in scale painting work and take into account losses and wastage. They are not optimum figures based upon ideal conditions of surface, nor minimum figures reflecting the reverse of these conditions.

There will be instances when the figures indicated by paint manufacturers in their literature will be higher than those shown in the schedule. The committee realise that under ideal conditions of application, and depending on such factors as the skill of the applicator and the type and quality of the product, better covering figures can be achieved.

The figures given below are for application by brush and to appropriate systems on each surface. They are given for guidance and are qualified to allow for variation depending on certain factors.

Type of surface

Coating (m2 per litre)	Finishing plaster	Wood floated rendering	Smooth concrete/ cement	Fair faced brickwork	Fair faced blockwork	Roughcast/ Pebbledash	Hard board	Soft fibre insulating board
Water thinned primer/under-coat								
as primer	13-15	-	-	-	-	-	10-12	7-10
as undercoat	-	-	-	-	-	-	-	7-10
Plaster primer (including building board)	9-11	8-12	9-11	7-9	5-7	2-4	8-10	7-9
Alkali resistant primer	7-11	6-8	7-11	6-8	4-6	2-4		
External wall primer sealer	6-8	6-7	6-8	5-7	4-6	2-4		
Undercoat	11-14	7-9	7-9	6-8	6-8	3-4	11-14	7-10
Gloss finish	11-14	8-10	8-10	7-9	6-8	-	11-14	7-10
Eggshell /semi-gloss finish (oil based)	11-14	9-11	11-14	8-10	7-9	-	10-13	7-10
Emulsion paint:								
Standard	12-15	8-12	11-14	8-12	6-10	2-4	12-15	8-10
Contract	10-12	7-11	10-12	7-10	5-9	2-4	10-12	7-9
Heavy textured coating	2-4	2-4	2-4	2-4	2-4	-	2-4	2-4
Masonry paint	5-7	4-6	5-7	4-6	3-5	2-4	-	-
Cement based paint	-	4-6	6-7	3-6	3-6	2-3	-	-

Oil based thixotropic finish: Figures should be obtained from individual manufacturers

Glossy emulsion: Figures should be obtained from individual manufacturers

The texture of roughcast, Tyrolean and pebbledash can vary markedly and thus there can be significant variations in the coverage of paints applied to such surfaces. The figures given are thought to be typical but under some circumstances much lower coverage will be obtained.

Type of surface

Coating (m2 per litre)	Fire retardent fibre insulating board	Smooth paper faced board	Hard asbestos sheet	Structural steelwork	Metal sheeting	Joinery	Smooth primed surfaces	Smooth Under-coated surfaces
Woodprimer (oil based)	-	-	-	-	-	8-11	-	-
Water thinned primer undercoat								
as primer	-	8-11	7-10	-	-	10-14	-	-
as undercoat	-	10-12	-	-	-	12-15	12-15	-
Aluminium sealer:*								
spirit based	-	-	-	-	-	7-9	-	-
oil based	-	-	-	-	9-13	9-13	-	-
Metal primer:								
Conventional	-	-	-	7-10	10-13	-	-	-
Plaster primer (including building board)	8-10	10-12	10-12	-	-	-	-	-
Alkali resistant primer	-	-	8-10	-	-	-	-	-
External wall primer sealer	-	-	6-8	-	-	-	-	-
Undercoat	10-12	11-14	10-12	10-12	10-12	10-12	11-14	-
Gloss finish	10-12	11-14	10-12	10-12	10-12	10-12	11-14	11-14
Eggshell/ semi-gloss finish (oil based)	10-12	11-14	10-12	10-12	10-12	10-12	11-14	11-14
Emulsion paint:								
Standard	8-10	12-15	10-12	-	-	10-12	12-15	12-15
Contract	-	10-12	8-10	-	-	10-12	10-12	10-12
Heavy textured coating	2-4	2-4	2-4	2-4	2-4	2-4	2-4	2-4
Masonry paint	-	-	5-7	-	-	-	8-10	6-8
Cement based paint	-	-	4-6	-	-	-	-	-

*Aluminium primer/sealer is normally used over 'bitumen' painted surfaces.
Specialised: Figures should be obtained from individual manufacturers
Oil based thixotropic finish: Figures should be obtained from individual manufacturers
Glossy emulsion: Figures should be obtained from individual manufacturers
In many instances the coverages achieved will be affected by the suction and texture of the backing; for example, the suction and texture of brickwork can vary to such an extent that coverages outside those quoted may be on occasions obtained.
It is necessary to take these factors into account when using this table.

WEIGHTS OF BUILDING MATERIALS

Material	Weight	Unit
Aggregates:		
Coarse, natural materials	1500.0	kg/m3
Coarse, natural sands:		
dry	1600.0	kg/m3
moist	1280.0	kg/m3
Aluminium:		
Cast and wrought	2770.0	kg/m3
Corrugated sheets; thickness:		
0.87 mm	1.7	kg/m2
1.10 mm	2.4	kg/m2
1.42 mm	2.7	kg/m2
1.89 mm	3.7	kg/m2
flat sheets; thickness:		
0.87 mm	1.5	kg/m2
1.10 mm	2.0	kg/m2
1.42 mm	2.4	kg/m2
1.89 mm	3.4	kg/m2
Asbestos cement:		
corrugated sheets; profile:		
standard 3"	15.1	kg/m2
standard 6"	15.1	kg/m2
flat sheets 6.4 mm thick:		
wallboard	6.8	kg/m2
semi-compressed	11.2	kg/m2
fully-compressed	12.2	kg/m2

Material	Weight	Unit
Asphalt:		
damp proofing; thickness:		
20 mm	42.4	kg/m2
25 mm	53.0	kg/m2
30 mm	63.6	kg/m2
flooring; thickness:		
20 mm	42.4	kg/m2
roofing; thickness:		
20 mm	43.9	kg/m2
Bitumen:		
damp proof courses BS, 743:		
type A, hessian base	3.8	kg/m2
type B, fibre base	3.3	kg/m2
type C, asbestos base	3.8	kg/m2
type D, hessian base and lead	4.4	kg/m2
type E, fibre base and lead	4.4	kg/m2
type F, asbestos base and lead	4.9	kg/m2
roofing felts, BS 747:		
hessian base type:		
1B	1.4,1.8,2.5	kg/m2
1E	3.8	kg/m2
1F	1.5	kg/m2
asbestos base; type:		
2B	1.8	kg/m2
2E	3.8	kg/m2

Material	Weight	Unit
Asphalt: (continued)		
glass fibre base; type:		
3B	1.8	kg/m
3E	2.8	kg/m2
3G	3.2	kg/m2
3H	1.7	kg/m2
Aggregates:		
sheathing and hair felts:		
AA(i)	1.7	kg/m2
AA(ii)		
brown Nr.1	2.5	kg/m2
brown Nr.2	2.0	kg/m2
brown	1.7	kg/m2
4B(i)	4.1	kg/m2
4B(ii)	4.1	kg/m2
Bitumen macadam:		
per 25 mm thickness	57.70	kg/m2
Blockwork, per 25 mm thickness:		
clay, hollow	25.5	kg/m2
Blockwork, per 25 mm thickness:		
concrete, natural aggregate:		
cellular	39.9	kg/m2
hollow	34.2	kg/m2
solid	53.8	kg/m2
concrete, lightweight aggregate:		
cellular	28.3	kg/m2
hollow	25.5	kg/m2
solid	31.7	kg/m2
Blockboard	450.0	kg/m3
Brass	8500.0	kg/m3
Brickwork, per 25 mm thickness:		
clay solid:		
low density	50.0	kg/m2
medium density	53.8	kg/m2
high density	58.2	kg/m2
clay perforated, 20% voids:		
low density	40.1	kg/m2
medium density	43.0	kg/m2
high density	46.1	kg/m2
concrete solid	57.7	kg/m2
calcium silicate, solid	50.0	kg/m2
Building boards, fibre:		
insulating, 12.7 mm thick	3.4	kg/m2
hardboard, 3.2 mm thick	3.4	kg/m2
Carpet	1.9 - 3.4	kg/m2
Cast stone	2240.0	kg/m3
Cement	1440.0	kg/m3
Concrete, plain:		
natural aggregates	2300.0	kg/m3
lightweight aggregates	1760.0	kg/m3
Concrete reinforced:		
natural aggregates	2450.0	kg/m3
lightweight aggregates	1900.0	kg/m3
Copper:		
cast	8730.0	kg/m3
wrought	8940.0	kg/m3
sheet and strip; thickness:		
0.87 mm	4.9	kg/m2
1.10 mm	6.3	kg/m2
1.42 mm	8.3	kg/m2
1.89 mm	10.8	kg/m2
Cork:		
loose granular	120.0	kg/m3
board compressed per 25 mm thick	7.2	kg/m2
flooring per 25 mm thickness	9.7	kg/m2

Material	Weight	Unit
Glass, float and plate:		
3 mm	7.71	kg/m2
4 mm	10.3	kg/m2
5 mm	12.8	kg/m2
6 mm	15.4	kg/m2
12 mm	30.8	kg/m2
25 mm	64.1	kg/m2
Glazing, patent:		
lead covered steel bars at 600 mm centres and 6 mm wired glass	26.0	kg/m2
aluminium bars at 600 mm centres and 6 mm wired glass	20.0	kg/m2
Lead:		
cast	11325.00	kg/m3
sheet, code:		
3	14.20	kg/m2
4	20.40	kg/m2
5	25.40	kg/m2
6	28.40	kg/m2
7	35.70	kg/m2
8	40.30	kg/m2
Lime, hydrated	720.00	kg/m3
Linoleum flooring:		
3.2 mm	4.40	kg/m2
4.5 mm	5.90	kg/m2
6.7 mm	9.80	kg/m2
Plasterboard:		
9.5 mm	8.30	kg/m2
12.7 mm	11.20	kg/m2
19.1 mm	17.10	kg/m2
Plywood, per 25 mm thickness	15.00	kg/m2
Rendering, cement and sand (1:3):		
12 mm thick	27.70	kg/m2
18 mm thick	41.60	kg/m2
Sand:		
dry	1600.00	kg/m3
moist	1280.00	kg/m3
Screeds, cement and sand (1:3):		
25 mm	57.70	kg/m2
50 mm	115.40	kg/m2
Slate Westmorland	2880.00	kg/m3
Soil, compact:		
sands and gravels	2080.0	kg/m3
silts and clays	2000.0	kg/m3
Steel, mild and cast	7850.0	kg/m3
Stone, natural:		
Bath	2080.0	kg/m3
Darley Dale	2320.0	kg/m3
Granite, Cornish	2640.0	kg/m3
Mantle	2720.0	kg/m3
Portland	2240.0	kg/m3
Terrazzo paving:		
per 25 mm thickness	49.5	kg/m2
Thatch, Norfolk reed:		
per 300 mm thickness	40.9	kg/m2
Timber:		
softwoods	500.0	kg/m3
hardwoods	800.0	kg/m3
Water	1000.0	kg/m3
Wood wool slabs:		
per 25 mm thickness	14.4	kg/m2

Dispute Resolution Service

Diploma in Adjudication in the Construction Industry

Comprised of four units, this qualification is designed for those **seeking to become an adjudicator**, and provides a pathway towards potential entry onto the **RICS Panel of Adjudicators**.

With a focus on contract and tort law and how they apply to adjudication, this course is designed to prepare you to progress to practice as an adjudicator. This course is suitable for those with experience in dispute resolution procedures with an understanding of the general principles of construction adjudication. The course content will focus on the format and content of an enforceable decision.

Learning Outcomes:

- Knowledge and understanding of the nature of law and its' place in society
- How the law of contract is applied to the practice of adjudication
- How the law of tort is applied to the practice of adjudication
- The practical application in the production of an enforceable decision.

Attainment of the learning outcomes will be assessed by a case study, whereby candidates will be required to produce an enforceable reasoned decision, based on material supplied in the case study.

To book or for further information, please contact DRS Training;

t **02476 868 584**　　e **drstraining@rics.org**　　w **rics.org/drs**

Trade & Government Information

BCIS
Independent cost information
for the built environment

CONSTRUCTION

LESS DESK TIME
MORE FREE TIME

THE REVOLUTION OF THE PRICE BOOK IS HERE
BCIS ONLINE RATES DATABASE

What the service can do for you:

Accuracy: You can benchmark against 18500 separate Supply Prices of which there are over 9,000 material costs and over 8000 specialist prices collected from independent suppliers. It will ensure that your information is accurate and reliable, reducing the margin of error.

Futureproof: You can adjust the prices using industry standard BCIS Tender Price Index and Location Factor adjustments so you can forecast your figures for projects up to two years ahead, putting you a step ahead of your competitors. It makes your project cost predictions more robust.

Value for money: It provides an expert opinion at your fingertips to give you the confidence that you are not over or underestimating quotes and costs. It could mean the difference between winning or losing a tender or being over charged for your works.

Saves time: The easy navigation system helps you find what you are looking for quickly and effortlessly. Add the information you want to a list for download to Excel.

Flexible: With a subscription to suit your job, you can access a variety of new and historical price data. This allows you to build up your own prices from individual elements so you can make your own decisions about how you cost your projects.

Customise: Adjust your data to your location and time frame and it will do the calculations for you. You can download the results, keep track of your adjustments and reduce your margin of error.

Portable: This service can be accessed on your computer and just as easily on your iPad or netbook on site.

Comprehensive: Everything you need is in one place; you have a full library of information at your disposal.

Offering immediate online access to independent BCIS resource rates data, quantity surveyors and others in the construction industry can have all the information needed to compile and check estimates on their desktops. You won't need to worry about being able to lay your hands on the office copy of the latest price books, all of the information is now easily accessible online.

For a **FREE TRIAL** of BCIS online rates database register at
www.bcis.co.uk/ordbdemo

BCIS is the Building Cost Information Service of **RICS** the mark of property professionalism worldwide

TRADE AND GOVERNMENT ORGANISATIONS

Asbestos Removal Contractors Association (ARCA)
Unit 1, Stretton Business Park 2
Brunel Drive
Stretton
Burton Upon Trent
Staffordshire
DE13 0BY

☎: 01283 566467
🖷: 01283 505770
✉: info@arca.org.uk
🕸: www.arca.org.uk

Association of Plumbing and Heating Contractors (APHC)
12 The Pavilions
Cranmore Drive
Solihull
B90 4SB

☎: 0121 711 5030
🖷: 0121 705 7871
🕸: www.competentpersonsscheme.co.uk

ASTA BEAB Certification Services
1 Station View
Guildford
Surrey
GU1 4JY

☎: 01483 455466
🖷: 01483 455477
🕸: www.engineeringtalk.com

British Approvals for Fire Equipment (BAFE)
Bridges 2
The Fire Service College
London Road
Morton in Marsh
Gloucestershire
GL56 0RH

☎: 0844 335 0897
🖷: 01608 653359
✉: info@bafe.org.uk
🕸: www.bafe.org.uk

British Approvals Service for Cables (BASEC)
23 Presley Way
Crownhill
Milton Keynes
MK8 0ES

☎: 01908 267300
🖷: 01908 267255
✉: mail@basec.org.uk
🕸: www.basec.org.uk

British Architectural Library
Royal Institute of British Architects (RIBA)
66 Portland Place
London
W1B 1AD

☎: 020 7580 5533
🖷: 020 7 255 1541
✉: info@riba.org
🕸: www.architecture.com

British Board of Agrément (BBA)
Bucknalls Lane
Garston
Watford
Herts
WD25 9BA

☎: 01923 665300
🖷: 01923 665301
✉: contact@bba.star.co.uk
🕸: www.bbacerts.co.uk

British Constructional Steelwork Association Ltd (BCSA)
4 Whitehall Court
Westminster
London
SW1A 2ES

☎: 020 7839 8566
🖷: 020 7976 1634
✉: gillian.mitchell@steelconstruction.org
🕸: www.steelconstruction.org

British Pest Control Association (BPCA)
4A Mallard Way
Pride Park
Derby
DE24 8GX

☎: 01332 294288
✉: enquiry@bpca.org.uk
🕸: www.bpca.org.uk

Building & Engineering Services Association (B&ES)
ESCA House
34 Palace Court
Bayswater
London
W2 4JG

☎: 020 7313 4900
🖷: 020 7727 9268
✉: contact@b-es.org
★: www.b-es.org

Builders Merchants Federation (BMF)
15 Soho Square
London
W1D 3HL

☎: 020 7439 1753
🖷: 020 7734 2766
✉: info@bmf.org.uk
★: www.bmf.org.uk

Building and Allied Trades Joint Industrial Council
Gordon Fisher House
14 - 15 Great James Street
London
WC1N 3DP

☎: 020 7242 7583
🖷: 020 7404 0296
✉: central@fmb.org.uk
★: www.fmb.org.uk

Building Cost Information Service (BCIS)
Parliament Square
London
SW1P 3AD

☎: 0870 333 1600
🖷: 020 7695 1501
✉: contact@bcis.co.uk
★: www.bcis.co.uk

Building Maintenance Information (BMI)
Parliament Square
London
SW1P 3AD

☎: 0870 333 1600
✉: contact@bcis.co.uk
★: www.bcis.co.uk

BRE
Orion House
Bucknalls Lane
Garston
Watford
WD25 9XX

☎:01923 664000
✉: enquiries@bre.co.uk
★: www.bre.co.uk

BRE Scotland
Orion House
Scottish Enterprise Technology Park
East Kilbride
Glasgow
G75 0RZ

☎: 01355 576200
🖷: 01355 576210
✉: eastkilbride@bre.co.uk
★: www.bre.co.uk

BSRIA Ltd
Old Bracknell Lane West
Bracknell
Berkshire
RG12 7AH

☎: 01344 465600
🖷: 01344 465626
✉: bsria@bsria.co.uk
★: www.bsria.co.uk

Chartered Institute of Arbitrators (CIArb)
12 Bloomsbury Square
London
WC1A 2LP

☎: 020 7421 7444
🖷: 020 7404 4023
✉: info@ciarb.org
★: www.ciarb.org

Chartered Institute of Architectural Technologists (CIAT)
397 City Road
London
EC1V 1NH

☎: 020 7278 2206
🖷: 020 7837 3194
✉: info@ciat.org.uk
★: www.ciat.org.uk

Chartered Institute of Building (CIOB)
Englemere
Kings Ride
Ascot
Berkshire
SL5 7TB

☎:01344 630700
🖷: 01344 630777
✉: reception@ciob.org.uk
🕸: www.ciob.org.uk

Chartered Institution of Building Service Engineers (CIBSE)
222 Balham High Road
London
SW12 9BS

☎: 020 8675 5211
🖷: 020 8675 5449
✉: enquiries@cibse.org
🕸: www.cibse.org

CBI
Centre Point
103 New Oxford Street
London
WC1A 1DU

☎: 020 7379 7400
🕸: www.cbi.org.uk

Construction Industry Research & Information Association (CIRIA)
Classic House
174-180 Old Street
London
EC1V 9BP

☎: 020 7549 3300
🖷: 020 7253 0523
✉: enquiries@ciria.org
🕸: www.ciria.org

Construction Industry Training Board (CITB)
Head Office
Bircham Newton
Kings Lynn
Norfolk
PE31 6RH

☎: 0344 994 4455
🖷: 0300 456 7587
✉: levy.grant@cskills.org
🕸: www.cskills.org

Construction Plant Hire Association
27-28 Newbury Street
Barbican
London
EC1A 7HU

☎: 020 7796 3366
🖷: 020 7796 3399
✉: enquiries@cpa.uk.net
🕸: www.cpa.uk.net

Construction Products Association
The Building Centre
26 Store Street
London
WC1E 7BT

☎: 020 7323 3770
🖷: 020 7323 0307
✉: enquiries@constructionproducts.org.uk
🕸: www.constructionproducts.org.uk

Contract Flooring Association Limited (CFA)
4c St Mary's Place
The Lace Market
Nottingham
NG1 1PH

☎: 0115 941 1126
🖷: 0115 941 2238
✉: info@cfa.org.uk
🕸: www.cfa.org.uk

Electrical Contractors Association (ECA)
ESCA House
34 Palace Court
Bayswater
London
W2 4HY

☎: 020 7313 4800
🖷: 020 7221 7344
✉: info@eca.co.uk
🕸: www.eca.co.uk

Electrical Contractors Association of Scotland (SELECT)
The Walled Garden
Bush Estate
Midlothian
EH26 0SB

☎: 0131 445 5577
🖷: 0131 445 5548
✉: admin@select.org.uk
🕸: www.select.org.uk

Federation of Master Builders (FMB)
Gordon Fisher House
14-15 Great James Street
London
WC1N 3DP

☎: 020 7242 7583
🖷: 020 7404 0296
✉: central@fmb.org.uk
★: www.fmb.org.uk

Fire Industry Association (FIA)
Tudor House
Kingsway Business Park
Oldfield Road
Hampton
Middlesex
TW12 2HD

☎: 020 3 166 5002
🖷: 020 8 941 0972
✉: info@fia.uk.com
★: www.fia.uk.com

Gas Safe Register
PO Box 6804
Basingstoke
RG24 4NB

☎: 0800 408 5500
✉: enquiries@gassaferegister.co.uk
★: www.gassaferegister.co.uk

Glass and Glazing Federation (GGF)
54 St Ayres Street
London
SE1 1EU

☎: 020 7939 9101
🖷: 0870 042 4266
✉: info@ggf.org.uk
★: www.ggf.org.uk

Institution of Civil Engineers (ICE)
1 Great George Street
Westminster
London
SW1P 3AA

☎: 020 7222 7722
🖷: 020 7222 7500
✉: library@ice.org.uk (library Enq's only)
★: www.ice.org.uk

Institution of Gas Engineers and Managers (IGEM)
IGEM House
High Street
Kegworth
Derbyshire
DE74 2DA

☎: 0844 375 4436
🖷: 01509 678 198
✉: general@igem.org.uk
★: www.igem.org.uk

Joint Industry Board for the Electrical Contracting Industry (JIB)
Kingswood House
47-51 Sidcup Hill
Sidcup
Kent
DA14 6HP

☎: 020 8302 0031
🖷: 020 8309 1103
✉: administration@jib.org.uk
★: www.jib.org.uk

Joint Industry Board for Plumbing and Mechanical Engineering Services in England and Wales (JIB-PMES)
PO Box 267
St Neots
Cambridgeshire
PE19 9DN

☎: 01480 476925
🖷: 01480 403081
✉: info@jib-pmes.org.uk
★: www.jib-pmes.org.uk

LASSCO
Brunswick House
30 Wandsworth Road
Vauxhall
London
SW8 2LG

☎: 020 7394 2100
🖷: 020 7501 7797
✉: brunswick@lassco.co.uk
★: www.lassco.co.uk

National Approval Council for Security Systems (NACOSS) / National Security Inspectorate (NSI)
Sentinel House
5 Reform Road
Maidenhead
Berkshire
SL6 8BY

☎: 01628 637512
🖷: 01628 773367
✉: nsi@nsi.org.uk
★: www.nsi.org.uk

National Association of Scaffolding Contractors (NASC)
4ᵗʰ Floor
Bridewell Place
London
EC4V 6AP

☎: 020 7822 7400
🖷: 020 7822 7401
✉: enquiries@nasc.org.uk
🕮: www.nasc.org.uk

National Federation of Builders Limited (NFB)
B & CE Building
Manor Royal
Crawley
West Sussex
RH10 9QP

☎: 08450 578160
🖷: 08450 578161
✉: national@builders.org.uk
🕮: www.builders.org.uk

National House Building Council (NHBC)
NHBC House
Davey Avenue
Knowlhill
Milton Keynes
MK5 8FP

☎: 0844 633 1000
🖷: 01908 747255
✉: esupport@nhbc.co.uk
🕮: www.nhbc.co.uk

National Inspection Council for Electrical Installation Contracting (NICEIC)
Warwick House
Houghton Hall Park
Houghton Regis
Dunstable
LU5 5ZX

☎: 0870 013 0382
🖷: 01582 556024
✉: enquiries@niceic.com
🕮: www.niceic.com

National Statistics Library and Information Service
Government Buildings
Cardiff Road
Newport
NP10 8XG

☎: 0845 601 3034
🖷: 01633 652747
✉: info@statistics.gov.uk
🕮: www.statistics.gov.uk

Natural England
Foundry House
3 Millsands
Riverside Exchange
Sheffield
S3 8NH

☎: 0845 600 3078
🖷: 0300 060 1622
✉: enquiries@naturalengland.org.uk
🕮: www.naturalengland.org.uk

Painting & Decorating Association
32 Coton Road
Nuneaton
Warwickshire
CV11 5TW

☎: 024 7635 3776
🖷: 024 7635 4513
✉: info@paintingdecoratingassopciation.co.uk
🕮: www.paintingdecoratingassociation.co.uk

Plastics Window Federation
Federation House
85-87 Wellington Street
Luton
LU1 5AF

☎: 01582 456147
🖷: 01582 412215
✉: ins@pwfed.co.uk
🕮: www.pwfed.co.uk

Royal Incorporation of Architects in Scotland (RIAS)
15 Rutland Square
Edinburgh
EH1 2BE

☎: 0131 229 7545
🖷: 0131 228 2188
✉: info@rias.org.uk
🕮: www.rias.org.uk

Royal Institute of British Architects (RIBA)
66 Portland Place
London
W1B 1AD

☎: 020 7580 5533
🖷: 020 7255 1541
✉: info@riba.org
🕮: www.architecture.com

Royal Institution of Chartered Surveyors (RICS)
Surveyor Court
Westwood Way
Coventry
CV4 8JE

☎: 0870 3331600
🖷: 020 7334 3811
✉: contactrics@rics.org.uk
🕸: www.rics.org

Royal Town Planning Institute (RTPI)
41 Botolph Lane
London
EC3R 8DL

☎: 020 7929 9494
🖷: 020 7929 9490
✉: online@rtpi.org.uk
🕸: www.rtpi.org.uk

Scottish Building Federation
Crichton House
4 Crichton's Close
Holyrood, Edinburgh
EH7 7SH

☎: 0131 556 8866
✉: info@scottish-building.co.uk
🕸: www.scottish-building.co.uk

Scottish Decorators' Federation
Castlecraig Business Park
Players Road
Stirling
FK7 7SH

☎: 01786 448838
🖷: 01786 450541
✉: info@scottishdecorators.co.uk
🕸: www.scottishdecorators.co.uk

Scottish and Northern Ireland Plumbing Employers Federation (SNIPEF)
Bellevue House
22 Hopetoun Street
Edinburgh
EH7 4GH

☎: 0131 556 0600
🖷: 0131 557 8409
✉: info@snipef.org
🕸: www.snipef.org

SSAIB
7 – 11 Earsdon Road
West Monkseaton
Whitley Bay
Tyne & Wear
NE25 9SX

☎: 0191 296 3242
🖷: 0191 296 2667
✉: ssaib@ssaib.co.uk
🕸: www.ssaib.co.uk

Society of Construction Law (UK)
The Cottage
Bullfurlong Lane
Burbage
Hinkley
LE10 2HQ

☎: 07730 474074
✉: admin@scl.org.uk
🕸: www.scl.org.uk

The Association of Building Engineers (ABE)
Lutens House
Billing Brook Road
Weston Favell
Northampton
Northamptonshire
NN3 8NW

☎: 0845 126 1058
🖷: 01604 784220
✉: building.engineers@abe.org.uk
🕸: www.abe.org.uk

The British Library
St Pancras
96 Euston Road
London
NW1 2DB

☎: 0843 2081144
✉: Customer-Services@bl.uk
🕸: www.bl.uk

The British Plastics Federation (BPF)
5 - 6 Bath Place
Rivington Street
London
EC2A 3JE

☎: 020 7457 5000
🖷: 020 7457 5020
✉: reception@bpf.co.uk
🕸: www.bpf.co.uk

The Building Centre (Exhibitions and Bookshop)
26 Store Street
London
WC1E 7BT

☎: 020 7692 4000
🖷: 020 7580 9641
✉: reception@buildingcentre.co.uk
🕸: www.buildingcentre.co.uk

The Chartered Institute of Highways and Transportation (CIHT)
19 Britannia Walk
London
N1 7JE

☎: 020 7336 1555
🖷: 020 7336 1556
✉: info@ciht.org.uk
🕸: www.ciht.org.uk

The Guild of Master Craftsmen
Castle Place
166 High Street
Lewes
East Sussex
BN7 1XU

☎: 01273 478449
🖷: 01273 478606
✉: theguild@thegmcgroup.com
🕸: www.guildmc.com

The National Federation of Roofing Contractors Ltd (NFRC)
Roofing House
31 Worship Street
London
EC2A 2DY

☎: 020 7638 7663
🖷: 020 7256 2125
✉: info@nfrc.co.uk
🕸: www.nfrc.co.uk

Town and Country Planning Association (TCPA)
17 Carlton House Terrace
London
SW1Y 5AS

☎: 020 7930 8903
🖷: 020 7930 3280
✉: tcpa@tcpa.org.uk
🕸: www.tcpa.org.uk

The Wood Protection Association
5 Flemming Court
Castleford
West Yorkshire
WF10 5HW

☎: 01977 558274
✉: info@wood-protection.org
🕸: www.wood-protection.org

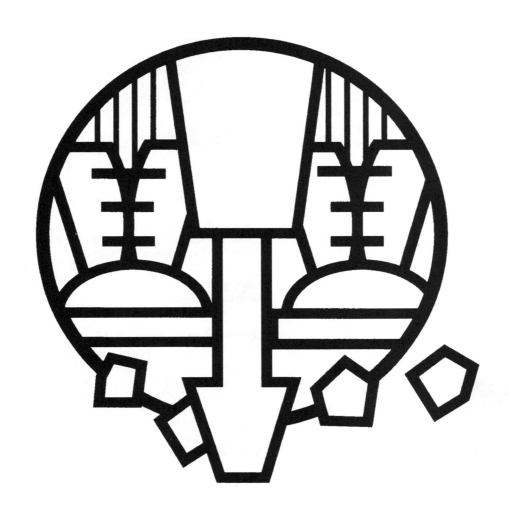

Dayworks

Independent cost information
for the built environment

Comprehensive Building Price Book 2013
Major and Minor Works dataset

The Major Works dataset focuses predominantly on large 'new build' projects reflecting the economies of scale found in these forms of construction. The Minor Works Estimating Dataset focuses on small to medium sized 'new build' projects reflecting the increase in costs brought about the reduced output, less discounts, increased carriage and supervision, to the similar items in the Major Works dataset. The dataset is presented in trade order. Revised and reworked items in underpinning composites; flue linings and rainwater goods.

Item code: 19215   **Price: £165.99**

SMM7 Estimating Price Book 2013

The SMM7 Estimating dataset focuses predominantly on large 'new build' projects reflecting the economies of scale found in these forms of construction. The dataset is presented in SMM7 grouping and order in accordance with the Common Arrangement of Work Sections. It is compiled using the latest independent costing information from manufacturers, material and plant suppliers, legislation effects and working rule agreements. Revised and reworked items in underpinning composites; flue linings and rainwater goods.

Item code: 19216   **Price: £139.99**

Alterations and Refurbishment Price Book 2013

The Alterations & Refurbishment dataset focuses on small to medium sized projects, generally working within an existing building and reflecting the increase in costs brought about the reduction in output, smaller discounts, increased carriage, increased supervision, and less productivity brought about by smaller economies of scale, increased production costs, more difficult access and the possibility of working in occupied premises. The dataset is presented in trade order. Revised and reworked items in underpinning composites; flue linings and rainwater goods.

Item code: 19217   **Price £109.99**

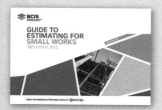

BCIS Guide to Estimating for Small Works 2012

The BCIS Guide to Estimating for Small Works 2012 is a unique dataset which shows the true power of resource based estimating. A set of composite built-up measured items are used to build up priced estimates for a large number of common specification extensions. The intention is to show estimating techniques in use and allow users to build up accurate estimates for their own projects, simply and easily, with up-to-date and independent cost information.

Item code: 19064   **Price: £59.99**

BCIS Painting and Decorating Price Book 2012

The BCIS Painting and Decorating dataset is the most handy pricing tool available to the painting and decorating sector of the industry, suitable for all projects needing more than a 'guess-timate'. Using this dataset a more accurate calculation based quotation or variation can be prepared. From these calculations an assessment of labour, plant and material content can be produced. This in turn enables the contractor to negotiate discounts on known material requirements and the effect of this workload on the availability of labour.

Item code: 19065   **Price: £39.99**

For more information call **0870 333 1600** email **contact@bcis.co.uk** or visit **www.bcis.co.uk**

BCIS is the Building Cost Information Service of **RICS** — the mark of property professionalism worldwide

DAYWORK

DEFINITION OF PRIME COST OF DAYWORK CARRIED OUT UNDER A BUILDING CONTRACT

There is no mandatory definition of Prime Cost of Daywork and contractors are not in any way debarred from defining Prime Cost and rendering their accounts for work carried out on a Daywork basis in any way they choose. Building owners/employers are advised to reach agreement with contractors on the Definition of Prime Cost to be used, prior to issuing instructions for work.

BUILD UP OF STANDARD HOURLY BASE RATES FOR DAYWORK USE

Model calculation of standard working hours per year

52 weeks at 39 hours	=	2028
Less 163 hours annual holiday		
63 hours public holiday	=	226

Net annual working hours	1802 hours	

Calculation of hourly rate

This calculation is based on the BATJIC agreed pay scales which become operative as of the 12th September 2011. Due to the current economic conditions no further settlements are expected during 2012.

		Craftsman		**Labourer**
BASIC AND GUARANTEED WAGES:	46.2 weeks at 418.47	19333.31	46.2 weeks at 310.44	14342.33
EXTRA PAYMENTS:	where applicable	-	where applicable	-
SUB TOTAL:		19333.31		14342.33
NATIONAL INSURANCE:	13.80% above ST	1634.65	13.80% above ST	945.90
WELFARE BENEFIT:	52 stamps at 11.00	572.00	52 stamps at 11.00	572.00
HOLIDAYS WITH PAY:	12.5% of PAYE	2416.66	12.5% of PAYE	1792.79
TRAINING ALLOWANCE:	0.50% of (PAYE + Hol)	108.75	0.50% of (PAYE + Hol)	80.68
ANNUAL LABOUR COST:		24065.37		17733.70
HOURLY BASE RATE:	**(divided by 1802)**	**13.35**	**(divided by 1802)**	**9.84**

Notes:
1. The RICS/BCIS calculations for the Guide to Daywork Rates 4th Edition provides the principles of calculation for the rates shown.
2. As of June 10th 2002 the Holiday Credit System ceased and was replaced with the Building and Civil Engineering Benefits Scheme - Holiday Pay Scheme. This sets out the percentage of PAYE to allow for holiday pay.

SCHEDULE OF BASIC PLANT CHARGES

Sixth Revision – July 2010
Reproduced with permission of The Royal Institution of Chartered Surveyors

Explanatory Notes
1. The rates in the Schedule are intended to apply solely to daywork carried out under and incidental to a Building Contract. They are NOT intended to apply to:
    (i) Jobbing or any other work carried out as a main or separate contract; or
    (ii) Work carried out after the date of commencement of the Defects Liability Period.
2. The rates apply to plant and machinery not hired by the Contractor and already on site. Where the plant is not hired, and needs to be bought to site specifically for work carried out on daywork basis, allowance should be made for transport/delivery to and from site, and erection and dismantling where applicable.
3. The rates, unless otherwise stated, include the cost of fuel and power of every description, lubricating oils, grease, maintenance, sharpening of tools, replacement of spare parts, all consumable stores, and licences and insurances applicable to items of plant.
4. The rates, unless otherwise stated, do not include the cost of drivers and attendants.
5. The rates do not include for any possible discounts which may be given to the Contractor if the plant or machinery was hired.
6. The rates are base costs and may be subject to the overall adjustment for price movement, overheads and profit quoted by the Contractor prior to the placing of the Contract.
7. The rates should be applied to the time during which the plant is actually engaged in daywork.
8. Whether or not plant is chargeable on daywork depends on the daywork agreement in use and the inclusion of an item of plant in this Schedule does not necessarily indicate that the item is chargeable.
9. Rates for plant not included in the Schedule and not hired, shall be settled at prices which are reasonably related to the rates in the Schedule, having regard to any overall adjustment quoted by the Contractor in the Conditions of Contract.

Item of Plant	Size/Rating	Unit	Rate/hr
PUMPS			
Mobile Pumps			
Including pump hoses, valves and strainers etc.			
Diaphragm	50 mm dia.	Each	1.17
Diaphragm	76 mm dia.	Each	1.89
Diaphragm	102 mm dia.	Each	3.54
Submersible	50 mm dia.	Each	0.76
Submersible	76 mm dia.	Each	0.86
Submersible	102 mm dia.	Each	1.03
Induced flow	50 mm dia.	Each	0.77
Induced flow	76 mm dia.	Each	1.67
Centrifugal, self priming	25 mm dia.	Each	1.30
Centrifugal, self priming	50 mm dia.	Each	1.92
Centrifugal, self priming	75 mm dia.	Each	2.74
Centrifugal, self priming	102 mm dia.	Each	3.35
Centrifugal, self priming	152 mm dia.	Each	4.27
SCAFFOLDING, SHORING, FENCING			
Complete Scaffolding			
Mobile working tower, single width	2.0 m x 0.72 m base x 7.45 m high	Each	3.36
Mobile working tower, single width	2.0 m x 0.72 m base x 8.84 m high	Each	3.79
Mobile working tower, double width	2.0 m x 1.35 m base x 7.45 m high	Each	3.79

Item of Plant	Size/Rating	Unit	Rate/hr
Complete Scaffolding (Continued)			
Mobile working tower, double width	2.0 m x 1.35 m base x 15.8 m high	Each	7.13
Chimney scaffold, single unit		Each	1.92
Chimney scaffold, twin unit		Each	3.59
Push along access platform	1.63 m – 3.1 m	Each	5.00
Push along access platform	1.8 m x 0.70 m	Each	1.79
Trestles			
Trestle, adjustable	Any height	Pair	0.14
Trestle, painters	1.8 m high	Pair	0.31
Trestle, painters	2.4 m high	Pair	0.36
Shoring, Planking and Strutting			
'Acrow' adjustable prop	Sizes up to 4.9 m (open)	Each	0.06
'Strong boy' support attachment		Each	0.22
Adjustable trench struts	Sizes up to 1.67 m (open)	Each	0.16
Trench sheet		Metre	0.03
Backhoe trench box	Base unit	Each	1.23
Backhoe trench box	Top unit	Each	0.87
Temporary Fencing			
Including block and coupler			
Site fencing steel grid panel	3.5 m x 2.0 m	Each	0.05
Anti-climb site steel grid fence panel	3.5 m x 2.0 m	Each	0.08
Solid panel Heras	2.0 m x 2.0 m	Each	0.09
Pedestrian gate		Each	0.36
Roadway gate		Each	0.60
LIFTING APPLIANCES AND CONVEYORS			
Cranes			
Mobile cranes			
Rates are inclusive of drivers			
Lorry mounted, telescopic jib			
Two wheel drive	5 tonnes	Each	19.00
Two wheel drive	8 tonnes	Each	42.00
Two wheel drive	10 tonnes	Each	50.00
Two wheel drive	12 tonnes	Each	77.00
Two wheel drive	20 tonnes	Each	89.69
Four wheel drive	18 tonnes	Each	46.51
Four wheel drive	25 tonnes	Each	35.90
Four wheel drive	30 tonnes	Each	38.46
Four wheel drive	45 tonnes	Each	46.15
Four wheel drive	50 tonnes	Each	53.85
Four wheel drive	60 tonnes	Each	61.54
Four wheel drive	70 tonnes	Each	71.79
Static tower cranes			
Rates inclusive of driver			

Note: *Capacity equals maximum lift in tonnes x maximum radius at which it can be lifted*

Item of Plant	Capacity (m.t) up to	Height under hook above ground (m) up to	Unit	Rate/hr
Tower crane	30	22	Each	22.23
Tower crane	40	22	Each	26.62
Tower crane	40	30	Each	33.33
Tower crane	50	22	Each	29.16
Tower crane	60	22	Each	35.90
Tower crane	60	36	Each	35.90
Tower crane	70	22	Each	41.03
Tower crane	80	22	Each	39.12
Tower crane	90	42	Each	37.18
Tower crane	110	36	Each	47.62
Tower crane	140	36	Each	55.77
Tower crane	170	36	Each	64.11
Tower crane	200	36	Each	71.95
Tower crane	250	36	Each	84.77
Tower crane with luffing jib	30	25	Each	22.23
Tower crane with luffing jib	40	30	Each	26.62
Tower crane with luffing jib	50	30	Each	29.16
Tower crane with luffing jib	60	36	Each	41.03
Tower crane with luffing jib	65	30	Each	33.13
Tower crane with luffing jib	80	22	Each	48.72
Tower crane with luffing jib	100	45	Each	48.72
Tower crane with luffing jib	125	30	Each	53.85
Tower crane with luffing jib	160	50	Each	53.85
Tower crane with luffing jib	200	50	Each	74.36
Tower crane with luffing jib	300	60	Each	100.00
Crane Equipment			
Muck tipping skip	Up to 200 litres	Each	0.67
Muck tipping skip	500 litres	Each	0.82
Muck tipping skip	750 litres	Each	1.08
Muck tipping skip	1000 litres	Each	1.28
Muck tipping skip	1500 litres	Each	1.41
Muck tipping skip	2000 litres	Each	1.67
Mortar skips	250 litres, plastic	Each	0.41
Mortar skips	350 litres, steel	Each	0.77
Boat skips	250 litres	Each	0.92
Boat skips	500 litres	Each	1.08
Boat skips	750 litres	Each	1.23
Boat skip	1000 litres	Each	1.38
Boat skip	1500 litres	Each	1.64
Boat skip	2000 litres	Each	1.90
Boat skip	3000 litres	Each	2.82
Boat skip	4000 litres	Each	3.23
Master flow skip	250 litres	Each	0.77

Item of Plant	Size/Rating	Unit	Rate/hr
Crane Equipment (Continued)			
Master flow skip	500 litres	Each	1.03
Master flow skip	750 litres	Each	1.28
Master flow skip	1000 litres	Each	1.44
Master flow skip	1500 litres	Each	1.69
Master flow skip	2000 litres	Each	1.85
Grand master flow skip	500 litres	Each	1.28
Grand master flow skip	750 litres	Each	1.64
Grand master flow skip	1000 litres	Each	1.69
Grand master flow skip	1500 litres	Each	1.95
Grand master flow skip	2000 litres	Each	2.21
Cone flow skip	500 litres	Each	1.33
Cone flow skip	1000 litres	Each	1.69
Geared rollover skip	500 litres	Each	1.28
Geared rollover skip	750 litres	Each	1.64
Geared rollover skip	1000 litres	Each	1.69
Geared rollover skip	1500 litres	Each	1.95
Geared rollover skip	2000 litres	Each	2.21
Multi skip, rope operated	200 mm outlet size, 500 litres	Each	1.49
Multi skip, rope operated	200 mm outlet size, 750 litres	Each	1.64
Multi skip, rope operated	200 mm outlet size, 1000 litres	Each	1.74
Multi skip, rope operated	200 mm outlet size, 1500 litres	Each	2.00
Multi skip, rope operated	200 mm outlet size, 2000 litres	Each	2.26
Multi skip, man riding	200 mm outlet size, 1000 litres	Each	2.00
Multi skip	4 point lifting frame	Each	0.90
Multi skip	Chain brothers	Set	0.87
<u>Crane Accessories</u>			
Multi-purpose crane forks	1.5 and 2 tonnes S.W.L.	Each	1.13
Self levelling crane forks		Each	1.28
Man cage	1 man, 230 kg S.W.L.	Each	1.90
Man cage	2 man, 500 kg S.W.L.	Each	1.95
Man cage	4 man, 750 kg S.W.L.	Each	2.15
Man cage	8 man, 1000 kg S.W.L.	Each	3.33
Stretcher cage	500 kg, S.W.L.	Each	2.69
Goods carrying cage	1500 kg, S.W.L.	Each	1.33
Goods carrying cage	3000 kg, S.W.L.	Each	1.85
Builders' skip lifting cradle	12 tonnes, S.W.L.	Each	2.31
Board/pallet fork	1600 kg, S.W.L.	Each	1.90
Gas bottle carrier	500 kg, S.W.L.	Each	0.92
Hoists			
Scaffold hoists	200 kg	Each	2.46
Rack and pinion (goods only)	500 kg	Each	4.56
Rack and pinion (goods only)	1100 kg	Each	5.90
Rack and pinion (goods and passenger)	8 person, 800 kg	Each	7.44
Rack and pinion (goods and passenger)	14 person, 1400 kg	Each	8.72
Wheelbarrow chain sling		Each	1.67
Conveyors			
<u>Belt conveyors</u>			
Conveyor	8 m long x 450 mm wide	Each	5.90
Miniveyor, control box and loading hopper	3 m unit	Each	4.49
<u>Other Conveying Equipment</u>			
Wheelbarrow		Each	0.62
Hydraulic superlift		Each	4.56
Pavac slab lifter (tile hoist)		Each	4.49
High lift pallet truck		Each	3.08

Lifting Trucks	Payload	Maximum Lift		
Fork lift, two wheel drive	1100 kg	up to 3.0 m	Each	5.64
Fork lift, two wheel drive	2540 kg	up to 3.7 m	Each	5.64
Fork lift, four wheel drive	1524 kg	up to 6.0 m	Each	5.64
Fork lift, four wheel drive	2600 kg	up to 5.4 m	Each	7.44
Fork lift, four wheel drive	4000 kg	Up to 17 m	Each	10.77

Lifting Platforms			
Hydraulic platform (Cherry picker)	9 m	Each	4.62
Hydraulic platform (Cherry picker)	12 m	Each	7.56
Hydraulic platform (Cherry picker)	15 m	Each	10.13
Hydraulic platform (Cherry picker)	17 m	Each	15.63
Hydraulic platform (Cherry picker)	20 m	Each	18.13
Hydraulic platform (Cherry picker)	25.6 m	Each	32.38
Scissor lift	7.6 m, electric	Each	3.85
Scissor lift	7.8 m, electric	Each	5.13
Scissor lift	9.7 m, electric	Each	4.23
Scissor lift	10 m, diesel	Each	6.41
Telescopic handler	7 m, 2 tonnes	Each	5.13
Telescopic handler	13 m, 3 tonnes	Each	7.18
Lifting and Jacking Gear			
Pipe winch including gantry	1 tonne	Set	1.92
Pipe winch including gantry	3 tonnes	Set	3.21
Chain block	1 tonne	Each	0.35
Chain block	2 tonnes	Each	0.58
Chain block	5 tonnes	Each	1.14
Pull lift (Tirfor winch)	1 tonne	Each	0.64
Pull lift (Tirfor winch)	1.6 tonnes	Each	0.90
Pull lift (Tirfor winch)	3.2 tonnes	Each	1.15
Brother or chain sling, two legs	not exceeding 3.1 tonnes	Set	0.21
Brother or chain sling, two legs	not exceeding 4.25 tonnes	Set	0.31
Brother or chain sling, four legs	not exceeding 11.2 tonnes	Set	1.09
CONSTRUCTION VEHICLES			
Lorries *(Plated lorries Rates are inclusive of driver)*			
Platform lorry	7.5 tonnes	Each	16.21
Platform lorry	17 tonnes	Each	22.90
Platform lorry	24 tonnes	Each	30.68

Item of Plant	Size/Rating	Unit	Rate/hr
Lorries (Continued)			
Extra for lorry with crane attachment	up to 2.5 tonnes	Each	3.25
Extra for lorry with crane attachment	up to 5 tonnes	Each	6.00
Extra for lorry with crane attachment	up to 7.5 tonnes	Each	9.10
Tipper lorries *(Rates are inclusive of driver)*			
Tipper lorry	up to 11 tonnes	Each	15.78
Tipper lorry	up to 17 tonnes	Each	23.95
Tipper lorry	up to 25 tonnes	Each	31.35
Tipper lorry	up to 31 tonnes	Each	37.79
Dumpers			
Site use only (excluding tax, insurance and extra cost of DERV etc. when operating on highway)	Makers capacity		
Two wheel drive	1 tonne	Each	1.71
Four wheel drive	2 tonnes	Each	2.43
Four wheel drive	3 tonnes	Each	2.44
Four wheel drive	5 tonnes	Each	3.08
Four wheel drive	6 tonnes	Each	3.85
Four wheel drive	9 tonnes	Each	5.65
Tracked	0.5 tonnes	Each	3.33
Tracked	1.5 tonnes	Each	4.23
Tracked	3.0 tonnes	Each	8.33
Tracked	6.0 tonnes	Each	16.03
Dumper Trucks *(Rates are inclusive of drivers)*			
Dumper truck	up to 15 tonnes	Each	28.56
Dumper truck	up to 17 tonnes	Each	32.82
Dumper truck	up to 23 tonnes	Each	54.64
Dumper truck	up to 30 tonnes	Each	63.50
Dumper truck	up to 35 tonnes	Each	73.02
Dumper truck	up to 40 tonnes	Each	87.84
Dumper truck	up to 50 tonnes	Each	133.44
Tractors			
<u>Agricultural type</u>			
Wheeled, rubber-clad tyred	up to 40 kW	Each	8.63
Wheeled, rubber-clad tyred	up to 90 kW	Each	25.31
Wheeled, rubber-clad tyred	up to 140 kW	Each	36.49
<u>Crawler tractors</u>			
With bull or angle dozer	up to 70 kW	Each	29.38
With bull or angle dozer	up to 85 kW	Each	38.63
With bull or angle dozer	up to 100 kW	Each	52.59
With bull or angle dozer	up to 115 kW	Each	55.85
With bull or angle dozer	up to 135 kW	Each	60.43
With bull or angle dozer	up to 185 kW	Each	76.44
With bull or angle dozer	up to 200 kW	Each	96.43
With bull or angle dozer	up to 250 kW	Each	117.68
With bull or angle dozer	up to 350 kW	Each	160.03
With bull or angle dozer	up to 450 kW	Each	219.86
With loading shovel	0.8 m3	Each	26.92
With loading shovel	1.0 m3	Each	32.59
With loading shovel	1.2 m3	Each	37.53
With loading shovel	1.4 m3	Each	42.89
With loading shovel	1.8 m3	Each	52.22
With loading shovel	2.0 m3	Each	57.22
With loading shovel	2.1 m3	Each	60.12
With loading shovel	3.5 m3	Each	87.26
Light vans			
VW Caddivan or the like		Each	5.26
VW Transport transit or the like	1.0 tonnes	Each	6.03
Luton Box Van or the like	1.8 tonnes	Each	9.87
Water/Fuel Storage			
Mobile water container	110 litres	Each	0.62
Water bowser	1100 litres	Each	0.72
Water bowser	3000 litres	Each	0.87
Mobile fuel container	110 litres	Each	0.62
Fuel bowser	1100 litres	Each	1.23
Fuel bowser	3000 litres	Each	1.87
EXCAVATORS AND LOADERS			
Excavators			
Wheeled, hydraulic	up to 11 tonnes	Each	25.86
Wheeled, hydraulic	up to 14 tonnes	Each	30.82
Wheeled, hydraulic	up to 16 tonnes	Each	34.50
Wheeled, hydraulic	up to 21 tonnes	Each	39.10
Wheeled, hydraulic	up to 25 tonnes	Each	43.81
Wheeled, hydraulic	up to 30 tonnes	Each	55.30
Crawler, hydraulic	up to 11 tonnes	Each	25.86
Crawler, hydraulic	up to 14 tonnes	Each	30.82
Crawler, hydraulic	up to 17 tonnes	Each	34.50
Crawler, hydraulic	up to 23 tonnes	Each	39.10
Crawler, hydraulic	up to 30 tonnes	Each	43.81
Crawler, hydraulic	up to 35 tonnes	Each	55.30
Crawler, hydraulic	up to 38 tonnes	Each	71.73
Crawler, hydraulic	up to 55 tonnes	Each	95.63
Mini excavator	1000/1500 kg	Each	4.87
Mini excavator	2150/2400 kg	Each	6.67
Mini excavator	2700/3500 kg	Each	7.31
Mini excavator	3500/4500 kg	Each	8.21
Mini excavator	4500/6000 kg	Each	9.23
Mini excavator	7000 kg	Each	14.10
Micro excavator	725 mm wide	Each	5.13

Item of Plant	Size/Rating	Unit	Rate/hr
Loaders			
Shovel loader	0.4 m3	Each	7.69
Shovel loader	1.57 m3	Each	8.97
Shovel loader, four wheel drive	1.7 m3	Each	4.83
Shovel loader, four wheel drive	2.3 m3	Each	4.38
Shovel loader, four wheel drive	3.3 m3	Each	5.06
Skid steer loader, wheeled	300/400 kg payload	Each	7.31
Skid steer loader, wheeled	625 kg payload	Each	7.67
Tracked skip loader	650 kg	Each	4.42
Excavator Loaders			
Wheeled tractor type with back-hoe excavator			
Four wheel drive			
Four wheel drive, 2 wheel steer	6 tonnes	Each	6.41
Four wheel drive, 4 wheel steer	8 tonnes	Each	8.59
Attachments			
Breakers for excavator		Each	8.72
Breakers for mini excavator		Each	1.75
Breakers for back-hoe excavator/loader		Each	5.13
COMPACTION EQUIPMENT			
Rollers			
Vibrating roller	368 kg - 420 kg	Each	1.43
Single roller	533 kg	Each	1.94
Single roller	750 kg	Each	3.43
Twin roller	up to 650 kg	Each	6.03
Twin roller	up to 950 kg	Each	6.62
Twin roller with seat end steering wheel	up to 1400 kg	Each	7.68
Twin roller with seat end steering wheel	up to 2500 kg	Each	10.61
Pavement roller	3 - 4 tonnes dead weight	Each	6.00
Pavement roller	4 - 6 tonnes	Each	6.86
Pavement roller	6 - 10 tonnes	Each	7.17
Pavement roller	10 – 13 tonnes	Each	19.86
Rammers			
Tamper rammer 2 stroke-petrol	225 mm - 275 mm	Each	1.52
Soil Compactors			
Plate compactor	75 mm - 400 mm	Each	1.53
Plate compactor rubber pad	375 mm - 1400 mm	Each	1.53
Plate compactor reversible plate - petrol	400 mm	Each	2.24
CONCRETE EQUIPMENT			
Concrete/Mortar Mixers			
Open drum without hopper	0.09/0.06 m3	Each	0.61
Open drum without hopper	0.12/0.09 m3	Each	1.22
Open drum without hopper	0.15/0.10 m3	Each	0.72
Concrete/Mortar Transport Equipment			
Concrete pump including hose, valve and couplers			
Lorry mounted concrete pump	24 m max. distance	Each	50.00
Lorry mounted concrete pump	34 m max. distance	Each	66.00
Lorry mounted concrete pump	42 m max. distance	Each	91.50
Concrete Equipment			
Vibrator, poker, petrol type	up to 75 mm dia.	Each	0.69
Air vibrator (excluding compressor and hose)	up to 75 mm dia.	Each	0.64
Extra poker heads	25/36/60 mm dia.	Each	0.76
Vibrating screed unit with beam	5 m	Each	2.48
Vibrating screed unit with adjustable beam	3 m - 5 m	Each	3.54
Power float	725 mm - 900 mm	Each	2.56
Power float finishing pan		Each	0.62
Floor grinder	660 x 1016 mm, 110V electric	Each	4.31
Floor plane	450 x 1100 mm	Each	4.31
TESTING EQUIPMENT			
Pipe Testing Equipment			
Pressure testing pump, electric		Set	2.19
Pressure test pump		Set	0.80
SITE ACCOMMODATION AND TEMPORARY SERVICES			
Heating Equipment			
Space heater, propane	80,000 Btu/hr	Each	1.03
Space heater, propane/electric	125,000 Btu/hr	Each	2.09
Space heater, propane/electric	250,000 Btu/hr	Each	2.33
Space heater, propane	125,000 Btu/hr	Each	1.54
Space heater, propane	260,000 Btu/hr	Each	1.88
Cabinet heater		Each	0.82
Cabinet heater catalytic		Each	0.57
Electric halogen heater		Each	1.27
Ceramic heater	3 kW	Each	0.99
Fan heater	3 kW	Each	0.66
Cooling fan		Each	1.92
Mobile cooling unit, small		Each	3.60
Mobile cooling unit, large		Each	4.98
Air conditioning unit		Each	2.81
Site Lighting and Equipment			
Tripod floodlight	500 W	Each	0.48
Tripod floodlight	1000 W	Each	0.62
Towable floodlight	4 x 1000 W	Each	3.85
Hand held floodlight	500 W	Each	0.51
Rechargeable light		Each	0.41
Inspection light		Each	0.37
Plasterer's light		Each	0.65
Lighting mast		Each	2.87
Festoon light string	25 m	Each	0.55

Item of Plant	Size/Rating	Unit	Rate/hr
Site Electrical Equipment			
Extension lead	240V/14 m	Each	0.26
Extension lead	110V/14 m	Each	0.36
Cable reel	25 m 110V/240V	Each	0.46
Cable reel	50 m 110V/240V	Each	0.88
4 way junction box	110V	Each	0.56
Power Generating Units			
Generator, petrol	2 kVA	Each	1.23
Generator, silenced petrol	2 kVA	Each	2.87
Generator, petrol	3 kVA	Each	1.47
Generator, diesel	5 kVA	Each	2.44
Generator, silenced diesel	10 kVA	Each	1.90
Generator, silenced diesel	15 kVA	Each	2.26
Generator, silenced diesel	30 kVA	Each	3.33
Generator, silenced diesel	50 kVA	Each	4.10
Generator, silenced diesel	75 kVA	Each	4.62
Generator, silenced diesel	100 kVA	Each	5.64
Generator, silenced diesel	150 kVA	Each	7.18
Generator, silenced diesel	200 kVA	Each	9.74
Generator, silenced diesel	250 kVA	Each	11.28
Generator, silenced diesel	350 kVA	Each	14.36
Generator, silenced diesel	500 kVA	Each	15.38
Tail adaptor	240 V	Each	0.10
Transformers			
Transformer	3 kVA	Each	0.32
Transformer	5 kVA	Each	1.23
Transformer	7.5 kVA	Each	0.59
Transformer	10 kVA	Each	2.00
Rubbish Collection and Disposal Equipment			
Rubbish chutes			
Standard plastic module	1 m section	Each	0.15
Steel insert liner		Each	0.30
Steel top hopper		Each	0.22
Plastic side entry hopper		Each	0.22
Plastic side entry hopper liner		Each	0.22
Dust Extraction Plant			
Dust extraction unit, light duty		Each	2.97
Dust extraction unit, heavy duty		Each	2.97
SITE EQUIPMENT			
Welding Equipment			
Arc-(electric) complete with leads			
Welder generator, petrol	200 amp	Each	3.53
Welder generator, diesel	300/350 amp	Each	3.78
Welder generator, diesel	4000 amp	Each	7.92
Extra welding lead sets		Each	0.69
Gas-oxy welder			
Welding and cutting set (including oxygen and acetylene, excluding underwater equipment and thermic boring)			
Small		Each	2.24
Large		Each	3.75
Lead burning gun		Each	0.50
Mig welder		Each	1.38
Fume extractor		Each	2.46
Road Works Equipment			
Traffic lights, mains/generator	2-way	Set	10.94
Traffic lights, mains/generator	3-way	Set	11.56
Traffic lights, mains/generator	4-way	Set	12.19
Flashing light		Each	0.10
Road safety cone	450 mm	Each	0.08
Safety cone	750 mm	Each	0.10
Safety barrier plank	1.25 m	Each	0.13
Safety barrier plank	2 m	Each	0.15
Safety barrier plank post		Each	0.13
Safety barrier plank post base		Each	0.10
Safety four gate barrier	1 m each gate	Set	0.77
Guard barrier	2 m	Each	0.19
Road sign	750 mm	Each	0.23
Road sign	900 mm	Each	0.31
Road sign	1200 mm	Each	0.42
Speed ramp/cable protection	500 mm section	Each	0.14
Hose ramp open top	3 m section	Each	0.07
DPC Equipment			
Damp proofing injection machine		Each	2.56
Cleaning Equipment			
Vacuum cleaner (industrial wet) single motor		Each	1.08
Vacuum cleaner (industrial wet) twin motor	30 litre capacity	Each	1.79
Vacuum cleaner (industrial wet) twin motor	70 litre capacity	Each	2.21
Steam cleaner	Diesel/electric 1 phase	Each	3.33
Steam cleaner	Diesel/electric 3 phase	Each	3.85
Pressure washer, light duty, electric	1450 PSI	Each	0.72
Pressure washer, heavy duty, diesel	2500 PSI	Each	1.33
Pressure washer, heavy duty, diesel	4000 PSI	Each	2.18
Cold pressure washer, electric		Each	2.39
Hot pressure washer, petrol		Each	4.19
Hot pressure washer, electric		Each	5.13
Cold pressure washer, petrol		Each	2.92
Sandblast attachment to last washer		Each	1.23
Drain cleaning attachment to last washer		Each	1.03

Item of Plant	Size/Rating	Unit	Rate/hr
Surface Preparation Equipment			
Rotavator	5 h.p.	Each	2.46
Rotavator	9 h.p.	Each	5.00
Scabbler, up to three heads		Each	1.53
Scabbler, pole		Each	2.68
Scabbler, multi-headed floor		Each	3.89
Floor preparation machine		Each	1.05
Compressors and Equipment			
Portable compressors			
Compressors, electric	4 cfm	Each	1.36
Compressors, electric	8 cfm lightweight	Each	1.31
Compressors, electric	8 cfm	Each	1.36
Compressors, electric	14 cfm	Each	1.56
Compressors, petrol	24 cfm	Each	2.15
Compressors, electric	25 cfm	Each	2.10
Compressors, electric	30 cfm	Each	2.36
Compressors, diesel	100 cfm	Each	2.56
Compressors, diesel	250 cfm	Each	5.54
Compressors, diesel	400 cfm	Each	8.72
Mobile compressors			
Lorry mounted compressor			
(machine plus lorry only)	up to 3 m3	Each	41.47
(machine plus lorry only)	up to 5 m3	Each	48.94
Tractor mounted compressors			
(machine plus rubber tyred tractor)	up to 4 m3	Each	21.03
Accessories (pneumatic tools)			
(with and including up to 15 m of air hose)			
Demolition pick, medium duty		Each	0.90
Demolition pick, heavy duty		Each	1.03
Breakers (with six steels) light	up to 150 kg	Each	1.19
Breakers (with six steels) medium	295 kg	Each	1.24
Breakers (with six steels) heavy	386 kg	Each	1.44
Rock drill (for use with compressor) hand held		Each	1.18
Additional hoses	15 m	Each	0.09
Breakers			
Demolition hammer drill, heavy duty, electric		Each	1.54
Road breaker, electric		Each	2.41
Road breaker, 2 stroke, petrol		Each	4.06
Hydraulic breaker unit, light duty, petrol		Each	3.06
Hydraulic breaker unit, heavy duty, petrol		Each	3.46
Hydraulic breaker unit, heavy duty, diesel		Each	4.62
Quarrying and Tooling Equipment			
Block and stone splitter, hydraulic	600 mm x 600 mm	Each	1.90
Block and slab splitter, manual		Each	1.64
Steel Reinforcement Equipment			
Bar bending machine, manual	up to 13 mm dia. rods	Each	1.03
Bar bending machine, manual	up to 20 mm dia. rods	Each	1.41
Bar shearing machine, electric	up to 38 mm dia. rods	Each	3.08
Bar shearing machine, electric	up to 40 mm dia. rods	Each	4.62
Bar cropper machine, electric	up to 13 mm dia. rods	Each	2.05
Bar cropper machine, electric	up to 20 mm dia rods	Each	2.56
Bar cropper machine, electric	up to 40 mm dia. rods	Each	4.62
Bar cropper machine, 3 phase	up to 40 mm dia. rods	Each	4.62
Dehumidifiers			
110/240V Water	68 litres extraction per 24 hrs	Each	2.46
110/240V Water	90 litres extraction per 24 hrs	Each	3.38
SMALL TOOLS			
Saws			
Masonry bench saw	350 mm - 500 mm dia.	Each	1.13
Floor saw	125 mm max. cut	Each	1.15
Floor saw	150 mm max. cut	Each	3.83
Floor saw, reversible	350 mm max. cut	Each	3.32
Wall saw, electric		Each	2.05
Chop/cut off saw, electric	350 mm dia.	Each	1.79
Circular saw, electric	230 mm dia.	Each	0.72
Tyrannosaw		Each	1.74
Reciprocating saw		Each	0.79
Door trimmer		Each	1.17
Stone saw	300 mm	Each	1.44
Chainsaw, petrol	500 mm	Each	3.92
Full chainsaw safety kit		Each	0.41
Worktop jig		Each	1.08
PipeWork Equipment			
Pipe bender	15 mm - 22 mm	Each	0.92
Pipe bender, hydraulic	50 mm	Each	1.76
Pipe bender, electric	50 mm - 150 mm dia.	Each	2.19
Pipe cutter, hydraulic		Each	0.46
Tripod pipe vice		Set	0.75
Ratchet threader	12 mm - 32 mm	Each	0.93
Pipe threading machine, electric	12 mm - 75 mm	Each	3.07
PipeWork Equipment			
Pipe threading machine, electric	12 mm - 100 mm	Each	4.93
Impact wrench, electric		Each	1.33
Hand-held Drills and Equipment			
Impact or hammer drill	up to 25 mm dia.	Each	1.03
Impact or hammer drill	35 mm dia.	Each	1.29
Dry diamond core cutter		Each	0.99
Angle head drill		Each	0.90
Stirrer, mixer drill		Each	1.13

Item of Plant	Size/Rating	Unit	Rate/hr
Paint, Insulation Application Equipment			
Airless spray unit		Each	4.13
Portaspray unit		Each	1.16
HVLP turbine spray unit		Each	2.23
Compressor and spray gun		Each	1.91
Other Handtools			
Staple gun		Each	0.96
Air nail gun	110V	Each	1.01
Cartridge hammer		Each	1.08
Tongue & groove nailer complete with mallet		Each	1.59
Diamond wall chasing machine		Each	2.63
Masonry chain saw	300 mm	Each	5.49
Floor grinder		Each	3.99
Floor plane		Each	1.79
Diamond concrete planer		Each	1.93
Autofeed screwdriver, electric		Each	1.38
Laminate trimmer		Each	0.91
Biscuit jointer		Each	1.49
Random orbital sander		Each	0.97
Floor sander		Each	1.54
Palm, delta, flap or belt sander		Each	0.75
Disk cutter, electric	300 mm	Each	1.49
Disk cutter, 2 stroke petrol	300 mm	Each	1.24
Dust suppressor for petrol disc cutter		Each	0.51
Cutter cart for petrol disc cutter		Each	1.21
Grinder, angle or cutter	up to 225 mm	Each	0.50
Grinder, angle or cutter	300 mm	Each	1.41
Motor raking tool attachment		Each	0.19
Floor polisher/scrubber	325 mm	Each	1.76
Floor tile stripper		Each	2.44
Wallpaper stripper, electric		Each	0.81
Hot air paint stripper		Each	0.50
Electric diamond tile cutter	all sizes	Each	2.42
Hand tile cutter		Each	0.82
Electric needle gun		Each	1.29
Needle chipping gun		Each	1.85
Pedestrian floor sweeper	250 mm dia.	Each	0.82
Pedestrian floor sweeper	petrol	Each	2.20
Diamond tile saw		Each	1.84
Blow lamp equipment and glass		Set	0.50

Introduction

INTRODUCTION
BCIS ALTERATIONS AND REFURBISHMENT ESTIMATING PRICE BOOK FOR SMALL PROJECTS

AA   GENERAL

001 **Basis of Pricing**

002 The aim of this book is to provide builders and building Consultants with a **GUIDE** to the current (net cost) unit prices for building alterations and refurbishment work at competitive rates.

003 The prices in this book are intended for projects consisting entirely or substantially of alterations and improvements to existing buildings, from simple operations such as taking out a door and blocking up the opening to complete refurbishment projects up to a value of £150,000.

004 This Database has been created on a nationally averaged 'best price' basis. For an indication of regional differentials, please refer to sub-section AF - 'Regional Variations'. These factors should be considered if local rates of labour and material are not known at the time of estimating.

005 The Database prices represent the net cost of labour, plant and materials, without additions for site overheads (examples of which are shown separately in section B - Preliminaries) or for off-site office overheads or profit, as such additions fluctuate with market conditions and require management policy decisions at the time of tender.

006 Prices for work which is normally executed under the Builder's direct control, whether employing in-house labour or labour only sub-contractors, are broken down into 'Net Labour', 'Net Plant' and 'Net Materials', with the aggregate of these separate prices given in bold type under the heading of 'NET UNIT PRICE'.

007 Work normally undertaken by specialist sub-contract firms has been priced by specialist firms and the prices given are total 'Net Unit Prices' inclusive of labour, plant, materials and the specialists' overheads and profit. The prices are inclusive of 2.5% cash discount to the Builder but are exclusive of the Builder's own overheads and profit, general and special attendance.

008 **Guide prices**

009 It must be stressed that the prices in the book are **GUIDE** prices. Quotations for materials and specialists' work should be obtained for particular projects as the prices cannot be guaranteed. The nature of the publication, which is intended to be a guide to building prices throughout the United Kingdom, precludes the possibility of firm prices for all situations. Regional price variations, qualities and quantities of materials and work, availability of skilled labour, location of sites and individual project requirements all have a bearing on prices for building work.

010 **Descriptions**

011 Descriptions of work are based upon the Sixth Edition of the Standard Method of Measurement for Building Works (SMM6).

012 **Value Added Tax**

013 The prices throughout the book are EXCLUSIVE of Value Added Tax.

AB   BASIC MATERIAL PRICES

001 **Base date of prices**

002 The supply prices of materials, as shown in 'Basic Prices of Materials' at the beginning of each work section were current during the second quarter of 2012.

003 **Delivery**

004 The supply prices of major items of building materials are given as "delivered to site" (unless otherwise stated) with allowance for delivery charges, if applicable, being made in rates to "average" sites, typically in an area of a conurbation (e.g. Greater London area) up to about 50 miles from the source of supply. Deliveries to city centre sites (particularly central London) and to more remote rural sites may attract delivery surcharges and additional allowance in such cases will need to be made in "overheads". The supply of ancillary materials is taken to be ex Builders Merchants, with site delivery or collection.

005 **Trade and quantity discounts**

006 The supply prices of materials generally are net Trade prices and are for part loads or small quantities.

007 **Waste factors**

008 Waste percentages added to the supply prices of materials are generally for handling wastage, for such materials as cement, sand and lime. The percentages added to other materials are generally for waste in use and in order to simplify the computation of the material constants used in the calculations of the Net Unit Prices.

009 **Unloading Costs**

010 Where materials are not supplied crated or palletised, the cost of site labour and plant in unloading materials has been shown separately, where applicable, and added to the supply prices.

011 **Crates and pallets**

012 Surcharges for returnable crates and pallets have been excluded from the supply prices of the materials.

AC   PLANT COSTS

001 Plant hire charges are applicable to the second quarter of 2012 and are typical rates obtained from plant hire companies. The hire charges for plant show hourly rates which have been calculated based upon **DAILY** hire charges, due to the intermittent short-term usage to be expected in alteration and refurbishment works. If sustained, longer-term use of any items of plant can be justified for the works, considerable savings in hire charges may be anticipated.

At the time of publication prices for plant hire were very competitive and Contractors are advised to obtain competitive quotations at the time of preparing tenders.

002 **Idle time**

003 Allowances have been made against the hire charges to allow for idle or standing time so that the hourly constants shown in the build-up of prices are for the actual working time of the plant.

004 **Operators**

005 Weekly hire charges for mechanical equipment are exclusive of operators. The costs of operators are shown separately and are calculated in accordance with the build-up of labour rates shown in Sub-Section AD.

006 Daily or hourly hire charges for mechanical equipment are inclusive of operators where indicated.

007 **Fuel etc.**

008 The hire charges for mechanical equipment exclude the provision of fuel but include maintenance and services charges. Unit rate build-ups include for fuel costs.

009 **Constants**

010 The constants, in the form of hours, against the items of plant have been rounded off to two decimal places after calculation.

AD   LABOUR COSTS

001 **Generally**

002 Labour costs have been calculated in accordance with the recommendations of the Code of Estimating Practice published by the Chartered Institute of Building.

003 **Base date of pricing**

004 Labour costs are based upon the operative rates of wages and allowances effective from 12th September 2011. Due to the current economic conditions no further settlements are expected during 2012.

005 **Hourly rates**

006 The hourly rates used for the calculations **in this book** are as follows:

Craftsman BATJIC = £15.20per hour   Labourer BATJIC = £11.22 per hour
Labourer BATJIC (skill rate A) = £11.82 per hour   Labourer BATJIC (semi-skilled A) = £14.02 per hour
Labourer BATJIC (skill rate B) = £12.12 per hour   Labourer BATJIC (semi-skilled B) = £14.38 per hour
Labourer BATJIC (skill rate C) = £12.45 per hour   Labourer BATJIC (semi-skilled C) = £14.74 per hour
Technican PHMES Operative = £21.80 per hour   Advanced PHMES Operative = £19.59 per hour
PHMES Operative = £16.73 per hour   Apprentice Plumber (3rd year) JIBPMES = £12.01 per hour

007 The Total Cost per Hour figures have been corrected to the nearest whole penny and are based on a 39 hour working week. However, the detailed calculations have been made using several places of decimal which may give rise to apparent 1p differences in some printed figures.

008 **Plus rates**

009 An enhanced 'plus rate' has been inserted in the calculation to allow for the more costly labour element of refurbishment work.

010 **Travelling allowances**

011 As travelling allowances vary with the distance of building sites from the Builder's office they have been excluded from the calculation of the hourly labour costs. Allowances for travelling time and/or expenses should be made in Preliminaries.

012 **Trade supervision**

013 Trade supervision has been excluded from the calculation of the hourly labour costs. Where trade supervision is required, particularly on larger projects, separate allowances should be made in Preliminaries.

014 **Overtime**

015 Allowance for overtime in the calculation of the hourly labour costs has been based on an average of 5 hours overtime per operative per week during British Summer Time. The non-productive element in the overtime amounts to an average of 65.5 hours per operative per annum.

016 **Other Emoluments**

017 With effect from 15th June 1998, tool allowances have been consolidated into the basic rate of pay.

018 **Constants**

019 The constants, in the form of hours, against each item in the price book have been rounded off to two decimal places after calculation.

020 **Calculation of hours worked per annum: Craftsmen and Labourers**

	hours	hours	hours
(a) Summertime working: 30 weeks of British Summertime at 44 hours per week Monday to Friday			
30 Weeks at 44 hours		1320.0	
Less annual holidays (14 days)	123.2		
public holidays (5 days)	44.0	167.2	1152.8
	-----	------	
(b) Winter working: 22 weeks at 39 hours per week			
22 Weeks at 39 hours		858.0	
Less annual holidays (7 days)	54.6		
public holidays (3 days)	23.4		
Sick leave (8 days NB 3 days unpaid)	39.0	117.0	741.0
	-----	-----	------
Total Number of paid working hours during year			1893.8
Less Allowance for inclement weather (2%)			37.8

TOTAL NUMBER OF PRODUCTIVE HOURS WORKED PER ANNUM			1856.0
			------

021 Calculation of Labour Costs - BATJIC award

The hourly cost of wages based upon the rates of wages and allowances agreed by the Building and Allied Trades Joint Industry Council is calculated as follows:

Annual cost of wages		Craftsman		Labourer
		£		£
Flat time	1893.8 hours at 10.73	20320.47	at 7.96	15074.65
Non-productive overtime	65.5 hours at 10.73	702.82	at 7.96	521.38
Public holidays	63.0 hours at 10.73	675.99	at 7.96	501.48
Sick Pay	5.0 days at 23.61	118.05	at 23.61	118.05
Plus rate (See notes below)	2022.3 hours at 0.10	202.23	at 0.10	202.23
		--------		--------
		22019.56		16417.79
Employer's National Insurance Contribution – Above ST	13.80%	2005.36	13.80%	1232.31
Training Allowance	(0.50% of PAYE)	110.10		82.09
Holiday credits	(12.6% of PAYE)	2774.46		2068.64
Retirement benefit	52.0 weeks at 3.00	156.00	at 3.00	156.00
Death benefit	12.0 months at 4.33	51.99	at 4.33	52.00
		--------		--------
		27117.47		20008.83
Severance pay and other statutory costs	2.00%	542.35	2.00%	400.18
		--------		--------
		27659.82		20409.01
Employer's liability insurance	2.00%	553.20	2.00%	408.18
		--------		--------
TOTAL COST OF 1856 PRODUCTIVE HOURS		28213.02		20817.19
		--------		--------
Total Labour Cost per hour		**15.20**		**11.22**
		========		========
Effect of 10p/hr plus rate on total cost per hour (see note 2 below)		0.1439		0.1439

PLEASE READ CAREFULLY THE NOTES PRECEDING THE FOREGOING CALCULATION AND AS FOLLOWS:-

1. Sources - BATJIC Agreement effective from 12th September 2011. Due to the current economic conditions no further settlements are expected during 2012. NI revisions as at 6th April 2012.

2. As previously stated, a 10p plus rate has been allowed and the effect of a further 10p variation is shown above.

3. Travelling, subsistence and trade supervision should be calculated as project overhead or preliminary items.

4. The CITB advise a levy of 0.50% of PAYE payroll and 1.50% of labour-only sub-contract costs. The training allowance above was agreed in November 2000. Each variation of £20 per annum would equate to approximately 1p variation of the total hourly cost.

5. USERS OF THIS GUIDE SHOULD SATISFY THEMSELVES AS TO THE BASIS OF CALCULATION OF PAYMENTS TO OPERATIVES, RELATED COSTS, WORKING AND PRODUCTIVE TIME ETC., WITHIN THEIR OWN ORGANISATION AND REGION, BEFORE APPLYING ANY LABOUR RATES WITHIN THIS GUIDE. PARTICULAR ATTENTION IS DRAWN TO THE CHANGE IN RULES CONCERNING RECOVERY OF STATUTORY SICK PAY. ALTHOUGH NO ALLOWANCE HAS BEEN MADE IN THESE CALCULATIONS FOR RECOVERY OF SSP, IT SHOULD BE NOTED THAT THE RATES OF NATIONAL INSURANCE CONTRIBUTION WERE REDUCED FOR 1994/5 IN ORDER TO ALLOW FOR POSSIBLE INCREASED OVERALL SICKNESS COSTS, AND THAT THESE REDUCTIONS **ARE** INCORPORATED IN THE CALCULATION.

6. With effect from 15th June 1998, tool allowances have been consolidated into the basic rate of pay.

7. With effect from 11th June 2001 the Holiday Credit and Retirement Benefit System ceased and was replaced with the Building and Civil Engineering Benefits Scheme. Holiday Pay Scheme - This sets out the percentage of PAYE to allow for holiday pay. The retirement benefit is accrued according to the stake-holders' pension scheme using the recommended allowance of £3.00 per week. However, if the employee chooses to pay a higher amount, up to £13.50, then this must be matched by the employer.

022 Calculation of Labour Costs - JIBPMES award

The hourly cost of wages for Plumbers based upon the rates of wages and allowances agreed by the Joint Industry Board for Plumbing and Mechanical Engineering Services in England and Wales is calculated as follows:

Annual Cost of Wages			Technican PHMES Operative £		Advanced PHMES Operative £		PHMES Operative £		Apprentice Plumber 3rd Year £
Flat time	1870.4 hours at	14.99	28037.30	13.50	25250.40	11.58	21659.23	7.26	13579.10
Non-productive overtime	65.5 hours at	14.99	981.84	13.50	884.25	11.58	758.49	0.00	0.00
Non-productive overtime	41.0 hours at	0.00	0.00	0.00	0.00	0.00	0.00	0.00	0.00
Sick pay	0.00 days at	0.00	0.00	0.00	0.00	0.00	0.00	0.00	0.00
Plus rate	2025.6 hours at	0.10	202.56	0.10	202.56	0.10	202.56	0.10	202.56
			29221.70		26337.21		22620.28		13781.66
National Insurance Employers Contribution – Above ST		13.80%	2999.25	13.80%	2601.19	13.80%	2088.26	13.80%	868.53
Training Allowance	(0.50% of PAYE)		146.11	0.50%	131.69	0.50%	113.10	0.00%	0.00
Holiday credit (Public & annual)	60 weeks at	59	3540.00	53.10	3186.00	45.55	2733.00	25.55	1533.00
			35907.06		32256.09		27554.64		16183.19
Severance pay and other statutory costs		1.50%	538.61	1.50%	483.84	1.50%	413.32	1.50%	242.75
			36445.67		32739.93		27967.96		16425.94
Employers liability etc.		2.00%	728.91	2.00%	654.80	2.00%	559.36	2.00%	328.52
			37174.58		33394.73		28527.32		16754.46
Industry Pension Scheme		7.50%	2788.09	7.50%	2504.60	7.50%	2139.55	7.50%	1256.58
TOTAL COST OF 1832.99 PRODUCTIVE HOURS			39962.67		35899.33		30666.87		
TOTAL COST OF 1499.79 PRODUCTIVE HOURS									18011.04
Total labour cost per hour			**21.80**		**19.59**		**16.73**		**12.01**

PLEASE READ CAREFULLY THE NOTES PRECEDING THE FOREGOING CALCULATION AND AS FOLLOWS:-

1. Sources - JIBPMES Promulgation No 163 & 164 effective from 2nd January 2012. NI revisions as at 6th April 2012.

AE   UNITS USED IN THE PRICING SECTIONS OF THIS BOOK

The Units have been abbreviated as follows:-

m - linear metre	kg - kilogram	Nr - number	mm - millimetre
m2 - square metre	t - tonne	Ft - feet	ml - millilitre
m3 - cubic metre	ltr - litre		

AF   REGIONAL VARIATIONS

001 The prices generally are based upon nationally averaged 'best prices' with a Factor of 1.00.

002 Individual prices may be calculated by applying the relevant local rates obtainable for labour and plant to the hourly constants indicated against each item, and then applying the local cost of materials to the quantities given, using the methods described in this book.

003 An indication of the possible level of **overall** pricing in areas of the United Kingdom compared to this Database may be obtained by reference to Regional Factors map shown here. 'Regional Factors' are taken from the BCIS Quarterly Review of Building Prices.

004 However, as the BCIS Quarterly Review is based upon total tender prices, it is stressed that this can only provide an approximate overall guide to the level of pricing and the figures in the guide should **never** be applied to individual prices under any circumstances.

REGIONAL FACTORS MAP

STANDARD STATISTICAL REGIONS
SHOWING REGIONAL FACTORS
BASED ON A NATIONAL AVERAGE = 1.00

Scotland
0.97

Northern Ireland
0.58

Northern
0.92

Yorkshire & Humberside
0.98

North West
0.91

East Midlands
0.97

West Midlands
0.98

East Anglia
1.05

Wales
0.94

South East
1.07

G.L.
1.12

South West
1.03

ISLANDS (Man, Scilly and Channel)
1.74

AG
HM REVENUE & CUSTOMS - LANDFILL TAX

Foreword This notice cancels and replaces Notice LFT1 (April 2011).

This notice provides a general guide to landfill tax. This is a tax on the disposal of waste to landfill. As such, it encourages efforts to minimise the amount of waste produced and the use of non-landfill waste management options, which might include recycling, composting and recovery. This notice deals with requirements under landfill tax legislation. Nothing in this notice changes your obligations under environmental law.

This notice, dated May 2012, replaces the edition of April 2011. We have rewritten the notice owing to changes in the law, most notably relating to ending the exemption for waste arising from the reclamation of contaminated land from 1 April 2012 and a minor update to the Landfill Tax (Qualifying Material) Order 2011

This notice is primarily for landfill site operators but will also be of interest to waste producers, others involved in the waste management industry and environmental bodies under the Landfill Communities Fund. Where we refer to site operators in this notice we mean the licence or permit holder of the landfill site. Unless indicated to the contrary, where we say 'you' or 'your' in this notice, we mean the landfill site operator and where we say 'we', 'our' or 'us' we mean HM Revenue & Customs.

1.1 Law

The primary law on landfill tax and the Landfill Communities Fund is contained in the Finance Act 1996 (sections 39 to 71 inclusive, and schedule 5), as amended. This Act also provides for the following secondary legislation:

*   the Landfill Tax Regulations 1996 (SI 1996 No. 1527), as amended - deal with the more detailed implementation aspects of the tax, such as registration, information gathering requirements and accounting procedures, and cover the Landfill Communities Fund (see section 11)
*   the Landfill Tax (Qualifying Material) Order 2011 (SI 2011 No. 1017) - defines the categories of waste to which the lower rate of tax applies, and
*   the Landfill Tax (Prescribed Landfill Activities) Order 2009 – lists certain activities on a landfill site that are subject to tax.

The landfill tax return (form LT100 Landfill Tax Return) is no longer determined by legislation and is instead determined by section 20.

2. Scope of the tax

2.1 What is landfill tax paid on?

Unless it is specifically exempt (see section 4), landfill tax applies to all material disposed of:

*   as waste (see paragraph 2.2)
*   by way of landfill (see paragraph 2.3), and
*   at a landfill site that is required to have a licence or permit under specific environmental legislation (see paragraph 2.4).

It also applies to the prescribed landfill activities relating to use of material on site that are listed in paragraph 2.5 (subject to the site being covered by paragraph 2.4).

2.2 What is disposal of material as waste?

A disposal of material is a disposal of it as waste if the person making the disposal does so with the intention of discarding the material.
In 2008, the Court of Appeal in the Commissioners for Her Majesty's Revenue & Customs v Waste Recycling Group Limited [2008] EWCA Civ 849, (the WRG case), ruled to the effect that material received on a landfill site which is put to a use on the site is not taxable. This is because there is not, at the relevant time, a disposal with the intention of discarding the material. However, legislation which came into effect on 1 September 2009 brought prescribed "landfill site activities" relating to use of material on site into the scope of the tax (see paragraph 2.5)

2.3 What is a disposal by way of landfill?

Disposal of waste by way of landfill takes place where material is deposited:

*   on the surface of the land
*   on a structure set into the surface of the land, or
*   under the surface of the land (land includes land covered by water which is above the low water mark of ordinary spring tides).

Whether the material is placed in a container before it is deposited is irrelevant. It is still a disposal for the purposes of the tax if the material is covered with earth or similar material straight away or if it is deposited in a cavity such as a cavern or mine. If material is deposited with a view to being covered at a later stage with earth, the disposal is made when the material is deposited, not when it is covered.

2.4 Which landfill sites are relevant for tax?

A site is relevant for the purposes of the tax if there is a licence or permit authorising disposals in or on the land under:

*   Part II of the Environmental Protection Act 1990
*   Regulations made under section 2 of the Pollution Prevention and Control Act 1999
*   Part II of the Pollution Control and Local Government (Northern Ireland) Order 1978 (SI 1978 No. 1049 (N.I. 9))
*   Regulations under Article 4 of the Environment (Northern Ireland) Order 2002 (SI 2002 No. 3153 (N.I. 7)).

Any material which is deposited at a site which is not subject to a waste management licence or permit under environmental law is not liable to tax.

2.5 Which landfill site activities are prescribed as being subject to tax?

The prescribed landfill site activities referred to in paragraphs 2.1 and 2.2 are set out in column B of the following table. They are subject to tax on or after 1 September 2009. Column C provides further detail about the taxable activities and column D sets out related activities that are not taxable.
While no tax is due on waste which is subject to processing or sorting in the area of a landfill site prior to the waste being subject to recovery, tax will be due if the site operator does not supply us with the information described in section 7 (requirements of an information area account).

Column A	Column B	Column C	Column D
Activity number	Description	What is taxable	What is not taxable
1	The use of material to cover the disposal area during a short-term cessation in landfill disposal activity. The disposal area, usually the landfill void, is any area where disposals of material as waste and by way of landfill take place (see paragraphs 2.2 and 2.3).	The placing of any material on the disposal area for mainly health or environmental reasons (such as reducing nuisance and disturbance by vermin, birds or insects) as opposed to for engineering reasons (such as the exclusion of water). This placing of material may be described as 'daily cover'.	The use of mineral material, including clay: • as a permanent cap or geological barrier on the bottom or sides of a disposal area, and • as a permanent cap on the top of the disposal area on completion of landfilling operations (an engineered layer used to stop ingress of water into the finished landfill). The use of material that meets all the conditions of one of the landfill tax exemptions set out in section 4.
2	The use of material to create or maintain a temporary haul road.	The use of material for the construction or maintenance of roads, either within the disposal area or adjacent to it. Such roads do not have engineered features (which may include kerbs or drains) and may be made from crushed or re-used materials, such as concrete or tarmac and may be eventually subsumed into the landfill site.	The use of material for construction or maintenance of permanent site roads. These have engineered features (which may include kerbs or drains) and have a surface that is prepared and/or finished. Permanent site roads are likely to have been constructed prior to the start of tipping operations on the site. The use of material that meets all the conditions of one of the landfill tax exemptions set out in section 4.
3	The use of material to create or maintain temporary hard standing.	The use of material for the construction or maintenance of a base on which activities such as waste recycling or treatment take place. Such bases do not have engineered features (which may include sealed drainage) and may be made from crushed or re-used materials, such as concrete or tarmac and may be eventually subsumed into the landfill site.	The use of material for construction or maintenance of permanent hard standing. These have engineered features (which may include sealed drainage) and have a surface that is prepared and/or finished. Permanent hard standing is likely to have been constructed prior to the start of tipping operations on the site. The use of material that meets all the conditions of one of the landfill tax exemptions set out in section 4.
4	The use of material to create or maintain a cell bund.	The use of material to form a structure within the disposal area to separate units of waste, for example, to identify the operational area.	The use of mineral material, including clay, to form separate cells on the edge of the landfill as part of the engineered containment. The use of material that meets all the conditions of one of the landfill tax exemptions set out in section 4.
5	The use of material to create or maintain a temporary screening bund.	The use of any material to create or maintain a structure, either below or above ground, with the purpose of reducing the visual or noise impact of discrete activities on a landfill site, where those activities will cease, while the wider site continues to operate.	The use of material to create or maintain a structure that performs a function in relation to the landfill site as a whole. It is likely that this will be in place during the entire period of operation of the site as a whole. Naturally occurring material derived from the site it is used at, when used to create or maintain a temporary screening bund. The use of material that meets all the conditions of one of the landfill tax exemptions set out in section 4.
6	The use of material placed against the drainage layer or liner of the disposal area to prevent damage to that layer or liner.	The placing of soft material, for example household waste, to prevent damage to the drainage layer / blanket or the liner. Such material may have been sorted / processed to remove sharp or hard objects.	The use of material that meets all the conditions of one of the landfill tax exemptions set out in section 4.
7	The temporary storage of ashes (including pulverised fuel ash and furnace bottom ash).	The storage of ashes from power generation in a facility, such as a lagoon, designed so that the ashes can be retrieved for use or for permanent disposal.	The use of material that meets all the conditions of one of the landfill tax exemptions set out in section 4.
8	The restoration of a landfill site.	The use of material (including site derived material) for site restoration purposes if you fail to notify us in writing of the intention to commence restoration or if the material is not deposited in the pre-notified area	The use of material (including site derived material) for site restoration purposes if you notify us in writing of the intention to commence restoration (see paragraph 2.5.2) and the material is deposited in the pre-notified area (see paragraph 2.5.1 regarding what is restoration).The use of material that meets all the conditions of one of the landfill tax exemptions set out in section 4.

For activities 1 to 6, tax is due regardless of whether the material was bought for the purpose or was otherwise obtained.

If material is used for the above activities and has previously been the subject of a taxable disposal, tax is due only on the material that has not borne tax. For example, of material used to cover waste, if 40% of the material has been taxed before and 60% is new material, tax is only due on the 60%.

Where material is taxable because it has been subjected to a landfill site activity which is temporary (activities 2, 3 and 5 in the table above) and that material is subsequently put to a non-taxable use (but not on a landfill site except when reusing it as restoration material), the crediting provisions described in section 10 apply.

2.6 Who is liable to pay landfill tax?

2.6.1 The landfill site operator

You are liable to pay tax on a taxable disposal if you are the licence or permit holder for a landfill site.

If you operate a licensed or permitted landfill site, any waste deposited in it, including waste which you have produced, will be liable to tax unless it is exempt from tax. This includes in-house sites where waste producers dispose of their own waste.

2.6.2 The controller of the landfill site

In some cases, the licence or permit holder for the landfill site has no direct involvement in operating the site. Where this is the case, the liability to pay tax is extended to the 'controller' of the site. This means that if the person named on the licence or permit fails to pay the tax, the controller will be jointly and severally liable for the debt.

The controller of a landfill site is a person, other than the licence or permit holder, who determines what materials (if any) are disposed of at the site, or part of the site. A person who is purely acting as an agent or employee of someone else is not a controller.

The controller of the site must notify us that they are the controller but does not have to register for landfill tax – that remains the responsibility of the site operator. If a person becomes, or ceases to be a controller, both you and the controller must notify us within 30 days of the change. If you both fail to do so then that person is liable to a penalty of £250. Notifications about becoming, or ceasing to become, the controller must include the:

- name and (if different) trading name of the operator and controller
- landfill tax registration number of the operator
- address of the landfill site for which there is a controller
- VAT registration number (if applicable) of the controller
- address (including postcode) of the principal place of business in the UK of the controller
- phone number of the controller, and
- date the controller became, or ceased to be, a controller at the site named.

3. Rates of tax

3.1 Two rates of tax

The tax is chargeable by weight and there are two rates:

- the lower rate applies to those less polluting wastes listed in the Landfill Tax (Qualifying Material) Order 2011, the relevant extract of which is set out in section 18, and
- the standard rate applies to all other taxable waste. The rates of tax since the introduction of the tax in October 1996 have been:

Date of change	Standard rate (£ per tonne)	Lower rate (£ per tonne)
01.10.96	7	2
01.04.99	10	2
01.04.00	11	2
01.04.01	12	2
01.04.02	13	2
01.04.03	14	2
01.04.04	15	2
01.04.05	18	2
01.04.06	21	2
01.04.07	24	2
01.04.08	32	2.50
01.04.09	40	2.50
01.04.10	48	2.50
01.04.11	56	2.50
01.04.12	64	2.50
01.04.13	72	2.50
01.04.14 (see note 1)	80	To be announced

Note 1: Budget 2010 announced that the standard rate of landfill tax would increase by £8 per tonne each year from 1 April 2011 until at least 2014. There will be a floor under the standard rate, so that the rate will not fall below £80 per tonne from 2014-15 to 2019-20.

3.2 Evidence for lower rate

You must keep sufficient evidence to substantiate applying the lower rate of tax to any particular disposal of waste.

To qualify for the lower rate the waste transfer note, which is required to accompany most movements of waste in the UK, must accurately describe the waste so that it can be related to the terms used in the Landfill Tax (Qualifying Material) Order 2011. The waste transfer note may cover individual loads or it may be a 'season ticket' covering a number of loads sent for disposal to your site over a period of time.

If you operate an in-house site and have applied the lower rate to waste which you have disposed of in that site you will need to provide evidence that the waste qualifies for that rate.

The requirements relating to the waste transfer note described above are for tax purposes. They in no way override or affect your obligations in relation to the waste transfer note in environmental protection law including the requirement to define the waste source by reference to the European Waste Catalogue codes.

Note: The only determining factor as to whether waste is lower rated is whether it is listed in the Landfill Tax (Qualifying Material) Order 2011. Whether or not waste is considered to be inert for environmental protection purposes is not relevant to matters of tax liability. Equally, the fact that waste is listed in the Landfill Tax (Qualifying Material) Order 2011 does not mean that the waste is inert for environmental protection purposes.

3.3 Mixed loads

Where a disposal to landfill contains both standard rated and lower rated materials, tax is due on the whole load at the standard rate. However, you may ignore the presence of an incidental amount of standard rated waste in a mainly lower rated load, and treat the whole load as taxable at the lower rate. For example, we would accept as qualifying for the lower rate:

- a load of bricks, stone and concrete from the demolition of a building that has small pieces of wood in it and small quantities of plaster attached to bricks as it would have not been feasible for a contractor to separate them
- a load of sub-soil that contains small quantities of grass
- waste such as mineral dust packaged in polythene bags for disposal, and
- a load of sub-soil and stone from street works containing tarmac (however, a load of tarmac containing soil and stone would not qualify).

It is not possible for us to advise you on every disposal. It is your responsibility to decide whether a particular load disposed of at your site contains a reasonable incidental amount of standard rated waste -you need to satisfy yourself that the load contains only a small quantity of such waste. The difficulty in separating the standard rated components from the lower rated waste is a factor that you can take into account, but this cannot be used to justify applying the lower rate of tax if the standard rated waste is more than a small amount of the total load. You will need to justify your decisions to us.

4. Exemptions

4.1 Dredgings - material removed from water

Waste removed from inland waterways and harbours by dredging and disposed of to landfill is exempt from landfill tax.
The circumstances under which dredging material qualifies for the exemption as originally introduced are shown below:

If	then
material is removed from the bed of the water (including the banks of canals and rivers) and has been dredged from: • a river, canal, watercourse, dock or harbour, or • the approaches to a harbour and removed in the interests of navigation, (to qualify as a watercourse it must be possible to show that a body of water has a: • natural source of surface or underground water • flow, under the action of gravity • reasonably well defined channel of bed and banks, and • meeting point with another watercourse or tidal waters.)	The disposal will qualify for exemption
Sand, gravel or other materials are any naturally occurring substances extracted from the seabed as part commercial operation	Any naturally occurring substances which result from this operation that are disposed of to landfill will qualify for the exemption.

The exemption was extended from 30 October 2007 to ensure compliance with the European Council Directive (99/31/EC) on the landfill of waste. This Directive requires those landfilling waste removed from water either to add material to the waste or remove the water from it. Since 30 October 2007, the exemption has applied to disposals of waste where we are satisfied that all of the disposal comprises material removed from the bed of the water (including the banks) and other material which has been added to it in order to ensure that it is no longer liquid waste.

Liquid waste is:
(i) any waste that immediately flows into a space made in its surface, or
(ii) any waste load containing more than 250 litres of free draining liquid or 10% of the load volume, whichever is the lesser amount. 'Free draining' means a liquid as defined in (i), whether or not it is in a container.

To qualify for the extended exemption, the additive used must have dehydrating properties or bind the excess moisture content within the waste and, in either case, produce a material that is not liquid waste. Additives such as sand and sawdust absorb liquid temporarily but release it again as waste is compressed within the landfill. Accordingly, these additives are not acceptable for the purposes of the exemption.

This extension to the scope of the exemption does not absolve waste producers and landfill site operators from fulfilling their obligations incurred under environmental regulations. If you have any doubts about those obligations, you should seek advice from:

- The Environment Agency (for England and Wales)
- The Scottish Environment Protection Agency (for Scotland), or
- The Northern Ireland Environment Agency (for Northern Ireland).

You do not need a certificate from us to apply this exemption but you should keep commercial documents that show the source of the waste and, where relevant, the nature and effect of the treatment it has undergone.

4.2 Mining and quarrying waste

Waste arising from mining and quarrying operations and disposed of to landfill is exempt from landfill tax.
To qualify for exemption the waste must:

- be naturally occurring in the course of a commercial mining or quarrying operation, including the reworking of tailings to extract further minerals. The term 'commercial' does not mean that a profit has to be made, but the operation has to be a business activity
- have the same chemical composition as it had when it was in the ground, and
- not be produced from a process separate from the mining/quarrying operation, so the exemption can apply to waste arising from winning the primary material from the spoil, but it does not apply to waste arising from the working of minerals from mines/quarries.

You do not need a certificate from us to qualify for this exemption but you must keep commercial documents showing the source of the waste.

4.3 Pet cemeteries

Pet cemeteries may be treated as landfill sites under environmental law. However, burials of dead pets at such sites are not taxable. To qualify for exemption the site must be used solely for the burial of dead domestic pets. In these circumstances the operator of the site is not required to register with us for landfill tax.

4.4 Filling of quarries

4.4.1 Conditions

Lower rated waste which is used for the purposes of filling existing or former quarries may qualify for exemption. The following table provides a summary of the conditions that must be met to qualify for exemption.

If	and	then
• the waste disposed of consists only of material listed in the Landfill Tax (Qualifying Material) Order 2011, a summary of which is set out in section 18, or • the waste disposed of consists mainly of material listed in the Landfill Tax (Qualifying Material) Order 2011 save for an incidental amount of standard rated waste as described in paragraph 3.3.	• the disposal takes place at a quarry • there is planning consent in place to fill (or partially fill) the quarry, and • the waste management licence or permit only authorises the disposal of qualifying material,	the disposal of waste is exempt.

4.4.2 What is a quarry?

We depend on common usage of the term quarry. For example, the Quarries Regulations 1999 defines a quarry as:
"an excavation or system of excavations made for the purpose of, or in connection with, the extraction of minerals (whether in their natural state or in solution or suspension) or products of minerals, being neither a mine nor merely a well or borehole or a well and borehole combined'.

We therefore see the term quarry as also applying to sand, gravel and clay pits and to other surface mineral workings.

4.4.3 'Old quarries'

Where a quarry was in existence before 1 October 1999 and quarrying operations ceased before then and there is not a planning consent in place either on or before 1 October 1999 to fill the quarry, it will not qualify for the exemption.

4.4.4 Variation of licence or permit to comply with the exemption

Many quarries taking only lower rated material may still have waste management licences or permits that authorise the disposal of other wastes. You may treat such licences/permits as being ones which only authorise the disposal of lower rated material for the period between the making of an application for the amendment of the licence/permit to authorise the disposal only of 'qualifying material' and the final resolution of that application, subject to that period not exceeding two years.

An application for amendment of a licence or permit is resolved if it is:

- granted
- withdrawn, or
- refused and a time limit for appeal against refusal expires without an appeal having been commenced.

Where an application to alter the waste management licence or permit has been made, disposals of material that were exempted from tax during the period between the making of the application and its resolution (or the two year period from the making of the application if that is the shorter period) remain exempt even if the application is unsuccessful. However, any disposals of material at the site after the end of that period will not qualify for exemption unless the application was granted.

Where an application is not resolved within two years but is ultimately granted, disposals made during the period between the end of the two years and the date on which the application is granted will not qualify for exemption.

4.5 Waste from visiting forces

Visiting NATO forces are exempt from paying landfill tax if relevant conditions are met.

To supply waste disposal services to visiting forces without charging landfill tax, a waste disposal contractor must have an official contract with the force authority showing:

- how long the contract will last
- the bases the contractor will cover, and
- the type and the amount of waste to be removed.

The contractor must also obtain an exemption certificate from the base Civil Engineer's office who will issue a certificate each month indicating the tonnage of waste to be removed and placed in landfill. This amount is the Approved Monthly Tonnage (AMT). The certificate must state the base where the contractor will collect the waste and the landfill site where it is to be deposited. In the case of landfilled waste from US visiting forces, the exemption certificate must contain the following declaration:

'The landfill tax liable on the disposal of active waste under this contract by landfill is to be relieved under the arrangements agreed between the appropriate authorities of the US visiting forces and HM Revenue & Customs reference: RDM 428/601/01. I hereby certify that this is official US forces active waste'.

In the case of landfilled waste from other NATO visiting forces, the exemption certificate must contain a similar declaration referring to an agreement between the force concerned and us, and certifying that this is visiting forces' waste.

The contractor must pass the certificate to you and you should use it to claim a reduction on your landfill tax return. You must keep the original certificates for our inspection.

5. Calculating the weight of waste

5.1 Sites with a weighbridge

The basic method of calculating the weight of waste is by weighing it at the time of disposal. If there is a weighbridge at your landfill site, we would expect you to use it. Weighbridges used at landfill sites to calculate weight for the purposes of the landfill tax must comply with the relevant weights and measures legislation.

You can ask us to agree an alternative method of calculating the weight if:

- using the weighbridge would involve a costly change to your current practices (for example, because the waste does not normally pass near the weighbridge), or
- your weighbridge has broken down.

5.2 Sites without a weighbridge

If there is no weighbridge at your site, you can use one or a mixture of three specified methods of calculating the weight of waste. A summary of the specified methods for such sites can be found at paragraph 5.3 and details of the methods can be found in paragraphs 5.4, 5.5 and 5.6.

If you cannot operate a specified method you can propose another method (a 'bespoke method'). You must be able to satisfy us that this will produce a fair and reasonable calculation of weight. Once satisfied, we will agree in writing and normally this agreement will run for 12 months. You must notify us of any changes to your business practices which will affect the reliability of this method. You must also notify us if you wish to change from a bespoke method to weighing the waste. On occasions we may wish to have an independent check (for example, by test weighing loads) on the accuracy of the method used. In addition, you must satisfy the weights and measures legislation.

5.3 Specified methods for sites without weighbridges

The conditions specified in paragraphs 5.4, 5.5 and 5.6 have the force of law under the Landfill Tax Regulations 1996 and remain in force until withdrawn by a further notice. If you wish to use any of the specified methods detailed in paragraphs 5.4, 5.5 and 5.6, you must abide by all the conditions specified under the relevant method.

You can use the specified methods without our agreement. You do not need to notify us that you have started to use a specified method unless you wish to:

- change from a bespoke method prior to the expiry of the current agreement, or
- agree a bespoke method as well.

However, once you have started to use a specified method you will not normally be allowed to change it except at the end of any complete year of operating it, reckoned from the beginning of the tax period in which you first start to use a specified method.

You can use a mixture of specified methods for different waste streams or for different customers but you must be consistent, that is, when you have started using a method for a particular waste stream or customer you must continue to do so.

5.4 Specified method 1: maximum permitted weight of container

5.4.1 Description of method

This method involves recording the maximum weight that a lorry, skip, rail wagon, etc. is permitted to carry and applying the appropriate rate of tax.

5.4.2 Maximum weights

You can use either the maximum plated weight that the vehicle can carry or the weights specified in the three tables below.
You should use the gross plated weight of the vehicle/container less its tare weight.
Any vehicles that are partially filled must be treated as full for your tax calculation purposes.

Lorries without cranes or buckets

Vehicle type	Maximum weight
4 axle lorry	20 tonnes
3 axle lorry	15 tonnes
2 axle lorry	10 tonnes

Lorries with cranes or buckets

If a crane or bucket is fitted to a vehicle the maximum weight that can be carried is reduced by 2 tonnes.

Vehicle type	Maximum weight
4 axle lorry with grab	18 tonnes
3 axle lorry with grab	13 tonnes
2 axle lorry with grab	8 tonnes

Light goods vehicles/vans/cars

Vehicle type	Maximum weight
Light goods vehicles,	The manufacturer's plate, usually in the passenger door well, shows the maximum gross weight

Vehicle type	Maximum weight
Other cars and vans	The vehicle handbook shows the maximum gross vehicle weight of the vehicle. Deduct from this the unladen weight shown in the vehicle handbook to give you the weight that can be carried by the vehicle.

5.4.3 What records do I need to keep?

To operate this method you must record all waste brought onto your site(s), showing the identifying number and type of vehicle/container, a description of the waste carried, and the date the waste was disposed at your site. You must also establish an audit trail or register which records the gross weight, net tare weight and maximum carrying weight for each vehicle/container using your site(s) for waste disposal.

5.5 Specified method 2 - volume to weight conversion

5.5.1 Description of method

To operate this method you will need to know the cubic capacity of the vehicles (lorry, skip, rail wagon, barge, etc.) that deliver waste to your site. These should be used with the categories of waste and the conversion factors in paragraph 5.5.2.

To comply with weights and measures legislation the maximum cubic capacity of the container must be a multiple of 0.1 cubic metres. Measurement can only go to one decimal place.

If the calculation results in a tonnage which is greater than the legal carrying capacity of the vehicle, it is to your benefit to use the maximum permitted weight of the container method (see paragraph 5.4). Your tax calculations must be based on all containers and vehicles being full.

5.5.2 Conversion factors

Note: If the waste falls into more than one category, the higher conversion factor applies to all of the waste.

Waste category	Typical waste types	Cubic metres to tonnes - multiply by:	Cubic yards to tonnes - multiply by:
Inactive or inert waste	Largely water insoluble and non or very slowly biodegradable, for example, sand, subsoil, concrete, bricks, mineral fibres, fibreglass etc.	1.5	1.15
General industrial waste: non-special, not compacted. (As compaction can significantly increase the density of this category of waste, if you accept compacted wastes you will need to uplift the conversion factor accordingly)	Paper and plastics	0.15	0.11
	Card, pallets, plasterboard, canteen waste, sawdust, textiles, leather	0.4	0.3
	Timber, building and construction wastes, factory waste and sweepings, etc.	0.6	0.46
	Foundary sands, slags, pulverised fuel ash, ashes from waste incineration.	1.5	1.15
Household waste – not compacted	Non-special, non inert wastes from domestic premises, including collected household waste.	0.2	0.15
Household waste – compacted (includes all bulk disposals)	Non-special, non inert wastes from domestic premises, including collected household waste.	0.4	0.30
Commercial waste – not compacted. (As compaction can significantly increase the density of this category of waste, if you accept compacted wastes you will need to uplift the conversion factor accordingly)	Non-special, non inert wastes from shops, hospitals, leisure centres, offices, etc, including civic amenity waste, parks and gardens waste, street litter, supermarket, shop and restaurant waste, general office waste.	0.2	0.15
Special waste	Defined by environmental regulations – broadly equivalent to hazardous waste.	1.0	0.76

5.5.3 What records do I need to keep?

You must record all waste brought onto your site(s), showing the identifying number and type of vehicle/container, a description of the waste carried, and the date disposed at your site. The volume of the vehicle/container must be recorded and evidenced with whatever documentation is available from the haulier.

5.6 Specified method 3 - weighing the waste prior to receipt at the site

5.6.1 Description of method

You may accept waste that is weighed away from your landfill site. If there is a clear audit trail including a record of weights for each vehicle, container, wagon, etc. and they go directly to the site, then this scheme can be used to calculate landfill tax.

5.6.2 What records do I need to keep?

To operate this method you must record all waste brought onto your site(s), showing where the waste was weighed, the identifying number and type of vehicle/container, a description of the waste, and the date disposed at your site. You must also record and retain the weighbridge tickets.

5.7 Discounting water

5.7.1 What are the qualifying conditions?

In certain circumstances, you can apply to discount the water content of waste (but only where it is not present naturally) when calculating the taxable weight of the waste. The circumstances under which you can and cannot apply to discount the water content of the waste are set out below.

If the water has	and	then
• been added to allow transportation for disposal, or • been used for the extraction of minerals or • arisen or been added or both, in the course of an industrial process	is 25% or more of the waste, by weight,	you can apply to discount the water content of the waste.

You will not be able to discount water where:

- it is present naturally in the waste (although you may agree a scheme to discount water up to, but not beyond, the amount present naturally)
- it is present because of rain or snow
- it was added to waste to damp it down to prevent it blowing away and the added water is less than 25% of the waste, by weight, or
- any of the water is capable of escaping from the landfill site by leaching. (This restriction does not apply if the only water that can escape is pure water or if the leachate is collected on site and treated in order to eliminate any potential it has to cause harm.)

For effluent or sewage sludge from waste water treatment works/sewage disposal works, you can apply to discount the water content, but:

- water which is present naturally cannot be discounted, and
- any water which has been extracted prior to disposal is treated as added water in preference to water present naturally in the material.

5.7.2 How do I apply to discount water?

Waste producers may propose schemes to quantify the water content of their waste, based, for example, on their production records. They will need to complete an application form LT 1WD Application for discounting of water content of waste which they can get from our website or by phoning the Excise Helpline, on 0845 010 9000.

If we are satisfied that the application qualifies for a scheme for discounting water, we will send written approval to you and the waste producer. However, we will not approve such schemes unless the waste producers have your prior agreement, which you gave using form LT4WD.

12. Registration

12.1 Who has to be registered for landfill tax?

If you are a landfill site operator (see paragraphs 2.4 and 2.6.1) and you are or have the intention of making taxable disposals (see paragraphs 2.1 and 12.2) you are liable to be registered. You must notify us of your liability to register within 30 days of making taxable disposals, or forming the intention to make taxable disposals. If you fail to notify us on time you may be liable to a penalty for failure to notify (see paragraph 16.1).

This applies even if you, as licence or permit holder, allow the site to be operated by someone else. We cannot register a site operator who is not the licence or permit holder. Unlike VAT, there is no registration threshold for landfill tax.

The registered person can be a:

Sole Proprietor	
Partnership	Each partner is liable for all the obligations and liabilities of the partnership in relation to landfill tax, including telling us about any liability to be registered.
Limited company	In certain circumstances: • associated companies can apply for group treatment -this will enable a group of companies to account for landfill tax under a single registration, or • a company can apply for divisional registration - this will enable its divisions to account for tax under separate registrations.

18. Summary of the Landfill Tax (Qualifying Material) Order 2011

18.1 Extract from the Order Qualifying material

Group	Description of material	Conditions	Notes
1	Rocks and soils	Naturally occurring	Group 1 comprises only i. rock, ii. clay, iii. sand, iv. gravel, v. sandstone, vi. limestone, vii. crushed stone, viii. china clay, ix. construction stone, x. stone from the demolition of buildings or structures, xi. slate, xii. sub-soil, xiii. silt, xiv. dredgings.
2	Ceramic or concrete materials		Group 2 comprises only i. glass, including fritted enamel, ii. ceramics, including bricks, bricks and mortar, tiles, clay ware, pottery, china and refractories, iii. concrete, including reinforced concrete, concrete blocks, breeze blocks and aircrete blocks Group 2 does not include i. glass fibre and glass-reinforced plastic, and ii. concrete plant washings.
3	Minerals	Processed or prepared, not used	Group 3 comprises only i. moulding sands, including used foundry sand, ii. clays, including moulding clays and clay absorbents (including Fuller's earth and bentonite), iii. mineral absorbents, iv. man-made mineral fibres, including glass fibres, v. silica, vi. mica, vii. mineral abrasives. Group 3 does not include i. moulding sands containing organic binders, ii. man-made mineral fibres made from glass-reinforced plastic and asbestos.
4	Furnace slags		Group 4 comprises only i. vitrified wastes and residues from thermal processing of minerals where, in either case, the residue is both fused and insoluble, and ii. slag from waste incineration
5	Ash		Group 5 comprises only i. bottom ash and fly ash produced only from the combustion of wood, of waste or of both, ii. bottom ash and fly ash from the combustion of coal, of petroleum coke or of both, deposited in a cell containing the product of that combustion alone, and, iii. bottom ash and fly ash from the combustion of coal, of petroleum coke or of both, burnt together with biomass and deposited in a cell containing the product of that combustion and burning alone. Group 5 does not include fly ash from sewage sludge, municipal, clinical and hazardous waste incinerators.

Group	Description of material	Conditions	Notes
6	Low activity inorganic compounds		Group 6 comprises only i. calcium based reaction wastes from titanium dioxide production, ii. calcium carbonate, iii. magnesium carbonate, iv. magnesium oxide, v. magnesium hydroxide, vi. iron oxide, vii. ferric hydroxide, viii. aluminium oxide, ix. aluminium hydroxide, x. zirconium dioxide.
7	Calcium sulphate	Disposed of in landfills for non-hazardous waste in a cell where no biodegradable waste is accepted	Group 7 includes i. calcium sulphate, ii. gypsum, iii. calcium sulphate based plasters, Group 7 does not include plasterboard.
8	Calcium hydroxide and brine	Deposited in brine cavity.	

AH
LANDFILL TAX EXEMPTION

1.1 This notice explains the circumstances under which waste arising from the reclamation of contaminated land is exempt from landfill tax. To gain the exemption the person carrying out the reclamation must apply to us. If the reclamation qualifies we will issue an exemption certificate. This notice also details the procedures for this. A separate Notice LFT1 A general guide to landfill tax is available detailing the circumstances when landfill tax applies to disposals of waste.

If you need general advice or copies of Customs and Excise notices, please ring the **National Advice Service** on **0845 010 9000, Monday to Friday from 8.00 a.m. to 8.00 p.m**. If you have **hearing difficulties** - please ring the **Textphone** service on **0845 000 0200**. If you would like to speak to someone in **Welsh** - please ring **0845 010 0300, Monday to Friday from 8.00 a.m. to 6.00 p.m**. All calls are charged at the local rate within the UK. Charges may differ for mobile phones.

See Section AH (above) for extracts from LFT1

This notice cancels and replaces Notice LFT2 (April 2003).

1 Introduction

1.2 This notice is for anyone (landowners, developers or contractors) carrying out a reclamation of contaminated land. It will also be of interest to landfill site operators who expect to receive waste from reclamation sites.

1.3 Sections 43A and 43B of the Finance Act 1996 as inserted by The Landfill Tax (Contaminated Land) Order 1996 (SI 1996 No. 1529) exempt the disposal to landfill of waste resulting from the reclamation of contaminated land.

Nothing in this notice changes your obligations under environmental law.

2. Eligibility for exemption

2.1 What is a qualifying reclamation?

A reclamation will qualify for exemption if it is or will be carried out with the object of:

(a) facilitating development, conservation, the provision of a public park or other amenity, or the use of the land for agriculture or forestry, or
(b) reducing or removing the potential of pollutants to cause harm.

The reclamation must also meet certain conditions in order to qualify for the exemption - see paragraph 2.2 for details of these conditions.

Note: Where we refer to reclamation for the purpose of "development" in this notice, we mean any reclamation falling within category (a) above.

2.2 What are the conditions?

2.2.1 General conditions

For both categories of reclamation, the following conditions must be met.

Condition	
1. Reclamation must involve clearing the land of pollutants that are causing harm or have the potential to cause harm.	You must be able to demonstrate that there are pollutants present which are: • polluting ground or surface water; or • harming the health of people, animals or plants; or • damaging the fabric of structures or services; or have the potential to do so. Reclamation of land which is merely derelict but not polluted will not qualify for exemption. You do not necessarily need to be clearing all of the pollutants from the land to qualify for exemption.
2. The cause of the pollution must have ceased.	The only exception to this is where the pollution is being caused by someone or something outside your control. In such cases you should contact the **Excise Helpline**, phone **0845 010 9000**.
3.The land is not subject to a works or remediation notice.	The exemption will not apply where the removal of the material is required in order to comply with a notice or order **unless** the reclamation is being undertaken by or on behalf of certain bodies – see paragraph 2.3 for further details.

2.2.2 Additional condition

Where the purpose of the reclamation is development, the following condition must also be met:

Condition	
The reclamation constitutes or includes clearing the land of pollutants which would (unless cleared) prevent the land being put to the intended use.	You must be able to demonstrate that the pollutants have to be removed because their potential to cause harm (see condition 1 of paragraph 2.2.1) would prevent the land being put to the intended use, were they to remain. We will not accept claims that, though the pollutants fall below the limits generally recognised as safe for the intended use for the land, they have to be removed for other reasons, for example, because: • the soil structure is unsuitable for buildings • those providing the financial backing for the development demand their removal • the waste can not be used on-site for landscaping/backfilling, or • the site level needs reducing.

2.3 What if material is removed to comply with a notice or order?

The exemption does not apply where the removal of material is required to comply with:

- a works notice served under section 46A of the Control of Pollution Act 1974
- a remediation notice served under section 78E of the Environmental Protection Act 1990
- an enforcement notice served under section 90B of the Water Resources Act 1991
- a works notice served under section 161A of the Water Resources Act 1991
- an enforcement notice served under regulation 24 of the Pollution Prevention and Control (England and Wales) Regulations 2000
- a suspension notice served under regulation 25 of those Regulations
- an order under regulation 35 of those Regulations
- an enforcement notice served under regulation 19 of the Pollution Prevention and Control (Scotland) Regulations 2000
- a suspension notice served under regulation 20 of those Regulations, or
- an order under regulation 33 of those Regulations.

However, this condition does not apply to land being reclaimed by or on behalf of any of the following:

- a local authority
- a development corporation
- the Environment Agency
- the Scottish Environment Protection Agency
- English Partnerships
- Scottish Enterprise
- Highlands and Islands Enterprise, or
- the Welsh Development Agency.

Any applications from the above organisations will have to satisfy all the other qualifying conditions in this section for the exemption to apply.

2.4 What is the definition of land for the purpose of the exemption?

The definition of land includes buildings standing on contaminated land and contaminated buildings themselves (whether or not they stand on contaminated land). You can therefore apply for exemption certificates for land, buildings and land, and buildings only.

2.5 Reclamation or construction?

Only waste arising from reclamation qualifies for exemption. Waste arising from construction activity does not qualify. Sometimes it may not be clear whether the activity which will give rise to the waste amounts to reclamation, prior to construction, or to construction activity itself. In these cases we will take various factors into account in determining the extent to which reclamation is taking place.

These include:

- whether the developer's plans identify a clear intention to remediate prior to the commencement of construction
- whether the amount of material being removed relates to that necessary to deal with any pollutants or only to that which needs to be removed for other reasons, for example reducing site levels or instability of made ground, and
- whether material is to be removed only from the construction area itself, leaving similar pollutants below or alongside, without dealing with them in some way, or from an area sufficient to remove any potential for harm.

Some examples of projects that we would and would not regard as reclamation can be found in sections 7 and 8 to assist you.

In many projects of reclamation, spoil is removed in order to remove pollutants which would have to have been excavated in any case to level land or to dig foundations or service trenches. If we are satisfied that what is taking place is reclamation, then the waste arising from that work would all be exempt, even though it would have been removed in any case as part of the later construction.

2.6 How to identify reclamation wastes

The exemption only applies to reclamation wastes. Once the qualifying conditions have been met you will need to identify and quantify these wastes. The following general rules apply.

If	Then
Pollutants are present in only part (or parts) of the site	Only the wastes arising from reclamation of this area qualify for exemption. The contaminated area and amounts of waste arising from its clearance should be clearly identified when applying for exemption.
Pollutants are present throughout the site but not all need to be removed for development to proceed	If: • reclamation is taking place with a view to development, and • the nature of the intended development is such that the level of pollutants would (unless cleared) prevent it proceeding in some areas but not others (for example they are above thresholds for garden or open space areas but not those for buildings) then only the wastes from areas where it is necessary to remove the pollutants will qualify for exemption.
Pollutants are present throughout the whole site at a level where reclamation is necessary in all areas	If the nature of the development is such that the level of pollutants would prevent the development from proceeding in all areas of the site, all wastes arising from the reclamation will qualify for exemption.
There are small areas of non qualifying land present on the site	We recognise that there may be instances where there are small areas of: • clean material, or • land which is contaminated, but not to a level that requires its removal, dispersed between areas of contamination and it would not be practicable to separate wastes arising from such land during the reclamation. You can include such wastes in your application, provided that they amount to less than a quarter of the total waste applied for.
It is necessary to remove clean or non qualifying land in order to get to the pollutants	If you can prove to us that as part of the reclamation, in order to get to the pollutants, you must remove clean land, or land which is contaminated but not to a level that requires its removal, you can include these wastes in your application.
The only practical or safe way to remove pollutants is to add materials to them, for example adding ash to tar to bind it	You can include the weight of these materials in your application.

3. Expiry of the exemption

3.1 General

The exemption automatically expires once pollutants have been cleared to the extent that they no longer prevent development, conservation, provision of a public park etc. or the potential for harm has been removed. Where a reclamation is carried out to facilitate construction of a building or civil engineering work, the exemption will automatically expire, in respect of that part of the land which relates to the construction, when the construction commences.

3.2 Phased developments

If construction has commenced on one phase, it will not prevent waste produced during the clearing of pollutants from a later phase from qualifying for exemption, provided that the clearance is necessary to facilitate further development. In the case of large developments involving several phases over a long period we request that you submit separate applications for each phase (apply separately for each phase at least 30 days prior to its commencement).

3.3 Discovery of further pollutants

There may be occasions where you discover further unexpected pollutants that make further reclamation necessary before construction can proceed. In such a case you should make application for an extension to your certificate to cover the additional waste that has to be removed to landfill (see paragraph 5.2). You will need to submit a revised plan and calculations which clearly show how the new figure has been arrived at.

4.1. Who should apply?

The person carrying out, or intending to carry out the reclamation of the contaminated land should apply for the exemption. This would normally be the landowner, developer or main contractor. If you appoint an agent to act on your behalf, the application must be completed in your name and be accompanied by your written authority.

4.2. How do I apply?

Please phone the Excise Helpline on 0845 010 9000 who will send you form LT1C Contaminated land - application for a certificate of exemption. Form LT1C is also available on our website, go to www.hmrc.gov.uk.

Once you have completed form LT1C please send it with the required evidence (see paragraph 4.4) to the Landfill Tax Processing Unit at:

HM Revenue & Customs
Dobson House
Regent Centre
Gosforth
Newcastle-upon-Tyne
NE3 3PF

4.3. When should I apply?

Step	Action
1	Apply at least 30 days before you intend to start removing the waste to landfill
2	If you have to clear the land within 30 days, for example if you uncover pollutants on a site you believed to be clean, you should mark your application clearly showing the deadlines you are hoping to meet and explaining why you have been unable to make the normal thirty day application. In such cases we will make every effort to assist you.
Note	To enable us to process your application quickly, you must supply all the information requested on the form and all the accompanying evidence to support it (see paragraph 4.4).

Remember: the law does not allow Customs to issue backdated certificates and any waste removed before a certificate is issued will not be exempted.

4.4 Evidence to support your application

You will need to provide the following evidence with your application. We may also request further information. If you do not provide all the information we need, issue of the certificate will be delayed.

	Evidence required	Including
1	Details of the pollutants	Evidence to demonstrate that there are pollutants that are causing or have the potential to cause harm. If reclamation is for the purpose of development then evidence must also demonstrate that failure to remove the pollutants would prevent that development from taking place. Such evidence could include: • site investigation report, detailing pollutants, potential pathways and targets • reference to recognised guidance on contaminated land redevelopment, and • any correspondence with environmental agencies.
2	Calculation of the weight of waste which has to be removed	• Full details of how the weight of waste to be removed has been calculated. These should be clearly linked to the recommendations of the site investigation report and the plan of the contaminated area (see 3 below). • Evidence to demonstrate that this is only waste arising from the reclamation stage and does not include any waste produced after the pollutants have been cleared.
3	Location of the contaminated land	• Copy of the site plan with full postal address, Ordnance Survey grid reference and Land Registry number (if applicable). The boundaries of the site and the areas of contamination within it should be clearly identified on the plan. • Cross-sections of the land, showing the extent, type and depth of pollutants throughout the site, if available
4	Action plan for development	For reclamations that involve development, showing: • A simple action plan showing a clear intention to remediate. • Estimates of expected dates that each stage will begin and end, the work involved and the amount of waste attributable to each.

4.5 What happens after I submit my application?

On receipt of your application we will take the following action:

Step	We Will
1	Allocate it a unique reference number which you should quote in any further correspondence.
2	Send you an acknowledgement and tell you which office is dealing with your application.
3	Contact you and may ask for additional information. We may also visit the site of the reclamation and make any other enquiries.
4	Issue the certificates once we are satisfied that the reclamation qualifies for exemption. (See section 5 for further information about certificates.)
5	Write to you explaining the reasons if we find it necessary to refuse your application or reduce the tonnage requested.

If you have any queries regarding the details of your application you should contact the officer dealing with it.

4.6 What if I don't know the details of the landfill sites and dates of reclamation?

This table shows what you need to do and what happens then.

Step	Who	Does What
1	**You**	• make the application without delay **This is important because the law does not allow us to backdate certificates, so any waste removed before a certificate is issued cannot be exempted.** • photocopy section 3 of form LT1C • complete and sign form LT1C, and • send it to the address in paragraph 4.2, enclosing all the supporting evidence with it.
2	**We** will then	• follow the procedure in paragraph 4.5, and as long as all the other essential information is produced • issue Part A of the certificate
3	**You** - once you know details of the landfill sites	Use the photocopy of section 3 of form LT1C to notify the officer who dealt with the application of: • the designated landfill sites and details of the operator • the weight of waste to be disposed of at each site, and • the dates from which disposals authorised under the exemption will commence.
4	**We** will then	Issue Part B certificates to the nominated site(s).

5. Certificates

5.1 Issue of certificates

The certificate is in two parts:

Part A (issued to the applicant). This certifies that the land identified in the application is deemed to be contaminated for the purposes of landfill tax. Our office dealing with your application should already have written to you advising the areas of the site and types and amounts of waste arising from reclamation to which the exemption will apply.

PART A OF THE CERTIFICATE DOES NOT BY ITSELF ENTITLE A SITE OPERATOR TO EXEMPT THE DISPOSAL OF WASTE.

Part B (issued to each of the landfill site operators nominated by you). You will also receive a copy of each Part B. The original Part B authorises the site operator(s) to exempt waste from a specified area of contaminated land.

It will detail:

- the contaminated land
- the landfill site authorised to accept the waste
- the date from which waste may be exempted, and
- the maximum weight of waste from the reclamation that may be exempted at that landfill site.

Do not move waste to landfill until you have told us which sites you have nominated to receive the waste and certificates have been issued to these sites advising them of what tonnages they can accept for exemption. You will receive copies of these certificates to let you know this has been done.

5.2 Amendments to certificates

It may become necessary to amend the Part B certificates at some stage because:

- you have discovered further pollutants giving rise to additional waste
- changes in the proposed end use of the site, mean that you need to remove pollutants from areas that would not otherwise have required it, or
- you need to amend the details of landfill sites to be used.

Any changes that will need an amendment to a Part B certificate must be notified in writing to the officer who dealt with your application. You should do this before any additional waste is landfilled at any of the nominated sites. Provided that the officer is satisfied with the information received, he/she will authorise the issue of a variation certificate. We do not require a further period of thirty days to make such amendments; we will normally process an amendment within five working days of receiving your notification.

YOU MUST INFORM US IMMEDIATELY OF ANY CHANGES THAT COULD AFFECT THE VALIDITY OF THE CERTIFICATE, QUOTING THE NUMBER OF YOUR ORIGINAL CERTIFICATE.

5.3 Completion statements

As soon as the reclamation is finished you must send the officer who dealt with your application a completion statement summarising, by each landfill site used:

- the start and finish dates of the qualifying disposals, and
- the total tonnage disposed of.

We periodically review exemption certificates to ensure applications are finalised within an identified period of exemption.

5.4 Withdrawal of certificates

We can withdraw certificates where:

- it is necessary to protect the revenue
- we discover the reclamation did not in fact qualify for the exemption
- no disposals of the material from the certified land take place, or
- an enforcement notice is served and the certificate holder is not one of the bodies listed (see paragraph 2.3).

However we would only refuse to issue a certificate for land that meets the qualifying conditions for the protection of the revenue, or where an enforcement notice is in force.

5.5 Reviews and appeals

If we decide to:

- refuse the issue of a certificate
- limit your certificate to only part of the land covered by your application, or
- withdraw your certificate,

You can seek a review (and subsequently appeal to a VAT and Duties Tribunal if necessary). The procedure is explained in the reviews and appeals section of Notice LFT1 A general guide to landfill tax.

6. If you are a landfill site operator

6.1 Issue of certificate

We will issue the relevant Part B of the certificate to each nominated landfill site operator.

6.2 What the certificate authorises

This authorises the maximum weight of waste from the contaminated land that can be exempted upon disposal at that particular site. The certificate will also specify the date from which the certificate is effective.

Any waste received prior to this date is not subject to exemption and you must account for tax on it.

6.3 Your responsibilities as a landfill site operator

If you have been authorised to exempt waste from an area of contaminated land, you must agree procedures with those reclaiming that land to ensure that only qualifying waste is exempted.

For example, by ensuring:

- waste transfer notes/weighbridge tickets identify the reclamation site that the waste comes from, and
- waste transfer notes include a cross reference to the exemption certificates.

You can find further details of your responsibilities in Notice LFT1 A general guide to landfill tax.

6.4 What happens when the authorised amount is exhausted?

Once this amount has been exhausted you must charge tax unless you have received an amended certificate from us.

Once a reclamation of contaminated land has taken place, the applicant is required to provide us with a statement detailing the quantity of qualifying waste which has been disposed of at your landfill site. We will expect this to accord with your exemption disposal record.

7. Examples of eligible reclamation projects

7.1 About these examples

Please note that these examples are only to be taken as illustrative of ones where exemption may apply. Each case will be treated on its own merits and similarity to your circumstances is not to be taken as an indication that exemption will apply.

7.2 Example 1

A football pitch is being developed on the site of a disused cokeworks. The area to be developed contains a number of pollutants (including various metals, polyaromatic hydrocarbons and tar). These exceed the threshold levels for parks and open spaces throughout the site and a condition of the planning approval is that they must be cleared before any development can take place. The consultant surveyors have recommended that material be removed to a depth of 1.5 metres to remove the potential for harm, a strategy agreed by the planning authority. This will take place before any construction work commences.

The waste removed will qualify for exemption. It is clear that a reclamation of contaminated land is taking place. This involves the removal of pollutants which, if not cleared, would prevent the development from proceeding.

7.3 Example 2

An industrial unit is to be constructed on the site of a former unlicensed tip which contains domestic waste. Surveys commissioned by the developer show that due to the lack of control over tipping at the site when it was operational there is a danger of leachate polluting the groundwater and gas emissions which could present a real danger to future employees unless the pollutants are removed.

The waste removed in clearing the land of pollutants will qualify for exemption. It is clear there is a potential for harm and that the development cannot proceed without removal of the pollutants. It does not matter in these circumstances whether or not the developer had to remove more waste than would have been removed in any case to reduce site levels.

7.4 Example 3

A housing development is to be constructed on a site polluted by previous industrial use. The whole site is contaminated with polyaromatic hydrocarbons, which exceed the ICRCL levels for gardens/play areas but not those for buildings, landscaped areas or hard cover.

The site qualifies for the issue of an exemption certificate because removal of the waste from gardens/play areas is necessary for development to proceed. However, we would restrict the exemption to only the gardens/play areas as removal from other areas is not required as a result of the presence of pollutants. But if the vast majority of the site is covered by the reclamation of the gardens/play areas, we would grant exemption to the whole site.

7.5 Example 4

A disused factory is being demolished prior to development of the site for sheltered housing with landscaped areas. Asbestos is found in the roof and internal walls of the factory.

In this case the asbestos waste cleared from the building will qualify for exemption.

8. Examples of ineligible projects

8.1 Example 1

A site to be developed was formerly used as a tip for construction waste. The waste is largely inert and there is no evidence that there are pollutants present with a potential to cause harm but the waste is to be removed anyway because the ground is too unstable to support the planned construction.

This will not qualify for exemption as it does not involve the removal of pollutants with the potential to cause harm.

8.2 Example 2

A motorway is being constructed through an area of land that contains contamination. This exceeds threshold levels for domestic gardens but not those for buildings or hard cover. Planning conditions dictate that in order to "hide" the road from view of local residents it will be built in a deep cutting. No more waste is being removed than is required to meet this condition and similar contamination is being left on either side of the section being removed.

This will not qualify for exemption because there is no evidence that removal of pollutants is necessary before construction can commence.

Diploma in Adjudication in the Construction Industry

Comprised of four units, this qualification is designed for those **seeking to become an adjudicator**, and provides a pathway towards potential entry onto the **RICS Panel of Adjudicators**.

With a focus on contract and tort law and how they apply to adjudication, this course is designed to prepare you to progress to practice as an adjudicator. This course is suitable for those with experience in dispute resolution procedures with an understanding of the general principles of construction adjudication. The course content will focus on the format and content of an enforceable decision.

Learning Outcomes:

- Knowledge and understanding of the nature of law and its' place in society
- How the law of contract is applied to the practice of adjudication
- How the law of tort is applied to the practice of adjudication
- The practical application in the production of an enforceable decision.

Attainment of the learning outcomes will be assessed by a case study, whereby candidates will be required to produce an enforceable reasoned decision, based on material supplied in the case study.

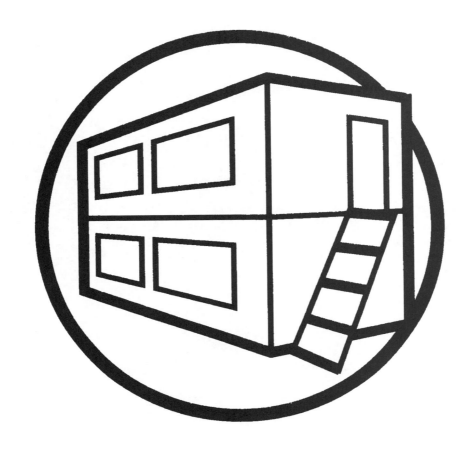

Preliminaries

BCIS

Independent cost information
for the built environment

CONSTRUCTION

LESS DESK TIME
MORE FREE TIME

THE REVOLUTION OF THE PRICE BOOK IS HERE
BCIS ONLINE RATES DATABASE

What the service can do for you:

Accuracy: You can benchmark against 18500 separate Supply Prices of which there are over 9,000 material costs and over 8000 specialist prices collected from independent suppliers. It will ensure that your information is accurate and reliable, reducing the margin of error.

Futureproof: You can adjust the prices using industry standard BCIS Tender Price Index and Location Factor adjustments so you can forecast your figures for projects up to two years ahead, putting you a step ahead of your competitors. It makes your project cost predictions more robust.

Value for money: It provides an expert opinion at your fingertips to give you the confidence that you are not over or underestimating quotes and costs. It could mean the difference between winning or losing a tender or being over charged for your works.

Saves time: The easy navigation system helps you find what you are looking for quickly and effortlessly. Add the information you want to a list for download to Excel.

Flexible: With a subscription to suit your job, you can access a variety

of new and historical price data. This allows you to build up your own prices from individual elements so you can make your own decisions about how you cost your projects.

Customise: Adjust your data to your location and time frame and it will do the calculations for you. You can download the results, keep track of your adjustments and reduce your margin of error.

Portable: This service can be accessed on your computer and just as easily on your iPad or netbook on site.

Comprehensive: Everything you need is in one place; you have a full library of information at your disposal.

Offering immediate online access to independent BCIS resource rates data, quantity surveyors and others in the construction industry can have all the information needed to compile and check estimates on their desktops. You won't need to worry about being able to lay your hands on the office copy of the latest price books, all of the information is now easily accessible online.

For a **FREE TRIAL** of BCIS online rates database register at
www.bcis.co.uk/ordbdemo

BCIS is the Building Cost Information Service of **RICS** the mark of property professionalism worldwide

PRELIMINARIES

BA		**GENERAL**		

001 | The prices in the Work or Trade Sections of the price book only allow for the cost of labour, plant and materials in each item of work.

The Cost of supervision, administration, scaffolding, insurances, small tools, temporary services etc., which are applicable to many items rather than a particular item are usually costed separately under the heading of 'Preliminaries'.

002 | The number of different items and the costs of each item in Preliminaries will vary from project to project as such factors as contract conditions, design, locality, and overall value all have their effect on Preliminaries.

BB		**PRICING EXAMPLE**	£	£
		Contract Conditions		

001 | Based upon a total Tender price of 165,000 the following is an example of the cost of items which should be considered in Preliminaries. The contract period is assumed at 12 weeks.

002 | **Supervision and administration**

003 | A full time foreman may not be economic and some jobs will not even have a working foreman. The leading tradesman on site may be required to supervise from time to time. Otherwise, supervision and administration is organised by office personnel.

A possible allowance could be an average of one day per week for entire contract period by office personnel.

		12 weeks at £135.00		**1,620**

004 | **Insurances**

005 | Building Employer's Liability and Public Liability is allowed for in the calculation of the total hourly rate (see Introduction sub-section AD Labour Costs).

006 | If the builder is required to insure the new building works in a contract of all new works then an allowance should be made as follows:

Contract value - say	£150,000		
Allowance for demolitions	£15,000		

	£165,000		
Professional fees (say) 12.5%	£20,625		

	£185,625		
Premium allowance (average)	0.30% of £185,625 = £556.88		**557**

007 | In a contract for alterations, extensions and renovations to existing buildings, it is usual for the building owner to insure the existing building and the improvements, but if the contract requires the builder to insure, then the replacement value of the existing building must be established and added to the cost of the improvements, with increased allowances for demolitions and fees calculated in a similar way to the above. | - | -

008 | **Increased costs**

009 | If the contract is for a short period of a few weeks, then increased costs will not be significant, but any longer period may see increases which could be substantial especially on a particular material forming a large part of the contract. | - | -

010 | The contract completion time will be the governing factor in determining whether or not to allow for this item. An overall allowance based on 10% per annum would not be unreasonable in the current economic climate. | - | -

011 | **Transport and haulage**

| 500 kg van and driver: | 12 weeks at £400 | 4,800 | |
| Running expenses say 40 miles per day for 12 weeks: | 40 x 5 x 12 x £0.35 | 840 | **5,640** |

012 | **Plant and small tools**

Concrete mixer:	7 weeks at £20.00	140	
Small tools allowances:	12 weeks at £35.00	420	
Sundry haulage of plant not covered in unit rates (say):	3 at £75.00	225	**785**
		---------	

013 | **Scaffolding**

Scaffolding to new extension:			
externally:	(say):	1,200	
internal, trestles, staging etc:	(say):	200	**1,400**
		---------	

014 | **Temporary buildings**

Site offices are not usually required on extension work but may be needed on all new work.

Storage sheds, if required, should be allowed at lump sums of (say) £175 each: | - | -

| | | | --------- | |
| | | Carried forward | | **10,002** |

	£	£
Brought forward		10,002

015 Temporary services

Connections are not normally required on extension work but water charges may be imposed at rates per 100 of the cost of the new building work.

If existing services are not available, then allowance for connections should be made, a typical charge for each service is shown:

water	£250.00
electricity	£350.00
telephone	£132.00

(**Note:** a minimum of 4 quarters rental is required by British Telecom)   -   -

Allowances for the cost of electricity should be allowed when separately metered:

(say) £27.50 per week   -   -

016 Cleaning

Sundry cleaning up of building and surrounds during the contract:

12 weeks at:	(say) £35.00	420	
cleaning up on completion:	(say)	100	**520**

017 Temporary fencing and screens

Such temporary fencing and screens as are required should be allowed:

fencing at:	(say) £11.00 per m		
temporary screens at:	(say) £16.50 per m	-	-

018 Summary of preliminary costs

Total estimated cost of foregoing example :   **10,522**

The total cost represents 14.57% of the remaining net cost of the works, calculated as follows:

Total Tender cost	£165,000
Less profit and off-site overheads	
(say 15% on nett costs)	£21,522
	£143,478
Less preliminaries	£10,522
	£132,956

$$\frac{10,522}{132,956} \times 100 = 7.91\%$$

being the percentage addition required for Preliminaries for a building project of the size and type stated.

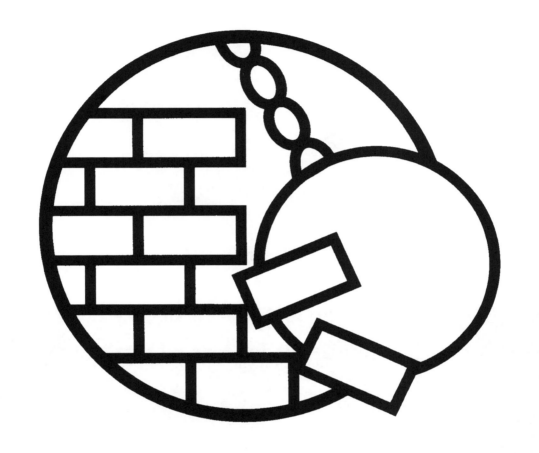

Demolition

ASBESTOS IN BUILDINGS

The following information on Asbestos Risk Management and on Asbestos Remediation Costs is reproduced with the kind permission of EC Harris LLP, ECHQ, 34 York Way, London N1 9AB Tel +44 (0)20 7812 2000, in whom the sole copyright is vested.

EC Harris is a Global Built Asset Consultancy, acting as trusted advisors to clients, in planning and executing strategies that optimise the construction, operation, use and ownership of built assets."

Introduction

Asbestos is a term used to describe the fibrous forms of a number of naturally occurring minerals (fibrous silicates). In its three common forms (Cocidolite, Grunerite and Chysotile) asbestos was used in insulation products and in building materials from the early 1900s (The other types of asbestos not commercially used are Actinolite, Anthophyllite, and Tremolite). Usage of asbestos containing materials (ACM's) continued until:

- The importation, use in manufacture and marketing of crocidolite (blue asbestos) and grunerite (brown asbestos also known as amosite) and products containing them was prohibited in 1985 and;

- The importation, supply and use of chrysotile (white asbestos) and all products containing it was prohibited, with few specific exceptions, in 1999.

It is nevertheless possible that some asbestos materials might still be being unknowingly imported into the UK in manufactured equipment and machinery and that Buildings constructed after the above dates might still comprise asbestos materials that have been used illegally (particularly in the early years).

The material was widely used in the construction industry from the 1920s onwards, with peak usage during the late 1960s to early 1970s.

Asbestos is, without doubt, a hazardous material, but it will only become a risk where the asbestos fibres become airborne and are inhaled. For this to happen there must be either significant degradation or physical disturbance of the material so that, in essence, the key to the avoidance of risk is:

- Maintenance of asbestos materials in good condition and;

- Prevention of disturbance.

Dangers of Asbestos

HSE figures indicate that asbestos related diseases currently kill around 4,000 people a year in the UK and that the number is set to rise and not peak until around 2020. Those that are now suffering, were, in the majority, exposed during the 1970's when the risks were, perhaps, less well understood and before the current asbestos regulations were introduced. They were employed in building and associated trades, for example, maintenance operatives, gas fitters and shop fitters and ancillary trades such as scaffolders and laundries etc. This is by no means exhaustive.

The dangers of asbestos are manifested when the fibres are released into the atmosphere in, for example, an enclosed space such as a building.

Fibres will be released when the material is damaged or disturbed. Provided the asbestos remains in good condition and is undamaged and undisturbed, the danger to health (risk) will be low.

Damage and disturbance to asbestos will occur when, for example, the material is:

- Subjected to unknowing or accidental and direct mechanical action, for example, cutting, drilling or breaking as might otherwise occur in connection with the repair, maintenance, refurbishment or demolition of a building;

- Removed. The removal of asbestos materials will, by its very nature, involve disturbance of the material. A high degree of control will be required and asbestos removal should only be carried out where necessary. Removal should not be carried out simply because asbestos materials are present.

- Subjected to vibration or strong air currents. This will be particularly significant where the material is either damaged or has low internal integrity.

- Subjected to minimal, but repeated mechanical action. An example of this would be accidental abrasion of door or wall panels.

In summary, the risks associated with asbestos containing materials revolve around the ability of the material to release fibres and the probability of those fibres being released. This, in turn, will be dependent upon such factors as the mechanical condition and integrity of the material (its softness and friability) and its liability to future physical disturbance and/or damage. Some materials, e.g. sprayed limpet asbestos fire insulation are soft and liable to break up readily, releasing fibres into the atmosphere. Others, such as asbestos cement panels are hard and unlikely, in most circumstances, to give off significant amounts of fibres. Note, however, that even for these relatively hard materials, care should be taken in, for example, maintenance or other activities that may give rise to disturbance. Specialist training will be necessary and sanding or wire brushing must, for example, be prohibited.

Uses of Asbestos

If we ignore the potential health risk, then at some point in time we may be susceptible to asbestos related illnesses, from pleural plaques and thickening to asbestosis, lung cancer or mesothelioma. The risks of all forms of asbestos related diseases are increased by smoking.

Asbestos was a very cheap and an extremely versatile material. For these reasons it was used in a wide range of applications and in many forms. The following is a summary of the primary uses of asbestos in buildings, but covers only a small selection of the actual asbestos materials (products) that were available and the applications to which they were put: -

1) **Loose fill insulation:**

   Loose insulation has been used (often in paper bags) between floors as acoustic insulation and as loft insulation. The material can also be found within, for example, the construction of fire doors, around electrical cables and in mattresses (manufactured for thermal insulation).

2) **Sprayed coatings:**

   Containing up to 85% fibre, sprayed coatings were primarily applied from the 1940s to the 1970s. Sprayed limpet asbestos was used as, for example, fire protection on structural steelwork and can be found in fire protecting lightweight roof structures where large open spans are required, for example, cinemas, shopping centres and swimming pools. Additional applications included both acoustic and thermal insulation, anti – condensation and decorative purposes.

3) **Thermal insulation (lagging):**

   This is a term covering many asbestos materials, for example, in situ applied insulation, pre-formed sections, rope etc. Crocidolite (blue) asbestos rope was used for lagging from the 1880s, although the more common form of pipe and boiler lagging consisting of 85% magnesia and 15% asbestos fibre was used from the 1920s to the late 1960s. Pipe and other forms of lagging can be found in all types of public and private buildings including residential, commercial, industrial, health care, hotels, etc.

4) Millboard:

These low density boards were relatively soft and of low cost. They can be found where good fire, insulation, thermal or electrical properties were specified (generally in industrial uses, but also in such applications as the inner panels to fire doors).

5) Insulating Boards (AIB):

Developed in the early 1950s to provide a fire resisting insulating material, insulation boards have in the range of 15 – 40% asbestos fibre mixed with hydrated Portland cement or calcium silicate. Again, insulating boards can be found in all types of public and private buildings in fire protection, acoustic and thermal insulation in the form of, for example, fire-breaks, wall linings, ceiling linings, tiles and upstands, and as a core for other products (e.g. fire doors). Insulating boards were also formed into composite materials, for example, sandwiched between non asbestos products such as plywood, straw board, metal and plasterboard.

6) Paper, paper products, felt and cardboard:

These have an asbestos content, which might be close to 100%. Used to provide acoustic and thermal insulation, the materials have found use in, for example, fireproof facings to other materials and have been incorporated into, for example, lagging to pipework and air conditioning ductwork.

7) Textiles, ropes and yarns:

These were manufactured, primarily for application in situations where thermal insulation or fire protection properties were required. Examples include, tape, flexible couplings, fire blankets, string (for sealing pipe threads etc) and rope (for pipe etc insulation).

8) Gaskets and washers:

Gaskets have been used for sealing pipe and valve joints in applications in all forms of buildings. Strings have generally been used for sealing screw thread joints.

9) Cement products:

Having a density approximate double that of insulating board, asbestos cement products typically contain 10 – 25% asbestos fibre mixed with Portland cement or autoclaved calcium silicate. Manufactured from the early 1950s to the late 1970s, asbestos cement products may be either profiled; semi or fully compressed or moulded. Profiled sheeting was often used as external roof and wall coverings, while semi and fully compressed sheets were used in, for example, panelling and partitions. Pre-formed moulded products included, for example, cable troughs and conduits, cisterns, tanks and rainwater goods.

Care must be taken to ensure that asbestos cement samples undergo a test to identify the material density. This is to confirm that the product is not, in fact, asbestos insulation board (AIB).

10) General building products:

Historically, asbestos has been incorporated into a variety of other building products. Examples would include:

- Textured coatings, paints and plasters (used for decorative finishes);

- Bitumen products, for example, roofing felts, damp-proof courses and associated mastics;

- Flooring products, for example, thermoplastic floor tiles, sheet floor coverings and associated mastics;

- Plastic / resin composites and friction products, for example, windowsills, toilet seats and cisterns etc;

- Metal-asbestos flues and other composites such as "Durasteel";

- Wall jointing tapes and fillers.

11) Domestic appliances and products:

Asbestos has been used in the construction of many domestic appliances and products. These have included, for example, ironing boards, hairdryers, cookers, hot plates, gas and electric fires and night storage radiators.

12) Industrial buildings:

Industrial buildings, for example power stations, will often comprise a very significant presence of asbestos materials, many of which have been mentioned above. Additionally, asbestos materials may also be present in machinery and with the higher electrical loads associated with industrial buildings, increased use of asbestos materials was made in electrical cables and switchgear.

13) Dust and Debris:

Asbestos dust and debris may be present where asbestos materials have been allowed to become damaged or where there has been removal carried out to poor standards. Where present, dust and debris will often be located in the least accessible locations.

<u>Responsibility / Legislation</u>

There are in existence many health and safety regulations that protect employees and other building users from exposure to the dangers presented by asbestos.

The Health and Safety at Work etc Act 1974 places a general duty on employers to provide a safe work environment and to provide information to others where their health and safety might be affected.

The Management of Health and Safety at Work Regulations 1999 requires an employer to assess risks, and to make appropriate arrangements to protect those who might otherwise be at risk.

The Workplace (Health Safety and Welfare) Regulations (1992) requires that a workplace building / premises is maintained such that occupants and workers are protected.

The Construction (Design and Management) Regulations 2007 require that information (including information about the presence of asbestos materials) is provided by the Client to the CDM Co-ordinator before the commencement of any works. This information will then be made available to all who may need it.

Defective Premises Act 1972 require that Landlords to take reasonable care to see that tenants and others are safe from injury or disease from defects in the state of premises.

This has particular relevance in respect of any risks to tenants from asbestos materials in council domestic properties and;

The Control of Asbestos Regulations 2012 (CAR) require, in summary, that:

- asbestos materials in non domestic premises are managed;

- risk assessments are undertaken before work is commenced;

- plans of work are produced detailing how work is to be carried out; and

- exposure to asbestos is either prevented or reduced to as low as is reasonably practicable

The Regulations also include a range of other requirements, for example, a duty to prevent the spread of asbestos.

<u>Identification, Assessment, Recording and Management of Asbestos Materials in Buildings</u>

Specific legal duty:

The CAR Regulations require every person who has an obligation by virtue of contract or tenancy in relation to the maintenance or repair of non-domestic premises or alternatively, who has control of part of those premises or of any means of access thereto or egress therefrom ("the dutyholder") to make assessments of, and to manage the risks from, asbestos materials. Clearly, the risks will vary as a building moves from cycles of normal occupation and maintenance, through refurbishment and perhaps alteration and ultimately, to demolition. Each situation will need to be separately assessed and from these assessments, plans will need to be formulated for the reduction of risk and for the management of the asbestos materials.

From a practical point of view, this means that the dutyholder (who might, for example, be either an employer or a tenant or a building owner) will need to undertake a number of tasks. These tasks will include:

- Taking reasonable steps to identify asbestos materials within the structure and fabric of a building, and/or perhaps presuming materials to contain asbestos.

- Work of this nature must be carried out by a competent asbestos surveyor (competence to be demonstrated either through an accredited organisation or for individual surveyors, through personnel certification), who should carry out a survey in line with the requirements of HSG 264 and with the intended activities to take place within the building (whether this be simple occupation and maintenance, or perhaps the more intrusive activities of, repairs and refurbishment and ultimately demolition).

- Making and keeping an up to date assessment of the risk of exposure from identified asbestos and presumed asbestos materials.

- Making and keeping an up to date written records of the location and condition of asbestos materials within the building.

- Preparing a plan to manage the assessed risks and the putting of this into effect to ensure that:

  - any material known or presumed is kept in a good state of repair;

  - any material that contains or is presumed to contain asbestos is, because of the risks associated with its location or condition, repaired or if necessary removed.

    Where removal, repair, encasement or encapsulation of asbestos materials is necessary, this work will generally need to be notified to the appropriate enforcing authority and undertaken by a licensed and competent asbestos contractor. (There are specific exceptions to the licensing and notification requirements and these are set out in Regulation 3(2) of the Control of Asbestos Regulations 2012).

  - information on the location and condition of the material is given to anyone potentially at risk.

  The Plan will need to be regularly reviewed and updated and will need to include procedures for, for example, regular monitoring of the identified asbestos materials and for the prevention of disturbance in connection with activities such as repair and maintenance.

Probability of Presence of Asbestos Materials:

The first question that will need to be answered by dutyholders is whether or not there is a possibility of asbestos being present within a building.

For buildings constructed prior to 2000, the presence of asbestos is, to a greater or lesser extent, almost universal. In addition, it is known that asbestos removal work carried out throughout the 1980s was often not undertaken to the standards required today. The consequence of this may be a presence of asbestos debris or perhaps that replacement material, for example man made mineral fibre pipe insulation, will conceal friable asbestos residue materials. In either case, these are materials that could be liable to disturbance during maintenance, refurbishment or demolition activities.

In order to identify asbestos materials in buildings, the surveyor must be competent to carry out the work required. To be competent, HSG 264 published by the Health and Safety Executive states that the "surveyor" must:

- Have sufficient training, qualifications, knowledge, experience and ability to carry out their duties in relation to the survey and to recognise their limitations;
- Have sufficient knowledge of the specific tasks to be undertaken and the risks which the work will entail;
- Be able to demonstrate independence, impartiality and integrity;
- Have an adequate quality management system; and
- Carry out the survey in accordance with HSG 264.

In addition, the surveyor should have training and experience in all aspects of survey work and a knowledge of;

- Asbestos products;
- Building construction, construction methods, fire protection and uses of buildings;
- Different forms of building construction (system build; traditional, framed etc.);
- The various uses and variations of use of asbestos materials, for example, pipe insulation tended to be used in three distinctly separate ways: -

  1) Plant, pipes, calorifiers, etc, within the boiler room only would be insulated (lagged), together with the general hot water distribution pipework.

  2) The boiler room, together with the general basement area (which was seen as a service area) and the vertical risers would be lagged. This was the most common use of asbestos lagging.

  3) Total lagging – all pipes lagged including horizontal runs, sometimes even up to the radiators.

- The extensive range of asbestos products for use in virtually all elements of building construction from, for example, roof coverings to damp proof courses.

It is only through experience, diligence and an understanding of the manner in which asbestos materials were used that the extent and scope of asbestos materials within a building can be truly identified. Some materials may be obvious, others will be hidden; some may be ad hoc or random in their application whilst others may have given rise to contamination by virtue of poor application (overspray), poor removal work (residues and debris) and mechanical disturbance (debris).

Procedures:

So, in the majority of cases, it is likely that asbestos materials will be present in your building. Now what do you do?

In the briefest terms, you will need to **identify**, **assess**, **record** and **manage** the materials and this will be achieved most readily through a considered and stepped approach. The steps that are likely to be required are set out in detail in the HSE publication "A comprehensive guide to Managing Asbestos in premises" and for ease of reference, they are summarised as follows:

- Step 1: Review the information that you already have on asbestos materials in your premises and the action that you currently take in order to manage risks.

- Step 2: Prevent any work that may disturb the fabric of the building until the presence or otherwise of asbestos materials has been established.

- Step 3: Carry out an initial inspection for any damaged asbestos materials or asbestos materials that could be easily disturbed. Take immediate action to control any identified risks.

- Step 4: Plan a strategy for compliance including further inspections and assessments of materials that could contain asbestos.

- Step 5: Carry out risk assessments of identified asbestos materials in order to set priorities.

- Step 6: Develop a long term management plan which might include, for example, information on:

  - The location and condition of asbestos materials;
  - Risk assessments (Initial, Continuing and Special);
  - Mechanisms for the provision of information about asbestos materials to those who need it;
  - Training;
  - Decisions about management options e.g. removal or encapsulation, labelling and management;
  - Timetables for action;
  - Safe Systems of Work;
  - Roles and Responsibilities;
  - A procedure for monitoring and review of the plan; and
  - Emergency Procedures.

- Step 7: Monitor and review the management plan.

Costs

Where asbestos materials are present within a building, the basic risk management options will be either: -

     a)   Removal; or

     b)   Treatment (Clean up, Repair, Encapsulate, Enclose, Label etc) followed by;

     c)   Ongoing management of the asbestos materials.

Removal will represent a capital cost likely to be significantly in excess of possible treatment costs. However, removal will be a one-off cost as against the ongoing cost of both treatment and subsequent management works and actions. In some situations removal may be the only option because of, for example, either:

- the physical condition of the asbestos;
- its location and exposure to physical damage; or perhaps
- unavoidable disturbance as a consequence of proposed maintenance, alteration and refurbishment or demolition activities.

The cost of removal of any particular item of asbestos will vary enormously and each application will need to be separately estimated.

For example, if we consider the cost of removing individual lengths of high-level pipe lagging, there will be the associated costs of setting up on site, providing access platforms and constructing a sealed enclosure. These are Preliminaries costs, which are always likely to be incurred.

Where the amount of asbestos to be removed is small, the resultant cost per metre run of pipe insulation, may run to thousands of pounds.

In other circumstances, the set up and enclosure costs may be less onerous and be diluted by long pipe runs. In these circumstances the resultant cost per metre run of pipe may be only in the order of tens of pounds.

Similarly for remediation, the costs will be lower, but equally variable. At the cheapest level it may, for example, be necessary only to seal small areas of the asbestos surface with encapsulant paint. Conversely, it may be necessary for the asbestos to be boarded in, and decontamination (clean up) works undertaken. In terms of the ongoing management costs, these will again reflect the individual circumstances, but the maintenance of records, labelling, periodic inspection (monitoring condition), provision of information, training and awareness procedures will need to be included as part of the building management costs.

A schedule of typical rates for both asbestos survey works and asbestos remediation works follows this section and this has been jointly prepared by E C Harris LLP and European Asbestos Services Ltd. The schedule includes typical rates for, for example, asbestos surveys, environmental cleaning, removal of fire protection, thermal insulation, insulation boarding, cement products, decorative finishes, thermoplastic products and encapsulation etc.

The units of measurement included in the schedule are those upon which a specialist contractor might be expected to price the works and the rates are those that are current at May 2012 for works to be undertaken in London and the South East.

The schedule includes preliminary costs, for example, the provision of decontamination facilities, enclosures etc, but excludes associated costs which might otherwise be incurred on particular projects, for example, the provision of scaffolding and bird cages, opening up works etc. so that care must always be taken when considering any individual project.

A final consideration is that, in certain circumstances, Tax Relief may be available on any survey, abatement and reinstatement costs. Separate, specialist advice should however be sought on this particular aspect.

EC Harris Services:

EC Harris is experienced in all aspects of asbestos management consultancy. Where asbestos materials are likely or suspected, EC Harris can provide a comprehensive service to clients covering the following: -

- Regulation 4 Asbestos Management Consultancy;
- Specialist estimating services;
- Procurement of Surveys, Reinspections and Asbestos Removal and Remediation Works;
- Specialist Project Management / Contract Administration;
- Expert witness service - matters of quantum; and
- Tax remediation.

European Asbestos Services (Co-Authors of the following Schedule of Asbestos Rates):

European Asbestos Services are a long established organisation having extensive experience in all aspects of asbestos surveying and remediation work. They are able to provide a complete HSE licensed asbestos service both nationally and internationally through their network of local offices in London, Somerset and Stoke on Trent. They are able to provide bespoke solutions to asbestos issues throughout the world and take pride in delivering projects on time and on budget.

EC Harris / European Asbestos Services Schedule of Asbestos Rates

		Base Date: May 2012
	Unit	Rate

Surveys

Asbestos surveys are required to be undertaken in accordance with the guidance set out in HSG264 - Asbestos: The survey guide published by the Health and Safety Executive.

Management Surveys:

Management surveys are undertaken in respect of the normal occupation and use, including foreseeable maintenance and installation, of a building in order to ensure the continued management of asbestos containing materials present within that building. They will often include minor intrusive investigations (for example above false ceilings and inside risers, service ducts, lift shafts etc) and some disturbance. Areas not accessed will need to be presumed to contain asbestos materials.

Normal Working Hours Including Sample Analysis and Report Preparation.

	Unit	Rate
Non Domestic Building Structures up to 2000 m² Gross Floor Area (Based on Two Man Team).	Item	£1000 - £1400
Non Domestic Building Structures greater than 2000 m² Gross Floor Area (Based on Two Man Team).	m²	£0.60 - £1.00
Typical Domestic Property (Average 75 square metres Gross Floor Area).	Item	£475
Out of Normal Working Hours Including Sample Analysis and Report Preparation.		Add 20% to 30% Uplift to the above rates.

Refurbishment and Demolition Surveys:

Refurbishment and demolition surveys become necessary when a building (or perhaps part of a building) is to be altered, refurbished or demolished. They will be intrusive and include destructive investigations so that all areas that will be subjected alteration, refurbishment and demolition works will be accessed and inspected (including areas that may be difficult to reach).

Normal Working Hours Including Sample Analysis and Report Preparation.

	Unit	Rate
Non Domestic Building Structures up to 1200 m² Gross Floor Area (Based on Two Man Team).	Item	£1000 - £1400
Non Domestic Building Structures greater than 1200 m² Gross Floor Area (Based on Two Man Team).	m²	£0.85 - £1.50
Typical Domestic Property (Average 75 square metres Gross Floor Area).	Item	£700
Out of Normal Working Hours Including Sample Analysis and Report Preparation.		Add 20% to 30% Uplift to the above rates.

Analytical Attendance:

Background, Leak Test and Reassurance Monitoring and Four Stage Clearance Procedures.

	Unit	Rate
Normal Working Hours - Provide Analyst per 8 Hour shift.	Day	£400 - £500
Out of Normal Working Hours - Provide Analyst per 8 Hour shift.	Day	£450 - £600

Four Stage Clearance Procedure Only (Small Works):

Normal Working Hours - Provide Analyst to undertake Four stage clearance procedure:, ,

	Unit	Rate
Enclosure up to 10m² (Half Day Visit).	Item	£280
Enclosure 10m² to 20m² (One Day Visit).	Item	£500
Enclosures greater than 20m².		See Above
Out of Normal Working Hours - Provide Analyst to undertake Four stage clearance procedure:		Add 20% to 30% Uplift to the above rates.

Asbestos Remediation Works:

Note: The following asbestos remediation costs are based on work during normal working hours. Where the work is to be undertaken out of hours, an uplift of up to 30% may be charged.

Environmental Cleaning:

	Unit	Rate
Occupied building spaces (dependent on specification and level of contamination). Minimum 35m² Gross Floor Area.	m²	£30 - £100
Plant Rooms (dependent on specification and level of contamination). Minimum 20m² Gross Floor Area.	m²	£50 - £200
Building Voids (dependent on specification and level of contamination). Minimum 15m² Gross Floor Area.	m²	£75 - £300

Removal of Sprayed Asbestos Fire Protection:

	Unit	Rate
Up to 5m²	Item	£2400
5m² to 10m²	m²	£425
10m² to 20m²	m²	£275
20m² to 100m²	m²	£250
100m² to 250m²	m²	£200
Greater than 250m²	m²	£130

Removal of Asbestos Thermal Insulation

Pipes up to 50mm Diameter:

	Unit	Rate
Up to 1 linear metre	Item	£800
1 to 10 metres	Item	£1600
10 to 20 metres	m	£160.00
20 to 50 metres	m	£140.00
50 to 100 metres	m	£100.00
Greater than 100 metres	m	£65.00

Pipes 50mm to 200 mm Diameter:

Up to 1 linear metre	Item	£1000
1 to 10 metres	Item	£2000
10 to 20 metres	m	£170.00
20 to 50 metres	m	£150.00
50 to 100 metres	m	£110.00
Greater than 100 metres	m	£75.00

Pipes Greater than 200mm Diameter:

Up to 1 linear metre	Item	£2000
1 to 10 metres	Item	£3000
10 to 20 metres	m	£185.00
20 to 50 metres	m	£160.00
50 to 100 metres	m	£120.00
Greater than 100 metres	m	£90.00

Removal of Asbestos Insulation Boarding:

Up to 1 m2	Item	£500
1 to 10 m2	Item	£1000
10 to 20 m2	Item	£2000
20 to 50 m2	m²	£85.00
50 to 100 m2	m²	£75.00
100 to 200 m2	m²	£65.00
Greater than 200m2	m²	£50.00

Removal of Asbestos Cement Corrugated Sheeting:

Up to 1 m2	Item	£500
1 to 10 m2	Item	£1,000
10 to 20 m2	Item	£1,200
20 to 50 m2	m²	£35.00
50 to 100 m2	m²	£30.00
Greater than 100m2	m²	£27.00
Removal of Associated Asbestos Cement Gutters / Downpipes etc	m	£16.00

Note:
The above rates for removal of asbestos cement corrugated sheeting are based on removal by hand. Where mechanical removal is undertaken (i.e. drenching, cutting and collapsing), tendered rates will be considerably lower.

Removal of Artex Decorative Finishes to Plasterboard Walls and Ceilings:

Up to 20m2	Item	£800
20 to 50 m2	Item	£1600
50 to 75m2	m²	£35.00
75 to 100 m2	m²	£30.00
Greater than 100 m2	m²	£25.00

Removal of Artex Decorative Finishes to Structural Walls and Ceilings:

Up to 10m2	Item	£800
10 to 25m2	Item	£1600
25 to 50m2	m²	£65.00
50 to 752m2	m²	£60.00
75 to 100m2	m²	£55.00
Greater than 100m2	m²	£50.00

Removal of Asbestos Containing Thermoplastic Products

Floor Tiles:

Up to 10m2	Item	£500
10 to 15m2	m²	£50.00
15 to 20m2	m²	£35.00
20 to 30m2	m²	£30.00
30to 50m2	m²	£25.00
50 to 75m2	m²	£20.00
Greater than 75m2	m²	£15.00

Encapsulation of Asbestos Materials:

Up to 25m2	Item	£400
25 to 50m2	m²	£16.00
50 to100m2	m²	£15.00
Greater than 100m2	m²	£14.00

Daywork Rates:

Where the work cannot be measured or quantified, then the following all inclusive daywork rates may be applied:

Foreman / Supervisor	Day	£400 - £450
Removal Operative	Day	£375 - £400

Pricing Notes:

The above rates are current at May 2012 for work undertaken in London and the South East and are based on the mid point where ranges of quantities are shown.

The above rates exclude:-1) Associated costs of, for example, access scaffolding and bird cages etc. 2) Any opening up or reinstatement costs. 3) Exceptional pricing factors which may occur during the present recession.

Notes

The term "demolition" in this context means the removal of relatively small parts of an existing building preparatory to subsequent alteration works. Such demolitions are expected to be carried out "by hand" using light (normally hand held) tools and plant and the loading of debris into skips etc. would similarly be expected to be carried out by hand. Labour hours, plant usage etc. used in this book are therefore based upon this method of working.

Where whole buildings or substantial parts of buildings are to be demolished, it should be possible to employ suitable heavy plant and equipment to carry out the demolition and subsequent removal of debris "by machine". In suitable cases, explosives may be used for the initial demolition. These substantial demolition works are normally carried out by the firms specialising in the work at the prices quoted for specific jobs using appropriate techniques. The cost of the demolition works may, in fact, be partly or entirely offset by the specialist's allowance for salvageable materials. Such works are outside the scope of this book and rates/allowances/prices included here must not be used in pricing them.

Demolitions are assumed to be carried out within single storey heights of about 3 metres and rates should be adjusted to take account of demolition, removal etc. from greater heights in auditoria, sports halls etc.

Rates for demolition of walls, slabs, columns etc. in this book include for the simultaneous removal of associated finishings (plaster, rendering etc.) unless otherwise stated. Rates have also been included for stripping finishings independently of the structure in various trade or work sections.

No allowance has been made in the rates for credits for old materials removed during demolition works but in estimating for such work, allowances may need to be made for items such as scrap metal, stone, slate etc. On the other hand, the contract may call for certain of the materials removed to remain the property of the building owner and costs of storage or transporting may have to be allowed for.

Plant Hire Charges		Daily Hire Charge £	Pro-ductive Hours Hrs	Cost Per Hour £	Operator Per Hour £	Fuel Per Hour £	Total Cost Per Hour £
	The hire charges shown exclude the cost of operators and fuel but are inclusive of oil, grease and the like. Fuel costs have been added in the following table as appropriate. The operator costs are either added in the table below or, where no operator shown, have been allowed for in the rates given in the individual items of work.						
	The cost of delivery to, or collection from site is EXCLUDED and allowance for this should be made in Preliminaries.						
A0191	Oxy-acetylene equipment and gas	19.50	4.00	4.88	-	4.6	**9.48**
A0111	Adjustable steel prop to 3 m long (per week)	2.20	1.00	2.20	-	-	**2.20**
A0091	Grinder and cutting discs	7.20	6.00	1.20	-	-	**1.20**
A0066	Compressor 250 cfm and two hammers	72.00	6.00	12.00	-	1.33	**13.33**
A0075	Kango hammer	25.00	6.00	4.17	-	-	**4.17**
A0195	Fuel for mechanical plant	-	-	-	-	-	**1.46**
A0196	Gas for blow lamps - Calor bottle	-	-	-	-	-	**1.97**
A0197	Gas for oxy-acetylene 2x1.3 m3	-	-	-	-	-	**23.00**

Basic Prices of Materials		Supply Price £	Waste Factor %	Unload. Labour £	Unload. Plant £	Total Unit Cost £	Unit
A0361	Sawn softwood for temporary works (earthwork support, propping and the like) divided by 6 for 6 uses	280.30	5%	11.22	-	**306.09**	m3
	Precast reinforced concrete lintels:						
C0116	215 x 215 mm	35.39	-	2.58	-	**37.97**	m
C0117	327.5 x 215 mm	44.96	-	3.93	-	**48.89**	m
C0218	IKOpro synthaprufe LAC	7.39	10%	-	-	**8.13**	ltr
C0314	Single door with frame and ironmongery (second hand)	30.00	-	-	-	**30.00**	nr
C0315	Pair of doors with frame and ironmongery (second hand)	55.00	-	-	-	**55.00**	nr

Unit Rates	Man-Hours	Plant Hours	Net Labour Price £	Net Plant Price £	Net Mats Price £	Net Unit Price £	Unit

	UNIT RATES **CONCRETE WORK**							

CA

001 Remove the following and load into skips

002 Reinforced concrete walls, including any plasterwork etc.:

	Man-Hours	Plant Hours	Net Labour Price £	Net Plant Price £	Net Mats Price £	Net Unit Price £	Unit
unrestricted demolition:							
100 mm thick	1.39	0.60	15.62	7.93	-	**23.55**	m2
150 mm thick	2.09	0.89	23.44	11.90	-	**35.34**	m2
200 mm thick	2.79	1.15	31.25	15.30	-	**46.55**	m2
taking down with care:							
100 mm thick	2.09	0.92	23.44	12.24	-	**35.68**	m2
150 mm thick	3.14	1.36	35.21	18.13	-	**53.34**	m2
200 mm thick	4.18	1.83	46.87	24.37	-	**71.24**	m2
003 Reinforced concrete solid floor slabs on ground:							
100 mm thick	0.93	0.38	10.41	5.11	-	**15.52**	m2
150 mm thick	1.39	0.58	15.62	7.70	-	**23.32**	m2
200 mm thick	1.86	0.77	20.82	10.20	-	**31.02**	m2
004 Reinforced concrete suspended floor or roof slabs:							
150 mm thick	2.32	1.00	26.04	13.37	-	**39.41**	m2
200 mm thick	3.25	1.40	36.45	18.70	-	**55.15**	m2
300 mm thick	3.71	1.57	41.66	20.97	-	**62.63**	m2
005 Reinforced concrete landings or balcony slabs:							
600 mm projection:							
150 mm thick	1.57	0.60	17.62	7.93	-	**25.55**	m
200 mm thick	2.09	0.91	23.44	12.13	-	**35.57**	m
1000 mm projection:							
150 mm thick	2.55	1.11	28.64	14.73	-	**43.37**	m
200 mm thick	3.48	1.51	39.07	20.17	-	**59.24**	m
006 Reinforced concrete beams:							
200 x 300 mm	0.74	0.32	8.34	4.20	-	**12.54**	m
300 x 400 mm	1.49	0.63	16.66	8.38	-	**25.04**	m
300 x 600 mm	2.23	0.94	25.00	12.46	-	**37.46**	m
007 **Extra over** for cutting off ends flush with wall face:							
200 x 300 mm	0.23	0.21	2.61	0.26	-	**2.87**	Nr
300 x 400 mm	0.42	0.38	4.70	0.46	-	**5.16**	Nr
300 x 600 mm	0.65	0.60	7.29	0.71	-	**8.00**	Nr
008 **Extra over** cutting out ends from walls:							
200 x 300 mm	0.14	-	1.57	-	-	**1.57**	Nr
300 x 400 mm	0.33	-	3.66	-	-	**3.66**	Nr
300 x 600 mm	0.56	-	6.25	-	-	**6.25**	Nr
009 Reinforced concrete columns:							
200 x 200 mm	0.56	0.24	6.25	3.17	-	**9.42**	m
300 x 300 mm	1.26	0.60	14.14	7.93	-	**22.07**	m
400 x 400 mm	2.24	0.91	25.13	12.13	-	**37.26**	m
010 **Extra over** cutting off flush with floor surface:							
200 x 200 mm	0.23	0.21	2.61	0.26	-	**2.87**	Nr
300 x 300 mm	0.37	0.34	4.16	0.41	-	**4.57**	Nr
400 x 400 mm	0.56	0.51	6.25	0.61	-	**6.86**	Nr
011 Reinforced concrete staircase 2650 mm rise and 2200 mm going with metal or timber balustrade on one side and all finishings:							
straight flight:							
900 mm wide	9.28	4.25	104.14	56.65	-	**160.79**	Nr
1200 mm wide	12.53	5.10	140.60	67.98	-	**208.58**	Nr
two flights and half space landing:							
900 mm wide	11.14	5.95	124.97	79.31	-	**204.28**	Nr
1200 mm wide	14.85	6.80	166.63	90.64	-	**257.27**	Nr
012 Cutting out precast concrete or reconstructed stone sills 150 mm thick:							
not exceeding 150 mm wide	0.25	-	5.22	-	-	**5.22**	m
150 - 300 mm wide	0.42	-	8.72	-	-	**8.72**	m
300 - 600 mm wide	0.67	-	13.90	-	-	**13.90**	m
013 Cutting back attached plain or lightly reinforced concrete plinth courses, band courses, pilasters, attached piers and the like, including finishings; flush with wall face:							
150 mm projection:							
over 1000 mm wide	1.02	0.47	11.46	6.24	-	**17.70**	m2
up to 250 mm wide	0.28	0.13	3.12	1.71	-	**4.83**	m
250 - 500 mm wide	0.52	0.24	5.83	3.17	-	**9.00**	m
500 - 1000 mm wide	1.02	0.47	11.46	6.24	-	**17.70**	m
300 mm projection:							
over 1000 mm wide	3.90	1.66	43.74	22.10	-	**65.84**	m2
up to 250 mm wide	0.93	0.39	10.41	5.21	-	**15.62**	m
250 - 500 mm wide	1.95	0.83	21.87	11.10	-	**32.97**	m
500 - 1000 mm wide	3.90	1.66	43.74	22.10	-	**65.84**	m

		Man-Hours	Net Labour Price £	Net Mats Price £	Net Unit Price £	Unit
Unit Rates						
CB	**BRICKWORK**					
001	**Remove the following and load into skips**					
002	Brick walls, including plasterwork where applicable:					
	unrestricted demolition:					
	in gauged mortar:					
	half brickwall	0.42	4.70	-	**4.70**	m2
	one brickwall	0.55	6.15	-	**6.15**	m2
	one and a half brickwall	0.84	9.37	-	**9.37**	m2
	in cement mortar:					
	half brickwall	0.55	6.15	-	**6.15**	m2
	one brickwall	0.84	9.37	-	**9.37**	m2
	one and a half brickwall	1.40	15.71	-	**15.71**	m2
	taking down with care:					
	in gauged mortar:					
	half brickwall	0.63	7.09	-	**7.09**	m2
	one brickwall	0.84	9.37	-	**9.37**	m2
	one and a half brickwall	1.25	14.07	-	**14.07**	m2
	in cement mortar:					
	half brickwall	0.84	9.37	-	**9.37**	m2
	one brickwall	1.25	14.07	-	**14.07**	m2
	one and a half brickwall	2.10	23.56	-	**23.56**	m2
003	Cutting out flush brick-on-edge sills:					
	common brickwork or facing brickwork in gauged mortar:					
	not exceeding half brick wide	0.33	6.95	-	**6.95**	m
	half brick to one brick wide	0.50	10.43	-	**10.43**	m
	one brick to one and a half brick wide	0.84	17.38	-	**17.38**	m
	engineering brickwork in cement mortar:					
	not exceeding half brick wide	0.50	10.43	-	**10.43**	m
	half brick to one brick wide	0.75	15.67	-	**15.67**	m
	one brick to one and a half brick wide	1.25	26.10	-	**26.10**	m
004	Cutting out projecting brick-on-edge sills:					
	common brickwork or facing brickwork in gauged mortar:					
	not exceeding 250 mm wide	0.25	5.22	-	**5.22**	m
	250 - 500 mm wide	0.42	8.72	-	**8.72**	m
	engineering brickwork in cement mortar:					
	not exceeding 250 mm wide	0.42	8.72	-	**8.72**	m
	250 - 500 mm wide	0.59	12.17	-	**12.17**	m
005	Fire place surround and hearth:					
	surround 1000 x 900 mm, hearth 1000 x 600 mm:					
	timber	0.34	3.86	-	**3.86**	Nr
	cast iron	0.42	4.70	-	**4.70**	Nr
	tiled concrete	0.70	7.82	-	**7.82**	Nr
	surround 1200 x 1000 mm, hearth 1200 x 600 mm:					
	timber	0.42	4.70	-	**4.70**	Nr
	cast iron	0.56	6.25	-	**6.25**	Nr
	tiled concrete	0.84	9.37	-	**9.37**	Nr
006	**Remove the following, clean off and set aside for reuse; load mortar and debris into skips**					
007	Brickwall in facing bricks in gauged mortar:					
	half brick thick	1.16	13.03	-	**13.03**	m2
	one brick thick	2.23	25.00	-	**25.00**	m2
	one and a half brick thick	3.43	38.53	-	**38.53**	m2
008	Fire place surround and hearth:					
	surround 1000 x 900 mm, hearth 1000 x 600 mm:					
	timber	0.46	5.21	-	**5.21**	Nr
	cast iron	0.56	6.25	-	**6.25**	Nr
	tiled concrete	0.93	10.41	-	**10.41**	Nr
	surround 1200 x 1000 mm, hearth 1200 x 600 mm:					
	timber	0.56	6.25	-	**6.25**	Nr
	cast iron	0.74	8.34	-	**8.34**	Nr
	tiled concrete	1.11	12.50	-	**12.50**	Nr
CC	**BLOCKWORK**					
001	**Remove the following and load into skips**					
002	Concrete block walls, including any plasterwork etc.:					
	unrestricted demolition:					
	75 mm thick	0.23	2.61	-	**2.61**	m2
	100 mm thick	0.28	3.12	-	**3.12**	m2
	150 mm thick	0.37	4.16	-	**4.16**	m2
	200 mm thick	0.46	5.21	-	**5.21**	m2
	taking down with care:					
	75 mm thick	0.35	3.96	-	**3.96**	m2
	100 mm thick	0.42	4.70	-	**4.70**	m2
	150 mm thick	0.56	6.25	-	**6.25**	m2
	200 mm thick	0.70	7.82	-	**7.82**	m2

	Unit Rates	Man-Hours	Net Labour Price £	Net Mats Price £	Net Unit Price £	Unit
003	**Remove the following, clean off and set aside for re-use; load mortar and debris into skips**					
004	Concrete block walls:					
	75 mm thick	0.56	6.25	-	**6.25**	m2
	100 mm thick	0.74	8.34	-	**8.34**	m2
	150 mm thick	0.93	10.41	-	**10.41**	m2
	200 mm thick	1.16	13.03	-	**13.03**	m2
CD	**RUBBLE WALLING**					
001	**Remove the following and load into skips**					
002	Random rubble stone wall in gauged mortar:					
	unrestricted demolition:					
	300 mm thick	0.56	6.25	-	**6.25**	m2
	450 mm thick	0.70	7.81	-	**7.81**	m2
	600 mm thick	0.92	10.30	-	**10.30**	m2
	taking down with care:					
	300 mm thick	0.70	7.81	-	**7.81**	m2
	450 mm thick	0.92	10.30	-	**10.30**	m2
	600 mm thick	1.39	15.62	-	**15.62**	m2
003	**Remove the following, clean off and set aside for re-use; load mortar and debris into skips**					
004	Random rubble stone walling in gauged mortar:					
	300 mm thick	0.84	9.38	-	**9.38**	m2
	450 mm thick	1.05	11.75	-	**11.75**	m2
	600 mm thick	1.35	15.17	-	**15.17**	m2
CE	**MASONRY**					
001	**Remove the following and load into skips**					
002	Ashlar stone walls in gauged mortar:					
	unrestricted demolition:					
	150 mm thick	0.37	4.16	-	**4.16**	m2
	300 mm thick	0.65	7.29	-	**7.29**	m2
	taking down with care:					
	150 mm thick	0.46	5.21	-	**5.21**	m2
	300 mm thick	0.74	8.34	-	**8.34**	m2
003	Cutting out flush stone sills:					
	150 x 150 mm	0.67	13.90	-	**13.90**	m
	150 x 250 mm	0.84	17.38	-	**17.38**	m
004	Cutting out projecting stone sills:					
	150 x 150 mm	0.50	10.43	-	**10.43**	m
	150 x 250 mm	0.67	13.90	-	**13.90**	m
005	**Remove the following, clean off and set aside for re-use; load mortar and debris into skips**					
006	Ashlar stone walls in gauged mortar:					
	150 mm thick	0.56	11.59	33.68	**45.27**	m2
	300 mm thick	0.74	15.46	67.24	**82.70**	m2
CF	**ASPHALT WORK**					
001	**Hack up the following and load into skips**					
002	Tanking, floor or roof covering on loose underlay to screed or concrete:					
	two coats, 20 mm thick	0.09	1.04	-	**1.04**	m2
	three coats, 30 mm thick	0.12	1.36	-	**1.36**	m2
	Tanking or floor covering keyed to concrete or screed:					
	horizontal:					
	two coats, 20 mm thick	0.46	5.21	-	**5.21**	m2
	three coats, 30 mm thick	0.56	6.25	-	**6.25**	m2
	vertical:					
	two coats, 20 mm thick	0.42	4.70	-	**4.70**	m2
	three coats, 30 mm thick	0.46	5.21	-	**5.21**	m2
003	Skirtings, flashings, coverings to kerbs and the like associated with roof coverings, up to 200 mm girth:					
	keyed to concrete or brickwork:					
	two coats, 20 mm thick	0.09	1.04	-	**1.04**	m
	three coats, 30 mm thick	0.14	1.57	-	**1.57**	m
	on expanded metal reinforcement:					
	two coats, 20 mm thick	0.05	0.53	-	**0.53**	m
	three coats, 30 mm thick	0.07	0.74	-	**0.74**	m
CG	**ROOFING**					
001	**Remove the following and load into skips**					
002	Roof coverings and the like:					
	slates	0.14	1.57	-	**1.57**	m2
	tiles	0.09	1.04	-	**1.04**	m2
	battens	0.05	0.53	-	**0.53**	m2
	counter battens	0.05	0.53	-	**0.53**	m2
	underfelting	0.02	0.20	-	**0.20**	m2

Unit Rates	Man-Hours	Net Labour Price £	Net Mats Price £	Net Unit Price £	Unit
timber boarding	0.14	1.57	-	**1.57**	m2
corrugated sheet coverings	0.09	1.04	-	**1.04**	m2
bituminous felt coverings	0.09	1.04	-	**1.04**	m2
lead coverings	0.23	2.61	-	**2.61**	m2
zinc coverings	0.19	2.09	-	**2.09**	m2
copper covering	0.19	2.09	-	**2.09**	m2
wood wool decking	0.19	2.09	-	**2.09**	m2
fibre cement decking	0.19	2.09	-	**2.09**	m2
firring pieces	0.09	1.04	-	**1.04**	m2
fibreboard insulation	0.09	1.04	-	**1.04**	m2
003 Skirtings, flashings, coverings to kerbs and the like associated with roofing; up to 200 mm girth:					
felt	0.02	0.20	-	**0.20**	m
lead	0.05	0.53	-	**0.53**	m
zinc	0.04	0.42	-	**0.42**	m
copper	0.04	0.42	-	**0.42**	m
aluminium	0.04	0.42	-	**0.42**	m
004 **Remove the following, set aside sound materials for re-use; load broken materials into skips**					
005 Slates	0.28	7.34	-	**7.34**	m2
006 Tiles	0.19	4.91	-	**4.91**	m2
CH **WOODWORK**					
001 **Remove the following and load into skips**					
002 Softwood beams:					
200 x 300 mm	0.09	0.98	-	**0.98**	m
300 x 400 mm	0.13	1.49	-	**1.49**	m
Extra over for cutting off ends flush with wall face:					
200 x 300 mm	0.46	7.05	-	**7.05**	Nr
300 x 400 mm	0.86	13.07	-	**13.07**	Nr
Extra over for disconnecting ends from timber column:					
200 x 300 mm	0.31	4.67	-	**4.67**	Nr
300 x 400 mm	0.55	8.36	-	**8.36**	Nr
Extra over for cutting out ends from walls:					
200 x 300 mm	0.23	2.61	-	**2.61**	Nr
300 x 400 mm	0.43	4.82	-	**4.82**	Nr
Note: 003 - 005 not used					
006 Softwood columns:					
200 x 200 mm	0.07	0.76	-	**0.76**	m
250 x 250 mm	0.09	0.98	-	**0.98**	m
300 x 300 mm	0.11	1.19	-	**1.19**	m
Extra over for cutting off flush with floor surface:					
200 x 200 mm	0.31	4.67	-	**4.67**	Nr
250 x 250 mm	0.42	6.38	-	**6.38**	Nr
300 x 300 mm	0.60	9.12	-	**9.12**	Nr
007 Softwood board and joist floors and roofs:					
150 mm thick	0.27	3.03	-	**3.03**	m2
200 mm thick	0.33	3.70	-	**3.70**	m2
300 mm thick	0.39	4.38	-	**4.38**	m2
008 Softwood stud partition walls including plasterboard finish both sides:					
unrestricted demolition:					
75 mm thick	0.24	2.65	-	**2.65**	m2
100 mm thick	0.25	2.85	-	**2.85**	m2
taking down with care:					
75 mm thick	0.36	4.04	-	**4.04**	m2
100 mm thick	0.40	4.49	-	**4.49**	m2
009 Eaves boarding, not exceeding 500 mm girth:					
softwood fascia board and fibre cement sheet soffit including bearers	0.18	2.02	-	**2.02**	m
heavy softwood moulded fascia and soffit boards	0.24	2.69	-	**2.69**	m
010 Wall lining and battening:					
plywood or similar	0.16	1.80	-	**1.80**	m2
matchboarding	0.17	1.86	-	**1.86**	m2
insulating board	0.15	1.65	-	**1.65**	m2
011 Ceiling lining and battening:					
plywood or similar	0.20	2.24	-	**2.24**	m2
matchboarding	0.21	2.36	-	**2.36**	m2
insulating board	0.19	2.13	-	**2.13**	m2
012 Softwood doors from frame or lining to remain; removing old ironmongery; piece out frames or linings:					
single door	0.70	10.59	0.95	**11.54**	Nr
pair of doors	0.93	14.11	1.58	**15.69**	Nr
013 Softwood doors, together with frames, linings, architraves, ironmongery and the like:					
single door	0.28	3.12	-	**3.12**	Nr
pair of door	0.46	5.20	-	**5.20**	Nr

Unit Rates

		Man-Hours	Net Labour Price £	Net Mats Price £	Net Unit Price £	Unit
014	Softwood windows together with frames, linings, ironmongery and the like:					
	casement windows:					
	not exceeding 1.00 m2	0.25	2.81	-	**2.81**	Nr
	1.00 - 2.00 m2	0.35	3.93	-	**3.93**	Nr
	2.00 - 4.00 m2	0.45	5.05	-	**5.05**	Nr
	sash windows:					
	not exceeding 1.00 m2	0.27	3.03	-	**3.03**	Nr
	1.00 - 2.00 m2	0.37	4.16	-	**4.16**	Nr
	2.00 - 4.00 m2	0.47	5.27	-	**5.27**	Nr
	borrowed light:					
	not exceeding 1.00 m2	0.20	2.24	-	**2.24**	Nr
	1.00 - 2.00 m2	0.30	3.37	-	**3.37**	Nr
	2.00 - 4.00 m2	0.40	4.49	-	**4.49**	Nr
015	Glazed softwood screens together with frames, linings, ironmongery and the like:					
	1.00 - 2.00 m2	0.30	3.37	-	**3.37**	Nr
	2.00 - 4.00 m2	0.40	4.49	-	**4.49**	Nr
	4.00 - 6.00 m2	0.50	5.61	-	**5.61**	Nr
016	Softwood frame or lining from blank openings, together with architraves and the like both sides:					
	1.00 - 2.00 m2	0.25	2.81	-	**2.81**	Nr
	2.00 - 4.00 m2	0.35	3.93	-	**3.93**	Nr
	4.00 - 6.00 m2	0.45	5.05	-	**5.05**	Nr
017	Softwood picture rails:					
	not exceeding 50 mm high	0.03	0.31	-	**0.31**	m
	50 - 100 mm high	0.04	0.45	-	**0.45**	m
018	Softwood dado rails:					
	not exceeding 50 mm high	0.03	0.31	-	**0.31**	m
	50 - 100 mm high	0.04	0.45	-	**0.45**	m
019	Softwood skirting including grounds:					
	not exceeding 100 mm high	0.04	0.45	-	**0.45**	m
	100 - 200 mm high	0.06	0.67	-	**0.67**	m
	200 - 300 mm high	0.08	0.90	-	**0.90**	m
020	Softwood fittings including associated bearers, cover fillets, architraves and the like:					
	wall cupboards not exceeding 500 mm deep:					
	750 x 500 mm	0.25	2.81	-	**2.81**	Nr
	1500 x 500 mm	0.30	3.37	-	**3.37**	Nr
	floor cupboards 500 - 1000 mm deep:					
	500 x 900 mm	0.30	3.37	-	**3.37**	Nr
	1000 x 900 mm	0.35	3.93	-	**3.93**	Nr
	1800 x 900 mm	0.40	4.49	-	**4.49**	Nr
	counters 500 - 1000 mm deep:					
	2000 x 900 mm	0.40	4.49	-	**4.49**	Nr
	2500 x 900 mm	0.45	5.05	-	**5.05**	Nr
	3000 x 900 mm	0.50	5.61	-	**5.61**	Nr
	draining boards 500 - 1000 mm deep:					
	500 mm	0.03	0.31	-	**0.31**	Nr
	1000 mm	0.04	0.42	-	**0.42**	Nr
	under sink units 500 - 1000 mm deep:					
	600 x 900 mm	0.30	3.37	-	**3.37**	Nr
	1200 x 900 mm	0.35	3.93	-	**3.93**	Nr
	shelving units not exceeding 300 mm deep:					
	1000 x 1000 mm	0.15	1.68	-	**1.68**	Nr
	2000 x 1500 mm	0.22	2.47	-	**2.47**	Nr
	shelving:					
	not exceeding 300 mm deep	0.03	0.37	-	**0.37**	m
	300 - 500 mm deep	0.04	0.45	-	**0.45**	m
021	Softwood staircase 2500 - 3000 mm rise and 2500 - 3000 mm going, with 12 - 15 treads and risers complete with wall strings and outer strings and handrail, balusters and newels and with finished plasterboard soffit:					
	straight flight:					
	600 mm wide	1.80	27.36	-	**27.36**	Nr
	900 mm wide	2.20	33.44	-	**33.44**	Nr
	1200 mm wide	2.50	38.00	-	**38.00**	Nr
	two flights with quarter space landing:					
	600 mm wide	2.00	30.40	-	**30.40**	Nr
	900 mm wide	2.50	38.00	-	**38.00**	Nr
	1200 mm wide	3.00	45.60	-	**45.60**	Nr
	two flights with half space landing:					
	600 mm wide	2.10	31.92	-	**31.92**	Nr
	900 mm wide	2.60	39.52	-	**39.52**	Nr
	1200 mm wide	3.10	47.12	-	**47.12**	Nr
022	Ironmongery; including piecing out softwood doors, windows, frames or linings:					
	butt hinge up to 100 mm	0.28	4.23	0.63	**4.86**	Nr
	tee hinge up to 450 mm	0.19	2.83	-	**2.83**	Nr
	barrel bolt up to 200 mm	0.28	4.23	0.32	**4.55**	Nr
	flush bolt up to 200 mm	0.46	7.05	0.63	**7.68**	Nr
	garage bolt up to 600 mm	0.19	2.83	-	**2.83**	Nr
	panic bolt, single	0.46	7.05	0.95	**8.00**	Nr
	panic bolt, double	0.56	8.47	1.26	**9.73**	Nr
	indicating bolt	0.37	5.64	0.63	**6.27**	Nr
	cabin hook and eye	0.09	1.41	-	**1.41**	Nr
	door safety chain	0.09	1.41	-	**1.41**	Nr

Unit Rates	Man-Hours	Net Labour Price £	Net Mats Price £	Net Unit Price £	Unit
rim lock and furniture	0.37	5.64	0.63	6.27	Nr
mortice lock and furniture	0.37	5.64	0.63	6.27	Nr
mortice dead lock	0.37	5.64	0.63	6.27	Nr
sliding door lock/latch and furniture	0.37	5.64	0.63	6.27	Nr
cylinder lock/latch and furniture	0.37	5.64	0.63	6.27	Nr
letter plate	0.46	7.05	0.95	8.00	Nr
push plate	0.09	1.41	-	1.41	Nr
pull handle	0.09	1.41	-	1.41	Nr
kicking plate	0.09	1.41	-	1.41	Nr
overhead door closer	0.19	2.83	0.32	3.15	Nr
floor spring	0.46	7.05	0.63	7.68	Nr
casement stay	0.09	1.41	-	1.41	Nr
casement fastener	0.09	1.41	-	1.41	Nr
sash lift	0.09	1.41	-	1.41	Nr
sash centre	0.09	1.41	-	1.41	Nr
023 Ironmongery; including piecing out softwood doors, windows, frames or linings:					
sash fastener	0.09	1.41	-	1.41	Nr
window pivot	0.19	2.83	0.32	3.15	Nr
window lock	0.19	2.83	0.32	3.15	Nr
fanlight stay	0.09	1.41	-	1.41	Nr
shelf bracket	0.09	1.41	-	1.41	Nr
hat or coat hook	0.09	1.41	-	1.41	Nr
curtain track	0.09	1.41	-	1.41	Nr
draught excluder	0.14	2.13	-	2.13	Nr
towel roller	0.09	1.41	-	1.41	Nr
toilet roll holder	0.09	1.41	-	1.41	Nr
024 Ironmongery; including piecing out hardwood doors, windows, frames or linings:					
butt hinge up to 100 mm	0.31	4.67	0.63	5.30	Nr
tee hinge up to 450 mm	0.20	3.10	-	3.10	Nr
barrel bolt up to 200 mm	0.31	4.67	0.32	4.99	Nr
flush bolt up to 200 mm	0.51	7.77	0.63	8.40	Nr
garage bolt up to 600 mm	0.20	3.10	-	3.10	Nr
panic bolt, single	0.51	7.77	0.95	8.72	Nr
panic bolt, double	0.61	9.30	1.26	10.56	Nr
indicating bolt	0.41	6.22	0.63	6.85	Nr
cabin hook and eye	0.09	1.41	-	1.41	Nr
door safety chain	0.09	1.41	-	1.41	Nr
rim lock and furniture	0.41	6.22	0.63	6.85	Nr
mortice lock and furniture	0.41	6.22	0.63	6.85	Nr
mortice dead lock	0.41	6.22	0.63	6.85	Nr
sliding door lock/latch and furniture	0.41	6.22	0.63	6.85	Nr
cylinder lock/latch and furniture	0.41	6.22	0.63	6.85	Nr
letter plate	0.56	8.47	0.95	9.42	Nr
pull handle	0.09	1.41	-	1.41	Nr
kicking plate	0.09	1.41	-	1.41	Nr
overhead door closer	0.20	3.10	-	3.10	Nr
floor spring	0.51	7.77	0.63	8.40	Nr
casement stay	0.09	1.41	-	1.41	Nr
casement fastener	0.09	1.41	-	1.41	Nr
sash lift	0.09	1.41	-	1.41	Nr
sash centre	0.09	1.41	-	1.41	Nr
sash fastener	0.09	1.41	-	1.41	Nr
window pivot	0.20	3.10	0.32	3.42	Nr
025 Ironmongery; including piecing out hardwood doors, windows, frames or linings:					
window lock	0.20	3.10	0.32	3.42	Nr
fanlight stay	0.09	1.41	-	1.41	Nr
shelf bracket	0.09	1.41	-	1.41	Nr
hat and coat hook	0.09	1.41	-	1.41	Nr
curtain track	0.09	1.41	-	1.41	Nr
draught excluder	0.14	2.13	-	2.13	Nr
towel roller	0.09	1.41	-	1.41	Nr
toilet roll holder	0.09	1.41	-	1.41	Nr
026 **Remove the following and set aside for re-use**					
027 Softwood doors from frame or lining to remain, removing old ironmongery; piece out doors and frames:					
single door (up to about 2.00 m2)	1.10	16.72	1.26	17.98	Nr
pair of doors (2.00 - 4.00 m2)	1.50	22.80	1.89	24.69	Nr
028 Softwood doors together with frames, linings and architraves; removing old ironmongery; piece out doors and frames:					
single door (up to about 2.00 m2)	1.40	21.28	1.26	22.54	Nr
pair of doors (2.00 - 4.00 m2)	1.90	28.88	1.89	30.77	Nr
029 Softwood windows together with frames, linings, ironmongery and the like:					
casement windows:					
not exceeding 1.00 m2	0.55	8.36	-	8.36	Nr
1.00 - 2.00 m2	0.75	11.40	-	11.40	Nr
2.00 - 4.00 m2	0.95	14.44	-	14.44	Nr
sash windows:					
not exceeding 1.00 m2	0.65	9.88	-	9.88	Nr
1.00 - 2.00 m2	0.85	12.92	-	12.92	Nr
2.00 - 4.00 m2	1.05	15.96	-	15.96	Nr
borrowed lights:					
not exceeding 1.00 m2	0.40	6.08	-	6.08	Nr

Unit Rates

	Man-Hours	Net Labour Price £	Net Mats Price £	Net Unit Price £	Unit
1.00 - 2.00 m2	0.60	9.12	-	**9.12**	Nr
2.00 - 4.00 m2	0.80	12.16	-	**12.16**	Nr
030 Glazed softwood screens together with frames, linings, ironmongery and the like:					
1.00 - 2.00 m2	0.70	10.64	-	**10.64**	Nr
2.00 - 4.00 m2	0.90	13.68	-	**13.68**	Nr
4.00 - 6.00 m2	1.10	12.34	-	**12.34**	Nr
031 Softwood frame or lining from blank openings, together with architraves and the like both sides:					
1.00 - 2.00 m2	0.60	9.12	-	**9.12**	Nr
2.00 - 4.00 m2	0.80	12.16	-	**12.16**	Nr
4.00 - 6.00 m2	1.00	11.22	-	**11.22**	Nr
032 Softwood fittings including associated bearers, cover fillets, architraves and the like:					
wall cupboards not exceeding 500 mm deep:					
750 x 500 mm	0.60	9.12	-	**9.12**	Nr
1500 x 500 mm	0.70	10.64	-	**10.64**	Nr
floor cupboards 500 - 1000 mm deep:					
500 x 900 mm	0.70	10.64	-	**10.64**	Nr
1000 x 900 mm	0.75	11.40	-	**11.40**	Nr
1800 x 900 mm	0.80	12.16	-	**12.16**	Nr
counters 500 - 1000 mm deep:					
2000 x 900 mm	0.80	12.16	-	**12.16**	Nr
2500 x 900 mm	0.85	12.92	-	**12.92**	Nr
3000 x 900 mm	0.90	13.68	-	**13.68**	Nr
draining boards 500 - 1000 mm deep:					
500 mm	0.09	1.41	-	**1.41**	Nr
1000 mm	0.10	1.52	-	**1.52**	Nr
under sink units 500 - 1000 mm deep:					
600 x 900 mm	0.70	10.64	-	**10.64**	Nr
1200 x 900 mm	0.80	12.16	-	**12.16**	Nr
shelving units not exceeding 300 mm deep:					
1000 x 1000 mm	0.35	5.32	-	**5.32**	Nr
2000 x 1500 mm	0.50	7.60	-	**7.60**	Nr
shelving:					
not exceeding 300 mm deep	0.08	1.22	-	**1.22**	m
300 - 500 mm deep	0.10	1.52	-	**1.52**	m

	Man-Hours	Plant Hours	Net Labour Price £	Net Plant Price £	Net Mats Price £	Net Unit Price £	Unit
CI STRUCTURAL STEELWORK							
001 Remove the following and load into skips							
002 Universal beams:							
254 x 146 mm (43 Kg/m)	0.33	-	3.66	-	-	**3.66**	m
305 x 165 mm (54 Kg/m)	0.42	-	4.70	-	-	**4.70**	m
406 x 178 mm (74 Kg/m)	0.56	-	6.25	-	-	**6.25**	m
003 Extra over for burning off ends flush with wall face:							
254 x 146 mm (43 Kg/m)	0.93	0.93	14.11	8.79	-	**22.90**	Nr
305 x 165 mm (54 Kg/m)	1.21	1.21	18.35	11.44	-	**29.79**	Nr
406 x 178 mm (74 Kg/m)	1.30	1.30	19.74	12.31	-	**32.05**	Nr
004 Extra over for disconnecting ends from steel columns:							
254 x 146 mm (43 Kg/m)	0.93	-	10.41	-	-	**10.41**	Nr
305 x 165 mm (54 Kg/m)	0.93	-	10.41	-	-	**10.41**	Nr
406 x 178 mm (74 Kg/m)	0.93	-	10.41	-	-	**10.41**	Nr
005 Extra over for cutting out ends from walls:							
254 x 146 mm (43 Kg/m)	0.93	-	10.41	-	-	**10.41**	Nr
305 x 165 mm (54 Kg/m)	0.93	-	10.41	-	-	**10.41**	Nr
406 x 178 mm (74 Kg/m)	0.93	-	10.41	-	-	**10.41**	Nr
006 Steel section columns:							
152 x 152 mm (30 Kg/m)	0.28	-	3.12	-	-	**3.12**	m
203 x 203 mm (60 Kg/m)	0.56	-	6.25	-	-	**6.25**	m
254 x 254 mm (107 Kg/m)	1.02	-	11.46	-	-	**11.46**	m
007 Extra over for burning off ends flush with floor surface:							
152 x 152 mm (30 Kg/m)	0.80	1.02	12.16	9.67	-	**21.83**	Nr
203 x 203 mm (60 Kg/m)	1.34	1.39	20.37	13.19	-	**33.56**	Nr
254 x 254 mm (107 Kg/m)	2.10	1.76	31.92	16.71	-	**48.63**	Nr
008 Extra over for disconnecting from base including breaking up concrete floor and excavating to expose base:							
152 x 152 mm (30 Kg/m)	5.57	0.64	62.48	8.50	-	**70.98**	Nr
203 x 203 mm (60 Kg/m)	5.57	0.64	62.48	8.50	-	**70.98**	Nr
254 x 254 mm (107 Kg/m)	5.57	0.64	62.48	8.50	-	**70.98**	Nr
009 Extra over for disconnecting from base including taking up timber flooring and excavating to expose base:							
152 x 152 mm (30 Kg/m)	4.64	-	52.07	-	-	**52.07**	Nr
203 x 203 mm (60 Kg/m)	4.64	-	52.07	-	-	**52.07**	Nr
254 x 254 mm (107 Kg/m)	4.64	-	52.07	-	-	**52.07**	Nr

	Unit Rates	Man-Hours	Net Labour Price £	Net Mats Price £	Net Unit Price £	Unit
CJ	**METALWORK**					
001	**Remove the following and load into skips**					
002	Metal windows together with frames, ironmongery and the like:					
	not exceeding 1.00 m2	0.34	7.10	1.76	**8.86**	Nr
	1.00 - 2.00 m2	0.46	9.47	1.76	**11.23**	Nr
	2.00 - 4.00 m2	0.23	4.74	1.76	**6.50**	Nr
003	Metal doors together with frames, linings, ironmongery and the like:					
	not exceeding 1.00 m2	1.00	11.22	-	**11.22**	Nr
	1.00 - 2.00 m2	1.30	14.59	-	**14.59**	Nr
	2.00 - 4.00 m2	2.00	22.44	-	**22.44**	Nr
004	Metal doors from frame or lining to remain; removing old ironmongery:					
	not exceeding 1.00 m2	0.85	9.54	-	**9.54**	Nr
	1.00 - 2.00 m2	1.00	11.22	-	**11.22**	Nr
	2.00 - 4.00 m2	1.50	16.83	-	**16.83**	Nr
005	Galvanised steel overhead garage doors together with frames ironmongery and the like:					
	single	1.80	20.20	-	**20.20**	Nr
	double	2.80	31.42	-	**31.42**	Nr
006	Galvanised steel overhead garage doors from frames to remain; removing old ironmongery:					
	single	1.50	16.83	-	**16.83**	Nr
	double	2.50	28.05	-	**28.05**	Nr
007	Mild steel staircase 2500 - 3000 mm rise and 2000 - 2500 mm going with 180 x 10 mm flat strings, about 12 - 15 treads in 6 mm chequer plate, balusters and hand rail:					
	straight flight:					
	900 mm wide	4.50	50.49	-	**50.49**	Nr
	1200 mm wide	5.50	61.71	-	**61.71**	Nr
	two flights with quarter space landing:					
	900 mm wide	5.50	61.71	-	**61.71**	Nr
	1200 mm wide	6.50	72.93	-	**72.93**	Nr
	two flights with half space landing:					
	900 mm wide	6.00	67.32	-	**67.32**	Nr
	1200 mm wide	7.00	78.54	-	**78.54**	Nr
	in two flights with half space landing together with supporting steelwork for fire escape staircase:					
	900 mm wide	11.00	123.42	-	**123.42**	Nr
	1200 mm wide	13.00	145.86	-	**145.86**	Nr
008	Galvanised tubular steel guard railing 1000 mm high consisting of two horizontal tubes spaced approximately 800 mm apart; vertical tubes at 2000 mm centres infilled with welded mesh panels, with all necessary fittings	0.50	5.61	-	**5.61**	m
009	**Remove the following and set aside for re-use**					
010	Metal windows together with frames, ironmongery and the like:					
	not exceeding 1.00 m2	1.50	16.83	-	**16.83**	Nr
	1.00 - 2.00 m2	2.20	24.68	-	**24.68**	Nr
	2.00 - 4.00 m2	3.50	39.27	-	**39.27**	Nr
011	Metal doors together with frames or linings, ironmongery and the like:					
	not exceeding 1.00 m2	2.00	22.44	-	**22.44**	Nr
	1.00 - 2.00 m2	2.50	28.05	-	**28.05**	Nr
	2.00 - 4.00 m2	4.00	44.88	-	**44.88**	Nr
012	Metal doors, frame and lining to remain; removing old ironmongery:					
	not exceeding 1.00 m2	1.80	20.20	-	**20.20**	Nr
	1.00 - 2.00 m2	2.20	24.68	-	**24.68**	Nr
	2.00 - 4.00 m2	3.50	39.27	-	**39.27**	Nr
013	Galvanised steel overhead garage doors together with frames, ironmongery and the like:					
	single	2.50	28.05	-	**28.05**	Nr
	double	3.50	39.27	-	**39.27**	Nr
014	Mild steel staircase 2500 - 3000 mm rise and 2000 - 2500 mm going with 180 x 10 mm flat strings, about 12 - 15 treads in 6 mm chequer plate, balusters and handrail:					
	straight flight:					
	900 mm wide	5.50	61.71	-	**61.71**	Nr
	1200 mm wide	6.50	72.93	-	**72.93**	Nr
	two flights with quarter space landing:					
	900 mm wide	6.50	72.93	-	**72.93**	Nr
	1200 mm wide	7.50	84.15	-	**84.15**	Nr
	two flights with half space landing:					
	900 mm wide	7.00	78.54	-	**78.54**	Nr
	1200 mm wide	8.00	89.76	-	**89.76**	Nr
015	Galvanised tubular steel guard railing 1000 mm high consisting of two horizontal tubes spaced approximately 800 mm apart, vertical tubes at 2000 centres infilled with welded mesh panels, with all necessary fittings	0.75	8.42	-	**8.42**	m

			Man-Hours	Net Labour Price £	Net Mats Price £	Net Unit Price £	Unit
CK		**PLUMBING**					
	001	**Remove the following and load into skips**					
	002	Eaves guttering and brackets:					
		PVC	0.09	1.04	-	**1.04**	m
		cast iron	0.11	1.25	-	**1.25**	m
		fibre cement	0.10	1.12	-	**1.12**	m
	003	Rainwater pipes and branches:					
		PVC	0.09	1.04	-	**1.04**	m
		cast iron	0.11	1.25	-	**1.25**	m
		fibre cement	0.10	1.12	-	**1.12**	m
	004	Sanitary fittings and appliances, together with taps and trap:					
		including service and waste pipes (up to 3 m length):					
		WC suite	0.45	5.05	-	**5.05**	Nr
		wash hand basin	0.40	4.49	-	**4.49**	Nr
		bath	0.60	6.73	-	**6.73**	Nr
		sink unit	0.40	4.49	-	**4.49**	Nr
		shower	0.20	2.24	-	**2.24**	Nr
		service and waste pipes remaining:					
		WC suite	0.35	3.93	-	**3.93**	Nr
		wash hand basin	0.30	3.37	-	**3.37**	Nr
		bath	0.50	5.61	-	**5.61**	Nr
		sink unit	0.30	3.37	-	**3.37**	Nr
		shower	0.15	1.68	-	**1.68**	Nr
	005	Soil and ventilation pipes and branches:					
		PVC	0.56	6.25	-	**6.25**	Nr
		cast iron	0.65	7.29	-	**7.29**	Nr
		lead	0.74	8.34	-	**8.34**	Nr
	006	Hot and cold water installation comprising, back boiler, cylinder, feed and expansion tank; cold water supply from entry of rising main to tank and to 14 No fittings; hot water supply to 10 No fittings	6.00	67.32	-	**67.32**	Nr
		The price for the above item is made up of the following separate prices for removal of:					
		back boiler	0.93	10.41	-	**10.41**	Nr
		feed and expansion tank	0.46	5.21	-	**5.21**	Nr
		cold water storage tank	0.56	6.25	-	**6.25**	Nr
		cylinder	0.37	4.16	-	**4.16**	Nr
		pipe work to fittings (per 5 m of pipework)	0.23	2.61	-	**2.61**	Nr
	007	Central heating installation comprising boiler with 3.00 m length of cast iron flue pipe, oil tank and oil supply pipe, feed and expansion tank, 10 Nr radiators, circulating pumps; pumped heating circuit pipework serving radiators; gravity heating pipework serving cylinder and cold water supply pipe from tee on rising main	9.50	106.59	-	**106.59**	Nr
		The price for the above item is made up of the following separate prices for removal of:					
		boiler and flue pipe	1.39	15.62	-	**15.62**	Nr
		oil tank and oil supply pipe	1.39	15.62	-	**15.62**	Nr
		feed and expansion tank	0.46	5.21	-	**5.21**	Nr
		radiators	0.23	2.61	-	**2.61**	Nr
		circulating pump	0.09	1.04	-	**1.04**	Nr
		pipework (per 5 m run)	0.23	2.61	-	**2.61**	Nr
CL		**ELECTRICAL INSTALLATION**					
	001	**Remove the following and load into skips**					
	002	Electrical installations comprising main switch board, distribution boards, meters, light fittings, power outlets, exposed conduits and trunking, wiring and switches; disconnecting mains power supply and making safe:					
		main switch board	1.21	18.35	-	**20.24**	Nr
		distribution board	0.97	14.68	-	**15.63**	Nr
		meter	0.81	12.24	-	**13.19**	Nr
		light fittings	0.17	2.62	-	**3.04**	Nr
		power outlets and short length of cable	0.29	4.37	-	**4.79**	Nr
		exposed conduits and trunking (per 5 m run)	0.58	8.74	-	**8.92**	Nr
		switches and short length of cable	0.29	4.37	-	**4.55**	Nr
		disconnecting mains power supply	2.88	43.70	-	**43.70**	Nr

			Man-Hours	Plant Hours	Net Labour Price £	Net Plant Price £	Net Mats Price £	Net Unit Price £	Unit
CM		**FLOOR WALL AND CEILING FINISHINGS**							
	001	**Remove the following and load into skips**							
	002	Wall finishes:							
		wall plaster:							
		cement and sand	0.70	0.70	7.85	2.92	-	**10.77**	m2
		lime or gypsum plaster	0.50	0.50	5.61	2.08	-	**7.69**	m2
		lath and plaster	0.40	0.40	4.49	1.67	-	**6.16**	m2

Unit Rates	Man-Hours	Plant Hours	Net Labour Price £	Net Plant Price £	Net Mats Price £	Net Unit Price £	Unit
applied finishings (backings to remain):							
Tyrolean render	0.30	0.30	3.37	1.25	-	**4.62**	m2
pebble dash or rough cast render	0.35	0.35	3.93	1.46	-	**5.39**	m2
ceramic wall tiles	0.50	0.50	5.61	2.08	-	**7.69**	m2
applied finishings (including cement and sand backing):							
Tyrolean render	0.85	0.85	9.54	3.54	-	**13.08**	m2
pebble dash or rough cast render	0.90	0.90	10.10	3.75	-	**13.85**	m2
ceramic wall tiles	1.10	1.10	12.34	4.58	-	**16.92**	m2
003 Ceiling finishes:							
solid plaster	0.60	0.60	6.73	2.50	-	**9.23**	m2
plasterboard	0.37	-	4.16	-	-	**4.16**	m2
lath and plaster	0.50	-	5.61	-	-	**5.61**	m2
suspended ceilings, including suspension system and all supports:							
plaster	0.60	-	6.73		-	**6.73**	m2
mineral fibre tile	0.50	-	5.61	-	-	**5.61**	m2
timber batten	0.50	-	5.61	-	-	**5.61**	m2
004 Floor finishes:							
applied floor finishes (screed to remain):							
linoleum, PVC or other sheet or tile flooring	0.19	-	2.09	-	-	**2.09**	m2
quarry or ceramic tiles	0.93	0.85	10.41	3.54	-	**13.95**	m2
applied floor coverings (including screed total 50 mm thick):							
linoleum, PVC or other sheet or tile flooring	1.02	0.94	11.46	3.90	-	**15.36**	m2
quarry or ceramic tiles	1.39	1.39	15.60	5.79	-	**21.39**	m2
in situ floor coverings:							
cement and sand screed 50 mm thick	0.93	0.85	10.41	3.54	-	**13.95**	m2
granolithic paving 50 mm thick	1.11	1.02	12.50	4.25	-	**16.75**	m2

CN　CUTTING OPENINGS ETC. IN WALLING

In order to provide flexible pricing for the infinite variations in cutting openings of different sizes, wall thicknesses, finishes etc., the prices have been broken down into operations to allow composite prices to be built up. The total net price should be composed of some or all of the following component operations:

1 Needling propping and supports
2 Cutting out walling
3 Making good jambs
4 Inserting lintels, arch bars and forming arches
5 Forming sills to openings cut in old walls
6 Building in damp proof courses
7 Making good wall finishes and extending to jambs

Examples of pricing composite items are given in Section Z

NEEDLING, PROPPING AND SUPPORTS

Note: net materials price allows for 6 uses of timber

001 **Sawn timber needles and props (not exceeding 3000 mm above floor level); cutting holes for needles and making good wall after removal (per needle and pair of props) for:**

	Man-Hours	Plant Hours	Net Labour Price £	Net Plant Price £	Net Mats Price £	Net Unit Price £	Unit
002 Brick walls:							
Half brick thick	1.11	2.00	23.18	4.40	3.71	**31.29**	Nr
one brick thick	1.67	2.00	34.77	4.40	5.59	**44.76**	Nr
one-and-a-half brickwall	2.28	2.00	47.34	4.40	9.00	**60.74**	Nr
003 Blockwork walls:							
75 mm thick	1.02	2.00	21.25	4.40	3.29	**28.94**	Nr
100 mm thick	1.21	2.00	25.12	4.40	3.30	**32.82**	Nr
140 mm thick	1.49	2.00	30.90	4.40	4.65	**39.95**	Nr
004 Stone rubble walling:							
300 mm thick	1.72	2.00	45.39	4.40	12.40	**62.19**	Nr
450 mm thick	2.23	2.00	58.86	4.40	18.14	**81.40**	Nr
600 mm thick	2.60	2.00	68.67	4.40	21.52	**94.59**	Nr
005 Stone ashlar walling:							
150 mm thick	1.67	2.00	34.77	4.40	8.74	**47.91**	Nr
200 mm thick	2.18	2.00	45.41	4.40	13.73	**63.54**	Nr
300 mm thick	2.74	2.00	57.00	4.40	17.48	**78.88**	Nr
006 Cavity walling comprising facing brick outer skin and concrete block inner skin:							
250 mm thick (100 mm inner skin)	2.51	2.00	52.15	4.40	8.02	**64.57**	Nr
300 mm thick (140 mm inner skin)	2.69	2.00	56.02	4.40	2.02	**62.44**	Nr

CUTTING OUT WALLING

007 **Cutting out walling to form new openings and for new lintels, removing debris and loading into skips**

	Man-Hours	Plant Hours	Net Labour Price £	Net Plant Price £	Net Mats Price £	Net Unit Price £	Unit
008 Common brickwork:							
Half brick thick	0.63	-	13.15	-	-	**13.15**	m2
one brick thick	0.84	-	17.38	-	-	**17.38**	m2
one-and-a-half brick thick	1.25	-	26.10	-	-	**26.10**	m2

	Unit Rates	Man-Hours	Plant Hours	Net Labour Price £	Net Plant Price £	Net Mats Price £	Net Unit Price £	Unit
009	Engineering brickwork:							
	Half brick thick	1.00	-	20.87		-	**20.87**	m2
	one brick thick	1.42	-	29.57	-	-	**29.57**	m2
	one-and-a-half brick thick	2.05	-	42.66	-	-	**42.66**	m2
010	Facing brickwork:							
	Half brick thick	0.84	-	17.38		-	**17.38**	m2
	one brick thick	1.25	-	26.10	-	-	**26.10**	m2
	one-and-a-half brick thick	1.70	-	35.38	-	-	**35.38**	m2
011	Blockwork walls:							
	75 mm thick	0.23	-	4.85	-	-	**4.85**	m2
	100 mm thick	0.37	-	7.72	-	-	**7.72**	m2
	150 mm thick	0.46	-	9.57	-	-	**9.57**	m2
012	Stone rubble walling:							
	300 mm thick	0.42	-	11.07	-	-	**11.07**	m2
	450 mm thick	0.55	-	14.48	-	-	**14.48**	m2
	600 mm thick	0.84	-	22.06	-	-	**22.06**	m2
013	Stone ashlar walling:							
	150 mm thick	0.42	-	8.72	-	-	**8.72**	m2
	200 mm thick	0.55	-	11.40	-	-	**11.40**	m2
	300 mm thick	0.67	-	13.90	-	-	**13.90**	m2
014	Reinforced concrete wall:							
	100 mm thick	2.09	0.92	23.44	12.24	-	**35.68**	m2
	150 mm thick	3.14	1.36	35.21	18.13	-	**53.34**	m2
	200 mm thick	4.18	1.83	46.87	24.37	-	**71.24**	m2
015	Cavity walling comprising facing brick outer skin and concrete block inner skin:							
	250 mm thick (100 mm inner skin)	1.15	-	23.93	-	-	**23.93**	m2
	300 mm thick (150 mm inner skin)	1.35	-	28.09	-	-	**28.09**	m2
016	**Cutting away walling at jambs, sills and heads of existing opening to enlarge openings; removing debris and loading into skips**							
017	Common brickwork:							
	Half brick thick	1.26	-	26.26	-	-	**26.26**	m2
	one brick thick	1.67	-	34.77	-	-	**34.77**	m2
	one-and-a-half brick thick	2.51	-	52.15	-	-	**52.15**	m2
018	Engineering brickwork:							
	Half brick thick	2.01	-	41.72	-	-	**41.72**	m2
	one brick thick	2.84	-	59.10	-	-	**59.10**	m2
	one-and-a-half brick thick	4.10	-	85.32	-	-	**85.32**	m2
019	Facing brickwork:							
	Half brick thick	1.67	-	34.77	-	-	**34.77**	m2
	one brick thick	2.51	-	52.15	-	-	**52.15**	m2
	one-and-a-half brick thick	3.40	-	70.75	-	-	**70.75**	m2
020	Blockwork walls:							
	75 mm thick	0.46	-	9.57	-	-	**9.57**	m2
	100 mm thick	0.74	-	15.40	-	-	**15.40**	m2
	150 mm thick	0.92	-	19.15	-	-	**19.15**	m2
021	Stone rubble walling:							
	300 mm thick	0.84	-	22.06	-	-	**22.06**	m2
	450 mm thick	1.09	-	28.72	-	-	**28.72**	m2
	600 mm thick	1.67	-	44.15	-	-	**44.15**	m2
022	Stone ashlar walling:							
	150 mm thick	0.84	-	17.38	-	-	**17.38**	m2
	200 mm thick	1.09	-	22.62	-	-	**22.62**	m2
	300 mm thick	1.34	-	27.82	-	-	**27.82**	m2
023	Reinforced concrete wall:							
	100 mm thick	2.32	1.06	26.04	14.17	-	**40.21**	m2
	150 mm thick	3.34	1.53	37.50	20.39	-	**57.89**	m2
	200 mm thick	4.46	2.04	49.99	27.19	-	**77.18**	m2
024	Cavity walling comprising facing brick outer skin and concrete block inner skin:							
	250 mm thick (100 mm inner skin)	2.30	-	47.86	-	-	**47.86**	m2
	300 mm thick (150 mm inner skin)	2.70	-	56.19	-	-	**56.19**	m2

		Man-Hours	Net Labour Price £	Net Mats Price £	Net Unit Price £	Unit
CR	**REMOVING CHIMNEY BREASTS AND STACKS**					
	This section provides detailed prices needed for pricing the removal of chimney breasts and stacks and the subsequent making good of walls, floors, roofs and finishings. The total net prices should be composed of some or all of the following component operations:					
	1. Removing fireplaces and hearths.					
	2. Cutting away breasts, demolishing stacks and removing pots.					
	3. Making good walls, floors, ceilings and roofs.					
	4. Making good finishings and skirtings.					
	Examples of pricing composite items are given in Section Z					
	REMOVING FIREPLACES AND HEARTHS					
001	**Remove the following and load into skips**					
002	Fireplace surround and hearth:					
	surround 1000 x 900 mm, hearth 1000 x 600 mm:					
	timber	0.35	7.26	-	**7.26**	Nr
	cast iron	0.42	8.72	-	**8.72**	Nr
	stone	0.56	11.59	-	**11.59**	Nr
	tiled concrete	0.70	14.50	-	**14.50**	Nr
	surround 1200 x 1000 mm, hearth 1200 x 600 mm:					
	timber	0.42	8.72	-	**8.72**	Nr
	cast iron	0.56	11.59	-	**11.59**	Nr
	stone	0.70	14.50	-	**14.50**	Nr
	tiled concrete	0.84	17.38	-	**17.38**	Nr
	surround 1500 x 1200 mm, hearth 1500 x 900 mm:					
	timber	0.56	11.59	-	**11.59**	Nr
	stone	0.84	17.38	-	**17.38**	Nr
	tiled concrete	0.93	19.31	-	**19.31**	Nr
003	**Remove the following and set aside for re-use**					
004	Fireplace surround and hearth:					
	surround 1000 x 900 mm, hearth 1000 x 600 mm:					
	timber	0.46	9.66	-	**9.66**	Nr
	cast iron	0.56	11.59	-	**11.59**	Nr
	stone	0.74	15.46	-	**15.46**	Nr
	tiled concrete	0.93	19.31	-	**19.31**	Nr
	surround 1200 x 1000 mm, hearth 1200 x 600 mm:					
	timber	0.56	11.59	-	**11.59**	Nr
	cast iron	0.74	15.46	-	**15.46**	Nr
	stone	0.93	19.31	-	**19.31**	Nr
	tiled concrete	1.11	23.18	-	**23.18**	Nr
	surround 1500 x 1200 mm, hearth 1500 x 900 mm:					
	timber	0.74	15.46	-	**15.46**	Nr
	stone	1.11	23.18	-	**23.18**	Nr
	tiled concrete	1.30	27.03	-	**27.03**	Nr
	CUTTING AWAY CHIMNEY BREASTS, DEMOLISHING STACKS					
005	**Cutting back projecting chimney breasts plastered all round; loading into skips**					
006	Common brickwork:					
	half brick projection	0.61	12.74	-	**12.74**	m2
	one brick projection	0.93	19.31	-	**19.31**	m2
	one and a half brick projection	1.40	29.13	-	**29.13**	m2
	two brick projection	1.70	35.38	-	**35.38**	m2
007	Engineering brickwork:					
	half brick projection	0.98	20.31	-	**20.31**	m2
	one brick projection	1.49	30.90	-	**30.90**	m2
	one and a half brick projection	2.25	46.82	-	**46.82**	m2
	two brick projection	2.80	58.27	-	**58.27**	m2
008	Concrete blockwork:					
	100 mm projection	0.70	14.50	-	**14.50**	m2
	200 mm projection	1.11	23.18	-	**23.18**	m2
	300 mm projection	1.49	30.90	-	**30.90**	m2
	400 mm projection	1.86	38.62	-	**38.62**	m2
009	Rubble walling:					
	100 mm projection	0.65	17.17	-	**17.17**	m2
	200 mm projection	1.02	26.97	-	**26.97**	m2
	300 mm projection	1.39	36.78	-	**36.78**	m2
	400 mm projection	1.67	44.15	-	**44.15**	m2
010	Masonry walling:					
	100 mm projection	0.84	17.38	-	**17.38**	m2
	200 mm projection	1.30	27.03	-	**27.03**	m2
	300 mm projection	1.76	36.71	-	**36.71**	m2
	400 mm projection	2.14	44.43	-	**44.43**	m2

		Man-Hours	Net Labour Price £	Net Mats Price £	Net Unit Price £	Unit
	Unit Rates					
011	**Demolishing 'back-to-back' chimney breasts and party walls in common chimneys; loading into skips**					
012	Common brickwork	3.70	77.00	-	**77.00**	m3
013	Engineering brickwork	5.80	120.70	-	**120.70**	m3
014	Concrete blockwork	3.60	74.92	-	**74.92**	m3
015	Rubble walling	3.00	79.26	-	**79.26**	m3
016	Masonry walling	4.00	83.24	-	**83.24**	m3
017	**Demolishing isolated chimney stacks; loading into skips (scaffolding excluded)**					
018	In roof space:					
	Common brickwork	5.57	115.89	-	**115.89**	m3
	Engineering brickwork	9.47	197.03	-	**197.03**	m3
	Concrete blockwork	5.29	110.11	-	**110.11**	m3
	Rubble walling	3.90	102.99	-	**102.99**	m3
	Masonry walling	4.18	86.92	-	**86.92**	m3
019	Projecting above roof slopes:					
	Facing brickwork	4.64	96.58	-	**96.58**	m3
	Engineering brickwork	7.89	164.19	-	**164.19**	m3
	Concrete blockwork	4.34	90.32	-	**90.32**	m3
	Rubble walling	3.25	85.84	-	**85.84**	m3
	Masonry walling	3.48	72.46	-	**72.46**	m3
020	Remove chimney pot, flaunching and chimney capping (per pot)	0.37	7.72	-	**7.72**	Nr
CT	**TEMPORARY SCREENS AND TEMPORARY ROOFS**					
	The 'Net Materials' prices assume FOUR uses where indicated					
001	**Temporary dustproof screens**					
002	Dustproof screen comprising sheet lining nailed to and including 50 x 100 mm sawn softwood framework; assumed 4 uses; sealing joints between sheets with self-adhesive PVC tape:					
	3 mm hardboard	0.46	7.05	3.79	**10.84**	m2
	12 mm insulation board	0.46	7.05	3.76	**10.81**	m2
	6 mm plywood	0.46	7.05	5.09	**12.14**	m2
003	Sealing perimeter at junction with structure with self-adhesive PVC tape	0.03	0.43	0.24	**0.67**	m
004	**Extra over** for; Waterproofing temporary screen with:					
	1200 gauge polythene sheet with sealed laps (one use only allowed)	0.09	1.41	1.09	**2.50**	m2
	IKOpro or equal waterproofing compound	0.14	2.13	4.88	**7.01**	m2
	one layer fibre based roofing felt (one use only allowed)	0.14	2.13	2.25	**4.38**	m2
005	**Extra over** for screen for forming access with door and frame complete with ironmongery (assumed 4 uses):					
	single door	1.39	21.16	9.75	**30.91**	Nr
	pair of doors	2.32	35.28	17.88	**53.16**	Nr
006	**Temporary waterproof screens**					
007	Waterproof screen comprising sheet linings nailed to and including 50 x 100 mm sawn softwood framework (assumed 4 uses):					
	standard corrugated galvanised steel sheeting (4 uses)	0.51	7.77	7.52	**15.29**	m2
	translucent corrugated PVC sheeting (4 uses)	0.51	7.77	5.44	**13.21**	m2
	two layers 1200 gauge polythene (1 use only)	0.46	7.05	3.67	**10.72**	m2
008	**Temporary roofs**					
009	Temporary roof comprising sheeting laid to slope and fixed with nails to 50 x 150 mm bearers and 100 x 100 mm posts (assumed 4 uses):					
	standard corrugated:					
	fibre cement	0.68	10.31	12.08	**22.39**	m2
	galvanised steel	0.70	10.59	8.99	**19.58**	m2
	translucent PVC	0.65	9.88	6.92	**16.80**	m2
010	100 mm half round PVC eaves gutter on brackets to 25 x 200 mm fascia including stop ends outlets and the like; (assumed 4 uses)	0.46	7.05	2.61	**9.66**	m
011	75 mm PVC down pipe and brackets including shoes, offsets and the like; (assumed 4 uses)	0.28	4.23	1.07	**5.30**	m

Unit Rates		Man-Hours	Net Labour Price £	Net Mats Price £	Net Unit Price £	Unit
CU	**SHORING**					
	The 'Net Material' prices allow ONE use of timber; where shoring is of a temporary nature to suit building operations, the 'Net materials' prices should be divided by the number of uses possible					
001	**Timber dead shores comprising 200 x 200 mm shores 250 x 50 mm floor plates, 200 x 200 mm head plates and 50 x 200 mm braces**					
002	Shoring to floors 3000 mm high with shoring centres one-way of:					
	1500 mm	2.97	45.14	46.35	**91.49**	m2
	2000 mm	2.23	33.87	34.77	**68.64**	m2
	3000 mm	1.49	22.57	23.19	**45.76**	m2
003	**Timber raking and flying shores comprising 200 x 200 mm shores, 250 x 50 mm floor plates, 250 x 50 mm wall plates 200 x 50 mm braces, struts and sole plates; together with timber cleats and needles; cutting holes in existing structure and later making good**					
004	Raking shore to suit two-storey building having first floor 4000 mm above ground and eaves 7500 mm above ground	17.64	268.07	277.86	**545.93**	Nr
005	Raking shore to suit three-storey building having first floor 4000 mm above ground, second floor 7500 mm above ground and eaves 10500 mm above ground	31.56	479.70	494.37	**974.07**	Nr
006	Flying shore between buildings 12 m apart having:					
	single horizontal shore	22.28	338.61	342.81	**681.42**	Nr
	two horizontal shores 3000 mm apart	62.19	945.27	974.31	**1919.58**	Nr

RIPAC

The total cost control and contract administration system that maximises performance and flexibility from minimised input

QS's, Consulting Engineers, Contractors, Project Managers, Developers and Client Bodies

- Budget estimates
- Cost planning
- Bills of quantities
- Measurement from CAD
- Tender pricing and appraisal
- E-tendering
- Resource analysis
- Programme planning links
- Post contract administration
- Payments
- Cash flow
- Whole life costing

Integrated cost control through all project stages.
Easy manipulation of data.
Outputs in user defined formats.
Speedy revisions and updates.
Previous projects available for re-use, analysis and benchmarking.

Various standard libraries of descriptions and price data bases including :

BCIS Price Books

29 London Road
Bromley Kent BR1 1DG
Tel   020 8460 0022
Fax   020 8460 1196
Email enq@cssp.co.uk
www.cssp.co.uk

CSSP
CONSTRUCTION SOFTWARE

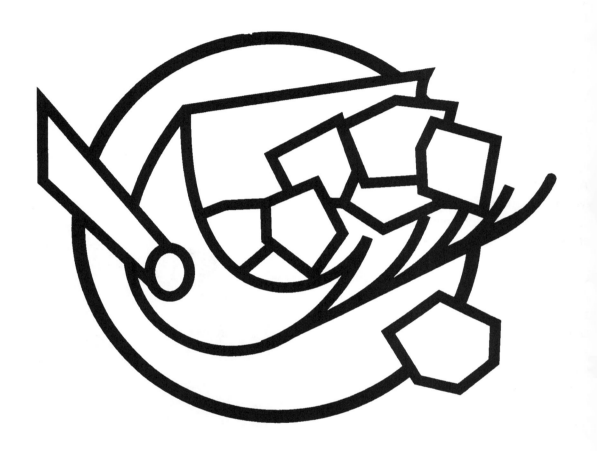

Excavations &
Earthworks

QSToolbox™

THE Weapons grade QS software suite

There are no prizes for second place in business - coming first is the only option. Lose or win, sink or swim, it's your choice so make it QSToolbox™. Designed, engineered and supported here in the UK, our software is at the heart of hundreds of businesses and thousands of seats in over 25 countries including, PQS's, Contractors, Specialists, and Freelancers in both the Civil Engineering and Building Sectors.

Whether you want to cherry pick just one solution, or employ a complete suite of programs, QSToolbox™ offers praise winning, profit making solutions for everyone. From early stage Feasibility Estimating through advanced Cost Planning, Resource Tender Estimating, BQ production and drawing measurement (in paper, scanned image. PDF, CAD and other file formats), QSToolbox™ really delivers. There's even an easy to use Cut & Fill solution!

You've heard all the names before; OnSight™, EasyGrid™ QSExpress™, LaunchSite™, DimSheet-Pro™ and EasyEarthworks™. Now's the time to find out what the buzz is all about.

If you want to move up a gear, call us now for your DVD and brochure pack - it's FREE!

⊕ **LaunchSite™** Estimating

⊕ **LaunchSite™** Cost Planning

⊕ **OnSight™** CAD Measurement

⊕ **EasyGrid™** Digitiser

⊕ **EasyEarthworks™** Cut & Fill

⊕ **QSExpress™** BQ take-off

⊕ **DimSheet-Pro™** for Excel™

QSToolbox™ - future changing technology

Go on-line or call now to receive your free demonstration DVD and brochure pack.

CALL NOW | 01543 262 222

Visual Precision

2 Sycamore Tree · Elmhurst Business Park
Park Lane · Elmhurst · Staffordshire · WS13 8EX
Tel: 01543 262 222 Fax: 01543 262 777
Email: sales@visualprecision.co.uk
Web: http://www.visualprecision.co.uk

LaunchSite™ | EasyGrid™ EVO3 | EasyEarthworks™ | OnSight™ | QSExpress™ | DimSheet-Pro™ | bespoke

EXCAVATION AND EARTHWORK
Notes

It is assumed that any excavation required will be carried out on sites within the confines of the existing buildings. On most sites this will probably entail carrying out excavating and associated work by hand under restricted working conditions and consequently a selection of price build-ups for the most common hand excavation items has been included with appropriate allowances for "average" site conditions built in. However, some sites will accommodate the use of light machinery (mini-excavators, dumpers etc.) and a selection of items has also been included to enable estimates to be prepared where such machinery can be fully or partially utilised.

Occasionally where, for example, the existing buildings are of clear span type construction (e.g. of the factory or warehouse type) it may be possible to use larger machinery for excavation work but this is considered to be outside the intended scope of this book.

Rates for machine work have therefore been based upon the smaller items of plant and readers will need to modify the rates to suit site conditions, particularly if the larger items of plant can be utilised.

Labour Rates

Excavation generally
Labourer (BATJIC Oper. Rate) - £11.22 per hour

Labourers using air or electric percussion drills, hammers, rammers etc.
Labourer (skill rate A) - £11.82 per hour

Earthwork support
Labourer (semi skill A) - £14.02 per hour

Plant Hire Charges

		Daily Hire Charge £	Productive Hours Hrs	Cost Per Hour £	Operator Per Hour £	Fuel Per Hour £	Total Cost Per Hour £
	The hire charges shown exclude the cost of operators and fuel but are inclusive of oil, grease and the like. The cost of delivery to, or collection from, site is EXCLUDED and allowance for this should be made in Preliminaries.						
A0025	Mini-excavator (hydraulic)	60.00	6.00	10.00	14.38	4.31	28.69
A0026	Hydraulic breaking equipment for mini-excavator	45.00	6.00	7.50	-	-	7.50
A0032	Small dumper (up to 1 tonne)	25.00	6.00	4.17	11.82	1.59	17.58
A0041	16 Tonne tipper truck (inclusive of driver and fuel)	224.00	8.00	28.00	-	-	28.00
A0052	Vibrating roller, 400 Kg	24.00	6.00	4.00	11.82	1.66	17.48
A0061	Whacker (hand held vibration rammer)	16.50	6.00	2.75	-	0.86	3.61
A0063	Compressor 100 cfm and one breaker	32.00	6.00	5.33	-	0.86	6.19
A0033	Skip hire charge (including removal etc.) £35.00 per m3 Allow for bulking 33.3% £11.66 -------- £46.66 --------	-	-	-	-	-	35.00
A0200	Tipping charges (per load)	110.00	1.00	110.00	-	-	110.00

The abbreviations under the headings on the succeeding pages have the following meanings:

    Excav   = Excavating plant (hydraulic excavator etc.)
    Brkng   = Breaking equipment (hydraulic breaker attachment or compressor and one breaker)
    Cmptg   = Compacting equipment (vibration rammer [Whacker type], vibrating roller etc.)
    Trans   = Transportation plant (Dumper, Lorry etc.)

Basic Prices of Materials

		Supply Price £	Waste Factor %	Unload. Labour £	Unload. Plant £	Total Unit Cost £	Unit
	The prices are for materials supplied in full loads to sites within 30 miles of the point of supply.						
A0331	Washed sand	29.64	10%	-	-	32.60	tonne
A0351	Hardcore (P.C. price)	18.11	-	-	-	18.11	m3
A0347	Gravel 20 mm down	32.38	10%	-	-	35.62	tonne
A0361	Timber for earthwork support	280.30	5%	11.22	-	306.09	m3

		Man-Hours	Net Labour Price £	Net Mats Price £	Net Unit Price £	Unit
	Unit Rates					
	UNIT RATES					
DA	**SITE PREPARATION BY HAND**					
001	Excavating over existing sub-floor or compacted fill to remove debris; average depth:					
	75 mm	0.20	2.24	-	**2.24**	m2
	100 mm	0.25	2.80	-	**2.80**	m2
DB	**EXCAVATION BY HAND**					
	Note: The rates for excavation in the work in this section allow for excavating in firm earth. For other types of ground the following additions should be made to prices for **hand excavation**.					
	Dry clay	20%				
	Wet clay	20%				
	Hard compact gravel	50%				
	Highly weathered rock not requiring breaking tools	75%				
	Running silt, running sand	100%				
	Running silt, running sand, below ground water level	200%				
	Note: 001 not used					
002	**Excavating starting at natural ground level or reduced ground level**					
003	Excavating to reduce levels, maximum depth not exceeding:					
	0.25 m	3.35	37.57	-	**37.57**	m3
	1.00 m	3.45	38.70	-	**38.70**	m3
004	Excavating for basements, maximum depth not exceeding:					
	0.25 m	3.35	37.57	-	**37.57**	m3
	1.00 m	3.45	38.70	-	**38.70**	m3
	2.00 m	4.25	47.67	-	**47.67**	m3
	4.00 m	6.80	76.27	-	**76.27**	m3
005	Excavating pits to receive bases of stanchions, isolated piers and the like, maximum depth not exceeding:					
	0.25 m	3.45	38.70	-	**38.70**	m3
	1.00 m	3.75	42.06	-	**42.06**	m3
	2.00 m	4.65	52.16	-	**52.16**	m3
	4.00 m	7.40	83.00	-	**83.00**	m3
006	Excavating pits to receive bases of stanchions, isolated piers and the like, having both plan dimensions less than 1.25 m, maximum depth not exceeding:					
	0.25 m	3.55	39.82	-	**39.82**	m3
	1.00 m	4.00	44.86	-	**44.86**	m3
	2.00 m	5.00	56.08	-	**56.08**	m3
	4.00 m	7.85	88.05	-	**88.05**	m3
007	Excavating trenches to receive foundations exceeding 0.30 m in width, maximum depth not exceeding:					
	0.25 m	3.35	37.57	-	**37.57**	m3
	1.00 m	3.75	42.06	-	**42.06**	m3
	2.00 m	4.65	52.16	-	**52.16**	m3
	4.00 m	7.40	83.00	-	**83.00**	m3
008	Excavating trenches to receive foundations not exceeding 0.30 m in width, maximum depth not exceeding:					
	0.25 m	0.26	2.92	-	**2.92**	m
	0.50 m	0.61	6.84	-	**6.84**	m
	0.75 m	0.91	10.21	-	**10.21**	m
	1.00 m	1.21	13.57	-	**13.57**	m
009	**Excavating starting 1.00 m below ground level**					
010	Excavating pits to receive bases of stanchions, isolated piers and the like maximum depth not exceeding:					
	0.25 m	3.80	42.62	-	**42.62**	m3
	1.00 m	4.70	52.72	-	**52.72**	m3
	2.00 m	5.90	66.18	-	**66.18**	m3
	4.00 m	9.60	107.68	-	**107.68**	m3
011	Excavating pits to receive bases of stanchions, isolated piers and the like, having both plan dimensions less than 1.25 m, maximum depth not exceeding:					
	0.25 m	4.05	45.43	-	**45.43**	m3
	1.00 m	5.00	56.08	-	**56.08**	m3
	2.00 m	6.22	69.76	-	**69.76**	m3
	4.00 m	10.15	113.84	-	**113.84**	m3
012	Excavating trenches to receive foundations exceeding 0.30 m in width, maximum depth not exceeding:					
	0.25 m	3.80	42.62	-	**42.62**	m3
	1.00 m	4.70	52.72	-	**52.72**	m3
	2.00 m	5.90	66.18	-	**66.18**	m3
	4.00 m	9.60	107.68	-	**107.68**	m3
013	Excavating trenches to receive foundations not exceeding 0.30 m width, maximum depth not exceeding:					
	0.25 m	0.29	3.25	-	**3.25**	m
	0.50 m	0.74	8.30	-	**8.30**	m
	0.75 m	1.15	12.90	-	**12.90**	m
	1.00 m	1.50	16.82	-	**16.82**	m

Unit Rates	Man-Hours	Excav Hours	Brkng Hours	Cmptg Hours	Trans Hours	Net Labour Price £	Net Plant Price £	Net Mats Price £	Net Unit Price £	Unit
DC **EXCAVATING (BY HAND) FOR WORKING SPACE, FILLING (BY HAND) WITH MATERIAL ARISING FROM EXCAVATIONS, COMPACTED WITH WHACKER IN 250 MM LAYERS**										
001 **Starting at natural ground or reduced ground level**										
002 Excavating for basements, maximum depth not exceeding:										
0.25 m	4.70	-	-	0.22	-	52.72	0.79	-	**53.51**	m3
1.00 m	4.85	-	-	0.22	-	54.40	0.79	-	**55.19**	m3
2.00 m	5.70	-	-	0.22	-	63.93	0.79	-	**64.72**	m3
4.00 m	8.50	-	-	0.22	-	95.34	0.79	-	**96.13**	m3
003 Excavating pits to receive bases of stanchions, isolated piers and the like, maximum depth not exceeding:										
0.25 m	4.85	-	-	0.22	-	54.40	0.79	-	**55.19**	m3
1.00 m	5.15	-	-	0.22	-	57.76	0.79	-	**58.55**	m3
2.00 m	6.10	-	-	0.22	-	68.42	0.79	-	**69.21**	m3
4.00 m	9.00	-	-	0.22	-	100.95	0.79	-	**101.74**	m3
004 Excavating pits to receive bases of stanchions, isolated piers and the like, having both plan dimensions less than 1.25 m, maximum depth not exceeding:										
0.25 m	4.90	-	-	0.22	-	54.96	0.79	-	**55.75**	m3
1.00 m	5.23	-	-	0.22	-	58.66	0.79	-	**59.45**	m3
2.00 m	6.20	-	-	0.22	-	69.54	0.79	-	**70.33**	m3
4.00 m	9.15	-	-	0.22	-	102.63	0.79	-	**103.42**	m3
005 Excavating trenches to receive foundations exceeding 0.30 m wide, maximum depth not exceeding:										
0.25 m	4.85	-	-	0.22	-	54.40	0.79	-	**55.19**	m3
1.00 m	5.15	-	-	0.22	-	57.76	0.79	-	**58.55**	m3
2.00 m	6.10	-	-	0.22	-	68.42	0.79	-	**69.21**	m3
4.00 m	9.00	-	-	0.22	-	100.95	0.79	-	**101.74**	m3
006 **Working space starting 1.00 m below ground level**										
007 Excavating pits to receive bases of stanchions, isolated piers and the like, maximum depth not exceeding:										
0.25 m	5.25	-	-	0.22	-	58.89	0.79	-	**59.68**	m3
1.00 m	6.00	-	-	0.22	-	67.30	0.79	-	**68.09**	m3
2.00 m	7.20	-	-	0.22	-	80.76	0.79	-	**81.55**	m3
4.00 m	11.00	-	-	0.22	-	123.38	0.79	-	**124.17**	m3
008 Excavating pits to receive bases of stanchions, isolated piers and the like, having both plan dimensions less than 1.25 m, maximum depth not exceeding:										
0.25 m	5.43	-	-	0.22	-	60.90	0.79	-	**61.69**	m3
1.00 m	6.20	-	-	0.22	-	69.54	0.79	-	**70.33**	m3
2.00 m	7.45	-	-	0.22	-	83.56	0.79	-	**84.35**	m3
4.00 m	11.35	-	-	0.22	-	127.30	0.79	-	**128.09**	m3
009 Excavating trenches to receive foundations exceeding 0.30 m wide, maximum depth not exceeding:										
0.25 m	5.25	-	-	0.22	-	58.89	0.79	-	**59.68**	m3
1.00 m	6.00	-	-	0.22	-	67.30	0.79	-	**68.09**	m3
2.00 m	7.20	-	-	0.22	-	80.76	0.79	-	**81.55**	m3
4.00 m	11.00	-	-	0.22	-	123.38	0.79	-	**124.17**	m3
010 **Extra over excavation (in any position) for working space and filling with excavated material, for filling with imported materials and depositing excavated material in spoil heaps or skips not exceeding 50 m from excavation**										
011 Filling with:										
Sand	2.20	0.22	-	-	0.27	24.68	28.29	59.98	**112.95**	m3
Hardcore	3.20	0.22	-	-	0.27	35.89	28.29	23.54	**87.72**	m3
Gravel (15 mm down)	2.40	0.22	-	-	0.27	26.92	28.29	66.96	**122.17**	m3
012 ADD for transporting excavated material to tip in urban areas rather than the rural areas allowed in the above prices, average distance from site:										
5 Km	-	-	-	-	0.03	-	0.81	-	**0.81**	m3
10 Km	-	-	-	-	0.06	-	1.65	-	**1.65**	m3
15 Km	-	-	-	-	0.09	-	2.46	-	**2.46**	m3
20 Km	-	-	-	-	0.12	-	3.30	-	**3.30**	m3

Unit Rates		Man-Hours	Excav Hours	Brkng Hours	Cmptg Hours	Trans Hours	Net Labour Price £	Net Plant Price £	Net Mats Price £	Net Unit Price £	Unit
DD	**BREAKING UP ROCK ETC., BREAKING OUT OBSTRUCTIONS MET WITH IN EXCAVATIONS**										
001	**Extra over**										
002	Excavations (in any position) for breaking up hard material (using hand held compressor tools):										
	soft rock or brickwork	3.50	3.50	-	-	-	41.37	21.68	-	**63.05**	m3
	hard rock	6.50	6.50	-	-	-	76.83	40.26	-	**117.09**	m3
	plain concrete	4.55	4.55	-	-	-	53.78	28.18	-	**81.96**	m3
	reinforced concrete	6.60	6.60	-	-	-	78.01	40.88	-	**118.89**	m3
003	Excavations for working space (in any position) for breaking up hard material (using hand-held compressor tools) filling (by hand) with material arising from the excavations; compacted with Whacker in 250 mm layers:										
	soft rock or brickwork	4.80	3.50	-	0.22	-	56.74	22.47	-	**79.21**	m3
	hard rock	7.80	6.50	-	0.22	-	92.20	41.05	-	**133.25**	m3
	plain concrete	5.85	4.55	-	0.22	-	69.15	28.97	-	**98.12**	m3
	reinforced concrete	7.90	6.60	-	0.22	-	93.38	41.67	-	**135.05**	m3

		Man-Hours	Plant Hours	Net Labour Price £	Net Plant Price £	Net Mats Price £	Net Unit Price £	Unit
DE	**BREAKING UP PAVINGS ETC. ON THE SURFACE OF THE GROUND**							
001	**Extra over excavations (in any position) for breaking up hard materials on the surface of the ground (using hand held compressor tools)**							
002	Tarmacadam paving:							
	50 mm thick	0.11	0.11	1.30	0.68	-	**1.98**	m2
	100 mm thick	0.22	0.22	2.60	1.36	-	**3.96**	m2
003	Plain concrete paving:							
	100 mm thick	0.45	0.45	5.32	2.79	-	**8.11**	m2
	150 mm thick	0.80	0.80	9.46	4.95	-	**14.41**	m2
	200 mm thick	1.15	1.15	13.59	7.12	-	**20.71**	m2
004	Reinforced concrete paving:							
	100 mm thick	0.80	0.80	9.46	4.95	-	**14.41**	m2
	150 mm thick	1.30	1.30	15.37	8.05	-	**23.42**	m2
	200 mm thick	1.85	1.85	21.87	11.46	-	**33.33**	m2
DF	**SITE PREPARATION BY MACHINE**							
001	Excavating over existing sub-floor or compacted fill to remove debris; average depth:							
	75 mm	-	0.02	-	0.57	-	**0.57**	m2
	100 mm	-	0.03	-	0.86	-	**0.86**	m2
DG	**EXCAVATION BY MACHINE**							
	Note: The rates for excavation in the work in this section allow for excavating in firm earth. For other types of ground the following additions should be made to prices for **machine excavation**.							
	Dry clay	15%						
	Hard compact gravel	20%						
	Highly weathered rock not requiring breaking tools	50%						
	Running silt, running sand	100%						
	Running silt, running sand, below ground water level	150%						
	Note: 001 not used							
002	**Excavating starting at natural ground level or reduced ground level**							
003	Excavating to reduce levels, maximum depth not exceeding:							
	0.25 m	-	0.15	-	4.30	-	**4.30**	m3
	1.00 m	-	0.14	-	4.02	-	**4.02**	m3
004	Excavating for basements, maximum depth not exceeding:							
	0.25 m	0.10	0.15	1.12	4.30	-	**5.42**	m3
	1.00 m	0.10	0.18	1.12	5.16	-	**6.28**	m3
	2.00 m	0.20	0.36	2.24	10.33	-	**12.57**	m3
	4.00 m	0.40	0.66	4.49	18.94	-	**23.43**	m3
005	Excavating pits to receive bases of stanchions, isolated piers and the like, maximum depth not exceeding:							
	0.25 m	0.25	0.45	2.81	12.91	-	**15.72**	m3
	1.00 m	0.20	0.35	2.24	10.04	-	**12.28**	m3
	2.00 m	0.25	0.50	2.81	14.35	-	**17.16**	m3
006	Excavating pits to receive bases of stanchions, isolated piers and the like, having both plan dimensions less than 1.25 m, maximum depth not exceeding:							
	0.25 m	0.25	0.48	2.81	13.77	-	**16.58**	m3
	1.00 m	0.20	0.38	2.24	10.90	-	**13.14**	m3
	2.00 m	0.25	0.50	2.81	14.35	-	**17.16**	m3

Unit Rates

		Man-Hours	Plant Hours	Net Labour Price £	Net Plant Price £	Net Mats Price £	Net Unit Price £	Unit
007	Excavating trenches to receive foundations exceeding 0.30 m in width, maximum depth not exceeding:							
	0.25 m	0.25	0.45	2.81	12.91	-	**15.72**	m3
	1.00 m	0.20	0.35	2.24	10.04	-	**12.28**	m3
	2.00 m	0.25	0.48	2.81	13.77	-	**16.58**	m3
008	Excavating trenches to receive foundations not exceeding 0.30 m in width, maximum depth not exceeding:							
	0.25 m	0.02	0.03	0.27	0.75	-	**1.02**	m
	0.50 m	0.05	0.05	0.50	1.43	-	**1.93**	m
	0.75 m	0.06	0.07	0.72	2.01	-	**2.73**	m
	1.00 m	0.08	0.09	0.90	2.52	-	**3.42**	m
009	**Excavating starting 1.00 m below ground level**							
010	Excavating pits to receive bases of stanchions, isolated piers and the like, maximum depth not exceeding:							
	0.25 m	0.30	0.55	3.37	15.78	-	**19.15**	m3
	1.00 m	0.25	0.45	2.81	12.91	-	**15.72**	m3
	2.00 m	0.35	0.60	3.93	17.21	-	**21.14**	m3
011	Excavating pits to receive bases of stanchions, isolated piers and the like, having both plan dimensions less than 1.25 m, maximum depth not exceeding:							
	0.25 m	0.30	0.60	3.37	17.21	-	**20.58**	m3
	1.00 m	0.25	0.50	2.81	14.35	-	**17.16**	m3
	2.00 m	0.35	0.65	3.93	18.65	-	**22.58**	m3
012	Excavating trenches to receive foundations exceeding 0.30 m in width, maximum depth not exceeding:							
	0.25 m	0.30	0.55	3.37	15.78	-	**19.15**	m3
	1.00 m	0.25	0.45	2.81	12.91	-	**15.72**	m3
	2.00 m	0.35	0.60	3.93	17.21	-	**21.14**	m3
013	Excavating trenches to receive foundations not exceeding 0.30 m width, maximum depth not exceeding:							
	0.25 m	0.03	0.04	0.28	1.15	-	**1.43**	m
	0.50 m	0.05	0.06	0.53	1.72	-	**2.25**	m
	0.75 m	0.07	0.08	0.74	2.30	-	**3.04**	m
	1.00 m	0.08	0.10	0.93	2.87	-	**3.80**	m

		Man-Hours	Excav Hours	Brkng Hours	Cmptg Hours	Trans Hours	Net Labour Price £	Net Plant Price £	Net Mats Price £	Net Unit Price £	Unit
DH	**EXCAVATING FOR WORKING SPACE (BY MACHINE), FILLING (BY HAND) WITH MATERIAL ARISING FROM EXCAVATIONS, COMPACTED WITH WHACKER IN 250 MM LAYERS**										
001	**Starting at natural ground or reduced ground level**										
002	Excavating for basements, maximum depth not exceeding:										
	0.25 m	1.25	0.15	-	0.22	-	14.03	5.09	-	**19.12**	m3
	1.00 m	1.25	0.18	-	0.22	-	14.03	5.95	-	**19.98**	m3
	2.00 m	1.31	0.36	-	0.22	-	14.70	11.12	-	**25.82**	m3
	4.00 m	1.40	0.66	-	0.22	-	15.71	19.73	-	**35.44**	m3
003	Excavating pits to receive bases of stanchions, isolated piers and the like, maximum depth not exceeding:										
	0.25 m	1.45	0.45	-	0.22	-	16.27	13.70	-	**29.97**	m3
	1.00 m	1.40	0.35	-	0.22	-	15.71	10.83	-	**26.54**	m3
	2.00 m	1.45	0.50	-	0.22	-	16.27	15.14	-	**31.41**	m3
004	Excavating pits to receive bases of stanchions, isolated piers and the like, having both plan dimensions less than 1.25 m, maximum depth not exceeding:										
	0.25 m	1.45	0.48	-	0.22	-	16.27	14.56	-	**30.83**	m3
	1.00 m	1.40	0.38	-	0.22	-	15.71	11.69	-	**27.40**	m3
	2.00 m	1.45	0.50	-	0.22	-	16.27	15.14	-	**31.41**	m3
005	Excavating trenches to receive foundations exceeding 0.30 m wide, maximum depth not exceeding:										
	0.25 m	1.45	0.45	-	0.22	-	16.27	13.70	-	**29.97**	m3
	1.00 m	1.40	0.35	-	0.22	-	15.71	10.83	-	**26.54**	m3
	2.00 m	1.45	0.48	-	0.22	-	16.27	14.56	-	**30.83**	m3

Unit Rates	Man-Hours	Excav Hours	Brkng Hours	Cmptg Hours	Trans Hours	Net Labour Price £	Net Plant Price £	Net Mats Price £	Net Unit Price £	Unit
006 **Working space starting 1.00 m below ground level**										
007 Excavating pits to receive bases of stanchions, isolated piers and the like, maximum depth not exceeding:										
0.25 m	1.50	0.55	-	0.22	-	16.83	16.57	-	**33.40**	m3
1.00 m	1.45	0.45	-	0.22	-	16.27	13.70	-	**29.97**	m3
2.00 m	1.55	0.60	-	0.22	-	17.39	18.00	-	**35.39**	m3
008 Excavating pits to receive bases of stanchions, isolated piers and the like, having both plan dimensions less than 1.25 m, maximum depth not exceeding:										
0.25 m	1.50	0.60	-	0.22	-	16.83	18.00	-	**34.83**	m3
1.00 m	1.45	0.50	-	0.22	-	16.27	15.14	-	**31.41**	m3
2.00 m	1.55	0.65	-	0.22	-	17.39	19.44	-	**36.83**	m3
009 Excavating trenches to receive foundations exceeding 0.30 m wide, maximum depth not exceeding:										
0.25 m	1.50	0.55	-	0.22	-	16.83	16.57	-	**33.40**	m3
1.00 m	1.45	0.45	-	0.22	-	16.27	13.70	-	**29.97**	m3
2.00 m	1.55	0.60	-	0.22	-	17.39	18.00	-	**35.39**	m3
010 **Extra over excavation (by machine in any position) for working space and filling with excavated material, for filling with imported materials and depositing excavated material in spoil heaps or skips not exceeding 50 m from excavation**										
011 Filling with:										
Sand	0.20	0.28	-	-	0.27	2.24	29.98	59.98	**92.20**	m3
Hardcore	0.20	0.39	-	-	0.27	2.24	33.16	23.54	**58.94**	m3
Gravel (15 mm down)	0.20	0.28	-	-	0.27	2.24	29.98	66.96	**99.18**	m3
012 ADD for transporting excavated material to tip in urban areas rather than the rural areas allowed in the above prices, average distance from site:										
5 Km	-	-	-	-	0.05	-	1.48	-	**1.48**	m3
10 Km	-	-	-	-	0.06	-	1.65	-	**1.65**	m3
15 Km	-	-	-	-	0.09	-	2.46	-	**2.46**	m3
20 Km	-	-	-	-	0.12	-	3.30	-	**3.30**	m3
DJ **BREAKING UP ROCK ETC., BREAKING OUT OBSTRUCTIONS MET WITH IN EXCAVATIONS**										
001 **Extra over**										
002 Excavations (in any position) for breaking up hard material (using hydraulic breaker equipment):										
soft rock or brickwork	2.40	2.40	-	-	-	28.37	14.86	-	**43.23**	m3
hard rock	3.85	3.85	-	-	-	45.51	23.84	-	**69.35**	m3
plain concrete	3.10	3.10	-	-	-	36.64	19.20	-	**55.84**	m3
reinforced concrete	4.00	4.00	-	-	-	47.28	24.77	-	**72.05**	m3
003 Excavations for working space (in any position) for breaking up hard material (using hydraulic breaker equipment); filling (by hand) with material arising from the excavations; compacted with Whacker in 250 mm layers:										
soft rock or brickwork	1.30	2.40	-	0.22	-	15.37	15.65	-	**31.02**	m3
hard rock	1.30	3.85	-	0.22	-	15.37	24.63	-	**40.00**	m3
plain concrete	1.30	3.10	-	0.22	-	15.37	19.99	-	**35.36**	m3
reinforced concrete	1.30	4.00	-	0.22	-	15.37	25.56	-	**40.93**	m3
DK **BREAKING UP PAVINGS ON THE SURFACE OF THE GROUND - MACHINE EXCAVATION**										
001 **Extra over excavations (in any position) for breaking up hard materials on the surface of the ground (using hydraulic breaker equipment)**										
002 Tarmacadam paving:										
50 mm thick	-	0.05	-	-	-	-	1.01	-	**1.01**	m2
100 mm thick	-	0.07	-	-	-	-	1.37	-	**1.37**	m2
003 **Breaking with compressor driven breaker, excavating by machine**										
004 Plain concrete paving:										
100 mm thick	0.05	0.06	-	-	0.20	0.56	6.65	-	**7.21**	m2
150 mm thick	0.08	0.08	-	-	0.26	0.90	8.68	-	**9.58**	m2
200 mm thick	0.10	0.10	-	-	0.32	1.12	10.70	-	**11.82**	m2

Unit Rates	Man-Hours	Excav Hours	Brkng Hours	Cmptg Hours	Trans Hours	Net Labour Price £	Net Plant Price £	Net Mats Price £	Net Unit Price £	Unit
005 Reinforced concrete paving:										
100 mm thick	0.09	0.10	-	-	0.26	1.01	9.02	-	**10.03**	m2
150 mm thick	0.14	0.12	-	-	0.30	1.57	10.49	-	**12.06**	m2
200 mm thick	0.20	0.16	-	-	0.40	2.24	13.99	-	**16.23**	m2

	Man-Hours	Net Labour Price £	Net Mats Price £	Net Unit Price £	Unit
DL **EARTHWORK SUPPORT**					
001 Timber earthwork support					
Note: The 'Net Material Price' allows for TEN (10) uses of timber. The 'Net Labour Price' allows for fixing once and striking once					
002 Earthwork support in **firm** ground, to opposing faces not exceeding 2.00 m apart, maximum depth not exceeding:					
1.00 m	0.20	2.80	0.61	**3.41**	m2
2.00 m	0.25	3.55	0.61	**4.16**	m2
4.00 m	0.35	4.91	0.61	**5.52**	m2
003 Earthwork support in **firm** ground, opposing faces 2.00 - 4.00 m apart, maximum depth not exceeding:					
1.00 m	0.22	3.08	0.61	**3.69**	m2
2.00 m	0.30	4.21	0.92	**5.13**	m2
4.00 m	0.40	5.61	0.92	**6.53**	m2
004 Earthwork support in **firm** ground, opposing faces exceeding 4.00 m apart, maximum depth not exceeding:					
1.00 m	0.25	3.51	0.92	**4.43**	m2
2.00 m	0.35	4.91	0.92	**5.83**	m2
4.00 m	0.45	6.31	1.22	**7.53**	m2
005 Earthwork support in **moderately firm** ground, opposing faces not exceeding 2.00 m apart, maximum depth not exceeding:					
1.00 m	0.57	7.99	1.84	**9.83**	m2
2.00 m	0.80	11.22	2.14	**13.36**	m2
4.00 m	1.00	14.02	2.45	**16.47**	m2
006 Earthwork support in **moderately firm** ground opposing faces 2.00 - 4.00 m apart, maximum depth not exceeding:					
1.00 m	0.62	8.69	2.14	**10.83**	m2
2.00 m	0.88	12.34	2.45	**14.79**	m2
4.00 m	1.10	15.42	2.75	**18.17**	m2
007 Earthwork support in **moderately firm** ground, opposing faces exceeding 4.00 m apart, maximum depth not exceeding:					
1.00 m	0.75	10.52	2.45	**12.97**	m2
2.00 m	1.05	14.72	2.45	**17.17**	m2
4.00 m	1.35	18.93	3.06	**21.99**	m2
008 Earthwork support in **loose ground**, running sand and the like, opposing faces not exceeding 2.00 m apart, maximum depth not exceeding:					
1.00 m	1.15	16.12	2.75	**18.87**	m2
2.00 m	1.70	23.84	3.06	**26.90**	m2
4.00 m	2.25	31.55	3.67	**35.22**	m2
009 Earthwork support in **loose ground**, running sand and the like, opposing faces 2.00 - 4.00 m apart, maximum depth not exceeding:					
1.00 m	1.25	17.53	3.37	**20.90**	m2
2.00 m	1.85	25.94	3.67	**29.61**	m2
4.00 m	2.45	34.35	4.29	**38.64**	m2
010 Earthwork support in **loose ground**, running sand and the like, opposing faces exceeding 4.00 m apart, maximum depth not exceeding:					
1.00 m	1.50	21.03	3.67	**24.70**	m2
2.00 m	2.25	31.55	3.98	**35.53**	m2
4.00 m	3.00	42.06	4.90	**46.96**	m2
011 Timber earthwork support left in					
The 'Net Material Price' for earthwork support items allows for (10) uses of timber. Therefore, where earthwork support is described as 'left in' the 'Net Material Price' should be multiplied by (10)					
As there will be no labour in striking earthwork support the labour price should be reduced by 20%					
012 Timber earthwork support below ground water level					
Allow an additional 10% to 'Net Labour Price' to cover the cost of working in wet ground conditions.					
013 Earthwork support next to roadways or existing buildings					
The advice of a structural engineer should be sought on the type and extent of support required to excavations next to roadways or existing buildings, as costs will vary from site to site due to ground conditions, amount of traffic on roads and heights stability or conditions of adjacent buildings					

Unit Rates	Man-Hours	Excav Hours	Brkng Hours	Cmptg Hours	Trans Hours	Net Labour Price £	Net Plant Price £	Net Mats Price £	Net Unit Price £	Unit
DM **DISPOSAL OF EXCAVATED MATERIAL**										
001 **Machine loading from spoil heaps or from side of excavation**										
002 Disposing of excavated material by depositing on site in temporary spoil heaps, average distance from excavation:										
25 m	-	0.09	-	-	-	-	2.58	-	**2.58**	m3
50 m	-	0.11	-	-	-	-	3.16	-	**3.16**	m3
100 m	-	0.16	-	-	-	-	4.59	-	**4.59**	m3
003 Disposing of excavated material by removing from site in skips (skip charges included under 'Net Materials Price'); transporting from excavation to skip by dumper, average distance:										
25 m	-	1.08	-	-	0.45	-	45.21	-	**45.21**	m3
50 m	-	1.08	-	-	0.55	-	46.97	-	**46.97**	m3
75 m	-	1.08	-	-	0.65	-	48.72	-	**48.72**	m3
100 m	-	1.08	-	-	0.75	-	50.48	-	**50.48**	m3
004 Disposing of excavated material by removing from site to tip and paying tipping charges, average distance from site:										
5 Km	-	0.26	-	-	0.18	-	28.34	-	**28.34**	m3
10 Km	-	0.26	-	-	0.22	-	29.60	-	**29.60**	m3
15 Km	-	0.26	-	-	0.27	-	30.86	-	**30.86**	m3
20 Km	-	0.26	-	-	0.31	-	32.09	-	**32.09**	m3
005 **Extra over** cost of transporting material in urban areas rather than the rural areas allowed in the previous prices, average distance from site:										
5 Km	-	-	-	-	0.03	-	0.81	-	**0.81**	m3
10 Km	-	-	-	-	0.06	-	1.65	-	**1.65**	m3
15 Km	-	-	-	-	0.09	-	2.46	-	**2.46**	m3
20 Km	-	-	-	-	0.12	-	3.30	-	**3.30**	m3
006 **Hand loading from spoil heaps or from side of excavations**										
007 Disposing of excavated material by depositing on site in temporary spoil heaps, average distance from excavation:										
25 m	2.10	-	-	-	-	23.55	-	-	**23.55**	m3
50 m	2.40	-	-	-	-	26.92	-	-	**26.92**	m3
75 m (transporting by dumper)	2.00	-	-	-	0.65	22.43	11.42	-	**33.85**	m3
100 m (transporting by dumper)	2.10	-	-	-	0.75	23.55	13.18	-	**36.73**	m3
008 Disposing of excavated material by depositing, spreading and levelling and compacting on site, by hand, in layers maximum 250 mm thick, average distance from excavation:										
25 m	3.00	-	-	-	-	33.65	-	-	**33.65**	m3
50 m	3.30	-	-	-	-	37.01	-	-	**37.01**	m3
75 m (transporting by dumper)	2.90	-	-	-	0.65	32.53	11.42	-	**43.95**	m3
100 m (transporting by dumper)	3.00	-	-	-	0.75	33.65	13.18	-	**46.83**	m3
009 Disposing of excavated material by removing from site in skips (skip charges included under 'Net Materials Price'); transporting from excavation to skip by dumper, average distance:										
25 m	1.55	1.00	-	-	0.45	17.39	42.91	-	**60.30**	m3
50 m	1.55	1.00	-	-	0.55	17.39	44.67	-	**62.06**	m3
75 m	1.55	1.00	-	-	0.65	17.39	46.42	-	**63.81**	m3
100 m	1.55	1.00	-	-	0.75	17.39	48.18	-	**65.57**	m3
010 Disposing of excavated material by removing from site to tip and paying tipping charges, average distance from site:										
5 Km	1.60	0.18	-	-	0.64	17.95	37.58	-	**55.53**	m3
10 Km	1.60	0.18	-	-	0.70	17.95	39.35	-	**57.30**	m3
15 Km	1.60	0.18	-	-	0.73	17.95	40.10	-	**58.05**	m3
20 Km	1.60	0.18	-	-	0.77	17.95	41.33	-	**59.28**	m3
011 **Extra over** cost of transporting material in urban areas rather than the rural areas allowed in the above prices, average distance from site:										
5 Km	-	-	-	-	0.03	-	0.81	-	**0.81**	m3
10 Km	-	-	-	-	0.06	-	1.54	-	**1.54**	m3
15 Km	-	-	-	-	0.09	-	2.46	-	**2.46**	m3
20 Km	-	-	-	-	0.12	-	3.30	-	**3.30**	m3
012 **Multiple handling of excavated material via spoil heaps**										
013 Machine loading and transporting and depositing in spoil heaps, average distance from excavations:										
25 m	-	0.09	-	-	-	-	4.22	-	**4.22**	m3

Unit Rates	Man-Hours	Excav Hours	Brkng Hours	Cmptg Hours	Trans Hours	Net Labour Price £	Net Plant Price £	Net Mats Price £	Net Unit Price £	Unit
50 m	-	0.11	-	-	-	-	5.15	-	**5.15**	m3
100 m	-	0.16	-	-	-	-	7.49	-	**7.49**	m3
014 Hand loading and transporting and depositing in spoil heaps, average distance from excavation:										
25 m	2.00	-	-	-	-	22.43	-	-	**22.43**	m3
50 m	2.40	-	-	-	-	26.92	-	-	**26.92**	m3
75 m (transporting by dumper)	2.00	-	-	-	0.65	22.43	11.42	-	**33.85**	m3
100 m (transporting by dumper)	2.10	-	-	-	0.75	23.55	13.18	-	**36.73**	m3
FILLING										
001 **Material arising from the excavations**										
002 Filling to excavations, by hand, compacting with Whacker in 250 mm layers	1.30	-	-	0.22	-	14.58	0.79	-	**15.37**	m3
003 Filling to make up levels by hand, wheeling average 25 m, compacting with a vibrating roller:										
over 250 mm thick	2.20	-	-	0.22	-	24.68	3.85	-	**28.53**	m3
average 100 mm thick	0.28	-	-	0.06	-	3.14	0.96	-	**4.10**	m2
average 150 mm thick	0.38	-	-	0.06	-	4.26	0.96	-	**5.22**	m2
average 200 mm thick	0.48	-	-	0.06	-	5.38	0.96	-	**6.34**	m2
Extra over wheeling beyond 25 m for each further 25 m	0.32	-	-	-	-	3.53	-	-	**3.53**	m3
004 Filling to make up levels by machine, transporting average 25 m, compacting with a vibrating roller:										
over 250 mm thick	0.23	0.11	-	0.22	-	2.58	7.01	-	**9.59**	m3
average 100 mm thick	0.05	0.02	-	0.06	-	0.56	1.59	-	**2.15**	m2
average 150 mm thick	0.06	0.03	-	0.06	-	0.67	1.76	-	**2.43**	m2
average 200 mm thick	0.07	0.03	-	0.06	-	0.80	1.88	-	**2.68**	m2
Extra over transporting beyond 25 m for each further 25 m	0.04	0.01	-	-	-	0.45	0.40	-	**0.85**	m3
005 **Imported sand filling**										
006 Filling to excavations, by hand, compacting with Whacker in 250 mm layers	1.10	-	-	0.22	-	12.34	0.79	59.98	**73.11**	m3
007 Filling to make up levels by hand, wheeling average 25 m, compacting with a vibrating roller:										
over 250 mm thick	2.00	-	-	0.22	-	22.43	3.85	59.98	**86.26**	m3
average 100 mm thick	0.26	-	-	0.06	-	2.92	0.96	6.00	**9.88**	m2
average 150 mm thick	0.34	-	-	0.06	-	3.81	0.96	9.00	**13.77**	m2
average 200 mm thick	0.44	-	-	0.06	-	4.94	0.96	12.00	**17.90**	m2
Extra over wheeling beyond 25 m for each further 25 m	0.35	-	-	-	-	3.93	-	-	**3.93**	m3
008 Filling to make up levels by machine, transporting average 25 m, compacting with a vibrating roller:										
over 250 mm thick	0.23	0.11	-	0.22	-	2.58	7.01	59.98	**69.57**	m3
average 100 mm thick	0.05	0.02	-	0.06	-	0.56	1.59	6.00	**8.15**	m2
average 150 mm thick	0.06	0.03	-	0.06	-	0.67	1.76	9.00	**11.43**	m2
average 200 mm thick	0.07	0.03	-	0.06	-	0.79	1.88	12.00	**14.67**	m2
Extra over transporting beyond 25 m for each further 25 m	0.04	0.01	-	-	-	0.45	0.40	-	**0.85**	m3
009 **Imported hardcore filling**										
010 Filling to excavations, by hand, compacting with Whacker in 250 mm layers	2.10	-	-	0.28	-	23.55	0.99	23.54	**48.08**	m3
011 Filling to make up levels by hand, wheeling average 25 m, compacting with a vibrating roller:										
over 250 mm thick	3.00	-	-	0.28	-	33.65	4.81	23.54	**62.00**	m3
average 100 mm thick	0.37	-	-	0.08	-	4.15	1.35	2.35	**7.85**	m2
average 150 mm thick	0.50	-	-	0.08	-	5.61	1.35	3.53	**10.49**	m2
average 200 mm thick	0.64	-	-	0.08	-	7.18	1.35	4.71	**13.24**	m2
Extra over wheeling beyond 25 m for each further 25 m	0.35	-	-	-	-	3.93	-	-	**3.93**	m3
012 Filling to make up levels by machine, transporting average 25 m, compacting with a vibrating roller:										
over 250 mm thick	0.42	0.22	-	0.28	-	4.71	11.12	23.54	**39.37**	m3
average 100 mm thick	0.09	0.04	-	0.07	-	1.01	2.41	2.35	**5.77**	m2
average 150 mm thick	0.11	0.06	-	0.07	-	1.23	2.73	3.53	**7.49**	m2
average 200 mm thick	0.13	0.06	-	0.07	-	1.46	2.96	4.71	**9.13**	m2
Extra over transporting beyond 25 m for each further 25 m	0.04	0.01	-	-	-	0.45	0.40	-	**0.85**	m3
013 Hand packing hardcore to form vertical or battering faces:										
over 250 mm thick	0.63	-	-	-	-	7.07	-	-	**7.07**	m2
average 100 mm thick	0.11	-	-	-	-	1.18	-	-	**1.18**	m
average 150 mm thick	0.15	-	-	-	-	1.65	-	-	**1.65**	m
average 200 mm thick	0.17	-	-	-	-	1.88	-	-	**1.88**	m

Unit Rates	Man-Hours	Excav Hours	Brkng Hours	Cmptg Hours	Trans Hours	Net Labour Price £	Net Plant Price £	Net Mats Price £	Net Unit Price £	Unit
DO										
SURFACE TREATMENTS										
001 Levelling and compacting bottoms of excavations	0.09	-	-	-	-	1.01	-	-	**1.01**	m2
002 Levelling and compacting with a mechanical rammer (Whacker):										
bottoms of excavations in trenches and the like	0.11	-	-	0.11	-	1.23	0.40	-	**1.63**	m2
surfaces of open excavation and filling	0.09	-	-	0.09	-	1.01	0.32	-	**1.33**	m2
003 Levelling and compacting with a vibrating roller:										
surfaces of open excavation and filling	0.15	-	-	0.08	-	1.68	1.40	-	**3.08**	m2
surfaces of open excavation and filling, including grading to falls	0.20	-	-	0.08	-	2.24	1.40	-	**3.64**	m2
surfaces of open excavation and filling, including grading to falls and crossfalls	0.25	-	-	0.08	-	2.80	1.40	-	**4.20**	m2
004 Levelling and trimming rock:										
in bottoms of excavations	0.55	-	-	-	-	6.17	-	-	**6.17**	m2
surfaces of open excavations	0.45	-	-	-	-	5.05	-	-	**5.05**	m2
surfaces of open excavations, including grading to falls	0.60	-	-	-	-	6.73	-	-	**6.73**	m2
surfaces of open excavations, including grading to falls and crossfalls	0.65	-	-	-	-	7.29	-	-	**7.29**	m2
005 Trimming sides of excavations in rock to produce fair exposed faces (hand held compressor tools):										
vertically	1.15	1.15	-	-	-	13.59	7.12	-	**20.71**	m2
sloping	1.40	1.40	-	-	-	16.55	8.67	-	**25.22**	m2
006 Blinding surfaces of earth filling or hardcore filling with sand and consolidating with a vibrating roller:										
25 mm thick	0.10	-	-	0.04	-	1.12	0.70	1.50	**3.32**	m2
50 mm thick	0.15	-	-	0.04	-	1.68	0.70	3.00	**5.38**	m2

Concrete Work

BCIS
Independent cost information
for the built environment

Comprehensive Building Price Book 2013
Major and Minor Works dataset

The Major Works dataset focuses predominantly on large 'new build' projects reflecting the economies of scale found in these forms of construction. The Minor Works Estimating Dataset focuses on small to medium sized 'new build' projects reflecting the increase in costs brought about the reduced output, less discounts, increased carriage and supervision, to the similar items in the Major Works dataset. The dataset is presented in trade order. Revised and reworked items in underpinning composites; flue linings and rainwater goods.

Item code: 19215   **Price: £165.99**

SMM7 Estimating Price Book 2013

The SMM7 Estimating dataset focuses predominantly on large 'new build' projects reflecting the economies of scale found in these forms of construction. The dataset is presented in SMM7 grouping and order in accordance with the Common Arrangement of Work Sections. It is compiled using the latest independent costing information from manufacturers, material and plant suppliers, legislation effects and working rule agreements. Revised and reworked items in underpinning composites; flue linings and rainwater goods.

Item code: 19216   **Price: £139.99**

Alterations and Refurbishment Price Book 2013

The Alterations & Refurbishment dataset focuses on small to medium sized projects, generally working within an existing building and reflecting the increase in costs brought about the reduction in output, smaller discounts, increased carriage, increased supervision, and less productivity brought about by smaller economies of scale, increased production costs, more difficult access and the possibility of working in occupied premises. The dataset is presented in trade order. Revised and reworked items in underpinning composites; flue linings and rainwater goods.

Item code: 19217   **Price £109.99**

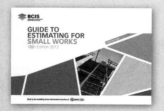

BCIS Guide to Estimating for Small Works 2012

The BCIS Guide to Estimating for Small Works 2012 is a unique dataset which shows the true power of resource based estimating. A set of composite built-up measured items are used to build up priced estimates for a large number of common specification extensions. The intention is to show estimating techniques in use and allow users to build up accurate estimates for their own projects, simply and easily, with up-to-date and independent cost information.

Item code: 19064   **Price: £59.99**

BCIS Painting and Decorating Price Book 2012

The BCIS Painting and Decorating dataset is the most handy pricing tool available to the painting and decorating sector of the industry, suitable for all projects needing more than a 'guess-timate'. Using this dataset a more accurate calculation based quotation or variation can be prepared. From these calculations an assessment of labour, plant and material content can be produced. This in turn enables the contractor to negotiate discounts on known material requirements and the effect of this workload on the availability of labour.

Item code: 19065   **Price: £39.99**

For more information call **0870 333 1600** email
contact@bcis.co.uk or visit **www.bcis.co.uk**

BCIS is the Building Cost Information Service of  RICS the mark of property professionalism worldwide

Labour Rates

Please note: The labour hours throughout this section are representative of the time required for one productive man to carry out the unit of work.

Gang rates are calculated as follows, by obtaining the overall gang cost and then dividing this by the number of productive members in the gang. The resulting rate is the Gang Cost per **Man - hour**. By using the same principle, any size gang may be built-up and used against the standard labour hours in this section.

The prices for labour in this section are as follows:

Plain concrete:
      Concretor = £11.22 per hour

A0201 Reinforced concrete - Gang rate of 4 labourers with one carpenter in attendance

Shuttering Carpenter	1.00	x £	15.20	= £	15.20
Concretor	4.00	x £	11.22	= £	44.88
Poker vibrator	3.00	x £	4.68	= £	14.04
Total hourly cost of gang				= £	74.12

Gang rate (divided by 4) = £18.53 per Man-hour

Reinforcement:
      Craftsman (BATJIC Craft Rate) = £15.20 per hour

Formwork (making):
      Craftsman (BATJIC Craft Rate) = £15.20 per hour

A0202 Precast concrete - gang rate of 2 craftsmen and one labourer

Ganger/Craftsman	2.00	x £	15.20	= £	30.40
Precast Concrete Labourer	1.00	x £	11.22	= £	11.22
Total hourly cost of gang				= £	41.62

Gang rate (divided by 2) = £20.81 per Man-hour

A0203 Formwork fix and strike gang - gang rate of 4 craftsmen and one labourer

Shuttering Carpenter	4.00	x £	15.20	= £	60.80
Formwork Labourer	1.00	x £	11.22	= £	11.22
Total hourly cost of gang				= £	72.02

Gang rate (divided by 4) = £18.01 per Man-hour

Plant Hire Charges

The hire charges shown exclude the cost of operators and fuel but are inclusive of oil, grease and the like. Fuel costs have been added in the following table as appropriate and the cost of operators has been allowed for in the labour rates given in the individual items of work.
The cost of delivery to, or collection from site is EXCLUDED and allowance for this should be made in Preliminaries.

		Daily Hire Charge £	Pro-ductive Hours Hrs	Cost Per Hour £	Operator Per Hour £	Fuel Per Hour £	Total Cost Per Hour £
A0064	250 cfm compressor	54.00	6.00	9.00	-	1.33	**10.33**
A0065	600 cfm compressor	102.00	6.00	17.00	-	2.52	**19.52**
A0071	Compressor hose	2.75	6.00	0.46	-	-	**0.46**
A0073	70 lb hammer	2.50	6.00	0.42	-	-	**0.42**
A0074	Concrete scabbler	21.00	6.00	3.50	-	-	**3.50**
A0075	Kango hammer	25.00	6.00	4.17	-	-	**4.17**
A0081	Power float (helicopter)	20.00	6.00	3.33	-	0.86	**4.19**
A0091	Grinder	7.20	6.00	1.20	-	-	**1.20**
A0101	Bar bending and shearing machine (diesel)	16.50	6.00	2.75	-	1.66	**4.41**
A0131	Melter pourer for expansion jointing	16.50	6.00	2.75	-	3.84	**6.59**
A0111	Adjustable steel prop to 3 m long	2.20	1.00	2.20	-	-	**2.20**
A0112	Adjustable steel prop to 6 m long	2.20	1.00	2.20	-	-	**2.20**
A0121	Column formwork clamp	5.00	1.00	5.00	-	-	**5.00**

Basic Prices of Materials

		Supply Price £	Waste Factor %	Unload. Labour £	Unload. Plant £	Total Unit Cost £	Unit
A0301	Portland Cement (bagged)	137.81	5%	11.22	-	**156.48**	tonne
A0331	Fine aggregate	29.64	10%	-	-	**32.60**	tonne
A0343	20 mm Aggregate	30.95	10%	-	-	**34.05**	tonne
A0342	40 mm Aggregate	31.05	10%	-	-	**34.15**	tonne
	'Aerofil' high density joint filler uncut boards:						
F0215	10 mm thick	8.54	5%	-	-	**8.97**	m2
F0234	'Vertiseal' polysulphide rubber gun grade sealant	12.72	10%	0.01	-	**14.00**	kg
F0236	PS primer (for `Paraseal' and `Vertiseal')	37.68	10%	-	-	**41.45**	ltr
F0517	Colorplete surface hardener	0.99	10%	-	-	**1.09**	kg
F0311	Visqueen polythene sheet, 300 mμ 25 m roll x 4 m wide	27.56	10%	-	-	**30.32**	roll
F0312	Black butyl jointing strip 19 mm wide	5.63	5%	-	-	**5.91**	roll

Basic Prices of Materials

		Supply Price £	Waste Factor %	Unload. Labour £	Unload. Plant £	Total Unit Cost £	Unit
F0313	RIW liquid asphaltic composition	7.14	5%	-	-	7.50	ltr
F0373	Synthaprufe waterproofer	4.01	5%	-	-	4.21	ltr
	Hyload tanking membranes and accessories:						
F0651	Hyload 1000 SA (15 m roll)	100.86	2%	0.37	-	103.26	roll
F0652	Hyload 2000 SA (15 m roll)	93.59	2%	0.37	-	95.84	roll
F0653	Hyload 3100, (10 m roll)	216.69	2%	0.40	-	221.43	roll
F0654	Hyload 3100 HD (7.5 m roll)	251.73	2%	0.40	-	257.17	roll
F0655	IKOpro Self Adhesive Primer	6.09	10%	0.01	-	6.71	ltr
F0657	IKOpro Stickall bitumen mastic	3.31	5%	0.06	-	3.54	m
F0656	Hyload reinforcing strip	4.26	5%	-	-	4.47	nr
	Hot rolled deformed high tensile steel reinforcement bars to BS 4449 in standard lengths (not exceeding 12 m) cut, bent, bundled and labelled (25 to under 100 tonnes):						
F0322	8 mm .395 kg per metre	875.00	2.5%	22.44	-	919.88	tonne
F0323	10 mm .616 kg per metre	854.00	2.5%	22.44	-	898.35	tonne
F0324	12 mm .888 kg per metre	831.00	2.5%	22.44	-	874.78	tonne
F0325	16 mm 1.579 kg per metre	788.00	2.5%	22.44	-	830.70	tonne
F0326	20 mm 2.466 kg per metre	766.00	2.5%	22.44	-	808.15	tonne
F0327	25 mm 3.854 kg per metre	750.00	2.5%	22.44	-	791.75	tonne
F0443	32 mm 6.313 kg per metre	750.00	2.5%	22.44	-	791.75	tonne
F0444	40 mm 9.864 kg per metre	750.00	2.5%	22.44	-	791.75	tonne
	Net deductions for stock bars:						
F0491	8 mm	126.00	2.5%	-	-	129.15	tonne
F0492	10 mm	80.50	2.5%	-	-	82.51	tonne
F0493	12 mm	56.00	2.5%	-	-	57.40	tonne
F0494	16 mm	31.50	2.5%	-	-	32.29	tonne
F0495	20 mm	19.60	2.5%	-	-	20.09	tonne
F0496	25 mm	14.00	2.5%	-	-	14.35	tonne
F0497	32 mm	14.00	2.5%	-	-	14.35	tonne
F0498	40 mm	14.00	2.5%	-	-	14.35	tonne
	Cutting, bending and labelling, cost only of reinforcing bars:						
F0329	8 mm	180.00	-	-	-	180.00	tonne
F0330	10 mm	115.00	-	-	-	115.00	tonne
F0331	12 mm	80.00	-	-	-	80.00	tonne
F0332	16 mm	45.00	-	-	-	45.00	tonne
F0333	20 mm	28.00	-	-	-	28.00	tonne
F0334	25 mm	20.00	-	-	-	20.00	tonne
	Steel fabric reinforcement to BS 4483, supplied in standard sheets, 8 to under 20 tonne loads, reference:						
F0462	A 142 2.22 kg per m2	2.05	2.5%	0.03	-	2.13	m2
F0463	A 193 3.02 kg per m2	2.60	2.5%	0.08	-	2.75	m2
F0464	A 252 3.95 kg per m2	3.47	2.5%	0.08	-	3.64	m2
F0465	A 393 6.16 kg per m2	5.21	2.5%	0.11	-	5.45	m2
F0466	B 196 3.05 kg per m2	2.90	2.5%	0.08	-	3.05	m2
F0467	B 283 3.73 kg per m2	3.54	2.5%	0.08	-	3.71	m2
F0468	B 385 4.53 kg per m2	3.91	2.5%	0.08	-	4.09	m2
F0469	B 503 5.93 kg per m2	4.95	2.5%	0.11	-	5.19	m2
F0470	B 785 8.14 kg per m2	7.73	2.5%	0.15	-	8.08	m2
F0336	B 1131 10.90 kg per m2	9.08	2.5%	0.22	-	9.53	m2
F0337	C 283 2.61 kg per m2	2.48	2.5%	0.03	-	2.57	m2
F0338	C 385 3.41 kg per m2	3.24	2.5%	0.08	-	3.40	m2
F0339	C 503 4.34 kg per m2	4.12	2.5%	0.08	-	4.31	m2
F0472	C 636 5.55 kg per m2	5.27	2.5%	0.11	-	5.51	m2
F0340	C 785 6.72 kg per m2	6.38	2.5%	0.15	-	6.69	m2
F0341	D 49 .77 kg per m2	1.83	2.5%	0.03	-	1.91	m2
	Reinforcement sundries:						
F0480	concrete block spacers C25/30	100.00	10%	0.19	-	110.21	1000
F0481	wheel spacers W12/25	27.70	10%	0.09	-	30.57	1000
F0482	grade plate spacers GP40/50	210.00	10%	0.04	-	231.04	1000
F0485	continuous high chairs CHL 150 (2.0m lengths)	2.30	5%	0.22	-	2.65	m
F0264	12 mm Dowel bars 400 mm long and PVC dowel caps	0.44	5%	-	-	0.46	nr
F0265	debond resin solution	1.76	10%	0.01	-	1.95	ltr
F0335	tying wire	1.38	10%	-	-	1.52	kg
F0266	formwork oil	1.54	20%	-	-	1.85	ltr
	Expamet Ref. 220 foundation bolt boxes:						
F0352	75 mm diameter x 150 mm long	2.42	2%	-	-	2.47	nr
F0356	75 mm diameter x 225 mm long	2.95	2%	-	-	3.00	nr
F0353	75 mm diameter x 300 mm long	3.91	2%	-	-	3.99	nr
F0357	100 mm diameter x 375 mm long	5.58	2%	-	-	5.69	nr
F0354	100 mm diameter x 450 mm long	6.29	2%	-	-	6.42	nr
F0355	100 mm diameter x 600 mm long	6.97	2%	-	-	7.11	nr
F0260	Sawn softwood for formwork	295.00	12.5%	11.22	-	344.50	m3
F0261	18 mm Plywood for formwork	8.60	10%	2.81	-	12.55	m2
F0263	Nails (mixed)	2.90	10%	-	-	3.19	kg
F0345	Oil Tempered hardboard 3.2 mm	2.82	7.5%	0.11	-	3.15	m2
F0347	25 mm Wrought face boarding	13.82	5%	0.26	-	14.78	m2
F0348	50 x 38 mm twice splayed timber fillets P.A.R.	0.86	5%	0.02	-	0.93	m
F0349	100 x 50 mm twice splayed timber fillets P.A.R.	1.78	5%	0.06	-	1.93	m
F0350	Release agent - Rheofinish 277	4.57	10%	-	-	5.03	ltr

Basic Prices of Materials	Supply Price £	Waste Factor %	Unload. Labour £	Unload. Plant £	Total Unit Cost £	Unit
Claymaster low density expanded polystyrene supplied 2.4m x 1.2m sheets in quantities 5-10 m3:						
F0636 50 mm thick	7.90	5%	0.11	-	8.41	m2
F0637 100 mm thick	11.88	5%	0.11	-	12.59	m2
F0638 150 mm thick	17.96	5%	0.11	-	18.97	m2
Polyfoam insulation board:						
F0960 25 mm thick	5.38	5%	-	-	5.65	m2
F0961 65 mm thick	8.83	5%	-	-	9.28	m2
Saddleback copings in precast concrete, double throated in 900 mm lengths:						
F0366 305 x 75 mm	9.28	2.5%	0.11	-	9.63	nr
F0369 356 x 75 mm	12.80	2.5%	0.15	-	13.27	nr
F0372 450 x 450 x 75 pier cap weathered four ways	10.35	2.5%	0.16	-	10.77	nr
Once splayed copings in precast concrete, double throated in 900 mm lengths:						
F0360 305 x 75 mm	8.07	2.5%	0.11	-	8.39	nr
F0363 450 x 75 mm	11.13	2.5%	0.15	-	11.56	nr
Precast concrete padstones; ordinary Portland cement C25/30; delivered to site up to 100 miles from point of supply:						
F0950 215 x 215 x 140 mm	8.06	2.5%	0.11	-	8.38	nr
F0951 300 x 215 x 100 mm	10.20	2.5%	0.11	-	10.57	nr
F0952 450 x 215 x 100 mm	13.58	2.5%	0.11	-	14.03	nr
F0953 450 x 300 x 150 mm	18.24	2.5%	0.11	-	18.81	nr
F0954 450 x 450 x 150 mm	21.37	2.5%	0.11	-	22.02	nr
Prestressed precast concrete lintels:						
F0702 100 x 65 mm	5.95	-	0.20	-	6.15	m
F0703 150 x 65 mm	8.59	-	0.28	-	8.87	m
F0705 220 x 65 mm	12.94	-	0.44	-	13.38	m
F0706 265 x 65 mm	17.36	-	0.50	-	17.86	m
F0707 100 x 150 mm	8.38	-	0.46	-	8.84	m
F0709 150 x 100 mm	8.02	-	0.46	-	8.48	m
F0710 150 x 140 mm	16.94	-	0.70	-	17.64	m
C0116 215 x 215 mm	35.39	-	2.58	-	37.97	m
C0117 327.5 x 215 mm	44.96	-	3.93	-	48.89	m
Ready Mixed concrete - Dense natural aggregate BS 8500; grade:						
F0451 C12/15	84.52	5%	-	-	88.75	m3
F0452 C16/20	87.45	5%	-	-	91.82	m3
F0453 C20/25	90.43	5%	-	-	94.95	m3
F0454 C25/30	93.79	5%	-	-	98.48	m3
F0455 C28/35	93.93	5%	-	-	98.63	m3
F0456 1 - 3 - 6	84.99	5%	-	-	89.24	m3
F0457 1 - 2 - 4	90.50	5%	-	-	95.03	m3
F0902 C20/25 P.C.	90.43	-	-	-	90.43	m3
Ready Mixed Concrete - Lightweight aggregate (Lytag) BS 8500; grade:						
F0500 LC16/18	143.81	5%	-	-	151.00	m3
F0501 LC20/22	147.40	5%	-	-	154.77	m3
F0502 LC25/28	152.93	5%	-	-	160.57	m3
F0503 LC30/33	156.30	5%	-	-	164.11	m3
F0504 LC35/38	163.73	5%	-	-	171.91	m3
F0903 LC25/28 P.C.	143.81	-	-	-	143.81	m3
Ready Mixed concrete - on - costs:						
F0505 Waiting time per hour	71.90	-	-	-	71.90	hour
F0506 Part load surcharge per m3 on part load not carried.	35.95	-	-	-	35.95	m3
F0507 Lean mix (1:12) concrete ready mixed	79.51	5%	-	-	83.49	m3
F0508 C16/20 concrete ready mixed	86.13	5%	-	-	90.44	m3
F0901 C16/20 concrete ready mixed P.C.	86.13	-	-	-	86.13	m3
Additives, special mixes						
The following additions should be made to the prices of lightweight aggregate grade LC25/28 concrete in this section, when required:						
F1500 Sulphate resisting cement	11.98	-	-	-	11.98	m3
F1501 Accelerating admixture	11.98	-	-	-	11.98	m3
F1502 Retarding admixture	11.98	-	-	-	11.98	m3
F1503 Normal water - reducing admixture	5.99	-	-	-	5.99	m3
F1504 Waterproof concrete	59.92	-	-	-	59.92	m3
F1505 Pumping grade concrete	11.98	-	-	-	11.98	m3
F1506 Minimum 360 kg cement	11.98	-	-	-	11.98	m3

Mortar Mix Analysis

A0622 Reconstructed stone mix comprising cement and Portland stone dust graded 6 mm down (1:3) comprising:

Cement (bagged)	0.42 tonne	x	£	156.48	=	£	65.72
Stone dust (bagged)	1.98 tonne	x	£	893.78	=	£	1769.68
Labourer	2.00 hour	x	£	11.22	=	£	22.44
						£	1857.84
Waste	10%				=	£	185.78
Cost per m3					=	£	**2043.62**

A0601 Cement and sand (1:2) grout

Cement (bagged)	0.59 tonne	x	£	156.48	=	£	92.32
Building sand	1.64 tonne	x	£	26.57	=	£	43.57
Labourer	2.00 hour	x	£	11.22	=	£	22.44
						£	158.33
Waste	10%				=	£	15.83
Cost per m3					=	£	**174.16**

A0611 Cement and sand (1:3) mortar

Cement (bagged)	0.44 tonne	x	£	156.48	=	£	68.85
Building sand	1.83 tonne	x	£	26.57	=	£	48.62
Labourer	2.00 hour	x	£	11.22	=	£	22.44
						£	139.91
Waste	10%				=	£	13.99
Cost per m3					=	£	**153.90**

A0563 Site concrete mix 25N/mm2

Cement (bagged)	0.33 tonne	x	£	156.48	=	£	51.64
Fine aggregate BS 882	0.90 tonne	x	£	32.60	=	£	29.34
20 mm Aggregate	1.30 tonne	x	£	34.05	=	£	44.27
						£	125.25
Waste	10%				=	£	12.53
Cost per m3					=	£	**137.78**

A0564 Site concrete weak mix (1:12)

Cement (bagged)	0.14 tonne	x	£	156.48	=	£	21.91
Coarse agg, nat, 40 mm BS 882	2.52 tonne	x	£	34.74	=	£	87.54
						£	109.45
Waste	10%				=	£	10.95
Cost per m3					=	£	**120.40**

Unit Rates	Man-Hours	Net Labour Price £	Net Mats Price £	Net Unit Price £	Unit

FA		UNIT RATES **DENSE AGGREGATE IN SITU CONCRETE**					
	001	**Basis of Prices**					
	002	**Note:** The prices of in situ concrete in this section are based upon ready mixed dense aggregate concrete grade C20/25 supplied to site at a price of £94.95 per m3. No allowance has been made for waiting time or part load surcharges. For every £1.00 per m3 difference in the supply price of the required grade of concrete ADD or DEDUCT £1.05 per m3 to, or from the 'Net Materials' prices and the 'NET UNIT' prices in this section.					
	003	**Additives, special mixes**					
	004	The following additions should be made to the prices of dense aggregate grade C20/25 concrete in this section, when required:					
		Sulphate resisting cement	-	-	11.98	**11.98**	Nr
		Accelerating admixture	-	-	11.98	**11.98**	Nr
		Retarding admixture	-	-	11.98	**11.98**	Nr
		Normal water - reducing admixture	-	-	5.99	**5.99**	Nr
		Waterproofing concrete	-	-	59.92	**59.92**	Nr
		Pumping grade concrete	-	-	11.98	**11.98**	Nr
		Minimum 360 kg cement	-	-	11.98	**11.98**	Nr
	005	**PLAIN dense aggregate concrete grade C20/25, filled into formwork**					
	006	Foundations in trenches:					
		not exceeding 100 mm thick	1.98	22.25	94.95	**117.20**	m3
		100 - 150 mm thick	1.93	21.61	94.95	**116.56**	m3
		150 - 300 mm thick	1.47	16.53	94.95	**111.48**	m3
		exceeding 300 mm thick	1.13	12.71	94.95	**107.66**	m3
	007	Isolated foundation bases to columns and piers	1.70	19.07	94.95	**114.02**	m3
	008	Beds:					
		not exceeding 100 mm thick	2.27	25.42	94.95	**120.37**	m3
		100 - 150 mm thick	1.70	19.07	94.95	**114.02**	m3
		150 - 300 mm thick	1.13	12.71	94.95	**107.66**	m3
		exceeding 300 mm thick	0.79	8.90	94.95	**103.85**	m3
	009	Steps	3.97	44.50	94.95	**139.45**	m3
	010	Filling to hollow walls:					
		not exceeding 100 mm thick	4.31	48.30	94.95	**143.25**	m3
		100 - 150 mm thick	3.85	43.22	94.95	**138.17**	m3
	011	Machine bases	1.98	22.25	94.95	**117.20**	m3
		Note: 012 - 014 not used					
	015	**REINFORCED dense aggregate concrete grade C20/25 filled into formwork**					
	016	Foundations in trenches:					
		not exceeding 100 mm thick	2.49	46.20	94.95	**141.15**	m3
		100 - 150 mm thick	2.38	44.08	94.95	**139.03**	m3
		150 - 300 mm thick	1.81	33.59	94.95	**128.54**	m3
		exceeding 300 mm thick	1.42	26.24	94.95	**121.19**	m3
	017	Isolated foundation bases to columns and piers	1.98	36.74	94.95	**131.69**	m3
	018	Beds:					
		not exceeding 100 mm thick	2.95	54.59	94.95	**149.54**	m3
		100 - 150 mm thick	2.27	41.99	94.95	**136.94**	m3
		150 - 300 mm thick	1.59	29.39	94.95	**124.34**	m3
		exceeding 300 mm thick	1.13	20.99	94.95	**115.94**	m3
	019	Suspended slabs:					
		not exceeding 100 mm thick	4.53	83.98	94.95	**178.93**	m3
		100 - 150 mm thick	3.40	62.98	94.95	**157.93**	m3
		150 - 300 mm thick	2.49	46.20	94.95	**141.15**	m3
		exceeding 300 mm thick	1.70	31.50	94.95	**126.45**	m3
	020	Upstands and kerbs, cross sectional area:					
		not exceeding 0.03 m2	7.93	146.96	94.95	**241.91**	m3
		0.03 - 0.10 m2	5.67	104.97	94.95	**199.92**	m3
		0.10 - 0.25 m2	4.42	81.88	94.95	**176.83**	m3
		exceeding 0.25 m2	3.97	73.49	94.95	**168.44**	m3
	021	Walls:					
		not exceeding 100 mm thick	4.87	90.28	94.95	**185.23**	m3
		100 - 150 mm thick	3.74	69.28	94.95	**164.23**	m3
		150 - 300 mm thick	3.29	60.89	94.95	**155.84**	m3
		exceeding 300 mm thick	2.27	41.99	94.95	**136.94**	m3
	022	Isolated beams, cross sectional area:					
		not exceeding 0.03 m2	6.23	115.48	94.95	**210.43**	m3
		0.03 - 0.10 m2	4.53	83.98	94.95	**178.93**	m3

			Man-Hours	Net Labour Price £	Net Mats Price £	Net Unit Price £	Unit
		Unit Rates					
		0.10 - 0.25 m2	3.97	73.49	94.95	**168.44**	m3
		exceeding 0.25 m2	3.40	62.98	94.95	**157.93**	m3
	023	Casings to isolated steel beams, cross sectional area:					
		not exceeding 0.03 m2	6.80	125.97	94.95	**220.92**	m3
		0.03 - 0.10 m2	4.87	90.28	94.95	**185.23**	m3
		0.10 - 0.25 m2	4.31	79.77	94.95	**174.72**	m3
		exceeding 0.25 m2	3.68	68.23	94.95	**163.18**	m3
	024	Deep beams, cross sectional area:					
		0.03 - 0.10 m2	5.10	94.48	94.95	**189.43**	m3
		0.10 - 0.25 m2	4.53	83.98	94.95	**178.93**	m3
		exceeding 0.25 m2	3.97	73.49	94.95	**168.44**	m3
	025	Deep casings to steel beams, cross sectional area:					
		0.03 - 0.10 m2	5.55	102.88	94.95	**197.83**	m3
		0.10 - 0.25 m2	4.87	90.28	94.95	**185.23**	m3
		exceeding 0.25 m2	4.31	79.77	94.95	**174.72**	m3
	026	Isolated columns, cross sectional area:					
		not exceeding 0.03 m2	6.80	125.97	94.95	**220.92**	m3
		0.03 - 0.10 m2	6.23	115.48	94.95	**210.43**	m3
		0.10 - 0.25 m2	5.67	104.97	94.95	**199.92**	m3
		exceeding 0.25 m2	5.10	94.48	94.95	**189.43**	m3
	027	Isolated casings to steel columns, cross sectional area:					
		not exceeding 0.03 m2	7.08	131.21	94.95	**226.16**	m3
		0.03 - 0.10 m2	6.52	120.72	94.95	**215.67**	m3
		0.10 - 0.25 m2	5.95	110.22	94.95	**205.17**	m3
		exceeding 0.25 m2	5.38	99.73	94.95	**194.68**	m3
	028	Lintels, cross sectional area:					
		not exceeding 0.03 m2	6.96	128.99	137.78	**266.77**	m3
		0.03 - 0.10 m2	5.11	94.60	137.78	**232.38**	m3
		0.10 - 0.25 m2	4.41	81.72	137.78	**219.50**	m3
		exceeding 0.25 m2	3.71	68.80	137.78	**206.58**	m3
	029	Steps and staircases	4.53	83.98	94.95	**178.93**	m3
	030	Machine bases	2.27	41.99	94.95	**136.94**	m3
FB		**LIGHTWEIGHT AGGREGATE IN SITU CONCRETE**					
	001	**Basis of Prices**					
	002	**Note:** The prices of in situ concrete in this section are based upon ready mixed lightweight aggregate (Lytag) concrete grade LC25/28 supplied to site at a price of £160.57 per m3. No allowance has been made for waiting time or part load surcharges. For every £1.00 per m3 difference in the supply price of the required grade of concrete ADD or DEDUCT £1.05 per m3 to, or from the 'Net Materials' prices and the 'NET UNIT' prices in this section.					
	003	**Additives, special mixes**					
	004	The following additions should be made to the prices of lightweight aggregate grade LC25/28 concrete in this section, when required:					
		Accelerating admixture	-	-	11.98	**11.98**	m3
		Retarding admixture	-	-	11.98	**11.98**	m3
		Normal water - reducing admixture	-	-	5.99	**5.99**	m3
		Waterproof concrete	-	-	59.92	**59.92**	m3
		Pumping grade concrete	-	-	11.98	**11.98**	m3
		Minimum 360 kg cement	-	-	11.98	**11.98**	m3
	005	**PLAIN lightweight aggregate concrete grade LC25/28, filled into formwork**					
	006	Beds:					
		not exceeding 100 mm thick	2.15	24.16	160.57	**184.73**	m3
		100 - 150 mm thick	1.62	18.18	160.57	**178.75**	m3
		150 - 300 mm thick	1.08	12.07	160.57	**172.64**	m3
		exceeding 300 mm thick	0.76	8.52	160.57	**169.09**	m3
	007	Steps	3.77	42.33	160.57	**202.90**	m3
	008	Filling to hollow walls:					
		not exceeding 100 mm thick	4.09	45.89	160.57	**206.46**	m3
		100 - 150 mm thick	3.66	41.07	160.57	**201.64**	m3
	009	Machine bases	1.89	21.23	160.57	**181.80**	m3
		Note: 010 not used					
	011	**REINFORCED lightweight aggregate concrete grade LC25/28 filled into formwork**					
	012	Beds:					
		not exceeding 100 mm thick	2.80	51.87	160.57	**212.44**	m3
		100 - 150 mm thick	2.15	39.90	160.57	**200.47**	m3
		150 - 300 mm thick	1.51	27.92	160.57	**188.49**	m3
		exceeding 300 mm thick	1.08	19.94	160.57	**180.51**	m3

	Unit Rates	Man-Hours	Net Labour Price £	Net Mats Price £	Net Unit Price £	Unit
013	Suspended slabs:					
	not exceeding 100 mm thick	4.31	79.77	160.57	**240.34**	m3
	100 - 150 mm thick	3.23	59.83	160.57	**220.40**	m3
	150 - 300 mm thick	2.37	43.88	160.57	**204.45**	m3
	exceeding 300 mm thick	1.62	30.02	160.57	**190.59**	m3
014	Upstands and kerbs, cross sectional area:					
	not exceeding 0.03 m2	7.53	139.61	160.57	**300.18**	m3
	0.03 - 0.10 m2	5.38	99.73	160.57	**260.30**	m3
	0.10 - 0.25 m2	4.20	77.88	160.57	**238.45**	m3
	exceeding 0.25 m2	3.77	69.91	160.57	**230.48**	m3
015	Walls:					
	not exceeding 100 mm thick	4.63	85.87	160.57	**246.44**	m3
	100 - 150 mm thick	3.56	65.93	160.57	**226.50**	m3
	150 - 300 mm thick	3.13	57.94	160.57	**218.51**	m3
	exceeding 300 mm thick	2.15	39.90	160.57	**200.47**	m3
016	Isolated beams, cross sectional area:					
	not exceeding 0.03 m2	5.93	109.81	160.57	**270.38**	m3
	0.03 - 0.10 m2	4.31	79.77	160.57	**240.34**	m3
	0.10 - 0.25 m2	3.77	69.91	160.57	**230.48**	m3
	exceeding 0.25 m2	3.23	59.83	160.57	**220.40**	m3
017	Casings to isolated steel beams, cross sectional area:					
	not exceeding 0.03 m2	6.46	119.67	160.57	**280.24**	m3
	0.03 - 0.10 m2	4.63	85.87	160.57	**246.44**	m3
	0.10 - 0.25 m2	4.09	75.79	160.57	**236.36**	m3
	exceeding 0.25 m2	3.50	64.87	160.57	**225.44**	m3
018	Deep beams, cross sectional area:					
	0.03 - 0.10 m2	4.85	89.85	160.57	**250.42**	m3
	0.10 - 0.25 m2	4.31	79.77	160.57	**240.34**	m3
	exceeding 0.25 m2	3.77	69.91	160.57	**230.48**	m3
019	Deep casings to steel beams, cross sectional area:					
	0.03 - 0.10 m2	5.28	97.84	160.57	**258.41**	m3
	0.10 - 0.25 m2	4.63	85.87	160.57	**246.44**	m3
	exceeding 0.25 m2	4.09	75.79	160.57	**236.36**	m3
020	Isolated columns, cross sectional area:					
	not exceeding 0.03 m2	6.46	119.67	160.57	**280.24**	m3
	0.03 - 0.10 m2	5.93	109.81	160.57	**270.38**	m3
	0.10 - 0.25 m2	5.38	99.73	160.57	**260.30**	m3
	exceeding 0.25 m2	4.85	89.85	160.57	**250.42**	m3
021	Isolated casings to steel columns, cross sectional area:					
	not exceeding 0.03 m2	6.73	124.71	160.57	**285.28**	m3
	0.03 - 0.10 m2	6.20	114.85	160.57	**275.42**	m3
	0.10 - 0.25 m2	5.65	104.77	160.57	**265.34**	m3
	exceeding 0.25 m2	5.12	94.89	160.57	**255.46**	m3
022	Steps and staircases	4.53	83.98	94.95	**178.93**	m3
023	Machine bases	2.15	39.90	160.57	**200.47**	m3

FC   **JOINTS IN CONCRETE**

The prices for 'making' allow for ONE use of timber formwork. Where multiple uses are possible the 'Net Labour, Net Materials and NET UNIT' prices should be divided by the number of uses and allowance made for waste in use of both labour and materials as follows:

Nr of uses	Waste in use
up to 4	Nil
5 to 6	10%
7 to 8	15%
9 to 10	17.5%
11 to 12	20%

No adjustment should be made to 'fixing' prices as these apply irrespective of the number of uses

		Man-Hours	Net Labour Price £	Net Mats Price £	Net Unit Price £	Unit
001	**Plain joints in concrete including formwork**					
002	Horizontal joints in beds:					
	75 mm deep:					
	making	0.23	3.45	1.95	**5.40**	m
	fixing	0.17	2.58	0.05	**2.63**	m
	100 mm deep:					
	making	0.28	4.30	6.28	**10.58**	m
	fixing	0.23	3.45	0.86	**4.31**	m
003	Horizontal joints in suspended slabs:					
	100 mm deep:					
	making	0.19	2.93	6.97	**9.90**	m
	fixing	0.28	4.30	0.86	**5.16**	m
	200 mm deep:					
	making	0.40	6.03	13.93	**19.96**	m
	fixing	0.57	8.62	1.73	**10.35**	m

Unit Rates	Man-Hours	Net Labour Price £	Net Mats Price £	Net Unit Price £	Unit
004 Vertical joints in walls:					
100 mm deep:					
making	0.14	2.07	6.09	**8.16**	m
fixing	0.09	1.38	0.93	**2.31**	m
200 mm deep:					
making	0.25	3.78	11.68	**15.46**	m
fixing	0.16	2.42	1.78	**4.20**	m
005 ADD to prices of joints for					
006 Notching formwork around reinforcing bars up to and including 25 mm diameter passing through joint at:					
150 mm centres:					
making	0.40	6.03	-	**6.03**	m
fixing	-	-	-	**0.00**	m
250 mm centres:					
making	0.25	3.78	-	**3.78**	m
fixing	-	-	-	**0.00**	m
007 12 mm diameter steel dowel bars 500 mm long cast into one side of joint and de-bonded for a length of 250 mm and capped with PVC dowel caps; notching formwork at:					
150 mm centres:					
making	0.40	6.03	-	**6.03**	m
fixing	0.63	9.64	3.14	**12.78**	m
250 mm centres:					
making	0.25	3.78	-	**3.78**	m
fixing	0.37	5.68	1.90	**7.58**	m
008 'Aerofil' high density fibre board joint filler and fixing in place in joint formwork					
009 10 mm thick cut to width on site:					
100 mm wide	0.04	0.67	0.90	**1.57**	m
150 mm wide	0.06	0.85	1.35	**2.20**	m
225 mm wide	0.11	1.73	2.02	**3.75**	m
300 mm wide	0.17	2.58	2.69	**5.27**	m
010 ADD to prices of 'Aerofil' for					
011 Notching any thickness around reinforcing bars up to and including 25 mm diameter passing through joint at:					
150 mm centres	0.40	6.03	-	**6.03**	m
250 mm centres	0.25	3.78	-	**3.78**	m
012 Joint sealants					
Note: 013 not used					
014 'Vertiseal' polysulphide rubber joint sealing compound applied by gun to joint:					
10 x 10 mm	0.05	0.68	0.87	**1.55**	m
Note: 015 - 016 not used					
017 Servicised PVC waterstops; casting into joints					
018 Centre bulb type:					
210 mm wide	0.19	2.93	9.97	**12.90**	m
FD FINISHES CAST ON TO CONCRETE					
001 Reconstructed stone, comprising cement and Portland Stone dust graded 6 mm down (1:3) 20 mm thick; cast on to concrete by lining formwork to					
002 Sides of:					
walls	2.83	43.06	40.38	**83.44**	m2
beams	4.53	68.89	40.38	**109.27**	m2
beds and suspended slabs	4.53	68.89	40.38	**109.27**	m2
isolated columns	5.67	86.11	40.38	**126.49**	m2
Soffits of:					
suspended slabs	1.70	25.84	40.38	**66.22**	m2
beams	3.40	51.66	40.38	**92.04**	m2
sloping staircases	2.83	43.06	40.38	**83.44**	m2
FE LABOURS ON CONCRETE					
001 Tamping surfaces of unset concrete, laid:					
level	0.03	0.38	-	**0.38**	m2
to falls	0.05	0.50	-	**0.50**	m2
to crossfalls	0.06	0.64	-	**0.64**	m2
to cambers	0.07	0.76	-	**0.76**	m2
to slopes not exceeding 15 degrees from horizontal	0.05	0.50	-	**0.50**	m2
002 Spade finishing surfaces of unset concrete, laid:					
level	0.10	1.14	-	**1.14**	m2
to falls	0.14	1.53	-	**1.53**	m2
to crossfalls	0.17	1.91	-	**1.91**	m2
to cambers	0.20	2.29	-	**2.29**	m2
to slopes not exceeding 15 degrees from horizontal	0.14	1.53	-	**1.53**	m2

Unit Rates

		Man-Hours	Net Labour Price £	Net Mats Price £	Net Unit Price £	Unit
003	Trowelling surfaces of unset concrete, laid:					
	level	0.17	1.91	-	**1.91**	m2
	to falls	0.23	2.55	-	**2.55**	m2
	to crossfalls	0.30	3.31	-	**3.31**	m2
	to cambers	0.35	3.94	-	**3.94**	m2
	to slopes not exceeding 15 degrees from horizontal	0.23	2.55	-	**2.55**	m2

		Man-Hours	Plant Hours	Net Labour Price £	Net Plant Price £	Net Mats Price £	Net Unit Price £	Unit
004	Power floating surfaces of unset concrete, laid:							
	level	0.13	0.11	1.40	0.46	-	**1.86**	m2
	to falls	0.16	0.14	1.78	0.59	-	**2.37**	m2
	to crossfalls	0.20	0.18	2.29	0.75	-	**3.04**	m2
	to cambers	0.24	0.21	2.67	0.88	-	**3.55**	m2
	to slopes not exceeding 15 degrees from horizontal	0.16	0.14	1.78	0.59	-	**2.37**	m2
005	**Extra over**; 'Colorplete' surface hardener applied at the rate of 4.9 kg per m2	0.15	-	1.65	-	5.34	**6.99**	m2
006	**Bush hammering concrete with Kango hammers**							
007	Vertical faces of:							
	walls	0.20	0.36	2.29	1.38	-	**3.67**	m2
	edges of slabs, attached beams, upstands and kerbs	0.23	0.40	2.55	1.53	-	**4.08**	m2
	isolated beams	0.68	1.20	7.63	4.60	-	**12.23**	m2
	isolated columns	0.45	0.80	5.08	3.07	-	**8.15**	m2
	walls in panels with margins of a different finish	0.28	0.50	3.17	1.92	-	**5.09**	m2
008	Soffits of:							
	suspended slabs	0.34	0.50	3.81	1.92	-	**5.73**	m2
	attached beams	0.45	0.80	5.08	3.07	-	**8.15**	m2
	isolated beams	0.68	1.20	7.63	4.60	-	**12.23**	m2
009	**Heavy bush hammering concrete with hand-held compressor tools**							
010	Vertical faces of:							
	walls	0.57	0.30	6.36	1.12	-	**7.48**	m2
	edges of slabs, attached beams, upstands and kerbs	0.62	3.30	6.99	12.33	-	**19.32**	m2
	isolated beams	0.85	4.50	9.53	16.81	-	**26.34**	m2
	isolated columns	0.74	4.50	8.26	16.81	-	**25.07**	m2
	walls in panels with margins of a different finish	0.62	3.30	6.99	12.33	-	**19.32**	m2
011	Soffits of:							
	suspended slabs	0.74	3.90	8.26	14.57	-	**22.83**	m2
	attached beams	0.79	4.20	8.89	15.69	-	**24.58**	m2
	isolated beams	1.08	5.70	12.07	21.29	-	**33.36**	m2
012	**Cuttings on concrete**							
013	Flush cut face of existing concrete walls after removal of plinth courses, band courses, pilasters, attached piers and the like, dressed with Kango hammer:							
	over 1000 mm wide	1.05	0.47	11.80	6.24	-	**18.04**	m2
	up to 250 mm wide	0.29	0.13	3.21	1.71	-	**4.92**	m
	250 - 500 mm wide	0.54	0.24	6.01	3.17	-	**9.18**	m
	500 - 1000 mm wide	1.05	0.47	11.80	6.24	-	**18.04**	m
014	Fair cutting with carborundum wheel both sides of wall prior to demolition:							
	100 mm thick	0.38	0.34	4.28	0.41	-	**4.69**	m
	150 mm thick	0.48	0.43	5.36	0.51	-	**5.87**	m
	200 mm thick	0.57	0.51	6.44	0.61	-	**7.05**	m
015	Cutting groove for water bar and running with cement	0.24	0.21	2.67	0.25	0.63	**3.55**	m
016	Cutting groove for turn in of lead flashings	0.19	0.17	2.16	0.20	-	**2.36**	m
017	Cutting mortices and running with cement for:							
	dowel	0.23	-	2.55	-	-	**2.55**	Nr
	ragbolt	0.28	-	3.17	-	-	**3.17**	Nr

		Man-Hours	Net Labour Price £	Net Mats Price £	Net Unit Price £	Unit
FF	**CONCRETE WORK SUNDRIES**					
001	Making good existing ground floor slabs in dense aggregate concrete grade 25N/mm2, after removal of columns:					
	solid concrete floors, 150 mm thick; area:					
	not exceeding 1.00 m2	0.43	4.85	20.67	**25.52**	Nr
	1.00 to 2.00 m2	0.70	7.85	41.33	**49.18**	Nr
	Extra over for trowelling smooth:					
	not exceeding 1.00 m2	0.48	5.36	-	**5.36**	Nr
	1.00 to 2.00 m2	0.72	8.06	-	**8.06**	Nr

Unit Rates	Man-Hours	Net Labour Price £	Net Mats Price £	Net Unit Price £	Unit
002 Making good jambs of openings cut in old reinforced concrete walls:					
with cement mortar (1:3) average 25 mm thick; wall:					
100 mm thick	0.24	4.99	0.39	**5.38**	m
150 mm thick	0.29	5.95	0.52	**6.47**	m
200 mm thick	0.34	6.99	0.65	**7.64**	m
003 Filling to make up levels with weak mix concrete (1:12)	1.91	21.45	120.40	**141.85**	m3
004 Prepare cut edge of existing reinforced concrete floor slab to receive new concrete:					
150 mm thick	0.16	1.83	-	**1.83**	m
200 mm thick	0.21	2.36	-	**2.36**	m
005 **Polyfoam insulation board, butt joints; laid on blinded hardcore or the like**					
006 Sheets laid horizontally under concrete slabs:					
25 mm thick	0.06	1.15	5.65	**6.80**	m2
65 mm thick	0.07	1.26	9.28	**10.54**	m2
FG **WATERPROOF MEMBRANES**					
001 **300 mμ (1200) gauge polythene sheet**					
002 Single layer with 150 mm side and end laps; laid:					
horizontally over 300 mm wide	0.03	0.38	0.30	**0.68**	m2
vertically not exceeding 150 mm wide	0.01	0.12	0.06	**0.18**	m
vertically 150 - 300 mm wide	0.02	0.20	0.09	**0.29**	m
003 **Extra over** last for:					
welted laps	0.03	0.38	-	**0.38**	m2
sealing laps with single sided adhesive tape and black butile jointing strip	0.01	0.12	0.13	**0.25**	m2
004 **RIW liquid asphaltic compound; first coat applied at the rate of 1.70 m2 per litre; second and subsequent coats at the rate of 2.5 m2 per litre per coat**					
005 Two coat membrane on concrete horizontal surfaces:					
over 300 mm wide	0.27	3.06	7.50	**10.56**	m2
not exceeding 150 mm wide	0.04	0.46	1.12	**1.58**	m
150 - 300 mm wide	0.08	0.91	2.25	**3.16**	m
006 Two coat membrane on concrete vertical surfaces:					
over 300 mm wide	0.21	2.31	7.50	**9.81**	m2
not exceeding 150 mm wide	0.03	0.35	1.12	**1.47**	m
150 - 300 mm wide	0.06	0.71	2.25	**2.96**	m
007 **Synthaprufe waterproofer**					
008 Two coat membrane on concrete; horizontal; first coat applied at the rate of 1.10 m2 per litre, second coat at the rate of 1.50 m2 per litre, final surface dusted with clean sharp sand:					
over 300 mm wide	0.30	3.32	6.96	**10.28**	m2
not exceeding 150 mm wide	0.04	0.49	1.01	**1.50**	m
150 - 300 mm wide	0.09	1.00	2.10	**3.10**	m
009 Three coat membrane on concrete; vertical; applied at the rate of 2.20 m2 per litre, final surfaces dusted with clean sharp sand:					
over 300 mm wide	0.32	3.56	6.21	**9.77**	m2
not exceeding 150 mm wide	0.05	0.50	0.91	**1.41**	m
150 - 300 mm wide	0.09	1.03	1.92	**2.95**	m
010 **Hyload tanking membranes; 100 mm side and end laps; priming surfaces with one coat plasprufe Quick Drying Primer**					
011 Hyload 1000 SA self bonded membranes:					
horizontal:					
over 300 mm wide	0.28	3.13	8.60	**11.73**	m2
not exceeding 150 mm wide	0.06	0.66	1.37	**2.03**	m
150 - 300 mm wide	0.11	1.22	2.57	**3.79**	m
vertical to upstands, turning over 50 mm wide at top, overlapping horizontal by 100 mm:					
not exceeding 300 mm girth	0.11	1.28	2.40	**3.68**	m
300 - 450 mm girth	0.15	1.68	3.60	**5.28**	m
012 Hyload 2000 SA self bonded membranes:					
horizontal:					
over 300 mm wide	0.28	3.13	8.10	**11.23**	m2
not exceeding 150 mm wide	0.06	0.66	1.29	**1.95**	m
150 - 300 mm wide	0.11	1.22	2.42	**3.64**	m
vertical:					
over 300 mm wide	0.27	3.06	8.10	**11.16**	m2
not exceeding 150 mm wide	0.06	0.71	1.29	**2.00**	m
150 - 300 mm wide	0.11	1.28	2.42	**3.70**	m
internal or external angle including reinforcing strip 350 mm wide	0.07	0.83	3.26	**4.09**	m
013 Hyload 3000 torch bonded membranes:					
horizontal, laid loose but with torch bonded laps and perimeters:					
over 300 mm wide	0.31	3.44	21.83	**25.27**	m2
not exceeding 150 mm wide	0.07	0.76	3.44	**4.20**	m
150 - 300 mm wide	0.13	1.40	6.04	**7.44**	m
vertical, torch bonded all over:					
over 300 mm wide	0.36	4.02	21.83	**25.85**	m2
not exceeding 150 mm wide	0.10	1.17	3.44	**4.61**	m

Unit Rates	Man-Hours	Net Labour Price £	Net Mats Price £	Net Unit Price £	Unit
150 - 300 mm wide	0.19	2.11	6.04	**8.15**	m
internal or external angle including reinforcing strip 350 mm wide	0.15	1.66	7.53	**9.19**	m
014 Hyload 3000 HD torch bonded membranes:					
horizontal, laid loose but with torch bonded laps and perimeters:					
over 300 mm wide	0.35	3.97	35.88	**39.85**	m2
not exceeding 150 mm wide	0.08	0.91	5.48	**6.39**	m
150 - 300 mm wide	0.15	1.67	9.76	**11.43**	m
vertical, torch bonded all over:					
150 - 300 mm wide	0.41	4.64	9.76	**14.40**	m
015 Hyload reinforcing stip 48 x 48 mm overall; bedding in mastic	0.23	2.55	4.09	**6.64**	m
016 **Extra over** for additional priming coat of IKOpro quick drying primer on porous surfaces:					
horizontal:					
over 300 mm wide	0.11	1.21	1.01	**2.22**	m2
not exceeding 150 mm wide	0.02	0.18	0.17	**0.35**	m
150 - 300 mm wide	0.03	0.37	0.34	**0.71**	m
vertical:					
over 300 mm wide	0.08	0.94	1.01	**1.95**	m2
not exceeding 150 mm wide	0.01	0.13	0.17	**0.30**	m
150 - 300 mm wide	0.03	0.29	0.34	**0.63**	m

FH **REINFORCEMENT**

Note: 001 – 003 not used

004 **Hot rolled deformed high yield steel bars BS 4449, supplied cut, bent and labelled**

	Man-Hours	Net Labour Price £	Net Mats Price £	Net Unit Price £	Unit
005 Straight and bent bars in any position:					
8 mm .395 kg per metre	0.06	0.94	0.95	**1.89**	Kg
10 mm .616 kg per metre	0.05	0.74	0.92	**1.66**	Kg
12 mm .888 kg per metre	0.04	0.65	0.89	**1.54**	Kg
16 mm 1.579 kg per metre	0.03	0.52	0.88	**1.40**	Kg
20 mm 2.466 kg per metre	0.03	0.46	0.85	**1.31**	Kg
25 mm 3.854 kg per metre	0.03	0.41	0.84	**1.25**	Kg
32 mm 6.313 kg per metre	0.02	0.32	0.84	**1.16**	Kg
40 mm 9.864 kg per metre	0.02	0.27	0.84	**1.11**	Kg
006 Links, stirrups, binders and special spacers in any position:					
8 mm .395 kg per metre	0.07	1.06	1.08	**2.14**	Kg
10 mm .616 kg per metre	0.06	0.87	1.00	**1.87**	Kg

	Man-Hours	Plant Hours	Net Labour Price £	Net Plant Price £	Net Mats Price £	Net Unit Price £	Unit
007 **ADD to above labour prices for cutting and bending on site (for bars purchased in straight standard lengths)**							
008 Straight and bent bars in any position:							
8 mm	0.04	-	0.59	-	-	**0.59**	Kg
10 mm	0.03	-	0.47	-	-	**0.47**	Kg
12 mm	0.03	-	0.41	-	-	**0.41**	Kg
16 mm	0.02	-	0.33	-	-	**0.33**	Kg
20 mm	0.02	-	0.27	-	-	**0.27**	Kg
25 mm (cutting and bending by machine)	0.01	0.01	0.15	0.04	-	**0.19**	Kg
32 mm (cutting and bending by machine)	0.01	0.01	0.11	0.03	-	**0.14**	Kg
40 mm (cutting and bending by machine)	0.01	0.01	0.08	0.02	-	**0.10**	Kg
009 Links, stirrups, binders and special spacers in any position:							
8 mm	0.06	-	0.88	-	-	**0.88**	Kg
10 mm	0.05	-	0.70	-	-	**0.70**	Kg

Note: 010 - 011 not used

	Man-Hours	Net Labour Price £	Net Mats Price £	Net Unit Price £	Unit
012 **Steel fabric reinforcement BS 4483, with one width mesh side laps and one width mesh end laps**					
013 Fabric reinforcement laid in ground slabs, reference:					
A 142, 200 mm side laps, 200 mm end laps	0.04	0.53	2.41	**2.94**	m2
A 193	0.05	0.73	3.05	**3.78**	m2
A 252	0.05	0.73	4.00	**4.73**	m2
A 393	0.06	0.87	5.94	**6.81**	m2
B 196, 100 mm side laps, 200 mm end laps	0.05	0.73	3.49	**4.22**	m2
B 283	0.05	0.73	4.06	**4.79**	m2
B 385	0.05	0.73	4.46	**5.19**	m2
B 503	0.06	0.87	5.58	**6.45**	m2
B 785	0.09	1.32	8.59	**9.91**	m2
B 1131	0.09	1.32	10.10	**11.42**	m2

Unit Rates	Man-Hours	Net Labour Price £	Net Mats Price £	Net Unit Price £	Unit
C 283, 100 mm side laps, 400 mm end laps	0.05	0.73	2.90	**3.63**	m2
C 385	0.05	0.73	3.77	**4.50**	m2
C 503	0.05	0.73	4.72	**5.45**	m2
C 636	0.05	0.81	5.99	**6.80**	m2
C 785	0.06	0.87	7.26	**8.13**	m2
014 Fabric reinforcement laid in suspended slabs, reference:					
A 142, 200 mm side laps, 200 mm end laps	0.04	0.53	2.41	**2.94**	m2
A 193	0.06	0.87	3.05	**3.92**	m2
A 252	0.06	0.87	4.00	**4.87**	m2
A 393	0.08	1.22	5.94	**7.16**	m2
B 196, 100 mm side laps, 200 mm end laps	0.06	0.87	3.39	**4.26**	m2
B 283	0.06	0.87	4.06	**4.93**	m2
B 385	0.06	0.87	4.46	**5.33**	m2
B 503	0.08	1.22	5.58	**6.80**	m2
B 785	0.11	1.72	8.59	**10.31**	m2
B 1131	0.11	1.72	10.10	**11.82**	m2
C 283, 100 mm side laps, 400 mm end laps	0.06	0.87	2.90	**3.77**	m2
C 385	0.06	0.87	3.77	**4.64**	m2
C 503	0.06	0.87	4.72	**5.59**	m2
C 636	0.07	1.03	5.99	**7.02**	m2
015 Fabric reinforcement laid in walls, reference:					
A 142, 200 mm side laps, 200 mm end laps	0.13	1.92	2.41	**4.33**	m2
A 193	0.16	2.48	3.05	**5.53**	m2
A 252	0.16	2.48	4.00	**6.48**	m2
A 393	0.19	2.89	5.94	**8.83**	m2
B 196, 100 mm side laps, 200 mm end laps	0.16	2.48	3.39	**5.87**	m2
B 283	0.16	2.48	4.06	**6.54**	m2
B 385	0.16	2.48	4.46	**6.94**	m2
B 503	0.19	2.89	5.58	**8.47**	m2
B 785	0.28	4.30	8.59	**12.89**	m2
B 1131	0.28	4.30	10.10	**14.40**	m2
C 283, 100 mm side laps, 400 mm end laps	0.16	2.48	2.90	**5.38**	m2
C 385	0.16	2.48	3.77	**6.25**	m2
C 503	0.16	2.48	4.72	**7.20**	m2
C 636	0.18	2.68	5.99	**8.67**	m2
016 Wrapping fabric in casings to steel columns and beams, reference:					
D 49, 100 mm side laps, 100 mm end laps	0.45	6.89	2.10	**8.99**	m2
017 **Cutting fabric reinforcement**					
018 Raking cutting fabric, reference:					
A 142	0.14	2.14	0.11	**2.25**	m
A 193	0.16	2.48	0.14	**2.62**	m
A 252	0.16	2.48	0.18	**2.66**	m
A 393	0.28	4.30	0.27	**4.57**	m
B 196	0.16	2.48	0.15	**2.63**	m
B 283	0.16	2.48	0.19	**2.67**	m
B 385	0.16	2.48	0.20	**2.68**	m
B 503	0.28	4.30	0.26	**4.56**	m
B 785	0.38	5.73	0.40	**6.13**	m
B 1131	0.38	5.73	0.48	**6.21**	m
C 283	0.16	2.48	0.13	**2.61**	m
C 385	0.16	2.48	0.17	**2.65**	m
C 503	0.16	2.48	0.22	**2.70**	m
C 636	0.22	3.40	0.28	**3.68**	m
C 785	0.28	4.30	0.33	**4.63**	m
D 49	0.14	2.14	0.10	**2.24**	m
019 Circular cutting fabric, reference:					
A 142	0.19	2.89	0.11	**3.00**	m
A 193	0.28	4.30	0.14	**4.44**	m
A 252	0.28	4.30	0.18	**4.48**	m
A 393	0.38	5.73	0.27	**6.00**	m
B 196	0.28	4.30	0.15	**4.45**	m
B 283	0.28	4.30	0.19	**4.49**	m
B 385	0.28	4.30	0.20	**4.50**	m
B 503	0.38	5.73	0.26	**5.99**	m
B 785	0.57	8.62	0.40	**9.02**	m
B 1131	0.57	8.62	0.48	**9.10**	m
C 283	0.28	4.30	0.13	**4.43**	m
C 385	0.28	4.30	0.17	**4.47**	m
C 503	0.28	4.30	0.22	**4.52**	m
C 636	0.33	5.02	0.28	**5.30**	m
C 785	0.38	5.73	0.33	**6.06**	m
D 49	0.19	2.89	0.10	**2.99**	m

	Unit Rates	Man-Hours	Plant Hours	Net Labour Price £	Net Plant Price £	Net Mats Price £	Net Unit Price £	Unit
FJ	**FORMWORK GENERALLY**							

The prices for 'making' formwork allow for ONE use of timber formwork.
Where multiple uses are possible the 'Net Labour, Material and TOTAL
UNIT' prices should be divided by the number of uses and allowance made
for waste in use of both labour and materials as follows:

Nr of uses	Waste in use
up to 4	Nil
5 to 6	10%
7 to 8	15%
9 to 10	17.5%
11 to 12	20%

No adjustment should be made to 'Fixing' formwork prices as these apply
irrespective of the number of uses.

Example
Formwork to soffit of slabs not exceeding 3.5 m high and not exceeding 200
mm thick, assuming 5 uses:

Item FJ004 **making** net labour (carpenter)	£ 8.62	
net materials	£ 24.14	
	-------	
one use	£ 32.76	
	-------	
5 uses (divide by 5)	£ 6.55	
Add waste 10%	£ 0.65	
fixing net labour (carpenter)	£ 20.82	
net plant	£ 6.60	
net materials	£ 0.99	

TOTAL NET PRICE FOR EACH USE	**£ 35.62**	

The prices for formwork are for horizontal or vertical straight or plain
surfaces, the following additions should be made for curved surfaces to both
`making' and 'fixing' prices:

Radius	Add to Labour	Add to Materials
1.5 m	200 %	100 %
3.0 m	150 %	75 %
6.0 m	100 %	50 %
9.0 m	70 %	35 %
12.0 m	50 %	25 %
15.0 m	30 %	15 %
18.0 m	20 %	10 %
21.0 m	15 %	7.5 %
24.0 m	10 %	5 %

		Man-Hours	Plant Hours	Net Labour Price £	Net Plant Price £	Net Mats Price £	Net Unit Price £	Unit
001	**Formwork to foundations and beds**							
002	Edges and faces of foundations, ground beams and beds:							
	exceeding 1.00 m high:							
	making	1.80	-	27.41	-	34.47	**61.88**	m2
	fixing	1.27	-	22.81	-	0.99	**23.80**	m2
	not exceeding 250 mm high:							
	making	0.93	-	14.09	-	8.70	**22.79**	m
	fixing	0.53	-	9.45	-	0.60	**10.05**	m
	250 - 500 mm high:							
	making	1.29	-	19.56	-	17.41	**36.97**	m
	fixing	0.79	-	14.28	-	0.75	**15.03**	m
	500 - 1000 mm high:							
	making	1.72	-	26.14	-	34.47	**60.61**	m
	fixing	1.20	-	21.52	-	0.99	**22.51**	m
003	**Formwork to slabs, staircases and associated faces**							
004	Soffits of slabs not exceeding 3.5 m high:							
	not exceeding 200 mm thick:							
	making	0.57	-	8.62	-	24.14	**32.76**	m2
	fixing	1.37	3.00	20.82	6.60	0.99	**28.41**	m2
	200 - 300 mm thick:							
	making	0.68	-	10.34	-	27.24	**37.58**	m2
	fixing	1.62	3.85	29.11	8.47	0.99	**38.57**	m2
	300 - 400 mm thick:							
	making	0.79	-	12.05	-	31.03	**43.08**	m2
	fixing	1.92	6.05	34.50	13.31	0.99	**48.80**	m2
005	Soffits of staircases; sloping over 15 degrees from horizontal, not exceeding 3.5 m high:							
	not exceeding 200 mm thick:							
	making	0.62	-	9.39	-	24.14	**33.53**	m2
	fixing	1.58	5.00	28.38	11.00	0.99	**40.37**	m2
006	Soffits of landings not exceeding 3.5 m high:							
	not exceeding 200 mm thick:							
	making	0.68	-	10.34	-	24.14	**34.48**	m2
	fixing	1.47	5.00	26.52	11.00	0.99	**38.51**	m2
007	Upper surfaces of slabs sloping more than 15 degrees from horizontal:							
	making	0.52	-	7.83	-	24.14	**31.97**	m2
	fixing	1.58	-	28.38	-	0.99	**29.37**	m2

		Man-Hours	Plant Hours	Net Labour Price £	Net Plant Price £	Net Mats Price £	Net Unit Price £	Unit
Unit Rates								
008	Soffits of attached beams or beam casings not exceeding 3.5 m high:							
	not exceeding 200 mm wide:							
	making	2.15	-	32.73	-	21.51	**54.24**	m
	fixing	1.03	6.00	18.55	13.20	0.52	**32.27**	m
	200 - 400 mm wide:							
	making	2.38	-	36.16	-	25.64	**61.80**	m
	fixing	1.24	6.00	22.25	13.20	0.65	**36.10**	m
	400 - 600 mm wide:							
	making	3.29	-	49.95	-	34.85	**84.80**	m
	fixing	1.65	9.00	29.67	19.80	0.80	**50.27**	m
	over 600 mm wide:							
	making	4.46	-	67.85	-	49.63	**117.48**	m2
	fixing	2.28	12.00	40.98	26.40	0.99	**68.37**	m2
009	Sides of attached beams, beam casings, upstands, kerbs and the like:							
	not exceeding 200 mm high:							
	making	1.25	-	18.94	-	13.89	**32.83**	m
	fixing	0.62	-	11.13	-	0.52	**11.65**	m
	200 - 400 mm high:							
	making	1.42	-	21.52	-	17.06	**38.58**	m
	fixing	0.72	-	12.98	-	0.65	**13.63**	m
	400 - 600 mm high:							
	making	1.59	-	24.11	-	20.66	**44.77**	m
	fixing	0.82	-	14.84	-	0.73	**15.57**	m
	over 600 mm high:							
	making	2.04	-	30.99	-	26.55	**57.54**	m2
	fixing	1.03	-	18.55	-	0.99	**19.54**	m2
010	Vertical edges of slabs:							
	not exceeding 250 mm deep:							
	making	0.48	-	7.24	-	4.88	**12.12**	m
	fixing	0.62	-	11.13	-	0.54	**11.67**	m
	250 - 500 mm deep:							
	making	0.91	-	13.77	-	9.41	**23.18**	m
	fixing	0.72	-	12.98	-	0.69	**13.67**	m
011	Risers of staircases:							
	not exceeding 250 mm deep:							
	making	0.80	-	12.13	-	2.81	**14.94**	m
	fixing	0.57	-	10.21	-	0.54	**10.75**	m
012	Edges of staircase flights, maximum:							
	200 mm wide:							
	making	1.13	-	17.22	-	4.88	**22.10**	m
	fixing	0.62	-	11.13	-	0.54	**11.67**	m
	300 mm wide:							
	making	1.36	-	20.67	-	5.65	**26.32**	m
	fixing	0.72	-	12.98	-	0.60	**13.58**	m
013	**Formwork to walls and associated features**							
014	Vertical faces of walls:							
	one side shuttered:							
	making	2.27	-	34.44	-	34.82	**69.26**	m2
	fixing	1.34	-	24.11	-	0.99	**25.10**	m2
	both sides shuttered (one side measured):							
	making	2.15	-	32.73	-	34.82	**67.55**	m2
	fixing	1.34	-	24.11	-	0.99	**25.10**	m2
015	Plain ends of walls, sides and soffits of openings in walls or sloping tops of walls:							
	100 mm thick:							
	making	0.25	-	3.78	-	4.14	**7.92**	m
	fixing	0.19	-	3.49	-	0.45	**3.94**	m
	100 - 200 mm thick:							
	making	0.45	-	6.89	-	7.47	**14.36**	m
	fixing	0.25	-	4.52	-	0.50	**5.02**	m
	200 - 300 mm thick:							
	making	0.60	-	9.17	-	13.01	**22.18**	m
	fixing	0.35	-	6.30	-	0.58	**6.88**	m
016	Face or side of rectangular projection on or recess in wall:							
	not exceeding 100 mm wide:							
	making	0.28	-	4.30	-	4.14	**8.44**	m
	fixing	0.21	-	3.71	-	0.44	**4.15**	m
	100 - 200 mm wide:							
	making	0.51	-	7.75	-	6.78	**14.53**	m
	fixing	0.36	-	6.48	-	0.52	**7.00**	m
	200 - 400 mm wide:							
	making	0.85	-	12.92	-	10.82	**23.74**	m
	fixing	0.57	-	10.21	-	0.65	**10.86**	m
	400 - 600 mm wide:							
	making	1.02	-	15.50	-	14.02	**29.52**	m
	fixing	0.72	-	12.98	-	0.76	**13.74**	m

	Unit Rates	Man-Hours	Plant Hours	Net Labour Price £	Net Plant Price £	Net Mats Price £	Net Unit Price £	Unit
017	**Formwork to isolated beams and columns**							
018	Soffits of isolated beams or beam casings not exceeding 3.5 m high:							
	not exceeding 200 mm wide:							
	making	2.15	-	32.73	-	16.61	**49.34**	m
	fixing	1.03	6.00	18.55	13.20	0.52	**32.27**	m
	200 - 400 mm wide:							
	making	2.72	-	41.33	-	25.48	**66.81**	m
	fixing	1.34	6.00	24.11	13.20	0.65	**37.96**	m
	400 - 600 mm wide:							
	making	3.29	-	49.95	-	34.54	**84.49**	m
	fixing	1.65	9.00	29.67	19.80	0.80	**50.27**	m
	over 600 mm wide:							
	making	4.42	-	67.17	-	49.63	**116.80**	m2
	fixing	2.28	12.00	40.98	26.40	0.99	**68.37**	m2
019	Sides of isolated beams or beam casings:							
	not exceeding 400 mm high:							
	making	1.25	-	18.94	-	14.77	**33.71**	m
	fixing	0.72	-	12.98	-	0.84	**13.82**	m
	400 - 600 mm high:							
	making	1.59	-	24.11	-	19.16	**43.27**	m
	fixing	0.93	-	16.69	-	0.95	**17.64**	m
	over 600 mm high:							
	making	2.04	-	30.99	-	26.20	**57.19**	m2
	fixing	1.34	-	24.11	-	0.99	**25.10**	m2
020	Sides of isolated rectangular columns or column casings including 'Acrow' props and clamps:							
	not exceeding 200 mm wide:							
	making	0.40	-	6.03	-	5.15	**11.18**	m
	fixing	0.21	2.51	3.71	10.20	0.52	**14.43**	m
	200 - 400 mm wide:							
	making	0.79	-	12.05	-	10.07	**22.12**	m
	fixing	0.41	2.51	7.42	10.20	0.84	**18.46**	m
	400 - 600 mm wide:							
	making	1.02	-	15.50	-	13.43	**28.93**	m
	fixing	0.62	2.51	11.13	10.20	0.95	**22.28**	m
	over 600 mm wide:							
	making	1.42	-	21.52	-	21.04	**42.56**	m2
	fixing	0.72	2.50	12.98	11.10	0.99	**25.07**	m2
021	Sides of isolated circular columns or column casings:							
	not exceeding 300 mm diameter:							
	making	6.12	-	92.99	-	39.54	**132.53**	m2
	fixing	1.96	10.50	35.24	42.70	0.99	**78.93**	m2
	300 - 600 mm diameter:							
	making	5.55	-	84.39	-	34.84	**119.23**	m2
	fixing	1.96	5.30	35.24	21.46	2.26	**58.96**	m2
	600 - 900 mm diameter:							
	making	4.87	-	74.05	-	33.58	**107.63**	m2
	fixing	1.96	3.60	35.24	14.64	0.99	**50.87**	m2
022	**Formwork to isolated lintels**							
023	Soffits of lintels not exceeding 3.5 m high:							
	not exceeding 200 mm wide:							
	making	2.73	-	41.42	-	10.50	**51.92**	m
	fixing	1.43	-	25.82	-	1.80	**27.62**	m
	200 - 400 mm wide:							
	making	3.01	-	45.80	-	20.99	**66.79**	m
	fixing	1.72	-	30.99	-	3.52	**34.51**	m
	400 - 600 mm wide:							
	making	4.16	-	63.23	-	31.48	**94.71**	m
	fixing	2.30	-	41.32	-	5.27	**46.59**	m
024	Sides of lintels:							
	not exceeding 200 mm high:							
	making	1.58	-	23.99	-	16.79	**40.78**	m
	fixing	1.01	-	18.10	-	2.77	**20.87**	m
	200 - 400 mm high:							
	making	2.01	-	30.51	-	27.28	**57.79**	m
	fixing	1.29	-	23.26	-	4.67	**27.93**	m
	400 - 600 mm high:							
	making	2.58	-	39.23	-	37.76	**76.99**	m
	fixing	1.58	-	28.41	-	6.37	**34.78**	m
025	**Formwork to form mortices for holding down bolts**							
026	Tapering mortices formed in plywood:							
	200 x 200 mm on surface, tapering to 50 x 50 mm at bottom and 200 mm deep:							
	making	0.85	-	12.92	-	2.53	**15.45**	Nr
	fixing	0.26	-	4.65	-	0.09	**4.74**	Nr
	200 x 200 mm on surface, tapering to 50 x 50 mm at bottom and 300 mm deep:							
	making	0.91	-	13.77	-	1.46	**15.23**	Nr
	fixing	0.31	-	5.56	-	0.19	**5.75**	Nr

Unit Rates	Man-Hours	Plant Hours	Net Labour Price £	Net Plant Price £	Net Mats Price £	Net Unit Price £	Unit
250 x 250 mm on surface, tapering to 50 x 50 mm at bottom and 600 mm deep:							
making	1.13	-	17.22	-	6.37	**23.59**	Nr
fixing	0.41	-	7.42	-	0.28	**7.70**	Nr
027 Cylindrical mortices formed with Expamet ref.: 220 foundation bolt boxes (making and fixing prices combined):							
150 mm long 75 mm diameter	0.28	-	4.30	-	3.51	**7.81**	Nr
300 mm long 75 mm diameter	0.28	-	4.30	-	5.02	**9.32**	Nr
450 mm long 100 mm diameter	0.28	-	4.30	-	7.45	**11.75**	Nr
600 mm long 100 mm diameter	0.28	-	4.30	-	8.14	**12.44**	Nr
028 Cylindrical mortices formed with Expamet ref.: 220 foundation bolt boxes (making and fixing prices combined):							
225 mm long 75 mm diameter	0.28	-	4.30	-	4.04	**8.34**	Nr
375 mm long 100 mm diameter	0.28	-	4.30	-	6.72	**11.02**	Nr
029 **Sundries**							
030 Raking cutting on formwork	0.28	-	4.30	-	0.63	**4.93**	m
031 Curved cutting on formwork	0.51	-	7.75	-	0.88	**8.63**	m
FK **FORMWORK TO PROVIDE FAIR FACE**							
001 **ADDITIONAL costs over 'making' prices in Formwork generally for the following**							
002 Fair face formed with:		•					
oil tempered hardboard lining	-	-	-	-	3.15	**3.15**	m2
wrought face timber 25 mm thick	-	-	-	-	6.17	**6.17**	m2
003 Ribbed face formed with 50 x 38 mm twice splayed timber fillets at 100 mm centres:							
large areas such as complete wall faces	0.76	-	11.54	-	12.46	**24.00**	m2
small areas such as edge beams	0.84	-	12.74	-	12.46	**25.20**	m2
panels not exceeding 1.00 m2	0.86	-	13.09	-	12.46	**25.55**	m2
panels 1.00 - 2.00 m2	0.83	-	12.57	-	12.46	**25.03**	m2
panels 2.00 - 5.00 m2	0.79	-	12.05	-	12.46	**24.51**	m2
004 Ribbed face formed with 100 x 50 mm twice splayed fillets at 200 mm centres:							
large areas such as complete wall faces	0.91	-	13.77	-	12.84	**26.61**	m2
small areas such as edge beams	1.00	-	15.15	-	12.84	**27.99**	m2
panels not exceeding 1.00 m2	1.13	-	17.22	-	12.84	**30.06**	m2
panels 1.00 - 2.00 m2	1.09	-	16.54	-	12.84	**29.38**	m2
panels 2.00 - 5.00 m2	1.04	-	15.84	-	12.84	**28.68**	m2
005 **ADDITIONAL costs over 'fixing' prices in Formwork generally for the following**							
006 Treating formwork with a release agent	0.37	-	5.68	-	0.90	**6.58**	m2
007 Rubbing down face of fair face concrete with a carborundum stone; filling blow holes with matching cement and sand mortar	0.15	-	2.23	-	0.13	**2.36**	m2
FM **PRECAST CONCRETE PERMANENT FORMWORK**							
001 **Precast concrete permanent formwork comprising 50 mm thick precast concrete panels 2400 mm wide and Omnia lattice girders and main steel reinforcement; C28/35 in situ concrete structural topping with tamped finish; temporary supports at maximum 1.5 m centres (fabric reinforcement priced separately)**							
002 Omnidec suspended floors or roofs with soffit not exceeding 3.50 m high above floor level; designed for finishes at 1.5 KN/m2 and superimposed loads of 2.5 KN/m2:							
135 mm thick comprising 50 mm units and 85 mm topping	1.06	0.68	19.57	6.53	86.23	**112.33**	m2
150 mm thick comprising 50 mm units and 100 mm topping	1.06	0.68	19.57	6.53	92.55	**118.65**	m2
175 mm thick comprising 50 mm units and 125 mm topping	1.11	0.68	20.59	6.66	102.95	**130.20**	m2
200 mm thick comprising 50 mm units and 150 mm topping	1.13	0.73	20.99	6.90	102.01	**129.90**	m2
225 mm thick comprising 50 mm units and 175 mm topping	1.27	0.74	23.44	6.96	113.55	**143.95**	m2
003 Omnicore suspended floors or roofs with soffit not exceeding 3.50 m high above floor level; designed for finishes at 1.5 KN/m2 and superimposed loads of 5.0 KN/m2; incorporating expanded polystyrene void formers:							
200 mm thick comprising 50 mm units and 150 mm topping	1.10	0.68	20.38	6.79	85.45	**112.62**	m2
225 mm thick comprising 50 mm units and 175 mm topping	1.16	0.69	21.40	6.85	78.59	**106.84**	m2
250 mm thick comprising 50 mm units and 200 mm topping	1.22	0.74	22.63	6.96	103.79	**133.38**	m2
300 mm thick comprising 50 mm units and 250 mm topping	1.30	0.74	24.05	6.96	115.03	**146.04**	m2

Unit Rates	Man-Hours	Plant Hours	Net Labour Price £	Net Plant Price £	Net Mats Price £	Net Unit Price £	Unit
FN PRECAST CONCRETE							
For precast concrete kerbs, edgings, bollards and the like, see Section Y - EXTERNAL WORKS.							
001 **Coping units; ordinary Portland cement; bedding jointing and pointing in cement mortar (1:3)**							
002 Splayed copings, double throated:							
305 x 75 mm	0.45	-	9.43	-	9.57	**19.00**	m
450 x 75 mm	0.68	-	14.15	-	13.23	**27.38**	m
003 Saddleback copings, double throated:							
305 x 75 mm	0.51	-	10.61	-	10.94	**21.55**	m
356 x 75 mm	0.79	-	16.50	-	15.12	**31.62**	m
004 Pier caps weathered four ways:							
450 x 450 x 75 mm	0.45	-	9.43	-	10.90	**20.33**	Nr
005 **Padstones; ordinary Portland cement 30 N/mm2; bedding in cement mortar (1:3)**							
006 215 x 215 x 140 mm	0.34	-	7.08	-	8.38	**15.46**	m
300 x 215 x 100 mm	0.34	-	7.08	-	10.57	**17.65**	m
450 x 215 x 100 mm	0.39	-	8.14	-	14.03	**22.17**	m
450 x 300 x 150 mm	0.45	-	9.43	-	18.81	**28.24**	m
450 x 450 x 150 mm	0.45	-	9.43	-	22.02	**31.45**	m
007 **Prestressed precast concrete lintels; bedding and pointing in cement mortar (1:3)**							
008 Standard composite sections for brickwork:							
100 x 65 mm	0.11	-	2.35	-	6.15	**8.50**	m
150 x 65 mm	0.17	-	3.54	-	8.87	**12.41**	m
220 x 65 mm	0.26	-	5.43	-	13.38	**18.81**	m
265 x 65 mm	0.29	-	6.12	-	17.86	**23.98**	m
100 x 150 mm	0.27	-	5.66	-	8.84	**14.50**	m
150 x 100 mm	0.27	-	5.66	-	8.48	**14.14**	m
150 x 140 mm	0.34	-	7.08	-	17.64	**24.72**	m

HOW LONG? HOW MUCH?

THE FASTEST, MOST UP-TO-DATE ANSWERS ARE AVAILABLE NOW

Cost information underpins every aspect of the built environment, from construction and rebuilding to maintenance and operation publications.

BCIS, the RICS' Building Cost Information Service, is the leading provider of cost information to the construction industry and anyone else who needs comprehensive, accurate and independent data.

For the past 50 years, BCIS has been collecting, collating, analysing, modelling and interpreting cost information.Today, BCIS make that information easily accessible through online applications, data licensing and publications.

For more information call **0870 333 1600** email **contact@bcis.co.uk** or visit **www.bcis.co.uk**

BCIS is the Building Cost Information Service of  **RICS** | the mark of property professionalism worldwide

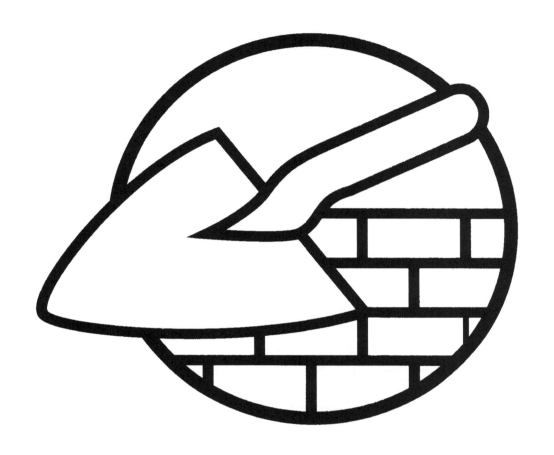

Brickwork & Blockwork

Diploma in Adjudication in the Construction Industry

Comprised of four units, this qualification is designed for those **seeking to become an adjudicator**, and provides a pathway towards potential entry onto the **RICS Panel of Adjudicators**.

With a focus on contract and tort law and how they apply to adjudication, this course is designed to prepare you to progress to practice as an adjudicator. This course is suitable for those with experience in dispute resolution procedures with an understanding of the general principles of construction adjudication. The course content will focus on the format and content of an enforceable decision.

Learning Outcomes:

- Knowledge and understanding of the nature of law and its' place in society

- How the law of contract is applied to the practice of adjudication

- How the law of tort is applied to the practice of adjudication

- The practical application in the production of an enforceable decision.

Attainment of the learning outcomes will be assessed by a case study, whereby candidates will be required to produce an enforceable reasoned decision, based on material supplied in the case study.

To book or for further information, please contact DRS Training;

t **02476 868 584**   e **drstraining@rics.org**   w **rics.org/drs**

Labour Rates

Please note: The labour hours throughout this section are representative of the time required for one productive man to carry out the unit of work.

Gang rates are calculated as follows by obtaining the overall gang cost and then dividing this by the number of productive members in the gang. The resulting rate is the Gang Cost per **Man - hour**. By using the same principle, any size gang may be built-up and used against the standard labour hours in this section.

The net labour prices in this section generally are based upon gang rates computed as follows:

A0204 BRICKLAYING

Brick/Block Layer	2.00	x	£	15.20	=	£	30.40
Brick/Blockwork Labourer	1.00	x	£	11.22	=	£	11.22
Total hourly cost of gang					=	£	41.62

Gang rate (divided by 2) = £20.81 per Man-hour

A0205 BLOCKLAYING

Brick/Block Layer	4.00	x	£	15.20	=	£	60.80
Brick/Blockwork Labourer	3.00	x	£	11.22	=	£	33.66
Total hourly cost of gang					=	£	94.46

Gang rate (divided by 4) = £23.62 per Man-hour

The labour constants reflect the employment of the Contractors own labour with good site supervision and the operation of suitable bonus schemes.

Where sub-contract labour-only prices are accepted for laying bricks, based upon a rate per 1000 bricks, the net labour prices should be calculated in accordance with the following table:

Rate for laying 1000 bricks

Cost per m2		£50	£60	£70	£80	£90	£100	£110	£120	£130	£140
102.5	mm wall	£ 3.00	£ 3.60	£ 4.20	£ 4.80	£ 5.40	£ 6.00	£ 6.60	£ 7.20	£ 7.80	£ 8.40
215	mm wall	£ 6.00	£ 7.20	£ 8.40	£ 9.60	£10.80	£12.00	£13.20	£14.40	£15.60	£16.80
327.5	mm wall	£ 9.00	£10.80	£12.60	£14.40	£16.20	£18.00	£19.80	£21.60	£23.40	£25.20
440	mm wall	£12.00	£14.40	£16.80	£19.20	£21.60	£24.00	£26.40	£28.80	£31.20	£33.60

As will be seen from the analysis of brickwork prices, substantially lower rates per thousand bricks could be negotiated for walls over 102.5 mm and 215 mm thick

The net labour prices for Centering are based upon the rate for carpenter: Cost per hour £15.20

Basic Prices of Materials

		Supply Price £	Waste Factor %	Unload. Labour £	Unload. Plant £	Total Unit Cost £	Unit
Note: All bricks are 215 x 102.5 x 65 mm; where no 'Labour unloading' prices are shown the materials are supplied palletised for crane unloading (surcharge for pallets excluded)							
Due to the wide range of facing bricks, special bricks etc., which are available, the following P.C. prices have been included to provide representative costs for these items.							
G0102	Common bricks	311.01	5%	-	-	**326.56**	1000
G0103	Class A engineering bricks	493.42	5%	-	-	**518.09**	1000
G0104	Class B engineering bricks	391.75	5%	-	-	**411.33**	1000
G0105	Facing bricks	351.38	5%	-	-	**368.95**	1000
G0106	Adjustment factor for price of facing bricks for bond	10.00	-	-	-	**10.00**	1000
G1001	Common bricks P.C.	311.01	-	-	-	**311.01**	1000
G1002	Class A engineering bricks P.C.	493.42	-	-	-	**493.42**	1000
G1003	Class B engineering bricks P.C.	391.75	-	-	-	**391.75**	1000
G1004	Facing bricks P.C.	351.38	-	-	-	**351.38**	1000
	Precast concrete blocks, BS 6073, natural aggregate, compressive strength 7 N/mm2 face size 440 x 215 mm, delivered to sites within about 25 miles of point of supply in 19 tonne loads:						
	solid blocks:						
G0111	75 mm	7.19	5%	-	-	**7.55**	m2
G0113	100 mm	7.74	5%	-	-	**8.12**	m2
G0116	140 mm	11.54	5%	-	-	**12.11**	m2
G0118	190 mm	17.69	5%	-	-	**18.57**	m2
G0120	215 mm	23.80	5%	-	-	**24.99**	m2
	hollow blocks:						
G0122	100 mm	7.71	5%	-	-	**8.09**	m2
G0125	140 mm	11.54	5%	-	-	**12.11**	m2
G0129	215 mm	16.20	5%	-	-	**17.01**	m2
G0130	**Extra over** for smooth face blocks, any thickness	1.44	5%	-	-	**1.51**	m2
	Precast concrete blocks, BS 6073, furnace clinker aggregate, compressive strength 3.5 N/mm2, face size 440 x 215 mm delivered to sites within about 25 miles of point of supply in 19 tonne loads:						
	solid blocks:						
G0134	100 mm	8.07	5%	-	-	**8.48**	m2
G0136	140 mm	12.46	5%	-	-	**13.08**	m2
G0194	**Extra over** for smooth face blocks, any thickness	1.44	5%	-	-	**1.51**	m2

Basic Prices of Materials	Supply Price £	Waste Factor %	Unload. Labour £	Unload. Plant £	Total Unit Cost £	Unit
Thermalite blocks, co-ordinating face size 440 x 215 mm delivered to sites within about 40 miles of point of supply in 15 tonne loads:						
Shield:						
G0153 100 mm	11.79	7.5%	-	-	12.67	m2
G0155 140 mm	16.50	7.5%	-	-	17.74	m2
G0157 190 mm	22.40	7.5%	-	-	24.08	m2
G0158 200 mm	23.58	7.5%	-	-	25.34	m2
Trenchblocks:						
G0159 275 mm	32.42	7.5%	-	-	34.86	m2
G0160 300 mm	35.36	7.5%	-	-	38.02	m2
Smooth Face Paint Grade blocks:						
G0163 100 mm	18.96	7.5%	-	-	20.38	m2
G0164 140 mm	26.53	7.5%	-	-	28.52	m2
G0167 200 mm	37.91	7.5%	-	-	40.75	m2
Turbo blocks:						
G0614 100 mm	11.72	7.5%	-	-	12.60	m2
Lignacite blocks, compressive strength 7 N/mm2, face size 440 x 215 mm delivered to sites within about 100-150 miles of point of supply in 25 tonne loads:						
solid blocks:						
G0169 75 mm	11.81	7.5%	-	-	12.69	m2
G0170 100 mm	15.32	7.5%	-	-	16.47	m2
G0171 140 mm	19.78	7.5%	-	-	21.26	m2
G0172 150 mm	23.77	7.5%	-	-	25.55	m2
G0181 190 mm	28.46	7.5%	-	-	30.60	m2
G0182 200 mm (special)	30.48	7.5%	-	-	32.77	m2
hollow blocks:						
G0173 140 mm	17.99	10%	-	-	19.79	m2
G0174 190 mm (special)	24.79	10%	-	-	27.27	m2
G0175 200 mm (special)	24.79	10%	-	-	27.27	m2
G0176 215 mm (special)	26.56	10%	-	-	29.21	m2
cellular blocks:						
G0178 100 mm	12.40	10%	-	-	13.64	m2
G0179 140 mm	17.01	10%	-	-	18.71	m2
G0180 **Extra over** for Fair Face blocks, any thickness	0.96	10%	-	-	1.06	m2
A0301 Portland cement delivered in bags	137.81	5%	11.22	-	156.48	tonne
A0311 Hydrated lime delivered in bags	216.00	5%	11.22	-	238.58	tonne
A0302 White Portland cement delivered in bags	314.16	5%	11.22	-	341.65	tonne
G0205 Colouring pigment (red, brown, yellow)	8.96	5%	-	-	9.41	kg
A0321 Building sand BS 1200	24.16	10%	-	-	26.57	tonne
A0331 Concreting sand (fine aggregate)	29.64	10%	-	-	32.60	tonne
A0342 19 mm Aggregate	31.05	10%	-	-	34.15	tonne
G0208 Refractory aggregate (crushed firebrick)	237.27	5%	11.22	-	260.92	tonne
G0209 Flue joint compound	4.92	10%	-	-	5.41	nr
Ready mixed mortars (**guide prices** based on London pricing levels) from Cemex:						
G0611 lime sand mortar (1:12)	44.98	5%	-	-	47.22	tonne
G0612 lime sand mortar (1:6)	46.09	5%	-	-	48.40	tonne
G0613 lime sand mortar (1:4.5)	47.21	5%	-	-	49.57	tonne
G0211 Granular faced concrete plain roofing tiles	633.00	-	-	-	633.00	1000
G0273 230 x 112.5 mm slates	477.25	10%	16.83	-	543.49	1000
G0274 230 x 225 mm slates	759.00	10%	18.51	-	855.26	1000
Damp proof courses to BS 6398, any standard width:						
G0269 Hessian base, ref A	9.25	5%	-	-	9.71	m2
G0270 Fibre base, ref B	7.28	5%	-	-	7.64	m2
Hyload damp proof courses:						
G0275 any standard width	6.17	5%	-	-	6.48	m2
G0276 internal corner cloak Type 8	3.33	2%	-	-	3.40	nr
G0277 external corner cloak Type 9	6.22	2%	-	-	6.35	nr
cavity corner cloak Type 7 (reversible):						
G0279 150 mm rise	14.27	2%	-	-	14.56	nr
G0280 225 mm rise	17.61	2%	-	-	17.96	nr
stop end cloak Type 3:						
G0282 150 mm rise	5.10	2%	-	-	5.21	nr
G0283 225 mm rise	9.45	2%	-	-	9.64	nr
change level cloak Type 1 (reversible):						
G0284 150 mm / 75 mm step on face	17.26	2%	-	-	17.61	nr
G0285 150 mm /225 mm step on face	19.42	2%	-	-	19.81	nr
G0286 225 mm / 75 mm step on face	19.74	2%	-	-	20.13	nr
G0288 225 mm /225 mm step on face	20.27	2%	-	-	20.68	nr
G0287 stop-end cloak Type 10	8.84	2%	-	-	9.01	nr
change level cloak Type 2:						
G0289 150 mm rise	16.99	2%	-	-	17.33	nr
G0290 225 mm rise	24.47	2%	-	-	24.96	nr
G0291 Polyethylene damp proof course, any standard width	0.86	5%	-	-	0.91	m2
G0292 Hyload contact adhesive	17.13	10%	-	-	18.84	ltr
G0293 Hyload mastic	14.70	10%	-	-	16.17	ltr
G0294 Hyload DPC jointing tape	2.20	-	-	-	2.20	m
G0295 Synthaprufe waterproofer and adhesive	2.95	5%	-	-	3.09	ltr

Basic Prices of Materials	Supply Price £	Waste Factor %	Unload. Labour £	Unload. Plant £	Total Unit Cost £	Unit
Cavity wall ties:						
G0311 200 mm stainless steel flat bar tie with expanded ends, type 1	0.27	10%	-	-	0.30	nr
G0312 200 mm stainless steel general purpose wire tie, type 2	0.12	10%	-	-	0.13	nr
G0313 200 mm stainless steel housing tie, type 4	0.06	10%	-	-	0.07	nr
G0314 75 mm stainless steel brick to timber tie	0.17	10%	-	-	0.18	nr
G0362 Retaining clip	0.06	-			0.06	nr
PIR Polyisocyanurate foam sheet insulation (1200 x 450 mm):						
G0315 40 mm	5.29	10%	-	-	5.82	m2
G0316 50 mm	6.48	15%	-	-	7.45	m2
Fibreglass Dritherm cavity wall insulation (1200 x 455 mm):						
G0317 75 mm	4.61	10%	-	-	5.07	m2
G0318 Gun-grade silicone sealant (400 ml cart.)	4.08	10%	-	-	4.49	nr
G0319 Fillcrete joint filler, 19 mm thick, cut to size	14.47	10%	-	-	15.92	m2
Expamet galvanised brickwork reinforcement:						
G0320 65 mm wide (100 metres)	62.64	10%	-	-	68.90	coil
G0321 115 mm wide (100 metres)	107.84	10%	-	-	118.62	coil
G0322 175 mm wide (100 metres)	169.02	10%	-	-	185.92	coil
G0323 Lead for running in mortices	2.15	5%	0.01	-	2.27	kg
Terracotta cavity wall liners for 275 mm wall:						
G0324 215 x 65 mm	1.49	5%	-	-	1.56	nr
G0325 215 x 140 mm	1.65	5%	-	-	1.73	nr
G0326 215 x 215 mm	4.57	5%	-	-	4.80	nr
Terracotta air bricks, square hole pattern:						
G0327 215 x 65 mm	0.89	5%	-	-	0.93	nr
G0328 215 x 140 mm	1.23	5%	-	-	1.29	nr
G0329 215 x 215 mm	3.31	5%	-	-	3.48	nr
Terracotta air bricks, louvre pattern:						
G0330 215 x 65 mm	1.02	5%	-	-	1.08	nr
G0331 215 x 140 mm	1.69	5%	-	-	1.77	nr
G0332 215 x 215 mm	3.97	5%	-	-	4.17	nr
Aluminium double soot doors:						
G0333 229 x 140 mm	41.66	5%	-	-	43.75	nr
G0334 229 x 229 mm	52.57	5%	-	-	55.19	nr
Hepworth circular clay flue linings BS EN 1457, class A1, 300 mm long:						
G0335 185 mm internal diameter	4.22	5%	-	-	4.43	nr
G0379 210 mm internal diameter	5.79	5%	-	-	6.08	nr
G0349 225 mm internal diameter	5.97	5%	-	-	6.27	nr
G0386 250 mm internal diameter	8.85	5%	-	-	9.29	nr
G0351 300 mm internal diameter	16.09	5%	-	-	16.89	nr
Circular bend 22.5 or 37.5 degrees:						
G0336 185 mm internal diameter	10.80	5%	-	-	11.34	nr
G0380 210 mm internal diameter	20.15	5%	-	-	21.16	nr
G0350 225 mm internal diameter	15.27	5%	-	-	16.03	nr
G0387 250 mm internal diameter	25.26	5%	-	-	26.53	nr
G0352 300 mm internal diameter	38.61	5%	-	-	40.54	nr
Hepworth square clay flue linings BS EN 1457, class A1, 300 mm long:						
G0337 185 x 185 mm internally	4.68	5%	-	-	4.92	nr
G0381 200 x 200 mm internally	8.29	5%	-	-	8.70	nr
G0353 225 x 225 mm internally	9.44	5%	-	-	9.91	nr
G0388 250 x 250 mm internally	11.18	5%	-	-	11.73	nr
G0390 300 x 300 mm internally	21.14	5%	-	-	22.20	nr
Square bend 22.5 or 37.5 degrees:						
G0338 185 x 185 mm internally	13.54	5%	-	-	14.22	nr
G0382 200 x 200 mm internally	14.97	5%	-	-	15.72	nr
G0354 225 x 225 mm internally	26.73	5%	-	-	28.06	nr
G0389 250 x 250 mm internally	34.94	5%	-	-	36.69	nr
G0391 300 x 300 mm internally	43.73	5%	-	-	45.92	nr
Flue adaptors for circular flue:						
G0544 185mm diameter flue	13.23	5%	-	-	13.90	nr
G0545 210 mm diameter flue, 550 x 100 x 450 mm	13.73	5%	-	-	14.42	nr
G0546 225 mm diameter flue, 560 x 100 x 450 mm	13.23	5%	-	-	13.90	nr
G0550 250 mm diameter flue, 560 x 100 x 450 mm	26.52	5%	-	-	27.85	nr
G0551 300 mm diameter flue, 560 x 100 x 450 mm	26.52	5%	-	-	27.85	nr
Flue adaptors for square flue:						
G0547 185 mm square flue, 580 x 100 x 450 mm	13.73	5%	-	-	14.42	nr
G0548 210 mm square flue, 560 x 100 x 450 mm	13.73	5%	-	-	14.42	nr
G0549 225 mm square flue, 560 x 100 x 450 mm	15.90	5%	-	-	16.69	nr
G0552 250 mm square flue, 560 x 100 x 450 mm	26.36	5%	-	-	27.68	nr
G0553 300 mm square flue, 560 x 100 x 450 mm	26.36	5%	-	-	27.68	nr
Schiedel twin wall aluminium flue, twist lock connection:						
G0561 125 mm nominal diameter flue	59.15	5%	-	-	62.11	nr
G0562 Flue block adaptor	40.08	5%	-	-	42.08	nr
G0563 Adjustable bend	39.38	5%	-	-	41.35	nr
G0564 Bracket	18.39	5%	-	-	19.31	nr

Basic Prices of Materials		Supply Price £	Waste Factor %	Unload. Labour £	Unload. Plant £	Total Unit Cost £	Unit
G0565	Terminal	43.16	5%	-	-	45.31	nr
G0566	Roof flashing	80.76	5%	-	-	84.80	nr
G0567	Ridge tile adaptor	43.66	5%	-	-	45.85	nr
	Dunbrik 'Mini Clearflow' gas flue block system:						
G0364	Standard recess starter block, 3 per flue, 1ZM	2.96	5%	-	-	3.10	nr
G0365	Gathering block for standard recess, 2GM	6.91	5%	-	-	7.26	nr
G0366	Straight bonded gas flue block, 225 mm high, 2M	4.65	5%	-	-	4.88	nr
G0367	Straight bonded gas flue block, 150 mm high, 2M/150	3.50	5%	-	-	3.67	nr
G0368	Straight bonded gas flue block, 75mm high, 2M/75	3.50	5%	-	-	3.67	nr
G0370	Straight gas flue block, 225 mm high, 2MN	4.65	5%	-	-	4.88	nr
G0371	Straight gas flue block, 150 mm high, 2MN/150	3.50	5%	-	-	3.67	nr
G0372	Straight gas flue block, 75mm high, 2MN/75	3.50	5%	-	-	3.67	nr
G0373	Side exit block, 5M	15.25	5%	-	-	16.01	nr
G0374	Back offset, 3MU	16.21	5%	-	-	17.03	nr
G0375	Top exit, 4M	10.42	5%	-	-	10.94	nr
G0376	Lateral offset, 3ME	5.22	5%	-	-	5.48	nr
G0377	Double tongue block, 2MDT190	4.65	5%	-	-	4.88	nr
G0378	Backset block, 125mm, 2BM	16.21	5%	-	-	17.03	nr
	Gas fired boiler recess components:						
G0403	Red set wide recess block, 3 per flue, 2GM	6.92	5%	-	-	7.27	nr
G0404	M set extra wide recess block, 3 per flue, MS	11.81	5%	-	-	12.40	nr
G0405	High density backup block	5.07	5%	-	-	5.33	nr
G0406	Damp proof membrane	7.61	5%	-	-	7.99	nr
G0407	Data plate	4.46	5%	-	-	4.68	nr
	Tapered roll chimney pots (red or buff):						
G0409	300 mm	9.72	-	-	-	9.72	nr
G0410	450 mm	11.59	-	-	-	11.59	nr
G0411	600 mm	17.75	-	-	-	17.75	nr
G0412	900 mm	33.57	-	-	-	33.57	nr
	Cannon head chimney pots (red or buff):						
G0413	300 mm	12.98	-	-	-	12.98	nr
G0414	450 mm	16.01	-	-	-	16.01	nr
G0415	600 mm	23.82	-	-	-	23.82	nr
	Ornamental chimney pots:						
G0417	Barrel top 600 mm	92.13	-	-	-	92.13	nr
G0418	Barrel top 750 mm	95.16	-	-	-	95.16	nr
G0419	Barrel top 900 mm	104.37	-	-	-	104.37	nr
G0420	Bishop pot 600 mm	147.98	-	-	-	147.98	nr
G0421	Bishop pot 750 mm	168.52	-	-	-	168.52	nr
	Stell 125 gas terminals:						
G0422	Terminal, 345 mm high x 160 mm diameter	22.81	-	-	-	22.81	nr
G0423	Standard base, 150 mm high x 180 mm diameter	17.06	-	-	-	17.06	nr
	Fire clay firebacks BS 1251:						
G0424	400 mm	21.03	-	-	-	21.03	nr
G0425	450 mm	25.31	-	-	-	25.31	nr
	Otty fireback hoods:						
G0426	400 mm	14.73	-	-	-	14.73	nr
G0427	450 mm	15.65	-	-	-	15.65	nr
	Fireplace components:						
G0396	Fire hearth, 910mm black granite fireplace hearth for solid fuel	48.28	5%	-	-	50.70	nr
G0397	Fire surround, plain limestone suitable for solid fuel	245.55	5%	-	-	257.83	nr
G0398	Fire surround, plain cast iron suitable for solid fuel	69.03	5%	-	-	72.48	nr
G0399	Fire surround, plain timber suitable for solid fuel	200.16	5%	-	-	210.17	nr
G0541	Fireplace lintel 800 x 215 x 600 mm	39.19	5%	-	-	41.15	nr
G0542	Fireplace corbel unit 1000 x 140 x 560 mm	35.37	5%	-	-	37.14	nr
G0543	Fireplace corbel unit 1200 x 140 x 560 mm	44.21	5%	-	-	46.43	nr
	Stoves and grates:						
	'Dauntless' cast iron bottom grate and vitreous enamel frets in copper lustre finish:						
G0428	400 mm	35.65	-	-	-	35.65	nr
G0429	450 mm	43.70	-	-	-	43.70	nr
	'Parkray' appliances:						
G0430	'Parkray Inset' fire to suit 400 mm opening	64.20	-	-	-	64.20	nr
	Extra over:						
G0431	overnight burning plate	14.96	-	-	-	14.96	nr
G0432	'Parkray 10' cast iron boiler and standard boiler unit	171.19	-	-	-	171.19	nr
	'Parkray 24' open fire high output boiler:						
G0433	400 mm	392.31	-	-	-	392.31	nr
G0437	'99G' Inset Room heater (Autumn Dusk)	822.25	-	-	-	822.25	nr
G0442	Sawn softwood for timber centering	339.25	12.5%	11.22	-	394.28	m3
G0443	Nails (100 mm x 4.50 mm round wire)	3.44	10%	-	-	3.78	kg
	Expamet stainless steel wall starters including fixings:						
G0450	Ref WS060, 60 - 75 mm	29.59	2.5%	-	-	30.33	nr
G0451	Ref WS090, 100 - 115 mm	23.01	2.5%	-	-	23.59	nr
G0452	Ref WS120, 125 - 180 mm	40.23	2.5%	-	-	41.24	nr
G0453	Ref WS185, 190 - 260 mm	49.93	2.5%	-	-	51.18	nr

Basic Prices of Materials

		Supply Price £	Waste Factor %	Unload. Labour £	Unload. Plant £	Total Unit Cost £	Unit
	Cavity Trays Ltd. preformed polypropylene/lead cavity trays:						
	15 degree pitch trays:						
G1102	Intermediate and Catchment Trays (short leads)	7.72	2%	-	-	**7.87**	nr
G1103	Intermediate and Catchment Trays (long leads)	11.00	2%	-	-	**11.22**	nr
G1104	Ridge Trays	13.69	2%	-	-	**13.96**	nr
	17 - 21 degree pitch trays:						
G1106	Intermediate and Catchment Trays (short leads)	6.20	2%	-	-	**6.32**	nr
G1107	Intermediate and Catchment Trays (long leads)	8.37	2%	-	-	**8.54**	nr
G1108	Ridge Trays	13.69	2%	-	-	**13.96**	nr
	22 - 26 degree pitch trays:						
G1110	Intermediate and Catchment Trays (short leads)	5.77	2%	-	-	**5.89**	nr
G1111	Intermediate and Catchment Trays (long leads)	7.70	2%	-	-	**7.85**	nr
G1112	Ridge Trays	12.69	2%	-	-	**12.94**	nr
	27 - 45 degree pitch trays:						
G1114	Intermediate and Catchment Trays (short leads)	5.51	2%	-	-	**5.62**	nr
G1115	Intermediate and Catchment Trays (long leads)	7.11	2%	-	-	**7.25**	nr
G1116	Ridge Trays	11.30	2%	-	-	**11.53**	nr
G1117	Angles (All pitches) short leads	11.80	2%	-	-	**12.04**	nr
G1118	Angles (All pitches) long leads	14.81	2%	-	-	**15.11**	nr
	Type E Trays:						
G1122	Standard 450 mm lengths	4.50	2%	-	-	**4.59**	nr
G1123	Standard 90 degree angles	6.54	2%	-	-	**6.67**	nr
G1124	Non-standard angles	11.49	2%	-	-	**11.72**	nr
G1125	Infill lengths	5.71	2%	-	-	**5.82**	nr
G1126	Lengths between 450 mm and 900 mm	11.43	2%	-	-	**11.66**	nr
G1127	Type W cavity weep/ventilator	0.50	2%	-	-	**0.51**	nr
G1128	Type W extension duct	0.89	2%	-	-	**0.91**	nr

Mortar Mix Analysis

The cost of labour in mixing mortar is included in the rate per hour of the gang. The cost of mixers or mortar mills should be costed in Preliminaries. The prices of 1 m3 of mortar are calculated as follows:

A0511 Cement mortar (1:3)

Cement (bagged)	0.44 tonne	x	£	156.48	=	£	68.85
Building sand	1.83 tonne	x	£	26.57	=	£	48.62
						£	117.47
Waste	10%				=	£	11.75
Cost per m3					=	£	**129.22**

A0542 Gauged mortar (1:2:9)

Cement (bagged)	0.16 tonne	x	£	156.48	=	£	25.04
Hydrated lime (del. in bags)	0.16 tonne	x	£	238.58	=	£	38.17
Building sand	1.98 tonne	x	£	26.57	=	£	52.61
						£	115.82
Waste	10%				=	£	11.58
Cost per m3					=	£	**127.40**

A0541 Gauged mortar (1:1:6)

Cement (bagged)	0.23 tonne	x	£	156.48	=	£	35.99
Hydrated lime (del. in bags)	0.12 tonne	x	£	238.58	=	£	28.63
Building sand	1.93 tonne	x	£	26.57	=	£	51.28
						£	115.90
Waste	10%				=	£	11.59
Cost per m3					=	£	**127.49**

A0531 Refractory mortar (1:4)

Cement (bagged)	0.37 tonne	x	£	156.48	=	£	57.90
Refractory agg/crush firebrick	1.11 tonne	x	£	260.92	=	£	289.62
						£	347.52
Waste	10%				=	£	34.75
Cost per m3					=	£	**382.27**

Mortar Mix Analysis

A0544 Coloured gauged mortar (1:2:9)

Cement (bagged)	0.16 tonne	x	£	156.48	=	£	25.04
Hydrated lime (del. in bags)	0.16 tonne	x	£	238.58	=	£	38.17
Building sand	1.98 tonne	x	£	26.57	=	£	52.61
Febtone colour pigment (red)	6.00 kg	x	£	7.82	=	£	46.92
						£	162.74
Waste	10%				=	£	16.27
Cost per m3					=	£	**179.01**

Concrete Mix Analysis

A0563 Concrete grade C25/30

Cement (bagged)	0.33 tonne	x	£	156.48	=	£	51.64
Fine aggregate BS 882	0.90 tonne	x	£	32.60	=	£	29.34
20 mm Aggregate	1.30 tonne	x	£	34.05	=	£	44.27
						£	125.25
Waste	10%				=	£	12.53
Cost per m3					=	£	**137.78**

Unit Rates

		Man-Hours	Net Labour Price £	Net Mats Price £	Net Unit Price £	Unit
GA	UNIT RATE **BRICKWORK IN CEMENT MORTAR**					
001	**Common bricks, BS 3921, P.C. £311.01 per 1000 in cement mortar (1:3)**					
002	Cut out vertical or raking cracks in existing brickwork and replace with new; average 45 mm wide; in:					
	half brickwall	1.67	34.77	10.17	**44.94**	m
	one brickwall	3.43	71.46	20.67	**92.13**	m
	one and a half brickwall	5.11	106.24	31.36	**137.60**	m
003	Cut out existing decayed or defective bricks, half brick deep; replacing with new brickwork:					
	area 0.50 m2 to 1.00 m2	3.30	68.67	23.87	**92.54**	Nr
	area up to 0.50 m2	1.70	35.38	11.93	**47.31**	Nr
	individual brick	0.15	3.12	0.59	**3.71**	Nr
004	Cut out existing defective arch and replace with new brickwork:					
	brick-on-end flat arch:					
	112.5 mm on soffit	0.82	17.00	5.03	**22.03**	m
	brick-on-edge flat arch:					
	112.5 mm on soffit	0.65	13.53	3.00	**16.53**	m
	225 mm on soffit	0.82	17.00	5.03	**22.03**	m
	segmental arch in two half brick-on-edge rings:					
	112.5 mm on soffit	1.30	27.03	6.33	**33.36**	m
	225 mm on soffit	1.63	33.98	10.50	**44.48**	m
	semi circular arch in two half brick-on-edge rings:					
	112.5 mm on soffit	1.63	33.98	6.33	**40.31**	m
	225 mm on soffit	2.04	42.49	10.50	**52.99**	m
GB	**BRICKWORK IN GAUGED MORTAR**					
001	**Common bricks, BS 3921, P.C. £311.01 per 1000 in cement mortar (1:2:9)**					
002	Filling to openings in existing brick walls; for plastering:					
	half brickwall	1.81	37.69	22.54	**60.23**	m2
	one brickwall	3.06	63.74	45.70	**109.44**	m2
	one and a half brickwall	3.62	75.33	69.06	**144.39**	m2
	Note: 003 - 007 not used					
008	Filling to openings in existing brick walls; finished fair and flush pointed one side; for plastering other side:					
	half brickwall	2.23	46.36	22.54	**68.90**	m2
	one brickwall	3.48	72.46	45.70	**118.16**	m2
	one and a half brickwall	4.04	84.05	69.06	**153.11**	m2
009	Filling to flue recess not exceeding 500 mm wide; bonding to existing both sides; half brick thick:					
	finished for plastering	1.50	31.22	11.58	**42.80**	m
	fair and flush pointed to match existing	2.75	57.23	15.35	**72.58**	m
010	Projections of attached piers, plinths, bands, oversailing courses and the like:					
	215 x 112.5 mm	0.48	9.95	5.66	**15.61**	m
	215 x 225 mm	1.24	25.80	10.41	**36.21**	m
	327.5 x 112.5 mm	0.68	14.19	7.88	**22.07**	m
	327.5 x 225 mm	1.87	38.81	15.05	**53.86**	m
	440 x 112.5 mm	0.91	18.92	10.54	**29.46**	m
	440 x 225 mm	2.48	51.59	20.76	**72.35**	m
	440 x 327.5 mm	2.97	61.76	28.45	**90.21**	m
011	Make good face of existing brickwork after removal of projecting chimney breasts:					
	with mortar to receive plaster	0.17	3.48	0.25	**3.73**	m2
	with new construction finished fair and flush pointed to match existing	2.32	48.30	23.82	**72.12**	m2
012	Make good face of existing brickwork after removal of plinth courses, band courses, pilasters, attached piers and the like with flush, matching construction, half brick thick:					
	over 1000 mm wide	2.32	48.30	23.82	**72.12**	m2
	up to 250 mm wide	0.60	12.57	6.11	**18.68**	m
	250 - 500 mm wide	1.16	24.16	11.90	**36.06**	m
	500 - 1000 mm wide	2.32	48.30	23.82	**72.12**	m
013	Make good jambs of openings cut in old brick walls with new brickwork; bonding to existing:					
	prepared for plastering:					
	half brickwall	0.28	5.79	3.59	**9.38**	m
	one brickwall	0.51	10.63	6.86	**17.49**	m
	one and a half brickwall	0.70	14.50	10.12	**24.62**	m
	finished fair and flush pointed:					
	half brickwall	0.59	12.17	3.59	**15.76**	m
	one brickwall	1.09	22.62	6.86	**29.48**	m
	one and a half brickwall	1.42	29.57	10.12	**39.69**	m
014	Brickwork half brick thick in making good to existing:					
	where cross wall removed:					
	half brick thick	0.25	5.22	2.54	**7.76**	m
	one brick thick	0.46	9.66	4.76	**14.42**	m
	one and a half brick thick	0.65	13.53	7.29	**20.82**	m
	where ends of joists removed:					
	50 x 200 mm x 450 mm centres	0.09	1.94	0.78	**2.72**	m
	50 x 250 mm x 450 mm centres	0.11	2.31	1.11	**3.42**	m

Unit Rates

	Man-Hours	Net Labour Price £	Net Mats Price £	Net Unit Price £	Unit
where ends of beams removed:					
200 x 300 mm	0.23	4.85	1.56	**6.41**	Nr
300 x 400 mm	0.28	5.79	2.67	**8.46**	Nr
300 x 600 mm	0.42	8.72	4.23	**12.95**	Nr
where brackets removed	0.09	1.94	0.46	**2.40**	Nr
015 Cut out vertical or raking cracks in existing brickwork and replace with new brick; average 450 mm wide; in:					
half brickwall	1.49	30.90	10.16	**41.06**	m
one brickwall	2.97	61.81	20.64	**82.45**	m
one and a half brickwall	4.46	92.71	31.30	**124.01**	m
016 Bonding end of brick walls 112.5 mm deep to existing; in alternate courses; cutting pockets in existing brickwork; extra material for bonding:					
half brickwall	0.56	11.59	1.11	**12.70**	m
one brickwall	0.79	16.44	2.21	**18.65**	m
one and a half brickwall	1.11	23.18	3.45	**26.63**	m
017 Cut out existing decayed or defective bricks, half brick deep; replace with new brickwork: Stretcher bond:					
area 0.50 m2 to 1.00 m2	2.90	60.35	23.82	**84.17**	Nr
area up to 0.50 m2	1.60	33.30	11.90	**45.20**	Nr
individual brick	0.12	2.50	0.58	**3.08**	Nr
018 Cut out existing defective arch and replace with new brickwork: brick-on-end flat arch:					
112.5 mm on soffit	0.70	14.50	5.01	**19.51**	m
brick-on-edge flat arch:					
112.5 mm on soffit	0.56	11.59	2.99	**14.58**	m
225 mm on soffit	0.70	14.50	5.01	**19.51**	m
segmental arch in two half brick-on-edge rings:					
112.5 mm on soffit	1.11	23.18	6.31	**29.49**	m
225 mm on soffit	1.39	28.97	10.48	**39.45**	m
semi circular arch in two half brick-on-edge rings:					
112.5 mm on soffit	1.39	28.97	6.31	**35.28**	m
225 mm on soffit	1.76	36.71	10.48	**47.19**	m
019 Flush cut faces of existing brickwork after removal of plinth courses, band courses, pilasters, attached piers and the like dressed with Kango hammer:					
over 1000 mm wide	0.33	3.75	-	**5.03**	m2
up to 250 mm wide	0.09	1.04	-	**1.39**	m
250 - 500 mm wide	0.19	2.09	-	**2.80**	m
500 - 1000 mm wide	0.33	3.75	-	**5.03**	m
020 Rough cutting to form: chamfered angles:					
50 mm wide	0.46	9.47	-	**9.47**	m
100 mm wide	0.57	11.84	-	**11.84**	m
rounded angles:					
50 mm radius	0.51	10.65	-	**10.65**	m
100 mm girth	0.57	11.84	-	**11.84**	m

GC CLASS A ENGINEERING BRICKS

001 **Class A Engineering Bricks to BS 3921 P.C. £493.42 per 1000 in cement mortar (1:3)**

Note: 002 - 009 not used

	Man-Hours	Net Labour Price £	Net Mats Price £	Net Unit Price £	Unit
010 Filling to openings in existing brick walls; for plastering:					
half brickwall	2.08	43.28	34.45	**77.73**	m2
one brickwall	3.50	72.84	69.15	**141.99**	m2
one and a half brickwall	3.99	83.03	104.24	**187.27**	m2
011 Filling to openings in existing brick walls; finished fair and flush pointed one side; for plastering other side:					
half brickwall	2.52	52.44	34.45	**86.89**	m2
one brickwall	3.84	79.91	69.15	**149.06**	m2
one and a half brickwall	4.21	87.61	104.24	**191.85**	m2
012 Projections of attached piers, plinths, bands, oversailing courses and the like:					
215 x 112.5 mm	0.55	11.45	8.55	**20.00**	m
215 x 225 mm	1.42	29.55	15.80	**45.35**	m
327.5 x 112.5 mm	0.78	16.23	11.91	**28.14**	m
327.5 x 225 mm	2.12	44.12	22.92	**67.04**	m
440 x 112.5 mm	1.04	21.64	15.93	**37.57**	m
440 x 225 mm	2.83	58.89	31.34	**90.23**	m
440 x 327.5 mm	3.41	70.96	41.56	**112.52**	m
013 Make good jambs of openings cut in old brick walls with new brickwork; bonding to existing: prepared for plastering:					
half brickwall	0.42	8.72	5.70	**14.42**	m
one brickwall	0.70	14.50	10.88	**25.38**	m
one and a half brickwall	1.02	21.25	16.06	**37.31**	m
finished fair and flush pointed:					
half brickwall	0.42	8.72	5.70	**14.42**	m
one brickwall	0.70	14.50	10.88	**25.38**	m
one and a half brickwall	1.02	21.25	16.06	**37.31**	m

	Unit Rates	Man-Hours	Net Labour Price £	Net Mats Price £	Net Unit Price £	Unit
014	Bonding end of brick walls 112.5 mm deep to existing; in alternate courses; cutting pockets in existing brickwork; extra material for bonding:					
	half brickwall	0.74	15.46	1.68	**17.14**	m
	one brickwall	1.07	22.23	3.37	**25.60**	m
	one and a half brickwall	1.49	30.90	5.18	**36.08**	m
015	Rough cutting to form:					
	chamfered angles:					
	50 mm wide	0.57	11.84	-	**11.84**	m
	100 mm wide	0.68	14.19	-	**14.19**	m
	rounded angles:					
	50 mm radius	0.63	13.03	-	**13.03**	m
	100 mm girth	0.68	14.19	-	**14.19**	m

GF **BRICK FACEWORK**

		Man-Hours	Net Labour Price £	Net Mats Price £	Net Unit Price £	Unit
001	**Extra over common bricks in any mortar for fair face**					
002	Flush pointing as the work proceeds in:					
	stretcher bond	0.34	7.10	-	**7.10**	m2
	Flemish bond	0.38	7.82	-	**7.82**	m2
	English bond	0.39	8.03	-	**8.03**	m2
003	Struck pointing as the work proceeds in:					
	stretcher bond	0.40	8.28	-	**8.28**	m2
	Flemish bond	0.43	9.01	-	**9.01**	m2
	English bond	0.44	9.22	-	**9.22**	m2
004	Bucket handle pointing as the work proceeds in:					
	stretcher bond	0.40	8.28	-	**8.28**	m2
	Flemish bond	0.43	9.01	-	**9.01**	m2
	English bond	0.44	9.22	-	**9.22**	m2
005	Pointing to margins	0.08	1.66	-	**1.66**	m
006	**Extra over Class A or Class B engineering bricks in cement mortar (1:3) for fair face**					
007	Flush pointing as the work proceeds in:					
	stretcher bond	0.40	8.28	-	**8.28**	m2
	Flemish bond	0.43	9.01	-	**9.01**	m2
	English bond	0.44	9.22	-	**9.22**	m2
008	Struck pointing as the work proceeds in:					
	stretcher bond	0.46	9.47	-	**9.47**	m2
	Flemish bond	0.49	10.18	-	**10.18**	m2
	English bond	0.51	10.65	-	**10.65**	m2
009	Bucket handle pointing as the work proceeds in:					
	stretcher bond	0.46	9.47	-	**9.47**	m2
	Flemish bond	0.49	10.18	-	**10.18**	m2
	English bond	0.51	10.65	-	**10.65**	m2
010	Pointing to margins	0.09	1.89	-	**1.89**	m
011	**Extra over common bricks in any mortar for facing bricks P.C. £351.38 per 1000 in the same mortar and flush pointing as the work proceeds**					
012	Walls and skins of hollow walls in:					
	stretcher bond	0.68	14.19	2.54	**16.73**	m2
	Flemish bond	0.91	18.92	3.43	**22.35**	m2
	English bond	1.02	21.31	3.90	**25.21**	m2
	Flemish garden wall bond	0.80	16.56	2.97	**19.53**	m2
	English garden wall bond	0.85	17.75	3.22	**20.97**	m2

GG **BRICKWORK BUILT FAIR BOTH SIDES**

		Man-Hours	Net Labour Price £	Net Mats Price £	Net Unit Price £	Unit
001	**Common bricks, BS 3921 P.C. £311.01 per 1000 in gauged mortar (1:2:9); flush pointing as the work proceeds**					
002	Filling to openings in existing brick walls; finishing fair and flush pointing both sides; to match existing walls:					
	half brickwall	2.65	55.06	22.54	**77.60**	m2
	one brickwall	3.90	81.12	45.70	**126.82**	m2
	one and a half brickwall	4.46	92.71	69.06	**161.77**	m2
003	**Class A engineering bricks, BS 3921, P.C. £493.42 per 1000, in cement mortar (1:3); flush pointing as the work proceeds**					
004	Filling to openings in existing brick walls; finishing fair and flush pointing both sides; to match existing walls:					
	half brickwall	2.94	61.18	34.45	**95.63**	m2
	one brickwall	4.28	89.07	69.15	**158.22**	m2
	one and a half brickwall	4.94	102.80	104.24	**207.04**	m2

	Unit Rates	Man-Hours	Net Labour Price £	Net Mats Price £	Net Unit Price £	Unit
005	**Class B engineering bricks BS 3921 P.C. £391.75 per 1000 in cement mortar (1:3); flush pointing as the work proceeds**					
006	Filling to openings in existing brick walls; finishing fair and flush pointing both sides; to match existing walls:					
	half brickwall	2.94	61.18	27.83	**89.01**	m2
	one brickwall	4.28	89.07	56.12	**145.19**	m2
	one and a half brickwall	4.94	102.80	84.70	**187.50**	m2
GH	**BRICKWORK BUILT ENTIRELY OF FACING BRICKS**					
001	**Facing bricks P.C. £351.38 per 1000 in gauged mortar (1:2:9); flush pointing as the work proceeds**					
	Note: 002 - 004 not used					
005	Filling to openings in existing brick walls; facing and pointing both sides; to match existing walls:					
	half brickwall	2.51	52.15	25.16	**77.31**	m2
	one brickwall	4.20	87.40	50.87	**138.27**	m2
	Note: 006 not used					
007	Facework 102.5 mm thick; in making good to match existing:					
	where cross wall removed:					
	half brick thick	0.32	6.58	2.09	**8.67**	m
	one brick thick	0.59	12.36	5.31	**17.67**	m
	one and a half brick thick	0.84	17.38	8.14	**25.52**	m
	where ends of joists removed:					
	50 x 200 mm x 450 mm centres	0.10	2.14	0.87	**3.01**	m
	50 x 250 mm x 450 mm centres	0.13	2.71	1.24	**3.95**	m
	where ends of beams removed:					
	200 x 300 mm	0.27	5.60	1.73	**7.33**	Nr
	300 x 400 mm	0.34	7.16	2.96	**10.12**	Nr
	300 x 600 mm	0.52	10.82	4.70	**15.52**	Nr
	where brackets removed	0.10	2.14	0.50	**2.64**	Nr
008	Make good existing facework after removal of plinth courses, band courses, pilasters, attached piers and the like with flush, matching facework, half brick thick:					
	over 1000 mm wide	2.32	48.30	26.44	**74.74**	m2
	up to 250 mm wide	0.60	12.57	6.79	**19.36**	m
	250 - 500 mm wide	1.16	24.16	13.22	**37.38**	m
	500 - 1000 mm wide	2.32	48.30	26.44	**74.74**	m
009	Make good jambs of openings cut in old brick walls with new facework; bonding to existing:					
	half brick thick	0.59	12.17	4.06	**16.23**	m
	one brick thick	1.09	22.62	7.75	**30.37**	m
	one and a half brick thick	1.42	29.57	11.44	**41.01**	m
010	Bonding ends of facing brick walls 112.5 mm deep to existing; in alternate courses; cutting pockets in existing facework; extra material for bonding:					
	half brick thick	0.70	14.50	1.24	**15.74**	m
	one brick thick	1.02	21.25	2.46	**23.71**	m
011	Cut out existing defective arch and replace with new facework:					
	brick-on-end flat arch:					
	112.5 mm on soffit	0.80	16.65	5.56	**22.21**	m
	brick-on-edge flat arch:					
	112.5 mm on soffit	0.65	13.53	3.33	**16.86**	m
	225 mm on soffit	0.80	16.65	5.56	**22.21**	m
	segmental arch in two half brick-on-edge rings:					
	112.5 mm on soffit	1.25	26.01	7.03	**33.04**	m
	225 mm on soffit	1.55	32.26	11.62	**43.88**	m
	semi circular arch in two half brick-on-edge rings:					
	112.5 mm on soffit	1.55	32.26	7.03	**39.29**	m
	225 mm on soffit	1.95	40.58	11.62	**52.20**	m
012	Fair returns:					
	not exceeding half brick wide	0.11	2.35	-	**2.35**	m
	over half brick, not exceeding one brick wide	0.17	3.56	-	**3.56**	m
013	Fair cutting on facings:					
	raking	1.08	22.47	1.48	**23.95**	m
	curved	1.65	34.32	1.48	**35.80**	m
014	**Extra over facing bricks in gauged mortar (1:2:9) flush pointed as the work proceeds for the following in the same facing bricks**					
	NB: Vertical items allow for fair straight cutting both sides					
015	Sunk plain bands set back 25 mm from general wall face:					
	85 mm wide:					
	horizontal	0.04	0.73	-	**0.73**	m
	raking	0.05	0.94	-	**0.94**	m
	vertical	0.76	15.86	-	**15.86**	m
	160 mm wide:					
	horizontal	0.07	1.42	-	**1.42**	m
	raking	0.10	2.14	-	**2.14**	m
	vertical	0.85	17.75	-	**17.75**	m

	Unit Rates	Man-Hours	Net Labour Price £	Net Mats Price £	Net Unit Price £	Unit
	235 mm wide:					
	horizontal	0.10	2.14	-	**2.14**	m
	raking	0.15	3.08	-	**3.08**	m
	vertical	0.93	19.39	-	**19.39**	m
016	Projecting plain bands set forward 25 mm from general wall face:					
	65 mm wide:					
	horizontal	0.05	0.94	2.34	**3.28**	m
	raking	0.07	1.42	2.34	**3.76**	m
	vertical	0.76	15.86	2.34	**18.20**	m
	140 mm wide:					
	horizontal	0.10	2.14	4.68	**6.82**	m
	raking	0.14	2.83	4.68	**7.51**	m
	vertical	0.85	17.75	4.68	**22.43**	m
	215 mm wide:					
	horizontal	0.15	3.08	6.89	**9.97**	m
	raking	0.21	4.27	6.89	**11.16**	m
	vertical	0.93	19.39	6.89	**26.28**	m
017	Sunk quoins set back 25 mm from general wall face:					
	317.5 mm girth	0.91	18.92	-	**18.92**	m
	486.25 mm girth	1.02	21.31	-	**21.31**	m
018	Projecting quoins set forward 25 mm from general wall face:					
	317.5 mm girth	1.14	23.66	7.76	**31.42**	m
	486.25 mm girth	1.54	31.96	11.45	**43.41**	m
019	Flush brick-on-edge bands formed entirely of headers:					
	112.5 mm wide:					
	horizontal	0.04	0.73	-	**0.73**	m
	raking	0.06	1.21	-	**1.21**	m
	vertical	0.77	16.11	-	**16.11**	m
	225 mm wide:					
	horizontal	0.08	1.66	-	**1.66**	m
	raking	0.11	2.35	-	**2.35**	m
	vertical	0.88	18.23	-	**18.23**	m
	327.5 mm wide:					
	horizontal	0.11	2.35	-	**2.35**	m
	raking	0.17	3.56	-	**3.56**	m
	vertical	0.97	20.12	-	**20.12**	m
020	**Extra over** for snapped headers in bands:					
	112.5 mm wide	0.28	5.91	1.11	**7.02**	m
	225 mm wide	0.57	11.84	2.58	**14.42**	m
	327.5 mm wide	0.85	17.75	3.69	**21.44**	m
021	Flush brick-on-end bands 225 mm wide:					
	horizontal	0.02	0.48	-	**0.48**	m
	raking	0.04	0.73	-	**0.73**	m
	vertical	0.74	15.38	-	**15.38**	m
022	Sunk brick-on-end bands 235 mm wide set back 25 mm from general wall face:					
	horizontal	0.06	1.21	-	**1.21**	m
	raking	0.07	1.42	-	**1.42**	m
	vertical	0.77	16.11	-	**16.11**	m
023	Projecting brick-on-end bands 215 mm wide set forward 25 mm from general wall face:					
	horizontal	0.13	2.60	5.42	**8.02**	m
	raking	0.15	3.08	5.42	**8.50**	m
	vertical	0.84	17.52	5.42	**22.94**	m
024	Flat arches formed entirely of headers-on-edge 112.5 mm wide on face 215 mm wide exposed soffit	0.38	7.82		**7.82**	m
025	Flat arches formed entirely of stretchers-on-end 225 mm wide on face 102.5 mm wide exposed soffit	0.63	13.03	-	**13.03**	m
	Note: 026 - 027 not used					
028	**Copings, sills and the like in facing bricks P.C. £351.38 per 1000 in cement mortar (1:3); flush pointing as the work proceeds**					
	Note: 029 not used					
030	Take down existing defective brick-on-edge coping to brick wall and replace with new coping 215 x 112.5 mm brick-on-edge to match existing:					
	facing bricks in gauged mortar (1:2:9):					
	plain coping	0.65	13.53	5.93	**19.46**	m
	coping with single course tile creasing	0.85	17.69	12.95	**30.64**	m
	coping with double course tile creasing	1.05	21.85	19.72	**41.57**	m
	Note: 031 not used					
032	**Arches, in facing bricks P.C. £351.38 per 1000 in gauged mortar (1:2:9); flush pointing where exposed; centering and supports**					
033	Flat arches:					
	brick-on-edge; 225 mm soffit, 112.5 mm high	2.69	55.98	12.66	**68.64**	m
	brick-on-end; 112.5 mm soffit, 225 mm high	1.91	39.75	9.29	**49.04**	m

	Unit Rates	Man-Hours	Net Labour Price £	Net Mats Price £	Net Unit Price £	Unit
034	Segmental arches:					
	brick-on-edge; 225 mm soffit, 112.5 mm high:					
	single course	2.83	58.93	12.66	**71.59**	m
	two courses	3.06	63.74	18.59	**82.33**	m
	brick-on-end; 112.5 mm soffit, 225 mm high	2.01	41.72	9.29	**51.01**	m
035	Semi-circular arches:					
	brick-on-edge; 225 mm soffit, 112.5 mm high:					
	single course	5.48	113.96	12.66	**126.62**	m
	two courses	5.71	118.80	18.59	**137.39**	m
	brick-on-end; 112.5 mm soffit, 225 mm high	4.92	102.36	9.29	**111.65**	m

GK

BLOCKWORK

001 **Precast concrete blocks, BS 6073, natural aggregates, compressive strength 7 N/mm2, face size 440 x 215 mm; in gauged mortar (1:2:9)**

Note: 002 - 006 not used

		Man-Hours	Net Labour Price £	Net Mats Price £	Net Unit Price £	Unit
007	Filling to openings in existing block walls; for plastering:					
	solid blocks; thickness:					
	75 mm	1.05	21.85	8.01	**29.86**	m2
	100 mm	1.25	26.10	8.76	**34.86**	m2
	140 mm	1.53	31.88	13.13	**45.01**	m2
	215 mm	1.86	38.62	26.39	**65.01**	m2
008	Filling to openings in existing block walls; finished fair and flush pointed one side; for plastering other side:					
	solid blocks; thickness:					
	75 mm	1.16	24.14	8.01	**32.15**	m2
	100 mm	1.36	28.30	8.76	**37.06**	m2
	140 mm	1.64	34.13	13.13	**47.26**	m2
	215 mm	1.97	41.00	26.39	**67.39**	m2
009	Filling to openings in existing block walls; finished fair and flush pointed both sides:					
	solid blocks; thickness:					
	75 mm	1.33	27.64	8.01	**35.65**	m2
	100 mm	1.53	31.88	8.76	**40.64**	m2
	140 mm	1.81	37.69	13.13	**50.82**	m2
	215 mm	2.14	44.53	26.39	**70.92**	m2
010	Filling to flue recess not exceeding 500 mm wide: bonding to existing both sides; solid blockwork 100 mm thick:					
	finished for plastering	1.20	24.97	11.58	**36.55**	m
	fair and flush pointed to match existing	1.90	39.54	6.02	**45.56**	m
011	Make good face of existing blockwork after removal of chimney breasts etc.:					
	with mortar to receive plaster	0.17	3.48	0.13	**3.61**	m2
	with new solid blockwork 100 mm thick finished fair and pointed to match existing	1.46	30.38	10.03	**40.41**	m2
012	Make good face of blockwork after removal of plinth courses, band courses, pilasters, attached piers and the like with flush, matching construction, 75 mm thick blocks in gauged mortar (1:2:9); fair facing and flush pointing:					
	over 1000 mm wide	1.11	23.18	8.01	**31.19**	m2
	up to 250 mm wide	0.33	6.95	2.42	**9.37**	m
	250 - 500 mm wide	0.56	11.59	4.45	**16.04**	m
	500 - 1000 mm wide	1.11	23.18	8.01	**31.19**	m
013	Make good jambs of openings cut in existing block walls with new blockwork; bonding to existing:					
	prepared for plastering:					
	100 mm thick	0.42	8.72	1.59	**10.31**	m
	140 mm thick	0.59	12.17	2.31	**14.48**	m
	215 mm thick	0.84	17.38	4.63	**22.01**	m
	finished fair and flush pointed:					
	100 mm thick	0.50	10.43	1.59	**12.02**	m
	140 mm thick	0.67	13.90	2.31	**16.21**	m
	215 mm thick	1.00	20.87	4.63	**25.50**	m
014	Blockwork 75 mm thick in making good:					
	where cross wall removed:					
	75 mm thick	0.19	3.87	0.51	**4.38**	m
	100 mm thick	0.23	4.85	1.06	**5.91**	m
	140 mm thick	0.37	7.72	2.08	**9.80**	m
	215 mm thick	0.46	9.66	5.01	**14.67**	m
	where ends of joists removed:					
	50 x 200 mm x 450 mm centres	0.09	1.94	0.45	**2.39**	m
	50 x 250 mm x 450 mm centres	0.11	2.31	0.62	**2.93**	m
	where ends of beams removed:					
	200 x 300 mm	0.19	3.87	1.70	**5.57**	Nr
	300 x 400 mm	0.23	4.85	3.55	**8.40**	Nr
	300 x 600 mm	0.33	6.78	5.25	**12.03**	Nr
015	Cut out vertical or raking cracks in existing blockwork and replace with new; average 450 mm wide:					
	75 mm thick	0.60	12.57	3.56	**16.13**	m
	100 mm thick	0.74	15.46	3.90	**19.36**	m
	140 mm thick	0.88	18.38	5.96	**24.34**	m
	190 mm thick	1.11	23.18	8.87	**32.05**	m

Unit Rates	Man-Hours	Net Labour Price £	Net Mats Price £	Net Unit Price £	Unit
016 Bonding ends of blockwork 150 mm deep to existing; in alternate block courses; cutting pockets in existing blockwork; extra material for bonding: solid blocks, thickness:					
75 mm thick	0.17	4.09	0.49	**4.58**	m
100 mm thick	0.19	4.37	0.53	**4.90**	m
140 mm thick	0.26	6.02	0.79	**6.81**	m
190 mm thick	0.28	6.68	1.34	**8.02**	m
017 Bonding ends of blockwork 112.5 mm deep to new brickwork in alternate group of three brick courses; forming pockets; extra material for bonding: solid blocks, thickness:					
75 mm thick	0.19	4.04	0.42	**4.46**	m
100 mm thick	0.21	4.27	0.45	**4.72**	m
140 mm thick	0.27	5.68	0.68	**6.36**	m
190 mm thick	0.30	6.16	1.17	**7.33**	m
215 mm thick	0.31	6.41	1.53	**7.94**	m
hollow blocks, thickness:					
100 mm thick	0.19	4.04	0.45	**4.49**	m
140 mm thick	0.26	5.45	0.68	**6.13**	m
215 mm thick	0.31	6.41	1.08	**7.49**	m
018 Cut out existing decayed or defective blockwork and replace with new: area 0.50 m2 to 1.00 m2:					
75 mm thick	1.39	28.97	8.01	**36.98**	Nr
100 mm thick	1.67	34.77	8.76	**43.53**	Nr
140 mm thick	1.95	40.56	13.13	**53.69**	Nr
215 mm thick	2.51	52.15	26.26	**78.41**	Nr
area up to 0.50 m2:					
75 mm thick	0.84	17.38	3.95	**21.33**	Nr
100 mm thick	1.02	21.25	4.44	**25.69**	Nr
140 mm thick	1.16	24.16	6.57	**30.73**	Nr
215 mm thick	1.49	30.90	13.14	**44.04**	Nr
individual block:					
75 mm thick	0.23	4.85	0.76	**5.61**	Nr
100 mm thick	0.28	5.79	0.94	**6.73**	Nr
140 mm thick	0.33	6.78	1.34	**8.12**	Nr
215 mm thick	0.37	7.72	2.63	**10.35**	Nr
019 **Extra over** for filling ends of hollow blocks with in situ concrete grade 25 N/mm2, thickness:					
100 mm	0.07	1.42	1.52	**2.94**	m
215 mm	0.14	2.83	3.31	**6.14**	m
020 Rough cutting to form: chamfered angles:					
50 mm wide	0.28	5.91	-	**5.91**	m
100 mm wide	0.40	8.28	-	**8.28**	m
rounded angles:					
50 mm radius	0.28	5.91	-	**5.91**	m
100 mm girth	0.68	14.19	-	**14.19**	m
021 Flush cut faces of blockwork after removal of plinth courses, band courses, pilasters, attached piers and the like dressed with Kango hammer:					
over 1000 mm wide	0.33	6.95	-	**8.23**	m2
up to 250 mm wide	0.09	1.94	-	**2.29**	m
250 - 500 mm wide	0.19	3.87	-	**4.58**	m
500 - 1000 mm wide	0.33	6.95	-	**8.23**	m
022 **Extra over** natural aggregate blockwork for fair face and flush pointing as the work proceeds, any thickness:					
one face	0.11	2.35	1.51	**3.86**	m2
both faces	0.28	5.91	1.51	**7.42**	m2
023 Fair returns:					
not exceeding 150 mm wide	0.11	2.35	-	**2.35**	m
150 - 300 mm wide	0.14	2.83	-	**2.83**	m
024 Fair cutting to form: chamfered angle:					
50 mm wide	0.34	7.10	-	**7.10**	m
100 mm wide	0.51	10.65	-	**10.65**	m
rounded angles:					
50 mm radius	0.57	11.84	-	**11.84**	m
100 mm girth	0.85	17.75	-	**17.75**	m
025 **Precast concrete blocks, BS 6073, furnace clinker aggregates, compressive strength 3.5 N/mm2; in gauged mortar (1:2:9)**					
026 Walls and partitions: solid blocks, thickness:					
100 mm	0.79	18.54	9.12	**27.66**	m2
140 mm	0.95	22.32	14.10	**36.42**	m2
027 Skins of hollow walls: solid blocks, thickness:					
100 mm	0.80	18.80	9.12	**27.92**	m2
140 mm	0.97	22.84	14.10	**36.94**	m2
Note: 028 - 031 not used					

	Unit Rates	Man-Hours	Net Labour Price £	Net Mats Price £	Net Unit Price £	Unit
032	Bonding ends of blockwork 112.5 mm deep to new brickwork in alternate group of three brick courses; forming pockets; extra material for bonding:					
	solid blocks, thickness:					
	100 mm	0.18	4.30	0.47	**4.77**	m
	140 mm	0.25	5.95	0.73	**6.68**	m
033	**Extra over** clinker aggregate blockwork for fair face and flush pointing as the work proceeds, any thickness:					
	one face	0.11	2.67	1.51	**4.18**	m2
	both faces	0.28	6.71	1.51	**8.22**	m2
034	Fair return:					
	not exceeding 150 mm wide	0.11	2.67	-	**2.67**	m
	150 - 300 mm wide	0.14	3.21	-	**3.21**	m
035	Fair cutting to form:					
	chamfered angle:					
	50 mm wide	0.28	6.71	-	**6.71**	m
	100 mm wide	0.46	10.74	-	**10.74**	m
	rounded angles:					
	50 mm radius	0.51	12.09	-	**12.09**	m
	100 mm girth	0.80	18.80	-	**18.80**	m
036	**Thermalite blocks face size 440 x 215 mm; in gauged mortar (1:2:9)**					
037	Walls and partitions:					
	100 mm	0.74	17.57	13.31	**30.88**	m2
	140 mm	0.86	20.24	18.76	**39.00**	m2
	200 mm	0.97	22.84	26.74	**49.58**	m2
038	Skins of hollow walls:					
	100 mm	0.79	18.61	13.31	**31.92**	m2
	140 mm	0.91	21.47	18.76	**40.23**	m2
	190 mm	0.91	21.47	25.35	**46.82**	m2
	100 mm turbo	0.72	17.03	13.24	**30.27**	m2
	190 mm turbo	0.83	19.60	24.82	**44.42**	m2
	200 mm turbo	0.89	21.02	26.21	**47.23**	m2
	Note: 039 - 042 not used					
043	Bonding ends of blockwork 112.5 mm deep to new brickwork in alternate group of three brick courses; forming pockets; extra material for bonding:					
	100 mm	0.18	4.30	0.71	**5.01**	m
	140 mm	0.24	5.62	0.99	**6.61**	m
	200 mm	0.25	5.90	1.55	**7.45**	m
044	**Extra over** Thermalite blockwork for smooth face blocks and pointing as the work proceeds:					
	one face:					
	100 mm	0.11	2.67	7.70	**10.37**	m2
	140 mm	0.11	2.67	10.78	**13.45**	m2
	200 mm	0.11	2.67	15.41	**18.08**	m2
	both faces:					
	100 mm	0.28	6.71	7.70	**14.41**	m2
	140 mm	0.28	6.71	10.78	**17.49**	m2
	200 mm	0.28	6.71	15.41	**22.12**	m2
045	Fair return:					
	not exceeding 150 mm wide	0.11	2.67	-	**2.67**	m
	150 - 300 mm wide	0.14	3.21	-	**3.21**	m
046	Fair cutting to form:					
	chamfered angle:					
	50 mm wide	0.23	5.38	-	**5.38**	m
	100 mm wide	0.46	10.74	-	**10.74**	m
	rounded angles:					
	50 mm radius	0.51	12.09	-	**12.09**	m
	100 mm girth	0.80	18.80	-	**18.80**	m
047	**Lignacite blocks, compressive strength 3.5 N/mm2 face size 440 x 215 mm; in gauged mortar (1:2:9)**					
048	Walls and partitions:					
	solid blocks:					
	75 mm	0.74	17.45	13.20	**30.65**	m2
	100 mm	0.80	18.80	17.11	**35.91**	m2
	140 mm	0.85	20.14	22.28	**42.42**	m2
	150 mm	0.85	20.14	26.57	**46.71**	m2
	hollow blocks:					
	100 mm	0.74	17.45	20.43	**37.88**	m2
	150 mm	0.80	18.80	28.29	**47.09**	m2
	200 mm	0.91	21.47	28.67	**50.14**	m2
	215 mm party wall	1.14	26.85	30.74	**57.59**	m2
	cellular blocks:					
	100 mm	0.74	17.45	14.28	**31.73**	m2
	150 mm	0.80	18.80	19.73	**38.53**	m2
049	Skins of hollow walls:					
	solid blocks:					
	100 mm	0.80	18.80	17.11	**35.91**	m2

Unit Rates	Man-Hours	Net Labour Price £	Net Mats Price £	Net Unit Price £	Unit
150 mm	0.85	20.14	26.57	**46.71**	m2
hollow blocks:					
100 mm	0.74	17.45	20.43	**37.88**	m2
150 mm	0.80	18.80	28.29	**47.09**	m2
cellular blocks:					
100 mm	0.74	17.45	14.28	**31.73**	m2
150 mm	0.80	18.80	19.73	**38.53**	m2
050 Bonding ends of blockwork 112.5 mm deep to new brickwork in alternate groups of three brick courses; forming pockets; extra material for bonding:					
solid blocks:					
100 mm	0.18	4.30	0.92	**5.22**	m
150 mm	0.24	5.62	1.43	**7.05**	m
hollow blocks:					
100 mm	0.17	4.04	1.11	**5.15**	m
150 mm	0.24	5.62	1.53	**7.15**	m
cellular blocks:					
100 mm	0.17	4.04	0.76	**4.80**	m
150 mm	0.24	5.62	1.05	**6.67**	m
051 **Extra over** Lignacite blockwork for fair face blocks and flush pointing as the work proceeds, any thickness:					
one face	0.11	2.67	1.06	**3.73**	m2
both faces	0.28	6.71	1.06	**7.77**	m2
052 Fair return:					
not exceeding 150 mm wide	0.11	2.67	-	**2.67**	m
150 - 300 mm wide	0.14	3.21	-	**3.21**	m
053 Fair cutting to form:					
chamfered angle:					
50 mm wide	0.23	5.38	-	**5.38**	m
100 mm wide	0.46	10.74	-	**10.74**	m
rounded angles:					
50 mm radius	0.51	12.09	-	**12.09**	m
100 mm girth	0.80	18.80	-	**18.80**	m
GM **DAMP PROOF COURSES**					
001 **Bitumen damp proof courses, BS 6398; 100 mm laps; in cement mortar (1:3), pointing where exposed**					
002 Hessian base, ref A:					
horizontal:					
over 225 mm wide	0.23	4.74	11.00	**15.74**	m2
75 mm wide	0.02	0.48	0.86	**1.34**	m
100 mm wide	0.02	0.48	1.10	**1.58**	m
150 mm wide	0.04	0.73	1.72	**2.45**	m
225 mm wide	0.06	1.21	2.58	**3.79**	m
vertical:					
75 mm wide	0.05	0.94	0.86	**1.80**	m
100 mm wide	0.05	0.94	1.10	**2.04**	m
150 mm wide	0.07	1.42	1.72	**3.14**	m
003 Fibre base, ref B:					
horizontal:					
over 225 mm wide	0.23	4.74	8.93	**13.67**	m2
75 mm wide	0.02	0.48	0.70	**1.18**	m
100 mm wide	0.02	0.48	0.89	**1.37**	m
150 mm wide	0.04	0.73	1.41	**2.14**	m
225 mm wide	0.06	1.21	2.11	**3.32**	m
vertical:					
75 mm wide	0.05	0.94	0.70	**1.64**	m
100 mm wide	0.05	0.94	0.89	**1.83**	m
150 mm wide	0.07	1.42	1.41	**2.83**	m
Note: 004 – 005 not used					
006 **Hyload pitch polymer damp proof course; 100 mm laps sealed with Hyload contact adhesive; in cement mortar (1:3) pointing where exposed**					
007 Horizontal damp proof course:					
over 225 mm wide	0.25	5.20	8.53	**13.73**	m2
75 mm wide	0.02	0.48	0.68	**1.16**	m
100 mm wide	0.02	0.48	0.85	**1.33**	m
150 mm wide	0.04	0.73	1.36	**2.09**	m
225 mm wide	0.06	1.21	2.04	**3.25**	m
008 Vertical damp proof course:					
75 mm wide	0.06	1.21	0.68	**1.89**	m
100 mm wide	0.06	1.21	0.85	**2.06**	m
150 mm wide	0.08	1.66	1.36	**3.02**	m
009 Horizontal damp proof course forming cavity gutters in hollow walls:					
over 225 mm wide	0.57	11.84	11.32	**23.16**	m2
010 Hyload pitch polymer cloaks:					
internal corner	0.17	3.56	4.00	**7.56**	Nr
external corner	0.17	3.56	7.10	**10.66**	Nr

Unit Rates	Man-Hours	Net Labour Price £	Net Mats Price £	Net Unit Price £	Unit
cavity corner:					
150 mm rise	0.23	4.74	15.79	**20.53**	Nr
225 mm rise	0.23	4.74	19.45	**24.19**	Nr
stop end (brick-cavity-brick):					
150 mm rise	0.23	4.74	5.89	**10.63**	Nr
225 mm rise	0.23	4.74	10.46	**15.20**	Nr
change level (brick-cavity-brick):					
150 mm/ 75 mm step on face	0.34	7.10	18.62	**25.72**	Nr
150 mm/ 225 mm step on face	0.34	7.10	21.04	**28.14**	Nr
225 mm/ 75 mm step on face	0.34	7.10	21.63	**28.73**	Nr
225 mm/ 225 mm step on face	0.34	7.10	21.91	**29.01**	Nr
stop end cloak (block-cavity-brick)	0.34	9.62	9.62	**16.72**	Nr
change level cloak (block-cavity-brick):					
150 mm rise	0.34	7.10	18.69	**25.79**	Nr
225 mm rise	0.34	7.10	26.41	**33.51**	Nr

011 **Polyethylene damp proof course; 100 mm laps sealed with adhesive tape; in cement mortar (1:3) pointing where exposed**

012 Horizontal:

over 225 mm wide	0.23	4.74	2.59	**7.33**	m2
75 mm wide	0.02	0.48	0.26	**0.74**	m
100 mm wide	0.02	0.48	0.29	**0.77**	m
150 mm wide	0.04	0.73	0.46	**1.19**	m
225 mm wide	0.06	1.21	0.73	**1.94**	m

013 Vertical:

75 mm wide	0.05	0.94	0.26	**1.20**	m
100 mm wide	0.05	0.94	0.29	**1.23**	m
150 mm wide	0.06	1.21	0.46	**1.67**	m

014 Horizontal, forming cavity gutters in hollow walls:

over 225 mm wide	0.46	9.47	2.59	**12.06**	m2

015 **Slate damp proof courses, BS 743; bedding and pointing in cement mortar (1:3)**

016 Single course slates:

horizontal:					
over 225 mm wide	0.91	18.92	18.40	**37.32**	m2
112.5 mm wide	0.15	3.08	2.98	**6.06**	m
225 mm wide	0.28	5.91	4.67	**10.58**	m
vertical:					
over 225 mm wide	1.14	23.66	18.40	**42.06**	m2
112.5 mm wide	0.19	4.04	2.98	**7.02**	m
225 mm wide	0.34	7.10	4.67	**11.77**	m

017 Two course slates:

horizontal:					
over 225 mm wide	1.88	39.04	35.94	**74.98**	m2
112.5 mm wide	0.32	6.62	5.28	**11.90**	m
225 mm wide	0.57	11.84	8.35	**20.19**	m
vertical:					
over 225 mm wide	2.27	47.32	35.94	**83.26**	m2
112.5 mm wide	0.40	8.28	5.28	**13.56**	m
225 mm wide	0.68	14.19	8.35	**22.54**	m

018 **Synthaprufe damp proof courses**

019 Three coats waterproofer on vertical brickwork or blockwork surfaces; each coat applied at the rate of 2.2 m2 per litre; final surface dusted with clean sharp sand:

over 300 mm wide	0.36	7.57	4.68	**12.25**	m2
not exceeding 150 mm wide	0.06	1.21	0.68	**1.89**	m
150-300 mm wide	0.11	2.35	1.44	**3.79**	m

020 **Preformed polypropylene/lead gable abutment cavity wall trays Type X by Cavity Trays Ltd; built into standard stepped brick courses and flush pointing as the work proceeds; including short lead flashings set projecting for dressing by others**

021 For 15 degree roof pitch:

Intermediate and catchment tray	0.09	1.94	8.00	**9.94**	Nr
Ridge tray	0.10	2.14	14.09	**16.23**	Nr

022 For 17 - 21 degree roof pitch:

Intermediate and catchment tray	0.09	1.94	6.45	**8.39**	Nr
Ridge tray	0.10	2.14	14.09	**16.23**	Nr

023 For 22 - 26 degree roof pitch:

Intermediate and catchment tray	0.08	1.71	6.02	**7.73**	Nr
Ridge tray	0.10	2.14	13.07	**15.21**	Nr

024 For 27 - 45 degree roof pitch:

Intermediate and catchment tray	0.08	1.71	5.75	**7.46**	Nr
Ridge tray	0.10	2.14	11.66	**13.80**	Nr

025 Corner catchment angle tray:

(all roof pitches)	0.10	2.14	12.17	**14.31**	Nr

Unit Rates

		Man-Hours	Net Labour Price £	Net Mats Price £	Net Unit Price £	Unit
026	**Preformed polypropylene/lead gable abutment cavity wall trays Type X by Cavity Trays Ltd; built into standard stepped brick courses and flush pointing as the work proceeds; including long lead flashings set projecting for dressing by others**					
027	For 15 degree roof pitch:					
	Intermediate and catchment tray	0.09	1.94	11.35	**13.29**	Nr
	Ridge tray	0.10	2.14	14.09	**16.23**	Nr
028	For 17 - 21 degree roof pitch:					
	Intermediate and catchment tray	0.09	1.94	8.67	**10.61**	Nr
	Ridge tray	0.10	2.14	14.09	**16.23**	Nr
029	For 22 - 26 degree roof pitch:					
	Intermediate and catchment tray	0.08	1.71	7.98	**9.69**	Nr
	Ridge tray	0.10	2.14	13.07	**15.21**	Nr
030	For 27 - 45 degree roof pitch:					
	Intermediate and catchment tray	0.08	1.71	7.38	**9.09**	Nr
	Ridge tray	0.10	2.14	11.66	**13.80**	Nr
031	Corner catchment angle tray:					
	(all roof pitches)	0.10	2.14	15.24	**17.38**	Nr
032	**Milled lead sheet code 4 to BS EN 12588:2006, (P.C. £2121.00 per tonne); bedded in cement mortar (1:3); pointing where exposed**					
033	Chimney tray:					
	Size 700 x 700 mm overall: hole for single flue with 25 mm welded turn ups: dressing down where exposed	2.40	47.00	27.66	**97.40**	Nr
	Size 1250 x 700 mm overall: hole for two flues with 25 mm welded turn ups: dressing down where exposed	4.20	82.26	49.44	**171.50**	Nr

		£	Unit
GM	**BRICKWORK**		
034	**Damp proofing existing walls**		
	The following **Specialist** Guide prices were provided by Croft Preservation Ltd, Unit 1, 14 Broom Road, Poole, Dorset, BH12 4NL (Telephone: 01202 737739, Fax: 01202 737735, E-mail: enquiries@croftpreservation.co.uk, Internet: www.croftpreservation.com)		
035	Damp proofing existing brick wall by aluminium sterate injection method (not including removal and making good plastered walls):		
	half brick wall	20.00	m
	one brick wall	28.00	m
	one and a half brick wall	32.00	m
036	Hack off and replaster wall internally to a height of 1000 mm above floor level	68.00	m

		Man-Hours	Net Labour Price £	Net Mats Price £	Net Unit Price £	Unit
037	Cut out one course of existing brickwork in alternate lengths not exceeding 1.00 m and insert damp proof course and replace with new brickwork:					
	common brickwork in gauged mortar (1:2:9):					
	half brickwall:					
	pitch polymer	1.63	33.82	3.43	**37.25**	m
	bituminous hessian based	1.63	33.82	3.54	**37.36**	m
	one brickwall:					
	pitch polymer	3.83	79.79	5.97	**85.76**	m
	bituminous hessian based	3.83	79.79	6.07	**85.86**	m
	one and a half brickwall:					
	pitch polymer	5.57	115.89	8.83	**124.72**	m
	bituminous hessian based	5.57	115.89	9.03	**124.92**	m
	common brickwork in gauged mortar (1:3):					
	half brickwall:					
	pitch polymer	1.90	39.54	3.45	**42.99**	m
	bituminous hessian based	1.90	39.54	3.56	**43.10**	m
	one brickwall:					
	pitch polymer	4.40	91.56	5.98	**97.54**	m
	bituminous hessian based	4.40	91.56	6.08	**97.64**	m
	one and a half brickwall:					
	pitch polymer	6.50	135.20	8.85	**144.05**	m
	bituminous hessian based	6.50	135.20	9.05	**144.25**	m
	facing brickwork to match existing in gauged mortar (1:2:9):					
	half brickwall:					
	pitch polymer	1.79	37.21	3.65	**40.86**	m
	bituminous hessian based	1.79	37.21	3.75	**40.96**	m
	one brickwall:					
	pitch polymer	4.20	87.40	6.40	**93.80**	m
	bituminous hessian based	4.20	87.40	6.49	**93.89**	m

Unit Rates

		Man-Hours	Net Labour Price £	Net Mats Price £	Net Unit Price £	Unit
038	Cut out one course of existing half-brick skin of cavity wall in short lengths (approx. 675 mm) and insert standard pre-formed polypropylene Type E cavitrays by Cavity Trays Ltd bedded in mortar and replace with new brickwork including wedging and pinning up with slates and inserting Type W cavity weep/ventilators at about 450 mm centres:					
	in common brickwork in cement mortar	2.20	45.78	18.71	**64.49**	m
	in facing brickwork to match existing in gauged mortar (1:2:9)	2.10	43.64	18.91	**62.55**	m
	Extra over for:					
	standard 90 degree angle	0.10	2.08	6.67	**8.75**	m
039	Cut chase 25 mm high through base of existing concrete block wall in alternate lengths not exceeding 1.00 m and insert damp proof course in gauged mortar (1:2:9):					
	75 mm thick:					
	pitch polymer	0.60	12.57	1.30	**14.22**	m
	bituminous hessian based	0.56	11.59	0.51	**12.45**	m
	100 mm thick:					
	pitch polymer	0.70	14.50	2.54	**17.55**	m
	bituminous hessian based	0.64	13.32	1.01	**14.84**	m
	150 mm thick:					
	pitch polymer	0.93	19.31	3.84	**23.82**	m
	bituminous hessian based	0.84	17.38	1.53	**19.58**	m
	200 mm thick:					
	pitch polymer	1.16	24.16	5.15	**30.17**	m
	bituminous hessian based	1.07	22.23	2.04	**25.13**	m

GN SUNDRIES

		Man-Hours	Net Labour Price £	Net Mats Price £	Net Unit Price £	Unit
001	Forming cavities not exceeding 75 mm wide; with:					
	No wall ties	0.02	0.48	-	**0.48**	m2
	3 Nr wall ties per m2:					
	200 mm stainless steel flat bar tie with expanded ends, type 1	0.04	0.73	0.90	**1.63**	m2
	200 mm stainless steel general purpose wire tie, type 2	0.04	0.73	0.39	**1.12**	m2
	200 mm stainless steel housing tie, type 4	0.04	0.73	0.20	**0.93**	m2
	75 mm stainless steel brick to timber tie	0.05	0.94	0.55	**1.49**	m2
	5 Nr wall ties per m2:					
	200 mm stainless steel flat bar tie with expanded ends, type 1	0.05	0.94	1.51	**2.45**	m2
	200 mm stainless steel general purpose wire tie, type 2	0.05	0.94	0.65	**1.59**	m2
	200 mm stainless steel housing tie, type 4	0.05	0.94	0.34	**1.28**	m2
	75 mm stainless steel brick to timber tie	0.06	1.21	0.92	**2.13**	m2
002	Closing cavities not exceeding 75 mm wide by returning:					
	102.5 mm common brickwork:					
	at jamb or end of wall	0.34	7.10	1.76	**8.86**	m
	at sill	0.46	9.47	1.76	**11.23**	m
	at top of wall	0.23	4.74	1.76	**6.50**	m
	102.5 mm Class A engineering brickwork:					
	at jamb or end of wall	0.40	8.28	2.72	**11.00**	m
	at sill	0.51	10.65	2.72	**13.37**	m
	at top of wall	0.28	5.91	2.72	**8.63**	m
	102.5 mm Class B engineering brickwork:					
	at jamb or end of wall	0.36	7.57	2.19	**9.76**	m
	at sill	0.48	9.95	2.19	**12.14**	m
	at top of wall	0.25	5.20	2.19	**7.39**	m
	102.5 mm facing brickwork:					
	at jamb or end of wall	0.46	9.47	1.97	**11.44**	m
	at sill	0.63	13.03	1.97	**15.00**	m
	at top of wall	0.34	7.10	1.97	**9.07**	m
	100 mm natural aggregate concrete blockwork:					
	at jamb or end of wall	0.23	4.74	0.78	**5.52**	m
	at sill	0.34	7.10	0.78	**7.88**	m
	at top of wall	0.17	3.56	0.78	**4.34**	m
	100 mm Thermalite blockwork:					
	at jamb or end of wall	0.17	3.56	1.14	**4.70**	m
	at sill	0.23	4.74	1.14	**5.88**	m
	at top of wall	0.11	2.35	1.14	**3.49**	m
003	**Cavity wall insulation, wedging in position between wall ties; fixing with insulation clips/discs**					
004	PIR Polyisocyanurate foam slab insulation:					
	40 mm thick	0.14	2.83	6.04	**8.87**	m2
	50 mm thick	0.14	2.83	7.67	**10.50**	m2
005	Fibreglass Drytherm fibreglass batts:					
	75 mm thick	0.14	2.83	5.07	**7.90**	m2
006	**Keying for plaster or similar in situ finishings**					
007	Raking out joints 10 mm deep as the work proceeds:					
	new brickwork	0.08	1.66	-	**1.66**	m2
	new concrete blockwork	0.04	0.73	-	**0.73**	m2
008	Rake out joints of existing brickwork 10 mm deep and hack face to form key for new plaster finish:					
	in gauged mortar	0.20	2.20	-	**2.20**	m2
	in cement mortar	0.29	3.23	-	**3.23**	m2
	Extra over:					
	hack off plaster	0.09	1.04	-	**1.04**	m2
	hack off cement rendering	0.19	2.09	-	**2.09**	m2

Unit Rates

	Man-Hours	Net Labour Price £	Net Mats Price £	Net Unit Price £	Unit
009 Rake out joints of existing brickwork 10 mm deep and repoint in gauged mortar (1:2:9):					
flush pointing in:					
Stretcher bond	0.88	18.38	0.25	**18.63**	m2
English bond	0.98	20.31	0.25	**20.56**	m2
Flemish bond	0.95	19.69	0.25	**19.94**	m2
struck pointing or bucket handle pointing in:					
Stretcher bond	0.93	19.31	0.25	**19.56**	m2
English bond	1.02	21.25	0.25	**21.50**	m2
Flemish bond	0.99	20.69	0.25	**20.94**	m2
Extra over for coloured mortar in:					
Stretcher bond	-	-	0.10	**0.10**	m2
English bond	-	-	0.10	**0.10**	m2
Flemish bond	-	-	0.10	**0.10**	m2
010 Rake out joints of existing blockwork 10 mm deep and hack face to form key for new plaster finish	0.11	1.24	-	**1.24**	m2
Extra over:					
hack off plaster	0.09	1.04	-	**1.04**	m2
hack off cement rendering	0.19	2.09	-	**2.09**	m2
011 Rake out joints of existing blockwork 10 mm deep and repoint in gauged mortar (1:2:9):					
flush pointing	0.46	9.66	0.13	**9.79**	m2
struck pointing or bucket handle pointing	0.51	10.63	0.13	**10.76**	m2
012 **Bedding in cement mortar (1:3)**					
013 Plates:					
100 mm wide	0.08	1.66	0.13	**1.79**	m
150 mm wide	0.11	2.35	0.25	**2.60**	m
014 Corrugated sheeting and the like:					
not exceeding 150 mm wide	0.16	3.33	0.38	**3.71**	m
150-300 mm wide	0.23	4.74	0.76	**5.50**	m
015 Wood frames and sills	0.23	4.74	0.13	**4.87**	m
016 Metal frames and sills	0.28	5.91	0.13	**6.04**	m
017 Pointing edges in gun-grade silicone sealant:					
one side	0.23	4.74	1.30	**6.04**	m
both sides	0.46	9.47	2.56	**12.03**	m
018 **Cutting grooves**					
019 Cutting groove for water bars and the like; grouting with cement mortar (1:3):					
new common brickwork	0.19	4.04	0.39	**4.43**	m
new engineering brickwork	0.28	5.91	0.39	**6.30**	m
new facing brickwork	0.28	5.91	0.39	**6.30**	m
new concrete blockwork	0.23	4.74	0.39	**5.13**	m
020 **Expansion joints; filling with Fillcrete joint filler**					
021 20 mm wide expansion joint in:					
common brickwork:					
102.5 mm wide	0.34	7.10	2.73	**9.83**	m
225 mm wide	0.57	11.84	5.29	**17.13**	m
engineering brickwork:					
102.5 mm wide	0.46	9.47	3.31	**12.78**	m
225 mm wide	0.85	17.75	6.25	**24.00**	m
facing brickwork:					
102.5 mm wide	0.46	9.47	2.86	**12.33**	m
225 mm wide	0.85	17.75	5.51	**23.26**	m
concrete blockwork:					
100 mm wide	0.28	5.91	2.40	**8.31**	m
140 mm wide	0.40	8.28	3.60	**11.88**	m
022 Pointing edges in gun-grade silicone sealant:					
one side	0.34	7.10	2.56	**9.66**	m
both sides	0.68	14.19	5.16	**19.35**	m
023 **Preparing for flashings and skirtings**					
024 Raking out horizontal joints for turned-in edges of flashings in new:					
brickwork	0.01	0.23	-	**0.23**	m
concrete blockwork	0.01	0.23	-	**0.23**	m
Extra over for pointing edges in cement mortar (1:3)	0.06	1.21	0.13	**1.34**	m
025 Raking out and enlarging horizontal joints for nibs of asphalt in new:					
common brickwork	0.23	4.74	-	**4.74**	m
engineering brickwork	0.28	5.91	-	**5.91**	m
facing brickwork	0.28	5.91	-	**5.91**	m
concrete blockwork	0.23	4.74	-	**4.74**	m
Extra over for pointing edges in cement mortar (1:3)	0.06	1.21	0.13	**1.34**	m
026 **Preparing old surfaces for raising**					
027 Concrete surfaces:					
not exceeding 250 mm wide	0.11	2.35	-	**2.35**	m
250 - 500 mm wide	0.11	2.35	-	**2.35**	m
500 - 1000 mm wide	0.14	2.83	-	**2.83**	m

Unit Rates

		Man-Hours	Net Labour Price £	Net Mats Price £	Net Unit Price £	Unit
028	Brickwork surfaces:					
	half brick wide	0.06	1.21	-	**1.21**	m
	one brick wide	0.08	1.66	-	**1.66**	m
	one-and-a-half brick wide	0.11	2.35	-	**2.35**	m
	two brick wide	0.15	3.08	-	**3.08**	m
029	Concrete blockwork surfaces:					
	not exceeding 150 mm wide	0.06	1.21	-	**1.21**	m
	150 - 300 mm wide	0.11	2.35	-	**2.35**	m
030	**Wedging and pinning up concealed work with slates in cement mortar (1:3)**					
031	Brick walls:					
	half brick thick	0.26	5.49	5.26	**10.75**	m
	one brick thick	0.44	9.16	7.96	**17.12**	m
	one and a half brick thick	0.68	14.19	8.94	**23.13**	m
032	Concrete block walls:					
	75 mm walls	0.22	4.58	4.41	**8.99**	m
	100 mm walls	0.26	5.49	5.26	**10.75**	m
	140 mm walls	0.36	7.55	6.25	**13.80**	m
	190 mm walls	0.47	9.84	7.10	**16.94**	m
033	Top of new lintels and underside of existing construction; thickness:					
	50 mm	0.05	0.98	4.41	**5.39**	m
	100 and 102.5 mm	0.05	0.98	5.26	**6.24**	m
	150 mm	0.07	1.37	6.25	**7.62**	m
	200 mm	0.08	1.75	7.10	**8.85**	m
	215 mm	0.09	1.94	7.96	**9.90**	m
	300 mm	0.13	2.71	8.94	**11.65**	m
	327.5 mm	0.14	2.91	8.94	**11.85**	m
	450 mm	0.19	3.87	10.06	**13.93**	m
	600 mm	0.25	5.22	11.04	**16.26**	m
034	**Wedging and pinning up exposed work with slates in cement mortar (1:3) and pointing to match existing**					
035	Fair faced brick work:					
	half brick thick	0.37	7.78	5.26	**13.04**	m
	one brick thick	0.55	11.45	7.96	**19.41**	m
	one and a half brick thick	0.79	16.48	8.94	**25.42**	m
036	Fair faced blockwork:					
	75 mm walls	0.33	6.87	4.41	**11.28**	m
	100 mm walls	0.37	7.78	5.26	**13.04**	m
	140 mm walls	0.47	9.84	6.25	**16.09**	m
	190 mm walls	0.58	12.13	7.10	**19.23**	m
037	Face brick walls:					
	half brick thick	0.39	8.01	5.26	**13.27**	m
	one brick thick	0.56	11.67	7.96	**19.63**	m
038	**Brick reinforcement and wall starters**					
039	Expamet 24 gauge galvanised brick reinforcement:					
	65 mm wide	0.23	4.74	0.69	**5.43**	m
	115 mm wide	0.28	5.91	1.19	**7.10**	m
	175 mm wide	0.28	5.91	1.86	**7.77**	m
040	Expamet stainless steel wall starters; plugging to brickwork with plugs and screws provided; bending out tie arms at 225 mm centres and building in to joints of new walls:					
	60 - 75 mm	0.14	3.00	12.92	**15.92**	m
	110 - 115 mm	0.14	3.00	10.05	**13.05**	m
	125 - 180 mm	0.27	5.58	17.57	**23.15**	m
	190 - 260 mm	0.27	5.58	21.80	**27.38**	m
041	**Building in metal windows, metal doors and the like, complete with frames; filling backs of frames and bedding in cement mortar (1:3)**					
042	Windows 300 mm high, length:					
	300 mm	0.80	16.56	0.13	**16.69**	Nr
	600 mm	0.91	18.92	0.13	**19.05**	Nr
	900 mm	0.91	18.92	0.26	**19.18**	Nr
	1200 mm	1.37	28.41	0.26	**28.67**	Nr
043	Windows 600 mm high, length:					
	300 mm	1.14	23.66	0.13	**23.79**	Nr
	600 mm	1.14	23.66	0.26	**23.92**	Nr
	900 mm	1.48	30.76	0.26	**31.02**	Nr
	1200 mm	1.71	35.50	0.39	**35.89**	Nr
	1500 mm	1.93	40.23	0.39	**40.62**	Nr
	1800 mm	2.05	42.60	0.39	**42.99**	Nr
044	Windows 900 mm high, length:					
	300 mm	1.14	23.66	0.26	**23.92**	Nr
	600 mm	1.25	26.01	0.26	**26.27**	Nr
	900 mm	1.93	40.23	0.39	**40.62**	Nr
	1200 mm	2.16	44.97	0.39	**45.36**	Nr
	1500 mm	2.27	47.32	0.39	**47.71**	Nr

	Unit Rates	Man-Hours	Net Labour Price £	Net Mats Price £	Net Unit Price £	Unit
	1800 mm	2.39	49.69	0.52	**50.21**	Nr
045	Windows 1200 mm high, length:					
	300 mm	1.25	26.01	0.26	**26.27**	Nr
	600 mm	1.37	28.41	0.39	**28.80**	Nr
	900 mm	2.05	42.60	0.39	**42.99**	Nr
	1200 mm	2.39	49.69	0.39	**50.08**	Nr
	1500 mm	2.50	52.07	0.52	**52.59**	Nr
	1800 mm	2.73	56.81	0.52	**57.33**	Nr
046	Windows 1500 mm high, length:					
	300 mm	1.37	28.41	0.39	**28.80**	Nr
	600 mm	1.59	33.13	0.39	**33.52**	Nr
	900 mm	2.39	49.69	0.39	**50.08**	Nr
	1200 mm	2.84	59.16	0.52	**59.68**	Nr
	1500 mm	3.07	63.89	0.52	**64.41**	Nr
	1800 mm	3.30	68.63	0.52	**69.15**	Nr
	2100 mm	3.64	75.73	0.65	**76.38**	Nr
047	Door frames and sidelights 2200 mm high, width:					
	900 mm	2.96	61.51	0.52	**62.03**	Nr
	1200 mm	3.07	63.89	0.65	**64.54**	Nr
	1500 mm	3.30	68.63	0.65	**69.28**	Nr
	1800 mm	3.64	75.73	0.65	**76.38**	Nr
	2100 mm	3.98	82.82	0.78	**83.60**	Nr
	2400 mm	4.55	94.64	0.78	**95.42**	Nr
048	Pointing edges of frames in silicone sealant	0.34	7.10	0.54	**7.64**	m
049	**Holes for pipes, tubes, bars, cables, conduits and the like; making good**					
050	Small pipes in new:					
	common brickwork:					
	102.5 mm	0.34	7.10	0.65	**7.75**	Nr
	215 mm	0.57	11.84	0.90	**12.74**	Nr
	327.5 mm	0.68	14.19	1.16	**15.35**	Nr
	engineering brickwork:					
	102.5 mm	0.46	9.47	0.65	**10.12**	Nr
	215 mm	0.68	14.19	0.90	**15.09**	Nr
	327.5 mm	0.80	16.56	1.16	**17.72**	Nr
	facing brickwork:					
	102.5 mm	0.57	11.84	0.64	**12.48**	Nr
	215 mm	0.80	16.56	0.89	**17.45**	Nr
	concrete blockwork:					
	75 mm	0.46	9.47	0.38	**9.85**	Nr
	100 mm	0.46	9.47	0.64	**10.11**	Nr
	150 mm	0.46	9.47	0.76	**10.23**	Nr
	200 mm	0.57	11.84	0.89	**12.73**	Nr
051	Large pipes in new:					
	common brickwork:					
	102.5 mm	0.46	9.47	0.64	**10.11**	Nr
	215 mm	0.68	14.19	0.89	**15.08**	Nr
	327.5 mm	0.80	16.56	1.15	**17.71**	Nr
	engineering brickwork:					
	102.5 mm	0.57	11.84	0.65	**12.49**	Nr
	215 mm	0.80	16.56	0.90	**17.46**	Nr
	327.5 mm	0.91	18.92	1.16	**20.08**	Nr
	facing brickwork:					
	102.5 mm	0.68	14.19	0.64	**14.83**	Nr
	215 mm	1.02	21.31	0.89	**22.20**	Nr
	concrete blockwork:					
	75 mm	0.46	9.47	0.38	**9.85**	Nr
	100 mm	0.46	9.47	0.64	**10.11**	Nr
	150 mm	0.57	11.84	0.76	**12.60**	Nr
	200 mm	0.68	14.19	0.89	**15.08**	Nr
052	Extra large pipes in new:					
	common brickwork:					
	102.5 mm	0.68	14.19	0.76	**14.95**	Nr
	215 mm	0.91	18.92	1.15	**20.07**	Nr
	327.5 mm	1.14	23.66	1.78	**25.44**	Nr
	engineering brickwork:					
	102.5 mm	0.68	14.19	0.78	**14.97**	Nr
	215 mm	1.02	21.31	1.16	**22.47**	Nr
	327.5 mm	1.37	28.41	1.81	**30.22**	Nr
	facing brickwork:					
	102.5 mm	0.91	18.92	0.76	**19.68**	Nr
	215 mm	1.14	23.66	1.15	**24.81**	Nr
	concrete blockwork:					
	75 mm	0.57	11.84	0.76	**12.60**	Nr
	100 mm	0.57	11.84	0.89	**12.73**	Nr
	150 mm	0.91	18.92	1.02	**19.94**	Nr
	200 mm	1.14	23.66	1.27	**24.93**	Nr
053	**Extra over** for building in pipe sleeves (supplied by others) into brick or block walls:					
	small	0.11	2.35	-	**2.35**	Nr
	large	0.11	2.35	-	**2.35**	Nr
	extra large	0.11	2.35	-	**2.35**	Nr

Unit Rates

		Man-Hours	Net Labour Price £	Net Mats Price £	Net Unit Price £	Unit
054	**Holes for gratings, ducting, trunking, trays and the like; making good**					
055	Holes not exceeding 0.10 m2 sectional area in new:					
	common brickwork:					
	102.5 mm	0.91	18.92	0.25	**19.17**	Nr
	215 mm	1.14	23.66	0.38	**24.04**	Nr
	327.5 mm	1.48	30.76	0.51	**31.27**	Nr
	engineering brickwork:					
	102.5 mm	1.14	23.66	0.26	**23.92**	Nr
	215 mm	1.48	30.76	0.39	**31.15**	Nr
	327.5 mm	1.93	40.23	0.52	**40.75**	Nr
	facing brickwork:					
	102.5 mm	1.14	23.66	0.25	**23.91**	Nr
	215 mm	1.48	30.76	0.38	**31.14**	Nr
	concrete blockwork:					
	75 mm	0.57	11.84	0.13	**11.97**	Nr
	100 mm	0.80	16.56	0.25	**16.81**	Nr
	150 mm	0.91	18.92	0.25	**19.17**	Nr
	200 mm	1.14	23.66	0.38	**24.04**	Nr
056	Holes 0.10 - 0.20 m2 sectional area in new:					
	common brickwork:					
	102.5 mm	1.14	23.66	0.25	**23.91**	Nr
	215 mm	1.48	30.76	0.51	**31.27**	Nr
	327.5 mm	1.71	35.50	0.76	**36.26**	Nr
	engineering brickwork:					
	102.5 mm	1.48	30.76	0.26	**31.02**	Nr
	215 mm	1.93	40.23	0.52	**40.75**	Nr
	327.5 mm	2.27	47.32	0.78	**48.10**	Nr
	facing brickwork:					
	102.5 mm	1.48	30.76	0.25	**31.01**	Nr
	215 mm	1.93	40.23	0.51	**40.74**	Nr
	concrete blockwork:					
	75 mm	0.80	16.56	0.13	**16.69**	Nr
	100 mm	1.02	21.31	0.25	**21.56**	Nr
	150 mm	1.14	23.66	0.38	**24.04**	Nr
	200 mm	1.37	28.41	0.51	**28.92**	Nr
057	Holes 0.20 - 0.30 m2 sectional area in new:					
	common brickwork:					
	102.5 mm	1.37	28.41	0.38	**28.79**	Nr
	215 mm	1.71	35.50	0.64	**36.14**	Nr
	327.5 mm	1.93	40.23	1.02	**41.25**	Nr
	engineering brickwork:					
	102.5 mm	1.71	35.50	0.39	**35.89**	Nr
	215 mm	2.16	44.97	0.65	**45.62**	Nr
	327.5 mm	2.50	52.07	1.03	**53.10**	Nr
	facing brickwork:					
	102.5 mm	1.71	35.50	0.38	**35.88**	Nr
	215 mm	2.16	44.97	0.64	**45.61**	Nr
	concrete blockwork:					
	75 mm	1.02	21.31	0.25	**21.56**	Nr
	100 mm	1.14	23.66	0.38	**24.04**	Nr
	150 mm	1.37	28.41	0.51	**28.92**	Nr
	200 mm	1.59	33.13	0.64	**33.77**	Nr
058	**Mortices; making good**					
059	Mortices in new common brickwork:					
	50 x 50 x 100 mm deep	0.23	4.74	-	**4.74**	Nr
	75 x 75 x 150 mm deep	0.28	5.91	-	**5.91**	Nr
	100 mm deep for 12 mm diameter Rawlbolts	0.11	2.35	-	**2.35**	Nr
060	Mortices in new engineering brickwork:					
	50 x 50 x 100 mm deep	0.34	7.10	-	**7.10**	Nr
	75 x 75 x 150 mm deep	0.46	9.47	-	**9.47**	Nr
	100 mm deep for 12 mm diameter Rawlbolts	0.17	3.56	-	**3.56**	Nr
061	Mortices in new facing brickwork:					
	50 x 50 x 100 mm deep	0.34	7.10	-	**7.10**	Nr
	75 x 75 x 150 mm deep	0.46	9.47	-	**9.47**	Nr
	100 mm deep for 12 mm diameter Rawlbolts	0.11	2.35	-	**2.35**	Nr
062	Mortices in new concrete blockwork:					
	50 x 50 x 100 mm deep	0.28	5.91	-	**5.91**	Nr
	75 x 75 x 150 mm deep	0.34	7.10	-	**7.10**	Nr
	100 mm deep for 12 mm diameter Rawlbolts	0.11	2.35	-	**2.35**	Nr
063	Grouting mortices in cement and sand (1:3):					
	50 x 50 x 100 mm deep	0.17	3.56	0.13	**3.69**	Nr
	75 x 75 x 150 mm deep	0.23	4.74	1.03	**5.77**	Nr
064	Running mortices with lead:					
	50 x 50 x 100 mm deep	0.34	7.10	3.97	**11.07**	Nr
	75 x 75 x 150 mm deep	0.46	9.47	14.18	**23.65**	Nr

Unit Rates	Man-Hours	Net Labour Price £	Net Mats Price £	Net Unit Price £	Unit
065 **Cut and pin ends of new lintels, arch bars, steps etc. to existing walls in**					
066 common brickwork	0.33	6.95	-	**6.95**	Nr
engineering brickwork	0.57	11.80	-	**11.80**	Nr
facing brickwork	0.50	10.43	-	**10.43**	Nr
blockwork	0.25	5.22	-	**5.22**	Nr
067 **Forming openings; slate lintel over**					
068 Opening 225 x 75 mm in new:					
brickwork:					
102.5 mm	0.23	4.74	0.54	**5.28**	Nr
215 mm	0.34	7.10	0.86	**7.96**	Nr
327.5 mm	0.46	9.47	1.71	**11.18**	Nr
concrete blockwork:					
75 mm	0.46	9.47	0.54	**10.01**	Nr
100 mm	0.57	11.84	0.54	**12.38**	Nr
150 mm	0.68	14.19	0.86	**15.05**	Nr
200 mm	0.91	18.92	0.86	**19.78**	Nr
069 Opening 225 x 150 mm in new:					
brickwork:					
102.5 mm	0.34	7.10	0.54	**7.64**	Nr
215 mm	0.46	9.47	0.86	**10.33**	Nr
327.5 mm	0.57	11.84	1.71	**13.55**	Nr
concrete blockwork:					
75 mm	0.46	9.47	0.54	**10.01**	Nr
100 mm	0.57	11.84	0.54	**12.38**	Nr
150 mm	0.68	14.19	0.86	**15.05**	Nr
200 mm	0.91	18.92	0.86	**19.78**	Nr
070 Opening 225 x 225 mm in new:					
brickwork:					
102.5 mm	0.57	11.84	0.54	**12.38**	Nr
215 mm	0.68	14.19	0.86	**15.05**	Nr
327.5 mm	0.80	16.56	1.71	**18.27**	Nr
concrete blockwork:					
75 mm	0.57	11.84	0.54	**12.38**	Nr
100 mm	0.68	14.19	0.54	**14.73**	Nr
150 mm	0.80	16.56	0.86	**17.42**	Nr
200 mm	1.02	21.31	0.86	**22.17**	Nr
071 Opening in cavity wall 275 mm thick comprising brickwork outer skin and concrete block inner skin; sealing 50 mm cavity with slates in cement mortar (1:3):					
225 x 75 mm	1.71	35.50	4.46	**39.96**	Nr
225 x 150 mm	2.05	42.60	5.54	**48.14**	Nr
225 x 225 mm	2.27	47.32	7.23	**54.55**	Nr
072 Opening in cavity wall 275 mm thick comprising brickwork outer skin and concrete block inner skin; building in terracotta cavity wall liner:					
225 x 75 mm	1.14	23.66	1.81	**25.47**	Nr
225 x 150 mm	1.48	30.76	1.98	**32.74**	Nr
225 x 225 mm	1.71	35.50	5.18	**40.68**	Nr
073 **Forming sills to openings cut in existing walls with granular faced concrete plain roofing tiles (P.C. £633.00 per 1000) bedded, jointed and pointed in cement mortar (1:3)**					
074 Double course tiles laid breaking joint:					
150 mm wide set to project 25 mm	0.70	14.50	4.11	**18.61**	m
265 mm wide set to project 50 mm	0.90	18.73	6.70	**25.43**	m
075 **Air bricks, ventilating gratings and soot doors; building in to prepared openings; pointing with cement mortar (1:3)**					
076 Terracotta air bricks, square hole pattern:					
215 x 65 mm	0.07	1.42	0.93	**2.35**	Nr
215 x 140 mm	0.08	1.66	1.29	**2.95**	Nr
215 x 215 mm	0.11	2.35	3.48	**5.83**	Nr
077 Terracotta air bricks, louvre pattern:					
215 x 65 mm	0.07	1.42	1.08	**2.50**	Nr
215 x 140 mm	0.08	1.66	1.77	**3.43**	Nr
215 x 215 mm	0.11	2.35	4.17	**6.52**	Nr
078 Cut out defective air brick and replace with new; make good; bed and point in cement mortar (1:3):					
cast iron:					
225 x 75 mm	0.33	6.78	1.21	**7.99**	Nr
225 x 150 mm	0.42	8.72	1.90	**10.62**	Nr
terracotta:					
220 x 70 mm	0.33	6.78	1.06	**7.84**	Nr
220 x 145 mm	0.42	8.72	1.42	**10.14**	Nr
fibrous plaster:					
225 x 75 mm	0.28	5.79	1.22	**7.01**	Nr
225 x 150 mm	0.37	7.72	2.14	**9.86**	Nr
079 Aluminium double soot doors:					
229 x 150 mm	0.17	3.56	43.75	**47.31**	Nr
229 x 229 mm	0.28	5.91	55.19	**61.10**	Nr

	Unit Rates	Man-Hours	Net Labour Price £	Net Mats Price £	Net Unit Price £	Unit
GO						
	FLUES, LININGS, CHIMNEY POTS, FIREBACKS ETC.					
001	**Flue linings, clay, BS EN1457**					
002	Class A1: rebated joints in refactory mortar (1:4):					
	185 mm diameter	0.30	6.24	29.03	**35.27**	m
	Extra over for:					
	bend	0.18	3.75	11.34	**15.09**	Nr
	185 x 185 mm square	0.30	6.24	24.18	**30.42**	m
	Extra over for:					
	bend	0.18	3.75	14.22	**17.97**	Nr
	200 x 200 mm square	0.32	6.56	36.78	**43.34**	m
	Extra over for:					
	bend	0.19	3.93	15.72	**19.65**	Nr
	210 mm diameter	0.32	6.56	36.02	**42.58**	m
	Extra over for:					
	bend	0.19	3.93	21.16	**25.09**	Nr
	225 mm diameter	0.33	6.88	37.43	**44.31**	m
	Extra over for:					
	bend	0.20	4.13	16.03	**20.16**	Nr
	225 x 225 mm square	0.35	7.23	43.88	**51.11**	m
	Extra over for:					
	bend	0.21	4.34	28.06	**32.40**	Nr
	250 mm diameter	0.36	7.59	47.52	**55.11**	m
	Extra over for:					
	bend	0.22	4.55	26.53	**31.08**	Nr
	250 x 250 mm square	0.38	7.97	49.94	**57.91**	m
	Extra over for:					
	bend	0.23	4.78	36.69	**41.47**	Nr
	300 mm diameter	0.38	7.97	75.35	**83.32**	m
	Extra over for:					
	bend	0.23	4.78	40.54	**45.32**	Nr
	300 x 300 mm square	0.38	7.97	84.79	**92.76**	m
	Extra over for:					
	bend	0.23	4.78	45.92	**50.70**	Nr
003	Precast concrete fireplace units: bedded and jointed in refactory cement mortar (1:4):					
	Lintel	0.48	9.89	58.55	**68.44**	Nr
	Corbel Unit:					
	800 mm	0.48	9.89	53.74	**63.63**	Nr
	1000 mm	0.48	9.89	64.88	**74.77**	Nr
	Flue adaptor for circular flue:					
	185 mm diameter	0.48	9.89	25.85	**35.74**	Nr
	210 mm diameter	0.48	9.89	26.48	**36.37**	Nr
	225 mm diameter	0.48	9.89	25.85	**35.74**	Nr
	250 mm diameter	0.48	9.89	42.59	**52.48**	Nr
	300 mm diameter	0.48	9.89	42.39	**52.28**	Nr
	Flue adaptor for square flue:					
	185 x 185 mm	0.48	9.89	26.48	**36.37**	Nr
	210 x 210 mm	0.48	9.89	26.48	**36.37**	Nr
	225 x 225 mm	0.48	9.89	29.20	**39.09**	Nr
	250 x 250 mm	0.48	9.89	42.39	**52.28**	Nr
	300 x 300 mm	0.48	9.89	42.59	**52.48**	Nr
004	**Dunbrik 'Mini Clearflow' flue blocks for for gas appliances; bedding and jointing together with Fluejoint compound; building in to brick-work or block walls**					
005	Gas Flue Blocks:					
	Standard recess starter block, 3 per flue, 1ZM	0.30	6.24	4.01	**10.25**	Nr
	Gathering block for standard recess, 2GM	0.36	7.49	8.16	**15.65**	Nr
	Straight bonded gas flue block, 225 mm high, 2M	0.18	3.75	5.78	**9.53**	Nr
	Straight bonded gas flue block, 150 mm high, 2M/150	0.12	2.50	4.57	**7.07**	Nr
	Straight bonded gas flue block, 75mm high, 2M/75	0.12	2.50	4.57	**7.07**	Nr
	Straight gas flue block, 225 mm high, 2MN	0.18	3.75	5.78	**9.53**	Nr
	Straight gas flue block, 150 mm high, 2MN/150	0.18	3.75	4.57	**8.32**	Nr
	Straight gas flue block, 75mm high, 2MN/75	0.18	3.75	4.57	**8.32**	Nr
	Side exit block, 5M	0.24	4.99	16.92	**21.91**	Nr
	Back offset, 3MU	0.24	4.99	17.93	**22.92**	Nr
	Top exit, 4M	0.24	4.99	11.84	**16.83**	Nr
	Lateral offset, 3ME	0.30	6.24	6.39	**12.63**	Nr
	Double tongue block, 2MDT190	0.18	3.75	5.78	**9.53**	Nr
	Backset block, 125mm, 2BM	0.18	3.75	17.93	**21.68**	Nr
	Insulated damp proofing mat fixed in cavity	0.21	4.37	7.99	**12.36**	m2
006	**Chimney pots; setting and flaunching in cement mortar (1:3)**					
007	Tapered roll top chimney pot:					
	300 mm long	0.36	7.49	12.30	**19.79**	Nr
	450 mm long	0.36	7.49	14.17	**21.66**	Nr
	600 mm long	0.36	7.49	20.33	**27.82**	Nr
	900 mm long	0.36	7.49	36.15	**43.64**	Nr
008	Canon head chimney pot:					
	300 mm long	0.36	7.49	15.56	**23.05**	Nr
	450 mm long	0.36	7.49	18.59	**26.08**	Nr
	600 mm long	0.36	7.49	26.40	**33.89**	Nr

Unit Rates

		Man-Hours	Net Labour Price £	Net Mats Price £	Net Unit Price £	Unit
009	Ornamental chimney pots:					
	Barrel top 600 mm	0.36	7.49	94.71	**102.20**	Nr
	Barrel top 750 mm	0.36	7.49	97.74	**105.23**	Nr
	Barrel top 900 mm	0.36	7.49	106.95	**114.44**	Nr
	Bishop pot 600 mm	0.36	7.49	150.56	**158.05**	Nr
	Bishop pot 750 mm	0.36	7.49	171.10	**178.59**	Nr
010	Stell 125 gas terminal:					
	Pot insert	0.60	12.49	45.03	**57.52**	Nr
011	**Fire clay firebacks; bedding solidly in refractory mortar (1:4)**					
012	Firebacks to BS 1251:					
	400 mm	1.20	24.97	28.68	**53.65**	Nr
	450 mm	1.20	24.97	32.96	**57.93**	Nr
013	Otty fireback hoods:					
	400 mm	0.36	7.49	15.11	**22.60**	Nr
	450 mm	0.36	7.49	16.03	**23.52**	Nr
014	**Fireplaces**					
015	Fire surrounds and hearths:					
	910 mm long granite hearth bedded in cement mortar (1:3)	0.80	16.66	51.81	**68.47**	Nr
	Plain limestone fire surround, assembled and fixed to masonry	2.70	56.19	258.09	**314.28**	Nr
	Plain cast iron fire surround, assembled and fixed to masonry	2.10	43.70	72.74	**116.44**	Nr
	Ornate timber fire surround, assembled and fixed to masonry	2.10	43.70	210.43	**254.13**	Nr
016	**Stoves and grates: setting in fireplace openings: jointing components in fire cement**					
017	'Ashton' cast iron bottom grates and vitreous enamel frets in copper lustre finish:					
	400 mm	0.12	2.50	35.65	**38.15**	Nr
	450 mm	0.18	3.75	43.70	**47.45**	Nr
018	'Parkray' appliances:					
	'Parkray Inset' fire to suit 400 mm opening with overnight burning plate	0.30	6.24	79.17	**85.41**	Nr
	'Parkray 10' open fire cast iron boiler and standard boiler unit	3.60	74.92	171.19	**246.11**	Nr
	'Parkray 24' open fire high output boiler unit 400 mm	4.80	99.89	392.31	**492.20**	Nr
	'77 Inset Roomheater Consort' with high output boiler	6.00	124.86	822.25	**947.11**	Nr

GP

CENTERING

The prices for **making** centering allow for ONE use of materials and where multiple uses are possible the Net Labour, Material and Total Unit Prices should be divided by the number of uses and allowance made for waste in use of both labour and materials as follows

Nr of uses	Waste in use
up to 4	Nil
5 to 6	10%
7 to 8	15%
9 to 10	17.5%
11 to 12	20%

No adjustment should be made to **fixing** prices as these apply irrespective of the number of uses.

		Man-Hours	Net Labour Price £	Net Mats Price £	Net Unit Price £	Unit
001	Centering to flat soffits:					
	not exceeding 2.00 m span, over 0.30 m wide:					
	making	0.57	8.65	66.60	**75.25**	m2
	fixing	1.34	20.35	9.46	**29.81**	m2
	2.50 m span, 0.30 m wide:					
	making	0.68	10.37	63.05	**73.42**	Nr
	fixing	1.55	23.48	9.46	**32.94**	Nr
	2.50 m span, 0.60 m wide:					
	making	1.02	15.57	76.85	**92.42**	Nr
	fixing	1.85	28.18	9.46	**37.64**	Nr
	3.00 m span, 0.30 m wide:					
	making	0.91	13.82	76.45	**90.27**	Nr
	fixing	1.65	25.05	9.46	**34.51**	Nr
	3.00 m span, 0.60 m wide:					
	making	1.14	17.28	101.68	**118.96**	Nr
	fixing	2.06	31.31	18.91	**50.22**	Nr
002	Centering to segmental arches:					
	900 mm span, 112.5 mm wide, 50 mm rise:					
	making	0.34	5.18	10.56	**15.74**	Nr
	fixing	0.52	7.83	-	**7.83**	Nr
	1200 mm span, 112.5 mm wide, 75 mm rise:					
	making	0.46	6.92	12.30	**19.22**	Nr
	fixing	0.62	9.39	-	**9.39**	Nr
	1500 mm span, 112.5 mm wide, 100 mm rise:					
	making	0.51	7.78	15.37	**23.15**	Nr
	fixing	0.93	14.09	-	**14.09**	Nr
	900 mm span, 225 mm wide, 50 mm rise:					
	making	0.57	8.65	21.12	**29.77**	Nr
	fixing	1.03	15.66	-	**15.66**	Nr
	1200 mm span, 225 mm wide, 75 mm rise:					
	making	0.68	10.37	25.54	**35.91**	Nr
	fixing	1.24	18.79	-	**18.79**	Nr
	1500 mm span, 225 mm wide, 100 mm rise:					
	making	0.85	12.97	31.69	**44.66**	Nr
	fixing	1.55	23.48	-	**23.48**	Nr

Unit Rates	Man-Hours	Net Labour Price £	Net Mats Price £	Net Unit Price £	Unit
003 Centering to semi-circular arches:					
900 mm diameter, 112.5 mm wide:					
making	3.07	46.67	10.56	**57.23**	Nr
fixing	1.34	20.35	-	**20.35**	Nr
1200 mm diameter, 112.5 mm wide:					
making	3.53	53.58	21.12	**74.70**	Nr
fixing	1.85	28.18	-	**28.18**	Nr
900 mm diameter, 225 mm wide:					
making	4.09	62.22	31.69	**93.91**	Nr
fixing	2.37	36.01	-	**36.01**	Nr
1200 mm diameter, 225 mm wide:					
making	4.55	69.13	42.25	**111.38**	Nr
fixing	2.78	42.27	-	**42.27**	Nr
004 Centering to bullseye arches and surrounds:					
600 mm diameter, 112.5 mm wide:					
making	3.41	51.85	10.56	**62.41**	Nr
fixing	1.03	15.66	-	**15.66**	Nr
900 mm diameter, 112.5 mm wide:					
making	3.98	60.50	16.32	**76.82**	Nr
fixing	1.55	23.48	-	**23.48**	Nr
600 mm diameter, 225 mm wide:					
making	4.55	69.13	21.12	**90.25**	Nr
fixing	1.24	18.79	-	**18.79**	Nr
900 mm diameter, 225 mm wide:					
making	5.69	86.43	26.88	**113.31**	Nr
fixing	1.85	28.18	-	**28.18**	Nr

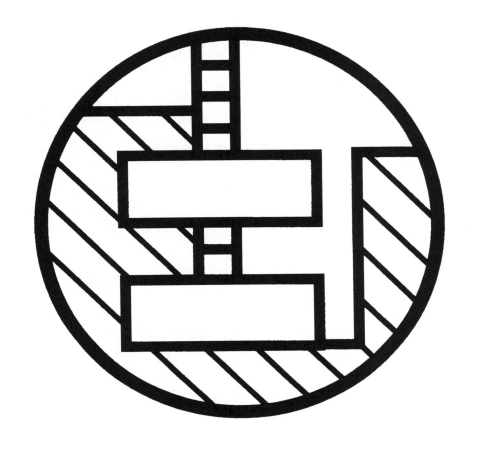

Underpinning

BCIS

Independent cost information
for the built environment

BCIS is the Building Cost Information Service of  **RICS** the mark of property professionalism worldwide

UNDERPINNING
Notes

The prices in this section are for underpinning work carried out in sections not exceeding 1200 mm long with no more than three sections being worked at one time. The prices apply to work carried out on one or both sides of the work being underpinned, within or immediately adjacent to the existing buildings with restricted working space. Such work will normally be carried out under the supervision of a structural engineer. On most sites, the conditions will entail the excavating and associated works being carried out by hand but since some sites may accommodate the use of light machinery (mini-excavators, dumpers etc.) a selection of items has been included to enable estimates to be prepared where such machinery can be fully or partially utilised. (See also notes included under Section D - Excavation and Earthwork). The rates for excavation work in this Section allow for excavating in firm earth. For other types of ground, additions should be made to prices for hand excavation and for machine excavation respectively. (See items DB001 and DG001 in Section D - Excavation and Earthwork).

Labour Rates

Please note: The labour hours throughout this section are representative of the time required for one productive man to carry out the unit of work.

Gang rates are calculated as follows by obtaining the overall gang cost and then dividing this by the number of productive members in the gang. The resulting rate is the Gang Cost per **Man - hour**. By using the same principle, any size gang may be built-up and used against the standard labour hours in this section.

Excavation generally
Labourer (BATJIC Oper. Rate) - £11.22 per hour

Labourers using air or electric percussion drills, hammers, rammers etc.
Labourer (skill rate A) - £11.82 per hour

Earthwork support
Labourer (semi skill A) - £14.02 per hour

Plain concrete
Concretor - £11.22 per hour

A0201 Reinforced concrete

Shuttering Carpenter	1.00	x	£	15.20	=	£	15.20
Concretor	4.00	x	£	11.22	=	£	44.88
Poker vibrator	3.00	x	£	4.68	=	£	14.04
Total hourly cost of gang					=	£	74.12

Gang rate (divided by 4) = £18.53 per Man-hour

Reinforcement
Craftsman (BATJIC Craft Rate) - £15.20 per hour

Formwork (making)
Shuttering Carpenter - £15.20 per hour

A0203 Formwork (fixing and striking)

Shuttering Carpenter	4.00	x	£	15.20	=	£	60.80
Formwork Labourer	1.00	x	£	11.22	=	£	11.22
Total hourly cost of gang					=	£	72.02

Gang rate (divided by 4) = £18.01 per Man-hour

A0204 Brickwork

Brick/Block Layer	2.00	x	£	15.20	=	£	30.40
Brick/Blockwork Labourer	1.00	x	£	11.22	=	£	11.22
Total hourly cost of gang					=	£	41.62

Gang rate (divided by 2) = 20.81 per Man-hour

Plant Hire Charges

		Daily Hire Charge £	Pro-ductive Hours Hrs	Cost Per Hour £	Operator Per Hour £	Fuel Per Hour £	Total Cost Per Hour £
	The hire charges shown exclude the cost of operators and fuel but are inclusive of oil, grease and the like. Fuel costs have been added in the following table as appropriate and the cost of operators has been allowed for in the labour rates given in the individual items of work.						
	The cost of delivery to, or collection from site is EXCLUDED and allowance for this should be made in Preliminaries.						
A0025	Mini-excavator (hydraulic)	60.00	6.00	10.00	14.38	4.31	**28.69**
A0026	Hydraulic breaking equipment for mini-excavator	45.00	6.00	7.50	-	-	**7.50**
A0041	16 Tonne tipper truck (inclusive of driver and fuel)	224.00	8.00	28.00	-	-	**28.00**
A0061	Whacker (hand held vibration rammer)	16.50	6.00	2.75	-	0.86	**3.61**
A0063	Compressor 100 cfm and one breaker	32.00	6.00	5.33	-	0.86	**6.19**
A0101	Bar bending and shearing machine (diesel)	16.50	6.00	2.75	-	1.66	**4.41**
A0200	Tipping charges (per load)	110.00	1.00	110.00	-	-	**110.00**

Basic Prices of Materials

		Supply Price £	Waste Factor %	Unload. Labour £	Unload. Plant £	Total Unit Cost £	Unit
	Basic Prices of Materials						
A0331	Fine aggregate	29.64	10%	-	-	32.60	tonne
A0351	Hardcore (P.C. price)	18.11	-	-	-	18.11	m3
A0347	Gravel 20 mm down	32.38	10%	-	-	35.62	tonne
A0361	Timber for earthwork support	280.30	5%	11.22	-	306.09	m3
F0453	Concrete grade C20/25	90.43	5%	-	-	94.95	m3
	Hot rolled deformed high tensile steel reinforcement bars to BS 4449 in standard lengths (not exceeding 12m), cut, bent, bundled and labelled (25 to under 100 tonnes):						
F0322	8 mm	875.00	2.5%	22.44	-	919.88	tonne
F0323	10 mm	854.00	2.5%	22.44	-	898.35	tonne
F0324	12 mm	831.00	2.5%	22.44	-	874.78	tonne
F0325	16 mm	788.00	2.5%	22.44	-	830.70	tonne
F0326	20 mm	766.00	2.5%	22.44	-	808.15	tonne
F0327	25 mm	750.00	2.5%	22.44	-	791.75	tonne
	Cutting, bending and labelling, cost only of reinforcing bars:						
F0329	8 mm	180.00	-	-	-	180.00	tonne
F0330	10 mm	115.00	-	-	-	115.00	tonne
F0331	12 mm	80.00	-	-	-	80.00	tonne
F0332	16 mm	45.00	-	-	-	45.00	tonne
F0333	20 mm	28.00	-	-	-	28.00	tonne
F0334	25 mm	20.00	-	-	-	20.00	tonne
F0335	Tying wire	1.38	10%	-	-	1.52	kg
F0260	Sawn softwood for formwork	295.00	12.5%	11.22	-	344.50	m3
F0261	19 mm plywood for formwork	8.60	10%	2.81	-	12.55	m2
F0263	Nails	2.90	10%	-	-	3.19	kg
F0266	Formwork oil	1.54	20%	-	-	1.85	ltr
F0491	Net deduct for stock bars 8 mm	126.00	2.5%	-	-	129.15	tonne
F0492	Net deduct for stock bars 10 mm	80.50	2.5%	-	-	82.51	tonne
F0493	Net deduct for stock bars 12 mm	56.00	2.5%	-	-	57.40	tonne
F0494	Net deduct for stock bars 16 mm	31.50	2.5%	-	-	32.29	tonne
F0495	Net deduct for stock bars 20 mm	19.60	2.5%	-	-	20.09	tonne
F0496	Net deduct for stock bars 25 mm	14.00	2.5%	-	-	14.35	tonne
G0102	Common bricks	311.01	5%	-	-	326.56	1000
G0103	Class A engineering bricks	493.42	5%	-	-	518.09	1000
G0104	Class B engineering bricks	391.75	5%	-	-	411.33	1000
G0269	Hessian base dpc	9.25	5%	-	-	9.71	m2
G0270	Fibre base dpc	7.28	5%	-	-	7.64	m2
G0274	230 x 225 mm slates	759.00	10%	18.51	-	855.26	1000
G0275	Hyload dpc	6.17	5%	-	-	6.48	m2
G0292	Hyload contact adhesive	17.13	10%	-	-	18.84	ltr
G0293	Hyload mastic	14.70	10%	-	-	16.17	ltr
G0295	Synthaprufe waterproofer	2.95	5%	-	-	3.09	ltr
F0516	Conbextra GP grout	0.34	10%	0.04	-	0.42	kg

Plant and Equipment Hours

The abbreviations under the headings on the succeeding pages have the following meanings:

    Excav = Excavating plant (JCB, Cat, etc.)
    Brkng = Breaking equipment (Hymac 580, breaker etc.)
    Cmptg = Compacting equipment (Whacker, roller etc.)
    Trans = Transportation plant (Dumper, lorry etc.)

Mortar Mix Analysis

Mortar Mix Analysis

The cost of labour in mixing mortar is included in the rate per hour of the gang. The cost of mixers or mortar mills should be costed in Preliminaries. The prices of 1 m3 of mortar are calculated as follows:

A0511 Cement mortar (1:3)

Cement (bagged)	0.44 tonne	x	£	156.48	=	£	68.85
Building sand	1.83 tonne	x	£	26.57	=	£	48.62
						£	117.47
Waste	10%				=	£	11.75
Cost per m3					=	£	**129.22**

Unit Rates	Man-Hours	Net Labour Price £	Net Mats Price £	Net Unit Price £	Unit
UNIT RATES					
EXCAVATION BY HAND					
001 **Excavating starting at natural or reduced ground level**					
002 Excavating preliminary trenches down to the level of the base of the existing foundation, maximum depth not exceeding:					
0.25 m	3.60	40.38	-	**40.38**	m3
1.00 m	3.96	44.42	-	**44.42**	m3
2.00 m	4.98	55.86	-	**55.86**	m3
4.00 m	6.23	69.82	-	**69.82**	m3
003 Excavating below the level of the base of the existing foundation, commencing depth below surface level:					
0.25 m, maximum depth not exceeding:					
0.25 m	4.50	50.47	-	**50.47**	m3
1.00 m	5.64	63.26	-	**63.26**	m3
2.00 m	7.14	80.08	-	**80.08**	m3
1.00 m, maximum depth not exceeding:					
0.25 m	5.64	63.26	-	**63.26**	m3
1.00 m	5.64	63.26	-	**63.26**	m3
2.00 m	7.14	80.08	-	**80.08**	m3
2.00 m, maximum depth not exceeding:					
0.25 m	7.14	80.08	-	**80.08**	m3
1.00 m	7.14	80.08	-	**80.08**	m3
2.00 m	9.30	104.31	-	**104.31**	m3
004 **Excavating starting 1.00 m below general ground level**					
005 Excavating preliminary trenches down to the level of the base of the existing foundation, maximum depth not exceeding:					
0.25 m	3.96	44.42	-	**44.42**	m3
1.00 m	4.98	55.86	-	**55.86**	m3
2.00 m	6.30	70.66	-	**70.66**	m3
4.00 m	10.50	117.77	-	**117.77**	m3
006 Excavating below the level of the base of the existing foundation, commencing depth below surface level:					
0.25 m, maximum depth not exceeding:					
0.25 m	5.64	63.26	-	**63.26**	m3
1.00 m	7.14	80.08	-	**80.08**	m3
2.00 m	9.30	104.31	-	**104.31**	m3
1.00 m, maximum depth not exceeding:					
0.25 m	7.14	80.08	-	**80.08**	m3
1.00 m	7.14	80.08	-	**80.08**	m3
2.00 m	9.30	104.31	-	**104.31**	m3
2.00 m, maximum depth not exceeding:					
0.25 m	9.30	104.31	-	**104.31**	m3
1.00 m	9.30	104.31	-	**104.31**	m3
2.00 m	11.88	133.25	-	**133.25**	m3
007 **Excavating starting 2.00 m below general ground level**					
008 Excavating preliminary trenches down to the level of the base of the existing foundation, maximum depth not exceeding:					
0.25 m	4.98	55.86	-	**55.86**	m3
1.00 m	6.30	70.66	-	**70.66**	m3
2.00 m	8.16	91.52	-	**91.52**	m3
4.00 m	13.74	154.11	-	**154.11**	m3
009 Excavating below the level of the base of the existing foundation, commencing depth below surface level:					
0.25 m, maximum depth not exceeding:					
0.25 m	7.14	80.08	-	**80.08**	m3
1.00 m	9.30	104.31	-	**104.31**	m3
2.00 m	11.88	133.25	-	**133.25**	m3
1.00 m, maximum depth not exceeding:					
0.25 m	9.30	104.31	-	**104.31**	m3
1.00 m	9.30	104.31	-	**104.31**	m3
2.00 m	11.88	133.25	-	**133.25**	m3
2.00 m, maximum depth not exceeding:					
0.25 m	11.88	133.25	-	**133.25**	m3
1.00 m	11.88	133.25	-	**133.25**	m3
2.00 m	15.60	174.97	-	**174.97**	m3
010 **Excavating starting 3.00 m below general ground level**					
011 Excavating preliminary trenches down to the level of the base of the existing foundation, maximum depth not exceeding:					
0.25 m	6.24	69.93	-	**69.93**	m3
1.00 m	7.79	87.35	-	**87.35**	m3
2.00 m	10.12	113.55	-	**113.55**	m3
4.00 m	16.91	189.63	-	**189.63**	m3
012 Excavating below the level of the base of the existing foundation, commencing depth below surface level:					
0.25 m, maximum depth not exceeding:					
0.25 m	7.85	88.04	-	**88.04**	m3
1.00 m	10.20	114.46	-	**114.46**	m3

Unit Rates

	Man-Hours	Net Labour Price £	Net Mats Price £	Net Unit Price £	Unit
2.00 m	13.01	145.93	-	**145.93**	m3
1.00 m, maximum depth not exceeding:					
0.25 m	10.20	114.46	-	**114.46**	m3
1.00 m	13.01	145.93	-	**145.93**	m3
2.00 m	16.59	186.07	-	**186.07**	m3
2.00 m, maximum depth not exceeding:					
0.25 m	13.01	145.93	-	**145.93**	m3
1.00 m	16.59	186.07	-	**186.07**	m3
2.00 m	21.15	237.23	-	**237.23**	m3

	Man-Hours	Excav Hours	Brkng Hours	Cmptg Hours	Trans Hours	Net Labour Price £	Net Plant Price £	Net Mats Price £	Net Unit Price £	Unit
013 Working space										
014 Excavating for working space (in any position); filling (by hand) with material arising from the excavations compacted with Whacker in 250 mm layers; maximum depth not exceeding:										
0.25 m	5.25	-	-	0.22	-	58.89	0.79	-	**59.68**	m3
1.00 m	6.00	-	-	0.22	-	67.30	0.79	-	**68.09**	m3
2.00 m	7.20	-	-	0.22	-	80.76	0.79	-	**81.55**	m3
015 **Extra over** excavating and back-filling working space (in any position) for filling with imported materials and depositing excavated material in spoil heaps or skips not exceeding 50 m from excavation:										
sand	2.20	0.22	-	-	0.27	24.68	28.29	59.98	**112.95**	m3
hardcore	3.20	0.22	-	-	0.27	35.89	28.29	23.54	**87.72**	m3
gravel (15 mm down)	2.40	0.22	-	-	0.27	26.92	28.29	66.96	**122.17**	m3

		Man-Hours	Plant Hours	Net Labour Price £	Net Plant Price £	Net Mats Price £	Net Unit Price £	Unit
HB	**BREAKING UP PAVINGS ON THE SURFACE OF THE GROUND BY HAND**							
001	**Extra over excavations (in any position) for breaking up hard materials on the surface of the ground (using hand held compressor tools)**							
002	Tarmacadam paving:							
	50 mm	0.11	0.11	1.30	0.68	-	**1.98**	m2
	100 mm	0.22	0.22	2.60	1.36	-	**3.96**	m2
003	Plain concrete paving:							
	100 mm	0.45	0.45	5.32	2.79	-	**8.11**	m2
	150 mm	0.80	0.80	9.46	4.95	-	**14.41**	m2
	200 mm	1.15	1.15	13.59	7.12	-	**20.71**	m2
004	Reinforced concrete paving:							
	100 mm	0.80	0.80	9.46	4.95	-	**14.41**	m2
	150 mm	1.30	1.30	15.37	8.05	-	**23.42**	m2
	200 mm	1.85	1.85	21.87	11.46	-	**33.33**	m2
HC	**EXCAVATING IN ROCK; BREAKING OUT OBSTRUCTIONS MET WITH IN EXCAVATIONS (BY HAND USING HAND HELD COMPRESSOR TOOLS)**							
	Note: The following prices are given 'Full value'. If items in Bills of Quantities are described as **'Extra over** excavation in normal ground' the prices for items under sections HA and HD should be DEDUCTED from the following prices:							
001	**Excavating starting at natural ground or reduced ground level**							
002	Excavating in SOFT ROCK or BRICKWORK in any position, maximum depth not exceeding:							
	0.25 m	7.08	2.40	83.69	14.86	-	**98.55**	m3
	1.00 m	7.20	2.50	85.11	15.48	-	**100.59**	m3
	2.00 m	8.58	2.65	101.42	16.41	-	**117.83**	m3
	4.00 m	12.42	2.90	146.81	17.96	-	**164.77**	m3
	6.00 m	18.66	3.10	220.57	19.20	-	**239.77**	m3
003	**Excavating starting 1.00 m below general ground level**							
004	Excavating in SOFT ROCK or BRICKWORK in any position, maximum depth not exceeding:							
	0.25 m	8.46	2.55	100.00	15.79	-	**115.79**	m3
	1.00 m	8.58	2.65	101.42	16.41	-	**117.83**	m3
	2.00 m	10.14	2.75	119.86	17.03	-	**136.89**	m3
	4.00 m	15.00	3.00	177.31	18.58	-	**195.89**	m3
	6.00 m	23.76	3.25	280.85	20.13	-	**300.98**	m3

Unit Rates	Man-Hours	Plant Hours	Net Labour Price £	Net Plant Price £	Net Mats Price £	Net Unit Price £	Unit
005 **Excavating starting 2.00 m below general ground level**							
006 Excavating in SOFT ROCK or BRICKWORK in any position, maximum depth not exceeding:							
0.25 m	10.02	2.65	118.44	16.41	-	**134.85**	m3
1.00 m	10.14	2.75	119.86	17.03	-	**136.89**	m3
2.00 m	12.42	2.90	146.81	17.96	-	**164.77**	m3
4.00 m	18.66	3.10	220.57	19.20	-	**239.77**	m3
6.00 m	30.60	3.35	361.70	20.75	-	**382.45**	m3
007 **Excavating starting 3.00 m below general ground level**							
008 Excavating in SOFT ROCK or BRICKWORK in any position, maximum depth not exceeding:							
0.25 m	12.30	2.80	145.39	17.34	-	**162.73**	m3
1.00 m	12.42	2.90	146.81	17.96	-	**164.77**	m3
2.00 m	15.00	3.00	177.31	18.58	-	**195.89**	m3
4.00 m	23.76	3.25	280.85	20.13	-	**300.98**	m3
6.00 m	40.14	3.50	474.47	21.68	-	**496.15**	m3

	Man-Hours	Excav Hours	Brkng Hours	Cmptg Hours	Trans Hours	Net Labour Price £	Net Plant Price £	Net Mats Price £	Net Unit Price £	Unit
009 **Extra over** excavations for working space (in any position) for breaking up hard material (using hand held compressor tools) filling (by hand) with material arising from the excavations; compacted with Whacker in 250 mm layers:										
soft rock or brickwork	4.80	3.50	-	0.22	-	56.74	22.47	-	**79.21**	m3

	Man-Hours	Plant Hours	Net Labour Price £	Net Plant Price £	Net Mats Price £	Net Unit Price £	Unit
HD **EXCAVATION BY MACHINE**							
001 **Excavating starting at natural or reduced ground level**							
002 Excavating preliminary trenches down to the level of the base of the existing foundation, maximum depth not exceeding:							
0.25 m	0.32	0.26	3.55	8.99	-	**12.54**	m3
1.00 m	0.21	0.18	2.36	5.98	-	**8.34**	m3
2.00 m	0.22	0.19	2.49	6.32	-	**8.81**	m3
003 **Excavating starting 1.00 m below general ground level**							
004 Excavating preliminary trenches down to the level of the base of the existing foundation, maximum depth not exceeding:							
0.25 m	0.41	0.34	4.62	11.72	-	**16.34**	m3
1.00 m	0.30	0.25	3.38	8.58	-	**11.96**	m3
2.00 m	0.31	0.26	3.51	8.92	-	**12.43**	m3
005 **Excavating starting 2.00 m below general ground level**							
006 Excavating preliminary trenches down to the level of the base of the existing foundation, maximum depth not exceeding:							
0.25 m	0.45	0.37	5.02	12.75	-	**17.77**	m3
1.00 m	0.33	0.28	3.71	9.43	-	**13.14**	m3
2.00 m	0.35	0.29	3.87	9.81	-	**13.68**	m3
Note: 007 - 008 not used							
009 **Working space**							
010 Excavating for working space (in any position); filling (by hand) with material arising from the excavations compacted with Whacker in 250 mm layers; maximum depth not exceeding:							
0.25 m	14.10	5.75	166.67	35.61	-	**202.28**	m3
1.00 m	14.22	5.85	168.09	36.23	-	**204.32**	m3
2.00 m	16.44	6.10	194.33	37.78	-	**232.11**	m3

	Man-Hours	Excav Hours	Brkng Hours	Cmptg Hours	Trans Hours	Net Labour Price £	Net Plant Price £	Net Mats Price £	Net Unit Price £	Unit
011 **Extra over** excavating and back-filling working space (in any position) for filling with imported materials and depositing excavated material in spoil heaps or skips not exceeding 50 m from excavation:										
sand	2.20	0.22	-	-	0.27	24.68	28.29	59.98	**112.95**	m3
hardcore	3.20	0.22	-	-	0.27	35.89	28.29	23.54	**87.72**	m3
gravel (15 mm down)	2.40	0.22	-	-	0.27	26.92	28.29	66.96	**122.17**	m3

Unit Rates	Man-Hours	Excav Hours	Brkng Hours	Cmptg Hours	Trans Hours	Net Labour Price £	Net Plant Price £	Net Mats Price £	Net Unit Price £	Unit
HE BREAKING UP PAVINGS ON THE SURFACE OF THE GROUND BY MACHINE										
001 **Extra over excavations (in any position) for breaking up hard materials on the surface of the ground (using hydraulic breaker equipment)**										
002 Tarmacadam paving:										
50 mm	-	0.05	-	-	-	-	1.01	-	**1.01**	m2
100 mm	-	0.07	-	-	-	-	1.37	-	**1.37**	m2
003 Plain concrete paving:										
100 mm	0.05	0.06	-	-	0.20	0.56	6.65	-	**7.21**	m2
150 mm	0.08	0.08	-	-	0.26	0.90	8.68	-	**9.58**	m2
200 mm	0.10	0.10	-	-	0.32	1.12	10.70	-	**11.82**	m2
004 Reinforced concrete paving:										
100 mm	0.09	0.10	-	-	0.26	1.01	9.02	-	**10.03**	m2
150 mm	0.14	0.12	-	-	0.30	1.57	10.49	-	**12.06**	m2
200 mm	0.20	0.16	-	-	0.40	2.24	13.99	-	**16.23**	m2
HF BREAKING UP ROCK ETC.; BREAKING OUT OBSTRUCTIONS MET WITH IN EXCAVATIONS BY MACHINE										
001 **Extra over** excavations (in any position) for breaking up hard material (using hydraulic breaker equipment):										
soft rock or brickwork	2.40	2.40	-	-	-	28.37	14.86	-	**43.23**	m3
hard rock	3.85	3.85	-	-	-	45.51	23.84	-	**69.35**	m3
plain concrete	3.10	3.10	-	-	-	36.64	19.20	-	**55.84**	m3
reinforced concrete	4.00	4.00	-	-	-	47.28	24.77	-	**72.05**	m3
002 **Extra over** excavations for working space (in any position) for breaking up hard material (using hydraulic breaker equipment) filling (by hand) with material arising from the excavations; compacted with Whacker in 250 mm layers:										
soft rock or brickwork	1.30	2.40	-	0.22	-	15.37	15.65	-	**31.02**	m3
hard rock	1.30	3.85	-	0.22	-	15.37	24.63	-	**40.00**	m3
plain concrete	1.30	3.10	-	0.22	-	15.37	19.99	-	**35.36**	m3
reinforced concrete	1.30	4.00	-	0.22	-	15.37	25.56	-	**40.93**	m3

	Man-Hours	Net Labour Price £	Net Mats Price £	Net Unit Price £	Unit
HG EARTHWORK SUPPORT					
001 **Timber earthwork support**					
Note: The 'Net Material' price allows for TEN (10) uses of timber. The 'Net Labour' price allows for fixing and striking once.					
002 Earthwork support in firm ground to opposing faces not exceeding 2.00 m apart:					
to preliminary trenches, maximum depth not exceeding:					
1.00 m	0.25	3.44	0.61	**4.05**	m2
2.00 m	0.38	5.26	0.61	**5.87**	m2
to excavation below the level of the base of the existing foundations, maximum depth not exceeding:					
1.00 m	0.38	5.33	0.92	**6.25**	m2
2.00 m	0.50	7.01	0.92	**7.93**	m2
003 Earthwork support in moderately firm ground to opposing faces not exceeding 2.00 m apart:					
to preliminary trenches, maximum depth not exceeding:					
1.00 m	1.08	15.14	1.84	**16.98**	m2
2.00 m	1.20	16.83	2.14	**18.97**	m2
to excavations below the level of the base of the existing foundations, maximum depth not exceeding:					
1.00 m	1.32	18.51	2.14	**20.65**	m2
2.00 m	1.44	20.19	2.45	**22.64**	m2
004 Earthwork support in loose ground, running sand and the like to opposing faces not exceeding 2.00 m apart:					
to preliminary trenches, maximum depth not exceeding:					
1.00 m	1.80	25.24	2.75	**27.99**	m2
2.00 m	2.64	37.02	3.06	**40.08**	m2
to excavations below the level of the base of the existing foundations, maximum depth not exceeding:					
1.00 m	2.16	30.29	3.67	**33.96**	m2
2.00 m	3.00	42.06	4.59	**46.65**	m2
HH DISPOSAL OF EXCAVATED MATERIALS					
See Section DM					

Unit Rates	Man-Hours	Net Labour Price £	Net Mats Price £	Net Unit Price £	Unit
HJ **FILLING**					
See Section DN					
HK **SURFACE TREATMENTS**					
See Section DO					

		Man-Hours	Plant Hours	Net Labour Price £	Net Plant Price £	Net Mats Price £	Net Unit Price £	Unit
HL	**PREPARING EXISTING FOUNDATIONS**							
001	Cutting away projecting brick footings:							
	one course	0.06	0.03	0.67	0.19	-	**0.86**	m
	two courses	0.22	0.07	2.42	0.43	-	**2.85**	m
	three courses	0.43	0.17	4.85	1.05	-	**5.90**	m
002	Cutting away projecting concrete foundation:							
	100 mm projection:							
	100 mm thick	0.12	0.05	1.35	0.31	-	**1.66**	m
	150 mm thick	0.18	0.07	2.02	0.43	-	**2.45**	m
	200 mm thick	0.24	0.09	2.69	0.56	-	**3.25**	m
	200 mm projection:							
	100 mm thick	0.30	0.13	3.36	0.81	-	**4.17**	m
	150 mm thick	0.42	0.18	4.71	1.11	-	**5.82**	m
	200 mm thick	0.66	0.26	7.40	1.61	-	**9.01**	m
	300 mm projection:							
	200 mm thick	0.60	0.25	6.73	1.55	-	**8.28**	m
	300 mm thick	0.96	0.40	10.77	2.48	-	**13.25**	m
003	Preparing underside of existing foundation to receive new pinning up:							
	concrete:							
	300 mm thick	0.10	-	1.08	-	-	**1.08**	m
	450 mm thick	0.13	-	1.48	-	-	**1.48**	m
	600 mm thick	0.18	-	2.02	-	-	**2.02**	m
	brickwork:							
	300 mm thick	0.12	-	1.35	-	-	**1.35**	m
	450 mm thick	0.18	-	2.02	-	-	**2.02**	m
	600 mm thick	0.24	-	2.69	-	-	**2.69**	m
	stonework:							
	300 mm thick	0.18	-	2.02	-	-	**2.02**	m
	450 mm thick	0.28	-	3.10	-	-	**3.10**	m
	600 mm thick	0.36	-	4.04	-	-	**4.04**	m
HM	**IN SITU CONCRETE IN UNDERPINNING**							
001	**PLAIN concrete grade C20/25 filled into formwork**							
002	Foundations in trenches:							
	not exceeding 100 mm thick	4.20	-	47.12	-	94.95	**142.07**	m3
	100 - 150 mm thick	4.08	-	45.78	-	94.95	**140.73**	m3
	150 - 300 mm thick	3.12	-	35.01	-	94.95	**129.96**	m3
	exceeding 300 mm thick	2.40	-	26.93	-	94.95	**121.88**	m3
003	**REINFORCED concrete grade C20/25 filled into formwork**							
004	Foundations in trenches:							
	not exceeding 100 mm thick	5.28	-	97.84	-	94.95	**192.79**	m3
	100 - 150 mm thick	5.04	-	93.39	-	94.95	**188.34**	m3
	150 - 300 mm thick	3.84	-	71.16	-	94.95	**166.11**	m3
	exceeding 300 mm thick	3.00	-	55.59	-	94.95	**150.54**	m3
HN	**REINFORCEMENT IN UNDERPINNING**							
	Note: 001 – 003 not used							
004	**Hot rolled deformed high yield steel bars to BS 4449, supplied in straight lengths, cut and bent on site**							
005	Straight and bent bars in foundations:							
	8 mm	0.14	-	2.10	-	0.82	**2.92**	Kg
	10 mm	0.11	-	1.69	-	0.84	**2.53**	Kg
	12 mm	0.10	-	1.46	-	0.83	**2.29**	Kg
	16 mm	0.08	-	1.17	-	0.84	**2.01**	Kg
	20 mm	0.07	-	0.99	-	0.83	**1.82**	Kg
	25 mm (cutting and bending by machine)	0.05	0.01	0.81	0.04	0.82	**1.67**	Kg
006	Links, stirrups, binders and special spacers in foundations:							
	8 mm	0.18	-	2.78	-	0.82	**3.60**	Kg
	10 mm	0.15	-	2.26	-	0.84	**3.10**	Kg

Unit Rates	Man-Hours	Net Labour Price £	Net Mats Price £	Net Unit Price £	Unit
HO **FORMWORK GENERALLY IN UNDERPINNING**					
Note: For explanation of the prices for formwork see Section FJ					
001 **Formwork to foundations**					
002 Edges and faces of foundations:					
exceeding 1.00 m high:					
making (one use allowed)	1.75	26.60	34.47	**61.07**	m2
fixing	1.86	33.49	0.99	**34.48**	m2
not exceeding 250 mm high:					
making (one use allowed)	0.90	13.68	8.70	**22.38**	m
fixing	0.78	14.04	0.60	**14.64**	m
250 - 500 mm high:					
making (one use allowed)	1.30	19.76	17.41	**37.17**	m
fixing	1.14	20.53	0.75	**21.28**	m
500 - 1000 mm high:					
making (one use allowed)	1.64	24.93	34.47	**59.40**	m
fixing	1.84	33.13	0.99	**34.12**	m
HP **BRICKWORK IN UNDERPINNING**					
001 **Brickwork in cement mortar (1:3) in walls in**					
002 Common bricks P.C. £311.01 per 1000:					
215 mm	5.28	109.88	45.78	**155.66**	m2
327.5 mm	6.24	129.85	69.19	**199.04**	m2
440 mm	7.68	159.82	91.88	**251.70**	m2
003 Class A Engineering bricks P.C. £493.42 per 1000:					
215 mm	5.40	112.37	69.15	**181.52**	m2
327.5 mm	6.48	134.85	104.24	**239.09**	m2
440 mm	7.92	164.82	138.04	**302.86**	m2
004 Class B Engineering bricks P.C. £391.75 per 1000:					
215 mm	5.28	109.88	56.12	**166.00**	m2
327.5 mm	6.24	129.85	84.70	**214.55**	m2
440 mm	7.68	159.82	112.31	**272.13**	m2
HQ **BRICK FACEWORK IN UNDERPINNING**					
001 **Extra over brickwork in cement mortar (1:3) for fair face and flush pointing as the work proceeds**					
002 Common brickwork in:					
Stretcher bond	0.72	14.98	-	**14.98**	m2
Flemish bond	0.78	16.23	-	**16.23**	m2
English bond	0.84	17.48	-	**17.48**	m2
003 Class A or Class B engineering brickwork in:					
Stretcher bond	0.84	17.48	-	**17.48**	m2
Flemish bond	0.90	18.73	-	**18.73**	m2
English bond	0.96	19.98	-	**19.98**	m2
HR **DAMP PROOF COURSES IN UNDERPINNING**					
001 **Bitumen damp proof courses, BS 6398; 100 mm laps; in cement mortar (1:3); pointing where exposed; horizontal**					
002 Hessian base, ref A:					
over 225 mm wide	0.30	6.24	11.00	**17.24**	m2
225 mm wide	0.07	1.50	2.58	**4.08**	m
003 Fibre base, ref B:					
over 225 mm wide	0.30	6.24	8.93	**15.17**	m2
225 mm wide	0.07	1.50	2.11	**3.61**	m
Note: 004 – 005 not used					
006 **Hyload pitch polymer damp proof course; 100 mm laps sealed with Hyload contact adhesive; in cement mortar (1:3) pointing where exposed**					
007 Horizontal damp proof course:					
over 225 mm wide	0.34	6.99	8.53	**15.52**	m2
225 mm wide	0.07	1.50	2.04	**3.54**	m
008 **Slate damp proof courses, BS 743; bedding and pointing in cement mortar (1:3)**					
009 Single course slates; horizontal:					
over 225 mm wide	1.20	24.97	18.40	**43.37**	m2
225 mm wide	0.36	7.49	4.67	**12.16**	m
010 Two courses slates, laid breaking joint; horizontal:					
over 225 mm wide	2.46	51.19	35.94	**87.13**	m2
225 mm wide	0.78	16.23	8.35	**24.58**	m

Unit Rates	Man-Hours	Net Labour Price £	Net Mats Price £	Net Unit Price £	Unit
011	**Synthaprufe damp proof courses**					
012	Three coats Synthaprufe waterproofer to vertical face of brickwork:					
	over 300 mm wide	0.58	11.99	4.25	**16.24**	m2
HS	**BRICKWORK SUNDRIES IN UNDERPINNING**					
001	**Wedging and pinning up with slates in cement mortar (1:3)**					
002	Wedging and pinning up new work to underside of existing construction:					
	215 mm	0.08	1.75	4.67	**6.42**	m
	327.5 mm	0.12	2.50	6.64	**9.14**	m
	440 mm	0.16	3.25	8.60	**11.85**	m
003	**Conbextra GP grout between new brickwork and underside of old foundations**					
004	Grouting 25 mm thick:					
	215 mm	0.60	12.49	4.52	**17.01**	m
	327.5 mm	0.72	14.98	6.58	**21.56**	m
	440 mm	0.90	18.73	8.84	**27.57**	m

Rubble Walling

Independent cost information
for the built environment

Comprehensive Building Price Book 2013
Major and Minor Works dataset

The Major Works dataset focuses predominantly on large 'new build' projects reflecting the economies of scale found in these forms of construction. The Minor Works Estimating Dataset focuses on small to medium sized 'new build' projects reflecting the increase in costs brought about the reduced output, less discounts, increased carriage and supervision, to the similar items in the Major Works dataset. The dataset is presented in trade order. Revised and reworked items in underpinning composites; flue linings and rainwater goods.

Item code: 19215　　**Price: £165.99**

SMM7 Estimating Price Book 2013

The SMM7 Estimating dataset focuses predominantly on large 'new build' projects reflecting the economies of scale found in these forms of construction. The dataset is presented in SMM7 grouping and order in accordance with the Common Arrangement of Work Sections. It is compiled using the latest independent costing information from manufacturers, material and plant suppliers, legislation effects and working rule agreements. Revised and reworked items in underpinning composites; flue linings and rainwater goods.

Item code: 19216　　**Price: £139.99**

Alterations and Refurbishment Price Book 2013

The Alterations & Refurbishment dataset focuses on small to medium sized projects, generally working within an existing building and reflecting the increase in costs brought about the reduction in output, smaller discounts, increased carriage, increased supervision, and less productivity brought about by smaller economies of scale, increased production costs, more difficult access and the possibility of working in occupied premises. The dataset is presented in trade order. Revised and reworked items in underpinning composites; flue linings and rainwater goods.

Item code: 19217　　**Price £109.99**

BCIS Guide to Estimating for Small Works 2012

The BCIS Guide to Estimating for Small Works 2012 is a unique dataset which shows the true power of resource based estimating. A set of composite built-up measured items are used to build up priced estimates for a large number of common specification extensions. The intention is to show estimating techniques in use and allow users to build up accurate estimates for their own projects, simply and easily, with up-to-date and independent cost information.

Item code: 19064　　**Price: £59.99**

BCIS Painting and Decorating Price Book 2012

The BCIS Painting and Decorating dataset is the most handy pricing tool available to the painting and decorating sector of the industry, suitable for all projects needing more than a 'guess-timate'. Using this dataset a more accurate calculation based quotation or variation can be prepared. From these calculations an assessment of labour, plant and material content can be produced. This in turn enables the contractor to negotiate discounts on known material requirements and the effect of this workload on the availability of labour.

Item code: 19065　　**Price: £39.99**

For more information call **0870 333 1600** email
contact@bcis.co.uk or visit **www.bcis.co.uk**

BCIS is the Building Cost Information Service of **RICS** | the mark of property professionalism worldwide

Labour Rates

Please note: The labour hours throughout this section are representative of the time required for one productive man to carry out the unit of work.

Gang rates are calculated as follows by obtaining the overall gang cost and then dividing this by the number of productive members in the gang. The resulting rate is the Gang Cost per **Man - hour**. By using the same principle, any size gang may be built-up and used against the standard labour hours in this section.

A0206 Walling generally

Rubble Wall Layer	1.00	x	£	15.20	= £	15.20
Rubble Walling Labourer	1.00	x	£	11.22	= £	11.22
Total hourly cost of gang					= £	26.42

Gang rate (divided by 1) = £26.42 per Man-hour

Mortar Mix Analysis

The cost of labour in mixing is included in the gang rate per hour for plastering. The cost of mixers or mortar mills should be costed in preliminaries.

A0511 Cement mortar (1:3)

Cement (bagged)	0.44 tonne	x	£	156.48	= £	68.85
Building sand	1.83 tonne	x	£	26.57	= £	48.62
					£	117.47
Waste	10%				= £	11.75
Cost per m3					= £	**129.22**

A0542 Cement lime sand mortar (1:2:9)

Cement (bagged)	0.16 tonne	x	£	156.48	= £	25.04
Hydrated lime (del. in bags)	0.16 tonne	x	£	238.58	= £	38.17
Building sand	1.98 tonne	x	£	26.57	= £	52.61
					£	115.82
Waste	10%				= £	11.58
Cost per m3					= £	**127.40**

A0544 Coloured cement lime sand mortar (1:2:9)

Cement (bagged)	0.16 tonne	x	£	156.48	= £	25.04
Hydrated lime (del. in bags)	0.16 tonne	x	£	238.58	= £	38.17
Building sand	1.98 tonne	x	£	26.57	= £	52.61
Febtone colour pigment (red)	6.00 kg	x	£	7.82	= £	46.92
					£	162.74
Waste	10%				= £	16.27
Cost per m3					= £	**179.01**

Basic Prices of Materials

		Supply Price £	Waste Factor %	Unload. Labour £	Unload. Plant £	Total Unit Cost £	Unit
J0101	Cotswold limestone, Farmington quarry, in full loads ex quarry: random rubble walling stone 75 - 150 mm course height	194.25	15%	-	-	223.39	tonne
J0102	Cotswold limestone, Farmington quarry, in full loads ex quarry: rough dressed light and dark cream building stone in random lengths and rises, sawn on back to give: 125 mm bed	204.75	15%	-	-	235.46	tonne
A0301	Portland cement, delivered in bags	137.81	5%	11.22	-	156.48	tonne
A0302	White Portland cement, delivered in bags	314.16	5%	11.22	-	341.65	tonne
A0311	Hydrated lime, delivered in bags	216.00	5%	11.22	-	238.58	tonne
A0321	Building sand BS 1200	24.16	10%	-	-	26.57	tonne
A0372	Febtone colouring pigment (Red)	7.45	5%	-	-	7.82	kg
G0318	Gun-grade silicone sealant (400 ml cart.)	4.08	10%	-	-	4.49	nr
G0323	Lead for running mortices	2.15	5%	0.01	-	2.27	kg

		Man-Hours	Net Labour Price £	Net Mats Price £	Net Unit Price £	Unit
	Unit Rates					
JA	UNIT RATES **STONE RUBBLE WORK**					
001	**Cotswold limestone, Farmington quarry, uncoursed random rubble walling; 75 - 150 mm high with natural exposed faces; laid dry**					
002	Walls; facing both side:					
	450 mm thick	3.24	85.60	158.61	**244.21**	m2
	412.5 mm thick (average) one face battering at the rate of 1:20	3.42	90.36	145.20	**235.56**	m2
	375 mm thick (average) both faces battering at the rate of 1:20	3.54	93.53	131.80	**225.33**	m2
003	Fair cutting on rubble work:					
	450 mm wide	1.20	31.70	-	**31.70**	m
	412.5 mm wide (average)	1.20	31.70	-	**31.70**	m
	375 mm wide (average)	1.20	31.70	-	**31.70**	m
004	Fair returns:					
	450 mm wide	0.24	6.34	-	**6.34**	m
	412.5 mm wide (average)	0.24	6.34	-	**6.34**	m
	375 mm wide (average)	0.24	6.34	-	**6.34**	m
005	Fair:					
	squint angles	0.18	4.76	-	**4.76**	m
	birdsmouth angles	0.12	3.17	-	**3.17**	m
	battered internal angles	0.18	4.76	-	**4.76**	m
	battered external angles	0.24	6.34	-	**6.34**	m
	Note: 006 - 021 not used					
022	**Cotswold limestone, Farmington quarry, light and dark cream, rough dressed random rubble walling sawn on back to provide uniform bed thickness; natural exposed faces; in cement lime mortar (1:2:9); joints recessed 12 mm deep as the work proceeds**					
023	Walls in skins of cavity walls; facing and pointing one side: 125 mm thick:					
	random coursing	2.40	63.41	49.64	**113.05**	m2
	random coursing brought to courses at average 500 mm vertical intervals	2.70	71.33	49.64	**120.97**	m2
	coursed in minimum 100 mm, maximum 180 mm courses	3.24	85.60	49.64	**135.24**	m2
	coursed in diminishing courses 180 mm maximum, 100 mm minimum high	3.48	91.94	49.64	**141.58**	m2
024	**Extra over** for: flat arches:					
	200 mm wide on face, 125 mm wide exposed soffit	0.12	3.17	11.77	**14.94**	m
	segmental arches:					
	200 mm wide on face, 125 mm wide exposed soffit	0.18	4.76	11.77	**16.53**	m
025	Fair cutting on rubble work: 125 mm wide	0.72	19.02	-	**19.02**	m
026	Fair returns not exceeding: 125 mm wide	0.18	4.76	-	**4.76**	m
027	Dressed margins:					
	50 mm wide	0.12	3.17	-	**3.17**	m
	100 mm wide	0.18	4.76	-	**4.76**	m
028	**ADDITIONAL COSTS to rough dressed random rubble walling sawn on back in cement lime mortar for the following**					
029	Flush pointing as the work proceeds	0.42	11.10	-	**11.10**	m2
030	Joints raked out 12 mm as the work proceeds; re-filling with coloured cement lime mortar (1:2:9) and flush pointing as a separate operation	0.72	19.02	0.36	**19.38**	m2
JB	**SUNDRIES**					
001	**Grooves**					
002	Grooves in rubble work for water bars	0.60	15.85	-	**15.85**	m
003	Grooves in rubble work; dressing face of rubble work below groove for:					
	turned-in edges of flashings	0.60	15.85	-	**15.85**	m
	nibs of asphalt	0.72	19.02	-	**19.02**	m
004	Pointing in cement mortar (1:3):					
	turned-in edges of flashings	0.06	1.59	0.13	**1.72**	m
	nibs of asphalt	0.06	1.59	0.13	**1.72**	m
005	**Building in metal windows, metal doors and the like complete with frames; filling backs of frames and bedding in cement mortar (1:3)**					
006	Windows 300 mm high, length:					
	600 mm	1.08	28.53	0.13	**28.66**	Nr
	1200 mm	1.68	44.39	0.26	**44.65**	Nr
007	Windows 600 mm high, length:					
	600 mm	1.38	36.46	0.26	**36.72**	Nr
	1200 mm	2.40	63.41	0.39	**63.80**	Nr
	1800 mm	2.52	66.58	0.39	**66.97**	Nr

	Unit Rates	Man-Hours	Net Labour Price £	Net Mats Price £	Net Unit Price £	Unit
008	Windows 900 mm high, length:					
	600 mm	1.50	39.63	0.26	**39.89**	Nr
	1200 mm	2.64	69.75	0.39	**70.14**	Nr
	1800 mm	2.88	76.09	0.52	**76.61**	Nr
009	Windows 1200 mm high, length:					
	600 mm	1.68	44.39	0.39	**44.78**	Nr
	1200 mm	2.88	76.09	0.39	**76.48**	Nr
	1800 mm	3.30	87.19	0.52	**87.71**	Nr
010	Door frames and side lights 2200 mm high, length:					
	900 mm	2.40	63.41	0.52	**63.93**	Nr
	1200 mm	2.52	66.58	0.65	**67.23**	Nr
	1800 mm	3.24	85.60	0.65	**86.25**	Nr
	2400 mm	4.32	114.13	0.78	**114.91**	Nr
011	Pointing edges of frames in silicone sealant:					
	one side	0.06	1.59	0.54	**2.13**	Nr
	both sides	0.12	3.17	1.08	**4.25**	Nr
012	**Building in**					
013	Ends of steel sections to rubble work:					
	small	1.20	31.70	-	**31.70**	Nr
	large	1.80	47.56	-	**47.56**	Nr
	extra large	2.40	63.41	-	**63.41**	Nr
014	**Holes for pipes, tubes, bars, cables, conduits and the like, making good**					
015	Small pipes in:					
	rubble walling:					
	450 mm thick	1.08	28.53	1.55	**30.08**	Nr
	600 mm thick	1.44	38.04	1.94	**39.98**	Nr
	facework:					
	200 mm thick	0.84	22.19	0.90	**23.09**	Nr
	300 mm thick	0.96	25.36	1.29	**26.65**	Nr
	skins of hollow walls:					
	125 mm thick	0.48	12.68	0.65	**13.33**	Nr
	150 mm thick	0.60	15.85	0.78	**16.63**	Nr
016	Large pipes in:					
	rubble walling:					
	450 mm thick	1.20	31.70	1.68	**33.38**	Nr
	600 mm thick	1.56	41.22	2.07	**43.29**	Nr
	facework:					
	200 mm thick	0.96	25.36	1.03	**26.39**	Nr
	300 mm thick	1.08	28.53	1.42	**29.95**	Nr
	skins of hollow walls:					
	125 mm thick	0.60	15.85	0.78	**16.63**	Nr
	150 mm thick	0.72	19.02	0.90	**19.92**	Nr
017	Extra large pipes in-					
	rubble walling:					
	450 mm thick	1.44	38.04	1.81	**39.85**	Nr
	600 mm thick	1.80	47.56	2.20	**49.76**	Nr
	facework:					
	200 mm thick	1.20	31.70	1.16	**32.86**	Nr
	300 mm thick	1.32	34.87	1.55	**36.42**	Nr
	skins of hollow walls:					
	125 mm thick	0.84	22.19	0.90	**23.09**	Nr
	150 mm thick	0.96	25.36	1.03	**26.39**	Nr
018	**Extra over** for building in pipe sleeves (supplied by others):					
	small; length:					
	not exceeding 200 mm	0.12	3.17	-	**3.17**	Nr
	200 - 400 mm	0.12	3.17	-	**3.17**	Nr
	400 - 600 mm	0.12	3.17	-	**3.17**	Nr
	large; length:					
	not exceeding 200 mm	0.12	3.17	-	**3.17**	Nr
	200 - 400 mm	0.12	3.17	-	**3.17**	Nr
	400 - 600 mm	0.12	3.17	-	**3.17**	Nr
	extra large; length:					
	not exceeding 200 mm	0.12	3.17	-	**3.17**	Nr
	200 - 400 mm	0.12	3.17	-	**3.17**	Nr
	400 - 600 mm	0.12	3.17	-	**3.17**	Nr
019	**Holes for gratings, ducting, trunking, trays and the like; making good**					
020	Holes not exceeding 0.10 m2 sectional area in:					
	rubble walling:					
	450 mm thick	2.40	63.41	0.90	**64.31**	Nr
	600 mm thick	2.64	69.75	1.29	**71.04**	Nr
	facework:					
	200 mm thick	1.92	50.73	0.65	**51.38**	Nr
	300 mm thick	2.64	69.75	1.29	**71.04**	Nr
	skins of hollow walls:					
	125 mm thick	1.44	38.04	0.39	**38.43**	Nr
	150 mm thick	1.56	41.22	0.52	**41.74**	Nr

Unit Rates	Man-Hours	Net Labour Price £	Net Mats Price £	Net Unit Price £	Unit
021 Holes 0.10 - 0.20 m2 sectional area in:					
rubble walling:					
450 mm thick	2.88	76.09	0.90	**76.99**	Nr
600 mm thick	3.12	82.43	1.29	**83.72**	Nr
facework:					
200 mm thick	2.40	63.41	0.65	**64.06**	Nr
300 mm thick	2.52	66.58	0.78	**67.36**	Nr
skins of hollow walls:					
125 mm thick	1.92	50.73	0.39	**51.12**	Nr
150 mm thick	2.28	60.24	0.52	**60.76**	Nr
022 Holes 0.20 - 0.30 m2 sectional area in:					
rubble walling:					
450 mm thick	3.60	95.11	1.03	**96.14**	Nr
600 mm thick	3.96	104.62	1.55	**106.17**	Nr
facework:					
200 mm thick	2.88	76.09	0.78	**76.87**	Nr
300 mm thick	3.00	79.26	0.90	**80.16**	Nr
skins of hollow walls:					
125 mm thick	2.16	57.07	0.52	**57.59**	Nr
150 mm thick	2.28	60.24	0.65	**60.89**	Nr
023 **Mortices; making good**					
024 Mortices in rubble work:					
50 x 50 x 100 mm deep	0.60	15.85	-	**15.85**	Nr
75 x 75 x 150 mm deep	0.78	20.61	-	**20.61**	Nr
100 mm deep for 12 mm diameter Rawlbolt	0.24	6.34	-	**6.34**	Nr
025 Grouting mortices in cement and sand (1:3):					
50 x 50 x 100 mm deep	0.18	4.76	0.13	**4.89**	Nr
75 x 75 x 150 mm deep	0.24	6.34	1.03	**7.37**	Nr
026 Running mortices with lead:					
50 x 50 x 100 mm deep	0.36	9.51	4.54	**14.05**	Nr
75 x 75 x 150 mm deep	0.38	10.15	17.01	**27.16**	Nr
027 **Flues, chimney pots, centering**					
028 See section GO for flues and chimney pots					
029 See section GP for centering					

Masonry

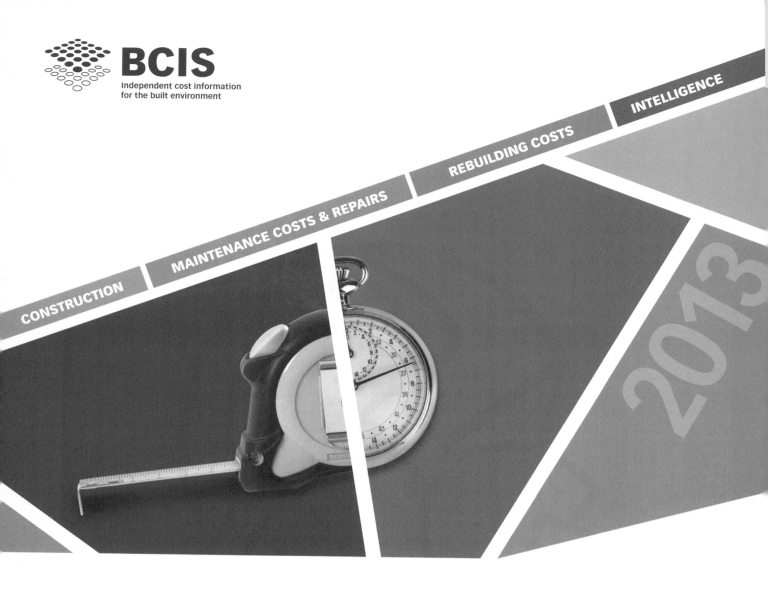

HOW LONG? HOW MUCH?
THE FASTEST, MOST UP-TO-DATE ANSWERS ARE AVAILABLE NOW

Cost information underpins every aspect of the built environment, from construction and rebuilding to maintenance and operation publications.

BCIS, the RICS' Building Cost Information Service, is the leading provider of cost information to the construction industry and anyone else who needs comprehensive, accurate and independent data.

For the past 50 years, BCIS has been collecting, collating, analysing, modelling and interpreting cost information. Today, BCIS make that information easily accessible through online applications, data licensing and publications.

For more information call **0870 333 1600** email **contact@bcis.co.uk** or visit **www.bcis.co.uk**

BCIS is the Building Cost Information Service of  **RICS** the mark of property professionalism worldwide

Labour Rates

Please note: The labour hours throughout this section are representative of the time required for one productive man to carry out the unit of work.

Gang rates are calculated as follows by obtaining the overall gang cost and then dividing this by the number of productive members in the gang. The resulting rate is the Gang Cost per **Man - hour.** By using the same principle, any size gang may be built-up and used against the standard labour hours in this section.

A0207 Reconstructed stonework

Stone Blocklayer	2.00	x	£	15.20	=	£	30.40
Recon. Stonework Labourer	1.00	x	£	11.22	=	£	11.22
Total hourly cost of gang					=	£	41.62

Gang rate (divided by 2) = £20.81 per Man-hour

Plant Hire Charges

		Daily Hire Charge £	Pro-ductive Hours Hrs	Cost Per Hour £	Operator Per Hour £	Fuel Per Hour £	Total Cost Per Hour £
	The hire charges shown exclude the cost of operators and fuel but are inclusive of oil, grease and the like. Fuel costs have been added in the following table as appropriate. The operator costs are either added in the table below or, where no operator shown, have been allowed for in the rates given in the individual items of work. The cost of delivery to, or collection from site is EXCLUDED and allowance for this should be made in Preliminaries.						
A0150	Hire of 5 tonne mobile crane	188.05	7.00	26.86	-	-	**26.86**

Basic Prices of Materials

		Supply Price £	Waste Factor %	Unload. Labour £	Unload. Plant £	Total Unit Cost £	Unit
	Note: The materials in this section are supplied palletised and prices allow for crane off-loading. No allowance has been made for pallet charges. Precast reconstructed stone components, P.C. prices:						
C0166	150 x 75 mm sill	63.00	-	-	-	**63.00**	m
C0167	200 x 75 mm sill	79.80	-	-	-	**79.80**	m
A0301	Portland cement (bagged)	137.81	5%	11.22	-	**156.48**	tonne
A0302	White Portland cement (bagged)	314.16	5%	11.22	-	**341.65**	tonne
A0311	Hydrated lime (bagged)	216.00	5%	11.22	-	**238.58**	tonne
A0321	Building sand	24.16	10%	-	-	**26.57**	tonne
K0189	Stone dust (bagged)	840.00	5%	11.22	-	**893.78**	tonne
A0361	Sawn softwood for temporary strutting (cost divided by 6 for 6 uses)	280.30	5%	11.22	-	**306.09**	m3

Mortar Mix Analysis

Note: The labour cost of mixing is included in the gang rate per hour. Mixers or mortar mills should be costed in preliminaries.

A0542 Cement lime mortar (1:2:9)
Cement (bagged)	0.16 tonne	x	£	156.48	=	£	25.04
Hydrated lime (del. in bags)	0.16 tonne	x	£	238.58	=	£	38.17
Building sand	1.98 tonne	x	£	26.57	=	£	52.61
						£	115.82
Waste	£10%				=	£	11.58
Cost per m3					=	£	**127.40**

A0541 Cement lime mortar (1:1:6)
Cement (bagged)	0.23 tonne	x	£	156.48	=	£	35.99
Hydrated lime (del. in bags)	0.12 tonne	x	£	238.58	=	£	28.63
Building sand	1.93 tonne	x	£	26.57	=	£	51.28
						£	115.90
Waste	10%				=	£	11.59
Cost per m3					=	£	**127.49**

A0523 Waterproof cement and sand mortar (1:6)
Cement (bagged)	0.25 tonne	x	£	156.48	=	£	39.12
Building sand	2.07 tonne	x	£	26.57	=	£	55.00
Pudlo waterproofer	10.00 kg	x	£	6.34	=	£	63.40
						£	157.52
Waste	10%				=	£	15.75
Cost per m3					=	£	**173.27**

A0524 Waterproof white cement and stone dust mortar (1:6)
White Portland cement in bags	0.24 tonne	x	£	341.65	=	£	82.00
Stone dust (bagged)	2.20 tonne	x	£	893.78	=	£	1966.32
Pudlo waterproofer	10.00 kg	x	£	6.34	=	£	63.40
						£	115.82
Waste	10%				=	£	211.17
Cost per m3					=	£	**2322.89**

Unit Rates	Man-Hours	Net Labour Price £	Net Mats Price £	Net Unit Price £	Unit
UNIT RATES					
KA **WORK TO EXISTING STONEWORK**					
001 Ashlar walling stone salvaged from demolition in making good jambs of cut openings in white cement lime putty mortar (2:5:7) with crushed stone dust:					
prepared for plastering:					
150 mm thick	1.72	35.81	0.13	**35.94**	m
200 mm thick	2.07	42.97	0.13	**43.10**	m
300 mm thick	2.41	50.13	0.13	**50.26**	m
finished fair and flush pointed:					
150 mm thick	1.80	37.40	0.13	**37.53**	m
200 mm thick	2.24	46.55	0.13	**46.68**	m
300 mm thick	2.58	53.71	0.13	**53.84**	m
002 Ashlar walling stone (P.C. £2122.44 per m3) in making good existing ashlar walls in white cement lime putty mortar (2:5:7) with crushed stone dust, flush pointing to match existing:					
where cross-wall removed:					
150 mm thick	0.57	11.94	33.68	**45.62**	m
300 mm thick	0.77	15.92	67.24	**83.16**	m
where ends of joists removed:					
50 x 200 mm x 450 centres	0.24	4.99	4.59	**9.58**	m
50 x 250 mm x 450 centres	0.29	5.95	6.82	**12.77**	m
where ends of beams removed:					
200 x 300 mm	0.57	11.94	13.75	**25.69**	Nr
300 x 400 mm	0.67	13.92	27.50	**41.42**	Nr
300 x 600 mm	0.96	19.89	41.26	**61.15**	Nr
where brackets removed	0.19	4.00	-	**4.00**	Nr

	£	Unit
The prices in this section are **Specialist** prices for natural stonework labour and materials fixed in position. The prices are for full load quantities delivered to sites within 60 miles of the stone-masons' yards and have been quoted by Farmington Natural Stone Ltd, Farmington, Northleach, Cheltenham, Gloucs, GL54 3NZ (Telephone: 01451 860280, Fax: 01451 860318, E-mail: cotswold stone@farmington.co.uk, web site: www.farmington.co.uk/stone)		
003 **Stone restoration - Hard Limestones**		
004 Cut out decayed and damaged stonework and replace with new matching stone walling with smooth finish:		
50 mm thick; area on face:		
not exceeding 0.05 m2	186.24	Nr
0.05 - 0.10 m2	297.91	Nr
0.10 - 0.25 m2	521.38	Nr
0.25 - 0.50 m2	893.77	Nr
100 mm thick; area on face:		
not exceeding 0.05 m2	248.29	Nr
0.05 - 0.10 m2	354.93	Nr
0.10 - 0.25 m2	567.73	Nr
0.25 - 0.50 m2	958.20	Nr
150 mm thick; area on face:		
not exceeding 0.05 m2	321.79	Nr
0.05 - 0.10 m2	429.03	Nr
0.10 - 0.25 m2	636.74	Nr
0.25 - 0.50 m2	1072.62	Nr
005 Cut out small defective section from face of plain column, pilaster, mullion or jamb; piece in new; 50 mm deep:		
rectangular section member; area on face:		
not exceeding 0.05 m2	186.24	Nr
0.05 - 0.10 m2	297.91	Nr
circular section member; area on face:		
not exceeding 0.05 m2	221.13	Nr
0.05 - 0.10 m2	372.57	Nr
006 Cut out section of damaged moulded coping, string course, band course, sill or the like; piece in new:		
50 mm deep; area on face:		
not exceeding 0.05 m2	238.44	Nr
0.05 - 0.10 m2	402.22	Nr
100 mm deep; area on face:		
not exceeding 0.05 m2	300.45	Nr
0.05 - 0.10 m2	459.25	Nr
007 Cut out complete section of moulded coping, string course, band course, sill or the like; build in new:		
200 x 100 mm; length:		
not exceeding 250 mm	260.66	Nr
250 - 500 mm	469.27	Nr
500 - 750 mm	744.78	Nr
750 - 1000 mm	1005.42	Nr
300 x 150 mm; length:		
not exceeding 250 mm	446.82	Nr
250 - 500 mm	804.60	Nr
500 - 750 mm	1288.44	Nr
750 - 1000 mm	1005.42	Nr
Angle section of member:		
200 x 200 x 100 mm	243.67	Nr
300 x 300 x 150 mm	521.38	Nr

		£	Unit
	Specialist		
008	**Stone restoration - Soft Limestones**		
009	Cut out decayed and damaged stonework and replace with new matching stone walling with smooth finish:		
	50 mm thick; area on face:		
	not exceeding 0.05 m2	178.80	Nr
	0.05 - 0.10 m2	283.18	Nr
	0.10 - 0.25 m2	491.41	Nr
	0.25 - 0.50 m2	833.98	Nr
	100 mm thick; area on face:		
	not exceeding 0.05 m2	245.01	Nr
	0.05 - 0.10 m2	350.10	Nr
	0.10 - 0.25 m2	559.97	Nr
	0.25 - 0.50 m2	955.24	Nr
	150 mm thick; area on face:		
	not exceeding 0.05 m2	315.12	Nr
	0.05 - 0.10 m2	420.04	Nr
	0.10 - 0.25 m2	623.52	Nr
	0.25 - 0.50 m2	1050.22	Nr
010	Cut out small defective section from face of plain column, pilaster, mullion or jamb; piece in new; 50 mm deep:		
	rectangular section member; area on face:		
	not exceeding 0.05 m2	178.80	Nr
	0.05 - 0.10 m2	283.18	Nr
	circular section member; area on face:		
	not exceeding 0.05 m2	213.69	Nr
	0.05 - 0.10 m2	357.82	Nr
011	Cut out section of damaged moulded coping, string course, band course, sill or the like; piece in new:		
	50 mm deep; area on face:		
	not exceeding 0.05 m2	231.00	Nr
	0.05 - 0.10 m2	387.50	Nr
	100 mm deep; area on face:		
	not exceeding 0.05 m2	297.16	Nr
	0.05 - 0.10 m2	454.41	Nr
012	Cut out complete section of moulded coping, string course, band course, sill or the like; build in new:		
	200 x 100 mm; length:		
	not exceeding 250 mm	253.31	Nr
	250 - 500 mm	446.87	Nr
	500 - 750 mm	714.89	Nr
	750 - 1000 mm	983.00	Nr
	300 x 150 mm; length:		
	not exceeding 250 mm	432.15	Nr
	250 - 500 mm	774.69	Nr
	500 - 750 mm	1236.11	Nr
	750 - 1000 mm	983.00	Nr
	Angle section of member:		
	200 x 200 x 100 mm	215.97	Nr
	300 x 300 x 150 mm	506.55	Nr
013	**Stone restoration - Sandstones**		
014	Cut out decayed and damaged stonework and replace with new matching stone walling with smooth finish:		
	50 mm thick; area on face:		
	not exceeding 0.05 m2	193.57	Nr
	0.05 - 0.10 m2	312.55	Nr
	0.10 - 0.25 m2	536.07	Nr
	0.25 - 0.50 m2	931.05	Nr
	100 mm thick; area on face:		
	not exceeding 0.05 m2	268.02	Nr
	0.05 - 0.10 m2	387.12	Nr
	0.10 - 0.25 m2	640.43	Nr
	0.25 - 0.50 m2	1042.72	Nr
	150 mm thick; area on face:		
	not exceeding 0.05 m2	342.58	Nr
	0.05 - 0.10 m2	461.34	Nr
	0.10 - 0.25 m2	714.89	Nr
	0.25 - 0.50 m2	1154.27	Nr
015	Cut out small defective section from face of plain column, pilaster, mullion or jamb; piece in new; 50 mm deep:		
	rectangular section member; area on face:		
	not exceeding 0.05 m2	193.57	Nr
	0.05 - 0.10 m2	312.55	Nr
	circular section member; area on face:		
	not exceeding 0.05 m2	228.45	Nr
	0.05 - 0.10 m2	387.18	Nr
016	Cut out section of damaged moulded coping, string course, band course, sill or the like; piece in new:		
	50 mm deep; area on face:		
	not exceeding 0.05 m2	245.73	Nr
	0.05 - 0.10 m2	416.84	Nr
	100 mm deep; area on face:		
	not exceeding 0.05 m2	320.18	Nr
	0.05 - 0.10 m2	491.41	Nr
017	Cut out complete section of moulded coping, string course, band course, sill or the like; build in new:		
	200 x 100 mm; length:		
	not exceeding 250 mm	268.02	Nr
	250 - 500 mm	484.13	Nr
	500 - 750 mm	774.69	Nr

Specialist	£	Unit

	£	Unit
750 - 1000 mm	1042.64	Nr
300 x 150 mm; length:		
not exceeding 250 mm	461.59	Nr
250 - 500 mm	834.06	Nr
500 - 750 mm	1333.12	Nr
750 - 1000 mm	1042.72	Nr
Angle section of member:		
200 x 200 x 100 mm	230.85	Nr
300 x 300 x 150 mm	536.07	Nr

Note: 018 - 019 not used

		Man-Hours	Net Labour Price £	Net Mats Price £	Net Unit Price £	Unit
020	**Repairs and renovations**					
021	Hack face of existing ashlar stone wall and rake out joints as key for new plaster finish	0.29	3.21	-	**3.21**	m2
022	Rake out joints 6 mm deep in existing ashlar stone wall and repoint in white cement lime putty mortar (2:5:7) with crushed stone dust; flush pointing	0.72	14.94	3.56	**18.50**	m2
023	Flush cut face of ashlar stone wall after removal of plinth courses, band courses, pilasters, attached piers and the like; dressed with Kango hammer:					
	over 1000 mm wide	0.34	3.86	-	**5.25**	m2
	up to 250 mm wide	0.10	1.09	-	**1.48**	m
	250 - 500 mm wide	0.19	2.15	-	**2.93**	m
	500 - 1000 mm wide	0.34	3.86	-	**5.25**	m
024	Prepare for raising; top of existing ashlar stone walling:					
	100 mm wide	0.10	2.14	-	**2.14**	m
	150 mm wide	0.14	3.00	-	**3.00**	m
	200 mm wide	0.19	3.85	-	**3.85**	m
025	Making good face of ashlar stone wall after removal of plinth courses, band courses, pilasters, attached piers and the like; with flush matching construction 50 mm thick:					
	over 1000 mm wide	1.91	39.79	28.96	**68.75**	m2
	up to 250 mm wide	0.57	11.94	7.58	**19.52**	m
	250 - 500 mm wide	0.96	19.89	15.60	**35.49**	m
	500 - 1000 mm wide	1.91	39.79	28.96	**68.75**	m
026	Making good face of existing ashlar stone walling after removal of projecting chimney breasts, piers etc.:					
	concealed work; to receive plaster	0.34	3.81	-	**5.19**	m2
	exposed work; in new ashlar 100 mm thick; finished fair and flush pointed to match existing	1.39	15.60	0.64	**17.62**	m2
027	Wedge and pin up new ashlar stone walling to existing; with slates in cement mortar (1:3): exposed work:					
	75 mm thick	0.49	10.13	4.41	**14.54**	m
	100 mm thick	0.51	10.61	5.26	**15.87**	m
	150 mm thick	0.54	11.32	6.25	**17.57**	m
	200 mm thick	0.57	11.80	7.10	**18.90**	m
028	**Bonding ends of ashlar stone walls to existing; average 100 mm deep in average 150 mm high alternate courses; cutting pockets in existing structure; extra material for bonding**					
029	Walls:					
	150 mm thick	0.62	12.94	6.69	**19.63**	m
	200 mm thick	0.81	16.94	8.91	**25.85**	m
030	Facework:					
	75 mm thick	0.43	8.99	6.24	**15.23**	m
	100 mm thick	0.53	10.95	8.47	**19.42**	m
031	**Cut and pin ends of new lintels and arch bars to openings in existing ashlar stone wall**					
032	150 mm thick	0.26	5.39	-	**5.39**	Nr
	200 mm thick	0.60	12.42	-	**12.42**	Nr
	300 mm thick	1.03	21.43	-	**21.43**	Nr

Specialist	£	Unit

KD STONE CLEANING

Specialist prices include for sealing doors, windows and other openings, provision of protective dust and spray sheeting and for cleaning up on completion. The prices are applicable to buildings up to 5 storeys in height above ground level, but are exclusive of scaffolding. Repointing **is not** included.

001 **Stone cleaning - Light griminess**

002 Cleaning wall surfaces with water sprays and light brushing:
   stone walls:

	£	Unit
plain (few mouldings)	289.85	10 m2
ornate (many mouldings)	404.07	10 m2
brick walls with stone dressings:		
plain dressings	275.46	10 m2
ornate dressings	398.45	10 m2

003 Cleaning wall surfaces with chemical solvents:
   stone walls:

	£	Unit
plain (few mouldings)	300.76	10 m2
ornate (many mouldings)	451.11	10 m2
brick walls with stone dressings:		
plain dressings	285.84	10 m2
ornate dressings	413.47	10 m2

004 Cleaning wall surfaces by sand blasting:
   stone walls:

	£	Unit
plain (few mouldings)	523.61	10 m2
ornate (many mouldings)	676.69	10 m2
brick walls with stone dressings:		
plain dressings	488.69	10 m2
ornate dressings	639.02	10 m2

005 **Stone cleaning - Medium griminess**

006 Cleaning wall surfaces with water sprays and light brushing:
   stone walls:

	£	Unit
plain (few mouldings)	362.28	10 m2
ornate (many mouldings)	579.61	10 m2
brick walls with stone dressings:		
plain dressings	340.38	10 m2
ornate dressings	536.26	10 m2

007 Cleaning wall surfaces with chemical solvents:
   stone walls:

	£	Unit
plain (few mouldings)	375.96	10 m2
ornate (many mouldings)	601.46	10 m2
brick walls with stone dressings:		
plain dressings	353.25	10 m2
ornate dressings	556.35	10 m2

008 Cleaning wall surfaces by sand blasting:
   stone walls:

	£	Unit
plain (few mouldings)	601.46	10 m2
ornate (many mouldings)	827.05	10 m2
brick walls with stone dressings:		
plain dressings	564.08	10 m2
ornate dressings	766.72	10 m2

009 **Stone cleaning - Heavy griminess**

010 Cleaning wall surfaces with water sprays and light brushing:
   stone walls:

	£	Unit
plain (few mouldings)	434.78	10 m2
ornate (many mouldings)	688.32	10 m2
brick walls with stone dressings:		
plain dressings	398.45	10 m2
ornate dressings	637.69	10 m2

011 Cleaning wall surfaces with chemical solvents:
   stone walls:

	£	Unit
plain (few mouldings)	451.11	10 m2
ornate (many mouldings)	714.30	10 m2
brick walls with stone dressings:		
plain dressings	413.52	10 m2
ornate dressings	661.77	10 m2

012 Cleaning wall surfaces by sand blasting:
   stone walls:

	£	Unit
plain (few mouldings)	676.69	10 m2
ornate (many mouldings)	939.91	10 m2
brick walls with stone dressings:		
plain dressings	624.23	10 m2
ornate dressings	864.76	10 m2

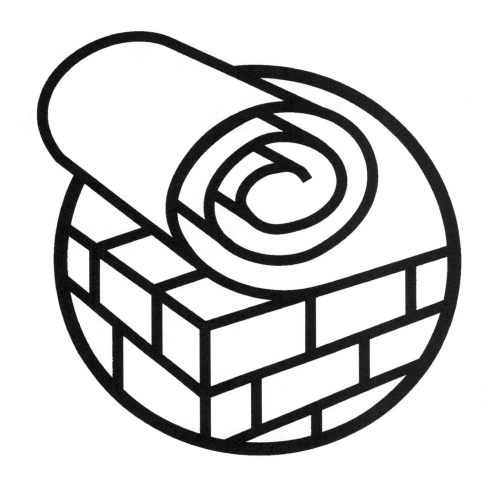

Asphalt Work

Dispute Resolution Service

Diploma in Adjudication in the Construction Industry

Comprised of four units, this qualification is designed for those **seeking to become an adjudicator**, and provides a pathway towards potential entry onto the **RICS Panel of Adjudicators**.

With a focus on contract and tort law and how they apply to adjudication, this course is designed to prepare you to progress to practice as an adjudicator. This course is suitable for those with experience in dispute resolution procedures with an understanding of the general principles of construction adjudication. The course content will focus on the format and content of an enforceable decision.

Learning Outcomes:

● Knowledge and understanding of the nature of law and its' place in society

● How the law of contract is applied to the practice of adjudication

● How the law of tort is applied to the practice of adjudication

● The practical application in the production of an enforceable decision.

Attainment of the learning outcomes will be assessed by a case study, whereby candidates will be required to produce an enforceable reasoned decision, based on material supplied in the case study.

To book or for further information, please contact DRS Training;

t **02476 868 584**   e **drstraining@rics.org**   w **rics.org/drs**

Specialist	Main Areas			Unit
	10 - 30 m2 £	30 - 100 m2 £	Over 100 m2 £	

SPECIALIST ASPHALT WORK
UNIT RATES
LA   ASPHALT WORK

The following **specialist** guide prices were provided by Pure Asphalt Company Limited, Burnden Works, Burnden Road, Bolton, Lancashire, BL3 2RD (Telephone: 01204 523244, Fax: 01204 395394, E-mail: enquiries@pureasphalt.co.uk, Internet: www.pureasphalt.co.uk)

The prices for work in this section are **specialist** guide prices, inclusive of labour and materials; and are applicable to sites over 30 miles but not exceeding 60 miles from the point of supply.

DAMP PROOFING AND TANKING

		10-30	30-100	Over 100	Unit
001	**Mastic asphalt BS 6925: 1988, T1097; PVA Keying mix and rubber based bitumen emulsion primer on vertical concrete surfaces**				
002	20 mm Two coat work subsequently covered including edges and arrises:				
	flat coverings to concrete base:				
	over 300 mm wide	35.45	30.47	24.80	m2
	not exceeding 150 mm wide	5.72	5.72	5.72	m
	150 - 300 mm wide	9.54	9.54	9.54	m
	sloping coverings over 10 degrees but not exceeding 45 degrees from horizontal to concrete base:				
	over 300 mm wide	43.63	39.70	35.77	m2
	not exceeding 150 mm wide	8.07	8.07	8.07	m
	150 - 300 mm wide	12.11	12.11	12.11	m
	sloping coverings over 45 degrees from horizontal and vertical coverings to concrete base:				
	over 300 mm wide	49.80	44.85	39.84	m2
	not exceeding 150 mm wide	10.70	10.70	10.70	m
	150 - 300 mm wide	15.17	15.17	15.17	m
	vertical coverings to brickwork base:				
	over 300 mm wide	49.80	44.85	39.84	m2
	not exceeding 150 mm wide	10.70	10.70	10.70	m
	150 - 300 mm wide	15.17	15.17	15.17	m
003	30 mm Three coat work subsequently covered including edges and arrises:				
	flat coverings to concrete base:				
	over 300 mm wide	50.67	45.60	40.70	m2
	not exceeding 150 mm wide	11.47	11.47	11.47	m
	150 - 300 mm wide	16.42	16.42	16.42	m
	sloping coverings over 10 degrees but not exceeding 45 degrees from horizontal to concrete base:				
	over 300 mm wide	55.68	52.34	45.54	m2
	not exceeding 150 mm wide	11.75	11.75	11.75	m
	150 - 300 mm wide	15.47	15.47	15.47	m
	sloping coverings over 45 degrees from horizontal and vertical coverings to concrete base:				
	over 300 mm wide	87.21	78.36	71.51	m2
	not exceeding 150 mm wide	15.20	15.20	15.20	m
	150 - 300 mm wide	21.02	21.02	21.02	m
	vertical coverings to brickwork base:				
	over 300 mm wide	87.21	78.36	71.51	m2
	not exceeding 150 mm wide	15.20	15.20	15.20	m
	150 - 300 mm wide	21.02	21.02	21.02	m
004	Internal angle fillets in two coats	5.88	5.88	5.88	m
005	Internal angle fillets in three coats	9.26	9.26	9.26	m
006	Turning nibs of asphalt into grooves	2.00	2.00	2.00	m
007	20 mm Two coat coverings to kerbs subsequently covered including fair edges and arrises:				
	to concrete base; two internal angle fillets, girth on face:				
	300 mm	29.29	26.36	23.43	m
	450 mm	36.37	32.73	29.10	m
	600 mm	43.35	39.00	34.68	m
	to brickwork base; two internal angle fillets, girth on face:				
	300 mm	29.29	26.36	23.43	m
	450 mm	36.37	32.73	29.10	m
	600 mm	43.35	39.00	34.68	m
008	20 mm Two coat linings to sumps subsequently covered including edges and arrises; to concrete base; internal angle fillets:				
	200 x 200 x 200 mm	49.70	49.70	49.70	Nr
	200 x 200 x 300 mm	49.70	49.70	49.70	Nr
	300 x 300 x 300 mm	69.60	69.60	69.60	Nr
	300 x 300 x 600 mm	88.14	88.14	88.14	Nr

Specialist	Main Areas			
	10 - 30 m2 £	30 - 100 m2 £	Over 100 m2 £	Unit

LB   **PAVINGS AND SUB - FLOORS**

The following **specialist** guide prices were provided by J&J Asphalt, 47 Kingsfield Drive, Enfield, Middlesex, EN3 6UA (Telephone: 01922 638 824, Fax: 01922 638 825, Internet: www.jandjasphalt.co.uk)

001 | **Mastic asphalt BS 6925: 1988, T1076**

002 | 20 mm Two coat coverings rubbed with fine sand; to concrete base:

	10 - 30 m2	30 - 100 m2	Over 100 m2	Unit
flat coverings:				
over 300 mm wide	31.44	29.22	27.01	m2
not exceeding 150 mm wide	8.97	8.97	8.97	m
150 - 300 mm wide	11.11	11.11	11.11	m
sloping coverings over 10 degrees but not exceeding 45 degrees from horizontal:				
over 300 mm wide	40.43	38.16	33.68	m2
not exceeding 150 mm wide	11.11	11.11	11.11	m
150 - 300 mm wide	13.49	13.49	13.49	m

003 | **Extra over** for working into recessed duct covers and the like 30 mm deep:

	10 - 30 m2	30 - 100 m2	Over 100 m2	Unit
not exceeding 150 mm wide	6.65	6.65	6.65	m
150 - 300 mm wide	10.08	10.08	10.08	m
300 - 450 mm wide	13.49	13.49	13.49	m
450 - 600 mm wide	17.86	17.86	17.86	m
600 - 750 mm wide	21.35	21.35	21.35	m
750 - 900 mm wide	24.77	24.77	24.77	m

004 | **Extra over** for working into:

	10 - 30 m2	30 - 100 m2	Over 100 m2	Unit
shallow channels; two arrises; girth on face:				
300 mm	26.96	24.72	22.47	m
600 mm	31.44	29.22	27.01	m
shallow channels to falls; two arrises; average girth on face:				
300 mm	26.96	24.72	22.47	m
600 mm	31.44	29.22	27.01	m

	10 - 30 m2	30 - 100 m2	Over 100 m2	Unit
005 Fair edges	-	-	-	m
006 Rounded edges	-	-	-	m
007 Arrises	-	-	-	m
008 Turning nibs of asphalt into grooves	2.22	2.22	2.22	m
009 Working asphalt into outlet pipes, dishing to gulleys and the like	44.43	44.43	34.17	Nr

010 | 15 mm Two coat skirtings; one internal angle fillet; one nib turned into groove:

	10 - 30 m2	30 - 100 m2	Over 100 m2	Unit
to brickwork base; width on face:				
100 mm	21.42	18.86	16.21	m
150 mm (average)	21.42	18.86	16.21	m
200 mm	21.42	18.86	16.21	m
to concrete base; width on face:				
100 mm	21.42	18.86	16.21	m
150 mm (average)	21.42	18.86	16.21	m
200 mm	21.42	18.86	16.21	m
angle on skirting; width on face:				
100 mm	-	-	-	Nr
150 mm (average)	-	-	-	Nr
200 mm	-	-	-	Nr
stopped end with internal angle fillet on skirting; width on face:				
100 mm	-	-	-	Nr
150 mm (average)	-	-	-	Nr
200 mm	-	-	-	Nr

011 | **Coloured mastic asphalt BS 6925: 1988, T1451 (Brown/Red)**

012 | 20 mm Two coat coverings rubbed with fine sand; to concrete base:

	10 - 30 m2	30 - 100 m2	Over 100 m2	Unit
flat coverings:				
over 300 mm wide	48.51	43.14	40.41	m2
not exceeding 150 mm wide	13.33	13.33	13.33	m
150 - 300 mm wide	16.21	16.21	16.21	m
sloping coverings over 10 degrees but not exceeding 45 degrees from horizontal:				
over 300 mm wide	53.91	51.27	40.41	m2
not exceeding 150 mm wide	13.33	13.33	13.33	m
150 - 300 mm wide	16.21	16.21	16.21	m

013 | **Extra over** for working into recessed duct covers and the like 30 mm deep:

	10 - 30 m2	30 - 100 m2	Over 100 m2	Unit
not exceeding 150 mm wide	10.79	10.79	10.79	m
150 - 300 mm wide	13.54	13.54	13.54	m
300 - 450 mm wide	17.43	17.43	17.43	m
450 - 600 mm wide	28.30	28.30	28.30	m
600 - 750 mm wide	32.35	32.35	32.35	m
750 - 900 mm wide	37.73	37.73	37.73	m

014 | **Extra over** for working into:

	10 - 30 m2	30 - 100 m2	Over 100 m2	Unit
shallow channels; two arrises; girth on face:				
300 mm	35.07	35.07	32.39	m
600 mm	37.73	37.73	37.73	m
shallow channels to falls; two arrises; average girth on face:				
300 mm	35.07	35.07	32.39	m
600 mm	37.73	37.73	37.73	m

Specialist	Main Areas			Unit
	10 - 30 m2 £	30 - 100 m2 £	Over 100 m2 £	
015 Fair edges	-	-	-	m
016 Rounded edges	-	-	-	m
017 Arrises	-	-	-	m
018 Turning nibs of asphalt into grooves	2.22	2.22	2.22	m
019 Working asphalt into outlet pipes, dishing to gulleys and the like	49.94	45.79	43.75	Nr
020 15 mm Two coat skirtings; one internal angle fillet; one nib turned into groove:				
to brickwork base; width on face:				
100 mm	21.42	18.86	16.21	m
150 mm (average)	21.42	18.86	16.21	m
200 mm	21.42	18.86	16.21	m
to concrete base; width on face:				
100 mm	21.42	18.86	16.21	m
150 mm (average)	21.42	18.86	16.21	m
200 mm	21.42	18.86	16.21	m
angle on skirting; width on face:				
100 mm	-	-	-	Nr
150 mm (average)	-	-	-	Nr
200 mm	-	-	-	Nr
stopped end with internal angle fillet on skirting; width on face:				
100 mm	-	-	-	Nr
150 mm (average)	-	-	-	Nr
200 mm	-	-	-	Nr

LC   **ROOFING**

001   **Mastic asphalt BS 6925: 1988, R988; black sheathing felt isolating membrane BS 747, Type 4A (i) weighing 17 Kg per roll with 50 mm lapped joints, laid loose**

	10 - 30 m2 £	30 - 100 m2 £	Over 100 m2 £	Unit
002 20 mm Two coat work rubbed with fine sand; to concrete base:				
flat coverings:				
over 300 mm wide	40.24	35.76	26.83	m2
not exceeding 150 mm wide	6.83	6.83	6.83	m
150 - 300 mm wide	10.24	10.24	10.24	m
sloping coverings over 10 degrees but not exceeding 45 degrees from horizontal:				
over 300 mm wide	44.72	40.24	31.31	m2
not exceeding 150 mm wide	7.68	7.68	7.68	m
150 - 300 mm wide	11.11	11.11	11.11	m
sloping coverings over 45 degrees from horizontal and vertical coverings; PVA Keying mix and rubber based bitumen emulsion primer (no underlay):				
over 300 mm wide	53.66	49.21	44.94	m2
not exceeding 150 mm wide	8.55	8.55	8.55	m
150 - 300 mm wide	11.96	11.96	11.96	m
003 20 mm Two coat work rubbed with fine sand; to timber base, underlay fixed with nails:				
flat coverings:				
over 300 mm wide	35.76	31.31	26.83	m2
not exceeding 150 mm wide	6.83	6.83	6.83	m
150 - 300 mm wide	10.24	10.24	10.24	m
sloping coverings over 10 degrees but not exceeding 45 degrees from horizontal expanded metal reinforcement:				
over 300 mm wide	55.87	53.66	49.21	m2
not exceeding 150 mm wide	11.16	11.16	11.16	m
150 - 300 mm wide	13.67	13.67	13.67	m
sloping coverings over 45 degrees from horizontal and vertical coverings; expanded metal reinforcement fixed with nails:				
over 300 mm wide	75.12	68.43	59.07	m2
not exceeding 150 mm wide	13.33	13.33	13.33	m
150 - 300 mm wide	16.40	16.40	16.40	m
004 **Extra over** for working two coat covering into:				
shallow channels; two arrises; girth on face:				
200 mm	26.83	26.83	26.83	m
300 mm	31.31	29.05	26.83	m
shallow channels to falls; two arrises; average girth on face:				
200 mm	31.31	29.05	26.83	m
300 mm	33.54	31.31	26.83	m
ends on shallow channels:				
200 mm girth	11.11	11.11	11.11	Nr
300 mm girth	11.11	11.11	11.11	Nr
intersections on shallow channels:				
200 mm girth	-	-	-	Nr
300 mm girth	-	-	-	Nr
angles on shallow channels:				
200 mm girth	-	-	-	Nr
300 mm girth	-	-	-	Nr
005 Internal angle fillets	7.86	7.86	7.86	m
006 Internal angle fillets in three coats	10.08	10.08	10.08	m
007 Fair edges	-	-	-	m
008 Rounded edges	-	-	-	m
009 Drips	-	-	-	m
010 Arrises	-	-	-	m

Specialist	Main Areas			Unit
	10 - 30 m2 £	30 - 100 m2 £	Over 100 m2 £	
011 Turning nibs of asphalt into grooves	2.22	2.22	2.22	m
012 Working asphalt to outlet pipes, gulleys and the like	26.83	24.60	22.38	Nr
013 15 mm Two coat skirtings; one internal angle fillet; one nib turned into groove:				
to concrete base:				
horizontal; width on face:				
100 mm	21.52	18.86	16.21	m
200 mm	21.52	18.86	16.21	m
300 mm	21.52	18.86	16.21	m
raking; width on face:				
100 mm	21.52	18.86	16.21	m
200 mm	21.52	18.86	16.21	m
300 mm	21.52	18.86	16.21	m
to brickwork base:				
horizontal; width on face:				
100 mm	21.52	18.86	16.21	m
200 mm	21.52	18.86	16.21	m
300 mm	21.52	18.86	16.21	m
stepped; overall width on face:				
300 mm	21.52	18.86	16.21	m
400 mm	24.19	21.52	18.86	m
angle on skirting; width on face:				
100 mm	-	-	-	Nr
200 mm	-	-	-	Nr
300 mm	-	-	-	Nr
400 mm	-	-	-	Nr
stopped end with angle fillet on skirting; width on face:				
100 mm	-	-	-	Nr
200 mm	-	-	-	Nr
300 mm	-	-	-	Nr
400 mm	-	-	-	Nr
014 20 mm Two coat linings to gutters to falls rubbed with fine sand; two arrises; two internal angle fillets:				
to concrete base; average girth on face:				
300 mm	34.82	33.54	29.05	m
450 mm	38.02	34.82	33.54	m
600 mm	40.24	38.02	34.82	m
to timber base; expanded metal reinforcement fixed with nails; average girth on face:				
300 mm	40.24	40.24	38.02	m
450 mm	44.43	41.01	40.24	m
600 mm	47.85	44.43	41.01	m
angles on gutters:				
300 mm	-	-	-	Nr
450 mm	-	-	-	Nr
600 mm	-	-	-	Nr
ends on gutters:				
300 mm	11.11	11.11	11.11	Nr
450 mm	11.11	11.11	11.11	Nr
600 mm	11.11	11.11	11.11	Nr
outlets on gutters	17.08	17.08	17.08	Nr
015 20 mm Two coat linings to sumps rubbed with fine sand; arrises and internal angle fillets; dressing to outlets:				
to concrete base:				
200 x 200 x 200 mm	26.83	22.38	17.95	Nr
200 x 200 x 300 mm	26.83	22.38	17.95	Nr
300 x 300 x 300 mm	26.83	22.38	17.95	Nr
300 x 300 x 600 mm	26.83	22.38	17.95	Nr
to timber base; expanded metal reinforcement fixed with nails:				
200 x 200 x 200 mm	29.05	24.77	20.51	Nr
200 x 200 x 300 mm	29.05	24.77	20.51	Nr
300 x 300 x 300 mm	29.05	24.77	20.51	Nr
300 x 300 x 600 mm	33.33	29.05	24.77	Nr
016 **Alternative and additional items**				
017 **Extra over** surface rubbed with fine sand for:				
painting with two coats solar reflective paint	5.81	5.12	4.46	m2
covering with 12 mm limestone chippings in hot bitumen dressing compound	5.81	5.12	4.46	m2
priming with bitumen primer and covering with slabs similarly primed and bedded in proprietary bonding compound:				
300 x 300 x 8 mm glass reinforced concrete tiles	64.93	61.52	59.81	m2
018 Insulation underlays:				
12 mm bitumen impregnated boards:				
laid loose	11.14	8.97	8.97	m2
bedded overall in hot bitumen	11.14	8.97	8.97	m2
25 mm polystyrene slabs:				
laid loose	14.52	14.52	11.96	m2
bedded overall in hot bitumen	14.52	14.52	11.96	m2
50 mm polystyrene slabs:				
laid loose	20.51	18.79	17.08	m2
bedded overall in hot bitumen	20.51	18.79	17.08	m2
019 Vapour barriers:				
bitumen felt BS 747 type 3B weighing 18 Kg/10 m2 with sealed joints:				
fully bonded in hot bitumen bonding compound	7.68	6.83	5.99	m2

Specialist	£	Unit
LD **REPAIRS**		
001 **The following prices are specialist guide prices only**		
002 Cut out crack and make good with new asphalt to match existing, not exceeding 1 metre:		
two coat work	9.30	m
three coat work	10.22	m
003 Cut out blister not exceeding 0.50 m2 and make good with new asphalt to match existing:		
two coat work	16.73	Nr
three coat work	18.59	Nr
004 Cut out defective horizontal area not exceeding 1.00 m2 and make good with new asphalt to match existing:		
two coat work	59.50	Nr
three coat work	83.67	Nr
005 Cut out defective vertical area not exceeding 1.00 m2 and make good with new asphalt to match existing:		
two coat work	85.53	Nr
three coat work	115.29	Nr

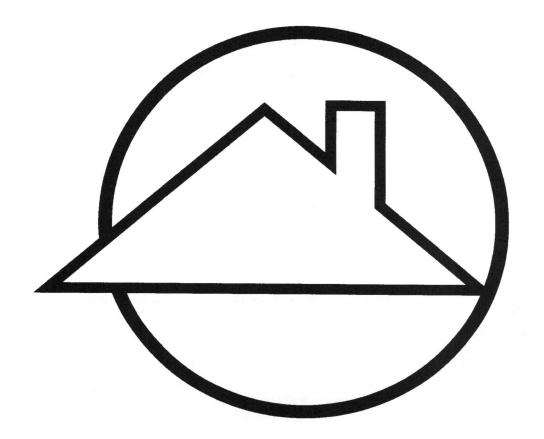

Roofing

Labour Rates

Please note: The labour hours throughout this section are representative of the time required for one productive man to carry out the unit of work.

Gang rates are calculated as follows by obtaining the overall gang cost and then dividing this by the number of productive members in the gang. The resulting rate is the Gang Cost per **Man - hour.** By using the same principle, any size gang may be built-up and used against the standard labour hours in this section.

A0208 Roof slating and tiling
Roof Slater/Tiler	1.00	x	£	15.20	= £	15.20
Roof Slating/Tiling Labourer	1.00	x	£	11.22	= £	11.22
Total hourly cost of gang				= £		26.42

Gang rate (divided by 1) = £26.42 per Man-hour

A0211 Roofing (sheet metal - plumbing gang)
Advanced PHMES Operative	1.00	x	£	19.59	= £	19.59
Apprentice Plumber (3rd Year)	1.00	x	£	12.01	= £	12.01
Total hourly cost of gang				= £		31.60

Gang rate (divided by 1) = £31.60 per Man-hour

A0209 Roof decking
Carpenter	1.00	x	£	15.20	= £	15.20
Roof Decking Labourer	1.00	x	£	11.22	= £	11.22
Total hourly cost of gang				= £		26.42

Gang rate (divided by 1) = £26.42 per Man-hour

Basic Prices of Materials

	Supply Price £	Waste Factor %	Unload. Labour £	Unload. Plant £	Total Unit Cost £	Unit
Note: Where no 'Labour Unloading' prices are shown the materials are supplied palletised for crane unloading (surcharge for pallets excluded). The cost of hoisting roofing materials to roof level is allowed in Preliminaries (plant and attendance).						
Burlington slates (quarry prices plus average £45.00 per tonne delivery):						
Blue/grey slates Type 1 - Patterns of uniform length and width:						
M0021 610 x 305 mm	4945.50	5%	-	-	**5192.78**	1000
M0022 510 x 255 mm	2110.50	5%	-	-	**2216.03**	1000
M0023 405 x 205 mm	1354.50	5%	-	-	**1422.23**	1000
Blue/grey slates Type 2 - Sized of uniform length and random widths:						
M0024 610 mm long	1176.00	5%	-	-	**1234.80**	tonne
M0025 510 mm long	887.25	5%	-	-	**931.61**	tonne
M0026 405 mm long	845.25	5%	-	-	**887.51**	tonne
Blue/grey random slates, random lengths, proportionate and random widths:						
M0027 1200 - 765 mm lengths (best mixed)	2021.25	5%	-	-	**2122.31**	tonne
M0028 710 - 560 mm lengths (best mixed)	1097.25	5%	-	-	**1152.11**	tonne
M0029 550 - 305 mm lengths (best mixed)	887.25	5%	-	-	**931.61**	tonne
M0030 355 - 255 mm lengths (best mixed)	651.00	5%	-	-	**683.55**	tonne
Marley Eternit roof tiles and accessories delivered to sites in the Greater London area:						
M0103 Ludlow Major granular/smooth	946.00	5%	-	-	**993.30**	1000
M0105 Mendip granular/smooth	962.00	5%	-	-	**1010.10**	1000
M0107 Modern smooth	982.00	5%	-	-	**1031.10**	1000
M0108 Wessex smooth	1459.00	5%	-	-	**1531.95**	1000
M0109 Malvern smooth	1055.00	5%	-	-	**1107.75**	1000
M0110 Melbourn smooth slates	2109.00	5%	-	-	**2214.45**	1000
M0111 Ludlow Plus granular/smooth	664.94	5%	-	-	**698.18**	1000
M0165 Anglia Plus granular/smooth	698.18	5%	-	-	**733.09**	1000
M0113 Pascoll roll granular	3.90	5%	-	-	**4.09**	nr
M0114 segmental ridge granular/smooth	4.39	5%	-	-	**4.61**	nr
M0115 Modern ridge granular/smooth	4.61	5%	-	-	**4.84**	nr
M0116 Modern mono ridge granular/smooth	8.23	5%	-	-	**8.64**	nr
M0117 segmental mono ridge granular/smooth	8.23	5%	-	-	**8.64**	nr
M0118 trough valleys smooth	8.23	5%	-	-	**8.64**	nr
M0119 dentil slips and verge slips	0.22	5%	-	-	**0.23**	nr
M0120 low resistance gas vent ridge with extension piece and gasket set	54.37	2.5%	-	-	**55.73**	nr
M0121 ventilating ridge	39.14	2.5%	-	-	**40.12**	nr
M0122 soffit strip 1220 x 150 mm	1.13	5%	-	-	**1.19**	nr
tile clips:						
M0133 Modern tile	0.05	5%	-	-	**0.05**	nr
M0134 Modern eave	0.04	5%	-	-	**0.04**	nr
M0135 Modern verge	0.35	5%	-	-	**0.36**	nr
M0136 Wessex tile	0.05	5%	-	-	**0.05**	nr
M0137 Wessex eave	0.20	5%	-	-	**0.21**	nr
M0138 Wessex verge	0.35	5%	-	-	**0.36**	nr
M0139 Mendip eave	0.04	5%	-	-	**0.04**	nr
M0140 Melbourn slate (clip and nail)	0.03	5%	-	-	**0.03**	nr
M0167 Melbourn eave (clip and nail)	0.31	5%	-	-	**0.33**	nr
M0168 Melbourn verge (clip and nail)	0.21	5%	-	-	**0.22**	nr
M0141 Ludlow major eave	0.04	5%	-	-	**0.04**	nr
M0142 Malvern tile	0.05	5%	-	-	**0.05**	nr
M0143 Malvern eave	0.04	5%	-	-	**0.04**	nr
M0144 Malvern verge	0.35	5%	-	-	**0.36**	nr

Basic Prices of Materials

		Supply Price £	Waste Factor %	Unload. Labour £	Unload. Plant £	Total Unit Cost £	Unit
	profiled eaves fillers:						
M0146	Mendip / Double Roman	0.31	5%	-	-	0.33	nr
M0147	Malvern	0.31	5%	-	-	0.33	nr
M0148	aluminium nails	2.93	5%	-	-	3.07	kg
M0149	wire nails	2.88	10%	-	-	3.16	kg
M0150	galvanised wire nails	2.92	10%	-	-	3.21	kg
M0151	annular ring shank nails	3.05	10%	-	-	3.36	kg
M0166	sheradised annular ring shank nails	0.22	5%	-	-	0.23	nr
M0152	4 mm hip irons	2.50	5%	-	-	2.62	nr
M0153	6 mm hip irons	2.94	5%	-	-	3.08	nr
M0154	tilers colour (black)	3.52	5%	-	-	3.70	ltr
	interlocking dry verge system:						
M0155	L.H. or R.H. verge unit	4.20	5%	-	-	4.41	nr
M0156	L.H. or R.H. stop end unit	3.81	5%	-	-	4.00	nr
M0157	Segmental or Modern ridge end cap	8.18	5%	-	-	8.58	nr
M0158	L.H. or R.H. monoridge end caps	8.18	5%	-	-	8.58	nr
	dry ridge system:						
M0159	batten section	14.90	5%	-	-	15.64	nr
M0160	Segmental or Modern ridge union	1.71	5%	-	-	1.80	nr
M0161	Modern filler unit Ludlow Major, Mendip, Malvern, Wessex or Double Roman	0.70	5%	-	-	0.74	nr
M0162	soil vent pipe ridge terminal	39.14	5%	-	-	41.10	nr
M0163	gas vent ridge adaptor unit for dry ridge	4.26	5%	-	-	4.47	nr
M0164	dry ridge setting out gauge	8.01	5%	-	-	8.41	nr
M0169	Melbourn dry verge system (5 m length) with union and fixing kit	57.74	5%	-	-	60.63	nr
	Redland roof tiles and accessories delivered to sites in the Greater London area:						
M0214	Plain tiles	443.10	5%	-	-	465.26	1000
M0216	Ornamental tiles	821.10	5%	-	-	862.16	1000
	Extra over for:						
M0241	bonnet hips	3.78	5%	-	-	3.97	nr
M0249	vertical angle tiles (internal and external)	3.78	5%	-	-	3.97	nr
M0299	aluminium alloy nails (1500 carton) 60 mm x 3.35	12.74	10%	-	-	14.01	nr
	Protimised sawn softwood battens:						
M0361	36 x 22 mm	0.36	5%	0.01	-	0.39	m
M0362	36 x 25 mm	0.36	5%	0.01	-	0.39	m
M0363	36 x 36 mm	0.55	5%	0.01	-	0.59	m
M0364	38 x 19 mm	0.36	5%	0.01	-	0.39	m
M0365	38 x 25 mm	0.36	5%	0.01	-	0.39	m
M0366	38 x 38 mm	0.55	5%	0.02	-	0.60	m
M0367	44 x 25 mm	0.48	5%	0.01	-	0.51	m
M0368	44 x 38 mm	0.71	5%	0.02	-	0.76	m
	Protimised sawn softwood ridge battens:						
M0380	50 x 20 mm	0.48	5%	0.01	-	0.51	m
M0381	50 x 25 mm	0.48	5%	0.01	-	0.51	m
M0382	50 x 30 mm	0.71	5%	0.02	-	0.76	m
M0383	50 x 35 mm	0.71	5%	0.02	-	0.76	m
M0384	50 x 40 mm	0.77	5%	0.02	-	0.83	m
M0385	50 x 45 mm	0.77	5%	0.02	-	0.83	m
M0386	50 x 50 mm	0.77	5%	0.03	-	0.84	m
M0387	50 x 75 mm	0.99	5%	0.04	-	1.08	m
M0388	50 x 100 mm	1.30	5%	0.06	-	1.43	m
M0369	50 - 75 mm Galvanised nails for battens	2.13	10%	-	-	2.35	kg
M0370	Hardened steel masonry nails 50 x 2.5 mm diameter	0.01	10%	-	-	0.02	nr
	Underslating:						
M0371	Rubershield – Pro breathable membrane (50 m2 roll)	97.54	12.5%	1.12	-	110.99	nr
M0372	Zylex reinforced felt - standard (15 m2 roll)	32.68	12.5%	1.12	-	38.03	nr
M0373	Roofguard SB non-breathable membrane (45 m2 roll)	62.14	12.5%	1.12	-	71.17	nr
A0301	Portland cement delivered in bags	137.81	5%	11.22	-	156.48	tonne
A0321	Building sand BS 1200	24.16	10%	-	-	26.57	tonne
M0379	Unibond PVA adhesive	2.80	10%	-	-	3.08	ltr
	Cartridge assisted fasteners (Hilti); for:						
M0455	75 mm material fixed to concrete NK72 S12	0.36	2.5%	-	-	0.37	nr
M0456	100 mm material fixed to concrete NK97 D12	0.46	2.5%	-	-	0.47	nr
M0457	fixing metal straps to steel ENK19 512	0.25	2.5%	-	-	0.26	nr
M0458	cartridges (red)	0.15	2.5%	-	-	0.15	nr
M0480	Bitumen bonding compound 105/35 (45 kg keg)	36.24	10%	-	-	39.87	nr
	Hambleside Danelaw Ltd GRP roofing accessories:						
M0500	GRP valley trough 400 mm girth	6.16	-	-	-	6.16	m
M0501	GRP valley trough 360 mm girth	5.51	-	-	-	5.51	m
M0502	GRP bonding gutter 225 mm wide	5.51	-	-	-	5.51	m
M0503	GRP continuous soaker for tiled roof 160 x 150 mm	5.19	-	-	-	5.19	m
M0504	GRP continuous soaker for slate roof 150 x 160 mm	5.19	-	-	-	5.19	m
M0505	SRV Universal roof vent 600 x 300 mm or 500 x 250 mm	11.15	-	-	-	11.15	nr

		Man-Hours	Net Labour Price £	Net Mats Price £	Net Unit Price £	Unit
	Unit Rates					

UNIT RATES
MA **SLATE ROOFING AND CLADDING**

NATURAL SLATES

		Man-Hours	Net Labour Price £	Net Mats Price £	Net Unit Price £	Unit
001	**Burlington blue/grey natural slates; fixing each slate with two aluminium alloy nails to 75 mm lap; 38 x 25 mm treated sawn softwood battens**					
	Note: 002 - 019 not used					
020	Remove decayed or defective battens, and replace with new:					
	38 x 25 mm in lengths:					
	not exceeding 1.00 m	0.14	3.70	0.40	**4.10**	Nr
	1.00 - 2.00 m	0.28	7.34	0.80	**8.14**	Nr
	over 2.00 m	0.08	1.98	0.40	**2.38**	m
	50 x 25 mm in lengths:					
	not exceeding 1.00 m	0.14	3.70	0.52	**4.22**	Nr
	1.00 - 2.00 m	0.28	7.34	1.04	**8.38**	Nr
	over 2.00 m	0.08	2.22	0.52	**2.74**	m
021	Remove damaged slates and replace with new, sloping or vertical:					
	610 x 305 mm:					
	single slate	0.23	6.16	5.20	**11.36**	Nr
	area not exceeding 1.00 m2	0.93	24.52	67.66	**92.18**	Nr
	area 1.00 - 2.00 m2	1.49	39.23	135.32	**174.55**	Nr
	510 x 255 mm:					
	single slate	0.23	6.16	2.23	**8.39**	Nr
	area not exceeding 1.00 m2	1.21	31.89	46.78	**78.67**	Nr
	area 1.00 - 2.00 m2	1.86	49.04	93.57	**142.61**	Nr
	405 x 205 mm:					
	single slate	0.23	6.16	1.43	**7.59**	Nr
	area not exceeding 1.00 m2	1.81	47.85	61.66	**109.51**	Nr
	area 1.00 - 2.00 m2	2.88	76.01	123.32	**199.33**	Nr
022	Refix slates previously removed and stacked; lay with 75 mm lap and fix each slate with two aluminium alloy nails:					
	610 x 305 mm:					
	single slate	0.19	4.91	0.01	**4.92**	Nr
	area not exceeding 1.00 m2	0.84	22.06	0.15	**22.21**	Nr
	area 1.00 - 2.00 m2	1.30	34.32	0.30	**34.62**	Nr
	510 x 255 mm:					
	single slate	0.19	4.91	0.01	**4.92**	Nr
	area not exceeding 1.00 m2	1.09	28.72	0.25	**28.97**	Nr
	area 1.00 - 2.00 m2	1.67	44.15	0.49	**44.64**	Nr
	405 x 205 mm:					
	single slate	0.19	4.91	0.01	**4.92**	Nr
	area not exceeding 1.00 m2	1.63	42.93	0.50	**43.43**	Nr
	area 1.00 - 2.00 m2	2.60	68.67	1.01	**69.68**	Nr
023	Remove double course at eaves and refix with new nails and 10% new slates:					
	610 x 305 mm in lengths:					
	not exceeding 1.00 m	0.14	3.70	5.23	**8.93**	Nr
	1.00 - 2.00 m	0.28	7.34	9.16	**16.50**	Nr
	over 2.00 m	0.14	3.70	5.23	**8.93**	m
	510 x 255 mm in lengths:					
	not exceeding 1.00 m	0.14	3.70	3.95	**7.65**	Nr
	1.00 - 2.00 m	0.28	7.34	6.60	**13.94**	Nr
	over 2.00 m	0.14	3.70	3.95	**7.65**	m
	405 x 205 mm in lengths:					
	not exceeding 1.00 m	0.14	3.70	2.65	**6.35**	Nr
	1.00 - 2.00 m	0.28	7.34	5.31	**12.65**	Nr
	over 2.00 m	0.14	3.70	2.65	**6.35**	m
024	Remove verge slates and replace with new; bedded and pointed in coloured cement mortar (1:3); each slate fixed with two new nails; 10% new slates:					
	610 x 305 mm in lengths:					
	not exceeding 1.00 m	0.28	7.34	11.32	**18.66**	Nr
	1.00 - 2.00 m	0.56	14.72	22.66	**37.38**	Nr
	over 2.00 m	0.24	6.37	11.32	**17.69**	m
	510 x 255 mm in lengths:					
	not exceeding 1.00 m	0.32	8.35	7.98	**16.33**	Nr
	1.00 - 2.00 m	0.63	16.70	15.95	**32.65**	Nr
	over 2.00 m	0.26	6.87	7.98	**14.85**	m
	405 x 205 mm in lengths:					
	not exceeding 1.00 m	0.33	8.82	8.92	**17.74**	Nr
	1.00 - 2.00 m	0.67	17.65	17.84	**35.49**	Nr
	over 2.00 m	0.28	7.34	8.92	**16.26**	m
025	Slating to match existing on and including 38 x 25 mm treated sawn softwood battens, underfelting and 50 x 150 mm treated softwood infill rafters (where chimney stack or bulkhead removed); to area:					
	not exceeding 1.00 m2:					
	610 x 305 mm in lengths	2.95	77.99	83.23	**161.22**	Nr
	510 x 255 mm in lengths	3.16	83.38	65.18	**148.56**	Nr
	405 x 205 mm in lengths	3.56	94.16	81.99	**176.15**	Nr
	1.00 - 2.00 m2:					
	610 x 305 mm in lengths	4.42	116.72	163.98	**280.70**	Nr
	510 x 255 mm in lengths	4.78	126.31	125.65	**251.96**	Nr
	405 x 205 mm in lengths	5.32	140.58	159.98	**300.56**	Nr

	Man-Hours	Net Labour Price £	Net Mats Price £	Net Unit Price £	Unit
Unit Rates					
2.00 - 3.00 m2:					
610 x 305 mm in lengths	5.53	146.16	245.41	**391.57**	Nr
510 x 255 mm in lengths	5.99	158.20	189.03	**347.23**	Nr
405 x 205 mm in lengths	6.60	174.37	240.17	**414.54**	Nr

MB   **TILE ROOFING AND CLADDING**

CONCRETE TILES

001 | **Marley concrete tiles; all perimeter tiles mechanically fixed; main body of tiles not fixed; 38 x 25 mm treated sawn softwood battens**

Note: 002 - 025 not used

	Man-Hours	Net Labour Price £	Net Mats Price £	Net Unit Price £	Unit
026 Remove damaged tiles and replace with new; sloping or vertical:					
Marley concrete tiles:					
413 x 330 mm (Ludlow):					
single tile	0.23	6.16	1.01	**7.17**	Nr
area not exceeding 1.00 m2	0.33	8.61	10.05	**18.66**	Nr
area 1.00 - 2.00 m2	0.54	14.24	20.10	**34.34**	Nr
420 x 330 mm (Malvern):					
single tile	0.23	6.16	1.12	**7.28**	Nr
area not exceeding 1.00 m2	0.32	8.35	11.19	**19.54**	Nr
area 1.00 - 2.00 m2	0.54	14.24	22.39	**36.63**	Nr
380 x 230 mm (Ludlow Plus):					
single tile	0.23	6.16	0.71	**6.87**	Nr
area not exceeding 1.00 m2	0.46	12.26	11.36	**23.62**	Nr
area 1.00 - 2.00 m2	0.78	20.61	22.72	**43.33**	Nr
265 x 165 mm (Plain tiles):					
single tile	0.23	6.16	0.64	**6.80**	Nr
area not exceeding 1.00 m2	2.28	60.32	41.26	**101.58**	Nr
area 1.00 - 2.00 m2	3.81	100.55	82.52	**183.07**	Nr
027 Refix tiles previously removed and stacked; lay with 75 mm lap and fix with aluminium alloy nails:					
Marley concrete tiles:					
413 x 330 mm (Ludlow):					
single tile	0.23	6.16	0.01	**6.17**	Nr
area not exceeding 1.00 m2	0.30	7.85	0.12	**7.97**	Nr
area 1.00 - 2.00 m2	0.48	12.73	0.23	**12.96**	Nr
420 x 330 mm (Malvern):					
single tile	0.23	6.16	0.01	**6.17**	Nr
area not exceeding 1.00 m2	0.30	7.85	0.12	**7.97**	Nr
area 1.00 - 2.00 m2	0.48	12.73	0.23	**12.96**	Nr
380 x 230 mm (Ludlow Plus):					
single tile	0.23	6.16	0.01	**6.17**	Nr
area not exceeding 1.00 m2	0.42	11.07	0.19	**11.26**	Nr
area 1.00 - 2.00 m2	0.71	18.63	0.37	**19.00**	Nr
265 x 165 mm (Plain tiles):					
single tile	0.23	6.16	0.01	**6.17**	Nr
area not exceeding 1.00 m2	2.05	54.21	0.75	**54.96**	Nr
area 1.00 - 2.00 m2	3.43	90.49	1.50	**91.99**	Unit
028 Remove eaves course of tiles and replace with new, fixed with aluminium nails, including eaves filler units and eave clips where necessary:					
Marley concrete tiles:					
413 x 330 mm (Ludlow):					
single tile	0.14	3.70	3.13	**6.83**	Nr
area not exceeding 1.00 m2	0.23	6.16	6.26	**12.42**	Nr
area 1.00 - 2.00 m2	0.12	3.20	3.13	**6.33**	m
420 x 330 mm (Malvern):					
single tile	0.14	3.70	3.47	**7.17**	Nr
area not exceeding 1.00 m2	0.23	6.16	6.94	**13.10**	Nr
area 1.00 - 2.00 m2	0.12	3.20	3.47	**6.67**	m
380 x 230 mm (Ludlow Plus):					
single tile	0.20	5.39	3.74	**9.13**	Nr
area not exceeding 1.00 m2	0.33	8.82	6.73	**15.55**	Nr
area 1.00 - 2.00 m2	0.17	4.41	3.74	**8.15**	m
265 x 165 mm (Plain tiles):					
single tile	0.19	4.91	6.45	**11.36**	Nr
area not exceeding 1.00 m2	0.31	8.11	12.89	**21.00**	Nr
area 1.00 - 2.00 m2	0.16	4.17	6.45	**10.62**	m
029 Remove verge tiles and replace with new, fixed with aluminium nails or clips bedded and pointed in coloured cement mortar (1:3):					
Marley concrete tiles:					
413 x 330 mm (Ludlow):					
single tile	0.80	21.08	3.43	**24.51**	Nr
area not exceeding 1.00 m2	1.30	34.32	6.59	**40.91**	Nr
area 1.00 - 2.00 m2	0.66	17.44	3.43	**20.87**	m
420 x 330 mm (Malvern):					
single tile	0.80	21.08	3.77	**24.85**	Nr
area not exceeding 1.00 m2	1.30	34.32	7.28	**41.60**	Nr
area 1.00 - 2.00 m2	0.66	17.44	3.77	**21.21**	m
380 x 230 mm (Ludlow Plus):					
single tile	0.92	24.28	2.55	**26.83**	Nr
area not exceeding 1.00 m2	1.54	40.71	4.82	**45.53**	Nr
area 1.00 - 2.00 m2	0.77	20.37	2.55	**22.92**	m

	Unit Rates	Man-Hours	Net Labour Price £	Net Mats Price £	Net Unit Price £	Unit
	265 x 165 mm (Plain tiles):					
	single tile	0.72	18.89	7.36	**26.25**	Nr
	area not exceeding 1.00 m2	1.19	31.39	14.71	**46.10**	Nr
	area 1.00 - 2.00 m2	0.59	15.69	7.36	**23.05**	m
030	Refixing ridge cappings previously removed; edge bedding and pointing in coloured cement mortar (1:3):					
	angular, in lengths:					
	not exceeding 1.00 m	0.74	19.63	0.27	**19.90**	Nr
	1.00 - 2.00 m	1.08	28.53	0.53	**29.06**	Nr
	over 2.00 m	0.56	14.72	0.27	**14.99**	m
	half round, in lengths:					
	not exceeding 1.00 m	0.74	19.63	0.27	**19.90**	Nr
	1.00 - 2.00 m	1.08	28.53	0.53	**29.06**	Nr
	over 2.00 m	0.56	14.72	0.27	**14.99**	m
031	Remove decayed and defective tiles and provide new:					
	half round ridge or hip tiles edge bedded in coloured cement mortar (1:3)	0.56	14.72	11.80	**26.52**	m
	bonnet hip tiles	0.42	11.07	39.11	**50.18**	m
	trough valley tiles	0.38	10.07	24.74	**34.81**	m
	vertical angle tiles	0.46	12.02	35.20	**47.22**	m
032	Rake out defective pointing to hip or ridge tiles and repoint in coloured cement mortar (1:3)	0.30	7.85	0.27	**8.12**	m
033	Remove defective hip iron and replace with new	0.23	6.16	2.62	**8.78**	Nr
034	Tiling to match existing on and including 38 x 25 mm treated sawn softwood battens, underfelting and 50 x 150 mm treated softwood infill rafters (where chimney stack or bulkhead removed); to area:					
	not exceeding 1.00 m2:					
	413 x 330 mm (Ludlow)	2.58	68.19	26.24	**94.43**	Nr
	420 x 330 mm (Malvern)	2.56	67.69	26.35	**94.04**	Nr
	380 x 230 mm (Ludlow Plus)	2.67	70.65	27.30	**97.95**	Nr
	265 x 165 mm (Plain tiles)	4.03	106.45	59.79	**166.24**	Nr
	1.00 - 2.00 m2:					
	413 x 330 mm (Ludlow)	3.99	105.44	48.93	**154.37**	Nr
	420 x 330 mm (Malvern)	3.96	104.73	50.18	**154.91**	Nr
	380 x 230 mm (Ludlow Plus)	4.18	110.36	51.97	**162.33**	Nr
	265 x 165 mm (Plain tiles)	6.24	164.78	117.05	**281.83**	Nr
	2.00 - 3.00 m2:					
	413 x 330 mm (Ludlow)	4.69	123.86	72.37	**196.23**	Nr
	420 x 330 mm (Malvern)	4.65	122.88	75.84	**198.72**	Nr
	380 x 230 mm (Ludlow Plus)	4.90	129.48	77.43	**206.91**	Nr
	265 x 165 mm (Plain tiles)	7.89	208.45	175.03	**383.48**	Nr
MC	**PLAIN TILE ROOFING AND CLADDING**					
001	**Plain tiling; 265 x 165 mm machine made tiles laid with maximum 100 mm gauge and minimum 65 mm lap; each tile in every fifth course and all perimeter tiles secured with two aluminium nails; 38 x 19 mm treated sawn softwood battens**					
002	Remove damaged tiles and replace with new:					
	concrete plain tiles:					
	single tile	0.25	6.61	0.47	**7.08**	Nr
	area not exceeding 1.00 m2	0.95	25.10	28.05	**53.15**	Nr
	area 1.00 - 2.00 m2	1.90	50.20	56.10	**106.30**	Nr
	plain red clay tiles:					
	single tile	0.25	6.61	0.62	**7.23**	Nr
	area not exceeding 1.00 m2	0.95	25.10	36.86	**61.96**	Nr
	area 1.00 - 2.00 m2	1.90	50.20	73.72	**123.92**	Nr
003	Refix tiles previously removed and stacked; lay with 65 mm lap and fix with aluminium alloy nails:					
	concrete plain tiles:					
	single tile	0.20	5.28	0.01	**5.29**	Nr
	area not exceeding 1.00 m2	0.90	23.78	0.13	**23.91**	Nr
	area 1.00 - 2.00 m2	1.80	47.56	0.27	**47.83**	Nr
	plain red clay tiles:					
	single tile	0.20	5.28	0.01	**5.29**	Nr
	area not exceeding 1.00 m2	0.90	23.78	0.13	**23.91**	Nr
	area 1.00 - 2.00 m2	1.80	47.56	0.27	**47.83**	Nr
004	Remove eaves double course of tiles and replace with new, fixed with aluminium nails:					
	concrete plain tiles; in lengths:					
	not exceeding 1.00 m	0.45	11.89	2.80	**14.69**	Nr
	1.00 - 2.00 m	0.90	23.78	5.65	**29.43**	Nr
	over 2.00 m	0.40	10.57	2.80	**13.37**	m
	plain red clay tiles; in lengths:					
	not exceeding 1.00 m	0.45	11.89	3.68	**15.57**	Nr
	1.00 - 2.00 m	0.90	23.78	7.41	**31.19**	Nr
	over 2.00 m	0.40	10.57	3.68	**14.25**	m
005	Remove verge tiles and replace with new, fixed with aluminium nails or clips bedded and pointed in coloured cement mortar (1:3):					
	concrete plain tiles; in lengths:					
	not exceeding 1.00 m	0.70	18.49	4.41	**22.90**	Nr
	1.00 - 2.00 m	1.20	31.70	8.82	**40.52**	Nr
	over 2.00 m	0.55	14.53	4.41	**18.94**	m
	plain red clay tiles; in lengths:					
	not exceeding 1.00 m	0.70	18.49	13.12	**31.61**	Nr

Unit Rates	Man-Hours	Net Labour Price £	Net Mats Price £	Net Unit Price £	Unit
1.00 - 2.00 m	1.20	31.70	26.24	**57.94**	Nr
over 2.00 m	0.55	14.53	13.12	**27.65**	m
006 Refixing ridge and hip tiles previously removed; edge bedding and pointing in coloured cement mortar (1:3):					
concrete plain tiles; in lengths:					
not exceeding 1.00 m	0.74	19.55	17.74	**37.29**	Nr
1.00 - 2.00 m	1.38	36.46	53.49	**89.95**	Nr
over 2.00 m	0.56	14.80	17.74	**32.54**	m
plain red clay tiles; in lengths:					
not exceeding 1.00 m	0.74	19.55	17.74	**37.29**	Nr
1.00 - 2.00 m	1.38	36.46	53.49	**89.95**	Nr
over 2.00 m	0.56	14.80	17.74	**32.54**	m
007 Remove decayed and defective ridge or hip tiles and provide new; bedded in coloured cement mortar (1:3):					
concrete plain tiles	0.90	23.78	49.69	**73.47**	m
plain red clay tiles	0.90	23.78	55.48	**79.26**	m
008 Rake out defective pointing to hip or ridge tiles and repoint in coloured cement mortar (1:3)	0.30	7.93	0.27	**8.20**	m
009 Remove defective hip iron and replace with new	0.24	6.34	2.62	**8.96**	Nr
010 Tiling to match existing on and including 38 x 25 mm treated sawn softwood battens, underfelting and 50 x 150 mm treated softwood infill rafters (where chimney stack or bulkhead removed); to area:					
not exceeding 1.00 m2:					
concrete plain tiles	2.60	68.69	43.23	**111.92**	Nr
plain red clay tiles	2.60	68.69	52.04	**120.73**	Nr
1.00 - 2.00 m2:					
concrete plain tiles	4.00	105.68	83.90	**189.58**	Nr
plain red clay tiles	4.00	105.68	101.52	**207.20**	Nr
2.00 - 3.00 m2:					
concrete plain tiles	4.70	124.17	125.32	**249.49**	Nr
plain red clay tiles	4.70	124.17	151.76	**275.93**	Nr
MD COUNTER-BATTENS AND UNDERSLATING					
001 **Treated sawn softwood counter-battens**					
002 Fixing with galvanised nails to softwood:					
38 x 19 mm:					
450 mm centres	0.06	1.59	0.98	**2.57**	m2
600 mm centres	0.04	1.16	0.73	**1.89**	m2
750 mm centres	0.04	0.95	0.57	**1.52**	m2
38 x 25 mm:					
450 mm centres	0.08	2.06	0.98	**3.04**	m2
600 mm centres	0.06	1.59	0.73	**2.32**	m2
750 mm centres	0.05	1.24	0.57	**1.81**	m2
38 x 38 mm:					
450 mm centres	0.12	3.12	1.44	**4.56**	m2
600 mm centres	0.09	2.35	1.08	**3.43**	m2
750 mm centres	0.07	1.90	0.84	**2.74**	m2
44 x 38 mm:					
450 mm centres	0.14	3.65	1.80	**5.45**	m2
600 mm centres	0.10	2.75	1.36	**4.11**	m2
750 mm centres	0.08	2.19	1.05	**3.24**	m2
003 Fixing direct with masonry nails to blockwork, brickwork or concrete:					
38 x 19 mm:					
450 mm centres	0.07	1.96	0.99	**2.95**	m2
600 mm centres	0.06	1.48	0.76	**2.24**	m2
750 mm centres	0.04	1.16	0.59	**1.75**	m2
38 x 25 mm:					
450 mm centres	0.10	2.59	0.99	**3.58**	m2
600 mm centres	0.07	1.96	0.76	**2.72**	m2
750 mm centres	0.06	1.56	0.59	**2.15**	m2
38 x 38 mm:					
450 mm centres	0.15	3.91	1.44	**5.35**	m2
600 mm centres	0.11	2.93	1.11	**4.04**	m2
750 mm centres	0.09	2.35	0.86	**3.21**	m2
44 x 38 mm:					
450 mm centres	0.17	4.57	1.80	**6.37**	m2
600 mm centres	0.13	3.43	1.39	**4.82**	m2
750 mm centres	0.10	2.75	1.07	**3.82**	m2
004 Individual counter-battens:					
fixing with galvanised nails to softwood:					
38 x 19 mm	0.03	0.74	0.45	**1.19**	m
38 x 25 mm	0.04	0.95	0.45	**1.40**	m
38 x 38 mm	0.05	1.43	0.66	**2.09**	m
44 x 38 mm	0.06	1.64	0.82	**2.46**	m
fixing direct with masonry nails to blockwork, brickwork or concrete:					
38 x 19 mm	0.03	0.90	0.44	**1.34**	m
38 x 25 mm	0.04	1.16	0.44	**1.60**	m
38 x 38 mm	0.07	1.77	0.65	**2.42**	m
44 x 38 mm	0.08	2.06	0.81	**2.87**	m

Unit Rates	Man-Hours	Net Labour Price £	Net Mats Price £	Net Unit Price £	Unit
005	**Underslating with 150 mm laps, secured with battens**					
006	Rubershield – Pro breathable membrane	0.03	0.66	2.33	**2.99**	m2
007	Zylex reinforced slaters felt to BS 747 Type 1F: standard	0.03	0.66	2.55	**3.21**	m2
008	Roofguard SB non-breathable membrane	0.03	0.66	1.59	**2.25**	m2

		Man-Hours	Plant Hours	Net Labour Price £	Net Plant Price £	Net Mats Price £	Net Unit Price £	Unit
MG	**BITUMINOUS BUILT UP FELT ROOFING**							
	Note: 001 - 020 not used							
021	Remove defective layer of bituminous felt roofing; prepare under layer and provide and lay new fine granular surface felt to BS 747:							
	fibre based bitumen felt type 1B:							
	one layer	0.14	0.13	3.70	0.58	4.41	**8.69**	m2
	two layers	0.23	0.21	6.16	0.96	8.88	**16.00**	m2
	glass fibre based bitumen felt, talc finish:							
	one layer	0.14	0.13	3.70	0.58	4.41	**8.69**	m2
	two layers	0.23	0.21	6.16	0.96	8.88	**16.00**	m2
	glass fibre based bitumen felt type 3B:							
	one layer	0.14	0.13	3.70	0.58	4.41	**8.69**	m2
	two layers	0.23	0.21	6.16	0.96	8.88	**16.00**	m2
022	**Extra over** felt roofing for top layer in mineral surfaced felt, in lieu of fine granular surface felt:							
	fibre based bitumen felt type 1E	0.09	0.09	2.46	0.38	2.91	**5.75**	m2
	polyester based bitumen felt, aluminium faced	0.09	0.09	2.46	0.38	35.51	**38.35**	m2
	glass fibre based bitumen felt type 3E	0.09	0.09	2.46	0.38	2.89	**5.73**	m2
023	**Extra over** for layer of stone chippings in hot bitumen	0.09	0.09	2.46	0.38	3.68	**6.52**	m2

		Man-Hours	Net Labour Price £	Net Mats Price £	Net Unit Price £	Unit
MJ	**SHEET METAL ROOFING GUTTERS AND FLASHINGS - LEAD**					
	Note: 001 - 037 not used					
038	Remove decayed or defective cover flashing and supply and fix new; wedge into groove:					
	not exceeding 150 mm girth:					
	BS Code 4	0.46	14.66	9.75	**24.41**	m
	BS Code 5	0.48	15.23	12.14	**27.37**	m
	BS Code 6	0.50	15.83	13.58	**29.41**	m
	150 - 300 mm girth:					
	BS Code 4	0.70	22.03	19.44	**41.47**	m
	BS Code 5	0.72	22.88	24.21	**47.09**	m
	BS Code 6	0.76	24.05	27.08	**51.13**	m
039	Remove decayed or defective apron flashing and supply and fix new; wedge into groove or copper nail on one edge:					
	not exceeding 150 mm girth:					
	BS Code 4	0.70	22.03	19.44	**41.47**	m
	BS Code 5	0.72	22.88	24.21	**47.09**	m
	BS Code 6	0.76	24.05	27.08	**51.13**	m
	150 - 300 mm girth:					
	BS Code 4	0.88	27.90	29.18	**57.08**	m
	BS Code 5	0.93	29.32	36.35	**65.67**	m
	BS Code 6	1.00	31.69	40.66	**72.35**	m
040	Remove decayed or defective stepped flashing and supply and fix new; wedge into groove one side:					
	not exceeding 150 mm girth:					
	BS Code 4	1.67	52.80	9.75	**62.55**	m
	BS Code 5	1.90	60.17	12.14	**72.31**	m
	BS Code 6	2.14	67.47	13.58	**81.05**	m
	150 - 300 mm girth:					
	BS Code 4	2.09	66.01	19.44	**85.45**	m
	BS Code 5	2.32	73.34	24.21	**97.55**	m
	BS Code 6	2.55	80.67	27.08	**107.75**	m
041	Remove decayed or defective gutter lining; supply and fix new:					
	not exceeding 500 mm girth:					
	BS Code 4	3.25	102.67	32.43	**135.10**	m
	BS Code 5	3.48	110.03	40.39	**150.42**	m
	BS Code 6	3.71	117.33	45.19	**162.52**	m
	500 - 1000 mm girth:					
	BS Code 4	6.50	205.31	64.87	**270.18**	m
	BS Code 5	6.96	219.97	80.79	**300.76**	m
	BS Code 6	7.43	234.66	90.37	**325.03**	m

	Unit Rates	Man-Hours	Net Labour Price £	Net Mats Price £	Net Unit Price £	Unit
042	Turn back lead flashing and redress to roof sheets or tiles:					
	along the slope of:					
	glass and glazing bars	0.26	8.15	-	**8.15**	m
	corrugated roofing	0.29	9.10	-	**9.10**	m
	Plain tiling	0.27	8.47	-	**8.47**	m
	Roman tiling	0.28	8.78	-	**8.78**	m
	Pantiling	0.28	8.78	-	**8.78**	m
	across the slope of:					
	glass and glazing bars	0.36	11.38	-	**11.38**	m
	corrugated roofing	0.39	12.36	-	**12.36**	m
	Plain tiling	0.37	11.72	-	**11.72**	m
	Roman tiling	0.38	12.04	-	**12.04**	m
	Pantiling	0.38	12.04	-	**12.04**	m
043	Repair crack in lead sheet; clean out crack and fill with solder:					
	not exceeding 150 mm long	0.46	14.66	4.53	**19.19**	Nr
	150 - 300 mm long	0.70	22.03	9.06	**31.09**	Nr
	over 300 mm long	1.05	33.18	27.19	**60.37**	m
MK	**SHEET METAL ROOFING, GUTTERS AND FLASHINGS - COPPER**					
	Note: 001 - 033 not used					
034	Remove decayed or defective flashing and supply and fix new; wedge one edge into groove:					
	cover flashing:					
	not exceeding 150 mm girth	0.37	11.72	2.20	**13.92**	m
	150 - 300 mm girth	0.56	17.60	4.39	**21.99**	m
	apron flashing:					
	not exceeding 150 mm girth	0.56	17.60	4.39	**21.99**	m
	150 - 300 mm girth	0.74	23.48	6.59	**30.07**	m
	stepped flashing:					
	not exceeding 150 mm girth	1.35	42.57	2.20	**44.77**	m
	150 - 300 mm girth	2.00	63.11	4.39	**67.50**	m
035	Remove decayed or defective gutter lining; supply and fix new:					
	not exceeding 500 mm average girth	2.60	82.13	7.32	**89.45**	m
	500 - 1000 mm average girth	5.20	164.26	14.64	**178.90**	m
ML	**SUNDRY WORK TO EXISTING ROOFS**					
001	Clean off existing roof covering and apply one coat liquid bitumen:					
	felt roofing	0.19	2.15	6.10	**8.25**	m2
	corrugated sheet roofing	0.29	3.21	4.88	**8.09**	m2
002	Remove decayed or defective cover flashing and supply and fix new self-adhesive metalised flashing:					
	150 mm girth	0.51	13.47	1.54	**15.01**	m
	300 mm girth	0.72	19.02	3.23	**22.25**	m
	450 mm girth	0.93	24.57	5.16	**29.73**	m

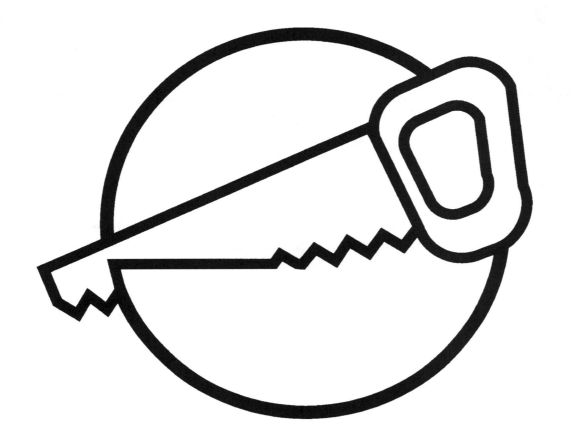

Woodwork

Labour Rates

Woodwork:

Carpenter = £15.20 per hour

Wood Machinist = £15.20 per hour

Workshop Joiner = £15.20 per hour

Labour unloading
Unloading cost includes for distributing materials around the site. Where no cost has been included for unloading the cost is deemed to be included in the cost of labour for handling and fixing.

Basic Prices of Materials		Supply Price £	Waste Factor %	Unload. Labour £	Unload. Plant £	Total Unit Cost £	Unit
Ancillary materials, (e.g. nails, screws, glue) Prices of materials include for ordinary wire nails, glue and the like according to description and waste allowances etc. All items are deemed fixed with ordinary nails; **Extra over** prices are given in the SUNDRIES section, for fixing with other types of nail, screws, plugs etc.							
	Material						
	Sawn softwood, Building quality, untreated:						
N0001	13 x 25 mm	0.15	7.5%	-	-	0.16	m
N0002	13 x 38 mm	0.22	7.5%	0.01	-	0.24	m
N0003	13 x 50 mm	0.24	7.5%	0.01	-	0.26	m
N0004	13 x 75 mm	0.36	7.5%	0.01	-	0.40	m
N0005	13 x 100 mm	0.48	7.5%	0.01	-	0.53	m
N0006	19 x 100 mm	0.73	7.5%	0.02	-	0.80	m
N0007	19 x 150 mm	1.09	7.5%	0.03	-	1.20	m
N0008	25 x 25 mm	0.24	7.5%	0.01	-	0.27	m
N0009	25 x 38 mm	0.37	7.5%	0.01	-	0.41	m
N0010	25 x 50 mm	0.49	7.5%	0.01	-	0.53	m
N0011	25 x 63 mm	0.61	7.5%	0.02	-	0.68	m
N0012	25 x 75 mm	0.72	7.5%	0.02	-	0.80	m
N0013	25 x 100 mm	0.86	7.5%	0.03	-	0.96	m
N0056	25 x 150 mm	1.30	7.5%	0.04	-	1.44	m
N0057	25 x 175 mm	1.55	7.5%	0.05	-	1.72	m
N0058	32 x 150 mm	2.09	7.5%	0.05	-	2.30	m
N0059	32 x 200 mm	2.79	7.5%	0.07	-	3.08	m
N0014	38 x 38 mm	0.55	7.5%	0.02	-	0.61	m
N0015	38 x 50 mm	0.73	7.5%	0.02	-	0.81	m
N0016	38 x 63 mm	0.92	7.5%	0.03	-	1.02	m
N0017	38 x 75 mm	1.09	7.5%	0.03	-	1.20	m
N0018	38 x 100 mm	1.40	7.5%	0.04	-	1.55	m
N0019	38 x 150 mm	2.09	7.5%	0.06	-	2.31	m
N0021	50 x 50 mm	0.68	7.5%	0.03	-	0.76	m
N0022	50 x 63 mm	0.92	7.5%	0.04	-	1.03	m
N0023	50 x 75 mm	0.99	7.5%	0.04	-	1.11	m
N0024	50 x 100 mm	1.32	7.5%	0.06	-	1.48	m
N0025	50 x 125 mm	1.65	7.5%	0.07	-	1.85	m
N0026	50 x 150 mm	1.98	7.5%	0.08	-	2.22	m
N0027	50 x 175 mm	2.31	7.5%	0.10	-	2.59	m
N0028	50 x 200 mm	2.64	7.5%	0.11	-	2.96	m
N0029	50 x 225 mm	2.97	7.5%	0.13	-	3.33	m
N0030	50 x 250 mm	4.04	7.5%	0.14	-	4.50	m
N0031	50 x 275 mm	4.61	7.5%	0.15	-	5.12	m
N0032	50 x 300 mm	5.03	7.5%	0.17	-	5.59	m
N0033	75 x 75 mm	1.71	7.5%	0.06	-	1.90	m
N0034	75 x 100 mm	2.28	7.5%	0.08	-	2.54	m
N0035	75 x 125 mm	2.85	7.5%	0.11	-	3.18	m
N0036	75 x 150 mm	3.42	7.5%	0.13	-	3.82	m
N0037	75 x 175 mm	3.99	7.5%	0.15	-	4.45	m
N0038	75 x 200 mm	4.56	7.5%	0.17	-	5.09	m
N0039	75 x 225 mm	5.13	7.5%	0.19	-	5.72	m
N0040	75 x 250 mm	6.45	7.5%	0.21	-	7.16	m
N0041	75 x 275 mm	7.10	7.5%	0.23	-	7.88	m
N0042	75 x 300 mm	7.75	7.5%	0.25	-	8.60	m
N0043	100 x 100 mm	3.36	7.5%	0.11	-	3.73	m
N0044	100 x 150 mm	5.04	7.5%	0.17	-	5.60	m
N0045	100 x 200 mm	6.72	7.5%	0.22	-	7.46	m
N0046	100 x 225 mm	7.56	7.5%	0.25	-	8.40	m
N0047	100 x 250 mm	8.93	7.5%	0.28	-	9.91	m
N0048	100 x 300 mm	10.71	7.5%	0.34	-	11.88	m
N0049	38 x 38 mm angle fillets	0.34	7.5%	0.02	-	0.39	m
N0050	50 x 50 mm angle fillets	0.70	7.5%	0.03	-	0.78	m
N0051	75 x 75 mm angle fillets	1.11	7.5%	0.06	-	1.26	m
N0052	25 x 50 mm tilting fillets	0.53	7.5%	0.01	-	0.59	m
N0053	38 x 75 mm tilting fillets	1.25	7.5%	0.03	-	1.38	m
N0054	50 x 50 mm rolls	1.11	7.5%	0.03	-	1.23	m
N0055	50 x 75 mm rolls	1.67	7.5%	0.04	-	1.83	m

Basic Prices of Materials

		Supply Price £	Waste Factor %	Unload. Labour £	Unload. Plant £	Total Unit Cost £	Unit
	firring pieces:						
N0061	50 x average 25 mm	0.31	7.5%	0.01	-	0.34	m
N0062	50 x average 50 mm	0.56	7.5%	0.03	-	0.63	m
N0063	50 x average 63 mm	0.70	7.5%	0.04	-	0.79	m
N0064	50 x average 75 mm	0.82	7.5%	0.04	-	0.93	m
N0065	75 x average 25 mm	0.39	7.5%	0.02	-	0.44	m
N0066	75 x average 50 mm	0.82	7.5%	0.03	-	0.92	m
N0067	75 x average 63 mm	1.04	7.5%	0.05	-	1.17	m
N0068	75 x average 75 mm	1.17	7.5%	0.06	-	1.32	m
N0069	100 x average 25 mm	0.60	7.5%	0.03	-	0.67	m
N0070	100 x average 50 mm	1.10	7.5%	0.06	-	1.25	m
N0071	100 x average 63 mm	1.39	7.5%	0.07	-	1.57	m
N0072	100 x average 75 mm	1.46	7.5%	0.08	-	1.66	m
N0081	19 mm square edge boarding 150 mm wide	1.10	7.5%	0.03	-	1.21	m
N0082	25 mm square edge boarding 150 mm wide	1.29	7.5%	0.04	-	1.43	m
	Wrought softwood, untreated:						
N0083	13 x 19 mm	0.30	7.5%	0.03	-	0.36	m
N0084	13 x 25 mm	0.41	7.5%	-	-	0.44	m
N0085	13 x 32 mm	0.54	7.5%	-	-	0.58	m
N0091	13 x 50 mm	0.53	7.5%	0.01	-	0.58	m
N0092	19 x 25 mm	0.58	7.5%	0.01	-	0.63	m
N0086	19 x 32 mm	0.75	7.5%	0.01	-	0.81	m
N0093	19 x 38 mm	0.73	7.5%	0.01	-	0.79	m
N0094	19 x 50 mm	0.82	7.5%	0.01	-	0.90	m
N0095	19 x 75 mm	1.22	7.5%	0.02	-	1.33	m
N0096	19 x 100 mm	1.62	7.5%	0.02	-	1.76	m
N0097	19 x 125 mm	2.02	7.5%	0.03	-	2.21	m
N0098	19 x 150 mm	2.43	7.5%	0.03	-	2.65	m
N0099	19 x 175 mm	2.84	7.5%	0.04	-	3.09	m
N0100	19 x 200 mm	3.24	7.5%	0.04	-	3.53	m
N0101	22 x 75 mm	1.42	7.5%	0.02	-	1.55	m
N0102	25 x 38 mm	0.92	7.5%	0.01	-	1.00	m
N0103	25 x 50 mm	0.95	7.5%	0.01	-	1.03	m
N0104	25 x 75 mm	1.42	7.5%	0.02	-	1.55	m
N0105	25 x 100 mm	1.77	7.5%	0.03	-	1.93	m
N0106	25 x 125 mm	2.22	7.5%	0.03	-	2.42	m
N0107	25 x 150 mm	2.66	7.5%	0.04	-	2.90	m
N0108	25 x 175 mm	3.10	7.5%	0.05	-	3.39	m
N0109	25 x 200 mm	4.18	7.5%	0.06	-	4.56	m
N0110	25 x 225 mm	4.89	7.5%	0.06	-	5.32	m
N0111	25 x 250 mm	4.92	7.5%	0.07	-	5.36	m
N0112	32 x 63 mm	1.47	7.5%	0.02	-	1.60	m
N0113	32 x 75 mm	1.76	7.5%	0.03	-	1.92	m
N0114	32 x 100 mm	2.20	7.5%	0.04	-	2.41	m
N0115	32 x 150 mm	3.30	7.5%	0.05	-	3.60	m
N0116	38 x 50 mm	1.30	7.5%	0.02	-	1.41	m
N0119	38 x 100 mm	2.36	7.5%	0.04	-	2.58	m
N0117	38 x 115 mm	2.75	7.5%	0.05	-	3.01	m
N0120	38 x 125 mm	2.95	7.5%	0.05	-	3.22	m
N0118	38 x 150 mm	3.53	7.5%	0.06	-	3.86	m
N0121	50 x 50 mm	1.40	7.5%	0.03	-	1.54	m
N0122	50 x 75 mm	2.10	7.5%	0.04	-	2.30	m
N0123	50 x 100 mm	2.70	7.5%	0.06	-	2.97	m
N0124	50 x 150 mm	5.05	7.5%	0.08	-	5.51	m
N0125	63 x 75 mm	3.35	7.5%	0.05	-	3.65	m
N0126	63 x 100 mm	4.24	7.5%	0.07	-	4.63	m
N0127	63 x 115 mm	5.01	7.5%	0.08	-	5.47	m
N0128	63 x 125 mm	5.30	7.5%	0.09	-	5.80	m
N0129	63 x 150 mm	6.36	7.5%	0.11	-	6.96	m
N0130	63 x 175 mm	7.42	7.5%	0.12	-	8.11	m
N0131	75 x 75 mm	3.00	7.5%	0.06	-	3.29	m
N0132	75 x 100 mm	5.05	7.5%	0.08	-	5.51	m
N0133	75 x 150 mm	7.57	7.5%	0.13	-	8.28	m
N0134	100 x 100 mm	6.98	7.5%	0.11	-	7.62	m
	Wrought softwood boarding, untreated, 125 mm wide:						
N0135	19 mm square edged	1.62	7.5%	0.03	-	1.77	m
N0136	22 mm square edged	1.83	7.5%	0.03	-	2.00	m
N0137	25 mm square edged	1.83	7.5%	0.03	-	2.00	m
N0138	19 mm tongued and grooved	1.62	7.5%	0.03	-	1.77	m
N0139	22 mm tongued and grooved	2.22	7.5%	0.03	-	2.42	m
N0140	25 mm tongued and grooved	2.22	7.5%	0.03	-	2.42	m
N0141	19 mm shiplap weatherboarding (150 mm wide)	2.22	7.5%	0.03	-	2.42	m
N0142	25 mm shiplap weatherboarding (150 mm wide)	2.92	7.5%	0.04	-	3.18	m
N0143	13 mm tongued, grooved and V-jointed (100 mm wide)	0.97	7.5%	0.01	-	1.06	m
N0144	19 mm tongued, grooved and V-jointed (100 mm wide)	1.48	7.5%	0.02	-	1.62	m

Basic Prices of Materials

		Supply Price £	Waste Factor %	Unload. Labour £	Unload. Plant £	Total Unit Cost £	Unit
N0145	16 mm cross-tongued (450 mm wide)	6.75	7.5%	0.08	-	7.34	m
N0146	19 mm cross-tongued (450 mm wide)	8.21	7.5%	0.11	-	8.95	m
N0147	25 mm cross-tongued (450 mm wide)	10.27	7.5%	0.11	-	11.16	m
	Machine shop labours on timber, per labour:						
N0231	softwood	2.47	7.5%	-	-	2.66	m
N0232	hardwood	3.08	7.5%	-	-	3.31	m
	Wrought Softwood standard mouldings:						
	quadrant:						
N0241	13 mm	0.67	7.5%	-	-	0.72	m
N0242	19 mm	0.75	7.5%	-	-	0.81	m
N0243	25 mm	1.30	7.5%	-	-	1.40	m
	scotia mould:						
N0244	19 mm	0.83	7.5%	-	-	0.89	m
N0245	25 mm	1.43	7.5%	-	-	1.53	m
	half round:						
N0246	25 mm	1.43	7.5%	-	-	1.53	m
	cover strip:						
N0247	13 x 50 mm	1.28	7.5%	0.01	-	1.39	m
	picture rail, moulded:						
N0248	19 x 50 mm	1.87	7.5%	0.01	-	2.02	m
	dado rail, moulded:						
C0237	25 x 50 mm	0.87	5%	-	-	0.91	m
C0238	25 x 75 mm	1.52	5%	-	-	1.60	m
	architrave:						
N0249	19 x 50 mm, bullnosed	0.77	7.5%	0.01	-	0.84	m
N0250	19 x 50 mm, chamfered and rounded	0.77	7.5%	0.01	-	0.84	m
N0251	25 x 75 mm, ogee or torus	1.57	7.5%	0.02	-	1.71	m
	skirting:						
N0252	19 x 75 mm, bullnosed	1.16	7.5%	0.02	-	1.27	m
N0253	19 x 100 mm, bullnosed	1.51	7.5%	0.02	-	1.64	m
N0254	19 x 75 mm, chamfered or rounded	1.16	7.5%	0.02	-	1.27	m
N0255	19 x 100 mm, chamfered or rounded	1.51	7.5%	0.02	-	1.64	m
N0256	19 x 100 mm, ogee or torus	1.51	7.5%	0.02	-	1.64	m
N0257	25 x 175 mm, ogee or torus	3.44	7.5%	0.05	-	3.75	m
	handrails:						
N0258	50 x 50 mm, mopstick	3.03	7.5%	0.03	-	3.29	m
N0259	50 x 75 mm, toad's back	4.54	7.5%	0.04	-	4.92	m
N0260	50 x 100 mm, sow's ear	6.44	7.5%	0.06	-	6.99	m
	weatherboard; throated:						
N0261	50 x 50 mm	3.02	7.5%	-	-	3.25	m
N0262	50 x 75 mm	4.54	7.5%	-	-	4.88	m
N0263	63 x 75 mm	5.45	7.5%	-	-	5.86	m
	windowboards, rebated and rounded:						
N0264	25 x 150 mm	5.25	7.5%	0.04	-	5.69	m
N0265	25 x 200 mm	6.14	7.5%	0.06	-	6.67	m
N0266	25 x 225 mm	9.75	7.5%	0.06	-	10.54	m
	dowels (Ramin):						
N0267	6 mm	0.54	7.5%	-	-	0.58	m
N0268	9 mm	0.99	7.5%	-	-	1.06	m
N0269	12 mm	1.76	7.5%	-	-	1.89	m
N0270	14 mm	2.11	7.5%	-	-	2.27	m
N0271	18 mm	2.42	7.5%	-	-	2.60	m
N0272	23 mm	2.73	7.5%	-	-	2.93	m
N0273	29 mm	4.46	7.5%	0.01	-	4.80	m
	stop fillets:						
N0274	13 x 25 mm	0.87	7.5%	-	-	0.94	m
N0275	13 x 38 mm	1.00	7.5%	0.01	-	1.09	m
N0276	16 x 50 mm	0.98	7.5%	0.01	-	1.07	m
N0278	25 x 25 mm	0.61	7.5%	0.01	-	0.67	m
N0279	25 x 38 mm	0.93	7.5%	0.01	-	1.01	m
N0280	25 x 50 mm	0.96	7.5%	0.01	-	1.04	m
	Wrought hardwood standard mouldings:						
N0281	architrave, moulded, 25 x 75 mm	5.47	7.5%	0.02	-	5.90	m
N0282	skirting, moulded, 25 x 125 mm	7.89	7.5%	0.03	-	8.52	m
N0283	weatherboard, moulded, 50 x 63 mm, 838 mm long	7.82	-	-	-	7.82	m
N0284	windowboard, nosed and tongued, 32 x 225 mm	25.95	7.5%	0.08	-	27.98	m
	Stop fillets:						
N0285	13 x 25 mm	2.60	7.5%	-	-	2.80	m
N0286	13 x 38 mm	2.92	7.5%	0.01	-	3.15	m
N0287	16 x 50 mm	3.48	7.5%	0.01	-	3.75	m
N0288	25 x 25 mm	3.16	7.5%	0.01	-	3.41	m
N0289	25 x 38 mm	3.76	7.5%	0.01	-	4.05	m
N0290	25 x 50 mm	4.31	7.5%	0.01	-	4.65	m
N0291	pellets	0.10	10%	-	-	0.11	nr
	Wrought hardwood shelf lipping:						
N0292	6 x 9 mm	1.43	7.5%	-	-	1.54	m
N0293	6 x 12 mm	1.47	7.5%	-	-	1.58	m
N0294	6 x 15 mm	1.51	7.5%	-	-	1.62	m
N0295	6 x 18 mm	1.53	7.5%	-	-	1.65	m
N0296	6 x 25 mm	1.62	7.5%	-	-	1.74	m
	Medium density fibreboard standard mouldings:						
	skirtings:						
N0495	14.5 x 100 mm, bullnosed	1.87	7.5%	-	-	2.01	m
N0496	14.5 x 100 mm, chamfered and rounded	1.87	7.5%	-	-	2.01	m

Basic Prices of Materials

		Supply Price £	Waste Factor %	Unload. Labour £	Unload. Plant £	Total Unit Cost £	Unit
N0497	18 x 125 mm, torus	2.64	7.5%	-	-	2.84	m
N0498	18 x 150 mm, ogee	3.17	7.5%	-	-	3.41	m
	windowboards, rebated and rounded:						
N0499	25 x 225 mm	4.76	7.5%		-	5.12	m
N0500	25 x 250 mm	5.29	7.5%	-	-	5.69	m
	Wrought softwood special mouldings:						
	ramp with handrail screws on moulded handrail:						
N0297	50 x 100 mm	42.68	-	-	-	42.68	nr
N0298	63 x 100 mm	42.68	-	-	-	42.68	nr
N0299	75 x 100 mm	42.68	-	-	-	42.68	nr
	wreath with handrail screws on moulded handrail:						
N0368	50 x 100 mm	84.10	-	-	-	84.10	nr
N0369	63 x 100 mm	84.10	-	-	-	84.10	nr
N0370	75 x 100 mm	84.10	-	-	-	84.10	nr
	Wrought Utile mahogany special mouldings:						
	ramp with handrail screws on moulded handrail:						
N0371	44 x 93 mm	50.58	-	-	-	50.58	nr
N0372	56 x 93 mm	50.58	-	-	-	50.58	nr
N0373	68 x 93 mm	50.58	-	-	-	50.58	nr
	wreath with handrail screws on moulded handrail:						
N0374	44 x 93 mm	116.41	-	-	-	116.41	nr
N0375	56 x 93 mm	116.41	-	-	-	116.41	nr
N0376	68 x 93 mm	116.41	-	-	-	116.41	nr
	Sheet products, delivered in full pallets						
	Standard quality hardboard:						
	plain:						
N0301	3.2 mm	1.56	5%	0.03	-	1.67	m2
N0302	4.8 mm	2.75	5%	0.06	-	2.95	m2
N0303	6.0 mm	3.90	5%	0.08	-	4.17	m2
	perforated:						
N0304	3.2 mm	2.41	5%	0.03	-	2.56	m2
N0305	6.0 mm	5.14	5%	0.08	-	5.48	m2
	tempered:						
N0306	3.2 mm	2.66	5%	0.03	-	2.83	m2
N0308	6.0 mm	3.80	5%	0.08	-	4.07	m2
	Class 1 flame retardant quality hardboard to BS 476:						
N0309	3.2 mm	3.96	5%	0.03	-	4.19	m2
	Painted hardboard:						
N0311	3.2 mm	2.27	5%	0.03	-	2.42	m2
	Medium quality hardboard:						
	interior quality (Sundeala K):						
N0312	6.4 mm	5.14	5%	0.02	-	5.42	m2
N0313	9.5 mm	7.58	5%	0.02	-	7.98	m2
	Flame retardant to BS 476 - class 1:						
N0318	6.4 mm	8.38	5%	0.03	-	8.83	m2
N0319	9.5 mm	10.38	5%	0.03	-	10.93	m2
	Building board (Promat Monolux):						
	natural finish:						
N0320	12.7 mm	63.09	5%	0.04	-	66.29	m2
N0321	19.0 mm	80.20	5%	0.06	-	84.27	m2
N0322	25.0 mm	96.16	5%	0.08	-	101.05	m2
	Insulation board ivory finish (Softboard):						
N0323	12.0 mm	2.75	5%	0.04	-	2.93	m2
	Chipboard:						
	plain:						
N0324	12 mm	2.56	5%	0.08	-	2.78	m2
N0325	15 mm	3.08	5%	0.10	-	3.34	m2
N0326	18 mm	3.70	5%	0.12	-	4.01	m2
N0327	25 mm	5.12	5%	0.17	-	5.55	m2
	moisture resistant:						
N0328	18 mm	5.29	5%	0.12	-	5.68	m2
	flooring grade, square edged:						
N0329	18 mm	4.87	5%	0.12	-	5.24	m2
N0330	22 mm	6.11	5%	0.15	-	6.58	m2
	flooring grade, tongued and grooved:						
N0331	18 mm	5.50	5%	0.12	-	5.90	m2
N0332	22 mm	8.55	5%	0.15	-	9.14	m2
	melamine faced both sides; white, unlipped:						
N0333	15 mm	5.01	5%	0.10	-	5.37	m2
N0334	18 mm	5.29	5%	0.12	-	5.68	m2
	Blockboard:						
	Finnish Birch faced:						
N0336	18 mm	15.31	5%	0.12	-	16.20	m2
N0338	25 mm	19.71	5%	0.17	-	20.88	m2
	Brazilian Virola faced:						
N0339	18 mm	9.90	5%	0.08	-	10.48	m2
N0341	25 mm	14.60	5%	0.12	-	15.45	m2

	Basic Prices of Materials	Supply Price £	Waste Factor %	Unload. Labour £	Unload. Plant £	Total Unit Cost £	Unit
	Plywood:						
	Internal quality, MR bonding, Far Eastern, red/white:						
N0344	4 mm	2.95	5%	0.02	-	3.11	m2
N0345	6 mm	3.28	5%	0.04	-	3.49	m2
N0346	9 mm	4.97	5%	0.06	-	5.28	m2
N0347	12 mm	6.44	5%	0.08	-	6.85	m2
	External quality, WBP bonding, Finnish Birch faced:						
N0348	4 mm	5.65	5%	0.02	-	5.95	m2
N0349	6 mm	6.63	5%	0.04	-	7.00	m2
N0350	9 mm	8.79	5%	0.06	-	9.29	m2
N0351	12 mm	10.75	5%	0.08	-	11.37	m2
	Floor panels, grade BB/WG, Birch faced:						
N0356	12 mm	13.57	5%	0.08	-	14.33	m2
N0357	15 mm	16.48	5%	0.10	-	17.41	m2
N0358	18 mm	20.13	5%	0.12	-	21.26	m2
	Plywood to BS 5268 PT2:						
	WBP BB/BB, exterior grade:						
N0352	12 mm	12.61	5%	0.08	-	13.32	m2
N0353	15 mm	15.37	5%	0.10	-	16.24	m2
N0354	18 mm	18.29	5%	0.12	-	19.33	m2
N0355	25 mm	23.78	5%	0.17	-	25.15	m2
	Non-asbestos boards, fire resisting Class 0:						
	Masterboard:						
N0359	6 mm	12.43	5%	0.04	-	13.09	m2
N0360	9 mm	21.56	5%	0.06	-	22.70	m2
N0361	12 mm	27.20	5%	0.08	-	28.64	m2
	sanded finish Supalux:						
N0362	6 mm	17.55	5%	0.04	-	18.47	m2
N0363	9 mm	24.48	5%	0.06	-	25.77	m2
N0364	12 mm	31.01	5%	0.08	-	32.64	m2
	Laminboard:						
	Birch faced:						
N0365	19 mm	17.20	5%	0.11	-	18.18	m2
N0366	22 mm	19.44	5%	0.15	-	20.57	m2
N0367	25 mm	20.08	5%	0.17	-	21.26	m2
N0381	0.9 mm plastic laminate 3 m x 1.2 m sheet (standard range)	50.47	5%	-	-	53.00	nr
N0391	0.9 mm plastic laminate edging up to 18 mm wide	0.86	5%	-	-	0.90	m
	15 mm chipboard shelving with facings both sides:						
	white melamine facing lipped on 2 edges:						
N0382	152 mm wide	1.05	5%	-	-	1.10	m
N0383	305 mm wide	2.10	5%	0.05	-	2.26	m
N0384	457 mm wide	3.15	5%	0.05	-	3.36	m
N0385	610 mm wide	4.20	5%	0.09	-	4.50	m
	teak melamine lacquer facing lipped on 2 edges:						
N0386	152 mm wide	1.74	5%	-	-	1.83	m
N0387	305 mm wide	3.63	5%	0.05	-	3.86	m
N0388	457 mm wide	5.99	5%	0.05	-	6.34	m
N0389	610 mm wide	6.62	5%	0.09	-	7.05	m
N0390	White or teak lipping 18 mm wide	0.86	5%	-	-	0.90	m
	Medium density fibreboard:						
	Standard grade:						
N0395	6 mm	3.57	5%	-	-	3.75	m2
N0396	9 mm	4.47	5%	-	-	4.69	m2
N0397	12 mm	5.55	5%	-	-	5.83	m2
N0398	18 mm	6.78	5%	-	-	7.12	m2
	ROOF WINDOWS						
	Velux 3059 varient roof windows factory finished and glazed with sealed double glazing units having 4mm Low-E float inner pane, 16 mm gas filled cavity, 4 mm toughened outer pane. Roof windows with obscure, toughened and laminated glazing and electrical operation are also available at extra cost						
	Centre pivot:						
	wide high						
N1231	GGL-M04 780 x 980	220.00	-	-	-	220.00	nr
N1232	GGL-M08 780 x 1400	275.00	-	-	-	275.00	nr
N1233	GGL-P10 940 x 1600	340.00	-	-	-	340.00	nr
N1234	GGL-S06 1140 x 1180	330.00	-	-	-	330.00	nr
N1235	GGL-C04 550 x 980	205.00	-	-	-	205.00	nr
N1236	GGL-C02 550 x 780	195.00	-	-	-	195.00	nr
N1239	GGL-F06 660 x 1180	240.00	-	-	-	240.00	nr
	Top-hung:						
N1242	GHL-M04 780 x 980	280.00	-	-	-	280.00	nr
N1244	GHL-S06 1140 x 1180	420.00	-	-	-	420.00	nr
N1245	GHL-C04 550 x 980	260.00	-	-	-	260.00	nr
	Note: Combined vertical and sloping roof windows include flashings						
N1251	GGL-SFOL122-M06 780 x 600 and 780 x 1180	654.50	-	-	-	654.50	nr
N1252	GGL-SFOL122-M08 780 x 600 and 780 x 1400	684.25	-	-	-	684.25	nr
N1253	GGL-SFOW122-M06 780 x 950 and 780 x 1180	684.25	-	-	-	684.25	nr
N1255	GGL-SFOW122-M08 780 x 950 and 780 x 1400	714.00	-	-	-	714.00	nr

	Basic Prices of Materials	Supply Price £	Waste Factor %	Unload. Labour £	Unload. Plant £	Total Unit Cost £	Unit
	Type EDZ; single flashing units for tiles to suit Velux window, reference:						
N1264	M04	37.50	-	-	-	37.50	nr
N1265	M08	47.60	-	-	-	47.60	nr
N1266	P10	54.40	-	-	-	54.40	nr
N1267	S06	52.70	-	-	-	52.70	nr
N1268	C04	39.10	-	-	-	39.10	nr
N1269	C02	37.40	-	-	-	37.40	nr
N1272	F06	45.00	-	-	-	45.00	nr
	Type EDW; single flashing units for tiles to suit Velux window, reference:						
N1330	C02	55.34	-	-	-	55.34	nr
N1331	C04	58.91	-	-	-	58.91	nr
N1332	F06	64.26	-	-	-	64.26	nr
N1333	M04	62.48	-	-	-	62.48	nr
N1334	M08	69.61	-	-	-	69.62	nr
N1335	P10	80.33	-	-	-	80.33	nr
N1336	S06	78.54	-	-	-	78.54	nr
	Type EDL; single flashing units for slates to suit Velux window, reference:						
N1275	M04	37.50	-	-	-	37.50	nr
N1276	M08	47.60	-	-	-	47.60	nr
N1277	P10	56.70	-	-	-	56.70	nr
N1278	S06	54.40	-	-	-	54.40	nr
N1279	C04	39.10	-	-	-	39.10	nr
N1280	C02	37.40	-	-	-	37.40	nr
N1283	F06	45.00	-	-	-	45.00	nr
	Type EBW; twin flashing units for tiles to suit Velux window, reference:						
N1286	C02	112.20	-	-	-	112.20	nr
N1287	C04	120.70	-	-	-	120.70	nr
N1288	F06	132.60	-	-	-	132.60	nr
N1289	M04	127.50	-	-	-	127.50	nr
N1290	M08	142.80	-	-	-	142.80	nr
N1291	P10	164.90	-	-	-	164.90	nr
N1292	S06	161.50	-	-	-	161.50	nr
	Standard range roller blinds RFL to suit Velux roof window reference:						
N1297	C02	42.50	-	-	-	42.50	nr
N1298	C04	44.20	-	-	-	44.20	nr
N1299	F06	52.70	-	-	-	52.70	nr
N1300	M04	51.00	-	-	-	51.00	nr
N1301	M08	59.50	-	-	-	59.50	nr
N1302	P10	68.00	-	-	-	68.00	nr
N1303	S06	66.30	-	-	-	66.30	nr
	Standard range venetian blinds PAL to suit Velux roof window reference:						
N1308	C02	60.69	-	-	-	60.69	nr
N1309	C04	67.83	-	-	-	67.83	nr
N1310	F06	76.75	-	-	-	76.76	nr
N1311	M04	73.19	-	-	-	73.19	nr
N1312	M08	85.68	-	-	-	85.68	nr
N1313	P10	98.17	-	-	-	98.18	nr
N1314	S06	94.61	-	-	-	94.61	nr
	Velux roof window accessories:						
	portable rod opening gear; type:						
N1320	ZCT200 - telescopic 1000 - 1800 mm	22.31	-	-	-	22.31	nr
N1321	ZCT100 - 1000 mm extension	13.39	-	-	-	13.39	nr
	accessories:						
N2000	ZOZ012 window lock for GGL/GGU	34.00	-	-	-	34.00	nr
N2001	ZOZ010 window opening restrictor for GGL/GGU	34.00	-	-	-	34.00	nr
	Smoke ventilation system complete with window (s), flashing (s), control panel, motors, smoke detectors and break glass for site fitting						
N2005	GGL S06 SD0L1 for slates providing 1m2 smoke vent area	1207.54	-	-	-	1207.54	nr
N2006	GGL S06 SD0W1 for tiles providing 1m2 smoke vent area	1235.83	-	-	-	1235.83	nr
N2007	GGL U08 SD0L1 for slates providing 1.5m2 smoke vent area	1265.89	-	-	-	1265.89	nr
N2008	GGL U08 SD0W1 for tiles providing 1.5m2 smoke vent area	1297.71	-	-	-	1297.71	nr
	Softwood staircases:						
	single straight flight 2700 mm going 2600 mm rise, 12 treads, 13 risers:						
N1401	864 mm wide	397.36	-	3.37	-	400.73	nr
	single straight flight 3150 mm going 3000 mm rise, 14 treads, 15 risers:						
N1403	864 mm wide	511.67	-	3.37	-	515.04	nr
	single half flight 1350 mm going 1400 mm rise, 6 treads, 7 risers:						
N1405	864 mm wide	225.64	-	2.24	-	227.88	nr
	Balustrades in Hemlock:						
N1421	moulded handrail 2400 mm long for 41 mm spindles	57.78	-	-	-	57.78	nr
	turned balusters 41 x 41 mm:						
N1427	900 mm high	3.55	-	-	-	3.55	nr
N1428	1100 mm high	6.92	-	-	-	6.92	nr
	newel posts 82 x 82 mm:						
N1429	1360 mm high with turned cap	35.07	-	-	-	35.07	nr
N1430	1640 mm high with turned cap	42.26	-	-	-	42.26	nr
	SUNDRIES AND INSULATION						
N1501	Proprietary plugs 'Rawlplug' plastic type; No 8 x 38 mm	0.02	10%	-	-	0.02	nr
N1502	Steel wood screws No 8 x 38 mm	0.02	10%	-	-	0.02	nr
N1503	Brass screws; self colour No 8 x 38 mm	0.03	10%	-	-	0.04	nr

Basic Prices of Materials

		Supply Price £	Waste Factor %	Unload. Labour £	Unload. Plant £	Total Unit Cost £	Unit
N1504	Brass countersunk screw cups 8 gauge, recess type	0.06	10%	-	-	0.07	nr
N1505	Cut steel clasp nails 75 mm	3.25	10%	-	-	3.58	kg
N1506	Hardened steel masonry nails 50 mm x 2.5 mm diameter	0.01	10%	-	-	0.01	nr
	Black coach screws, square head:						
N1507	1/4" x 2"	0.02	2.5%	-	-	0.02	nr
N1508	5/16" x 2"	0.04	2.5%	-	-	0.04	nr
N1509	3/8" x 2"	0.07	2.5%	-	-	0.07	nr
N1510	3/8" x 3"	0.08	2.5%	-	-	0.08	nr
N1511	3/8" x 4"	0.11	2.5%	-	-	0.11	nr
N1512	3/8" x 5"	0.12	2.5%	-	-	0.13	nr
N1513	Evomastic general purpose mastic, 370 ml C30 cartridge	2.65	2.5%	-	-	2.72	nr
N1514	Evo-stik 528 contact adhesive	11.55	2.5%	-	-	11.84	ltr
V0405	Intumescent paint	18.34	7.5%	-	-	19.71	ltr
	PIR Polyisocyanurate foam insulation:						
	Type XR:						
N1539	100 mm thick	11.77	5%	-	-	12.36	m2
N1540	130 mm thick	15.73	5%	-	-	16.52	m2
	Type GA:						
N1545	35 mm thick	4.84	5%	-	-	5.08	m2
	Glass fibre loft insulating mat 1200 mm wide:						
N1552	100 mm thick (split 3 x 400 mm) (9.17 m roll)	27.84	5%	0.22	-	29.46	roll
N1553	100 mm thick (split 2 x 600 mm) (9.17 m roll)	27.84	5%	0.22	-	29.46	roll
N1550	150 mm thick (split 2 x 580 mm) (6.03 m roll)	23.22	5%	0.22	-	24.61	roll
N1549	200 mm thick (3.88 m roll)	23.22	5%	0.22	-	24.61	roll
	Glass fibre sound-deadening quilt type PF 1200 wide:						
N1554	13 mm thick (16 m roll)	25.92	5%	0.22	-	27.44	roll
	CARPENTER'S METALWORK						
	Galvanised mild steel dowels:						
N1561	8 x 100 mm	0.36	5%	-	-	0.38	nr
N1562	10 x 50 mm	0.29	5%	-	-	0.30	nr
	Black hexagon head bolts and nuts, grade 4.6 to BS 4190 including one nut and one washer:						
N1563	M6 x 25 mm	0.06	2.5%	-	-	0.06	nr
N1564	M6 x 50 mm	0.08	2.5%	-	-	0.08	nr
N1565	M6 x 80 mm	0.10	2.5%	-	-	0.10	nr
N1566	M6 x 100 mm	0.11	2.5%	-	-	0.11	nr
N1567	M8 x 25 mm	0.09	2.5%	-	-	0.09	nr
N1568	M8 x 50 mm	0.12	2.5%	-	-	0.12	nr
N1569	M10 x 50 mm	0.14	2.5%	-	-	0.15	nr
N1570	M10 x 80 mm	0.18	2.5%	-	-	0.18	nr
N1571	M10 x 100 mm	0.22	2.5%	-	-	0.22	nr
N1572	M10 x 140 mm	0.32	2.5%	-	-	0.33	nr
N1573	M12 x 50 mm	0.24	2.5%	-	-	0.25	nr
N1574	M12 x 80 mm	0.30	2.5%	-	-	0.31	nr
N1575	M12 x 100 mm	0.37	2.5%	-	-	0.38	nr
N1576	M12 x 140 mm	0.51	2.5%	-	-	0.53	nr
N1577	M12 x 200 mm	1.56	2.5%	-	-	1.60	nr
N1578	M12 x 260 mm	1.77	2.5%	-	-	1.81	nr
N1579	M12 x 300 mm	1.94	2.5%	-	-	1.99	nr
N1580	M16 x 50 mm	0.66	2.5%	-	-	0.68	nr
N1581	M16 x 80 mm	0.80	2.5%	-	-	0.82	nr
N1582	M16 x 100 mm	0.89	2.5%	-	-	0.91	nr
N1584	M20 x 100 mm	1.65	2.5%	-	-	1.69	nr
	Black cup square hexagon carriage bolts and nuts, grade 4.6 to BS 4933, including one nut and one washer:						
N1585	M6 x 50 mm	0.03	2.5%	-	-	0.03	nr
N1586	M6 x 75 mm	0.04	2.5%	-	-	0.04	nr
N1587	M6 x 100 mm	0.05	2.5%	-	-	0.05	nr
N1588	M8 x 50 mm	0.07	2.5%	-	-	0.07	nr
N1589	M8 x 75 mm	0.07	2.5%	-	-	0.07	nr
N1590	M8 x 100 mm	0.08	2.5%	-	-	0.08	nr
N1591	M10 x 50 mm	0.11	2.5%	-	-	0.12	nr
N1592	M10 x 75 mm	0.12	2.5%	-	-	0.13	nr
N1593	M10 x 100 mm	0.15	2.5%	-	-	0.15	nr
N1594	M12 x 75 mm	0.29	2.5%	-	-	0.30	nr
N1595	M12 x 100 mm	0.38	2.5%	-	-	0.39	nr
N1596	M12 x 150 mm	0.41	2.5%	-	-	0.42	nr
	Expanding bolts with plated finish to BS 1706, Class C, bolt projecting type unit, one nut and one washer:						
N1597	M6 10P	0.70	2.5%	-	-	0.72	nr
N1598	M6 25P	0.81	2.5%	-	-	0.83	nr
N1599	M6 60P	0.82	2.5%	-	-	0.84	nr
N1600	M8 25P	0.96	2.5%	-	-	0.98	nr
N1601	M8 60P	1.04	2.5%	-	-	1.07	nr
N1602	M10 15P	1.09	2.5%	-	-	1.12	nr
N1603	M10 30P	1.14	2.5%	-	-	1.17	nr
N1604	M10 60P	1.11	2.5%	-	-	1.14	nr
N1605	M12 15P	1.77	2.5%	-	-	1.82	nr
N1606	M12 30P	1.86	2.5%	-	-	1.91	nr
N1607	M12 75P	2.30	2.5%	-	-	2.36	nr

Basic Prices of Materials		Supply Price £	Waste Factor %	Unload. Labour £	Unload. Plant £	Total Unit Cost £	Unit
N1608	M16 35P	4.26	2.5%	-	-	**4.37**	nr
N1609	M16 75P	4.40	2.5%	-	-	**4.51**	nr
	Expanded bolts with plated finish to BS 1706, Class C loose bolt type:						
N1610	M6 10L	0.76	2.5%	-	-	**0.77**	nr
N1611	M6 25L	0.76	2.5%	-	-	**0.77**	nr
N1612	M6 40L	0.89	2.5%	-	-	**0.91**	nr
N1613	M8 10L	0.89	2.5%	-	-	**0.91**	nr
N1614	M8 25L	0.96	2.5%	-	-	**0.98**	nr
N1615	M8 40L	1.03	2.5%	-	-	**1.05**	nr
N1616	M10 25L	1.14	2.5%	-	-	**1.17**	nr
N1617	M10 50L	1.17	2.5%	-	-	**1.19**	nr
N1618	M10 75L	1.26	2.5%	-	-	**1.29**	nr
N1619	M12 25L	2.07	2.5%	-	-	**2.12**	nr
N1620	M12 60L	2.59	2.5%	-	-	**2.66**	nr
N1621	M16 30L	4.36	2.5%	-	-	**4.47**	nr
N1622	M16 60L	5.10	2.5%	-	-	**5.23**	nr
	3 mm Black steel square plate washers to BS 3410 table 11, for 12 mm diameter bolts:						
N1628	38 x 38 x 3 mm	0.14	2.5%	-	-	**0.14**	nr
N1629	50 x 50 x 3 mm	0.25	2.5%	-	-	**0.25**	nr
	Galvanised mild steel single sided round toothed plate connectors to BS 1579 table 4 for 9 - 12 mm bolts:						
N1631	50 mm diameter for 12 mm bolt single	0.48	2.5%	-	-	**0.49**	nr
N1632	63 mm diameter for 12 mm bolt single	0.70	2.5%	-	-	**0.72**	nr
N1633	75 mm diameter for 12 mm bolt single	1.03	2.5%	-	-	**1.06**	nr
	Galvanised mild steel double sided round toothed plate connectors to BS 1579 table 4:						
N1635	50 mm diameter for 12 mm bolt double	0.54	2.5%	-	-	**0.55**	nr
N1636	63 mm diameter for 12 mm bolt double	0.78	2.5%	-	-	**0.80**	nr
N1637	75 mm diameter for 12 mm bolt double	1.08	2.5%	-	-	**1.10**	nr
	Galvanised mild steel split ring connectors to BS 1579 table 1:						
N1638	63 mm diameter	2.25	2.5%	-	-	**2.30**	nr
N1639	101 mm diameter	6.00	2.5%	-	-	**6.15**	nr
	Galvanised mild steel shear plate connectors to BS 1579 table 2:						
N1640	67 mm diameter pressed steel	3.60	2.5%	-	-	**3.69**	nr
N1641	101 mm malleable cast iron	15.59	2.5%	-	-	**15.98**	nr
	Galvanised mild steel safe edge pattern frame ties:						
N1642	200 x 25 x 3 mm	0.70	2.5%	-	-	**0.72**	nr
N1643	250 x 25 x 3 mm	0.70	2.5%	-	-	**0.72**	nr
	Galvanised steel standard restraint straps; 30 x 2.5 mm section with staggered 6 mm diameter holes:						
N1644	30 x 2.5 x 400 mm long	1.14	2.5%	-	-	**1.17**	nr
N1645	30 x 2.5 x 600 mm long	1.59	2.5%	-	-	**1.63**	nr
N1646	30 x 2.5 x 800 mm long	2.35	2.5%	-	-	**2.41**	nr
N1647	30 x 2.5 x 1000 mm long	3.05	2.5%	-	-	**3.13**	nr
N1648	30 x 2.5 x 1200 mm long	3.71	2.5%	-	-	**3.81**	nr
	Heavy duty 30 x 5 mm section:						
N1649	700 mm girth bent at 75 mm	2.37	2.5%	-	-	**2.43**	nr
N1650	800 mm girth bent at 100 mm	3.25	2.5%	-	-	**3.34**	nr
N1651	1000 mm girth bent at 100 mm	3.95	2.5%	-	-	**4.05**	nr
N1652	1200 mm girth bent at 100 mm	4.77	2.5%	-	-	**4.89**	nr
N1653	1500 mm girth bent at 100 mm	6.33	2.5%	-	-	**6.49**	nr
N1654	1300 mm girth bent at 300 mm	5.16	2.5%	-	-	**5.28**	nr
N1655	1700 mm girth bent at 300 mm	6.75	2.5%	-	-	**6.92**	nr
N1656	500 mm straight strap with twist at 100 mm	2.96	2.5%	-	-	**3.04**	nr
N1657	700 mm straight strap with twist at 100 mm	4.12	2.5%	-	-	**4.22**	nr
	Galvanised steel water bar:						
N1669	25 x 3 mm in 3 m lengths	8.45	2.5%	-	-	**8.66**	nr
N1671	25 x 6 mm in 4 m lengths	9.12	2.5%	-	-	**9.35**	nr
N1672	40 x 6 mm in 4 m lengths	11.46	2.5%	-	-	**11.74**	nr
	The Expanded Metal Co.; SPH joist hangers:						
	type 'S' standard for 38 mm joists; depth:						
N1701	100 mm	3.24	2.5%	-	-	**3.32**	nr
N1702	125 mm	3.25	2.5%	-	-	**3.33**	nr
N1703	150 mm	3.05	2.5%	-	-	**3.13**	nr
N1704	175 mm	3.20	2.5%	-	-	**3.28**	nr
N1705	200 mm	3.54	2.5%	-	-	**3.63**	nr
N1706	225 mm	3.76	2.5%	-	-	**3.85**	nr
N1707	250 mm	5.13	2.5%	-	-	**5.26**	nr
	type 'S' standard for 50 mm joists; depth:						
N1708	100 mm	3.24	2.5%	-	-	**3.32**	nr
N1709	125 mm	3.25	2.5%	-	-	**3.33**	nr
N1710	150 mm	3.05	2.5%	-	-	**3.13**	nr
N1711	175 mm	3.20	2.5%	-	-	**3.28**	nr
N1712	200 mm	3.54	2.5%	-	-	**3.63**	nr
N1713	225 mm	3.76	2.5%	-	-	**3.85**	nr
N1714	250 mm	5.13	2.5%	-	-	**5.26**	nr

Basic Prices of Materials

		Supply Price £	Waste Factor %	Unload. Labour £	Unload. Plant £	Total Unit Cost £	Unit
	type 'S' standard for 75 mm joists; depth:						
N1715	100 mm	4.02	2.5%	-	-	4.12	nr
N1716	125 mm	4.11	2.5%	-	-	4.22	nr
N1717	150 mm	4.70	2.5%	-	-	4.82	nr
N1718	175 mm	4.42	2.5%	-	-	4.53	nr
N1719	200 mm	4.70	2.5%	-	-	4.82	nr
N1720	225 mm	5.04	2.5%	-	-	5.17	nr
N1721	250 mm	5.34	2.5%	-	-	5.47	nr
	type 'S' standard for 100 mm joists; depth:						
N1722	100 mm	5.13	2.5%	-	-	5.26	nr
N1723	125 mm	5.37	2.5%	-	-	5.51	nr
N1724	150 mm	5.66	2.5%	-	-	5.80	nr
N1725	175 mm	6.14	2.5%	-	-	6.29	nr
N1726	200 mm	5.85	2.5%	-	-	6.00	nr
N1727	225 mm	6.20	2.5%	-	-	6.35	nr
N1728	250 mm	6.57	2.5%	-	-	6.74	nr
	type 'ST' straddle for 38 mm joists; depth:						
N1729	100 mm	10.11	2.5%	-	-	10.36	nr
N1730	125 mm	10.19	2.5%	-	-	10.44	nr
N1731	150 mm	9.60	2.5%	-	-	9.84	nr
N1732	175 mm	10.07	2.5%	-	-	10.32	nr
N1733	200 mm	10.94	2.5%	-	-	11.21	nr
N1734	225 mm	11.53	2.5%	-	-	11.82	nr
N1735	250 mm	15.10	2.5%	-	-	15.48	nr
	type 'ST' straddle for 50 mm joists; depth:						
N1736	100 mm	10.11	2.5%	-	-	10.36	nr
N1737	125 mm	10.19	2.5%	-	-	10.44	nr
N1738	150 mm	9.60	2.5%	-	-	9.84	nr
N1739	175 mm	10.07	2.5%	-	-	10.32	nr
N1740	200 mm	10.94	2.5%	-	-	11.21	nr
N1741	225 mm	11.53	2.5%	-	-	11.82	nr
N1742	250 mm	15.10	2.5%	-	-	15.48	nr
	type 'ST' straddle for 75 mm joists; depth:						
N1743	100 mm	12.24	2.5%	-	-	12.55	nr
N1744	125 mm	12.41	2.5%	-	-	12.73	nr
N1745	150 mm	13.95	2.5%	-	-	14.30	nr
N1746	175 mm	13.25	2.5%	-	-	13.58	nr
N1747	200 mm	13.95	2.5%	-	-	14.30	nr
N1748	225 mm	14.85	2.5%	-	-	15.22	nr
N1749	250 mm	15.61	2.5%	-	-	16.00	nr
	type 'ST' straddle for 100 mm joists; depth:						
N1751	100 mm	15.10	2.5%	-	-	15.48	nr
N1752	125 mm	15.65	2.5%	-	-	16.04	nr
N1753	150 mm	16.48	2.5%	-	-	16.89	nr
N1754	175 mm	17.74	2.5%	-	-	18.19	nr
N1755	200 mm	16.98	2.5%	-	-	17.40	nr
N1756	225 mm	17.85	2.5%	-	-	18.29	nr
N1757	250 mm	18.81	2.5%	-	-	19.28	nr
	type 'R' return flange for 38 mm joists; depth:						
N1758	100 mm	5.87	2.5%	-	-	6.02	nr
N1759	125 mm	5.89	2.5%	-	-	6.03	nr
N1760	150 mm	5.63	2.5%	-	-	5.77	nr
N1761	175 mm	5.86	2.5%	-	-	6.01	nr
N1762	200 mm	6.28	2.5%	-	-	6.43	nr
N1763	225 mm	6.59	2.5%	-	-	6.75	nr
N1764	250 mm	8.35	2.5%	-	-	8.55	nr
	type 'R' return flange for 50 mm joists; depth:						
N1765	100 mm	5.87	2.5%	-	-	6.02	nr
N1766	125 mm	5.89	2.5%	-	-	6.03	nr
N1767	150 mm	5.63	2.5%	-	-	5.77	nr
N1768	175 mm	5.86	2.5%	-	-	6.01	nr
N1769	200 mm	6.28	2.5%	-	-	6.43	nr
N1770	225 mm	6.59	2.5%	-	-	6.75	nr
N1771	250 mm	8.35	2.5%	-	-	8.55	nr
	type 'R' return flange for 75 mm joists; depth:						
N1772	100 mm	6.93	2.5%	-	-	7.10	nr
N1773	125 mm	7.04	2.5%	-	-	7.22	nr
N1774	150 mm	7.77	2.5%	-	-	7.97	nr
N1775	175 mm	7.44	2.5%	-	-	7.63	nr
N1776	200 mm	7.77	2.5%	-	-	7.97	nr
N1777	225 mm	8.22	2.5%	-	-	8.43	nr
N1778	250 mm	8.62	2.5%	-	-	8.83	nr
	type 'R' return flange for 100 mm joists; depth:						
N1779	100 mm	8.35	2.5%	-	-	8.55	nr
N1780	125 mm	8.62	2.5%	-	-	8.84	nr
N1781	150 mm	9.02	2.5%	-	-	9.25	nr
N1782	175 mm	9.69	2.5%	-	-	9.93	nr
N1783	200 mm	9.32	2.5%	-	-	9.55	nr
N1784	225 mm	9.75	2.5%	-	-	9.99	nr
N1785	250 mm	10.22	2.5%	-	-	10.48	nr
	The Expanded Metal Co. Speedy joist hangers:						
	type Maxi face fixing, all 185 deep for joist width 38 - 100 mm:						
N1786	type 335	3.24	2.5%	-	-	3.33	nr
N1787	type 380	4.14	2.5%	-	-	4.24	nr
N1788	type 500	4.82	2.5%	-	-	4.94	nr
N1789	type 560	5.65	2.5%	-	-	5.79	nr

Basic Prices of Materials	Supply Price £	Waste Factor %	Unload. Labour £	Unload. Plant £	Total Unit Cost £	Unit
P C Henderson Ltd Sliding Door Gear						
'Slipper' cupboard door gear sets for 2 doors:						
N1801 SS4	21.12	-	-	-	**21.12**	nr
N1802 SS5	24.83	-	-	-	**24.83**	nr
N1803 SS6	27.74	-	-	-	**27.74**	nr
'Loretto' cupboard door gear sets for 2 doors:						
N1804 D4	35.77	-	-	-	**35.77**	nr
N1805 D5	39.80	-	-	-	**39.80**	nr
N1806 D6	45.00	-	-	-	**45.00**	nr
'Single Top' wardrobe door gear sets for single doors:						
N1807 ST12	17.46	-	-	-	**17.46**	nr
N1808 ST15	19.67	-	-	-	**19.67**	nr
N1809 ST18	22.26	-	-	-	**22.26**	nr
'Double Top' wardrobe door gear sets for bi-parting doors:						
N1810 W12 for 2 doors	29.94	-	-	-	**29.94**	nr
N1811 W15 for 2 doors	33.39	-	-	-	**33.39**	nr
N1812 W18 for 2 doors	37.02	-	-	-	**37.02**	nr
N1813 W24 for 3 doors	48.56	-	-	-	**48.56**	nr
'Bi-fold' wardrobe door gear sets:						
N1815 B10/2 for 2 doors	27.54	-	-	-	**27.54**	nr
N1816 B15/4 for 4 doors	46.69	-	-	-	**46.69**	nr
N1817 B20/4 for 4 doors	51.14	-	-	-	**51.14**	nr
'Marathon Junior'						
N1821 J2	42.90	-	-	-	**42.90**	nr
N1822 J3	45.29	-	-	-	**45.29**	nr
N1823 J4	49.01	-	-	-	**49.01**	nr
N1824 J5	55.39	-	-	-	**55.39**	nr
'Marathon Senior'						
N1825 S3	60.76	-	-	-	**60.76**	nr
N1826 S6	119.32	-	-	-	**119.32**	nr
N1827 'Phantom' P9	46.15	-	-	-	**46.15**	nr
Pelmets for Marathon:						
N1829 40P-1850 mm long	22.76	-	-	-	**22.76**	nr
N1830 cap ends EC40P	2.48	-	-	-	**2.48**	pair
Industrial top hung sliding door gear						
Galvanised steel track:						
N1851 type 290	18.89	-	-	-	**18.89**	m
N1852 type 301	25.52	-	-	-	**25.52**	m
N1853 type 301H	40.20	-	-	-	**40.20**	m
N1854 type 305	51.55	-	-	-	**51.55**	m
Galvanised steel channel with lugs for concrete:						
N1855 type 89	17.60	-	-	-	**17.60**	m
N1856 type 97	26.20	-	-	-	**26.20**	m
Single track support brackets; aluminium sidewall pattern:						
N1857 1A/290 open and closed	7.87	-	-	-	**7.87**	nr
N1858 1AX/290 jointing	9.62	-	-	-	**9.62**	nr
N1859 1A/301 open and closed	12.72	-	-	-	**12.72**	nr
N1860 1AX/301 jointing	17.56	-	-	-	**17.56**	nr
N1861 1A/305 open and closed	26.32	-	-	-	**26.32**	nr
N1862 1AX/305 jointing	31.87	-	-	-	**31.87**	nr
Single track support brackets; steel fascia sidewall pattern:						
N1863 9A/290 open and closed	13.45	-	-	-	**13.45**	nr
N1864 9A/301S open	20.53	-	-	-	**20.53**	nr
N1865 9A/305 open	39.11	-	-	-	**39.11**	nr
Single track support brackets; aluminium side ear soffit pattern:						
N1866 3A/290	10.91	-	-	-	**10.91**	nr
N1867 3A/301	22.66	-	-	-	**22.66**	nr
N1868 3A/305	44.52	-	-	-	**44.52**	nr
Single track support brackets; aluminium parallel ear soffit pattern:						
N1869 4A/290	10.91	-	-	-	**10.91**	nr
N1870 4A/301	24.31	-	-	-	**24.31**	nr
N1871 4A/305	44.52	-	-	-	**44.52**	nr
Double track brackets; aluminium sidewall pattern:						
N1872 5/290 open	25.18	-	-	-	**25.18**	nr
N1873 5/301 open	34.93	-	-	-	**34.93**	nr
N1874 5/305 open	75.41	-	-	-	**75.41**	nr
Double track brackets; aluminium soffit pattern:						
N1875 6/301 open	43.71	-	-	-	**43.71**	nr
Hangers for wood doors; four-wheel type:						
N1876 53K/N	33.38	-	-	-	**33.38**	nr
N1877 53A/S or 53A/N	58.78	-	-	-	**58.78**	nr
N1878 53C	74.78	-	-	-	**74.78**	nr
Bottom roller guides for wood doors:						
N1879 102/97	16.29	-	-	-	**16.29**	nr
N1881 105R/97	13.22	-	-	-	**13.22**	nr
N1882 105R/89	12.43	-	-	-	**12.43**	nr
Bottom guide ground stay rollers:						
N1883 126	11.50	-	-	-	**11.50**	nr
N1884 126H	36.95	-	-	-	**36.95**	nr
Accessories:						
N1885 bow handle, 463	8.75	-	-	-	**8.75**	nr
N1887 flush pull, 414	8.40	-	-	-	**8.40**	nr
N1888 surface bolt 380 mm long, 994	19.42	-	-	-	**19.42**	nr
N1889 flush bolt, 333	30.30	-	-	-	**30.30**	nr
N1890 flush bolt, 454	43.89	-	-	-	**43.89**	nr
N1892 single buffer wall stop, 109	16.75	-	-	-	**16.75**	nr

Unit Rates	Man-Hours	Net Labour Price £	Net Mats Price £	Net Unit Price £	Unit

UNIT RATES

NA   **CARCASSING ITEMS**

Note: The prices for softwood in this section allow for untreated timber; the following allowances should be made to material prices for preservative treatment, special qualities and special sawings etc.:

       preservative treatment + 15%
       stress grading - GS + 7%
       stress grading - SS + 25%
       gauging + 6%
       special sawing + 15%
       long lengths = 5.1 - 6.0 m + 8%
                     6.3 - 7.2 m + 15%
                     7.5 and over + 20%

		Man-Hours	Net Labour Price £	Net Mats Price £	Net Unit Price £	Unit
001	**Sawn softwood, Building quality, untreated**					
002	Floors:					
	50 x 100 mm	0.14	2.16	1.48	**3.64**	m
	50 x 150 mm	0.16	2.36	2.22	**4.58**	m
	50 x 200 mm	0.17	2.52	2.96	**5.48**	m
	75 x 150 mm	0.18	2.71	3.82	**6.53**	m
	75 x 200 mm	0.24	3.60	5.09	**8.69**	m
	75 x 250 mm	0.30	4.51	7.16	**11.67**	m
	75 x 300 mm	0.36	5.40	8.60	**14.00**	m
	100 x 200 mm	0.32	4.86	7.46	**12.32**	m
	100 x 250 mm	0.36	5.40	9.91	**15.31**	m
	100 x 300 mm	0.43	6.48	11.88	**18.36**	m
003	Partitions:					
	38 x 50 mm	0.20	2.98	0.81	**3.79**	m
	38 x 100 mm	0.28	4.32	1.55	**5.87**	m
	50 x 50 mm	0.20	2.98	0.76	**3.74**	m
	50 x 75 mm	0.28	4.32	1.11	**5.43**	m
	50 x 100 mm	0.28	4.32	1.48	**5.80**	m
	75 x 75 mm	0.30	4.51	1.90	**6.41**	m
	75 x 100 mm	0.33	5.05	2.54	**7.59**	m
	100 x 100 mm	0.38	5.76	3.73	**9.49**	m
004	Flat roofs:					
	38 x 100 mm	0.12	1.79	1.55	**3.34**	m
	38 x 150 mm	0.18	2.71	2.31	**5.02**	m
	50 x 100 mm	0.14	2.16	1.48	**3.64**	m
	50 x 150 mm	0.16	2.43	2.22	**4.65**	m
	50 x 200 mm	0.17	2.61	2.96	**5.57**	m
	50 x 250 mm	0.21	3.24	4.50	**7.74**	m
	75 x 150 mm	0.19	2.89	3.82	**6.71**	m
	75 x 200 mm	0.21	3.24	5.09	**8.33**	m
	75 x 225 mm	0.23	3.42	5.72	**9.14**	m
	75 x 250 mm	0.26	3.97	7.16	**11.13**	m
	75 x 300 mm	0.31	4.68	8.60	**13.28**	m
	100 x 200 mm	0.26	3.97	7.46	**11.43**	m
	100 x 250 mm	0.33	5.05	9.91	**14.96**	m
	100 x 300 mm	0.39	5.94	11.88	**17.82**	m
005	Pitched roofs including ceiling joists:					
	25 x 100 mm	0.15	2.25	0.96	**3.21**	m
	25 x 150 mm	0.23	3.42	1.44	**4.86**	m
	25 x 175 mm	0.26	3.97	1.72	**5.69**	m
	32 x 150 mm	0.26	3.97	2.30	**6.27**	m
	32 x 200 mm	0.26	3.97	3.08	**7.05**	m
	38 x 100 mm	0.18	2.71	2.31	**5.02**	m
	38 x 150 mm	0.24	3.60	2.31	**5.91**	m
	50 x 50 mm	0.15	2.25	0.76	**3.01**	m
	50 x 100 mm	0.22	3.33	1.48	**4.81**	m
	50 x 150 mm	0.26	3.97	2.22	**6.19**	m
	50 x 200 mm	0.39	5.94	2.96	**8.90**	m
	50 x 225 mm	0.45	6.84	3.33	**10.17**	m
	75 x 100 mm	0.33	5.05	2.54	**7.59**	m
	75 x 150 mm	0.47	7.20	3.82	**11.02**	m
	75 x 200 mm	0.59	9.00	5.09	**14.09**	m
	75 x 250 mm	0.74	11.25	7.16	**18.41**	m
	75 x 300 mm	0.89	13.48	8.60	**22.08**	m
	100 x 100 mm	0.41	6.29	3.73	**10.02**	m
	100 x 150 mm	0.62	9.36	5.60	**14.96**	m
	100 x 200 mm	0.78	11.89	7.46	**19.35**	m
	100 x 225 mm	0.88	13.42	8.40	**21.82**	m
	100 x 250 mm	0.98	14.91	9.91	**24.82**	m
	100 x 300 mm	1.17	17.83	11.88	**29.71**	m
006	Kerbs, bearers and the like:					
	19 x 100 mm	0.08	1.17	0.80	**1.97**	m
	19 x 150 mm	0.12	1.75	1.20	**2.95**	m
	25 x 50 mm	0.07	0.99	0.53	**1.52**	m
	25 x 75 mm	0.08	1.17	0.80	**1.97**	m
	25 x 100 mm	0.10	1.55	0.96	**2.51**	m
	38 x 50 mm	0.08	1.17	0.81	**1.98**	m
	38 x 75 mm	0.12	1.75	1.20	**2.95**	m
	38 x 100 mm	0.15	2.31	1.55	**3.86**	m

Unit Rates	Man-Hours	Net Labour Price £	Net Mats Price £	Net Unit Price £	Unit
50 x 50 mm	0.10	1.55	0.76	2.31	m
50 x 75 mm	0.15	2.30	1.11	3.41	m
50 x 100 mm	0.20	3.07	1.48	4.55	m
75 x 75 mm	0.23	3.47	1.90	5.37	m
75 x 100 mm	0.30	4.61	2.54	7.15	m
75 x 150 mm	0.46	6.93	3.82	10.75	m
75 x 200 mm	0.61	9.23	5.09	14.32	m
100 x 100 mm	0.39	5.94	3.73	9.67	m
100 x 150 mm	0.59	8.91	5.60	14.51	m
100 x 200 mm	0.78	11.89	7.46	19.35	m
100 x 250 mm	0.98	14.85	9.91	24.76	m
100 x 300 mm	1.17	17.83	11.88	29.71	m
007 Solid strutting to joists:					
50 x 150 mm	0.38	5.81	2.22	8.03	m
50 x 200 mm	0.39	5.91	2.96	8.87	m
50 x 225 mm	0.40	6.03	3.33	9.36	m
50 x 250 mm	0.41	6.16	4.50	10.66	m
50 x 275 mm	0.41	6.29	5.12	11.41	m
50 x 300 mm	0.42	6.44	5.59	12.03	m
008 Herring bone strutting:					
38 x 38 mm to joists:					
150 mm deep	0.39	5.99	1.23	7.22	m
200 mm deep	0.39	5.99	1.23	7.22	m
250 mm deep	0.39	5.99	1.23	7.22	m
300 mm deep	0.39	5.99	1.23	7.22	m
50 x 50 mm to joists:					
150 mm deep	0.47	7.08	1.53	8.61	m
200 mm deep	0.47	7.08	1.53	8.61	m
250 mm deep	0.47	7.08	1.53	8.61	m
300 mm deep	0.47	7.08	1.53	8.61	m
009 Cleats; two out of:					
50 x 100 mm x 200 mm long	0.39	5.99	0.30	6.29	Nr
75 x 150 mm x 300 mm long	0.47	7.20	1.15	8.35	Nr
100 x 200 mm x 400 mm long	0.59	9.00	2.99	11.99	Nr
010 Wrought face by hand	0.36	5.40	-	5.40	m2
011 Notching and fitting timber to metal	0.33	5.05	-	5.05	Nr
012 Trimming around openings:					
50 x 100 mm members; opening:					
500 x 1000 mm	4.15	63.02	-	63.02	Nr
750 x 1250 mm	4.15	63.02	-	63.02	Nr
50 x 150 mm members; opening:					
600 x 1200 mm	4.74	72.02	-	72.02	Nr
900 x 1500 mm	4.98	75.62	-	75.62	Nr
50 x 200 mm members; opening:					
600 x 1200 mm	5.33	81.02	-	81.02	Nr
900 x 1500 mm	5.63	85.53	-	85.53	Nr
75 x 250 mm members; opening:					
600 x 1200 mm	6.40	97.22	-	97.22	Nr
900 x 1500 mm	6.75	102.63	-	102.63	Nr
1000 x 2000 mm	7.11	108.03	-	108.03	Nr
75 x 300 mm members; opening:					
600 x 1200 mm	7.58	115.23	-	115.23	Nr
900 x 1500 mm	8.06	122.44	-	122.44	Nr
1000 x 2000 mm	8.53	129.63	-	129.63	Nr
1500 x 3000 mm	9.95	151.24	-	151.24	Nr
013 Raking cutting on softwood:					
38 mm thick	0.12	1.79	0.20	1.99	m
50 mm thick	0.12	1.79	0.52	2.31	m
75 mm thick	0.14	2.16	1.02	3.18	m
100 mm thick	0.18	2.71	1.49	4.20	m
014 Curved cutting on softwood:					
38 mm thick	0.53	8.12	0.20	8.32	m
50 mm thick	0.53	8.12	0.52	8.64	m
75 mm thick	0.59	9.00	1.02	10.02	m
100 mm thick	0.66	10.08	1.49	11.57	m
015 Scribing softwood:					
38 mm thick	0.57	8.65	0.20	8.85	m
50 mm thick	0.57	8.65	0.52	9.17	m
75 mm thick	0.65	9.91	1.02	10.93	m
100 mm thick	0.71	10.81	1.49	12.30	m
016 Hand labours on softwood:					
rounds	0.24	3.60	-	3.60	m
rebates	0.36	5.40	-	5.40	m
grooves	0.34	5.23	-	5.23	m
chamfers	0.18	2.71	-	2.71	m
throats	0.36	5.40	-	5.40	m
mouldings; per 25 mm girth	1.07	16.20	-	16.20	m

Note: 017 - 028 not used

	Unit Rates	Man-Hours	Net Labour Price £	Net Mats Price £	Net Unit Price £	Unit
029	**Work to existing carcassing items**					
030	Remove decayed or defective floor joists; ceiling joists, rafters and the like and replace with new:					
	50 x 75 mm	0.29	4.35	1.44	**5.79**	m
	50 x 100 mm	0.29	4.35	1.44	**5.79**	m
	50 x 150 mm	0.42	6.40	2.89	**9.29**	m
	50 x 225 mm	0.73	11.04	4.33	**15.37**	m
	75 x 100 mm	0.54	8.15	2.89	**11.04**	m
	75 x 150 mm	0.77	11.63	4.33	**15.96**	m
	75 x 225 mm	1.01	15.28	6.50	**21.78**	m
	75 x 250 mm	1.26	19.18	7.22	**26.40**	m
031	Cutting back eaves of pitched timber roof up to 500 mm projection from wall face, including stripping off roof tiles or slates, battens and underfelt, not exceeding 1000 mm on slope; removing timber fascia, asbestos free cement sheet soffit and bearers up to 1000 mm girth; cutting off rafters flush with wall face; reforming eaves course at higher level with new treated sawn softwood tilting fillet	1.91	29.06	6.13	**35.19**	m
	BOARDING AND FLOORING					
	Note: The prices for softwood in this section allow for untreated timber; allowances should be made to material prices for the following: preservative treatment + 15%					
001	**Sawn softwood, untreated**					
002	Square edged boarding to roofs; in 150 mm widths:					
	laid flat to falls:					
	19 mm thick	0.65	9.91	8.38	**18.29**	m2
	25 mm thick	0.65	9.91	9.85	**19.76**	m2
	laid to slope:					
	19 mm thick	0.71	10.81	8.38	**19.19**	m2
	25 mm thick	0.71	10.81	9.85	**20.66**	m2
	laid diagonally, flat to falls:					
	19 mm thick	0.83	12.60	8.38	**20.98**	m2
	25 mm thick	0.83	12.60	9.85	**22.45**	m2
	laid diagonally, to slope:					
	19 mm thick	0.88	13.33	8.38	**21.71**	m2
	25 mm thick	0.88	13.33	9.85	**23.18**	m2
	laid to tops and cheeks of dormers:					
	19 mm thick	1.19	18.01	8.38	**26.39**	m2
	25 mm thick	1.19	18.01	9.85	**27.86**	m2
	Note: 003 - 006 not used					
007	**Wrought softwood, untreated**					
008	Square edged boarding to floors; 125 mm widths:					
	19 mm thick	0.79	12.01	14.72	**26.73**	m2
	22 mm thick	0.79	12.01	16.56	**28.57**	m2
	25 mm thick	0.79	12.01	16.56	**28.57**	m2
	ADD for laying diagonally	0.26	4.01	-	**4.01**	m2
009	Tongued and grooved boarding to floors; 125 mm widths:					
	19 mm thick	0.89	13.50	14.72	**28.22**	m2
	22 mm thick	0.89	13.50	20.07	**33.57**	m2
	25 mm thick	0.89	13.50	20.07	**33.57**	m2
	ADD for laying diagonally	0.30	4.51	-	**4.51**	m2
010	Tongued and grooved boarding to roofs:					
	laid flat to falls:					
	19 mm thick	0.83	12.60	14.72	**27.32**	m2
	25 mm thick	0.83	12.60	20.07	**32.67**	m2
	ADD for laying diagonally	0.30	4.51	-	**4.51**	m2
	laid to slope:					
	19 mm thick	0.86	13.06	14.72	**27.78**	m2
	25 mm thick	0.86	13.06	20.07	**33.13**	m2
	ADD for laying diagonally	0.30	4.51	-	**4.51**	m2
	laid to tops and cheeks of dormers:					
	19 mm thick	0.89	13.50	14.72	**28.22**	m2
	25 mm thick	0.89	13.50	20.07	**33.57**	m2
	ADD for laying diagonally	0.30	4.51	-	**4.51**	m2
	Note: 011 - 012 not used					
013	Tongued and grooved boarding to gutter bottoms and sides; in 125 mm widths:					
	19 mm	3.02	45.92	16.85	**62.77**	m2
	25 mm	3.32	50.42	22.97	**73.39**	m2
014	Shiplap weatherboarding, in 150 mm widths to sloping or vertical surfaces:					
	19 mm	0.65	9.91	20.07	**29.98**	m2
	25 mm	0.65	9.91	26.37	**36.28**	m2
015	Tongued and grooved, V-jointed one side matchboarding in 100 mm widths:					
	to walls:					
	13 mm thick	0.73	11.16	11.72	**22.88**	m2
	19 mm thick	0.73	11.16	17.93	**29.09**	m2
	ADD for laying diagonally	0.30	4.51	-	**4.51**	m2

	Man-Hours	Net Labour Price £	Net Mats Price £	Net Unit Price £	Unit
to ceilings:					
13 mm thick	0.85	12.89	11.72	**24.61**	m2
19 mm thick	0.85	12.89	17.93	**30.82**	m2
ADD for laying diagonally	0.30	4.51	-	**4.51**	m2
Note: 016 not used					
017 Cross-tongued boarding to eaves and verges, fascias and barge boards:					
16 mm thick:					
over 300 mm wide	1.36	20.72	16.31	**37.03**	m2
150 mm wide	0.34	5.23	2.69	**7.92**	m
200 mm wide	0.34	5.23	3.59	**8.82**	m
225 mm wide	0.36	5.40	4.03	**9.43**	m
250 mm wide	0.41	6.29	4.49	**10.78**	m
19 mm thick:					
over 300 mm wide	1.48	22.51	19.89	**42.40**	m2
150 mm wide	0.38	5.76	3.27	**9.03**	m
200 mm wide	0.38	5.76	4.37	**10.13**	m
225 mm wide	0.41	6.29	4.91	**11.20**	m
250 mm wide	0.45	6.84	5.48	**12.32**	m
25 mm thick:					
over 300 mm wide	1.52	23.04	24.80	**47.84**	m2
150 mm wide	0.44	6.67	4.08	**10.75**	m
200 mm wide	0.44	6.67	5.46	**12.13**	m
225 mm wide	0.49	7.37	6.12	**13.49**	m
250 mm wide	0.51	7.75	6.83	**14.58**	m
018 Tongued and grooved, V-jointed matchboarding to eaves and verges, fascias and barge boards:					
13 mm thick:					
over 300 mm wide	1.71	25.93	11.72	**37.65**	m2
150 mm wide	0.43	6.48	1.90	**8.38**	m
200 mm wide	0.43	6.48	2.53	**9.01**	m
225 mm wide	0.47	7.20	2.85	**10.05**	m
250 mm wide	0.51	7.75	3.27	**11.02**	m
19 mm thick:					
over 300 mm wide	1.85	28.09	17.93	**46.02**	m2
150 mm wide	0.46	7.01	2.91	**9.92**	m
200 mm wide	0.46	7.01	3.88	**10.89**	m
225 mm wide	0.51	7.75	4.36	**12.11**	m
250 mm wide	0.56	8.47	5.01	**13.48**	m
Note: 019 not used					
020 Hand labours on boarding:					
15 mm thick:					
rounded edges	0.24	3.60	-	**3.60**	m
chamfered edges	0.12	1.79	-	**1.79**	m
19 mm thick:					
rounded edges	0.30	4.51	-	**4.51**	m
chamfered edges	0.18	2.71	-	**2.71**	m
25 mm thick:					
rounded edges	0.36	5.40	-	**5.40**	m
chamfered edges	0.24	3.60	-	**3.60**	m
any thickness:					
grooves	0.36	5.40	-	**5.40**	m
throatings	0.36	5.40	-	**5.40**	m
mouldings, per 25 mm girth	1.07	16.20	-	**16.20**	m
021 Raking cutting on boarding and boundary cutting on diagonal boarding:					
15 mm thick	0.12	1.79	0.04	**1.83**	m
19 mm thick	0.12	1.79	0.05	**1.84**	m
25 mm thick	0.12	1.79	0.07	**1.86**	m
022 Curved cutting on boarding:					
15 mm thick	0.30	4.51	0.04	**4.55**	m
19 mm thick	0.30	4.51	0.05	**4.56**	m
25 mm thick	0.30	4.51	0.07	**4.58**	m
023 Scribing on boarding:					
15 mm thick	0.36	5.40	0.04	**5.44**	m
19 mm thick	0.36	5.40	0.05	**5.45**	m
25 mm thick	0.36	5.40	0.07	**5.47**	m
024 Tongued edges on boarding:					
15 mm thick	0.41	6.29	0.04	**6.33**	m
19 mm thick	0.41	6.29	0.05	**6.34**	m
25 mm thick	0.41	6.29	0.07	**6.36**	m
025 Mitred angles on boarding:					
15 mm thick	0.58	8.74	0.04	**8.78**	m
19 mm thick	0.58	8.74	0.05	**8.79**	m
25 mm thick	0.58	8.74	0.07	**8.81**	m
026 Notches; per 25 mm girth on boarding:					
15 mm thick	0.05	0.81	-	**0.81**	Nr
19 mm thick	0.05	0.81	-	**0.81**	Nr
25 mm thick	0.05	0.81	-	**0.81**	Nr

Unit Rates

		Man-Hours	Net Labour Price £	Net Mats Price £	Net Unit Price £	Unit
027	Rounded corners; per 25 mm girth on boarding:					
	15 mm thick	0.06	0.91	-	**0.91**	Nr
	19 mm thick	0.06	0.91	-	**0.91**	Nr
	25 mm thick	0.06	0.91	-	**0.91**	Nr
028	Sinkings; per 25 mm deep:					
	25 x 50 mm	0.30	4.51	-	**4.51**	Nr
	50 x 50 mm	0.41	6.29	-	**6.29**	Nr
	50 x 100 mm	0.71	10.81	-	**10.81**	Nr
029	Cutting and fitting around obstructions; per 25 mm girth on boarding:					
	15 mm thick	0.07	1.09	-	**1.09**	Nr
	19 mm thick	0.08	1.25	-	**1.25**	Nr
	25 mm thick	0.09	1.41	-	**1.41**	Nr
030	Access traps; 25 mm boarding on 38 x 50 mm wrought softwood bearers:					
	400 x 400 mm	0.43	6.48	4.43	**10.91**	Nr
	600 x 600 mm	0.78	11.89	9.19	**21.08**	Nr
	900 x 900 mm	1.62	24.67	20.07	**44.74**	Nr
031	Cesspools; 25 mm boarding on 25 x 25 mm sawn softwood bearers to bottom and sides:					
	300 x 300 x 200 mm deep	2.07	31.51	7.30	**38.81**	Nr
	450 x 300 x 200 mm deep	2.67	40.51	9.77	**50.28**	Nr
	600 x 300 x 300 mm deep	4.15	63.02	15.82	**78.84**	Nr
	Note: 032 - 042 not used					
043	**Plywood BS 5268 PT2 WBP BB/BB exterior grade**					
044	Boarding to floors or roofs; butt joints:					
	18 mm	0.39	5.94	19.33	**25.27**	m2
	25 mm	0.44	6.67	25.15	**31.82**	m2
045	Boarding to floors or roofs; tongued and grooved joints:					
	12 mm	0.36	5.40	14.33	**19.73**	m2
	15 mm	0.39	5.94	17.41	**23.35**	m2
	18 mm	0.50	7.55	21.26	**28.81**	m2
046	Boarding to gutter bottoms and sides:					
	18 mm	2.37	36.01	19.33	**55.34**	m2
	25 mm	2.70	41.06	25.15	**66.21**	m2
047	Boarding to gutter bottoms and sides:					
	150 mm wide:					
	18 mm	0.65	9.91	2.90	**12.81**	m
	25 mm	0.77	11.69	3.77	**15.46**	m
	225 mm wide:					
	18 mm	0.77	11.69	4.45	**16.14**	m
	25 mm	0.81	12.24	5.78	**18.02**	m
048	Eaves and verge boarding, fascias and barge boards:					
	12 mm thick:					
	over 300 mm wide	1.16	17.65	13.32	**30.97**	m2
	150 mm wide	0.28	4.32	2.00	**6.32**	m
	200 mm wide	0.30	4.58	2.66	**7.24**	m
	225 mm wide	0.33	4.94	3.06	**8.00**	m
	250 mm wide	0.36	5.40	3.33	**8.73**	m
	15 mm thick:					
	over 300 mm wide	1.19	18.01	16.24	**34.25**	m2
	150 mm wide	0.30	4.59	2.44	**7.03**	m
	200 mm wide	0.32	4.86	3.25	**8.11**	m
	225 mm wide	0.36	5.40	3.74	**9.14**	m
	250 mm wide	0.40	6.08	4.06	**10.14**	m
	18 mm thick:					
	over 300 mm wide	1.36	20.72	19.33	**40.05**	m2
	150 mm wide	0.33	5.05	2.90	**7.95**	m
	200 mm wide	0.36	5.40	3.87	**9.27**	m
	225 mm wide	0.40	6.03	4.45	**10.48**	m
	250 mm wide	0.43	6.58	4.83	**11.41**	m
	25 mm thick:					
	over 300 mm wide	1.48	22.51	25.15	**47.66**	m2
	150 mm wide	0.36	5.40	3.77	**9.17**	m
	200 mm wide	0.39	5.85	5.03	**10.88**	m
	225 mm wide	0.40	6.13	5.78	**11.91**	m
	250 mm wide	0.44	6.67	6.29	**12.96**	m
049	Raking cutting on plywood boarding:					
	12 mm thick	0.30	4.51	2.00	**6.51**	m
	15 mm thick	0.33	4.94	2.44	**7.38**	m
	18 mm thick	0.36	5.40	2.90	**8.30**	m
	25 mm thick	0.39	5.85	3.77	**9.62**	m
050	Curved cutting on plywood boarding:					
	12 mm thick	0.83	12.60	2.00	**14.60**	m
	15 mm thick	0.89	13.50	2.44	**15.94**	m
	18 mm thick	0.95	14.41	2.90	**17.31**	m
	25 mm thick	1.01	15.31	3.77	**19.08**	m

Unit Rates

		Man-Hours	Net Labour Price £	Net Mats Price £	Net Unit Price £	Unit
051	Scribing on plywood boarding:					
	12 mm thick	1.01	15.31	2.00	**17.31**	m
	15 mm thick	1.07	16.20	2.44	**18.64**	m
	18 mm thick	1.13	17.12	2.90	**20.02**	m
	25 mm thick	1.19	18.01	3.77	**21.78**	m
052	**Chipboard to BS 5669; flooring grade**					
053	Boarding to floors; butt joints:					
	18 mm	0.33	5.05	5.24	**10.29**	m2
	22 mm	0.39	5.94	6.58	**12.52**	m2
054	Boarding to floors; tongued and grooved joints:					
	18 mm	0.41	6.29	5.90	**12.19**	m2
	22 mm	0.45	6.84	9.14	**15.98**	m2
055	Boarding to roofs; butt joints:					
	12 mm flat to falls (standard grade)	0.30	4.59	2.78	**7.37**	m2
	12 mm sloping (standard grade)	0.30	4.59	2.78	**7.37**	m2
	15 mm flat to falls (standard grade)	0.30	4.59	3.34	**7.93**	m2
	15 mm sloping (standard grade)	0.34	5.14	3.34	**8.48**	m2
	18 mm flat to falls	0.33	5.05	4.01	**9.06**	m2
	18 mm sloping	0.39	5.94	4.01	**9.95**	m2
	22 mm flat to falls	0.39	5.94	5.55	**11.49**	m2
	22 mm sloping	0.49	7.37	5.55	**12.92**	m2
056	Raking cutting on chipboard boarding:					
	12 mm thick	0.30	4.51	0.42	**4.93**	m
	15 mm thick	0.30	4.51	0.50	**5.01**	m
	18 mm thick	0.30	4.51	0.60	**5.11**	m
	22 mm thick	0.30	4.51	0.83	**5.34**	m
057	Curved cutting on chipboard boarding:					
	12 mm thick	0.65	9.91	0.42	**10.33**	m
	15 mm thick	0.71	10.81	0.50	**11.31**	m
	18 mm thick	0.83	12.60	0.60	**13.20**	m
	22 mm thick	0.89	13.50	0.83	**14.33**	m
058	Scribing on chipboard boarding:					
	12 mm thick	0.78	11.89	0.42	**12.31**	m
	15 mm thick	0.85	12.97	0.50	**13.47**	m
	18 mm thick	1.00	15.12	0.60	**15.72**	m
	22 mm thick	1.07	16.20	0.83	**17.03**	m
059	**Non-asbestos boards to BS 476, flameproof to class 1; 'Supalux', natural finish**					
060	Eaves and verge boarding:					
	6 mm thick:					
	over 300 mm wide	1.78	27.01	18.47	**45.48**	m2
	150 mm wide	0.43	6.48	2.77	**9.25**	m
	200 mm wide	0.45	6.84	3.69	**10.53**	m
	225 mm wide	0.50	7.55	4.25	**11.80**	m
	250 mm wide	0.53	8.12	4.62	**12.74**	m
	9 mm thick:					
	over 300 mm wide	1.90	28.80	25.77	**54.57**	m2
	150 mm wide	0.45	6.84	3.87	**10.71**	m
	200 mm wide	0.47	7.20	5.15	**12.35**	m
	225 mm wide	0.53	8.12	5.93	**14.05**	m
	250 mm wide	0.57	8.65	6.44	**15.09**	m
	12 mm thick:					
	over 300 mm wide	2.01	30.61	32.64	**63.25**	m2
	150 mm wide	0.49	7.37	4.90	**12.27**	m
	200 mm wide	0.51	7.75	6.53	**14.28**	m
	225 mm wide	0.57	8.65	7.51	**16.16**	m
	250 mm wide	0.61	9.20	8.16	**17.36**	m
061	Raking cutting on 'Supalux' boarding:					
	6 mm thick	0.30	4.51	2.77	**7.28**	m
	9 mm thick	0.30	4.51	3.87	**8.38**	m
	12 mm thick	0.30	4.51	4.90	**9.41**	m
062	Curved cutting on 'Supalux' boarding:					
	6 mm thick	0.83	12.60	2.77	**15.37**	m
	9 mm thick	0.83	12.60	3.87	**16.47**	m
	12 mm thick	0.95	14.41	4.90	**19.31**	m
063	Scribing on 'Supalux' boarding:					
	6 mm thick	1.01	15.31	2.77	**18.08**	m
	9 mm thick	1.01	15.31	3.87	**19.18**	m
	12 mm thick	1.13	17.12	4.90	**22.02**	m
064	**Work to existing boarding and flooring**					
065	Make good boarded floor where cross wall removed; 50 x 50 mm sawn softwood bearers:					
	25 mm tongued and grooved wrought softwood:					
	not exceeding 100 mm wide	0.31	4.70	2.96	**7.66**	m
	100 - 200 mm wide	0.46	7.04	5.56	**12.60**	m
	200 - 300 mm wide	0.62	9.39	7.44	**16.83**	m
	300 - 400 mm wide	0.77	11.75	9.32	**21.07**	m

	Unit Rates	Man-Hours	Net Labour Price £	Net Mats Price £	Net Unit Price £	Unit
	400 - 500 mm wide	0.93	14.09	11.56	**25.65**	m
	500 - 600 mm wide	1.08	16.43	13.44	**29.87**	m
	18 mm flooring grade chipboard:					
	not exceeding 100 mm wide	0.29	4.38	1.79	**6.17**	m
	100 - 200 mm wide	0.43	6.58	3.23	**9.81**	m
	200 - 300 mm wide	0.58	8.77	3.94	**12.71**	m
	300 - 400 mm wide	0.72	10.96	4.65	**15.61**	m
	400 - 500 mm wide	0.87	13.15	5.72	**18.87**	m
	500 - 600 mm wide	1.01	15.34	6.43	**21.77**	m
066	Make good boarded floors where piers etc. are removed:					
	not exceeding 0.50 m2; 50 x 100 mm joists at 400 mm centres:					
	25 mm square edged wrought softwood	1.15	17.43	14.38	**31.81**	Nr
	25 mm tongued and grooved wrought softwood	1.15	17.43	14.89	**32.32**	Nr
	18 mm flooring grade chipboard	1.15	17.43	10.02	**27.45**	Nr
	0.50 - 1.00 m2; 50 x 100 mm joists at 400 mm centres:					
	25 mm square edged wrought softwood	1.82	27.62	28.11	**55.73**	Nr
	25 mm tongued and grooved wrought softwood	1.82	27.62	29.12	**56.74**	Nr
	18 mm flooring grade chipboard	1.82	27.62	19.38	**47.00**	Nr
	not exceeding 0.50 m2; 50 x 200 mm joists at 400 mm centres:					
	25 mm square edged wrought softwood	1.20	18.18	16.19	**34.37**	Nr
	25 mm tongued and grooved wrought softwood	1.20	18.18	16.69	**34.87**	Nr
	18 mm flooring grade chipboard	1.20	18.18	11.82	**30.00**	Nr
	0.50 - 1.00 m2; 50 x 200 mm joists at 400 mm centres:					
	25 mm square edged wrought softwood	1.91	28.96	31.72	**60.68**	Nr
	25 mm tongued and grooved wrought softwood	1.91	28.96	32.72	**61.68**	Nr
	18 mm flooring grade chipboard	1.91	28.96	22.99	**51.95**	Nr
067	Make good boarded floor where columns etc. removed; 50 x 50 mm sawn softwood bearers:					
	25 mm tongued and grooved wrought softwood:					
	not exceeding 1.00 m2	1.96	29.75	19.20	**48.95**	Nr
	1.00 - 2.00 m2	3.04	46.19	38.08	**84.27**	Nr
	18 mm flooring grade chipboard:					
	not exceeding 1.00 m2	1.13	17.22	9.47	**26.69**	Nr
	1.00 - 2.00 m2	1.70	25.84	12.69	**38.53**	Nr
068	Make good boarded floors where staircases etc. removed:					
	not exceeding 2.00 m2; 50 x 150 mm joists at 400 mm centres:					
	25 mm square edged wrought softwood	2.78	42.27	42.92	**85.19**	Nr
	25 mm tongued and grooved wrought softwood	3.04	46.19	44.93	**91.12**	Nr
	18 mm flooring grade chipboard	1.70	25.84	25.47	**51.31**	Nr
	2.00 - 3.00 m2; 50 x 175 mm joists at 400 mm centres:					
	25 mm square edged wrought softwood	3.50	53.23	67.08	**120.31**	Nr
	25 mm tongued and grooved wrought softwood	3.81	57.93	70.11	**128.04**	Nr
	18 mm flooring grade chipboard	2.27	34.44	40.91	**75.35**	Nr
069	Take up decayed or defective floor boarding and replace with new wrought softwood boarding:					
	tongued and grooved:					
	25 mm thick:					
	single board 125 x 500 mm	0.10	1.46	1.08	**2.54**	Nr
	area not exceeding 1.00 m2	1.43	21.80	17.22	**39.02**	Nr
	area 1.00 - 2.00 m2	2.57	38.99	34.45	**73.44**	Nr
	32 mm thick:					
	single board 125 x 500 mm	0.10	1.57	1.56	**3.13**	Nr
	area not exceeding 1.00 m2	1.55	23.48	24.94	**48.42**	Nr
	area 1.00 - 2.00 m2	2.58	39.14	49.88	**89.02**	Nr
	square edged:					
	25 mm thick:					
	single board 125 x 500 mm	0.10	1.46	1.01	**2.47**	Nr
	area not exceeding 1.00 m2	1.28	19.47	16.12	**35.59**	Nr
	area 1.00 - 2.00 m2	2.31	35.07	32.23	**67.30**	Nr
	32 mm thick:					
	single board 125 x 500 mm	0.10	1.57	1.34	**2.91**	Nr
	area not exceeding 1.00 m2	1.39	21.14	21.42	**42.56**	Nr
	area 1.00 - 2.00 m2	2.52	38.36	42.83	**81.19**	Nr
070	Level up existing joists after removal of decayed or defective boarding and prepare to receive new boarding	0.19	2.92	-	**2.92**	m2
071	Remove tacks from existing softwood flooring, punch down nails etc. and fill nail holes	0.13	1.90	-	**1.90**	m2
072	Cut out decayed softwood timber fascia board and piece in new wrought softwood fascia to match existing:					
	25 x 250 mm in lengths:					
	up to 500 mm	0.98	14.87	3.68	**18.55**	Nr
	500 - 1000 mm	1.19	18.01	4.05	**22.06**	Nr
	32 x 350 mm in lengths:					
	up to 500 mm	1.09	16.60	5.52	**22.12**	Nr
	500 - 1000 mm	1.34	20.35	6.08	**26.43**	Nr
073	Cut out decayed soffits and piece in new to match existing:					
	wrought softwood 25 x 150 mm in lengths:					
	up to 500 mm	0.67	10.17	2.26	**12.43**	Nr
	500 - 1000 mm	0.86	13.07	2.49	**15.56**	Nr
	wrought softwood 25 x 250 mm in lengths:					
	up to 500 mm	0.72	10.96	3.68	**14.64**	Nr
	500 - 1000 mm	0.96	14.53	4.05	**18.58**	Nr
	fibre cement 6 x 150 mm in lengths:					
	up to 500 mm	0.62	9.39	2.53	**11.92**	Nr

Unit Rates	Man-Hours	Net Labour Price £	Net Mats Price £	Net Unit Price £	Unit
500 - 1000 mm	0.79	12.05	2.78	**14.83**	Nr
fibre cement 6 x 300 mm in lengths:					
up to 500 mm	0.85	12.84	5.06	**17.90**	Nr
500 - 1000 mm	1.08	16.43	5.57	**22.00**	Nr

NC — FILLETS, ROLLS AND THE LIKE

Note: Prices for softwood in this section are for untreated timber; allowances should be made to material prices for the following:
preservative treatment + 15%

001 Sawn softwood, untreated

	Man-Hours	Net Labour Price £	Net Mats Price £	Net Unit Price £	Unit
002 Angle fillets:					
38 x 38 mm	0.18	2.71	0.39	**3.10**	m
50 x 50 mm	0.19	2.89	0.78	**3.67**	m
75 x 75 mm	0.20	3.07	1.26	**4.33**	m
003 Tilting fillets:					
25 x 50 mm	0.11	1.63	0.59	**2.22**	m
38 x 75 mm	0.13	1.98	1.38	**3.36**	m
004 Rolls:					
50 x 50 mm	0.21	3.24	1.23	**4.47**	m
50 x 75 mm	0.24	3.60	1.83	**5.43**	m
005 Firring pieces:					
50 mm wide; average depth:					
25 mm	0.02	0.35	0.34	**0.69**	m
50 mm	0.05	0.68	0.63	**1.31**	m
63 mm	0.06	0.85	0.79	**1.64**	m
75 mm	0.07	1.00	0.93	**1.93**	m
75 mm wide; average depth:					
25 mm	0.03	0.50	0.44	**0.94**	m
50 mm	0.07	1.00	0.92	**1.92**	m
63 mm	0.08	1.28	1.17	**2.45**	m
75 mm	0.10	1.52	1.32	**2.84**	m
100 mm wide; average depth:					
25 mm	0.05	0.68	0.67	**1.35**	m
50 mm	0.09	1.35	1.25	**2.60**	m
63 mm	0.11	1.70	1.57	**3.27**	m
75 mm	0.13	2.04	1.66	**3.70**	m
006 Wrought softwood					
007 Rounded nosings tongued to edge of boarding:					
19 x 75 mm	0.57	8.65	1.60	**10.25**	m
19 x 75 mm; crossgrain	0.65	9.91	1.60	**11.51**	m
22 x 75 mm	0.59	9.00	1.86	**10.86**	m
22 x 75 mm; crossgrain	0.68	10.28	1.86	**12.14**	m
25 x 75 mm	0.65	9.91	1.86	**11.77**	m
25 x 75 mm; crossgrain	0.73	11.16	1.86	**13.02**	m

ND — GROUNDS, BATTENS AND FRAMEWORK

Note: Prices for softwood in this section are for untreated timber; allowances should be made to material prices for the following:
preservative treatment + 15%

001 Sawn softwood, untreated

	Man-Hours	Net Labour Price £	Net Mats Price £	Net Unit Price £	Unit
002 Open spaced battening one way at:					
300 mm centres:					
13 x 50 mm	0.44	6.67	0.87	**7.54**	m2
25 x 50 mm	0.51	7.75	1.76	**9.51**	m2
38 x 50 mm	0.58	8.83	2.66	**11.49**	m2
400 mm centres:					
13 x 50 mm	0.33	5.05	0.66	**5.71**	m2
25 x 50 mm	0.38	5.76	1.33	**7.09**	m2
38 x 50 mm	0.44	6.67	2.02	**8.69**	m2
600 mm centres:					
13 x 50 mm	0.23	3.42	0.45	**3.87**	m2
25 x 50 mm	0.25	3.77	0.91	**4.68**	m2
38 x 50 mm	0.30	4.51	1.37	**5.88**	m2
900 mm centres:					
13 x 50 mm	0.14	2.16	0.29	**2.45**	m2
25 x 50 mm	0.17	2.52	0.59	**3.11**	m2
38 x 50 mm	0.19	2.89	0.89	**3.78**	m2
003 Open spaced battening both ways at:					
300 mm centres:					
13 x 50 mm	1.03	15.66	1.77	**17.43**	m2
25 x 50 mm	1.15	17.46	3.57	**21.03**	m2
38 x 50 mm	1.29	19.64	5.40	**25.04**	m2
400 mm centres:					
13 x 50 mm	0.77	11.69	1.32	**13.01**	m2
25 x 50 mm	0.87	13.15	2.66	**15.81**	m2
38 x 50 mm	0.97	14.76	4.03	**18.79**	m2

Unit Rates	Man-Hours	Net Labour Price £	Net Mats Price £	Net Unit Price £	Unit
600 mm centres:					
13 x 50 mm	0.51	7.75	0.87	**8.62**	m2
25 x 50 mm	0.58	8.83	1.76	**10.59**	m2
38 x 50 mm	0.65	9.91	2.66	**12.57**	m2
900 mm centres:					
13 x 50 mm	0.34	5.23	0.58	**5.81**	m2
25 x 50 mm	0.38	5.76	1.17	**6.93**	m2
38 x 50 mm	0.43	6.48	1.77	**8.25**	m2
004 Individual grounds and battens:					
13 x 25 mm	0.13	1.98	0.16	**2.14**	m
13 x 38 mm	0.13	1.98	0.24	**2.22**	m
13 x 50 mm	0.13	1.98	0.26	**2.24**	m
13 x 75 mm	0.14	2.16	0.40	**2.56**	m
13 x 100 mm	0.16	2.36	0.53	**2.89**	m
25 x 38 mm	0.16	2.36	0.41	**2.77**	m
25 x 50 mm	0.16	2.36	0.53	**2.89**	m
38 x 50 mm	0.18	2.71	0.81	**3.52**	m
005 Framework to receive sheet finish:					
to steel beams with 50 x 75 mm horizontal members and 25 x 50 mm vertical and cross members at 400 mm centres	2.78	42.30	3.01	**45.31**	m2
to false ceilings, 50 x 50 mm both ways at 300 mm centres	2.72	41.40	5.12	**46.52**	m2
to bath panels, 38 x 50 mm at 450 mm centres vertically, 500 mm centres horizontally	2.32	35.29	4.76	**40.05**	m2
006 Framework to receive pipe casing; 25 x 38 mm horizontal members at 600 mm centres; 25 x 38 mm vertical members at sides; 38 x 38 mm vertical members at angles:					
to one side of pipe:					
150 mm wide	0.33	5.05	0.93	**5.98**	m
300 mm wide	0.38	5.76	1.05	**6.81**	m
to two adjacent sides of pipe:					
300 mm girth	0.57	8.65	1.63	**10.28**	m
450 mm girth	0.59	9.00	1.71	**10.71**	m
600 mm girth	0.64	9.73	1.83	**11.56**	m
to three sides of pipe:					
450 mm girth	0.81	12.24	2.36	**14.60**	m
600 mm girth	0.84	12.77	2.44	**15.21**	m
750 mm girth	0.88	13.33	2.56	**15.89**	m
900 mm girth	0.91	13.86	2.64	**16.50**	m
NE UNFRAMED SECOND FIXINGS					
001 Standard mouldings in wrought softwood					
002 Quadrant:					
13 mm	0.13	1.98	0.72	**2.70**	m
19 mm	0.14	2.16	0.81	**2.97**	m
25 mm	0.16	2.36	1.40	**3.76**	m
003 Scotia mould:					
19 mm	0.14	2.16	0.72	**2.88**	m
25 mm	0.16	2.36	1.53	**3.89**	m
004 Half round:					
25 mm	0.16	2.36	1.53	**3.89**	m
005 Cover strip:					
13 x 50 mm	0.14	2.16	1.39	**3.55**	m
006 Picture rail, moulded:					
19 x 50 mm	0.41	6.29	2.02	**8.31**	m
007 Architrave, bullnosed:					
19 x 50 mm	0.18	2.71	0.84	**3.55**	m
008 Architrave, chamfered and rounded:					
19 x 50 mm	0.18	2.71	0.84	**3.55**	m
009 Architrave, moulded:					
25 x 75 mm	0.24	3.60	1.71	**5.31**	m
010 Skirting, bullnosed:					
19 x 75 mm	0.41	6.29	1.27	**7.56**	m
19 x 100 mm	0.41	6.29	1.64	**7.93**	m
011 Skirting, chamfered and rounded:					
19 x 75 mm	0.41	6.29	1.27	**7.56**	m
19 x 100 mm	0.41	6.29	1.64	**7.93**	m
012 Skirting, dual purpose:					
19 x 100 mm	0.41	6.29	1.64	**7.93**	m
013 Skirting, torus moulded:					
25 x 175 mm	0.47	7.20	3.75	**10.95**	m
returned end	0.18	2.71	-	**2.71**	Nr
mitre	0.30	4.51	-	**4.51**	Nr
014 Handrail, mopstick:					
50 x 50 mm	0.24	3.60	3.29	**6.89**	m
returned end	0.36	5.40	3.29	**8.69**	Nr
015 Handrail, moulded:					
50 x 75 mm	0.30	4.51	4.92	**9.43**	m
50 x 100 mm	0.33	5.05	6.99	**12.04**	m
returned end	0.47	7.20	-	**7.20**	Nr

	Unit Rates	Man-Hours	Net Labour Price £	Net Mats Price £	Net Unit Price £	Unit
	mitre	0.59	9.00	-	**9.00**	Nr
016	Weatherboard 828 mm long; screwed and bedded in mastic:					
	50 x 50 mm	0.36	5.40	3.66	**9.06**	Nr
	50 x 75 mm	0.36	5.40	5.29	**10.69**	Nr
	63 x 75 mm	0.36	5.40	6.27	**11.67**	Nr
017	Window boards, nosed and tongued:					
	25 x 150 mm	0.71	10.81	5.69	**16.50**	m
	25 x 200 mm	0.77	11.69	6.67	**18.36**	m
	25 x 225 mm; in one width	0.81	12.24	10.54	**22.78**	m
	returned and notched end	0.24	3.60	-	**3.60**	Nr
018	Dowels (Ramin):					
	6 mm	0.12	1.79	0.58	**2.37**	m
	9 mm	0.12	1.79	1.06	**2.85**	m
	12 mm	0.12	1.79	1.89	**3.68**	m
	15 mm	0.12	1.79	2.27	**4.06**	m
	18 mm	0.13	1.98	2.60	**4.58**	m
	21 mm	0.14	2.16	2.93	**5.09**	m
	25 mm	0.14	2.16	4.80	**6.96**	m
019	Stop fillets:					
	13 x 25 mm	0.16	2.36	0.94	**3.30**	m
	13 x 38 mm	0.16	2.36	1.09	**3.45**	m
	16 x 50 mm	0.17	2.52	1.07	**3.59**	m
	25 x 25 mm	0.18	2.71	0.67	**3.38**	m
	25 x 38 mm	0.20	3.07	1.01	**4.08**	m
	25 x 50 mm	0.20	3.07	1.04	**4.11**	m
020	Stop fillets; fixing with screws:					
	25 x 25 mm	0.27	4.15	0.73	**4.88**	m
	25 x 38 mm	0.30	4.51	1.07	**5.58**	m
	25 x 50 mm	0.30	4.51	1.10	**5.61**	m
021	**Standard mouldings in wrought hardwood**					
022	Architrave, moulded:					
	25 x 75 mm	0.36	5.40	5.90	**11.30**	m
023	Skirting, moulded:					
	25 x 125 mm	0.57	8.65	8.52	**17.17**	m
024	Weatherboard, moulded 828 mm long; screwed and pellated, bedded in mastic:					
	50 x 63 mm	0.53	8.12	8.55	**16.67**	Nr
025	Window boards, nosed and tongued:					
	32 x 225 mm; in one width	0.95	14.41	27.98	**42.39**	m
	returned and notched end	0.30	4.51	-	**4.51**	Nr
026	Stop fillets:					
	13 x 25 mm	0.27	4.15	2.80	**6.95**	m
	13 x 38 mm	0.27	4.15	3.15	**7.30**	m
	16 x 50 mm	0.30	4.51	3.75	**8.26**	m
	25 x 25 mm	0.32	4.86	3.41	**8.27**	m
	25 x 38 mm	0.36	5.40	4.05	**9.45**	m
	25 x 50 mm	0.36	5.40	4.65	**10.05**	m
027	Stop fillets; screwed and pellated:					
	25 x 25 mm	0.47	7.20	3.81	**11.01**	m
	25 x 38 mm	0.52	7.92	4.46	**12.38**	m
	25 x 50 mm	0.52	7.92	5.05	**12.97**	m
028	**Standard mouldings in Medium density fibreboard**					
029	Skirting, bullnosed:					
	14.5 x 100 mm	0.40	6.14	2.01	**8.15**	m
030	Skirting, chamfered and rounded:					
	14.5 x 100 mm	0.40	6.14	2.01	**8.15**	m
031	Skirting, torus moulded:					
	18 x 125 mm	0.46	7.02	2.84	**9.86**	m
032	Skirting, ogee moulded:					
	18 x 125 mm	0.46	7.02	3.41	**10.43**	m
033	Windowboards, nosed and tongued:					
	25 x 225; in one width	0.79	11.93	5.12	**17.05**	m
	25 x 250; in one width	0.81	12.30	5.69	**17.99**	m
	returned and notched ends	0.24	3.68	-	**3.68**	Nr
034	**Wrought softwood; non-standard mouldings**					
035	Glazing beads; splayed or chamfered or rounded; including mitres:					
	13 x 19 mm	0.21	3.24	3.01	**6.25**	m
	13 x 25 mm	0.19	2.89	3.10	**5.99**	m
	13 x 32 mm	0.14	2.16	3.24	**5.40**	m
	19 x 25 mm	0.20	3.07	3.29	**6.36**	m

Unit Rates	Man-Hours	Net Labour Price £	Net Mats Price £	Net Unit Price £	Unit
19 x 32 mm	0.18	2.71	3.47	6.18	m
036 Glazing beads; splayed or chamfered or rounded; including mitres; fixing with screws and cups:					
13 x 19 mm	0.32	4.86	3.36	8.22	m
13 x 25 mm	0.28	4.32	3.44	7.76	m
13 x 32 mm	0.21	3.24	3.58	6.82	m
19 x 25 mm	0.31	4.68	3.63	8.31	m
19 x 32 mm	0.27	4.15	3.81	7.96	m
037 Architrave, twice rounded:					
19 x 75 mm	0.19	2.89	6.64	9.53	m
19 x 100 mm	0.20	3.07	7.07	10.14	m
25 x 50 mm	0.18	2.71	6.34	9.05	m
25 x 75 mm	0.19	2.89	6.86	9.75	m
25 x 100 mm	0.20	3.07	7.24	10.31	m
25 x 125 mm	0.21	3.24	7.73	10.97	m
25 x 150 mm	0.23	3.42	8.21	11.63	m
25 x 175 mm	0.24	3.60	8.70	12.30	m
mitres on:					
25 x 100 mm	0.24	3.60	-	3.60	Nr
25 x 125 mm	0.25	3.77	-	3.77	Nr
25 x 150 mm	0.26	3.97	-	3.97	Nr
25 x 175 mm	0.27	4.15	-	4.15	Nr
038 Architrave, moulded:					
19 x 50 mm	0.18	2.71	6.21	8.92	m
19 x 75 mm	0.19	2.89	6.64	9.53	m
19 x 100 mm	0.20	3.07	7.07	10.14	m
25 x 50 mm	0.18	2.71	6.34	9.05	m
25 x 75 mm	0.19	2.89	6.86	9.75	m
25 x 100 mm	0.20	3.07	7.24	10.31	m
25 x 125 mm	0.21	3.24	7.73	10.97	m
25 x 150 mm	0.23	3.42	8.21	11.63	m
25 x 175 mm	0.24	3.60	8.70	12.30	m
mitres on:					
25 x 100 mm	0.26	3.97	-	3.97	Nr
25 x 125 mm	0.27	4.15	-	4.15	Nr
25 x 150 mm	0.28	4.32	-	4.32	Nr
25 x 175 mm	0.30	4.51	-	4.51	Nr
039 Skirting, rounded:					
25 x 75 mm	0.41	6.29	4.21	10.50	m
25 x 100 mm	0.44	6.67	4.59	11.26	m
25 x 125 mm	0.46	7.01	5.07	12.08	m
25 x 150 mm	0.49	7.37	5.56	12.93	m
25 x 175 mm	0.51	7.75	6.04	13.79	m
25 x 200 mm	0.53	8.12	7.22	15.34	m
returned ends on:					
25 x 100 mm	0.14	2.16	-	2.16	Nr
25 x 125 mm	0.16	2.36	-	2.36	Nr
25 x 150 mm	0.17	2.52	-	2.52	Nr
25 x 175 mm	0.18	2.71	-	2.71	Nr
25 x 200 mm	0.19	2.89	-	2.89	Nr
mitres on:					
25 x 100 mm	0.26	3.97	-	3.97	Nr
25 x 125 mm	0.27	4.15	-	4.15	Nr
25 x 150 mm	0.28	4.32	-	4.32	Nr
25 x 175 mm	0.30	4.51	-	4.51	Nr
25 x 200 mm	0.31	4.68	-	4.68	Nr
040 Skirting, moulded:					
25 x 75 mm	0.41	6.29	6.86	13.15	m
25 x 100 mm	0.44	6.67	7.24	13.91	m
25 x 125 mm	0.46	7.01	7.73	14.74	m
25 x 150 mm	0.49	7.37	8.21	15.58	m
25 x 175 mm	0.51	7.75	8.70	16.45	m
25 x 200 mm	0.53	8.12	9.87	17.99	m
returned ends on:					
25 x 100 mm	0.16	2.36	-	2.36	Nr
25 x 125 mm	0.17	2.52	-	2.52	Nr
25 x 150 mm	0.18	2.71	-	2.71	Nr
25 x 175 mm	0.19	2.89	-	2.89	Nr
25 x 200 mm	0.20	3.07	-	3.07	Nr
mitres on:					
25 x 100 mm	0.28	4.32	-	4.32	Nr
25 x 125 mm	0.30	4.51	-	4.51	Nr
25 x 150 mm	0.31	4.68	-	4.68	Nr
25 x 175 mm	0.32	4.86	-	4.86	Nr
25 x 200 mm	0.33	5.05	-	5.05	Nr
041 Picture rail, moulded:					
25 x 75 mm	0.44	6.67	6.86	13.53	m
25 x 100 mm	0.46	7.01	7.24	14.25	m
32 x 75 mm	0.50	7.55	7.23	14.78	m
32 x 100 mm	0.52	7.92	7.72	15.64	m
returned ends on:					
25 x 100 mm	0.24	3.60	-	3.60	Nr
32 x 100 mm	0.27	4.15	-	4.15	Nr

	Unit Rates	Man-Hours	Net Labour Price £	Net Mats Price £	Net Unit Price £	Unit
	mitres on:					
	25 x 100 mm	0.28	4.32	-	**4.32**	Nr
	32 x 100 mm	0.32	4.86	-	**4.86**	Nr
042	Handrail, moulded:					
	50 x 100 mm	0.33	5.05	10.93	**15.98**	m
	63 x 100 mm	0.38	5.76	12.60	**18.36**	m
	75 x 100 mm	0.43	6.48	13.48	**19.96**	m
	returned ends on:					
	50 x 100 mm	0.59	9.00	-	**9.00**	Nr
	63 x 100 mm	0.71	10.81	-	**10.81**	Nr
	75 x 100 mm	0.83	12.60	-	**12.60**	Nr
	ramp with handrail screws on:					
	50 x 100 mm	1.19	18.01	42.68	**60.69**	Nr
	63 x 100 mm	1.30	19.81	42.68	**62.49**	Nr
	75 x 100 mm	1.42	21.60	42.68	**64.28**	Nr
	wreath with handrail screws on:					
	50 x 100 mm	1.90	28.80	84.10	**112.90**	Nr
	63 x 100 mm	2.01	30.61	84.10	**114.71**	Nr
	75 x 100 mm	2.13	32.41	84.10	**116.51**	Nr
043	Solid shelving, table tops, seats and the like:					
	19 mm cross tongued; over 300 mm wide	1.19	18.01	19.89	**37.90**	m2
	19 x 150 mm	0.21	3.24	3.44	**6.68**	m
	19 x 200 mm	0.24	3.60	4.56	**8.16**	m
	25 mm cross tongued; over 300 mm wide	1.30	19.81	24.80	**44.61**	m2
	25 x 150 mm	0.24	3.60	3.44	**7.04**	m
	25 x 200 mm	0.26	3.97	4.56	**8.53**	m
	25 x 250 mm, in on width	0.30	4.51	5.36	**9.87**	m
044	Slatted shelving; over 300 mm wide:					
	19 x 38 mm slats at 75 mm centres	1.58	23.96	10.53	**34.49**	m2
	25 x 50 mm slats at 75 mm centres	1.75	26.65	13.76	**40.41**	m2
	25 x 50 mm slats at 100 mm centres	1.32	19.99	10.35	**30.34**	m2
045	Slatted shelving; removable on and including cross-bearers at 900 mm centres; over 300 mm wide:					
	19 x 38 mm slats at 75 mm centres; 19 x 38 mm cross-bearers	1.71	25.95	11.40	**37.35**	m2
	25 x 50 mm slats at 75 mm centres; 25 x 50 mm cross-bearers	1.91	29.00	14.90	**43.90**	m2
	25 x 50 mm slats at 100 mm centres; 25 x 50 mm cross-bearers	1.47	22.33	11.48	**33.81**	m2
046	Shelving bearers:					
	19 x 25 mm	0.11	1.63	0.63	**2.26**	m
	19 x 38 mm	0.12	1.79	0.79	**2.58**	m
	25 x 38 mm	0.13	1.98	1.00	**2.98**	m
	25 x 50 mm	0.14	2.16	1.03	**3.19**	m
047	Shelving bearers and legs; framed:					
	25 x 50 mm	0.30	4.51	1.03	**5.54**	m
	38 x 50 mm	0.32	4.86	1.41	**6.27**	m
	50 x 50 mm	0.71	10.79	3.08	**13.87**	m
	50 x 75 mm	0.41	6.29	2.30	**8.59**	m
	75 x 75 mm	0.47	7.20	3.29	**10.49**	m
	75 x 100 mm	0.53	8.12	5.51	**13.63**	m
	100 x 100 mm	0.59	9.00	7.62	**16.62**	m
048	Labours on shelving and bearers:					
	rounding 10 mm radius	0.30	4.51	-	**4.51**	m
	chamfer 10 mm wide	0.24	3.60	-	**3.60**	m
	notching per 25 mm girth:					
	19 mm thick	0.24	3.60	-	**3.60**	Nr
	25 mm thick	0.27	4.15	-	**4.15**	Nr
	Note: 049 - 056 not used					
057	**Board and sheet solid shelving, table tops, seats and the like**					
058	Chipboard, BS 5669:					
	12 mm:					
	over 300 mm wide	0.71	10.81	2.78	**13.59**	m2
	not exceeding 150 mm wide	0.12	1.79	0.42	**2.21**	m
	150 - 300 mm wide	0.24	3.60	0.83	**4.43**	m
	15 mm:					
	over 300 mm wide	0.77	11.69	3.34	**15.03**	m2
	not exceeding 150 mm wide	0.14	2.16	0.50	**2.66**	m
	150 - 300 mm wide	0.28	4.32	1.00	**5.32**	m
	18 mm:					
	over 300 mm wide	0.95	14.41	4.01	**18.42**	m2
	not exceeding 150 mm wide	0.18	2.71	0.60	**3.31**	m
	150 - 300 mm wide	0.36	5.40	1.20	**6.60**	m
059	Blockboard, BS 3444, Bonding BR, grade SI, birch faced:					
	18 mm:					
	over 300 mm wide	0.71	10.81	16.20	**27.01**	m2
	not exceeding 150 mm wide	0.11	1.72	2.43	**4.15**	m
	150 - 300 mm wide	0.24	3.60	6.26	**9.86**	m
	25 mm:					
	over 300 mm wide	1.19	18.01	20.88	**38.89**	m2
	not exceeding 150 mm wide	0.21	3.24	3.13	**6.37**	m

Unit Rates	Man-Hours	Net Labour Price £	Net Mats Price £	Net Unit Price £	Unit
150 - 300 mm wide	0.43	6.48	6.26	**12.74**	m
060 Plywood, BS 1455, grade BB, birch faced, internal quality:					
6 mm:					
over 300 mm wide	0.53	8.12	3.49	**11.61**	m2
not exceeding 150 mm wide	0.10	1.44	0.56	**2.00**	m
150 - 300 mm wide	0.19	2.89	1.12	**4.01**	m
9 mm:					
over 300 mm wide	0.65	9.91	5.28	**15.19**	m2
not exceeding 150 mm wide	0.12	1.79	0.84	**2.63**	m
150 - 300 mm wide	0.24	3.60	1.69	**5.29**	m
12 mm:					
over 300 mm wide	0.77	11.69	6.85	**18.54**	m2
not exceeding 150 mm wide	0.14	2.16	1.10	**3.26**	m
150 - 300 mm wide	0.28	4.32	2.19	**6.51**	m
061 1.3 mm plastic laminate (standard range) facing to shelving secured with adhesive:					
over 300 mm wide	2.37	36.01	18.99	**55.00**	m2
not exceeding 150 mm wide	0.41	6.29	3.25	**9.54**	m
150 - 300 mm wide	0.83	12.60	6.56	**19.16**	m
edging with chamfer to shelf facing:					
9 - 25 mm wide	0.24	3.60	1.02	**4.62**	m
062 UBM board, 15 mm chipboard faced both sides:					
white melamine facing both sides and lipped on two edges:					
150 mm wide	0.12	1.79	1.47	**3.26**	m
300 mm wide	0.24	3.60	3.01	**6.61**	m
450 mm wide	0.36	5.40	4.48	**9.88**	m
600 mm wide	0.47	7.20	6.01	**13.21**	m
teak melanite lacquer to both sides and lipped on two edges:					
150 mm wide	0.12	1.79	2.44	**4.23**	m
300 mm wide	0.24	3.60	5.16	**8.76**	m
450 mm wide	0.36	5.40	8.46	**13.86**	m
600 mm wide	0.47	7.20	9.41	**16.61**	m
lipping to cut edges 17 mm wide with chamfer both sides, white or teak finish	0.24	3.60	0.90	**4.50**	m
063 Labours on shelving:					
notching per 25 mm girth:					
chipboard 12-18 mm thick	0.20	3.07	-	**3.07**	Nr
blockboard 12-25 mm thick	0.24	3.60	-	**3.60**	Nr
plywood 9-18 mm thick	0.18	2.71	-	**2.71**	Nr
decorative laminate facing 1.5 mm thick	0.24	3.60	-	**3.60**	Nr
UBM board 17 mm thick	0.30	4.51	-	**4.51**	Nr
rounded corner 150 mm radius:					
chipboard 12-18 mm thick	0.36	5.40	-	**5.40**	Nr
blockboard 12-25 mm thick	0.41	6.29	-	**6.29**	Nr
plywood 9-18 mm thick	0.30	4.51	-	**4.51**	Nr
decorative laminate facing 1.5 mm thick	0.41	6.29	-	**6.29**	Nr
UBM board 17 mm thick	0.53	8.12	-	**8.12**	Nr
064 Wrought hardwood lipping pinned and glued to edge of shelving:					
6 x 9 mm	0.20	3.07	1.54	**4.61**	m
6 x 12 mm	0.20	3.07	1.58	**4.65**	m
6 x 15 mm	0.20	3.07	1.62	**4.69**	m
6 x 18 mm	0.20	3.07	1.65	**4.72**	m
6 x 25 mm	0.20	3.07	1.74	**4.81**	m
lipping to rounded corner 150 mm radius:					
6 x 9 mm	0.36	5.40	0.46	**5.86**	Nr
6 x 12 mm	0.36	5.40	0.47	**5.87**	Nr
6 x 15 mm	0.36	5.40	0.49	**5.89**	Nr
6 x 18 mm	0.36	5.40	0.49	**5.89**	Nr
6 x 25 mm	0.36	5.40	0.52	**5.92**	Nr
065 **Work to existing unframed second fixings**					
066 Making good with new 25 mm wrought softwood dado rail to match existing where cross-walls, wall cupboards and the like removed:					
not exceeding 600 mm lengths with two splayed heading joints:					
50 mm high	0.59	8.92	0.91	**9.83**	Nr
75 mm high	0.62	9.39	1.60	**10.99**	Nr
in long lengths:					
50 mm high	0.43	6.58	0.95	**7.53**	m
75 mm high	0.45	6.89	1.68	**8.57**	m
067 Making good with new 25 mm wrought softwood picture rail to match existing where cross-walls, beams, wall cupboards and the like removed:					
not exceeding 600 mm lengths with two splayed heading joints:					
50 mm high	0.59	8.92	0.91	**9.83**	Nr
75 mm high	0.62	9.45	1.36	**10.81**	Nr
in long lengths:					
50 mm high	0.44	6.63	0.95	**7.58**	m
75 mm high	0.45	6.89	1.43	**8.32**	m
068 Making good with new 25 mm wrought softwood skirting to match existing, where cross-walls, wall cupboards and the like removed:					
not exceeding 600 mm lengths with two splayed heading joints:					
300 mm high	0.61	9.24	1.36	**10.60**	Nr
100 mm high	0.64	9.71	1.69	**11.40**	Nr
75 mm high	0.93	14.09	13.57	**27.66**	Nr

	Unit Rates	Man-Hours	Net Labour Price £	Net Mats Price £	Net Unit Price £	Unit
	in long lengths:					
	300 mm high	0.45	6.89	1.43	**8.32**	m
	100 mm high	0.47	7.20	1.77	**8.97**	m
	75 mm high	0.62	9.39	14.25	**23.64**	m
069	Cut out decayed 25 mm wrought softwood dado rail and replace with new to match existing including splayed heading joints:					
	not exceeding 600 mm lengths:					
	50 mm high	0.64	9.71	0.91	**10.62**	Nr
	75 mm high	0.67	10.17	1.60	**11.77**	Nr
	in long lengths:					
	50 mm high	0.47	7.20	0.95	**8.15**	m
	75 mm high	0.49	7.51	1.68	**9.19**	m
070	Cut out decayed 25 mm wrought softwood picture rail and replace with new to match existing including splayed heading joints:					
	not exceeding 600 mm lengths:					
	50 mm high	0.64	9.71	0.91	**10.62**	Nr
	75 mm high	0.67	10.17	1.36	**11.53**	Nr
	in long lengths:					
	50 mm high	0.47	7.20	0.95	**8.15**	m
	75 mm high	0.49	7.51	1.43	**8.94**	m
071	Cut out decayed 25 mm wrought softwood skirting and replace with new to match existing, including splayed heading joints:					
	not exceeding 600 mm lengths:					
	75 mm high	0.67	10.17	1.36	**11.53**	Nr
	100 mm high	0.72	10.91	1.69	**12.60**	Nr
	300 mm high	0.96	14.56	13.57	**28.13**	Nr
	in long lengths:					
	75 mm high	0.49	7.51	1.49	**9.00**	m
	100 mm high	0.53	8.00	1.86	**9.86**	m
	300 mm high	0.67	10.17	14.93	**25.10**	m
072	Wrought softwood skirting; fixing direct with hardened steel masonry nails; in extending skirtings to match existing:					
	19 x 100 mm once rounded	0.46	7.04	1.58	**8.62**	m
	25 x 125 mm moulded	0.46	7.04	2.15	**9.19**	m
	25 x 250 mm moulded	0.52	7.83	12.74	**20.57**	m
NF	**SHEET LININGS AND CASINGS**					
001	**Standard quality hardboard**					
002	3.2 mm linings or casings:					
	over 300 mm wide	0.58	8.74	1.67	**10.41**	m2
	not exceeding 100 mm wide	0.18	2.71	0.17	**2.88**	m
	100 - 200 mm wide	0.24	3.60	0.33	**3.93**	m
	200 - 300 mm wide	0.30	4.51	0.50	**5.01**	m
003	6.0 mm linings or casings:					
	over 300 mm wide	0.59	9.00	4.17	**13.17**	m2
	not exceeding 100 mm wide	0.21	3.24	0.42	**3.66**	m
	100 - 200 mm wide	0.27	4.15	0.83	**4.98**	m
	200 - 300 mm wide	0.33	5.05	1.25	**6.30**	m
004	**Perforated hardboard**					
005	3.2 mm linings or casings:					
	over 300 mm wide	0.58	8.74	2.56	**11.30**	m2
	not exceeding 100 mm wide	0.18	2.71	0.26	**2.97**	m
	100 - 200 mm wide	0.24	3.60	0.51	**4.11**	m
	200 - 300 mm wide	0.30	4.51	0.77	**5.28**	m
006	6.0 mm linings or casings:					
	over 300 mm wide	0.59	9.00	5.48	**14.48**	m2
	not exceeding 100 mm wide	0.21	3.24	0.55	**3.79**	m
	100 - 200 mm wide	0.27	4.15	1.10	**5.25**	m
	200 - 300 mm wide	0.33	5.05	1.64	**6.69**	m
007	**Hardboard; flameproofed in accordance with BS 476, Class 1**					
008	3.2 mm linings or casings:					
	over 300 mm wide	0.58	8.74	4.19	**12.93**	m2
	not exceeding 100 mm wide	0.18	2.71	0.42	**3.13**	m
	100 - 200 mm wide	0.24	3.60	0.84	**4.44**	m
	200 - 300 mm wide	0.30	4.51	1.26	**5.77**	m
	Note: 009 not used					
010	**Hardboard; stove enamel finish one side**					
011	3.2 mm linings or casings:					
	over 300 mm wide	0.59	9.00	2.42	**11.42**	m2
	not exceeding 100 mm wide	0.21	3.24	0.24	**3.48**	m
	100 - 200 mm wide	0.27	4.15	0.48	**4.63**	m
	200 - 300 mm wide	0.33	5.05	0.73	**5.78**	m

Unit Rates	Man-Hours	Net Labour Price £	Net Mats Price £	Net Unit Price £	Unit
012 **Building board (Promat Monolux)**					
013 12.7 mm linings or casings; natural finish:					
over 300 mm wide	0.33	5.05	66.29	**71.34**	m2
not exceeding 100 mm wide	0.10	1.44	6.63	**8.07**	m
100 - 200 mm wide	0.14	2.16	13.26	**15.42**	m
200 - 300 mm wide	0.18	2.71	19.89	**22.60**	m
014 19 mm linings or casings; natural finish:					
over 300 mm wide	0.36	5.40	84.27	**89.67**	m2
not exceeding 100 mm wide	0.12	1.79	8.43	**10.22**	m
100 - 200 mm wide	0.17	2.52	16.85	**19.37**	m
200 - 300 mm wide	0.20	3.07	25.28	**28.35**	m
015 25 mm linings or casings; natural finish:					
over 300 mm wide	0.41	6.29	101.05	**107.34**	m2
not exceeding 100 mm wide	0.14	2.16	10.10	**12.26**	m
100 - 200 mm wide	0.19	2.89	20.21	**23.10**	m
200 - 300 mm wide	0.23	3.42	30.31	**33.73**	m
Note: 016 not used					
017 **Chipboard**					
018 12 mm linings or casings:					
over 300 mm wide	0.47	7.20	2.78	**9.98**	m2
not exceeding 100 mm wide	0.19	2.89	0.28	**3.17**	m
100 - 200 mm wide	0.21	3.24	0.56	**3.80**	m
200 - 300 mm wide	0.24	3.60	0.83	**4.43**	m
019 15 mm linings or casings:					
over 300 mm wide	0.50	7.55	3.34	**10.89**	m2
not exceeding 100 mm wide	0.20	3.07	0.33	**3.40**	m
100 - 200 mm wide	0.24	3.60	0.67	**4.27**	m
200 - 300 mm wide	0.26	3.97	1.00	**4.97**	m
020 18 mm linings or casings:					
over 300 mm wide	0.64	9.73	4.01	**13.74**	m2
not exceeding 100 mm wide	0.26	3.97	0.40	**4.37**	m
100 - 200 mm wide	0.28	4.32	0.80	**5.12**	m
200 - 300 mm wide	0.31	4.68	1.20	**5.88**	m
021 **Plastics laminate faced chipboard with balancing veneer**					
022 15 mm linings and casings:					
over 300 mm wide	0.60	9.07	53.69	**62.76**	m2
not exceeding 100 mm wide	0.24	3.63	5.37	**9.00**	m
100 - 200 mm wide	0.27	4.10	10.74	**14.84**	m
200 - 300 mm wide	0.29	4.41	16.11	**20.52**	m
023 18 mm linings or casings:					
over 300 mm wide	0.77	11.66	56.84	**68.50**	m2
not exceeding 100 mm wide	0.31	4.68	5.68	**10.36**	m
100 - 200 mm wide	0.33	5.05	11.37	**16.42**	m
200 - 300 mm wide	0.37	5.61	17.05	**22.66**	m
024 **Insulation board**					
025 12 mm linings or casings; ivory finish:					
over 300 mm wide	0.33	5.05	2.93	**7.98**	m2
not exceeding 100 mm wide	0.10	1.44	0.29	**1.73**	m
100 - 200 mm wide	0.14	2.16	0.59	**2.75**	m
200 - 300 mm wide	0.18	2.71	0.88	**3.59**	m
Note: 026 - 027 not used					
028 **Blockboard, Finnish Birch 5 ply, grade BB**					
029 18 mm linings or casings:					
over 300 mm wide	0.64	9.73	16.20	**25.93**	m2
not exceeding 100 mm wide	0.26	3.97	1.62	**5.59**	m
100 - 200 mm wide	0.28	4.32	3.24	**7.56**	m
200 - 300 mm wide	0.31	4.68	4.86	**9.54**	m
030 25 mm linings or casings:					
over 300 mm wide	0.78	11.89	20.88	**32.77**	m2
not exceeding 100 mm wide	0.31	4.76	2.09	**6.85**	m
100 - 200 mm wide	0.34	5.12	4.18	**9.30**	m
200 - 300 mm wide	0.36	5.40	6.26	**11.66**	m
031 **Blockboard, Brazilian Virola 5 ply, bonding MR, grade B/BB**					
032 18 mm casings to pipes:					
over 300 mm wide	0.47	7.20	10.48	**17.68**	m2
not exceeding 100 mm wide	0.19	2.89	1.05	**3.94**	m
100 - 200 mm wide	0.21	3.24	2.10	**5.34**	m
200 - 300 mm wide	0.24	3.60	3.14	**6.74**	m

		Man-Hours	Net Labour Price £	Net Mats Price £	Net Unit Price £	Unit
033	25 mm casings to pipes:					
	over 300 mm wide	0.64	9.73	15.45	**25.18**	m2
	not exceeding 100 mm wide	0.26	3.97	1.55	**5.52**	m
	100 - 200 mm wide	0.28	4.32	3.09	**7.41**	m
	200 - 300 mm wide	0.31	4.68	4.64	**9.32**	m
034	**Extra over** for forming access panels 300 x 400 mm:					
	18 mm	1.42	21.60	-	**21.60**	Nr
	22 mm	1.42	21.60	-	**21.60**	Nr
	25 mm	1.42	21.60	-	**21.60**	Nr
035	**Laminboard; Birch faced**					
036	19 mm linings or casings:					
	over 300 mm wide	0.62	9.36	18.18	**27.54**	m2
	not exceeding 100 mm wide	0.25	3.77	1.82	**5.59**	m
	100 - 200 mm wide	0.27	4.15	3.64	**7.79**	m
	200 - 300 mm wide	0.30	4.51	5.45	**9.96**	m
037	22 mm linings or casings:					
	over 300 mm wide	0.70	10.61	20.57	**31.18**	m2
	not exceeding 100 mm wide	0.28	4.32	2.06	**6.38**	m
	100 - 200 mm wide	0.30	4.51	4.11	**8.62**	m
	200 - 300 mm wide	0.31	4.68	6.17	**10.85**	m
038	25 mm linings or casings:					
	over 300 mm wide	0.78	11.89	21.26	**33.15**	m2
	not exceeding 100 mm wide	0.31	4.76	2.13	**6.89**	m
	100 - 200 mm wide	0.34	5.12	4.25	**9.37**	m
	200 - 300 mm wide	0.36	5.40	6.38	**11.78**	m
039	**Plywood, MR Bonding, grade B/BB, Far Eastern Hardwood, red/white, internal quality**					
040	4 mm linings or casings:					
	over 300 mm wide	0.36	5.40	3.11	**8.51**	m2
	not exceeding 100 mm wide	0.14	2.16	0.31	**2.47**	m
	100 - 200 mm wide	0.17	2.52	0.62	**3.14**	m
	200 - 300 mm wide	0.19	2.89	0.93	**3.82**	m
041	6 mm linings or casings:					
	over 300 mm wide	0.36	5.40	3.49	**8.89**	m2
	not exceeding 100 mm wide	0.14	2.16	0.35	**2.51**	m
	100 - 200 mm wide	0.17	2.52	0.70	**3.22**	m
	200 - 300 mm wide	0.19	2.89	1.05	**3.94**	m
042	9 mm linings or casings:					
	over 300 mm wide	0.41	6.29	5.28	**11.57**	m2
	not exceeding 100 mm wide	0.17	2.52	0.53	**3.05**	m
	100 - 200 mm wide	0.19	2.89	1.06	**3.95**	m
	200 - 300 mm wide	0.21	3.24	1.58	**4.82**	m
043	12 mm linings or casings:					
	over 300 mm wide	0.45	6.84	6.85	**13.69**	m2
	not exceeding 100 mm wide	0.18	2.71	0.69	**3.40**	m
	100 - 200 mm wide	0.20	3.07	1.37	**4.44**	m
	200 - 300 mm wide	0.23	3.42	2.06	**5.48**	m
044	**Extra over** for forming access panels 300 x 400 mm:					
	4 mm	1.42	21.60	-	**21.60**	Nr
	6 mm	1.42	21.60	-	**21.60**	Nr
	9 mm	1.42	21.60	-	**21.60**	Nr
	12 mm	1.42	21.60	-	**21.60**	Nr
045	**Plywood, WBP Bonding, grade BB, Finish Birch Faced, external quality**					
046	4 mm linings or casings:					
	over 300 mm wide	0.36	5.40	5.95	**11.35**	m2
	not exceeding 100 mm wide	0.14	2.16	0.60	**2.76**	m
	100 - 200 mm wide	0.17	2.52	1.19	**3.71**	m
	200 - 300 mm wide	0.19	2.89	1.79	**4.68**	m
047	6 mm linings or casings:					
	over 300 mm wide	0.36	5.40	7.00	**12.40**	m2
	not exceeding 100 mm wide	0.14	2.16	0.70	**2.86**	m
	100 - 200 mm wide	0.17	2.52	1.40	**3.92**	m
	200 - 300 mm wide	0.19	2.89	2.10	**4.99**	m
048	9 mm linings or casings:					
	over 300 mm wide	0.41	6.29	9.29	**15.58**	m2
	not exceeding 100 mm wide	0.17	2.52	0.93	**3.45**	m
	100 - 200 mm wide	0.19	2.89	1.86	**4.75**	m
	200 - 300 mm wide	0.21	3.24	2.79	**6.03**	m
049	12 mm linings or casings:					
	over 300 mm wide	0.45	6.84	11.37	**18.21**	m2
	not exceeding 100 mm wide	0.18	2.71	1.14	**3.85**	m
	100 - 200 mm wide	0.20	3.07	2.27	**5.34**	m
	200 - 300 mm wide	0.23	3.42	3.41	**6.83**	m

Unit Rates

	Man-Hours	Net Labour Price £	Net Mats Price £	Net Unit Price £	Unit
Unit Rates					
050	**Non-asbestos boards, fire resisting Class 0; 'Masterboard'**					
051	6 mm linings or casings:					
	over 300 mm wide	0.59	9.00	13.09	**22.09**	m2
	not exceeding 100 mm wide	0.24	3.60	1.31	**4.91**	m
	100 - 200 mm wide	0.26	3.97	2.62	**6.59**	m
	200 - 300 mm wide	0.28	4.32	3.93	**8.25**	m
052	9 mm linings or casings:					
	over 300 mm wide	0.65	9.91	22.70	**32.61**	m2
	not exceeding 100 mm wide	0.26	3.97	2.27	**6.24**	m
	100 - 200 mm wide	0.28	4.32	4.54	**8.86**	m
	200 - 300 mm wide	0.31	4.68	6.81	**11.49**	m
053	12 mm linings or casings:					
	over 300 mm wide	0.77	11.69	28.64	**40.33**	m
	not exceeding 100 mm wide	0.31	4.68	2.86	**7.54**	m
	100 - 200 mm wide	0.33	5.05	5.73	**10.78**	m
	200 - 300 mm wide	0.36	5.40	8.59	**13.99**	m
054	**Non-asbestos boards, fire resisting Class 0; 'Supalux' sanded finish**					
055	6 mm linings or casings:					
	over 300 mm wide	0.59	9.00	18.47	**27.47**	m2
	not exceeding 100 mm wide	0.24	3.60	1.85	**5.45**	m
	100 - 200 mm wide	0.26	3.97	3.69	**7.66**	m
	200 - 300 mm wide	0.28	4.32	5.54	**9.86**	m
056	9 mm linings or casings:					
	over 300 mm wide	0.65	9.91	25.77	**35.68**	m2
	not exceeding 100 mm wide	0.26	3.97	2.58	**6.55**	m
	100 - 200 mm wide	0.28	4.32	5.15	**9.47**	m
	200 - 300 mm wide	0.31	4.68	7.73	**12.41**	m
057	12 mm linings or casings:					
	over 300 mm wide	0.77	11.69	32.64	**44.33**	m2
	not exceeding 100 mm wide	0.31	4.68	3.26	**7.94**	m
	100 - 200 mm wide	0.33	5.05	6.53	**11.58**	m
	200 - 300 mm wide	0.36	5.40	9.79	**15.19**	m
058	**Medium density fibreboard, standard grade to BS EN622**					
059	6 mm linings or casings:					
	over 300 mm wide	0.35	5.27	3.75	**9.02**	m2
	not exceeding 100 mm wide	0.14	2.11	0.37	**2.48**	m
	100 - 200 mm wide	0.16	2.46	0.75	**3.21**	m
	200 - 300 mm wide	0.19	2.81	1.12	**3.93**	m
060	9 mm linings or casings:					
	over 300 mm wide	0.40	6.14	4.69	**10.83**	m2
	not exceeding 100 mm wide	0.16	2.46	0.47	**2.93**	m
	100 - 200 mm wide	0.19	2.81	0.94	**3.75**	m
	200 - 300 mm wide	0.21	3.16	1.41	**4.57**	m
061	12 mm linings or casings:					
	over 300 mm wide	0.44	6.67	5.83	**12.50**	m2
	not exceeding 100 mm wide	0.17	2.63	0.58	**3.21**	m
	100 - 200 mm wide	0.20	2.98	1.17	**4.15**	m
	200 - 300 mm wide	0.22	3.33	1.75	**5.08**	m
062	18 mm linings or casings:					
	over 300 mm wide	0.50	7.55	7.12	**14.67**	m2
	not exceeding 100 mm wide	0.20	2.98	0.71	**3.69**	m
	100 - 200 mm wide	0.22	3.33	1.42	**4.75**	m
	200 - 300 mm wide	0.24	3.69	2.14	**5.83**	m
063	**Labours on sheet linings and casings**					
064	Rounded edges:					
	12 mm chipboard	0.10	1.49	-	**1.49**	m
	15 mm chipboard	0.14	2.08	-	**2.08**	m
	18 mm chipboard	0.16	2.36	-	**2.36**	m
	15 mm plastics laminate faced chipboard	0.14	2.08	-	**2.08**	m
	18 mm plastics laminate faced chipboard	0.16	2.40	-	**2.40**	m
	12 mm blockboard	0.10	1.49	-	**1.49**	m
	18 mm blockboard	0.14	2.08	-	**2.08**	m
	25 mm blockboard	0.14	2.08	-	**2.08**	m
	9 mm plywood	0.10	1.49	-	**1.49**	m
	12 mm plywood	0.10	1.49	-	**1.49**	m
	9 mm medium density fibreboard	0.09	1.40	-	**1.40**	m
	12 mm medium density fibreboard	0.10	1.46	-	**1.46**	m
	18 mm medium density fibreboard	0.15	2.28	-	**2.28**	m

		Man-Hours	Net Labour Price £	Net Mats Price £	Net Unit Price £	Unit
Unit Rates						
065	Raking cutting:					
	3.2 mm hardboard	0.14	2.16	0.25	**2.41**	m
	6.4 mm hardboard	0.14	2.16	0.63	**2.79**	m
	3.2 mm stove enamelled one sided hardboard	0.14	2.16	0.36	**2.52**	m
	12 mm building board	0.22	3.36	9.94	**13.30**	m
	19 mm building board	0.26	3.92	12.64	**16.56**	m
	25 mm building board	0.28	4.27	15.16	**19.43**	m
	12 mm chipboard	0.30	4.51	0.42	**4.93**	m
	15 mm chipboard	0.30	4.51	0.50	**5.01**	m
	18 mm chipboard	0.30	4.51	0.60	**5.11**	m
	15 mm plastics laminate faced chipboard	0.30	4.51	0.81	**5.32**	m
	18 mm plastics laminate faced chipboard	0.30	4.51	0.85	**5.36**	m
	18 mm blockboard	0.30	4.51	2.43	**6.94**	m
	25 mm blockboard	0.30	4.51	3.13	**7.64**	m
	4 mm plywood	0.24	3.60	0.47	**4.07**	m
	6 mm plywood	0.24	3.60	0.52	**4.12**	m
	9 mm plywood	0.24	3.60	0.79	**4.39**	m
	12 mm plywood	0.30	4.51	1.03	**5.54**	m
	6 mm non-asbestos board	0.30	4.51	1.96	**6.47**	m
	9 mm non-asbestos board	0.30	4.51	3.41	**7.92**	m
	12 mm non-asbestos board	0.30	4.51	4.30	**8.81**	m
	12 mm insulation board	0.12	1.79	0.44	**2.23**	m
	6 mm medium density fibreboard	0.25	3.86	0.56	**4.42**	m
	9 mm medium density fibreboard	0.25	3.86	0.70	**4.56**	m
	12 mm medium density fibreboard	0.29	4.39	0.87	**5.26**	m
	18 mm medium density fibreboard	0.29	4.39	1.07	**5.46**	m
066	Curved cutting:					
	3.2 mm hardboard	0.47	7.20	0.25	**7.45**	m
	6.4 mm hardboard	0.47	7.20	0.63	**7.83**	m
	3.2 mm stove enamelled one side hardboard	0.47	7.20	0.36	**7.56**	m
	12 mm building board	0.97	14.79	9.94	**24.73**	m
	19 mm building board	0.97	14.79	12.64	**27.43**	m
	25 mm building board	0.93	14.12	15.16	**29.28**	m
	12 mm chipboard	0.65	9.91	0.42	**10.33**	m
	15 mm chipboard	0.71	10.81	0.50	**11.31**	m
	18 mm chipboard	0.89	13.50	0.60	**14.10**	m
	15 mm plastics laminate faced chipboard	0.65	9.91	0.81	**10.72**	m
	18 mm plastics laminate faced chipboard	0.89	13.50	0.85	**14.35**	m
	12 mm blockboard	0.65	9.91	2.43	**12.34**	m
	25 mm blockboard	0.89	13.50	5.11	**18.61**	m
	4 mm plywood	0.53	8.12	0.47	**8.59**	m
	6 mm plywood	0.53	8.12	0.52	**8.64**	m
	9 mm plywood	0.83	12.60	0.79	**13.39**	m
	12 mm plywood	0.83	12.60	1.03	**13.63**	m
	6 mm non-asbestos board	0.83	12.60	1.96	**14.56**	m
	9 mm non-asbestos board	0.83	12.60	3.41	**16.01**	m
	12 mm non-asbestos board	0.95	14.41	4.30	**18.71**	m
	12 mm insulation board	0.36	5.40	0.44	**5.84**	m
	6 mm medium density fibreboard	0.64	9.65	0.56	**10.21**	m
	9 mm medium density fibreboard	0.69	10.53	0.70	**11.23**	m
	12 mm medium density fibreboard	0.75	11.42	0.87	**12.29**	m
	18 mm medium density fibreboard	0.81	12.30	1.07	**13.37**	m
067	Notches per 25 mm girth:					
	3.2 mm hardboard	0.10	1.44	-	**1.44**	Nr
	6.4 mm hardboard	0.12	1.79	-	**1.79**	Nr
	3.2 mm stove enamelled one side hardboard	0.11	1.63	-	**1.63**	Nr
	12 mm building board	0.16	2.48	-	**2.48**	Nr
	19 mm building board	0.20	3.01	-	**3.01**	Nr
	25 mm building board	0.22	3.36	-	**3.36**	Nr
	12 mm chipboard	0.18	2.71	-	**2.71**	Nr
	15 mm chipboard	0.18	2.71	-	**2.71**	Nr
	18 mm chipboard	0.20	3.07	-	**3.07**	Nr
	15 mm plastics laminate faced chipboard	0.20	3.07	-	**3.07**	Nr
	18 mm plastics laminate faced chipboard	0.24	3.60	-	**3.60**	Nr

Unit Rates	Man-Hours	Net Labour Price £	Net Mats Price £	Net Unit Price £	Unit
12 mm blockboard	0.18	2.71	-	2.71	Nr
18 mm blockboard	0.20	3.07	-	3.07	Nr
25 mm blockboard	0.24	3.60	-	3.60	Nr
4 mm plywood	0.14	2.16	-	2.16	Nr
6 mm plywood	0.14	2.16	-	2.16	Nr
9 mm plywood	0.14	2.16	-	2.16	Nr
12 mm plywood	0.18	2.71	-	2.71	Nr
6 mm non-asbestos board	0.19	2.89	-	2.89	Nr
9 mm non-asbestos board	0.19	2.89	-	2.89	Nr
12 mm non-asbestos board	0.19	2.89	-	2.89	Nr
12 mm insulation board	0.06	0.91	-	0.91	Nr
6 mm medium density fibreboard	0.12	1.76	-	1.76	Nr
9 mm medium density fibreboard	0.15	2.28	-	2.28	Nr
12 mm medium density fibreboard	0.17	2.63	-	2.63	Nr
18 mm medium density fibreboard	0.20	2.98	-	2.98	Nr
068 Forming openings not exceeding 0.50 m2:					
3.2 mm hardboard	0.30	4.51	-	4.51	Nr
6.4 mm hardboard	0.30	4.51	-	4.51	Nr
3.2 mm stove enamelled one side hardboard	0.33	5.05	-	5.05	Nr
12 mm building board	0.44	6.73	-	6.73	Nr
19 mm building board	0.44	6.73	-	6.73	Nr
25 mm building board	0.47	7.10	-	7.10	Nr
12 mm chipboard	0.36	5.40	-	5.40	Nr
15 mm chipboard	0.36	5.40	-	5.40	Nr
18 mm chipboard	0.38	5.76	-	5.76	Nr
15 mm plastics laminate faced chipboard	0.36	5.40	-	5.40	Nr
18 mm plastics laminate faced chipboard	0.38	5.76	-	5.76	Nr
12 mm blockboard	0.36	5.40	-	5.40	Nr
18 mm blockboard	0.38	5.76	-	5.76	Nr
25 mm blockboard	0.41	6.29	-	6.29	Nr
4 mm plywood	0.36	5.40	-	5.40	Nr
6 mm plywood	0.36	5.40	-	5.40	Nr
9 mm plywood	0.38	5.76	-	5.76	Nr
12 mm plywood	0.41	6.29	-	6.29	Nr
6 mm non-asbestos board	0.39	5.94	-	5.94	Nr
9 mm non-asbestos board	0.39	5.94	-	5.94	Nr
12 mm non-asbestos board	0.41	6.29	-	6.29	Nr
12 mm insulation board	0.24	3.60	-	3.60	Nr
6 mm medium density fibreboard	0.29	4.39	-	4.39	Nr
9 mm medium density fibreboard	0.31	4.74	-	4.74	Nr
12 mm medium density fibreboard	0.35	5.27	-	5.27	Nr
18 mm medium density fibreboard	0.37	5.62	-	5.62	Nr

NG

DOORS

INTERNAL DOORS

Note: Because of the very wide variety of door types available, supply prices have not been given. The following prices are for **fixing only** doors.

001 Wrought softwood interior casement and panel doors

	Man-Hours	Net Labour Price £	Net Mats Price £	Net Unit Price £	Unit
002 35 mm thick doors:					
610 x 1981 mm	0.95	14.41	-	14.41	Nr
686 x 1981 mm	0.95	14.41	-	14.41	Nr
762 x 1981 mm	0.95	14.41	-	14.41	Nr
838 x 1981 mm	0.95	14.41	-	14.41	Nr
003 40 mm thick doors:					
726 x 2040 mm	0.95	14.41	-	14.41	Nr
826 x 2040 mm	0.95	14.41	-	14.41	Nr

004 Wrought softwood flush doors

	Man-Hours	Net Labour Price £	Net Mats Price £	Net Unit Price £	Unit
005 35 mm thick doors:					
610 x 1829 mm	0.95	14.41	-	14.41	Nr
381 x 1981 mm	0.95	14.41	-	14.41	Nr
457 x 1981 mm	0.95	14.41	-	14.41	Nr
533 x 1981 mm	0.95	14.41	-	14.41	Nr
610 x 1981 mm	0.95	14.41	-	14.41	Nr
686 x 1981 mm	0.95	14.41	-	14.41	Nr
762 x 1981 mm	0.95	14.41	-	14.41	Nr
838 x 1981 mm	0.95	14.41	-	14.41	Nr

Unit Rates

		Man-Hours	Net Labour Price £	Net Mats Price £	Net Unit Price £	Unit
006	40 mm thick doors:					
	526 x 2040 mm	0.95	14.41	-	**14.41**	Nr
	626 x 2040 mm	0.95	14.41	-	**14.41**	Nr
	726 x 2040 mm	0.95	14.41	-	**14.41**	Nr
	826 x 2040 mm	0.95	14.41	-	**14.41**	Nr
007	**Wrought hardwood doors**					
008	35 mm thick doors:					
	610 x 1981 mm	1.30	19.81	-	**19.81**	Nr
	686 x 1981 mm	1.30	19.81	-	**19.81**	Nr
	762 x 1981 mm	1.30	19.81	-	**19.81**	Nr
009	Fire check doors 44 mm thick:					
	762 x 1981 mm	1.42	21.60	-	**21.60**	Nr
	838 x 1981 mm	1.42	21.60	-	**21.60**	Nr
	526 x 2040 mm	1.42	21.60	-	**21.60**	Nr
	626 x 2040 mm	1.42	21.60	-	**21.60**	Nr
	726 x 2040 mm	1.42	21.60	-	**21.60**	Nr
	826 x 2040 mm	1.42	21.60	-	**21.60**	Nr
	EXTERNAL DOORS					
	Note: The following prices are for **fixing only** doors					
010	**Matchboarded doors**					
011	38 mm thick doors:					
	686 x 1981 mm	1.07	16.20	-	**16.20**	Nr
	762 x 1981 mm	1.07	16.20	-	**16.20**	Nr
	838 x 1981 mm	1.07	16.20	-	**16.20**	Nr
012	44 mm thick doors:					
	686 x 1981 mm	1.30	19.81	-	**19.81**	Nr
	762 x 1981 mm	1.30	19.81	-	**19.81**	Nr
	838 x 1981 mm	1.30	19.81	-	**19.81**	Nr
013	Wrought softwood casement and panel doors					
014	44 mm thick doors:					
	762 x 1981 mm	0.95	14.41	-	**14.41**	Nr
	838 x 1981 mm	0.95	14.41	-	**14.41**	Nr
	807 x 2000 mm	0.95	14.41	-	**14.41**	Nr
NH	**DOOR FRAMES AND LININGS**					
	Note: 001 - 089 not used					
090	**Wrought softwood door frame and lining sets**					
091	Frames, at jambs or heads:					
	32 x 63 mm	0.24	3.60	1.60	**5.20**	m
	32 x 100 mm	0.24	3.60	2.41	**6.01**	m
	32 x 150 mm	0.24	3.60	3.60	**7.20**	m
	50 x 75 mm	0.26	3.97	2.30	**6.27**	m
	50 x 100 mm	0.26	3.97	2.97	**6.94**	m
	50 x 150 mm	0.26	3.97	5.51	**9.48**	m
092	Frames, once rebated, at jambs or heads:					
	50 x 75 mm	0.26	3.97	4.96	**8.93**	m
	50 x 100 mm	0.26	3.97	5.62	**9.59**	m
	50 x 150 mm	0.28	4.32	8.17	**12.49**	m
	63 x 75 mm	0.28	4.32	6.31	**10.63**	m
	63 x 100 mm	0.33	5.05	7.29	**12.34**	m
	63 x 125 mm	0.33	5.05	8.45	**13.50**	m
	63 x 150 mm	0.33	5.05	9.61	**14.66**	m
093	Frames, once rebated and once grooved, at jambs or heads:					
	50 x 100 mm	0.26	3.97	8.28	**12.25**	m
	50 x 125 mm	0.26	3.97	13.79	**17.76**	m
	50 x 150 mm	0.28	4.32	10.82	**15.14**	m
	63 x 75 mm	0.33	5.05	8.96	**14.01**	m
	63 x 100 mm	0.33	5.05	9.94	**14.99**	m
	63 x 125 mm	0.33	5.05	11.11	**16.16**	m
	63 x 150 mm	0.33	5.05	12.27	**17.32**	m
094	Frames, at mullions or transoms:					
	32 x 63 mm	0.18	2.71	1.60	**4.31**	m
	32 x 100 mm	0.18	2.71	2.41	**5.12**	m
	32 x 150 mm	0.18	2.71	3.60	**6.31**	m
095	Frames, twice rebated at mullions or transoms:					
	38 x 115 mm	0.26	3.97	8.32	**12.29**	m
	38 x 150 mm	0.26	3.97	9.17	**13.14**	m
	50 x 100 mm	0.26	3.97	8.28	**12.25**	m
	63 x 115 mm	0.33	5.05	10.78	**15.83**	m
	63 x 150 mm	0.33	5.05	12.27	**17.32**	m

	Unit Rates	Man-Hours	Net Labour Price £	Net Mats Price £	Net Unit Price £	Unit
096	Frames, once sunk weathered, once rebated and three times grooved, at sills:					
	63 x 175 mm	0.33	5.05	21.38	**26.43**	m
	75 x 150 mm	0.33	5.05	21.55	**26.60**	m
097	Linings; tongued at angles:					
	25 x 75 mm	0.24	3.60	1.55	**5.15**	m
	25 x 100 mm	0.24	3.60	1.93	**5.53**	m
	25 x 125 mm	0.24	3.60	2.42	**6.02**	m
	25 x 150 mm	0.24	3.60	2.90	**6.50**	m
	32 x 100 mm	0.24	3.60	2.41	**6.01**	m
	32 x 125 mm	0.24	3.60	3.00	**6.60**	m
	32 x 150 mm	0.24	3.60	3.60	**7.20**	m
098	Linings; once rebated and tongued at angles:					
	38 x 100 mm	0.26	3.97	5.23	**9.20**	m
	38 x 125 mm	0.26	3.97	5.87	**9.84**	m
	38 x 150 mm	0.26	3.97	6.52	**10.49**	m
099	**Wrought hardwood door frame and lining sets**					
100	Frames, at jambs or heads:					
	26 x 56 mm	0.36	5.40	5.06	**10.46**	m
	26 x 93 mm	0.36	5.40	6.99	**12.39**	m
	26 x 143 mm	0.36	5.40	9.58	**14.98**	m
	44 x 68 mm	0.39	5.94	8.13	**14.07**	m
	44 x 93 mm	0.39	5.94	10.33	**16.27**	m
	44 x 143 mm	0.39	5.94	15.44	**21.38**	m
101	Frames, once rebated at jambs or heads:					
	44 x 68 mm	0.39	5.94	11.44	**17.38**	m
	44 x 93 mm	0.39	5.94	13.64	**19.58**	m
	44 x 143 mm	0.39	5.94	18.75	**24.69**	m
	56 x 68 mm	0.45	6.84	13.07	**19.91**	m
	56 x 93 mm	0.45	6.84	15.87	**22.71**	m
	56 x 143 mm	0.45	6.84	18.30	**25.14**	m
102	Frames, once rebated and once grooved, at jambs or heads:					
	44 x 93 mm	0.39	5.94	16.95	**22.89**	m
	44 x 143 mm	0.39	5.94	22.07	**28.01**	m
	56 x 68 mm	0.45	6.84	16.39	**23.23**	m
	56 x 93 mm	0.45	6.84	19.18	**26.02**	m
	56 x 143 mm	0.45	6.84	21.61	**28.45**	m
103	Frames, at mullions and transoms:					
	26 x 56 mm	0.33	5.02	5.06	**10.08**	m
	26 x 93 mm	0.33	5.02	6.99	**12.01**	m
	26 x 143 mm	0.33	5.02	9.58	**14.60**	m
104	Frames, twice rebated at mullions or transoms:					
	32 x 118 mm	0.36	5.47	16.32	**21.79**	m
	32 x 143 mm	0.36	5.47	17.92	**23.39**	m
	44 x 93 mm	0.36	5.47	16.95	**22.42**	m
	56 x 143 mm	0.43	6.48	21.61	**28.09**	m
105	Frames, once sunk-weathered, once rebated and three times grooved, at sills:					
	56 x 168 mm	0.43	6.48	42.90	**49.38**	m
	68 x 143 mm	0.43	6.48	43.68	**50.16**	m
106	Linings; tongued at angles:					
	20 x 68 mm	0.28	4.32	4.88	**9.20**	m
	20 x 93 mm	0.28	4.32	5.86	**10.18**	m
	20 x 118 mm	0.28	4.32	7.66	**11.98**	m
	20 x 143 mm	0.28	4.32	8.58	**12.90**	m
	26 x 93 mm	0.28	4.32	6.99	**11.31**	m
	26 x 118 mm	0.28	4.32	8.27	**12.59**	m
	26 x 143 mm	0.28	4.32	9.58	**13.90**	m
107	Linings; once rebated, tongued at angles:					
	32 x 93 mm	0.31	4.68	11.40	**16.08**	m
	32 x 118 mm	0.31	4.68	13.01	**17.69**	m
	32 x 143 mm	0.31	4.68	14.61	**19.29**	m
	Note: 108 - 123 not used					
124	**Work to existing doors, frames etc.**					
125	Ease and adjust doors and windows, oil locks, hinges and the like:					
	single timber doors	0.23	3.54	-	**3.54**	Nr
	pair of timber doors	0.46	7.05	-	**7.05**	Nr
126	Cut out decayed softwood from door frames etc., piece in, or frame in, new wrought softwood to match existing:					
	door frame up to 1000 mm long:					
	100 x 50 mm	0.70	10.59	13.40	**23.99**	Nr
	150 x 75 mm	0.75	11.40	16.60	**28.00**	Nr
	door lining up to 1000 mm long:					
	100 x 25 mm	0.56	8.47	2.84	**11.31**	Nr
	250 x 25 mm	0.60	9.12	4.97	**14.09**	Nr

Unit Rates	Man-Hours	Net Labour Price £	Net Mats Price £	Net Unit Price £	Unit
architrave up to 1000 mm long:					
25 x 50 mm	0.23	3.54	1.18	**4.72**	Nr
38 x 75 mm	0.25	3.80	2.26	**6.06**	Nr
50 x 100 mm	0.30	4.56	3.34	**7.90**	Nr

NJ **WINDOWS, FRAMES ETC.**

Note: Because of the very wide variety of window types available, supply prices have not been given. The following prices are for **fixing only** windows.

001 | Fix only standard windows:

	Man-Hours	Net Labour Price £	Net Mats Price £	Net Unit Price £	Unit
488 x 750 mm	0.29	4.41	-	**4.41**	Nr
488 x 900 mm	0.31	4.71	-	**4.71**	Nr
488 x 1050 mm	0.33	5.02	-	**5.02**	Nr
488 x 1200 mm	0.36	5.47	-	**5.47**	Nr
631 x 750 mm	0.36	5.47	-	**5.47**	Nr
631 x 1050 mm	0.41	6.23	-	**6.23**	Nr
631 x 1200 mm	0.47	7.14	-	**7.14**	Nr
915 x 900 mm	0.64	9.73	-	**9.73**	Nr
915 x 1050 mm	0.76	11.55	-	**11.55**	Nr
915 x 1200 mm	0.93	14.14	-	**14.14**	Nr
1200 x 900 mm	0.87	13.22	-	**13.22**	Nr
1200 x 1050 mm	0.99	15.05	-	**15.05**	Nr
1200 x 1200 mm	1.16	17.63	-	**17.63**	Nr
1200 x 1350 mm	1.33	20.22	-	**20.22**	Nr
1200 x 1500 mm	1.51	22.95	-	**22.95**	Nr
1524 x 1050 mm	1.33	20.22	-	**20.22**	Nr
1524 x 1200 mm	1.56	23.71	-	**23.71**	Nr
1524 x 1350 mm	1.79	27.21	-	**27.21**	Nr
1769 x 900 mm	1.33	20.22	-	**20.22**	Nr
1769 x 1050 mm	1.56	23.71	-	**23.71**	Nr
1769 x 1200 mm	1.79	27.21	-	**27.21**	Nr
1769 x 1350 mm	2.02	30.70	-	**30.70**	Nr
2338 x 1050 mm	2.20	33.44	-	**33.44**	Nr
2338 x 1200 mm	2.49	37.85	-	**37.85**	Nr
2338 x 1350 mm	2.78	42.26	-	**42.26**	Nr
2338 x 1500 mm	3.07	46.66	-	**46.66**	Nr

Note: 002 - 031 not used

VELUX ROOF WINDOWS

032 | **Velux roof windows in laminated pre-finished softwood construction; anodised aluminium external facing; pre-glazed with sealed double glazed units with 4 mm Low-E float inner pane, 16 mm gas filled cavity, 4 mm toughened outer pane; screwing to softwood**

033 | Velux windows, type:

		Man-Hours	Net Labour Price £	Net Mats Price £	Net Unit Price £	Unit
GGL-C02	550 x 780 mm	0.95	14.41	195.29	**209.70**	Nr
GGL-C04	550 x 980 mm	1.19	18.01	205.29	**223.30**	Nr
GGL-F06	660 x 1180 mm	0.71	10.81	240.22	**251.03**	Nr
GGL-M04	780 x 980 mm	1.19	18.01	220.29	**238.30**	Nr
GGL-M08	780 x 1400 mm	1.42	21.60	275.36	**296.96**	Nr
GGL-P10	940 x 1600 mm	1.78	27.01	340.36	**367.37**	Nr
GGL-S06	1140 x 1180 mm	1.54	23.41	330.29	**353.70**	Nr
GHL-C04	550 x 980 mm	1.19	18.01	260.29	**278.30**	Nr
GHL-M04	780 x 980 mm	1.19	18.01	280.29	**298.30**	Nr
GHL-S06	1140 x 1180 mm	1.19	18.01	420.29	**438.30**	Nr

Velux window types GGL and GHL may also be glazed with Obscure; Anti-sun; Toughened clear; and Laminated and electrical operation at extra cost.

034 | Velux combined sloping and vertical windows; clear glazed; screwed to softwood (includes flashings):

		Man-Hours	Net Labour Price £	Net Mats Price £	Net Unit Price £	Unit
GGL-M06-SFOL122	780 x 600 and 780 x 1180	3.50	53.20	654.79	**707.99**	Nr
GGL-M08-SFOL122	780 x 600 and 780 x 1400	3.70	56.24	684.54	**740.78**	Nr
GGL-M06-SFOW122	780 x 950 and 780 x 1180	1.42	21.60	684.61	**706.21**	Nr
GGL-M08-SFOW122	780 x 950 and 780 x 1400	1.19	18.01	714.29	**732.30**	Nr

035 | **Velux flashing units to suit Velux roof windows**

036 | Flashing type EDW; single unit for tiles, to suit windows type:

	Man-Hours	Net Labour Price £	Net Mats Price £	Net Unit Price £	Unit
C02	1.19	18.01	55.34	**73.35**	Nr
C04	1.42	21.60	58.91	**80.51**	Nr
F06	1.78	27.09	64.26	**91.35**	Nr
M04	1.55	23.48	62.48	**85.96**	Nr
M08	1.19	18.01	69.62	**87.63**	Nr
P10	0.95	14.41	80.33	**94.74**	Nr
S06	1.66	25.20	78.54	**103.74**	Nr

037 | Flashing unit type EDZ; single unit for tiles to suit windows type:

	Man-Hours	Net Labour Price £	Net Mats Price £	Net Unit Price £	Unit
C02	0.95	14.41	37.40	**51.81**	Nr
C04	1.19	18.01	39.10	**57.11**	Nr
F06	0.71	10.81	45.00	**55.81**	Nr
M04	1.19	18.01	37.50	**55.51**	Nr
M08	1.42	21.60	47.60	**69.20**	Nr
P10	1.78	27.01	54.40	**81.41**	Nr
S06	1.54	23.41	52.70	**76.11**	Nr

Unit Rates	Man-Hours	Net Labour Price £	Net Mats Price £	Net Unit Price £	Unit
038 Flashing type EDL; single unit for slates to suit windows type:					
C02	0.95	14.41	37.40	**51.81**	Nr
C04	1.19	18.01	39.10	**57.11**	Nr
F06	0.71	10.81	45.00	**55.81**	Nr
M04	1.19	18.01	37.50	**55.51**	Nr
M08	1.42	21.60	47.60	**69.20**	Nr
P10	1.78	27.01	56.70	**83.71**	Nr
S06	1.54	23.41	54.40	**77.81**	Nr
039 Flashing type EBW; twin unit for tiles to suit pair of coupled windows type:					
C02	2.13	32.41	112.20	**144.61**	Nr
C04	2.37	36.01	120.70	**156.71**	Nr
F06	3.32	50.42	132.60	**183.02**	Nr
M04	2.84	43.21	127.50	**170.71**	Nr
M08	2.13	32.41	142.80	**175.21**	Nr
P10	1.66	25.20	164.90	**190.10**	Nr
S06	3.08	46.82	161.50	**208.32**	Nr
040 Velux sun protection; blinds and awnings screwed to softwood					
041 Standard range roller blinds RFL; to suit windows type:					
C02	0.41	6.29	42.50	**48.79**	Nr
C04	0.47	7.20	44.20	**51.40**	Nr
F06	0.59	9.00	52.70	**61.70**	Nr
M04	0.53	8.12	51.00	**59.12**	Nr
M08	0.53	8.12	59.50	**67.62**	Nr
P10	0.32	4.86	68.00	**72.86**	Nr
S06	0.56	8.47	66.30	**74.77**	Nr
042 Standard venetian blinds PAL; to suit window type:					
C02	0.59	9.00	60.69	**69.69**	Nr
C04	0.71	10.81	67.83	**78.64**	Nr
F06	0.89	13.50	76.76	**90.26**	Nr
M04	0.77	11.69	73.19	**84.88**	Nr
M08	0.59	9.00	85.68	**94.68**	Nr
P10	0.47	7.20	98.18	**105.38**	Nr
S06	0.83	12.60	94.61	**107.21**	Nr
043 Velux roof windows accessories					
044 Portable rod opening gear; type:					
ZCT200 - telescopic 1000 mm - 1800 mm	0.20	3.07	22.31	**25.38**	Nr
ZCT100 - 1000 mm extension	0.20	3.07	13.39	**16.46**	Nr
045 Window lock ZOZ012	0.35	5.24	34.00	**39.24**	Nr
Window opening restrictor ZOZ010	0.35	5.24	34.00	**39.24**	Nr
046 Smoke ventilation system complete with window(s), flashing(s), control panel, motors, smoke detectors and 'break glass:'					
047 Fixing into tiled roofs:					
GGL S06 SD0W1; providing 1m2 smoke vent area	4.90	74.48	1235.83	**1310.31**	Nr
GGL U08 SD0W1; providing 1.5m2 smoke vent area	5.10	77.52	1297.71	**1375.23**	Nr
048 Fixing into slate roofs:					
GGL S06 SD0L1; providing 1m2 smoke vent area	4.90	74.48	1207.54	**1282.02**	Nr
GGL U08 SD0L1; providing 1.5m2 smoke vent area	5.10	77.52	1265.89	**1343.41**	Nr
Note: 049 not used					
050 Work to existing windows, frames, etc.					
051 Ease and adjust windows, oil fasteners, hinges and the like:					
casement window	0.56	8.47	-	**8.47**	Nr
sash window	0.70	10.59	-	**10.59**	Nr
Extra over for renewing sash cord	0.93	14.11	0.71	**14.82**	Nr
052 Cut out decayed timber from windows and frames, piecing in or frame in new wrought softwood to match existing:					
frame up to 1000 mm long:					
100 x 50 mm	0.70	10.59	13.40	**23.99**	Nr
150 x 75 mm	0.75	11.40	16.60	**28.00**	Nr
053 Renew decayed wrought softwood casement window sill 150 x 75 mm, rebated, grooved, weathered and throated, including removing window and frame from opening and later refixing, including bedding and pointing in cement mortar (1:3):					
600 mm wide	3.71	56.44	9.95	**66.39**	Nr
900 mm wide	4.64	70.54	14.92	**85.46**	Nr
1200 mm wide	5.57	84.65	19.89	**104.54**	Nr
1500 mm wide	6.50	98.75	24.86	**123.61**	Nr

	Unit Rates	Man-Hours	Net Labour Price £	Net Mats Price £	Net Unit Price £	Unit
NK	**STAIRCASES**					
001	**Standard staircases in wrought softwood**					
002	Straight flight stairs in one flight 2700 mm going, 2600 mm rise, 12 treads, 13 risers:					
	864 mm wide	17.77	270.07	400.73	**670.80**	Nr
003	Straight flight stairs in one flight 3150 mm going, 3000 mm rise, 14 treads, 15 risers:					
	864 mm wide	20.14	306.08	515.04	**821.12**	Nr
004	Half flight stairs in one straight flight 1350 mm going, 1400 mm rise, 6 treads, 7 risers:					
	864 mm wide	7.70	117.02	227.88	**344.90**	Nr
	Note: 005 - 006 not used					
	STAIRCASE BALUSTRADES					
007	**Balustrades in wrought Hemlock; 75 x 75 mm moulded handrails; 41 x 41 mm turned balusters at 150 mm centres housed each end; 57 x 27 mm string capping**					
008	Horizontal balustrades; overall height:					
	900 mm	3.32	50.42	49.75	**100.17**	m
	1000 mm	3.32	50.42	72.22	**122.64**	m
009	Raking balustrades; overall height:					
	900 mm	3.73	56.73	42.50	**99.23**	m
	1000 mm	3.73	56.73	58.10	**114.83**	m
	Note: 010 not used					
011	82 x 82 mm Newel posts, turned:					
	1360 mm long with base and turned cap	0.59	9.00	35.07	**44.07**	Nr
	1640 mm long with base and turned cap	0.59	9.00	42.26	**51.26**	Nr
012	DEDUCT from above prices if balusters nailed and NOT housed:					
	horizontal balustrade	2.37	36.01	-	**36.01**	m
	raking balustrade	2.49	37.80	-	**37.80**	m
	Note: 013 - 017 not used					
018	**Work to existing staircases and balustrades**					
019	Cutting out decayed or defective members of softwood staircase and piecing in new:					
	tread 25 x 275 mm, in lengths:					
	not exceeding 300 mm	0.93	14.11	6.57	**20.68**	Nr
	300 - 600 mm	1.16	17.65	13.13	**30.78**	Nr
	600 - 900 mm	1.39	21.16	13.13	**34.29**	Nr
	900 - 1200 mm	1.63	24.70	17.07	**41.77**	Nr
	tread 32 x 275 mm, in lengths:					
	not exceeding 300 mm	0.95	14.44	8.40	**22.84**	Nr
	300 - 600 mm	1.18	17.94	16.80	**34.74**	Nr
	600 - 900 mm	1.42	21.58	16.80	**38.38**	Nr
	900 - 1200 mm	1.67	25.31	21.84	**47.15**	Nr
	riser 19 x 210 mm, in lengths:					
	not exceeding 300 mm	0.46	7.05	3.09	**10.14**	Nr
	300 - 600 mm	0.70	10.59	6.17	**16.76**	Nr
	600 - 900 mm	0.93	14.11	6.17	**20.28**	Nr
	900 - 1200 mm	1.16	17.65	8.03	**25.68**	Nr
	riser 25 x 210 mm, in lengths:					
	not exceeding 300 mm	0.48	7.30	5.78	**13.08**	Nr
	300 - 600 mm	0.72	10.94	11.57	**22.51**	Nr
	600 - 900 mm	0.96	14.59	11.57	**26.16**	Nr
	900 - 1200 mm	1.19	18.09	15.03	**33.12**	Nr
020	Cut back old softwood tread for a width of 200 mm and provide and fix new rounded or moulded nosing with glued and dowelled joints to old tread:					
	32 mm thick, in lengths:					
	not exceeding 300 mm	1.00	15.20	5.09	**20.29**	Nr
	300 - 600 mm	1.25	19.00	10.19	**29.19**	Nr
	600 - 900 mm	1.45	22.04	10.19	**32.23**	Nr
	900 - 1200 mm	1.65	25.08	13.24	**38.32**	Nr
	25 mm thick, in lengths:					
	not exceeding 300 mm	1.02	15.50	4.22	**19.72**	Nr
	300 - 600 mm	1.27	19.30	8.43	**27.73**	Nr
	600 - 900 mm	1.47	22.34	8.43	**30.77**	Nr
	900 - 1200 mm	1.67	25.38	10.96	**36.34**	Nr
021	Cut out decayed or defective wrought softwood baluster 950 mm high and piece in new:					
	turned:					
	25 mm diameter	0.23	3.54	3.69	**7.23**	Nr
	32 mm diameter	0.23	3.54	3.12	**6.66**	Nr
	square bar:					
	25 x 25 mm	0.23	3.54	1.65	**5.19**	Nr
	32 x 32 mm	0.23	3.54	1.91	**5.45**	Nr
022	Replacing missing baluster with new wrought softwood baluster 950 mm high; cleaning out existing mortices; piece in to match existing:					
	turned:					
	25 mm diameter	0.22	3.34	3.69	**7.03**	Nr

	Man-Hours	Net Labour Price £	Net Mats Price £	Net Unit Price £	Unit
Unit Rates					
32 mm diameter	0.22	3.34	3.12	**6.46**	Nr
square bar:					
25 x 25 mm	0.22	3.34	1.65	**4.99**	Nr
32 x 32 mm	0.22	3.34	1.91	**5.25**	Nr
023 Cut out decayed or defective wrought softwood handrail and piece in new 1000 mm lengths to match existing:					
mopstick, 38 mm	0.95	14.44	4.30	**18.74**	Nr
moulded, 75 x 100 mm	1.40	21.31	6.44	**27.75**	Nr

NL

KITCHEN FITTINGS

Note: Because of the very wide variation in design and quality of kitchen fittings, supply prices have not been given. The following prices are for **fixing only** kitchen units

001 **Fixing only kitchen fittings; ready assembled and shrink wrapped**

002 Floor cupboard units, 500 or 600 mm deep, 900 mm high:

	Man-Hours	Net Labour Price £	Net Mats Price £	Net Unit Price £	Unit
base units:					
300 mm long	0.71	10.81	-	**10.81**	Nr
500 mm long	0.89	13.50	-	**13.50**	Nr
1000 mm long	1.48	22.51	-	**22.51**	Nr
1500 mm long	1.78	27.01	-	**27.01**	Nr
sink base units:					
1000 mm long	1.48	22.51	-	**22.51**	Nr
1500 mm long	1.78	27.01	-	**27.01**	Nr
corner units:					
1000 mm long	1.78	27.01	-	**27.01**	Nr
1200 mm long	2.07	31.51	-	**31.51**	Nr

003 Oven and tall storage units, 500 or 600 mm deep, 2100 mm high:

	Man-Hours	Net Labour Price £	Net Mats Price £	Net Unit Price £	Unit
500 or 600 mm long	1.78	27.01	-	**27.01**	Nr

004 Wall cupboard units 300 mm deep:

	Man-Hours	Net Labour Price £	Net Mats Price £	Net Unit Price £	Unit
600 mm high:					
300 mm long	0.89	13.50	-	**13.50**	Nr
500 mm long	1.19	18.01	-	**18.01**	Nr
600 mm long	1.42	21.60	-	**21.60**	Nr
1000 mm long	2.07	31.51	-	**31.51**	Nr
600 x 600 mm corner unit	2.37	36.01	-	**36.01**	Nr
900 mm high:					
300 mm long	0.89	13.50	-	**13.50**	Nr
500 mm long	1.19	18.01	-	**18.01**	Nr
600 mm long	1.42	21.60	-	**21.60**	Nr
1000 mm long	2.07	31.51	-	**31.51**	Nr
600 x 600 mm corner unit	2.37	36.01	-	**36.01**	Nr

005 Sundry accessories:

	Man-Hours	Net Labour Price £	Net Mats Price £	Net Unit Price £	Unit
end panels 500 x 600 mm wide x 900 mm high	0.59	9.00	-	**9.00**	Nr
leg support 900 mm high	0.30	4.51	-	**4.51**	Nr
tray space up to 300 mm wide	0.89	13.50	-	**13.50**	Nr
cornices	0.30	4.51	-	**4.51**	m
lighting pelmets	0.18	2.71	-	**2.71**	m
tidy bins, vegetable racks and the like	0.24	3.60	-	**3.60**	Nr

006 **Fixing only kitchen fittings; self-assembly units supplied boxed in packs with assembly instructions**

007 Floor cupboard units, 500 or 600 mm deep, 900 mm high:

	Man-Hours	Net Labour Price £	Net Mats Price £	Net Unit Price £	Unit
base units:					
300 mm long	1.07	16.20	-	**16.20**	Nr
500 mm long	1.48	22.51	-	**22.51**	Nr
1000 mm long	2.19	33.32	-	**33.32**	Nr
1500 mm long	2.67	40.51	-	**40.51**	Nr
sink base units:					
1000 mm long	2.19	33.32	-	**33.32**	Nr
1500 mm long	2.67	40.51	-	**40.51**	Nr
corner units:					
1000 mm long	2.67	40.51	-	**40.51**	Nr
1200 mm long	2.96	45.01	-	**45.01**	Nr

008 Oven and tall storage units, 500 or 600 mm deep, 2100 mm high:

	Man-Hours	Net Labour Price £	Net Mats Price £	Net Unit Price £	Unit
500 or 600 mm long	2.67	40.51	-	**40.51**	Nr

009 Wall cupboard units 300 mm deep:

	Man-Hours	Net Labour Price £	Net Mats Price £	Net Unit Price £	Unit
600 mm high:					
300 mm long	1.48	22.51	-	**22.51**	Nr
500 mm long	1.78	27.01	-	**27.01**	Nr
600 mm long	2.01	30.61	-	**30.61**	Nr
1000 mm long	2.67	40.51	-	**40.51**	Nr
600 x 600 mm corner unit	2.96	45.01	-	**45.01**	Nr
900 mm high:					
300 mm long	1.48	22.51	-	**22.51**	Nr
500 mm long	1.78	27.01	-	**27.01**	Nr
600 mm long	2.01	30.61	-	**30.61**	Nr
1000 mm long	2.67	40.51	-	**40.51**	Nr
600 x 600 mm corner unit	2.96	45.01	-	**45.01**	Nr

		Man-Hours	Net Labour Price £	Net Mats Price £	Net Unit Price £	Unit
Unit Rates						
010	Sundry accessories:					
	end panels 500 x 600 mm wide x 900 mm high	0.71	10.81	-	**10.81**	Nr
	leg support 900 mm high	0.41	6.29	-	**6.29**	Nr
	tray space up to 300 mm wide	1.07	16.20	-	**16.20**	Nr
	cornices	0.30	4.51	-	**4.51**	m
	lighting pelmets	0.18	2.71	-	**2.71**	m
	tidy bins, vegetable racks and the like	0.24	3.60	-	**3.60**	Nr
011	Work tops, 500 and 600 mm wide:					
	300 mm long	0.30	4.51	-	**4.51**	Nr
	500 mm long	0.36	5.40	-	**5.40**	Nr
	1000 mm long	0.59	9.00	-	**9.00**	Nr
	1500 mm long	0.71	10.81	-	**10.81**	Nr
	2000 mm long	0.89	13.50	-	**13.50**	Nr
	3000 mm long	1.07	16.20	-	**16.20**	Nr
NM	**SUNDRIES**					
	SCREWS					
001	**Extra over for fixing timber with screws**					
002	Steel slotted head countersunk wood screws (No. 8 x 38 mm):					
	flush with surface:					
	300 mm centres	0.27	4.15	0.06	**4.21**	m
	400 mm centres	0.20	3.07	0.04	**3.11**	m
	600 mm centres	0.13	1.98	0.02	**2.00**	m
	900 mm centres	0.10	1.44	0.02	**1.46**	m
	1200 mm centres	0.07	1.08	0.01	**1.09**	m
	countersunk; filling heads:					
	300 mm centres	0.30	4.51	0.06	**4.57**	m
	400 mm centres	0.23	3.42	0.04	**3.46**	m
	600 mm centres	0.16	2.36	0.02	**2.38**	m
	900 mm centres	0.10	1.44	0.02	**1.46**	m
	1200 mm centres	0.07	1.08	0.01	**1.09**	m
	countersunk; pellating heads:					
	300 mm centres	0.36	5.40	0.06	**5.46**	m
	400 mm centres	0.28	4.32	0.04	**4.36**	m
	600 mm centres	0.19	2.89	0.02	**2.91**	m
	900 mm centres	0.12	1.79	0.02	**1.81**	m
	1200 mm centres	0.10	1.44	0.01	**1.45**	m
003	Brass raised countersunk wood screws (No. 8 x 38 mm); brass screwcups:					
	flush with surface:					
	300 mm centres	0.30	4.51	0.35	**4.86**	m
	400 mm centres	0.23	3.42	0.27	**3.69**	m
	600 mm centres	0.16	2.36	0.16	**2.52**	m
	900 mm centres	0.10	1.44	0.12	**1.56**	m
	1200 mm centres	0.07	1.08	0.08	**1.16**	m
	PLUGGING					
004	Plugging to receive screws (priced elsewhere); No. 8 x 38 mm plastic plugs in:					
	concrete:					
	300 mm centres	0.21	3.24	0.07	**3.31**	m
	400 mm centres	0.17	2.52	0.06	**2.58**	m
	600 mm centres	0.11	1.63	0.04	**1.67**	m
	900 mm centres	0.07	1.08	0.02	**1.10**	m
	1200 mm centres	0.06	0.91	0.02	**0.93**	m
	300 mm centres one way, 600 mm centres other way	0.36	5.40	0.12	**5.52**	m2
	Isolated	0.10	1.44	0.02	**1.46**	Nr
	brickwork or blockwork:					
	300 mm centres	0.19	2.89	0.07	**2.96**	m
	400 mm centres	0.14	2.16	0.06	**2.22**	m
	600 mm centres	0.10	1.44	0.04	**1.48**	m
	900 mm centres	0.06	0.91	0.02	**0.93**	m
	1200 mm centres	0.05	0.71	0.02	**0.73**	m
	300 mm centres one way, 600 mm centres other way	0.32	4.86	0.12	**4.98**	m2
	Isolated	0.08	1.26	0.02	**1.28**	Nr
005	**Fixing with nails**					
006	Fixing direct with 75 mm cut steel clasp nails (no plugging) in:					
	concrete	0.12	1.79	0.18	**1.97**	m
	brickwork or blockwork	0.10	1.44	0.18	**1.62**	m
007	Fixing direct with 50 x 2.5 mm hardened masonry nails (no plugging) in:					
	concrete	0.12	1.79	0.03	**1.82**	m
	brickwork or blockwork	0.10	1.44	0.03	**1.47**	m
	HOLES IN TIMBER					
008	**Holes in Timber**					
009	Holes for bolts and the like:					
	12 mm softwood	0.06	0.91	-	**0.91**	Nr
	25 mm softwood	0.10	1.44	-	**1.44**	Nr
	50 mm softwood	0.14	2.16	-	**2.16**	Nr
	12 mm hardwood	0.07	1.08	-	**1.08**	Nr

	Unit Rates	Man-Hours	Net Labour Price £	Net Mats Price £	Net Unit Price £	Unit
	25 mm hardwood	0.12	1.79	-	**1.79**	Nr
	50 mm hardwood	0.17	2.52	-	**2.52**	Nr
010	Countersinking:					
	softwood	0.04	0.55	-	**0.55**	Nr
	hardwood	0.05	0.71	-	**0.71**	Nr
011	Countersinking and pellating:					
	softwood	0.22	3.28	-	**3.28**	Nr
	hardwood	0.26	3.97	-	**3.97**	Nr
012	Holes for ducting, trunking and the like in softwood:					
	12 mm thick timber:					
	not exceeding 0.025 m2	0.20	2.99	-	**2.99**	Nr
	0.025 - 0.05 m2	0.24	3.60	-	**3.60**	Nr
	0.05 - 0.075 m2	0.30	4.51	-	**4.51**	Nr
	25 mm thick timber:					
	not exceeding 0.025 m2	0.22	3.33	-	**3.33**	Nr
	0.025 - 0.05 m2	0.26	3.97	-	**3.97**	Nr
	0.05 - 0.075 m2	0.32	4.86	-	**4.86**	Nr
	50 mm thick timber:					
	not exceeding 0.025 m2	0.30	4.51	-	**4.51**	Nr
	0.025 - 0.05 m2	0.36	5.40	-	**5.40**	Nr
	0.05 - 0.075 m2	0.41	6.29	-	**6.29**	Nr
013	Holes for ducting, trunking and the like in hardwood:					
	12 mm thick timber:					
	not exceeding 0.025 m2	0.24	3.60	-	**3.60**	Nr
	0.025 - 0.05 m2	0.28	4.32	-	**4.32**	Nr
	0.05 - 0.075 m2	0.36	5.40	-	**5.40**	Nr
	25 mm thick timber:					
	not exceeding 0.025 m2	0.26	3.97	-	**3.97**	Nr
	0.025 - 0.05 m2	0.31	4.68	-	**4.68**	Nr
	0.05 - 0.075 m2	0.38	5.76	-	**5.76**	Nr
	50 mm thick timber:					
	not exceeding 0.025 m2	0.36	5.40	-	**5.40**	Nr
	0.025 - 0.05 m2	0.43	6.48	-	**6.48**	Nr
	0.05 - 0.075 m2	0.50	7.55	-	**7.55**	Nr
	INSULATION					
014	**Insulation**					
015	Glass fibre insulating mat 1200 mm wide laid in position:					
	100 mm thick	0.19	2.89	3.27	**6.16**	m2
016	Glass fibre insulating mat 1200 mm wide fixed vertically with battens (battens measured separately):					
	100 mm thick	0.36	5.40	3.27	**8.67**	m2
017	Glass fibre roof insulation 600 mm wide; laid in position between joists:					
	100 mm thick	0.19	2.89	3.27	**6.16**	m2
	200 mm thick	0.20	3.04	6.15	**9.19**	m2
018	Glass fibre sound deadening quilt type PF; 1200 mm wide:					
	laid in position:					
	13 mm thick	0.14	2.16	1.43	**3.59**	m2
	fixed vertically between battens:					
	13 mm thick	0.14	2.16	1.43	**3.59**	m2
019	PIR Polyisocyanurate foam insulation; cut and fitted between joist/rafters:					
	35 mm thick	0.25	3.80	5.08	**8.88**	m2
	100 mm thick	0.36	5.47	12.36	**17.83**	m2
	130 mm thick	0.40	6.08	16.52	**22.60**	m2
020	Expanded polystyrene boards; fixed with adhesive to walls:					
	12 mm standard grade	0.36	5.40	1.15	**6.55**	m2
	25 mm standard grade	0.41	6.29	2.31	**8.60**	m2
	50 mm standard grade	0.47	7.20	4.61	**11.81**	m2
	12 mm fire-resisting grade	0.36	5.40	2.31	**7.71**	m2
021	Raking or curved cutting:					
	100 mm glass fibre	0.07	1.08	0.44	**1.52**	m
	150 mm glass fibre	0.08	1.22	0.37	**1.59**	m
	200 mm glass fibre	0.09	1.37	0.37	**1.74**	m
	25 mm expanded polystyrene	0.10	1.44	0.03	**1.47**	m
	50 mm expanded polystyrene	0.12	1.79	0.07	**1.86**	m
	Note: 022 not used					
	CARPENTER'S METALWORK					
023	**Carpenter's metalwork**					
024	Galvanised mild steel dowels:					
	8 mm diameter x 100 mm long	0.10	1.44	0.30	**1.74**	Nr
	10 mm diameter x 50 mm long	0.10	1.44	0.38	**1.82**	Nr

	Unit Rates	Man-Hours	Net Labour Price £	Net Mats Price £	Net Unit Price £	Unit
025	Black hexagon head bolts and nuts, Grade 4.6 to BS 4190 including one nut and one washer:					
	M6 x 25 mm	0.12	1.79	0.06	**1.85**	Nr
	M6 x 50 mm	0.12	1.79	0.08	**1.87**	Nr
	M6 x 80 mm	0.12	1.79	0.10	**1.89**	Nr
	M6 x 100 mm	0.12	1.79	0.11	**1.90**	Nr
	M8 x 25 mm	0.12	1.79	0.09	**1.88**	Nr
	M8 x 50 mm	0.12	1.79	0.12	**1.91**	Nr
	M10 x 50 mm	0.12	1.79	0.15	**1.94**	Nr
	M10 x 80 mm	0.12	1.79	0.18	**1.97**	Nr
	M10 x 100 mm	0.14	2.16	0.22	**2.38**	Nr
	M10 x 140 mm	0.17	2.52	0.33	**2.85**	Nr
	M12 x 50 mm	0.12	1.79	0.25	**2.04**	Nr
	M12 x 80 mm	0.12	1.79	0.31	**2.10**	Nr
	M12 x 100 mm	0.14	2.16	0.38	**2.54**	Nr
	M12 x 140 mm	0.17	2.52	0.53	**3.05**	Nr
	M12 x 200 mm	0.18	2.71	1.60	**4.31**	Nr
	M12 x 260 mm	0.19	2.89	1.81	**4.70**	Nr
	M12 x 300 mm	0.19	2.89	1.99	**4.88**	Nr
	M16 x 50 mm	0.14	2.16	0.68	**2.84**	Nr
	M16 x 80 mm	0.14	2.16	0.82	**2.98**	Nr
	M16 x 100 mm	0.14	2.16	0.91	**3.07**	Nr
	M20 x 100 mm	0.17	2.52	1.69	**4.21**	Nr
026	Black cup square hexagon carriage bolts and nuts, Grade 4.6 to BS 4933 including one nut and one washer:					
	M6 x 50 mm	0.12	1.79	0.03	**1.82**	Nr
	M6 x 75 mm	0.12	1.79	0.04	**1.83**	Nr
	M6 x 100 mm	0.12	1.79	0.05	**1.84**	Nr
	M8 x 50 mm	0.12	1.79	0.07	**1.86**	Nr
	M8 x 75 mm	0.12	1.79	0.07	**1.86**	Nr
	M8 x 100 mm	0.12	1.79	0.08	**1.87**	Nr
	M10 x 50 mm	0.12	1.79	0.12	**1.91**	Nr
	M10 x 75 mm	0.12	1.79	0.13	**1.92**	Nr
	M10 x 100 mm	0.14	2.16	0.15	**2.31**	Nr
	M12 x 75 mm	0.12	1.79	0.30	**2.09**	Nr
	M12 x 100 mm	0.14	2.16	0.39	**2.55**	Nr
	M12 x 150 mm	0.17	2.52	0.42	**2.94**	Nr
027	Expanding bolts with plated finish to BS 1706 Class C, bolt projecting type with one nut and one washer:					
	M6 10P	0.18	2.71	0.72	**3.43**	Nr
	M6 25P	0.18	2.71	0.83	**3.54**	Nr
	M6 60P	0.18	2.71	0.84	**3.55**	Nr
	M8 25P	0.21	3.24	0.98	**4.22**	Nr
	M8 60P	0.21	3.24	1.07	**4.31**	Nr
	M10 15P	0.24	3.60	1.12	**4.72**	Nr
	M10 30P	0.26	3.97	1.17	**5.14**	Nr
	M10 60P	0.30	4.51	1.14	**5.65**	Nr
	M12 15P	0.21	3.24	1.82	**5.06**	Nr
	M12 30P	0.24	3.60	1.91	**5.51**	Nr
	M12 75P	0.33	5.05	2.36	**7.41**	Nr
	M16 35P	0.36	5.40	4.37	**9.77**	Nr
	M16 75P	0.38	5.76	4.51	**10.27**	Nr
028	Expanding bolts with plated finish to BS 1706 Class C, loose bolt type:					
	M6 10L	0.18	2.71	0.77	**3.48**	Nr
	M6 25L	0.18	2.71	0.77	**3.48**	Nr
	M6 40L	0.18	2.71	0.91	**3.62**	Nr
	M8 10L	0.18	2.71	0.91	**3.62**	Nr
	M8 25L	0.21	3.24	0.98	**4.22**	Nr
	M8 40L	0.24	3.60	1.05	**4.65**	Nr
	M10 25L	0.24	3.60	1.17	**4.77**	Nr
	M10 50L	0.26	3.97	1.19	**5.16**	Nr
	M10 75L	0.26	3.97	1.29	**5.26**	Nr
	M12 25L	0.21	3.24	2.12	**5.36**	Nr
	M12 60L	0.30	4.51	2.66	**7.17**	Nr
	M16 30L	0.33	5.05	4.47	**9.52**	Nr
	M16 60L	0.36	5.40	5.23	**10.63**	Nr
029	3 mm black steel square plate washers to BS 3410 Table 11, for 12 mm diameter bolts:					
	38 x 38 mm	0.04	0.59	0.14	**0.73**	Nr
	50 x 50 mm	0.04	0.59	0.25	**0.84**	Nr
030	Galvanised mild steel single sided round toothed plate connectors to BS 1579 Table 4:					
	50 mm diameter for 12 mm bolt	0.06	0.91	0.49	**1.40**	Nr
	63 mm diameter for 12 mm bolt	0.07	1.08	0.72	**1.80**	Nr
	75 mm diameter for 12 mm bolt	0.07	1.08	1.06	**2.14**	Nr
031	Galvanised mild steel double sided round toothed plate connectors to BS 1579 Table 4:					
	50 mm diameter for 12 mm bolt	0.08	1.26	0.55	**1.81**	Nr
	63 mm diameter for 12 mm bolt	0.10	1.44	0.80	**2.24**	Nr
	75 mm diameter for 12 mm bolt	0.10	1.44	1.10	**2.54**	Nr
032	Galvanised mild steel split ring connectors to BS 1579 Table 1:					
	64 mm diameter; parallel sides	0.20	2.99	2.30	**5.29**	Nr
	102 mm diameter; parallel sides	0.22	3.34	6.15	**9.49**	Nr
033	Galvanised mild steel shear plate connectors to BS 1579 Table 2:					
	67 mm diameter pressed steel	0.20	2.99	3.69	**6.68**	Nr

Unit Rates	Man-Hours	Net Labour Price £	Net Mats Price £	Net Unit Price £	Unit
102 mm diameter malleable cast iron	0.22	3.34	15.98	**19.32**	Nr
034 Galvanised mild steel safe edge door frame ties:					
200 x 25 x 3 mm	0.14	2.16	0.72	**2.88**	Nr
250 x 25 x 3 mm	0.14	2.16	0.72	**2.88**	Nr
035 Galvanised steel standard restraint straps; 30 x 2.5 mm section with staggered 6 mm diameter holes; fixing to softwood with screws:					
30 x 2.5 x 400 mm long	0.38	5.76	1.17	**6.93**	Nr
30 x 2.5 x 600 mm long	0.41	6.29	1.63	**7.92**	Nr
30 x 2.5 x 800 mm long	0.45	6.84	2.41	**9.25**	Nr
30 x 2.5 x 1000 mm long	0.56	8.47	3.13	**11.60**	Nr
30 x 2.5 x 1200 mm long	0.59	9.00	3.81	**12.81**	Nr
036 Galvanised steel heavy duty restraint straps, 30 x 5 mm section with staggered 6 mm diameter holes:					
700 mm girth bent at 75 mm	0.18	2.71	2.43	**5.14**	Nr
800 mm girth bent at 100 mm	0.18	2.71	3.34	**6.05**	Nr
1000 mm girth bent at 100 mm	0.21	3.24	4.05	**7.29**	Nr
1200 mm girth bent at 100 mm	0.21	3.24	4.89	**8.13**	Nr
1500 mm girth bent at 100 mm	0.24	3.60	6.49	**10.09**	Nr
1300 mm girth bent at 300 mm	0.24	3.60	5.28	**8.88**	Nr
1700 mm girth bent at 300 mm	0.26	3.97	6.92	**10.89**	Nr
500 mm straight strap with twist at 100 mm	0.18	2.71	3.04	**5.75**	Nr
700 mm straight strap with twist at 100 mm	0.18	2.71	4.22	**6.93**	Nr
037 Galvanised mild steel water bars, bedding in white lead in groove in timber:					
3 x 25 mm	0.33	5.05	2.86	**7.91**	m
6 x 25 mm	0.38	5.76	2.34	**8.10**	m
6 x 40 mm	0.40	6.13	2.94	**9.07**	m
038 **The Expanded Metal Co. SPH joist hangers; building in to brickwork or blockwork**					
039 Type 'S' standard for 38 mm joists; depth:					
100 mm	0.10	1.44	3.32	**4.76**	Nr
125 mm	0.10	1.44	3.33	**4.77**	Nr
150 mm	0.10	1.44	3.13	**4.57**	Nr
175 mm	0.10	1.44	3.28	**4.72**	Nr
200 mm	0.10	1.44	3.63	**5.07**	Nr
225 mm	0.10	1.44	3.85	**5.29**	Nr
250 mm	0.10	1.44	5.26	**6.70**	Nr
040 Type 'S' standard for 50 mm joists; depth:					
100 mm	0.10	1.44	3.32	**4.76**	Nr
125 mm	0.10	1.44	3.33	**4.77**	Nr
150 mm	0.10	1.44	3.13	**4.57**	Nr
175 mm	0.10	1.44	3.28	**4.72**	Nr
200 mm	0.10	1.44	3.63	**5.07**	Nr
225 mm	0.10	1.44	3.85	**5.29**	Nr
250 mm	0.10	1.44	5.26	**6.70**	Nr
041 Type 'S' standard for 75 mm joists; depth:					
100 mm	0.12	1.79	4.12	**5.91**	Nr
125 mm	0.12	1.79	4.22	**6.01**	Nr
150 mm	0.12	1.79	4.82	**6.61**	Nr
175 mm	0.12	1.79	4.53	**6.32**	Nr
200 mm	0.12	1.79	4.82	**6.61**	Nr
225 mm	0.12	1.79	5.17	**6.96**	Nr
250 mm	0.12	1.79	5.47	**7.26**	Nr
042 Type 'S' standard for 100 mm joists; depth:					
100 mm	0.12	1.79	5.26	**7.05**	Nr
125 mm	0.12	1.79	5.51	**7.30**	Nr
150 mm	0.12	1.79	5.80	**7.59**	Nr
175 mm	0.12	1.79	6.29	**8.08**	Nr
200 mm	0.12	1.79	6.00	**7.79**	Nr
225 mm	0.12	1.79	6.35	**8.14**	Nr
250 mm	0.12	1.79	6.74	**8.53**	Nr
043 Type 'ST' straddle for 38 mm joists; depth:					
100 mm	0.14	2.16	10.36	**12.52**	Nr
125 mm	0.14	2.16	10.44	**12.60**	Nr
150 mm	0.14	2.16	9.84	**12.00**	Nr
175 mm	0.14	2.16	10.32	**12.48**	Nr
200 mm	0.14	2.16	11.21	**13.37**	Nr
225 mm	0.14	2.16	11.82	**13.98**	Nr
044 Type 'ST' straddle for 50 mm joists; depth:					
100 mm	0.14	2.16	10.36	**12.52**	Nr
125 mm	0.14	2.16	10.44	**12.60**	Nr
150 mm	0.14	2.16	9.84	**12.00**	Nr
175 mm	0.14	2.16	10.32	**12.48**	Nr
200 mm	0.14	2.16	11.21	**13.37**	Nr
225 mm	0.14	2.16	11.82	**13.98**	Nr
250 mm	0.14	2.16	15.48	**17.64**	Nr
045 Type 'ST' straddle for 75 mm joists; depth:					
100 mm	0.16	2.36	12.55	**14.91**	Nr
125 mm	0.16	2.36	12.73	**15.09**	Nr

	Unit Rates	Man-Hours	Net Labour Price £	Net Mats Price £	Net Unit Price £	Unit
	150 mm	0.16	2.36	14.30	**16.66**	Nr
	175 mm	0.16	2.36	13.58	**15.94**	Nr
	200 mm	0.16	2.36	14.30	**16.66**	Nr
	225 mm	0.16	2.36	15.22	**17.58**	Nr
	250 mm	0.16	2.36	16.00	**18.36**	Nr
046	Type 'ST' straddle for 100 mm joists; depth:					
	100 mm	0.16	2.36	15.48	**17.84**	Nr
	125 mm	0.16	2.36	16.04	**18.40**	Nr
	150 mm	0.16	2.36	16.89	**19.25**	Nr
	175 mm	0.16	2.36	18.19	**20.55**	Nr
	200 mm	0.16	2.36	17.40	**19.76**	Nr
	225 mm	0.16	2.36	18.29	**20.65**	Nr
	250 mm	0.16	2.36	19.28	**21.64**	Nr
047	Type 'R' return flange for 38 mm joists; depth:					
	100 mm	0.14	2.16	6.02	**8.18**	Nr
	125 mm	0.14	2.16	6.03	**8.19**	Nr
	150 mm	0.14	2.16	5.77	**7.93**	Nr
	175 mm	0.14	2.16	6.01	**8.17**	Nr
	200 mm	0.14	2.16	6.43	**8.59**	Nr
	225 mm	0.14	2.16	6.75	**8.91**	Nr
	250 mm	0.14	2.16	8.55	**10.71**	Nr
048	Type 'R' return flange for 50 mm joists; depth:					
	100 mm	0.14	2.16	6.02	**8.18**	Nr
	125 mm	0.14	2.16	6.03	**8.19**	Nr
	150 mm	0.14	2.16	5.77	**7.93**	Nr
	175 mm	0.14	2.16	6.01	**8.17**	Nr
	200 mm	0.14	2.16	6.43	**8.59**	Nr
	225 mm	0.14	2.16	6.75	**8.91**	Nr
	250 mm	0.14	2.16	8.55	**10.71**	Nr
049	Type 'R' return flange for 75 mm joists; depth:					
	100 mm	0.16	2.36	7.10	**9.46**	Nr
	125 mm	0.16	2.36	7.22	**9.58**	Nr
	150 mm	0.16	2.36	7.97	**10.33**	Nr
	175 mm	0.16	2.36	7.63	**9.99**	Nr
	200 mm	0.16	2.36	7.97	**10.33**	Nr
	225 mm	0.16	2.36	8.43	**10.79**	Nr
	250 mm	0.16	2.36	8.83	**11.19**	Nr
050	Type 'R' return flange for 100 mm joists; depth:					
	100 mm	0.16	2.36	8.55	**10.91**	Nr
	125 mm	0.16	2.36	8.84	**11.20**	Nr
	150 mm	0.16	2.36	9.25	**11.61**	Nr
	175 mm	0.16	2.36	9.93	**12.29**	Nr
	200 mm	0.16	2.36	9.55	**11.91**	Nr
	225 mm	0.16	2.36	9.99	**12.35**	Nr
	250 mm	0.16	2.36	10.48	**12.84**	Nr
051	**The Expanded Metal Co. SPW joist hangers type FF for face fixing; fixing with 2 Nr 12 mm expanded bolts; loose bolt type; drilling concrete**					
052	Type 'FF' face fixing; joist width:					
	38 mm	0.71	10.81	8.64	**19.45**	Nr
	50 mm	0.71	10.81	9.56	**20.37**	Nr
	75 mm	0.71	10.81	10.26	**21.07**	Nr
	100 mm	0.71	10.81	11.11	**21.92**	Nr
NN	**IRONMONGERY**					
	Note: Hanging doors priced separately; see section NG 001 et seq.					
	Note: 001 not used					
002	**Fixing only ironmongery; to softwood and the like**					
003	Hinges:					
	light steel butts	0.21	3.24	-	**3.24**	Pair
	medium steel butts	0.24	3.60	-	**3.60**	Pair
	heavy steel butts	0.26	3.97	-	**3.97**	Pair
	100 mm 'Parliament' hinges	0.36	5.40	-	**5.40**	Pair
	rising/falling butts:					
	75 mm	1.42	21.60	-	**21.60**	Pair
	100 mm	1.45	21.96	-	**21.96**	Pair
	125 mm	1.48	22.51	-	**22.51**	Pair
	backflap hinges	1.01	15.31	-	**15.31**	Pair
	'T' hinges:					
	300 mm	0.59	9.00	-	**9.00**	Pair
	400 mm	0.83	12.60	-	**12.60**	Pair
	500 mm	0.89	13.50	-	**13.50**	Pair
	hook and band hinges:					
	450 mm	1.30	19.81	-	**19.81**	Pair
	600 mm	1.36	20.72	-	**20.72**	Pair
	750 mm	1.48	22.51	-	**22.51**	Pair
	900 mm	1.78	27.01	-	**27.01**	Pair

Unit Rates	Man-Hours	Net Labour Price £	Net Mats Price £	Net Unit Price £	Unit
single action spring hinges:					
75 mm	0.83	12.60	-	**12.60**	Pair
100 mm	0.89	13.50	-	**13.50**	Pair
double action spring hinges:					
75 mm	1.19	18.01	-	**18.01**	Pair
100 mm	1.48	22.51	-	**22.51**	Pair
004 Floor springs:					
single action; setting in floor (prepared mortice)	2.07	31.51	-	**31.51**	Nr
double action; setting in floor (prepared mortice)	2.37	36.01	-	**36.01**	Nr
005 Locks, latches and furniture:					
rim latch	1.19	18.01	-	**18.01**	Nr
mortice latch	0.89	13.50	-	**13.50**	Nr
rebated mortice latch	1.01	15.31	-	**15.31**	Nr
night latch	1.48	22.51	-	**22.51**	Nr
cylinder night latch	1.78	27.01	-	**27.01**	Nr
Norfolk/Suffolk latch	1.19	18.01	-	**18.01**	Nr
thumb latch	0.89	13.50	-	**13.50**	Nr
gate latch	0.30	4.51	-	**4.51**	Nr
rim dead lock	0.89	13.50	-	**13.50**	Nr
mortice dead lock	1.07	16.20	-	**16.20**	Nr
rebated mortice dead lock	1.54	23.41	-	**23.41**	Nr
mortice cupboard lock	0.59	9.00	-	**9.00**	Nr
rebated mortice cupboard lock	0.83	12.60	-	**12.60**	Nr
cupboard catch	0.36	5.40	-	**5.40**	Nr
ball catch	0.36	5.40	-	**5.40**	Nr
lever lock/latch furniture	0.47	7.20	-	**7.20**	Set
knob lock/latch furniture	0.41	6.29	-	**6.29**	Set
escutcheons	0.18	2.71	-	**2.71**	Nr
006 Door closers:					
overhead door, single action	1.30	19.81	-	**19.81**	Nr
overhead door, double action	1.42	21.60	-	**21.60**	Nr
coil spring closer, 150 mm	0.39	5.94	-	**5.94**	Nr
door selector	0.41	6.29	-	**6.29**	Nr
'Perko' closer	0.59	9.00	-	**9.00**	Nr
007 Bolts:					
barrel or tower:					
100 mm	0.24	3.60	-	**3.60**	Nr
150 mm	0.30	4.51	-	**4.51**	Nr
200 mm	0.36	5.40	-	**5.40**	Nr
225 mm	0.41	6.29	-	**6.29**	Nr
250 mm	0.47	7.20	-	**7.20**	Nr
300 mm	0.53	8.12	-	**8.12**	Nr
450 mm	0.59	9.00	-	**9.00**	Nr
monkey tail:					
450 mm	1.19	18.01	-	**18.01**	Nr
600 mm	1.48	22.51	-	**22.51**	Nr
1500 mm	1.78	27.01	-	**27.01**	Nr
flush:					
100 mm	0.71	10.81	-	**10.81**	Nr
150 mm	0.95	14.41	-	**14.41**	Nr
200 mm	1.19	18.01	-	**18.01**	Nr
225 mm	1.42	21.60	-	**21.60**	Nr
250 mm	1.66	25.20	-	**25.20**	Pair
300 mm	1.90	28.80	-	**28.80**	Nr
450 mm	2.13	32.41	-	**32.41**	Nr
WC indicator	1.19	18.01	-	**18.01**	Nr
single door, panic bolt	2.13	32.41	-	**32.41**	Nr
double door, panic bolt	3.32	50.42	-	**50.42**	Nr
easy clean bolt socket (mortice measured separately)	0.24	3.60	-	**3.60**	Nr
008 Handles and pulls:					
cupboard knobs	0.14	2.16	-	**2.16**	Nr
door pull handles:					
150 mm	0.30	4.51	-	**4.51**	Nr
225 mm	0.36	5.40	-	**5.40**	Nr
300 mm	0.39	5.94	-	**5.94**	Nr
450 mm	0.41	6.29	-	**6.29**	Nr
600 mm	0.47	7.20	-	**7.20**	Nr
flush handles:					
150 mm	0.39	5.94	-	**5.94**	Nr
225 mm	0.41	6.29	-	**6.29**	Nr
300 mm	0.47	7.20	-	**7.20**	Nr
009 Plates:					
door push plates:					
200 mm	0.24	3.60	-	**3.60**	Nr
300 mm	0.24	3.60	-	**3.60**	Nr
600 mm	0.30	4.51	-	**4.51**	Nr
kicking plates:					
450 x 225 mm	0.41	6.29	-	**6.29**	Nr
600 x 225 mm	0.45	6.84	-	**6.84**	Nr
750 x 225 mm	0.47	7.20	-	**7.20**	Nr
900 x 225 mm	0.50	7.55	-	**7.55**	Nr
letter plate including 125 mm slot	1.48	22.51	-	**22.51**	Nr

	Man-Hours	Net Labour Price £	Net Mats Price £	Net Unit Price £	Unit
010 Window fittings:					
casement stay:					
250 mm	0.30	4.51	-	**4.51**	Nr
450 mm	0.39	5.94	-	**5.94**	Nr
casement fastener	0.30	4.51	-	**4.51**	Nr
quadrant stay	0.36	5.40	-	**5.40**	Nr
fanlight catch	0.30	4.51	-	**4.51**	Nr
sash fastener	0.30	4.51	-	**4.51**	Nr
sash lift	0.18	2.71	-	**2.71**	Nr
sash centre set	0.24	3.60	-	**3.60**	Nr
sash pulley	0.36	5.40	-	**5.40**	Nr
011 Sundry items:					
towel rail or roller	0.36	5.40	-	**5.40**	Nr
hat and coat hook	0.18	2.71	-	**2.71**	Nr
cabin hook and eye	0.24	3.60	-	**3.60**	Nr
padlock hasp and staple	0.36	5.40	-	**5.40**	Nr
rubber door stop	0.12	1.79	-	**1.79**	Nr
shelf bracket	0.36	5.40	-	**5.40**	Nr
curtain track	0.79	12.07	-	**12.07**	m
draught excluder	0.39	5.94	-	**5.94**	m
stair nosing	0.77	11.69	-	**11.69**	m
hanging rail	0.12	1.79	-	**1.79**	m
Extra over for:					
sockets	0.18	2.71	-	**2.71**	Nr
centre bracket	0.24	3.60	-	**3.60**	Nr
012 Fixing only ironmongery; to hardwood and the like					
013 Hinges:					
light steel butts	0.30	4.51	-	**4.51**	Pair
medium steel butts	0.32	4.86	-	**4.86**	Pair
heavy steel butts	0.36	5.40	-	**5.40**	Pair
100 mm 'Parliament' hinges	0.41	6.29	-	**6.29**	Pair
rising/falling butts:					
75 mm	2.61	39.61	-	**39.61**	Pair
100 mm	2.65	40.33	-	**40.33**	Pair
125 mm	2.96	45.01	-	**45.01**	Pair
backflap hinges	2.01	30.61	-	**30.61**	Pair
'T' hinges:					
300 mm	0.83	12.60	-	**12.60**	Pair
400 mm	1.07	16.20	-	**16.20**	Pair
500 mm	1.13	17.12	-	**17.12**	Pair
hook and band hinges:					
450 mm	1.54	23.41	-	**23.41**	Pair
600 mm	1.60	24.32	-	**24.32**	Pair
750 mm	1.78	27.01	-	**27.01**	Pair
900 mm	2.01	30.61	-	**30.61**	Pair
single action, spring hinges:					
75 mm	1.24	18.89	-	**18.89**	Pair
100 mm	1.36	20.72	-	**20.72**	Pair
double action, spring hinges:					
75 mm	2.07	31.51	-	**31.51**	Pair
100 mm	2.37	36.01	-	**36.01**	Pair
014 Floor springs:					
single action; setting box in floor (prepared mortice)	2.37	36.01	-	**36.01**	Nr
double action; setting box in floor (prepared mortice)	2.67	40.51	-	**40.51**	Nr
015 Locks, latches and furniture:					
rim latch	1.48	22.51	-	**22.51**	Nr
mortice latch	1.19	18.01	-	**18.01**	Nr
rebated mortice latch	1.19	18.01	-	**18.01**	Nr
night latch	1.78	27.01	-	**27.01**	Nr
cylinder night latch	1.78	27.01	-	**27.01**	Nr
Norfolk/Suffolk latch	1.48	22.51	-	**22.51**	Nr
thumb latch	1.19	18.01	-	**18.01**	Nr
gate latch	0.36	5.40	-	**5.40**	Nr
rim dead lock	1.19	18.01	-	**18.01**	Nr
mortice dead lock	1.30	19.81	-	**19.81**	Nr
rebated mortice dead lock	1.78	27.01	-	**27.01**	Nr
mortice cupboard lock	0.89	13.50	-	**13.50**	Nr
rebated mortice cupboard lock	1.19	18.01	-	**18.01**	Nr
cupboard catch	0.47	7.20	-	**7.20**	Nr
ball catch	0.47	7.20	-	**7.20**	Nr
lever lock/latch furniture	0.59	9.00	-	**9.00**	Set
knob lock/latch furniture	0.53	8.12	-	**8.12**	Set
escutcheons	0.24	3.60	-	**3.60**	Nr
016 Door closers:					
overhead door, single action	1.78	27.01	-	**27.01**	Nr
overhead door, double action	2.01	30.61	-	**30.61**	Nr
coil spring closer; 150 mm	0.59	9.00	-	**9.00**	NN
door selector	0.71	10.81	-	**10.81**	Nr
'Perko' closer	0.95	14.41	-	**14.41**	Nr

Unit Rates

		Man-Hours	Net Labour Price £	Net Mats Price £	Net Unit Price £	Unit
017	Bolts:					
	barrel or tower:					
	100 mm	0.47	7.20	-	7.20	Nr
	150 mm	0.59	9.00	-	9.00	Nr
	200 mm	0.71	10.81	-	10.81	Nr
	225 mm	0.83	12.60	-	12.60	Nr
	250 mm	0.95	14.41	-	14.41	Nr
	300 mm	1.07	16.20	-	16.20	Nr
	450 mm	1.19	18.01	-	18.01	Nr
	monkey tail:					
	450 mm	1.78	27.01	-	27.01	Nr
	600 mm	1.90	28.80	-	28.80	Nr
	1500 mm	2.37	36.01	-	36.01	Nr
	flush:					
	100 mm	0.95	14.41	-	14.41	Nr
	150 mm	1.19	18.01	-	18.01	Nr
	200 mm	1.42	21.60	-	21.60	Nr
	225 mm	1.66	25.20	-	25.20	Nr
	250 mm	2.13	32.41	-	32.41	Nr
	300 mm	2.37	36.01	-	36.01	Nr
	450 mm	2.61	39.61	-	39.61	Nr
	WC indicator	1.78	27.01	-	27.01	Nr
	single door, panic bolt	2.72	41.40	-	41.40	Nr
	double door, panic bolt	4.03	61.21	-	61.21	Nr
	easy clean bolt socket (mortice measured separately)	0.36	5.40	-	5.40	Nr
018	Handles and pulls:					
	cupboard knob	0.18	2.71	-	2.71	Nr
	door pull handle:					
	150 mm	0.36	5.40	-	5.40	Nr
	225 mm	0.38	5.76	-	5.76	Nr
	300 mm	0.41	6.29	-	6.29	Nr
	450 mm	0.44	6.67	-	6.67	Nr
	600 mm	0.50	7.55	-	7.55	Nr
	flush handles:					
	150 mm	0.59	9.00	-	9.00	Nr
	225 mm	0.71	10.81	-	10.81	Nr
	300 mm	0.95	14.41	-	14.41	Nr
019	Plates:					
	door push plate:					
	200 mm	0.36	5.40	-	5.40	Nr
	300 mm	0.47	7.20	-	7.20	Nr
	600 mm	0.59	9.00	-	9.00	Nr
	kicking plate:					
	450 x 225 mm	0.47	7.20	-	7.20	Nr
	600 x 225 mm	0.49	7.37	-	7.37	Nr
	750 x 225 mm	0.50	7.55	-	7.55	Nr
	900 x 225 mm	0.51	7.75	-	7.75	Nr
	letter plate including 125 mm slot	2.37	36.01	-	36.01	Nr
020	Window fittings:					
	casement stay:					
	250 mm	0.36	5.40	-	5.40	Nr
	450 mm	0.40	6.13	-	6.13	Nr
	casement fastener	0.36	5.40	-	5.40	Nr
	quadrant stay	0.38	5.76	-	5.76	Nr
	fanlight catch	0.36	5.40	-	5.40	Nr
	sash fastener	0.36	5.40	-	5.40	Nr
	sash lift	0.24	3.60	-	3.60	Nr
	sash centre set	0.26	3.97	-	3.97	Nr
	sash pulley	0.38	5.76	-	5.76	Nr
021	Sundry items:					
	towel rail or roller	0.47	7.20	-	7.20	Nr
	hat and coat hook	0.24	3.60	-	3.60	Nr
	cabin hook	0.26	3.97	-	3.97	Nr
	padlock hasp and staple	0.38	5.76	-	5.76	Nr
	rubber door stop	0.14	2.16	-	2.16	Nr
	shelf bracket	0.38	5.76	-	5.76	Nr
	curtain track	0.89	13.50	-	13.50	m
	draught excluder	0.41	6.29	-	6.29	m
	stair nosing	0.89	13.50	-	13.50	m
	hanging rail	0.18	2.71	-	2.71	m
	Extra over for:					
	sockets	0.21	3.15	-	3.15	Nr
	centre bracket	0.26	3.97	-	3.97	Nr
022	**Fixing only ironmongery**					
023	To concrete:					
	Towel rail or roller	0.47	7.20	0.09	7.29	Nr
	Hat and coat hook	0.30	4.51	0.04	4.55	Nr
	Cabin hook and eye	0.30	4.51	0.04	4.55	Nr
	Rubber door stop	0.18	2.71	0.02	2.73	Nr
	Shelf bracket	0.41	6.29	0.09	6.38	Nr
	Curtain track	1.19	18.01	0.04	18.05	m
	Stair nosing	1.19	18.01	0.04	18.05	m

Unit Rates	Man-Hours	Net Labour Price £	Net Mats Price £	Net Unit Price £	Unit
To brickwork or blockwork:					
Towel rail or roller	0.41	6.29	0.09	**6.38**	Nr
Hat and coat hook	0.24	3.60	0.04	**3.64**	Nr
Cabin hook and eye	0.26	3.97	0.04	**4.01**	Nr
Padlock, hasp and staple	0.38	5.76	0.07	**5.83**	Nr
Rubber door stop	0.14	2.16	0.02	**2.18**	Nr
Shelf bracket	0.38	5.76	0.09	**5.85**	Nr
Curtain track	0.89	13.50	0.04	**13.54**	m
Hanging rail	0.18	2.71	-	**2.71**	m
Extra over for:					
sockets	0.21	3.15	0.04	**3.19**	Nr
centre brackets	0.26	3.97	0.04	**4.01**	Nr

024   **Supplying and fixing P C Henderson Ltd, sliding door gear to softwood and hardwood**

Note: Sets normally include top tracks, bottom guides, hangers, stops, flush pulls, screws, and fixing instructions; refer to manufacturer's catalogue for full details. Hanging and adjusting doors priced separately, see section NG 001 et seq.

025   'Slipper' cupboard door gear sets for 2 doors:

	Man-Hours	Net Labour Price £	Net Mats Price £	Net Unit Price £	Unit
SS4 for 1200 mm opening	1.01	15.31	21.12	**36.43**	Nr
SS5 for 1500 mm opening	1.13	17.12	24.83	**41.95**	Nr
SS6 for 1800 mm opening	1.24	18.89	27.74	**46.63**	Nr

026   'Loretto' cupboard door gear sets for 2 doors (grooves for top track priced elsewhere):

4D for 1200 mm opening	3.08	46.82	35.77	**82.59**	Nr
5D for 1500 mm opening	3.32	50.42	39.80	**90.22**	Nr
6D for 1800 mm opening	3.55	54.02	45.00	**99.02**	Nr

027   'Single Top' wardrobe door gear sets for single doors:

ST4 for 600 mm opening	1.13	17.12	17.46	**34.58**	Nr
ST5 for 750 mm opening	1.24	18.89	19.67	**38.56**	Nr
ST6 for 900 mm opening	1.36	20.72	22.26	**42.98**	Nr

028   'Double Top' wardrobe door gear sets for bi-passing doors:

4W for 2 doors in 1200 mm opening	1.90	28.80	29.94	**58.74**	Nr
5W for 2 doors in 1500 mm opening	2.01	30.61	33.39	**64.00**	Nr
6W for 2 doors in 1800 mm opening	2.13	32.41	37.02	**69.43**	Nr
8W for 3 doors in 2400 mm opening	2.72	41.40	48.56	**89.96**	Nr

029   'Bi-Fold' wardrobe door gear sets:

B302 for 2 doors in 915 mm opening	1.42	21.60	27.54	**49.14**	Nr
B404 for 4 doors in 1220 mm opening	2.49	37.80	46.69	**84.49**	Nr
B504 for 4 doors in 1525 mm opening	2.61	39.61	51.14	**90.75**	Nr

030   Single door gear sets:
    'Marathon Junior' (groove for bottom channel included):

J2 for doors to 600 mm wide	2.49	37.80	42.90	**80.70**	Nr
J3 for doors to 750 mm wide	2.61	39.61	45.29	**84.90**	Nr
J4 for doors to 900 mm wide	2.72	41.40	49.01	**90.41**	Nr
J5 for doors to 1050 mm wide	2.84	43.21	55.39	**98.60**	Nr
'Marathon Senior' (groove for bottom channel included):					
S3 for doors to 900 mm wide	2.61	39.61	60.76	**100.37**	Nr
S6 for doors to 1200 mm wide	2.96	45.01	119.32	**164.33**	Nr
'Phantom' (groove for bottom channel included)	2.61	39.61	46.15	**85.76**	Nr
Pelmets to suit 'Marathon' and 'Phantom':					
1855 mm long	0.39	5.94	25.24	**31.18**	Nr

031   **Supplying and fixing P C Henderson Ltd's 'Straight Run' industrial sliding door gear**

032   Galvanised steel track; brackets priced separately:

290	0.30	4.51	18.87	**23.38**	m
301	0.30	4.51	25.50	**30.01**	m
301H	0.36	5.40	40.16	**45.56**	m
305	0.41	6.29	51.50	**57.79**	m

033   Galvanised steel channel with lugs; casting into concrete:

89C	0.36	5.40	17.58	**22.98**	m
97C	0.36	5.40	26.17	**31.57**	m

034   Single track support brackets, side wall pattern; fixing with loose-bolt type Rawlbolts:

1A/290, open or closed	0.47	7.20	8.92	**16.12**	Nr
1AX/290, jointing	0.47	7.20	10.67	**17.87**	Nr
1A/301, open or closed	0.53	8.12	15.38	**23.50**	Nr
1AX/301, jointing	0.53	8.12	17.56	**25.68**	Nr
1A/305, open or closed	0.59	9.00	31.55	**40.55**	Nr
1AX/305, jointing	0.59	9.00	37.10	**46.10**	Nr

035   Single track support brackets, fascia sidewall pattern; fixing with 2 Nr loose-bolt Rawlbolts:

9A/290, open	0.71	10.81	15.55	**26.36**	Nr
9/301/S, open	0.83	12.60	25.85	**38.45**	Nr
9A/305, open	0.95	14.41	49.57	**63.98**	Nr

036   Single track support brackets; fixing with 2 Nr loose-bolt Rawlbolts:
    side ear soffit pattern:

3A/290	0.71	10.81	13.02	**23.83**	Nr
3A/301	0.83	12.60	27.98	**40.58**	Nr
3A/305	0.95	14.41	54.98	**69.39**	Nr

Unit Rates	Man-Hours	Net Labour Price £	Net Mats Price £	Net Unit Price £	Unit
parallel ear soffit pattern:					
4A/290	0.71	10.81	13.02	**23.83**	Nr
4A/301	0.83	12.60	29.62	**42.22**	Nr
4A/305	0.95	14.41	54.98	**69.39**	Nr
037 Double track brackets:					
sidewall pattern; fixing with 1 Nr loose-bolt Rawlbolts:					
5/290, open	0.53	8.12	26.23	**34.35**	Nr
5/301, open	0.59	9.00	37.58	**46.58**	Nr
5/305, open	0.65	9.91	80.64	**90.55**	Nr
soffit pattern; fixing with 4 Nr loose-bolt Rawlbolts:					
6/301, open	1.42	21.60	54.34	**75.94**	Nr
038 Hangers for wood doors:					
53K/N for track 290	0.59	9.00	33.38	**42.38**	Nr
53A for track 301 and 301H	0.59	9.00	58.78	**67.78**	Nr
53C for track 305	0.59	9.00	74.78	**83.78**	Nr
039 Bottom roller guides for wood doors:					
102/97 for channel 97C	0.59	9.00	16.29	**25.29**	Nr
105R/97 for channel 97C	0.59	9.00	13.22	**22.22**	Nr
105R/89 for channel 89	0.47	7.20	12.43	**19.63**	Nr
040 Bottom guide ground stay rollers; grouting into mortices:					
126	0.36	5.40	11.50	**16.90**	Nr
126H	0.47	7.20	36.95	**44.15**	Nr
041 Accessories:					
Bow handle, 463	0.36	5.40	8.75	**14.15**	Nr
flush pull, 414	0.71	10.81	8.40	**19.21**	Nr
Surface bolt 380 mm long, 994; socket set in concrete	1.07	16.20	19.42	**35.62**	Nr
flush bolt 333	2.13	32.41	30.30	**62.71**	Nr
flush bolt 454	2.37	36.01	43.89	**79.90**	Nr
single ground or wall stop; 109.5; fixing with 2 Nr bolt projecting Rawlbolts	0.59	9.00	19.33	**28.33**	Nr

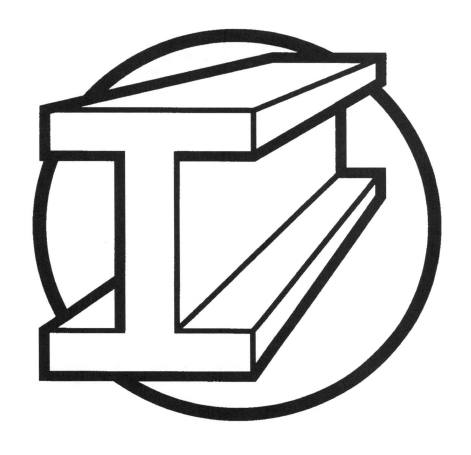

Structural Steelwork/
Mezzanine Flooring

Comprehensive Building Price Book 2013
Major and Minor Works dataset

The Major Works dataset focuses predominantly on large 'new build' projects reflecting the economies of scale found in these forms of construction. The Minor Works Estimating Dataset focuses on small to medium sized 'new build' projects reflecting the increase in costs brought about the reduced output, less discounts, increased carriage and supervision, to the similar items in the Major Works dataset. The dataset is presented in trade order. Revised and reworked items in underpinning composites; flue linings and rainwater goods.

Item code: 19215   **Price: £165.99**

SMM7 Estimating Price Book 2013

The SMM7 Estimating dataset focuses predominantly on large 'new build' projects reflecting the economies of scale found in these forms of construction. The dataset is presented in SMM7 grouping and order in accordance with the Common Arrangement of Work Sections. It is compiled using the latest independent costing information from manufacturers, material and plant suppliers, legislation effects and working rule agreements. Revised and reworked items in underpinning composites; flue linings and rainwater goods.

Item code: 19216   **Price: £139.99**

Alterations and Refurbishment Price Book 2013

The Alterations & Refurbishment dataset focuses on small to medium sized projects, generally working within an existing building and reflecting the increase in costs brought about the reduction in output, smaller discounts, increased carriage, increased supervision, and less productivity brought about by smaller economies of scale, increased production costs, more difficult access and the possibility of working in occupied premises. The dataset is presented in trade order. Revised and reworked items in underpinning composites; flue linings and rainwater goods.

Item code: 19217   **Price £109.99**

BCIS Guide to Estimating for Small Works 2012

The BCIS Guide to Estimating for Small Works 2012 is a unique dataset which shows the true power of resource based estimating. A set of composite built-up measured items are used to build up priced estimates for a large number of common specification extensions. The intention is to show estimating techniques in use and allow users to build up accurate estimates for their own projects, simply and easily, with up-to-date and independent cost information.

Item code: 19064   **Price: £59.99**

BCIS Painting and Decorating Price Book 2012

The BCIS Painting and Decorating dataset is the most handy pricing tool available to the painting and decorating sector of the industry, suitable for all projects needing more than a 'guess-timate'. Using this dataset a more accurate calculation based quotation or variation can be prepared. From these calculations an assessment of labour, plant and material content can be produced. This in turn enables the contractor to negotiate discounts on known material requirements and the effect of this workload on the availability of labour.

Item code: 19065   **Price: £39.99**

For more information call **0870 333 1600** email **contact@bcis.co.uk** or visit **www.bcis.co.uk**

BCIS is the Building Cost Information Service of  RICS | the mark of property professionalism worldwide

Labour Rates

Please note: The labour hours throughout this section are representative of the time required for one productive man to carry out the unit of work.

Gang rates are calculated as follows by obtaining the overall gang cost and then dividing this by the number of productive members in the gang. The resulting rate is the Gang Cost per **Man - hour.** By using the same principle, any size gang may be built-up and used against the standard labour hours in this section.

Unframed steelwork prices are based upon a gang rate comprising 4 labourers and craftsman, together with simple lifting tackle as follows:

A0210 Unframed steelwork:

Steelwork Labourer	4.00	x	£	11.22	=	£	44.88
Ganger/Craftsman	1.00	x	£	15.20	=	£	15.20
Block and tackle 2 tonne	1.00	x	£	1.38	=	£	1.38
Total hourly cost of gang					=	£	61.46

Gang rate (divided by 1) = £61.46 per Man-hour

Fixing bolts
  Steelfixer - £15.20 per hour

Basic Prices of Materials	Supply Price £	Waste Factor %	Unload. Labour £	Unload. Plant £	Total Unit Cost £	Unit
Basic prices for rolled steel to BS EN 10025 grade S275JR						
Prices for universal beams, universal columns, joists, channels, angles and tees have been obtained from stockholders and reflect the small quantities of steel likely to be required in the smaller refurbishment works. For works involving larger quantities, direct from the mills prices should be obtained.						
Universal Beams						
Size 914 x 419 (mm):						
P0010 388 (kg/m)	1138.00	2.5%	2.81	16.59	1186.34	tonne
P0011 343 (kg/m)	1138.00	2.5%	2.81	16.59	1186.34	tonne
Size 914 x 305 (mm):						
P0012 289 (kg/m)	1138.00	2.5%	2.81	16.59	1186.34	tonne
P0013 253 (kg/m)	1138.00	2.5%	2.81	16.59	1186.34	tonne
P0014 224 (kg/m)	1138.00	2.5%	2.81	16.59	1186.34	tonne
P0015 201 (kg/m)	1138.00	2.5%	2.81	16.59	1186.34	tonne
Size 838 x 292 (mm):						
P0016 226 (kg/m)	1128.00	2.5%	2.81	16.59	1176.09	tonne
P0017 194 (kg/m)	1128.00	2.5%	2.81	16.59	1176.09	tonne
P0018 176 (kg/m)	1128.00	2.5%	2.81	16.59	1176.09	tonne
Size 762 x 267 (mm):						
P0019 197 (kg/m)	1128.00	2.5%	2.81	16.59	1176.09	tonne
P0020 173 (kg/m)	1128.00	2.5%	2.81	16.59	1176.09	tonne
P0021 147 (kg/m)	1128.00	2.5%	2.81	16.59	1176.09	tonne
Size 686 x 254 (mm):						
P0022 170 (kg/m)	1128.00	2.5%	2.81	16.59	1176.09	tonne
P0023 152 (kg/m)	1128.00	2.5%	2.81	16.59	1176.09	tonne
P0024 140 (kg/m)	1128.00	2.5%	2.81	16.59	1176.09	tonne
P0025 125 (kg/m)	1128.00	2.5%	2.81	16.59	1176.09	tonne
Size 610 x 305 (mm):						
P0026 238 (kg/m)	1118.00	2.5%	2.81	16.59	1165.84	tonne
P0027 179 (kg/m)	1118.00	2.5%	2.81	16.59	1165.84	tonne
P0028 149 (kg/m)	1118.00	2.5%	2.81	16.59	1165.84	tonne
Size 610 x 229 (mm):						
P0029 140 (kg/m)	1096.00	2.5%	2.81	16.59	1143.29	tonne
P0030 125 (kg/m)	1096.00	2.5%	2.81	16.59	1143.29	tonne
P0031 113 (kg/m)	1096.00	2.5%	2.81	16.59	1143.29	tonne
P0032 101 (kg/m)	1096.00	2.5%	2.81	16.59	1143.29	tonne
Size 533 x 210 (mm):						
P0033 122 (kg/m)	1096.00	2.5%	2.81	16.59	1143.29	tonne
P0034 109 (kg/m)	1096.00	2.5%	2.81	16.59	1143.29	tonne
P0035 101 (kg/m)	1096.00	2.5%	2.81	16.59	1143.29	tonne
P0036 92 (kg/m)	1096.00	2.5%	2.81	16.59	1143.29	tonne
P0037 82 (kg/m)	1096.00	2.5%	2.81	16.59	1143.29	tonne
Size 457 x 191 (mm):						
P0038 98 (kg/m)	1086.00	2.5%	2.81	16.59	1133.04	tonne
P0039 89 (kg/m)	1086.00	2.5%	2.81	16.59	1133.04	tonne
P0040 82 (kg/m)	1086.00	2.5%	2.81	16.59	1133.04	tonne
P0041 74 (kg/m)	1086.00	2.5%	2.81	16.59	1133.04	tonne
P0042 67 (kg/m)	1086.00	2.5%	2.81	16.59	1133.04	tonne
Size 457 x 152 (mm):						
P0043 82 (kg/m)	1096.00	2.5%	2.81	16.59	1143.29	tonne
P0044 74 (kg/m)	1096.00	2.5%	2.81	16.59	1143.29	tonne
P0045 67 (kg/m)	1096.00	2.5%	2.81	16.59	1143.29	tonne
P0046 60 (kg/m)	1096.00	2.5%	2.81	16.59	1143.29	tonne
P0047 52 (kg/m)	1096.00	2.5%	2.81	16.59	1143.29	tonne
Size 406 x 178 (mm):						
P0048 74 (kg/m)	1096.00	2.5%	2.81	16.59	1143.29	tonne
P0049 67 (kg/m)	1096.00	2.5%	2.81	16.59	1143.29	tonne
P0050 60 (kg/m)	1096.00	2.5%	2.81	16.59	1143.29	tonne
P0051 54 (kg/m)	1096.00	2.5%	2.81	16.59	1143.29	tonne

Basic Prices of Materials

		Supply Price £	Waste Factor %	Unload. Labour £	Unload. Plant £	Total Unit Cost £	Unit
	Size 406 x 140 (mm):						
P0052	46 (kg/m)	1096.00	2.5%	2.81	16.59	1143.29	tonne
P0053	39 (kg/m)	1096.00	2.5%	2.81	16.59	1143.29	tonne
	Size 356 x 171 (mm):						
P0054	67 (kg/m)	1096.00	2.5%	2.81	16.59	1143.29	tonne
P0055	57 (kg/m)	1096.00	2.5%	2.81	16.59	1143.29	tonne
P0056	51 (kg/m)	1096.00	2.5%	2.81	16.59	1143.29	tonne
P0057	45 (kg/m)	1096.00	2.5%	2.81	16.59	1143.29	tonne
	Size 356 x 127 (mm):						
P0058	39 (kg/m)	1096.00	2.5%	2.81	16.59	1143.29	tonne
P0059	33 (kg/m)	1096.00	2.5%	2.81	16.59	1143.29	tonne
	Size 305 x 165 (mm):						
P0060	54 (kg/m)	1086.00	2.5%	2.81	16.59	1133.04	tonne
P0061	46 (kg/m)	1086.00	2.5%	2.81	16.59	1133.04	tonne
P0062	40 (kg/m)	1086.00	2.5%	2.81	16.59	1133.04	tonne
	Size 305 x 127 (mm):						
P0063	48 (kg/m)	1086.00	2.5%	2.81	16.59	1133.04	tonne
P0064	42 (kg/m)	1086.00	2.5%	2.81	16.59	1133.04	tonne
P0065	37 (kg/m)	1086.00	2.5%	2.81	16.59	1133.04	tonne
	Size 305 x 102 (mm):						
P0066	33 (kg/m)	1086.00	2.5%	2.81	16.59	1133.04	tonne
P0067	28 (kg/m)	1086.00	2.5%	2.81	16.59	1133.04	tonne
P0068	25 (kg/m)	1086.00	2.5%	2.81	16.59	1133.04	tonne
	Size 254 x 146 (mm):						
P0069	43 (kg/m)	1096.00	2.5%	2.81	16.59	1143.29	tonne
P0070	37 (kg/m)	1096.00	2.5%	2.81	16.59	1143.29	tonne
P0071	31 (kg/m)	1096.00	2.5%	2.81	16.59	1143.29	tonne
	Size 254 x 102 (mm):						
P0072	28 (kg/m)	1096.00	2.5%	2.81	16.59	1143.29	tonne
P0073	25 (kg/m)	1096.00	2.5%	2.81	16.59	1143.29	tonne
P0074	22 (kg/m)	1096.00	2.5%	2.81	16.59	1143.29	tonne
	Size 203 x 133 (mm):						
P0075	30 (kg/m)	1096.00	2.5%	2.81	16.59	1143.29	tonne
P0076	25 (kg/m)	1096.00	2.5%	2.81	16.59	1143.29	tonne
	Universal columns						
	Size 356 x 406 (mm):						
P0077	634 (kg/m)	1154.00	2.5%	2.81	16.59	1202.74	tonne
P0078	551 (kg/m)	1154.00	2.5%	2.81	16.59	1202.74	tonne
P0079	467 (kg/m)	1154.00	2.5%	2.81	16.59	1202.74	tonne
P0080	393 (kg/m)	1144.00	2.5%	2.81	16.59	1192.49	tonne
P0081	340 (kg/m)	1144.00	2.5%	2.81	16.59	1192.49	tonne
P0082	287 (kg/m)	1144.00	2.5%	2.81	16.59	1192.49	tonne
P0083	235 (kg/m)	1144.00	2.5%	2.81	16.59	1192.49	tonne
	Size 356 x 368 (mm):						
P0084	202 (kg/m)	1144.00	2.5%	2.81	16.59	1192.49	tonne
P0085	177 (kg/m)	1144.00	2.5%	2.81	16.59	1192.49	tonne
P0086	153 (kg/m)	1144.00	2.5%	2.81	16.59	1192.49	tonne
P0087	129 (kg/m)	1144.00	2.5%	2.81	16.59	1192.49	tonne
	Size 305 x 305 (mm):						
P0088	283 (kg/m)	1096.00	2.5%	2.81	16.59	1143.29	tonne
P0089	240 (kg/m)	1096.00	2.5%	2.81	16.59	1143.29	tonne
P0090	198 (kg/m)	1096.00	2.5%	2.81	16.59	1143.29	tonne
	Size 305 x 305 (mm):						
P0091	158 (kg/m)	1096.00	2.5%	2.81	16.59	1143.29	tonne
P0092	137 (kg/m)	1096.00	2.5%	2.81	16.59	1143.29	tonne
P0093	118 (kg/m)	1096.00	2.5%	2.81	16.59	1143.29	tonne
P0094	97 (kg/m)	1096.00	2.5%	2.81	16.59	1143.29	tonne
	Size 254 x 254 (mm):						
P0095	167 (kg/m)	1086.00	2.5%	2.81	16.59	1133.04	tonne
P0096	132 (kg/m)	1086.00	2.5%	2.81	16.59	1133.04	tonne
P0097	107 (kg/m)	1086.00	2.5%	2.81	16.59	1133.04	tonne
P0098	89 (kg/m)	1086.00	2.5%	2.81	16.59	1133.04	tonne
P0099	73 (kg/m)	1086.00	2.5%	2.81	16.59	1133.04	tonne
	Size 203 x 203 (mm):						
P0100	86 (kg/m)	1086.00	2.5%	2.81	16.59	1133.04	tonne
P0101	71 (kg/m)	1086.00	2.5%	2.81	16.59	1133.04	tonne
P0102	60 (kg/m)	1086.00	2.5%	2.81	16.59	1133.04	tonne
P0103	52 (kg/m)	1086.00	2.5%	2.81	16.59	1133.04	tonne
P0104	46 (kg/m)	1086.00	2.5%	2.81	16.59	1133.04	tonne
	Size 152 x 152 (mm):						
P0105	37 (kg/m)	1076.00	2.5%	2.81	16.59	1122.79	tonne
P0106	30 (kg/m)	1076.00	2.5%	2.81	16.59	1122.79	tonne
P0107	23 (kg/m)	1076.00	2.5%	2.81	16.59	1122.79	tonne
	Joists						
P0108	254 x 203 (mm) 81.85 (kg/m)	1250.00	2.5%	2.81	16.59	1301.14	tonne
P0109	254 x 114 (mm) 37.20 (kg/m)	1250.00	2.5%	2.81	16.59	1301.14	tonne
P0110	203 x 152 (mm) 52.09 (kg/m)	1250.00	2.5%	2.81	16.59	1301.14	tonne
P0111	203 x 102 (mm) 25.33 (kg/m)	1250.00	2.5%	2.81	16.59	1301.14	tonne
P0113	152 x 127 (mm) 37.20 (kg/m)	1250.00	2.5%	2.81	16.59	1301.14	tonne
P0114	152 x 89 (mm) 17.09 (kg/m)	1250.00	2.5%	2.81	16.59	1301.14	tonne
P0116	127 x 114 (mm) 29.76 (kg/m)	1250.00	2.5%	2.81	16.59	1301.14	tonne
P0117	127 x 114 (mm) 26.79 (kg/m)	1250.00	2.5%	2.81	16.59	1301.14	tonne
P0118	127 x 76 (mm) 16.37 (kg/m)	1250.00	2.5%	2.81	16.59	1301.14	tonne
P0120	114 x 114 (mm) 26.79 (kg/m)	1250.00	2.5%	2.81	16.59	1301.14	tonne
P0121	102 x 102 (mm) 23.06 (kg/m)	1250.00	2.5%	2.81	16.59	1301.14	tonne
P0122	89 x 89 (mm) 19.35 (kg/m)	1250.00	2.5%	2.81	16.59	1301.14	tonne

Basic Prices of Materials

		Supply Price £	Waste Factor %	Unload. Labour £	Unload. Plant £	Total Unit Cost £	Unit
P0123	76 x 76 (mm) 12.65 (kg/m)	1250.00	2.5%	2.81	16.59	**1301.14**	tonne
	Channels						
P0124	430 x 100 (mm) 64.40 (kg/m)	1341.00	2.5%	2.81	15.92	**1393.72**	tonne
P0125	380 x 100 (mm) 54.00 (kg/m)	1203.00	2.5%	2.81	16.59	**1252.96**	tonne
P0126	300 x 100 (mm) 45.50 (kg/m)	1171.00	2.5%	2.81	16.59	**1220.16**	tonne
P0127	300 x 90 (mm) 41.40 (kg/m)	1171.00	2.5%	2.81	16.59	**1220.16**	tonne
P0128	260 x 90 (mm) 34.80 (kg/m)	1171.00	2.5%	2.81	16.59	**1220.16**	tonne
P0129	260 x 75 (mm) 27.60 (kg/m)	1171.00	2.5%	2.81	16.59	**1220.16**	tonne
P0130	230 x 90 (mm) 32.20 (kg/m)	1171.00	2.5%	2.81	16.59	**1220.16**	tonne
P0131	230 x 75 (mm) 25.70 (kg/m)	1171.00	2.5%	2.81	16.59	**1220.16**	tonne
P0132	200 x 90 (mm) 29.70 (kg/m)	1096.00	2.5%	2.81	16.59	**1143.29**	tonne
P0133	200 x 75 (mm) 23.40 (kg/m)	1060.00	2.5%	2.81	16.59	**1106.39**	tonne
P0134	180 x 90 (mm) 26.10 (kg/m)	1096.00	2.5%	2.81	16.59	**1143.29**	tonne
P0135	180 x 75 (mm) 20.30 (kg/m)	1060.00	2.5%	2.81	16.59	**1106.39**	tonne
P0136	150 x 90 (mm) 23.90 (kg/m)	1096.00	2.5%	2.81	16.59	**1143.29**	tonne
P0137	150 x 75 (mm) 17.90 (kg/m)	1060.00	2.5%	2.81	16.59	**1106.39**	tonne
P0138	125 x 65 (mm) 14.80 (kg/m)	1060.00	2.5%	2.81	16.59	**1106.39**	tonne
P0139	100 x 50 (mm) 10.20 (kg/m)	1060.00	2.5%	2.81	16.59	**1106.39**	tonne
P0140	75 x 50 (mm) 9.30 (kg/m)	880.09	2.5%	2.81	16.59	**921.98**	tonne
P0141	75 x 35 (mm) 6.60 (kg/m)	880.09	2.5%	2.81	16.59	**921.98**	tonne
P0143	50 x 35 (mm) 5.70 (kg/m)	880.09	2.5%	2.81	16.59	**921.98**	tonne
P0144	50 x 25 (mm) 4.50 (kg/m)	880.09	2.5%	2.81	16.59	**921.98**	tonne
	Equal Angles						
	Size 200 x 200 (mm); Thickness:						
P0146	16 (mm)	1138.00	2.5%	2.81	16.59	**1186.34**	tonne
P0147	18 (mm)	1138.00	2.5%	2.81	16.59	**1186.34**	tonne
P0148	20 (mm)	1138.00	2.5%	2.81	16.59	**1186.34**	tonne
P0149	24 (mm)	1138.00	2.5%	2.81	16.59	**1186.34**	tonne
	Size 150 x 150 (mm); Thickness:						
P0150	10 (mm)	1054.00	2.5%	2.81	16.59	**1100.24**	tonne
P0151	12 (mm)	1054.00	2.5%	2.81	16.59	**1100.24**	tonne
P0152	15 (mm)	1054.00	2.5%	2.81	16.59	**1100.24**	tonne
P0153	18 (mm)	1054.00	2.5%	2.81	16.59	**1100.24**	tonne
	Size 120 x 120 (mm); Thickness:						
P0154	8 (mm)	1044.00	2.5%	2.81	16.59	**1089.99**	tonne
P0155	10 (mm)	1044.00	2.5%	2.81	16.59	**1089.99**	tonne
P0156	12 (mm)	1044.00	2.5%	2.81	16.59	**1089.99**	tonne
P0157	15 (mm)	1044.00	2.5%	2.81	16.59	**1089.99**	tonne
	Size 100 x 100 (mm); Thickness:						
P0158	8 (mm)	1034.00	2.5%	2.81	16.59	**1079.74**	tonne
P0159	10 (mm)	1034.00	2.5%	2.81	16.59	**1079.74**	tonne
P0160	12 (mm)	1034.00	2.5%	2.81	16.59	**1079.74**	tonne
P0161	15 (mm)	1034.00	2.5%	2.81	16.59	**1079.74**	tonne
	Size 90 x 90 (mm); Thickness:						
P0162	6 (mm)	1034.00	2.5%	2.81	16.59	**1079.74**	tonne
P0163	8 (mm)	1034.00	2.5%	2.81	16.59	**1079.74**	tonne
P0164	10 (mm)	1034.00	2.5%	2.81	16.59	**1079.74**	tonne
P0165	12 (mm)	1034.00	2.5%	2.81	16.59	**1079.74**	tonne
	Size 80 x 80 (mm); Thickness:						
P0166	6 (mm)	825.82	2.5%	2.81	16.59	**866.36**	tonne
P0167	8 (mm)	825.82	2.5%	2.81	16.59	**866.36**	tonne
P0168	10 (mm)	825.82	2.5%	2.81	16.59	**866.36**	tonne
	Size 70 x 70 (mm); Thickness:						
P0169	6 (mm)	825.82	2.5%	2.81	16.59	**866.36**	tonne
P0170	8 (mm)	825.82	2.5%	2.81	16.59	**866.36**	tonne
P0171	10 (mm)	825.82	2.5%	2.81	16.59	**866.36**	tonne
	Size 60 x 60 (mm); Thickness:						
P0172	5 (mm)	825.82	2.5%	2.81	16.59	**866.36**	tonne
P0173	6 (mm)	825.82	2.5%	2.81	16.59	**866.36**	tonne
P0174	8 (mm)	825.82	2.5%	2.81	16.59	**866.36**	tonne
P0175	10 (mm)	825.82	2.5%	2.81	16.59	**866.36**	tonne
	Size 50 x 50 (mm); Thickness:						
P0176	5 (mm)	825.82	2.5%	2.81	16.59	**866.36**	tonne
P0177	6 (mm)	825.82	2.5%	2.81	16.59	**866.36**	tonne
P0178	8 (mm)	825.82	2.5%	2.81	16.59	**866.36**	tonne
	Size 45 x 45 (mm); Thickness:						
P0179	4 (mm)	825.82	2.5%	2.81	16.59	**866.36**	tonne
P0180	5 (mm)	825.82	2.5%	2.81	16.59	**866.36**	tonne
P0181	6 (mm)	825.82	2.5%	2.81	16.59	**866.36**	tonne
	Size 40 x 40 (mm); Thickness:						
P0182	5 (mm)	825.82	2.5%	2.81	16.59	**866.36**	tonne
P0183	6 (mm)	825.82	2.5%	2.81	16.59	**866.36**	tonne
	Size 30 x 30 (mm); Thickness:						
P0185	5 (mm)	825.82	2.5%	2.81	16.59	**866.36**	tonne
P0186	6 (mm)	825.82	2.5%	2.81	16.59	**866.36**	tonne
	Unequal Angles						
	Size 200 x 150 (mm); Thickness:						
P0187	12 (mm)	1563.00	2.5%	2.81	16.59	**1621.96**	tonne
P0188	15 (mm)	1563.00	2.5%	2.81	16.59	**1621.96**	tonne
P0189	18 (mm)	1563.00	2.5%	2.81	16.59	**1621.96**	tonne
	Size 200 x 100 (mm); Thickness:						
P0190	10 (mm)	1138.00	2.5%	2.81	16.59	**1186.34**	tonne
P0191	12 (mm)	1138.00	2.5%	2.81	16.59	**1186.34**	tonne
P0192	15 (mm)	1138.00	2.5%	2.81	16.59	**1186.34**	tonne

Basic Prices of Materials		Supply Price £	Waste Factor %	Unload. Labour £	Unload. Plant £	Total Unit Cost £	Unit
	Size 150 x 90 (mm); Thickness:						
P0193	10 (mm)	1096.00	2.5%	2.81	16.59	1143.29	tonne
P0194	12 (mm)	1096.00	2.5%	2.81	16.59	1143.29	tonne
P0195	15 (mm)	1096.00	2.5%	2.81	16.59	1143.29	tonne
	Size 150 x 75 (mm); Thickness:						
P0196	10 (mm)	1060.00	2.5%	2.81	16.59	1106.39	tonne
P0197	12 (mm)	1060.00	2.5%	2.81	16.59	1106.39	tonne
P0198	15 (mm)	1060.00	2.5%	2.81	16.59	1106.39	tonne
	Size 125 x 75 (mm); Thickness:						
P0199	8 (mm)	1060.00	2.5%	2.81	16.59	1106.39	tonne
P0200	10 (mm)	1060.00	2.5%	2.81	16.59	1106.39	tonne
P0201	12 (mm)	1060.00	2.5%	2.81	16.59	1106.39	tonne
	Size 100 x 75 (mm); Thickness:						
P0202	8 (mm)	1060.00	2.5%	2.81	16.59	1106.39	tonne
P0203	10 (mm)	1060.00	2.5%	2.81	16.59	1106.39	tonne
P0204	12 (mm)	1060.00	2.5%	2.81	16.59	1106.39	tonne
	Size 100 x 65 (mm); Thickness:						
P0205	7 (mm)	1060.00	2.5%	2.81	16.59	1106.39	tonne
P0206	8 (mm)	1060.00	2.5%	2.81	16.59	1106.39	tonne
P0207	10 (mm)	1060.00	2.5%	2.81	16.59	1106.39	tonne
	Size 80 x 60 (mm); Thickness:						
P0208	6 (mm)	825.82	2.5%	2.81	16.59	866.36	tonne
P0209	7 (mm)	825.82	2.5%	2.81	16.59	866.36	tonne
P0210	8 (mm)	825.82	2.5%	2.81	16.59	866.36	tonne
	Size 75 x 50 (mm); Thickness:						
P0211	6 (mm)	825.82	2.5%	2.81	16.59	866.36	tonne
P0212	8 (mm)	825.82	2.5%	2.81	16.59	866.36	tonne
	Size 65 x 50 (mm); Thickness:						
P0213	5 (mm)	825.82	2.5%	2.81	16.59	866.36	tonne
P0214	6 (mm)	825.82	2.5%	2.81	16.59	866.36	tonne
P0215	8 (mm)	825.82	2.5%	2.81	16.59	866.36	tonne
	Size 60 x 30 (mm); Thickness:						
P0216	5 (mm)	825.82	2.5%	2.81	16.59	866.36	tonne
P0217	6 (mm)	825.82	2.5%	2.81	16.59	866.36	tonne
	Size 50 x 40 (mm); Thickness:						
P0218	5 (mm)	825.82	2.5%	2.81	16.59	866.36	tonne
P0219	6 (mm)	825.82	2.5%	2.81	16.59	866.36	tonne
	Tees						
	Size 51 x 51 (mm); Thickness:						
P0220	6 (mm)	1761.08	2.5%	2.81	16.59	1825.00	tonne
	Extra over basic prices for stockholders margins or small quantities:						
P0227	Up to 5 kg	594.59	-	-	-	594.59	tonne
P0228	5 - 25 kg	495.50	-	-	-	495.50	tonne
P0229	25 - 50 kg	495.50	-	-	-	495.50	tonne
P0230	50 - 100 kg	297.30	-	-	-	297.30	tonne
P0231	Over 100 kg	297.30	-	-	-	297.30	tonne
P0240	**Extra over** for shot blasting and priming steel sections (average mix) before delivery	120.00	-	-	-	120.00	tonne
	Metsec joists with end fixing						
	Guide prices provided by Metal Sections Limited for supply and delivery to site:						
P0278	B30 Metsec with end fixing	32.29	-	0.24	0.56	33.09	m
P0279	B35 Metsec with end fixing	33.83	-	0.25	0.59	34.67	m
P0280	D35 Metsec with end fixing	44.59	-	0.29	0.70	45.58	m
	Extra over for timber inserts:						
P0282	B and D Types (per chord)	4.25	-	-	-	4.25	m
P0232	M12 x 160 mm indented bolts	0.76	5%	-	-	0.79	nr
P0233	M16 x 140 mm indented bolts	0.71	5%	-	-	0.75	nr

Unit Rates	Man-Hours	Net Labour Price £	Net Mats Price £	Net Unit Price £	Unit
UNIT RATES					
PA UNFABRICATED STEELWORK					
001 **Weldable structural steel to BS EN 10025 in beams, in single members cut to length, primed with one coat of red oxide primer at works; ends built into structure**					
002 Universal beams:					
fixing at ground level:					
457 x 191 mm 82 Kg/m	2.27	139.27	1430.33	**1569.60**	tonne
406 x 178 mm 60 Kg/m	2.27	139.27	1440.58	**1579.85**	tonne
356 x 171 mm 51 Kg/m	2.27	139.27	1440.58	**1579.85**	tonne
305 x 165 mm 46 Kg/m	2.83	174.12	1628.53	**1802.65**	tonne
254 x 146 mm 37 Kg/m	2.83	174.12	1638.78	**1812.90**	tonne
fixing at 3 m above ground level:					
457 x 191 mm 82 Kg/m	2.83	174.12	1430.33	**1604.45**	tonne
406 x 178 mm 60 Kg/m	2.83	174.12	1440.58	**1614.70**	tonne
356 x 171 mm 51 Kg/m	2.83	174.12	1440.58	**1614.70**	tonne
305 x 165 mm 46 Kg/m	3.40	208.90	1628.53	**1837.43**	tonne
254 x 146 mm 37 Kg/m	3.40	208.90	1638.78	**1847.68**	tonne
003 Joists:					
fixing at ground level:					
254 x 114 mm 37.20 Kg/m	2.83	174.12	1796.63	**1970.75**	tonne
203 x 102 mm 25.33 Kg/m	2.83	174.12	1796.63	**1970.75**	tonne
fixing at 3 m above ground level:					
254 x 114 mm 37.20 Kg/m	3.40	208.90	1796.63	**2005.53**	tonne
203 x 102 mm 25.33 Kg/m	3.40	208.90	1796.63	**2005.53**	tonne
004 Channels:					
fixing at ground level:					
260 x 75 mm 27.6 Kg/m	2.83	174.12	1715.66	**1889.78**	tonne
200 x 90 mm 29.7 Kg/m	2.83	174.12	1638.78	**1812.90**	tonne
180 x 90 mm 26.1 Kg/m	2.83	174.12	1638.78	**1812.90**	tonne
150 x 75 mm 17.9 Kg/m	3.97	243.75	1601.88	**1845.63**	tonne
100 x 50 mm 10.2 Kg/m	3.97	243.75	1601.88	**1845.63**	tonne
fixing at 3 m above ground level:					
260 x 75 mm 27.6 Kg/m	3.40	208.90	1715.66	**1924.56**	tonne
200 x 90 mm 29.7 Kg/m	3.40	208.90	1638.78	**1847.68**	tonne
180 x 90 mm 26.1 Kg/m	3.40	208.90	1638.78	**1847.68**	tonne
150 x 75 mm 17.9 Kg/m	4.53	278.54	1601.88	**1880.42**	tonne
100 x 50 mm 10.2 Kg/m	4.53	278.54	1601.88	**1880.42**	tonne
005 Unequal angles:					
fixing at ground level:					
200 x 150 mm 15 mm thick	2.83	174.12	2117.46	**2291.58**	tonne
150 x 90 mm 10 mm thick	3.97	243.75	1638.78	**1882.53**	tonne
125 x 75 mm 8 mm thick	3.97	243.75	1601.88	**1845.63**	tonne
100 x 65 mm 7 mm thick	4.53	278.54	1601.88	**1880.42**	tonne
75 x 50 mm 6 mm thick	4.53	278.54	1361.85	**1640.39**	tonne
fixing at 3 m above ground level:					
200 x 150 mm 15 mm thick	3.40	208.90	2117.46	**2326.36**	tonne
150 x 90 mm 10 mm thick	4.53	278.54	1638.78	**1917.32**	tonne
125 x 75 mm 8 mm thick	4.53	278.54	1601.88	**1880.42**	tonne
100 x 65 mm 7 mm thick	5.10	313.38	1601.88	**1915.26**	tonne
75 x 50 mm 6 mm thick	5.10	313.38	1361.85	**1675.23**	tonne
006 **Metsec steel joists with end fixings, in single members, primed with one coat of red oxide primer at, works; ends built into structure**					
007 Fixing at 3 m above ground level:					
NBS30 10.3 Kg/m	0.05	2.77	33.09	**35.86**	m
NBS35 11.2 Kg/m	0.06	3.50	34.67	**38.17**	m
D35 12.8 Kg/m	0.06	3.50	45.58	**49.08**	m

HOW LONG? HOW MUCH?

THE FASTEST, MOST UP-TO-DATE ANSWERS ARE AVAILABLE NOW

Cost information underpins every aspect of the built environment, from construction and rebuilding to maintenance and operation publications.

BCIS, the RICS' Building Cost Information Service, is the leading provider of cost information to the construction industry and anyone else who needs comprehensive, accurate and independent data.

For the past 50 years, BCIS has been collecting, collating, analysing, modelling and interpreting cost information.Today, BCIS make that information easily accessible through online applications, data licensing and publications.

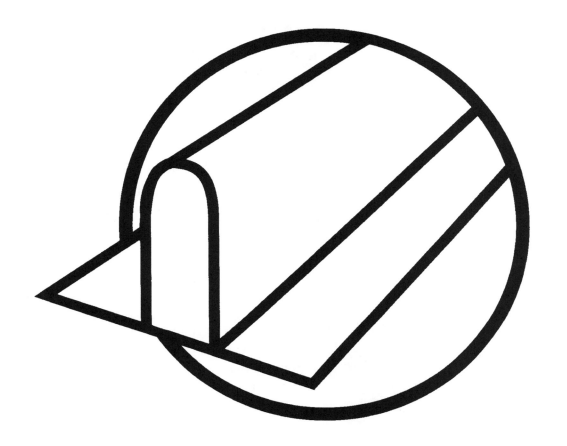

Metalwork

Diploma in Adjudication in the Construction Industry

Comprised of four units, this qualification is designed for those **seeking to become an adjudicator**, and provides a pathway towards potential entry onto the **RICS Panel of Adjudicators**.

With a focus on contract and tort law and how they apply to adjudication, this course is designed to prepare you to progress to practice as an adjudicator. This course is suitable for those with experience in dispute resolution procedures with an understanding of the general principles of construction adjudication. The course content will focus on the format and content of an enforceable decision.

Learning Outcomes:

- Knowledge and understanding of the nature of law and its' place in society
- How the law of contract is applied to the practice of adjudication
- How the law of tort is applied to the practice of adjudication
- The practical application in the production of an enforceable decision.

Attainment of the learning outcomes will be assessed by a case study, whereby candidates will be required to produce an enforceable reasoned decision, based on material supplied in the case study.

Labour Rates

Please note: The labour hours throughout this section are representative of the time required for one productive man to carry out the unit of work.

Gang rates are calculated as follows by obtaining the overall gang cost and then dividing this by the number of productive members in the gang. The resulting rate is the Gang Cost per **Man - hour**. By using the same principle, any size gang may be built-up and used against the standard labour hours in this section.

A0204 Fixing arch bars, lintels and the like:

Brick/Block Layer	2.00	x	£	15.20	= £	30.40
Brick/Blockwork Labourer	1.00	x	£	11.22	= £	11.22
Total hourly cost of gang					= £	41.62

Gang rate (divided by 2) = £20.81 per Man-hour

Fixing steel and aluminium windows to timber surrounds
Craftsman (BATJIC Craft Rate) - £15.20 per hour

	Basic Prices of Materials	Supply Price £	Waste Factor %	Unload. Labour £	Unload. Plant £	Total Unit Cost £	Unit
	Prices for 'labour unloading' include for distributing materials around the site to locations adjacent to positions where the items are fixed.						
	Plain steel sections:						
	flats:						
Q0001	25 x 10 mm	1.75	5%	0.02	-	**1.86**	m
Q0002	50 x 10 mm	3.36	5%	0.04	-	**3.57**	m
Q0003	80 x 10 mm	5.44	5%	0.07	-	**5.78**	m
Q0004	100 x 10 mm	6.80	5%	0.09	-	**7.24**	m
	equal angles:						
Q0005	50 x 50 x 6 mm	4.02	5%	0.07	-	**4.29**	m
Q0006	80 x 80 x 8 mm	9.07	5%	0.11	-	**9.64**	m
Q0007	100 x 100 x 8 mm	10.13	5%	0.13	-	**10.78**	m
Q0008	150 x 150 x 10 mm	22.84	5%	0.26	-	**24.25**	m
	unequal angles:						
Q0009	125 x 75 x 8 mm	10.63	5%	0.19	-	**11.36**	m
Q0010	150 x 75 x 10 mm	16.63	5%	0.22	-	**17.70**	m
Q0011	200 x 100 x 10 mm	23.79	5%	0.26	-	**25.25**	m
	Metric black hexagon bolts and nuts, BS 4190 (add 20% for BZP):						
Q0012	M6 x 50 mm	0.09	2.5%	-	-	**0.09**	nr
Q0013	M6 x 100 mm	0.17	2.5%	-	-	**0.18**	nr
Q0014	M8 x 50 mm	0.14	2.5%	-	-	**0.15**	nr
Q0015	M10 x 50 mm	0.23	2.5%	-	-	**0.24**	nr
Q0016	M10 x 100 mm	0.39	2.5%	-	-	**0.40**	nr
Q0017	M12 x 75 mm	0.43	2.5%	-	-	**0.44**	nr
Q0018	M12 x 130 mm	0.63	2.5%	-	-	**0.65**	nr
Q0019	M16 x 50 mm	0.60	2.5%	-	-	**0.61**	nr
Q0020	M16 x 80 mm	0.76	2.5%	-	-	**0.78**	nr
	Rawlbolts, bolt projecting type; corrosion resisting; reference:						
Q0030	M6 25P	0.81	2.5%	-	-	**0.83**	nr
Q0031	M6 60P	0.82	2.5%	-	-	**0.84**	nr
Q0032	M8 25P	0.96	2.5%	-	-	**0.98**	nr
Q0033	M8 60P	1.04	2.5%	-	-	**1.07**	nr
Q0034	M10 30P	1.14	2.5%	-	-	**1.17**	nr
Q0035	M10 60P	1.11	2.5%	-	-	**1.14**	nr
Q0036	M12 30P	1.86	2.5%	-	-	**1.91**	nr
Q0037	M12 75P	2.30	2.5%	-	-	**2.36**	nr
Q0038	M16 35P	4.26	2.5%	-	-	**4.37**	nr
	Rawlbolts, loose bolt type; corrosion resisting; reference:						
Q0041	M6 25L	0.76	2.5%	-	-	**0.77**	nr
Q0042	M6 40L	0.89	2.5%	-	-	**0.91**	nr
Q0043	M8 25L	0.96	2.5%	-	-	**0.98**	nr
Q0044	M8 40L	1.03	2.5%	-	-	**1.05**	nr
Q0045	M10 25L	1.14	2.5%	-	-	**1.17**	nr
Q0046	M10 75L	1.26	2.5%	-	-	**1.29**	nr
Q0047	M12 25L	2.07	2.5%	-	-	**2.12**	nr
Q0048	M16 30L	4.36	2.5%	-	-	**4.47**	nr
	Steel lintels by Catnic Limited, delivered to site:						
	Type CG50/100; 243 mm wide; suitable for use in external walls having a 50 - 65 mm wide cavity and 100 mm inner skin:						
	length:						
Q0121	750 mm	25.25	-	0.04	-	**25.29**	nr
Q0122	900 mm	30.31	-	0.07	-	**30.38**	nr
Q0123	1200 mm	39.28	-	0.10	-	**39.38**	nr
Q0124	1500 mm	50.77	-	0.13	-	**50.90**	nr
Q0125	1800 mm	63.10	-	0.19	-	**63.29**	nr
Q0126	2100 mm	72.45	-	0.26	-	**72.71**	nr
Q0127	2400 mm	88.81	-	0.30	-	**89.11**	nr
Q0128	2700 mm	100.80	-	0.43	-	**101.23**	nr
Q0129	3000 mm	139.56	-	0.47	-	**140.03**	nr
Q0130	3300 mm	155.79	-	0.57	-	**156.36**	nr
Q0131	3600 mm	170.95	-	0.63	-	**171.58**	nr
Q0132	3900 mm	272.95	-	0.74	-	**273.69**	nr

Basic Prices of Materials	Supply Price £	Waste Factor %	Unload. Labour £	Unload. Plant £	Total Unit Cost £	Unit
Type CX50/100; 243 mm wide; suitable for use in external walls having a 50 - 65 mm wide cavity and 100 mm inner skin:						
length:						
Q0181 2400 mm	139.51	-	0.53	-	140.04	nr
Q0182 2700 mm	163.50	-	0.58	-	164.08	nr
Q0183 3000 mm	189.02	-	0.65	-	189.67	nr
Q0184 3300 mm	217.73	-	0.72	-	218.45	nr
Q0185 3600 mm	237.09	-	0.79	-	237.88	nr
Q0186 3900 mm	272.95	-	0.85	-	273.80	nr
Q0133 4200 mm	302.98	-	0.80	-	303.78	nr
Q0134 4575 mm	339.77	-	0.98	-	340.75	nr
Q0135 4800 mm	356.09	-	1.04	-	357.13	nr
Type CG50/125; 263 mm wide; suitable for use in external walls having a 50 mm wide cavity and 140 mm inner skin:						
length:						
Q0141 750 mm	24.49	-	0.09	-	24.58	nr
Q0142 900 mm	29.40	-	0.15	-	29.55	nr
Q0143 1200 mm	39.22	-	0.19	-	39.41	nr
Q0144 1500 mm	50.40	-	0.24	-	50.64	nr
Q0145 1800 mm	62.60	-	0.28	-	62.88	nr
Q0146 2100 mm	72.27	-	0.34	-	72.61	nr
Q0147 2400 mm	88.11	-	0.45	-	88.56	nr
Q0148 2700 mm	100.80	-	0.50	-	101.30	nr
Q0149 3000 mm	139.24	-	0.56	-	139.80	nr
Type CX50/125; 263 mm wide; suitable for use in external walls having a 50 mm wide cavity and 140 mm inner skin:						
length:						
Q0150 3300 mm	268.45	-	0.62	-	269.07	nr
Q0151 3600 mm	292.85	-	0.67	-	293.52	nr
Type CG70/100; 263 mm wide; suitable for use in external walls having a 70 - 85 mm wide cavity:						
length:						
Q0101 750 mm	24.62	-	0.07	-	24.69	nr
Q0102 900 mm	29.40	-	0.10	-	29.50	nr
Q0103 1200 mm	39.22	-	0.12	-	39.34	nr
Q0104 1500 mm	49.00	-	0.16	-	49.16	nr
Q0105 1800 mm	61.33	-	0.19	-	61.52	nr
Q0106 2100 mm	70.14	-	0.26	-	70.40	nr
Q0107 2400 mm	83.16	-	0.38	-	83.54	nr
Q0108 2700 mm	95.97	-	0.43	-	96.40	nr
Q0109 3000 mm	136.58	-	0.47	-	137.05	nr
Q0110 3300 mm	151.56	-	0.57	-	152.13	nr
Q0111 3600 mm	165.30	-	0.63	-	165.93	nr
Q0112 3900 mm	179.08	-	0.74	-	179.82	nr
Type CH70/100; 263 mm wide; suitable for use in external walls having a 70 - 85 mm wide cavity and 100 mm inner skin; heavy duty loading:						
length:						
Q0162 900 mm	34.51	-	0.15	-	34.66	nr
Q0163 1200 mm	45.91	-	0.19	-	46.10	nr
Q0164 1500 mm	65.84	-	0.24	-	66.08	nr
Q0165 1800 mm	86.70	-	0.28	-	86.98	nr
Q0166 2100 mm	108.73	-	0.34	-	109.07	nr
Q0167 2400 mm	135.31	-	0.45	-	135.76	nr
Type CX70/100; 263 mm wide; suitable for use in external walls having a 70 - 85 mm wide cavity:						
length:						
Q0168 2700 mm	177.56	-	0.50	-	178.06	nr
Q0169 3000 mm	197.44	-	0.56	-	198.00	nr
Q0170 3300 mm	230.19	-	0.62	-	230.81	nr
Q0171 3600 mm	251.58	-	0.67	-	252.25	nr
Q0113 4200 mm	312.72	-	0.80	-	313.52	nr
Q0114 4575 mm	341.35	-	0.98	-	342.33	nr
Q0115 4800 mm	362.18	-	1.04	-	363.22	nr
Type CTF5;142 mm wide; suitable for use with timber frame construction, also provides support for brick veneer over openings; depth:						
128 mm; length:						
Q0191 750 mm	8.44	-	0.02	-	8.46	nr
Q0192 900 mm	10.07	-	0.03	-	10.10	nr
Q0193 1200 mm	13.50	-	0.04	-	13.54	nr
Q0194 1500 mm	17.39	-	0.08	-	17.47	nr
183 mm; length:						
Q0195 1800 mm	23.51	-	0.10	-	23.61	nr
Q0196 2100 mm	29.03	-	0.12	-	29.15	nr
Q0197 2400 mm	38.93	-	0.15	-	39.08	nr
Q0198 2700 mm	45.20	-	0.21	-	45.41	nr
Q0199 3000 mm	62.78	-	0.24	-	63.02	nr
218 mm; length:						
Q0200 3300 mm	69.82	-	0.26	-	70.08	nr
Q0201 3600 mm	104.43	-	0.39	-	104.82	nr
256 mm; length:						
Q0202 3900 mm	113.17	-	0.43	-	113.60	nr
Q0203 4200 mm	121.88	-	0.46	-	122.34	nr
Q0204 4575 mm	130.56	-	0.49	-	131.05	nr
Q0205 4800 mm	137.25	-	0.53	-	137.78	nr

Basic Prices of Materials	Supply Price £	Waste Factor %	Unload. Labour £	Unload. Plant £	Total Unit Cost £	Unit
Type CN100 Box beam; 100 mm wide; suitable for use in 100 mm wide internal walls:						
50 mm deep; length:						
Q0213 1200 mm	15.90	-	0.09	-	**15.99**	nr
75 mm deep; length:						
Q0214 1500 mm	19.65	-	0.11	-	**19.76**	nr
Type CN5XA Box beam; 100 mm wide; suitable for use in 100 mm wide internal walls:						
143 mm deep; length:						
Q0215 1800 mm	38.58	-	0.17	-	**38.75**	nr
Q0216 2100 mm	44.09	-	0.19	-	**44.28**	nr
Q0217 2400 mm	52.92	-	0.22	-	**53.14**	nr
Q0218 2700 mm	60.62	-	0.25	-	**60.87**	nr
Type CN6XB Box beam; 100 mm wide; suitable for use in 100 mm wide internal walls:						
219 mm deep; length:						
Q0221 3000 mm	105.23	-	0.46	-	**105.69**	nr
Q0222 3300 mm	116.18	-	0.50	-	**116.68**	nr
Q0223 3600 mm	127.09	-	0.55	-	**127.64**	nr
CN5XA:						
C0302 1050 mm long	36.34	-	0.19	-	**36.53**	nr
C0303 1200 mm long	37.28	-	0.29	-	**37.57**	nr
C0304 1500 mm long	41.89	-	0.34	-	**42.23**	nr
C0305 2400 mm long	79.61	-	0.34	-	**79.95**	nr
CN6XB:						
C0306 2700 mm long	147.63	-	0.37	-	**148.00**	nr
C0307 3000 mm long	158.29	-	0.40	-	**158.69**	nr
CN56XA:						
C0308 1050 mm long	33.14	-	0.29	-	**33.43**	nr
C0309 1200 mm long	39.23	-	0.34	-	**39.57**	nr
C0310 1500 mm long	49.00	-	0.37	-	**49.37**	nr
C0311 2400 mm long	88.23	-	0.37	-	**88.60**	nr
The following prices, supplied by Crittall Windows Ltd, include for delivery to site on the UK mainland. Supply prices include for all necessary lugs or fixing screws.						
Crittall Homelight window range; steel windows constructed in accordance with BS 6510, galvanised after fabrication and finished with Duralife polyester powder coating in white; all opening lights weather-stripped in PVC or neoprene; clip-on channel section beads for single glazing:						
fixed light windows in one pane; reference:						
Q0301 NG5	49.18	-	1.12	-	**50.30**	nr
Q0302 NC5	68.90	-	1.12	-	**70.02**	nr
Q0303 ND5	79.06	-	2.02	-	**81.08**	nr
Q0304 ZNG5	55.52	-	1.12	-	**56.64**	nr
Q0305 ZNC5	79.07	-	2.02	-	**81.09**	nr
Q0306 ZND5	92.97	-	2.02	-	**94.99**	nr
Q0307 NG13	75.44	-	1.12	-	**76.56**	nr
Q0308 NC13	100.98	-	2.02	-	**103.00**	nr
Q0309 ND13	115.51	-	3.03	-	**118.54**	nr
Q0310 ZNG13	84.78	-	1.12	-	**85.90**	nr
Q0311 ZNC13	109.73	-	3.03	-	**112.76**	nr
Q0312 ZND13	124.70	-	4.15	-	**128.85**	nr
Q0313 NG14	90.51	-	1.12	-	**91.63**	nr
Q0314 NC14	119.69	-	3.03	-	**122.72**	nr
Q0315 ND14	134.79	-	5.27	-	**140.06**	nr
Q0316 ZNG14	107.80	-	1.12	-	**108.92**	nr
Q0317 ZNC14	135.50	-	4.15	-	**139.65**	nr
Q0318 ZND14	149.77	-	5.27	-	**155.04**	nr
top hung windows in one pane; reference:						
Q0321 NG1	123.74	-	1.12	-	**124.86**	nr
Q0322 NE1	149.76	-	1.12	-	**150.88**	nr
Q0323 ZNG1	135.75	-	1.12	-	**136.87**	nr
Q0324 ZNE1	156.68	-	1.12	-	**157.80**	nr
side hung windows in one pane; reference:						
Q0325 NC1	173.75	-	1.12	-	**174.87**	nr
Q0326 ND1	197.27	-	2.02	-	**199.29**	nr
Q0327 ZNC1	187.86	-	1.12	-	**188.98**	nr
Q0328 ZND1	218.38	-	2.02	-	**220.40**	nr
horizontal pivoted windows in one pane; reference:						
Q0331 NC13R	549.35	-	4.15	-	**553.50**	nr
Q0332 ND13R	596.72	-	4.15	-	**600.87**	nr
Q0333 ZNC13R	576.13	-	6.17	-	**582.30**	nr
Q0334 ZND13R	619.88	-	6.17	-	**626.05**	nr
two light windows comprising fixed light with top hung fanlight over; reference:						
Q0341 NE5F	157.94	-	1.12	-	**159.06**	nr
Q0342 NC5F	167.34	-	1.12	-	**168.46**	nr
Q0343 ND5F	177.91	-	2.02	-	**179.93**	nr
Q0344 ZNE5F	173.28	-	1.12	-	**174.40**	nr
Q0345 ZNC5F	186.18	-	2.02	-	**188.20**	nr
Q0346 ZND5F	196.73	-	2.02	-	**198.75**	nr
Q0347 NC13F	245.55	-	2.02	-	**247.57**	nr
Q0348 ND13F	261.81	-	3.03	-	**264.84**	nr

Basic Prices of Materials

		Supply Price £	Waste Factor %	Unload. Labour £	Unload. Plant £	Total Unit Cost £	Unit
Q0349	ZNC13F	272.83	-	3.03	-	**275.86**	nr
Q0350	ZND13F	286.58	-	4.15	-	**290.73**	nr
	two light windows comprising fixed light with adjacent top hung casement; reference:						
Q0361	NG2	170.88	-	1.12	-	**172.00**	nr
Q0362	NE2	201.38	-	3.03	-	**204.41**	nr
Q0363	ZNG2	187.43	-	1.12	-	**188.55**	nr
Q0364	ZNE2	214.78	-	3.03	-	**217.81**	nr
	three light windows comprising fixed light with top hung fanlight over and adjacent side hung casement; reference:						
Q0371	NC2F	331.40	-	3.03	-	**334.43**	nr
Q0372	ND2F	367.58	-	3.03	-	**370.61**	nr
Q0373	ZNC2F	359.98	-	3.03	-	**363.01**	nr
Q0374	ZND2F	400.80	-	4.15	-	**404.95**	nr
Q0375	NC10F	432.98	-	3.03	-	**436.01**	nr
Q0376	ND10F	467.11	-	5.27	-	**472.38**	nr
Q0377	ZNC10F	450.59	-	4.15	-	**454.74**	nr
Q0378	ZND10F	498.77	-	5.27	-	**504.04**	nr
	three light windows comprising top hung fanlight over all fixed light and adjacent side hung casement; reference:						
Q0381	ZNC2V	396.88	-	3.03	-	**399.91**	nr
Q0382	ZND2V	435.02	-	4.15	-	**439.17**	nr
	four light windows comprising central fixed light with top hung fanlight over and two side hung casements; reference:						
Q0391	NC4F	504.46	-	3.03	-	**507.49**	nr
Q0392	ND4F	694.18	-	5.27	-	**699.45**	nr
Q0393	ZNC4F	530.79	-	4.15	-	**534.94**	nr
Q0394	ZND4F	593.21	-	5.27	-	**598.48**	nr
Q0395	NC11F	540.39	-	4.15	-	**544.54**	nr
Q0396	ND11F	589.78	-	6.17	-	**595.95**	nr
	single side hung door in three panes; reference:						
Q0397	NA15	1561.51	-	4.15	-	**1565.66**	nr
	pair of side hung doors each leaf in three panes; reference:						
Q0398	NA25	2382.42	-	6.17	-	**2388.59**	nr
	Controlair ventilators; width:						
Q0401	508 mm	54.73	-	-	-	**54.73**	nr
Q0402	628 mm	56.66	-	-	-	**56.66**	nr
Q0403	997 mm	69.20	-	-	-	**69.20**	nr
Q0404	1237 mm	129.09	-	-	-	**129.09**	nr
Q0405	1486 mm	154.83	-	-	-	**154.83**	nr
Q0406	1846 mm	180.54	-	-	-	**180.54**	nr
	pressed steel sills; width:						
Q0411	508 mm	52.76	-	-	-	**52.76**	nr
Q0412	628 mm	55.41	-	-	-	**55.41**	nr
Q0413	997 mm	66.54	-	-	-	**66.54**	nr
Q0414	1237 mm	69.33	-	-	-	**69.33**	nr
Q0415	1486 mm	76.37	-	-	-	**76.37**	nr
Q0416	1846 mm	82.53	-	-	-	**82.53**	nr
Q0417	1994 mm	84.28	-	-	-	**84.28**	nr
	transoms; width:						
Q0421	508 mm	32.20	-	-	-	**32.20**	nr
Q0422	628 mm	37.41	-	-	-	**37.41**	nr
Q0423	997 mm	54.47	-	-	-	**54.47**	nr
Q0424	1237 mm	64.98	-	-	-	**64.98**	nr
Q0425	1486 mm	75.70	-	-	-	**75.70**	nr
Q0426	1846 mm	92.35	-	-	-	**92.35**	nr
	mullions; height:						
Q0431	292 mm	20.95	-	-	-	**20.95**	nr
Q0432	628 mm	35.09	-	-	-	**35.09**	nr
Q0433	923 mm	47.33	-	-	-	**47.33**	nr
Q0434	1218 mm	60.68	-	-	-	**60.68**	nr
	Henderson 'Merlin' one-piece up-and-over garage doors factory assembled with gear attached ready to install; overhead pre-tensioned spring operation complete with guides and rollers; steel sub-frame; canopy action.						
	Doors are subject to the following charges for delivery (Double door = 2 single).						
	- 1 door = £27.00						
	- 2 doors = £32.00						
	- 3 doors = £37.00						
	- 4 doors = £42.00						
	- 5 doors = FREE						
	galvanised primed finish:						
Q0901	2134 x 1981 mm high	479.60	-	1.91	-	**481.51**	nr
Q0902	2134 x 2134 mm high	536.80	-	2.24	-	**539.04**	nr
	galvanised, primed and colour coated finish:						
Q0903	2134 x 1981 mm high	479.60	-	2.24	-	**481.84**	nr
Q0904	2286 x 1981 mm high	567.60	-	2.69	-	**570.29**	nr
Q0905	2438 x 1981 mm high	643.50	-	3.03	-	**646.53**	nr
Q0906	2134 x 2134 mm high	536.80	-	2.24	-	**539.04**	nr
Q0907	2286 x 2134 mm high	638.00	-	2.69	-	**640.69**	nr
Q0908	2438 x 2134 mm high	655.60	-	3.37	-	**658.97**	nr
	Sundries						
N1513	Evomastic general purpose mastic, 370 ml cartridge	2.65	2.5%	-	-	**2.72**	nr

Unit Rates	Man-Hours	Net Labour Price £	Net Mats Price £	Net Unit Price £	Unit

		Man-Hours	Net Labour Price £	Net Mats Price £	Net Unit Price £	Unit
QA	UNIT RATES **GENERAL METALWORK**					
001	**Plain steel sections**					
002	Flat section arch bars, bearers and the like; building in to brickwork, blockwork or stonework:					
	25 x 10 mm	0.07	1.48	1.86	**3.34**	m
	50 x 10 mm	0.10	1.98	3.57	**5.55**	m
	80 x 10 mm	0.12	2.46	5.78	**8.24**	m
	100 x 10 mm	0.14	2.96	7.24	**10.20**	m
003	Angle section arch bars, bearers and the like; building in to brickwork, blockwork or stonework:					
	50 x 50 x 6 mm	0.12	2.46	4.29	**6.75**	m
	80 x 80 x 8 mm	0.18	3.70	9.64	**13.34**	m
	100 x 100 x 8 mm	0.24	4.93	10.78	**15.71**	m
	125 x 75 x 8 mm	0.21	4.43	11.36	**15.79**	m
	150 x 150 x 10 mm	0.47	9.86	24.25	**34.11**	m
	150 x 75 x 10 mm	0.38	7.89	17.70	**25.59**	m
	200 x 100 x 10 mm	0.47	7.21	25.25	**32.46**	m
	fixing with bolts (measured separately):					
	50 x 50 x 8 mm	0.04	0.53	4.29	**4.82**	m
	80 x 80 x 8 mm	0.06	0.88	9.64	**10.52**	m
	100 x 100 x 8 mm	0.07	1.08	10.78	**11.86**	m
	150 x 150 x 10 mm	0.14	2.16	24.25	**26.41**	m
	100 x 75 x 8 mm	0.06	0.91	11.36	**12.27**	m
	150 x 75 x 10 mm	0.11	1.63	17.70	**19.33**	m
	200 x 100 x 10 mm	0.14	2.16	25.25	**27.41**	m
004	**Metric Black hexagon bolts and nuts, BS 4190**					
005	Bolts, each with one nut and one washer:					
	M6 x 50 mm	0.12	1.79	0.09	**1.88**	Nr
	M6 x 100 mm	0.12	1.79	0.18	**1.97**	Nr
	M8 x 50 mm	0.12	1.79	0.15	**1.94**	Nr
	M10 x 50 mm	0.12	1.79	0.24	**2.03**	Nr
	M10 x 100 mm	0.14	2.16	0.40	**2.56**	Nr
	M12 x 75 mm	0.12	1.79	0.44	**2.23**	Nr
	M12 x 130 mm	0.16	2.36	0.65	**3.01**	Nr
	M16 x 50 mm	0.14	2.16	0.61	**2.77**	Nr
	M16 x 80 mm	0.14	2.16	0.78	**2.94**	Nr
006	Rawlbolts, bolt projecting type; corrosion resistant; drilling concrete:					
	6 x 70 mm, ref M625P	0.18	2.71	0.83	**3.54**	Nr
	6 x 105 mm, ref M660P	0.24	3.60	0.84	**4.44**	Nr
	8 x 80 mm, ref M825P	0.24	3.60	0.98	**4.58**	Nr
	8 x 115 mm, ref M860P	0.26	3.97	1.07	**5.04**	Nr
	10 x 90 mm, ref M1030P	0.33	5.05	1.17	**6.22**	Nr
	10 x 120 mm, ref M1060P	0.36	5.40	1.14	**6.54**	Nr
	12 x 105 mm, ref M1230P	0.36	5.40	1.91	**7.31**	Nr
	12 x 150 mm, ref M1275P	0.38	5.76	2.36	**8.12**	Nr
	16 x 150 mm, ref M1635P	0.41	6.29	4.37	**10.66**	Nr
007	Rawlbolts, loose bolt type; corrosion resistant; drilling concrete:					
	6 x 70 mm, ref M625L	0.18	2.71	0.77	**3.48**	Nr
	6 x 85 mm, ref M640L	0.21	3.24	0.91	**4.15**	Nr
	8 x 80 mm, ref M825L	0.24	3.60	0.98	**4.58**	Nr
	8 x 95 mm, ref M840L	0.25	3.77	1.05	**4.82**	Nr
	10 x 85 mm, ref M1025L	0.33	5.05	1.17	**6.22**	Nr
	10 x 135 mm, ref M1075L	0.37	5.59	1.29	**6.88**	Nr
	12 x 100 mm, ref M1225L	0.36	5.40	2.12	**7.52**	Nr
	16 x 145 mm, ref M1630L	0.41	6.29	4.47	**10.76**	Nr
008	**Drilling steel for bolts**					
009	Drill holes in steel to suit bolts; steel thickness:					
	8 mm; for bolt diameter:					
	M6 or M8	0.30	4.51	-	**4.51**	Nr
	M10 or M12	0.41	6.29	-	**6.29**	Nr
	M16	0.59	9.00	-	**9.00**	Nr
	10 mm; for bolt diameter:					
	M6 or M8	0.36	5.40	-	**5.40**	Nr
	M10 or M12	0.47	7.20	-	**7.20**	Nr
	M16	0.65	9.91	-	**9.91**	Nr
010	**Work to existing metalwork**					
011	Cut out defective metal balusters and replace with new; including welded joints:					
	710 mm in length:					
	12 mm diameter	0.50	7.60	0.94	**13.28**	Nr
	16 mm diameter	0.70	10.59	1.57	**18.76**	Nr
	20 mm diameter	0.90	13.68	2.39	**24.60**	Nr
	12 x 12 mm	0.60	9.12	1.48	**16.29**	Nr
	16 x 16 mm	0.80	12.16	2.32	**22.06**	Nr
	20 x 20 mm	1.00	15.20	4.14	**28.82**	Nr
	915 mm in length:					
	12 mm diameter	0.50	5.61	1.03	**11.38**	Nr
	16 mm diameter	0.70	10.64	1.73	**19.00**	Nr
	20 mm diameter	0.90	13.68	2.63	**24.84**	Nr
	12 x 12 mm	0.60	9.12	1.63	**16.44**	Nr

Unit Rates	Man-Hours	Net Labour Price £	Net Mats Price £	Net Unit Price £	Unit
16 x 16 mm	0.80	12.16	2.55	**22.29**	Nr
20 x 20 mm	1.00	15.20	4.56	**29.24**	Nr
012 Make good damaged weld including removing remains of weld, wire brushing and hacking surface and rewelding connection to metal rail:					
12 mm diameter rail	0.35	5.32	0.09	**8.73**	Nr
16 mm diameter rail	0.45	6.84	0.16	**11.26**	Nr
20 mm diameter rail	0.55	8.36	0.24	**13.81**	Nr
12 x 12 mm bar	0.40	6.08	0.15	**10.02**	Nr
16 x 16 mm bar	0.50	7.60	0.23	**12.57**	Nr
20 x 20 mm bar	0.60	9.12	0.41	**15.22**	Nr
013 Remove defective arch bar including cutting out from brickwork and replace with new primed mild steel bar; make good brickwork; allow for temporary supports:					
flat arch bars up to 1.50 m long:					
25 x 6 mm	1.90	39.54	4.62	**44.16**	Nr
35 x 6 mm	1.90	39.54	5.72	**45.26**	Nr
51 x 10 mm	1.90	39.54	8.23	**47.77**	Nr
angle arch bars up to 1.50 m long:					
100 x 50 x 8 mm	2.35	48.90	21.29	**70.19**	Nr
150 x 75 x 10 mm	2.35	48.90	41.38	**90.28**	Nr
QB **STEEL LINTELS**					
001 **Catnic Steel lintels; building into brickwork or blockwork**					
002 Steel lintel type CG70/100; 263 mm wide lintel:					
length:					
750 mm	0.11	2.23	24.69	**26.92**	Nr
900 mm	0.12	2.46	29.50	**31.96**	Nr
1200 mm	0.14	2.96	39.34	**42.30**	Nr
1500 mm	0.16	3.23	49.16	**52.39**	Nr
1800 mm	0.18	3.70	61.52	**65.22**	Nr
2100 mm	0.21	4.43	70.40	**74.83**	Nr
2400 mm	0.27	5.68	83.54	**89.22**	Nr
2700 mm	0.30	6.18	96.40	**102.58**	Nr
3000 mm	0.32	6.66	137.05	**143.71**	Nr
3300 mm	0.34	7.16	152.13	**159.29**	Nr
3600 mm	0.37	7.66	165.93	**173.59**	Nr
3900 mm	0.45	9.36	179.82	**189.18**	Nr
003 Steel lintel type CX70/100; 263 mm wide lintel:					
length:					
2700 mm	0.32	6.58	178.06	**184.64**	Nr
3000 mm	0.34	7.05	198.00	**205.05**	Nr
3300 mm	0.36	7.55	230.81	**238.36**	Nr
3600 mm	0.39	8.03	252.25	**260.28**	Nr
4200 mm	0.49	10.09	313.52	**323.61**	Nr
4500 mm	0.59	12.32	342.33	**354.65**	Nr
4800 mm	0.63	13.05	363.22	**376.27**	Nr
004 Steel lintel type CG50/100; 243 mm wide lintel:					
length:					
750 mm	0.10	1.98	25.29	**27.27**	Nr
900 mm	0.11	2.23	30.38	**32.61**	Nr
1200 mm	0.13	2.71	39.38	**42.09**	Nr
1500 mm	0.14	2.96	50.90	**53.86**	Nr
1800 mm	0.18	3.70	63.29	**66.99**	Nr
2100 mm	0.21	4.43	72.71	**77.14**	Nr
2400 mm	0.23	4.68	89.11	**93.79**	Nr
2700 mm	0.30	6.18	101.23	**107.41**	Nr
3000 mm	0.32	6.66	140.03	**146.69**	Nr
3300 mm	0.34	7.16	156.36	**163.52**	Nr
3600 mm	0.37	7.66	171.58	**179.24**	Nr
3900 mm	0.46	9.59	273.69	**283.28**	Nr
005 Steel lintel type CX50/100; 243 mm wide lintel:					
length:					
2400 mm	0.25	5.16	140.04	**145.20**	Nr
2700 mm	0.27	5.68	164.08	**169.76**	Nr
3000 mm	0.30	6.18	189.67	**195.85**	Nr
3300 mm	0.32	6.66	218.45	**225.11**	Nr
3600 mm	0.33	6.91	237.88	**244.79**	Nr
3900 mm	0.36	7.39	273.80	**281.19**	Nr
4200 mm	0.49	10.09	303.78	**313.87**	Nr
4500 mm	0.59	12.32	340.75	**353.07**	Nr
4800 mm	0.63	13.05	357.13	**370.18**	Nr
006 Steel lintel type CG50/125; 268 mm wide lintel:					
length:					
750 mm	0.12	2.46	24.58	**27.04**	Nr
900 mm	0.14	2.96	29.55	**32.51**	Nr
1200 mm	0.18	3.70	39.41	**43.11**	Nr
1500 mm	0.20	4.20	50.64	**54.84**	Nr
1800 mm	0.24	4.93	62.88	**67.81**	Unr
2100 mm	0.26	5.43	72.61	**78.04**	Nr
2400 mm	0.33	6.91	88.56	**95.47**	Nr
2700 mm	0.37	7.66	101.30	**108.96**	Nr
3000 mm	0.39	8.14	139.80	**147.94**	Nr

Unit Rates	Man-Hours	Net Labour Price £	Net Mats Price £	Net Unit Price £	Unit
007 Steel lintel type CX50/125; 268 mm wide lintel:					
length:					
3300 mm	0.45	9.36	269.07	**278.43**	Nr
3600 mm	0.49	10.09	293.52	**303.61**	Nr
008 Steel lintel type CH70/100; 263 mm wide lintel:					
length:					
900 mm	0.13	2.66	34.66	**37.32**	Nr
1200 mm	0.15	3.14	46.10	**49.24**	Nr
1500 mm	0.16	3.41	66.08	**69.49**	Nr
1800 mm	0.20	4.12	86.98	**91.10**	Nr
2100 mm	0.22	4.62	109.07	**113.69**	Nr
2400 mm	0.29	6.10	135.76	**141.86**	Nr
Note: 009 - 010 not used					
011 Steel lintels type CN100 box beam; 100 mm wide:					
50 mm deep; length:					
1200 mm	0.12	2.46	15.99	**18.45**	Nr
75 mm deep; length:					
1500 mm	0.13	2.71	19.76	**22.47**	Nr
012 Steel lintels type CN5XA box beam; 100 mm wide:					
143 mm deep; length:					
1800 mm	0.16	3.23	38.75	**41.98**	Nr
2100 mm	0.18	3.70	44.28	**47.98**	Nr
2400 mm	0.19	3.95	53.14	**57.09**	Nr
2700 mm	0.20	4.20	60.87	**65.07**	Nr
013 Steel lintels type CN6XB box beam; 100 mm wide:					
219 mm deep; length:					
3000 mm	0.31	6.41	105.69	**112.10**	Nr
3300 mm	0.34	7.16	116.68	**123.84**	Nr
3600 mm	0.37	7.66	127.64	**135.30**	Nr
Note: 014 not used					
015 Steel lintel type CTF5; 142 mm wide lintel; fixing with retaining clips nailed at 500 mm centres:					
length:					
750 mm	0.01	0.23	8.46	**8.69**	Nr
900 mm	0.02	0.50	10.10	**10.60**	Nr
1200 mm	0.02	0.50	13.54	**14.04**	Nr
1500 mm	0.05	0.98	17.47	**18.45**	Nr
1800 mm	0.05	0.98	23.61	**24.59**	Nr
2100 mm	0.07	1.48	29.15	**30.63**	Nr
2400 mm	0.07	1.48	39.08	**40.56**	Nr
2700 mm	0.12	2.46	45.41	**47.87**	Nr
3000 mm	0.13	2.71	63.02	**65.73**	Nr
3300 mm	0.14	2.96	70.08	**73.04**	Nr
3600 mm	0.21	4.43	104.82	**109.25**	Nr
3900 mm	0.23	4.68	113.60	**118.28**	Nr
4200 mm	0.25	5.16	122.34	**127.50**	Nr
4500 mm	0.26	5.43	131.05	**136.48**	Nr
4800 mm	0.27	5.68	137.78	**143.46**	Nr
016 **Catnic lintels; bedding ends in cement mortar (1:3)**					
017 Type CG50/100 for use in cavity walls with 50-65 mm cavity; 100 mm inner skin:					
900 mm long	0.38	7.93	30.38	**38.31**	Nr
1200 mm long	0.42	8.72	39.38	**48.10**	Nr
1500 mm long	0.46	9.66	50.90	**60.56**	Nr
018 Type CU70/100 for use in cavity walls with 70-85 mm cavity; 100 mm inner skin:					
2400 mm long	0.66	13.73	83.54	**97.27**	Nr
2700 mm long	0.70	14.50	96.40	**110.90**	Nr
3000 mm long	0.74	15.46	137.05	**152.51**	Nr
019 Type CN5XA for use in internal 100 mm walls; 100 x 143 mm deep:					
1050 mm long	0.27	5.60	36.53	**42.13**	Nr
1200 mm long	0.31	6.39	37.57	**43.96**	Nr
1500 mm long	0.35	7.35	42.23	**49.58**	Nr
2400 mm long	0.47	9.86	79.95	**89.81**	Nr
020 Type CN6XB for use in internal 100 mm walls; 100 x 219 mm deep:					
2700 mm long	0.52	10.82	148.00	**158.82**	Nr
3000 mm long	0.56	11.59	158.69	**170.28**	Nr
021 Type CN56XA for use in internal 150 mm walls; 150 x 143 mm deep:					
1050 mm long	0.33	6.95	33.43	**40.38**	Nr
1200 mm long	0.38	7.93	39.57	**47.50**	Nr
1500 mm long	0.42	8.72	49.37	**58.09**	Nr
2400 mm long	0.55	11.40	88.60	**100.00**	Nr

Unit Rates	Man-Hours	Net Labour Price £	Net Mats Price £	Net Unit Price £	Unit
QC **WINDOWS AND DOORS**					

Note: The labour hours and prices which follow are for fixing windows to timber surrounds, for building in windows to Brickwork, Blockwork or Stonework see Sections GJ or JB.

STEEL WINDOWS AND DOORS

	Man-Hours	Net Labour Price £	Net Mats Price £	Net Unit Price £	Unit
001 **Crittall Duralife Homelight window range; steel windows constructed and finished with Duralife polyester powder coating in white; all opening lights weatherstripped in PVC or neoprene; clip-on channel section glazing beads; bedding frames in mastic and pointing one side**					
002 Fixed light windows in one pane; width:					
508 mm; height and type:					
292 mm, NG5	0.47	9.86	50.44	**60.30**	Nr
923 mm, NC5	0.65	13.57	70.27	**83.84**	Nr
1218 mm, ND5	0.71	14.80	81.39	**96.19**	Nr
628 mm; height and type:					
292 mm, ZNG5	0.53	11.11	56.81	**67.92**	Nr
923 mm, ZNC5	0.71	14.80	81.37	**96.17**	Nr
1218 mm, ZND5	0.89	18.48	95.32	**113.80**	Nr
997 mm; height and type:					
292 mm, NG13	0.59	12.32	76.78	**89.10**	Nr
923 mm, NE13	0.77	16.00	103.29	**119.29**	Nr
1218 mm, ND13	1.13	23.43	118.93	**142.36**	Nr
1237 mm; height and type:					
292 mm, ZNG13	0.65	13.57	86.17	**99.74**	Nr
923 mm, ZNC13	0.89	18.48	113.09	**131.57**	Nr
1218 mm, ZND13	1.24	25.87	129.28	**155.15**	Nr
1486 mm; height and type:					
292 mm, NG14	0.71	14.80	91.95	**106.75**	Nr
923 mm, NC14	1.19	24.66	123.14	**147.80**	Nr
1218 mm, ND14	1.48	30.82	140.54	**171.36**	Nr
1846 mm; height and type:					
292 mm, ZNG14	0.83	17.25	109.30	**126.55**	Nr
923 mm, ZNC14	1.54	32.05	140.14	**172.19**	Nr
1218 mm, ZND14	1.78	36.98	155.59	**192.57**	Nr
003 Top hung windows in one pane; width:					
508 mm; height and type:					
292 mm, NG1	0.47	9.86	125.00	**134.86**	Nr
628 mm, NE1	0.59	12.32	151.08	**163.40**	Nr
628 mm; height and type:					
292 mm, ZNG1	0.53	11.11	137.03	**148.14**	Nr
628 mm, ZNE1	0.65	13.57	158.02	**171.59**	Nr
004 Side hung casement windows in one pane; width:					
508 mm; height and type:					
923 mm, NC1	0.65	13.57	175.13	**188.70**	Nr
1218 mm, ND1	0.71	14.80	199.60	**214.40**	Nr
628 mm; height and type:					
923 mm, ZNC1	0.71	14.80	189.25	**204.05**	Nr
1218 mm, ZND1	0.89	18.48	220.72	**239.20**	Nr
005 Horizontally pivot hung windows in one pane; width:					
997 mm; height and type:					
923 mm, NC13R	0.95	19.73	553.84	**573.57**	Nr
1218 mm, ND13R	1.13	23.43	601.26	**624.69**	Nr
1237 mm; height and type:					
923 mm, ZNC13R	1.07	22.18	582.69	**604.87**	Nr
1218 mm, ZND13R	1.24	25.87	626.49	**652.36**	Nr
006 Two light windows comprising fixed light with top hung fanlight over; width:					
508 mm; height and type:					
628 mm, NE5F	0.59	12.32	159.26	**171.58**	Nr
923 mm, NC5F	0.65	13.57	168.71	**182.28**	Nr
1218 mm, ND5F	0.71	14.80	180.23	**195.03**	Nr
628 mm; height and type:					
628 mm, ZNE5F	0.65	13.57	174.62	**188.19**	Nr
923 mm, ZNC5F	0.71	14.80	188.47	**203.27**	Nr
1218 mm, ZND5F	0.89	18.48	199.08	**217.56**	Nr
997 mm; height and type:					
923 mm, NC13F	0.95	19.73	247.91	**267.64**	Nr
1218 mm, ND13F	1.13	23.43	265.23	**288.66**	Nr
1237 mm; height and type:					
923 mm, ZNC13F	1.07	22.18	276.25	**298.43**	Nr
1218 mm, ZND13F	1.24	25.87	291.17	**317.04**	Nr
007 Two light windows comprising fixed light with adjacent top hung casement; width:					
997 mm; height and type:					
292 mm, NG2	0.59	12.32	172.23	**184.55**	Nr
628 mm, NE2	0.77	16.00	204.70	**220.70**	Nr
1237 mm; height and type:					
292 mm, ZNG2	0.65	13.57	188.82	**202.39**	Nr
628 mm, ZNE2	0.89	18.48	218.14	**236.62**	Nr

Unit Rates

		Man-Hours	Net Labour Price £	Net Mats Price £	Net Unit Price £	Unit
008	Three light windows comprising fixed light with fanlight over and adjacent side hung casement; width:					
	997 mm; height and type:					
	923 mm, NC2F	0.95	19.73	334.77	**354.50**	Nr
	1218 mm, ND2F	1.13	23.43	371.01	**394.44**	Nr
	1237 mm; height and type:					
	923 mm, ZNC2F	1.07	22.18	363.39	**385.57**	Nr
	1218 mm, ZND2F	1.24	25.87	405.38	**431.25**	Nr
	1486 mm; height and type:					
	923 mm, NC10F	1.19	24.66	436.44	**461.10**	Nr
	1218 mm, ND10F	1.48	30.82	472.86	**503.68**	Nr
	1846 mm; height and type:					
	923 mm, ZNC10F	1.54	32.05	455.23	**487.28**	Nr
	1218 mm, ZND10F	1.78	36.98	504.58	**541.56**	Nr
009	Three light windows comprising wide fanlight over fixed light and adjacent side hung casement; width:					
	1237; height and type:					
	923 mm, NC4F	1.07	22.18	400.29	**422.47**	Nr
	1218 mm, ND4F	1.24	25.87	439.61	**465.48**	Nr
010	Four light windows comprising wide fanlight over fixed light between Nr side hung casement; width:					
	1486 mm; height and type:					
	923 mm, NC4F	1.19	24.66	507.92	**532.58**	Nr
	1218 mm, ND4F	1.48	30.82	699.93	**730.75**	Nr
	1846 mm; height and type:					
	923 mm, ZNC4F	1.54	32.05	535.42	**567.47**	Nr
	1218 mm, ZND4F	1.78	36.98	599.03	**636.01**	Nr
	1994 mm; height and type:					
	923 mm, NC11F	1.78	36.98	545.06	**582.04**	Nr
	1218 mm, ND11F	2.13	44.37	596.52	**640.89**	Nr
011	Single side hung door in three panes:					
	761 mm x 2056 mm high, type NA15	1.54	23.41	1566.15	**1589.56**	Nr
012	Pair of side hung doors each leaf in three panes:					
	1143 mm x 2056 mm high, type NA25	1.60	24.32	2389.16	**2413.48**	Nr
013	**Extra over** windows for Controlair ventilators; width:					
	508 mm	-	-	54.80	**54.80**	Nr
	628 mm	-	-	56.73	**56.73**	Nr
	997 mm	-	-	69.31	**69.31**	Nr
	1237 mm	-	-	129.22	**129.22**	Nr
	1486 mm	-	-	154.99	**154.99**	Nr
	1846 mm	-	-	180.74	**180.74**	Nr
014	**Extra over** windows for pressed steel sills; bedding in cement mortar (1:3); width:					
	508 mm	0.19	3.95	52.94	**56.89**	Nr
	628 mm	0.23	4.68	55.60	**60.28**	Nr
	997 mm	0.36	7.39	66.89	**74.28**	Nr
	1237 mm	0.45	9.36	69.70	**79.06**	Nr
	1486 mm	0.53	11.11	63.27	**74.38**	Nr
	1846 mm	0.66	13.80	83.08	**96.88**	Nr
	1994 mm	0.71	14.80	84.85	**99.65**	Nr
015	**Extra over** windows for transoms; width:					
	508 mm	0.31	4.68	32.24	**36.92**	Nr
	628 mm	0.38	5.76	37.46	**43.22**	Nr
	997 mm	0.59	9.00	54.56	**63.56**	Nr
	1237 mm	0.73	11.16	65.09	**76.25**	Nr
	1486 mm	0.89	13.50	75.83	**89.33**	Nr
	1846 mm	1.10	16.75	92.51	**109.26**	Nr
016	**Extra over** windows for mullions; height:					
	292 mm	0.18	2.71	20.98	**23.69**	Nr
	628 mm	0.38	5.76	35.14	**40.90**	Nr
	923 mm	0.56	8.47	47.41	**55.88**	Nr
	1218 mm	0.72	10.99	60.79	**71.78**	Nr
	STEEL GARAGE DOORS					
017	**Henderson 'Merlin' one piece up-and-over garage doors factory assembled with gear attached ready to install; overhead pre-tensioned spring operation complete with guide frames and rollers; fixing with screws to timber sub-frames (measured separately)**					
018	Galvanised finish:					
	2134 x 1981 mm	4.74	72.02	481.51	**553.53**	Nr
	2134 x 2134 mm	5.33	81.02	539.04	**620.06**	Nr
019	Galvanised, primed and colour coated:					
	2134 x 1981 mm	4.74	72.02	481.84	**553.86**	Nr
	2286 x 1981 mm	5.33	81.02	570.29	**651.31**	Nr
	2438 x 1981 mm	5.92	90.01	646.53	**736.54**	Nr
	2134 x 2134 mm	5.33	81.02	539.04	**620.06**	Nr
	2286 x 2134 mm	5.92	90.01	640.69	**730.70**	Unit
	2438 x 2134 mm	6.52	99.03	658.97	**758.00**	Nr

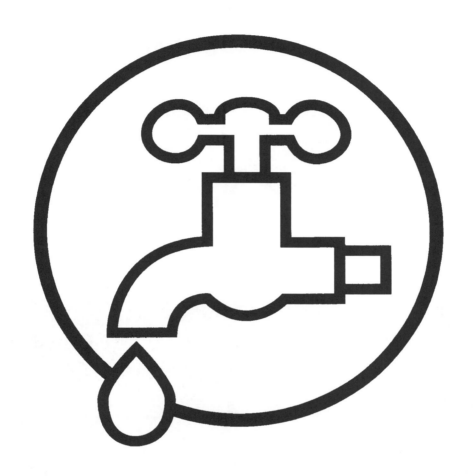

Plumbing and Engineering Installations

Labour Rates

Please note: The labour hours throughout this section are representative of the time required for one productive man to carry out the unit of work.

Gang rates are calculated as follows by obtaining the overall gang cost and then dividing this by the number of productive members in the gang. The resulting rate is the Gang Cost per **Man - hour.** By using the same principle, any size gang may be built-up and used against the standard labour hours in this section.

A0211 General plumbing work:

Advanced PHMES Operative	1.00	x	£	19.59	= £	19.59
Apprentice Plumber (3rd Year)	1.00	x	£	12.01	= £	12.01
Total hourly cost of gang					= £	31.60

Gang rate (divided by 1) = £31.60 per Man-hour

A0204 Builders work in connection with plumbing installations:

Brick/Block Layer	2.00	x	£	15.20	= £	30.40
Brick/Blockwork Labourer	1.00	x	£	11.22	= £	11.22
Total hourly cost of gang					= £	41.62

Gang rate (divided by 2) = £20.81 per Man-hour

Basic Prices of Materials

		Supply Price £	Waste Factor %	Unload. Labour £	Unload. Plant £	Total Unit Cost £	Unit
	The cost of unloading materials is included in the price for fixing the materials.						
	Cast iron eaves gutters and fittings						
R0111	100 mm half round	16.35	5%	-	-	**17.17**	m
	Extra over for:						
R0112	stopped end	4.19	2.5%	-	-	**4.30**	nr
R0113	angle/nozzle outlet	12.46	2.5%	-	-	**12.77**	nr
R0114	fascia bracket	3.51	2.5%	-	-	**3.59**	nr
R0115	150 mm half round	34.05	5%	-	-	**35.75**	m
	Extra over for:						
R0116	stopped end	7.53	2.5%	-	-	**7.71**	nr
R0117	angle/nozzle outlet	27.63	2.5%	-	-	**28.33**	nr
R0118	fascia bracket	4.45	2.5%	-	-	**4.56**	nr
R0119	100 mm ogee	17.10	5%	-	-	**17.96**	m
	Extra over for:						
R0120	stopped end	4.01	2.5%	-	-	**4.11**	nr
R0121	angle/nozzle outlet	12.20	2.5%	-	-	**12.50**	nr
R0122	fascia bracket	3.57	2.5%	-	-	**3.66**	nr
R0123	125 mm ogee	19.73	5%	-	-	**20.72**	m
	Extra over for:						
R0124	stopped end	5.20	2.5%	-	-	**5.33**	nr
R0125	angle/nozzle outlet	14.45	2.5%	-	-	**14.81**	nr
R0126	fascia bracket	4.04	2.5%	-	-	**4.14**	nr
	Cast aluminium eaves gutters and fittings; plain mill finish						
R0131	100 mm half round	10.85	5%	-	-	**11.39**	m
	Extra over for:						
R0132	stopped end	3.23	2.5%	-	-	**3.31**	nr
R0133	angle, 90° / 135°	6.67	2.5%	-	-	**6.84**	nr
R0134	outlet, 63 mm drop	7.67	2.5%	-	-	**7.86**	nr
R1583	union clip	3.29	2.5%	-	-	**3.38**	nr
R0135	fascia bracket	1.92	2.5%	-	-	**1.96**	nr
R1503	113 mm half round	11.70	5%	-	-	**12.28**	m
	Extra over for:						
R1505	stopped end	3.38	2.5%	-	-	**3.46**	nr
R1509	angle 90°	7.74	2.5%	-	-	**7.93**	nr
R1510	angle 135°	7.51	2.5%	-	-	**7.70**	nr
R1506	outlet, 63 mm diameter	8.31	2.5%	-	-	**8.52**	nr
R1507	outlet, 76 mm diameter	8.07	2.5%	-	-	**8.27**	nr
R1508	outlet, 76 x 76 mm	20.62	2.5%	-	-	**21.13**	nr
R1504	union clip	3.28	2.5%	-	-	**3.36**	nr
R1511	fascia bracket	1.97	2.5%	-	-	**2.02**	nr
R0136	125 mm half round	13.54	5%	-	-	**14.22**	m
	Extra over for:						
R0137	stopped end	4.29	2.5%	-	-	**4.39**	nr
R0138	square angle	8.52	2.5%	-	-	**8.73**	nr
R0139	outlet, 63/76 mm diameter	8.77	2.5%	-	-	**8.99**	nr
R1584	union clip	4.70	2.5%	-	-	**4.82**	nr
R0140	fascia bracket	3.49	2.5%	-	-	**3.58**	nr
R0141	100 mm ogee	14.27	5%	-	-	**14.98**	m
	Extra over for:						
R0142	stopped end	3.53	2.5%	-	-	**3.62**	nr
R0143	angle, 90°/135°	7.41	2.5%	-	-	**7.59**	nr
R0144	outlet, 63/76 mm diameter	9.21	2.5%	-	-	**9.44**	nr
R1585	union clip	3.87	2.5%	-	-	**3.97**	nr
R0145	fascia bracket	3.53	2.5%	-	-	**3.62**	nr
R1512	113 mm ogee	14.15	5%	-	-	**14.86**	m
	Extra over for:						
R1514	stopped end	3.70	2.5%	-	-	**3.79**	nr
R1518	angle, 90°	9.07	2.5%	-	-	**9.30**	nr
R1519	angle, 135°	9.07	2.5%	-	-	**9.30**	nr
R1515	outlet, 63 mm diameter	9.27	2.5%	-	-	**9.50**	nr

Basic Prices of Materials

		Supply Price £	Waste Factor %	Unload. Labour £	Unload. Plant £	Total Unit Cost £	Unit
R1516	outlet, 76 mm diameter	27.83	2.5%	-	-	28.53	nr
R1517	outlet, 76 x 76 mm	27.83	2.5%	-	-	28.53	nr
R1513	union clip	3.70	2.5%	-	-	3.79	nr
R1520	fascia bracket	3.70	2.5%	-	-	3.79	nr
R0146	125 mm ogee	18.86	5%	-	-	19.80	m
	Extra over for:						
R0147	stopped end	4.01	2.5%	-	-	4.11	nr
R0148	angle, 90°/135°	10.91	2.5%	-	-	11.18	nr
R0149	outlet, 76 mm diameter	10.80	2.5%	-	-	11.07	nr
R1574	union clip	6.41	2.5%	-	-	6.57	nr
R0150	fascia bracket	4.01	2.5%	-	-	4.11	nr
	Cast aluminium eaves gutters and fittings; polyester powder coated						
R1531	100 mm half round	25.37	5%	-	-	26.64	m
	Extra over for:						
R1534	stopped end	6.87	2.5%	-	-	7.04	nr
R1535	angle, 90°	13.40	2.5%	-	-	13.74	nr
R1536	angle, 135°	13.46	2.5%	-	-	13.80	nr
R1537	outlet, 63/76 mm diameter	14.57	2.5%	-	-	14.93	nr
R1538	outlet, 76 x 76 mm	31.38	2.5%	-	-	32.17	nr
R1539	outlet, 102 x 102 mm	32.90	2.5%	-	-	33.72	nr
R1532	union clip	6.74	2.5%	-	-	6.91	nr
R1533	fascia bracket	3.51	2.5%	-	-	3.60	nr
R1540	113 mm half round	26.06	5%	-	-	27.36	m
	Extra over for:						
R1543	stopped end	7.09	2.5%	-	-	7.27	nr
R1544	angle, 90°	15.56	2.5%	-	-	15.95	nr
R1545	angle, 135°	15.11	2.5%	-	-	15.49	nr
R1546	outlet, 63/76 mm diameter	15.82	2.5%	-	-	16.21	nr
R1547	outlet, 76 x 76 mm	33.02	2.5%	-	-	33.85	nr
R1541	union clip	7.09	2.5%	-	-	7.27	nr
R1542	fascia bracket	3.55	2.5%	-	-	3.64	nr
R1548	125 mm half round	29.83	5%	-	-	31.33	m
	Extra over for:						
R1551	stopped end	8.81	2.5%	-	-	9.03	nr
R1552	angle, 90°	17.69	2.5%	-	-	18.13	nr
R1553	angle, 135°	17.27	2.5%	-	-	17.70	nr
R1556	outlet, 63/76 mm diameter	14.63	2.5%	-	-	14.99	nr
R1841	outlet, 76 x 76 mm	33.04	2.5%	-	-	33.86	nr
R1555	outlet, 102 mm	17.63	2.5%	-	-	18.07	nr
R1549	union clip	8.64	2.5%	-	-	8.86	nr
R1550	fascia bracket	6.84	2.5%	-	-	7.01	nr
R1557	100 mm ogee	21.71	5%	-	-	22.80	m
	Extra over for:						
R1560	stopped end	4.97	2.5%	-	-	5.10	nr
R1561	angle, 90°	10.33	2.5%	-	-	10.59	nr
R1562	angle, 135°	10.33	2.5%	-	-	10.59	nr
R1563	outlet, 63/76 mm diameter	12.26	2.5%	-	-	12.56	nr
R1564	outlet, 76 x 76 mm	27.67	2.5%	-	-	28.36	nr
R1558	union clip	4.97	2.5%	-	-	5.10	nr
R1559	fascia bracket	4.97	2.5%	-	-	5.10	nr
R1565	113 mm ogee	24.15	5%	-	-	25.35	m
	Extra over for:						
R1568	stopped end	2.81	2.5%	-	-	2.88	nr
R1569	angle, 90°	12.32	2.5%	-	-	12.62	nr
R1570	angle, 135°	12.32	2.5%	-	-	12.62	nr
R1571	outlet, 63/76 mm diameter	30.39	2.5%	-	-	31.14	nr
R1572	outlet, 76 x 76 mm	30.39	2.5%	-	-	31.14	nr
R1566	union clip	5.32	2.5%	-	-	5.45	nr
R1567	fascia bracket	5.32	2.5%	-	-	5.45	nr
R1573	125 mm ogee	27.35	5%	-	-	28.72	m
	Extra over for:						
R1576	stopped end	6.41	2.5%	-	-	6.57	nr
R1577	angle, 90°	14.30	2.5%	-	-	14.65	nr
R1578	angle, 135°	14.72	2.5%	-	-	15.09	nr
R1579	outlet, 63/76 mm diameter	14.52	2.5%	-	-	14.88	nr
R1580	outlet, 76 x 76 mm	34.11	2.5%	-	-	34.97	nr
R1574	union clip	6.41	2.5%	-	-	6.57	nr
R1575	fascia bracket	5.80	2.5%	-	-	5.94	nr
	PVCu gutters and fittings						
R0181	112 mm half round	2.00	5%	-	-	2.10	m
	Extra over for:						
R0182	stopped end	1.20	2.5%	-	-	1.23	nr
R0183	angle, 90°	2.47	2.5%	-	-	2.53	nr
R0184	outlet	2.14	2.5%	-	-	2.19	nr
R0185	gutter jointing bracket	1.38	2.5%	-	-	1.41	nr
R0186	gutter support bracket	0.73	2.5%	-	-	0.74	nr
R0187	150 mm half round	5.63	5%	-	-	5.91	m
	Extra over for:						
R0188	stopped end	3.62	2.5%	-	-	3.71	nr
R0189	angle, 90°	10.44	2.5%	-	-	10.70	nr
R0190	outlet	7.91	2.5%	-	-	8.11	nr
R0191	gutter jointing bracket	4.09	2.5%	-	-	4.19	nr
R0192	gutter support bracket	2.43	2.5%	-	-	2.49	nr

Basic Prices of Materials		Supply Price £	Waste Factor %	Unload. Labour £	Unload. Plant £	Total Unit Cost £	Unit
R0193	112 mm square section	2.00	5%	-	-	2.10	m
	Extra over for:						
R0194	stopped end	1.10	2.5%	-	-	1.13	nr
R0195	angle, 90°	3.01	2.5%	-	-	3.08	nr
R0196	outlet	3.08	2.5%	-	-	3.16	nr
R0197	gutter jointing bracket	1.77	2.5%	-	-	1.81	nr
R0198	gutter support bracket	0.78	2.5%	-	-	0.80	nr
	Cast iron rainwater pipes and fittings						
R1601	63 mm nominal size pipes; eared	33.29	2.5%	-	-	34.12	m
	Extra over for:						
R1602	shoe, eared	29.22	2.5%	-	-	29.96	nr
R1603	bend	17.89	2.5%	-	-	18.34	nr
R1604	offset, 150 mm projection	27.37	2.5%	-	-	28.06	nr
R1605	offset, 300 mm projection	37.33	2.5%	-	-	38.26	nr
R1606	branch	35.15	2.5%	-	-	36.03	nr
R0225	75 mm nominal size pipes; eared	29.74	5%	-	-	31.23	m
	Extra over for:						
R0226	shoe, eared	26.12	2.5%	-	-	26.77	nr
R0227	bend	19.40	2.5%	-	-	19.89	nr
R0228	offset, 150 mm projection	24.46	2.5%	-	-	25.07	nr
R0229	offset, 300 mm projection	35.00	2.5%	-	-	35.88	nr
R0230	branch	34.63	2.5%	-	-	35.50	nr
R0231	100 mm nominal size pipes; eared	39.95	5%	-	-	41.95	m
	Extra over for:						
R0232	shoe, eared	34.67	2.5%	-	-	35.53	nr
R0233	bend	27.39	2.5%	-	-	28.08	nr
R0234	offset, 150 mm projection	46.14	2.5%	-	-	47.29	nr
R0235	offset, 300 mm projection	56.99	2.5%	-	-	58.41	nr
R0236	branch	40.35	2.5%	-	-	41.36	nr
R0237	100 x 75 mm rectangular pipes; eared	80.33	5%	-	-	84.35	m
	Extra over for:						
R0238	shoe, eared	97.78	2.5%	-	-	100.22	nr
R0239	bend	93.09	2.5%	-	-	95.42	nr
R0240	offset, 150 mm projection	124.55	2.5%	-	-	127.66	nr
R0241	offset, 300 mm projection	144.85	2.5%	-	-	148.47	nr
R0242	branch	157.92	2.5%	-	-	161.87	nr
R0245	Rainwater head, hopper type, flat, eared, 75 mm outlet	104.19	2.5%	-	-	106.80	nr
R0246	Rainwater head, rectangular, 250 x 175 x 175 mm	123.50	2.5%	-	-	126.58	nr
R0247	Rainwater head, rectangular, 300 x 250 x 200 mm	188.16	2.5%	-	-	192.86	nr
	Cast aluminium rainwater pipes and fittings; plain mill finish						
R0250	63 mm nominal size pipes	11.00	5%	-	-	11.55	m
	Extra over for:						
R0251	shoe, eared	6.59	2.5%	-	-	6.76	nr
R1821	loose socket	5.64	2.5%	-	-	5.78	nr
R0252	bend	7.55	2.5%	-	-	7.74	nr
R0253	offset, 152 mm projection	17.99	2.5%	-	-	18.44	nr
R0254	offset, 304 mm projection	20.39	2.5%	-	-	20.90	nr
R0255	offset, 609 mm projection	22.82	2.5%	-	-	23.39	nr
R0256	branch	9.89	5%	-	-	10.38	nr
R1818	clip	3.39	2.5%	-	-	3.47	nr
R0257	76 mm nominal size pipes	12.75	2.5%	-	-	13.07	m
	Extra over for:						
R0258	shoe, eared	9.14	2.5%	-	-	9.37	nr
R1822	loose socket	6.60	2.5%	-	-	6.77	nr
R0259	bend	12.27	2.5%	-	-	12.58	nr
R0260	offset, 152 mm projection	20.21	2.5%	-	-	20.71	nr
R0261	offset, 304 mm projection	22.53	2.5%	-	-	23.09	nr
R0262	offset, 609 mm projection	37.36	2.5%	-	-	38.30	nr
R0263	branch	12.27	2.5%	-	-	12.58	nr
R1819	clip	3.81	2.5%	-	-	3.90	nr
R0264	102 mm nominal size pipes	21.99	5%	-	-	23.09	m
	Extra over for:						
R0265	shoe, eared	10.93	2.5%	-	-	11.20	nr
R1823	loose socket	13.28	2.5%	-	-	13.62	nr
R0266	bend	14.44	2.5%	-	-	14.81	nr
R0267	offset, 152 mm projection	23.09	2.5%	-	-	23.67	nr
R0268	offset, 304 mm projection	29.17	2.5%	-	-	29.90	nr
R0269	offset, 609 mm projection	43.25	2.5%	-	-	44.33	nr
R0270	branch	17.09	2.5%	-	-	17.51	nr
R1820	clip	4.31	2.5%	-	-	4.41	nr
	Cast aluminium rainwater pipes and fittings; polyester powder coated						
R1774	63 mm pipe; eared	15.20	5%	-	-	15.96	m
	Extra over for:						
R1777	shoe	10.11	2.5%	-	-	10.36	nr
R1786	loose socket	7.46	2.5%	-	-	7.65	nr
R1780	bend	19.18	2.5%	-	-	19.66	nr
R1789	150 mm offset	21.31	2.5%	-	-	21.84	nr
R1792	300 mm offset	26.94	2.5%	-	-	27.61	nr
R1795	600 mm offset	39.35	2.5%	-	-	40.33	nr
R1798	branch	13.66	2.5%	-	-	14.00	nr
R1783	clip	4.39	2.5%	-	-	4.50	nr

Basic Prices of Materials

		Supply Price £	Waste Factor %	Unload. Labour £	Unload. Plant £	Total Unit Cost £	Unit
R1775	76 mm pipe; eared	17.70	5%	-	-	18.59	m
	Extra over for:						
R1778	shoe	24.70	2.5%	-	-	25.31	nr
R1787	loose socket	8.74	2.5%	-	-	8.96	nr
R1781	bend	13.65	2.5%	-	-	13.99	nr
R1790	150 mm offset	23.89	2.5%	-	-	24.49	nr
R1793	300 mm offset	30.46	2.5%	-	-	31.22	nr
R1796	600 mm offset	43.88	2.5%	-	-	44.98	nr
R1798	branch	13.66	2.5%	-	-	14.00	nr
R1784	clip	4.91	2.5%	-	-	5.03	nr
R1776	102 mm pipe; eared	30.12	5%	-	-	31.63	m
	Extra over for:						
R1779	shoe	16.73	2.5%	-	-	17.15	nr
R1788	loose socket	17.69	2.5%	-	-	18.13	nr
R1782	bend	19.00	2.5%	-	-	19.47	nr
R1791	150 mm offset	27.39	2.5%	-	-	28.07	nr
R1794	300 mm offset	35.36	2.5%	-	-	36.24	nr
R1797	600 mm offset	50.47	2.5%	-	-	51.73	nr
R1800	branch	22.69	2.5%	-	-	23.26	nr
R1785	clip	5.55	2.5%	-	-	5.69	nr
	Cast accessories; plain mill finish						
R0271	Rainwater head, hopper type, flat, 63 mm outlet	16.76	2.5%	-	-	17.18	nr
R1802	Rainwater head, hopper type, for 76 mm diameter pipe	18.84	2.5%	-	-	19.31	nr
R1803	Rainwater head, hopper type, for 102 mm diameter pipe	47.71	2.5%	-	-	48.91	nr
R0272	Rainwater head, rectangular, 250 x 180 x 180 mm, 63 mm outlet	25.08	2.5%	-	-	25.71	nr
R0273	Rainwater head, rectangular, 250 x 180 x 180 mm, 102 mm outlet	26.83	2.5%	-	-	27.50	nr
R1804	Rainwater head, hopper type, square outlet	39.24	2.5%	-	-	40.22	nr
R1805	Rainwater head, triangular, for 63 mm diameter pipe	19.59	2.5%	-	-	20.08	nr
R1806	Rainwater head, triangular, for 76 mm diameter pipe	18.88	2.5%	-	-	19.35	nr
R1807	Rainwater head, triangular square outlet	43.43	2.5%	-	-	44.51	nr
R1808	Rainwater head, ornamental all types and sizes	137.08	2.5%	-	-	140.50	nr
	Cast accessories; polyester powder coated						
R1809	Rainwater head, hopper type, for 63 mm diameter pipe	34.81	2.5%	-	-	35.68	nr
R1810	Rainwater head, hopper type, for 76 mm diameter pipe	36.11	2.5%	-	-	37.01	nr
R1811	Rainwater head, hopper type, for 102 mm diameter pipe	32.40	2.5%	-	-	33.21	nr
R1812	Rainwater head, hopper type, square outlet	33.35	2.5%	-	-	34.18	nr
R1813	Rainwater head, triangular, for 63 mm diameter pipe	26.90	2.5%	-	-	27.58	nr
R1814	Rainwater head, triangular, for 76 mm diameter pipe	22.57	2.5%	-	-	23.14	nr
R1815	Rainwater head, triangular square outlet	51.41	2.5%	-	-	52.69	nr
R1816	Rainwater head, ornamental all types and sizes	148.50	2.5%	-	-	152.21	nr
	PVCu rainwater pipes and fittings						
R0306	61 mm x 61 mm nominal size pipe	1.99	5%	-	-	2.09	m
	Extra over for:						
R0307	shoe, and fixing bracket	2.28	2.5%	-	-	2.34	nr
R0308	bend	3.28	2.5%	-	-	3.36	nr
R0309	offset bend	2.84	2.5%	-	-	2.91	nr
R0310	branch	5.82	2.5%	-	-	5.96	nr
R0311	pipe clip	0.77	2.5%	-	-	0.79	nr
R0312	drain connector	2.38	2.5%	-	-	2.44	nr
R0292	68 mm nominal size pipe	1.82	2.5%	-	-	1.87	m
	Extra over for:						
R0293	shoe	1.55	2.5%	-	-	1.59	nr
R0294	bend	2.63	2.5%	-	-	2.70	nr
R0295	offset bend	1.43	2.5%	-	-	1.46	nr
R0296	branch	4.68	2.5%	-	-	4.80	nr
R0297	pipe clip	0.94	2.5%	-	-	0.96	nr
R0298	drain connector	2.38	2.5%	-	-	2.44	nr
R0299	110 mm nominal size ring seal pipe	4.06	5%	-	-	4.26	m
	Extra over for:						
R0300	shoe	4.31	2.5%	-	-	4.42	nr
R0301	bend	6.30	2.5%	-	-	6.46	nr
R0302	offset bend	6.51	2.5%	-	-	6.67	nr
R0303	branch	8.60	2.5%	-	-	8.82	nr
R0304	pipe clip	2.39	2.5%	-	-	2.45	nr
R0305	drain connector	5.19	2.5%	-	-	5.32	nr
R0313	Rainwater head, rectangular, 236 x 152 x 187 mm, 68 mm outlet	5.97	2.5%	-	-	6.12	nr
R0314	Rainwater head, rectangular, 252 x 195 x 210 mm, 110 mm outlet	13.90	2.5%	-	-	14.25	nr
R0315	Rainwater head, rectangular, 254 x 178 x 137 mm, 61 mm square outlet	7.34	2.5%	-	-	7.53	nr
	Cast iron soil pipes and fittings, BS 416 (uneared)						
R0339	75 mm nominal size pipe	42.16	5%	-	-	44.27	m
	Extra over for:						
R0340	access pipe, oval door	71.42	2.5%	-	-	73.21	nr
R0341	bend	41.59	2.5%	-	-	42.63	nr
R0342	offset, 150 mm projection	50.97	2.5%	-	-	52.24	nr
R0343	offset, 300 mm projection	72.07	2.5%	-	-	73.88	nr
R0344	bossed pipe, one boss, 150 mm long	58.87	2.5%	-	-	60.34	nr
R0345	branch	58.87	2.5%	-	-	60.34	nr
R0346	double branch	109.69	2.5%	-	-	112.43	nr
R0347	roof connector	113.95	2.5%	-	-	116.80	nr
R0348	cast iron holderbat	22.51	2.5%	-	-	23.08	nr

Basic Prices of Materials

		Supply Price £	Waste Factor %	Unload. Labour £	Unload. Plant £	Total Unit Cost £	Unit
R0349	100 mm nominal size pipe	53.71	5%	-	-	56.40	m
	Extra over for:						
R0350	W.C. connector, effective length 300 mm	89.71	2.5%	-	-	91.95	nr
R0351	W.C. connector, effective length 450 mm	89.71	2.5%	-	-	91.95	nr
R0352	access pipe, oval door	106.33	2.5%	-	-	108.99	nr
R0353	bend	50.41	2.5%	-	-	51.67	nr
R0354	offset, 150 mm projection	74.51	2.5%	-	-	76.37	nr
R0355	offset, 300 mm projection	99.11	2.5%	-	-	101.59	nr
R0356	bossed pipe, one boss, 150 mm long	128.75	2.5%	-	-	131.97	nr
R0357	branch	129.04	2.5%	-	-	132.26	nr
R0358	double branch	143.54	2.5%	-	-	147.13	nr
R0359	roof connector	113.95	2.5%	-	-	116.80	nr
R0360	cast iron holderbat	22.51	2.5%	-	-	23.08	nr
R0361	reducer, 100 x 75 mm	60.05	2.5%	-	-	61.55	nr
R0362	75 mm galvanised wire balloon grating	27.01	2.5%	-	-	27.68	nr
R0363	100 mm galvanised wire balloon grating	27.01	2.5%	-	-	27.68	nr
R0364	Lead wool	4.09	5%	-	-	4.30	kg
R0365	Gaskin yarn	0.77	10%	-	-	0.84	m
	Copper pipes BS EN1057						
	Table X:						
R0369	15 mm nominal size pipe	2.22	5%	-	-	2.33	m
R0370	22 mm nominal size pipe	4.44	5%	-	-	4.66	m
R0371	28 mm nominal size pipe	5.60	5%	-	-	5.88	m
R0372	35 mm nominal size pipe	11.08	5%	-	-	11.63	m
R0373	42 mm nominal size pipe	13.29	5%	-	-	13.96	m
R0374	54 mm nominal size pipe	17.49	5%	-	-	18.37	m
	Table Z:						
R0375	15 mm nominal size pipe	2.68	5%	-	-	2.82	m
R0376	22 mm nominal size pipe	5.31	5%	-	-	5.58	m
R0377	28 mm nominal size pipe	6.71	5%	-	-	7.05	m
R0378	35 mm nominal size pipe	13.39	5%	-	-	14.06	m
R0379	42 mm nominal size pipe	15.95	5%	-	-	16.75	m
R0380	54 mm nominal size pipe	20.99	5%	-	-	22.04	m
	Table Y:						
R0381	15 mm nominal size pipe	4.18	5%	-	-	4.39	m
R0382	22 mm nominal size pipe	7.13	5%	-	-	7.49	m
R0383	28 mm nominal size pipe	9.47	5%	-	-	9.94	m
	Two piece copper spacing clips:						
R0384	15 mm	0.19	5%	-	-	0.20	nr
R0385	22 mm	0.21	5%	-	-	0.22	nr
R0386	28 mm	0.22	5%	-	-	0.24	nr
R0387	35 mm	0.38	5%	-	-	0.40	nr
R0388	42 mm	0.84	5%	-	-	0.88	nr
R0389	54 mm	1.11	5%	-	-	1.17	nr
	Capillary fittings for copper pipes, BS EN1254, Part 1						
	Straight coupling:						
R0390	15 mm	0.28	2.5%	-	-	0.29	nr
R0391	22 mm	0.75	2.5%	-	-	0.76	nr
R0392	28 mm	1.73	2.5%	-	-	1.78	nr
R0393	35 mm	5.86	2.5%	-	-	6.01	nr
R0394	42 mm	9.79	2.5%	-	-	10.03	nr
R0395	54 mm	18.05	2.5%	-	-	18.50	nr
	Tank connector with back nut:						
R0396	15 mm	9.09	2.5%	-	-	9.32	nr
R0397	22 mm	13.84	2.5%	-	-	14.19	nr
R0398	28 mm	18.20	2.5%	-	-	18.65	nr
R0399	35 mm	24.22	2.5%	-	-	24.82	nr
R0400	42 mm	31.75	2.5%	-	-	32.54	nr
R0401	54 mm	48.51	2.5%	-	-	49.72	nr
	Straight tap connector:						
R0402	15 mm	5.67	2.5%	-	-	5.81	nr
R0403	22 mm	2.92	2.5%	-	-	3.00	nr
	Elbow:						
R0404	15 mm	0.50	2.5%	-	-	0.51	nr
R0405	22 mm	1.32	2.5%	-	-	1.35	nr
R0406	28 mm	2.78	2.5%	-	-	2.85	nr
R0407	35 mm	12.55	2.5%	-	-	12.86	nr
R0408	42 mm	20.73	2.5%	-	-	21.25	nr
R0409	54 mm	42.82	2.5%	-	-	43.89	nr
	Overflow bend:						
R0981	22 mm	18.83	2.5%	-	-	19.31	nr
	Tee:						
R0410	15 mm	0.96	2.5%	-	-	0.98	nr
R0411	22 mm	3.04	2.5%	-	-	3.12	nr
R0412	28 mm	7.72	2.5%	-	-	7.91	nr
R0413	35 mm	20.43	2.5%	-	-	20.95	nr
R0414	42 mm	32.77	2.5%	-	-	33.59	nr
R0415	54 mm	66.08	2.5%	-	-	67.73	nr
	Reducing tee:						
R0416	22 x 22 x 15 mm	2.42	2.5%	-	-	2.48	nr
R0417	28 x 28 x 22 mm	11.41	2.5%	-	-	11.69	nr
R0418	35 x 35 x 28 mm	27.32	2.5%	-	-	28.01	nr
R0419	42 x 42 x 35 mm	61.86	2.5%	-	-	63.40	nr
R0420	54 x 54 x 42 mm	103.94	2.5%	-	-	106.54	nr

Basic Prices of Materials		Supply Price £	Waste Factor %	Unload. Labour £	Unload. Plant £	Total Unit Cost £	Unit
	Sweep tee:						
R0982	35 mm	41.09	2.5%	-	-	42.12	nr
R0983	42 mm	60.91	2.5%	-	-	62.43	nr
	Reducing sweep tee:						
R0984	35 x 35 x 22 mm	41.09	2.5%	-	-	42.12	nr
	Straight male connector:						
R0421	15 mm x 1/2" BSP	3.63	2.5%	-	-	3.72	nr
R0422	22 mm x 3/4" BSP	6.49	2.5%	-	-	6.65	nr
R0423	28 mm x 1" BSP	10.49	2.5%	-	-	10.75	nr
R0424	35 mm x 1.1/4" BSP	19.11	2.5%	-	-	19.58	nr
R0425	42 mm x 1.1/2" BSP	24.61	2.5%	-	-	25.22	nr
R0426	54 mm x 2" BSP	37.36	2.5%	-	-	38.30	nr
	Straight female connector:						
R0427	15 mm x 1/2" BSP	4.28	2.5%	-	-	4.38	nr
R0428	22 mm x 3/4" BSP	6.18	2.5%	-	-	6.34	nr
R0429	28 mm x 1" BSP	11.69	2.5%	-	-	11.98	nr
R0430	35 mm x 1.1/4" BSP	20.97	2.5%	-	-	21.49	nr
R0431	42 mm x 1.1/2" BSP	27.21	2.5%	-	-	27.89	nr
R0432	54 mm x 2" BSP	43.15	2.5%	-	-	44.23	nr
	Straight union adaptor:						
R0433	15 mm x 1/2" BSP	7.51	2.5%	-	-	7.70	nr
R0434	22 mm x 3/4" BSP	9.59	2.5%	-	-	9.83	nr
	Compression fittings for copper pipes, BS EN1254, Part 2, Type A						
	Straight couplings:						
R0440	15 mm	3.83	2.5%	-	-	3.92	nr
R0441	22 mm	6.59	2.5%	-	-	6.75	nr
R0442	28 mm	20.79	2.5%	-	-	21.31	nr
R0443	35 mm	22.61	2.5%	-	-	23.17	nr
R0444	42 mm	29.73	2.5%	-	-	30.47	nr
R0445	54 mm	44.45	2.5%	-	-	45.56	nr
	Tank connector:						
R0446	15 mm	3.45	2.5%	-	-	3.54	nr
R0447	22 mm	3.71	2.5%	-	-	3.80	nr
R0448	28 mm	13.49	2.5%	-	-	13.83	nr
	Straight swivel tap connector:						
R0449	15 mm	3.30	2.5%	-	-	3.39	nr
R0450	22 mm	8.60	2.5%	-	-	8.82	nr
	Elbow:						
R0451	15 mm	1.87	2.5%	-	-	1.92	nr
R0452	22 mm	3.20	2.5%	-	-	3.28	nr
R0453	28 mm	10.81	2.5%	-	-	11.08	nr
R0454	35 mm	30.52	2.5%	-	-	31.28	nr
R0455	42 mm	41.33	2.5%	-	-	42.36	nr
R0456	54 mm	71.12	2.5%	-	-	72.89	nr
	Tee:						
R0457	15 mm	2.66	2.5%	-	-	2.72	nr
R0458	22 mm	4.47	2.5%	-	-	4.58	nr
R0459	28 mm	20.36	2.5%	-	-	20.86	nr
R0460	35 mm	39.69	2.5%	-	-	40.68	nr
R0461	42 mm	62.40	2.5%	-	-	63.96	nr
R0462	54 mm	100.25	2.5%	-	-	102.76	nr
	Reducing tee:						
R0463	22 mm	11.51	2.5%	-	-	11.80	nr
R0464	28 mm	20.46	2.5%	-	-	20.97	nr
	Straight female coupling:						
R0465	15 mm x 1/2" BSP	1.75	2.5%	-	-	1.80	nr
R0466	22 mm x 3/4" BSP	2.52	2.5%	-	-	2.58	nr
R0467	28 mm x 1" BSP	7.30	2.5%	-	-	7.48	nr
R0468	35 mm x 1.1/4" BSP	20.63	2.5%	-	-	21.14	nr
R0469	42 mm x 1.1/2" BSP	27.74	2.5%	-	-	28.44	nr
R0470	54 mm x 2" BSP	40.69	2.5%	-	-	41.71	nr
	Female reducing coupling:						
R0471	15 mm x 3/4" BSP	6.91	2.5%	-	-	7.09	nr
R0472	22 mm x 1" BSP	9.99	2.5%	-	-	10.24	nr
R0473	28 mm x 1" BSP	9.44	2.5%	-	-	9.68	nr
	Gunmetal compression fittings, BS EN1254, Part 2, Type B						
	Straight coupling:						
R0480	15 mm	2.79	2.5%	-	-	2.86	nr
R0481	22 mm	4.53	2.5%	-	-	4.64	nr
R0482	28 mm	10.30	2.5%	-	-	10.55	nr
	Elbow:						
R0483	15 mm	3.35	2.5%	-	-	3.44	nr
R0484	22 mm	5.34	2.5%	-	-	5.48	nr
R0485	28 mm	13.29	2.5%	-	-	13.62	nr
	Tee:						
R0486	15 mm	4.70	2.5%	-	-	4.82	nr
R0487	22 mm	7.77	2.5%	-	-	7.96	nr
R0488	28 mm	21.19	2.5%	-	-	21.72	nr
	Reducing tee:						
R0489	22 mm	12.42	2.5%	-	-	12.74	nr
R0490	28 mm	20.46	2.5%	-	-	20.97	nr
	Female coupling:						
R0491	15 mm x 1/2" BSP	2.98	2.5%	-	-	3.06	nr
R0493	22 mm x 3/4" BSP	4.37	2.5%	-	-	4.48	nr
R0494	28 mm x 1" BSP	9.44	2.5%	-	-	9.68	nr

Basic Prices of Materials

		Supply Price £	Waste Factor %	Unload. Labour £	Unload. Plant £	Total Unit Cost £	Unit
	PVCu pipes and fittings, BS 3505, Class E						
R0501	1/2" nominal size pipe	1.32	5%	-	-	**1.38**	m
R0502	3/4" nominal size pipe	1.86	5%	-	-	**1.95**	m
R0503	1" nominal size pipe	2.60	5%	-	-	**2.73**	m
R0504	1.1/4" nominal size pipe	3.99	5%	-	-	**4.19**	m
R0505	1.1/2" nominal size pipe	5.19	5%	-	-	**5.45**	m
	Tank connector:						
R0506	1/2"	8.74	2.5%	-	-	**8.96**	nr
R0507	3/4"	10.01	2.5%	-	-	**10.26**	nr
	Straight tap connector:						
R0508	1/2"	4.79	2.5%	-	-	**4.91**	nr
R0509	3/4"	5.21	2.5%	-	-	**5.34**	nr
	Elbow:						
R0511	1/2"	2.27	2.5%	-	-	**2.33**	nr
R0512	3/4"	2.72	2.5%	-	-	**2.79**	nr
R0513	1"	3.79	2.5%	-	-	**3.88**	nr
R0514	1.1/4"	6.62	2.5%	-	-	**6.79**	nr
R0515	1.1/2"	8.53	2.5%	-	-	**8.74**	nr
	Tees:						
R0517	1/2"	2.63	2.5%	-	-	**2.69**	nr
R0518	3/4"	3.31	2.5%	-	-	**3.39**	nr
R0519	1"	5.00	2.5%	-	-	**5.13**	nr
R0520	1.1/4"	7.09	2.5%	-	-	**7.26**	nr
R0521	1.1/2"	10.23	2.5%	-	-	**10.48**	nr
	Reducing bush:						
R0522	1/2"	1.30	2.5%	-	-	**1.33**	nr
R0523	3/4"	1.71	2.5%	-	-	**1.75**	nr
R0524	1"	2.21	2.5%	-	-	**2.26**	nr
R0525	1.1/4"	2.98	2.5%	-	-	**3.05**	nr
R0526	1.1/2"	3.51	2.5%	-	-	**3.60**	nr
	Coupling:						
R0528	1/2"	1.71	2.5%	-	-	**1.75**	nr
R0529	3/4"	1.90	2.5%	-	-	**1.95**	nr
R0530	1"	2.21	2.5%	-	-	**2.26**	nr
R0531	1.1/4"	3.99	2.5%	-	-	**4.09**	nr
R0532	1.1/2"	4.67	2.5%	-	-	**4.79**	nr
	Union connector:						
R0533	1/2"	8.77	2.5%	-	-	**8.99**	nr
R0534	3/4"	10.04	2.5%	-	-	**10.29**	nr
R0535	1"	13.00	2.5%	-	-	**13.33**	nr
R0536	1.1/4"	16.19	2.5%	-	-	**16.59**	nr
R0537	1.1/2"	22.19	2.5%	-	-	**22.75**	nr
	Pipe clip:						
R0539	1/2"	0.77	2.5%	-	-	**0.79**	nr
R0540	3/4"	0.82	2.5%	-	-	**0.84**	nr
R0541	1"	0.91	2.5%	-	-	**0.93**	nr
R0542	1/1/4"	1.22	2.5%	-	-	**1.25**	nr
R0543	1.1/2"	1.33	2.5%	-	-	**1.36**	nr
	PVCu overflow pipes and fittings						
R0550	19 mm nominal size pipe	0.41	2.5%	-	-	**0.42**	m
	Extra over for:						
R0551	Pipe clip	0.19	2.5%	-	-	**0.19**	nr
R0552	Double socket	0.48	2.5%	-	-	**0.49**	nr
R0553	Straight tank connector	0.51	2.5%	-	-	**0.52**	nr
R0554	Bent tank connector	0.64	2.5%	-	-	**0.65**	nr
R0555	Bend	0.48	2.5%	-	-	**0.50**	nr
R0556	Tee	0.57	2.5%	-	-	**0.59**	nr
	PVCu soil and vent pipes and fittings, BS 4514						
R0560	82 mm nominal size pipe	4.38	5%	-	-	**4.60**	m
	Extra over for:						
R0561	holderbat	1.45	2.5%	-	-	**1.49**	nr
R0562	W.C. connector	4.40	2.5%	-	-	**4.51**	nr
R0563	W.C. connecting bend	5.79	2.5%	-	-	**5.94**	nr
R0564	access pipe door	11.96	2.5%	-	-	**12.26**	nr
R0565	bend	7.49	2.5%	-	-	**7.68**	nr
R0566	boss pipe and waste adaptor	7.43	2.5%	-	-	**7.61**	nr
R0567	branch	10.64	2.5%	-	-	**10.91**	nr
R0569	drain connector	4.40	2.5%	-	-	**4.51**	nr
R0570	balloon grating	2.10	2.5%	-	-	**2.15**	nr
R0571	weathering collar	2.30	2.5%	-	-	**2.36**	nr
R0572	110 mm nominal size pipe	4.44	5%	-	-	**4.67**	m
	Extra over for:						
R0573	holderbat	1.35	2.5%	-	-	**1.39**	nr
R0574	W.C. connector	6.44	2.5%	-	-	**6.61**	nr
R0575	W.C. connecting bend	6.44	2.5%	-	-	**6.61**	nr
R0576	access pipe door	6.98	2.5%	-	-	**7.15**	nr
R0577	bend	8.10	2.5%	-	-	**8.30**	nr
R0578	boss pipe and waste adaptor	3.74	2.5%	-	-	**3.84**	nr
R0579	branch	12.95	2.5%	-	-	**13.27**	nr
R0580	double branch	28.67	2.5%	-	-	**29.38**	nr
R0581	access branch	21.73	2.5%	-	-	**22.27**	nr
R0583	drain connector	8.53	2.5%	-	-	**8.74**	nr
R0584	balloon grating	1.90	2.5%	-	-	**1.95**	nr
R0585	weathering collar	2.66	2.5%	-	-	**2.73**	nr

Basic Prices of Materials

		Supply Price £	Waste Factor %	Unload. Labour £	Unload. Plant £	Total Unit Cost £	Unit
	Weathering slate, aluminium base:						
R0587	450 x 450 mm	20.56	2.5%	-	-	21.07	nr
R0588	450 x 600 mm	26.94	2.5%	-	-	27.61	nr
	Polyethylene Cold water pipes, blue or black, coiled M.D.P.E. pipes to BS 6572/BS 6730						
R0598	20 mm nominal size	1.65	5%	-	-	1.73	m
R0599	25 mm nominal size	2.09	5%	-	-	2.19	m
R0611	32 mm nominal size	3.50	5%	-	-	3.68	m
R0612	50 mm nominal size	8.41	5%	-	-	8.83	m
	Galvanised steel pipe brackets:						
R0613	3/8" nominal size	0.45	2.5%	-	-	0.46	nr
R0614	1/2" nominal size	0.45	2.5%	-	-	0.46	nr
R0615	3/4" nominal size	0.64	2.5%	-	-	0.65	nr
R0616	1" nominal size	0.82	2.5%	-	-	0.84	nr
R0617	1.1/4" nominal size	1.07	2.5%	-	-	1.10	nr
R0618	2" nominal size	2.17	2.5%	-	-	2.22	nr
	Gunmetal and brass compression fittings, BS EN1254 , Part 3 for polythene pipes						
	Straight tap connector:						
R0621	1/2" x 1/2" BSP	13.34	2.5%	-	-	13.67	nr
R0622	3/4" x 3/4" BSP	23.41	2.5%	-	-	23.99	nr
	Elbow:						
R0625	20 mm	10.53	2.5%	-	-	10.79	nr
R0626	25 mm	15.89	2.5%	-	-	16.28	nr
R0627	32 mm	30.46	2.5%	-	-	31.22	nr
R0628	50 mm	72.38	2.5%	-	-	74.19	nr
	Tee:						
R0631	20 mm	14.11	2.5%	-	-	14.46	nr
R0632	25 mm	22.93	2.5%	-	-	23.51	nr
R0633	32 mm	37.76	2.5%	-	-	38.70	nr
R0634	50 mm	95.03	2.5%	-	-	97.41	nr
	Reducing tee:						
R0635	25 mm	24.51	2.5%	-	-	25.12	nr
R0636	32 mm	37.76	2.5%	-	-	38.70	nr
R0637	50 mm	95.03	2.5%	-	-	97.41	nr
R0638	63 mm	144.99	2.5%	-	-	148.62	nr
	Straight coupling, PE x copper (table X):						
R0640	20 mm	8.15	2.5%	-	-	8.35	nr
R0641	25 mm	12.05	2.5%	-	-	12.36	nr
R0642	32 mm	23.17	2.5%	-	-	23.75	nr
	Straight coupling, PE x FI:						
R0643	32 mm	17.79	2.5%	-	-	18.23	nr
R0644	50 mm	46.43	2.5%	-	-	47.59	nr
	Female coupling, PE x BSP thread:						
R0648	20 mm	7.99	2.5%	-	-	8.19	nr
R0649	25 mm	11.33	2.5%	-	-	11.62	nr
R0650	32 mm	17.79	2.5%	-	-	18.23	nr
R0651	50 mm	46.43	2.5%	-	-	47.59	nr
	Copper liner:						
R0654	20 mm	0.98	2.5%	-	-	1.00	nr
R0655	25 mm	1.19	2.5%	-	-	1.22	nr
R0656	32 mm	1.43	2.5%	-	-	1.46	nr
R0657	50 mm	3.44	2.5%	-	-	3.53	nr
R0658	63 mm	4.17	2.5%	-	-	4.27	nr
	MuPVC waste pipes and fittings, BS 5255						
R0660	1.1/4" (32) nominal size pipe	3.44	5%	-	-	3.62	m
R0661	1.1/2" (40) nominal size pipe	3.98	5%	-	-	4.17	m
R0662	2" (50) nominal size pipe	6.13	5%	-	-	6.44	m
	Pipe clip:						
R0663	1.1/4" (32)	0.41	2.5%	-	-	0.42	nr
R0664	1.1/2" (40)	0.45	2.5%	-	-	0.46	nr
R0665	2" (50)	0.79	2.5%	-	-	0.81	nr
	Double socket:						
R0666	1.1/4" (32)	1.81	2.5%	-	-	1.85	nr
R0667	1.1/2" (40)	1.81	2.5%	-	-	1.85	nr
R0668	2" (50)	2.48	2.5%	-	-	2.54	nr
	Elbow:						
R0669	1.1/4" (32)	1.84	2.5%	-	-	1.88	nr
R0670	1.1/2" (40)	1.92	2.5%	-	-	1.97	nr
R0671	2" (50)	2.53	2.5%	-	-	2.59	nr
	Tee:						
R0672	1.1/4" (32)	1.92	2.5%	-	-	1.97	nr
R0673	1.1/2" (40)	1.92	2.5%	-	-	1.97	nr
R0674	2" (50)	2.65	2.5%	-	-	2.72	nr
	Straight tank connector:						
R0675	1.1/4" (32)	1.64	2.5%	-	-	1.68	nr
R0676	1.1/2" (40)	1.64	2.5%	-	-	1.68	nr
	Expansion socket:						
R0677	1.1/4" (32)	2.04	2.5%	-	-	2.09	nr
R0678	1.1/2" (40)	2.04	2.5%	-	-	2.09	nr
R0679	2" (50)	2.92	2.5%	-	-	2.99	nr

Basic Prices of Materials

		Supply Price £	Waste Factor %	Unload. Labour £	Unload. Plant £	Total Unit Cost £	Unit
	Connector:						
R0680	1.1/4" (32) to copper	2.71	2.5%	-	-	2.78	nr
R0681	1.1/2" (40) to copper	2.71	2.5%	-	-	2.78	nr
R0682	1.1/4" (32) to steel	2.71	2.5%	-	-	2.78	nr
R0683	1.1/2" (40) to steel	2.71	2.5%	-	-	2.78	nr
R0684	2" (50) to steel	4.39	2.5%	-	-	4.50	nr
	Rubber reducer:						
R0686	1.1/4" (32)	1.90	2.5%	-	-	1.95	nr
R0687	1.1/2" (40)	2.36	2.5%	-	-	2.42	nr
	Polypropylene traps						
	Bottle 'P' trap, 38 mm seal:						
R0690	1.1/4" (32) nominal size	4.14	2.5%	-	-	4.24	nr
R0691	1.1/2" (40) nominal size	4.75	2.5%	-	-	4.87	nr
	Bottle 'P' trap, 76 mm seal:						
R0692	1.1/4" (32) nominal size	4.51	2.5%	-	-	4.63	nr
R0693	1.1/2" (40) nominal size	5.27	2.5%	-	-	5.40	nr
R0694	1.1/4" (32) nominal size, anti-syphon	6.67	2.5%	-	-	6.84	nr
R0695	1.1/2" (40) nominal size, anti-syphon	7.34	2.5%	-	-	7.53	nr
	Tubular trap, 76 mm seal:						
R0696	1.1/4" (32) nominal size, 'P' trap	4.75	2.5%	-	-	4.87	nr
R0697	1.1/2" (40) nominal size, 'P' trap	5.27	2.5%	-	-	5.40	nr
R0698	1.1/4" (32) nominal size, 'S' trap	5.53	2.5%	-	-	5.67	nr
R0699	1.1/2" (40) nominal size, 'S' trap	6.17	2.5%	-	-	6.32	nr
	Three-piece running 'P' trap, 76 mm seal:						
R0700	1.1/4" (32) nominal size	6.67	2.5%	-	-	6.84	nr
R0701	1.1/2" (40) nominal size	6.99	2.5%	-	-	7.16	nr
	1.1/2" (40) nominal size bath trap, complete with flexible pipe for over flow connection:						
R0702	'P' trap	10.78	2.5%	-	-	11.05	nr
	Copper traps						
	'P' trap, 38 mm seal						
R0991	35 mm	28.09	2.5%	-	-	28.79	nr
R0992	42 mm	41.56	2.5%	-	-	42.60	nr
	'S' trap, 76 mm seal						
R0993	35 mm	29.95	2.5%	-	-	30.70	nr
R0994	42 mm	43.09	2.5%	-	-	44.17	nr
	Galvanised steel pipes, BS 1387						
	Medium grade:						
R0705	15 mm nominal size pipe screwed & socketed	5.02	5%	-	-	5.27	m
R0706	20 mm nominal size pipe screwed & socketed	5.33	5%	-	-	5.60	m
R0707	25 mm nominal size pipe screwed & socketed	7.82	5%	-	-	8.21	m
R0708	32 mm nominal size pipe screwed & socketed	9.31	5%	-	-	9.78	m
R0709	40 mm nominal size pipe screwed & socketed	10.75	5%	-	-	11.28	m
R0710	50 mm nominal size pipe screwed & socketed	15.88	5%	-	-	16.67	m
	Heavy grade:						
R0711	15 mm nominal size pipe screwed & socketed	6.03	5%	-	-	6.33	m
R0712	20 mm nominal size pipe screwed & socketed	6.39	5%	-	-	6.71	m
R0713	25 mm nominal size pipe screwed & socketed	9.07	5%	-	-	9.53	m
R0714	32 mm nominal size pipe screwed & socketed	11.18	5%	-	-	11.74	m
R0715	40 mm nominal size pipe screwed & socketed	12.90	5%	-	-	13.54	m
R0716	50 mm nominal size pipe screwed & socketed	19.06	5%	-	-	20.01	m
R0717	2" galvanised steel pipe clips	0.38	5%	-	-	0.40	nr
	Galvanised malleable iron fittings for steel pipes BS 143 and BS 1256						
	Elbow:						
R0720	15 mm	0.61	2.5%	-	-	0.63	nr
R0721	20 mm	0.73	2.5%	-	-	0.75	nr
R0722	25 mm	1.04	2.5%	-	-	1.07	nr
R0723	32 mm	1.85	0.5%	-	-	1.86	nr
R0724	40 mm	3.13	2.5%	-	-	3.21	nr
R0725	50 mm	3.60	2.5%	-	-	3.69	nr
	Tee:						
R0726	15 mm	0.74	2.5%	-	-	0.76	nr
R0727	20 mm	0.98	2.5%	-	-	1.01	nr
R0728	25 mm	1.50	2.5%	-	-	1.54	nr
R0729	32 mm	2.45	2.5%	-	-	2.51	nr
R0730	40 mm	3.72	2.5%	-	-	3.82	nr
R0731	50 mm	5.62	2.5%	-	-	5.76	nr
	Reducing tee:						
R0732	20 mm	2.64	2.5%	-	-	2.70	nr
R0733	25 mm	1.42	2.5%	-	-	1.45	nr
R0734	32 mm	2.09	2.5%	-	-	2.14	nr
R0735	40 mm	2.88	2.5%	-	-	2.95	nr
R0736	50 mm	3.97	2.5%	-	-	4.07	nr
	Gunmetal and brass stop valves, BS 1010						
	Stopcock, copper x copper, compression joints:						
R0740	15 mm nominal size	10.70	2.5%	-	-	10.96	nr
R0741	22 mm nominal size	18.79	2.5%	-	-	19.26	nr

Basic Prices of Materials

		Supply Price £	Waste Factor %	Unload. Labour £	Unload. Plant £	Total Unit Cost £	Unit
R0742	28 mm nominal size	49.02	2.5%	-	-	50.24	nr
	Stopcock, PVC x PVC:						
R0743	3/8" nominal size	28.42	2.5%	-	-	29.13	nr
R0744	1/2" nominal size	29.31	2.5%	-	-	30.04	nr
	Stopcock, polythene x polythene:						
R0745	3/8" nominal size	28.42	2.5%	-	-	29.13	nr
R0746	1/2" nominal size	29.31	2.5%	-	-	30.04	nr
R0747	3/4" nominal size	44.00	2.5%	-	-	45.10	nr
	Stopcock, female threaded ends:						
R0749	15 mm nominal size	25.36	2.5%	-	-	25.99	nr
R0750	22 mm nominal size	35.67	2.5%	-	-	36.56	nr
R0751	28 mm nominal size	63.45	2.5%	-	-	65.04	nr
R0752	35 mm nominal size	156.73	2.5%	-	-	160.65	nr
R0753	42 mm nominal size	215.11	2.5%	-	-	220.48	nr
R0754	54 mm nominal size	338.38	2.5%	-	-	346.83	nr
	Gunmetal gatevalve, BS 5154 copper x copper, capillary ends:						
R0755	15 mm nominal size	19.66	2.5%	-	-	20.15	nr
R0756	22 mm nominal size	34.05	2.5%	-	-	34.91	nr
R0757	28 mm nominal size	57.96	2.5%	-	-	59.41	nr
R0758	35 mm nominal size	89.02	2.5%	-	-	91.24	nr
R0759	42 mm nominal size	118.21	2.5%	-	-	121.17	nr
R0760	54 mm nominal size	176.58	2.5%	-	-	180.99	nr
	Brass wheelvalve, BS 5154, female threaded ends:						
R0761	15 mm nominal size	24.52	2.5%	-	-	25.13	nr
R0762	20 mm nominal size	28.39	2.5%	-	-	29.10	nr
R0763	25 mm nominal size	39.54	2.5%	-	-	40.53	nr
R0764	32 mm nominal size	27.54	2.5%	-	-	28.23	nr
R0765	40 mm nominal size	110.27	2.5%	-	-	113.03	nr
R0766	50 mm nominal size	159.97	2.5%	-	-	163.97	nr
	Brass drain cocks, threaded end:						
R0767	15 mm nominal size	57.60	2.5%	-	-	59.04	nr
	Brass draw-off elbow, copper x copper, compression ends:						
R0769	15 mm nominal size	15.88	2.5%	-	-	16.27	nr
R0770	22 mm nominal size	18.20	2.5%	-	-	18.66	nr
R0771	28 mm nominal size	28.02	2.5%	-	-	28.72	nr
	Radiator valves, wheel head, matt brass:						
R0772	15 mm nominal size, for copper	2.16	2.5%	-	-	2.22	nr
R0773	22 mm nominal size, for copper	18.29	2.5%	-	-	18.75	nr
R0774	15 mm nominal size, for iron	10.39	2.5%	-	-	10.65	nr
R0775	20 mm nominal size, for iron	25.30	2.5%	-	-	25.94	nr
	Thermostatic radiator valves, chromium plated:						
R0776	15 mm nominal size, for copper	11.23	2.5%	-	-	11.52	nr
R0777	15 mm nominal size, for iron	13.62	2.5%	-	-	13.96	nr
R0778	20 mm nominal size, for iron	34.57	2.5%	-	-	35.43	nr
	Ball valves, BS 1212:						
R0779	15 mm nominal size, piston type	29.42	2.5%	-	-	30.15	nr
R0780	22 mm nominal size, piston type	45.20	2.5%	-	-	46.33	nr
R0781	28 mm nominal size, piston type	88.34	2.5%	-	-	90.55	nr
R0782	15 mm nominal size, diaphragm type	10.95	2.5%	-	-	11.22	nr
	Copper float, BS 1968:						
R0783	4.1/2"	11.17	2.5%	-	-	11.45	nr
R0784	5"	15.23	2.5%	-	-	15.61	nr
R0785	6"	16.27	2.5%	-	-	16.68	nr
	Floor, wall and ceiling plates, chrome effect polypropylene for pipe:						
R0790	15 mm nominal size	0.42	2.5%	-	-	0.43	nr
R0791	22 mm nominal size	0.48	2.5%	-	-	0.49	nr
R0792	28 mm nominal size	0.60	2.5%	-	-	0.61	nr
R0793	35 mm nominal size	0.78	2.5%	-	-	0.80	nr
R0794	42 mm nominal size	1.02	2.5%	-	-	1.04	nr
R0795	54 mm nominal size	1.26	2.5%	-	-	1.29	nr

Sanitary Fittings

With a wide variation of prices over the range of sanitary fittings and accessories available on the market, the following P.C. prices have been included as representative of the fittings which might be used in commercial work.

Sinks

		Supply Price £	Waste Factor %	Unload. Labour £	Unload. Plant £	Total Unit Cost £	Unit
	Fireclay sink, Belfast pattern, BS 1206:						
R0800	610 x 455 x 255 mm	205.99	-	-	-	205.99	nr
R0801	760 x 455 x 255 mm	399.77	-	-	-	399.77	nr
	Stainless steel sink:						
R0802	1000 x 600 mm (single drainer)	82.69	-	-	-	82.69	nr
R0803	1500 x 600 mm (double drainer)	169.81	-	-	-	169.81	nr

Baths, nominal sizes

		Supply Price £	Waste Factor %	Unload. Labour £	Unload. Plant £	Total Unit Cost £	Unit
	Cast iron, porcelain enamelled, rectangular, white:						
R0805	1500 mm long	366.45	-	-	-	366.45	nr
R0806	1700 mm long	366.45	-	-	-	366.45	nr
	Pressed steel, vitreous enamelled, rectangular:						
R0807	1500 mm long, white	141.04	-	-	-	141.04	nr
R0808	1700 mm long, white	141.04	-	-	-	141.04	nr
R0809	1700 mm long, coloured	141.04	-	-	-	141.04	nr
	5 mm glass fibre reinforced acrylic:						
R0810	1700 mm long, white	139.89	-	-	-	139.89	nr
R0811	1700 mm long, coloured	139.89	-	-	-	139.89	nr

Basic Prices of Materials	Supply Price £	Waste Factor %	Unload. Labour £	Unload. Plant £	Total Unit Cost £	Unit
Lavatory basins						
Vitreous china:						
R0812 560 x 405 mm, white	39.90	-	-	-	**39.90**	nr
R0813 560 x 405 mm, coloured	52.50	-	-	-	**52.50**	nr
R0814 635 x 455 mm, white	82.69	-	-	-	**82.69**	nr
R0815 635 x 455 mm, coloured	82.69	-	-	-	**82.69**	nr
Pedestal stand:						
R0816 white	22.16	-	-	-	**22.16**	nr
R0817 coloured	22.16	-	-	-	**22.16**	nr
WC suites						
Vitreous china, close coupled, washdown, dual flush syphon:						
R0820 white	150.71	-	-	-	**150.71**	nr
R0821 coloured	150.71	-	-	-	**150.71**	nr
Vitreous china, close coupled, syphonic, double trap:						
R0822 white	160.82	-	-	-	**160.82**	nr
R0823 coloured	160.82	-	-	-	**160.82**	nr
Solid plastic seat and cover:						
R0824 white	12.73	-	-	-	**12.73**	nr
R0825 coloured	12.73	-	-	-	**12.73**	nr
Urinals						
R0826 Single stall urinal, white glazed fireclay, complete with automatic flushing cistern and supports, stainless steel flush pipe and spreader, and domed outlet grating	915.60	-	-	-	**915.60**	nr
Slab urinal, white glazed fireclay, complete with back slabs, separate return ends, waterway channel, dome outlet grating, automatic flushing cistern and supports, stainless steel flushpipes, sparge pipe and clips:						
R0827 2 persons	1358.70	-	-	-	**1358.70**	nr
R0828 3 persons	1765.05	-	-	-	**1765.05**	nr
R0829 4 persons	2189.25	-	-	-	**2189.25**	nr
Bowl urinal, white vitreous china, complete with flushing cistern with automatic syphon, drip trap and wall hanger, stainless steel flush pipes with spreaders and clips, domed outlet grating:						
R0830 1 person	222.54	-	-	-	**222.54**	nr
R0831 2 persons	269.04	-	-	-	**269.04**	nr
R0832 3 persons	444.06	-	-	-	**444.06**	nr
R0833 Division	82.33	-	-	-	**82.33**	nr
Sundries						
Bib tap, BS 5412, chromium plated:						
R0835 13 mm nominal size	9.90	2.5%	-	-	**10.15**	nr
R0836 19 mm nominal size	17.67	2.5%	-	-	**18.11**	nr
Pillar tap, BS 5412, chromium plated:						
R0837 13 mm nominal size	9.79	2.5%	-	-	**10.03**	nr
R0838 19 mm nominal size	14.47	2.5%	-	-	**14.84**	nr
Chromium plated waste:						
R0840 32 mm basin waste	3.72	2.5%	-	-	**3.82**	nr
R0841 38 mm bath waste	3.57	2.5%	-	-	**3.66**	nr
R0842 38 mm sink waste	4.17	2.5%	-	-	**4.27**	nr
R0843 38 mm steel sink waste	3.87	2.5%	-	-	**3.96**	nr
Chromium plated waste chain:						
R0844 12" for lavatory basin	0.96	2.5%	-	-	**0.98**	nr
R0845 12" for metal sink	0.96	2.5%	-	-	**0.98**	nr
R0846 18" for sink	1.12	2.5%	-	-	**1.15**	nr
R0847 18" for bath	1.12	2.5%	-	-	**1.15**	nr
R0848 Bath overflow, chromium plated grid	6.46	2.5%	-	-	**6.62**	nr
Rubber plug:						
R0849 1.1/2"	0.49	2.5%	-	-	**0.51**	nr
R0850 1.3/4"	0.73	2.5%	-	-	**0.75**	nr
R0851 Cast iron screw to wall sink support bracket and leg	16.54	2.5%	-	-	**16.95**	set
R0852 Wall hangers for lavatory basins, aluminium alloy	5.93	2.5%	-	-	**6.08**	pair
Cast iron towel rail brackets:						
R0853 12" painted	6.62	2.5%	-	-	**6.78**	pair
R0854 12" plastic coated	13.26	2.5%	-	-	**13.59**	pair
Enamelled hardboard bath panel:						
R0855 760 x 610 x 3.2 mm thick end panel	2.53	2.5%	-	-	**2.60**	nr
R0856 1830 x 610 x 3.2 mm thick side panel	6.12	2.5%	-	-	**6.27**	nr
R0857 Polished aluminium angle strip 560 mm long	1.00	2.5%	-	-	**1.02**	nr
R0858 Detachable dome headed wood screws, chromium plated 3/4" x No. 8	0.60	2.5%	-	-	**0.61**	nr
Cisterns and cylinders						
Plastic water storage cistern, BS 4213, complete with lids and insulation:						
R0867 18 ltr capacity, type PC 4	41.17	-	-	-	**41.17**	nr
R0868 114 ltr capacity, type PC 25	45.81	-	-	-	**45.81**	nr
R0869 227 ltr capacity, type PC 50	71.72	-	-	-	**71.72**	nr
R0870 455 ltr capacity, type PC 100	148.06	-	-	-	**148.06**	nr
Copper hot water cylinder, direct pattern, BS 1566 Part 1, pre foamed						
Direct pattern:						
R0884 117 ltr capacity	135.52	-	-	-	**135.52**	nr
R0885 140 ltr capacity	184.37	-	-	-	**184.37**	nr
R0886 162 ltr capacity	195.83	-	-	-	**195.83**	nr
R0887 206 ltr capacity	276.22	-	-	-	**276.22**	nr

Basic Prices of Materials	Supply Price £	Waste Factor %	Unload. Labour £	Unload. Plant £	Total Unit Cost £	Unit
indirect pattern:						
R0888 117 ltr capacity	148.07	-	-	-	148.07	nr
R0889 140 ltr capacity	204.22	-	-	-	204.22	nr
R0890 162 ltr capacity	226.23	-	-	-	226.23	nr
R0891 206 ltr capacity	288.31	-	-	-	288.31	nr
Copper hot water cylinder, solar twin coil, pre-foamed:						
R0892 140 ltr capacity	378.55	-	-	-	378.55	nr
R0893 206 ltr capacity	397.25	-	-	-	397.25	nr
Copper combination hot water storage unit, direct pattern BS 3198, pre foamed:						
450 mm dia. x 1075 mm high:						
R0894 115 ltr hot water, 20 ltr cold water	236.99	-	-	-	236.99	nr
450 mm dia. x 1200 mm high:						
R0895 115 ltr hot water, 40 ltr cold water	252.43	-	-	-	252.43	nr
Copper combination hot water storage unit, indirect pattern, BS 3198, pre foamed:						
450 mm dia. x 1200 mm high:						
R0896 115 ltr hot water, 40 ltr cold water	317.26	-	-	-	317.26	nr
Mild steel oil storage tank, primed finish:						
R0897 300 gallon capacity, 2mm thick	490.88	-	-	-	490.88	nr
R0898 600 gallon capacity, 2.5mm thick	560.17	-	-	-	560.18	nr
Steel panel radiators, primed finish						
Single panel radiator with one convector surface, 450 mm high:						
R0900 600 mm long	33.59	-	-	-	33.59	nr
R0901 900 mm long	45.57	-	-	-	45.57	nr
R0902 1200 mm long	57.38	-	-	-	57.38	nr
R0903 1600 mm long	74.56	-	-	-	74.56	nr
R0904 2000 mm long	91.42	-	-	-	91.42	nr
R0905 2400 mm long	146.53	-	-	-	146.53	nr
Single panel radiator with one convector surface, 600 mm high:						
R0906 600 mm long	35.44	-	-	-	35.44	nr
R0907 900 mm long	52.50	-	-	-	52.50	nr
R0908 1200 mm long	68.25	-	-	-	68.25	nr
R0909 1600 mm long	92.42	-	-	-	92.42	nr
R0910 2000 mm long	114.11	-	-	-	114.11	nr
R0911 2400 mm long	183.37	-	-	-	183.37	nr
Single panel radiator with one convector surface, 700 mm high:						
R0912 600 mm long	45.51	-	-	-	45.51	nr
R0913 900 mm long	62.71	-	-	-	62.71	nr
R0914 1200 mm long	79.78	-	-	-	79.78	nr
R0915 1600 mm long	104.10	-	-	-	104.10	nr
R0916 2000 mm long	128.85	-	-	-	128.85	nr
R0917 2400 mm long	207.31	-	-	-	207.31	nr
Double panel radiator, with one convector surface, 450 mm high:						
R0918 600 mm long	50.80	-	-	-	50.80	nr
R0919 900 mm long	71.52	-	-	-	71.52	nr
R0920 1200 mm long	91.78	-	-	-	91.78	nr
R0921 1600 mm long	120.79	-	-	-	120.79	nr
R0922 2000 mm long	149.73	-	-	-	149.73	nr
R0923 2400 mm long	242.15	-	-	-	242.15	nr
Double panel radiator, with one convector surface, 600 mm high:						
R0924 600 mm long	61.68	-	-	-	61.68	nr
R0925 900 mm long	89.11	-	-	-	89.11	nr
R0926 1200 mm long	115.06	-	-	-	115.06	nr
R0927 1600 mm long	151.72	-	-	-	151.73	nr
R0928 2000 mm long	189.02	-	-	-	189.02	nr
R0929 2400 mm long	306.31	-	-	-	306.31	nr
Double panel radiator, with one convector surface, 700 mm high:						
R0930 600 mm long	70.58	-	-	-	70.58	nr
R0931 900 mm long	100.60	-	-	-	100.60	nr
R0932 1200 mm long	130.18	-	-	-	130.18	nr
R0933 1600 mm long	171.93	-	-	-	171.93	nr
R0934 2000 mm long	214.41	-	-	-	214.41	nr
R0935 2400 mm long	347.72	-	-	-	347.72	nr
Solid fuel boilers						
For domestic hot water, up to 5.90/2.60 kWh room heater:						
R0936 open flue	848.92	-	-	-	848.93	nr
For central heating and indirect hot water supply:						
R0937 output 13.2 kWh	1670.29	-	-	-	1670.29	nr
R0938 output 17.6 kWh	1941.97	-	-	-	1941.98	nr
R0939 output 23.5 kWh	2158.54	-	-	-	2158.54	nr
Oil fired boilers						
For central heating only, SEDBUK Band A:						
R0940 output 15.0 - 26.0 kWh	1416.45	-	-	-	1416.45	nr
R0941 output 26.0 - 36.0 kWh	1548.75	-	-	-	1548.75	nr
R0942 output 36.0 - 46.0 kWh	1959.30	-	-	-	1959.30	nr

Basic Prices of Materials	Supply Price £	Waste Factor %	Unload. Labour £	Unload. Plant £	Total Unit Cost £	Unit
Gas fired boilers						
For central heating and indirect hot water supply, floor standing, SEDBUK Band A:						
R0943 output 8.8 - 14.6 kWh, fan assisted flue	774.90	-	-	-	**774.90**	nr
R0945 output 8.8 - 23.4 kWh, fan assisted flue	1086.75	-	-	-	**1086.75**	nr
R0946 output 10.6 - 30.1 kWh, fan assisted flue	1338.75	-	-	-	**1338.75**	nr
For central heating and indirect hot water supply, floor standing combi, with storage cylinder, SEDBUK Band A:						
R0947 output 8.8 - 23.4 kWh; DHW 35 Ltr/min, 80 Ltr storage, fan assisted flue - condensing	1582.09	-	-	-	**1582.09**	nr
R0948 output 8.8 - 23.4 kWh, DHW 35 Ltr/min, 120 Ltr storage, fan assisted flue - condensing	1722.00	-	-	-	**1722.00**	nr
For central heating and indirect hot water supply, wall mounted, SEDBUK Band A:						
R0951 output 9.2 - 15.2 kWh, fan assisted flue - condensing	635.10	-	-	-	**635.10**	nr
R0952 output 9.2 - 22.0 kWh, fan assisted flue - condensing	691.60	-	-	-	**691.60**	nr
R0953 output 9.2 - 30.2 kWh, fan assisted flue - condensing	742.45	-	-	-	**742.45**	nr
For central heating and direct hot water supply, wall mounted combi, SEDBUK Band A:						
R0954 output 9.8 - 24.0 kWh; DHW 9.8 Ltr/min, fan assisted flue	675.78	-	-	-	**675.78**	nr
R0955 output 8.7 - 24.0 kWh; DHW 11.5 Ltr/min, fan assisted flue	723.24	-	-	-	**723.24**	nr
R0956 output 9.4 - 28.0 kWh; DHW 13.5 Ltr/min, fan assisted flue	743.58	-	-	-	**743.58**	nr
Lagging and insulation						
R0960 Polypropylene backed hair felt pipe lagging, 100 mm wide x 5 mm thick	1.16	5%	-	-	**1.22**	roll
Preformed sectional pipe insulation, wall thickness 9 mm:						
R0961 for 15 mm copper tube	1.90	5%	-	-	**1.99**	m
R0962 for 22 mm copper tube	2.73	5%	-	-	**2.87**	m
R0963 for 28 mm copper tube	3.09	5%	-	-	**3.25**	m
R0964 for 35 mm copper tube	3.85	5%	-	-	**4.04**	m
R0965 for 42 mm copper tube	4.61	5%	-	-	**4.84**	m
R0966 for 54 mm copper tube	5.95	5%	-	-	**6.25**	m
R0967 Adhesive tape, 25 mm wide	2.60	5%	-	-	**2.73**	roll
Cylinder insulating jackets, BS 5615, 80 mm glass fibre insulation encased in flame-retardant PVC, complete with two fixing bands for cylinder:						
R0968 450 mm dia. x 900 mm high	15.28	2.5%	-	-	**15.66**	nr
R0969 450 mm dia. x 1050 mm high	16.55	2.5%	-	-	**16.97**	nr
R0970 450 mm dia. x 1200 mm high	17.83	2.5%	-	-	**18.27**	nr
Electric water heaters						
Santon electric water heaters:						
Aquarius standard over sink type:						
R1001 A7/3	88.45	-	-	-	**88.45**	nr
Aquarius under sink type:						
R1003 AU7	91.09	-	-	-	**91.09**	nr
Aquaheat point of use heater type:						
R1004 AH7	145.84	-	-	-	**145.84**	nr
Storage water heaters type:						
R1006 R45	551.11	-	-	-	**551.11**	nr
R1007 DFB50	932.83	-	-	-	**932.83**	nr
R1008 Automatic water heater, cylindrical, PP150B	573.31	-	-	-	**573.31**	nr
Instantaneous shower heaters:						
R1010 7.2 kW	107.25	-	-	-	**107.25**	nr
R1011 8.5 kW	141.12	-	-	-	**141.12**	nr
R1012 9.5 kW	168.17	-	-	-	**168.17**	nr
Circulator pumps						
Myson domestic circulator pumps type:						
R1032 CP53, 3 speed	44.21	-	-	-	**44.21**	nr
R1033 CP63, 3 speed	53.14	-	-	-	**53.14**	nr
Wilo commercial circulator pumps type:						
R1041 SE 125 bare pump	204.97	-	-	-	**204.97**	nr
R1042 SE 150 bare pump	337.05	-	-	-	**337.05**	nr
R1043 SE 200 bare pump	427.35	-	-	-	**427.35**	nr
Grundfos domestic circulator pumps type:						
R1051 UPS15/50, three speed	73.56	-	-	-	**73.56**	nr
R1052 UPS15/60, high head	88.77	-	-	-	**88.77**	nr
Honeywell motorised valve packs complete with room thermostat and cylinder thermostat; sundial plan model:						
R1061 'S' reference T6060 with 22 mm outlets (without Programmer)	160.38	-	-	-	**160.38**	nr
R1062 'Y', with 22 mm outlets (without Programmer)	124.76	-	-	-	**124.76**	nr
R1063 'Y', with 1" outlets (without Programmer)	149.87	-	-	-	**149.87**	nr
R1064 'Y' timed reference Y603A/1075 with 22 mm outlets on 3-way valve with Programmer and 10-way junction box	220.69	-	-	-	**220.69**	nr

Basic Prices of Materials

		Supply Price £	Waste Factor %	Unload. Labour £	Unload. Plant £	Total Unit Cost £	Unit
	Fire fighting equipment						
	Automatic fire hose reels; wall mounted; 19 mm hose, 30 m long:						
R1072	fixed reel on circular drum	199.47	-	-	-	**199.47**	nr
R1073	swinging reel	207.87	-	-	-	**207.87**	nr
R1074	recessed reel	136.47	-	-	-	**136.47**	nr
R1076	concealed hose reel	184.77	-	-	-	**184.77**	nr
	Fire extinguishers complete with wall brackets:						
	water type; capacity:						
R1092	9 litres	29.40	-	-	-	**29.40**	nr
	CO2 type; capacity:						
R1095	2 kg	32.55	-	-	-	**32.55**	nr
	Foam type; capacity:						
R1101	6 litres	36.75	-	-	-	**36.75**	nr
	Dry powder type; capacity:						
R1122	6 Kg	38.85	-	-	-	**38.85**	nr
	Wet chemical type; capacity:						
R1131	6 litres	43.05	-	-	-	**43.05**	nr

Unit Rates	Man-Hours	Net Labour Price £	Net Mats Price £	Net Unit Price £	Unit
UNIT RATES					
RA **RAINWATER PIPEWORK AND GUTTERS**					
GUTTERWORK					
001 **Work to existing rainwater installations**					
002 Clean out existing guttering; flush:					
any type, any size, flush using hose pipe	0.08	2.37	-	**2.37**	m
003 Take off gutter (up to 152 mm diameter), securely fix brackets and refix gutter including remaking joints:					
PVCu	0.48	15.17	-	**15.17**	Nr
cast iron or aluminium	0.53	16.68	-	**16.68**	Nr
004 Cut out defective 102 mm half round guttering and renew with joints to existing, both ends:					
PVCu:					
gutter not exceeding 1.20 m long	0.41	13.02	5.51	**18.53**	Nr
stopped ends	0.20	6.32	2.64	**8.96**	Nr
outlets	0.30	9.48	5.02	**14.50**	Nr
angles	0.23	7.36	2.53	**9.89**	Nr
cast iron or aluminium:					
gutter not exceeding 1.20 m long	0.62	19.66	36.48	**56.14**	m
stopped ends	0.18	5.53	-	**5.53**	m
outlets	0.48	15.10	3.66	**18.76**	m
angles	0.48	15.10	12.77	**27.87**	m
005 Rod and clear existing rainwater pipe; including any hopper head; flush:					
not exceeding 10m in length, any type, any size	0.33	10.43	-	**10.43**	Nr
Extra over for cleaning out rainwater gulley	0.33	10.43	-	**10.43**	Nr
006 Take off rainwater pipe (up to 110 mm diameter), securely fix brackets and refix pipe, including remaking joints:					
PVCu	0.41	13.02	-	**13.02**	m
cast iron	0.55	17.25	-	**17.25**	m
007 Cut out defective 75 mm rainwater pipe and renew:					
PVCu:					
pipe not exceeding 1.20 m long	0.54	16.94	7.57	**24.51**	Nr
offsets	0.42	13.27	1.46	**14.73**	Nr
shoes	0.21	6.64	1.59	**8.23**	Nr
junctions	0.63	19.91	4.80	**24.71**	Nr
cast iron:					
pipe not exceeding 1.20 m long	0.66	20.82	39.98	**60.80**	Nr
offsets	0.48	15.17	33.36	**48.53**	Nr
shoes	0.24	7.58	26.77	**34.35**	Nr
junctions	0.71	22.44	35.50	**57.94**	Nr
008 **Gutters and fittings; PVCu, BS EN 12200-1:2000; fixing with standard brackets**					
009 112 mm nominal half round eaves gutters	0.23	7.30	3.28	**10.58**	m
Extra over for:					
stopped ends	0.08	2.43	1.23	**3.66**	Nr
90 degree angles	0.15	4.87	3.27	**8.14**	Nr
outlets	0.23	7.30	2.94	**10.24**	Nr
010 150 mm nominal half round eaves gutters	0.25	8.03	9.72	**17.75**	m
Extra over for:					
stopped ends	0.12	3.89	3.71	**7.60**	Nr
90 degree angles	0.24	7.58	13.19	**20.77**	Nr
outlets	0.36	11.38	10.60	**21.98**	Nr
011 112 mm square eaves gutters	0.23	7.27	3.15	**10.42**	m
Extra over for:					
stopped ends	0.08	2.43	1.13	**3.56**	Nr
90 degree angles	0.15	4.87	3.88	**8.75**	Nr
outlets	0.23	7.30	3.96	**11.26**	Nr
012 **Gutters and fittings; cast iron, BS ISO 4525:2003; fixing with standard brackets**					
013 100 mm diameter half round eaves gutters	0.34	10.68	21.16	**31.84**	m
Extra over for:					
stopped ends	0.08	2.43	4.30	**6.73**	Nr
90 degree angles	0.15	4.87	16.76	**21.63**	Nr
outlets	0.23	7.30	16.76	**24.06**	Nr
014 150 mm diameter half round eaves gutters	0.39	12.32	40.82	**53.14**	m
Extra over for:					
stopped ends	0.09	2.78	7.71	**10.49**	Nr
90 degree angles	0.18	5.59	33.39	**38.98**	Nr
outlets	0.27	8.37	33.39	**41.76**	Nr
015 100 mm diameter ogee eaves gutters	0.34	10.68	22.02	**32.70**	Nr
Extra over for:					
stopped ends	0.08	2.43	4.11	**6.54**	Nr
90 degree angles	0.15	4.87	16.56	**21.43**	Nr
outlets	0.23	7.30	16.56	**23.86**	Nr

Unit Rates

		Man-Hours	Net Labour Price £	Net Mats Price £	Net Unit Price £	Unit
016	125 mm ogee eaves gutters	0.37	11.76	25.31	**37.07**	m
	Extra over for:					
	stopped ends	0.09	2.69	5.33	**8.02**	Nr
	90 degree angles	0.17	5.34	19.40	**24.74**	Nr
	outlets	0.25	8.03	19.40	**27.43**	Nr
	Note: 017 – 030 not used					
031	**Gutters and fittings; cast aluminium, BS EN 573-3:2009; plain mill finish; fixing with standard brackets**					
032	100 mm diameter half round eaves gutters	0.34	10.68	15.45	**26.13**	m
	Extra over for:					
	stopped ends	0.08	2.43	3.31	**5.74**	Nr
	square or obtuse angles	0.15	4.87	12.18	**17.05**	Nr
	outlets	0.23	7.30	13.20	**20.50**	Nr
033	113 mm diameter half round eaves gutters	0.36	11.38	16.40	**27.78**	m
	Extra over for:					
	stopped ends	0.08	2.56	3.46	**6.02**	Nr
	square or obtuse angles	0.16	5.12	13.31	**18.43**	Nr
	outlets	0.24	7.65	26.52	**34.17**	Nr
034	125 mm diameter half round eaves gutters	0.37	11.69	20.87	**32.56**	m
	Extra over for:					
	stopped ends	0.09	2.69	4.39	**7.08**	m
	square or obtuse angles	0.17	5.37	17.13	**22.50**	Nr
	outlets	0.27	8.53	17.39	**25.92**	Nr
035	100 mm ogee eaves gutters	0.34	10.68	21.21	**31.89**	m
	Extra over for:					
	stopped ends	0.08	2.43	3.62	**6.05**	Nr
	square or obtuse angles	0.15	4.87	15.18	**20.05**	Nr
	outlets	0.23	7.30	17.02	**24.32**	Nr
036	113 mm ogee eaves gutters	0.36	11.38	21.18	**32.56**	m
	Extra over for:					
	stopped ends	0.08	2.56	3.79	**6.35**	Nr
	square or obtuse angles	0.16	5.12	21.18	**26.30**	Nr
	outlets	0.24	7.65	34.85	**42.50**	Nr
037	125 mm ogee eaves gutters	0.37	11.69	26.57	**38.26**	Nr
	Extra over for:					
	stopped ends	0.09	2.69	4.11	**6.80**	Nr
	square or obtuse angles	0.17	5.37	19.72	**25.09**	Nr
	outlets	0.28	8.85	19.15	**28.00**	Nr
038	**Gutters and fittings; cast aluminium, BS EN 573-3:2009; polyester powder coated; fixing with standard brackets**					
039	100 mm diameter half round eaves gutters	0.34	10.68	34.47	**45.15**	m
	Extra over for:					
	stopped ends	0.08	2.43	7.04	**9.47**	Nr
	square or obtuse angles	0.15	4.87	24.24	**29.11**	Nr
	outlets	0.23	7.30	18.36	**25.66**	Nr
040	113 mm diameter half round eaves gutters	0.36	11.25	35.45	**46.70**	m
	Extra over for:					
	stopped ends	0.08	2.56	3.31	**5.87**	Nr
	square or obtuse angles	0.16	5.12	26.39	**31.51**	Nr
	outlets	0.24	7.65	44.75	**52.40**	Nr
041	125 mm diameter half round eaves gutters	0.37	11.79	44.04	**55.83**	m
	Extra over for:					
	stopped ends	0.09	2.69	9.03	**11.72**	m
	square or obtuse angles	0.17	5.37	34.00	**39.37**	Nr
	outlets	0.25	8.03	34.00	**42.03**	Nr
042	100 mm ogee eaves gutters	0.34	10.68	31.30	**41.98**	m
	Extra over for:					
	stopped ends	0.08	2.43	5.10	**7.53**	Nr
	square or obtuse angles	0.15	4.87	20.79	**25.66**	Nr
	outlets	0.23	7.30	22.76	**30.06**	Nr
043	113 mm ogee eaves gutters	0.36	11.25	34.44	**45.69**	m
	Extra over for:					
	stopped ends	0.08	2.43	2.88	**5.31**	Nr
	square or obtuse angles	0.16	5.06	23.53	**28.59**	Nr
	outlets	0.24	7.58	42.05	**49.63**	Nr
044	125 mm ogee eaves gutters	0.37	11.79	29.21	**41.00**	Nr
	Extra over for:					
	stopped ends	0.09	2.84	6.57	**9.41**	Nr
	square or obtuse angles	0.17	5.37	50.38	**55.75**	Nr
	outlets	0.28	8.85	50.17	**59.02**	Nr

	Unit Rates	Man-Hours	Net Labour Price £	Net Mats Price £	Net Unit Price £	Unit
	RAINWATER PIPEWORK					
045	**Rainwater Pipes and fittings; PVCu, BS EN 12200-1:2000; fixing with standard brackets vertically to masonry**					
046	68 mm nominal size pipes	0.25	7.77	2.35	**10.12**	m
	Extra over for:					
	shoes	0.13	4.04	2.55	**6.59**	Nr
	bends	0.18	5.66	2.70	**8.36**	Nr
	offsets, 150 mm projection	0.23	7.30	2.92	**10.22**	Nr
	offsets, 300 mm projection	0.23	7.30	2.92	**10.22**	Nr
	branches	0.28	8.91	4.80	**13.71**	Nr
047	110 mm nominal size pipes	0.43	13.62	5.64	**19.26**	m
	Extra over for:					
	shoes	0.14	4.42	6.87	**11.29**	m
	bends	0.18	5.69	6.46	**12.15**	Nr
	offsets, 150 mm projection	0.23	7.30	13.34	**20.64**	Nr
	offsets, 300 mm projection	0.23	7.30	13.34	**20.64**	Nr
	branches	0.28	8.91	8.82	**17.73**	Nr
048	Connections between rainwater pipes and 100 mm nominal size clay drain pipes; drain connectors; joints in cement mortar (1:3):					
	68 mm nominal size pipes	0.15	4.87	2.75	**7.62**	Nr
	110 mm nominal size pipes	0.15	4.87	5.63	**10.50**	Nr
	Note: 049 not used					
050	61 mm Squareline pipes	0.25	7.90	2.46	**10.36**	m
	Extra over for:					
	shoes	0.14	4.42	2.34	**6.76**	Nr
	bends	0.18	5.69	3.36	**9.05**	Nr
	offsets, 150 mm projection	0.23	7.27	5.83	**13.10**	Nr
	offsets, 300 mm projection	0.23	7.27	0.47	**7.74**	Nr
	branches	0.28	8.85	5.96	**14.81**	Nr
	connections between 61 mm Squareline pipes and 100 mm nominal size clay drain pipes; adaptors, drain connectors; joints in cement mortar (1:3)	0.21	6.48	2.75	**9.23**	Nr
051	Rainwater heads; PVCu:					
	flat type, eared, plain mill finish	-	-	6.12	**6.12**	Nr
	rectangular, 252 x 195 x 210 mm, 110 mm outlet	0.51	16.21	14.25	**30.46**	Nr
	rectangular, 254 x 148 x 137 mm, 61 mm square outlet	0.51	16.21	7.53	**23.74**	Nr
052	**Rainwater pipes and fittings; cast iron, BS ISO 4525:2003, ears cast on; fixing with pipe nails and hardwood distance pieces; fixed vertically to masonry**					
053	63 mm nominal size pipes	0.32	10.18	34.12	**44.30**	m
	Extra over for:					
	shoes	0.15	4.87	29.96	**34.83**	Nr
	bends	0.15	4.87	18.34	**23.21**	Nr
	offsets, 150 mm projection	0.23	7.30	28.06	**35.36**	Nr
	offsets, 300 mm projection	0.23	7.30	38.26	**45.56**	Nr
	branches	0.28	8.91	36.03	**44.94**	Nr
054	75 mm nominal size pipes	0.34	10.68	31.23	**41.91**	m
	Extra over for:					
	shoes	0.15	4.87	26.77	**31.64**	Nr
	bends	0.18	5.66	19.89	**25.55**	Nr
	offsets, 150 mm projection	0.23	7.30	25.07	**32.37**	Nr
	offsets, 300 mm projection	0.23	7.30	35.88	**43.18**	Nr
	branches	0.34	10.68	35.50	**46.18**	Nr
055	100 mm nominal size pipes	0.36	11.25	41.95	**53.20**	m
	Extra over for:					
	shoes	0.16	5.12	35.53	**40.65**	Nr
	bends	0.19	5.97	28.08	**34.05**	Nr
	offsets, 150 mm projection	0.24	7.65	47.29	**54.94**	Nr
	offsets, 300 mm projection	0.24	7.65	58.41	**66.06**	Nr
	branches	0.36	11.25	41.36	**52.61**	Nr
056	75 x 100 mm nominal size rectangular pipes	0.37	11.79	84.35	**96.14**	m
	Extra over for:					
	shoes	0.17	5.37	100.22	**105.59**	Nr
	bends	0.20	6.26	95.42	**101.68**	Nr
	offsets, 150 mm projection	0.25	8.03	127.66	**135.69**	Nr
	offsets, 300 mm projection	0.25	8.03	148.47	**156.50**	Nr
	branches	0.37	11.79	161.87	**173.66**	Nr
057	Connections between rainwater pipes and 100 mm nominal size clay drain pipes; joints in cement mortar (1:3):					
	63 mm nominal size pipes	0.15	4.87	1.63	**6.50**	Nr
	100 mm nominal size pipes	0.21	6.48	0.46	**6.94**	Nr
	75 x 100 mm nominal size pipes	0.23	7.30	0.46	**7.76**	Nr
058	Rainwater heads; cast iron:					
	flat type, eared, plain mill finish	0.33	10.43	106.80	**117.23**	Nr
	rectangular, 250 x 175 x 175 mm, 75 mm outlet, plain mill finish	0.39	12.17	126.58	**138.75**	Nr
	rectangular, 300 x 250 x 200 mm, 100 mm outlet, plain mill finish	0.44	13.90	192.86	**206.76**	Nr

Unit Rates

		Man-Hours	Net Labour Price £	Net Mats Price £	Net Unit Price £	Unit
	Note: 059 - 066 not used					
067	**Rainwater pipes and fittings; cast aluminium, BS EN 573-3:2009; ears cast on; plain mill finish; fixing with expanding bolts vertically to masonry**					
068	63 mm nominal size pipes	0.26	8.22	15.02	**23.24**	m
	Extra over for:					
	shoes	0.15	4.87	10.23	**15.10**	Nr
	bends	0.18	5.66	14.68	**20.34**	Nr
	offsets, 150 mm projection	0.23	7.30	21.91	**29.21**	Nr
	offsets, 300 mm projection	0.23	7.30	24.37	**31.67**	Nr
	offsets, 600 mm projection	0.28	8.91	26.87	**35.78**	Nr
	branches	0.28	8.91	20.80	**29.71**	Nr
069	76 mm nominal size pipes	0.34	10.68	17.00	**27.68**	m
	Extra over for:					
	shoes	0.16	5.12	13.27	**18.39**	Nr
	bends	0.19	5.97	20.39	**26.36**	Nr
	offsets, 150 mm projection	0.24	7.65	24.62	**32.27**	Nr
	offsets, 300 mm projection	0.24	7.65	27.00	**34.65**	Nr
	offsets, 600 mm projection	0.30	9.35	42.20	**51.55**	Nr
	branches	0.30	9.35	24.29	**33.64**	Nr
070	102 mm nominal size pipes	0.36	11.25	28.13	**39.38**	m
	Extra over for:					
	shoes	0.17	5.37	15.61	**20.98**	Nr
	bends	0.20	6.26	23.63	**29.89**	Nr
	offsets, 150 mm projection	0.25	8.03	28.08	**36.11**	Nr
	offsets, 300 mm projection	0.25	8.03	34.31	**42.34**	Nr
	offsets, 600 mm projection	0.31	9.83	48.75	**58.58**	Nr
	branches	0.31	9.83	30.75	**40.58**	Nr
071	**Rainwater pipes and fittings; cast aluminium, BS EN 573-3:2009; ears cast on; polyester powder coated; fixing with expanding bolts vertically to masonry**					
072	63 mm nominal size pipes	0.26	8.22	20.47	**28.69**	m
	Extra over for:					
	shoes	0.15	4.87	14.86	**19.73**	Nr
	bends	0.15	4.87	28.65	**33.52**	Nr
	offsets, 150 mm projection	0.23	7.30	26.34	**33.64**	Nr
	offsets, 300 mm projection	0.23	7.30	32.11	**39.41**	Nr
	offsets, 600 mm projection	0.23	7.30	44.83	**52.13**	Nr
	branches	0.28	8.91	27.50	**36.41**	Nr
073	76 mm nominal size pipes	0.34	10.68	23.67	**34.35**	Nr
	Extra over for:					
	shoes	0.16	5.12	29.50	**34.62**	Nr
	bends	0.16	5.12	24.05	**29.17**	Nr
	offsets, 150 mm projection	0.24	7.65	29.52	**37.17**	Nr
	offsets, 300 mm projection	0.24	7.65	36.25	**43.90**	Nr
	offsets, 600 mm projection	0.24	7.65	60.07	**67.72**	Nr
	branches	0.30	9.35	32.46	**41.81**	Nr
074	102 mm nominal size pipes	0.36	11.25	38.18	**49.43**	m
	Extra over for:					
	shoes	0.17	5.37	22.84	**28.21**	Nr
	bends	0.17	5.37	30.86	**36.23**	Nr
	offsets, 150 mm projection	0.25	8.03	33.77	**41.80**	Nr
	offsets, 300 mm projection	0.25	8.03	41.93	**49.96**	Nr
	offsets, 600 mm projection	0.25	8.03	57.42	**65.45**	Nr
	branches	0.31	9.83	40.34	**50.17**	Nr
	Note: 075 - 082 not used					
083	Connections between rainwater pipes and 100 mm nominal size clay drain pipes; joints in cement mortar (1:3):					
	63 mm nominal size pipes	0.15	4.87	0.62	**5.49**	Nr
	76 mm nominal size pipes	0.18	5.66	0.62	**6.28**	Nr
	102 mm nominal size pipes	0.21	6.48	0.46	**6.94**	Nr
084	Rainwater heads; hopper type, aluminium:					
	flat, 63 mm outlet, plain mill finish	0.46	14.57	17.18	**31.75**	Nr
	flat, 63 mm outlet, polyester powder coated	0.46	14.57	35.68	**50.25**	Nr
	flat, 76 mm outlet, plain mill finish	0.46	14.57	19.31	**33.88**	Nr
	flat, 76 mm outlet, polyester powder coated	0.46	14.57	37.01	**51.58**	Nr
	flat, 102 mm outlet, plain mill finish	0.46	14.57	48.91	**63.48**	Nr
	flat, 102 mm outlet, polyester powder coated	0.46	14.57	33.21	**47.78**	Nr
	flat, square outlet, plain mill finish	0.46	14.57	40.22	**54.79**	Nr
	flat, square outlet, polyester powder coated	0.46	14.57	34.18	**48.75**	Nr
	rectangular, 250 x 180 x 180 mm, 63 mm outlet	0.49	15.55	25.71	**41.26**	Nr
	rectangular, 250 x 180 x 180 mm, 102 mm outlet	0.49	15.55	27.50	**43.05**	Nr
	triangular, 63 mm diameter outlet, plain mill finish	0.49	15.55	20.08	**35.63**	Nr
	triangular, 63 mm diameter outlet, polyester powder coated	0.49	15.55	27.58	**43.13**	Nr
	triangular, 76 mm diameter outlet, plain mill finish	0.49	15.55	19.35	**34.90**	Nr
	triangular, 76 mm diameter outlet, polyester powder coated	0.49	15.55	23.14	**38.69**	Nr
	triangular, square outlet, plain mill finish	0.49	15.55	44.51	**60.06**	Nr
	triangular, square outlet, polyester powder coated	0.49	15.55	52.69	**68.24**	Nr
	ornamental, any outlet, plain mill finish	0.49	15.55	140.50	**156.05**	Nr
	ornamental, any outlet, polyester powder coated	0.49	15.55	152.21	**167.76**	Nr

Unit Rates	Man-Hours	Net Labour Price £	Net Mats Price £	Net Unit Price £	Unit
RB SANITARY INSTALLATIONS					
PIPEWORK					
001 **Pipes and fittings, cast iron, BS 416; spigot and socket joints caulked in lead; cast iron holderbats**					
002 75 mm nominal size pipes	0.52	16.46	58.68	**75.14**	m
Extra over for:					
access pipes with oval doors	0.62	19.69	78.42	**98.11**	Nr
bends	0.62	19.69	47.85	**67.54**	Nr
offsets, 150 mm projection	0.65	20.41	57.46	**77.87**	Nr
offsets, 300 mm projection	0.68	21.49	79.09	**100.58**	Nr
single 50 mm BSP bossed pipe	0.74	23.26	38.84	**62.10**	Nr
branches	0.86	27.21	65.56	**92.77**	Nr
double branches	1.13	35.80	122.87	**158.67**	Nr
roof connectors	0.65	20.41	122.01	**142.42**	Nr
003 100 mm nominal size pipes	0.63	20.03	71.70	**91.73**	m
Extra over for:					
W.C. connectors, effective length 300 mm	0.77	24.33	98.77	**123.10**	Nr
W.C. connectors, effective length 450 mm	0.77	24.33	98.77	**123.10**	Nr
access pipes with oval doors	0.79	25.06	115.81	**140.87**	Nr
bends	0.79	25.06	58.50	**83.56**	Nr
offsets, 150 mm projection	0.79	25.06	83.19	**108.25**	Nr
offsets, 300 mm projection	0.85	26.86	108.41	**135.27**	Nr
single 50 mm BSP bossed pipes	0.93	29.36	104.76	**134.12**	Nr
branches	0.97	30.78	139.08	**169.86**	Nr
double branches	1.30	41.17	160.76	**201.93**	Nr
roof connectors	0.79	25.06	123.62	**148.68**	Nr
100 x 75 mm nominal size reducing connectors	0.79	25.06	68.37	**93.43**	Nr
004 Connections between 100 mm nominal size pipes and 100 mm nominal size clay drain pipes; joints in cement mortar (1:3)	0.20	6.45	0.46	**6.91**	Nr
005 Galvanised wire balloon gratings, fitted to pipes:					
75 mm nominal size	0.11	3.57	27.68	**31.25**	Nr
100 mm nominal size	0.11	3.57	27.68	**31.25**	Nr
006 **Pipes and fittings; PVCu soil and vent system; BS 4514; solvent welded joints in the running length; standard pipe brackets at 1500 mm centres**					
007 82 mm nominal size pipes	0.23	7.17	5.59	**12.76**	m
Extra over for:					
straight w.c. connectors	0.34	10.74	4.51	**15.25**	Nr
w.c. connecting bends	0.48	15.04	5.94	**20.98**	Nr
access doors	0.96	30.43	12.26	**42.69**	Nr
bends	0.45	14.31	7.68	**21.99**	Nr
boss connectors	0.62	19.69	7.61	**27.30**	Nr
branches	0.57	17.92	10.91	**28.83**	Nr
008 110 mm nominal size pipes	0.26	8.25	5.59	**13.84**	m
Extra over for:					
straight w.c. connectors	0.37	11.82	6.61	**18.43**	Nr
w.c. connecting bends	0.51	16.12	6.61	**22.73**	Nr
access doors	0.96	30.43	7.15	**37.58**	Nr
bends	0.51	16.12	8.30	**24.42**	Nr
boss connectors	0.66	20.76	3.84	**24.60**	Nr
branches	0.62	19.69	13.27	**32.96**	Nr
double branches	0.74	23.26	29.38	**52.64**	Nr
access branches	0.62	19.69	22.27	**41.96**	Nr
Note: 009 not used					
010 Connections between PVCu pipes and 100 mm nominal size clay drain pipes; drain connectors; gaskin yarn and cement joints:					
82 mm nominal size pipes	0.20	6.45	5.35	**11.80**	Nr
110 mm nominal size pipes	0.20	6.45	9.57	**16.02**	Nr
011 Balloon gratings:					
82 mm nominal size pipes	0.25	7.87	2.15	**10.02**	Nr
110 mm nominal size pipes	0.25	7.87	1.95	**9.82**	Nr
012 Weathering collars:					
82 mm nominal size pipes	0.23	7.17	2.36	**9.53**	Nr
110 mm nominal size pipes	0.23	7.17	2.73	**9.90**	Nr
013 Weathering slates, aluminium base:					
450 x 450 mm	0.32	10.02	21.07	**31.09**	Nr
600 x 600 mm	0.32	10.02	27.61	**37.63**	Nr
014 **Pipes and fittings, MuPVC waste pipes, BS 5255; solvent welded joints in the running length; standard pipe clips at 500 mm centres**					
015 1.1/4" (32) nominal size pipes	0.45	14.31	4.02	**18.33**	m
Extra over for:					
straight tank connectors	0.40	12.55	1.68	**14.23**	Nr
elbows	0.32	10.02	1.88	**11.90**	Nr
tees	0.43	13.62	1.97	**15.59**	Nr

Unit Rates

		Man-Hours	Net Labour Price £	Net Mats Price £	Net Unit Price £	Unit
016	1.1/2" (40) nominal size pipes	0.48	15.04	4.52	**19.56**	m
	Extra over for:					
	straight tank connectors	0.43	13.62	1.68	**15.30**	Nr
	elbows	0.37	11.82	1.97	**13.79**	Nr
	tees	0.48	15.04	1.97	**17.01**	Nr
017	2" (50) nominal size pipes	0.52	16.46	7.09	**23.55**	m
	Extra over for:					
	elbows	0.43	13.62	2.59	**16.21**	Nr
	tees	0.57	17.92	2.72	**20.64**	Nr
018	Expansion compensators; one solvent welded joint, one ring seal joint:					
	1.1/4" (32) nominal size pipes	0.32	10.02	2.09	**12.11**	Nr
	1.1/2" (40) nominal size pipes	0.37	11.82	2.09	**13.91**	Nr
	2" (50) nominal size pipes	0.43	13.62	2.99	**16.61**	Nr
019	Connections between pipes of differing materials:					
	1.1/4" (32) MuPVC x 35 mm copper	0.28	8.94	2.78	**11.72**	Nr
	1.1/2" (40) MuPVC x 42 mm copper	0.34	10.74	2.78	**13.52**	Nr
	1.1/4" (32) MuPVC x 32 mm steel	0.32	10.02	2.78	**12.80**	Nr
	1.1/2" (40) MuPVC x 40 mm steel	0.37	11.82	2.78	**14.60**	Nr
	2" (50) MuPVC x 50 mm steel	0.43	13.62	4.50	**18.12**	Nr
	1.1/4" (32) MuPVC x PVCu soil and vent pipe, boss adaptor	0.23	7.17	1.95	**9.12**	Nr
	1.1/2" (40) MuPVC x PVCu SVP, boss adaptor	0.25	7.87	2.42	**10.29**	Nr
020	**Pipework ancillaries, polypropylene; jointing to outlets and to plastic pipes**					
021	Bottle 'P' traps, 38 mm seal:					
	1.1/4" (32) nominal size	0.32	10.02	4.24	**14.26**	Nr
	1.1/2" (40) nominal size	0.40	12.55	4.87	**17.42**	Nr
022	Bottle 'P' traps, 76 mm seal:					
	1.1/4" (32) nominal size	0.32	10.02	4.63	**14.65**	Nr
	1.1/2" (40) nominal size	0.40	12.55	5.40	**17.95**	Nr
023	Bottle 'P' traps, 76 mm seal, anti-syphon:					
	1.1/4" (32) nominal size	0.32	10.02	6.84	**16.86**	Nr
	1.1/2" (40) nominal size	0.40	12.55	7.53	**20.08**	Nr
024	Tubular 'P' traps, 76 mm seal:					
	1.1/4" (32) nominal size	0.32	10.02	4.87	**14.89**	Nr
	1.1/2" (40) nominal size	0.40	12.55	5.40	**17.95**	Nr
025	Tubular 'S' traps, 76 mm seal:					
	1.1/4" (32) nominal size	0.32	10.02	5.67	**15.69**	Nr
	1.1/2" (40) nominal size	0.40	12.55	6.32	**18.87**	Nr
026	Three-piece running 'P' traps, 76 mm seal:					
	1.1/4" (32) nominal size	0.32	10.02	6.84	**16.86**	Nr
	1.1/2" (40) nominal size	0.40	12.55	7.16	**19.71**	Nr
027	1.1/2" (40) nominal size bath traps, complete with flexible pipe for overflow connection:					
	'P' trap	0.59	18.61	11.05	**29.66**	Nr
028	**Pipes and fittings, PVCu overflow system; solvent welded joints in the running length; standard pipe clips at 500 mm centres**					
029	19 mm nominal size pipes	0.23	7.17	0.94	**8.11**	m
	Extra over for:					
	straight tank connectors	0.34	10.74	0.52	**11.26**	Nr
	bent tank connectors	0.34	10.74	0.65	**11.39**	Nr
	elbows	0.24	7.52	0.50	**8.02**	Nr
	tees	0.31	9.67	0.59	**10.26**	Nr
	splay cut ends	0.06	1.80	-	**1.80**	Nr
030	**Pipes and fittings; copper tubes BS EN1057, Table X; capillary fittings, BS EN1254 Part 1; capillary joints in the running length; two piece copper spacing clips at 1500 mm centres**					
031	22 mm nominal size overflow pipes	0.32	10.02	5.05	**15.07**	m
	Extra over for:					
	elbows	0.28	8.94	1.35	**10.29**	Nr
	tees	0.32	10.02	3.12	**13.14**	Nr
	made bends	0.17	5.37	-	**5.37**	Nr
032	28 mm nominal size overflow pipes	0.40	12.55	6.58	**19.13**	m
	Extra over for:					
	elbows	0.30	9.32	2.85	**12.17**	Nr
	tees	0.40	12.55	7.91	**20.46**	Nr
	reducing tees	0.40	12.55	11.69	**24.24**	Nr
	made bends	0.25	7.87	-	**7.87**	Nr
033	35 mm nominal size waste pipes	0.45	14.31	13.72	**28.03**	m
	Extra over for:					
	elbows	0.36	11.47	12.86	**24.33**	Nr
	tees	0.45	14.31	20.95	**35.26**	Nr
	pitcher tees	0.45	14.31	42.12	**56.43**	Nr
	made bends	0.40	12.55	-	**12.55**	Nr

Unit Rates

		Man-Hours	Net Labour Price £	Net Mats Price £	Net Unit Price £	Unit
034	42 mm nominal size waste pipes	0.51	16.12	17.58	**33.70**	m
	Extra over for:					
	elbows	0.40	12.55	21.25	**33.80**	Nr
	tees	0.51	16.12	33.59	**49.71**	Nr
	reducing tees	0.51	16.12	63.40	**79.52**	Nr
	pitcher tees	0.51	16.12	62.43	**78.55**	Nr
	reducing pitcher tees	0.51	16.12	42.12	**58.24**	Nr
035	Connections of overflow pipes to cisterns:					
	22 mm nominal size:					
	tank connector	0.40	12.55	14.19	**26.74**	Nr
	overflow bend	0.40	12.55	19.31	**31.86**	Nr
036	**Pipework ancillaries, copper; joints to appliances and to copper pipes**					
037	'P' trap 38 mm seal, adjustable for depth and direction:					
	35 mm	0.45	14.31	28.79	**43.10**	Nr
	42 mm	0.57	17.92	42.60	**60.52**	Nr
038	'S' trap 76 mm seal, adjustable for depth and direction:					
	35 mm	0.45	14.31	30.70	**45.01**	Nr
	42 mm	0.57	17.92	44.17	**62.09**	Nr
	Note: 039 not used					
	EQUIPMENT AND ANCILLARIES					
040	**Sanitary fittings; Sinks, assembling and jointing component parts, bedding taps and outlets in white lead**					
041	Fireclay sinks, Belfast pattern, BS 1206, white fireclay; 38 mm chromium plated waste, plug, chain and stay; pair wall brackets fixed with screws to brickwork:					
	610 x 455 x 255 mm	2.78	87.72	229.11	**316.83**	Nr
	760 x 455 x 255 mm	2.78	87.72	422.88	**510.60**	Nr
042	Bib taps, BS 5412, chromium plated; screwed joint to pipe:					
	13 mm nominal size	0.20	6.45	20.30	**26.75**	Nr
	19 mm nominal size	0.23	7.17	36.23	**43.40**	Nr
043	Stainless steel sinks; 38 mm chromium plated waste, plug, chain and stay; fixing on sink base unit (measured separately):					
	1000 x 600 mm (single drainer)	3.17	100.24	88.38	**188.62**	Nr
	1500 x 600 mm (double drainer)	3.40	107.41	175.50	**282.91**	Nr
044	Pillar taps, BS 5412, chromium plated; fixing to sink top, connecting to pipe:					
	13 mm nominal size	0.20	6.45	20.06	**26.51**	Nr
	19 mm nominal size	0.23	7.17	29.67	**36.84**	Nr
045	**Sanitary fittings; Baths, nominal size, assembling and jointing component parts, bedding taps and outlets in white lead**					
046	Baths, cast iron, porcelain enamelled, rectangular; 38 mm chromium plated waste, plug, chain and overflow fitting; pair 19 mm chromium plated pillar taps:					
	1500 mm long, white	4.25	134.27	408.29	**542.56**	Nr
	1700 mm long, white	4.25	134.27	408.29	**542.56**	Nr
047	Baths, pressed steel, vitreous enamelled, rectangular; 38 mm chromium plated waste, plug, chain and overflow fitting; pair 19 mm chromium plated pillar taps:					
	1500 mm long, white	4.25	134.27	182.88	**317.15**	Nr
	1700 mm long, white	4.25	134.27	182.88	**317.15**	Nr
	1700 mm long, coloured	4.25	134.27	182.88	**317.15**	Nr
048	Baths, 3 mm glass fibre reinforced acrylic; 38 mm chromium plated waste, plug, chain and overflow fitting; pair 19 mm chromium plated pillar taps:					
	1700 mm long, white	3.68	116.35	181.74	**298.09**	Nr
	1700 mm long, coloured	3.68	116.35	181.74	**298.09**	Nr
049	Bath panels, enamelled hardboard; cutting to required size, fixing with chromium plated dome headed screws:					
	760 x 610 x 3.2 mm thick, end panels	0.40	12.55	5.05	**17.60**	Nr
	1830 x 610 x 3.2 mm thick, side panels	0.62	19.69	8.72	**28.41**	Nr
050	Angle strips, polished chromium; fixing with screws:					
	560 x 25 x 25 mm angle	0.23	7.17	1.02	**8.19**	Nr
051	**Sanitary fittings; Lavatory basins, assembling and jointing component parts, bedding taps and outlets in white lead**					
052	Lavatory basins, vitreous china; 32 mm chromium plated waste, plug, chain and stay; pair 13 mm chromium plated pillar taps; pair wall hanging brackets, fixing with screws to brickwork:					
	560 x 405 mm white	2.95	93.09	71.35	**164.44**	Nr
	560 x 405 mm coloured	2.95	93.09	83.95	**177.04**	Nr
	635 x 455 mm white	2.95	93.09	114.14	**207.23**	Nr
	635 x 455 mm coloured	2.95	93.09	114.14	**207.23**	Nr
053	**Extra over** for pedestal stand; fixing with screws to concrete:					
	white	0.62	19.69	16.07	**35.76**	Nr
	coloured	0.62	19.69	16.07	**35.76**	Nr

Unit Rates

		Man-Hours	Net Labour Price £	Net Mats Price £	Net Unit Price £	Unit
054	**Extra over** for towel rail brackets, cast iron; fixing with screws to brickwork:					
	painted	0.28	8.94	0.70	**9.64**	Nr
	plastic coated	0.02	0.73	7.51	**8.24**	Nr
055	**Sanitary fittings; W.C. suites, assembling and jointing component parts, bedding taps and outlets in white lead**					
056	W.C. suites, vitreous china, close coupled, washdown; 'S' or 'P' trap pan, 9 litre cistern, flushing bend and connector, plastic ring seat; fixing pan with screws to concrete floor, fixing cistern brackets with screws to brickwork:					
	white	2.72	85.92	163.43	**249.35**	Nr
	coloured	2.72	85.92	163.43	**249.35**	Nr
057	W.C. suites, vitreous china, close coupled syphonic; 'S' or 'P' trap pan, 9 litre cistern, flushing bend and connector, plastic ring seat; fixing pan with screws to concrete floor, fixing cistern brackets with screws to brickwork:					
	white	2.83	89.52	173.54	**263.06**	Nr
	coloured	2.83	89.52	173.54	**263.06**	Nr
058	**Sanitary fittings; Urinals, assembling and jointing component parts, bedding taps and outlets in white lead**					
059	Single stall urinals, white glazed fireclay, 610 mm wide x 1061 mm high; vitreous china automatic flushing cistern and supports, stainless steel flush pipe and spreader, domed outlet grating; fixing in position, fixing cistern supports with screws to brickwork	4.31	136.04	915.60	**1051.64**	Nr
060	Slab urinals, white glazed fireclay, 1061 mm high, with 305 mm wide return ends; 150 mm waterway channel with domed grating, automatic flushing cistern and supports, stainless steel flush pipe with perforated sparge pipe and clips; fixing in position, fixing cistern support with screws to brickwork:					
	2 persons, 1220 mm wide	5.44	171.84	1358.70	**1530.54**	Nr
	3 persons, 1830 mm wide	6.69	211.25	1765.05	**1976.30**	Nr
	4 persons, 2440 mm wide	7.93	250.62	2189.25	**2439.87**	Nr
061	Bowl urinals, white vitreous china; vitreous china flushing cistern with automatic syphon, drip tap and wall hanger, stainless steel flush pipes with spreaders and clips, domed outlet gratings; fixing wall hangers with screws to brickwork:					
	1 person	2.55	80.55	222.54	**303.09**	Nr
	2 persons	3.97	125.33	269.04	**394.37**	Nr
	3 persons	5.38	170.07	444.06	**614.13**	Nr
	Extra for division	0.91	28.63	82.33	**110.96**	Nr
062	**Work to existing sanitary installations**					
063	Take off soil and vent pipe (up to 110 mm diameter) securely fix brackets and refix pipe including remaking joints:					
	PVC	0.38	12.04	-	**12.04**	m
	cast iron	0.62	19.66	8.30	**27.96**	Nr
064	Cut out defective 100 mm diameter soil and vent pipe and renew:					
	PVC:					
	pipe not exceeding 1.50 m long	0.48	15.10	7.28	**22.38**	Nr
	offset	0.62	19.66	8.30	**27.96**	Nr
	junction	0.77	24.17	13.27	**37.44**	Nr
	cast iron:					
	pipe not exceeding 1.50 m long	1.43	45.31	88.71	**134.02**	Nr
	offset	1.13	35.80	101.59	**137.39**	Nr
	junction	1.24	39.28	132.26	**171.54**	Nr
065	Take off waste pipe (up to 54 mm diameter) securely fix brackets and refix pipe including remaking joints:					
	PVC	0.67	21.14	-	**21.14**	m
	copper	0.81	25.72	-	**25.72**	m
066	Cut out defective waste pipe and renew:					
	PVC:					
	50 mm pipe not exceeding 1.50 m long	0.80	25.25	12.93	**38.18**	Nr
	'P' trap	0.51	15.99	5.40	**21.39**	Nr
	elbow	0.52	16.27	2.72	**18.99**	Nr
	copper:					
	54 mm pipe not exceeding 1.50 m long	0.41	13.05	2.15	**15.20**	Nr
	'P' trap	0.93	29.29	83.98	**113.27**	Nr
	'S' trap	0.62	19.53	92.48	**112.01**	Nr
	tee	0.62	19.53	149.32	**168.85**	Nr
	elbow	0.62	19.53	194.74	**214.27**	Nr
067	Cut out joint to back inlet gully and renew mortar, collar etc.	0.28	8.78	-	**8.78**	Nr
068	Remove old sanitary fittings and provide and fix new, including reconnecting waste services and overflows:					
	fireclay sink, Belfast pattern BS 1206, white fireclay, 38 mm chromium plated waste, plug, chain, stay:					
	610 x 455 x 255 mm	3.59	113.32	217.90	**331.22**	Nr
	760 x 455 x 255 mm	3.59	113.32	411.67	**524.99**	Nr
	stainless steel sink, 38 mm chromium plated waste, plug, chain, stay:					
	1000 x 600 (single drainer)	4.02	126.87	94.59	**221.46**	Nr
	1500 x 600 (double drainer)	4.30	135.94	181.71	**317.65**	Nr

Unit Rates

		Man-Hours	Net Labour Price £	Net Mats Price £	Net Unit Price £	Unit
	cast iron bath, porcelain enamelled, rectangular, 38 mm chromium plated waste, plug, chain and overflow fittings:					
	1500 mm long, white	5.67	179.01	378.36	**557.37**	Nr
	1700 mm long, white	5.67	179.01	378.36	**557.37**	Nr
	3 mm glass fibre reinforced acrylic bath, 38 mm chromium plated waste, plug, chain and overflow fittings:					
	1700 mm long, white	4.74	149.72	151.80	**301.52**	Nr
	vitreous china lavatory basin, 32 mm chromium plated waste, plug, chain and stay and pair of cast iron wall hanging brackets:					
	560 x 405 mm	3.71	117.17	51.81	**168.98**	Nr
	635 x 455 mm	3.71	117.17	94.59	**211.76**	Nr
	single stall urinals, white glazed fire clay including vitreous china automatic flushing cistern and supports, stainless steel flush pipe and spreader, domed outlet grating:					
	610 mm wide x 1065 mm high	5.46	172.50	923.54	**1096.04**	Nr
	vitreous china w.c. suite, close coupled washdown 'S' or 'P' trap pan, glass fibre cistern, flushing bend and connector, plastic ring seat	3.61	113.92	158.64	**272.56**	Nr
	remove old high level cistern and provide and fix new low level 9 litre cistern; adapting service and overflow pipes	1.24	39.06	71.17	**110.23**	Nr
069	Take off old W.C. seat and provide and fix new ring pattern plastic seat and cover	0.31	9.76	12.73	**22.49**	Nr
RC	**COLD WATER INSTALLATIONS**					
	PIPEWORK					
001	**Pipes and fittings; copper tubes, BS EN1057, Table X; capillary fittings, BS EN1254, Part 1; capillary joints in the running length; two piece copper spacing clips at 1500 mm centres**					
002	15 mm nominal size pipes	0.30	9.32	2.56	**11.88**	m
	Extra over for:					
	tank connectors	0.34	10.74	9.32	**20.06**	Nr
	straight tap connectors	0.25	7.87	5.81	**13.68**	Nr
	elbows	0.25	7.87	0.51	**8.38**	Nr
	tees	0.28	8.94	0.98	**9.92**	Nr
	made bends	0.14	4.30	-	**4.30**	Nr
	made offsets, 100 mm projection	0.28	8.94	-	**8.94**	Nr
003	22 mm nominal size pipes	0.32	10.02	5.05	**15.07**	m
	Extra over for:					
	tank connectors	0.36	11.47	14.19	**25.66**	Nr
	straight tap connectors	0.28	8.94	3.00	**11.94**	Nr
	elbows	0.28	8.94	1.35	**10.29**	Nr
	tees	0.32	10.02	3.12	**13.14**	Nr
	reducing tees	0.32	10.02	2.48	**12.50**	Nr
	made bends	0.17	5.37	-	**5.37**	Nr
	made offsets, 100 mm projection	0.32	10.02	-	**10.02**	Nr
004	28 mm nominal size pipes	0.40	12.55	6.58	**19.13**	m
	Extra over for:					
	tank connectors	0.45	14.31	18.65	**32.96**	Nr
	elbows	0.30	9.32	2.85	**12.17**	Nr
	tees	0.40	12.55	7.91	**20.46**	Nr
	reducing tees	0.40	12.55	11.69	**24.24**	Nr
	made bends	0.25	7.87	-	**7.87**	Nr
	made offsets, 100 mm projection	0.45	14.31	-	**14.31**	Nr
005	35 mm nominal size pipes	0.45	14.31	13.72	**28.03**	m
	Extra over for:					
	tank connectors	0.51	16.12	24.82	**40.94**	Nr
	elbows	0.36	11.47	12.86	**24.33**	Nr
	tees	0.45	14.31	20.95	**35.26**	Nr
	reducing tees	0.45	14.31	28.01	**42.32**	Nr
	made bends	0.40	12.55	-	**12.55**	Nr
006	42 mm nominal size pipes	0.51	16.12	17.58	**33.70**	m
	Extra over for:					
	tank connectors	0.59	18.61	32.54	**51.15**	Nr
	elbows	0.40	12.55	21.25	**33.80**	Nr
	tees	0.51	16.12	33.59	**49.71**	Nr
	reducing tees	0.51	16.12	63.40	**79.52**	Nr
	made bends	0.48	15.04	-	**15.04**	Nr
007	54 mm nominal size pipes	0.63	20.03	24.73	**44.76**	m
	Extra over for:					
	tank connectors	0.68	21.49	49.72	**71.21**	Nr
	elbows	0.45	14.31	43.89	**58.20**	Nr
	tees	0.62	19.69	67.73	**87.42**	Nr
	reducing tees	0.62	19.69	106.54	**126.23**	Nr
	made bends	0.59	18.61	-	**18.61**	Nr
008	Connections between pipes of differing materials:					
	15 mm copper x 15 mm steel	0.40	12.55	4.38	**16.93**	Nr
	15 mm copper x 20 mm steel, reducing connector	0.45	14.31	7.70	**22.01**	Nr
	22 mm copper x 20 mm steel	0.51	16.12	6.34	**22.46**	Nr
	22 mm copper x 15 mm steel, reducing connector	0.51	16.12	9.83	**25.95**	Nr
	35 mm copper x 32 mm steel	0.57	17.92	21.49	**39.41**	Nr
	54 mm copper x 50 mm steel	0.62	19.69	44.23	**63.92**	Nr

	Unit Rates	Man-Hours	Net Labour Price £	Net Mats Price £	Net Unit Price £	Unit
009	Connections between pipes and copper cylinders:					
	15 mm x 1/2" BSP straight male connectors	0.36	11.47	3.72	**15.19**	Nr
	22 mm x 3/4" BSP straight male connectors	0.40	12.55	6.65	**19.20**	Nr
	28 mm x 1" BSP straight male connectors	0.40	12.55	10.75	**23.30**	Nr
	35 mm x 1.1/4" BSP straight male connectors	0.45	14.31	19.58	**33.89**	Nr
	42 mm x 1.1/2" BSP straight male connectors	0.51	16.12	25.22	**41.34**	Nr
	54 mm x 2" BSP straight male connectors	0.57	17.92	38.30	**56.22**	Nr
010	**Pipes and fittings, copper tubes, BS EN1057, Table X compression fittings, BS EN1254, Part 2; compression joints in the running length; two piece copper spacing clips at 1500 mm centres**					
011	15 mm nominal size pipes	0.30	9.32	3.65	**12.97**	m
	Extra over for:					
	tank connectors	0.26	8.25	3.54	**11.79**	Nr
	straight tap connectors	0.19	6.10	3.39	**9.49**	Nr
	elbows	0.19	6.10	1.92	**8.02**	Nr
	tees	0.22	6.79	2.72	**9.51**	Nr
012	22 mm nominal size pipes	0.32	10.02	6.84	**16.86**	m
	Extra over for:					
	tank connectors	0.24	7.52	3.80	**11.32**	Nr
	straight tap connectors	0.22	6.79	8.82	**15.61**	Nr
	elbows	0.22	6.79	3.28	**10.07**	Nr
	tees	0.24	7.52	4.58	**12.10**	Nr
	reducing tees	0.24	7.52	11.80	**19.32**	Nr
013	28 mm nominal size pipes	0.40	12.55	12.44	**24.99**	m
	Extra over for:					
	tank connectors	0.34	10.74	13.83	**24.57**	Nr
	elbows	0.23	7.17	11.08	**18.25**	Nr
	tees	0.30	9.32	20.86	**30.18**	Nr
	reducing tees	0.30	9.32	20.97	**30.29**	Nr
014	35 mm nominal size pipes	0.45	14.31	18.86	**33.17**	m
	Extra over for:					
	elbows	0.27	8.60	31.28	**39.88**	Nr
	tees	0.34	10.74	40.68	**51.42**	Nr
015	42 mm nominal size pipes	0.51	16.12	23.71	**39.83**	m
	Extra over for:					
	elbows	0.30	9.32	42.36	**51.68**	Nr
	tees	0.39	12.17	63.96	**76.13**	Nr
016	54 mm nominal size pipes	0.63	20.03	32.85	**52.88**	m
	Extra over for:					
	elbows	0.34	10.74	72.89	**83.63**	Nr
	tees	0.45	14.31	102.76	**117.07**	Nr
017	Connections between pipes of differing materials:					
	15 mm copper x 15 mm steel	0.20	6.45	1.80	**8.25**	Nr
	15 mm copper x 20 mm steel, reducing connector	0.23	7.17	7.09	**14.26**	Nr
	22 mm copper x 20 mm steel	0.24	7.52	2.58	**10.10**	Nr
	22 mm copper x 25 mm steel, reducing connector	0.27	8.60	10.24	**18.84**	Nr
	28 mm copper x 25 mm steel	0.30	9.32	7.48	**16.80**	Nr
	42 mm copper x 40 mm steel	0.34	10.74	28.44	**39.18**	Nr
	15 mm copper x 20 mm polythene	0.20	6.45	8.35	**14.80**	Nr
	28 mm copper x 32 mm polythene	0.30	9.32	23.75	**33.07**	Nr
018	**Pipes and fittings, copper tubes, BS EN1057, Table Z, capillary fittings, BS EN1254, Part 1; capillary joints in the running length; two piece copper spacing clips at 1500 mm centres**					
019	15 mm nominal size pipes	0.30	9.32	3.05	**12.37**	m
020	22 mm nominal size pipes	0.32	10.02	5.96	**15.98**	m
021	28 mm nominal size pipes	0.40	12.55	7.74	**20.29**	m
022	35 mm nominal size pipes	0.45	14.31	16.14	**30.45**	m
023	42 mm nominal size pipes	0.51	16.12	20.37	**36.49**	m
024	54 mm nominal size pipes	0.63	20.03	28.40	**48.43**	m
	For fittings see copper tubes, BS EN1057, Table X items RC001 - RC009					
025	**Pipes and fittings, copper tubes, BS EN1057, Table Z, compression fittings, BS EN1254, Part 2; compression joints in the running length; two piece copper spacing clips at 1500 mm centres**					
026	15 mm nominal size pipes	0.30	9.32	4.14	**13.46**	m
027	22 mm nominal size pipes	0.32	10.02	7.76	**17.78**	m
028	28 mm nominal size pipes	0.40	12.55	13.60	**26.15**	m
029	35 mm nominal size pipes	0.45	14.31	21.29	**35.60**	m
030	42 mm nominal size pipes	0.51	16.12	26.50	**42.62**	m
031	54 mm nominal size pipes	0.63	20.03	36.52	**56.55**	m
	For fittings see copper tubes, BS EN1057, Table X, items RC011 - RC017					
032	**Pipes and fittings, copper tubes, BS EN1057, Table Y, gunmetal compression fittings, BS EN1254, Part 2; compression joints in the running length**					
033	15 mm nominal size pipes; laying in trenches	0.14	4.30	5.25	**9.55**	m

Unit Rates

		Man-Hours	Net Labour Price £	Net Mats Price £	Net Unit Price £	Unit
	Extra over for:					
	elbows	0.30	9.32	3.44	**12.76**	Nr
	tees	0.40	12.55	4.82	**17.37**	Nr
034	22 mm nominal size pipes; laying in trenches	0.16	5.02	8.88	**13.90**	m
	Extra over for:					
	elbows	0.40	12.55	5.48	**18.03**	Nr
	tees	0.50	15.77	7.96	**23.73**	Nr
	reducing tees	0.50	15.77	12.74	**28.51**	Nr
035	28 mm nominal size pipes; laying in trenches	0.20	6.45	13.11	**19.56**	m
	Extra over for:					
	elbows	0.42	13.24	13.62	**26.86**	Nr
	tees	0.59	18.61	21.72	**40.33**	Nr
	reducing tees	0.59	18.61	20.97	**39.58**	Nr
036	Connections between pipes of differing materials:					
	15 mm copper x 15 mm steel	0.20	6.45	3.06	**9.51**	Nr
	22 mm copper x 20 mm steel	0.24	7.52	4.48	**12.00**	Nr
	28 mm copper x 25 mm steel	0.30	9.32	9.68	**19.00**	Nr
037	**Pipes and fittings, PVCu, BS 3505 Class E; solvent welded joints in the running length; standard pipe clips at 1500 mm centres**					
	Note: 038 not used					
039	1/2" nominal size pipes	0.36	11.47	2.25	**13.72**	m
	Extra over for:					
	tank connectors	0.34	10.74	8.96	**19.70**	Nr
	straight tap connectors	0.20	6.45	4.91	**11.36**	Nr
	elbows	0.24	7.52	2.33	**9.85**	Nr
	tees	0.30	9.32	2.69	**12.01**	Nr
	reducing bushes	0.23	7.17	1.33	**8.50**	Nr
040	3/4" nominal size pipes	0.41	12.89	2.91	**15.80**	m
	Extra over for:					
	straight tap connectors	0.39	12.17	10.26	**22.43**	Nr
	elbows	0.26	8.25	2.79	**11.04**	Nr
	tees	0.34	10.74	3.39	**14.13**	Nr
	reducing bushes	0.27	8.60	1.75	**10.35**	Nr
041	1" nominal size pipes	0.48	15.04	3.83	**18.87**	m
	Extra over for:					
	elbows	0.30	9.32	3.88	**13.20**	Nr
	tees	0.40	12.55	5.13	**17.68**	Nr
	reducing bushes	0.32	10.02	2.26	**12.28**	Nr
042	1.1/4" nominal size pipes	0.54	17.19	5.86	**23.05**	m
	Extra over for:					
	elbows	0.36	11.47	6.79	**18.26**	Nr
	tees	0.48	15.04	7.26	**22.30**	Nr
	reducing bushes	0.37	11.82	3.05	**14.87**	Nr
043	1.1/2" nominal size pipes	0.62	19.69	7.36	**27.05**	m
	Extra over for:					
	elbows	0.42	13.24	8.74	**21.98**	Nr
	tees	0.57	17.92	10.48	**28.40**	Nr
	reducing bushes	0.43	13.62	3.60	**17.22**	Nr
044	Connections between pipes of differing materials:					
	1/2" PVCu x 15 mm steel	0.20	6.45	8.99	**15.44**	Nr
	1" PVCu x 25 mm steel	0.28	8.94	13.33	**22.27**	Nr
	1.1/2" PVCu x 40 mm steel	0.34	10.74	22.75	**33.49**	Nr
	Note: 045 - 051 not used					
052	**Pipes medium density polythene for cold water services; brass and gunmetal compression fittings, BS EN1254 Part 3; compression joints in the running length**					
053	Pipes to BS 6572, laying in trenches:					
	20 mm nominal size	0.09	2.88	1.73	**4.61**	m
	25 mm nominal size	0.12	3.92	2.19	**6.11**	m
	32 mm nominal size	0.19	5.85	3.68	**9.53**	m
	50 mm nominal size	0.27	8.47	8.83	**17.30**	m
	Note: 054 not used					
055	Pipes to BS 6730, fixing with galvanised brackets to brickwork:					
	20 mm nominal size	0.50	15.77	2.38	**18.15**	m
	25 mm nominal size	0.54	17.19	3.04	**20.23**	m
	32 mm nominal size	0.62	19.69	4.78	**24.47**	m
	50 mm nominal size	0.70	22.18	11.05	**33.23**	m
056	**Extra over** for polythene pipes for 'Kuterlite 700' compression fittings:					
	20 mm elbow	0.37	11.72	12.79	**24.51**	Nr
	25 mm elbow	0.41	13.02	18.73	**31.75**	Nr
	32 mm elbow	0.45	14.31	34.14	**48.45**	Nr
	50 mm elbow	0.56	17.57	81.25	**98.82**	Nr

Unit Rates

	Man-Hours	Net Labour Price £	Net Mats Price £	Net Unit Price £	Unit
20 mm tee	0.46	14.63	17.47	**32.10**	Nr
25 mm tee	0.49	15.61	27.18	**42.79**	Nr
32 mm tee	0.54	16.94	43.08	**60.02**	Nr
50 mm tee	0.64	20.19	108.00	**128.19**	Nr
25 mm reducing tee	0.46	14.63	28.57	**43.20**	Nr
32 mm reducing tee	0.49	15.61	42.62	**58.23**	Nr
50 mm reducing tee	0.54	16.94	105.69	**122.63**	Nr
63 mm reducing tee	0.64	20.19	158.38	**178.57**	Nr
25 mm straight coupling x copper	0.21	6.51	13.58	**20.09**	Nr
32 mm straight coupling x copper	0.28	8.78	25.21	**33.99**	Nr
32 mm straight coupling x F.I.	0.35	11.06	19.69	**30.75**	Nr
50 mm straight coupling x F.I.	0.47	14.98	51.12	**66.10**	Nr
20 mm female coupling x BSP	0.41	13.02	9.19	**22.21**	Nr
25 mm female coupling x BSP	0.45	14.31	12.84	**27.15**	Nr
32 mm female coupling x BSP	0.49	15.61	19.69	**35.30**	Nr
50 mm female coupling x BSP	0.62	19.53	51.12	**70.65**	Nr

057   **Pipes, galvanised steel, BS 1387, medium grade, malleable iron fittings, BS 143 and 1256, screwed and socketed joints in red lead; galvanised steel brackets at 2000 mm centres**

	Man-Hours	Net Labour Price £	Net Mats Price £	Net Unit Price £	Unit
058 15 mm nominal size pipes	0.36	11.47	5.50	**16.97**	m
Extra over for:					
elbows	0.40	12.55	0.63	**13.18**	Nr
tees	0.48	15.04	0.76	**15.80**	Nr
059 20 mm nominal size pipes	0.43	13.62	5.91	**19.53**	m
Extra over for:					
elbows	0.49	15.39	0.75	**16.14**	Nr
tees	0.59	18.61	1.01	**19.62**	Nr
reducing tees	0.59	18.61	2.70	**21.31**	Nr
060 25 mm nominal size pipes	0.53	16.84	8.62	**25.46**	m
Extra over for:					
elbows	0.59	18.61	1.07	**19.68**	Nr
tees	0.74	23.26	1.54	**24.80**	Nr
reducing tees	0.74	23.26	1.45	**24.71**	Nr
061 32 mm nominal size pipes	0.66	20.76	10.31	**31.07**	m
Extra over for:					
elbows	0.74	23.26	1.86	**25.12**	Nr
tees	0.93	29.36	2.51	**31.87**	Nr
reducing tees	0.93	29.36	2.14	**31.50**	Nr
062 40 mm nominal size pipes	0.77	24.33	12.37	**36.70**	m
Extra over for:					
elbows	0.93	29.36	3.21	**32.57**	Nr
tees	1.19	37.60	3.82	**41.42**	Nr
reducing tees	1.19	37.60	2.95	**40.55**	Nr
063 50 mm nominal size pipes	0.88	27.93	16.84	**44.77**	m
Extra over for:					
elbows	1.19	37.60	3.69	**41.29**	Nr
tees	1.45	45.82	5.76	**51.58**	Nr
reducing tees	1.45	45.82	4.07	**49.89**	Nr

064   **Pipes, galvanised steel, BS 1387, heavy grade, malleable iron fittings, BS 143 and 1256; screwed and socketed joints in red lead**

	Man-Hours	Net Labour Price £	Net Mats Price £	Net Unit Price £	Unit
065 Pipes, laying in trenches:					
15 mm nominal size	0.17	5.37	6.32	**11.69**	m
20 mm nominal size	0.20	6.45	6.70	**13.15**	m
25 mm nominal size	0.25	7.87	9.51	**17.38**	m
066 Pipes, fixing with galvanised steel brackets at 2000 mm centres:					
15 mm nominal size	0.36	11.47	6.55	**18.02**	m
20 mm nominal size	0.43	13.62	7.02	**20.64**	m
25 mm nominal size	0.53	16.84	9.93	**26.77**	m
32 mm nominal size	0.66	20.76	12.27	**33.03**	m
40 mm nominal size	0.77	24.33	14.63	**38.96**	m
50 mm nominal size	0.88	27.93	20.17	**48.10**	m
For fittings see galvanised steel pipes, medium grade items RC058 - RC063					
067 Connections between pipes of differing materials:					
20 mm steel x 28 mm copper (Table X), reducing connector, compression fitting	0.54	17.19	9.68	**26.87**	Nr
25 mm steel x 28 mm copper (Table X), capillary fitting	0.61	19.34	11.98	**31.32**	Nr
32 mm steel x 35 mm copper (Table X), compression fitting	0.66	20.76	21.14	**41.90**	Nr
40 mm steel x 42 mm copper (Table X), capillary fitting	0.73	22.91	27.89	**50.80**	Nr
50 mm steel x 54 mm copper (Table X), compression fitting	0.85	26.86	41.71	**68.57**	Nr
20 mm steel x 3/4" PVCu (BS 3505)	0.34	10.74	10.29	**21.03**	Nr
32 mm steel x 1.1/4" PVCu (BS 3505)	0.43	13.62	16.59	**30.21**	Unit
20 mm steel x 20 mm polythene	0.32	10.02	9.19	**19.21**	Nr
32 mm steel x 32 mm polythene	0.41	12.89	19.69	**32.58**	Nr

Unit Rates	Man-Hours	Net Labour Price £	Net Mats Price £	Net Unit Price £	Unit
PIPEWORK ANCILLARIES					
068 Pipework ancillaries; gunmetal and brass, BS 1010					
069 Stop valves; jointing to copper pipes:					
15 mm nominal size	0.27	8.60	10.96	**19.56**	Nr
22 mm nominal size	0.31	9.67	19.26	**28.93**	Nr
28 mm nominal size	0.34	10.74	50.24	**60.98**	Nr
070 Stop valves; jointing to PVCu pipes:					
3/8" nominal size	0.20	6.45	29.13	**35.58**	Nr
1/2" nominal size	0.23	7.17	30.04	**37.21**	Nr
071 Stop valves; jointing to polythene pipes:					
3/8" nominal size	0.28	8.94	29.13	**38.07**	Nr
1/2" nominal size	0.32	10.02	30.04	**40.06**	Nr
3/4" nominal size	0.40	12.55	45.10	**57.65**	Nr
072 Stop valves; jointing to steel pipes:					
15 mm nominal size	0.40	12.55	25.99	**38.54**	Nr
22 mm nominal size	0.48	15.04	36.56	**51.60**	Nr
28 mm nominal size	0.59	18.61	65.04	**83.65**	Nr
35 mm nominal size	0.74	23.26	160.65	**183.91**	Nr
42 mm nominal size	0.95	30.08	220.48	**250.56**	Nr
54 mm nominal size	1.19	37.60	346.83	**384.43**	Nr
073 Pipework ancillaries; gunmetal, BS 5154					
074 Wheelvalves; jointing to copper pipes:					
15 mm nominal size	0.27	8.60	20.15	**28.75**	Nr
22 mm nominal size	0.31	9.67	34.91	**44.58**	Nr
28 mm nominal size	0.34	10.74	59.41	**70.15**	Nr
35 mm nominal size	0.39	12.17	91.24	**103.41**	Nr
42 mm nominal size	0.45	14.31	121.17	**135.48**	Nr
54 mm nominal size	0.51	16.12	180.99	**197.11**	Nr
075 Pipework ancillaries; brass					
076 Wheelvalves; jointing to steel pipes:					
15 mm nominal size	0.40	12.55	25.13	**37.68**	Nr
22 mm nominal size	0.48	15.04	29.10	**44.14**	Nr
28 mm nominal size	0.59	18.61	40.53	**59.14**	Nr
35 mm nominal size	0.74	23.26	28.23	**51.49**	Nr
42mm nominal size	0.95	30.08	113.03	**143.11**	Nr
54 mm nominal size	1.19	37.60	163.97	**201.57**	Nr
Note: 077 not used					
078 Drain cocks; jointing to steel pipes:					
15 mm nominal size	0.17	5.37	59.04	**64.41**	Nr
079 Draw-off elbows; jointing to copper pipes:					
15 mm nominal size	0.17	5.37	16.27	**21.64**	Nr
22 mm nominal size	0.20	6.45	18.66	**25.11**	Nr
28 mm nominal size	0.23	7.17	28.72	**35.89**	Nr
EQUIPMENT					
080 Pipework ancillaries; BS 1212					
081 Ball valves, piston type, and copper floats, BS 1968; jointing to tanks:					
15 mm nominal size, 4.1/2" float	0.20	6.45	41.60	**48.05**	Nr
22 mm nominal size, 5" float	0.25	7.87	61.94	**69.81**	Nr
28 mm nominal size, 8" float	0.32	10.02	107.22	**117.24**	Nr
082 Ball valves, diaphragm type, and copper floats, BS 1968; jointing to tanks:					
15 mm nominal size, 4.1/2" float	0.20	6.45	22.67	**29.12**	Nr
Note: 083 - 085 not used					
086 Plastic water storage cisterns, BS 4213					
087 Cisterns; complete with lids and insulation; hoisting and placing in position:					
18 ltr capacity, type PC 4	0.45	14.31	41.17	**55.48**	Nr
114 ltr capacity, type PC 25	0.57	17.92	45.81	**63.73**	Nr
227 ltr capacity, type PC 50	0.79	25.06	71.72	**96.78**	Nr
455 ltr capacity, type PC 100	1.02	32.23	148.06	**180.29**	Nr
088 Drilling holes for pipe connections:					
19 mm diameter	0.14	4.30	-	**4.30**	Nr
28 mm diameter	0.14	4.30	-	**4.30**	Nr
42 mm diameter	0.20	6.45	-	**6.45**	Nr
Note: 089 - 090 not used					

		Man-Hours	Net Labour Price £	Net Mats Price £	Net Unit Price £	Unit
	Unit Rates					
	INSULATION					
091	**Insulation to pipework, polypropylene backed hair felt; secured with galvanised wire**					
092	10 mm insulation to copper pipework, including working over pipe fittings:					
	15 mm nominal size pipes	0.14	4.30	0.19	**4.49**	m
	22 mm nominal size pipes	0.15	4.65	0.24	**4.89**	m
	28 mm nominal size pipes	0.16	5.02	0.29	**5.31**	m
	35 mm nominal size pipes	0.17	5.37	0.34	**5.71**	m
	42 mm nominal size pipes	0.19	6.10	0.40	**6.50**	m
	54 mm nominal size pipes	0.22	6.79	0.49	**7.28**	m
093	**Insulation to pipework, preformed sectional pipe insulation; jointing with adhesive, securing with adhesive tape at 600 mm centres**					
094	9 mm insulation to copper pipework:					
	15 mm nominal size pipes	0.09	2.88	2.04	**4.92**	m
	22 mm nominal size pipes	0.09	2.88	2.92	**5.80**	m
	28 mm nominal size pipes	0.10	3.22	3.31	**6.53**	m
	35 mm nominal size pipes	0.10	3.22	4.12	**7.34**	m
	42 mm nominal size pipes	0.11	3.57	4.93	**8.50**	m
	54 mm nominal size pipes	0.11	3.57	6.35	**9.92**	m
095	**Extra over** for fitting insulation around:					
	elbows	0.05	1.42	-	**1.42**	Nr
	tees	0.07	2.15	-	**2.15**	Nr
	valves	0.06	1.80	-	**1.80**	Nr
RD	**FIRE FIGHTING INSTALLATIONS**					
	EQUIPMENT					
	Note: 001 - 041 not used					
042	**Automatic fire hose reels; 30 m of 19 mm nominal size reinforced rubber hose; fixing with expansion type bolts including drilling structure; connections to services measured separately**					
043	Wall mounted hose reels:					
	fixed reel on circular drum with simple fixing	0.68	21.49	199.47	**220.96**	Nr
	swinging reel	0.74	23.26	207.87	**231.13**	Nr
	recessed reel	0.85	26.86	136.47	**163.33**	Nr
	concealed hose reel	1.42	44.75	184.77	**229.52**	Nr
044	**Fire extinguishers; fixing on brackets plugged and screwed to brickwork, blockwork or concrete**					
045	Water extinguisher; capacity:					
	9 litres	0.37	5.68	29.40	**35.08**	Nr
046	CO2 extinguisher; capacity:					
	2 Kg	0.37	5.68	32.55	**38.23**	Nr
047	Foam extinguisher; capacity:					
	6 litres	0.37	5.68	36.75	**42.43**	Nr
	Note: 048 not used					
049	Dry powder extinguisher; capacity:					
	6 Kg	0.37	5.68	38.85	**44.53**	Nr
050	Wet chemical type extinguisher; capacity:					
	6 litres	0.37	5.68	43.05	**48.73**	Nr
RE	**HOT WATER INSTALLATIONS**					
	Note: 001 - 055 not used					
	EQUIPMENT (connections to services not included)					
056	**Copper hot water cylinders, direct pattern, BS 1566 Part 1, pre foamed**					
057	Cylinders with 4 pipe bosses and immersion heater boss; placing in position:					
	117 ltr capacity	0.45	14.31	135.52	**149.83**	Nr
	140 ltr capacity	0.45	14.31	184.37	**198.68**	Nr
	162 ltr capacity	0.57	17.92	195.83	**213.75**	Nr
	206 ltr capacity	0.68	21.49	276.22	**297.71**	Nr
058	**Copper hot water cylinders, indirect pattern, BS 1566 Part 1, pre foamed**					
059	Cylinders with 4 pipe bosses and immersion heater boss; placing in position:					
	117 ltr capacity	0.45	14.31	148.07	**162.38**	Nr
	140 ltr capacity	0.45	14.31	204.22	**218.53**	Nr
	162 ltr capacity	0.57	17.92	226.23	**244.15**	Nr
	206 ltr capacity	0.68	21.49	288.31	**309.80**	Nr

	Unit Rates	Man-Hours	Net Labour Price £	Net Mats Price £	Net Unit Price £	Unit
060	**Copper hot water cylinders, solar twin coil, pre foamed**					
061	Cylinders with 6 pipe bosses and immersion heater boss; placing in position:					
	140 ltr capacity	0.68	21.33	378.55	**399.88**	Nr
	206 ltr capacity	0.77	24.27	397.25	**421.52**	Nr
062	**Fortic type copper combination lagged hot water storage units, floor mounted cylindrical units with 4 pipe bosses**					
063	115 litres hot water, 20 litres cold water capacity, direct pattern	0.62	19.53	236.99	**256.52**	Nr
	115 litres hot water, 40 litres cold water capacity, direct pattern	0.67	21.14	252.43	**273.57**	Nr
	115 litres hot water, 40 litres cold water capacity, indirect pattern	0.72	22.78	317.26	**340.04**	Nr
	Note: 064 - 065 not used					
066	**Santon electric water heaters; fixing to walls by plugging and screwing**					
067	Aquarius over sink heater type:					
	A7/3, capacity 7 litres, loading 3 kW	0.57	17.92	88.45	**106.37**	Nr
068	Aquarius under sink heater type:					
	AU7, capacity 7 litres, loading 3 kW	0.57	17.92	91.09	**109.01**	Nr
	Aquaheat point of use heater type:					
	AH7, capacity 7 litres, loading 2.2 kW	0.57	17.92	145.84	**163.76**	Nr
069	Storage water heaters:					
	R45, capacity, 45 litres, loading 3 kW	0.68	21.49	551.11	**572.60**	Nr
	DFB50, capacity 50 litres, loading 3 kW	0.68	21.49	932.83	**954.32**	Nr
070	**Santon electric water heaters; floor mounting units; placing in position**					
071	Automatic water heaters, PP150B, cylindrical, 150 litres, loading 3 kW	0.57	17.92	573.31	**591.23**	Nr
072	**Redring instantaneous shower heaters; plugging and screwing to walls**					
073	Wall mounted units complete with hose, handset, bracket and riser rail; model:					
	Active 300, 7.2kW	0.57	17.92	107.25	**125.17**	Nr
	Expression 500, 8.5kW	0.57	17.92	141.12	**159.04**	Nr
	Expression 500, 9.5kW	0.57	17.92	168.17	**186.09**	Nr
	Note: 074 - 079 not used					
080	**Cylinder sectional insulating jackets, BS 5615, glass fibre encased in flame retardant PVC; securing with PVC bands; fitting around pipes and immersion heaters**					
081	80 mm jackets to suit copper cylinder:					
	450 mm dia. x 900 mm high	0.68	21.49	15.66	**37.15**	Nr
	450 mm dia. x 1050 mm high	0.68	21.49	16.97	**38.46**	Nr
	450 mm dia. x 1200 mm high	0.68	21.49	18.27	**39.76**	Nr
	Note: 082 not used					
083	**Work to existing water installations**					
084	Drain down cold water and hot water system prior to repairs, later refill and test system	2.06	65.10	-	**65.10**	item
085	Remove defective and supply and fix new ancillaries with joints to copper:					
	stop valves, nominal size:					
	15 mm	0.34	10.87	10.96	**21.83**	Nr
	22 mm	0.38	12.07	19.26	**31.33**	Nr
	28 mm	0.43	13.65	20.15	**33.80**	Nr
	wheel valves, nominal size:					
	15 mm	0.34	10.87	20.15	**31.02**	Nr
	22 mm	0.38	12.07	34.91	**46.98**	Nr
	28 mm	0.43	13.65	59.41	**73.06**	Nr
	35 mm	0.48	15.10	91.24	**106.34**	Nr
	42 mm	0.57	18.14	121.17	**139.31**	Nr
	54 mm	0.65	20.57	180.99	**201.56**	Nr
	draw off elbows, nominal size:					
	15 mm	0.22	6.95	16.27	**23.22**	Nr
	22 mm	0.26	8.18	18.66	**26.84**	Nr
	28 mm	0.29	9.04	28.72	**37.76**	Nr
	radiator valves, nominal size:					
	15 mm	0.51	15.99	2.22	**18.21**	Nr
	22 mm	0.65	20.57	18.75	**39.32**	Nr
	ball valves, piston type BS 1968 with copper floats, nominal size:					
	15 mm	0.29	9.04	30.15	**39.19**	Nr
	22 mm	0.34	10.62	46.33	**56.95**	Nr
086	Cut out and renew lengths of 15 mm diameter pipe up to 1 m long and supply and fix new copper pipe with two straight couplers to old pipe:					
	copper	0.77	24.17	60.26	**84.43**	Nr
	lead	0.98	30.90	42.69	**73.59**	Nr

	Unit Rates	Man-Hours	Net Labour Price £	Net Mats Price £	Net Unit Price £	Unit
RF	**CENTRAL HEATING INSTALLATIONS**					
	Note: 001 - 050 not used					
051	**Pipework ancillaries; brass**					
052	Radiator valves, jointing to radiators and:					
	15 mm copper pipes	0.40	12.55	2.22	**14.77**	Nr
	22 mm copper pipes	0.51	16.12	18.75	**34.87**	Nr
	15 mm steel pipes	0.45	14.31	10.65	**24.96**	Nr
	20 mm steel pipes	0.57	17.92	25.94	**43.86**	Nr
053	Radiator valves, thermostatic pattern, jointing to radiators and:					
	15 mm copper pipes	0.40	12.55	11.52	**24.07**	Nr
	15 mm steel pipes	0.45	14.31	13.96	**28.27**	Nr
	20 mm steel pipes	0.57	17.92	35.43	**53.35**	Nr
	Note: 054 - 059 not used					
	EQUIPMENT					
060	**Plastic water storage cisterns, BS 4213, complete with lid, insulation and Byelaw kit**					
061	Cisterns; hoisting and placing in position:					
	type PC4 18 ltr capacity	0.45	14.31	41.17	**55.48**	Nr
062	Drilling holes for pipe connections:					
	19 mm diameter	0.14	4.30	-	**4.30**	Nr
	28 mm diameter	0.14	4.30	-	**4.30**	Nr
063	**Mild steel oil storage tanks, primed finish**					
064	Tanks with fill and vent holes, or draw-off, drain and contents indicator; placing in position:					
	2mm steel, 300 gallon capacity	0.91	28.63	490.88	**519.51**	Nr
	2.5mm steel, 600 gallon capacity	1.36	42.98	560.18	**603.16**	Nr
065	**Steel panel radiators; primed finish, complete with air vent plug and concealed fixing brackets; fixing brackets with screws to brickwork**					
066	Single panel radiators with one convector surface, 450 mm high:					
	640 mm long	1.70	53.72	33.59	**87.31**	Nr
	960 mm long	1.70	53.72	45.57	**99.29**	Nr
	1280 mm long	1.70	53.72	57.38	**111.10**	Nr
	1600 mm long	1.70	53.72	74.56	**128.28**	Nr
	1920 mm long	2.04	64.43	91.42	**155.85**	Nr
	2400 mm long	2.04	64.43	146.53	**210.96**	Nr
067	Single panel radiators with one convector surface, 600 mm high:					
	640 mm long	1.70	53.72	35.44	**89.16**	Nr
	960 mm long	1.70	53.72	52.50	**106.22**	Nr
	1280 mm long	1.70	53.72	68.25	**121.97**	Nr
	1600 mm long	1.70	53.72	92.42	**146.14**	Nr
	1920 mm long	2.04	64.43	114.11	**178.54**	Nr
	2400 mm long	2.04	64.43	183.37	**247.80**	Nr
068	Single panel radiators with one convector surface, 750 mm high:					
	640 mm long	1.70	53.72	45.51	**99.23**	Nr
	960 mm long	1.70	53.72	62.71	**116.43**	Nr
	1280 mm long	1.70	53.72	79.78	**133.50**	Nr
	1600 mm long	1.70	53.72	104.10	**157.82**	Nr
	1920 mm long	2.04	64.43	128.85	**193.28**	Nr
	2400 mm long	2.04	64.43	207.31	**271.74**	Nr
069	Double panel radiators with one convector surface, 450 mm high:					
	640 mm long	1.81	57.29	50.80	**108.09**	Nr
	960 mm long	1.81	57.29	71.52	**128.81**	Nr
	1280 mm long	1.81	57.29	91.78	**149.07**	Nr
	1600 mm long	1.81	57.29	120.79	**178.08**	Nr
	1920 mm long	2.15	68.03	149.73	**217.76**	Nr
	2400 mm long	2.15	68.03	242.15	**310.18**	Nr
070	Double panel radiators with one convector surface, 600 mm high:					
	640 mm long	1.81	57.29	61.68	**118.97**	Nr
	960 mm long	1.81	57.29	89.11	**146.40**	Nr
	1280 mm long	1.81	57.29	115.06	**172.35**	Nr
	1600 mm long	1.81	57.29	151.73	**209.02**	Nr
	1920 mm long	2.15	68.03	189.02	**257.05**	Nr
	2400 mm long	2.15	68.03	306.31	**374.34**	Nr
071	Double panel radiators with one convector surface, 700 mm high:					
	640 mm long	1.81	57.29	70.58	**127.87**	Nr
	960 mm long	1.81	57.29	100.60	**157.89**	Nr
	1280 mm long	1.81	57.29	130.18	**187.47**	Nr
	1600 mm long	1.81	57.29	171.93	**229.22**	Nr
	1920 mm long	2.15	68.03	214.41	**282.44**	Nr
	2400 mm long	2.15	68.03	347.72	**415.75**	Nr

Unit Rates

		Man-Hours	Net Labour Price £	Net Mats Price £	Net Unit Price £	Unit
072	**Solid fuel boilers**					
073	Boilers for domestic hot water, brown enamelled finish; rated up to 5.90/2.60 kWh room heater, open flue; placing in position	3.68	116.35	848.93	**965.28**	Nr
074	Boilers, central heating and indirect hot water supply, white stove enamelled finish; thermostat, open flue; placing in position:					
	output 13.2 kWh	5.67	179.01	1670.29	**1849.30**	Nr
	output 17.6 kWh	5.67	179.01	1941.98	**2120.99**	Nr
	output 23.5 kWh	5.67	179.01	2158.54	**2337.55**	Nr
075	**Oil fired boilers**					
076	Boilers, central heating and indirect hot water supply, SEDBUK Band A, stainless steel heat exchanger, white stove enamelled finish; fully automatic, with open flue; placing in position:					
	output 15.0 - 26.06 kWh	4.53	143.21	1416.45	**1559.66**	Nr
	output 26.0 - 36.0 kWh	4.53	143.21	1548.75	**1691.96**	Nr
	output 36.0 - 46.0 kWh	4.53	143.21	1959.30	**2102.51**	Nr
077	**Gas fired boilers**					
078	Boilers, central heating and indirect hot water supply, floor standing SEDBUK Band A, white stove enamelled finish; fan assisted flue; placing in position:					
	output 8.8 - 14.6 kWh	3.97	125.33	774.90	**900.23**	Nr
	output 8.8 - 23.4 kWh	3.97	125.33	1086.75	**1212.08**	Nr
	output 10.6 - 30.1 kWh	3.97	125.33	1338.75	**1464.08**	Nr
079	Boilers, central heating and direct hot water supply, floor standing combi with storage cylinder, SEDBUK Band A, white stove enamelled finish; fan assisted flue condensing; placing in position:					
	output 8.8 - 23.4 kWh; DHW 35 Ltr/min, 80 Ltr storage	4.82	152.15	1582.09	**1734.24**	Nr
	output 8.8 - 23.4 kWh, DHW 35 Ltr/min, 120 Ltr storage	4.82	152.15	1722.00	**1874.15**	Nr
080	Boilers, central heating and indirect hot water supply, wall mounted, SEDBUK Band A, white stove enamelled finish; fan assisted flue-condensing; fixing with screws to brickwork:					
	output 9.2 - 15.2 kWh	3.40	107.41	635.10	**742.51**	Nr
	output 9.2 - 22.0 kWh	3.40	107.41	691.60	**799.01**	Nr
	output 9.2 - 30.2 kWh	3.40	107.41	742.45	**849.86**	Nr
081	Boilers, central heating and direct hot water supply, wall mounted combi, SEDBUK Band A,white stove enamelled finish; fan assisted flue; fixing with screws to brickwork:					
	output 9.8 - 24.0 kWh; DHW 9.8 Ltr/min	4.82	152.15	675.78	**827.93**	Nr
	output 8.7 - 24.0 kWh; DHW 11.5 Ltr/min	4.82	152.15	723.24	**875.39**	Nr
	output 9.4 - 28.0 kWh; DHW 13.5 Ltr/min	4.82	152.15	743.58	**895.73**	Nr
	Note: 082 - 084 not used					
085	**Circulator pumps; connections to services measured separately; excluding valves**					
086	Myson domestic circulator pumps:					
	CP53, 3 speed	0.91	28.63	44.21	**72.84**	Nr
	CP63, 3 speed	1.02	32.23	53.14	**85.37**	Nr
087	Wilo commercial circulator pumps:					
	SE 125 bare pump	1.13	35.80	204.97	**240.77**	Nr
	SE 150 bare pump	1.42	44.75	337.05	**381.80**	Nr
	SE 200 bare pump	1.70	53.72	427.35	**481.07**	Nr
088	Grundfos domestic circulator pumps:					
	UPS15/50, three speed	0.91	28.63	73.56	**102.19**	Nr
	UPS15/60, high head	0.91	28.63	88.77	**117.40**	Nr
089	**Motorised valves; connections to services measured separately**					
090	Honeywell motorised valves, room thermostats and cylinder thermostats; Sundial Plan model:					
	'S' with 22 mm outlets	1.02	32.23	160.38	**192.61**	Nr
	'Y' with 22 mm outlets	1.02	32.23	124.76	**156.99**	Nr
	'Y' with 1 inch outlets	1.02	32.23	149.87	**182.10**	Nr
	'Y' timed, reference Y603A/1075	1.13	35.80	220.69	**256.49**	Nr
	Note: 091 - 096 not used					
097	**Work to existing central heating systems**					
098	Drain down existing central heating system prior to repairs, later refill and test system:					
	up to 20 radiators	2.06	65.10	-	**65.10**	item
	20 - 50 radiators	6.18	195.29	-	**195.29**	item
099	Remove defective and supply and fix new ancillaries with joints to copper:					
	stop valves, nominal size:					
	15 mm	0.34	10.87	10.96	**21.83**	Nr
	22 mm	0.38	12.07	19.26	**31.33**	Nr
	28 mm	0.43	13.65	20.15	**33.80**	Nr
	wheel valves, nominal size:					
	15 mm	0.34	10.87	20.15	**31.02**	Nr
	22 mm	0.38	12.07	34.91	**46.98**	Nr
	28 mm	0.43	13.65	59.41	**73.06**	Nr
	35 mm	0.48	15.10	91.24	**106.34**	Nr
	42 mm	0.57	18.14	121.17	**139.31**	Nr
	54 mm	0.65	20.57	180.99	**201.56**	Nr

Unit Rates

	Man-Hours	Net Labour Price £	Net Mats Price £	Net Unit Price £	Unit
draw off elbows, nominal size:					
15 mm	0.26	8.18	18.66	**26.84**	Nr
22 mm	0.26	8.18	18.66	**26.84**	Nr
28 mm	0.29	9.04	28.72	**37.76**	Nr
radiator valves, nominal size:					
15 mm	0.51	15.99	2.22	**18.21**	Nr
22 mm	0.65	20.57	18.75	**39.32**	Nr
ball valves, piston type BS 1968 with copper floats, nominal size:					
15 mm	0.29	9.04	30.15	**39.19**	Nr
22 mm	0.34	10.62	46.33	**56.95**	Nr

RG   **PLUMBING SUNDRIES**

001   **Supplying pipe sleeves for fixing by other trades; steel**

002   Sleeves 100 mm long to suit nominal size pipes:

	Man-Hours	Net Labour Price £	Net Mats Price £	Net Unit Price £	Unit
15 mm	0.19	6.10	0.57	**6.67**	Nr
20 mm	0.23	7.17	0.84	**8.01**	Nr
22 mm	0.23	7.17	0.84	**8.01**	Nr
25 mm	0.28	8.94	1.00	**9.94**	Nr
28 mm	0.28	8.94	1.00	**9.94**	Nr
32 mm	0.37	11.82	1.16	**12.98**	Nr
35 mm	0.37	11.82	1.16	**12.98**	Nr
40 mm	0.45	14.31	1.71	**16.02**	Nr
42 mm	0.45	14.31	1.71	**16.02**	Nr
50 mm	0.57	17.92	2.45	**20.37**	Nr
54 mm	0.57	17.92	2.45	**20.37**	Nr

003   Sleeves 200 mm long to suit nominal size pipes:

	Man-Hours	Net Labour Price £	Net Mats Price £	Net Unit Price £	Unit
15 mm	0.19	6.10	1.15	**7.25**	Nr
20 mm	0.23	7.17	1.68	**8.85**	Nr
22 mm	0.23	7.17	1.68	**8.85**	Nr
25 mm	0.28	8.94	2.00	**10.94**	Nr
28 mm	0.28	8.94	2.00	**10.94**	Nr
32 mm	0.37	11.82	2.31	**14.13**	Nr
35 mm	0.37	11.82	2.31	**14.13**	Nr
40 mm	0.45	14.31	3.41	**17.72**	Nr
42 mm	0.45	14.31	3.41	**17.72**	Nr
50 mm	0.57	17.92	4.80	**22.72**	Nr
54 mm	0.57	17.92	4.80	**22.72**	Nr

004   Sleeves 300 mm long to suit nominal size pipes:

	Man-Hours	Net Labour Price £	Net Mats Price £	Net Unit Price £	Unit
15 mm	0.19	6.10	1.68	**7.78**	Nr
20 mm	0.23	7.17	2.47	**9.64**	Nr
22 mm	0.23	7.17	2.47	**9.64**	Nr
25 mm	0.28	8.94	2.94	**11.88**	Nr
28 mm	0.28	8.94	2.94	**11.88**	Nr
32 mm	0.37	11.82	3.39	**15.21**	Nr
35 mm	0.37	11.82	3.39	**15.21**	Nr
40 mm	0.45	14.31	5.01	**19.32**	Nr
42 mm	0.45	14.31	5.01	**19.32**	Nr
50 mm	0.57	17.92	7.04	**24.96**	Nr
54 mm	0.57	17.92	7.04	**24.96**	Nr

005   **Floor, wall and ceiling plates**

006   Chrome effect polypropylene for pipe:

	Man-Hours	Net Labour Price £	Net Mats Price £	Net Unit Price £	Unit
15 mm nominal size	0.09	2.88	0.43	**3.31**	Nr
22 mm nominal size	0.09	2.88	0.49	**3.37**	Nr
28 mm nominal size	0.09	2.88	0.61	**3.49**	Nr
35 mm nominal size	0.11	3.57	0.80	**4.37**	Nr
42 mm nominal size	0.11	3.57	1.04	**4.61**	Nr
54 mm nominal size	0.11	3.57	1.29	**4.86**	Nr

RH   **BUILDERS WORK IN CONNECTION WITH PLUMBING AND MECHANICAL ENGINEERING INSTALLATIONS**

001   **Bedding in cement mortar (1:3) and pointing**

002   Components, units of equipment, ancillaries and the like:

	Man-Hours	Net Labour Price £	Net Mats Price £	Net Unit Price £	Unit
500 x 400 mm horizontally	0.36	7.39	0.46	**7.85**	Nr

003   **Cutting and pinning to new or existing structure**

004   Ends of supports for pipes not exceeding 55 mm nominal size spaced at 1000 mm centres to:

	Man-Hours	Net Labour Price £	Net Mats Price £	Net Unit Price £	Unit
concrete	0.36	7.39	-	**7.39**	m
brickwork	0.30	6.18	-	**6.18**	m
blockwork	0.26	5.43	-	**5.43**	m
stonework	0.36	7.39	-	**7.39**	m

005   Ends of 50 x 50 mm supports for equipment, ancillaries and the like to:

	Man-Hours	Net Labour Price £	Net Mats Price £	Net Unit Price £	Unit
concrete	0.45	9.36	-	**9.36**	Nr
brickwork	0.36	7.39	-	**7.39**	Nr
blockwork	0.30	6.18	-	**6.18**	Nr
stonework	0.45	9.36	-	**9.36**	Nr

Note: 006 not used

	Man-Hours	Net Labour Price £	Net Mats Price £	Net Unit Price £	Unit
007 **Extra over** for making good fair face or facing bricks	0.18	3.70	-	**3.70**	Nr

Unit Rates	Man-Hours	Net Labour Price £	Net Mats Price £	Net Unit Price £	Unit
008	Lifting and replacing existing floorboards for:					
	50 mm nominal size pipes	0.47	7.20	-	7.20	m
	300 mm diameter ducts	1.01	15.31	-	15.31	m
009	**Cutting chases in new or existing structure**					
010	Cutting chases for 22 mm nominal size pipes in:					
	concrete	0.71	7.97	-	7.97	m
	brickwork	0.59	6.64	-	6.64	m
	blockwork	0.57	6.38	-	6.38	m
	stonework	0.71	7.97	-	7.97	m

RIPAC

The total cost control and contract administration system that maximises performance and flexibility from minimised input

QS's, Consulting Engineers, Contractors, Project Managers, Developers and Client Bodies

- Budget estimates
- Cost planning
- Bills of quantities
- Measurement from CAD
- Tender pricing and appraisal
- E-tendering
- Resource analysis
- Programme planning links
- Post contract administration
- Payments
- Cash flow
- Whole life costing

Integrated cost control through all project stages.
Easy manipulation of data.
Outputs in user defined formats.
Speedy revisions and updates.
Previous projects available for re-use, analysis and benchmarking.

Various standard libraries of descriptions and price data bases including :

BCIS Price Books

29 London Road
Bromley Kent BR1 1DG
Tel   020 8460 0022
Fax   020 8460 1196
Email enq@cssp.co.uk
www.cssp.co.uk

CSSP
CONSTRUCTION SOFTWARE

Electrical
Installations

Labour Rates

ELECTRICAL INSTALLATIONS

Please note: The labour hours throughout this section are representative of the time required for one productive man to carry out the unit of work.
Gang rates are calculated as follows by obtaining the overall gang cost and then dividing this by the number of productive members in the gang. The resulting rate is the Gang Cost per **Man - hour.** By using the same principle, any size gang may be built-up and used against the standard labour hours in this section.

Electrical:
   Craftsman (BATJIC Craft Rate) = £15.20 per hour

   Labourer (BATJIC Oper. Rate) - £11.22 per hour

Note: The labour rate shown below is used in the items for making good surface finishes.

Labourer (skill rate A) - £11.82 per hour

A0212 Solid plasterwork, screeds, in situ flooring:

Plasterer	4.00	x	£	15.20	=	£	60.80
Plastering Labourer	3.00	x	£	11.22	=	£	33.66
Total hourly cost of gang					=	£	94.46

Gang rate (divided by 4) = £23.62 per Man-hour

Mortar Mix Analysis

The cost of labour in mixing is included in the gang rate per hour for plastering.
The cost of mixers or mortar mills should be costed in preliminaries.

A0511 Cement mortar (1:3)

Cement (bagged)	0.44 tonne	x	£	156.48	=	£	68.85
Building sand	1.83 tonne	x	£	26.57	=	£	48.62
						£	117.47
Waste	10%				=	£	11.75
Cost per m3					=	£	**129.22**

Plant Hire Charges		Daily Hire Charge £	Pro-ductive Hours Hrs	Cost Per Hour £	Operator Per Hour £	Fuel Per Hour £	Total Cost Per Hour £
	The hire charges shown exclude the cost of operators and fuel but are inclusive of oil, grease and the like. Fuel costs have been added in the following table as appropriate. The operator costs are either added in the table below or, where no operator shown, have been allowed for in the rates given in the individual items of work.						
	The cost of delivery to, or collection from site is EXCLUDED and allowance for this should be made in Preliminaries.						
A0075	Kango hammer	25.00	6.00	4.17	-	-	**4.17**
A0076	Petrol driven hammer - rig and adaptor	28.00	6.00	4.67	-	-	**4.67**
A0102	Conduit bender	27.00	6.00	4.50	-	-	**4.50**
A0104	Conduit threader	24.00	6.00	4.00	-	-	**4.00**

Basic Prices of Materials		Supply Price £	Waste Factor %	Unload. Labour £	Unload. Plant £	Total Unit Cost £	Unit
	The cost of carriage and delivery has not been included in the material prices.						
	The cost of manual unloading has been allowed in the price for fixing the materials.						
	The cost of any craneage is EXCLUDED and allowance for this should be made in Preliminaries.						
	Ready mixed concrete - Dense natural aggregate BS 8500; grade:						
F0451	C12/15	84.52	5%	-	-	**88.75**	m3
	Cable, standard:						
	2 core and earth:						
S0100	1.0 mm2	0.24	-	-	-	**0.24**	m
S0101	1.5 mm2	0.32	-	-	-	**0.32**	m
S0102	2.5 mm2	0.47	-	-	-	**0.47**	m
S0103	4.0 mm2	0.97	5%	-	-	**1.02**	m
S0104	6.0 mm2	1.02	5%	-	-	**1.07**	m
S0105	10.0 mm2	1.83	5%	-	-	**1.92**	m
S0106	16.0 mm2	4.17	5%	-	-	**4.38**	m
	3 core and earth:						
S0112	1.5 mm2	0.58	5%	-	-	**0.61**	m
S0113	2.5 mm2	0.88	5%	-	-	**0.92**	m

	Basic Prices of Materials	Supply Price £	Waste Factor %	Unload. Labour £	Unload. Plant £	Total Unit Cost £	Unit
	Cable, PVC insulated:						
	2 core and earth:						
S0122	1.0 mm2	0.33	5%	-	-	**0.35**	m
S0123	1.5 mm2	0.53	5%	-	-	**0.56**	m
S0124	2.5 mm2	0.58	5%	-	-	**0.61**	m
S0125	4.0 mm2	0.77	5%	-	-	**0.80**	m
	4 core and earth:						
S0131	1.0 mm2	0.61	5%	-	-	**0.64**	m
S0132	1.5 mm2	0.99	5%	-	-	**1.04**	m
S0133	2.5 mm2	1.50	5%	-	-	**1.58**	m
	Cable, Firesure tri-rated:						
	2 core:						
S0140	1.0 mm2	0.82	5%	-	-	**0.86**	m
S0141	1.5 mm2	0.96	5%	-	-	**1.00**	m
S0142	2.5 mm2	1.79	5%	-	-	**1.87**	m
S0143	4.0 mm2	2.23	5%	-	-	**2.34**	m
	3 core:						
S0144	1.0 mm2	1.57	5%	-	-	**1.65**	m
S0145	1.5 mm2	1.83	5%	-	-	**1.93**	m
S0146	2.5 mm2	3.43	5%	-	-	**3.60**	m
S0147	4.0 mm2	4.29	5%	-	-	**4.50**	m
	4 core:						
S0148	1.0 mm2	1.80	5%	-	-	**1.89**	m
S0149	1.5 mm2	2.12	5%	-	-	**2.23**	m
S0150	2.5 mm2	3.94	5%	-	-	**4.14**	m
S0151	4.0 mm2	4.93	5%	-	-	**5.18**	m
	Cable, MICC:						
	2 core:						
S0160	1.5 mm2	4.00	5%	-	-	**4.20**	m
S0161	2.5 mm2	5.05	5%	-	-	**5.31**	m
S0162	4.0 mm2	7.60	5%	-	-	**7.98**	m
	3 core:						
S0163	1.5 mm2	5.34	5%	-	-	**5.60**	m
S0164	2.5 mm2	7.98	5%	-	-	**8.38**	m
	4 core:						
S0165	1.5 mm2	6.31	5%	-	-	**6.63**	m
S0166	2.5 mm2	9.52	5%	-	-	**10.00**	m
	Cable, SWA/PVC/PVC:						
	2 core:						
S0176	1.5 mm2	0.89	5%	-	-	**0.93**	m
S0177	2.5 mm2	1.07	5%	-	-	**1.13**	m
S0178	4.0 mm2	1.46	5%	-	-	**1.54**	m
S0179	6.0 mm2	2.17	5%	-	-	**2.28**	m
S0180	10.0 mm2	2.76	5%	-	-	**2.90**	m
S0181	16.0 mm2	4.61	5%	-	-	**4.85**	m
	3 core:						
S0182	1.5 mm2	1.11	5%	-	-	**1.17**	m
S0183	2.5 mm2	1.48	5%	-	-	**1.56**	m
S0184	4.0 mm2	1.82	5%	-	-	**1.91**	m
S0185	6.0 mm2	2.22	5%	-	-	**2.34**	m
S0186	10.0 mm2	3.58	5%	-	-	**3.76**	m
S0187	16.0 mm2	4.91	5%	-	-	**5.16**	m
	4 core:						
S0188	1.5 mm2	1.32	5%	-	-	**1.38**	m
S0189	2.5 mm2	1.91	5%	-	-	**2.00**	m
S0190	4.0 mm2	2.04	5%	-	-	**2.14**	m
S0191	6.0 mm2	3.26	5%	-	-	**3.42**	m
S0192	10.0 mm2	4.71	5%	-	-	**4.94**	m
S0193	16.0 mm2	6.75	5%	-	-	**7.08**	m
	Cable, SY flexible control:						
	3 core:						
S0201	1.0 mm2	0.55	5%	-	-	**0.58**	m
S0202	1.5 mm2	0.79	5%	-	-	**0.83**	m
S0203	2.5 mm2	1.37	5%	-	-	**1.44**	m
S0204	4.0 mm2	2.00	5%	-	-	**2.10**	m
S0205	6.0 mm2	2.76	5%	-	-	**2.90**	m
	4 core:						
S0206	1.0 mm2	0.82	5%	-	-	**0.86**	m
S0207	1.5 mm2	0.99	5%	-	-	**1.04**	m
S0208	2.5 mm2	1.53	5%	-	-	**1.60**	m
S0209	4.0 mm2	2.61	5%	-	-	**2.74**	m
S0210	6.0 mm2	3.46	5%	-	-	**3.63**	m
	5 core:						
S0211	1.0 mm2	1.06	5%	-	-	**1.12**	m
S0212	1.5 mm2	1.12	5%	-	-	**1.18**	m
S0213	2.5 mm2	1.86	5%	-	-	**1.95**	m
S0214	4.0 mm2	3.05	5%	-	-	**3.20**	m
S0215	6.0 mm2	4.09	5%	-	-	**4.29**	m
	7 core:						
S0216	0.75 mm2	1.09	5%	-	-	**1.14**	m
S0217	1.0 mm2	1.34	5%	-	-	**1.41**	m
S0218	1.5 mm2	1.65	5%	-	-	**1.73**	m
S0219	2.5 mm2	2.45	5%	-	-	**2.57**	m

Basic Prices of Materials	Supply Price £	Waste Factor %	Unload. Labour £	Unload. Plant £	Total Unit Cost £	Unit
Cable, YY flexible control:						
3 core:						
S0221 0.75 mm2	0.33	5%	-	-	0.35	m
S0222 1.0 mm2	0.39	5%	-	-	0.41	m
4 core:						
S0227 1.5 mm2	0.72	5%	-	-	0.76	m
S0228 2.5 mm2	1.22	5%	-	-	1.28	m
5 core:						
S0229 0.75 mm2	0.51	5%	-	-	0.53	m
S0230 1.0 mm2	0.63	5%	-	-	0.67	m
S0231 1.5 mm2	0.93	5%	-	-	0.97	m
S0232 2.5 mm2	1.51	5%	-	-	1.59	m
12 core:						
S0237 1.5 mm2	1.39	5%	-	-	1.46	m
S0238 2.5 mm2	2.37	5%	-	-	2.49	m
S0246 Cable, satellite, digital	0.20	5%	-	-	0.21	m
Cable, telephone:						
S0247 2 pair	0.13	5%	-	-	0.13	m
S0248 3 pair	0.18	5%	-	-	0.19	m
S0249 4 pair	0.29	5%	-	-	0.30	m
Cable, aerial:						
S0251 co-axial	0.11	5%	-	-	0.11	m
Cable, communication:						
S0252 speaker/bell	0.07	5%	-	-	0.07	m
Cable gland kit:						
indoor:						
S0301 20 mm	0.52	2.5%	-	-	0.53	nr
S0302 25 mm	1.03	2.5%	-	-	1.06	nr
S0303 32 mm	1.61	2.5%	-	-	1.65	nr
S0304 40 mm	1.92	2.5%	-	-	1.97	nr
outdoor:						
S0307 20 mm	0.93	2.5%	-	-	0.95	nr
S0308 25 mm	1.99	2.5%	-	-	2.04	nr
S0309 32 mm	2.76	2.5%	-	-	2.83	nr
S0310 40 mm	7.16	2.5%	-	-	7.34	nr
Cable gland:						
fire rated:						
S0152 20 mm	0.50	2.5%	-	-	0.51	nr
S0169 MICC pyro, plain seal	1.71	2.5%	-	-	1.76	nr
Cable clip:						
round:						
S0330 10 mm	0.02	2.5%	-	-	0.02	nr
S0331 15 mm	0.02	2.5%	-	-	0.03	nr
S0332 20 mm	0.05	2.5%	-	-	0.05	nr
S0154 insulated	0.13	5%	-	-	0.14	nr
S0167 insulated, MICC	0.58	5%	-	-	0.61	nr
Consumer unit, 100 AMP main switch, bare:						
S0401 6 way	29.73	2.5%	-	-	30.47	nr
S0402 9 way	34.93	2.5%	-	-	35.80	nr
S0403 12 way	43.85	2.5%	-	-	44.94	nr
S0404 Consumer unit, split load, insulated 15 way twin RCD flexible with 1 x 63A 30mA RCD's, 1 x 80A 30mA RCD's and 100A switch disconnect or isolator, MK Sentry	111.08	2.5%	-	-	113.86	nr
Modules						
RCD, 2 module:						
double pole:						
S0410 16A 230V 10mA	66.10	2.5%	-	-	67.75	nr
S0411 16A 230V 30mA	40.56	2.5%	-	-	41.58	nr
S0412 32A 230V 30mA	41.38	2.5%	-	-	42.42	nr
S0413 40A 230V 30mA	42.63	2.5%	-	-	43.69	nr
S0414 63A 230V 30mA	46.12	2.5%	-	-	47.27	nr
S0415 80A 230V 30mA	51.69	2.5%	-	-	52.98	nr
S0416 100A 230V 30mA	63.77	2.5%	-	-	65.37	nr
S0417 63A 230V 100mA	60.02	2.5%	-	-	61.52	nr
S0418 100A 230V 100mA	71.29	2.5%	-	-	73.07	nr
S0419 MCB type B/C, 1 module, single pole 6 to 50A	2.96	2.5%	-	-	3.03	nr
DP switch connector, 2 module:						
S0420 63A	6.75	2.5%	-	-	6.92	nr
S0421 100A	7.44	2.5%	-	-	7.62	nr
S0422 RCBO, single pole, type B, 6 - 50A, 1 module	38.93	2.5%	-	-	39.90	nr
RCD, double pole, time delayed, 1 module:						
S0423 80A 100mA	83.10	2.5%	-	-	85.18	nr
S0424 100A 100mA	79.51	2.5%	-	-	81.49	nr
S0425 Contactor, double pole, 20A, 1 module	34.00	2.5%	-	-	34.85	nr
S0426 Contactor, four pole, 20A, 2 module	27.21	2.5%	-	-	27.89	nr

	Basic Prices of Materials	Supply Price £	Waste Factor %	Unload. Labour £	Unload. Plant £	Total Unit Cost £	Unit
S0427	Bell transformer, 2 module	17.71	2.5%	-	-	18.15	nr
	Time switch:						
S0428	electromechanical, no power failure reserve, weekly programme, 3 module	56.75	2.5%	-	-	58.17	nr
S0429	electromechanical, power failure reserve 150Hr, weekly programme, 3 module	88.18	2.5%	-	-	90.38	nr
S0430	digital, multiple programming, one channel, 2 module	79.61	2.5%	-	-	81.60	nr
	Luminaires						
	Fluorescent batten, single tube, Thorn EMI popular range, lamps included:						
S0601	600 mm, 18 Watt ref PP20	10.69	2.5%	-	-	10.96	nr
S0602	1200 mm, 36 Watt, ref PP40	8.90	2.5%	-	-	9.12	nr
S0603	1500 mm, 58 Watt, ref PP65	10.07	2.5%	-	-	10.32	nr
S0604	1800 mm 70 Watt ref PP675	13.79	2.5%	-	-	14.13	nr
S0605	2400 mm, 100 Watt, ref PP100	24.86	2.5%	-	-	25.48	nr
	Fluorescent batten, twin tube, Thorn EMI popular range, lamps included:						
S0606	600 mm 18 Watt ref PP220	16.23	2.5%	-	-	16.64	nr
S0607	1200 mm 36 Watt ref PP240	20.26	2.5%	-	-	20.77	nr
S0608	1500 mm 58 Watt ref PP265	21.11	2.5%	-	-	21.64	nr
S0609	1800 mm 70 Watt ref PP2675	23.98	2.5%	-	-	24.58	nr
S0610	2400 mm 100 Watt ref PP2100	43.66	2.5%	-	-	44.75	nr
	Fluorescent batten, single tube, opal diffusers, Thorn EMI popular range:						
S0611	1200 mm, 36 Watt	7.99	2.5%	-	-	8.19	nr
S0612	1500 mm, 58 Watt	9.54	2.5%	-	-	9.77	nr
S0613	1800 mm, 70 Watt	12.42	2.5%	-	-	12.73	nr
S0614	2400 mm, 100 Watt	18.64	2.5%	-	-	19.10	nr
	Fluorescent batten, twin tube, opal diffusers, Thorn EMI popular range:						
S0615	1200 mm, 36 Watt	12.16	2.5%	-	-	12.47	nr
S0616	1500 mm, 58 Watt	13.98	2.5%	-	-	14.33	nr
S0617	1800 mm, 70 Watt	17.08	2.5%	-	-	17.51	nr
S0618	2400 mm, 100 Watt	22.77	2.5%	-	-	23.34	nr
	Fluorescent batten, single tube, prismatic diffusers, , Thorn EMI popular range:						
S0619	1200 mm, 36 Watt	10.35	2.5%	-	-	10.61	nr
S0620	1500 mm, 58 Watt,	11.65	2.5%	-	-	11.94	nr
S0621	1800 mm, 70 Watt	12.94	2.5%	-	-	13.27	nr
S0622	2400 mm, 100 Watt	19.15	2.5%	-	-	19.63	nr
	Fluorescent batten, twin tube, prismatic diffusers, Thorn EMI popular range:						
S0623	600 mm, 18 Watt	9.83	2.5%	-	-	10.08	nr
S0624	1200 mm, 36 Watt	12.68	2.5%	-	-	13.00	nr
S0625	1500 mm, 58 Watt	14.50	2.5%	-	-	14.86	nr
S0626	1800 mm, 70 Watt	17.60	2.5%	-	-	18.04	nr
S0627	2400 mm, 100 Watt	23.81	2.5%	-	-	24.41	nr
	Recessed modular fluorescent fitting lamps, Dextra:						
S0636	600 x 600 mm, 3 x 18 Watt	15.93	2.5%	-	-	16.33	nr
S0637	600 x 600 mm, 4 x 18 Watt	14.47	2.5%	-	-	14.83	nr
S0638	600 x 1200 mm, 3 x 36 Watt	22.17	2.5%	-	-	22.72	nr
S0639	600 x 1200 mm, 4 x 36 Watt	22.67	2.5%	-	-	23.23	nr
	Attachments						
	Louvre, Cat2:						
S0640	600 x 600 mm	10.85	2.5%	-	-	11.12	nr
S0641	600 x 1200 mm	21.32	2.5%	-	-	21.85	nr
	Louvre, low brightness:						
S0642	600 x 600 mm	9.24	2.5%	-	-	9.48	nr
S0643	600 x 1200 mm	14.46	2.5%	-	-	14.82	nr
	Prismatic panel:						
S0644	600 x 600 mm	1.94	2.5%	-	-	1.99	nr
S0645	600 x 1200 mm	3.87	2.5%	-	-	3.96	nr
	Fire retardant diffuser:						
S0646	600 x 600 mm	7.69	2.5%	-	-	7.89	nr
S0647	600 x 1200 mm	15.38	2.5%	-	-	15.76	nr
	Lamps						
	Fluorescent tube:						
	T8 standard:						
	cool white:						
S0651	240V, 18 Watt, 600 mm	1.47	2.5%	-	-	1.50	nr
S0654	240V, 36 Watt, 1200 mm	1.86	2.5%	-	-	1.90	nr
S0657	240V, 58 Watt, 1500 mm	1.92	2.5%	-	-	1.97	nr
S0660	240V, 70 Watt x 1800 mm	3.18	2.5%	-	-	3.26	nr
S0663	240V, 100 Watt, 2400 mm	4.43	2.5%	-	-	4.54	nr
	white:						
S0652	240V, 18 Watt, 600 mm	1.31	2.5%	-	-	1.34	nr
S0655	240V, 36 Watt, 1200 mm	1.86	2.5%	-	-	1.34	nr
S0658	240V, 58 Watt, 1500 mm	1.92	2.5%	-	-	1.90	nr
S0661	240V, 70 Watt x 1800 mm	2.75	2.5%	-	-	2.82	nr
S0664	240V, 100 Watt, 2400 mm	3.66	2.5%	-	-	3.76	nr
	warm white:						
S0653	240V, 18 Watt, 600 mm	1.65	2.5%	-	-	1.69	nr

	Basic Prices of Materials	Supply Price £	Waste Factor %	Unload. Labour £	Unload. Plant £	Total Unit Cost £	Unit
S0656	240V, 36 Watt, 1200 mm	1.86	2.5%	-	-	**1.90**	nr
S0659	240V, 58 Watt, 1500 mm	1.92	2.5%	-	-	**1.97**	nr
S0662	240V, 70 Watt x 1800 mm	2.82	2.5%	-	-	**2.89**	nr
S0665	240V, 100 Watt, 2400 mm	3.78	2.5%	-	-	**3.87**	nr
	T12 Standard:						
	daylight:						
S0666	240V, 20 Watt, 600 mm	3.87	2.5%	-	-	**3.96**	nr
S0668	240V, 40 Watt, 1200 mm	4.95	2.5%	-	-	**5.08**	nr
S0670	240V, 65/80 Watt, 1500 mm	8.21	2.5%	-	-	**8.42**	nr
	white:						
S0667	240V, 20 Watt, 600 mm	3.87	2.5%	-	-	**3.96**	nr
S0669	240V, 40 Watt, 1200 mm	4.95	2.5%	-	-	**5.08**	nr
S0671	240V, 65/80 Watt, 1500 mm	8.21	2.5%	-	-	**8.42**	nr
S0672	240V, 75/80 Watt, 1800 mm	9.77	2.5%	-	-	**10.01**	nr
	cool white:						
S0673	240V 85 Watt x 1800 mm	9.34	2.5%	-	-	**9.57**	nr
S0674	240V, 100 Watt, 2400 mm	10.70	2.5%	-	-	**10.96**	nr
S0675	240V, 125 Watt, 2400 mm	10.70	2.5%	-	-	**10.96**	nr
	FITTINGS						
S0701	Lampholder, straight batten with home office shield 2 terminal body and 3 terminal earth base	2.68	2.5%	-	-	**2.75**	nr
S0702	Pendant set with ceiling rose and lampholder, T2 rated 6 inch	1.24	2.5%	-	-	**1.27**	nr
S0703	Luminaire, low energy circular fitting IP44, glass diffuser, 16 Watt 2D lamp included, stainless steel	27.14	2.5%	-	-	**27.82**	nr
S0704	Ceiling globe luminaire with opal glass diffuser IP43 60w GLS BC 240v 145 mm diameter x 200 mm high	13.45	2.5%	-	-	**13.79**	nr
S0705	Luminaire, ceiling globe fitting IP43, opal glass diffuser, 145 mm diameter x 200 mm high, 100W GLS BC lamp included	15.28	2.5%	-	-	**15.67**	nr
S0706	Showerlight, polished chrome low voltage cast pack with transformer and lamp IP65 50 Watt MR16 GX5.3 12V	10.78	2.5%	-	-	**11.05**	nr
S0707	Shaver light, dual voltage 110V/240V, white with chrome décor, pullcord, IP21, 60 Watt S15 240V, 80 x 417 x 74 mm	30.35	2.5%	-	-	**31.11**	nr
S0708	Spotlight, single, matt chrome mains voltage, with lamp 40 Watt G9 240V, 125 x 140 mm, Massive Titania series	10.03	2.5%	-	-	**10.28**	nr
S0709	Spotlight, twin, matt chrome mains voltage, with lamps 2 x 40 Watt G9 240V, 135 x 145 mm, Massive Titania series	19.53	2.5%	-	-	**20.02**	nr
	Downlight:						
S0710	adjustable, mains voltage low energy fire rated with 11 Watt SGU 10 lamp 240V, polished brass die-cast	14.58	2.5%	-	-	**14.94**	nr
S0711	fixed, low voltage fire rated with 50 Watt MR16 12V lamp, polished brass die-cast	13.41	2.5%	-	-	**13.75**	nr
	eyeball:						
S0712	mains voltage with lamp 50 Watt GU10 240V, brass pressed steel	3.82	2.5%	-	-	**3.92**	nr
S0713	low voltage with lamp 50 Watt MR16 12V, brass pressed steel	3.68	2.5%	-	-	**3.78**	nr
S0714	Wall light, spot, IP54 rated, stainless steel with clear glass, cool white LEDs, 3 x 1 Watt 350mA	75.40	2.5%	-	-	**77.28**	nr
	Highbay architectural, integral gear, lamp IP20 included, Dextra:						
	SON-T:						
S0715	150 Watt	66.45	2.5%	-	-	**68.11**	nr
S0716	250 Watt	70.88	2.5%	-	-	**72.65**	nr
S0717	400 Watt	74.97	2.5%	-	-	**76.84**	nr
	HQI-T included:						
S0718	250 Watt	79.08	2.5%	-	-	**81.06**	nr
S0719	400 Watt	83.19	2.5%	-	-	**85.27**	nr
	MBF included:						
S0720	250 Watt	58.56	2.5%	-	-	**60.02**	nr
S0721	400 Watt	63.91	2.5%	-	-	**65.51**	nr
	Floodlight:						
	medium beam economy discharge, toughened glass diffuser, integral gear, timed ignitor and lamp included, black aluminium:						
	SON-T:						
S0726	150 Watt	75.11	2.5%	-	-	**76.98**	nr
S0727	250 Watt	81.48	2.5%	-	-	**83.52**	nr
S0728	400 Watt	90.34	2.5%	-	-	**92.59**	nr
	MBF:						
S0729	250 Watt	66.25	2.5%	-	-	**67.91**	nr
S0730	400 Watt	72.80	2.5%	-	-	**74.62**	nr
	HQI-T:						
S0731	150 Watt	89.45	2.5%	-	-	**91.69**	nr
S0732	250 Watt	80.77	2.5%	-	-	**82.79**	nr
S0733	400 Watt	84.67	2.5%	-	-	**86.79**	nr
	low Wattage discharge:						
S0741	80 Watt MBF, clear polycarbonate diffuser, integral gear and lamp included, black	33.57	2.5%	-	-	**34.41**	nr
S0742	70 Watt SON-T, clear polycarbonate diffuser, integral gear (no ignitor) and ignitor lamp included, black	24.89	2.5%	-	-	**25.51**	nr
S0743	70 Watt HQI-T, clear polycarbonate diffuser, integral gear, timed ignitor and open fixture rated lamp included, black	58.45	2.5%	-	-	**59.91**	nr
S0744	IP65 70 Watt SON-T, clear polycarbonate diffuser, photocell, integral gear (no ignitor) and ignitor lamp included, black	41.54	2.5%	-	-	**42.58**	nr
S0745	IP65 70 Watt HQI-T, clear polycarbonate diffuser, photocell, integral gear, timed ignitor and open fixture rated lamp, black	75.28	2.5%	-	-	**77.16**	nr

Basic Prices of Materials

		Supply Price £	Waste Factor %	Unload. Labour £	Unload. Plant £	Total Unit Cost £	Unit
	Under cabinet light, T5 fluorescent tube 240V, polycarbonate diffuser, switch, linkable, white:						
S0751	245 mm, 6 Watt	9.11	2.5%	-	-	9.34	nr
S0752	580 mm, 14 Watt	12.14	2.5%	-	-	12.44	nr
S0753	880 mm, 21 Watt	15.18	2.5%	-	-	15.56	nr
	Striplight, T4 240V, linkable, white:						
S0754	275 mm, electronic, IP20 6 Watt	10.14	2.5%	-	-	10.39	nr
S0755	400 mm, electronic, IP20 8 Watt	10.70	2.5%	-	-	10.96	nr
S0756	630 mm, electronic, IP20 20 Watt	12.10	2.5%	-	-	12.40	nr
S0757	815 mm, electronic, IP20 30 Watt	15.84	2.5%	-	-	16.24	nr
	Cabinet downlight, LV C/W capsule lamp for surface/recessed mounting, 12V:						
S0758	black	3.52	2.5%	-	-	3.61	nr
S0759	brushed nickel	3.97	2.5%	-	-	4.07	nr
S0760	polished brass	4.10	2.5%	-	-	4.21	nr
S0761	Fluorescent kitchen rail light, 580 x 57x 130 mm, 10 Watt T4 240V, IP20, acrylic diffuser and 5 hanging hooks, brushed nickel	32.01	2.5%	-	-	32.81	nr
S0762	Fluorescent glass shelf light, 547x 95 x 186mm, 13 Watt T5 240V, IP20, brushed nickel	49.52	2.5%	-	-	50.76	nr
	Mirror light:						
S0763	opalite, 60 Watt, unswitched, IP20, white	21.34	2.5%	-	-	21.87	nr
S0764	chrome scallop end with opal diffuser and pullcord, IP44, 24 Watt Pll 2G11 240V	67.91	2.5%	-	-	69.61	nr
S0765	fluorescent with pullcord, silver backed circular, IP44, 40 Watt T8 G10Q 240V	103.75	2.5%	-	-	106.35	nr
S0766	Showerlight, die cast low voltage, IP65, 50 Watt MR16 12V, 85 mm diameter x 130 mm recess depth x 72 mm cut out, polished chrome	13.86	2.5%	-	-	14.20	nr
S0767	Downlight, fire rated, pressed steel adjustable, 50 Watt MR16 12V, 90mm diameter x 115 mm recess depth x 75 mm cut out, satin nickel	7.17	2.5%	-	-	7.35	nr
	Transformer:						
	self monitoring:						
S0768	20VA - 60VA, electronic, dimmable	7.88	2.5%	-	-	8.07	nr
S0769	35VA - 105VA, electronic, dimmable	9.96	2.5%	-	-	10.21	nr
	submersible:						
S0770	IP68, 20VA - 60VA, electronic, dimmable	9.96	2.5%	-	-	10.21	nr
S0771	IP68, 35VA - 105VA, electronic, dimmable	11.39	2.5%	-	-	11.67	nr
	Emergency bulkhead luminaire:						
	internal:						
S0776	3 hour non-maintained, IP40, 8 Watt T5 240V	58.70	2.5%	-	-	60.17	nr
S0777	3 hour maintained, IP20, 8 Watt T5 240V, opal polycarbonate diffuser, Slimlite	119.23	2.5%	-	-	122.21	nr
S0778	Self adhesive legend kit for Slimlite bulkhead luminaire	6.27	2.5%	-	-	6.43	nr
	weatherproof:						
S0779	3 hour non-maintained, IP65, 8 Watt T5 240V	25.48	2.5%	-	-	26.12	nr
S0780	3 hour maintained, IP65, 8 Watt T5 240V	33.80	2.5%	-	-	34.65	nr
S0781	Self adhesive legend kit for bulkhead luminaire	4.58	2.5%	-	-	4.70	nr
	Track lighting						
	Single circuit mains voltage track:						
	dead end, 16A 240V:						
S0791	1.2 m	13.25	2.5%	-	-	13.58	nr
S0792	2 m	18.56	2.5%	-	-	19.02	nr
	connector:						
S0793	4 mm	2.15	2.5%	-	-	2.20	nr
S0794	adjustable, 120 mm	7.52	2.5%	-	-	7.70	nr
S0795	T 65 x 95 mm	7.52	2.5%	-	-	7.70	nr
S0796	X 95 x 95 mm	12.82	2.5%	-	-	13.14	nr
S0797	live end, 65 mm	3.23	2.5%	-	-	3.31	nr
S0798	flexible, 160 mm	10.38	2.5%	-	-	10.64	nr
S0799	Surface mounting base for single circuit mains voltage track, 120 mm cutout	7.10	2.5%	-	-	7.27	nr
	Track pack, 3 light track pack with 1m track, live and dead ends, 3 x GU10 spotlights and lamps IP20 3 x 50 Watt GU10 240V:						
S0801	white	39.54	2.5%	-	-	40.52	nr
S0802	brushed chrome	50.30	2.5%	-	-	51.56	nr
	Spotlight, IP20 50 Watt GU10 240V:						
S0803	acorn white	13.27	2.5%	-	-	13.60	nr
S0804	brushed chrome	13.43	2.5%	-	-	13.77	nr
	Compact fluorescent lamp:						
	6000 Hr:						
S0811	240V BC 5 and 7 Watt	2.47	2.5%	-	-	2.53	nr
S0812	240V BC 9 - 11 Watt	3.02	2.5%	-	-	3.10	nr
S0813	240V BC 15 and 18 Watt	3.27	2.5%	-	-	3.35	nr
S0814	240V BC 20 - 23 Watt	3.27	2.5%	-	-	3.35	nr
	10000 Hr:						
S0815	240V G23 2 pin 5 - 11 Watt	1.42	2.5%	-	-	1.46	nr
S0816	240V 2G11 4 pin 9 - 11 Watt	1.81	2.5%	-	-	1.85	nr
S0817	240V 2G11 4 pin 18 - 36 Watt	2.61	2.5%	-	-	2.67	nr

Basic Prices of Materials	Supply Price £	Waste Factor %	Unload. Labour £	Unload. Plant £	Total Unit Cost £	Unit
Halogen lamp, 50 mm, low voltage dichroic reflector lamp, 12V, GU5.3 cap, 4000 Hr, tungsten:						
S0818 10° beam angle, 35 - 50 Watt,	2.82	2.5%	-	-	2.89	nr
S0819 38° beam angle, 20 - 50 Watt,	0.61	2.5%	-	-	0.62	nr
S0820 Halogen lamp, 50 mm, dichroic reflector lamp, 25° beam angle, 35 - 50 Watt, 240V, GU10, 2500 Hr, tungsten	1.01	2.5%	-	-	1.04	nr
S0821 Standard GLS lamp, 40 - 100 Watt BC 240V	0.51	2.5%	-	-	0.52	nr
S0822 Golf ball lamp, 25 - 60 Watt BC 240V, 45 mm	0.51	2.5%	-	-	0.52	nr
S0823 Service lamp, pearl rough 60 to 100 Watt BC 110/240V 60 mm x 103 mm	0.82	2.5%	-	-	0.84	nr
S0824 Reflector lamp, internally silvered R80 blown bulb 60 Watt BC 240V	0.85	2.5%	-	-	0.87	nr
Switches and sockets						
Plateswitch:						
S0831 1 gang 1 way, single pole 10 AMP, white moulded, MK 4870 Logic Plus	0.98	2.5%	-	-	1.00	nr
S0832 1 gang 2 way, single pole 10 AMP, white moulded, MK 4871 Logic Plus	1.20	2.5%	-	-	1.23	nr
S0833 1 gang intermediate, 10A, white moulded, MK 4875 Logic Plus	5.81	2.5%	-	-	5.95	nr
S0834 2 gang 2 way, single pole 10 AMP, white moulded, MK 4872 Logic Plus	2.05	2.5%	-	-	2.10	nr
S0835 3 gang 2 way, single pole 10 AMP, white moulded, MK 4873 Logic Plus	4.70	2.5%	-	-	4.81	nr
S0836 4 gang 2 way, single pole 10 AMP, white moulded, MK 4874 Logic Plus	10.25	2.5%	-	-	10.51	nr
S0837 6 gang 2 way, single pole, 10A, white moulded, MK 4879 Logic Plus	22.31	2.5%	-	-	22.87	nr
Architrave switch:						
S0838 1 gang 2 way, single pole, 10A, white moulded, MK 4841 Logic Plus	2.28	2.5%	-	-	2.33	nr
S0839 2 gang 2 way, single pole, 10A, white moulded, MK 4842 Logic Plus	5.85	2.5%	-	-	6.00	nr
Pullcord ceiling switch:						
S0841 single pole, 1 way, with mounting block, white, 6A, MK	3.55	2.5%	-	-	3.64	nr
S0842 2 way, single pole, white with mounting block 6 AMP, MK	4.09	2.5%	-	-	4.19	nr
S0843 double pole, 1 way, flush mounting, white with neon 50A, MK	10.28	2.5%	-	-	10.54	nr
Dimmer switch:						
S0844 1 gang 1 way, white moulded, 40 - 250 Watt, MK Logic Plus	12.62	2.5%	-	-	12.94	nr
S0845 1 gang 1 way, white moulded, 65- 450 Watt, MK Logic Plus	16.85	2.5%	-	-	17.27	nr
S0846 1 gang 2 way, white moulded, 2 x 40 Watt - 250 Watt, MK Logic Plus	18.96	2.5%	-	-	19.43	nr
S0847 1 gang 2 way, white moulded, 2 x 40 Watt - 300 Watt, MK Logic Plus	38.68	2.5%	-	-	39.64	nr
Surface mounting box:						
S0851 1 gang, white moulded, 16 mm, MK Logic Plus	0.83	2.5%	-	-	0.85	nr
S0852 2 gang, white moulded, 16 mm, MK Logic Plus	3.20	2.5%	-	-	3.28	nr
S0853 1 gang architrave, white moulded, 87 x 33 x 16mm, MK Logic Plus	1.18	2.5%	-	-	1.21	nr
S0854 2 gang architrave, white moulded, 148 x 33 x 16 mm, MK Logic Plus	3.34	2.5%	-	-	3.42	nr
Switch module:						
S0861 1 way 20A, 1 module single pole, white, MK Grid Plus	2.27	2.5%	-	-	2.32	nr
S0862 2 way 20A, 1 module single pole, white, MK Grid Plus	2.96	2.5%	-	-	3.03	nr
Frontplate, white:						
S0871 1 module 86 x 86 mm, MK Logic Plus	0.90	2.5%	-	-	0.92	nr
S0872 2 module 86 x 86 mm, MK Logic Plus	0.90	2.5%	-	-	0.92	nr
S0873 3 module 86 x 146 mm, MK Logic Plus	2.17	2.5%	-	-	2.23	nr
S0874 4 module 86 x 146 mm, MK Logic Plus	2.21	2.5%	-	-	2.26	nr
S0875 6 module 146 x 146 mm, MK Logic Plus	3.93	2.5%	-	-	4.03	nr
S0876 8 module 146 x 146 mm, MK Logic Plus	3.93	2.5%	-	-	4.03	nr
S0877 12 module, 206 x 146 mm, MK Logic Plus	6.81	2.5%	-	-	6.98	nr
Switched socket:						
S0881 1 gang, double pole, white moulded, 13 AMP, MK Logic Plus	2.02	2.5%	-	-	2.07	nr
S0882 2 gang, double pole, white moulded, 13 AMP, MK Logic Plus	2.64	2.5%	-	-	2.71	nr
S0883 Switched connection unit with flex outlet in base, 13 AMP, double pole, white moulded, MK Logic Plus	4.31	2.5%	-	-	4.42	nr
S0884 Switched socket flush mounting cooker control unit, 45 AMP with 13 AMP socket, double pole, white moulded, MK Logic Plus	12.01	2.5%	-	-	12.31	nr
S0885 Cooker connection unit, white moulded, 86 mm x 86 mm, MK Logic Plus	3.36	2.5%	-	-	3.44	nr
S0886 Shaver socket, dual voltage 115V/230V, white moulded, MK Logic Plus	19.88	2.5%	-	-	20.38	nr
S0887 TV/FM co-axial socket, single outlet non-isolated, white moulded, MK Logic Plus	4.34	2.5%	-	-	4.45	nr
Telephone socket, BT:						
S0891 master, single flush mounting, IDC terminals, white moulded	6.05	2.5%	-	-	6.20	nr
S0892 secondary, single flush mounting, IDC terminals, white moulded	4.00	2.5%	-	-	4.10	nr
Telephone module, BT:						
S0893 master, white moulded, MK Logic Plus	7.82	2.5%	-	-	8.02	nr
S0894 secondary, white moulded, MK Logic Plus	5.45	2.5%	-	-	5.59	nr
S0895 Frontplate for telephone module, 2 gang, 3 module, white moulded, MK Logic Plus	3.80	2.5%	-	-	3.89	nr
Equipment						
Window fan:						
S0901 6"/150 mm 278m3/Hr, dark grey external grille and automatic thermo-activated internal shutters	46.36	2.5%	-	-	47.52	nr
S0902 9"/230 mm 668m3/Hr, dark grey external grille and automatic thermo-activated internal shutters	110.47	2.5%	-	-	113.23	nr

Basic Prices of Materials	Supply Price £	Waste Factor %	Unload. Labour £	Unload. Plant £	Total Unit Cost £	Unit
S0903 12"/300 mm 1021 m3/Hr, with dark grey external grille and automatic thermo-activated internal shutters	247.22	2.5%	-	-	253.40	nr
Wall or ceiling:						
S0904 bathroom fan, white recessed with Iris shutter, 197 x 40 mm 240V	33.79	2.5%	-	-	34.63	nr
S0905 bathroom fan, white recessed with Iris shutter 225 mm x 43 mm 240v	69.04	2.5%	-	-	70.77	nr
S0906 kitchen fan, white recessed with Iris shutter, 280 x 55 mm 240V	81.13	2.5%	-	-	83.16	nr
S0907 shower fan with in-line PVC ducting kit and grille 100 mm 240V	102.06	2.5%	-	-	104.61	nr
Extractor fan, white:						
S0908 for remote switching with automatic shutter, 100 mm/4 inch 240V	15.62	2.5%	-	-	16.01	nr
S0909 with adjustable electronic timer and automatic shutter, 100 mm/4 inch 240V	17.68	2.5%	-	-	18.13	nr
Wall/ceiling fan, commercial surface:						
S0910 pullcord operated internal shutters, 12"/300 mm, 1021 m3/Hr	204.60	2.5%	-	-	209.72	nr
S0911 automatic thermo-activated internal shutters, 12"/300 mm, 1021 m3/Hr	235.34	2.5%	-	-	241.22	nr
Fan fixing kit:						
S0912 for glass	8.25	2.5%	-	-	8.46	nr
S0913 for cavity wall	16.84	2.5%	-	-	17.26	nr
Alarm systems						
Conventional fire panel with 24 hour battery standby, EN54:						
S0921 2 zone	109.20	2.5%	-	-	111.93	nr
S0922 4 zone	135.66	2.5%	-	-	139.05	nr
S0923 8 zone	213.37	2.5%	-	-	218.71	nr
S0924 Fire alarm contractor kit, 4 zone bi-wire with 1 x 4 zone fire panel and batteries, 6 x multipoint detectors C/W sounder, 2 x manual call points, 1 x detector head/sounder removal tool 230V	542.28	2.5%	-	-	555.84	nr
Smoke detector:						
S0925 optical, battery, interlinkable, 9V	17.57	2.5%	-	-	18.01	nr
S0926 optical with hush, mains powered, alkaline battery back up and mounting plate 240V	25.68	2.5%	-	-	26.33	nr
S0927 ionisation, alkaline battery and escape light 9V	11.44	2.5%	-	-	11.73	nr
S0928 ionisation with hush, mains powered, alkaline battery back up and mounting plate 240V	16.05	2.5%	-	-	16.45	nr
Heat detector:						
S0929 optical, 24V, DC	23.76	2.5%	-	-	24.35	nr
S0930 with hush, mains powered, alkaline battery back up and mounting plate, 240V	36.30	2.5%	-	-	37.20	nr
Security bell, 6 inch:						
S0931 12V AC	33.21	2.5%	-	-	34.04	nr
S0932 230V AC	33.21	2.5%	-	-	34.04	nr
Sounder:						
S0933 mains multi frequency IP54 230V	50.25	2.5%	-	-	51.50	nr
S0934 for conduit wiring, deep base, 102 dBA IP54 24V DC	20.47	2.5%	-	-	20.98	nr
S0935 and beacon combined 90 dBA IP54 24V DC	48.26	2.5%	-	-	49.47	nr
Call point:						
S0936 flush mounting break glass with resistor/diode	9.98	2.5%	-	-	10.23	nr
S0937 surface mounting break glass with resistor/diode	9.81	2.5%	-	-	10.06	nr
S0938 resettable manual break glass with backbox and bezel for surface/flush fitting 230V	13.91	2.5%	-	-	14.26	nr
S0939 weatherproof resettable manual break glass with backbox and bezel for surface/flush fitting IP55 230V	27.40	2.5%	-	-	28.08	nr
S0940 resettable manual break glass with integral alarm sounder, backbox and bezel for surface/flush fitting 90 dBA 230V	26.54	2.5%	-	-	27.20	nr
S0941 weatherproof resettable manual break glass with integral alarm sounder, backbox and bezel for surface/flush fitting 90 dBA IP55 230V	44.99	2.5%	-	-	46.11	nr
S0942 Disabled toilet alarm kit with single zone controller, ceiling pullcord, overdoor light with sounder, reset button and disabled WC sticker	94.46	2.5%	-	-	96.82	nr
S0943 Carbon monoxide alarm, mains powered with built-in pattress and memory feature 240V, Aico	32.27	2.5%	-	-	33.08	nr
S0946 Bell chime, fixed wall mounted, Friedland D107	11.17	2.5%	-	-	11.45	nr
Conduits						
Conduit, black enamel or galvanised steel:						
S1001 20 mm	1.32	2.5%	-	-	1.35	m
S1002 25 mm	1.63	2.5%	-	-	1.67	m
straight solid coupler for round steel conduit:						
S1003 20 mm	0.13	2.5%	-	-	0.13	nr
S1004 25 mm	0.17	2.5%	-	-	0.18	nr
spacer bar saddle for round steel conduit:						
S1005 20 mm	0.06	2.5%	-	-	0.06	nr
S1006 25 mm	0.08	2.5%	-	-	0.08	nr
distance saddles for round steel conduit:						
S1007 20 mm	0.25	2.5%	-	-	0.25	nr
S1008 25 mm	0.31	2.5%	-	-	0.31	nr
terminal box:						
S1010 1 way, 20 mm	0.87	2.5%	-	-	0.89	nr
S1011 1 way, 25 mm	1.27	2.5%	-	-	1.30	nr
S1012 2 way, 20 mm	0.87	2.5%	-	-	0.89	nr
S1013 2 way, 25 mm	1.27	2.5%	-	-	1.30	nr

BCIS

Basic Prices of Materials	Supply Price £	Waste Factor %	Unload. Labour £	Unload. Plant £	Total Unit Cost £	Unit
branch U box, 2 way:						
S1014 — 20 mm	1.13	2.5%	-	-	1.16	nr
S1015 — 25 mm	1.46	2.5%	-	-	1.50	nr
angle box, 2 way:						
S1016 — 20 mm	0.87	2.5%	-	-	0.89	nr
S1017 — 25 mm	1.27	2.5%	-	-	1.30	nr
tee box, 3 way:						
S1018 — 20 mm	0.95	2.5%	-	-	0.98	nr
S1019 — 25 mm	1.32	2.5%	-	-	1.35	nr
branch box, 3 way:						
S1020 — 20 mm	1.13	2.5%	-	-	1.16	nr
S1021 — 25 mm	1.69	2.5%	-	-	1.73	nr
intersection box, 4 way:						
S1022 — 20 mm	0.99	2.5%	-	-	1.02	nr
S1023 — 25 mm	1.37	2.5%	-	-	1.40	nr
through box H, 4 way:						
S1024 — 20 mm	2.13	2.5%	-	-	2.19	nr
S1025 — 25 mm	4.37	2.5%	-	-	4.48	nr
inspection bend:						
S1026 — 20 mm	1.44	2.5%	-	-	1.47	nr
S1027 — 25 mm	2.40	2.5%	-	-	2.46	nr
inspection elbow:						
S1028 — 20 mm	1.27	2.5%	-	-	1.30	nr
S1029 — 25 mm	2.11	2.5%	-	-	2.16	nr
inspection tee:						
S1030 — 20 mm	1.52	2.5%	-	-	1.56	nr
S1031 — 25 mm	2.50	2.5%	-	-	2.56	nr
gland, TRS weathertight, brass:						
S1032 — 20 mm	0.37	2.5%	-	-	0.38	nr
S1033 — 25 mm	0.56	2.5%	-	-	0.57	nr
adaptable box with knockouts, black enamel or galvanised:						
S1051 — 75 x 75 x 40 mm	1.78	2.5%	-	-	1.83	nr
S1052 — 75 x 75 x 50 mm	1.89	2.5%	-	-	1.94	nr
S1053 — 75 x 75 x 75 mm	2.29	2.5%	-	-	2.35	nr
S1054 — 100 x 100 x 40 mm	1.75	2.5%	-	-	1.79	nr
S1055 — 100 x 100 x 50 mm	2.18	2.5%	-	-	2.23	nr
S1056 — 100 x 100 x 75 mm	2.59	2.5%	-	-	2.65	nr
S1057 — 150 x 150 x 50 mm	3.42	2.5%	-	-	3.50	nr
S1058 — 150 x 150 x 75 mm	3.60	2.5%	-	-	3.69	nr
S1059 — 150 x 150 x 100 mm	4.54	2.5%	-	-	4.66	nr
S1060 — 225 x 225 x 75 mm	9.58	2.5%	-	-	9.82	nr
S1061 — 300 x 300 x 100 mm	11.52	2.5%	-	-	11.81	nr
brass female (ring) bush, (pack size 100):						
S1062 — 20 mm	0.08	2.5%	-	-	0.08	nr
S1063 — 25 mm	0.15	2.5%	-	-	0.15	nr
brass long male bush (pack size 100):						
S1064 — 20 mm	0.14	2.5%	-	-	0.14	nr
S1065 — 25 mm	0.20	2.5%	-	-	0.20	nr
Conduit, round PVC, lightweight:						
S1076 — 20 mm	0.25	2.5%	-	-	0.26	m
S1077 — 25 mm	0.36	2.5%	-	-	0.37	m
straight solid coupler:						
S1078 — 20 mm	0.09	2.5%	-	-	0.09	nr
S1079 — 25 mm	0.13	2.5%	-	-	0.13	nr
spacer bar saddle:						
S1080 — 20 mm	0.13	2.5%	-	-	0.13	nr
S1081 — 25 mm	0.13	2.5%	-	-	0.13	nr
terminal box, 1 way:						
S1085 — 20 mm	0.35	2.5%	-	-	0.35	nr
S1086 — 25 mm	0.68	2.5%	-	-	0.70	nr
terminal box, 2 way:						
S1087 — 20 mm	0.41	2.5%	-	-	0.42	nr
S1088 — 25 mm	0.75	2.5%	-	-	0.77	nr
branch U box, 2 way:						
S1089 — 20 mm	0.41	2.5%	-	-	0.42	nr
S1090 — 25 mm	0.75	2.5%	-	-	0.77	nr
angle box, 2 way:						
S1091 — 20 mm	0.44	2.5%	-	-	0.45	nr
S1092 — 25 mm	0.72	2.5%	-	-	0.74	nr
tee box, 3 way:						
S1093 — 20 mm	0.45	2.5%	-	-	0.46	nr
S1094 — 25 mm	1.01	2.5%	-	-	1.04	nr
branch box, 3 way:						
S1095 — 20 mm	0.45	2.5%	-	-	0.46	nr
S1096 — 25 mm	1.01	2.5%	-	-	1.04	nr
intersection box, 4 way:						
S1097 — 20 mm	0.39	2.5%	-	-	0.40	nr
S1098 — 25 mm	0.85	2.5%	-	-	0.87	nr
through box H, 4 way:						
S1099 — 20 mm	0.59	2.5%	-	-	0.60	nr
S1100 — 25 mm	0.68	2.5%	-	-	0.70	nr
inspection bend:						
S1101 — 20 mm	0.41	2.5%	-	-	0.42	nr
S1102 — 25 mm	0.78	2.5%	-	-	0.80	nr
inspection elbow:						
S1103 — 20 mm	0.30	2.5%	-	-	0.31	nr
S1104 — 25 mm	0.52	2.5%	-	-	0.53	nr
inspection tee:						
S1105 — 20 mm	0.39	2.5%	-	-	0.40	nr

Basic Prices of Materials		Supply Price £	Waste Factor %	Unload. Labour £	Unload. Plant £	Total Unit Cost £	Unit
S1106	25 mm	0.85	2.5%	-	-	0.87	nr
	plain bend, 20 mm:						
S1107	20 mm	0.40	2.5%	-	-	0.41	nr
S1108	25 mm	0.66	2.5%	-	-	0.67	nr
	threaded adaptor:						
S1109	20 mm	1.31	2.5%	-	-	1.34	nr
S1110	25 mm	1.97	2.5%	-	-	2.02	nr
	Conduit, PVC, round, heavy gauge:						
S1125	20 mm	0.34	2.5%	-	-	0.35	m
S1126	25 mm	0.48	2.5%	-	-	0.50	m
	Conduit, PVC, oval:						
S1131	13 mm	0.13	2.5%	-	-	0.13	m
S1132	16 mm	0.15	2.5%	-	-	0.15	m
S1133	20 mm	0.19	2.5%	-	-	0.19	m
S1134	25 mm	0.24	2.5%	-	-	0.25	m
S1135	30 mm	0.28	2.5%	-	-	0.28	m
	Conduit, steel, PVC covered, flexible:						
S1181	16 mm	2.10	2.5%	-	-	2.16	m
S1182	20 mm	2.35	2.5%	-	-	2.41	m
S1183	25 mm	3.66	2.5%	-	-	3.75	m
	fixed fitting:						
S1184	16 mm	1.66	2.5%	-	-	1.70	nr
S1185	20 mm	2.12	2.5%	-	-	2.17	nr
S1186	25 mm	3.86	2.5%	-	-	3.95	nr
	swivel fitting:						
S1187	16 mm	1.84	2.5%	-	-	1.89	nr
S1188	20 mm	2.50	2.5%	-	-	2.57	nr
S1189	25 mm	3.93	2.5%	-	-	4.02	nr
	clip:						
S1190	16 mm	0.41	2.5%	-	-	0.42	nr
S1191	20 mm	0.42	2.5%	-	-	0.44	nr
S1192	25 mm	0.43	2.5%	-	-	0.44	nr
Capping							
	Capping, PVC:						
S1136	13 mm	0.12	2.5%	-	-	0.12	m
S1137	16 mm	0.16	2.5%	-	-	0.16	m
S1138	38 mm	0.25	2.5%	-	-	0.25	m
Trunking							
	Mini trunking, PVC, self adhesive:						
S1141	16 x 16 mm	0.42	2.5%	-	-	0.43	m
S1142	16 x 25 mm	0.56	2.5%	-	-	0.58	m
S1143	16 x 40 mm	0.76	2.5%	-	-	0.77	m
S1144	25 x 40 mm	0.83	2.5%	-	-	0.85	m
	fittings for mini trunking, PVC:						
S1145	16 x 16mm	0.15	2.5%	-	-	0.15	nr
S1146	16 x 25 mm	0.17	2.5%	-	-	0.18	nr
S1147	16 x 40 mm	0.20	2.5%	-	-	0.20	nr
S1148	25 x 40 mm	0.32	2.5%	-	-	0.33	nr
	Trunking, PVC:						
S1151	50 x 50 mm	2.53	2.5%	-	-	2.60	m
S1152	50 x 75 mm	3.11	2.5%	-	-	3.18	m
S1153	75 x 75 mm	2.76	2.5%	-	-	2.83	m
S1154	50 x 100 mm	4.93	2.5%	-	-	5.05	m
S1155	100 x 100 mm	5.05	2.5%	-	-	5.18	m
	coupling:						
S1156	50 x 50 mm	0.61	2.5%	-	-	0.62	nr
S1157	50 x 75 mm	0.61	2.5%	-	-	0.62	nr
S1158	75 x 75 mm	0.63	2.5%	-	-	0.65	nr
S1159	50 x 100 mm	0.67	2.5%	-	-	0.69	nr
S1160	100 x 100 mm	1.41	2.5%	-	-	1.45	nr
	stopped end:						
S1161	50 x 50 mm	0.35	2.5%	-	-	0.36	nr
S1162	50 x 75 mm	0.48	2.5%	-	-	0.49	nr
S1163	75 x 75 mm	0.56	2.5%	-	-	0.57	nr
S1164	50 x 100 mm	0.69	2.5%	-	-	0.71	nr
S1165	100 x 100 mm	1.12	2.5%	-	-	1.15	nr
	angle:						
S1166	50 x 50 mm	3.08	2.5%	-	-	3.16	nr
S1167	50 x 75 mm	3.95	2.5%	-	-	4.05	nr
S1168	75 x 75 mm	4.92	2.5%	-	-	5.05	nr
S1169	50 x 100 mm	5.17	2.5%	-	-	5.30	nr
S1170	100 x 100 mm	9.47	2.5%	-	-	9.71	nr
	flat angle:						
S1171	50 x 50 mm	2.34	2.5%	-	-	2.40	nr
S1172	50 x 75 mm	2.80	2.5%	-	-	2.87	nr
S1173	75 x 75 mm	3.61	2.5%	-	-	3.70	nr
S1174	50 x 100 mm	4.72	2.5%	-	-	4.84	nr
S1175	100 x 100 mm	4.73	2.5%	-	-	4.85	nr
	flat tee:						
S1176	50 x 50 mm	3.29	2.5%	-	-	3.37	nr
S1177	50 x 75 mm	4.67	2.5%	-	-	4.79	nr
S1178	75 x 75 mm	5.08	2.5%	-	-	5.21	nr

Basic Prices of Materials	Supply Price £	Waste Factor %	Unload. Labour £	Unload. Plant £	Total Unit Cost £	Unit
S1179 50 x 100 mm	6.49	2.5%	-	-	6.65	nr
S1180 100 x 100 mm	8.75	2.5%	-	-	8.97	nr
Lighting trunking, galvanised steel, with steel lid:						
S1511 50 x 50 mm	3.52	2.5%	-	-	3.61	m
drop or riser:						
S1503 50 x 50 mm	7.40	2.5%	-	-	7.59	nr
4 way:						
S1504 50 x 50 mm	8.42	2.5%	-	-	8.63	nr
stopped end:						
S1505 50 x 50 mm	1.01	2.5%	-	-	1.04	nr
connector:						
S1506 50 x 50 mm	1.65	2.5%	-	-	1.70	nr
hanger:						
S1507 50 x 50 mm	1.85	2.5%	-	-	1.89	nr
angel:						
S1508 50 x 50 mm	7.25	2.5%	-	-	7.43	nr
Bracketry						
High tensile set bolt:						
S1268 M6 x 25	0.04	2.5%	-	-	0.05	nr
High tensile nut:						
S1280 M6	0.01	2.5%	-	-	0.01	nr
Shake proof washer:						
S1288 M6	0.01	2.5%	-	-	0.01	nr
Earthing systems						
Copper tape, bare, (priced based on LME rate £6000/tonne):						
S1351 3 x 25 mm	18.61	2.5%	-	-	19.08	m
S1352 4 x 25 mm	24.23	2.5%	-	-	24.83	m
S1353 3 x 40 mm	38.88	2.5%	-	-	39.85	m
S1354 4 x 40 mm	58.41	2.5%	-	-	59.87	m
S1355 6 x 50 mm	71.85	2.5%	-	-	73.65	m
Copper tape, PVC covered, (priced based on LME rate £6000/tonne):						
S1356 3 x 25 mm	20.79	2.5%	-	-	21.31	m
S1357 6 x 50 mm	80.21	2.5%	-	-	82.21	m
DC tape clip for bare copper:						
S1361 3 x 25 mm	3.14	2.5%	-	-	3.22	nr
S1362 4 x 25 mm	4.06	2.5%	-	-	4.16	nr
S1363 4 x 40 mm	8.76	2.5%	-	-	8.98	nr
DC tape clip for PVC covered copper:						
S1364 3 x 25 mm	3.14	2.5%	-	-	3.22	nr
S1365 4 x 25 mm	4.06	2.5%	-	-	4.16	nr
Test and junction clamp copper:						
S1366 25 mm	11.06	2.5%	-	-	11.34	nr
S1367 40 mm	41.34	2.5%	-	-	42.37	nr
S1369 Rod to tape coupling 15 mm copper	21.14	2.5%	-	-	21.67	nr
S1370 Puddle flange copper	116.68	2.5%	-	-	119.59	nr
S1372 Air terminal multipoint, 15 mm copper	54.05	2.5%	-	-	55.40	nr
S1373 Strike pad copper and stem	26.91	2.5%	-	-	27.58	nr
S1374 Air rod base, 15 mm copper	32.17	2.5%	-	-	32.98	nr
S1375 Air rod bracket, 15 mm copper (pair)	55.50	2.5%	-	-	56.88	nr
S1376 Water main bond	13.49	2.5%	-	-	13.83	nr
S1377 Tower earthing clamp	19.89	2.5%	-	-	20.39	nr
S1378 Rod to tape clamp 10 x 26 mm	10.19	2.5%	-	-	10.45	nr
S1379 Flexible copper braid 200 mm long	17.51	2.5%	-	-	17.94	nr
Earth rod unthreaded:						
S1391 14.2 mm diameter x 1200 mm long	16.99	2.5%	-	-	17.41	nr
S1393 17.2 mm diameter x 1200 mm long	21.80	2.5%	-	-	22.35	nr
Earth rod coupling:						
S1395 14.2 mm diameter	7.35	2.5%	-	-	7.54	nr
Earth rod driving head:						
S1397 14.2 mm diameter	1.86	2.5%	-	-	1.91	nr
S1398 17.2 mm diameter	3.07	2.5%	-	-	3.15	nr
Earth rod threaded:						
S1399 13 mm diameter x 1200 mm long	15.63	2.5%	-	-	16.02	nr
S1400 13 mm diameter x 1800 mm long	22.92	2.5%	-	-	23.50	nr
S1401 16 mm diameter x 1200 mm long	17.24	2.5%	-	-	17.67	nr
S1403 19 mm diameter x 1200 mm long	22.11	2.5%	-	-	22.66	nr
Earth rod coupling:						
S1405 13 mm diameter	7.96	2.5%	-	-	8.16	nr
S1406 16 mm diameter	7.35	2.5%	-	-	7.54	nr
S1407 19 mm diameter	10.83	2.5%	-	-	11.10	nr

	Basic Prices of Materials	Supply Price £	Waste Factor %	Unload. Labour £	Unload. Plant £	Total Unit Cost £	Unit
	Earth rod driving stud:						
S1408	13 mm diameter	4.39	2.5%	-	-	4.50	nr
S1409	16 mm diameter	1.60	2.5%	-		1.64	nr
S1410	19 mm diameter	3.41	2.5%	-	-	3.49	nr
	Inspection pit:						
S1423	concrete	52.01	2.5%	-	-	53.32	nr
	Equipotential earth bonding conductors:						
S1431	6 mm2	0.28	2.5%	-	-	0.28	m
S1432	10 mm2	0.51	2.5%	-	-	0.53	m
S1433	16 mm2	0.99	2.5%	-	-	1.01	m
S1434	25 mm2	1.89	2.5%	-	-	1.94	m
	Heaters						
	Immersion heater, copper sheathed:						
S1621	280 mm long	16.49	2.5%	-	-	16.90	nr
S1622	686 mm long	18.68	2.5%	-	-	19.14	nr
S1623	280 mm long, anti corrosive	19.78	2.5%	-	-	20.27	nr
S1631	Fan heater, 3.0kW wall mounted (warm air curtain), Dimplex AC range, white	128.47	2.5%	-	-	131.68	nr
S1632	Warm air curtain, Dimplex AC range white with adjustable air flow direction and integral controls for double doorways 6.0 kW	258.00	2.5%	-	-	264.45	nr
S1633	Unit heater, Dimplex BFH range brown base 2.4 kW for fitting into panelling etc	99.20	2.5%	-	-	101.68	nr
	Storage heater, with multi-sense two thermostatic sensor control system, Creda TSR Sensor Plus series white:						
S1641	0.9kW, 6 AW	155.91	2.5%	-	-	159.80	nr
S1642	1.7kW, 12 AW	226.06	2.5%	-	-	231.71	nr
S1643	2.5 kW, 18AW	300.21	2.5%	-	-	307.71	nr
S1644	3.4 kW, 24AW	365.78	2.5%	-	-	374.92	nr
	Note: The following material prices apply to section SH (making good) only						
	The following material prices have been calculated on a National Average 'best price' basis. Please refer to Introduction, General Item AA004						
T0064	Thistle Finish	226.51	5%	11.22	-	249.62	tonne

Unit Rates	Man-Hours	Plant Hours	Net Labour Price £	Net Plant Price £	Net Mats Price £	Net Unit Price £	Unit
SA **DOMESTIC AND INDUSTRIAL SWITCHGEAR**							
001 **MK Electric Sentry 17th edition consumer unit**							
002 Insulated enclosures 100A SP and N:							
with 5+5 way consumer unit, 100A isolator + 2 x 63A 30 mA split load RCDs and 10 MCBs	2.30	-	34.96	-	30.47	**65.43**	Nr
with 5+5 way consumer unit, 100A isolator + 1 x 63A 30 mA RCDs, 1 x 80A 30 mA RCDs and 10 MCBs	2.30	-	34.96	-	35.80	**70.76**	Nr
12 way twin RCD flexible split load consumer unit with 1 x 63A 30 mA RCDs, 1 x 80A 30 mA RCDs and 100A switch disconnector isolator	3.45	-	52.44	-	44.94	**97.38**	Nr
15 way twin RCD flexible split load consumer unit with 1 x 63A 30 mA RCDs, 1 x 100A 30 mA RCDs and 100A switch disconnector isolator	3.45	-	52.44	-	113.86	**166.30**	Nr
003 RCD earth leakage device, 2 module double pole:							
16A 230V 10 mA	0.40	-	6.12	-	67.75	**73.87**	Nr
16A 230V 30 mA	0.40	-	6.12	-	41.58	**47.70**	Nr
32A 230V 30 mA	0.40	-	6.12	-	42.42	**48.54**	Nr
40A 230V 30 mA	0.40	-	6.12	-	43.69	**49.81**	Nr
63A 230V 30 mA	0.40	-	6.12	-	47.27	**53.39**	Nr
80A 230V 30 mA	0.40	-	6.12	-	52.98	**59.10**	Nr
100A 230V 30 mA	0.40	-	6.12	-	65.37	**71.49**	Nr
63A 230V 100 mA	0.40	-	6.12	-	61.52	**67.64**	Nr
100A 230V 100 mA	0.40	-	6.12	-	73.07	**79.19**	Nr
single pole type B RCBO 6 to 50A - 1 module	0.25	-	3.85	-	3.03	**6.88**	Nr
double pole time delayed RCD 80A 100 mA	0.32	-	4.89	-	85.18	**90.07**	Nr
double pole time delayed RCD 100A 100 mA	0.32	-	4.89	-	81.49	**86.38**	Nr
004 Supplementary circuit protection and fitting into consumer unit:							
MCB type B/C single pole 6 to 50A - 1 module	0.25	-	3.85	-	3.03	**6.88**	Nr
double pole switch connector 63A - 2 module	0.32	-	4.89	-	6.92	**11.81**	Nr
double pole switch connector 100A - 2 module	0.32	-	4.89	-	7.62	**12.51**	Nr
single pole MCB 6 - 50A - 1 module	0.32	-	4.89	-	39.90	**44.79**	Nr
contactor double pole 20A - 1 module	0.32	-	4.89	-	34.85	**39.74**	Nr
contactor four pole 20A - 2 module	0.46	-	6.99	-	27.89	**34.88**	Nr
bell transformer - 2 module	0.25	-	3.85	-	18.15	**22.00**	Nr
electromechanical time switch no power failure reserve, weekly programme - 3 module	0.25	-	3.85	-	58.17	**62.02**	Nr
electromechanical time switch power failure reserve 150Hr , weekly programme - 3 module	0.25	-	3.85	-	90.38	**94.23**	Nr
digital time switch multiple programming one channel - 2 module	0.25	-	3.85	-	81.60	**85.45**	Nr
SB **LIGHTING LUMINAIRES AND ACCESSORIES**							
001 **Fluorescent fittings; Thorn EMI Popular Pack**							
002 Surface mounted; with tubes:							
single tube: 600 mm 18 Watt ref PP20	0.55	-	8.30	-	10.96	**19.26**	Nr
single tube: 1200 mm 36 Watt ref PP40	0.63	-	9.54	-	9.12	**18.66**	Nr
single tube: 1500 mm 58 Watt ref PP65	0.72	-	10.98	-	10.32	**21.30**	Nr
single tube: 1800 mm 70 Watt ref PP675	0.83	-	12.62	-	14.13	**26.75**	Nr
single tube: 2400 mm 100 Watt ref PP100	0.96	-	14.53	-	25.48	**40.01**	Nr
twin tube: 600 mm 18 Watt ref PP220	0.58	-	8.74	-	16.64	**25.38**	Nr
twin tube: 1200 mm 36 Watt ref PP240	0.66	-	10.05	-	20.77	**30.82**	Nr
twin tube: 1500 mm 58 Watt ref PP265	0.76	-	11.56	-	21.64	**33.20**	Nr
twin tube: 1800 mm 70 Watt ref PP2675	0.87	-	13.28	-	24.58	**37.86**	Nr
twin tube: 2400 mm 100 Watt ref PP2100	1.01	-	15.30	-	44.75	**60.05**	Nr
003 Fluorescent fittings surface modular type with tubes and diffusers, diffuser pack range:							
single tube: 1200 mm 36 Watt opal	0.63	-	9.54	-	8.19	**17.73**	Nr
single tube: 1500 mm 58 Watt opal	0.72	-	10.98	-	9.77	**20.75**	Nr
single tube: 1800 mm 70 Watt opal	0.83	-	12.62	-	12.73	**25.35**	Nr
single tube: 2400 mm 100 Watt opal	0.95	-	14.51	-	19.10	**33.61**	Nr
twin tube 1200 mm 36 Watt opal	0.76	-	11.56	-	12.47	**24.03**	Nr
twin tube 1500 mm 58 Watt opal	0.83	-	12.62	-	14.33	**26.95**	Nr
twin tube 1800 mm 70 Watt opal	0.95	-	14.51	-	17.51	**32.02**	Nr
twin tube 2400 mm 100 Watt opal	1.10	-	16.69	-	23.34	**40.03**	Nr
single tube: 1200 mm 36 Watt prismatic	0.63	-	9.54	-	10.61	**20.15**	Nr
single tube: 1500 mm 58 Watt prismatic	0.72	-	10.98	-	11.94	**22.92**	Nr
single tube: 1800 mm 70 Watt prismatic	0.83	-	12.62	-	13.27	**25.89**	Nr
single tube: 2400 mm 70 Watt prismatic	0.95	-	14.51	-	19.63	**34.14**	Nr
twin tube 600 mm 18 Watt prismatic	0.83	-	12.62	-	10.08	**22.70**	Nr
twin tube 1200 mm 36 Watt prismatic	0.95	-	14.51	-	13.00	**27.51**	Nr
twin tube 1500 mm 58 Watt prismatic	0.83	-	12.62	-	14.86	**27.48**	Nr
twin tube 1800 mm 70 Watt prismatic	0.95	-	14.51	-	18.04	**32.55**	Nr
twin tube 2400 mm 100 Watt prismatic	1.10	-	16.69	-	24.41	**41.10**	Nr
004 Fluorescent fittings recessed modular with tubes and diffusers for lay in grid ceilings supplied without lamps:							
600 x 600 mm 3 x 18 Watt lamps	0.60	-	9.18	-	16.33	**25.51**	Nr
600 x 600 mm 4 x 18 Watt lamps	0.60	-	9.18	-	14.83	**24.01**	Nr
600 x 1200 mm 3 x 36 Watt lamps	0.60	-	9.18	-	22.72	**31.90**	Nr
600 x 1200 mm 4 x 36 Watt tubes	0.60	-	9.18	-	23.23	**32.41**	Nr
Extra over for CAT2 louvre 600 x 600 mm	0.12	-	1.75	-	11.12	**12.87**	Nr
Extra over for CAT2 louvre 600 x 1200 mm	0.12	-	1.75	-	21.85	**23.60**	Nr
Extra over for low brightness louvre 600 x 600 mm	0.12	-	1.75	-	9.48	**11.23**	Nr
Extra over for low brightness louvre 600 x 1200 mm	0.12	-	1.75	-	14.82	**16.57**	Nr
Extra over for low prismatic louvre 600 x 600 mm	0.12	-	1.75	-	1.99	**3.74**	Nr

Unit Rates	Man-Hours	Plant Hours	Net Labour Price £	Net Plant Price £	Net Mats Price £	Net Unit Price £	Unit
Extra over for low prismatic louvre 600 x 1200 mm	0.12	-	1.75	-	3.96	**5.71**	Nr
Extra over for fire retardant diffuser 600 x 600 mm	0.12	-	1.75	-	7.89	**9.64**	Nr
Extra over for fire retardant diffuser 600 x 1200 mm	0.12	-	1.75	-	15.76	**17.51**	Nr
005 Fluorescent tubes:							
type T8 240V 18 Watt x 600 mm cool white	0.12	-	1.75	-	1.50	**3.25**	Nr
type T8 240V 18 Watt x 600 mm white	0.12	-	1.75	-	1.34	**3.09**	Nr
type T8 240V 18 Watt x 600 mm warm white	0.12	-	1.75	-	1.69	**3.44**	Nr
type T8 240V 36 Watt x 1200 mm cool white	0.12	-	1.75	-	1.90	**3.65**	Nr
type T8 240V 36 Watt x 1200 mm white	0.12	-	1.75	-	1.90	**3.65**	Nr
type T8 240V 36 Watt x 1200 mm warm white	0.12	-	1.75	-	1.90	**3.65**	Nr
type T8 240V 58 Watt x 1500 mm cool white	0.13	-	1.92	-	1.97	**3.89**	Nr
type T8 240V 58 Watt x 1500 mm white	0.13	-	1.92	-	1.97	**3.89**	Nr
type T8 240V 58 Watt x 1500 mm warm white	0.13	-	1.92	-	1.97	**3.89**	Nr
type T8 240V 70 Watt x 1800 mm cool white	0.14	-	2.10	-	3.26	**5.36**	Nr
type T8 240V 70 Watt x 1800 mm white	0.14	-	2.10	-	2.82	**4.92**	Nr
type T8 240V 70 Watt x 1800 mm warm white	0.14	-	2.10	-	2.89	**4.99**	Nr
type T8 240V 100 Watt x 2400 mm cool white	0.14	-	2.19	-	4.54	**6.73**	Nr
type T8 240V 100 Watt x 2400 mm white	0.14	-	2.19	-	3.76	**5.95**	Nr
type T8 240V 100 Watt x 2400 mm warm white	0.14	-	2.19	-	3.87	**6.06**	Nr
type 12 240V 20 Watt x 600 mm daylight	0.12	-	1.75	-	3.96	**5.71**	Nr
type 12 240V 20 Watt x 600 mm white	0.12	-	1.75	-	3.96	**5.71**	Nr
type 12 240V 40 Watt x 1200 mm daylight	0.12	-	1.75	-	5.08	**6.83**	Nr
type 12 240V 40 Watt x 1200 mm white	0.12	-	1.75	-	5.08	**6.83**	Nr
type 12 240V 65/80 Watt x 1500 mm daylight	0.13	-	1.92	-	8.42	**10.34**	Nr
type 12 240V 65/80 Watt x 1500 mm white	0.13	-	1.92	-	8.42	**10.34**	Nr
type 12 240V 75/80 Watt x 1800 mm white	0.14	-	2.10	-	10.01	**12.11**	Nr
type 12 240V 85 Watt x 1800 mm cool white	0.14	-	2.10	-	9.57	**11.67**	Nr
type 12 240V 100 Watt x 2400 mm cool white	0.14	-	2.19	-	10.96	**13.15**	Nr
type 12 240V 125 Watt x 2400 mm cool white	0.14	-	2.19	-	10.96	**13.15**	Nr
006 **Non-fluorescent fitting**							
007 Domestic light fittings:							
ceiling mounted batten holder	0.20	-	3.06	-	2.75	**5.81**	Nr
ceiling pendant fitting with flex and lampholders	0.20	-	3.06	-	1.27	**4.33**	Nr
stainless steel low energy circular luminaire with glass diffuser IP44 16 Watt 2D 240V	0.40	-	6.12	-	27.82	**33.94**	Nr
ceiling globe luminaire with opal glass diffuser IP43 60 Watt GLS BC 240V 145 mm diameter x 200 mm high	0.40	-	6.12	-	13.79	**19.91**	Nr
ceiling globe luminaire with opal glass diffuser IP43 100 Watt GLS BC 240V 145 mm diameter x 200 mm high	0.40	-	6.12	-	15.67	**21.79**	Nr
polished chrome low voltage cast showerlight pack with transformer and lamp IP65 50 Watt MR16 GX5.3 12V	0.40	-	6.12	-	11.05	**17.17**	Nr
110V/240V dual voltage shaver light with chrome décor and pullcord IP21 60 Watt S15 240V 80 x 417 x 74 mm deep	0.40	-	6.12	-	31.11	**37.23**	Nr
massive Titania series matt chrome mains voltage single spotlight with lamp 40 Watt G9 240V	0.40	-	6.12	-	10.28	**16.40**	Nr
massive Titania series matt chrome mains voltage twin light plate spotlight with lamps 2 x 40 Watt G9 240V 135 mm diameter x 145 mm high	0.49	-	7.43	-	20.02	**27.45**	Nr
polished brass die-cast mains voltage low energy fire rated adjustable downlight for 11 Watt SGU10 lamp 240V	0.29	-	4.37	-	14.94	**19.31**	Nr
polished brass die-cast low voltage fire rated fixed downlight with lamp 50 Watt MR16 12V	0.29	-	4.37	-	13.75	**18.12**	Nr
brass pressed steel mains voltage eyeball downlight with lamp 50 Watt GU10 240V	0.32	-	4.81	-	3.92	**8.73**	Nr
brass pressed steel low voltage eyeball downlight with lamp 50 Watt MR16 12V	0.32	-	4.81	-	3.78	**8.59**	Nr
stainless steel LED spot wall light with clear glass and cool white LEDs IP54 3 x 1 Watt 350 mA	0.32	-	4.81	-	77.28	**82.09**	Nr
008 Industrial lighting fittings; high bay type complete with reflector and lamp and gear:							
150 Watt sodium	1.58	-	24.04	-	68.11	**92.15**	Nr
250 Watt sodium	1.58	-	24.04	-	72.65	**96.69**	Nr
400 Watt sodium	1.58	-	24.04	-	76.84	**100.88**	Nr
250 Watt metal hallide	1.58	-	24.04	-	81.06	**105.10**	Nr
400 Watt metal hallide	1.58	-	24.04	-	85.27	**109.31**	Nr
250 Watt mercury discharge	1.58	-	24.04	-	60.02	**84.06**	Nr
400 Watt mercury discharge	1.58	-	24.04	-	65.51	**89.55**	Nr
009 Black aluminium medium beam economy discharge floodlight with toughened glass diffuser, integral gear, timed ignitor and lamp:							
150 Watt SON-T	1.44	-	21.85	-	76.98	**98.83**	Nr
250 Watt SON-T	1.44	-	21.85	-	83.52	**105.37**	Nr
400 Watt SON-T	1.44	-	21.85	-	92.59	**114.44**	Nr
250 Watt MBF	1.44	-	21.85	-	67.91	**89.76**	Nr
400 Watt MBF	1.44	-	21.85	-	74.62	**96.47**	Nr
150 Watt HQI-T	1.44	-	21.85	-	91.69	**113.54**	Nr
250 Watt HQI-T	1.44	-	21.85	-	82.79	**104.64**	Nr
450 Watt HQI-T	1.44	-	21.85	-	86.79	**108.64**	Nr
010 Black low Wattage discharge floodlight with clear polycarbonate diffuser, integral gear:							
lamp 80 Watt MBF	1.44	-	21.85	-	34.41	**56.26**	Nr
lamp 70 Watt SON-T no ignitor	1.44	-	21.85	-	25.51	**47.36**	Nr
lamp 70 Watt HQI-T	1.44	-	21.85	-	59.91	**81.76**	Nr
lamp 70 Watt SON-T no ignitor with photocell	1.67	-	25.35	-	42.58	**67.93**	Nr

Unit Rates	Man-Hours	Plant Hours	Net Labour Price £	Net Plant Price £	Net Mats Price £	Net Unit Price £	Unit
lamp IP65 70 Watt HQI-T with timed ignitor and photocell	1.67	-	25.35	-	77.16	**102.51**	Nr
011 Kitchen, bathroom lighting and transformers:							
white linkable under cabinet light with switch, polycarbonate diffuser and 6 Watt T5 fluorescent tube 240V length: 245 mm	0.40	-	6.12	-	9.34	**15.46**	Nr
white linkable under cabinet light with switch, polycarbonate diffuser and 6 Watt T5 fluorescent tube 240V length: 580 mm	0.40	-	6.12	-	12.44	**18.56**	Nr
white linkable under cabinet light with switch, polycarbonate diffuser and 6 Watt T5 fluorescent tube 240V length: 880 mm	0.40	-	6.12	-	15.56	**21.68**	Nr
white linkable electronic striplights IP20 6 Watt T4 240V 275 mm	0.40	-	6.12	-	10.39	**16.51**	Nr
white linkable electronic striplights IP20 6 Watt T4 240V 400 mm	0.40	-	6.12	-	10.96	**17.08**	Nr
white linkable electronic striplights IP20 6 Watt T4 240V 600 mm	0.40	-	6.12	-	12.40	**18.52**	Nr
white linkable electronic striplights IP20 6 Watt T4 240V 815 mm	0.40	-	6.12	-	16.24	**22.36**	Nr
black LV cabinet downlight c/w capsule lamp for surface/recessed mounting 12V	0.49	-	7.43	-	3.61	**11.04**	Nr
brushed nickel LV cabinet downlight c/w capsule lamp for surface/recessed mounting 12V	0.49	-	7.43	-	4.07	**11.50**	Nr
polished brass LV cabinet downlight c/w capsule lamp for surface/recessed mounting 12V	0.49	-	7.43	-	4.21	**11.64**	Nr
brushed nickel fluorescent kitchen rail light with acrylic diffuser and 5 hanging hooks IP20 10 Watt-T4 240V 580 x 57 x 130 mm projection	0.66	-	10.05	-	32.81	**42.86**	Nr
brushed nickel fluorescent glass shelf light IP20 1 x 13 Watt-T5 tube 240V 547 x 95 x 186 mm projection	0.66	-	10.05	-	50.76	**60.81**	Nr
white unswitched striplight with opal diffuser and lamp IP20 60 Watt	0.32	-	4.81	-	21.87	**26.68**	Nr
chrome scallop end bathroom mirror light with opal diffuser and pullcord IP44 24 Watt PLL 2G11 240V	0.40	-	6.12	-	69.61	**75.73**	Nr
silver backed circular bathroom fluorescent mirror light with pullcord IP44 40 Watt T8 G10q 240V	0.55	-	8.30	-	106.35	**114.65**	Nr
polished chrome low voltage cast showerlight with lamp IP65 50 Watt MR16 GX5.3 12V	0.40	-	6.12	-	14.20	**20.32**	Nr
satin nickel pressed steel low voltage fire rated adjustable downlight with 50 Watt MR16 lamp 12V	0.37	-	5.68	-	7.35	**13.03**	Nr
self monitoring electronic dimmable transformer 20VA - 60VA	0.29	-	4.37	-	8.07	**12.44**	Nr
self monitoring electronic dimmable transformer 35VA - 105VA	0.29	-	4.37	-	10.21	**14.58**	Nr
submersible electronic dimmable transformer IP68 20VA - 60VA	0.29	-	4.37	-	10.21	**14.58**	Nr
submersible electronic dimmable transformer IP68 35VA - 105VA	0.29	-	4.37	-	11.67	**16.04**	Nr
012 Emergency lighting luminaires:							
3 hour non-maintained emergency bulkhead luminaire IP40 8 watt T5 240V	0.40	-	6.12	-	60.17	**66.29**	Nr
white 3 hour maintained emergency bulkhead luminaire with opal polycarbonate diffuser IP20 8 Watt T5 240V	0.40	-	6.12	-	122.21	**128.33**	Nr
self adhesive legend kit for Slimlite luminaire range	0.14	-	2.19	-	6.43	**8.62**	Nr
weatherproof non-maintained emergency bulkhead luminaire IP65 8 Watt T5 240V	0.40	-	6.12	-	26.12	**32.24**	Nr
weatherproof maintained emergency bulkhead luminaire IP65 8 Watt T5 240V	0.40	-	6.12	-	34.65	**40.77**	Nr
self adhesive legend kit for bulkhead luminaire range	0.14	-	2.19	-	4.70	**6.89**	Nr
013 Mains voltage single circuit track 240V:							
16A 240V 1.2 m length	0.46	-	6.99	-	13.58	**20.57**	Nr
16A 240V 2 m length	0.60	-	9.18	-	19.02	**28.20**	Nr
4 mm straight connector 240V	0.06	-	0.87	-	2.20	**3.07**	Nr
120 mm adjustable connector 240V	0.09	-	1.31	-	7.70	**9.01**	Nr
track 65 x 95 mm T connector 240V	0.09	-	1.31	-	7.70	**9.01**	Nr
track 95 x 95 mm X connector 240V	0.09	-	1.31	-	13.14	**14.45**	Nr
track 65 mm live end connector 240V	0.06	-	0.87	-	3.31	**4.18**	Nr
track 160 mm flexible connector 240V	0.06	-	0.87	-	10.64	**11.51**	Nr
surface mounting base (120 mm cutout) 240V	0.32	-	4.81	-	7.27	**12.08**	Nr
white 3 light track pack with 1 m track, live and dead ends, 3 x GU10 spotlights and lamps IP20 3 x 50 Watt GU10 240V	1.09	-	16.61	-	40.52	**57.13**	Nr
brushed chrome 3 light track pack with 1 m track, live and dead ends, 3 x GU10 spotlights and lamps IP20 3 x 50 Watt GU10 240V	1.09	-	16.61	-	51.56	**68.17**	Nr
acorn white spotlight IP20 50 Watt GU10 240V	0.12	-	1.75	-	13.60	**15.35**	Nr
brushed chrome spotlight IP20 50 Watt GU10 240V	0.12	-	1.75	-	13.77	**15.52**	Nr
014 **Lamps**							
015 Energy saving, tungsten halogen and incandescent lamps:							
compact fluorescent lamp 6000 hours 240V Bc 5 and 7 Watt	0.12	-	1.75	-	2.53	**4.28**	Nr
compact fluorescent lamp 6000 hours 240V Bc 9 to 11 Watt	0.12	-	1.75	-	3.10	**4.85**	Nr
compact fluorescent lamp 6000 hours 240V Bc 15 and 18 Watt	0.12	-	1.75	-	3.35	**5.10**	Nr
compact fluorescent lamp 6000 hours 240V Bc 20 to 23 Watt	0.12	-	1.75	-	3.35	**5.10**	Nr
compact fluorescent lamp 10000 hours 240V G23 2-pin 5 to 11 Watt	0.12	-	1.75	-	1.46	**3.21**	Nr
compact fluorescent lamp 10000 hours 240V 2G11 4-pin 9 to 11 Watt	0.12	-	1.75	-	1.85	**3.60**	Nr
compact fluorescent lamp 10000 hours 240V 2G11 4-pin 18 to 36 Watt	0.12	-	1.75	-	2.67	**4.42**	Nr
tungsten halogen 50 mm dichroic reflector lamp with 10 degree beam angle 4000 hours 35 to 50 Watt Gu5.3 12V	0.12	-	1.75	-	2.89	**4.64**	Nr
tungsten halogen 50 mm dichroic reflector lamp with 38 degree beam angle 4000 hours 20 to 50 Watt Gu5.3 12V	0.12	-	1.75	-	0.62	**2.37**	Nr
tungsten halogen 50 mm dichroic reflector lamp with 25 degree beam angle 2500 hours 35 to 50 Watt Gu10 240V	0.12	-	1.75	-	1.04	**2.79**	Nr
standard Gls lamp 40 to 100 Watt Bc 240V	0.12	-	1.75	-	0.52	**2.27**	Nr
45 mm golf ball lamp 25 to 60 Watt Bc 240V	0.12	-	1.75	-	0.52	**2.27**	Nr
pearl rough service lamp 60 to 100 Watt Bc 110/240V 60 x 103 mm	0.12	-	1.75	-	0.84	**2.59**	Nr
internally silvered R80 blown bulb reflector lamp 60 Watt Bc 240V	0.12	-	1.75	-	0.87	**2.62**	Nr

	Man-Hours	Plant Hours	Net Labour Price £	Net Plant Price £	Net Mats Price £	Net Unit Price £	Unit
Unit Rates							
016	**MK lighting switches prices shown allow for surface or flush boxes terminated with switches or socket outlets as appropriate**						
017	Wall switches:						
1 gang type: 1 way SP MK 4870 white flush	0.20	-	3.06	-	1.00	**4.06**	Nr
1 gang type: 1 way SP MK 4870 white surface mounted	0.23	-	3.50	-	1.85	**5.35**	Nr
1 gang type: 2 way SP MK 4871 white flush	0.23	-	3.50	-	1.23	**4.73**	Nr
1 gang type: 2 way SP MK 4871 white surface mounted	0.26	-	3.93	-	2.07	**6.00**	Nr
1 gang type: intermediate MK 4875 white flush	0.20	-	3.06	-	5.95	**9.01**	Nr
1 gang type: intermediate MK 4875 white surface mounted	0.23	-	3.50	-	6.80	**10.30**	Nr
2 gang type: 2 way SP MK 4872 white flush	0.26	-	3.93	-	2.10	**6.03**	Nr
2 gang type: 2 way SP MK 4872 white surface mounted	0.29	-	4.37	-	5.38	**9.75**	Nr
3 gang type: 2 way SP MK 4873 white flush	0.29	-	4.37	-	4.81	**9.18**	Nr
3 gang type: 2 way SP MK 4873 white surface mounted	0.32	-	4.81	-	8.10	**12.91**	Nr
4 gang type: 2 way SP MK 4874 white flush	0.32	-	4.81	-	10.51	**15.32**	Nr
4 gang type: 2 way SP MK 4874 white surface mounted	0.35	-	5.24	-	13.79	**19.03**	Nr
6 gang type: 2 way SP MK 4879 white flush	0.35	-	5.24	-	22.87	**28.11**	Nr
6 gang type: 2 way SP MK 4879 white surface mounted	0.37	-	5.68	-	26.15	**31.83**	Nr
architrave switches: 1 gang 2 way SP MK 4841 white flush	0.20	-	3.06	-	2.33	**5.39**	Nr
architrave switches: 1 gang 2 way SP MK 4841 white surface mounted	0.23	-	3.50	-	3.55	**7.05**	Nr
architrave switches: 2 gang 2 way SP MK 4842 white flush	0.26	-	3.93	-	6.00	**9.93**	Nr
architrave switches: 2 gang 2 way SP MK 4842 white surface mounted	0.29	-	4.37	-	9.42	**13.79**	Nr
018	Ceiling switches:						
6A 1 way SP MK 3191	0.26	-	3.93	-	3.64	**7.57**	Nr
6A 2 way SP MK 3192	0.32	-	4.81	-	4.19	**9.00**	Nr
50A double pole (electric shower) MK 3164	0.37	-	5.68	-	10.54	**16.22**	Nr
019	Dimmer switches:						
white moulded 1 gang 1 way dimmer switch 40 Watt - 250 Watt flush	0.23	-	3.50	-	12.94	**16.44**	Nr
white moulded 1 gang 1 way dimmer switch 40 Watt - 250 Watt surface mounted	0.26	-	3.93	-	13.79	**17.72**	Nr
white moulded 1 gang 1 way dimmer switch 65 Watt - 450 Watt flush	0.26	-	3.93	-	17.27	**21.20**	Nr
white moulded 1 gang 1 way dimmer switch 65 Watt - 450 Watt surface mounted	0.29	-	4.37	-	18.12	**22.49**	Nr
white moulded 1 gang 2 way dimmer switch 2 x 40 Watt - 250 Watt flush	0.29	-	4.37	-	19.43	**23.80**	Nr
white moulded 1 gang 2 way dimmer switch 2 x 40 Watt - 250 Watt surface mounted	0.32	-	4.81	-	22.71	**27.52**	Nr
white moulded 1 gang 2 way dimmer switch 2 x 40 Watt - 300 Watt flush	0.32	-	4.81	-	39.64	**44.45**	Nr
white moulded 1 gang 2 way dimmer switch 2 x 40 Watt - 300 Watt surface mounted	0.35	-	5.24	-	42.93	**48.17**	Nr
020	Multigang grid switches; MK complete box with white grid and 20A 2 way grid switches fixed and terminated:						
1 gang	0.29	-	4.37	-	3.24	**7.61**	Nr
2 gang	0.46	-	6.99	-	5.56	**12.55**	Nr
3 gang	0.63	-	9.61	-	9.19	**18.80**	Nr
4 gang 2Nr 1 way 2Nr 2 way	0.86	-	13.11	-	12.97	**26.08**	Nr
6 gang 3Nr 1 way 3Nr 2 way	1.24	-	18.79	-	20.09	**38.88**	Nr
8 gang 4Nr 1 way 4Nr 2 way	1.61	-	24.47	-	25.44	**49.91**	Nr
12 gang 12Nr 1 way	2.19	-	33.21	-	34.84	**68.05**	Nr
12 gang 12Nr 2 way	2.53	-	38.46	-	43.33	**81.79**	Nr
12 gang 6Nr 1 way 6Nr 2 way	2.36	-	35.83	-	39.09	**74.92**	Nr
021	**Power accessories**						
022	MK power accessories; surface or flush boxes terminated with appropriate accessory:						
13A single switched socket outlet MK 2757 white	0.20	-	3.06	-	2.07	**5.13**	Nr
2 gang double pole switched socket 13A	0.26	-	3.93	-	2.71	**6.64**	Nr
double pole switched connection unit with flex outlet in base 13A	0.26	-	3.93	-	4.42	**8.35**	Nr
double pole flush mounting cooker control unit with 13A switch socket 45A	0.49	-	7.43	-	12.31	**19.74**	Nr
cooker connection unit 86 x 86 mm	0.32	-	4.81	-	3.44	**8.25**	Nr
twin switched socket outlet solid brass MK 4347	0.32	-	4.81	-	20.38	**25.19**	Nr
single outlet non-isolated TV/FM co-axial socket	0.32	-	4.81	-	4.45	**9.26**	Nr
double pole flush mounting ceiling switch with pullcord	0.32	-	4.81	-	10.54	**15.35**	Nr
023	**Communications accessories**						
024	BT accessories; telephone socket and mounting box:						
single flush mounting BT master telephone socket with IDC terminals	0.29	-	4.37	-	6.20	**10.57**	Nr
single flush mounting BT secondary telephone socket with IDC terminals	0.23	-	3.50	-	4.10	**7.60**	Nr
1 module BT master telephone socket module	0.26	-	3.93	-	8.02	**11.95**	Nr
1 module BT secondary telephone socket module	0.20	-	3.06	-	5.59	**8.65**	Nr
2 gang / 3 module frontplate one master to secondary socket module	0.46	-	6.99	-	23.08	**30.07**	Nr
Friedland white mains voltage doorchime contractor kit with chime, bellpush, transformer and 8 m bellwire cable	0.95	-	14.42	-	11.45	**25.87**	Nr

Unit Rates	Man-Hours	Plant Hours	Net Labour Price £	Net Plant Price £	Net Mats Price £	Net Unit Price £	Unit
025 **Ventilation equipment**							
026 Ventilation fans supply and installation to a precut aperture and connection to an adjacent electrical supply:							
window fan with dark grey external grille and automatic thermo-activated internal shutters 6"/150 mm 278 m3/Hr	1.55	-	23.60	-	47.52	**71.12**	Nr
window fan with dark grey external grille and automatic thermo-activated internal shutters 9"/230 mm 668 m3/Hr	1.67	-	25.35	-	113.23	**138.58**	Nr
window fan with dark grey external grille and automatic thermo-activated internal shutters 12"/300 mm 1021 m3/Hr	1.78	-	27.09	-	253.40	**280.49**	Nr
white recessed wall/ceiling bathroom fan with iris shutter 197 x 40 mm 240V	1.55	-	23.60	-	34.63	**58.23**	Nr
white recessed/surface wall/ceiling bathroom/utility room fan with iris shutter 225 x 43 mm 240V	1.67	-	25.35	-	70.77	**96.12**	Nr
white recessed/surface wall/ceiling kitchen fan with iris shutter 280 x 55 mm 240V	1.67	-	25.35	-	83.16	**108.51**	Nr
shower fan with in-line PVC ducting kit and grille 100 mm 240V	2.30	-	34.96	-	104.61	**139.57**	Nr
white wall / ceiling extractor fan for remote switching with automatic shutter 100 mm / 4 inch 240V	1.55	-	23.60	-	16.01	**39.61**	Nr
white wall / ceiling extractor fan with adjustable electronic timer and automatic shutter 100 mm / 4 inch 240V	1.55	-	23.60	-	18.13	**41.73**	Nr
commercial surface wall/ceiling fan with pullcord operated internal shutters 12"/300 mm 1021 m3/Hr	2.01	-	30.59	-	209.72	**240.31**	Nr
commercial surface wall/ceiling fan with automatic thermo-activated internal shutters 12"/300 mm 1021 m3/Hr	2.01	-	30.59	-	241.22	**271.81**	Nr
Extra over for window fixing kit and fitting	0.38	-	5.77	-	8.46	**14.23**	Nr
Extra over for wall fixing kit and fitting	0.38	-	5.77	-	17.26	**23.03**	Nr
dimplex AC range white warm air curtain with adjustable air flow direction and handheld remote control for single doorways 3.0kW	1.53	-	23.25	-	131.68	**154.93**	Nr
dimplex AC range white warm air curtain with adjustable air flow direction and integral controls for double doorways 6.0kW	1.92	-	29.19	-	264.45	**293.64**	Nr
dimplex BFH range brown base unit heater 2.4kW for fitting into panelling etc	1.53	-	23.25	-	101.68	**124.93**	Nr
027 **Fire alarm equipment to EN54 supply and connection to prewired MICC cable (see cables section for prices)**							
028 Control panels complete with standby power supply:							
EN54 2 zone conventional fire panel with 24 hour battery standby	1.73	-	26.22	-	111.93	**138.15**	Nr
EN54 4 zone conventional fire panel with 24 hour battery standby	2.59	-	39.33	-	139.05	**178.38**	Nr
EN54 8 zone conventional fire panel with 24 hour battery standby	5.18	-	78.66	-	218.71	**297.37**	Nr
4 zone bi-wire fire alarm contractor kit with 1 x 4 zone fire panel and batteries, 6 x multipoint detectors C/W sounder, 2 x manual call points, 1 x detector head/sounder removal tool 230V	7.25	-	110.12	-	555.84	**665.96**	Nr
disabled toilet alarm kit with single zone controller, ceiling pullcord, overdoor light with sounder, reset button and disabled WC sticker	3.05	-	46.32	-	96.82	**143.14**	Nr
029 Equipment:							
interlinkable battery optical smoke alarm 9V	0.43	-	6.56	-	18.01	**24.57**	Nr
mains optical smoke alarm with hush, alkaline battery back up and mounting plate 240V	0.52	-	7.87	-	26.33	**34.20**	Nr
ionisation smoke alarm with alkaline battery and escape light 9V	0.43	-	6.56	-	11.73	**18.29**	Nr
mains ionisation smoke alarm with hush, alkaline battery back up and mounting plate 240V	0.52	-	7.87	-	16.45	**24.32**	Nr
optical heat detector 24V DC	0.43	-	6.56	-	24.35	**30.91**	Nr
mains heat alarm with hush, alkaline battery back up and mounting plate 240V	0.52	-	7.87	-	37.20	**45.07**	Nr
6 inch security bell 12V AC	0.43	-	6.56	-	34.04	**40.60**	Nr
6 inch security bell 230V AC	0.43	-	6.56	-	34.04	**40.60**	Nr
mains multi frequency sounder IP54 230V	0.52	-	7.87	-	51.50	**59.37**	Nr
deep base sounder for conduit wiring 102dBA IP54 24V DC	0.52	-	7.87	-	20.98	**28.85**	Nr
combined sounder and beacon 90dBA IP54 24V DC	0.52	-	7.87	-	49.47	**57.34**	Nr
flush mounting break glass call point with resistor/diode	0.52	-	7.87	-	10.23	**18.10**	Nr
surface mounting break glass call point with resistor/diode	0.43	-	6.56	-	10.06	**16.62**	Nr
resettable manual break glass call point with backbox and bezel for surface/flush fitting 230V	0.52	-	7.87	-	14.26	**22.13**	Nr
weatherproof resettable manual break glass call point with backbox and bezel for surface/flush fitting IP55 230V	0.63	-	9.61	-	28.08	**37.69**	Nr
resettable manual break glass call point with integral alarm sounder, backbox and bezel for surface/flush fitting 90dBA 230V	0.52	-	7.87	-	27.20	**35.07**	Nr
weatherproof resettable manual break glass call point with integral alarm sounder, backbox and bezel for surface/flush fitting 90dBA IP55 230V	0.63	-	9.61	-	46.11	**55.72**	Nr
Aico mains powered carbon monoxide alarm with built-in pattress and memory feature 240V	0.63	-	9.61	-	33.08	**42.69**	Nr
SC **CONDUITS, TRUNKING AND FITTINGS**							
CONDUITS							
001 **Black enamel or galvanised conduit to BS 4568 with general fittings and fixings**							
002 Fixed to brickwork, blockwork or concrete in chases by others:							
20 mm diameter	0.26	0.45	3.93	1.91	1.49	**7.33**	m
25 mm diameter	0.29	0.50	4.37	2.13	1.86	**8.36**	m
003 Fixed to surfaces:							
20 mm diameter	0.31	0.54	4.72	2.30	1.70	**8.72**	m

	Unit Rates	Man-Hours	Plant Hours	Net Labour Price £	Net Plant Price £	Net Mats Price £	Net Unit Price £	Unit
	25 mm diameter	0.35	0.60	5.24	2.55	2.12	**9.91**	m
004	Embedded in concrete or screed:							
	20 mm diameter	0.23	0.41	3.55	1.73	1.49	**6.77**	m
	25 mm diameter	0.26	0.45	3.93	1.91	1.86	**7.70**	m
005	**Extra over** for 20 mm fittings:							
	made bend	0.09	-	1.31	-	-	**1.31**	Nr
	circular terminal box (1 way) 20 mm	0.20	0.18	3.06	0.70	0.89	**4.65**	Nr
	circular terminal box (2 way) 20 mm	0.29	0.25	4.37	1.00	0.89	**6.26**	Nr
	circular branch U box (2 way) 20 mm	0.29	0.25	4.37	1.00	1.16	**6.53**	Nr
	circular angle box (2 way) 20 mm	0.29	0.25	4.37	1.00	0.89	**6.26**	Nr
	circular tee box (3 way) 20 mm	0.37	0.33	5.68	1.30	0.98	**7.96**	Nr
	circular branch box (3 way) 20 mm	0.37	0.33	5.68	1.30	1.16	**8.14**	Nr
	circular intersection box (4 way) 20 mm	0.46	0.40	6.99	1.60	1.02	**9.61**	Nr
	circular twin through H box (4 way) 20 mm	0.46	0.40	6.99	1.60	2.19	**10.78**	Nr
	inspection bend 20 mm	0.29	0.25	4.37	1.00	1.47	**6.84**	Nr
	inspection elbow 20 mm	0.29	0.25	4.37	1.00	1.30	**6.67**	Nr
	inspection tee 20 mm	0.37	0.33	5.68	1.30	1.56	**8.54**	Nr
	brass TRS weathertight gland 20 mm	0.09	0.08	1.31	0.30	0.38	**1.99**	Nr
	brass TRS weathertight gland 25 mm	0.09	0.08	1.31	0.30	0.57	**2.18**	Nr
006	**Extra over** for 25 mm fittings:							
	made bend	0.10	-	1.45	-	-	**1.45**	Nr
	circular terminal box (1 way) 25 mm	0.22	0.19	3.37	0.77	1.30	**5.44**	Nr
	circular terminal box (2 way) 25 mm	0.32	0.28	4.81	1.10	1.30	**7.21**	Nr
	circular branch U box (2 way) 25 mm	0.32	0.28	4.81	1.10	1.50	**7.41**	Nr
	circular angle box (2 way) 25 mm	0.32	0.28	4.81	1.10	1.30	**7.21**	Nr
	circular tee box (3 way) 25 mm	0.41	0.36	6.26	1.43	1.35	**9.04**	Nr
	circular branch box (3 way) 25 mm	0.41	0.36	6.26	1.43	1.73	**9.42**	Nr
	circular intersection box (4 way) 25 mm	0.51	0.44	7.69	1.76	1.40	**10.85**	Nr
	circular twin through H box (4 way) 25 mm	0.51	0.44	7.69	1.76	4.48	**13.93**	Nr
	inspection bend 25 mm	0.32	0.28	4.81	1.10	2.46	**8.37**	Nr
	inspection elbow 25 mm	0.32	0.28	4.81	1.10	2.16	**8.07**	Nr
	inspection tee 25 mm	0.41	0.36	6.26	1.43	2.56	**10.25**	Nr
	brass TRS weathertight gland 20 mm	0.09	0.08	1.31	0.30	0.38	**1.99**	Nr
	brass TRS weathertight gland 25 mm	0.09	0.08	1.31	0.30	0.57	**2.18**	Nr
007	Adaptable boxes lid with knock outs:							
	BE or galv adaptable box with knockouts 75 x 75 x 40 mm	0.38	-	5.77	-	1.83	**7.60**	Nr
	BE or galv adaptable box with knockouts 75 x 75 x 50 mm	0.43	-	6.56	-	1.94	**8.50**	Nr
	BE or galv adaptable box with knockouts 75 x 75 x 75 mm	0.49	-	7.43	-	2.35	**9.78**	Nr
	BE or galv adaptable box with knockouts 100 x 100 x 40 mm	0.58	-	8.74	-	1.79	**10.53**	Nr
	BE or galv adaptable box with knockouts 100 x 100 x 50 mm	0.63	-	9.61	-	2.23	**11.84**	Nr
	BE or galv adaptable box with knockouts 100 x 100 x 75 mm	0.69	-	10.49	-	2.65	**13.14**	Nr
	BE or galv adaptable box with knockouts 150 x 150 x 50 mm	0.86	-	13.11	-	3.50	**16.61**	Nr
	BE or galv adaptable box with knockouts 150 x 150 x 75 mm	0.98	-	14.86	-	3.69	**18.55**	Nr
	BE or galv adaptable box with knockouts 150 x 150 x 100 mm	1.15	-	17.48	-	4.66	**22.14**	Nr
	BE or galv adaptable box with knockouts 225 x 225 x 75 mm	1.44	-	21.85	-	9.82	**31.67**	Nr
	BE or galv adaptable box with knockouts 300 x 300 x 100 mm	1.73	-	26.22	-	11.81	**38.03**	Nr
	20 mm brass female/male bush drilling into trunking or box	0.12	-	1.75	-	0.22	**1.97**	Nr
	25 mm brass female/male bush drilling into trunking or box	0.14	-	2.19	-	0.36	**2.55**	Nr
008	**Round PVC Conduit**							
009	Fixed to brickwork, blockwork or concrete in chases by others:							
	20 mm diameter light gauge	0.16	-	2.36	-	0.31	**2.67**	m
	20 mm diameter heavy gauge	0.16	-	2.36	-	0.40	**2.76**	m
	25 mm diameter light gauge	0.17	-	2.62	-	0.44	**3.06**	m
	25 mm diameter heavy gauge	0.17	-	2.62	-	0.57	**3.19**	m
010	Fixed to surfaces:							
	20 mm diameter light gauge	0.19	-	2.83	-	0.46	**3.29**	m
	20 mm diameter heavy gauge	0.19	-	2.83	-	0.55	**3.38**	m
	25 mm diameter light gauge	0.21	-	3.15	-	0.59	**3.74**	m
	25 mm diameter heavy gauge	0.21	-	3.15	-	0.72	**3.87**	m
011	Embedded in concrete or screed:							
	20 mm diameter light gauge	0.14	-	2.13	-	0.31	**2.44**	m
	20 mm diameter heavy gauge	0.14	-	2.13	-	0.57	**2.70**	m
	25 mm diameter light gauge	0.16	-	2.36	-	0.44	**2.80**	m
	25 mm diameter heavy gauge	0.16	-	2.36	-	0.72	**3.08**	m
012	**Extra over** for 20 mm fittings:							
	20 mm plain bend	0.29	-	4.37	-	0.41	**4.78**	Nr
	20 mm threaded adaptor	0.29	-	4.37	-	1.34	**5.71**	Nr
	circular terminal box (1 way) 20 mm	0.20	-	3.06	-	0.35	**3.41**	Nr
	circular terminal box (2 way) 20 mm	0.35	-	5.38	-	0.42	**5.80**	Nr
	circular branch U box (2 way) 20 mm	0.29	-	4.37	-	0.42	**4.79**	Nr
	circular angle box (2 way) 20 mm	0.29	-	4.37	-	0.45	**4.82**	Nr
	circular tee box (3 way) 20 mm	0.37	-	5.68	-	0.46	**6.14**	Nr
	circular branch box (3 way) 20 mm	0.37	-	5.68	-	0.46	**6.14**	Nr
	circular intersection box (4 way) 20 mm	0.46	-	6.99	-	0.40	**7.39**	Nr
	circular twin through H box (4 way) 20 mm	0.46	-	6.99	-	0.60	**7.59**	Nr
	inspection bend 20 mm	0.29	-	4.37	-	0.42	**4.79**	Nr
	inspection elbow 20 mm	0.29	-	4.37	-	0.31	**4.68**	Nr
	inspection tee 20 mm	0.37	-	5.68	-	0.40	**6.08**	Nr

Unit Rates	Man-Hours	Plant Hours	Net Labour Price £	Net Plant Price £	Net Mats Price £	Net Unit Price £	Unit
013 **Extra over** for 25 mm fittings:							
25 mm plain bend	0.29	-	4.37	-	0.67	**5.04**	Nr
25 mm threaded adaptor	0.29	-	4.37	-	2.02	**6.39**	Nr
circular terminal box (1 way) 25 mm	0.20	-	3.06	-	0.70	**3.76**	Nr
circular terminal box (2 way) 25 mm	0.29	-	4.37	-	0.77	**5.14**	Nr
circular branch U box (2 way) 25 mm	0.29	-	4.37	-	0.77	**5.14**	Nr
circular angle box (2 way) 25 mm	0.29	-	4.37	-	0.74	**5.11**	Nr
circular tee box (3 way) 25 mm	0.37	-	5.68	-	1.04	**6.72**	Nr
circular branch box (3 way) 25 mm	0.37	-	5.68	-	1.04	**6.72**	Nr
circular intersection box (4 way) 25 mm	0.46	-	6.99	-	0.87	**7.86**	Nr
circular twin through H box (4 way) 25 mm	0.46	-	6.99	-	0.70	**7.69**	Nr
inspection bend 25 mm	0.29	-	4.37	-	0.80	**5.17**	Nr
inspection elbow 25 mm	0.29	-	4.37	-	0.53	**4.90**	Nr
inspection tee 25 mm	0.37	-	5.68	-	0.87	**6.55**	Nr
014 **Oval PVC conduit**							
015 Fixed to brickwork, blockwork or concrete in chases by others:							
13 mm	0.09	-	1.31	-	0.13	**1.44**	Nr
16 mm	0.09	-	1.31	-	0.15	**1.46**	Nr
20 mm	0.10	-	1.49	-	0.19	**1.68**	Nr
25 mm	0.10	-	1.49	-	0.25	**1.74**	Nr
30 mm	0.10	-	1.57	-	0.28	**1.85**	Nr
016 **PVC Covered flexible steel conduit**							
017 Clipped to surface:							
16 mm diameter	0.20	-	3.06	-	2.62	**5.68**	Nr
20 mm diameter	0.20	-	3.06	-	2.89	**5.95**	Nr
25 mm diameter	0.20	-	3.06	-	4.25	**7.31**	Nr
16 mm diameter fixed fitting	0.29	-	4.37	-	1.70	**6.07**	Nr
20 mm diameter fixed fitting	0.29	-	4.37	-	2.17	**6.54**	Nr
25 mm diameter fixed fitting	0.29	-	4.37	-	3.95	**8.32**	Nr
16 mm diameter swivel fitting	0.29	-	4.37	-	1.89	**6.26**	Nr
20 mm diameter swivel fitting	0.29	-	4.37	-	2.57	**6.94**	Nr
25 mm diameter swivel fitting	0.29	-	4.37	-	4.02	**8.39**	Nr
018 **PVC capping**							
019 Fixed to brickwork, blockwork or concrete:							
13 mm	0.09	-	1.31	-	0.12	**1.43**	Nr
25 mm	0.10	-	1.49	-	0.16	**1.65**	Nr
38 mm	0.10	-	1.57	-	0.25	**1.82**	Nr
TRUNKING							
020 **Self adhesive PVC mini trunking including fittings**							
021 Fixed to brickwork, blockwork or concrete:							
16 x 16 mm	0.09	-	1.31	-	0.60	**1.91**	Nr
16 x 25 mm	0.09	-	1.31	-	0.77	**2.08**	Nr
16 x 40 mm	0.10	-	1.49	-	1.00	**2.49**	Nr
25 x 40 mm	0.10	-	1.57	-	1.22	**2.79**	Nr
022 **PVC trunking**							
023 Fixed to brickwork, blockwork or concrete:							
50 x 50 mm	0.23	-	3.50	-	3.29	**6.79**	Nr
50 x 75 mm	0.28	-	4.20	-	3.88	**8.08**	Nr
75 x 75 mm	0.33	-	5.03	-	3.56	**8.59**	Nr
50 x 100 mm	0.33	-	5.03	-	5.81	**10.84**	Nr
100 x 100 mm	0.40	-	6.05	-	6.79	**12.84**	Nr
50 x 50 mm stop end	0.09	-	1.31	-	0.36	**1.67**	Nr
50 x 75 mm stop end	0.09	-	1.31	-	0.49	**1.80**	Nr
75 x 75 mm stop end	0.09	-	1.31	-	0.57	**1.88**	Nr
50 x 100 mm stop end	0.09	-	1.31	-	0.71	**2.02**	Nr
100 x 100 mm stop end	0.09	-	1.31	-	1.15	**2.46**	Nr
50 x 50 mm angle	0.12	-	1.75	-	3.16	**4.91**	Nr
50 x 75 mm angle	0.12	-	1.75	-	4.05	**5.80**	Nr
75 x 75 mm angle	0.12	-	1.75	-	5.05	**6.80**	Nr
50 x 100 mm angle	0.12	-	1.75	-	5.30	**7.05**	Nr
100 x 100 mm angle	0.14	-	2.19	-	9.71	**11.90**	Nr
50 x 50 mm flat angle	0.12	-	1.75	-	2.40	**4.15**	Nr
50 x 75 mm flat angle	0.12	-	1.75	-	2.87	**4.62**	Nr
75 x 75 mm flat angle	0.12	-	1.75	-	3.70	**5.45**	Nr
50 x 100 mm flat angle	0.12	-	1.75	-	4.84	**6.59**	Nr
100 x 100 mm flat angle	0.14	-	2.19	-	4.85	**7.04**	Nr
50 x 50 mm flat tee	0.12	-	1.75	-	3.37	**5.12**	Nr
50 x 75 mm flat tee	0.12	-	1.75	-	4.79	**6.54**	Nr
75 x 75 mm flat tee	0.12	-	1.75	-	5.21	**6.96**	Nr
50 x 100 mm flat tee	0.12	-	1.75	-	6.65	**8.40**	Nr
100 x 100 mm flat tee	0.14	-	2.19	-	8.97	**11.16**	Nr
024 **Galvanised steel lighting trunking**							
025 Lighting trunking, 50 x 50 mm, including steel lid:							
fixed to wall	0.24	-	3.67	-	4.17	**7.84**	m
suspended from soffit	0.27	-	4.04	-	4.80	**8.84**	m
angle	0.12	-	1.75	-	14.61	**16.36**	m

Unit Rates	Man-Hours	Plant Hours	Net Labour Price £	Net Plant Price £	Net Mats Price £	Net Unit Price £	Unit
drop or riser	0.12	-	1.75	-	14.77	**16.52**	m
stop end	0.12	-	1.75	-	2.74	**4.49**	m
4 way	0.23	-	3.50	-	22.98	**26.48**	m
SE CABLES							
001 **Single core PVC insulated cable 6491X with strandedcopper conductors to BS 6004/6346 drawn into conduits or trunking**							
002 Single phase circuit; phase and neutral and earth conductors:							
1.0 mm2	0.06	-	0.87	-	0.24	**1.11**	m
1.5 mm2	0.07	-	1.05	-	0.32	**1.37**	m
2.5 mm2	0.12	-	1.75	-	0.47	**2.22**	m
4.0 mm2	0.14	-	2.19	-	1.02	**3.21**	m
6.0 mm2	0.17	-	2.62	-	1.07	**3.69**	m
10.0 mm2	0.20	-	3.06	-	1.92	**4.98**	m
16.0 mm2	0.26	-	3.93	-	4.38	**8.31**	m
003 Three phase circuit; three phases and neutral and earth conductors:							
1.0 mm2	0.06	-	0.96	-	0.64	**1.60**	m
1.5 mm2	0.08	-	1.15	-	1.04	**2.19**	m
2.5 mm2	0.13	-	1.92	-	1.58	**3.50**	m
004 Equipotential earth bonding conductors clipped to surfaces:							
6 mm2	0.16	-	2.36	-	0.28	**2.64**	m
10 mm2	0.17	-	2.61	-	0.53	**3.14**	m
16 mm2	0.19	-	2.85	-	1.01	**3.86**	m
25 mm2	0.21	-	3.15	-	1.94	**5.09**	m
005 **Twin and multicore PVC insulated and PVC sheathed cables to BS 6004/6346 with copper conductors and uninsulated earth continuity conductor 6242Y and 6243Y**							
006 Clipped to surfaces:							
1.0 mm2 twin and earth	0.06	-	0.87	-	0.35	**1.22**	m
1.5 mm2 twin and earth	0.07	-	1.05	-	0.56	**1.61**	m
2.5 mm2 twin and earth	0.12	-	1.75	-	0.61	**2.36**	m
4.0 mm2 twin and earth	0.14	-	2.19	-	0.80	**2.99**	m
1.0 mm2 3 core and earth	0.06	-	0.96	-	0.92	**1.88**	m
1.5 mm2 3 core and earth	0.08	-	1.15	-	0.61	**1.76**	m
2.5 mm2 3 core and earth	0.13	-	1.92	-	0.92	**2.84**	m
007 **Steel wire armoured cable PVC insulated and sheathed**							
008 2 core clipped to surface:							
1.5 mm2	0.07	-	1.05	-	0.98	**2.03**	m
2.5 mm2	0.12	-	1.75	-	1.18	**2.93**	m
4.0 mm2	0.14	-	2.19	-	1.59	**3.78**	m
6.0 mm2	0.17	-	2.62	-	2.33	**4.95**	m
10.0 mm2	0.20	-	3.06	-	2.98	**6.04**	m
16.0 mm2	0.26	-	3.93	-	4.99	**8.92**	m
009 3 core clipped to surface:							
1.5 mm2	0.08	-	1.15	-	1.22	**2.37**	m
2.5 mm2	0.13	-	1.92	-	1.61	**3.53**	m
4.0 mm2	0.16	-	2.41	-	1.96	**4.37**	m
6.0 mm2	0.19	-	2.88	-	2.38	**5.26**	m
10.0 mm2	0.22	-	3.37	-	3.83	**7.20**	m
16.0 mm2	0.29	-	4.34	-	5.30	**9.64**	m
010 4 core clipped to surface:							
1.5 mm2	0.08	-	1.28	-	1.43	**2.71**	m
2.5 mm2	0.14	-	2.12	-	2.05	**4.17**	m
4.0 mm2	0.17	-	2.64	-	2.19	**4.83**	m
6.0 mm2	0.21	-	3.18	-	3.47	**6.65**	m
10.0 mm2	0.24	-	3.71	-	5.02	**8.73**	m
16.0 mm2	0.31	-	4.75	-	7.23	**11.98**	m
011 SWA glands for cable termination with earth tags - internal:							
20 mm	0.09	-	1.31	-	0.53	**1.84**	Nr
25 mm	0.12	-	1.75	-	1.06	**2.81**	Nr
32 mm	0.14	-	2.19	-	1.65	**3.84**	Nr
40 mm	0.17	-	2.62	-	1.97	**4.59**	Nr
012 SWA glands for cable termination with earth tags - external:							
20 mm	0.10	-	1.45	-	0.95	**2.40**	Nr
25 mm	0.13	-	1.92	-	2.04	**3.96**	Nr
32 mm	0.16	-	2.41	-	2.83	**5.24**	Nr
40 mm	0.19	-	2.88	-	7.34	**10.22**	Nr
013 **Twin and multicore mineral insulated copper sheathed cables with copper conductors and PVC outer sheath; light duty 600V**							
014 2 core, screw clipped to surface:							
1.0 mm2	0.06	-	0.87	-	1.27	**2.14**	m
1.5 mm2	0.07	-	1.05	-	1.41	**2.46**	m
2.5 mm2	0.12	-	1.75	-	2.28	**4.03**	m
4.0 mm2	0.14	-	2.19	-	2.75	**4.94**	m

Unit Rates	Man-Hours	Plant Hours	Net Labour Price £	Net Plant Price £	Net Mats Price £	Net Unit Price £	Unit
015	3 core, screw clipped to surface:						
	1.0 mm2	0.06	-	0.96	-	2.06	**3.02**	m
	1.5 mm2	0.08	-	1.15	-	2.34	**3.49**	m
	2.5 mm2	0.13	-	1.92	-	4.01	**5.93**	m
	4.0 mm2	0.16	-	2.41	-	4.91	**7.32**	m
016	4 core, screw clipped to surface:						
	1.0 mm2	0.07	-	1.07	-	2.30	**3.37**	m
	1.5 mm2	0.08	-	1.28	-	2.64	**3.92**	m
	2.5 mm2	0.14	-	2.12	-	4.55	**6.67**	m
	4.0 mm2	0.17	-	2.64	-	5.59	**8.23**	m
	add for 20 mm fire rated cable gland	0.03	-	0.44	-	0.51	**0.95**	Nr
	add for 25 mm fire rated cable gland	0.03	-	0.52	-	0.51	**1.03**	Nr
017	**Mineral insulated copper cable - sheathed**						
018	2 core clipped to surface:						
	1.5 mm2	0.10	-	1.59	-	6.05	**7.64**	m
	2.5 mm2	0.17	-	2.64	-	7.15	**9.79**	m
	4.0 mm2	0.22	-	3.30	-	9.82	**13.12**	m
019	3 core clipped to surface:						
	1.5 mm2	0.12	-	1.75	-	7.45	**9.20**	m
	2.5 mm2	0.19	-	2.90	-	10.22	**13.12**	m
020	4 core clipped to surface:						
	1.5 mm2	0.13	-	1.92	-	8.47	**10.39**	m
	2.5 mm2	0.21	-	3.20	-	11.84	**15.04**	m
	compression terminations for MICC cables fitted and shrouded	0.12	-	1.75	-	1.76	**3.51**	Nr
	Note: 021 – 024 not used						
025	**YY flexible multicore control cable, numbered cores, unbraided**						
026	3 core clipped to surface:						
	0.75 mm2	0.04	-	0.61	-	0.40	**1.01**	m
	1.0 mm2	0.06	-	0.96	-	0.45	**1.41**	m
	1.5 mm2	0.08	-	1.15	-	0.05	**1.20**	m
	2.5 mm2	0.13	-	1.92	-	0.05	**1.97**	m
027	4 core clipped to surface:						
	0.75 mm2	0.04	-	0.68	-	0.05	**0.73**	m
	1.0 mm2	0.07	-	1.07	-	0.05	**1.12**	m
	1.5 mm2	0.08	-	1.28	-	0.81	**2.09**	m
	2.5 mm2	0.14	-	2.12	-	1.33	**3.45**	m
028	5 core clipped to surface:						
	0.75 mm2	0.05	-	0.73	-	0.58	**1.31**	m
	1.0 mm2	0.08	-	1.17	-	0.72	**1.89**	m
	1.5 mm2	0.09	-	1.40	-	1.02	**2.42**	m
	2.5 mm2	0.15	-	2.33	-	1.64	**3.97**	m
029	7 core clipped to surface:						
	0.75 mm2	0.05	-	0.82	-	0.58	**1.40**	m
	1.0 mm2	0.08	-	1.28	-	0.72	**2.00**	m
	1.5 mm2	0.10	-	1.54	-	1.02	**2.56**	m
	2.5 mm2	0.17	-	2.55	-	1.64	**4.19**	m
030	12 core clipped to surface:						
	1.5 mm2	0.11	-	1.70	-	1.53	**3.23**	m
	2.5 mm2	0.19	-	2.82	-	2.63	**5.45**	m
031	**SY flexible multicore control cable, numbered cores, braided**						
032	3 core clipped to surface:						
	1.0 mm2	0.06	-	0.96	-	0.63	**1.59**	m
	1.5 mm2	0.08	-	1.15	-	0.88	**2.03**	m
	2.5 mm2	0.13	-	1.92	-	1.49	**3.41**	m
	4.0 mm2	0.16	-	2.41	-	2.15	**4.56**	m
	6.0 mm2	0.19	-	2.88	-	2.98	**5.86**	m
033	4 core clipped to surface:						
	1.0 mm2	0.07	-	1.07	-	0.91	**1.98**	m
	1.5 mm2	0.08	-	1.28	-	1.09	**2.37**	m
	2.5 mm2	0.14	-	2.12	-	1.65	**3.77**	m
	4.0 mm2	0.17	-	2.64	-	2.82	**5.46**	m
	6.0 mm2	0.21	-	3.18	-	3.68	**6.86**	m
034	5 core clipped to surface:						
	1.0 mm2	0.08	-	1.17	-	1.16	**2.33**	m
	1.5 mm2	0.09	-	1.40	-	1.23	**2.63**	m
	2.5 mm2	0.15	-	2.33	-	2.00	**4.33**	m
	4.0 mm2	0.19	-	2.90	-	3.28	**6.18**	m
	6.0 mm2	0.23	-	3.50	-	4.34	**7.84**	m
035	7 core clipped to surface:						
	0.75 mm2	0.05	-	0.82	-	1.19	**2.01**	m
	1.0 mm2	0.08	-	1.28	-	1.46	**2.74**	m
	1.5 mm2	0.10	-	1.54	-	1.78	**3.32**	m

		Man-Hours	Plant Hours	Net Labour Price £	Net Plant Price £	Net Mats Price £	Net Unit Price £	Unit
	Unit Rates							
	2.5 mm2	0.17	-	2.55	-	2.62	**5.17**	m
036	**Miscellaneous communication cables or the like**							
037	Clipped to surface:							
	digital satallite cable	0.04	-	0.61	-	0.21	**0.82**	m
	2 pair telephone cable	0.04	-	0.61	-	0.13	**0.74**	m
	3 pair telephone cable	0.04	-	0.61	-	0.19	**0.80**	m
	4 pair telephone cable	0.04	-	0.61	-	0.30	**0.91**	m
	co-axial cable	0.04	-	0.61	-	0.11	**0.72**	m
	speaker/bell cable	0.03	-	0.52	-	0.07	**0.59**	m
SF	**LIGHTNING PROTECTION**							
001	**Tapes fixed to surfaces at 1.00 m intervals with spacer bar holdfast or similar**							
002	Fixing to horizontal surfaces:							
	bare copper tape 3 x 25 mm	0.26	-	3.93	-	26.07	**30.00**	m
	bare copper tape 4 x 25 mm	0.26	-	3.93	-	32.77	**36.70**	m
	bare copper tape 3 x 40 mm	0.29	-	4.37	-	62.94	**67.31**	m
	bare copper tape 4 x 40 mm	0.29	-	4.37	-	82.95	**87.32**	m
	bare copper tape 6 x 50 mm	0.35	-	5.24	-	91.92	**97.16**	m
	PVC covered copper tape 3 x 25 mm	0.26	-	3.93	-	28.30	**32.23**	m
	PVC covered copper tape 6 x 50 mm	0.35	-	5.24	-	90.15	**95.39**	m
003	Fixing to vertical surfaces:							
	bare copper tape 3 x 25 mm	0.29	-	4.34	-	26.07	**30.41**	m
	bare copper tape 4 x 25 mm	0.29	-	4.34	-	32.77	**37.11**	m
	bare copper tape 3 x 40 mm	0.32	-	4.81	-	62.94	**67.75**	m
	bare copper tape 4 x 40 mm	0.32	-	4.81	-	82.95	**87.76**	m
	bare copper tape 6 x 50 mm	0.38	-	5.77	-	91.92	**97.69**	m
	PVC covered copper tape 3 x 25 mm	0.29	-	4.34	-	28.30	**32.64**	m
	PVC covered copper tape 6 x 50 mm	0.38	-	5.77	-	90.52	**96.29**	m
004	Bonding tape to structure:							
	water main bond	0.17	-	2.62	-	31.90	**34.52**	Nr
	tower earthing clamp	0.17	-	2.62	-	38.47	**41.09**	Nr
	rod to tape clamp 10 x 26 mm	0.17	-	2.62	-	28.52	**31.14**	Nr
	puddle flange copper	0.17	-	2.62	-	137.54	**140.16**	Nr
005	Terminals:							
	air terminal comprising multiple pointed end, 15 mm rod, strike pad and stem, rod base and brackets fixed to masonry	1.44	-	21.85	-	194.64	**216.49**	Nr
006	Copper earth electrodes, extendable type including driving heads and couplers. mechanically driven into ground and connected to conductors with triangular pattern clamps; including fixing with bolts, screws and the like:							
	unthreaded copperbond earth rod 14.2 mm diameter x 1200 mm long	1.44	0.33	21.85	1.54	48.66	**72.05**	Nr
	add per 14.2 mm diameter section x 1200 mm long driven to a maximum of 6 m	0.38	0.33	5.77	1.54	24.95	**32.26**	Nr
	unthreaded copperbond earth rod 17.2 mm diameter x 1200 mm long	1.44	-	21.85	-	47.29	**69.14**	Nr
	add per 17.2 mm diameter section x 1200 mm long driven to a maximum of 6 m	0.44	0.38	6.64	1.77	29.88	**38.29**	Nr
	threaded copperbond earth rod 13 mm diameter x 1200 mm long	1.44	0.33	21.85	1.54	42.32	**65.71**	Nr
	add per 13 mm diameter section x 1200 mm long driven to a maximum of 6 m	0.50	0.44	7.62	2.03	24.18	**33.83**	Nr
	threaded copperbond earth rod 16 mm diameter x 1200 mm long	1.51	0.35	22.95	1.62	41.11	**65.68**	Nr
	add per 16 mm diameter section x 1200 mm long driven to a maximum of 6 m	0.42	0.36	6.36	1.70	31.03	**39.09**	Nr
	threaded copperbond earth rod 19 mm diameter x 1200 mm long	1.58	0.36	24.09	1.70	47.95	**73.74**	Nr
	add per 19 mm diameter section x 1200 mm long driven to a maximum of 6 m	0.44	0.38	6.68	1.78	33.76	**42.22**	Nr
	concrete inspection pit bedded and surrounded in concrete	0.38	-	4.26	-	55.53	**59.79**	Nr
SG	**HEATING AND HEATERS**							
001	Convection heater:							
	dimplex AC range white warm air curtain with adjustable air flow direction and handheld remote control for single doorways 3.0kW	1.15	-	17.48	-	131.68	**149.16**	Nr
	dimplex AC range white warm air curtain with adjustable air flow direction and integral controls for double doorways 6.0kW	1.44	-	21.85	-	264.45	**286.30**	Nr
	dimplex BFH range brown base unit heater 2.4kW for fitting into panelling etc	1.73	-	26.22	-	101.68	**127.90**	Nr
002	Night storage heater:							
	Creda TSR Sensor Plus series TSR6AW white storage heater with multi-sense two thermostatic sensor control system 0.9kW	2.10	-	30.48	-	159.80	**190.28**	Nr
	Creda TSR Sensor Plus series TSR12AW white storage heater with multi-sense two thermostatic sensor control system 1.7kW	2.10	-	30.48	-	231.71	**262.19**	Nr
	Creda TSR Sensor Plus series TSR18AW white storage heater with multi-sense two thermostatic sensor control system 2.5kW	2.32	-	33.52	-	307.71	**341.23**	Nr
	Creda TSR Sensor Plus series TSR18AW white storage heater with multi-sense two thermostatic sensor control system 3.4kW	2.55	-	36.88	-	374.92	**411.80**	Nr
	creda TSR sensor plus series TSR24AW white storage heater with multi-sense two thermostatic sensor control system 3.4kW	2.80	-	40.57	-	374.92	**415.49**	Nr
	copper sheathed immersion heater 280 mm long	0.86	-	13.11	-	16.90	**30.01**	Nr
	copper sheathed immersion heater 686 mm long	0.86	-	13.11	-	19.14	**32.25**	Nr
	copper sheathed immersion heater 280 mm long anti corrosive	0.86	-	13.11	-	20.27	**33.38**	Nr

Unit Rates		Man-Hours	Plant Hours	Net Labour Price £	Net Plant Price £	Net Mats Price £	Net Unit Price £	Unit

SH — **BUILDERS WORK IN CONNECTION WITH ELECTRICAL INSTALLATIONS**

001 Cutting away for and making good after electrician installing the following electrical points in new structures

Note: the following allowances have been made in calculating the prices per point.

		Chases m	Holes Nr	Man-Hours	Plant Hours	Net Labour Price £	Net Plant Price £	Net Mats Price £	Net Unit Price £	Unit
002	Concealed cables:									
	lighting point	0.50	2	1.61	1.40	19.03	5.83	1.87	**26.73**	Nr
	power point	0.50	3	2.30	2.00	27.19	8.33	2.78	**38.30**	Nr
	fitting outlet point	1.00	3	2.53	2.20	29.91	9.17	2.84	**41.92**	Nr
	equipment outlet point	1.25	4	3.34	2.90	39.42	12.08	3.79	**55.29**	Nr
003	Concealed conduits:									
	lighting point	2.00	2	2.30	2.00	27.19	8.33	2.07	**37.59**	Nr
	power point	1.50	3	2.76	2.40	32.62	10.00	2.91	**45.53**	Nr
	fitting outlet point	1.75	3	2.88	2.50	33.98	10.42	2.95	**47.35**	Nr
	equipment outlet point	2.00	4	3.68	3.20	43.50	13.33	3.88	**60.71**	Nr
004	Exposed cables and conduits:									
	lighting point	-	2	1.38	1.20	16.31	5.00	1.81	**23.12**	Nr
	power point	-	3	2.07	1.80	24.47	7.50	2.71	**34.68**	Nr
	fitting outlet point	-	3	2.07	1.80	24.47	7.50	2.71	**34.68**	Nr
	equipment outlet point	-	4	2.76	2.40	32.62	10.00	3.62	**46.24**	Nr

005 Cutting chases for cables and conduits in existing structures and making good with cement mortar (1:3)

006	Chase for one cable or conduit in existing:			Man-Hours	Plant Hours	Net Labour	Net Plant	Net Mats	Net Unit	Unit
	concrete			0.52	0.45	6.12	1.88	0.13	**8.13**	m
	common brickwork			0.38	0.33	4.49	1.38	0.13	**6.00**	m
	engineering brickwork			0.46	0.40	5.44	1.67	0.13	**7.24**	m
	concrete blockwork			0.40	0.35	4.76	1.46	0.13	**6.35**	m
	stonework			0.46	0.40	5.44	1.67	0.13	**7.24**	m
007	Chases for two cables or conduits in existing:									
	concrete			0.63	0.55	7.48	2.29	0.26	**10.03**	m
	common brickwork			0.52	0.45	6.12	1.88	0.26	**8.26**	m
	engineering brickwork			0.62	0.54	7.34	2.25	0.26	**9.85**	m
	concrete blockwork			0.58	0.50	6.80	2.08	0.26	**9.14**	m
	stonework			0.62	0.54	7.34	2.25	0.26	**9.85**	m
008	Chases for three cables or conduits in existing:									
	concrete			0.81	0.70	9.52	2.92	0.39	**12.83**	m
	common brickwork			0.63	0.55	7.48	2.29	0.39	**10.16**	m
	engineering brickwork			0.76	0.66	8.97	2.75	0.39	**12.11**	m
	concrete blockwork			0.69	0.60	8.16	2.50	0.39	**11.05**	m
	stonework			0.76	0.66	8.97	2.75	0.39	**12.11**	m
009	**Extra over** cutting chases in existing structure for cutting away existing plasterwork and making good with new Thistle plaster; for:									
	one cable or conduit			0.40	-	9.51	-	0.05	**9.56**	m
	two cables or conduits			0.46	-	10.86	-	0.10	**10.96**	m
	three cables or conduits			0.52	-	12.22	-	0.20	**12.42**	m

		Net Labour Price £	Net Plant Price £	Net Mats Price £	Net Unit Price £	Unit
SJ	**ELECTRICAL INSTALLATION**					
	Note: 001 – 002 not used					
003	**Repairs and renovations**					
004	Take out old wiring and rewire from point to consumer unit or distribution board; reconnecting to existing switches, socket outlets and the like: PVC insulated and sheathed cable: exposed cables surface fixed to:					
	switch point	1.67	25.35	4.90	**31.13**	Nr
	5A socket outlet	1.90	28.84	6.36	**36.08**	Nr
	13A socket outlet	2.82	42.83	9.47	**53.18**	Nr
	immersion heater	4.60	69.92	21.43	**93.10**	Nr
	cooker outlet	5.46	83.03	38.41	**123.19**	Nr
	door bell	1.04	15.73	-	**16.61**	Nr
	TV outlet	1.09	16.61	2.25	**20.61**	Nr
	shower	6.04	91.77	87.56	**354.33**	Nr
	night storage heater	4.31	65.55	21.43	**87.86**	Nr
	emergency lighting	1.90	28.84	6.36	**36.08**	Nr
	fans	2.82	42.83	9.47	**53.18**	Nr
	boiler control panels	4.40	66.86	6.36	**74.10**	Nr
	pumps 240V	2.82	42.83	9.47	**53.18**	Nr
	thermostats	0.86	13.11	1.38	**15.37**	Nr
	chiller 240V	2.82	42.83	9.47	**53.18**	Nr

Unit Rates	Net Labour Price £	Net Plant Price £	Net Mats Price £	Net Unit Price £	Unit
air handling equipment 415V	4.31	65.55	21.43	**87.86**	Nr
005 Take out old wiring and rewire from point to consumer unit or distribution board; reconnecting to existing switches, socket outlets and the like:					
concealed cables (chases excluded) to:					
switch point	1.75	26.62	4.90	**32.40**	Nr
5A socket outlet	1.99	30.29	6.36	**37.53**	Nr
13A socket outlet	2.96	44.98	9.47	**55.33**	Nr
immersion heater	4.83	73.42	21.43	**96.60**	Nr
cooker outlet	5.74	87.19	38.41	**127.35**	Nr
door bell	1.09	16.52	1.38	**18.78**	Nr
TV outlet	1.15	17.45	2.25	**21.45**	Nr
shower	6.34	96.37	87.56	**358.93**	Nr
night storage heater	4.53	68.84	21.43	**91.15**	Nr
emergency lighting	1.99	30.29	6.36	**37.53**	Nr
fans	2.96	44.98	9.47	**55.33**	Nr
boiler control panels	4.62	70.20	6.36	**77.44**	Nr
pumps 240V	2.96	44.98	9.47	**55.33**	Nr
thermostats	0.91	13.77	1.38	**16.03**	Nr
chiller 240V	2.96	44.98	9.47	**55.33**	Nr
air handling equipment 415V	4.53	68.84	21.43	**91.15**	Nr
006 Take out old wiring and rewire from point to consumer unit or distribution board; reconnecting to existing switches, socket outlets and the like:					
via existing cables and conduits to:					
switch point	1.93	29.28	4.90	**35.06**	Nr
5A socket outlet	2.19	33.32	6.36	**40.56**	Nr
13A socket outlet	3.25	49.47	9.47	**59.82**	Nr
immersion heater	5.31	80.76	21.43	**103.94**	Nr
cooker outlet	6.31	95.90	38.41	**136.06**	Nr
door bell	1.20	18.18	1.38	**20.44**	Nr
TV outlet	1.26	19.18	2.25	**23.18**	Nr
shower	6.97	106.00	87.56	**368.56**	Nr
night storage heater	4.98	75.71	21.43	**98.02**	Nr
emergency lighting	2.19	33.32	6.36	**40.56**	Nr
fans	3.25	49.47	9.47	**59.82**	Nr
boiler control panels	5.08	77.23	6.36	**84.47**	Nr
pumps 240V	3.25	49.47	9.47	**59.82**	Nr
thermostats	1.00	15.14	1.38	**17.40**	Nr
chiller 240V	3.25	49.47	9.47	**59.82**	Nr
air handling equipment 415V	4.98	75.71	21.43	**98.02**	Nr
mineral insulated copper cable (concealed or exposed):					
heat detector, smoke detector, alarm bell or break glass point	3.22	48.94	84.07	**133.89**	Nr
emergency lighting or the like	3.62	55.06	106.11	**162.05**	Nr
powered doors or the like	4.08	61.95	159.64	**222.47**	Nr
007 Remove damaged accessories and refit new:					
lighting points:					
one way switch plate	0.30	4.60	1.00	**5.60**	Nr
two way switch plate	0.35	5.24	1.23	**6.47**	Nr
three way switch plate	0.43	6.56	4.81	**11.37**	Nr
socket points:					
single 13A outlet	0.30	4.60	2.07	**6.67**	Nr
single outlet non-isolated TV/FM co-axial socket	0.48	7.22	4.45	**11.67**	Nr
double 13A outlet	0.39	5.91	2.71	**8.62**	Nr
equipment points:					
immersion heater switch	0.39	5.91	2.32	**8.23**	Nr
cooker control panel	0.60	9.18	12.31	**21.49**	Nr
door bell	1.04	15.79	12.31	**28.10**	Nr
TV outlet plate	0.41	6.17	4.45	**10.62**	Nr
fire protection points:					
emergency light fitting	0.46	7.05	60.17	**67.22**	Nr
heat detectors	0.46	7.05	24.35	**31.40**	Nr
smoke detectors	0.46	7.05	26.33	**33.38**	Nr
alarm bells	0.77	11.66	34.04	**45.70**	Nr
break glass points	0.77	11.66	10.06	**21.72**	Nr
008 Break into existing ring main circuit and provide new single switched socket outlets, together with 5 m length of cable fixed on surface:					
PVC insulated and sheathed cable:					
exposed cables surface fixed to:					
5A socket outlet	0.86	13.11	1.59	**15.58**	Nr
13A socket outlet	1.09	16.61	2.37	**19.86**	Nr

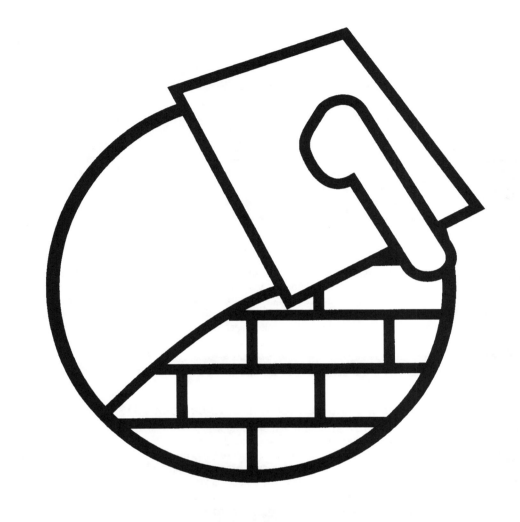

Floor, Wall and Ceiling Finishings

Comprehensive Building Price Book 2013
Major and Minor Works dataset

The Major Works dataset focuses predominantly on large 'new build' projects reflecting the economies of scale found in these forms of construction. The Minor Works Estimating Dataset focuses on small to medium sized 'new build' projects reflecting the increase in costs brought about the reduced output, less discounts, increased carriage and supervision, to the similar items in the Major Works dataset. The dataset is presented in trade order. Revised and reworked items in underpinning composites; flue linings and rainwater goods.

Item code: 19215   **Price: £165.99**

SMM7 Estimating Price Book 2013

The SMM7 Estimating dataset focuses predominantly on large 'new build' projects reflecting the economies of scale found in these forms of construction. The dataset is presented in SMM7 grouping and order in accordance with the Common Arrangement of Work Sections. It is compiled using the latest independent costing information from manufacturers, material and plant suppliers, legislation effects and working rule agreements. Revised and reworked items in underpinning composites; flue linings and rainwater goods.

Item code: 19216   **Price: £139.99**

Alterations and Refurbishment Price Book 2013

The Alterations & Refurbishment dataset focuses on small to medium sized projects, generally working within an existing building and reflecting the increase in costs brought about the reduction in output, smaller discounts, increased carriage, increased supervision, and less productivity brought about by smaller economies of scale, increased production costs, more difficult access and the possibility of working in occupied premises. The dataset is presented in trade order. Revised and reworked items in underpinning composites; flue linings and rainwater goods.

Item code: 19217   **Price £109.99**

BCIS Guide to Estimating for Small Works 2012

The BCIS Guide to Estimating for Small Works 2012 is a unique dataset which shows the true power of resource based estimating. A set of composite built-up measured items are used to build up priced estimates for a large number of common specification extensions. The intention is to show estimating techniques in use and allow users to build up accurate estimates for their own projects, simply and easily, with up-to-date and independent cost information.

Item code: 19064   **Price: £59.99**

BCIS Painting and Decorating Price Book 2012

The BCIS Painting and Decorating dataset is the most handy pricing tool available to the painting and decorating sector of the industry, suitable for all projects needing more than a 'guess-timate'. Using this dataset a more accurate calculation based quotation or variation can be prepared. From these calculations an assessment of labour, plant and material content can be produced. This in turn enables the contractor to negotiate discounts on known material requirements and the effect of this workload on the availability of labour.

Item code: 19065   **Price: £39.99**

For more information call **0870 333 1600** email
contact@bcis.co.uk or visit **www.bcis.co.uk**

BCIS is the Building Cost Information Service of  **RICS** | the mark of property professionalism worldwide

Labour Rates

Please note: The labour hours throughout this section are representative of the time required for one productive man to carry out the unit of work.

Gang rates are calculated as follows by obtaining the overall gang cost and then dividing this by the number of productive members in the gang. The resulting rate is the Gang Cost per **Man - hour**. By using the same principle, any size gang may be built-up and used against the standard labour hours in this section.

The prices for labour in this section are based upon the following rates:

A0212 Plastering and rendering:
Plasterer	4.00	x	£	15.20	=	£	60.80
Plastering Labourer	3.00	x	£	11.22	=	£	33.66
Total hourly cost of gang					=	£	94.46

Gang rate (divided by 4) = £23.62 per Man-hour

A0213 Wallboard, drylinings, partitions:
Plasterboard Tacker	2.00	x	£	15.20	=	£	30.40
Plasterboard Tacking Labourer	1.00	x	£	11.22	=	£	11.22
Total hourly cost of gang					=	£	41.62

Gang rate (divided by 2) = £20.81 per Man-hour

A0218 Flexible sheet and tile floor coverings:
Sheet/Flex. Tile Floorlayer	2.00	x	£	15.20	=	£	30.40
Floorlaying Labourer	1.00	x	£	11.22	=	£	11.22
Total hourly cost of gang					=	£	41.62

Gang rate (divided by 2) = £20.81 per Man-hour

A0219 Floor screeding:
Floor Screeder	4.00	x	£	15.20	=	£	60.80
Floor Screeding Labourer	3.00	x	£	11.22	=	£	33.66
Total hourly cost of gang					=	£	94.46

Gang rate (divided by 4) = £23.62 per Man-hour

Artexer
    Artexer = £15.20 per hour

Carpetlayer
    Carpetlayer = £15.20 per hour

Ceramic wall tiler
    Ceramic Wall Tiler = £15.20 per hour

Ceramic/Quarry floor tiler
    Ceramic/Quarry Floor Tiler = £15.20 per hour

Suspended ceiling fixer
    Suspended Ceiling Fixer = £15.20 per hour

Basic Prices of Materials

		Supply Price £	Waste Factor %	Unload. Labour £	Unload. Plant £	Total Unit Cost £	Unit
	The following material prices have been calculated on a National Average 'best price' basis. Please refer to Introduction, General Item AA004.						
A0301	Portland cement delivered in bags	137.81	5%	11.22	-	**156.48**	tonne
A0311	Hydrated lime delivered in bags	216.00	5%	11.22	-	**238.58**	tonne
A0323	Plastering sand	28.52	10%	-	-	**31.37**	tonne
A0331	Concrete sand (fine aggregate)	29.64	10%	-	-	**32.60**	tonne
T0055	Coarse aggregate 10 mm nominal size	24.15	10%		-	**26.57**	tonne
T0084	Crushed stone 14 - 6 mm	18.78	5%		-	**19.72**	tonne
T0085	Derbyshire spar chippings 3 - 12 mm	63.67	5%	-	-	**66.85**	tonne
T0091	Leicestershire granite chippings 14 mm	46.30	10%	-	-	**50.94**	tonne
T0141	Lytag lightweight aggregate pump grade (delivered full loads of approx. 24 m3)	119.25	10%	11.22	-	**143.52**	tonne
T0140	Vermiculite aggregate/insulation	149.90	10%	5.61	-	**171.06**	m3
T0092	Febproof plus waterproofer	1.56	10%	-	-	**1.72**	ltr
T0093	Polyurethane floor sealer	7.05	10%	-	-	**7.76**	ltr
A0371	Pudlo water proofer	6.04	5%	-	-	**6.34**	kg
T0096	Carborundum non-slip grains	4.51	10%	0.01	-	**4.97**	kg
	Galvanised wire netting 19 gauge:						
T0097	25 mm mesh, 900 mm wide	2.50	10%	-	-	**2.75**	m
T0098	50 mm mesh, 900 mm wide	2.14	10%	-	-	**2.35**	m
T0110	Newlath polypropylene fixing plugs	0.13	5%	-	-	**0.14**	nr
T0115	Newlath lathing 10 m x 1.5 m roll	9.43	10%	0.01	-	**10.39**	m2
T0142	Stopgap green bag powder	0.30	5%	0.01	-	**0.33**	kg
T0143	Stopgap liquid Latex No 128	1.80	5%	0.01	-	**1.90**	ltr
T0144	Unibond PVA adhesive and sealer	2.79	10%	0.02	-	**3.09**	ltr

Basic Prices of Materials

		Supply Price £	Waste Factor %	Unload. Labour £	Unload. Plant £	Total Unit Cost £	Unit
T0086	Cullamix Tyrolean render	836.00	10%	11.22	-	931.94	tonne
T0087	Cemrend textured surface coating	0.61	5%	0.01	-	0.65	kg
T0088	Surface primer	6.53	10%	0.02	-	7.21	ltr
T0090	Sandtex matt (white)	3.00	10%	0.02	-	3.32	ltr
	Limelite plasters (ex. works)						
T0040	Tarmac High Impact Finish	268.59	5%	11.22	-	293.81	tonne
T0041	Limelite Backing	343.00	5%	11.22	-	371.93	tonne
T0042	Whitewall High Impact Backing Browning	279.89	5%	11.22	-	305.67	tonne
T0043	Limelite Renovating	435.35	5%	11.22	-	468.90	tonne
	The following British Gypsum prices are based on full loads (22.5 tonnes) delivered to site. Full loads of plaster only orders are classified as 22.5 tonnes or 18 full pallets whichever is the lower weight. Prices are applicable to the whole of England, Wales and Scottish mainland. - Service charges may be applied for requirements outside a 'normal full load'.						
T0059	Thistle Browning	309.76	5%	11.22	-	337.03	tonne
T0061	Thistle Hardwall	275.88	5%	11.22	-	301.46	tonne
T0062	Thistle Bonding coat	307.82	5%	11.22	-	335.00	tonne
T0064	Thistle Multi-Finish	226.51	5%	11.22	-	249.62	tonne
T0056	Thistle Board finish	212.13	5%	11.22	-	234.51	tonne
T0058	Thistle Tough Coat	319.65	5%	11.22	-	347.41	tonne
T0066	Thistle Universal one coat plaster	356.44	5%	11.22	-	386.04	tonne
T0116	15 mm Gyproc Fireline	4.97	5%	0.17	-	5.40	m2
T0118	9.5 mm Gyproc wallboard	2.37	5%	0.10	-	2.59	m2
T0119	9.5 mm Gyproc Handi-board	2.73	5%	0.10	-	2.97	m2
T0120	12.5 mm Gyproc Handi-board	3.65	5%	0.13	-	3.97	m2
T0121	12.5 mm Gyproc wallboard	2.37	5%	0.13	-	2.62	m2
T0122	15 mm Gyproc wallboard	2.84	5%	0.10	-	3.09	m2
T0123	12.5 mm Gyproc Fireline board	2.88	5%	0.13	-	3.16	m2
T0124	19 mm Gyproc plank	4.91	5%	0.20	-	5.37	m2
T0125	**Extra over** cost for Duplex grade board	1.09	5%	-	-	1.15	m2
T0126	22 mm Gyproc ThermaLine Basic (loads of 500 m2)	4.61	5%	0.13	-	4.98	m2
T0127	30 mm Gyproc ThermaLine Basic (loads of 500 m2)	5.08	5%	0.13	-	5.47	m2
T0128	40 mm Gyproc ThermaLine Basic (loads of 500 - 959 m2)	5.83	5%	0.13	-	6.26	m2
T0129	50 mm Gyproc ThermaLine Basic VC (loads of 500 - 959 m2)	6.90	5%	0.13	-	7.38	m2
T0130	50 mm Gyproc ThermaLine super (loads of 499 m2)	13.96	5%	0.13	-	14.80	m2
T0131	60 mm Gyproc ThermaLine super (loads of 499 m2)	15.46	5%	0.13	-	16.37	m2
T0137	65 mm Gyproc ThermaLine super (loads of 499 m2)	16.75	5%	0.13	-	17.72	m2
T0147	42 mm Gyproc Tri-line (loads of 6-12 pallets)	12.81	5%	0.13	-	13.59	m2
T0148	52 mm Gyproc Tri-line (loads of 6-12 pallets)	15.18	5%	0.13	-	16.08	m2
T0138	**Extra over** cost for vapour check thermal board	1.09	5%	-	-	1.15	m2
T0081	Gyproc cove, 100 mm girth (loads of not less than 600 m)	1.02	5%	0.02	-	1.10	m
T0082	Gyproc cove, 127 mm girth (loads of not less than 600 m)	1.02	5%	0.01	-	1.08	m
T0083	Plaster cove adhesive	0.94	5%	0.01	-	1.00	kg
T0067	Thistle ProTape FT50	0.03	10%	0.11	-	0.15	m
T0136	Gyproc Dri-Wall adhesive	0.27	10%	0.01	-	0.31	kg
T0204	Gyproc Joint Filler	0.50	10%	0.01	-	0.56	kg
T0205	Gyproc Easi-Fill	1.02	10%	0.01	-	1.13	kg
T0206	Gyproc Joint Tape	0.03	10%	-	-	0.03	m
T0207	Gyproc Corner Tape	0.53	10%	-	-	0.58	m
T0208	Gyproc Drywall Sealer	2.62	10%	0.02	-	2.90	ltr
T0221	Gypframe metal C-stud 48 mm wide	1.29	10%	0.01	-	1.43	m
T0222	Gypframe metal floor and ceiling channel 50 mm wide	1.41	10%	0.01	-	1.57	m
T0223	Gyproc dry wall screws 32 mm long	4.06	10%	0.03	-	4.50	1000
T0224	Gyproc dry wall screws 36 mm long	4.76	10%	0.03	-	5.27	1000
T0244	Gyproc acoustic sealant, 900 ml (carton of 9 cartridges)	94.80	10%	0.15	-	104.45	carton
T0132	Gyproc Angle Bead (carton of 2400 mm x 50 lengths)	53.37	10%	0.29	-	59.02	carton
T0133	Gyproc acrylic sealant/adhesive	10.25	10%	0.02	-	11.29	ltr
T0250	Gyproc nailable plugs 60 x 6 mm	0.20	10%	-	-	0.22	nr
T0251	Gyproc nailable plugs 75 x 6 mm	0.22	10%	-	-	0.24	nr
T0252	Gyproc nailable plugs 100 x 6 mm	0.33	10%	-	-	0.36	nr
	Wrought softwood partition battens:						
T0209	19 x 30 mm	0.38	10%	-	-	0.41	m
T0210	19 x 37 mm	0.44	10%	-	-	0.48	m
T0211	19 x 50 mm	0.55	10%	-	-	0.61	m
T0212	19 x 57 mm	0.66	10%	-	-	0.72	m
T0213	19 x 36 mm	0.42	10%	-	-	0.47	m
T0214	25 x 38 mm	0.54	10%	-	-	0.60	m
T0215	30 x 37 mm	0.62	10%	-	-	0.69	m
T0216	37 x 37 mm	0.72	10%	-	-	0.79	m
T0217	38 x 48 mm	0.92	10%	-	-	1.01	m
	Gyproc galvanised nails:						
T0218	30 mm long	2.64	10%	0.02	-	2.93	kg
T0219	40 mm long	2.64	10%	0.02	-	2.93	kg
T0220	50 mm long	2.64	10%	0.02	-	2.93	kg
T0227	65 and 75 mm long	2.22	10%	0.02	-	2.46	kg
	Oval lost head nails, length:						
T0245	40 mm	2.88	10%	0.02	-	3.19	kg
T0246	50 mm	2.89	10%	0.02	-	3.20	kg
T0247	65 mm	2.81	10%	0.02	-	3.11	kg
	Hardened steel masonry nails:						
T0139	31 x 2.5 mm	0.01	10%	-	-	0.01	nr
T0117	50 x 2.5 mm	0.02	10%	-	-	0.02	nr

Basic Prices of Materials	Supply Price £	Waste Factor %	Unload. Labour £	Unload. Plant £	Total Unit Cost £	Unit
No 8 counter sunk wood screws, length:						
T0236 32 mm	0.01	10%	-	-	0.01	nr
T0237 40 mm	0.01	10%	-	-	0.01	nr
T0238 50 mm	0.02	10%	-	-	0.02	nr
No 10 counter sunk wood screws, length:						
T0239 60 mm	0.03	10%	-	-	0.03	nr
No 6 self-tapping screws, length:						
T0240 19 mm	0.01	10%	-	-	0.01	nr
T0241 32 mm	0.01	10%	-	-	0.01	nr
Zinc plated steel counter sunk screws, length:						
T0242 65 mm x 10 gauge	0.05	10%	-	-	0.06	nr
T0243 75 mm x 12 gauge	0.08	10%	-	-	0.08	nr
T0248 Hilti cartridges (red)	0.15	2.5%	-	-	0.15	nr
T0249 Hilti nails for fixing material to concrete	0.36	10%	-	-	0.40	nr
T0225 40 mm resin bonded glass fibre slab insulation (in 1200 x 455 mm sheets)	2.85	5%	-	-	3.00	m2
Supalux sheet, sanded finish:						
N0362 6 mm	17.55	5%	0.04	-	18.47	m2
N0363 9 mm	24.48	5%	0.06	-	25.77	m2
N0364 12 mm	31.01	5%	0.08	-	32.64	m2
Supalux fillets - 75 mm:						
T0232 6 mm	1.47	5%	0.01	-	1.55	m
T0233 9 mm	2.18	5%	0.02	-	2.31	m
T0234 12 mm	2.89	5%	0.02	-	3.06	m
Aluminium safety tread with carborundum insert strip:						
T0099 19 mm wide	18.92	5%	-	-	19.87	m
T0100 38 mm wide	22.35	5%	-	-	23.47	m
T0101 50 mm wide	28.92	5%	-	-	30.37	m
Gradus aluminium safety nosings:						
2mm gauge						
T0103 nosing with single insert (AS11)	9.75	5%	-	-	10.24	m
T0104 nosing with single insert (AR81)	11.87	5%	-	-	12.46	m
T0105 nosing with double insert (AS12)	13.50	5%	-	-	14.18	m
5mm gauge						
T0106 nosing with single insert (G11)	11.57	5%	-	-	12.15	m
T0107 nosing with single insert (GR81)	14.12	5%	-	-	14.83	m
T0108 nosing with single insert (G12)	15.89	5%	-	-	16.68	m
T0109 Thixotropic contact adhesive (370 ml cartridge)	3.69	10%	-	-	4.06	nr
Drilling nosings and provision of matching insert plugs:						
T0400 single infill nosings	0.55	5%	-	-	0.58	m
T0401 double infill nosings	0.66	5%	-	-	0.70	m
The following prices are for Expanded Metal Company products delivered to sites within the UK mainland.						
Expanded metal lath; galvanised:						
T0111 BB 263 9 mm mesh 0.500 mm material	5.67	10%	-	-	6.24	m2
T0113 BB 264 9 mm mesh 0.725 mm material	7.93	10%	-	-	8.73	m2
T0402 Riblath ref 269 0.300 material	10.08	10%	0.03	-	11.12	m2
T0403 Riblath ref 271 0.500 material	11.60	10%	0.03	-	12.79	m2
T0404 Spraylath ref 273 0.500 material	13.94	10%	0.03	-	15.37	m2
T0405 Red-rib lath ref 274 0.500 material	12.80	10%	-	-	14.08	m2
T0407 Strip mesh ref 584 for external use 100 mm wide	3.28	10%	-	-	3.61	m
T0409 Corner mesh ref 583 for external use 100 mm wide	1.27	10%	-	-	1.40	m
Expanded metal lath, stainless steel:						
T0410 ref. 267 Riblath 0.300 mm material	29.97	10%	-	-	32.97	m2
T0448 ref. 95S Spec.304.S.15 0.46 mm material	30.08	10%	-	-	33.08	m2
Stainless steel clamping system:						
T0112 standard band 1/2" wide ref RB112	1.06	10%	-	-	1.16	m
T0114 standard band 3/4" wide ref RB134	1.25	10%	-	-	1.37	m
T0406 standard buckle ref TB112	0.23	5%	-	-	0.24	nr
T0408 standard buckle ref TB134	0.34	5%	-	-	0.36	nr
Expamet beads for plaster, plasterboard and render:						
T0070 ref 550 angle bead	0.92	5%	-	-	0.97	m
T0411 ref 558 maxicon angle bead	0.73	5%	-	-	0.77	m
T0072 ref 588 movement bead, internal use	7.66	5%	-	-	8.05	m
T0412 ref 590 movement bead, external use	8.63	5%	-	-	9.06	m
T0413 ref 562 plaster stop bead 10 mm deep	1.16	5%	-	-	1.22	m
T0068 ref 563 plaster stop bead 13 mm deep	1.13	5%	-	-	1.19	m
T0414 ref 565 plaster stop bead 16 mm deep	1.61	5%	-	-	1.69	m
T0415 ref 566 plaster stop bead 19 mm deep	1.61	5%	-	-	1.69	m
T0073 ref 579 architrave bead	2.47	5%	-	-	2.59	m
T0074 ref 580 architrave bead	2.46	5%	-	-	2.58	m
T0416 ref 585 architrave bead	2.46	5%	-	-	2.58	m
T0417 ref 586 architrave bead	2.53	5%	-	-	2.66	m

Basic Prices of Materials

		Supply Price £	Waste Factor %	Unload. Labour £	Unload. Plant £	Total Unit Cost £	Unit
T0418	ref 569 depth gauge bead	1.52	5%	-	-	1.60	m
T0419	ref 559 square nose angle bead	1.65	5%	-	-	1.74	m
T0077	ref 570 external render stop	1.22	5%	-	-	1.28	m
T0079	ref 548 dry wall corner bead	1.03	5%	-	-	1.08	m
T0080	ref 567 plasterboard edging bead	2.78	5%	-	-	2.92	m
T0420	ref 568 plasterboard edging bead	2.85	5%	-	-	2.99	m
T0421	ref 553 thin-coat angle bead, 3 mm	0.88	5%	-	-	0.93	m
T0071	ref 554 thin-coat angle bead, 6 mm	0.86	5%	-	-	0.91	m
T0422	ref 560 thin-coat stop bead, 3 mm	1.34	5%	-	-	1.40	m
T0069	ref 561 thin-coat stop bead, 6 mm	1.30	5%	-	-	1.37	m
T0075	ref 545 external angle bead	3.91	5%	-	-	4.11	m
T0076	ref 546 external stop bead	3.48	5%	-	-	3.65	m
T0078	ref 533 external render stop type (2)	3.48	5%	-	-	3.65	m
	Expamet arch forms:						
	arch corner ref:						
T0423	EAC 15 radius 381 mm	35.56	-	-	-	35.56	nr
T0424	EAC 18 radius 457 mm	43.28	-	-	-	43.28	nr
T0425	EAC 24 radius 610 mm	52.82	-	-	-	52.82	nr
T0426	EAC 30 radius 762 mm	76.86	-	-	-	76.86	nr
	semicircle arches ref:						
T0427	ESC 30 for 762 mm opening	69.90	-	-	-	69.90	nr
T0428	ESC 32 for 812 mm opening	71.04	-	-	-	71.04	nr
T0429	ESC 33 for 838 mm opening	73.40	-	-	-	73.40	nr
T0430	ESC 36 for 914 mm opening	85.86	-	-	-	85.86	nr
	elliptical arches ref:						
T0431	EEL 48 for 1219 mm opening	135.95	-	-	-	135.95	nr
T0432	EEL 54 for 1372 mm opening	142.53	-	-	-	142.53	nr
T0433	EEL 60 for 1524 mm opening	151.38	-	-	-	151.38	nr
T0434	EEL 72 for 1829 mm opening	163.05	-	-	-	163.05	nr
T0435	EEL 84 for 2134 mm opening	178.87	-	-	-	178.87	nr
T0436	EEL 96 for 2438 mm opening	187.76	-	-	-	187.76	nr
T0437	EEL 120 for 3048 mm opening	191.60	-	-	-	191.60	nr
	spandrel arches ref:						
T0438	ESP 30 for 762 mm opening	89.01	-	-	-	89.01	nr
T0439	ESP 36 for 914 mm opening	99.48	-	-	-	99.48	nr
T0440	ESP 48 for 1219 mm opening	120.16	-	-	-	120.16	nr
T0441	ESP 60 for 1524 mm opening	133.68	-	-	-	133.68	nr
T0442	ESP 72 for 1829 mm opening	147.19	-	-	-	147.19	nr
T0443	ESP 84 for 2134 mm opening	160.33	-	-	-	160.33	nr
T0444	ESP 96 for 2438 mm opening	169.96	-	-	-	169.96	nr
T0445	ESP 120 for 3048 mm opening	196.34	-	-	-	196.34	nr
	bulls-eye ref:						
T0446	BE 18 radius 229 mm	91.64	-	-	-	91.64	nr
	lath soffit strip ref:						
T0447	LSS 6 length 1830 mm, width 155 mm	8.87	5%	-	-	9.31	nr

Wall and Floor Tiles

Due to the wide range of wall and floor tiles available the following P.C. sums have been included to provide representative prices for these items.

		Supply Price £	Waste Factor %	Unload. Labour £	Unload. Plant £	Total Unit Cost £	Unit
	Glazed wall tiles:						
T0151	100 x 100 x 6.5 mm	0.18	5%	-	-	0.19	nr
T0152	150 x 150 x 6.5 mm	0.35	5%	-	-	0.37	nr
T0154	Ceramic tile adhesive	0.70	10%	0.02	-	0.79	ltr
T0155	Ceramic tile grout	0.88	10%	0.01	-	0.98	kg
	Patterned glazed wall tiles:						
T0156	100 x 100 x 6.5 mm	0.23	5%	-	-	0.24	nr
T0157	152 x 152 x 5.5 mm	0.42	5%	-	-	0.44	nr
T0158	200 x 150 x 6.5 mm	0.88	5%	-	-	0.92	nr
	Quarry tiles - brown:						
T0160	150 x 150 x 12.5 mm	0.55	5%	-	-	0.58	nr
	Extra over:						
T0161	rounded edge tiles	0.97	5%	-	-	1.02	nr
T0192	double rounded edge tiles	3.01	5%	-	-	3.16	nr
T0162	194 x 194 x 25 mm	2.33	5%	-	-	2.45	nr
	Extra over:						
T0163	rounded edge tiles	3.04	5%	-	-	3.19	nr
T0193	double rounded edge tiles	6.88	5%	-	-	7.22	nr
T0164	150 x 150 mm cove skirting	1.44	5%	-	-	1.51	nr
	Extra over:						
T0165	internal angle	4.25	5%	-	-	4.46	nr
T0166	external angle	4.25	5%	-	-	4.46	nr
	Porcelain floor tiles:						
T0175	150 x 150 x 8.5 mm	0.53	5%	-	-	0.56	nr
T0177	200 x 200 x 8.5 mm	0.83	5%	-	-	0.87	nr
T0180	150 x 100 x 8.5 mm round top cove skirting	1.89	5%	-	-	1.99	nr
	Extra over:						
T0181	internal angle	3.41	5%	-	-	3.58	nr
T0182	external angle	3.41	5%	-	-	3.58	nr
T0183	200 x 100 x 8.5 mm square top cove skirting	3.64	5%	-	-	3.82	nr
	Extra over:						
T0184	internal angle	3.41	5%	-	-	3.58	nr
T0185	external angle	3.41	5%	-	-	3.58	nr

Basic Prices of Materials		Supply Price £	Waste Factor %	Unload. Labour £	Unload. Plant £	Total Unit Cost £	Unit
T0186	150 x 100 x 8.5 mm sit-on cove	1.89	5%	-	-	1.99	nr
	Extra over:						
T0188	external angle	3.41	5%	-	-	3.58	nr
T0194	Silicone sealant, white (400 ml cartridge)	2.90	5%	-	-	3.05	nr
	Ready mixed mortars (**Guide Prices** based on London pricing levels) from Cemex:						
	Paving mortars (lime:sand):						
T0501	1:2.5	54.56	5%	-	-	57.29	tonne
T0502	1:6	52.16	5%	-	-	54.77	tonne
T0503	1:12	49.60	5%	-	-	52.08	tonne
	Screed mortars (retarded cement:sand):						
T0504	1:3	79.36	5%	-	-	83.33	tonne
T0505	1:4	76.65	5%	-	-	80.48	tonne
	Plastering mortars (lime:sand):						
T0506	1:12	54.60	5%	-	-	57.33	tonne
T0507	1:9	54.09	5%	-	-	56.79	tonne
	Floor Coverings						
	Nairn Marmoleum marbled pattern linoleum:						
T0600	2.5 mm sheet	15.60	10%	0.11	-	17.28	m2
T0601	3.2 mm sheet	18.72	10%	0.17	-	20.78	m2
	Nairn Artoleum linoleum sheet:						
T0602	2.5 mm sheet	18.72	10%	0.11	-	20.71	m2
	Nairn Marmoleum Dual marbled pattern linoleum tiles:						
T0610	333 x 333 x 2.5 mm tiles	20.80	10%	0.17	-	23.07	m2
	Tarkett vinyl sheet flooring:						
T0620	2.0 mm IQ Granite sheet 2m x 20 m	15.49	10%	0.11	-	17.16	m2
T0622	2.0 mm Eclipse 2m x 20 m	11.99	10%	0.13	-	13.33	m2
T0624	2.0 mm Safetred Universal 2m x 20 m	14.49	10%	0.11	-	16.06	m2
T0625	2.0 mm Safetread Dimension 2m x 20 m	16.49	10%	0.11	-	18.26	m2
T0626	2.0 mm Safetread Aqua 2m x 20 m	22.49	10%	0.11	-	24.86	m2
	Tarkett vinyl tiles:						
T0630	2.0 mm Standard tiles	10.49	10%	0.11	-	11.66	m2
T0631	2.0 mm Vylon plus	8.99	10%	0.11	-	10.01	m2
T0633	2.0 mm Tarkett Premium Eclipse/Primo tiles	12.99	10%	0.11	-	14.41	m2
T0636	2.0 mm Tarkett 'iQ' collection 'Eminent' tiles	21.49	10%	0.11	-	23.76	m2
T0637	2.0 mm IQ Granite	16.49	10%	0.11	-	18.26	m2
T0638	2.0 mm Somplan Plus	11.49	10%	0.11	-	12.76	m2
	Tarkett flooring accessories:						
T0651	100 mm x 2 mm gauge sit-on vinyl skirting	3.34	10%	-	-	3.67	m
T0652	100 mm x 2 mm gauge set-in vinyl skirting	5.69	10%	-	-	6.26	m
T0654	4 mm rod for cold welding	0.32	10%	-	-	0.35	m
	Jaymart Synthetic Rubber floor tiles and accessories (supplier's references shown in brackets). "Prialpas Central" 500 mm x 500 mm x 4 mm tiles; low profile studded finish; indoor quality:						
T0670	black (Group 1)	23.66	10%	0.22	-	26.27	m2
T0671	brown (Group 2)	26.36	10%	0.22	-	29.24	m2
T0672	colours (Group 3)	27.98	10%	0.22	-	31.02	m2
	"Prialpas Central" one-piece combined stair finish 480 mm girth in 1285 mm lengths; studded tread / smooth riser / stair nosing; indoor quality:						
T0675	black (Group 1)	21.17	10%	0.06	-	23.35	m
T0680	brown (Group 2)	26.00	10%	0.06	-	28.67	m
T0681	colours (Group 3)	26.00	10%	0.06	-	28.67	m
	Pre-formed internal coved angle sections:						
T0690	60 mm sit-on skirting (FL60), black (Group 1)	4.88	10%	-	-	5.37	m
T0691	60 mm sit-on skirting (FL60), brown (Group 2)	5.18	10%	-	-	5.69	m
T0693	100 mm set-in skirting (FL100), black (Group 1)	7.50	10%	-	-	8.25	m
T0694	100 mm set-in skirting (FL100), brown (Group 2)	7.97	10%	-	-	8.77	m
	Cork tiles, supplied by Siesta Cork Tile Co.						
	300 mm x 300 mm heavy density cork floor tiles:						
	Unsealed:						
T0700	4.8 mm	9.31	10%	0.11	-	10.36	m2
T0701	6.0 mm	10.85	10%	0.11	-	12.05	m2
	Pre-sealed:						
T0704	3.2 mm	10.95	10%	0.11	-	12.17	m2
T0705	6.0 mm	13.72	10%	0.11	-	15.21	m2
T0708	Corktile adhesive	3.78	10%	-	-	4.16	ltr
T0709	Quick dry tile sealer	4.86	10%	-	-	5.35	ltr
	Flooring Adhesives						
T0661	Laybond Safety Fix PVC tile/sheet adhesive	3.59	10%	-	-	3.95	ltr
T0662	Laybond Gripfill Plus contact adhesive	5.50	10%	-	-	6.05	ltr

Mortar, Plaster & Screeds Mix Analysis

The cost of labour in mixing is included in the gang rate per hour for plastering.
The cost of mixers or mortar mills should be costed in preliminaries.

A0501 Cement mortar (1:2)

Cement (bagged)	0.59 tonne	x	£	156.48	=	£	92.32
Building sand	1.64 tonne	x	£	26.57	=	£	43.57
						£	135.89
Waste	10%				=	£	13.59
Cost per m3					=	£	**149.48**

A0511 Cement mortar (1:3)

Cement (bagged)	0.44 tonne	x	£	156.48	=	£	68.85
Building sand	1.83 tonne	x	£	26.57	=	£	48.62
						£	117.47
Waste	10%				=	£	11.75
Cost per m3					=	£	**129.22**

A0512 Cement mortar (1:3) screeds

Cement (bagged)	0.44 tonne	x	£	156.48	=	£	68.85
Sharp sand BS 882 Zone M	1.83 tonne	x	£	27.78	=	£	50.84
						£	119.69
Waste	10%				=	£	11.97
Cost per m3					=	£	**131.66**

A0521 Cement mortar (1:4)

Cement (bagged)	0.35 tonne	x	£	156.48	=	£	54.77
Sharp sand BS 882 Zone M	1.94 tonne	x	£	27.78	=	£	53.89
						£	108.66
Waste	10%				=	£	10.87
Cost per m3					=	£	**119.53**

A0541 Cement, lime and sand mortar (1:1:6)

Cement (bagged)	0.23 tonne	x	£	156.48	=	£	35.99
Hydrated lime (del. in bags)	0.12 tonne	x	£	238.58	=	£	28.63
Building sand	1.93 tonne	x	£	26.57	=	£	51.28
						£	115.90
Waste	10%				=	£	11.59
Cost per m3					=	£	**127.49**

A0542 Cement, lime and sand mortar (1:2:9)

Cement (bagged)	0.16 tonne	x	£	156.48	=	£	25.04
Hydrated lime (del. in bags)	0.16 tonne	x	£	238.58	=	£	38.17
Building sand	1.98 tonne	x	£	26.57	=	£	52.61
						£	115.82
Waste	10%				=	£	11.58
Cost per m3					=	£	**127.40**

A0561 Fine concrete (1:1.5:3)

Cement (bagged)	0.42 tonne	x	£	156.48	=	£	65.72
Fine aggregate BS 882	0.87 tonne	x	£	32.60	=	£	28.36
Coarse agg, nat, cr, 14 mm BS 882	1.25 tonne	x	£	33.92	=	£	42.40
						£	136.48
Waste	10%				=	£	13.65
Cost per m3					=	£	**150.13**

A0556 Rough cast finish (2:1:6:3)

Cement (bagged)	0.38 tonne	x	£	156.48	=	£	59.46
Hydrated lime (del. in bags)	0.09 tonne	x	£	238.58	=	£	21.47
Sharp sand BS 882 Zone M	1.57 tonne	x	£	27.78	=	£	43.61
Crushed stone 14 - 6 mm	0.57 tonne	x	£	19.72	=	£	11.24
						£	135.78
Waste	10%				=	£	13.58
Cost per m3					=	£	**149.36**

Mortar, Plaster & Screeds Mix Analysis

A0555 Granolithic paving (1:2.5)

Cement (bagged)	0.54 tonne	x	£	156.48	=	£	84.50
Leics. granite chips 14 mm	1.97 tonne	x	£	50.94	=	£	100.35
						£	184.85
Waste	10%				=	£	18.49
Cost per m3					=	£	**203.34**

A0553 Vermiculite lightweight screed (1:8)

Cement (bagged)	0.23 tonne	x	£	156.48	=	£	35.21
Vermiculite aggregate	1.20 m3	x	£	171.06	=	£	205.27
						£	240.48
Waste	10%				=	£	24.05
Cost per m3					=	£	**264.53**

A0554 Lightweight concrete screed (1:8)

Cement (bagged)	0.20 tonne	x	£	156.48	=	£	31.30
Lytag pump grade screed aggregate	0.78 tonne	x	£	143.52	=	£	111.95
						£	143.25
Waste	10%				=	£	14.33
Cost per m3					=	£	**157.58**

Analysis of plastering mortars using Cemex ready mixed mortars

X0542 Cement lime mortar (1:1/4:3)

Cement (bagged)	0.38 tonne	x	£	156.48	=	£	59.46
Cemex mortar plaster 1:12 (int)	1.52 tonne	x	£	57.33	=	£	87.14
						£	146.60
Waste	10%				=	£	14.66
Cost per m3					=	£	**161.26**

X0541 Cement lime mortar (1:1/2:4.1/2)

Cement (bagged)	0.28 tonne	x	£	156.48	=	£	43.81
Cemex mortar plaster 1:9 (ext)	1.63 tonne	x	£	56.79	=	£	92.57
						£	136.38
Waste	10%				=	£	13.64
Cost per m3					=	£	**150.02**

Unit Rates

	Man-Hours	Net Labour Price £	Net Mats Price £	Net Unit Price £	Unit
UNIT RATES					
TA **IN SITU FINISHINGS**					
GYPSUM PLASTERS					
001 **2 mm Thistle Multi- Finish on Thistle background plasters;**					
8 mm and 11 mm bonding;					
11 mm metal lathing (including pricking up coat);					
11 mm browning;					
002 To walls:					
10 mm two coat work, to concrete in extending/repairing existing finishes (Bonding):					
over 300 mm wide	0.60	14.10	2.84	**16.94**	m2
not exceeding 300 mm wide	1.19	27.98	2.84	**30.82**	m2
isolated areas not exceeding 1.00 m2 including flush joint to existing	0.70	16.53	2.84	**19.37**	m2
13 mm two coat work, to brick, block or stone walls, in extending/repairing existing finishes (Browning):					
over 300 mm wide	0.57	13.39	2.86	**16.25**	m2
not exceeding 300 mm wide	1.14	26.99	2.86	**29.85**	m2
isolated areas not exceeding 1.00 m2 including flush joint to existing	0.65	15.33	2.86	**18.19**	m2
Extra over for dubbing out plasterwork in extending/repairing existing finishes for each additional 10 mm thickness:					
over 300 mm wide	0.26	6.09	1.29	**7.38**	m2
not exceeding 300 mm wide	0.52	12.16	1.29	**13.45**	m2
isolated areas not exceeding 1.00 m2 including flush joint to existing	0.30	7.06	1.29	**8.35**	m2
Extra over for dubbing out plasterwork in extending/repairing existing finishes for each additional 12 mm thickness:					
over 300 mm wide	0.28	6.56	1.55	**8.11**	m2
not exceeding 300 mm wide	0.56	13.13	1.55	**14.68**	m2
isolated areas not exceeding 1.00 m2 including flush joint to existing	0.32	7.53	1.55	**9.08**	m2
003 To sides of isolated columns:					
10 mm two coat work, to concrete; (Bonding):					
over 300 mm wide	0.62	14.59	2.84	**17.43**	m2
not exceeding 300 mm wide	1.24	29.19	2.84	**32.03**	m2
10 mm two coat work, to plasterboard, including scrimming joints; (Bonding):					
over 300 mm wide	0.95	22.43	3.23	**25.66**	m2
not exceeding 300 mm wide	1.90	44.87	3.61	**48.48**	m2
13 mm two coat work, to low-suction surfaces; (Bonding):					
over 300 mm wide	0.60	14.10	4.18	**18.28**	m2
not exceeding 300 mm wide	1.19	27.98	4.18	**32.16**	m2
13 mm two coat work, to brick or block; (Browning):					
over 300 mm wide	0.59	13.86	2.86	**16.72**	m2
not exceeding 300 mm wide	1.17	27.72	2.86	**30.58**	m2
13 mm three coat work, to metal lathing; (Bonding):					
over 300 mm wide	0.70	16.41	5.52	**21.93**	m2
not exceeding 300 mm wide	1.39	32.85	5.52	**38.37**	m2
004 To ceilings:					
10 mm two coat work, to concrete in extending/repairing existing finishes (Bonding):					
over 300 mm wide	0.59	14.03	2.84	**16.87**	m2
not exceeding 300 mm wide	1.19	28.08	2.84	**30.92**	m2
isolated areas not exceeding 1.00 m2 including flush joint to existing	0.89	21.04	3.23	**24.27**	m2
13 mm two coat work, to low-suction surfaces, in extending/repairing existing finishes (Browning):					
over 300 mm wide	1.78	42.06	3.61	**45.67**	m2
not exceeding 300 mm wide	0.63	14.90	4.18	**19.08**	m2
isolated areas not exceeding 1.00 m2 including flush joint to existing	1.26	29.80	4.18	**33.98**	m2
Extra over for dubbing out plasterwork in extending/repairing existing finishes for each additional 10 mm thickness:					
over 300 mm wide	0.67	15.80	5.52	**21.32**	m2
not exceeding 300 mm wide	1.34	31.62	5.52	**37.14**	m2
isolated areas not exceeding 1.00 m2 including flush joint to existing	0.74	17.52	2.84	**20.36**	m2
Extra over for dubbing out plasterwork in extending/repairing existing finishes for each additional 12 mm thickness:					
over 300 mm wide	1.48	35.02	2.84	**37.86**	m2
not exceeding 300 mm wide	0.85	19.95	2.84	**22.79**	m2
isolated areas not exceeding 1.00 m2 including flush joint to existing	0.78	18.49	4.18	**22.67**	m2
005 To sides, soffits and tops of isolated beams:					
10 mm two coat work, to concrete in extending/repairing existing finishes (Bonding):					
over 300 mm wide	0.74	17.52	2.84	**20.36**	m2
not exceeding 300 mm wide	1.48	35.02	2.84	**37.86**	m2
isolated areas not exceeding 1.00 m2 including flush joint to existing	1.14	26.92	3.23	**30.15**	m2
13 mm two coat work, to brick, block or stone walls, in extending/repairing existing finishes (Browning):					
over 300 mm wide	2.28	53.84	3.61	**57.45**	m2
not exceeding 300 mm wide	0.72	17.03	4.18	**21.21**	m2
isolated areas not exceeding 1.00 m2 including flush joint to existing	1.44	34.05	4.18	**38.23**	m2
Extra over for dubbing out plasterwork in extending/repairing existing finishes for each additional 10 mm thickness:					
over 300 mm wide	0.83	19.69	5.52	**25.21**	m2
not exceeding 300 mm wide	1.67	39.41	5.52	**44.93**	m2
isolated areas not exceeding 1.00 m2 including flush joint to existing	0.93	21.89	2.84	**24.73**	m2
Extra over for dubbing out plasterwork in extending/repairing existing finishes for each additional 12 mm thickness:					
over 300 mm wide	1.85	43.78	2.84	**46.62**	m2
not exceeding 300 mm wide	1.07	25.29	2.84	**28.13**	m2

Unit Rates	Man-Hours	Net Labour Price £	Net Mats Price £	Net Unit Price £	Unit
isolated areas not exceeding 1.00 m2 including flush joint to existing	0.91	21.40	4.18	**25.58**	m2
006 Additions to Thistle Browning					
007 Extra over 13 mm two coat work if Thistle Tough Coat:					
over 300 mm wide	-	-	0.07	**0.07**	m2
not exceeding 300 mm wide	-	-	0.07	**0.07**	m2
in repairs in isolated areas not exceeding 1.00 m2 including flush joint to existing	-	-	0.07	**0.07**	m2
Note: 008 not used					
009 Thistle board finish plaster to plasterboard; 5 mm two coat work including scrimming joints					
010 To walls:					
over 300 mm wide	0.31	7.34	1.79	**9.13**	m2
not exceeding 300 mm wide	0.62	14.71	1.79	**16.50**	m2
in repairs in isolated areas not exceeding 1.00 m2 including flush joint to existing	0.36	8.57	1.79	**10.36**	m2
011 To sides of isolated columns:					
over 300 mm wide	0.40	9.42	1.79	**11.21**	m2
not exceeding 300 mm wide	0.80	18.80	1.79	**20.59**	m2
in repairs in isolated areas not exceeding 1.00 m2 including flush joint to existing	0.46	10.93	1.79	**12.72**	m2
012 To ceilings:					
over 300 mm wide	0.39	9.19	1.79	**10.98**	m2
not exceeding 300 mm wide	0.78	18.40	1.79	**20.19**	m2
in repairs in isolated areas not exceeding 1.00 m2 including flush joint to existing	0.45	10.70	1.79	**12.49**	m2
013 To sides, soffits and tops of isolated beams:					
over 300 mm wide	0.49	11.45	1.79	**13.24**	m2
not exceeding 300 mm wide	0.97	22.88	1.79	**24.67**	m2
in repairs in isolated areas not exceeding 1.00 m2 including flush joint to existing	0.56	13.18	1.79	**14.97**	m2
Note: 014-015 not used					
016 Thistle universal one coat plaster					
017 To brick or block walls 13 mm thick:					
over 300 mm wide	0.35	8.17	4.25	**12.42**	m2
not exceeding 300 mm wide	0.69	16.34	4.25	**20.59**	m2
018 To brick or block walls 19 mm thick:					
over 300 mm wide	0.43	10.23	6.18	**16.41**	m2
not exceeding 300 mm wide	0.87	20.43	6.18	**26.61**	m2
019 To brick or block walls 25 mm thick:					
over 300 mm wide	0.52	12.26	8.11	**20.37**	m2
not exceeding 300 mm wide	1.04	24.51	8.11	**32.62**	m2
020 To concrete walls 8 mm thick:					
over 300 mm wide	0.26	6.14	3.09	**9.23**	m2
not exceeding 300 mm wide	0.52	12.26	3.09	**15.35**	m2
021 To sides of isolated brick or block columns 13 mm thick:					
over 300 mm wide	0.43	10.23	4.25	**14.48**	m2
not exceeding 300 mm wide	0.87	20.43	4.25	**24.68**	m2
022 To sides of isolated concrete columns 8 mm thick:					
over 300 mm wide	0.35	8.17	3.09	**11.26**	m2
not exceeding 300 mm wide	0.69	16.34	3.09	**19.43**	m2
023 To concrete ceilings 8 mm thick:					
over 300 mm wide	0.37	8.78	3.09	**11.87**	m2
not exceeding 300 mm wide	0.75	17.59	3.09	**20.68**	m2
024 To plasterboard ceilings 5 mm thick including scrimming joints:					
over 300 mm wide	0.33	7.82	2.70	**10.52**	m2
not exceeding 300 mm wide	0.66	15.63	2.70	**18.33**	m2
025 To sides, soffits and tops of concrete beams 8 mm thick:					
over 300 mm wide	0.46	10.82	3.09	**13.91**	m2
not exceeding 300 mm wide	0.92	21.68	3.09	**24.77**	m2
026 To plasterboard sides, soffits and tops of isolated beams 5 mm thick including scrimming joints:					
over 300 mm wide	0.41	9.73	2.70	**12.43**	m2
not exceeding 300 mm wide	0.83	19.48	2.70	**22.18**	m2
027 Thistle Multi-Finish to (moist) sanded undercoats; 3 mm finishing coat					
028 To walls:					
over 300 mm wide	0.22	5.29	0.75	**6.04**	m2
not exceeding 300 mm wide	0.45	10.56	0.75	**11.31**	m2
in repairs in isolated areas not exceeding 1.00 m2 including flush joint to existing	0.26	6.09	0.50	**6.59**	m2
029 To sides of isolated columns:					
over 300 mm wide	0.29	6.73	0.75	**7.48**	m2
not exceeding 300 mm wide	0.57	13.51	0.75	**14.26**	m2
in repairs in isolated areas not exceeding 1.00 m2 including flush joint to existing	0.33	7.79	0.50	**8.29**	m2

		Man-Hours	Net Labour Price £	Net Mats Price £	Net Unit Price £	Unit
030	To ceilings:					
	over 300 mm wide	0.27	6.45	0.75	**7.20**	m2
	not exceeding 300 mm wide	0.55	12.89	0.75	**13.64**	m2
	in repairs in isolated areas not exceeding 1.00 m2 including flush joint to existing	0.31	7.30	0.50	**7.80**	m2
031	To sides, soffits and tops of isolated beams:					
	over 300 mm wide	0.30	7.04	0.75	**7.79**	m2
	not exceeding 300 mm wide	0.60	14.05	0.75	**14.80**	m2
	in repairs in isolated areas not exceeding 1.00 m2 including flush joint to existing	0.34	8.03	0.50	**8.53**	m2
032	**Thistle Multi-finish to mature concrete surfaces; one coat; 3 mm finished thickness**					
033	To walls:					
	over 300 mm wide	0.24	5.60	1.00	**6.60**	m2
	not exceeding 300 mm wide	0.47	11.19	1.00	**12.19**	m2
034	To sides of isolated columns:					
	over 300 mm wide	0.30	7.16	1.00	**8.16**	m2
	not exceeding 300 mm wide	0.61	14.33	1.00	**15.33**	m2
035	To ceilings:					
	over 300 mm wide	0.30	7.01	1.00	**8.01**	m2
	not exceeding 300 mm wide	0.59	14.00	1.00	**15.00**	m2
036	To sides, soffits and tops of isolated beams:					
	over 300 mm wide	0.37	8.71	1.00	**9.71**	m2
	not exceeding 300 mm wide	0.74	17.40	1.00	**18.40**	m2
	CEMENTITIOUS PLASTERS					
037	**1.5 mm TARMAC HIGH IMPACT plaster finish on LIMELITE background plasters**					
038	To walls:					
	13 mm two coat work, Cement Backing Plaster (Also `X ADDS'):					
	over 300 mm wide	0.41	9.71	3.56	**13.27**	m2
	not exceeding 300 mm wide	0.82	19.39	3.56	**22.95**	m2
	13 mm two coat work, Cement Browning Plaster:					
	over 300 mm wide	0.46	10.77	2.73	**13.50**	m2
	not exceeding 300 mm wide	0.91	21.56	2.73	**24.29**	m2
	14 mm three coat work, to metal lathing, Cement Browning:					
	over 300 mm wide	0.54	12.73	4.87	**17.60**	m2
	not exceeding 300 mm wide	1.08	25.46	4.87	**30.33**	m2
	13 mm two coat work, Cement Renovating Plaster:					
	over 300 mm wide	0.46	10.77	4.34	**15.11**	m2
	not exceeding 300 mm wide	0.91	21.56	4.34	**25.90**	m2
039	To sides of isolated columns:					
	13 mm two coat work, Cement Backing Plaster (Also 'X ADDS'):					
	over 300 mm wide	0.52	12.33	3.56	**15.89**	m2
	not exceeding 300 mm wide	1.04	24.65	3.56	**28.21**	m2
	13 mm two coat work, Cement Browning Plaster:					
	over 300 mm wide	0.58	13.72	2.73	**16.45**	m2
	not exceeding 300 mm wide	1.16	27.42	2.73	**30.15**	m2
	14 mm three coat work, to metal lathing, Cement Browning:					
	over 300 mm wide	0.69	16.20	4.87	**21.07**	m2
	not exceeding 300 mm wide	1.32	31.20	4.87	**36.07**	m2
	13 mm two coat work, Cement Renovating Plaster:					
	over 300 mm wide	0.58	13.72	4.34	**18.06**	m2
	not exceeding 300 mm wide	1.16	27.42	4.34	**31.76**	m2
040	To ceilings:					
	13 mm two coat work, Cement Backing Plaster (Also 'X ADDS'):					
	over 300 mm wide	0.51	12.11	3.56	**15.67**	m2
	not exceeding 300 mm wide	1.03	24.23	3.56	**27.79**	m2
	13 mm two coat work, Cement Browning Plaster:					
	over 300 mm wide	0.57	13.46	2.73	**16.19**	m2
	not exceeding 300 mm wide	1.14	26.90	2.73	**29.63**	m2
	14 mm three coat work, to metal lathing, Cement Browning:					
	over 300 mm wide	0.67	15.89	4.87	**20.76**	m2
	not exceeding 300 mm wide	1.35	31.81	4.87	**36.68**	m2
041	To sides, soffits and tops of isolated beams:					
	13 mm two coat work, Cement Backing Plaster (Also 'X ADDS'):					
	over 300 mm wide	0.64	15.09	3.56	**18.65**	m2
	not exceeding 300 mm wide	1.28	30.16	3.56	**33.72**	m2
	13 mm two coat work, Cement Browning Plaster:					
	over 300 mm wide	0.71	16.77	2.73	**19.50**	m2
	not exceeding 300 mm wide	1.42	33.51	2.73	**36.24**	m2
	14 mm three coat work, to metal lathing, Cement Browning:					
	over 300 mm wide	0.84	19.79	4.87	**24.66**	m2
	not exceeding 300 mm wide	1.68	39.60	4.87	**44.47**	m2

Unit Rates

		Man-Hours	Net Labour Price £	Net Mats Price £	Net Unit Price £	Unit
	CEMENT RENDERING (INTERNAL)					
042	**Cement and sand (1:3) trowelled finish to brickwork, blockwork or concrete**					
043	To walls in extending/repairing existing finishes:					
	12 mm one coat work:					
	over 300 mm wide	0.46	10.93	1.55	**12.48**	m2
	not exceeding 300 mm wide	0.94	22.13	1.55	**23.68**	m2
	isolated areas not exceeding 1.00 m2 including flush joint to existing	0.54	12.66	1.55	**14.21**	m2
	18 mm two coat work:					
	over 300 mm wide	0.68	16.06	2.33	**18.39**	m2
	not exceeding 300 mm wide	1.37	32.35	2.33	**34.68**	m2
	isolated areas not exceeding 1.00 m2 including flush joint to existing	0.78	18.49	2.33	**20.82**	m2
044	**Cement, lime and sand (1:1:6) trowelled finish to brickwork, blockwork or concrete**					
045	To walls in extending/repairing existing finishes:					
	12 mm one coat work:					
	over 300 mm wide	0.46	10.93	1.53	**12.46**	m2
	not exceeding 300 mm wide	0.94	22.13	1.53	**23.66**	m2
	isolated areas not exceeding 1.00 m2 including flush joint to existing	0.54	12.66	1.53	**14.19**	m2
	18 mm two coat work:					
	over 300 mm wide	0.68	16.06	2.29	**18.35**	m2
	not exceeding 300 mm wide	1.37	32.35	2.29	**34.64**	m2
	isolated areas not exceeding 1.00 m2 including flush joint to existing	0.78	18.49	2.29	**20.78**	m2
046	ADD TO THE FOREGOING PRICES for:					
	cement and sand (1:2) spatterdash applied to walls as key:					
	over 300 mm wide	0.17	4.09	0.75	**4.84**	m2
	not exceeding 300 mm wide	0.35	8.17	0.75	**8.92**	m2
	neat unibond adhesive applied to walls as key:					
	over 300 mm wide	0.13	3.07	3.63	**6.70**	m2
	not exceeding 300 mm wide	0.26	6.14	3.63	**9.77**	m2
047	**Dubbing out in cement and sand (1:3) on brick or block**					
048	To walls in extending/repairing existing finishes:					
	over 300 mm wide:					
	6 mm thick	0.18	4.13	0.78	**4.91**	m2
	12 mm thick	0.32	7.53	1.55	**9.08**	m2
	19 mm thick	0.43	10.23	2.33	**12.56**	m2
	not exceeding 300 mm wide:					
	6 mm thick	0.35	8.27	0.78	**9.05**	m2
	12 mm thick	0.65	15.33	1.55	**16.88**	m2
	19 mm thick	0.87	20.43	2.33	**22.76**	m2
	isolated areas not exceeding 1.00 m2:					
	6 mm thick	0.21	4.86	0.78	**5.64**	m2
	12 mm thick	0.37	8.76	1.55	**10.31**	m2
	19 mm thick	0.49	11.67	2.33	**14.00**	m2
049	**Labours on Plastering**					
050	External angles	0.16	3.80	-	**3.80**	m
051	Rounded internal angles:					
	not exceeding 10 mm radius	0.19	4.37	-	**4.37**	m
	10 - 100 mm radius	0.28	6.71	-	**6.71**	m
052	Rounded external angles:					
	not exceeding 10 mm radius	0.16	3.80	-	**3.80**	m
	10 - 100 mm radius	0.25	5.83	-	**5.83**	m
053	Fair joint to flush edges of existing finishes	0.06	1.46	-	**1.46**	m
054	Making good and labour finishing around steel joists, angles, pipes and the like:					
	over 2.00 m girth	0.07	1.75	-	**1.75**	m
	not exceeding 0.30 m girth	0.10	2.34	-	**2.34**	Nr
	0.30 - 1.00 m girth	0.12	2.93	-	**2.93**	Nr
	1.00 - 2.00 m girth	0.16	3.80	-	**3.80**	Nr
055	**Repairs to existing plastering**					
056	Cut out damaged plaster and make good in Thistle plaster with flush joints to existing all round:					
	to brick or block walls:					
	two coat work 13 mm thick (**Browning**):					
	not exceeding 1.00 m2	1.85	43.78	2.86	**46.64**	Nr
	1.00 - 2.00 m2	3.30	77.84	5.72	**83.56**	Nr
	setting coat only; 2 mm thick:					
	not exceeding 1.00 m2	1.19	27.98	0.50	**28.48**	Nr
	1.00 - 2.00 m2	2.27	53.51	1.00	**54.51**	Nr
	to concrete ceilings:					
	two coat work 13 mm thick (**Bonding**):					
	not exceeding 1.00 m2	2.73	64.47	2.86	**67.33**	Nr
	1.00 - 2.00 m2	4.48	105.80	5.38	**111.18**	Nr
	setting coat only; 2 mm thick:					
	not exceeding 1.00 m2	1.40	33.08	0.50	**33.58**	Nr
	1.00 - 2.00 m2	2.70	63.74	1.00	**64.74**	Nr

Unit Rates

		Man-Hours	Net Labour Price £	Net Mats Price £	Net Unit Price £	Unit
057	**Extra over** for dubbing out with Thistle bonding coat, if required, per 12 mm additional thickness:					
	not exceeding 1.00 m2	0.73	17.26	3.35	**20.61**	Nr
	1.00 - 2.00 m2	1.08	25.53	6.70	**32.23**	Nr
058	Cut out crack in plaster and make good with Thistle Tough Coat plaster with flush joints to both sides:					
	average 25 mm wide	0.19	4.37	0.25	**4.62**	m
	average 75 mm wide	0.26	6.09	0.25	**6.34**	m
059	Cut out damaged cement rendering and make good with cement and sand (1:3) trowelled smooth; all round fair flush joint to existing:					
	to walls:					
	one coat work 12 mm thick:					
	not exceeding 1.00 m2	1.75	41.35	1.55	**42.90**	Nr
	1.00 - 2.00 m2	3.04	71.77	3.10	**74.87**	Nr
	two coat work 18 mm thick:					
	not exceeding 1.00 m2	2.27	53.51	2.33	**55.84**	Nr
	1.00 - 2.00 m2	3.81	90.00	4.65	**94.65**	Nr
060	**Extra over** for dubbing out with cement and sand (1:3), if required, per 12 mm additional thickness:					
	not exceeding 1.00 m2	0.51	11.93	1.55	**13.48**	Nr
	1.00 - 2.00 m2	0.77	18.25	3.10	**21.35**	Nr
061	**Expamet internal beads fixed with plaster dabs**					
062	Ref 550 angle bead	0.16	3.66	0.97	**4.63**	m
063	Ref 558 maxicon angle bead	0.16	3.66	0.77	**4.43**	m
064	Ref 558 movement bead	0.16	3.66	8.05	**11.71**	m
065	Ref 562 plaster stop bead, 10 mm deep	0.12	2.93	1.22	**4.15**	m
066	Ref 563 plaster stop bead 13 mm deep	0.12	2.93	1.19	**4.12**	m
067	Ref 565 plaster stop bead 16 mm deep	0.12	2.93	1.69	**4.62**	m
068	Ref 566 plaster stop bead 19 mm deep	0.12	2.93	1.69	**4.62**	m
069	Ref 579 architrave bead	0.14	3.21	2.59	**5.80**	m
070	Ref 580 architrave bead	0.14	3.21	2.58	**5.79**	m
071	Ref 585 architrave bead	0.14	3.21	2.58	**5.79**	m
072	Ref 568 architrave bead	0.14	3.21	2.66	**5.87**	m
073	Ref 569 depth gauge bead	0.12	2.93	1.60	**4.53**	m
074	Ref 559 square nose angle bead	0.16	3.66	1.74	**5.40**	m
075	**Expamet dry wall beads fixed with nails to timber**					
076	Ref 548 corner bead	0.15	3.50	1.08	**4.58**	m
077	Ref 567 plasterboard edging bead	0.15	3.50	2.92	**6.42**	m
078	Ref 568 plasterboard edging bead	0.15	3.50	2.99	**6.49**	m
079	Ref 553 thin coat angle bead 3 mm	0.12	2.93	0.93	**3.86**	m
080	Ref 554 thin coat angle bead 16 mm	0.12	2.93	0.91	**3.84**	m
081	Ref 560 thin coat stop bead 3 mm	0.10	2.34	1.40	**3.74**	m
082	Ref 561 thin coat stop bead 6 mm	0.10	2.34	1.37	**3.71**	m
TB	**EXTERNAL RENDERING**					
	Note: prices for plain face cement and sand renderings are the same as for internal renderings - see items					
001	**External cement, lime and sand (1:1:6) rendering to brickwork, blockwork or concrete**					
002	12 mm one coat rendering to walls with:					
	wood float finish:					
	over 300 mm wide	0.35	8.17	1.53	**9.70**	m2
	not exceeding 300 mm wide	0.69	16.34	1.53	**17.87**	m2
	scraped finish:					
	over 300 mm wide	0.39	9.19	1.53	**10.72**	m2
	not exceeding 300 mm wide	0.78	18.40	1.53	**19.93**	m2
003	18 mm two coat rendering to walls with:					
	wood float finish:					
	over 300 mm wide	0.52	12.26	2.29	**14.55**	m2
	not exceeding 300 mm wide	1.04	24.51	2.29	**26.80**	m2
	scraped finish:					
	over 300 mm wide	0.56	13.27	2.29	**15.56**	m2
	not exceeding 300 mm wide	1.13	26.57	2.29	**28.86**	m2
004	ADD TO THE FOREGOING PRICES for:					
	integral waterproofer in rendering:					
	12 mm thick	-	-	0.34	**0.34**	m2
	18 mm thick	-	-	0.51	**0.51**	m2
	cement and sand (1:2) spatterdash coat to provide key:					
	over 300 mm wide	0.17	4.09	0.75	**4.84**	m2
	not exceeding 300 mm wide	0.35	8.17	0.75	**8.92**	m2

Unit Rates

		Man-Hours	Net Labour Price £	Net Mats Price £	Net Unit Price £	Unit
005	**Tyrolean rendering in three coats to finish 7 mm thick with honeycomb finish on and including cement, lime and sand (1:1:6) backing to brickwork, blockwork or concrete**					
006	Tyrolean rendering on 12 mm one coat backing to walls:					
	over 300 mm wide	0.56	13.27	6.19	**19.46**	m2
	not exceeding 300 mm wide	1.13	26.57	6.19	**32.76**	m2
	in repairs in isolated areas not exceeding 1.00 m2 including flush joint to existing	0.65	15.33	6.19	**21.52**	m2
007	Tyrolean rendering on 18 mm two coat backing to walls:					
	over 300 mm wide	0.74	17.36	6.95	**24.31**	m2
	not exceeding 300 mm wide	1.47	34.74	6.95	**41.69**	m2
	in repairs in isolated areas not exceeding 1.00 m2 including flush joint to existing	0.85	19.95	6.95	**26.90**	m2
008	ADD TO THE FOREGOING PRICES for rubbed finish to Tyrolean rendering before final set	0.13	3.07	-	**3.07**	m2
009	**Cemrend textured surface coating over Surface primer on and including cement, lime and sand (1:1:6:) backings to brickwork, blockwork or concrete**					
010	Cemrend coating on 12 mm one coat backing to walls:					
	over 300 mm wide	0.59	13.89	8.95	**22.84**	m2
	not exceeding 300 mm wide	1.18	27.77	8.95	**36.72**	m2
	Cemrend coating on 18 mm two coat backing to walls:					
	over 300 mm wide	0.76	17.97	9.71	**27.68**	m2
	not exceeding 300 mm wide	1.52	35.94	9.71	**45.65**	m2
011	**Roughcast external rendering on and including cement, lime and sand (1:2:9) backings to brickwork, blockwork or concrete**					
012	Roughcast on 12 mm one coat backing to walls:					
	over 300 mm wide	0.80	18.96	2.72	**21.68**	m2
	not exceeding 300 mm wide	1.61	37.95	2.72	**40.67**	m2
	in repairs in isolated areas not exceeding 1.00 m2 including joint to existing	0.93	21.89	2.72	**24.61**	m2
013	Roughcast on 18 mm two coat backing to walls:					
	over 300 mm wide	1.05	24.82	3.49	**28.31**	m2
	not exceeding 300 mm wide	2.10	49.62	3.49	**53.11**	m2
	in repairs in isolated areas not exceeding 1.00 m2 including joint to existing	1.21	28.46	3.49	**31.95**	m2
014	ADD TO THE FOREGOING PRICES for integral waterproofer in backing coats:					
	12 mm thick	-	-	0.25	**0.25**	m2
	18 mm thick	-	-	0.38	**0.38**	m2
015	**Drydash (pebbledash) finish of Derbyshire Spar chippings on and including cement, lime and sand (1:2:9) backings to brickwork, blockwork or concrete**					
016	Drydash finish on 18 mm two coat backing to walls:					
	over 300 mm wide	1.11	26.26	2.96	**29.22**	m2
	not exceeding 300 mm wide	2.23	52.54	2.96	**55.50**	m2
017	**Labours on external finishes**					
018	External angles	0.19	4.37	-	**4.37**	m
019	Fair joint to flush edges of existing finishes	0.06	1.46	-	**1.46**	m
020	Making good and labour finishing around steel joists, angles, pipes and the like:					
	over 2.00 m girth	0.09	2.05	-	**2.05**	m
	not exceeding 0.30 m girth	0.12	2.93	-	**2.93**	Nr
	0.30 - 1.00 m girth	0.15	3.50	-	**3.50**	Nr
	1.00 - 2.00 m girth	0.19	4.37	-	**4.37**	Nr
	EXTERNAL BEADS					
021	**Expamet external beads fixed with dabs of mortar**					
022	Ref 590 movement bead	0.16	3.80	9.06	**12.86**	m
023	Ref 570 render stop	0.15	3.50	1.28	**4.78**	m
024	Ref 545 angle bead	0.16	3.80	4.11	**7.91**	m
025	Ref 546 stop bead	0.15	3.50	3.65	**7.15**	m
026	Ref 533 render stop type 2	0.15	3.50	3.65	**7.15**	m
TC	**GRANOLITHIC**					
001	**Granolithic paving (1:2.5) trowelled finish laid level and to falls only**					
	Note: 002 not used					
003	To floors in extending/repairing existing paving:					
	over 300 mm wide:					
	25 mm thick	0.41	9.73	5.08	**14.81**	m2
	32 mm thick	0.43	10.23	6.51	**16.74**	m2
	38 mm thick	0.45	10.70	7.73	**18.43**	m2
	50 mm thick	0.49	11.67	10.17	**21.84**	m2
	not exceeding 300 mm wide:					
	25 mm thick	0.81	19.22	5.08	**24.30**	m2
	32 mm thick	0.86	20.19	6.51	**26.70**	m2
	38 mm thick	0.91	21.40	7.73	**29.13**	m2
	50 mm thick	0.99	23.36	10.17	**33.53**	m2

Unit Rates

	Man-Hours	Net Labour Price £	Net Mats Price £	Net Unit Price £	Unit
isolated areas not exceeding 1.00 m2 including flush joint to existing:					
25 mm thick	0.47	11.19	5.08	**16.27**	m2
32 mm thick	0.49	11.67	6.51	**18.18**	m2
38 mm thick	0.53	12.40	7.73	**20.13**	m2
50 mm thick	0.57	13.39	10.17	**23.56**	m2
Note: 004 not used					
005 To floors in extending/repairing existing paving:					
over 300 mm wide:					
25 mm thick	0.62	14.59	5.08	**19.67**	m2
32 mm thick	0.65	15.33	6.51	**21.84**	m2
38 mm thick	0.68	16.06	7.73	**23.79**	m2
50 mm thick	0.75	17.76	10.17	**27.93**	m2
not exceeding 300 mm wide:					
25 mm thick	1.23	28.95	5.08	**34.03**	m2
32 mm thick	1.30	30.65	6.51	**37.16**	m2
38 mm thick	1.37	32.35	7.73	**40.08**	m2
50 mm thick	1.50	35.52	10.17	**45.69**	m2
isolated areas not exceeding 1.00 m2 including flush joint to existing:					
25 mm thick	0.71	16.79	5.08	**21.87**	m2
32 mm thick	0.74	17.52	6.51	**24.03**	m2
38 mm thick	0.78	18.49	7.73	**26.22**	m2
50 mm thick	0.87	20.43	10.17	**30.60**	m2
006 To treads 250 mm wide:					
25 mm thick	0.25	5.93	1.22	**7.15**	m
32 mm thick	0.26	6.14	1.63	**7.77**	m
38 mm thick	0.28	6.56	2.03	**8.59**	m
007 To risers 175 mm wide:					
25 mm thick	0.28	6.56	1.02	**7.58**	m
32 mm thick	0.30	7.01	1.22	**8.23**	m
38 mm thick	0.32	7.44	1.42	**8.86**	m
008 To undercut risers 175 mm wide:					
25 mm thick	0.33	7.89	1.02	**8.91**	m
32 mm thick	0.35	8.31	1.22	**9.53**	m
38 mm thick	0.37	8.76	1.42	**10.18**	m
009 19 mm to side of open string 350 mm wide	0.54	12.70	1.42	**14.12**	m
010 19 mm to side of string average 150 mm wide including cove to treads and risers	0.41	9.63	0.61	**10.24**	m
011 19 mm to top of string including arris:					
100 mm wide	0.28	6.56	0.41	**6.97**	m
150 mm wide	0.30	7.01	0.61	**7.62**	m
012 19 mm to top of string including two arrises:					
100 mm wide	0.42	9.82	0.41	**10.23**	m
150 mm wide	0.44	10.30	0.61	**10.91**	m
013 19 x 50 mm wide to soffit of string including arris and fair edge	0.42	9.82	0.20	**10.02**	m
014 19 mm skirting with rounded top edge and cove to paving:					
150 mm high	0.46	10.93	0.61	**11.54**	m
Extra over for:					
ends	0.13	3.07	-	**3.07**	Nr
angles	0.14	3.28	-	**3.28**	Nr
225 mm (average) high and raking	0.51	12.04	0.81	**12.85**	m
Extra over for:					
ends	0.14	3.28	-	**3.28**	Nr
angles	0.15	3.50	-	**3.50**	Nr
ramp	0.14	3.28	-	**3.28**	Nr
015 19 mm covering to top and one side of kerb including one arris and one cove to paving:					
100 mm wide x 75 mm high	0.46	10.93	0.61	**11.54**	m
Extra over for:					
ends	0.13	3.07	-	**3.07**	Nr
angles	0.14	3.28	-	**3.28**	Nr
150 mm wide x 150 mm high	0.62	14.69	1.22	**15.91**	m
Extra over for:					
ends	0.15	3.50	-	**3.50**	Nr
angles	0.17	3.94	-	**3.94**	Nr
016 19 mm covering to top and two sides of kerb including two arrises and two coves to paving:					
100 mm wide x 75 mm high	0.81	19.03	1.02	**20.05**	m
Extra over for:					
ends	0.19	4.37	-	**4.37**	Nr
angles	0.23	5.50	-	**5.50**	Nr
150 mm wide x 150 mm high	1.08	25.60	1.83	**27.43**	m
Extra over for:					
ends	0.23	5.50	-	**5.50**	Nr
angles	0.28	6.56	-	**6.56**	Nr
017 **Extra over** working to shallow channels including:					
150 mm girth:					
25 mm thick	0.19	4.37	0.20	**4.57**	m

Unit Rates	Man-Hours	Net Labour Price £	Net Mats Price £	Net Unit Price £	Unit
32 mm thick	0.22	5.24	0.41	**5.65**	m
38 mm thick	0.26	6.14	0.41	**6.55**	m
50 mm thick	0.31	7.30	0.61	**7.91**	m
150 mm girth to falls:					
25 mm thick	0.21	4.96	0.20	**5.16**	m
32 mm thick	0.25	5.83	0.41	**6.24**	m
38 mm thick	0.27	6.42	0.41	**6.83**	m
50 mm thick	0.35	8.17	0.61	**8.78**	m
300 mm girth:					
25 mm thick	0.22	5.24	0.41	**5.65**	m
32 mm thick	0.25	5.83	0.41	**6.24**	m
38 mm thick	0.28	6.71	0.61	**7.32**	m
50 mm thick	0.37	8.76	0.61	**9.37**	m
300 mm girth to falls:					
25 mm thick	0.25	5.83	0.41	**6.24**	m
32 mm thick	0.27	6.42	0.41	**6.83**	m
38 mm thick	0.32	7.58	0.61	**8.19**	m
50 mm thick	0.41	9.63	0.81	**10.44**	m
Labours to shallow channels (all thicknesses):					
ends:					
150 mm girth	0.06	1.46	-	**1.46**	Nr
300 mm girth	0.09	2.05	-	**2.05**	Nr
angles:					
150 mm girth	0.07	1.75	-	**1.75**	Nr
300 mm girth	0.11	2.62	-	**2.62**	Nr
three-way intersections:					
150 mm girth	0.12	2.93	-	**2.93**	Nr
300 mm girth	0.19	4.37	-	**4.37**	Nr
018 **Extra over** for working into:					
recessed duct covers:					
150 mm wide	0.19	4.37	-	**4.37**	m
300 mm wide	0.31	7.30	-	**7.30**	m
450 mm wide	0.43	10.23	-	**10.23**	m
600 mm wide	0.56	13.13	-	**13.13**	m
recessed manhole covers:					
600 x 450 mm	0.25	5.83	-	**5.83**	Nr
600 x 600 mm	0.37	8.76	-	**8.76**	Nr
019 External angles	0.12	2.93	-	**2.93**	m
020 Rounded internal angles:					
not exceeding 10 mm radius	0.20	4.68	-	**4.68**	m
10 - 100 mm radius	0.25	5.83	-	**5.83**	m
021 Rounded external angles:					
not exceeding 10 mm radius	0.20	4.68	-	**4.68**	m
10 - 100 mm radius	0.25	5.83	-	**5.83**	m
022 Fair joints to flush edges of existing finishes	0.12	2.93	-	**2.93**	m
023 Making good and labour finishing around steel joists, angles, pipes and the like:					
over 2.00 m girth	0.25	5.83	-	**5.83**	m
not exceeding 0.30 m girth	0.12	2.93	-	**2.93**	Nr
0.30 - 1.00 m girth	0.25	5.83	-	**5.83**	Nr
1.00 - 2.00 m girth	0.49	11.67	-	**11.67**	Nr
024 ADD TO THE FOREGOING PRICES for:					
Laying to falls and cross falls and slopes not exceeding 15 degrees horizontal:					
over 300 mm wide	0.19	4.37	-	**4.37**	m2
not exceeding 300 mm wide	0.37	8.76	-	**8.76**	m2
Two coats Febco surface hardener and dust proofer brushed on	0.12	2.93	0.43	**3.36**	m2
Two coats polyurethane floor sealer brushed on	0.37	8.76	1.55	**10.31**	m2
Neat cement grout applied to concrete base as key	0.19	4.37	0.47	**4.84**	m2
Non-slip grit trowelled in (1 kg/m2):					
over 300 mm wide	0.06	1.46	4.97	**6.43**	m2
not exceeding 300 mm wide	0.12	2.93	4.97	**7.90**	m2
19 gauge galvanised wire netting laid in paving 50 mm lap:					
over 300 mm wide:					
25 mm mesh	0.04	0.87	3.30	**4.17**	m2
38 mm mesh	0.04	0.87	2.82	**3.69**	m2
not exceeding 300 mm wide:					
25 mm mesh	0.07	1.75	3.30	**5.05**	m2
38 mm mesh	0.07	1.75	2.82	**4.57**	m2
025 Cut out area of damaged granolithic paving and make good to match existing including flush joint to existing all round:					
25 mm paving to floors:					
not exceeding 1.00 m2	1.70	40.15	5.69	**45.84**	Nr
1.00 - 2.00 m2	3.14	74.17	11.39	**85.56**	Nr
32 mm paving to floors:					
not exceeding 1.00 m2	1.77	41.85	7.12	**48.97**	Nr
1.00 - 2.00 m2	3.30	77.84	14.23	**92.07**	Nr
38 mm paving to floors:					
not exceeding 1.00 m2	1.85	43.78	8.54	**52.32**	Nr
1.00 - 2.00 m2	3.50	82.70	17.08	**99.78**	Nr
50 mm paving to floors:					
not exceeding 1.00 m2	2.01	47.44	11.18	**58.62**	Nr

Unit Rates	Man-Hours	Net Labour Price £	Net Mats Price £	Net Unit Price £	Unit
1.00 - 2.00 m2	3.71	87.56	22.37	**109.93**	Nr
paving to tread 300 mm wide:					
25 mm thick:					
not exceeding 0.50 m long	0.48	11.29	0.81	**12.10**	Nr
0.50 - 1.00 m long	0.73	17.22	1.63	**18.85**	Nr
32 mm thick:					
not exceeding 0.50 m long	0.57	13.56	1.02	**14.58**	Nr
0.50 - 1.00 m long	0.92	21.75	2.24	**23.99**	Nr
facing to riser 175 mm high:					
19 mm thick:					
not exceeding 0.50 m long	0.43	10.20	0.41	**10.61**	Nr
0.50 - 1.00 m long	0.63	14.95	0.81	**15.76**	Nr
25 mm thick:					
not exceeding 0.50 m long	0.48	11.29	0.41	**11.70**	Nr
0.50 - 1.00 m long	0.73	17.22	1.02	**18.24**	Nr

026 Cut out crack in existing granolithic paving up to 50 mm thick and make good to match existing; fair flush joints to both sides:

average 25 mm wide	0.19	4.37	0.20	**4.57**	m
average 75 mm wide	0.26	6.09	0.61	**6.70**	m

TD LATHING AND BASEBOARDING

001 **Expamet 9 mm galvanised expanded metal lathing**

002 To walls; fixing to softwood with galvanised nails:

over 300 mm wide:					
BB 263 0.500 mm thick	0.16	3.23	6.37	**9.60**	m2
BB 264 0.725 mm thick	0.18	3.64	8.81	**12.45**	m2
not exceeding 300 mm wide:					
BB 263 0.500 mm thick	0.31	6.43	6.37	**12.80**	m2
BB 264 0.725 mm thick	0.35	7.28	8.86	**16.14**	m2

Note: 003 not used

004 To walls; to steel with tying wire:

over 300 mm wide:					
BB 263 0.500 mm thick	0.17	3.43	6.37	**9.80**	m2
BB 264 0.725 mm thick	0.19	3.85	8.81	**12.66**	m2
not exceeding 300 mm wide:					
BB 263 0.500 mm thick	0.33	6.87	6.37	**13.24**	m2
BB 264 0.725 mm thick	0.37	7.72	8.86	**16.58**	m2

005 To sides of isolated columns fixing with tying wire to stainless steel straps secured with clamping buckles:

over 300 mm wide:					
BB 263 0.500 mm thick	0.21	4.29	11.25	**15.54**	m2
BB 264 0.725 mm thick	0.24	4.93	13.74	**18.67**	m2
not exceeding 300 mm wide:					
BB 263 0.500 mm thick	0.31	6.43	10.31	**16.74**	m2
BB 264 0.725 mm thick	0.36	7.49	12.80	**20.29**	m2

006 To ceilings; fixing to softwood with galvanised nails:

over 300 mm wide:					
BB 263 0.500 mm thick	0.21	4.29	6.37	**10.66**	m2
BB 264 0.725 mm thick	0.24	4.93	8.81	**13.74**	m2
not exceeding 300 mm wide:					
BB 263 0.500 mm thick	0.41	8.57	6.37	**14.94**	m2
BB 264 0.725 mm thick	0.47	9.86	8.86	**18.72**	m2

007 To ceilings; to steel with tying wire:

over 300 mm wide:					
BB 263 0.500 mm thick	0.23	4.72	6.37	**11.09**	m2
BB 264 0.725 mm thick	0.26	5.37	8.81	**14.18**	m2
not exceeding 300 mm wide:					
BB 263 0.500 mm thick	0.45	9.43	6.37	**15.80**	m2
BB 264 0.725 mm thick	0.52	10.72	8.86	**19.58**	m2

008 To sides, soffits and tops of isolated beams fixing with tying wire to stainless steel straps secured with clamping buckles:

over 300 mm wide:					
BB 263 0.500 mm thick	0.29	5.99	11.25	**17.24**	m2
BB 264 0.725 mm thick	0.33	6.87	13.74	**20.61**	m2
not exceeding 300 mm wide:					
BB 263 0.500 mm thick	0.43	9.01	10.31	**19.32**	m2
BB 264 0.725 mm thick	0.49	10.28	12.80	**23.08**	m2

009 Raking cutting:

0.500 mm thick	0.10	2.14	0.94	**3.08**	m
0.725 mm thick	0.11	2.35	1.31	**3.66**	m

010 Curved cutting:

0.500 mm thick	0.16	3.23	0.94	**4.17**	m
0.725 mm thick	0.17	3.43	1.31	**4.74**	m

011 Stripmesh 100 mm wide; fixing to brickwork, blockwork or concrete with galvanised nails:

ref 584	0.05	1.08	3.65	**4.73**	m

Unit Rates

	Man-Hours	Net Labour Price £	Net Mats Price £	Net Unit Price £	Unit
012 Corner mesh 100 mm girth; fixing to brickwork, blockwork or concrete with galvanised nails:					
ref 583	0.06	1.29	1.44	**2.73**	m
METAL LATHING					
013 **Expamet Rib-lath and Spraylath**					
014 To walls fixing to softwood with galvanised nails:					
over 300 mm wide:					
Rib-lath ref 269 0.300 mm thick	0.14	3.00	11.25	**14.25**	m2
Rib-lath ref 271 0.508 mm thick	0.16	3.23	12.93	**16.16**	m2
Spraylath ref 273 0.508 mm thick	0.16	3.23	15.50	**18.73**	m2
Stainless steel:					
Rib-lath ref 267 0.300 mm thick	0.14	3.00	33.10	**36.10**	m2
Red-Rib-lath ref 274 0.500 mm thick	0.16	3.23	14.21	**17.44**	m2
not exceeding 300 mm wide:					
Rib-lath ref 269 0.300 mm thick	0.29	5.99	11.25	**17.24**	m2
Rib-lath ref 271 0.508 mm thick	0.31	6.43	12.93	**19.36**	m2
Spraylath ref 273 0.508 mm thick	0.31	6.43	15.50	**21.93**	m2
Stainless steel:					
Rib-lath ref 267 0.300 mm thick	0.29	5.99	33.10	**39.09**	m2
Red-Rib-lath ref 274 0.500 mm thick	0.31	6.43	14.21	**20.64**	m2
015 To walls; fixing to steel with tying wire:					
over 300 mm wide:					
Rib-lath ref 269 0.300 mm thick	0.16	3.23	11.25	**14.48**	m2
Rib-lath ref 271 0.508 mm thick	0.17	3.43	12.88	**16.31**	m2
Spraylath ref 273 0.508 mm thick	0.17	3.43	15.50	**18.93**	m2
Stainless steel:					
Rib-lath ref 267 0.300 mm thick	0.16	3.23	33.10	**36.33**	m2
Red-Rib-lath ref 274 0.500 mm thick	0.17	3.43	14.21	**17.64**	m2
not exceeding 300 mm wide:					
Rib-lath ref 269 0.300 mm thick	0.31	6.43	11.25	**17.68**	m2
Rib-lath ref 271 0.508 mm thick	0.33	6.87	12.93	**19.80**	m2
Spraylath ref 273 0.508 mm thick	0.33	6.87	15.50	**22.37**	m2
Stainless steel:					
Rib-lath ref 267 0.300 mm thick	0.31	6.43	33.10	**39.53**	m2
Red-Rib-lath ref 274 0.500 mm thick	0.33	6.87	14.21	**21.08**	m2
016 To walls; fixing to brickwork, blockwork stonework or concrete with cartridge fired nails:					
over 300 mm wide:					
Rib-lath ref 269 0.300 mm thick	0.09	1.94	16.61	**18.55**	m2
Rib-lath ref 271 0.508 mm thick	0.10	2.14	18.29	**20.43**	m2
Spraylath ref 273 0.508 mm thick	0.10	2.14	20.87	**23.01**	m2
Stainless steel:					
Rib-lath ref 267 0.300 mm thick	0.09	1.94	38.46	**40.40**	m2
Red-Rib-lath ref 274 0.500 mm thick	0.10	2.14	19.58	**21.72**	m2
not exceeding 300 mm wide:					
Rib-lath ref 269 0.300 mm thick	0.19	3.85	16.61	**20.46**	m2
Rib-lath ref 271 0.508 mm thick	0.21	4.29	18.29	**22.58**	m2
Spraylath ref 273 0.508 mm thick	0.21	4.29	20.87	**25.16**	m2
Stainless steel:					
Rib-lath ref 267 0.300 mm thick	0.19	3.85	38.46	**42.31**	m2
Red-Rib-lath ref 274 0.500 mm thick	0.21	4.29	19.58	**23.87**	m2
017 To ceilings; fixing to softwood with galvanised nails:					
over 300 mm wide:					
Rib-lath ref 269 0.300 mm thick	0.19	3.85	11.25	**15.10**	m2
Rib-lath ref 271 0.508 mm thick	0.21	4.29	12.93	**17.22**	m2
Spraylath ref 273 0.508 mm thick	0.21	4.29	15.50	**19.79**	m2
Stainless steel:					
Rib-lath ref 267 0.300 mm thick	0.19	3.85	33.10	**36.95**	m2
Red-Rib-lath ref 274 0.500 mm thick	0.21	4.29	14.21	**18.50**	m2
not exceeding 300 mm wide:					
Rib-lath ref 269 0.300 mm thick	0.37	7.72	11.25	**18.97**	m2
Rib-lath ref 271 0.508 mm thick	0.41	8.57	12.93	**21.50**	m2
Spraylath ref 273 0.508 mm thick	0.41	8.57	15.50	**24.07**	m2
Stainless steel:					
Rib-lath ref 267 0.300 mm thick	0.37	7.72	33.10	**40.82**	m2
Red-Rib-lath ref 274 0.500 mm thick	0.41	8.57	14.21	**22.78**	m2
018 To ceilings; fixing to steel with tying wire:					
over 300 mm wide:					
Rib-lath ref 269 0.300 mm thick	0.21	4.29	11.25	**15.54**	m2
Rib-lath ref 271 0.508 mm thick	0.23	4.72	12.93	**17.65**	m2
Spraylath ref 273 0.508 mm thick	0.23	4.72	15.50	**20.22**	m2
Stainless steel:					
Rib-lath ref 267 0.300 mm thick	0.21	4.29	33.10	**37.39**	m2
Red-Rib-lath ref 274 0.500 mm thick	0.23	4.72	14.21	**18.93**	m2
not exceeding 300 mm wide:					
Rib-lath ref 269 0.300 mm thick	0.41	8.57	11.25	**19.82**	m2
Rib-lath ref 271 0.508 mm thick	0.45	9.43	12.93	**22.36**	m2
Spraylath ref 273 0.508 mm thick	0.45	9.43	15.50	**24.93**	m2
Stainless steel:					
Rib-lath ref 267 0.300 mm thick	0.41	8.57	33.10	**41.67**	m2
Red-Rib-lath ref 274 0.500 mm thick	0.45	9.43	14.21	**23.64**	m2
019 Raking cutting:					
ref 269 0.300 mm thick	0.09	1.94	1.67	**3.61**	m

Unit Rates	Man-Hours	Net Labour Price £	Net Mats Price £	Net Unit Price £	Unit
ref 271 0.508 mm thick	0.10	2.14	1.92	**4.06**	m
ref 273 0.508 mm thick	0.10	2.14	2.31	**4.45**	m
ref 267 0.300 mm thick	0.09	1.94	4.94	**6.88**	m
ref 274 0.500 mm thick	0.10	2.14	2.11	**4.25**	m
020 Curved cutting:					
ref 269 0.300 mm thick	0.14	3.00	1.67	**4.67**	m
ref 271 0.508 mm thick	0.16	3.23	1.92	**5.15**	m
ref 273 0.508 mm thick	0.16	3.23	2.31	**5.54**	m
ref 267 0.300 mm thick	0.14	3.00	4.94	**7.94**	m
ref 274 0.500 mm thick	0.16	3.23	2.11	**5.34**	m
021 **Expamet Archforms fixed to brickwork, blockwork or concrete with galvanised nails and wired together at mid-point of soffit**					
022 Arch corners:					
ref EAC 15 radius 381 mm	0.52	10.72	35.56	**46.28**	Nr
ref EAC 18 radius 457 mm	0.57	11.80	43.28	**55.08**	Nr
ref EAC 24 radius 610 mm	0.62	12.86	52.82	**65.68**	Nr
ref EAC 30 radius 762 mm	0.67	13.92	76.86	**90.78**	Nr
023 Semi-circle arches:					
ref ESC 30 for 762 mm opening	1.03	21.43	69.90	**91.33**	Nr
ref ESC 32 for 812 mm opening	1.08	22.50	71.04	**93.54**	Nr
ref ESC 33 for 838 mm opening	1.13	23.58	73.40	**96.98**	Nr
ref ESC 36 for 914 mm opening	1.19	24.66	85.86	**110.52**	Nr
024 Elliptical arches:					
ref EEL 48 for 1219 mm opening	1.29	26.78	135.95	**162.73**	Nr
ref EEL 54 for 1372 mm opening	1.34	27.86	142.53	**170.39**	Nr
ref EEL 60 for 1524 mm opening	1.39	28.95	151.38	**180.33**	Nr
ref EEL 72 for 1829 mm opening	1.44	30.01	163.05	**193.06**	Nr
ref EEL 84 for 2134 mm opening	1.49	31.09	178.87	**209.96**	Nr
ref EEL 96 for 2438 mm opening	1.55	32.15	187.76	**219.91**	Nr
ref EEL 120 for 3048 mm opening	1.80	37.52	191.60	**229.12**	Nr
025 Spandrel arches:					
ref ESP 30 for 762 mm opening	1.03	21.43	89.01	**110.44**	Nr
ref ESP 36 for 914 mm opening	1.19	24.66	99.48	**124.14**	Nr
ref ESP 48 for 1219 mm opening	1.29	26.78	120.16	**146.94**	Nr
ref ESP 60 for 1524 mm opening	1.39	28.95	133.68	**162.63**	Nr
ref ESP 72 for 1829 mm opening	1.44	30.01	147.19	**177.20**	Nr
ref ESP 84 for 2134 mm opening	1.49	31.09	160.33	**191.42**	Nr
ref ESP 96 for 2438 mm opening	1.55	32.15	169.96	**202.11**	Nr
ref ESP 120 for 3048 mm opening	1.80	37.52	196.34	**233.86**	Nr
026 Bulls-eye:					
ref BE 18 radius 229 mm	0.77	16.09	91.64	**107.73**	Nr
027 Lath soffit strip wired to arch forms:					
ref LSS6 155 mm wide	0.10	2.14	5.59	**7.73**	m
028 **Newlath Lathing**					
029 To walls, brickwork, stonework or concrete; fixing with polypropylene fixing plugs:					
over 300 mm wide	0.18	3.64	33.38	**37.02**	m2
not exceeding 300 mm wide	0.33	6.87	36.83	**43.70**	m2
030 Raking cutting	0.05	1.08	4.67	**5.75**	m
031 Curved cutting	0.05	1.08	4.67	**5.75**	m
GYPROC HANDI-BOARD					
032 **Gypsum plasterboard fixed with galvanised nails to softwood**					
033 To walls in extending/repairing existing:					
9.5 mm wallboard:					
over 300 mm wide	0.26	5.37	2.64	**8.01**	m2
not exceeding 300 mm wide	0.52	10.72	2.68	**13.40**	m2
isolated areas not exceeding 1.00 m2 including flush joint to existing	0.29	5.99	2.68	**8.67**	m2
12.5 mm wallboard:					
over 300 mm wide	0.32	6.64	2.67	**9.31**	m2
not exceeding 300 mm wide	0.64	13.30	2.71	**16.01**	m2
isolated areas not exceeding 1.00 m2 including flush joint to existing	0.37	7.72	2.71	**10.43**	m2
9.5 mm lath:					
over 300 mm wide	0.26	5.37	3.03	**8.40**	m2
not exceeding 300 mm wide	0.52	10.72	3.09	**13.81**	m2
isolated areas not exceeding 1.00 m2 including flush joint to existing	0.29	5.99	3.20	**9.19**	m2
12.5 lath:					
over 300 mm wide	0.32	6.64	3.43	**10.07**	m2
not exceeding 300 mm wide	0.64	13.30	3.65	**16.95**	m2
isolated areas not exceeding 1.00 m2 including flush joint to existing	0.37	7.72	3.65	**11.37**	m2
034 To sides of isolated columns:					
9.5 mm wallboard:					
over 300 mm wide	0.31	6.43	2.64	**9.07**	m2
not exceeding 300 mm wide	0.46	9.64	2.68	**12.32**	m2
12.5 mm wallboard:					
over 300 mm wide	0.36	7.49	2.67	**10.16**	m2

Unit Rates	Man-Hours	Net Labour Price £	Net Mats Price £	Net Unit Price £	Unit
not exceeding 300 mm wide	0.49	10.28	2.71	**12.99**	m2
9.5 mm lath:					
over 300 mm wide	0.31	6.43	3.03	**9.46**	m2
not exceeding 300 mm wide	0.46	9.64	3.09	**12.73**	m2
12.5 lath:					
over 300 mm wide	0.36	7.49	3.43	**10.92**	m2
not exceeding 300 mm wide	0.49	10.28	3.65	**13.93**	m2
035 To ceilings in extending/repairing existing:					
9.5 mm wallboard in extending/repairing existing:					
over 300 mm wide	0.31	6.43	2.64	**9.07**	m2
not exceeding 300 mm wide	0.58	12.01	2.68	**14.69**	m2
isolated areas not exceeding 1.00 m2 including flush joint to existing	0.36	7.49	2.68	**10.17**	m2
12.5 mm wallboard:					
over 300 mm wide	0.37	7.72	2.67	**10.39**	m2
not exceeding 300 mm wide	0.62	12.86	2.71	**15.57**	m2
isolated areas not exceeding 1.00 m2 including flush joint to existing	0.42	8.78	2.71	**11.49**	m2
9.5 mm lath:					
over 300 mm wide	0.31	6.43	3.03	**9.46**	m2
not exceeding 300 mm wide	0.58	12.01	3.09	**15.10**	m2
isolated areas not exceeding 1.00 m2 including flush joint to existing	0.36	7.49	3.20	**10.69**	m2
12.5 lath:					
over 300 mm wide	0.37	7.72	3.43	**11.15**	m2
not exceeding 300 mm wide	0.62	12.86	3.65	**16.51**	m2
isolated areas not exceeding 1.00 m2 including flush joint to existing	0.42	8.78	3.65	**12.43**	m2
036 To sides, soffits and tops of isolated beams:					
9.5 mm wallboard:					
over 300 mm wide	0.31	6.43	2.64	**9.07**	m2
not exceeding 300 mm wide	0.46	9.64	2.68	**12.32**	m2
12.5 mm wallboard:					
over 300 mm wide	0.36	7.49	2.67	**10.16**	m2
not exceeding 300 mm wide	0.49	10.28	2.71	**12.99**	m2
9.5 mm lath:					
over 300 mm wide	0.31	6.43	3.03	**9.46**	m2
not exceeding 300 mm wide	0.46	9.64	3.09	**12.73**	m2
12.5 lath:					
over 300 mm wide	0.36	7.49	3.43	**10.92**	m2
not exceeding 300 mm wide	0.49	10.28	3.65	**13.93**	m2
037 ADD TO THE FOREGOING PRICES for:					
Duplex grade plasterboard	-	-	1.15	**1.15**	m2
12.5 mm Fireline board in lieu of 12.5 mm wallboard	-	-	0.53	**0.53**	m2
038 Raking cutting:					
9.5 mm wallboard	0.05	1.08	0.52	**1.60**	m
9.5 mm lath	0.05	1.08	0.59	**1.67**	m
12.5 mm wallboard	0.06	1.29	0.52	**1.81**	m
12.5 mm lath	0.06	1.29	0.62	**1.91**	m
039 Curved cutting:					
9.5 mm wallboard	0.07	1.50	0.52	**2.02**	m
9.5 mm lath	0.07	1.50	0.59	**2.09**	m
12.5 mm wallboard	0.08	1.71	0.52	**2.23**	m
12.5 mm lath	0.08	1.71	0.62	**2.33**	m
Note: 040 - 041 not used					
042 Flush joint to existing wallboard	0.05	1.08	-	**1.08**	m
043 Cutting around steel joists, angles, pipes and the like:					
over 2.00 m girth:					
9.5 mm wallboard	0.05	1.08	-	**1.08**	m
9.5 mm lath	0.05	1.08	-	**1.08**	m
12.5 mm wallboard	0.06	1.29	-	**1.29**	m
12.5 mm lath	0.06	1.29	-	**1.29**	m
not exceeding 0.30 m girth:					
9.5 mm wallboard	0.02	0.44	-	**0.44**	Nr
9.5 mm lath	0.02	0.44	-	**0.44**	Nr
12.5 mm wallboard	0.03	0.65	-	**0.65**	Nr
12.5 mm lath	0.03	0.65	-	**0.65**	Nr
0.30 - 1.00 m girth:					
9.5 mm wallboard	0.06	1.29	-	**1.29**	Nr
9.5 mm lath	0.06	1.29	-	**1.29**	Nr
12.5 mm wallboard	0.07	1.50	-	**1.50**	Nr
12.5 mm lath	0.07	1.50	-	**1.50**	Nr
1.00 - 2.00 m girth:					
9.5 mm wallboard	0.10	2.14	-	**2.14**	Nr
9.5 mm lath	0.10	2.14	-	**2.14**	Nr
12.5 mm wallboard	0.12	2.58	-	**2.58**	Nr
12.5 mm lath	0.12	2.58	-	**2.58**	Nr
044 Cut out damaged plasterboard and skim, make good with Gypsum lath with Thistle finish on Thistle bonding coat with scrimmed flush joints to existing all round:					
to walls:					
9.5 mm lath:					
not exceeding 1.00 m2	1.39	32.75	2.89	**35.64**	Nr
1.00 - 2.00 m2	2.55	60.12	5.79	**65.91**	Nr

Unit Rates	Man-Hours	Net Labour Price £	Net Mats Price £	Net Unit Price £	Unit
12.5 mm lath:					
not exceeding 1.00 m2	1.44	34.10	2.93	**37.03**	Nr
1.00 - 2.00 m2	2.66	62.82	5.86	**68.68**	Nr
finishing plaster:					
5 mm skimming coat:					
not exceeding 1.00 m2	0.62	14.59	2.07	**16.66**	Nr
1.00 - 2.00 m2	0.93	21.89	4.37	**26.26**	Nr
10 mm two coat work:					
not exceeding 1.00 m2	0.91	21.47	3.60	**25.07**	Nr
1.00 - 2.00 m2	1.59	37.55	7.53	**45.08**	Nr
to ceilings:					
9.5 mm lath:					
not exceeding 1.00 m2	1.61	37.95	2.89	**40.84**	Nr
1.00 - 2.00 m2	2.88	68.11	5.79	**73.90**	Nr
12.5 mm lath:					
not exceeding 1.00 m2	1.66	39.27	2.93	**42.20**	Nr
1.00 - 2.00 m2	0.92	21.75	2.24	**23.99**	Nr
finishing plaster:					
5 mm skimming coat:					
not exceeding 1.00 m2	0.74	17.52	2.07	**19.59**	Nr
1.00 - 2.00 m2	1.15	27.25	4.37	**31.62**	Nr
10 mm two coat work:					
not exceeding 1.00 m2	1.15	27.09	3.60	**30.69**	Nr
1.00 - 2.00 m2	2.07	48.84	7.53	**56.37**	Nr

TE · **BEDS AND BACKINGS**

001 · **Cement and sand (1:3) trowelled beds laid level and to falls only**

Note: 002 not used

	Man-Hours	Net Labour Price £	Net Mats Price £	Net Unit Price £	Unit
003 To floors in extending/repairing existing paving:					
over 300 mm wide:					
25 mm thick	0.35	8.27	3.23	**11.50**	m2
32 mm thick	0.37	8.76	4.13	**12.89**	m2
38 mm thick	0.39	9.23	4.91	**14.14**	m2
50 mm thick	0.46	10.93	6.46	**17.39**	m2
not exceeding 300 mm wide:					
25 mm thick	0.70	16.53	3.23	**19.76**	m2
32 mm thick	0.74	17.52	4.13	**21.65**	m2
38 mm thick	0.79	18.73	4.91	**23.64**	m2
50 mm thick	0.93	21.89	6.46	**28.35**	m2
isolated areas not exceeding 1.00 m2 including flush joint to existing:					
25 mm thick	0.40	9.49	3.23	**12.72**	m2
32 mm thick	0.42	9.97	4.13	**14.10**	m2
38 mm thick	0.45	10.70	4.91	**15.61**	m2
50 mm thick	0.53	12.40	6.46	**18.86**	m2
Note: 004 not used					
005 To landings in extending/repairing existing paving:					
over 300 mm wide:					
25 mm thick	0.53	12.40	3.23	**15.63**	m2
32 mm thick	0.56	13.13	4.13	**17.26**	m2
38 mm thick	0.60	14.10	4.91	**19.01**	m2
50 mm thick	0.69	16.29	6.46	**22.75**	m2
not exceeding 300 mm wide:					
25 mm thick	1.04	24.56	3.23	**27.79**	m2
32 mm thick	1.11	26.26	4.13	**30.39**	m2
38 mm thick	1.19	27.98	4.91	**32.89**	m2
50 mm thick	1.39	32.85	6.46	**39.31**	m2
isolated areas not exceeding 1.00 m2 including flush joint to existing:					
25 mm thick	0.61	14.36	3.23	**17.59**	m2
32 mm thick	0.64	15.09	4.13	**19.22**	m2
38 mm thick	0.68	16.06	4.91	**20.97**	m2
50 mm thick	0.79	18.73	6.46	**25.19**	m2
006 To treads 250 mm wide:					
25 mm thick	0.21	5.03	0.78	**5.81**	m
32 mm thick	0.22	5.24	1.03	**6.27**	m
38 mm thick	0.24	5.69	1.29	**6.98**	m
50 mm thick	0.28	6.56	1.68	**8.24**	m
007 To risers 175 mm wide:					
19 mm thick	0.21	5.03	0.52	**5.55**	m
25 mm thick	0.24	5.69	0.65	**6.34**	m
008 To undercut risers 175 mm wide:					
19 mm thick	0.28	6.56	0.52	**7.08**	m
25 mm thick	0.31	7.25	0.65	**7.90**	m
009 **Extra over** working to shallow channels including arrises:					
150 mm girth:					
25 mm thick	0.19	4.37	0.13	**4.50**	m
32 mm thick	0.22	5.24	0.26	**5.50**	m
38 mm thick	0.26	6.14	0.26	**6.40**	m
50 mm thick	0.31	7.30	0.39	**7.69**	m
150 mm girth to falls:					
25 mm thick	0.21	4.96	0.13	**5.09**	m

Unit Rates	Man-Hours	Net Labour Price £	Net Mats Price £	Net Unit Price £	Unit
32 mm thick	0.25	5.83	0.26	6.09	m
38 mm thick	0.27	6.42	0.26	6.68	m
50 mm thick	0.35	8.17	0.39	8.56	m
300 mm girth:					
25 mm thick	0.22	5.24	0.26	5.50	m
32 mm thick	0.25	5.83	0.26	6.09	m
38 mm thick	0.28	6.71	0.39	7.10	m
50 mm thick	0.37	8.76	0.52	9.28	m
300 mm girth to falls:					
25 mm thick	0.25	5.83	0.26	6.09	m
32 mm thick	0.27	6.42	0.26	6.68	m
38 mm thick	0.32	7.58	0.39	7.97	m
50 mm thick	0.41	9.63	0.52	10.15	m
Labours to shallow channels (all thicknesses):					
ends:					
150 mm girth	0.06	1.46	-	1.46	Nr
300 mm girth	0.09	2.05	-	2.05	Nr
angles:					
150 mm girth	0.07	1.75	-	1.75	Nr
300 mm girth	0.11	2.62	-	2.62	Nr
three-way intersections:					
150 mm girth	0.12	2.93	-	2.93	Nr
300 mm girth	0.19	4.37	-	4.37	Nr
010 **Extra over** for working into:					
recessed duct covers:					
150 mm wide	0.19	4.37	-	4.37	m
300 mm wide	0.31	7.30	-	7.30	m
450 mm wide	0.43	10.23	-	10.23	m
600 mm wide	0.56	13.13	-	13.13	m
recessed manhole covers:					
600 x 450 mm	0.25	5.83	-	5.83	Nr
600 x 600 mm	0.37	8.76	-	8.76	Nr
011 DEDUCT FROM THE FOREGOING PRICES for:					
screeded finish:					
over 300 mm wide	-0.15	-3.50	-	-3.50	m2
not exceeding 300 mm wide	-0.30	-7.01	-	-7.01	m2
floated finish:					
over 300 mm wide	-0.04	-0.87	-	-0.87	m2
not exceeding 300 mm wide	-0.07	-1.75	-	-1.75	m2
cement and sand (1:4) mix for each 25 mm thickness	-	-	-0.24	-0.24	m2
012 ADD TO THE FOREGOING PRICES for:					
Laying to falls and crossfalls and slopes not exceeding 15 degrees from horizontal:					
over 300 mm wide	0.19	4.37	-	4.37	m2
not exceeding 300 mm wide	0.37	8.76	-	8.76	m2
Three coats Febco surface hardener brushed on	0.12	2.93	0.43	3.36	m2
Two coat polyurethane floor sealer brushed on	0.37	8.76	1.55	10.31	m2
Neat cement grout applied to concrete base as key	0.19	4.37	0.47	4.84	m2
19 gauge galvanised wire netting laid in screed 50 mm lap:					
over 300 mm wide:					
25 mm mesh	0.04	0.87	3.30	4.17	m2
38 mm mesh	0.04	0.87	2.82	3.69	m2
not exceeding 300 mm wide:					
25 mm mesh	0.07	1.75	3.30	5.05	m2
38 mm mesh	0.07	1.75	2.82	4.57	m2
013 19 mm steel trowelled skirting with square top edge to brick or block wall:					
150 mm high	0.37	8.76	0.39	9.15	m
Extra over for:					
ends	0.13	3.07	-	3.07	Nr
angles	0.14	3.28	-	3.28	Nr
225 mm (average) high	0.42	9.82	0.52	10.34	m
Extra over for:					
ends	0.14	3.28	-	3.28	Nr
angles	0.15	3.50	-	3.50	Nr
ramps	0.14	3.28	-	3.28	Nr
014 25 mm lining to channel including two internal angles and two arrises:					
300 mm girth on face	0.46	10.93	1.03	11.96	m
300 mm girth to falls	0.56	13.13	1.03	14.16	m
Extra over for:					
ends	0.19	4.37	-	4.37	Nr
angles	0.23	5.50	-	5.50	Nr
intersections	0.23	5.50	-	5.50	Nr
500 mm girth on face	0.74	17.52	1.68	19.20	m
500 mm girth to falls	0.83	19.69	1.68	21.37	m
Extra over for:					
ends	0.23	5.50	-	5.50	Nr
angles	0.28	6.56	-	6.56	Nr
intersections	0.28	6.56	-	6.56	Nr
015 **Cement and sand (1:3) screeded finish to brickwork, blockwork or concrete**					
016 To walls:					
12 mm one coat work:					
over 300 mm wide	0.31	7.25	1.55	8.80	m2
not exceeding 300 mm wide	0.61	14.45	1.55	16.00	m2

	Unit Rates	Man-Hours	Net Labour Price £	Net Mats Price £	Net Unit Price £	Unit
	18 mm two coat work:					
	over 300 mm wide	0.51	12.04	2.33	**14.37**	m2
	not exceeding 300 mm wide	1.02	24.09	2.33	**26.42**	m2
017	To sides of isolated columns:					
	12 mm one coat work:					
	over 300 mm wide	0.65	15.33	1.55	**16.88**	m2
	not exceeding 300 mm wide	1.30	30.65	1.55	**32.20**	m2
	18 mm two coat work:					
	over 300 mm wide	0.68	16.01	2.33	**18.34**	m2
	not exceeding 300 mm wide	1.35	31.95	2.33	**34.28**	m2
018	DEDUCT FROM THE FOREGOING PRICES for:					
	cement and sand (1:4) 12 mm one coat work:					
	over 300 mm wide	-	-	-0.12	**-0.12**	m2
	not exceeding 300 mm wide	-	-	-0.12	**-0.12**	m2
	cement and sand (1:4) 18 mm two coat work:					
	over 300 mm wide	-	-	-0.17	**-0.17**	m2
	not exceeding 300 mm wide	-	-	-0.17	**-0.17**	m2
	cement, lime and sand (1:1:6) 12 mm one coat work:					
	over 300 mm wide	-	-	-0.02	**-0.02**	m2
	not exceeding 300 mm wide	-	-	-0.02	**-0.02**	m2
	cement, lime and sand (1:1:6) 18 mm two coat work:					
	over 300 mm wide	-	-	-0.03	**-0.03**	m2
	not exceeding 300 mm wide	-	-	-0.03	**-0.03**	m2
019	ADD TO THE FOREGOING PRICES for:					
	floated finish:					
	over 300 mm wide	0.08	1.98	-	**1.98**	m2
	not exceeding 300 mm wide	0.17	3.94	-	**3.94**	m2
	trowelled finish:					
	over 300 mm wide	0.11	2.62	-	**2.62**	m2
	not exceeding 300 mm wide	0.22	5.24	-	**5.24**	m2
	cement and sand (1:2) spatterdash applied to walls as key:					
	over 300 mm wide	0.19	4.37	0.75	**5.12**	m2
	not exceeding 300 mm wide	0.37	8.76	0.75	**9.51**	m2
020	**Fine concrete (1:1.5:3-10 mm aggregate) trowelled bed laid level and to falls only**					
021	To floors over 300 mm wide:					
	50 mm thick	0.37	8.76	7.51	**16.27**	m2
	63 mm thick	0.44	10.30	9.46	**19.76**	m2
	75 mm thick	0.50	11.83	11.26	**23.09**	m2
022	To floors not exceeding 300 mm wide:					
	50 mm thick	0.74	17.52	7.51	**25.03**	m2
	63 mm thick	0.87	20.57	9.46	**30.03**	m2
	75 mm thick	1.00	23.64	11.26	**34.90**	m2
023	**Lightweight screeds**					
024	Vermiculite screed (1 part cement to 8 parts vermiculite) finished with 13 mm cement and sand (1:4) screeded bed laid level and to falls only over 300 mm wide:					
	38 mm overall	0.33	7.67	7.88	**15.55**	m2
	50 mm overall	0.35	8.31	11.05	**19.36**	m2
	63 mm overall	0.40	9.45	14.49	**23.94**	m2
	75 mm overall	0.46	10.74	17.66	**28.40**	m2
025	ADD TO THE FOREGOING PRICES for:					
	laying to falls and crossfalls and slopes not exceeding 15 degrees from horizontal	0.14	3.28	-	**3.28**	m2
026	Lightweight concrete screed (1 part cement to 8 parts medium grade Aglite lightweight aggregate) finished with 13 mm cement and sand (1:4) screeded bed laid level and to falls only over 300 mm wide:					
	50 mm overall	0.35	8.31	7.31	**15.62**	m2
	63 mm overall	0.40	9.45	9.36	**18.81**	m2
	75 mm overall	0.46	10.74	11.25	**21.99**	m2
	100 mm overall	0.56	13.13	15.19	**28.32**	m2
027	ADD TO THE FOREGOING PRICES for:					
	laying to falls and crossfalls and slopes not exceeding 15 degrees from horizontal	0.19	4.37	-	**4.37**	m2
028	**Levelling screed**					
029	Stopgap screeding compound laid on existing concrete including cleaning surface of concrete:					
	over 300 mm wide:					
	3 mm thick	0.31	6.43	3.53	**9.96**	m2
	6 mm thick	0.43	9.01	7.06	**16.07**	m2
	not exceeding 300 mm wide:					
	3 mm thick	0.62	12.86	3.53	**16.39**	m2
	6 mm thick	0.87	18.00	7.06	**25.06**	m2

Unit Rates	Man-Hours	Net Labour Price £	Net Mats Price £	Net Unit Price £	Unit
TF **TILE SLAB AND BLOCK FINISHINGS**					
WALL TILING					
001 **Glazed wall tiling fixed with adhesive to floated backings and grouted with white cement**					
Note: 002 not used					
003 To walls in extending/repairing existing tiling:					
over 300 mm wide:					
100 x 100 x 6.5 mm	2.50	38.05	26.19	**64.24**	m2
150 x 150 x 6.5 mm	1.73	26.30	23.04	**49.34**	m2
200 x 150 x 6.5 mm (100% pattern)	1.86	28.33	37.05	**65.38**	m2
not exceeding 300 mm wide:					
100 x 100 x 6.5 mm	5.03	76.40	29.82	**106.22**	m2
150 x 150 x 6.5 mm	3.47	52.76	26.09	**78.85**	m2
200 x 150 x 6.5 mm (100% pattern)	3.73	56.68	42.90	**99.58**	m2
isolated areas not exceeding 1.00 m2 including flush joint to existing:					
100 x 100 x 6.5 mm	2.87	43.68	26.19	**69.87**	m2
150 x 150 x 6.5 mm	1.99	30.22	23.04	**53.26**	m2
200 x 150 x 6.5 mm (100% pattern)	2.14	32.56	37.05	**69.61**	m2
004 Raking cutting:					
100 x 100 x 6.5 mm	0.08	1.25	0.77	**2.02**	m
150 x 150 x 6.5 mm	0.09	1.41	0.77	**2.18**	m
005 Curved cutting:					
100 x 100 x 6.5 mm	0.17	2.51	1.17	**3.68**	m
150 x 150 x 6.5 mm	0.19	2.81	1.14	**3.95**	m
006 Fair joint to flush edges of existing finishes:					
100 x 100 x 6.5 mm	0.05	0.79	-	**0.79**	m
150 x 150 x 6.5 mm	0.05	0.79	-	**0.79**	m
200 x 150 x 6.5 mm (100% pattern)	0.05	0.79	-	**0.79**	m
007 Cut and fit wall tiles around steel joists, angles, pipes and the like:					
over 2.00 m girth:					
100 x 100 x 6.5 mm	0.12	1.88	-	**1.88**	m
150 x 150 x 6.5 mm	0.14	2.19	-	**2.19**	m
200 x 150 x 6.5 mm	0.16	2.36	-	**2.36**	m
not exceeding 0.30 m girth:					
100 x 100 x 6.5 mm	0.05	0.79	-	**0.79**	Nr
150 x 150 x 6.5 mm	0.06	0.94	-	**0.94**	Nr
200 x 150 x 6.5 mm	0.07	1.09	-	**1.09**	Nr
0.30 - 1.00 m girth:					
100 x 100 x 6.5 mm	0.08	1.25	-	**1.25**	Nr
150 x 150 x 6.5 mm	0.10	1.57	-	**1.57**	Nr
200 x 150 x 6.5 mm	0.11	1.72	-	**1.72**	Nr
1.00 - 2.00 m girth:					
100 x 100 x 6.5 mm	0.19	2.81	-	**2.81**	Nr
150 x 150 x 6.5 mm	0.22	3.28	-	**3.28**	Nr
200 x 150 x 6.5 mm	0.24	3.60	-	**3.60**	Nr
008 ADD TO THE FOREGOING PRICES for:					
patterned wall tiles (25% of area):					
100 x 100 x 6.5 mm	-	-	1.29	**1.29**	m2
150 x 150 x 6.5 mm	-	-	0.80	**0.80**	m2
patterned wall tiles (100% of area):					
100 x 100 x 6.5 mm	-	-	5.15	**5.15**	m2
150 x 150 x 6.5 mm	-	-	3.21	**3.21**	m2
009 Cut out existing damaged glazed wall tiles and provide and fix new bedded in adhesive and grouted in white cement to match existing; flush joint to existing all round:					
100 x 100 x 6.5 mm:					
individual tile	0.24	3.65	0.25	**3.90**	Nr
area not exceeding 0.50 m2	3.30	50.10	8.48	**58.58**	Nr
area 0.50 - 1.00 m2	4.74	72.02	16.97	**88.99**	Nr
area 1.00 - 2.00 m2	7.31	111.16	33.94	**145.10**	Nr
150 x 150 x 6.5 mm:					
individual tile	0.24	3.65	0.40	**4.05**	Nr
area not exceeding 0.50 m2	2.68	40.71	8.36	**49.07**	Nr
area 0.50 - 1.00 m2	3.81	57.93	16.72	**74.65**	Nr
area 1.00 - 2.00 m2	5.77	87.67	33.43	**121.10**	Nr
QUARRY TILING					
010 **Quarry tiles including 10 mm bed of cement mortar (1:3) and jointing and pointing in cement mortar (1:3) straight joints both ways**					
011 To floors level and to falls only in extending/repairing existing tiling:					
over 300 mm wide:					
150 x 150 x 12.5 mm	1.74	26.46	25.57	**52.03**	m2
194 x 194 x 25 mm	1.32	20.03	62.77	**82.80**	m2
not exceeding 300 mm wide:					
150 x 150 x 12.5 mm	3.47	52.76	30.37	**83.13**	m2
194 x 194 x 25 mm	2.89	43.99	75.01	**119.00**	m2
isolated areas not exceeding 1.00 m2 including flush joint to existing:					
150 x 150 x 12.5 mm	2.00	30.37	25.57	**55.94**	m2
194 x 194 x 25 mm	1.51	23.01	62.77	**85.78**	m2

Unit Rates

		Man-Hours	Net Labour Price £	Net Mats Price £	Net Unit Price £	Unit
012	To landings over 300 mm wide:					
	150 x 150 x 12.5 mm	2.01	30.54	25.57	**56.11**	m2
	194 x 194 x 25 mm	1.55	23.48	62.77	**86.25**	m2
013	To treads 250 mm wide with rounded edge:					
	150 x 150 x 12.5 mm	0.67	10.17	10.75	**20.92**	m
	194 x 194 x 25 mm	0.52	7.83	21.23	**29.06**	m
014	To risers 175 mm wide:					
	150 x 150 x 12.5 mm	0.52	7.83	5.92	**13.75**	m
	194 x 194 x 25 mm	0.36	5.47	12.50	**17.97**	m
015	**Extra over** for:					
	rounded edge tiles:					
	150 x 150 x 12.5 mm	0.02	0.32	2.85	**3.17**	m
	194 x 194 x 25 mm	0.02	0.32	4.80	**5.12**	m
	working into recessed duct covers:					
	150 mm wide:					
	150 x 150 x 12.5 mm	0.13	2.04	7.22	**9.26**	m
	194 x 194 x 25 mm	0.21	3.13	12.24	**15.37**	m
	300 mm wide:					
	150 x 150 x 12.5 mm	0.16	2.36	7.22	**9.58**	m
	194 x 194 x 25 mm	0.21	3.13	12.24	**15.37**	m
	450 mm wide:					
	150 x 150 x 12.5 mm	0.18	2.66	7.22	**9.88**	m
	194 x 194 x 25 mm	0.21	3.13	12.24	**15.37**	m
	600 mm wide:					
	150 x 150 x 12.5 mm	0.21	3.13	7.22	**10.35**	m
	194 x 194 x 25 mm	0.17	2.51	12.24	**14.75**	m
	working into recessed manhole covers:					
	600 x 450 mm:					
	150 x 150 x 12.5 mm	0.21	3.13	7.57	**10.70**	Nr
	194 x 194 x 25 mm	0.26	3.92	12.24	**16.16**	Nr
	600 x 600 mm:					
	150 x 150 x 12.5 mm	0.26	3.92	8.66	**12.58**	Nr
	194 x 194 x 25 mm	0.21	3.13	14.69	**17.82**	Nr
	Note: 016 not used					
017	Raking cutting:					
	150 x 150 x 12.5 mm	0.11	1.72	1.21	**2.93**	m
	194 x 194 x 25 mm	0.13	2.04	4.90	**6.94**	m
018	Curved cutting:					
	150 x 150 x 12.5 mm	0.23	3.45	1.79	**5.24**	m
	194 x 194 x 25 mm	0.27	4.07	7.35	**11.42**	m
019	Fair joint to flush edge of existing finishes:					
	150 x 150 x 12.5 mm	0.05	0.79	-	**0.79**	m
	194 x 194 x 25 mm	0.05	0.79	-	**0.79**	m
020	Cut and fit floor tiles around steel joists, angles, pipes and the like:					
	over 2.00 m girth:					
	150 x 150 x 12.5 mm	0.18	2.66	-	**2.66**	m
	194 x 194 x 25 mm	0.21	3.13	-	**3.13**	m
	not exceeding 0.30 m girth:					
	150 x 150 x 12.5 mm	0.08	1.25	-	**1.25**	Nr
	194 x 194 x 25 mm	0.09	1.41	-	**1.41**	Nr
	0.30 - 1.00 m girth:					
	150 x 150 x 12.5 mm	0.13	2.04	-	**2.04**	Nr
	194 x 194 x 25 mm	0.16	2.36	-	**2.36**	Nr
	1.00 - 2.00 m girth:					
	150 x 150 x 12.5 mm	0.26	3.92	-	**3.92**	Nr
	194 x 194 x 25 mm	0.31	4.70	-	**4.70**	Nr
021	Quarry tile skirting including 10 mm bed of cement mortar (1:3) and jointing and pointing with cement mortar (1:3):					
	150 x 150 mm cove skirting	0.41	6.26	10.10	**16.36**	m
	Extra over:					
	ends	0.05	0.79	-	**0.79**	Nr
	internal angle	0.10	1.57	4.46	**6.03**	Nr
	external angle	0.10	1.57	4.46	**6.03**	Nr
022	Quarry tile capping with two opposite rounded edges, including 10 mm bed of cement mortar (1:3) and jointing and pointing in cement mortar (1:3); full tile width:					
	150 x 150 x 12.5 mm	0.41	6.26	20.83	**27.09**	m
	194 x 194 x 25 mm	0.46	7.04	36.35	**43.39**	m
023	Cut out damaged quarry tiles and provide and fix new bedded in cement and sand (1:3) with joints grouted in cement and sand (1:3) to match existing; flush joint to existing all round:					
	150 x 150 x 12.5 mm:					
	individual tile	0.29	4.35	0.71	**5.06**	Nr
	area not exceeding 0.50 m2	1.80	27.41	12.91	**40.32**	Nr
	area 0.50 - 1.00 m2	3.91	59.49	25.81	**85.30**	Nr
	area 1.00 - 2.00 m2	6.08	92.37	51.61	**143.98**	Nr
	194 x 194 x 25 mm:					
	individual tile	0.29	4.38	2.58	**6.96**	Nr
	area not exceeding 0.50 m2	1.75	26.62	26.49	**53.11**	Nr
	area 0.50 - 1.00 m2	3.71	56.36	52.97	**109.33**	Nr

Unit Rates	Man-Hours	Net Labour Price £	Net Mats Price £	Net Unit Price £	Unit
area 1.00 - 2.00 m2	5.77	87.67	105.94	**193.61**	Nr

Note: 024 - 025 not used

CERAMIC FLOOR TILES

026 **Porcelain floor tiles including 10 mm bed of cement mortar (1:3) and jointing and pointing in cement mortar (1:3) straight joints both ways**

027 To floors, level and to falls only:

	Man-Hours	Net Labour Price £	Net Mats Price £	Net Unit Price £	Unit
over 300 mm wide:					
150 x 150 x 8.5 mm	1.24	18.79	24.76	**43.55**	m2
200 x 200 x 8.5 mm	1.08	16.43	28.18	**44.61**	m2
not exceeding 300 mm wide:					
150 x 150 x 8.5 mm	2.47	37.57	29.45	**67.02**	m2
200 x 200 x 8.5 mm	2.16	32.88	33.51	**66.39**	m2

028 To floors, to falls and crossfalls not exceeding 15 degrees from horizontal:

	Man-Hours	Net Labour Price £	Net Mats Price £	Net Unit Price £	Unit
over 300 mm wide:					
150 x 150 x 8.5 mm	1.29	19.56	24.76	**44.32**	m2
200 x 200 x 8.5 mm	1.13	17.22	28.18	**45.40**	m2
not exceeding 300 mm wide:					
150 x 150 x 8.5 mm	2.58	39.14	29.45	**68.59**	m2
200 x 200 x 8.5 mm	2.27	34.44	33.51	**67.95**	m2

029 To landings over 300 mm wide:

	Man-Hours	Net Labour Price £	Net Mats Price £	Net Unit Price £	Unit
150 x 150 x 8.5 mm	1.85	28.18	24.76	**52.94**	m2
200 x 200 x 8.5 mm	1.63	24.73	28.18	**52.91**	m2

030 To treads 250 mm wide:

	Man-Hours	Net Labour Price £	Net Mats Price £	Net Unit Price £	Unit
150 x 150 x 8.5 mm	0.62	9.39	4.02	**13.41**	m

031 To risers 175 mm high:

	Man-Hours	Net Labour Price £	Net Mats Price £	Net Unit Price £	Unit
150 x 150 x 8.5 mm	0.46	7.04	5.73	**12.77**	m
200 x 200 x 8.5 mm	0.38	5.79	5.41	**11.20**	m

032 **Extra over** for:

	Man-Hours	Net Labour Price £	Net Mats Price £	Net Unit Price £	Unit
For working into recessed duct covers:					
152 mm wide:					
150 x 150 x 8.5 mm	0.13	2.04	6.97	**9.01**	m
200 x 200 x 8.5 mm	0.16	2.36	8.03	**10.39**	m
300 mm wide:					
150 x 150 x 8.5 mm	0.16	2.36	6.97	**9.33**	m
200 x 200 x 8.5 mm	0.19	2.81	8.03	**10.84**	m
450 mm wide:					
150 x 150 x 8.5 mm	0.18	2.66	6.97	**9.63**	m
200 x 200 x 8.5 mm	0.21	3.13	8.03	**11.16**	m
600 mm wide:					
150 x 150 x 8.5 mm	0.21	3.13	6.97	**10.10**	m
200 x 200 x 8.5 mm	0.24	3.60	8.03	**11.63**	m
For working into recessed manhole covers:					
600 x 450 mm:					
150 x 150 x 8.5 mm	0.21	3.13	7.31	**10.44**	Nr
200 x 200 x 8.5 mm	0.24	3.60	8.47	**12.07**	Nr
600 x 600 mm:					
150 x 150 x 8.5 mm	0.26	3.92	8.37	**12.29**	Nr
200 x 200 x 8.5 mm	0.29	4.38	9.61	**13.99**	Nr

033 Raking cutting:

	Man-Hours	Net Labour Price £	Net Mats Price £	Net Unit Price £	Unit
150 x 150 x 8.5 mm	0.10	1.57	1.17	**2.74**	m
200 x 200 x 8.5 mm	0.08	1.25	1.31	**2.56**	m

034 Curved cutting:

	Man-Hours	Net Labour Price £	Net Mats Price £	Net Unit Price £	Unit
150 x 150 x 8.5 mm	0.21	3.13	1.73	**4.86**	m
200 x 200 x 8.5 mm	0.17	2.51	2.01	**4.52**	m

035 Fair joint to flush edge of existing finishes:

	Man-Hours	Net Labour Price £	Net Mats Price £	Net Unit Price £	Unit
150 x 150 x 8.5 mm	0.05	0.79	-	**0.79**	m
200 x 200 x 8.5 mm	0.05	0.79	-	**0.79**	m

036 Cut and fit floor tiles around steel joists, angles, pipes and the like:

	Man-Hours	Net Labour Price £	Net Mats Price £	Net Unit Price £	Unit
over 2.00 m girth:					
150 x 150 x 8.5 mm	0.16	2.36	-	**2.36**	m
200 x 200 x 8.5 mm	0.12	1.88	-	**1.88**	m
not exceeding 0.30 m girth:					
150 x 150 x 8.5 mm	0.07	1.09	-	**1.09**	Nr
200 x 200 x 8.5 mm	0.05	0.79	-	**0.79**	Nr
0.30 - 1.00 m girth:					
150 x 150 x 8.5 mm	0.11	1.72	-	**1.72**	Nr
200 x 200 x 8.5 mm	0.09	1.41	-	**1.41**	Nr
1.00 - 2.00 m girth:					
150 x 150 x 8.5 mm	0.24	3.60	-	**3.60**	Nr
200 x 200 x 8.5 mm	0.19	2.81	-	**2.81**	Nr

037 Porcelain tile skirting including 10 mm bed of cement mortar (1:3) and jointing and pointing with cement mortar (1:3):

	Man-Hours	Net Labour Price £	Net Mats Price £	Net Unit Price £	Unit
150 x 100 x 8.5 mm square/round top cove, 100 mm high	0.21	3.13	13.19	**16.32**	m
Extra over for:					
end	0.05	0.79	-	**0.79**	Nr

Unit Rates

	Man-Hours	Net Labour Price £	Net Mats Price £	Net Unit Price £	Unit
internal mitre	0.10	1.57	3.58	**5.15**	Nr
external angle	0.10	1.57	3.58	**5.15**	Nr
200 x 100 x 8.5 mm square/round top cove, 100 mm high	0.26	3.92	25.09	**29.01**	m
Extra over for:					
end	0.05	0.79	-	**0.79**	Nr
internal mitre	0.10	1.57	3.58	**5.15**	Nr
external angle	0.10	1.57	3.58	**5.15**	Nr
150 x 100 x 8.5 mm sit-on cove, 100 mm high	0.26	3.92	13.19	**17.11**	m
Extra over for:					
end	0.05	0.79	-	**0.79**	Nr
external angle	0.10	1.57	3.58	**5.15**	Nr

038 Cut out damaged glazed ceramic floor tiles and provide and fix new, bedded in cement and sand (1:3) with joints grouted in cement and sand (1:3); flush joint to existing all round:

	Man-Hours	Net Labour Price £	Net Mats Price £	Net Unit Price £	Unit
152 x 152 x 12 mm:					
individual tile	0.29	4.35	0.69	**5.04**	Nr
area not exceeding 0.50 m2	1.77	26.93	12.50	**39.43**	Nr
area 0.50 - 1.00 m2	3.88	59.02	24.98	**84.00**	Nr
area 1.00 - 2.00 m2	6.03	91.60	49.96	**141.56**	Nr
200 x 200 x 12 mm:					
individual tile	0.29	4.38	1.88	**6.26**	Nr
area not exceeding 0.50 m2	1.75	26.62	2.35	**28.97**	Nr
area 0.50 - 1.00 m2	3.76	57.15	4.61	**61.76**	Nr
area 1.00 - 2.00 m2	5.82	88.46	9.21	**97.67**	Nr

TG DRY LININGS

001 Gypsum plasterboard; tapered edges, fixed with galvanised nails to softwood; joints filled, taped and finished flush; holes filled with joint filler; surface finished with one coat Gyproc Drywall Sealer

Note: 002 - 005 not used

006 To walls in extending/repairing existing dry linings on and including 50 x 50 mm sawn softwood bearers at about 400 mm centres; flush joints to existing:

	Man-Hours	Net Labour Price £	Net Mats Price £	Net Unit Price £	Unit
9.5 mm wallboard:					
over 300 mm wide	0.58	12.01	3.33	**15.34**	m2
not exceeding 300 mm wide	1.15	24.01	3.50	**27.51**	m2
isolated areas not exceeding 1.00 m2	0.66	13.71	3.33	**17.04**	m2
12.5 mm wallboard:					
over 300 mm wide	0.65	13.51	3.36	**16.87**	m2
not exceeding 300 mm wide	1.31	27.22	3.53	**30.75**	m2
isolated areas not exceeding 1.00 m2	0.74	15.44	3.36	**18.80**	m2
15.0 mm wallboard:					
over 300 mm wide	0.72	15.00	3.82	**18.82**	m2
not exceeding 300 mm wide	1.45	30.22	4.00	**34.22**	m2
isolated areas not exceeding 1.00 m2	0.82	17.15	3.82	**20.97**	m2
19.0 mm plank:					
over 300 mm wide	0.80	16.71	6.12	**22.83**	m2
not exceeding 300 mm wide	1.39	28.95	6.29	**35.24**	m2
isolated areas not exceeding 1.00 m2	0.92	19.08	6.12	**25.20**	m2

007 To ceilings in extending/repairing existing dry linings on and including 50 x 50 mm sawn softwood bearers at about 400 mm centres; flush joints to existing:

	Man-Hours	Net Labour Price £	Net Mats Price £	Net Unit Price £	Unit
9.5 mm wallboard:					
over 300 mm wide	0.64	13.30	3.21	**16.51**	m2
not exceeding 300 mm wide	1.28	26.57	3.38	**29.95**	m2
isolated areas not exceeding 1.00 m2	0.73	15.21	3.21	**18.42**	m2
12.5 mm wallboard:					
over 300 mm wide	0.71	14.80	3.24	**18.04**	m2
not exceeding 300 mm wide	1.42	29.57	3.41	**32.98**	m2
isolated areas not exceeding 1.00 m2	0.81	16.94	3.24	**20.18**	m2
15.0 mm wallboard:					
over 300 mm wide	0.78	16.29	3.71	**20.00**	m2
not exceeding 300 mm wide	1.58	32.80	3.88	**36.68**	m2
isolated areas not exceeding 1.00 m2	0.90	18.65	3.71	**22.36**	m2
19.0 mm plank:					
over 300 mm wide	0.86	17.79	6.01	**23.80**	m2
not exceeding 300 mm wide	1.72	35.79	6.18	**41.97**	m2
isolated areas not exceeding 1.00 m2	0.98	20.35	6.01	**26.36**	m2

008 **Extra over** Gypsum wallboard for:

	Man-Hours	Net Labour Price £	Net Mats Price £	Net Unit Price £	Unit
Fireline board 12.5 mm	-	-	0.53	**0.53**	m2
Fireline board 15 mm	-	-	2.31	**2.31**	m2
Duplex grade (wallboard and Fireline board only)	-	-	1.15	**1.15**	m2
Fixing 9.5 and 12.5 mm wallboard by the Gyproc **Dri-wall** system using dabs and perimeter seal	0.12	2.58	1.84	**4.42**	m2

009 Angles:

	Man-Hours	Net Labour Price £	Net Mats Price £	Net Unit Price £	Unit
Internal angles including jointing tape	0.10	2.14	0.58	**2.72**	m
External angles including corner tape	0.18	3.70	0.58	**4.28**	m
External angles including dry wall angle bead	0.14	2.96	1.62	**4.58**	m

010 Cutting to profile of openings:

	Man-Hours	Net Labour Price £	Net Mats Price £	Net Unit Price £	Unit
9.5 mm wallboard	0.05	0.98	-	**0.98**	m
12.5 mm wallboard	0.06	1.25	-	**1.25**	m
15.0 mm wallboard	0.07	1.48	-	**1.48**	m
19.0 mm plank	0.07	1.48	-	**1.48**	m

		Man-Hours	Net Labour Price £	Net Mats Price £	Net Unit Price £	Unit
Unit Rates						
011	Raking cutting:					
	9.5 mm wallboard	0.04	0.85	0.26	**1.11**	m
	12.5 mm wallboard	0.05	1.08	0.26	**1.34**	m
	15.0 mm wallboard	0.06	1.29	0.31	**1.60**	m
	19.0 mm plank	0.07	1.50	0.54	**2.04**	m
012	Curved cutting:					
	9.5 mm wallboard	0.05	1.08	0.52	**1.60**	m
	12.5 mm wallboard	0.06	1.29	0.52	**1.81**	m
	15.0 mm wallboard	0.07	1.50	0.62	**2.12**	m
	19.0 mm plank	0.08	1.71	1.07	**2.78**	m
013	Cutting around steel joists, angles, pipes and the like:					
	over 2.00 m girth:					
	9.5 mm wallboard	0.05	1.08	-	**1.08**	m
	12.5 mm wallboard	0.06	1.29	-	**1.29**	m
	15.0 mm wallboard	0.07	1.50	-	**1.50**	m
	19.0 mm plank	0.08	1.73	-	**1.73**	m
	not exceeding 0.30 m girth:					
	9.5 mm wallboard	0.04	0.75	-	**0.75**	Nr
	12.5 mm wallboard	0.04	0.75	-	**0.75**	Nr
	15.0 mm wallboard	0.05	1.00	-	**1.00**	Nr
	19.0 mm plank	0.05	1.00	-	**1.00**	Nr
	0.30 - 1.00 m girth:					
	9.5 mm wallboard	0.05	1.00	-	**1.00**	Nr
	12.5 mm wallboard	0.05	1.00	-	**1.00**	Nr
	15.0 mm wallboard	0.06	1.25	-	**1.25**	Nr
	19.0 mm plank	0.06	1.25	-	**1.25**	Nr
	1.00 - 2.00 m girth:					
	9.5 mm wallboard	0.10	1.98	-	**1.98**	Nr
	12.5 mm wallboard	0.10	1.98	-	**1.98**	Nr
	15.0 mm wallboard	0.11	2.23	-	**2.23**	Nr
	19.0 mm plank	0.12	2.48	-	**2.48**	Nr
014	**Gyproc ThermaLine Basic thermal board; tapered edges, fixed to plastered or smooth faced surfaces with Gyproc acrylic adhesive and nailable plugs secondary fixing; joints filled, taped and finished flush; holes filled with joint filler; surface finished with one coat Gyproc Drywall Sealer**					
015	To walls:					
	over 300 mm wide:					
	22 mm thick	0.52	10.84	17.70	**28.54**	m2
	30 mm thick	0.52	10.84	18.26	**29.10**	m2
	40 mm thick	0.59	12.32	19.04	**31.36**	m2
	50 mm thick	0.59	12.32	20.53	**32.85**	m2
	not exceeding 300 mm wide:					
	22 mm thick	1.04	21.68	17.93	**39.61**	m2
	30 mm thick	1.04	21.68	18.43	**40.11**	m2
	40 mm thick	1.19	24.66	19.21	**43.87**	m2
	50 mm thick	1.19	24.66	20.70	**45.36**	m2
016	To ceilings:					
	over 300 mm wide:					
	22 mm thick	0.57	11.84	17.03	**28.87**	m2
	30 mm thick	0.57	11.84	17.53	**29.37**	m2
	40 mm thick	0.64	13.32	18.32	**31.64**	m2
	50 mm thick	0.64	13.32	19.44	**32.76**	m2
	not exceeding 300 mm wide:					
	22 mm thick	1.14	23.66	17.21	**40.87**	m2
	30 mm thick	1.14	23.66	17.70	**41.36**	m2
	40 mm thick	1.28	26.62	18.49	**45.11**	m2
	50 mm thick	1.28	26.62	19.61	**46.23**	m2
017	**Extra over** Gyproc thermal board for **ThermaLine Super:**					
	50 mm thick	0.02	0.44	9.82	**10.26**	m2
018	**Extra over** Gyproc thermal board for **Tri-line laminate board:**					
	40 mm thick	-	-	7.33	**7.33**	m2
	50 mm thick	-	-	8.69	**8.69**	m2
019	**Extra over** Gyproc thermal board or Gyproc Tri-line for **vapour check**	-	-	1.15	**1.15**	m2
	Note: 020 not used					
021	Internal angles including jointing tape	0.10	2.14	0.03	**2.17**	m
022	External angles including corner tape	0.12	2.58	0.58	**3.16**	m
023	External angles including dry wall angle bead	0.16	3.23	1.84	**5.07**	m
024	Cutting to profile of openings:					
	22 mm thick	0.06	1.29	-	**1.29**	m
	30 mm thick	0.06	1.29	-	**1.29**	m
	40 mm thick	0.06	1.29	-	**1.29**	m
	50 mm thick	0.06	1.29	-	**1.29**	m
025	Raking cutting:					
	22 mm thick	0.07	1.48	1.00	**2.48**	m
	30 mm thick	0.07	1.48	1.09	**2.57**	m
	40 mm thick	0.07	1.48	1.25	**2.73**	m
	50 mm thick	0.07	1.48	1.48	**2.96**	m

Unit Rates

		Man-Hours	Net Labour Price £	Net Mats Price £	Net Unit Price £	Unit
026	Curved cutting:					
	22 mm thick	0.08	1.71	1.00	**2.71**	m
	30 mm thick	0.08	1.71	1.09	**2.80**	m
	40 mm thick	0.09	1.94	1.25	**3.19**	m
	50 mm thick	0.09	1.94	1.48	**3.42**	m
027	Cutting around steel joists, angles, pipes and the like:					
	over 2.00 m girth:					
	22 mm thick	0.07	1.50	-	**1.50**	m
	30 mm thick	0.07	1.50	-	**1.50**	m
	40 mm thick	0.08	1.71	-	**1.71**	m
	50 mm thick	0.08	1.71	-	**1.71**	m
	not exceeding 0.30 m girth:					
	22 mm thick	0.04	0.85	-	**0.85**	Nr
	30 mm thick	0.04	0.85	-	**0.85**	Nr
	40 mm thick	0.05	1.08	-	**1.08**	Nr
	50 mm thick	0.05	1.08	-	**1.08**	Nr
	0.30 - 1.00 m girth:					
	22 mm thick	0.06	1.29	-	**1.29**	Nr
	30 mm thick	0.06	1.29	-	**1.29**	Nr
	40 mm thick	0.07	1.50	-	**1.50**	Nr
	50 mm thick	0.07	1.50	-	**1.50**	Nr
	1.00 - 2.00 m girth:					
	22 mm thick	0.10	2.14	-	**2.14**	Nr
	30 mm thick	0.10	2.14	-	**2.14**	Nr
	40 mm thick	0.12	2.58	-	**2.58**	Nr
	50 mm thick	0.12	2.58	-	**2.58**	Nr
028	**Non-asbestos boards (Supalux) with sanded finish; screwed to softwood, heads of screws sunk and filled**					
	Note: 029 - 032 not used					
033	To walls in extending/repairing existing boarding on and including 50 x 50 mm wrought softwood bearers at about 400 mm centres; fair flush joints to existing:					
	over 300 mm wide:					
	6 mm thick	0.89	13.47	18.72	**32.19**	m2
	9 mm thick	0.96	14.56	25.90	**40.46**	m2
	12 mm thick	1.03	15.66	32.78	**48.44**	m2
	not exceeding 300 mm wide:					
	6 mm thick	1.77	26.93	18.85	**45.78**	m2
	9 mm thick	1.92	29.12	25.97	**55.09**	m2
	12 mm thick	2.07	31.46	32.84	**64.30**	m2
	isolated areas not exceeding 1.00 m2:					
	6 mm thick	1.01	15.34	18.72	**34.06**	m2
	9 mm thick	1.01	15.34	25.90	**41.24**	m2
	12 mm thick	1.19	18.01	32.78	**50.79**	m2
034	To ceilings in extending/repairing existing boarding on and including 50 x 50 mm wrought softwood bearers at about 400 mm centres; fair flush joints to existing:					
	over 300 mm wide:					
	6 mm thick	0.97	14.71	18.72	**33.43**	m2
	9 mm thick	1.03	15.66	25.94	**41.60**	m2
	12 mm thick	1.09	16.60	32.82	**49.42**	m2
	not exceeding 300 mm wide:					
	6 mm thick	1.93	29.28	18.85	**48.13**	m2
	9 mm thick	2.06	31.31	26.02	**57.33**	m2
	12 mm thick	2.18	33.20	32.90	**66.10**	m2
	isolated areas not exceeding 1.00 m2:					
	6 mm thick	1.11	16.90	18.72	**35.62**	m2
	9 mm thick	1.19	18.01	25.94	**43.95**	m2
	12 mm thick	1.26	19.11	32.82	**51.93**	m2
035	75 mm Supalux fillets:					
	to face of vertical timbers at 450 mm centres:					
	6 mm thick	0.45	6.89	3.45	**10.34**	m2
	9 mm thick	0.51	7.68	5.14	**12.82**	m2
	12 mm thick	0.58	8.77	6.79	**15.56**	m2
	to face of vertical timbers at 600 mm centres:					
	6 mm thick	0.34	5.17	2.59	**7.76**	m2
	9 mm thick	0.38	5.79	3.86	**9.65**	m2
	12 mm thick	0.43	6.58	5.11	**11.69**	m2
	to soffit of timbers at 450 mm centres:					
	6 mm thick	0.58	8.77	3.45	**12.22**	m2
	9 mm thick	0.62	9.39	5.14	**14.53**	m2
	12 mm thick	0.69	10.49	6.79	**17.28**	m2
036	Raking cutting:					
	6 mm thick	0.07	1.09	2.77	**3.86**	m
	9 mm thick	0.07	1.09	3.87	**4.96**	m
	12 mm thick	0.08	1.25	4.90	**6.15**	m
037	Cutting around steel joists, angles, pipes and the like:					
	over 2.00 m girth:					
	6 mm thick	0.05	0.74	-	**0.74**	m
	9 mm thick	0.05	0.74	-	**0.74**	m
	12 mm thick	0.06	0.87	-	**0.87**	m
	not exceeding 0.30 m girth:					
	6 mm thick	0.02	0.35	-	**0.35**	Nr

Unit Rates	Man-Hours	Net Labour Price £	Net Mats Price £	Net Unit Price £	Unit
9 mm thick	0.02	0.35	-	0.35	Nr
12 mm thick	0.03	0.40	-	0.40	Nr
0.30 - 1.00 m girth:					
6 mm thick	0.04	0.55	-	0.55	Nr
9 mm thick	0.04	0.55	-	0.55	Nr
12 mm thick	0.05	0.70	-	0.70	Nr
1.00 - 2.00 m girth:					
6 mm thick	0.07	1.12	-	1.12	Nr
9 mm thick	0.07	1.12	-	1.12	Nr
12 mm thick	0.09	1.29	-	1.29	Nr

GYPROC COVE

038 | **Gypsum plaster core cove cornice fixed with adhesive**

039 100 mm Girth	0.11	2.67	1.27	**3.94**	m
Extra over:					
return end	0.16	3.66	0.77	**4.43**	Nr
angles	0.21	4.86	0.77	**5.63**	Nr
040 100 mm girth; in isolated lengths in making good including flush joint to existing each end:					
not exceeding 1.00 m long	0.14	3.40	11.14	**14.54**	m
1.00 - 2.00 m long	0.29	6.80	22.29	**29.09**	m
041 127 mm Girth	0.12	2.93	1.39	**4.32**	m
Extra over:					
return end	0.18	4.13	0.11	**4.24**	Nr
angles	0.26	6.09	0.11	**6.20**	Nr
042 127 mm girth; in isolated lengths in making good including flush joint to existing each end:					
not exceeding 1.00 m long	0.16	3.66	11.08	**14.74**	m
1.00 - 2.00 m long	0.31	7.30	22.16	**29.46**	m

TH | **PARTITIONS**

Note: 001 – 015 not used

LAMINATED PARTITIONS

016 | **Gyproc laminated partition; 50 mm thick partition comprising 19 mm Gyproc plank core faced both sides with 12.5 mm Gyproc wallboard bonded on; 65 mm thick partition comprising 19 mm Gyproc plank core faced both sides with 19 mm Gyproc tapered edge plank bonded on; joints filled, taped and finished flush; holes filled with joint filler; surface finished with one coat Gyproc Drywall Sealer**

017 Over 300 mm wide:					
50 mm thick	1.15	24.01	14.61	**38.62**	m2
65 mm thick	1.32	27.43	20.10	**47.53**	m2
018 Not exceeding 300 mm wide:					
50 mm thick	2.31	48.01	14.96	**62.97**	m2
65 mm thick	2.64	54.88	20.44	**75.32**	m2
019 Base/head fixing including 38 x 25 mm softwood batten fixed to softwood:					
50 mm thick	0.16	3.23	0.77	**4.00**	m
65 mm thick	0.16	3.23	0.77	**4.00**	m
020 End fixing including 38 x 25 mm softwood batten fixed to softwood:					
50 mm thick	0.16	3.23	0.77	**4.00**	m
65 mm thick	0.16	3.23	0.77	**4.00**	m
021 Square angle including 38 x 25 mm softwood batten and dry wall angle bead:					
50 mm thick	0.26	5.37	1.68	**7.05**	m
65 mm thick	0.26	5.37	1.68	**7.05**	m
022 Intersection:					
50 mm thick	0.16	3.23	-	**3.23**	m
65 mm thick	0.16	3.23	-	**3.23**	m
023 Exposed end including 38 x 25 mm softwood batten 9.5 mm plasterboard to end and two dry wall angle beads:					
50 mm thick	0.52	10.72	3.06	**13.78**	m
65 mm thick	0.52	10.72	3.06	**13.78**	m
024 Framing to openings including 38 x 25 mm softwood batten:					
50 mm thick	0.36	7.39	2.46	**9.85**	m
65 mm thick	0.36	7.39	3.28	**10.67**	m
025 Raking cutting:					
50 mm thick	0.19	3.95	1.86	**5.81**	m
65 mm thick	0.21	4.29	2.68	**6.97**	m
026 Cutting around steel joists, angles, pipes and the like including additional 38 x 25 mm softwood battens:					
over 2.00 m girth:					
50 mm thick	0.22	4.49	0.60	**5.09**	m
65 mm thick	0.22	4.49	0.60	**5.09**	m
not exceeding 0.30 m girth:					
50 mm thick	0.09	1.85	0.18	**2.03**	Nr

Unit Rates

		Man-Hours	Net Labour Price £	Net Mats Price £	Net Unit Price £	Unit
	65 mm thick	0.10	2.06	0.18	**2.24**	Nr
	0.30 - 1.00 m girth:					
	50 mm thick	0.14	2.98	0.51	**3.49**	Nr
	65 mm thick	0.16	3.29	0.51	**3.80**	Nr
	1.00 - 2.00 m girth:					
	50 mm thick	0.29	6.12	0.95	**7.07**	Nr
	65 mm thick	0.32	6.74	0.95	**7.69**	Nr
027	ADD TO THE FOREGOING PRICES for:					
	fixing battens direct with hardened steel masonry nails:					
	to brick or block	0.08	1.71	0.04	**1.75**	m2
	to concrete	0.10	2.14	0.04	**2.18**	m2
028	**Extra over** Gyproc laminated partition if **Duplex board**; per side	-	-	1.15	**1.15**	m2
	METAL STUD PARTITIONS					
029	**75 mm Gyproc metal stud partition; 48 mm studs 12.5 mm taper edge wallboard each side; joints filled, taped and finished flush; holes filled with joint filler; surface finished with one coat Gyproc Drywall Sealer**					
030	Over 300 mm wide	1.26	26.26	11.13	**37.39**	m2
031	Not exceeding 300 mm wide	3.61	75.02	12.66	**87.68**	m2
032	Base/head fixing to softwood	0.16	3.23	1.85	**5.08**	m
033	End fixing to softwood	0.16	3.23	1.72	**4.95**	m
034	Square angle including additional stud and dry wall angle bead	0.30	6.18	2.56	**8.74**	m
035	Intersection including additional stud	0.30	6.18	1.48	**7.66**	m
036	Exposed end including additional stud 9.5 mm plasterboard to end and two dry wall angle beads	0.58	11.97	3.94	**15.91**	m
037	Framing to openings including 38 x 25 mm softwood batten	0.36	7.39	2.08	**9.47**	m
038	Cutting around steel joists, angles, pipes and the like including additional studs:					
	over 2.00 m girth	0.30	6.18	1.48	**7.66**	m
	not exceeding 0.30 m girth	0.13	2.71	0.47	**3.18**	Nr
	0.30 - 1.00 m girth	0.21	4.43	1.05	**5.48**	Nr
	1.00 - 2.00 m girth	0.45	9.36	2.20	**11.56**	Nr
039	ADD TO THE FOREGOING PRICES for:					
	40 mm resin bonded glass wool slab in cavity	0.21	4.29	3.00	**7.29**	m2
	Additional 12.5 mm wallboard each side (100 mm overall):					
	over 300 mm wide	1.19	24.66	5.32	**29.98**	m2
	not exceeding 300 mm wide	2.37	49.30	5.36	**54.66**	m2
	Two 12.5 mm Fireline boards each side (100 mm overall) in lieu of one 12.5 mm wallboard each side:					
	over 300 mm wide	1.19	24.66	7.45	**32.11**	m2
	not exceeding 300 mm wide	2.37	49.30	7.49	**56.79**	m2
	Square edge panels with 5 mm two coat Thistle Board finish in lieu of taper edge panels finished for decoration:					
	over 300 mm wide:					
	one side	0.20	4.20	1.26	**5.46**	m2
	both sides	0.40	8.39	2.51	**10.90**	m2
	not exceeding 300 mm wide:					
	one side	0.40	8.39	1.09	**9.48**	m2
	both sides	0.81	16.75	2.17	**18.92**	m2
	fixing frames direct with hardened steel masonry nails:					
	to brick or block	0.08	1.71	-	**1.71**	m2
	to concrete	0.10	2.14	-	**2.14**	m2
040	38 x 48 mm softwood plate fixed to softwood	0.10	2.14	1.01	**3.15**	m
TM	**RUBBER FLOORING**					
001	**Jaymart "Prialpas Central" low profile studded finish synthetic rubber floor tiles 500 mm x 500 mm x 4 mm; indoor quality; fixed to prepared level cement and sand base with adhesive; straight butt jointed both ways to**					
002	Floors over 300 mm wide:					
	black (Group 1)	0.80	16.65	30.05	**46.70**	m2
	brown (Group 2)	0.80	16.65	33.02	**49.67**	m2
	colours (Group 3)	0.80	16.65	34.80	**51.45**	m2
003	Landings over 300 mm wide:					
	black (Group 1)	0.86	17.90	30.05	**47.95**	m2
	brown (Group 2)	0.86	17.90	33.02	**50.92**	m2
	colours (Group 3)	0.86	17.90	34.80	**52.70**	m2
	Note: 004 – 006 not used					
007	**Jaymart " Prialpas Central " synthetic rubber accessories; indoor quality; fixed to prepared cement and sand base with adhesive; butt jointed ends**					
008	One piece combined stair finish (9781N), 480 mm overall girth; studded tread / smooth riser / ribbed nosing:					
	black (Group 1)	0.61	12.69	25.26	**37.95**	m
	brown (Group 2)	0.61	12.69	30.57	**43.26**	m
	colours (Group 3)	0.61	12.69	30.57	**43.26**	m

Unit Rates	Man-Hours	Net Labour Price £	Net Mats Price £	Net Unit Price £	Unit
Note: 009 not used					
010 Pre-formed internal wall angle section coving including ends and angles:					
61 mm sit-on skirting (M691), black (Group 1)	0.39	8.12	5.76	**13.88**	m
61 mm sit-on skirting (M691), brown (Group 2)	0.39	8.12	6.09	**14.21**	m
100 mm set-in skirting (M686), black (Group 1)	0.39	8.12	8.82	**16.94**	m
100 mm set-in skirting (M686), brown (Group 2)	0.41	8.53	9.35	**17.88**	m
TN **LINOLEUM FLOORING**					
001 **Nairn Marmoleum Real marbled pattern sheet linoleum; BS 6826; fixed to prepared level cement and sand base with adhesive; butt jointed to**					
Note: 002 - 005 not used					
006 Floors; in extending/repairing existing sheeting:					
over 300 mm wide:					
2.5 mm	0.42	8.78	18.88	**27.66**	m2
3.2 mm	0.42	8.78	22.38	**31.16**	m2
not exceeding 300 mm wide:					
2.5 mm	0.83	17.36	18.88	**36.24**	m2
3.2 mm	0.82	17.15	22.38	**39.53**	m2
007 Cut out and remove defective sheet linoleum flooring; isolated areas; clean off screed and piece in new linoleum to match existing; fair flush butt joints to existing all round:					
areas not exceeding 0.50 m2:					
2.5 mm	1.55	32.15	10.39	**42.54**	Nr
3.2 mm	1.55	32.15	12.32	**44.47**	Nr
areas 0.50 - 1.00 m2:					
2.5 mm	2.58	53.59	19.92	**73.51**	Nr
3.2 mm	2.58	53.59	23.60	**77.19**	Nr
areas 1.00 - 2.00 m2:					
2.5 mm	4.89	101.82	39.84	**141.66**	Nr
3.2 mm	4.89	101.82	47.19	**149.01**	Nr
Note: 008 - 009 not used					
010 **Nairn Artoleum Scala sheet linoleum; BS 6826; fixed to prepared level cement and sand base with adhesive; butt jointed to**					
Note: 011 - 014 not used					
015 Floors; in extending/repairing existing sheeting:					
over 300 mm wide:					
2.5 mm	0.42	8.78	22.31	**31.09**	m2
not exceeding 300 mm wide:					
2.5 mm	0.82	17.15	22.31	**39.46**	m2
016 Cut out and remove defective sheet linoleum flooring; isolated areas; clean off screed and piece in new linoleum to match existing; fair flush butt joints to existing all round:					
areas not exceeding 0.50 m2:					
2.5 mm	1.55	32.15	12.28	**44.43**	Nr
areas 0.50 - 1.00 m2:					
2.5 mm	2.58	53.59	23.53	**77.12**	Nr
areas 1.00 - 2.00 m2:					
2.5 mm	4.89	101.82	47.05	**148.87**	Nr
Note: 017 - 019 not used					
020 **333 x 333 x 2.5 mm Nairn Marmoleum Dual marble pattern linoleum tiles; BS 6826; fixed to prepared level cement and sand base with adhesive; straight butt jointed both ways; to**					
Note: 021 - 024 not used					
025 Floors; in extending/repairing existing tiling:					
over 300 mm wide	0.49	10.28	24.84	**35.12**	m2
not exceeding 300 mm wide	0.93	19.29	24.84	**44.13**	m2
isolated areas not exceeding 1.00 m2 including fair flush butt joints to existing	0.05	1.08	-	**1.08**	m2
026 Cut out defective floor tiling and supply and fix new to match existing; fair flush butt joints to existing:					
individual tiles	0.41	8.57	2.48	**11.05**	Nr
area not exceeding 0.50 m2	1.49	31.09	13.58	**44.67**	Nr
area 0.50 - 1.00 m2	2.52	52.52	26.00	**78.52**	Nr
area 1.00 - 2.00 m2	4.79	99.68	51.99	**151.67**	Nr
TO **PVC VINYL AND THERMOPLASTIC FLOORING**					
001 **Tarkett flexible vinyl sheet flooring; BS 3261 (Part A); fixed to prepared level cement and sand base with adhesive; welded butt jointed to**					
Note: 002 - 005 not used					
006 Floors; in extending/repairing existing sheeting:					
over 300 mm wide:					
2.0 mm IQ Granite sheet	0.49	10.28	18.43	**28.71**	m2
2.0 mm Eclipse vinyl sheet	0.49	10.28	14.60	**24.88**	m2
2.0 mm Safetred Universal sheet	0.49	10.28	17.33	**27.61**	m2

		Man-Hours	Net Labour Price £	Net Mats Price £	Net Unit Price £	Unit
	Unit Rates					
	not exceeding 300 mm wide:					
	2.0 mm IQ Granite sheet	0.93	19.29	18.43	**37.72**	m2
	2.0 mm Eclipse vinyl sheet	0.93	19.29	14.60	**33.89**	m2
	2.0 mm Safetred Universal sheet	0.93	19.29	17.33	**36.62**	m2
007	Cut out and remove defective sheet linoleum flooring; isolated areas; clean off screed and piece in new linoleum to match existing; fair flush butt joints to existing all round:					
	areas not exceeding 0.50 m2:					
	2.0 mm IQ Granite sheet	1.55	32.15	10.19	**42.34**	Nr
	2.0 mm Eclipse vinyl sheet	1.55	32.15	8.08	**40.23**	Nr
	2.0 mm Safetred Universal sheet	1.55	32.15	9.58	**41.73**	Nr
	areas 0.50 - 1.00 m2:					
	2.0 mm IQ Granite sheet	2.58	53.59	19.51	**73.10**	Nr
	2.0 mm Eclipse vinyl sheet	2.58	53.59	15.50	**69.09**	Nr
	2.0 mm Safetred Universal sheet	2.58	53.59	18.36	**71.95**	Nr
	areas 1.00 - 2.00 m2:					
	2.0 mm IQ Granite sheet	4.89	101.82	39.03	**140.85**	Nr
	2.0 mm Eclipse vinyl sheet	4.89	101.82	30.99	**132.81**	Nr
	2.0 mm Safetred Universal sheet	4.89	101.82	36.72	**138.54**	Nr
008	**300 x 300 mm Tarkett flexible vinyl tile flooring; BS 3261 (Part A); fixed to prepared level cement and sand base with adhesive; straight butt jointed both ways to**					
	Note: 009 - 012 not used					
013	Floors; in extending/repairing existing tiling:					
	over 300 mm wide:					
	2.0 mm Standard tiles	0.42	8.78	12.67	**21.45**	m2
	2.0 mm Vylon Plus tiles	0.42	8.78	11.02	**19.80**	m2
	not exceeding 300 mm wide:					
	2.0 mm Standard tiles	0.82	17.15	12.67	**29.82**	m2
	2.0 mm Vylon Plus tiles	0.82	17.15	11.02	**28.17**	m2
	isolated areas not exceeding 1.00 m2 including fair flush butt joints to existing:					
	2.0 mm Standard tiles	0.48	10.07	12.67	**22.74**	m2
	2.0 mm Vylon Plus tiles	0.48	10.07	11.02	**21.09**	m2
014	Cut out and remove defective sheet linoleum flooring; isolated areas; clean off screed and piece in new linoleum to match existing; fair flush butt joints to existing all round:					
	individual tiles:					
	2.0 mm Standard tiles	0.41	8.57	1.28	**9.85**	Nr
	2.0 mm Vylon Plus tiles	0.41	8.57	1.12	**9.69**	Nr
	areas not exceeding 0.50 m2:					
	2.0 mm Standard tiles	1.55	32.15	7.01	**39.16**	Nr
	2.0 mm Vylon Plus tiles	1.55	32.15	6.10	**38.25**	Nr
	areas 0.50 - 1.00 m2:					
	2.0 mm Standard tiles	2.58	53.59	13.43	**67.02**	Nr
	2.0 mm Vylon Plus tiles	2.58	53.59	11.70	**65.29**	Nr
	areas 1.00 - 2.00 m2:					
	2.0 mm Standard tiles	4.89	101.82	26.86	**128.68**	Nr
	2.0 mm Vylon Plus tiles	4.89	101.82	23.39	**125.21**	Nr
015	**610 x 610 mm Tarkett Homogeneous Premium flooring; BS 3260; fixed to prepared level cement and sand base with adhesive; straight butt jointed both ways to**					
016	Floors over 300 mm wide:					
	2.0 mm Eclipse/Primo tiles	0.45	9.43	15.42	**24.85**	m2
017	Landings over 300 mm wide:					
	2.0 mm Eclipse/Primo tiles	0.49	10.28	15.42	**25.70**	m2
018	Treads 300 mm wide:					
	2.0 mm Eclipse/Primo tiles	0.34	7.08	4.68	**11.76**	m
019	Risers 150 mm high:					
	2.0 mm Eclipse/Primo tiles	0.30	6.22	2.34	**8.56**	m
	Note: 020 - 022 not used					
023	**610 x 610 x 2 mm Tarkett iQ collection – 'Eminent' ; fixed to prepared level cement and sand base with adhesive; welded straight butt jointed both ways; to**					
024	floors over 300 mm wide	0.86	17.79	25.81	**43.60**	m2
	landings over 300 mm wide	0.94	19.50	25.81	**45.31**	m2
	treads 300 mm wide	0.45	9.43	8.26	**17.69**	m
	risers 150 mm high	0.42	8.78	4.44	**13.22**	m
025	**610 x 610 mm Tarkett Homogeneous Plus tile flooring; fixed to prepared level cement and sand base with adhesive; straight butt jointed both ways; to**					
	Note: 026 - 028 not used					
029	Floors; in extending/repairing existing tiling:					
	over 300 mm wide:					
	2.0 mm IQ Granite tiles	0.57	11.80	19.27	**31.07**	m2
	2.0 mm Somplan Plus tiles	0.57	11.80	13.77	**25.57**	m2
	not exceeding 300 mm wide:					
	2.0 mm IQ Granite tiles	1.08	22.50	19.27	**41.77**	m2
	2.0 mm Somplan Plus tiles	1.08	22.50	13.77	**36.27**	m2

Unit Rates	Man-Hours	Net Labour Price £	Net Mats Price £	Net Unit Price £	Unit
isolated areas not exceeding 1.00 m2 including fair flush butt joints to existing:					
2.0 mm IQ Granite tiles	0.65	13.51	19.27	**32.78**	m2
2.0 mm Somplan Plus tiles	0.65	13.51	13.77	**27.28**	m2
030 Cut out defective floor tiling and supply and fix new to match existing; fair flush butt joints to existing:					
individual tiles:					
2.0 mm IQ Granite tiles	0.41	8.57	1.94	**10.51**	Nr
2.0 mm Somplan Plus tiles	0.41	8.57	1.39	**9.96**	Nr
area not exceeding 0.50 m2:					
2.0 mm IQ Granite tiles	1.55	32.15	10.64	**42.79**	Nr
2.0 mm Somplan Plus tiles	1.55	32.15	7.61	**39.76**	Nr
area 0.50 - 1.00 m2:					
2.0 mm IQ Granite tiles	2.58	53.59	20.36	**73.95**	Nr
2.0 mm Somplan Plus tiles	2.58	53.59	14.58	**68.17**	Nr
area 1.00 - 2.00 m2:					
2.0 mm IQ Granite tiles	4.89	101.82	40.72	**142.54**	Nr
2.0 mm Somplan Plus tiles	4.89	101.82	29.17	**130.99**	Nr
031 **2 mm thick Tarkett vinyl coved skirting; 2 metre lengths with butt end joints; fixed with adhesive to prepared cement and sand or plaster backing including ends and angles**					
032 100 mm high sit-on skirting	0.29	5.99	3.79	**9.78**	m
100 mm high set-in skirting with butt joint to sheet or tile flooring	0.29	5.99	6.38	**12.37**	m
100 mm high set-in skirting with welded butt joint to sheet or tile flooring	0.34	7.08	6.77	**13.85**	m
033 Fair flush butt joint of new sheet flooring to existing	0.05	1.08	-	**1.08**	m
034 Fair flush butt joint of new tile flooring to existing	0.05	1.08	-	**1.08**	m
035 Fair flush welded butt joint of new sheet flooring to existing	0.05	1.08	0.52	**1.60**	m
036 Fair flush welded butt joint of new tile flooring to existing	0.05	1.08	0.52	**1.60**	m
037 **Aluminium safety tread with carborundum insert**					
038 Safety tread set flush in and fixed with contact adhesive to paving including temporary batten insert:					
19 mm wide	0.19	3.85	20.78	**24.63**	m
38 mm wide	0.25	5.14	24.43	**29.57**	m
50 mm wide	0.27	5.66	31.82	**37.48**	m
039 **Aluminium safety nosings fixed with contact fixative**					
040 2mm gauge:					
Nosing with single insert (AS11)	0.25	5.14	11.05	**16.19**	m
Nosing with single insert (AR81)	0.27	5.66	13.28	**18.94**	m
Nosing with double insert (AS12)	0.26	5.41	15.39	**20.80**	m
041 5mm gauge:					
Nosing with single insert (G11)	0.28	5.72	13.37	**19.09**	m
Nosing with single insert (GR81)	0.28	5.72	16.04	**21.76**	m
Nosing with double insert (G12)	0.28	5.72	17.90	**23.62**	m
TP **CORK FLOORING**					
001 **Heavy density unsealed cork floor tiles; (supplied by Siesta Cork Tile Co.) 300 x 300 mm; fixed to prepared level cement and sand base with adhesive; straight butt jointed both ways to**					
002 Floors over 300 mm wide:					
4.8 mm	0.52	10.76	10.64	**21.40**	m2
6.0 mm	0.52	10.76	12.33	**23.09**	m2
003 Landings over 300 mm wide:					
4.8 mm	0.57	11.82	10.64	**22.46**	m2
6.0 mm	0.57	11.82	12.33	**24.15**	m2
004 Treads 300 mm wide:					
4.8 mm	0.38	7.95	3.20	**11.15**	m
6.0 mm	0.38	7.95	3.71	**11.66**	m
005 Risers 150 mm high:					
4.8 mm	0.36	7.51	1.60	**9.11**	m
6.0 mm	0.36	7.51	1.85	**9.36**	m
006 Prepare and apply two coats polyurethane sealer to sanded cork flooring	0.07	1.42	0.27	**1.69**	m2
Note: 007 - 009 not used					
010 **Heavy density pre-sealed cork floor tiles; (supplied by Siesta Cork Tile Co.) 300 x 300 mm; fixed to prepared level cement and sand base with adhesive**					
011 Floors over 300 mm wide:					
3.2 mm	0.52	10.76	12.45	**23.21**	m2
6.0 mm	0.52	10.76	15.49	**26.25**	m2
012 Landings over 300 mm wide:					
3.2 mm	0.57	11.82	12.45	**24.27**	m2
6.0 mm	0.57	11.82	15.49	**27.31**	m2

Unit Rates	Man-Hours	Net Labour Price £	Net Mats Price £	Net Unit Price £	Unit
013 Treads 300 mm wide:					
3.2 mm	0.38	7.95	3.74	**11.69**	m
6.0 mm	0.38	7.95	4.65	**12.60**	m
014 Risers 150 mm high:					
3.2 mm	0.35	7.30	1.87	**9.17**	m
6.0 mm	0.35	7.30	2.33	**9.63**	m

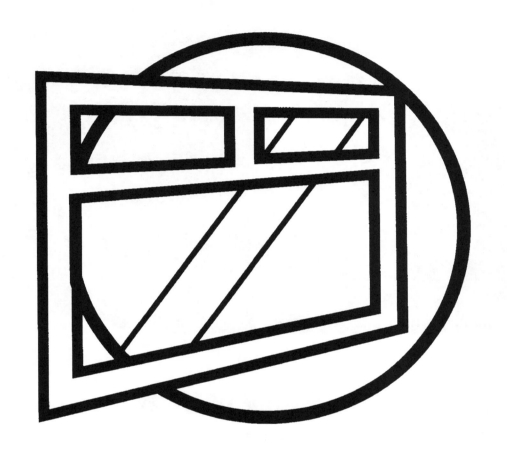

Glazing

HOW LONG? HOW MUCH?
THE FASTEST, MOST UP-TO-DATE ANSWERS ARE AVAILABLE NOW

Cost information underpins every aspect of the built environment, from construction and rebuilding to maintenance and operation publications.

BCIS, the RICS' Building Cost Information Service, is the leading provider of cost information to the construction industry and anyone else who needs comprehensive, accurate and independent data.

For the past 50 years, BCIS has been collecting, collating, analysing, modelling and interpreting cost information.Today, BCIS make that information easily accessible through online applications, data licensing and publications.

For more information call **0870 333 1600** email **contact@bcis.co.uk** or visit **www.bcis.co.uk**

BCIS is the Building Cost Information Service of  **RICS** | the mark of property professionalism worldwide

Labour Rates

Please note: The labour hours throughout this section are representative of the time required for one productive man to carry out the unit of work.

Gang rates are calculated as follows by obtaining the overall gang cost and then dividing this by the number of productive members in the gang. The resulting rate is the Gang Cost per **Man - hour.** By using the same principle, any size gang may be built-up and used against the standard labour hours in this section.

The prices for labour in this section are based upon the following rates:

A0214 Glazing:

Glazier	1.00	x	£	15.20	=	£	15.20
Glazing Labourer	1.00	x	£	11.22	=	£	11.22
Total hourly cost of gang					=	£	26.42

Gang rate (divided by 1) = £26.42 per Man-hour

Unloading

Unloading cost includes for the labour for getting in to a designated point and for temporary handling facilities and return of protective frames or crates.

Glazing generally

Glass suppliers generally classify pane sizes of the glass in common use into 2 broad groups - those not exceeding 0.10 m2 and those exceeding 0.10 m2 - and base prices on this division (plates under 0.10 m2 being charged as 0.10 m2). Similarly, tempered safety glass and other special glass is generally classified into pane sizes not exceeding 0.20 m2 and those exceeding 0.20 m2 (plates under 0.20 m2 being charged as 0.20 m2). All double glazed units less than 0.20 m2 in area are charged as 0.20 m2. Hence, prices in this section comply with this practice which departs from the more detailed requirements of SMM6. There are, however, 'normal' maximum sheet sizes (NMS) within each category and thickness of glass and any panes required to be above this standard maximum are subject to surcharge, which must be allowed for in addition to the prices given here. Prices given are for cut-to-size panes. Where estimates are being compiled for contracts involving large quantities of glass in identically sized panes or in panes outside the normal standard size range, readers are advised to consult their own particular suppliers for specific terms.

Prices do not allow for any preparation of rebates prior to glazing, such as priming or for treatment of timber surfaces which have been treated with water repellents or preservatives, nor for the supply of glazing beads.

Where glass is described as 'to metal with synthetic rubber extruded gaskets and clip-on metal beads', the gaskets are deemed to be provided by the manufacturer of the metal frames and are excluded from the glazing prices.

Basic Prices of Materials		Supply Price £	Waste Factor %	Unload. Labour £	Unload. Plant £	Total Unit Cost £	Unit
U0089	Non-setting glazing compound	1.50	5%	-	-	1.58	kg
U0090	Linseed oil putty	2.40	5%	-	-	2.52	kg
U0091	Metal casement putty	2.40	5%	-	-	2.52	kg
U0092	Silicone glazing compound	10.81	5%	-	-	11.35	ltr
	Imitation washleather or similar glazing strip:						
U0093	narrow	1.49	10%	-	-	1.64	m
U0094	broad	1.49	10%	-	-	1.64	m
	Clear float glass; GG Quality:						
U0100	3 mm	20.72	7.5%	0.11	-	22.40	m2
U0101	4 mm	24.07	7.5%	0.15	-	26.03	m2
U0102	5 mm	30.06	7.5%	0.19	-	32.52	m2
U0103	6 mm	32.57	7.5%	0.22	-	35.25	m2
U0104	10 mm	65.14	7.5%	0.37	-	70.43	m2
	Styppolyte glass:						
U0110	6 mm	38.50	7.5%	0.22	-	41.62	m2
	Wired glass:						
U0120	7 mm Georgian wired cast	75.00	7.5%	0.26	-	80.90	m2
U0121	Allowance for additional cutting cost for lining up wires on adjacent panes when glazed	3.50	7.5%	-	-	3.76	m2
U0122	6 mm Georgian wired polished	110.00	7.5%	0.22	-	118.49	m2
U0123	Allowance for additional cutting cost for lining up wires on adjacent panes when glazed	3.50	7.5%	-	-	3.76	m2
	Anti-sun float glass, tinted grey or bronze:						
U0125	4 mm	48.68	7.5%	0.15	-	52.50	m2
U0126	6 mm	70.91	7.5%	0.22	-	76.47	m2
U0127	10 mm	154.76	7.5%	0.37	-	166.76	m2
U0128	12 mm	195.17	7.5%	0.45	-	210.29	m2
U0129	6 mm Eclipse Advantage glass	102.11	7.5%	0.22	-	110.01	m2
	Patterned glass:						
	white:						
U0130	4 mm	25.16	7.5%	0.15	-	27.20	m2
U0131	6 mm	43.35	7.5%	0.22	-	46.84	m2
	tinted:						
U0132	4 mm	45.95	7.5%	0.15	-	49.56	m2
U0133	6 mm	56.93	7.5%	0.22	-	61.43	m2
	clear float:						
U0134	3 mm	44.46	7.5%	0.11	-	47.91	m2
U0135	4 mm	51.76	7.5%	0.15	-	55.80	m2
U0136	6 mm	54.82	7.5%	0.22	-	59.17	m2

	Basic Prices of Materials	Supply Price £	Waste Factor %	Unload. Labour £	Unload. Plant £	Total Unit Cost £	Unit
	tinted float:						
U0137	4 mm	79.24	7.5%	0.15	-	85.34	m2
U0138	6 mm	108.80	7.5%	0.22	-	117.20	m2
	Special glasses						
	Low emmissivity:						
U1304	4 mm	25.93	5%	-	-	27.23	m2
U1305	6 mm	45.38	5%	-	-	47.65	m2
	Self Cleaning:						
U1306	4 mm	36.64	5%	-	-	38.47	m2
U1307	6 mm	64.91	5%	-	-	68.16	m2
U1308	4 mm toughened	56.85	5%	-	-	59.69	m2
U1309	6 mm toughened	83.44	5%	-	-	87.62	m2
	Fire Resisting:						
U1310	7 mm 30/30	314.92	5%	-	-	330.66	m2
U1311	12 mm 60/60	388.43	5%	-	-	407.85	m2
U1312	16 mm 90/90	467.91	5%	-	-	491.30	m2
U1313	21 mm 120/120	648.51	5%	-	-	680.94	m2
U1316	Intumescent glazing tape	4.23	10%	-	-	4.65	m
	Anti-sun double glazing units:						
U1314	4mm Pilkington Suncool 66/33 and 4mm toughened DG unit	328.06	5%	-	-	344.47	m2
U1315	4mm Guardian Sunguard 61/32 and 4mm toughened DG unit	164.97	5%	-	-	173.22	m2
	Adjustments used to construct double glazed unit prices from glasses listed above						
U1300	Add for making double glazed unit	8.80	5%	-	-	9.24	m2
U1301	Add for making triple glazed unit	14.08	5%	-	-	14.78	m2
U1302	Add for argon filling between panes	5.89	5%	-	-	6.19	m2
U1303	Warm edge glazing spacer	2.65	5%	-	-	2.78	m
	As a general guide, the following are given as Extra over prices to those given for the corresponding thickness of						
	Clear float glass per leaf:						
U0498	4 mm glass with applied lead strip to form simulated rectangular pattern leaded lights	30.97	7.5%	-	-	33.29	m2
U0499	6 mm glass with applied lead strip to form simulated rectangular pattern leaded lights	30.97	7.5%	-	-	33.29	m2
	Glass louvres with long edges ground or smoothed:						
	blades 600 mm long x 102 mm wide:						
U0520	6 mm clear float	26.66	5%	0.02	-	28.01	nr
U0521	6 mm Styppolyte	26.73	5%	0.02	-	28.09	nr
U0522	7 mm wired cast	25.96	5%	0.02	-	27.28	nr
U0523	6 mm polished wired plate	29.40	5%	0.02	-	30.89	nr
	blades 600 mm long x 152 mm wide:						
U0524	6 mm clear float	28.74	5%	0.02	-	30.20	nr
U0525	6 mm Styppolyte	29.40	5%	0.02	-	30.89	nr
U0526	7 mm wired cast	28.55	5%	0.02	-	29.99	nr
U0527	6 mm polished wired plate	32.34	5%	0.02	-	33.98	nr
	4 mm silvered float glass mirrors, copper backed; polished edges; 4 drilled holes:						
U0530	350 x 255 mm	17.77	5%	0.06	-	18.72	nr
U0531	450 x 300 mm	17.77	5%	0.06	-	18.72	nr
U0532	600 x 450 mm	23.98	5%	0.06	-	25.24	nr
U0533	900 x 450 mm	35.97	5%	0.06	-	37.83	nr
U0534	900 x 600 mm	47.95	5%	0.06	-	50.41	nr
U0535	1200 x 300 mm	31.97	5%	0.06	-	33.63	nr
U0536	1200 x 450 mm	47.95	5%	0.06	-	50.41	nr
U0537	400 mm diameter	22.20	5%	0.06	-	23.37	nr
U0538	600 mm diameter	39.96	5%	0.06	-	42.02	nr
U0539	1 1/4" x No. 8 mirror screws with rubber washers and chromium plated dome caps	1.08	10%	-	-	1.19	nr
U0540	Plastic wall plugs for 1 1/4" x No. 8 mirror screws	-	10%	-	-	-	nr

Unit Rates	Man-Hours	Net Labour Price £	Net Mats Price £	Net Unit Price £	Unit
UNIT RATES					
UA **CLEAR, TINTED AND PATTERNED GLASS**					
001 **Clear float glass; GG Quality**					
002 To wood with putty and sprigs:					
3 mm in panes not exceeding 0.15 m2	1.02	15.50	30.58	**46.08**	m2
3 mm in panes 0.15 - 4.0 m2	0.54	8.22	23.66	**31.88**	m2
4 mm in panes not exceeding 0.15 m2	1.02	15.50	35.13	**50.63**	m2
4 mm in panes 0.15 - 4.0 m2	0.54	8.22	27.29	**35.51**	m2
5 mm in panes not exceeding 0.15 m2	1.02	15.50	43.24	**58.74**	m2
5 mm in panes 0.15 - 4.0 m2	0.54	8.22	33.78	**42.00**	m2
6 mm in panes not exceeding 0.15 m2	1.02	15.50	46.65	**62.15**	m2
6 mm in panes 0.15 - 4.0 m2	0.54	8.22	36.51	**44.73**	m2
10 mm in panes not exceeding 0.15 m2	1.20	18.24	90.61	**108.85**	m2
10 mm in panes 0.15 - 4.0 m2	0.64	9.67	71.69	**81.36**	m2
003 To wood with bradded wood beads (supplied cut to length by others):					
3 mm in panes not exceeding 0.15 m2	1.36	20.67	30.58	**51.25**	m2
3 mm in panes 0.15 - 4.0 m2	0.72	10.95	27.29	**38.24**	m2
4 mm in panes not exceeding 0.15 m2	1.36	20.67	35.13	**55.80**	m2
4 mm in panes 0.15 - 4.0 m2	0.72	10.95	27.29	**38.24**	m2
5 mm in panes not exceeding 0.15 m2	1.36	20.67	43.24	**63.91**	m2
5 mm in panes 0.15 - 4.0 m2	0.72	10.95	33.78	**44.73**	m2
6 mm in panes not exceeding 0.15 m2	1.36	20.67	46.65	**67.32**	m2
6 mm in panes 0.15 - 4.0 m2	0.72	10.95	36.51	**47.46**	m2
10 mm in panes not exceeding 0.15 m2	1.60	24.31	90.61	**114.92**	m2
10 mm in panes 0.15 - 4.0 m2	0.85	12.89	71.69	**84.58**	m2
004 To wood with screwed wood beads (supplied cut to length by others):					
3 mm in panes not exceeding 0.15 m2	2.04	31.01	30.58	**61.59**	m2
3 mm in panes 0.15 - 4.0 m2	1.08	16.43	23.66	**40.09**	m2
4 mm in panes not exceeding 0.15 m2	2.04	31.01	35.13	**66.14**	m2
4 mm in panes 0.15 - 4.0 m2	1.08	16.43	27.29	**43.72**	m2
5 mm in panes not exceeding 0.15 m2	2.04	31.01	43.24	**74.25**	m2
5 mm in panes 0.15 - 4.0 m2	1.08	16.43	33.78	**50.21**	m2
6 mm in panes not exceeding 0.15 m2	2.04	31.01	46.65	**77.66**	m2
6 mm in panes 0.15 - 4.0 m2	1.08	16.43	48.27	**64.70**	m2
10 mm in panes not exceeding 0.15 m2	2.40	36.48	90.61	**127.09**	m2
10 mm in panes 0.15 - 4.0 m2	1.27	19.33	71.69	**91.02**	m2
005 To metal with putty and clips:					
3 mm in panes not exceeding 0.15 m2	1.08	16.42	30.58	**47.00**	m2
3 mm in panes 0.15 - 4.0 m2	0.57	8.70	23.66	**32.36**	m2
4 mm in panes not exceeding 0.15 m2	1.08	16.42	35.13	**51.55**	m2
4 mm in panes 0.15 - 4.0 m2	0.57	8.70	27.29	**35.99**	m2
5 mm in panes not exceeding 0.15 m2	1.08	16.42	43.24	**59.66**	m2
5 mm in panes 0.15 - 4.0 m2	0.57	8.70	33.78	**42.48**	m2
6 mm in panes not exceeding 0.15 m2	1.08	16.42	46.65	**63.07**	m2
6 mm in panes 0.15 - 4.0 m2	0.57	8.70	36.51	**45.21**	m2
10 mm in panes not exceeding 0.15 m2	1.27	19.31	90.61	**109.92**	m2
10 mm in panes 0.15 - 4.0 m2	0.67	10.24	71.69	**81.93**	m2
006 To metal with screwed metal beads (supplied cut to length by others):					
3 mm in panes not exceeding 0.15 m2	1.98	30.10	30.58	**60.68**	m2
3 mm in panes 0.15 - 4.0 m2	1.05	15.95	23.66	**39.61**	m2
4 mm in panes not exceeding 0.15 m2	1.98	30.10	35.13	**65.23**	m2
4 mm in panes 0.15 - 4.0 m2	1.05	15.95	27.29	**43.24**	m2
5 mm in panes not exceeding 0.15 m2	1.98	30.10	43.24	**73.34**	m2
5 mm in panes 0.15 - 4.0 m2	1.05	15.95	33.78	**49.73**	m2
6 mm in panes not exceeding 0.15 m2	1.98	30.10	46.65	**76.75**	m2
6 mm in panes 0.15 - 4.0 m2	1.05	15.95	36.51	**52.46**	m2
10 mm in panes not exceeding 0.15 m2	2.33	35.41	90.61	**126.02**	m2
10 mm in panes 0.15 - 4.0 m2	1.23	18.77	71.69	**90.46**	m2
007 To metal with synthetic rubber extruded gaskets and clip-on metal beads (supplied cut to length by others):					
3 mm in panes not exceeding 0.15 m2	1.92	29.18	28.00	**57.18**	m2
3 mm in panes 0.15 - 4.0 m2	1.02	15.47	22.40	**37.87**	m2
4 mm in panes not exceeding 0.15 m2	1.92	29.18	32.54	**61.72**	m2
4 mm in panes 0.15 - 4.0 m2	1.02	15.47	26.03	**41.50**	m2
5 mm in panes not exceeding 0.15 m2	1.92	29.18	40.65	**69.83**	m2
5 mm in panes 0.15 - 4.0 m2	1.02	15.47	32.52	**47.99**	m2
6 mm in panes not exceeding 0.15 m2	1.92	29.18	44.06	**73.24**	m2
6 mm in panes 0.15 - 4.0 m2	1.02	15.47	35.25	**50.72**	m2
10 mm in panes not exceeding 0.15 m2	2.26	34.33	88.03	**122.36**	m2
10 mm in panes 0.15 - 4.0 m2	1.20	18.20	70.43	**88.63**	m2
008 **Styppolyte obscured and textured glass**					
009 To wood with putty and sprigs:					
6 mm in panes not exceeding 0.15 m2	1.02	15.50	54.61	**70.11**	m2
6 mm in panes 0.15 - 4.0 m2	0.54	8.22	42.88	**51.10**	m2
010 To wood with bradded wood beads (supplied cut to length by others):					
6 mm in panes not exceeding 0.15 m2	1.36	20.67	52.72	**73.39**	m2
6 mm in panes 0.15 - 4.0 m2	0.72	10.95	41.94	**52.89**	m2

Unit Rates	Man-Hours	Net Labour Price £	Net Mats Price £	Net Unit Price £	Unit
011	To wood with screwed wood beads (supplied cut to length by others):					
	6 mm in panes not exceeding 0.15 m2	2.04	31.01	52.72	**83.73**	m2
	6 mm in panes 0.15 - 4.0 m2	1.08	16.43	41.94	**58.37**	m2
012	To metal with putty and clips:					
	6 mm in panes not exceeding 0.15 m2	1.08	16.42	55.24	**71.66**	m2
	6 mm in panes 0.15 - 4.0 m2	0.57	8.70	43.20	**51.90**	m2
013	To metal with screwed metal beads (supplied cut to length by others):					
	6 mm in panes not exceeding 0.15 m2	1.98	30.10	52.85	**82.95**	m2
	6 mm in panes 0.15 - 4.0 m2	1.05	15.95	42.00	**57.95**	m2
014	To metal with synthetic rubber extruded gaskets and clip-on metal beads (supplied cut to length by others):					
	6 mm in panes not exceeding 0.15 m2	1.92	29.18	52.03	**81.21**	m2
	6 mm in panes 0.15 - 4.0 m2	1.02	15.47	41.62	**57.09**	m2
015	To wood with putty and sprigs:					
	4 mm in panes not exceeding 0.15 m2	1.02	15.50	36.59	**52.09**	m2
	4 mm in panes 0.15 - 4.0 m2	0.54	8.22	28.46	**36.68**	m2
	6 mm in panes not exceeding 0.15 m2	1.02	15.50	61.14	**76.64**	m2
	6 mm in panes 0.15 - 4.0 m2	0.54	8.22	48.10	**56.32**	m2
016	To wood with bradded wood beads (supplied cut to length by others):					
	4 mm in panes not exceeding 0.15 m2	1.36	20.67	34.70	**55.37**	m2
	4 mm in panes 0.15 - 4.0 m2	0.72	10.95	27.52	**38.47**	m2
	6 mm in panes not exceeding 0.15 m2	1.36	20.67	59.25	**79.92**	m2
	6 mm in panes 0.15 - 4.0 m2	0.72	10.95	47.16	**58.11**	m2
017	To wood with screwed wood beads (supplied cut to length by others):					
	4 mm in panes not exceeding 0.15 m2	2.04	31.01	34.70	**65.71**	m2
	4 mm in panes 0.15 - 4.0 m2	1.08	16.43	27.52	**43.95**	m2
	6 mm in panes not exceeding 0.15 m2	2.04	31.01	59.25	**90.26**	m2
	6 mm in panes 0.15 - 4.0 m2	1.08	16.43	47.16	**63.59**	m2
018	To metal with putty and clips:					
	4 mm in panes not exceeding 0.15 m2	1.08	16.42	37.22	**53.64**	m2
	4 mm in panes 0.15 - 4.0 m2	0.57	8.70	28.78	**37.48**	m2
	6 mm in panes not exceeding 0.15 m2	1.08	16.42	61.77	**78.19**	m2
	6 mm in panes 0.15 - 4.0 m2	0.57	8.70	48.42	**57.12**	m2
019	To metal with screwed metal beads (supplied cut to length by others):					
	4 mm in panes not exceeding 0.15 m2	1.98	30.10	34.82	**64.92**	m2
	4 mm in panes 0.15 - 4.0 m2	1.05	15.95	27.58	**43.53**	m2
	6 mm in panes not exceeding 0.15 m2	1.98	30.10	59.37	**89.47**	m2
	6 mm in panes 0.15 - 4.0 m2	1.05	15.95	47.22	**63.17**	m2
020	To metal with synthetic rubber extruded gaskets and clip-on metal beads (supplied cut to length by others):					
	4 mm in panes not exceeding 0.15 m2	1.92	29.18	34.00	**63.18**	m2
	4 mm in panes 0.15 - 4.0 m2	1.02	15.47	27.20	**42.67**	m2
	6 mm in panes not exceeding 0.15 m2	1.92	29.18	58.55	**87.73**	m2
	6 mm in panes 0.15 - 4.0 m2	1.02	15.47	46.84	**62.31**	m2
021	**Tinted patterned glass**					
022	To wood with putty and sprigs:					
	4 mm in panes not exceeding 0.15 m2	1.02	15.50	64.53	**80.03**	m2
	4 mm in panes 0.15 - 4.0 m2	0.54	8.22	50.82	**59.04**	m2
	6 mm in panes not exceeding 0.15 m2	1.02	15.50	79.38	**94.88**	m2
	6 mm in panes 0.15 - 4.0 m2	0.54	8.22	50.82	**59.04**	m2
023	To wood with bradded wood beads (supplied cut to length by others):					
	4 mm in panes not exceeding 0.15 m2	1.36	20.67	62.64	**83.31**	m2
	4 mm in panes 0.15 - 4.0 m2	0.72	10.95	49.88	**60.83**	m2
	6 mm in panes not exceeding 0.15 m2	1.36	20.67	77.49	**98.16**	m2
	6 mm in panes 0.15 - 4.0 m2	0.72	10.95	61.75	**72.70**	m2
024	To wood with screwed wood beads (supplied cut to length by others):					
	4 mm in panes not exceeding 0.15 m2	2.04	31.01	62.64	**93.65**	m2
	4 mm in panes 0.15 - 4.0 m2	1.08	16.43	49.88	**66.31**	m2
	6 mm in panes not exceeding 0.15 m2	2.04	31.01	77.49	**108.50**	m2
	6 mm in panes 0.15 - 4.0 m2	1.08	16.43	61.75	**78.18**	m2
025	To metal with putty and clips:					
	4 mm in panes not exceeding 0.15 m2	1.08	16.42	65.16	**81.58**	m2
	4 mm in panes 0.15 - 4.0 m2	0.57	8.70	51.14	**59.84**	m2
	6 mm in panes not exceeding 0.15 m2	1.08	16.42	80.01	**96.43**	m2
	6 mm in panes 0.15 - 4.0 m2	0.57	8.70	63.01	**71.71**	m2
026	To metal with screwed metal beads (supplied cut to length by others):					
	4 mm in panes not exceeding 0.15 m2	2.04	31.01	62.77	**93.78**	m2
	4 mm in panes 0.15 - 4.0 m2	1.08	16.43	49.94	**66.37**	m2
	6 mm in panes not exceeding 0.15 m2	2.04	31.01	77.61	**108.62**	m2
	6 mm in panes 0.15 - 4.0 m2	1.08	16.43	61.81	**78.24**	m2
027	To metal with synthetic rubber extruded gaskets and clip-on metal beads (supplied cut to length by others):					
	4 mm in panes not exceeding 0.15 m2	1.92	29.18	61.95	**91.13**	m2

Unit Rates	Man-Hours	Net Labour Price £	Net Mats Price £	Net Unit Price £	Unit
4 mm in panes 0.15 - 4.0 m2	1.02	15.47	49.56	**65.03**	m2
6 mm in panes not exceeding 0.15 m2	1.92	29.18	76.79	**105.97**	m2
6 mm in panes 0.15 - 4.0 m2	1.02	15.47	61.43	**76.90**	m2
028 Silvered clear float glass					
029 To wood with bradded wood beads (supplied cut to length by others):					
4 mm in panes not exceeding 0.15 m2	1.36	20.67	70.44	**91.11**	m2
4 mm in panes 0.15 - 4.0 m2	0.72	10.95	56.12	**67.07**	m2
6 mm in panes not exceeding 0.15 m2	1.36	20.67	74.65	**95.32**	m2
6 mm in panes 0.15 - 4.0 m2	0.72	10.95	59.48	**70.43**	m2
030 To wood with screwed wood beads (supplied cut to length by others):					
4 mm in panes not exceeding 0.15 m2	2.04	31.01	70.44	**101.45**	m2
4 mm in panes 0.15 - 4.0 m2	1.08	16.43	56.12	**72.55**	m2
6 mm in panes not exceeding 0.15 m2	2.04	31.01	74.65	**105.66**	m2
6 mm in panes 0.15 - 4.0 m2	1.08	16.43	59.48	**75.91**	m2
031 To metal with screwed metal beads (supplied cut to length by others):					
4 mm in panes not exceeding 0.15 m2	1.98	30.10	70.57	**100.67**	m2
4 mm in panes 0.15 - 4.0 m2	1.05	15.95	56.18	**72.13**	m2
6 mm in panes not exceeding 0.15 m2	1.98	30.10	74.78	**104.88**	m2
6 mm in panes 0.15 - 4.0 m2	1.05	15.95	59.55	**75.50**	m2
032 To metal with synthetic rubber extruded gaskets and clip-on metal beads (supplied cut to length by others):					
4 mm in panes not exceeding 0.15 m2	1.92	29.18	69.75	**98.93**	m2
4 mm in panes 0.15 - 4.0 m2	1.02	15.47	55.80	**71.27**	m2
6 mm in panes not exceeding 0.15 m2	1.92	29.18	73.96	**103.14**	m2
6 mm in panes 0.15 - 4.0 m2	1.02	15.47	59.17	**74.64**	m2
033 Silvered tinted float glass (bronze or grey)					
034 To wood with bradded wood beads (supplied cut to length by others):					
4 mm in panes not exceeding 0.15 m2	1.36	20.67	107.37	**128.04**	m2
4 mm in panes 0.15 - 4.0 m2	0.72	10.95	85.65	**96.60**	m2
6 mm in panes not exceeding 0.15 m2	1.36	20.67	147.19	**167.86**	m2
6 mm in panes 0.15 - 4.0 m2	0.72	10.95	117.51	**128.46**	m2
035 To wood with screwed wood beads (supplied cut to length by others):					
4 mm in panes not exceeding 0.15 m2	2.04	31.01	107.37	**138.38**	m2
4 mm in panes 0.15 - 4.0 m2	1.08	16.43	85.65	**102.08**	m2
6 mm in panes not exceeding 0.15 m2	2.04	31.01	147.19	**178.20**	m2
6 mm in panes 0.15 - 4.0 m2	1.08	16.43	117.51	**133.94**	m2
036 To metal with screwed metal beads (supplied cut to length by others):					
4 mm in panes not exceeding 0.15 m2	1.98	30.10	107.49	**137.59**	m2
4 mm in panes 0.15 - 4.0 m2	1.05	15.95	85.72	**101.67**	m2
6 mm in panes not exceeding 0.15 m2	1.98	30.10	147.32	**177.42**	m2
6 mm in panes 0.15 - 4.0 m2	1.05	15.95	117.58	**133.53**	m2
037 To metal with synthetic rubber extruded gaskets and clip-on metal beads (supplied cut to length by others):					
4 mm in panes not exceeding 0.15 m2	1.92	29.18	106.67	**135.85**	m2
4 mm in panes 0.15 - 4.0 m2	1.02	15.47	85.34	**100.81**	m2
6 mm in panes not exceeding 0.15 m2	1.92	29.18	146.50	**175.68**	m2
6 mm in panes 0.15 - 4.0 m2	1.02	15.47	117.20	**132.67**	m2
038 Anti-sun solar control glass, tinted grey or bronze					
039 To wood with putty and sprigs:					
4 mm in panes not exceeding 0.15 m2	1.02	15.50	68.20	**83.70**	m2
4 mm in panes 0.15 - 4.0 m2	0.54	8.22	53.76	**61.98**	m2
6 mm in panes not exceeding 0.15 m2	1.02	15.50	98.16	**113.66**	m2
6 mm in panes 0.15 - 4.0 m2	0.54	8.22	77.73	**85.95**	m2
10 mm in panes not exceeding 0.15 m2	1.20	18.24	211.04	**229.28**	m2
10 mm in panes 0.15 - 4.0 m2	0.64	9.67	168.02	**177.69**	m2
12 mm in panes not exceeding 0.15 m2	1.20	18.24	265.45	**283.69**	m2
12 mm in panes 0.15 - 4.0 m2	0.64	9.67	53.76	**63.43**	m2
040 To wood with bradded wood beads (supplied cut to length by others):					
4 mm in panes not exceeding 0.15 m2	1.36	20.67	66.31	**86.98**	m2
4 mm in panes 0.15 - 4.0 m2	0.72	10.95	52.81	**63.76**	m2
6 mm in panes not exceeding 0.15 m2	1.36	20.67	96.27	**116.94**	m2
6 mm in panes 0.15 - 4.0 m2	0.72	10.95	76.78	**87.73**	m2
10 mm in panes not exceeding 0.15 m2	1.60	24.26	209.15	**233.41**	m2
10 mm in panes 0.15 - 4.0 m2	0.85	12.86	167.08	**179.94**	m2
12 mm in panes not exceeding 0.15 m2	1.60	24.26	263.56	**287.82**	m2
12 mm in panes 0.15 - 4.0 m2	0.85	12.86	52.81	**65.67**	m2
041 To wood with screwed wood beads (supplied cut to length by others):					
4 mm in panes not exceeding 0.15 m2	2.04	31.01	66.31	**97.32**	m2
4 mm in panes 0.15 - 4.0 m2	1.08	16.43	52.81	**69.24**	m2
6 mm in panes not exceeding 0.15 m2	2.04	31.01	96.27	**127.28**	m2
6 mm in panes 0.15 - 4.0 m2	1.08	16.43	76.78	**93.21**	m2
10 mm in panes not exceeding 0.15 m2	2.40	36.48	209.15	**245.63**	m2
10 mm in panes 0.15 - 4.0 m2	1.27	19.33	167.08	**186.41**	m2
12 mm in panes not exceeding 0.15 m2	2.40	36.48	263.56	**300.04**	m2
12 mm in panes 0.15 - 4.0 m2	1.27	19.33	52.81	**72.14**	m2

Unit Rates	Man-Hours	Net Labour Price £	Net Mats Price £	Net Unit Price £	Unit
042 To metal with putty and clips:					
4 mm in panes not exceeding 0.15 m2	1.08	16.42	68.83	**85.25**	m2
4 mm in panes 0.15 - 4.0 m2	0.57	8.70	54.07	**62.77**	m2
6 mm in panes not exceeding 0.15 m2	1.08	16.42	98.79	**115.21**	m2
6 mm in panes 0.15 - 4.0 m2	0.57	8.70	78.04	**86.74**	m2
10 mm in panes not exceeding 0.15 m2	1.27	19.33	211.67	**231.00**	m2
10 mm in panes 0.15 - 4.0 m2	0.67	10.25	168.34	**178.59**	m2
12 mm in panes not exceeding 0.15 m2	1.27	19.33	266.08	**285.41**	m2
12 mm in panes 0.15 - 4.0 m2	0.67	10.25	54.07	**64.32**	m2
043 To metal with screwed metal beads (supplied cut to length by others):					
4 mm in panes not exceeding 0.15 m2	1.98	30.10	66.31	**96.41**	m2
4 mm in panes 0.15 - 4.0 m2	1.05	15.95	52.81	**68.76**	m2
6 mm in panes not exceeding 0.15 m2	1.98	30.10	96.27	**126.37**	m2
6 mm in panes 0.15 - 4.0 m2	1.05	15.95	76.78	**92.73**	m2
10 mm in panes not exceeding 0.15 m2	2.33	35.39	209.15	**244.54**	m2
10 mm in panes 0.15 - 4.0 m2	1.23	18.75	167.08	**185.83**	m2
12 mm in panes not exceeding 0.15 m2	2.33	35.39	263.56	**298.95**	m2
12 mm in panes 0.15 - 4.0 m2	1.23	18.75	52.81	**71.56**	m2
044 To metal with synthetic rubber extruded gaskets and clip-on metal beads (supplied cut to length by others):					
4 mm in panes not exceeding 0.15 m2	1.92	29.18	65.62	**94.80**	m2
4 mm in panes 0.15 - 4.0 m2	1.02	15.47	52.50	**67.97**	m2
6 mm in panes not exceeding 0.15 m2	1.92	29.18	95.58	**124.76**	m2
6 mm in panes 0.15 - 4.0 m2	1.02	15.47	76.47	**91.94**	m2
10 mm in panes not exceeding 0.15 m2	2.26	34.29	208.45	**242.74**	m2
10 mm in panes 0.15 - 4.0 m2	1.20	18.17	166.76	**184.93**	m2
12 mm in panes not exceeding 0.15 m2	2.26	34.29	262.87	**297.16**	m2
12 mm in panes 0.15 - 4.0 m2	1.20	18.17	210.29	**228.46**	m2
045 **'Eclipse Advantage' solar control glass**					
046 To wood with putty and sprigs:					
6 mm in panes not exceeding 0.15 m2	1.02	15.50	140.09	**155.59**	m2
6 mm in panes 0.15 - 4.0 m2	0.54	8.22	111.27	**119.49**	m2
047 To wood with bradded wood beads (supplied cut to length by others):					
6 mm in panes not exceeding 0.15 m2	1.36	20.61	138.20	**158.81**	m2
6 mm in panes 0.15 - 4.0 m2	0.72	10.92	110.32	**121.24**	m2
048 To wood with screwed wood beads (supplied cut to length by others):					
6 mm in panes not exceeding 0.15 m2	2.04	31.01	138.20	**169.21**	m2
6 mm in panes 0.15 - 4.0 m2	1.08	16.43	110.32	**126.75**	m2
049 To metal with putty and clips:					
6 mm in panes not exceeding 0.15 m2	1.08	16.42	140.72	**157.14**	m2
6 mm in panes 0.15 - 4.0 m2	0.57	8.70	111.58	**120.28**	m2
050 To metal with screwed metal beads (supplied cut to length by others):					
6 mm in panes not exceeding 0.15 m2	1.98	30.10	138.20	**168.30**	m2
6 mm in panes 0.15 - 4.0 m2	1.05	15.95	110.32	**126.27**	m2
051 To metal with synthetic rubber extruded gaskets and clip-on metal beads (supplied cut to length by others):					
6 mm in panes not exceeding 0.15 m2	1.92	29.18	137.51	**166.69**	m2
6 mm in panes 0.15 - 4.0 m2	1.02	15.47	110.01	**125.48**	m2
052 **Toughened clear float safety glass**					
053 To wood with putty and clips:					
4 mm in panes not exceeding 0.15 m2	1.02	15.50	70.31	**85.81**	m2
4 mm in panes 0.15 - 4.0 m2	0.54	8.22	55.44	**63.66**	m2
5 mm in panes not exceeding 0.15 m2	1.02	15.50	78.40	**93.90**	m2
5 mm in panes 0.15 - 4.0 m2	0.54	8.23	61.91	**70.14**	m2
6 mm in panes not exceeding 0.15 m2	1.02	15.50	81.83	**97.33**	m2
6 mm in panes 0.15 - 4.0 m2	0.54	8.23	64.65	**72.88**	m2
10 mm in panes not exceeding 0.15 m2	1.20	18.24	125.79	**144.03**	m2
10 mm in panes 0.15 - 4.0 m2	0.64	9.67	99.83	**109.50**	m2
054 To wood with bradded wood beads (supplied cut to length by others):					
4 mm in panes not exceeding 0.15 m2	1.36	20.67	68.42	**89.09**	m2
4 mm in panes 0.15 - 4.0 m2	0.72	10.95	54.49	**65.44**	m2
5 mm in panes not exceeding 0.15 m2	1.36	20.67	76.51	**97.18**	m2
5 mm in panes 0.15 - 4.0 m2	0.72	10.95	60.97	**71.92**	m2
6 mm in panes not exceeding 0.15 m2	1.36	20.67	79.94	**100.61**	m2
6 mm in panes 0.15 - 4.0 m2	0.72	10.95	63.71	**74.66**	m2
10 mm in panes not exceeding 0.15 m2	1.60	24.26	123.90	**148.16**	m2
10 mm in panes 0.15 - 4.0 m2	0.85	12.86	98.88	**111.74**	m2
055 To wood with screwed wood beads (supplied cut to length by others):					
4 mm in panes not exceeding 0.15 m2	2.04	31.01	68.42	**99.43**	m2
4 mm in panes 0.15 - 4.0 m2	1.08	16.43	54.49	**70.92**	m2
5 mm in panes not exceeding 0.15 m2	2.04	31.01	76.51	**107.52**	m2
5 mm in panes 0.15 - 4.0 m2	1.08	16.43	60.97	**77.40**	Un2
6 mm in panes not exceeding 0.15 m2	2.04	31.01	79.94	**110.95**	m2
6 mm in panes 0.15 - 4.0 m2	1.08	16.43	63.71	**80.14**	m2
10 mm in panes not exceeding 0.15 m2	2.40	36.48	123.90	**160.38**	m2
10 mm in panes 0.15 - 4.0 m2	1.27	19.33	98.88	**118.21**	m2

Unit Rates	Man-Hours	Net Labour Price £	Net Mats Price £	Net Unit Price £	Unit
056 To metal with screwed metal beads (supplied cut to length by others):					
4 mm in panes not exceeding 0.15 m2	1.98	30.10	68.54	**98.64**	m2
4 mm in panes 0.15 - 4.0 m2	1.05	15.95	54.56	**70.51**	m2
5 mm in panes not exceeding 0.15 m2	1.98	30.10	76.64	**106.74**	m2
5 mm in panes 0.15 - 4.0 m2	1.05	15.95	61.03	**76.98**	m2
6 mm in panes not exceeding 0.15 m2	1.98	30.10	80.06	**110.16**	m2
6 mm in panes 0.15 - 4.0 m2	1.05	15.95	63.77	**79.72**	m2
10 mm in panes not exceeding 0.15 m2	2.33	35.39	124.03	**159.42**	m2
10 mm in panes 0.15 - 4.0 m2	1.23	18.75	98.95	**117.70**	m2
057 To metal with synthetic rubber extruded gaskets and clip-on metal beads (supplied cut to length by others):					
4 mm in panes not exceeding 0.15 m2	1.92	29.18	67.72	**96.90**	m2
4 mm in panes 0.15 - 4.0 m2	1.02	15.47	54.18	**69.65**	m2
5 mm in panes not exceeding 0.15 m2	1.92	29.18	75.82	**105.00**	m2
5 mm in panes 0.15 - 4.0 m2	1.02	15.47	60.65	**76.12**	m2
6 mm in panes not exceeding 0.15 m2	1.92	29.18	79.24	**108.42**	m2
6 mm in panes 0.15 - 4.0 m2	1.02	15.47	63.39	**78.86**	m2
10 mm in panes not exceeding 0.15 m2	2.26	34.29	123.21	**157.50**	m2
10 mm in panes 0.15 - 4.0 m2	1.20	18.17	98.57	**116.74**	m2
058 **Anti-sun solar control toughened saftey glass, tinted bronze or grey**					
059 To wood with putty and sprigs:					
4 mm in panes not exceeding 0.15 m2	1.02	15.50	104.65	**120.15**	m2
4 mm in panes 0.15 - 4.0 m2	0.54	8.22	82.46	**90.68**	m2
6 mm in panes not exceeding 0.15 m2	1.02	15.50	134.05	**149.55**	m2
6 mm in panes 0.15 - 4.0 m2	0.54	8.22	106.43	**114.65**	m2
060 To wood with bradded wood beads (supplied cut to length by others):					
4 mm in panes not exceeding 0.15 m2	1.36	20.67	102.20	**122.87**	m2
4 mm in panes 0.15 - 4.0 m2	0.72	10.95	81.52	**92.47**	m2
6 mm in panes not exceeding 0.15 m2	1.36	20.67	132.16	**152.83**	m2
6 mm in panes 0.15 - 4.0 m2	0.72	10.95	105.49	**116.44**	m2
061 To wood with screwed wood beads (supplied cut to length by others):					
4 mm in panes not exceeding 0.15 m2	2.04	31.01	102.20	**133.21**	m2
4 mm in panes 0.15 - 4.0 m2	1.08	16.43	81.52	**97.95**	m2
6 mm in panes not exceeding 0.15 m2	2.04	31.01	132.16	**163.17**	m2
6 mm in panes 0.15 - 4.0 m2	1.08	16.43	105.49	**121.92**	m2
062 To metal with screwed metal beads (supplied cut to length by others):					
4 mm in panes not exceeding 0.15 m2	1.98	30.10	102.20	**132.30**	m2
4 mm in panes 0.15 - 4.0 m2	1.05	15.95	81.52	**97.47**	m2
6 mm in panes not exceeding 0.15 m2	1.98	30.10	132.16	**162.26**	m2
6 mm in panes 0.15 - 4.0 m2	1.05	15.95	105.49	**121.44**	m2
063 To metal with synthetic rubber extruded gaskets and clip-on metal beads (supplied cut to length by others):					
4 mm in panes not exceeding 0.15 m2	1.92	29.18	101.50	**130.68**	m2
4 mm in panes 0.15 - 4.0 m2	1.02	15.47	81.20	**96.67**	m2
6 mm in panes not exceeding 0.15 m2	1.92	29.18	131.46	**160.64**	m2
6 mm in panes 0.15 - 4.0 m2	1.02	15.47	105.17	**120.64**	m2
064 **White patterned toughened safety glass**					
065 To wood with putty and sprigs:					
4 mm in panes not exceeding 0.15 m2	1.02	15.50	72.47	**87.97**	m2
4 mm in panes 0.15 - 4.0 m2	0.54	8.22	57.17	**65.39**	m2
6 mm in panes not exceeding 0.15 m2	1.02	15.50	97.02	**112.52**	m2
6 mm in panes 0.15 - 4.0 m2	0.54	8.22	76.81	**85.03**	m2
066 To wood with bradded wood beads (supplied cut to length by others):					
4 mm in panes not exceeding 0.15 m2	1.36	20.67	70.58	**91.25**	m2
4 mm in panes 0.15 - 4.0 m2	0.72	10.95	56.22	**67.17**	m2
6 mm in panes not exceeding 0.15 m2	1.36	20.67	95.13	**115.80**	m2
6 mm in panes 0.15 - 4.0 m2	0.72	10.95	75.86	**86.81**	m2
067 To wood with screwed wood beads (supplied cut to length by others):					
4 mm in panes not exceeding 0.15 m2	2.04	31.01	70.58	**101.59**	m2
4 mm in panes 0.15 - 4.0 m2	1.08	16.43	56.22	**72.65**	m2
6 mm in panes not exceeding 0.15 m2	2.04	31.01	95.13	**126.14**	m2
6 mm in panes 0.15 - 4.0 m2	1.08	16.43	75.86	**92.29**	m2
068 To metal with screwed metal beads (supplied cut to length by others):					
4 mm in panes not exceeding 0.15 m2	1.98	30.10	70.58	**100.68**	m2
4 mm in panes 0.15 - 4.0 m2	1.05	15.95	56.22	**72.17**	m2
6 mm in panes not exceeding 0.15 m2	1.98	30.10	95.13	**125.23**	m2
6 mm in panes 0.15 - 4.0 m2	1.05	15.95	75.86	**91.81**	m2
069 To metal with synthetic rubber extruded gaskets and clip-on metal beads (supplied cut to length by others):					
4 mm in panes not exceeding 0.15 m2	1.92	29.18	69.89	**99.07**	m2
4 mm in panes 0.15 - 4.0 m2	1.02	15.47	55.91	**71.38**	m2
6 mm in panes not exceeding 0.15 m2	1.92	29.18	94.44	**123.62**	m2
6 mm in panes 0.15 - 4.0 m2	1.02	15.47	75.55	**91.02**	m2

	Unit Rates	Man-Hours	Net Labour Price £	Net Mats Price £	Net Unit Price £	Unit
070	**Tinted patterned toughened safety glass**					
071	To wood with putty and sprigs:					
	4 mm in panes not exceeding 0.15 m2	1.02	15.50	100.42	**115.92**	m2
	4 mm in panes 0.15 - 4.0 m2	0.54	8.22	79.53	**87.75**	m2
072	To wood with bradded wood beads (supplied cut to length by others):					
	4 mm in panes not exceeding 0.15 m2	1.36	20.67	98.53	**119.20**	m2
	4 mm in panes 0.15 - 4.0 m2	0.72	10.95	78.59	**89.54**	m2
073	To wood with screwed wood beads (supplied cut to length by others):					
	4 mm in panes not exceeding 0.15 m2	2.04	31.01	98.53	**129.54**	m2
	4 mm in panes 0.15 - 4.0 m2	1.08	16.43	78.59	**95.02**	m2
074	To metal with screwed metal beads (supplied cut to length by others):					
	4 mm in panes not exceeding 0.15 m2	1.98	30.10	98.53	**128.63**	m2
	4 mm in panes 0.15 - 4.0 m2	1.05	15.95	78.59	**94.54**	m2
075	To metal with synthetic rubber extruded gaskets and clip-on metal beads (supplied cut to length by others):					
	4 mm in panes not exceeding 0.15 m2	1.92	29.18	97.84	**127.02**	m2
	4 mm in panes 0.15 - 4.0 m2	1.02	15.47	78.27	**93.74**	m2
076	**Laminated clear safety glass (float quality)**					
077	To wood with bradded wood beads (supplied cut to length by others):					
	4 mm in panes not exceeding 0.15 m2	1.36	20.67	59.02	**79.69**	m2
	4 mm in panes 0.15 - 4.0 m2	0.72	10.95	46.98	**57.93**	m2
	5.4 mm in panes not exceeding 0.15 m2	1.36	20.67	66.92	**87.59**	m2
	5.4 mm in panes 0.15 - 4.0 m2	0.72	10.95	53.30	**64.25**	m2
	6.4 mm in panes not exceeding 0.15 m2	1.36	20.67	108.49	**129.16**	m2
	6.4 mm in panes 0.15 - 4.0 m2	0.72	10.95	86.55	**97.50**	m2
	6.8 mm in panes not exceeding 0.15 m2	1.36	20.67	108.55	**129.22**	m2
	6.8 mm in panes 0.15 - 4.0 m2	0.72	10.95	86.60	**97.55**	m2
	8.8 mm in panes not exceeding 0.15 m2	1.56	23.77	117.40	**141.17**	m2
	8.8 mm in panes 0.15 - 4.0 m2	0.83	12.60	93.68	**106.28**	m2
	10.8 mm in panes not exceeding 0.15 m2	1.56	23.77	139.73	**163.50**	m2
	10.8 mm in panes 0.15 - 4.0 m2	0.83	12.60	111.54	**124.14**	m2
078	To wood with screwed wood beads (supplied cut to length by others):					
	4 mm in panes not exceeding 0.15 m2	2.04	31.01	59.02	**90.03**	m2
	4 mm in panes 0.15 - 4.0 m2	1.08	16.43	46.98	**63.41**	m2
	5.4 mm in panes not exceeding 0.15 m2	2.04	31.01	66.92	**97.93**	m2
	5.4 mm in panes 0.15 - 4.0 m2	1.08	16.43	53.30	**69.73**	m2
	6.4 mm in panes not exceeding 0.15 m2	2.04	31.01	108.49	**139.50**	m2
	6.4 mm in panes 0.15 - 4.0 m2	1.08	16.43	86.55	**102.98**	m2
	6.8 mm in panes not exceeding 0.15 m2	2.04	31.01	108.55	**139.56**	m2
	6.8 mm in panes 0.15 - 4.0 m2	1.08	16.43	86.60	**103.03**	m2
	8.8 mm in panes not exceeding 0.15 m2	2.40	36.48	117.40	**153.88**	m2
	8.8 mm in panes 0.15 - 4.0 m2	1.27	19.33	93.68	**113.01**	m2
	10.8 mm in panes not exceeding 0.15 m2	2.40	36.48	139.73	**176.21**	m2
	10.8 mm in panes 0.15 - 4.0 m2	1.27	19.33	111.54	**130.87**	m2
079	To metal with screwed metal beads (supplied cut to length by others):					
	4 mm in panes not exceeding 0.15 m2	1.98	30.10	59.02	**89.12**	m2
	4 mm in panes 0.15 - 4.0 m2	1.05	15.95	46.98	**62.93**	m2
	5.4 mm in panes not exceeding 0.15 m2	1.98	30.10	66.92	**97.02**	m2
	5.4 mm in panes 0.15 - 4.0 m2	1.05	15.95	53.30	**69.25**	m2
	6.4 mm in panes not exceeding 0.15 m2	1.98	30.10	108.49	**138.59**	m2
	6.4 mm in panes 0.15 - 4.0 m2	1.05	15.95	86.55	**102.50**	m2
	6.8 mm in panes not exceeding 0.15 m2	1.98	30.10	108.55	**138.65**	m2
	6.8 mm in panes 0.15 - 4.0 m2	1.05	15.95	86.60	**102.55**	m2
	8.8 mm in panes not exceeding 0.15 m2	2.35	35.75	117.40	**153.15**	m2
	8.8 mm in panes 0.15 - 4.0 m2	1.25	18.95	93.68	**112.63**	m2
	10.8 mm in panes not exceeding 0.15 m2	2.35	35.75	139.73	**175.48**	m2
	10.8 mm in panes 0.15 - 4.0 m2	1.25	18.95	111.54	**130.49**	m2
080	To metal with synthetic rubber extruded gaskets and clip-on metal beads (supplied cut to length by others):					
	4 mm in panes not exceeding 0.15 m2	1.92	29.18	58.33	**87.51**	m2
	4 mm in panes 0.15 - 4.0 m2	1.02	15.47	46.66	**62.13**	m2
	5.4 mm in panes not exceeding 0.15 m2	1.92	29.18	66.23	**95.41**	m2
	5.4 mm in panes 0.15 - 4.0 m2	1.02	15.47	52.98	**68.45**	m2
	6.4 mm in panes not exceeding 0.15 m2	1.92	29.18	107.80	**136.98**	m2
	6.4 mm in panes 0.15 - 4.0 m2	1.02	15.47	86.24	**101.71**	m2
	6.8 mm in panes not exceeding 0.15 m2	1.92	29.18	107.86	**137.04**	m2
	6.8 mm in panes 0.15 - 4.0 m2	1.02	15.47	86.29	**101.76**	m2
	8.8 mm in panes not exceeding 0.15 m2	2.26	34.29	116.71	**151.00**	m2
	8.8 mm in panes 0.15 - 4.0 m2	1.20	18.17	93.36	**111.53**	m2
	10.8 mm in panes not exceeding 0.15 m2	2.26	34.29	139.03	**173.32**	m2
	10.8 mm in panes 0.15 - 4.0 m2	1.20	18.17	111.23	**129.40**	m2
081	**Laminated clear security glass (float quality)**					
082	To wood with bradded wood beads (supplied cut to length by others):					
	7.5 mm in panes not exceeding 0.15 m2	1.36	20.67	187.61	**208.28**	m2
	7.5 mm in panes 0.15 - 4.0 m2	0.72	10.95	149.85	**160.80**	m2
	9.5 mm in panes not exceeding 0.15 m2	1.56	23.77	192.22	**215.99**	m2
	9.5 mm in panes 0.15 - 4.0 m2	0.83	12.60	153.54	**166.14**	m2

Unit Rates	Man-Hours	Net Labour Price £	Net Mats Price £	Net Unit Price £	Unit
11.5 mm in panes not exceeding 0.15 m2	1.56	23.77	213.25	**237.02**	m2
11.5 mm in panes 0.15 - 4.0 m2	0.83	12.60	170.36	**182.96**	m2
083 To wood with bradded wood beads (supplied cut to length by others):					
7.5 mm in panes not exceeding 0.15 m2	2.04	31.01	187.61	**218.62**	m2
7.5 mm in panes 0.15 - 4.0 m2	1.08	16.43	149.85	**166.28**	m2
9.5 mm in panes not exceeding 0.15 m2	2.40	36.48	192.22	**228.70**	m2
9.5 mm in panes 0.15 - 4.0 m2	1.27	19.33	153.91	**173.24**	m2
11.5 mm in panes not exceeding 0.15 m2	2.40	36.48	212.87	**249.35**	m2
11.5 mm in panes 0.15 - 4.0 m2	1.27	19.33	170.36	**189.69**	m2
084 To wood with bradded wood beads (supplied cut to length by others):					
7.5 mm in panes not exceeding 0.15 m2	1.98	30.10	187.61	**217.71**	m2
7.5 mm in panes 0.15 - 4.0 m2	1.05	15.95	149.85	**165.80**	m2
9.5 mm in panes not exceeding 0.15 m2	2.33	35.39	192.22	**227.61**	m2
9.5 mm in panes 0.15 - 4.0 m2	1.23	18.75	153.54	**172.29**	m2
11.5 mm in panes not exceeding 0.15 m2	2.33	35.39	213.25	**248.64**	m2
11.5 mm in panes 0.15 - 4.0 m2	1.23	18.75	170.36	**189.11**	m2
085 To metal with synthetic rubber extruded gaskets and clip-on metal beads (supplied cut to length by others):					
7.5 mm in panes not exceeding 0.15 m2	1.92	29.18	186.91	**216.09**	m2
7.5 mm in panes 0.15 - 4.0 m2	1.02	15.47	149.53	**165.00**	m2
9.5 mm in panes not exceeding 0.15 m2	2.21	33.56	191.53	**225.09**	m2
9.5 mm in panes 0.15 - 4.0 m2	1.17	17.79	153.22	**171.01**	m2
11.5 mm in panes not exceeding 0.15 m2	2.26	34.29	212.56	**246.85**	m2
11.5 mm in panes 0.15 - 4.0 m2	1.17	17.79	170.05	**187.84**	m2
UB **FIRE RESISTING GLASS**					
001 **Laminated Fire Rated (30/30) glass, clear**					
002 To wood with bradded hardwood wood beads (supplied cut to length by others) and set in intumescent glazing tape:					
7 mm in panes not exceeding 0.15 m2	1.56	23.77	459.82	**483.59**	m2
7 mm in panes 0.15 - 4.0 m2	0.83	12.60	358.56	**371.16**	m2
003 **Laminated Fire Rated (60/60) glass, clear**					
004 To wood with screwed hardwood wood beads (supplied cut to length by others) and set in intumescent glazing tape:					
12 mm in panes not exceeding 0.15 m2	2.70	41.01	556.30	**597.31**	m2
12 mm in panes 0.15 - 4.0 m2	1.43	21.73	435.74	**457.47**	m2
16 mm in panes not exceeding 0.15 m2	2.97	45.11	660.62	**705.73**	m2
16 mm in panes 0.15 - 4.0 m2	1.57	23.91	495.95	**519.86**	m2
005 To metal with screwed metal beads (supplied cut to length by others):					
12 mm in panes not exceeding 0.15 m2	2.70	41.01	556.30	**597.31**	m2
12 mm in panes 0.15 - 4.0 m2	1.43	21.73	435.74	**457.47**	m2
16 mm in panes not exceeding 0.15 m2	2.97	45.11	660.62	**705.73**	m2
16 mm in panes 0.15 - 4.0 m2	1.57	23.91	495.95	**519.86**	m2
006 **Laminated solar control tinted safety glass**					
007 To wood with bradded wood beads (supplied cut to length by others):					
6.4 mm in panes not exceeding 0.15 m2	1.36	20.67	137.28	**157.95**	m2
6.4 mm in panes 0.15 - 4.0 m2	0.72	10.95	109.58	**120.53**	m2
008 To wood with screwed wood beads (supplied cut to length by others):					
6.4 mm in panes not exceeding 0.15 m2	2.04	31.01	137.28	**168.29**	m2
6.4 mm in panes 0.15 - 4.0 m2	1.08	16.43	109.58	**126.01**	m2
009 To metal with screwed metal beads (supplied cut to length by others):					
6.4 mm in panes not exceeding 0.15 m2	2.04	31.01	137.28	**168.29**	m2
6.4 mm in panes 0.15 - 4.0 m2	1.08	16.43	109.58	**126.01**	m2
010 To metal with synthetic rubber extruded gaskets and clip-on metal beads (supplied cut to length by others):					
6.4 mm in panes not exceeding 0.15 m2	1.92	29.18	136.59	**165.77**	m2
6.4 mm in panes 0.15 - 4.0 m2	1.02	15.47	109.27	**124.74**	m2
011 **Cast Georgian wired glass**					
012 To wood with putty and sprigs:					
7 mm in panes not exceeding 0.15 m2	1.02	15.50	103.71	**119.21**	m2
7 mm in panes 0.15 - 4.0 m2	0.54	8.22	82.16	**90.38**	m2
013 To wood with bradded wood beads (supplied cut to length by others):					
7 mm in panes not exceeding 0.15 m2	1.36	20.67	101.82	**122.49**	m2
7 mm in panes 0.15 - 4.0 m2	0.72	10.95	81.22	**92.17**	m2
014 To wood with screwed wood beads (supplied cut to length by others):					
7 mm in panes not exceeding 0.15 m2	2.04	31.01	101.82	**132.83**	m2
7 mm in panes 0.15 - 4.0 m2	1.08	16.43	81.22	**97.65**	m2
015 To metal with putty and clips:					
7 mm in panes not exceeding 0.15 m2	1.08	16.42	104.34	**120.76**	m2
7 mm in panes 0.15 - 4.0 m2	0.57	8.70	82.48	**91.18**	m2

Unit Rates

		Man-Hours	Net Labour Price £	Net Mats Price £	Net Unit Price £	Unit
016	To metal with screwed metal beads (supplied cut to length by others):					
	7 mm in panes not exceeding 0.15 m2	1.98	30.10	101.95	**132.05**	m2
	7 mm in panes 0.15 - 4.0 m2	1.05	15.95	81.28	**97.23**	m2
017	To metal with synthetic rubber extruded gaskets and clip-on metal beads (supplied cut to length by others):					
	7 mm in panes not exceeding 0.15 m2	1.92	29.18	101.13	**130.31**	m2
	7 mm in panes 0.15 - 4.0 m2	1.02	15.47	80.90	**96.37**	m2
018	**Cast Georgian wired glass with wires on adjacent panes lined up one way**					
019	To wood with putty and sprigs:					
	7 mm in panes not exceeding 0.15 m2	1.02	15.50	108.42	**123.92**	m2
	7 mm in panes 0.15 - 4.0 m2	0.59	8.95	85.93	**94.88**	m2
020	To wood with bradded wood beads (supplied cut to length by others):					
	7 mm in panes not exceeding 0.15 m2	1.46	22.13	106.53	**128.66**	m2
	7 mm in panes 0.15 - 4.0 m2	0.77	11.68	84.98	**96.66**	m2
021	To wood with screwed wood beads (supplied cut to length by others):					
	7 mm in panes not exceeding 0.15 m2	2.04	31.01	106.53	**137.54**	m2
	7 mm in panes 0.15 - 4.0 m2	1.08	16.43	84.98	**101.41**	m2
022	To metal with putty and clips:					
	7 mm in panes not exceeding 0.15 m2	1.08	16.42	109.05	**125.47**	m2
	7 mm in panes 0.15 - 4.0 m2	0.57	8.70	86.24	**94.94**	m2
023	To metal with screwed metal beads (supplied cut to length by others):					
	7 mm in panes not exceeding 0.15 m2	1.98	30.10	106.65	**136.75**	m2
	7 mm in panes 0.15 - 4.0 m2	1.05	15.95	85.05	**101.00**	m2
024	To metal with synthetic rubber extruded gaskets and clip-on metal beads (supplied cut to length by others):					
	7 mm in panes not exceeding 0.15 m2	1.92	29.18	105.83	**135.01**	m2
	7 mm in panes 0.15 - 4.0 m2	1.02	15.47	84.67	**100.14**	m2
025	**Polished Georgian wired glass**					
026	To wood with putty and sprigs:					
	6 mm in panes not exceeding 0.15 m2	1.02	15.50	121.07	**136.57**	m2
	6 mm in panes 0.15 - 4.0 m2	0.54	8.22	119.75	**127.97**	m2
027	To wood with bradded wood beads (supplied cut to length by others):					
	6 mm in panes not exceeding 0.15 m2	1.36	20.67	148.80	**169.47**	m2
	6 mm in panes 0.15 - 4.0 m2	0.72	10.95	118.80	**129.75**	m2
028	To wood with screwed wood beads (supplied cut to length by others):					
	6 mm in panes not exceeding 0.15 m2	2.04	31.01	148.80	**179.81**	m2
	6 mm in panes 0.15 - 4.0 m2	1.08	16.43	118.80	**135.23**	m2
029	To metal with putty and clips:					
	6 mm in panes not exceeding 0.15 m2	1.08	16.42	151.32	**167.74**	m2
	6 mm in panes 0.15 - 4.0 m2	0.57	8.70	120.06	**128.76**	m2
030	To metal with screwed metal beads (supplied cut to length by others):					
	6 mm in panes not exceeding 0.15 m2	1.98	30.10	148.93	**179.03**	m2
	6 mm in panes 0.15 - 4.0 m2	1.05	15.95	118.86	**134.81**	m2
031	To metal with synthetic rubber extruded gaskets and clip-on metal beads (supplied cut to length by others):					
	6 mm in panes not exceeding 0.15 m2	1.92	29.18	148.11	**177.29**	m2
	6 mm in panes 0.15 - 4.0 m2	1.02	15.47	118.49	**133.96**	m2
032	**Polished Georgian glass with wires on adjacent panes lined up one way**					
033	To metal with synthetic rubber extruded gaskets and clip-on metal beads (supplied cut to length by others):					
	6 mm in panes not exceeding 0.15 m2	1.02	15.50	155.39	**170.89**	m2
	6 mm in panes 0.15 - 4.0 m2	0.54	8.22	123.51	**131.73**	m2
034	To metal with synthetic rubber extruded gaskets and clip-on metal beads (supplied cut to length by others):					
	6 mm in panes not exceeding 0.15 m2	1.36	20.67	153.50	**174.17**	m2
	6 mm in panes 0.15 - 4.0 m2	0.72	10.95	122.56	**133.51**	m2
035	To metal with synthetic rubber extruded gaskets and clip-on metal beads (supplied cut to length by others):					
	6 mm in panes not exceeding 0.15 m2	2.04	31.01	153.50	**184.51**	m2
	6 mm in panes 0.15 - 4.0 m2	1.08	16.43	122.56	**138.99**	m2
036	To metal with synthetic rubber extruded gaskets and clip-on metal beads (supplied cut to length by others):					
	6 mm in panes not exceeding 0.15 m2	1.08	16.42	156.02	**172.44**	m2
	6 mm in panes 0.15 - 4.0 m2	0.57	8.70	123.82	**132.52**	m2
037	To metal with synthetic rubber extruded gaskets and clip-on metal beads (supplied cut to length by others):					
	6 mm in panes not exceeding 0.15 m2	1.98	30.10	153.63	**183.73**	m2
	6 mm in panes 0.15 - 4.0 m2	1.05	15.95	122.63	**138.58**	m2

Unit Rates		Man-Hours	Net Labour Price £	Net Mats Price £	Net Unit Price £	Unit
038	To metal with synthetic rubber extruded gaskets and clip-on metal beads (supplied cut to length by others):					
	6 mm in panes not exceeding 0.15 m2	1.92	29.18	152.81	**181.99**	m2
	6 mm in panes 0.15 - 4.0 m2	1.02	15.47	122.25	**137.72**	m2
UC	**HERMETICALLY SEALED DOUBLE GLAZED UNITS**					
001	**4 mm clear float glass, 4 mm low emissivity clear glass, cavity not exceeding 20 mm**					
002	To wood or metal with screwed beads and non-setting compound					
	in panes not exceeding 0.15 m2	2.45	37.21	106.56	**143.77**	m2
	in panes 0.15 - 4.0 m2	1.30	19.72	79.56	**99.28**	m2
003	To metal with synthetic rubber extruded gaskets and clip-on metal beads (supplied cut to length by others); unit size not exceeding:					
	in panes not exceeding 0.15 m2	2.30	35.02	106.56	**141.58**	m2
	in panes 0.15 - 4.0 m2	1.22	18.56	79.56	**98.12**	m2
004	**6 mm clear float glass, 6 mm low emissivity clear glass, cavity not exceeding 20 mm**					
005	To wood or metal with screwed beads and non-setting compound:					
	in panes not exceeding 0.15 m2	2.45	37.21	143.61	**180.82**	m2
	in panes 0.15 - 4.0 m2	1.30	19.72	109.20	**128.92**	m2
006	To metal with synthetic rubber extruded gaskets and clip-on metal beads (supplied cut to length by others); unit size not exceeding:					
	in panes not exceeding 0.15 m2	2.30	35.02	143.61	**178.63**	m2
	in panes 0.15 - 4.0 m2	1.22	18.56	109.20	**127.76**	m2
007	**3 x 4 mm clear float glass, cavity not exceeding 20 mm**					
008	To wood or metal with screwed beads and non-setting compound					
	in panes not exceeding 0.15 m2	2.45	37.21	168.84	**206.05**	m2
	in panes 0.15 - 4.0 m2	1.30	19.72	110.03	**129.75**	m2
009	To metal with synthetic rubber extruded gaskets and clip-on metal beads (supplied cut to length by others); unit size not exceeding:					
	in panes not exceeding 0.15 m2	2.30	35.02	168.84	**203.86**	m2
	in panes 0.15 - 4.0 m2	1.22	18.56	110.03	**128.59**	m2
010	**3 x 4 mm clear float glass, toughened, cavity not exceeding 20 mm**					
011	To wood or metal with screwed beads and non-setting compound					
	in panes not exceeding 0.15 m2	2.45	37.21	250.08	**287.29**	m2
	in panes 0.15 - 4.0 m2	1.30	19.72	140.20	**159.92**	m2
012	To metal with synthetic rubber extruded gaskets and clip-on metal beads (supplied cut to length by others); unit size not exceeding:					
	in panes not exceeding 0.15 m2	2.30	35.02	250.08	**285.10**	m2
	in panes 0.15 - 4.0 m2	1.22	18.56	209.66	**228.22**	m2
013	**6 mm clear float glass, 6 mm low emission clear glass, toughened, cavity not exceeding 20 mm**					
014	To wood or metal with screwed beads and non-setting compound					
	in panes not exceeding 0.15 m2	2.45	37.21	178.79	**216.00**	m2
	in panes 0.15 - 4.0 m2	1.30	19.72	178.79	**198.51**	m2
015	To wood or metal with screwed beads and non-setting compound					
	in panes not exceeding 0.15 m2	2.30	35.02	178.79	**213.81**	m2
	in panes 0.15 - 4.0 m2	1.22	18.56	178.79	**197.35**	m2
016	**3 x 4 mm clear float glass, cavity not exceeding 20 mm**					
017	To wood or metal with screwed beads and non-setting compound					
	in panes not exceeding 0.15 m2	2.45	37.21	274.38	**311.59**	m2
	in panes 0.15 - 4.0 m2	1.30	19.72	185.25	**204.97**	m2
018	To metal with synthetic rubber extruded gaskets and clip-on metal beads (supplied cut to length by others); unit size not exceeding:					
	in panes not exceeding 0.15 m2	2.45	37.21	436.91	**474.12**	m2
	in panes 0.15 - 4.0 m2	1.30	19.72	194.47	**214.19**	m2
019	**Most suppliers offer a range of alternative glass in making up double glazing units. As a general guide to the comparative prices of these alternatives, the following are given as EXTRA OVER prices to those given for 4 mm clear float glass**					
020	Extra over for filling glazing units with argon gas:					
	double glazing in panes not exceeding 0.15 m2	-	-	12.38	**12.38**	m2
	double glazing in panes 0.15 - 4.0 m2	-	-	6.19	**6.19**	m2
	triple glazing in panes not exceeding 0.15 m2	-	-	24.75	**24.75**	m2
	triple glazing in panes 0.15 - 4.0 m2	-	-	12.38	**12.38**	m2
021	Extra over toughening glass:					
	single glazing in panes not exceeding 0.15 m2	-	-	35.18	**35.18**	m2
	single glazing in panes 0.15 - 4.0 m2	-	-	28.14	**28.14**	m2
	double glazing in panes not exceeding 0.15 m2	-	-	70.36	**70.36**	m2
	double glazing in panes 0.15 - 4.0 m2	-	-	56.29	**56.29**	m2
	triple glazing in panes not exceeding 0.15 m2	-	-	105.54	**105.54**	m2

Unit Rates	Man-Hours	Net Labour Price £	Net Mats Price £	Net Unit Price £	Unit
triple glazing in panes 0.15 - 4.0 m2	-	-	84.43	**84.43**	m2
022 Extra over 4 mm clear float for 4 mm low emissivity glass:					
single glazing or inner leaf of insulating unit not exceeding 0.15m2	-	-	1.49	**1.49**	m2
single glazing or inner leaf of insulating unit 0.15 to 4 m2	-	-	1.19	**1.19**	m2
023 Extra over 4 mm clear float for 6 mm low emissivity glass:					
single glazing or inner leaf of insulating unit not exceeding 0.15m2	-	-	27.02	**27.02**	m2
single glazing or inner leaf of insulating unit 0.15 to 4 m2	-	-	21.62	**21.62**	m2
024 Extra over 4 mm clear float for 4 mm self cleaning glass:					
single glazing or inner leaf of insulating unit not exceeding 0.15m2	-	-	15.54	**15.54**	m2
single glazing or inner leaf of insulating unit 0.15 to 4 m2	-	-	12.43	**12.43**	m2
025 Extra over 4 mm clear float for 6 mm self cleaning glass:					
single glazing or inner leaf of insulating unit not exceeding 0.15m2	-	-	52.66	**52.66**	m2
single glazing or inner leaf of insulating unit 0.15 to 4 m2	-	-	42.13	**42.13**	m2
026 Extra over clear float for 4 mm white patterned glass:					
single glazing or inner leaf of insulating unit not exceeding 0.15m2	-	-	1.46	**1.46**	m2
single glazing or inner leaf of insulating unit 0.15 to 4 m2	-	-	1.17	**1.17**	m2
027 Extra over clear float for 6 mm white patterned glass:					
single glazing or inner leaf of insulating unit not exceeding 0.15m2	-	-	26.01	**26.01**	m2
single glazing or inner leaf of insulating unit 0.15 to 4 m2	-	-	11.59	**11.59**	m2
028 Extra over clear float for 4 mm bronze or grey tinted patterned glass:					
single glazing or inner leaf of insulating unit not exceeding 0.15m2	-	-	29.41	**29.41**	m2
single glazing or inner leaf of insulating unit 0.15 to 4 m2	-	-	23.53	**23.53**	m2
029 Extra over clear float for 4 mm bronze or grey tinted patterned glass:					
single glazing or inner leaf of insulating unit not exceeding 0.15m2	-	-	33.08	**33.08**	m2
single glazing or inner leaf of insulating unit 0.15 to 4 m2	-	-	26.46	**26.46**	m2
030 Extra over clear float for 6 mm anti-sun bronze or grey tinted glass:					
single glazing or inner leaf of insulating unit not exceeding 0.15m2	-	-	44.25	**44.25**	m2
single glazing or inner leaf of insulating unit 0.15 to 4 m2	-	-	35.40	**35.40**	m2
031 Extra over clear float for 6 mm Styppolyte glass:					
single glazing or inner leaf of insulating unit not exceeding 0.15m2	-	-	19.49	**19.49**	m2
single glazing or inner leaf of insulating unit 0.15 to 4 m2	-	-	15.59	**15.59**	m2
032 Extra over clear float for 7 mm Georgian wired cast glass					
single glazing or inner leaf of insulating unit not exceeding 0.15m2	-	-	68.59	**68.59**	m2
single glazing or inner leaf of insulating unit 0.15 to 4 m2	-	-	48.36	**48.36**	m2
033 Extra over clear float for 6 mm Georgian wired polished glass					
single glazing or inner leaf of insulating unit not exceeding 0.15m2	-	-	115.57	**115.57**	m2
single glazing or inner leaf of insulating unit 0.15 to 4 m2	-	-	92.45	**92.45**	m2
034 Extra over clear float for applied lead strip to form rectangular pattern leaded lights					
single glazing or inner leaf of insulating unit 0.15 to 4 m2	-	-	33.29	**33.29**	m2

UD   **PLASTICS SHEET GLAZING**

001   **Polycarbonate clear sheet**

002 To wood with bradded wood beads (supplied cut to length by others) and silicone:	Man-Hours	Net Labour Price £	Net Mats Price £	Net Unit Price £	Unit
3 mm in panes not exceeding 0.15 m2	1.36	20.67	26.37	**47.04**	m2
3 mm in panes 0.15 - 4.0 m2	0.72	10.95	24.61	**35.56**	m2
4 mm in panes not exceeding 0.15 m2	1.36	20.67	34.00	**54.67**	m2
4 mm in panes 0.15 - 4.0 m2	0.72	10.95	32.24	**43.19**	m2
5 mm in panes not exceeding 0.15 m2	1.36	20.67	41.62	**62.29**	m2
5 mm in panes 0.15 - 4.0 m2	0.72	10.95	39.87	**50.82**	m2
6 mm in panes not exceeding 0.15 m2	1.36	20.67	49.23	**69.90**	m2
6 mm in panes 0.15 - 4.0 m2	0.72	10.95	47.47	**58.42**	m2
8 mm in panes not exceeding 0.15m2	1.56	23.77	91.66	**115.43**	m2
8 mm in panes 0.15 - 4.0 m2	0.83	12.60	89.90	**102.50**	m2
9.5 mm in panes not exceeding 0.15 m2	1.56	23.77	130.79	**154.56**	m2
9.5 mm in panes 0.15 - 4.0 m2	0.83	12.60	129.03	**141.63**	m2
12 mm in panes not exceeding 0.15 m2	1.56	23.77	164.38	**188.15**	m2
12 mm in panes 0.15 - 4.0 m2	0.83	12.60	162.62	**175.22**	m2
003 To wood or metal with screwed beads and silicone:					
3 mm in panes not exceeding 0.15 m2	2.04	31.01	26.37	**57.38**	m2
3 mm in panes 0.15 - 4.0 m2	1.08	16.43	24.61	**41.04**	m2
4 mm in panes not exceeding 0.15 m2	2.04	31.01	34.00	**65.01**	m2
4 mm in panes 0.15 - 4.0 m2	1.08	16.43	32.24	**48.67**	m2
5 mm in panes not exceeding 0.15 m2	2.04	31.01	41.62	**72.63**	m2
5 mm in panes 0.15 - 4.0 m2	1.08	16.43	39.87	**56.30**	m2
6 mm in panes not exceeding 0.15 m2	2.04	31.01	49.23	**80.24**	m2
6 mm in panes 0.15 - 4.0 m2	1.08	16.43	47.47	**63.90**	m2
8 mm in panes not exceeding 0.15 m2	2.35	35.66	91.66	**127.32**	m2
8 mm in panes 0.15 - 4.0 m2	1.24	18.90	89.90	**108.80**	m2
9.5 mm in panes not exceeding 0.15 m2	2.35	35.66	130.79	**166.45**	m2
9.5 mm in panes 0.15 - 4.0 m2	1.24	18.90	129.03	**147.93**	m2
12 mm in panes not exceeding 0.15 m2	2.35	35.66	164.38	**200.04**	m2
12 mm in panes 0.15 - 4.0 m2	1.24	18.90	162.62	**181.52**	m2

Unit Rates	Man-Hours	Net Labour Price £	Net Mats Price £	Net Unit Price £	Unit
004 To metal with synthetic rubber extruded gaskets and clip-on metal beads (supplied cut to length by others):					
3 mm in panes not exceeding 0.15 m2	1.92	29.18	22.85	**52.03**	m2
3 mm in panes 0.15 - 4.0 m2	1.02	15.47	22.85	**38.32**	m2
4 mm in panes not exceeding 0.15 m2	1.92	29.18	30.48	**59.66**	m2
4 mm in panes 0.15 - 4.0 m2	1.02	15.47	30.48	**45.95**	m2
5 mm in panes not exceeding 0.15 m2	1.92	29.18	38.11	**67.29**	m2
5 mm in panes 0.15 - 4.0 m2	1.02	15.47	38.11	**53.58**	m2
6 mm in panes not exceeding 0.15 m2	1.92	29.18	45.71	**74.89**	m2
6 mm in panes 0.15 - 4.0 m2	1.02	15.47	45.71	**61.18**	m2
8 mm in panes not exceeding 0.15 m2	2.21	33.56	88.15	**121.71**	m2
8 mm in panes 0.15 - 4.0 m2	1.17	17.79	88.15	**105.94**	m2
9.5 mm in panes not exceeding 0.15 m2	2.21	33.56	127.27	**160.83**	m2
9.5 mm in panes 0.15 - 4.0 m2	1.17	17.79	127.27	**145.06**	m2
12 mm in panes not exceeding 0.15 m2	2.21	33.56	160.86	**194.42**	m2
12 mm in panes 0.15 - 4.0 m2	1.17	17.79	160.86	**178.65**	m2
005 **Polycarbonate coated clear sheet**					
006 To wood with bradded wood beads (supplied cut to length by others) and silicone:					
3 mm in panes not exceeding 0.15 m2	1.36	20.67	47.87	**68.54**	m2
3 mm in panes 0.15 - 4.0 m2	0.72	10.95	46.11	**57.06**	m2
4 mm in panes not exceeding 0.15 m2	1.36	20.67	62.62	**83.29**	m2
4 mm in panes 0.15 - 4.0 m2	0.72	10.95	60.86	**71.81**	m2
5 mm in panes not exceeding 0.15 m2	1.36	20.67	77.39	**98.06**	m2
5 mm in panes 0.15 - 4.0 m2	0.72	10.95	75.63	**86.58**	m2
6 mm in panes not exceeding 0.15 m2	1.36	20.67	91.97	**112.64**	m2
6 mm in panes 0.15 - 4.0 m2	0.72	10.95	90.21	**101.16**	m2
8 mm in panes not exceeding 0.15 m2	1.56	23.77	121.66	**145.43**	m2
8 mm in panes 0.15 - 4.0 m2	0.83	12.60	119.90	**132.50**	m2
9.5 mm in panes not exceeding 0.15 m2	1.56	23.77	143.83	**167.60**	m2
9.5 mm in panes 0.15 - 4.0 m2	0.83	12.60	142.07	**154.67**	m2
12 mm in panes not exceeding 0.15 m2	1.56	23.77	181.83	**205.60**	m2
12 mm in panes 0.15 - 4.0 m2	0.83	12.60	180.07	**192.67**	m2
007 To wood or metal with screwed beads and silicone:					
3 mm in panes not exceeding 0.15 m2	2.04	31.01	47.87	**78.88**	m2
3 mm in panes 0.15 - 4.0 m2	1.08	16.43	46.11	**62.54**	m2
4 mm in panes not exceeding 0.15 m2	2.04	31.01	62.62	**93.63**	m2
4 mm in panes 0.15 - 4.0 m2	1.08	16.43	60.86	**77.29**	m2
5 mm in panes not exceeding 0.15 m2	2.04	31.01	77.39	**108.40**	m2
5 mm in panes 0.15 - 4.0 m2	1.08	16.43	75.63	**92.06**	m2
6 mm in panes not exceeding 0.15 m2	2.04	31.01	91.97	**122.98**	m2
6 mm in panes 0.15 - 4.0 m2	1.08	16.43	90.21	**106.64**	m2
8 mm in panes not exceeding 0.15 m2	2.35	35.66	121.66	**157.32**	m2
8 mm in panes 0.15 - 4.0 m2	1.24	18.90	119.90	**138.80**	m2
9.5 mm in panes not exceeding 0.15 m2	2.35	35.66	143.83	**179.49**	m2
9.5 mm in panes 0.15 - 4.0 m2	1.24	18.90	142.07	**160.97**	m2
12 mm in panes not exceeding 0.15 m2	2.35	35.66	181.83	**217.49**	m2
12 mm in panes 0.15 - 4.0 m2	1.24	18.90	180.07	**198.97**	m2
008 To wood or metal with screwed beads and silicone:					
3 mm in panes not exceeding 0.15 m2	1.92	29.18	44.35	**73.53**	m2
3 mm in panes 0.15 - 4.0 m2	1.02	15.47	44.35	**59.82**	m2
4 mm in panes not exceeding 0.15 m2	1.92	29.18	59.10	**88.28**	m2
4 mm in panes 0.15 - 4.0 m2	1.02	15.47	59.10	**74.57**	m2
5 mm in panes not exceeding 0.15 m2	1.92	29.18	73.87	**103.05**	m2
5 mm in panes 0.15 - 4.0 m2	1.02	15.47	73.87	**89.34**	m2
6 mm in panes not exceeding 0.15 m2	1.92	29.18	88.45	**117.63**	m2
6 mm in panes 0.15 - 4.0 m2	1.02	15.47	88.45	**103.92**	m2
8 mm in panes not exceeding 0.15 m2	2.21	33.56	118.14	**151.70**	m2
8 mm in panes 0.15 - 4.0 m2	1.17	17.79	118.14	**135.93**	m2
9.5 mm in panes not exceeding 0.15 m2	2.21	33.56	140.31	**173.87**	m2
9.5 mm in panes 0.15 - 4.0 m2	1.17	17.79	140.31	**158.10**	m2
12 mm in panes not exceeding 0.15 m2	2.21	33.56	178.31	**211.87**	m2
12 mm in panes 0.15 - 4.0 m2	1.17	17.79	178.31	**196.10**	m2
Note: 009 - 013 not used					
014 **Glass louvres fitting to but not including frames**					
015 Louvre blades, with long edges ground or smoothed; fixed in metal clips:					
5 mm or 6 mm float glass: 600 mm x 102 mm wide louvres	0.12	1.82	28.01	**29.83**	Nr
5 mm or 6 mm float glass: 600 mm x 152 mm wide louvres	0.12	1.82	30.20	**32.02**	Nr
6 mm Styppolyte glass: 600 mm x 102 mm wide louvres	0.12	1.82	28.09	**29.91**	Nr
6 mm Styppolyte glass: 600 mm x 152 mm wide louvres	0.12	1.82	30.89	**32.71**	Nr
7 mm wired cast glass: 600 mm x 102 mm wide louvres	0.12	1.82	27.28	**29.10**	Nr
7 mm wired cast glass: 600 mm x 152 mm wide louvres	0.12	1.82	29.99	**31.81**	Nr
6 mm polished wired plate: 600 mm x 102 mm wide louvres	0.12	1.82	30.89	**32.71**	Nr
6 mm polished wired plate: 600 mm x 152 mm wide louvres	0.12	1.82	33.98	**35.80**	Nr
UE **WORK ON GLASS**					
001 **Drilling glass in panes not exceeding 1 m2; holes through glass not exceeding:**					
002 6 mm thick:					
6 - 15 mm diameter hole	0.12	1.82	-	**1.82**	Nr
16 - 25 mm diameter hole	0.30	4.56	-	**4.56**	Nr

Unit Rates		Man-Hours	Net Labour Price £	Net Mats Price £	Net Unit Price £	Unit
003	6-10 mm thick:					
	6 - 15 mm diameter hole	0.36	5.47	-	5.47	Nr
	16 - 25 mm diameter hole	0.45	6.84	-	6.84	Nr
004	**Drilling glass in panes over 1 m2; holes through glass not exceeding:**					
005	6 mm thick:					
	6 - 15 mm diameter hole	0.36	5.47	-	5.47	Nr
	16 - 25 mm diameter hole	0.45	6.84	-	6.84	Nr
006	6-10 mm thick:					
	6 - 15 mm diameter hole	0.54	8.21	-	8.21	Nr
	16 - 25 mm diameter hole	0.68	10.31	-	10.31	Nr
007	**Polishing edges of glass; straight work:**					
008	Panes not exceeding 2.50 m2:					
	3 mm clear float	0.72	10.94	-	10.94	m
	4 mm clear float	0.72	10.94	-	10.94	m
	6 mm clear float	0.84	12.77	-	12.77	m
	6 mm rough cast	0.96	14.59	-	14.59	m
	6 mm wired	1.44	21.89	-	21.89	m
	7 mm wired	1.80	27.36	-	27.36	m
009	**Bevelling edges of 6 mm float glass; straight work:**					
010	Panes not exceeding 1.00 m2; width of bevel not exceeding:					
	6 mm wide	0.96	14.59	-	14.59	m
	10 mm wide	1.08	16.42	-	16.42	m
	16 mm wide	1.80	27.36	-	27.36	m
011	**Sundry items**					
012	Bedding edges of panes in imitation washleather strip:					
	3 - 6 mm thick glass	0.06	0.91	1.64	2.55	m
	10 - 12 mm thick glass	0.07	1.09	1.64	2.73	m
013	Hacking out putty, preparing rebates:					
	for glass 3 - 6 mm thick in timber window	0.40	6.02	-	6.02	m
	for glass 7 - 12 mm thick in timber window	0.46	7.02	-	7.02	m
	for glass 3 - 6 mm thick in metal window	0.44	6.62	-	6.62	m
	for glass 7 - 12 mm thick in metal window	0.51	7.73	-	7.73	m
014	Carefully removing glazing bead, any type, set aside for re-use, remove broken glass:					
	for glass 3 - 6 mm thick in timber window	0.30	4.56	-	4.56	m
	for glass 7 - 12 mm thick in timber window	0.36	5.47	-	5.47	m
	for glass 3 - 6 mm thick in metal window	0.33	5.02	-	5.02	m
	for glass 7 - 12 mm thick in metal window	0.40	6.02	-	6.02	m
015	**Mirrors**					
016	4 mm silvered float glass mirrors, copper backed, with polished edges and 4 drilled holes; plugged and screwed to plastered brick or block wall with mirror screws, rubber washers and chromium plated domes:					
	300 x 255 mm	0.96	14.59	24.12	38.71	Nr
	450 x 300 mm	1.02	15.50	24.43	39.93	Nr
	600 x 450 mm	1.08	16.42	31.08	47.50	Nr
	900 x 450 mm	1.14	17.33	43.74	61.07	Nr
	900 x 600 mm	1.20	18.24	56.44	74.68	Nr
	1200 x 300 mm	1.14	17.33	39.53	56.86	Nr
	1200 x 450 mm	1.17	17.78	56.38	74.16	Nr
	400 mm diameter	1.02	15.50	29.09	44.59	Nr
	600 mm diameter	1.08	16.42	47.86	64.28	Nr
UF	**LEADED LIGHTS**					
001	**Leaded lights exceeding 0.15 m2 formed of lead cames; rectangular shaped panes average size 100 mm x 150 mm; clear float glass (GG quality)**					
002	To wood with putty and sprigs:					
	3 mm	1.02	15.50	166.81	182.31	m2
	4 mm	1.20	18.24	171.04	189.28	m2
003	To wood with bradded wood beads (supplied cut to length by others):					
	3 mm	1.36	20.67	165.86	186.53	m2
	4 mm	1.36	20.67	170.10	190.77	m2
004	To wood with screwed wood beads (supplied cut to length by others):					
	3 mm	2.04	31.01	165.86	196.87	m2
	4 mm	2.04	31.01	170.10	201.11	m2
005	To metal with putty and clips:					
	3 mm	1.02	15.50	165.86	181.36	m2
	4 mm	1.02	15.50	170.10	185.60	m2
006	To metal with screwed metal beads (supplied cut to length by others):					
	3 mm	1.36	20.67	165.86	186.53	m2
	4 mm	1.36	20.67	170.10	190.77	m2

Unit Rates	Man-Hours	Net Labour Price £	Net Mats Price £	Net Unit Price £	Unit
007	To metal with synthetic extruded rubber gaskets and clip-on metal beads (supplied cut to length by others):					
	3 mm	1.92	29.18	165.55	**194.73**	m2
	4 mm	1.92	29.18	169.78	**198.96**	m2
008	**Leaded lights exceeding 0.15 m2 formed of lead cames; diamond shaped panes average size 75 mm x 100 mm extreme; clear float glass (GG quality)**					
009	To wood with putty and sprigs:					
	3 mm	1.53	23.26	201.18	**224.44**	m2
	4 mm	1.53	23.26	205.41	**228.67**	m2
010	To wood with bradded wood beads (supplied cut to length by others):					
	3 mm	2.04	31.00	200.24	**231.24**	m2
	4 mm	2.04	31.00	204.47	**235.47**	m2
011	To wood with screwed wood beads (supplied cut to length by others):					
	3 mm	3.06	46.51	200.24	**246.75**	m2
	4 mm	3.06	46.51	204.47	**250.98**	m2
012	To metal with putty and clips:					
	3 mm	1.53	23.26	201.50	**224.76**	m2
	4 mm	1.53	23.26	205.73	**228.99**	m2
013	To metal with screwed metal beads (supplied cut to length by others):					
	3 mm	1.53	23.26	200.30	**223.56**	m2
	4 mm	1.53	23.26	204.53	**227.79**	m2
014	To metal with synthetic extruded rubber gaskets and clip-on metal beads (supplied cut to length by others):					
	3 mm	1.20	18.24	199.92	**218.16**	m2
	4 mm	1.20	18.24	204.15	**222.39**	m2
015	**Imitation leaded lights exceeding 0.15 m2 formed of applied lead strip to simulate rectangular shaped panes average size 100 mm x 150 mm; clear float glass (GG quality)**					
016	To wood with putty and sprigs:					
	3 mm	1.02	15.50	30.51	**46.01**	m2
	4 mm	1.02	15.50	34.15	**49.65**	m2
017	To wood with bradded wood beads (supplied cut to length by others):					
	3 mm	1.36	20.67	29.57	**50.24**	m2
	4 mm	1.36	20.67	33.20	**53.87**	m2
018	To wood with screwed wood beads (supplied cut to length by others):					
	3 mm	2.04	31.01	29.57	**60.58**	m2
	4 mm	2.04	31.01	33.20	**64.21**	m2
019	To metal with putty and clips:					
	3 mm	1.02	15.50	30.83	**46.33**	m2
	4 mm	1.02	15.50	34.46	**49.96**	m2
020	To metal with screwed metal beads (supplied cut to length by others):					
	3 mm	2.04	31.01	29.63	**60.64**	m2
	4 mm	2.04	31.01	33.27	**64.28**	m2
021	To metal with synthetic extruded rubber gaskets and clip-on metal beads (supplied cut to length by others):					
	3 mm	1.92	29.18	29.25	**58.43**	m2
	4 mm	1.92	29.18	32.89	**62.07**	m2
022	**Imitation leaded lights exceeding 0.15 m2 formed of applied lead strip to simulate diamond shaped panes average size 100 mm x 150 mm; clear float glass (GG quality)**					
023	To wood with putty and sprigs:					
	3 mm	1.07	16.28	33.25	**49.53**	m2
	4 mm	1.07	16.28	36.89	**53.17**	m2
024	To wood with bradded wood beads (supplied cut to length by others):					
	3 mm	1.43	21.70	32.31	**54.01**	m2
	4 mm	1.43	21.70	35.94	**57.64**	m2
025	To wood with screwed wood beads (supplied cut to length by others):					
	3 mm	2.14	32.56	32.31	**64.87**	m2
	4 mm	2.14	32.56	35.94	**68.50**	m2
026	To metal with putty and clips:					
	3 mm	1.07	16.28	33.57	**49.85**	m2
	4 mm	1.07	16.28	37.20	**53.48**	m2
027	To metal with screwed metal beads (supplied cut to length by others):					
	3 mm	2.14	32.56	32.37	**64.93**	m2
	4 mm	2.14	32.56	36.01	**68.57**	m2
028	To metal with synthetic extruded rubber gaskets and clip-on metal beads (supplied cut to length by others):					
	3 mm	2.02	30.64	31.99	**62.63**	m2
	4 mm	2.02	30.64	35.63	**66.27**	m2

Diploma in Adjudication in the Construction Industry

Comprised of four units, this qualification is designed for those **seeking to become an adjudicator**, and provides a pathway towards potential entry onto the **RICS Panel of Adjudicators**.

With a focus on contract and tort law and how they apply to adjudication, this course is designed to prepare you to progress to practice as an adjudicator. This course is suitable for those with experience in dispute resolution procedures with an understanding of the general principles of construction adjudication. The course content will focus on the format and content of an enforceable decision.

Learning Outcomes:

- Knowledge and understanding of the nature of law and its' place in society
- How the law of contract is applied to the practice of adjudication
- How the law of tort is applied to the practice of adjudication
- The practical application in the production of an enforceable decision.

Attainment of the learning outcomes will be assessed by a case study, whereby candidates will be required to produce an enforceable reasoned decision, based on material supplied in the case study.

Painting &
Decorating

Labour Rates

Artexer
   Artexer   £15.20 per hour

Paint sprayer
   Paint Sprayer   £15.20 per hour

Painter and decorator
   Painter and Decorator   £15.20 per hour

PAPERHANGING, sheet plastic and fabric linings
   Craftsman (BATJIC Craft Rate)   £15.20 per hour

SPRAY PAINTING, based upon the cost of labour plus spraying equipment calculated as follows:

COST PER WEEK	£
Hire of (2) gun electric spray equipment	180.00
Use of face masks etc.	4.45
Masking materials, tape etc.	6.50
Cleaning fluids	4.60
Painters (2) x £15.20 per hour x 39 hrs	1185.60
Total weekly cost	**£1381.15**

ACTUAL HOURS WORKED PER WEEK		Hours
(2) Painters at 39 hours		78 hrs
Less cleaning up time (half hr per day)	5 hrs	
masking time (1.5 hours per day)	15 hrs	20 hrs
NET hours worked per week		58 hrs

COST PER HOUR
Total weekly cost divided by Net Hours worked (£1381.15 divided by 58)

Cost per hour   £23.81

Adjustment for roller applied paints
The labour and material content of unit rates within this section are based upon paints applied by brush. For guidance to the cost of painting using a roller, the following percentage adjustments, obtained from industry specialists, should be applied:
a)   Net Labour Price   -   Reduce by 15%
b)   Net Material Price   -   Increase by 7.5%

Brush Allowance
Allowance has been made in the 'Net Materials' prices for brushes, rollers, pads, sandpaper, pumice stones and the like in accordance with the following table:

Surface	Allowance made per coat per m2 £
V0005 Plaster	0.02
V0006 Smooth concrete	0.03
V0007 Fibre cement	0.02
V0008 Textured paper	0.02
V0009 Cement render	0.02
V0010 Fair face brick	0.03
V0011 Fair face blockwork	0.05
V0012 Smooth timber	0.02
V0013 Sawn timber	0.03
V0014 Metalwork	0.02
V0015 Pebbledash	0.05
V0016 Rough cast	0.03
V0017 Tyrolean render	0.06
V0018 Plasterboard	0.02
V0019 Paperhanging (generally)	0.02

Thinners
Unless specifically stated in the descriptions, no thinning of paint has been allowed and the 'Net Materials' price is for neat paints.

Basic Prices of Materials		Supply Price £	Waste Factor %	Unload. Labour £	Unload. Plant £	Total Unit Cost £	Unit
	Primers:						
V0101	all purpose primer	15.43	2.5%	-	-	15.82	ltr
V0102	wood primer, white and pink	7.31	2.5%	-	-	7.49	ltr
V0103	metal primer, zinc phosphate	8.05	2.5%	-	-	8.25	ltr
V0104	metal primer, zinc chromate	7.44	2.5%	-	-	7.62	ltr
V0105	metal primer, zinc rich	39.37	2.5%	-	-	40.36	ltr
V0106	metal primer, red oxide	8.02	2.5%	-	-	8.22	ltr
V0107	alkali resisting primer	12.80	2.5%	-	-	13.12	ltr
V0108	aluminium wood primer	13.89	2.5%	-	-	14.24	ltr
V0109	acrylic primer undercoat (white)	7.31	2.5%	-	-	7.49	ltr
V0110	ICI quick drying wood primer	12.48	2.5%	-	-	12.79	ltr
V0111	etching primer (2 pack)	21.00	2.5%	-	-	21.53	ltr
V0112	thinners for etching primer	11.73	2.5%	-	-	12.03	ltr
V0113	preservative primer	12.29	2.5%	-	-	12.59	ltr
V0114	WSE primer / adhesion promoter high performance water-based anti bacterial, two component epoxy coating	15.10	7.5%	-	-	16.24	ltr

Basic Prices of Materials	Supply Price £	Waste Factor %	Unload. Labour £	Unload. Plant £	Total Unit Cost £	Unit
Undercoats:						
V0120 white	6.11	2.5%	-	-	6.26	ltr
V0121 brilliant white	6.11	2.5%	-	-	6.26	ltr
V0122 standard colours	6.73	2.5%	-	-	6.90	ltr
Eggshell paints:						
V0130 white	6.67	2.5%	-	-	6.84	ltr
V0131 brilliant white	6.67	2.5%	-	-	6.84	ltr
V0132 standard colours	7.34	2.5%	-	-	7.53	ltr
Gloss paints:						
V0140 white	6.11	2.5%	-	-	6.26	ltr
V0141 brilliant white	6.56	2.5%	-	-	6.73	ltr
V0142 standard colours	6.73	2.5%	-	-	6.90	ltr
Emulsion paints:						
silk:						
V0150 white	5.57	2.5%	-	-	5.71	ltr
V0151 brilliant white	5.80	2.5%	-	-	5.95	ltr
V0152 standard colours	6.11	2.5%	-	-	6.26	ltr
matt:						
V0153 white	4.81	2.5%	-	-	4.93	ltr
V0154 brilliant white	5.08	2.5%	-	-	5.20	ltr
V0155 standard colours	9.05	2.5%	-	-	9.28	ltr
Metal finish:						
V0160 Hammerite 'hammered' metal finish	10.34	2.5%	-	-	10.60	ltr
V0161 Hammerite 'smooth' metal finish	10.34	2.5%	-	-	10.60	ltr
V0162 Hammerite No. 1 metal primer	12.76	2.5%	-	-	13.08	ltr
V0163 Hammerite thinners	6.70	2.5%	-	-	6.87	ltr
Fire resisting paints:						
V0401 Thermoguard Thermocoat intumescent paint - high build primer	14.26	7.5%	-	-	15.33	ltr
V0402 Thermoguard Thermocoat intumescent paint - base coat	14.26	7.5%	-	-	15.33	ltr
V0403 Thermoguard Thermocoat intumescent paint - top coat	14.26	7.5%	-	-	15.33	ltr
V0404 Thermoguard Wallcoat - intumescent paint - top coat	18.34	7.5%	-	-	19.71	ltr
V0405 Thermoguard Timbercoat - intumescent paint	18.34	7.5%	-	-	19.71	ltr
V0406 Thermoguard fire varnish - intumescent varnish - coverage 6m2/1	14.26	7.5%	-	-	15.33	ltr
V0407 Thermoguard sealer for fire varnish basecoat. Available in matt, stain and gloss	16.17	7.5%	-	-	17.38	ltr
V0408 Thermoguard flame retardant acrylic matt	14.26	7.5%	-	-	15.33	ltr
Flooring Paints:						
V0166 non slip floor paint with bauxite aggregate	5.32	5%	-	-	5.59	ltr
V0167 Bartoline creosote d/brown 201	1.88	5%	-	-	1.98	ltr
V0168 quick drying Thermoplastic protective floor paint	4.30	5%	-	-	4.52	ltr
V0243 line marking paint - chlorinated rubber	8.07	7.5%	-	-	8.67	ltr
V0244 line paint thinners (th14) (1:10)	7.87	7.5%	-	-	8.46	ltr
Sundries:						
V0178 fungicidal solution	3.48	5%	-	-	3.65	ltr
V0179 paint stripper	7.09	5%	-	-	7.45	ltr
V0180 masonry stabilising sealer	9.03	5%	-	-	9.48	ltr
V0181 aluminium paint	14.02	2.5%	-	-	14.37	ltr
V0182 floor paint, tile red	6.49	2.5%	-	-	6.65	ltr
V0183 'Snowcem' cement based paint (white)	1.38	5%	-	-	1.44	kg
V0191 patent knotting	30.36	10%	-	-	33.39	ltr
V0185 boiled linseed oil	4.67	5%	-	-	4.90	ltr
V0186 raw linseed oil	4.16	5%	-	-	4.37	ltr
V0187 interior clear varnish (gloss, satin or matt)	11.96	2.5%	-	-	12.26	ltr
V0188 'Artex' AX compound	0.83	5%	-	-	0.88	kg
V0189 'Artex' joint tape 64 mm wide 180 m roll	9.70	10%	-	-	10.67	nr
V0190 'Artex' sealer	4.90	10%	-	-	5.39	ltr
V0192 masonry paint, brilliant white, smooth	8.78	10%	-	-	9.66	ltr
V0193 'Sandtex' Exterior Matt (white)	3.39	10%	-	-	3.73	ltr
V0194 masonry stabilising solution	6.34	10%	-	-	6.98	ltr
V0195 'Sandtex' Fine Build	2.88	10%	-	-	3.16	kg
V0196 'Sandtex' High Build	3.52	10%	-	-	3.87	kg
V0197 Fosroc 'Galvafroid' galvanising paint	35.73	5%	-	-	37.51	ltr
V0198 exterior varnish	16.67	2.5%	-	-	17.08	ltr
V0199 white spirit	3.57	5%	-	-	3.75	ltr
V0381 Aquagene hygiene paint water-based, two pack polyurethane system (8 m2/litre per coat)	22.03	7.5%	-	-	23.68	ltr
V0391 white peak Buxton limewash - white	1.90	7.5%	-	-	2.05	ltr
The following prices were supplied by ICI Paints						
Wood preservers:						
V0200 clear wood preserver	5.61	5%	-	-	5.89	ltr
V0201 light oak/dark oak preserver	5.61	5%	-	-	5.89	ltr
V0202 green wood preserver	5.61	5%	-	-	5.89	ltr
V0204 Ducksback	2.57	5%	-	-	2.70	ltr
Fencing treatments:						
V0203 exterior wood preserver	3.44	5%	-	-	3.61	ltr
V0205 Garden Timbercare	1.81	5%	-	-	1.90	ltr
V0206 Garden Shades	5.92	5%	-	-	6.22	ltr
V0207 Landscape Shades	14.61	5%	-	-	15.34	ltr
V0208 Landscape Stain	12.85	5%	-	-	13.49	ltr
V0210 decorative preserver (i.e. red cedar)	6.55	5%	-	-	6.87	ltr
Wood stains:						
V0211 Premier 5	14.89	5%	-	-	15.63	ltr
V0212 Select	14.27	5%	-	-	14.98	ltr
Interior floor finishes:						
V0217 Original Bourneseal (gloss)	13.21	2.5%	-	-	13.54	ltr
V0218 Quick drying Bourneseal (gloss/satin)	12.95	2.5%	-	-	13.28	ltr
Varnishes:						
V0213 Trade polyurethane clear (gloss/satin/matt)	9.22	2.5%	-	-	9.45	ltr
V0214 Trade Quick Dry clear (gloss/satin)	10.79	2.5%	-	-	11.06	ltr

Basic Prices of Materials	Supply Price £	Waste Factor %	Unload. Labour £	Unload. Plant £	Total Unit Cost £	Unit
V0216 Trade Quick Dry colours (satin)	12.97	2.5%	-	-	**13.30**	ltr
V0215 Yacht varnish (exterior - gloss)	9.74	2.5%	-	-	**9.99**	ltr
The following prices are indicative for Sadolin products:						
Wood preservers and stains:						
V0230 'Classic' clear base	11.18	5%	-	-	**11.74**	ltr
V0231 'Classic' decorative timber protection	11.18	5%	-	-	**11.74**	ltr
V0232 'Superdec' opaque wood protection	12.83	5%	-	-	**13.47**	ltr
V0233 'Extra' joinery protection	11.18	5%	-	-	**11.74**	ltr
The following prices were supplied by Arch Coatings Ltd						
V0237 Hardwood Finish	9.08	2.5%	-	-	**9.31**	ltr
V0238 Breather Paint	9.60	5%	-	-	**10.08**	ltr

Decorative paper and other wall coverings

The prices for "general wallpapers" are given as P.C. prices per standard roll of 5.3 m2. However due to the varying roll lengths and widths of other wall coverings, prices for these are given as P.C. prices per square metre. The P.C. prices are based on the price of an average quality material within each particular range of wallcovering.
Waste has been allowed in the constants used for calculating the 'Net Materials' prices. This waste factor may increase for pattern match materials. Check with manufacturer's literature for pattern repeats.

	Supply Price £	Waste Factor %	Unload. Labour £	Unload. Plant £	Total Unit Cost £	Unit
General wallpapers:						
V0250 lining paper	2.09	5%	-	-	**2.20**	nr
V0251 woodchip paper	2.09	-	-	-	**2.09**	nr
V0252 vinyl surfaced paper	12.13	10%	-	-	**13.34**	nr
V0253 ready pasted vinyl surfaced paper	15.43	10%	-	-	**16.98**	nr
V0254 mid-range quality paper	13.23	10%	-	-	**14.55**	nr
V0255 heavy embossed paper for painting	9.92	10%	-	-	**10.91**	nr
V0275 blown vinyl surface paper	8.26	10%	-	-	**9.08**	nr
V0350 lining paper P.C.	2.10	-	-	-	**2.10**	nr
V0351 woodchip paper P.C.	2.10	-	-	-	**2.10**	nr
V0352 vinyl surfaced paper P.C.	12.13	-	-	-	**12.13**	nr
V0353 ready pasted vinyl surfaced paper P.C.	15.43	-	-	-	**15.43**	nr
V0354 mid-range quality paper P.C.	13.23	-	-	-	**13.23**	nr
V0355 heavy embossed paper for painting P.C.	9.92	-	-	-	**9.92**	nr
V0375 blown vinyl surface paper P.C.	8.26	-	-	-	**8.26**	nr
Other wall coverings:						
(Wallcoverings i.e. wide width contract vinyls are supplied in 30 - 50 m rolls, but other lengths are available. Due to varying sizes, prices are quoted per m2; compiled from information given by Muraspec Ltd)						
V0258 high quality textile	32.06	10%	-	-	**35.27**	m2
V0259 mid-range textile	24.02	10%	-	-	**26.42**	m2
V0260 glass fibre	6.25	10%	-	-	**6.87**	m2
V0261 suede effect	25.42	10%	-	-	**27.96**	m2
V0262 fabric backed vinyl	11.66	10%	-	-	**12.83**	m2
V0263 paper backed vinyl	2.54	10%	-	-	**2.80**	m2
V0276 hessian wall covering	6.61	10%	-	-	**7.28**	m2
V0358 high quality textile P.C.	29.15	-	-	-	**29.15**	m2
V0359 mid-range textile P.C.	21.84	-	-	-	**21.84**	m2
V0360 glass fibre P.C.	5.68	-	-	-	**5.68**	m2
V0361 suede effect P.C.	23.11	-	-	-	**23.11**	m2
V0362 fabric backed vinyl P.C.	10.60	-	-	-	**10.60**	m2
V0363 paper backed vinyl P.C.	2.31	-	-	-	**2.31**	m2
Wallpaper paste and adhesives etc.:						
V0256 ordinary	0.53	10%	-	-	**0.58**	ltr
V0257 heavy duty	0.71	10%	-	-	**0.78**	ltr
V0269 standard adhesive	3.21	10%	-	-	**3.53**	kg
V0270 Grade 1 adhesive (heavy)	3.59	10%	-	-	**3.95**	kg
V0271 Grade 2 adhesive (medium)	3.21	10%	-	-	**3.53**	kg
V0272 Grade 3 adhesive (light)	2.11	10%	-	-	**2.32**	kg
V0273 size	2.38	10%	-	-	**2.61**	ltr

Unit Rates	Man-Hours	Net Labour Price £	Net Mats Price £	Net Unit Price £	Unit
VA	UNIT RATES **NEW WORK INTERNALLY**					

(SEE ALSO SECTION VZ FOR COMPOSITE EXAMPLES)

Prices are given separately for first or priming coats (which include for preparation of the surfaces to be painted), undercoats and finishing coats. The total cost of decoration will be combinations of these individual coat prices in accordance with the required specification. A large number of permutations for various specifications is therefore possible. Refer to Section VZ for examples of prices for composite painting and decorating items.

WALLS AND CEILINGS - INTERNALLY

EMULSION PAINT; VINYL SILK - INTERNALLY

		Man-Hours	Net Labour Price £	Net Mats Price £	Net Unit Price £	Unit
001	**One coat of emulsion paint, white; first coat to unprimed surfaces**					
002	Walls over 300 mm wide:					
	plastered	0.14	2.16	0.54	**2.70**	m2
	smooth concrete	0.16	2.46	0.55	**3.01**	m2
	fibre cement	0.16	2.46	0.65	**3.11**	m2
	embossed or textured papered	0.17	2.61	0.65	**3.26**	m2
	cement rendered	0.14	2.16	0.65	**2.81**	m2
	fair face brickwork	0.19	2.89	0.66	**3.55**	m2
	fair face blockwork	0.23	3.45	0.76	**4.21**	m2
	Note: 003 not used					
004	Walls in staircase areas over 300 mm wide:					
	plastered	0.15	2.20	0.54	**2.74**	m2
	smooth concrete	0.17	2.54	0.55	**3.09**	m2
	fibre cement	0.17	2.54	0.65	**3.19**	m2
	embossed or textured papered	0.18	2.69	0.65	**3.34**	m2
	cement rendered	0.15	2.20	0.65	**2.85**	m2
	fair face brickwork	0.19	2.95	0.66	**3.61**	m2
	fair face blockwork	0.23	3.54	0.76	**4.30**	m2
005	Ceilings over 300 mm wide:					
	plastered	0.15	2.25	0.54	**2.79**	m2
	smooth concrete	0.17	2.58	0.55	**3.13**	m2
	fibre cement	0.17	2.58	0.65	**3.23**	m2
	embossed or textured papered	0.18	2.74	0.65	**3.39**	m2
	cement rendered	0.15	2.25	0.65	**2.90**	m2
	Note: 006 not used					
007	Ceilings in staircase areas over 300 mm wide:					
	plastered	0.15	2.30	0.54	**2.84**	m2
	smooth concrete	0.17	2.63	0.55	**3.18**	m2
	fibre cement	0.17	2.63	0.65	**3.28**	m2
	embossed or textured papered	0.18	2.78	0.65	**3.43**	m2
	cement rendered	0.15	2.30	0.65	**2.95**	m2
008	**One coat of emulsion paint, white; second and subsequent coats**					
009	Walls over 300 mm wide:					
	plastered	0.10	1.55	0.48	**2.03**	m2
	smooth concrete	0.11	1.72	0.49	**2.21**	m2
	fibre cement	0.11	1.72	0.59	**2.31**	m2
	embossed or textured papered	0.12	1.88	0.54	**2.42**	m2
	cement rendered	0.10	1.55	0.54	**2.09**	m2
	fair face brickwork	0.14	2.16	0.60	**2.76**	m2
	fair face blockwork	0.16	2.42	0.67	**3.09**	m2
	Note: 010 not used					
011	Walls in staircase areas over 300 mm wide:					
	plastered	0.10	1.58	0.48	**2.06**	m2
	smooth concrete	0.12	1.76	0.49	**2.25**	m2
	fibre cement	0.12	1.76	0.59	**2.35**	m2
	embossed or textured papered	0.13	1.93	0.54	**2.47**	m2
	cement rendered	0.10	1.58	0.54	**2.12**	m2
	fair face brickwork	0.15	2.20	0.60	**2.80**	m2
	fair face blockwork	0.16	2.48	0.67	**3.15**	m2
012	Ceilings over 300 mm wide:					
	plastered	0.11	1.64	0.48	**2.12**	m2
	smooth concrete	0.12	1.79	0.49	**2.28**	m2
	fibre cement	0.12	1.79	0.59	**2.38**	m2
	embossed or textured papered	0.13	1.96	0.54	**2.50**	m2
	cement rendered	0.11	1.64	0.54	**2.18**	m2
	Note: 013 not used					
014	Ceilings in staircase areas over 300 mm wide:					
	plastered	0.11	1.67	0.48	**2.15**	m2
	smooth concrete	0.12	1.87	0.49	**2.36**	m2
	fibre cement	0.12	1.87	0.59	**2.46**	m2
	embossed or textured papered	0.13	2.02	0.54	**2.56**	m2

Unit Rates	Man-Hours	Net Labour Price £	Net Mats Price £	Net Unit Price £	Unit
cement rendered	0.11	1.67	0.54	**2.21**	m2

EMULSION PAINT; VINYL MATT - INTERNALLY

015	**One coat of emulsion paint, white; first coat to unprimed surfaces**				
016	Walls over 300 mm wide:				
	plastered	0.14	2.16	0.47	**2.63**	m2
	smooth concrete	0.16	2.46	0.48	**2.94**	m2
	fibre cement	0.16	2.46	0.56	**3.02**	m2
	embossed or textured papered	0.17	2.61	0.56	**3.17**	m2
	cement rendered	0.14	2.16	0.56	**2.72**	m2
	fair face brickwork	0.19	2.89	0.58	**3.47**	m2
	fair face blockwork	0.23	3.45	0.69	**4.14**	m2
	Note: 017 not used				
018	Walls in staircase areas over 300 mm wide:				
	plastered	0.15	2.20	0.47	**2.67**	m2
	smooth concrete	0.17	2.54	0.48	**3.02**	m2
	fibre cement	0.17	2.54	0.56	**3.10**	m2
	embossed or textured papered	0.18	2.69	0.56	**3.25**	m2
	cement rendered	0.15	2.20	0.56	**2.76**	m2
	fair face brickwork	0.19	2.95	0.58	**3.53**	m2
	fair face blockwork	0.23	3.54	0.69	**4.23**	m2
019	Ceilings over 300 mm wide:				
	plastered	0.15	2.25	0.47	**2.72**	m2
	smooth concrete	0.17	2.58	0.48	**3.06**	m2
	fibre cement	0.17	2.58	0.56	**3.14**	m2
	embossed or textured papered	0.18	2.74	0.56	**3.30**	m2
	cement rendered	0.15	2.25	0.56	**2.81**	m2
	Note: 020 not used				
021	Ceilings in staircase areas over 300 mm wide:				
	plastered	0.15	2.30	0.47	**2.77**	m2
	smooth concrete	0.17	2.63	0.48	**3.11**	m2
	fibre cement	0.17	2.63	0.56	**3.19**	m2
	embossed or textured papered	0.18	2.78	0.56	**3.34**	m2
	cement rendered	0.15	2.30	0.56	**2.86**	m2
022	**One coat of emulsion paint, white; second and subsequent coats**				
023	Walls over 300 mm wide:				
	plastered	0.10	1.55	0.42	**1.97**	m2
	smooth concrete	0.11	1.72	0.43	**2.15**	m2
	fibre cement	0.11	1.72	0.52	**2.24**	m2
	embossed or textured papered	0.12	1.88	0.47	**2.35**	m2
	cement rendered	0.10	1.55	0.47	**2.02**	m2
	fair face brickwork	0.14	2.16	0.53	**2.69**	m2
	fair face blockwork	0.16	2.42	0.59	**3.01**	m2
	Note: 024 not used				
025	Walls in staircase areas over 300 mm wide:				
	plastered	0.10	1.58	0.42	**2.00**	m2
	smooth concrete	0.12	1.76	0.43	**2.19**	m2
	fibre cement	0.12	1.76	0.52	**2.28**	m2
	embossed or textured papered	0.13	1.93	0.47	**2.40**	m2
	cement rendered	0.10	1.58	0.47	**2.05**	m2
	fair face brickwork	0.15	2.20	0.53	**2.73**	m2
	fair face blockwork	0.16	2.48	0.59	**3.07**	m2
026	Ceilings over 300 mm wide:				
	plastered	0.11	1.64	0.42	**2.06**	m2
	smooth concrete	0.12	1.79	0.43	**2.22**	m2
	fibre cement	0.12	1.79	0.52	**2.31**	m2
	embossed or textured papered	0.13	1.96	0.47	**2.43**	m2
	cement rendered	0.11	1.64	0.47	**2.11**	m2
	Note: 027 not used				
028	Ceilings in staircase areas over 300 mm wide:				
	plastered	0.11	1.67	0.42	**2.09**	m2
	smooth concrete	0.12	1.87	0.43	**2.30**	m2
	fibre cement	0.12	1.87	0.52	**2.39**	m2
	embossed or textured papered	0.13	2.02	0.47	**2.49**	m2
	cement rendered	0.11	1.67	0.47	**2.14**	m2

ARTEX FINISH - INTERNALLY

029	**One coat of Artex sealer and one coat of Artex standard compound; with stipple finish**				
030	Walls over 300 mm wide:				
	plastered	0.34	5.17	1.42	**6.59**	m2
	smooth concrete	0.39	5.85	1.44	**7.29**	m2
	fibre cement	0.34	5.17	1.42	**6.59**	m2
	plasterboard including scrimming joints	0.37	5.68	1.54	**7.22**	m2

		Man-Hours	Net Labour Price £	Net Mats Price £	Net Unit Price £	Unit
	Unit Rates					
	cement rendered	0.39	5.85	1.53	**7.38**	m2
	fair face brickwork	0.39	5.85	1.55	**7.40**	m2
	fair face blockwork	0.39	5.85	1.76	**7.61**	m2
	Note: 031 not used					
032	Walls in staircase areas over 300 mm wide:					
	plastered	0.35	5.34	1.42	**6.76**	m2
	smooth concrete	0.40	6.03	1.44	**7.47**	m2
	fibre cement	0.35	5.34	1.42	**6.76**	m2
	plasterboard including scrimming joints	0.39	5.85	1.54	**7.39**	m2
	cement rendered	0.40	6.03	1.53	**7.56**	m2
	fair face brickwork	0.40	6.03	1.55	**7.58**	m2
	fair face blockwork	0.40	6.03	1.76	**7.79**	m2
033	Ceilings over 300 mm wide:					
	plastered	0.36	5.52	1.42	**6.94**	m2
	smooth concrete	0.41	6.20	1.44	**7.64**	m2
	fibre cement	0.36	5.52	1.42	**6.94**	m2
	plasterboard including scrimming joints	0.40	6.03	1.54	**7.57**	m2
	cement rendered	0.41	6.20	1.53	**7.73**	m2
	Note: 034 not used					
035	Ceilings in staircase areas over 300 mm wide:					
	plastered	0.37	5.68	1.42	**7.10**	m2
	smooth concrete	0.42	6.37	1.44	**7.81**	m2
	fibre cement	0.37	5.68	1.42	**7.10**	m2
	plasterboard including scrimming joints	0.41	6.20	1.54	**7.74**	m2
	cement rendered	0.41	6.20	1.53	**7.73**	m2
	PRIMERS - INTERNALLY					
036	**One coat of alkali resisting primer on untreated surfaces**					
037	Walls over 300 mm wide:					
	plastered	0.19	2.89	1.47	**4.36**	m2
	smooth concrete	0.22	3.27	1.48	**4.75**	m2
	fibre cement	0.22	3.27	1.47	**4.74**	m2
	cement rendered	0.19	2.89	1.93	**4.82**	m2
	fair face brickwork	0.25	3.82	1.94	**5.76**	m2
	fair face blockwork	0.30	4.61	2.67	**7.28**	m2
	Note: 038 not used					
039	Walls in staircase areas over 300 mm wide:					
	plastered	0.19	2.95	1.47	**4.42**	m2
	smooth concrete	0.22	3.36	1.48	**4.84**	m2
	fibre cement	0.22	3.36	1.47	**4.83**	m2
	cement rendered	0.19	2.95	1.93	**4.88**	m2
	fair face brickwork	0.26	3.94	1.94	**5.88**	m2
	fair face blockwork	0.31	4.71	2.67	**7.38**	m2
040	Ceilings over 300 mm wide:					
	plastered	0.20	3.02	1.47	**4.49**	m2
	smooth concrete	0.23	3.45	1.48	**4.93**	m2
	fibre cement	0.23	3.45	1.47	**4.92**	m2
	cement rendered	0.20	3.02	1.93	**4.95**	m2
	Note: 041 not used					
042	Ceilings in staircase areas over 300 mm wide:					
	plastered	0.20	3.09	1.47	**4.56**	m2
	smooth concrete	0.23	3.54	1.48	**5.02**	m2
	fibre cement	0.23	3.54	1.47	**5.01**	m2
	cement rendered	0.20	3.09	1.93	**5.02**	m2
043	**One coat of all-purpose primer on untreated surfaces**					
044	Walls over 300 mm wide:					
	plastered	0.19	2.89	0.37	**3.26**	m2
	smooth concrete	0.22	3.27	0.38	**3.65**	m2
	fibre cement	0.22	3.27	0.37	**3.64**	m2
	embossed or textured papered	0.23	3.44	0.48	**3.92**	m2
	cement rendered	0.19	2.89	0.48	**3.37**	m2
	fair face brickwork	0.25	3.82	0.49	**4.31**	m2
	fair face blockwork	0.30	4.61	0.68	**5.29**	m2
	Note: 045 not used					
046	Walls in staircase areas over 300 mm wide:					
	plastered	0.19	2.95	0.37	**3.32**	m2
	smooth concrete	0.22	3.36	0.38	**3.74**	m2
	fibre cement	0.22	3.36	0.37	**3.73**	m2
	embossed or textured papered	0.23	3.53	0.48	**4.01**	m2
	cement rendered	0.19	2.95	0.48	**3.43**	m2
	fair face brickwork	0.26	3.94	0.49	**4.43**	m2
	fair face blockwork	0.31	4.71	0.68	**5.39**	m2

Unit Rates	Man-Hours	Net Labour Price £	Net Mats Price £	Net Unit Price £	Unit
047 Ceilings over 300 mm wide:					
plastered	0.20	3.02	0.37	**3.39**	m2
smooth concrete	0.23	3.45	0.38	**3.83**	m2
fibre cement	0.23	3.45	0.37	**3.82**	m2
embossed or textured papered	0.24	3.60	0.48	**4.08**	m2
cement rendered	0.20	3.02	0.48	**3.50**	m2
Note: 048 not used					
049 Ceilings in staircase areas over 300 mm wide:					
plastered	0.20	3.09	0.37	**3.46**	m2
smooth concrete	0.23	3.54	0.38	**3.92**	m2
fibre cement	0.23	3.54	0.37	**3.91**	m2
embossed or textured papered	0.24	3.69	0.48	**4.17**	m2
cement rendered	0.20	3.09	0.48	**3.57**	m2
ALKYD BASED PAINT; UNDERCOAT - INTERNALLY					
050 **One undercoat of alkyd based paint, white; on primed surfaces**					
051 Walls over 300 mm wide:					
plastered	0.10	1.57	0.49	**2.06**	m2
smooth concrete	0.11	1.72	0.82	**2.54**	m2
fibre cement	0.11	1.72	0.59	**2.31**	m2
embossed or textured papered	0.12	1.88	0.81	**2.69**	m2
cement rendered	0.10	1.57	0.81	**2.38**	m2
fair face brickwork	0.14	2.16	0.94	**3.10**	m2
fair face blockwork	0.16	2.46	0.95	**3.41**	m2
Note: 052 not used					
053 Walls in staircase areas over 300 mm wide:					
plastered	0.11	1.60	0.49	**2.09**	m2
smooth concrete	0.12	1.76	0.82	**2.58**	m2
fibre cement	0.12	1.76	0.59	**2.35**	m2
embossed or textured papered	0.13	1.93	0.81	**2.74**	m2
cement rendered	0.11	1.60	0.81	**2.41**	m2
fair face brickwork	0.15	2.20	0.94	**3.14**	m2
fair face blockwork	0.17	2.54	0.95	**3.49**	m2
054 Ceilings over 300 mm wide:					
plastered	0.11	1.66	0.49	**2.15**	m2
smooth concrete	0.12	1.79	0.82	**2.61**	m2
fibre cement	0.12	1.79	0.59	**2.38**	m2
embossed or textured papered	0.13	1.96	0.81	**2.77**	m2
cement rendered	0.11	1.66	0.81	**2.47**	m2
Note: 055 not used					
056 Ceilings in staircase areas over 300 mm wide:					
plastered	0.11	1.69	0.49	**2.18**	m2
smooth concrete	0.12	1.87	0.82	**2.69**	m2
fibre cement	0.12	1.87	0.59	**2.46**	m2
embossed or textured papered	0.13	2.02	0.81	**2.83**	m2
cement rendered	0.11	1.69	0.81	**2.50**	m2
Note: 057 - 070 not used					
ALKYD BASED PAINT; EGGSHELL FINISH - INTERNALLY					
071 **One coat of alkyd based paint, eggshell finish, first and subsequent coats**					
072 Walls over 300 mm wide:					
plastered	0.10	1.57	0.54	**2.11**	m2
smooth concrete	0.11	1.72	0.55	**2.27**	m2
fibre cement	0.11	1.72	0.64	**2.36**	m2
embossed or textured papered	0.12	1.88	0.71	**2.59**	m2
cement rendered	0.10	1.57	0.71	**2.28**	m2
fair face brickwork	0.10	1.57	0.79	**2.36**	m2
fair face blockwork	0.11	1.72	0.90	**2.62**	m2
Note: 073 not used					
074 Walls in staircase areas over 300 mm wide:					
plastered	0.11	1.60	0.54	**2.14**	m2
smooth concrete	0.12	1.76	0.55	**2.31**	m2
fibre cement	0.12	1.76	0.64	**2.40**	m2
embossed or textured papered	0.13	1.93	0.71	**2.64**	m2
cement rendered	0.11	1.60	0.71	**2.31**	m2
fair face brickwork	0.11	1.60	0.79	**2.39**	m2
fair face blockwork	0.12	1.76	0.90	**2.66**	m2
075 Ceilings over 300 mm wide:					
plastered	0.11	1.66	0.54	**2.20**	m2
smooth concrete	0.12	1.79	0.55	**2.34**	m2
fibre cement	0.12	1.79	0.64	**2.43**	m2
embossed or textured papered	0.13	1.96	0.71	**2.67**	m2
cement rendered	0.11	1.66	0.71	**2.37**	m2

Unit Rates

		Man-Hours	Net Labour Price £	Net Mats Price £	Net Unit Price £	Unit
	Note: 076 not used					
077	Ceilings in staircase areas over 300 mm wide:					
	plastered	0.11	1.69	0.54	**2.23**	m2
	smooth concrete	0.12	1.87	0.55	**2.42**	m2
	fibre cement	0.12	1.87	0.64	**2.51**	m2
	embossed or textured papered	0.13	2.02	0.71	**2.73**	m2
	cement rendered	0.11	1.69	0.71	**2.40**	m2
	Note: 078 - 081 not used					
	ALKYD BASED PAINT; GLOSS FINISH - INTERNALLY					
082	**One coat of alkyd based paint, gloss finish to undercoated surfaces**					
083	Walls over 300 mm wide:					
	plastered	0.11	1.60	0.49	**2.09**	m2
	smooth concrete	0.11	1.73	0.72	**2.45**	m2
	fibre cement	0.11	1.73	0.59	**2.32**	m2
	embossed or textured papered	0.13	1.93	0.71	**2.64**	m2
	cement rendered	0.11	1.60	0.71	**2.31**	m2
	fair face brickwork	0.11	1.73	0.82	**2.55**	m2
	fair face blockwork	0.13	1.92	0.95	**2.87**	m2
	Note: 084 not used					
085	Walls in staircase areas over 300 mm wide:					
	plastered	0.11	1.64	0.49	**2.13**	m2
	smooth concrete	0.12	1.78	0.72	**2.50**	m2
	fibre cement	0.12	1.78	0.59	**2.37**	m2
	embossed or textured papered	0.13	1.95	0.71	**2.66**	m2
	cement rendered	0.11	1.64	0.71	**2.35**	m2
	fair face brickwork	0.12	1.78	0.82	**2.60**	m2
	fair face blockwork	0.13	1.96	0.95	**2.91**	m2
086	Ceilings over 300 mm wide:					
	plastered	0.11	1.69	0.49	**2.18**	m2
	smooth concrete	0.12	1.84	0.72	**2.56**	m2
	fibre cement	0.12	1.84	0.59	**2.43**	m2
	embossed or textured papered	0.13	1.99	0.71	**2.70**	m2
	cement rendered	0.11	1.69	0.71	**2.40**	m2
	Note: 087 not used					
088	Ceilings in staircase areas over 300 mm wide:					
	plastered	0.11	1.72	0.49	**2.21**	m2
	smooth concrete	0.12	1.88	0.72	**2.60**	m2
	fibre cement	0.12	1.88	0.59	**2.47**	m2
	embossed or textured papered	0.13	2.04	0.71	**2.75**	m2
	cement rendered	0.11	1.72	0.71	**2.43**	m2
	SUNDRIES					
089	**Cutting in to line on flush surfaces**					
090	Flush surfaces:					
	1 Coat work	0.11	1.72	-	**1.72**	m
	2 Coat work	0.17	2.58	-	**2.58**	m
	3 Coat work	0.23	3.45	-	**3.45**	m
VB	ANTI-BACTERIAL PAINT SYSTEM - INTERNALLY					
	Note: 001 - 021 not used					
022	**Prepare; apply one coat primer/adhesive high performance water-based, two component epoxy coating**					
023	Walls over 300 mm wide:					
	plastered	0.12	1.80	2.06	**3.86**	m2
	smooth concrete	0.13	1.99	2.06	**4.05**	m2
	fibre cement	0.14	2.19	2.19	**4.38**	m2
	embossed or textured paper	0.14	2.19	2.19	**4.38**	m2
	cement render	0.16	2.41	2.19	**4.60**	m2
	fair face brickwork	0.17	2.65	2.19	**4.84**	m2
	fair face blockwork	0.19	2.91	2.19	**5.10**	m2
024	Walls 3.50 - 5.00 m high over 300 mm wide:					
	plastered	0.13	1.94	2.36	**4.30**	m2
	smooth concrete	0.14	2.14	2.19	**4.33**	m2
	fibre cement	0.16	2.36	2.19	**4.55**	m2
	embossed or textured paper	0.16	2.43	2.19	**4.62**	m2
	cement render	0.17	2.60	2.19	**4.79**	m2
	fair face brickwork	0.19	2.85	2.19	**5.04**	m2
	fair face blockwork	0.21	3.13	2.36	**5.49**	m2
025	Walls in staircase area over 300 mm girth:					
	plastered	0.14	2.08	2.06	**4.14**	m2
	smooth concrete	0.15	2.30	2.06	**4.36**	m2
	fibre cement	0.17	2.54	2.19	**4.73**	m2

Unit Rates	Man-Hours	Net Labour Price £	Net Mats Price £	Net Unit Price £	Unit
embossed or textured paper	0.03	0.47	2.19	**2.66**	m2
cement render	0.18	2.79	2.19	**4.98**	m2
fair face brickwork	0.20	3.07	2.19	**5.26**	m2
fair face blockwork	0.22	3.37	2.36	**5.73**	m2
026 Ceilings over 300 mm girth:					
plastered	0.13	1.99	2.06	**4.05**	m2
smooth concrete	0.14	2.19	2.06	**4.25**	m2
fibre cement	0.16	2.41	2.19	**4.60**	m2
cement render	0.17	2.65	2.19	**4.84**	m2
fair face brickwork	0.19	2.91	2.19	**5.10**	m2
fair face blockwork	0.21	3.21	2.36	**5.57**	m2
027 Ceilings over 300 mm girth 3.50- 5.00 m high:					
plastered	0.14	2.08	2.06	**4.14**	m2
smooth concrete	0.15	2.30	2.06	**4.36**	m2
fibre cement	0.17	2.54	2.19	**4.73**	m2
cement render	0.18	2.77	2.19	**4.96**	m2
fair face brickwork	0.20	3.05	2.19	**5.24**	m2
fair face blockwork	0.22	3.37	2.36	**5.73**	m2
028 Ceilings in staircase areas over 300 mm wide:					
plastered	0.14	2.08	2.06	**4.14**	m2
smooth concrete	0.15	2.30	2.06	**4.36**	m2
fibre cement	0.17	2.54	2.14	**4.68**	m2
cement render	0.18	2.77	2.14	**4.91**	m2
fair face brickwork	0.20	3.05	2.14	**5.19**	m2
fair face blockwork	0.22	3.37	2.36	**5.73**	m2
029 **One coat water based hygiene paint, two pack polyurethane system, to primed surface; and subsequent coats**					
030 Walls over 300 mm wide:					
plastered	0.10	1.57	2.66	**4.23**	m2
smooth concrete	0.11	1.72	2.66	**4.38**	m2
fibre cement	0.12	1.89	2.83	**4.72**	m2
embossed or textured paper	0.12	1.89	2.83	**4.72**	m2
cement render	0.14	2.08	2.83	**4.91**	m2
fair face brickwork	0.15	2.29	2.83	**5.12**	m2
fair face blockwork	0.17	2.52	2.99	**5.51**	m2
031 Walls 3.50 - 5.00 m high over 300 mm wide:					
plastered	0.11	1.69	2.66	**4.35**	m2
smooth concrete	0.12	1.85	2.66	**4.51**	m2
fibre cement	0.13	2.04	2.83	**4.87**	m2
embossed or textured paper	0.13	2.04	2.83	**4.87**	m2
cement render	0.15	2.24	2.83	**5.07**	m2
fair face brickwork	0.16	2.46	2.83	**5.29**	m2
fair face blockwork	0.18	2.71	2.99	**5.70**	m2
032 Walls in staircase area over 300 mm girth:					
plastered	0.12	1.82	2.66	**4.48**	m2
smooth concrete	0.13	1.99	2.66	**4.65**	m2
fibre cement	0.14	2.19	2.83	**5.02**	m2
embossed or textured paper	0.14	2.19	2.83	**5.02**	m2
cement render	0.16	2.41	2.83	**5.24**	m2
fair face brickwork	0.17	2.65	2.83	**5.48**	m2
fair face blockwork	0.19	2.91	2.99	**5.90**	m2
033 Ceilings over 300 mm girth:					
plastered	0.11	1.72	2.66	**4.38**	m2
smooth concrete	0.12	1.89	2.66	**4.55**	m2
fibre cement	0.14	2.08	2.83	**4.91**	m2
cement render	0.15	2.29	2.83	**5.12**	m2
fair face brickwork	0.17	2.52	2.83	**5.35**	m2
fair face blockwork	0.18	2.77	2.99	**5.76**	m2
034 Ceilings over 300 mm girth 3.50- 5.00 m high:					
plastered	0.11	1.72	2.66	**4.38**	m2
smooth concrete	0.12	1.89	2.66	**4.55**	m2
fibre cement	0.14	2.08	2.83	**4.91**	m2
cement render	0.15	2.29	2.83	**5.12**	m2
fair face brickwork	0.17	2.52	2.83	**5.35**	m2
fair face blockwork	0.18	2.77	2.99	**5.76**	m2
035 Ceilings in staircase areas over 300 mm wide:					
plastered	0.13	2.00	2.66	**4.66**	m2
smooth concrete	0.14	2.19	2.66	**4.85**	m2
fibre cement	0.16	2.41	2.83	**5.24**	m2
cement render	0.17	2.65	2.83	**5.48**	m2
fair face brickwork	0.19	2.91	2.83	**5.74**	m2
fair face blockwork	0.21	3.21	2.99	**6.20**	m2
INTUMESCENT PAINT - INTERNALLY					
036 **Prepare; one coat Thermoguard Wallcoat to painted**					
037 Walls over 300 mm wide:					
plastered	0.13	2.04	2.22	**4.26**	m2

Unit Rates	Man-Hours	Net Labour Price £	Net Mats Price £	Net Unit Price £	Unit
smooth concrete	0.15	2.24	2.50	**4.74**	m2
fibre cement	0.16	2.46	2.50	**4.96**	m2
embossed or textured paper	0.12	1.89	2.50	**4.39**	m2
cement render	0.18	2.71	2.50	**5.21**	m2
fair face brickwork	0.20	2.97	2.50	**5.47**	m2
fair face blockwork	0.22	3.27	2.85	**6.12**	m2
038 Walls 3.50 - 5.00 m high over 300 mm wide:					
plastered	0.14	2.14	2.22	**4.36**	m2
smooth concrete	0.16	2.41	2.50	**4.91**	m2
fibre cement	0.17	2.65	2.50	**5.15**	m2
embossed or textured paper	0.13	2.04	2.50	**4.54**	m2
cement render	0.19	2.91	2.50	**5.41**	m2
fair face brickwork	0.21	3.19	2.50	**5.69**	m2
fair face blockwork	0.23	3.52	2.50	**6.02**	m2
039 Walls in staircase area over 300 mm girth:					
plastered	0.15	2.30	2.22	**4.52**	m2
smooth concrete	0.17	2.60	2.50	**5.10**	m2
fibre cement	0.19	2.85	2.50	**5.35**	m2
embossed or textured paper	0.14	2.19	2.50	**4.69**	m2
cement render	0.21	3.13	2.50	**5.63**	m2
fair face brickwork	0.23	3.43	2.50	**5.93**	m2
fair face blockwork	0.25	3.79	2.50	**6.29**	m2
040 Ceilings over 300 mm girth:					
plastered	0.15	2.24	2.50	**4.74**	m2
smooth concrete	0.16	2.46	2.50	**4.96**	m2
fibre cement	0.18	2.71	2.50	**5.21**	m2
cement render	0.20	2.97	2.50	**5.47**	m2
fair face brickwork	0.22	3.27	2.50	**5.77**	m2
fair face blockwork	0.24	3.60	2.50	**6.10**	m2
041 Ceilings over 300 mm girth 3.50- 5.00 m high:					
plastered	0.15	2.35	2.22	**4.57**	m2
smooth concrete	0.17	2.58	2.50	**5.08**	m2
fibre cement	0.19	2.85	2.50	**5.35**	m2
cement render	0.21	3.13	2.50	**5.63**	m2
fair face brickwork	0.23	3.43	2.50	**5.93**	m2
fair face blockwork	0.25	3.79	2.50	**6.29**	m2
042 Ceilings in staircase areas over 300 mm wide:					
plastered	0.16	2.47	2.50	**4.97**	m2
smooth concrete	0.18	2.71	2.50	**5.21**	m2
fibre cement	0.20	2.99	2.50	**5.49**	m2
cement render	0.22	3.29	2.50	**5.79**	m2
fair face brickwork	0.24	3.60	2.50	**6.10**	m2
fair face blockwork	0.26	3.98	2.50	**6.48**	m2
043 **Prepare; second and subsequent coat 'Thermoguard flame retardant acrylic', matt/eggshell**					
044 Walls over 300 mm wide:					
plastered	0.11	1.72	1.57	**3.29**	m2
smooth concrete	0.12	1.89	1.57	**3.46**	m2
fibre cement	0.14	2.08	1.74	**3.82**	m2
embossed or textured paper	0.12	1.89	1.74	**3.63**	m2
cement render	0.15	2.29	1.74	**4.03**	m2
fair face brickwork	0.17	2.52	1.74	**4.26**	m2
fair face blockwork	0.18	2.77	1.95	**4.72**	m2
045 Walls 3.50 - 5.00 m high over 300 mm wide:					
plastered	0.12	1.82	1.57	**3.39**	m2
smooth concrete	0.13	2.04	1.57	**3.61**	m2
fibre cement	0.15	2.24	1.74	**3.98**	m2
embossed or textured paper	0.13	2.04	1.74	**3.78**	m2
cement render	0.16	2.46	1.74	**4.20**	m2
fair face brickwork	0.18	2.71	1.74	**4.45**	m2
fair face blockwork	0.20	2.97	1.95	**4.92**	m2
046 Walls in staircase area over 300 mm girth:					
plastered	0.13	1.96	1.57	**3.53**	m2
smooth concrete	0.14	2.19	1.57	**3.76**	m2
fibre cement	0.16	2.41	1.74	**4.15**	m2
embossed or textured paper	0.14	2.19	1.74	**3.93**	m2
cement render	0.17	2.65	1.74	**4.39**	m2
fair face brickwork	0.19	2.91	1.74	**4.65**	m2
fair face blockwork	0.21	3.19	1.95	**5.14**	m2
047 Ceilings over 300 mm girth:					
plastered	0.12	1.89	1.57	**3.46**	m2
smooth concrete	0.14	2.08	1.57	**3.65**	m2
fibre cement	0.15	2.29	1.74	**4.03**	m2
cement render	0.17	2.52	1.74	**4.26**	m2
fair face brickwork	0.18	2.77	1.74	**4.51**	m2
fair face blockwork	0.20	3.05	1.95	**5.00**	m2
048 Ceilings over 300 mm girth 3.50- 5.00 m high:					
plastered	0.13	1.99	1.57	**3.56**	m2
smooth concrete	0.14	2.19	1.57	**3.76**	m2

Unit Rates	Man-Hours	Net Labour Price £	Net Mats Price £	Net Unit Price £	Unit
fibre cement	0.16	2.40	1.74	**4.14**	m2
cement render	0.17	2.65	1.74	**4.39**	m2
fair face brickwork	0.19	2.91	1.74	**4.65**	m2
fair face blockwork	0.21	3.21	1.95	**5.16**	m2
049 Ceilings in staircase areas over 300 mm wide:					
plastered	0.14	2.08	1.57	**3.65**	m2
smooth concrete	0.15	2.30	1.57	**3.87**	m2
fibre cement	0.17	2.52	1.74	**4.26**	m2
cement render	0.18	2.77	1.74	**4.51**	m2
fair face brickwork	0.20	3.05	1.74	**4.79**	m2
fair face blockwork	0.22	3.37	1.95	**5.32**	m2

VC   NEW WORK INTERNALLY - FLOOR PAINTS

Note: 001 - 099 not used

100   **One coat semi-gloss floor paint**

	Man-Hours	Net Labour Price £	Net Mats Price £	Net Unit Price £	Unit
101 First coat to unprimed surfaces:					
over 300 mm girth	0.10	1.49	0.41	**1.90**	m2
not exceeding 150 mm girth	0.02	0.31	0.06	**0.37**	m
150 - 300 mm girth	0.04	0.55	0.12	**0.67**	m
102 Second and subsequent coats:					
over 300 mm girth	0.09	1.41	0.33	**1.74**	m2
not exceeding 150 mm girth	0.02	0.31	0.05	**0.36**	m
150 - 300 mm girth	0.04	0.55	0.10	**0.65**	m

103   **Prepare; one coat quick drying Thermoplastic Protective floor paint thinned by 10% with clean water**

	Man-Hours	Net Labour Price £	Net Mats Price £	Net Unit Price £	Unit
104 Floor, concrete or the like:					
over 300 mm girth	0.10	1.57	0.41	**1.98**	m2
not exceeding 150 mm girth	0.02	0.31	0.06	**0.37**	m
150 - 300 mm girth	0.04	0.55	0.12	**0.67**	m

105   **One coat quick drying floor paint and each subsequent coat**

	Man-Hours	Net Labour Price £	Net Mats Price £	Net Unit Price £	Unit
106 Floor, concrete or the like:					
over 300 mm girth	0.10	1.57	0.54	**2.11**	m2
not exceeding 150 mm girth	0.02	0.31	0.08	**0.39**	m
150 - 300 mm girth	0.04	0.55	0.16	**0.71**	m

107   **One coat anti-slip floor paint with bauxite aggregate and each subsequent coat on floor paint**

	Man-Hours	Net Labour Price £	Net Mats Price £	Net Unit Price £	Unit
108 Floor, concrete or the like:					
over 300 mm girth	0.10	1.57	0.73	**2.30**	m2
not exceeding 150 mm girth	0.02	0.31	1.07	**1.38**	m
150 - 300 mm girth	0.04	0.55	0.22	**0.77**	m

VD   **METALWORK - INTERNALLY**

METALWORK PRIMERS - INTERNALLY

001   **Prepare; one coat two-pack etching primer, metalwork surfaces, applied to a dry film thickness of 3 microns**

	Man-Hours	Net Labour Price £	Net Mats Price £	Net Unit Price £	Unit
002 General surfaces:					
over 300 mm girth	0.23	3.45	0.61	**4.06**	m2
not exceeding 150 mm girth	0.07	1.03	0.11	**1.14**	m
150 - 300 mm girth	0.10	1.55	0.22	**1.77**	m
isolated; not exceeding 0.50 m2	0.17	2.51	0.32	**2.83**	Nr
003 Glazed doors and screens in panes:					
small - not exceeding 0.10 m2	0.57	8.62	0.35	**8.97**	m2
medium - 0.10 - 0.50 m2	0.40	6.03	0.29	**6.32**	m2
large - 0.50 - 1.00 m2	0.37	5.68	0.24	**5.92**	m2
extra large - over 1.00 m2	0.34	5.17	0.24	**5.41**	m2
004 Windows in panes:					
small - not exceeding 0.10 m2	0.57	8.62	0.29	**8.91**	m2
medium - 0.10 - 0.50 m2	0.40	6.03	0.24	**6.27**	m2
large - 0.50 - 1.00 m2	0.37	5.68	0.24	**5.92**	m2
extra large - over 1.00 m2	0.34	5.17	0.18	**5.35**	m2
005 Structural members:					
over 300 mm girth	0.26	3.97	0.61	**4.58**	m2
not exceeding 150 mm girth	0.08	1.19	0.11	**1.30**	m
150 - 300 mm girth	0.12	1.78	0.22	**2.00**	m
006 Members of roof trusses:					
over 300 mm girth	0.34	5.17	0.78	**5.95**	m2
not exceeding 150 mm girth	0.10	1.55	0.11	**1.66**	m
150 - 300 mm girth	0.15	2.33	0.27	**2.60**	m
007 Radiators:					
over 300 mm girth	0.30	4.48	0.67	**5.15**	m2

		Man-Hours	Net Labour Price £	Net Mats Price £	Net Unit Price £	Unit
008	Pipes and conduits, ducting, trunking and the like:					
	over 300 mm girth	0.25	3.78	0.72	**4.50**	m2
	not exceeding 150 mm girth	0.08	1.14	0.11	**1.25**	m
	150 - 300 mm girth	0.11	1.70	0.22	**1.92**	m
009	Staircases:					
	over 300 mm girth	0.25	3.78	0.61	**4.39**	m2
	not exceeding 150 mm girth	0.08	1.14	0.11	**1.25**	m
	150 - 300 mm girth	0.11	1.70	0.22	**1.92**	m
010	**Prepare; one coat zinc phosphate primer, metalwork surfaces**					
011	General surfaces:					
	over 300 mm girth	0.23	3.45	1.01	**4.46**	m2
	not exceeding 150 mm girth	0.07	1.03	0.17	**1.20**	m
	150 - 300 mm girth	0.10	1.55	0.29	**1.84**	m
	isolated; not exceeding 0.50 m2	0.17	2.51	0.50	**3.01**	Nr
012	Glazed doors and screens in panes:					
	small - not exceeding 0.10 m2	0.57	8.62	0.52	**9.14**	m2
	medium - 0.10 - 0.50 m2	0.40	6.03	0.39	**6.42**	m2
	large - 0.50 - 1.00 m2	0.37	5.68	0.35	**6.03**	m2
	extra large - over 1.00 m2	0.34	5.17	0.31	**5.48**	m2
013	Windows in panes:					
	small - not exceeding 0.10 m2	0.57	8.62	0.39	**9.01**	m2
	medium - 0.10 - 0.50 m2	0.40	6.03	0.35	**6.38**	m2
	large - 0.50 - 1.00 m2	0.37	5.68	0.31	**5.99**	m2
	extra large - over 1.00 m2	0.34	5.17	0.27	**5.44**	m2
014	Structural members:					
	over 300 mm girth	0.26	3.97	1.01	**4.98**	m2
	not exceeding 150 mm girth	0.08	1.19	0.17	**1.36**	m
	150 - 300 mm girth	0.12	1.78	0.29	**2.07**	m
015	Members of roof trusses:					
	over 300 mm girth	0.34	5.17	1.30	**6.47**	m2
	not exceeding 150 mm girth	0.10	1.55	0.21	**1.76**	m
	150 - 300 mm girth	0.15	2.33	0.37	**2.70**	m
016	Radiators:					
	over 300 mm girth	0.30	4.48	1.14	**5.62**	m2
017	Pipes and conduits, ducting, trunking and the like:					
	over 300 mm girth	0.25	3.78	1.05	**4.83**	m2
	not exceeding 150 mm girth	0.08	1.14	0.17	**1.31**	m
	150 - 300 mm girth	0.11	1.70	0.33	**2.03**	m
018	Staircases:					
	over 300 mm girth	0.25	3.78	1.01	**4.79**	m2
	not exceeding 150 mm girth	0.08	1.14	0.17	**1.31**	m
	150 - 300 mm girth	0.11	1.70	0.29	**1.99**	m
019	**Prepare; one coat zinc chromate primer, metalwork surfaces**					
020	General surfaces:					
	over 300 mm girth	0.23	3.45	0.94	**4.39**	m2
	not exceeding 150 mm girth	0.07	1.03	0.15	**1.18**	m
	150 - 300 mm girth	0.10	1.55	0.27	**1.82**	m
	isolated; not exceeding 0.50 m2	0.17	2.51	0.46	**2.97**	Nr
021	Glazed doors and screens in panes:					
	small - not exceeding 0.10 m2	0.57	8.62	0.48	**9.10**	m2
	medium - 0.10 - 0.50 m2	0.40	6.03	0.37	**6.40**	m2
	large - 0.50 - 1.00 m2	0.37	5.68	0.33	**6.01**	m2
	extra large - over 1.00 m2	0.34	5.17	0.29	**5.46**	m2
022	Windows in panes:					
	small - not exceeding 0.10 m2	0.57	8.62	0.37	**8.99**	m2
	medium - 0.10 - 0.50 m2	0.40	6.03	0.33	**6.36**	m2
	large - 0.50 - 1.00 m2	0.37	5.68	0.29	**5.97**	m2
	extra large - over 1.00 m2	0.34	5.17	0.25	**5.42**	m2
023	Structural members:					
	over 300 mm girth	0.26	3.97	0.94	**4.91**	m2
	not exceeding 150 mm girth	0.08	1.19	0.15	**1.34**	m
	150 - 300 mm girth	0.12	1.78	0.27	**2.05**	m
024	Members of roof trusses:					
	over 300 mm girth	0.34	5.17	1.20	**6.37**	m2
	not exceeding 150 mm girth	0.10	1.55	0.19	**1.74**	m
	150 - 300 mm girth	0.15	2.33	0.34	**2.67**	m
025	Radiators:					
	over 300 mm girth	0.30	4.48	1.05	**5.53**	m2
026	Pipes and conduits, ducting, trunking and the like:					
	over 300 mm girth	0.25	3.78	0.98	**4.76**	m2
	not exceeding 150 mm girth	0.08	1.14	0.15	**1.29**	m

Unit Rates

Unit Rates	Man-Hours	Net Labour Price £	Net Mats Price £	Net Unit Price £	Unit
150 - 300 mm girth	0.11	1.70	0.30	**2.00**	m
027 Staircases:					
over 300 mm girth	0.25	3.78	0.94	**4.72**	m2
not exceeding 150 mm girth	0.08	1.14	0.15	**1.29**	m
150 - 300 mm girth	0.11	1.70	0.27	**1.97**	m
028 Prepare; one coat of zinc rich primer, metalwork surfaces					
029 General surfaces:					
over 300 mm girth	0.23	3.45	4.87	**8.32**	m2
not exceeding 150 mm girth	0.07	1.03	0.81	**1.84**	m
150 - 300 mm girth	0.10	1.55	1.41	**2.96**	m
isolated; not exceeding 0.50 m2	0.17	2.51	2.42	**4.93**	Nr
030 Glazed doors and screens in panes:					
small - not exceeding 0.10 m2	0.57	8.62	2.44	**11.06**	m2
medium - 0.10 - 0.50 m2	0.40	6.03	1.84	**7.87**	m2
large - 0.50 - 1.00 m2	0.37	5.68	1.64	**7.32**	m2
extra large - over 1.00 m2	0.34	5.17	1.43	**6.60**	m2
031 Windows in panes:					
small - not exceeding 0.10 m2	0.57	8.62	1.84	**10.46**	m2
medium - 0.10 - 0.50 m2	0.40	6.03	1.64	**7.67**	m2
large - 0.50 - 1.00 m2	0.37	5.68	1.43	**7.11**	m2
extra large - over 1.00 m2	0.34	5.17	1.23	**6.40**	m2
032 Structural members:					
over 300 mm girth	0.26	3.97	4.87	**8.84**	m2
not exceeding 150 mm girth	0.08	1.19	0.81	**2.00**	m
150 - 300 mm girth	0.12	1.78	1.41	**3.19**	m
033 Members of roof trusses:					
over 300 mm girth	0.34	5.17	6.28	**11.45**	m2
not exceeding 150 mm girth	0.10	1.57	1.01	**2.58**	m
150 - 300 mm girth	0.15	2.33	1.82	**4.15**	m
034 Radiators:					
over 300 mm girth	0.30	4.48	5.47	**9.95**	m2
035 Pipes and conduits, ducting, trunking and the like:					
over 300 mm girth	0.25	3.78	5.07	**8.85**	m2
not exceeding 150 mm girth	0.08	1.14	0.81	**1.95**	m
150 - 300 mm girth	0.11	1.70	1.61	**3.31**	m
036 Staircases:					
over 300 mm girth	0.25	3.78	4.87	**8.65**	m2
not exceeding 150 mm girth	0.08	1.14	0.81	**1.95**	m
150 - 300 mm girth	0.11	1.70	1.41	**3.11**	m
037 Prepare; one coat red oxide primer, metalwork surfaces					
038 General surfaces:					
over 300 mm girth	0.23	3.45	1.01	**4.46**	m2
not exceeding 150 mm girth	0.07	1.03	0.16	**1.19**	m
150 - 300 mm girth	0.10	1.55	0.29	**1.84**	m
isolated; not exceeding 0.50 m2	0.17	2.51	0.49	**3.00**	Nr
039 Glazed doors and screens in panes:					
small - not exceeding 0.10 m2	0.57	8.62	0.52	**9.14**	m2
medium - 0.10 - 0.50 m2	0.40	6.03	0.39	**6.42**	m2
large - 0.50 - 1.00 m2	0.37	5.68	0.35	**6.03**	m2
extra large - over 1.00 m2	0.34	5.17	0.31	**5.48**	m2
040 Windows in panes:					
small - not exceeding 0.10 m2	0.57	8.62	0.39	**9.01**	m2
medium - 0.10 - 0.50 m2	0.40	6.03	0.35	**6.38**	m2
large - 0.50 - 1.00 m2	0.37	5.68	0.31	**5.99**	m2
extra large - over 1.00 m2	0.34	5.17	0.27	**5.44**	m2
041 Structural members:					
over 300 mm girth	0.26	3.97	1.01	**4.98**	m2
not exceeding 150 mm girth	0.08	1.19	0.16	**1.35**	m
150 - 300 mm girth	0.12	1.78	0.29	**2.07**	m
042 Members of roof trusses:					
over 300 mm girth	0.34	5.17	1.30	**6.47**	m2
not exceeding 150 mm girth	0.10	1.55	0.21	**1.76**	m
150 - 300 mm girth	0.15	2.33	0.37	**2.70**	m
043 Radiators:					
over 300 mm girth	0.30	4.48	1.13	**5.61**	m2
044 Pipes and conduits, ducting, trunking and the like:					
over 300 mm girth	0.25	3.78	1.05	**4.83**	m2
not exceeding 150 mm girth	0.08	1.14	0.16	**1.30**	m
150 - 300 mm girth	0.11	1.70	0.33	**2.03**	m

		Man-Hours	Net Labour Price £	Net Mats Price £	Net Unit Price £	Unit
045	**Staircases:**					
	over 300 mm girth	0.25	3.78	1.01	**4.79**	m2
	not exceeding 150 mm girth	0.08	1.14	0.16	**1.30**	m
	150 - 300 mm girth	0.11	1.70	0.29	**1.99**	m
046	**Prepare; one coat of galvanising paint, metalwork surfaces, applied to a dry film thickness of 125 microns**					
047	General surfaces:					
	over 300 mm girth	0.20	2.98	1.90	**4.88**	m2
	not exceeding 150 mm girth	0.06	0.90	0.30	**1.20**	m
	150 - 300 mm girth	0.09	1.35	0.60	**1.95**	m
	isolated; not exceeding 0.50 m2	0.12	1.88	1.05	**2.93**	Nr
048	Glazed doors and screens in panes:					
	small - not exceeding 0.10 m2	0.56	8.45	1.07	**9.52**	m2
	medium - 0.10 - 0.50 m2	0.38	5.79	0.85	**6.64**	m2
	large - 0.50 - 1.00 m2	0.37	5.55	0.77	**6.32**	m2
	extra large - over 1.00 m2	0.33	4.97	0.62	**5.59**	m2
049	Windows in panes:					
	small - not exceeding 0.10 m2	0.56	8.45	0.85	**9.30**	m2
	medium - 0.10 - 0.50 m2	0.38	5.79	0.77	**6.56**	m2
	large - 0.50 - 1.00 m2	0.37	5.55	0.62	**6.17**	m2
	extra large - over 1.00 m2	0.33	4.97	0.55	**5.52**	m2
050	Structural members:					
	over 300 mm girth	0.26	3.97	1.90	**5.87**	m2
	not exceeding 150 mm girth	0.08	1.19	0.30	**1.49**	m
	150 - 300 mm girth	0.12	1.78	0.60	**2.38**	m
051	Members of roof trusses:					
	over 300 mm girth	0.33	5.02	2.35	**7.37**	m2
	not exceeding 150 mm girth	0.11	1.60	0.38	**1.98**	m
	150 - 300 mm girth	0.16	2.42	0.75	**3.17**	m
052	Radiators:					
	over 300 mm girth	0.29	4.38	2.12	**6.50**	m2
053	Pipes and conduits, ducting, trunking and the like:					
	over 300 mm girth	0.22	3.27	2.20	**5.47**	m2
	not exceeding 150 mm girth	0.07	1.00	0.38	**1.38**	m
	150 - 300 mm girth	0.10	1.47	0.75	**2.22**	m
054	Staircases:					
	over 300 mm girth	0.26	3.97	1.90	**5.87**	m2
	not exceeding 150 mm girth	0.08	1.19	0.30	**1.49**	m
	150 - 300 mm girth	0.12	1.78	0.60	**2.38**	m
055	**One coat of galvanising paint; second and subsequent coats to previously coated metalwork surfaces; applied to a dry film thickness of 125 microns**					
056	General surfaces:					
	over 300 mm girth	0.19	2.81	1.60	**4.41**	m2
	not exceeding 150 mm girth	0.05	0.81	0.23	**1.04**	m
	150 - 300 mm girth	0.08	1.25	0.53	**1.78**	m
	isolated; not exceeding 0.50 m2	0.14	2.19	0.75	**2.94**	Nr
057	Glazed doors and screens in panes:					
	small - not exceeding 0.10 m2	0.54	8.27	0.77	**9.04**	m2
	medium - 0.10 - 0.50 m2	0.36	5.44	0.62	**6.06**	m2
	large - 0.50 - 1.00 m2	0.33	5.05	0.55	**5.60**	m2
	extra large - over 1.00 m2	0.29	4.41	0.62	**5.03**	m2
058	Windows in panes:					
	small - not exceeding 0.10 m2	0.54	8.27	0.62	**8.89**	m2
	medium - 0.10 - 0.50 m2	0.37	5.61	0.55	**6.16**	m2
	large - 0.50 - 1.00 m2	0.34	5.20	0.47	**5.67**	m2
	extra large - over 1.00 m2	0.30	4.58	0.40	**4.98**	m2
059	Structural members:					
	over 300 mm girth	0.23	3.54	1.60	**5.14**	m2
	not exceeding 150 mm girth	0.07	1.08	0.23	**1.31**	m
	150 - 300 mm girth	0.10	1.57	0.53	**2.10**	m
060	Members of roof trusses:					
	over 300 mm girth	0.33	5.02	1.97	**6.99**	m2
	not exceeding 150 mm girth	0.09	1.41	0.30	**1.71**	m
	150 - 300 mm girth	0.15	2.22	0.68	**2.90**	m
061	Radiators:					
	over 300 mm girth	0.29	4.36	1.75	**6.11**	m2
062	Pipes and conduits, ducting, trunking and the like:					
	over 300 mm girth	0.21	3.13	1.90	**5.03**	m2
	not exceeding 150 mm girth	0.05	0.73	0.30	**1.03**	m
	150 - 300 mm girth	0.08	1.22	0.60	**1.82**	m

	Unit Rates	Man-Hours	Net Labour Price £	Net Mats Price £	Net Unit Price £	Unit
063	Staircases:					
	over 300 mm girth	0.24	3.69	1.60	**5.29**	m2
	not exceeding 150 mm girth	0.07	1.08	0.23	**1.31**	m
	150 - 300 mm girth	0.10	1.57	0.53	**2.10**	m
	METALWORK UNDERCOATS - INTERNALLY					
064	**One undercoat alkyd based paint; primed metalwork surfaces**					
065	General surfaces:					
	over 300 mm girth	0.17	2.58	0.56	**3.14**	m2
	not exceeding 150 mm girth	0.05	0.79	0.09	**0.88**	m
	150 - 300 mm girth	0.08	1.17	0.16	**1.33**	m
	isolated; not exceeding 0.50 m2	0.17	2.51	0.25	**2.76**	Nr
066	Glazed doors and screens in panes:					
	small - not exceeding 0.10 m2	0.51	7.75	0.27	**8.02**	m2
	medium - 0.10 - 0.50 m2	0.34	5.17	0.24	**5.41**	m2
	large - 0.50 - 1.00 m2	0.32	4.82	0.21	**5.03**	m2
	extra large - over 1.00 m2	0.28	4.30	0.18	**4.48**	m2
067	Windows in panes:					
	small - not exceeding 0.10 m2	0.51	7.75	0.24	**7.99**	m2
	medium - 0.10 - 0.50 m2	0.34	5.17	0.21	**5.38**	m2
	large - 0.50 - 1.00 m2	0.32	4.82	0.18	**5.00**	m2
	extra large - over 1.00 m2	0.28	4.30	0.15	**4.45**	m2
068	Structural members:					
	over 300 mm girth	0.23	3.45	0.56	**4.01**	m2
	not exceeding 150 mm girth	0.07	1.03	0.09	**1.12**	m
	150 - 300 mm girth	0.10	1.55	0.16	**1.71**	m
069	Members of roof trusses:					
	over 300 mm girth	0.31	4.65	0.71	**5.36**	m2
	not exceeding 150 mm girth	0.09	1.40	0.09	**1.49**	m
	150 - 300 mm girth	0.14	2.10	0.22	**2.32**	m
070	Radiators:					
	over 300 mm girth	0.27	4.13	0.59	**4.72**	m2
071	Pipes and conduits, ducting, trunking and the like:					
	over 300 mm girth	0.19	2.84	0.59	**3.43**	m2
	not exceeding 150 mm girth	0.06	0.87	0.09	**0.96**	m
	150 - 300 mm girth	0.08	1.26	0.19	**1.45**	m
072	Staircases:					
	over 300 mm girth	0.23	3.45	0.56	**4.01**	m2
	not exceeding 150 mm girth	0.07	1.03	0.09	**1.12**	m
	150 - 300 mm girth	0.10	1.55	0.16	**1.71**	m
	METALWORK GLOSS FINISH - INTERNALLY					
073	**One coat alkyd based paint, gloss finish; undercoated metalwork surfaces**					
074	General surfaces:					
	over 300 mm girth	0.19	2.93	0.56	**3.49**	m2
	not exceeding 150 mm girth	0.06	0.88	0.09	**0.97**	m
	150 - 300 mm girth	0.09	1.34	0.16	**1.50**	m
	isolated; not exceeding 0.50 m2	0.17	2.51	0.25	**2.76**	Nr
075	Glazed doors and screens in panes:					
	small - not exceeding 0.10 m2	0.53	8.10	0.27	**8.37**	m2
	medium - 0.10 - 0.50 m2	0.36	5.52	0.24	**5.76**	m2
	large - 0.50 - 1.00 m2	0.34	5.17	0.21	**5.38**	m2
	extra large - over 1.00 m2	0.31	4.65	0.18	**4.83**	m2
076	Windows in panes:					
	small - not exceeding 0.10 m2	0.53	8.10	0.24	**8.34**	m2
	medium - 0.10 - 0.50 m2	0.36	5.52	0.21	**5.73**	m2
	large - 0.50 - 1.00 m2	0.34	5.17	0.18	**5.35**	m2
	extra large - over 1.00 m2	0.31	4.65	0.15	**4.80**	m2
077	Structural members:					
	over 300 mm girth	0.25	3.78	0.56	**4.34**	m2
	not exceeding 150 mm girth	0.08	1.14	0.09	**1.23**	m
	150 - 300 mm girth	0.11	1.70	0.16	**1.86**	m
078	Members of roof trusses:					
	over 300 mm girth	0.32	4.82	0.71	**5.53**	m2
	not exceeding 150 mm girth	0.10	1.44	0.09	**1.53**	m
	150 - 300 mm girth	0.14	2.17	0.22	**2.39**	m
079	Radiators:					
	over 300 mm girth	0.28	4.30	0.59	**4.89**	m2
080	Pipes and conduits, ducting, trunking and the like:					
	over 300 mm girth	0.21	3.22	0.59	**3.81**	m2
	not exceeding 150 mm girth	0.06	0.97	0.09	**1.06**	m
	150 - 300 mm girth	0.10	1.44	0.16	**1.60**	m

	Unit Rates	Man-Hours	Net Labour Price £	Net Mats Price £	Net Unit Price £	Unit
081	Staircases:					
	over 300 mm girth	0.24	3.62	0.56	**4.18**	m2
	not exceeding 150 mm girth	0.07	1.08	0.09	**1.17**	m
	150 - 300 mm girth	0.11	1.64	0.16	**1.80**	m
VE	**METALWORK ALUMINIUM PAINT - INTERNALLY**					
	Note: 001 - 027 not used					
028	**Prepare; one coat aluminium paint, metalwork surfaces**					
029	Boilers, tanks, calorifiers and the like:					
	over 300 mm girth	0.27	4.13	1.24	**5.37**	m2
030	Pipes, conduits, ducting, trunking and the like:					
	over 300 mm girth	0.19	2.84	1.32	**4.16**	m2
	not exceeding 150 mm girth	0.06	0.87	0.22	**1.09**	m
	150 - 300 mm girth	0.08	1.26	0.43	**1.69**	m
	Note: 031 - 049 not used					
050	**Prepare; one coat Thermoguard high build primer, primed surfaces**					
051	Structural members:					
	over 300 mm girth	0.26	3.91	1.21	**5.12**	m2
	not exceeding 150 mm girth	0.08	1.25	0.19	**1.44**	m
	150 - 300 mm girth	0.11	1.72	0.36	**2.08**	m
052	Members of roof trusses:					
	over 300 mm girth	0.28	4.31	1.21	**5.52**	m2
	not exceeding 150 mm girth	0.08	1.25	0.19	**1.44**	m
	150 - 300 mm girth	0.11	1.72	0.36	**2.08**	m
053	**One coat 'Thermoguard Thermacoat W' intumescent paint to high build primer, protection given 30 minutes**					
054	Structural members:					
	over 300 mm girth	0.26	3.91	1.74	**5.65**	m2
	not exceeding 150 mm girth	0.08	1.25	0.27	**1.52**	m
	150 - 300 mm girth	0.11	1.72	0.52	**2.24**	m
055	Members of roof trusses:					
	over 300 mm girth	0.28	4.31	1.74	**6.05**	m2
	not exceeding 150 mm girth	0.09	1.38	0.27	**1.65**	m
	150 - 300 mm girth	0.12	1.89	0.52	**2.41**	m
056	**Subsequent coat 'Thermoguard Thermacoat W' intumescent paint giving extra protection of 30 minutes**					
057	Structural members:					
	over 300 mm girth	0.19	2.82	1.74	**4.56**	m2
	not exceeding 150 mm girth	0.08	1.25	0.27	**1.52**	m
	150 - 300 mm girth	0.11	1.72	0.52	**2.24**	m
058	Members of roof trusses:					
	over 300 mm girth	0.20	3.10	1.71	**4.81**	m2
	not exceeding 150 mm girth	0.09	1.38	0.27	**1.65**	m
	150 - 300 mm girth	0.12	1.89	0.52	**2.41**	m
059	**Prepare; second and subsequent coat 'Thermoguard flame retardant acrylic', matt/eggshell**					
060	Structural members:					
	over 300 mm girth	0.21	3.13	1.43	**4.56**	m2
	not exceeding 150 mm girth	0.09	1.41	0.22	**1.63**	m
	150 - 300 mm girth	0.13	1.96	0.42	**2.38**	m
061	Members of roof trusses:					
	over 300 mm girth	0.23	3.44	1.47	**4.91**	m2
	not exceeding 150 mm girth	0.10	1.55	0.22	**1.77**	m
	150 - 300 mm girth	0.14	2.16	0.45	**2.61**	m
VF	**WOODWORK - INTERNALLY**					
	WOODWORK PRIMERS					
001	**Prepare, knotting and stopping; one coat wood primer, wood surfaces**					
002	General surfaces:					
	over 300 mm girth	0.23	3.45	1.08	**4.53**	m2
	not exceeding 150 mm girth	0.07	1.03	0.18	**1.21**	m
	150 - 300 mm girth	0.10	1.55	0.29	**1.84**	m
	isolated; not exceeding 0.50 m2	0.17	2.51	0.55	**3.06**	Nr
003	Glazed doors and screens in panes:					
	small - not exceeding 0.10 m2	0.51	7.75	0.68	**8.43**	m2
	medium - 0.10 - 0.50 m2	0.37	5.68	0.57	**6.25**	m2
	large - 0.50 - 1.00 m2	0.34	5.17	0.42	**5.59**	m2
	extra large - over 1.00 m2	0.32	4.82	0.31	**5.13**	m2

Unit Rates

		Man-Hours	Net Labour Price £	Net Mats Price £	Net Unit Price £	Unit
004	Windows in panes:					
	small - not exceeding 0.10 m2	0.57	8.62	0.86	**9.48**	m2
	medium - 0.10 - 0.50 m2	0.40	6.03	0.78	**6.81**	m2
	large - 0.50 - 1.00 m2	0.37	5.68	0.68	**6.36**	m2
	extra large - over 1.00 m2	0.34	5.17	0.57	**5.74**	m2
005	Frames, linings and associated mouldings:					
	over 300 mm girth	0.23	3.45	1.08	**4.53**	m2
	not exceeding 150 mm girth	0.07	1.03	0.18	**1.21**	m
	150 - 300 mm girth	0.10	1.55	0.29	**1.84**	m
006	Cornices:					
	over 300 mm girth	0.27	4.13	1.08	**5.21**	m2
	not exceeding 150 mm girth	0.08	1.20	0.18	**1.38**	m
	150 - 300 mm girth	0.13	1.90	0.29	**2.19**	m
007	Skirtings, dado rails, picture rails and the like:					
	over 300 mm girth	0.25	3.78	1.08	**4.86**	m2
	not exceeding 150 mm girth	0.08	1.14	0.18	**1.32**	m
	150 - 300 mm girth	0.11	1.72	0.29	**2.01**	m
008	Staircases:					
	over 300 mm girth	0.24	3.62	1.08	**4.70**	m2
	not exceeding 150 mm girth	0.07	1.08	0.18	**1.26**	m
	150 - 300 mm girth	0.11	1.64	0.29	**1.93**	m
009	**Prepare, knotting, stopping; one coat aluminium wood primer, wood surfaces**					
010	General surfaces:					
	over 300 mm girth	0.23	3.45	1.04	**4.49**	m2
	not exceeding 150 mm girth	0.07	1.03	0.17	**1.20**	m
	150 - 300 mm girth	0.10	1.55	0.28	**1.83**	m
	isolated; not exceeding 0.50 m2	0.17	2.51	0.53	**3.04**	Nr
011	Glazed doors and screens in panes:					
	small - not exceeding 0.10 m2	0.51	7.75	0.65	**8.40**	m2
	medium - 0.10 - 0.50 m2	0.37	5.68	0.55	**6.23**	m2
	large - 0.50 - 1.00 m2	0.34	5.17	0.41	**5.58**	m2
	extra large - over 1.00 m2	0.32	4.82	0.30	**5.12**	m2
012	Windows in panes:					
	small - not exceeding 0.10 m2	0.57	8.62	0.83	**9.45**	m2
	medium - 0.10 - 0.50 m2	0.40	6.03	0.76	**6.79**	m2
	large - 0.50 - 1.00 m2	0.37	5.68	0.65	**6.33**	m2
	extra large - over 1.00 m2	0.34	5.17	0.55	**5.72**	m2
013	Frames, linings and associated mouldings:					
	over 300 mm girth	0.23	3.45	1.04	**4.49**	m2
	not exceeding 150 mm girth	0.07	1.03	0.17	**1.20**	m
	150 - 300 mm girth	0.10	1.55	0.28	**1.83**	m
014	Cornices:					
	over 300 mm girth	0.27	4.13	1.04	**5.17**	m2
	not exceeding 150 mm girth	0.08	1.20	0.17	**1.37**	m
	150 - 300 mm girth	0.13	1.90	0.28	**2.18**	m
015	Skirtings, dado rails, picture rails and the like:					
	over 300 mm girth	0.25	3.78	1.04	**4.82**	m2
	not exceeding 150 mm girth	0.08	1.14	0.17	**1.31**	m
	150 - 300 mm girth	0.11	1.72	0.28	**2.00**	m
016	Staircases:					
	over 300 mm girth	0.24	3.62	1.04	**4.66**	m2
	not exceeding 150 mm girth	0.07	1.08	0.17	**1.25**	m
	150 - 300 mm girth	0.11	1.64	0.28	**1.92**	m
017	**Prepare, knotting, stopping; one coat acrylic wood primer, wood surfaces**					
018	General surfaces:					
	over 300 mm girth	0.23	3.45	1.63	**5.08**	m2
	not exceeding 150 mm girth	0.07	1.03	0.26	**1.29**	m
	150 - 300 mm girth	0.10	1.55	0.45	**2.00**	m
	isolated; not exceeding 0.50 m2	0.17	2.51	0.84	**3.35**	Nr
019	Glazed doors and screens in panes:					
	small - not exceeding 0.10 m2	0.51	7.75	1.02	**8.77**	m2
	medium - 0.10 - 0.50 m2	0.37	5.68	0.86	**6.54**	m2
	large - 0.50 - 1.00 m2	0.34	5.17	0.63	**5.80**	m2
	extra large - over 1.00 m2	0.32	4.82	0.47	**5.29**	m2
020	Windows in panes:					
	small - not exceeding 0.10 m2	0.57	8.62	1.31	**9.93**	m2
	medium - 0.10 - 0.50 m2	0.40	6.03	1.18	**7.21**	m2
	large - 0.50 - 1.00 m2	0.37	5.68	1.02	**6.70**	m2
	extra large - over 1.00 m2	0.34	5.17	0.86	**6.03**	m2
021	Frames, linings and associated mouldings:					
	over 300 mm girth	0.23	3.45	1.63	**5.08**	m2
	not exceeding 150 mm girth	0.07	1.03	0.26	**1.29**	m

Unit Rates	Man-Hours	Net Labour Price £	Net Mats Price £	Net Unit Price £	Unit
150 - 300 mm girth	0.10	1.55	0.45	**2.00**	m
022 Cornices:					
over 300 mm girth	0.27	4.13	1.63	**5.76**	m2
not exceeding 150 mm girth	0.08	1.20	0.26	**1.46**	m
150 - 300 mm girth	0.13	1.90	0.45	**2.35**	m
023 Skirtings, dado rails, picture rails and the like:					
over 300 mm girth	0.25	3.78	1.63	**5.41**	m2
not exceeding 150 mm girth	0.08	1.14	0.26	**1.40**	m
150 - 300 mm girth	0.11	1.72	0.45	**2.17**	m
024 Staircases:					
over 300 mm girth	0.24	3.62	1.63	**5.25**	m2
not exceeding 150 mm girth	0.07	1.08	0.26	**1.34**	m
150 - 300 mm girth	0.11	1.64	0.45	**2.09**	m
WOODWORK UNDERCOAT - INTERNALLY					
025 **One undercoat alkyd based paint, white; primed wood surfaces**					
026 General surfaces:					
over 300 mm girth	0.17	2.58	0.56	**3.14**	m2
not exceeding 150 mm girth	0.05	0.79	0.09	**0.88**	m
150 - 300 mm girth	0.08	1.17	0.16	**1.33**	m
isolated; not exceeding 0.50 m2	0.17	2.51	0.25	**2.76**	Nr
027 Glazed doors and screens in panes:					
small - not exceeding 0.10 m2	0.45	6.89	0.34	**7.23**	m2
medium - 0.10 - 0.50 m2	0.32	4.82	0.27	**5.09**	m2
large - 0.50 - 1.00 m2	0.28	4.30	0.24	**4.54**	m2
extra large - over 1.00 m2	0.26	3.97	0.18	**4.15**	m2
028 Windows in panes:					
small - not exceeding 0.10 m2	0.51	7.75	0.43	**8.18**	m2
medium - 0.10 - 0.50 m2	0.34	5.17	0.40	**5.57**	m2
large - 0.50 - 1.00 m2	0.32	4.82	0.34	**5.16**	m2
extra large - over 1.00 m2	0.28	4.30	0.27	**4.57**	m2
029 Frames, linings and associated mouldings:					
over 300 mm girth	0.17	2.58	0.56	**3.14**	m2
not exceeding 150 mm girth	0.05	0.79	0.09	**0.88**	m
150 - 300 mm girth	0.08	1.17	0.16	**1.33**	m
030 Cornices:					
over 300 mm girth	0.20	3.10	0.56	**3.66**	m2
not exceeding 150 mm girth	0.06	0.93	0.09	**1.02**	m
150 - 300 mm girth	0.09	1.41	0.16	**1.57**	m
031 Skirtings, dado rails, picture rails and the like:					
over 300 mm girth	0.19	2.84	0.56	**3.40**	m2
not exceeding 150 mm girth	0.06	0.87	0.09	**0.96**	m
150 - 300 mm girth	0.09	1.29	0.16	**1.45**	m
032 Staircases:					
over 300 mm girth	0.18	2.72	0.56	**3.28**	m2
not exceeding 150 mm girth	0.05	0.82	0.09	**0.91**	m
150 - 300 mm girth	0.08	1.22	0.16	**1.38**	m
WOODWORK ALKYD BASED GLOSS FINISH					
033 **One coat alkyd based paint gloss finish; undercoated wood surfaces**					
034 General surfaces:					
over 300 mm girth	0.19	2.93	0.56	**3.49**	m2
not exceeding 150 mm girth	0.06	0.88	0.09	**0.97**	m
150 - 300 mm girth	0.09	1.34	0.16	**1.50**	m
isolated; not exceeding 0.50 m2	0.17	2.51	0.25	**2.76**	Nr
035 Glazed doors and screens in panes:					
small - not exceeding 0.10 m2	0.48	7.24	0.34	**7.58**	m2
medium - 0.10 - 0.50 m2	0.34	5.17	0.27	**5.44**	m2
large - 0.50 - 1.00 m2	0.31	4.65	0.24	**4.89**	m2
extra large - over 1.00 m2	0.28	4.30	0.18	**4.48**	m2
036 Windows in panes:					
small - not exceeding 0.10 m2	0.53	8.10	0.43	**8.53**	m2
medium - 0.10 - 0.50 m2	0.36	5.52	0.40	**5.92**	m2
large - 0.50 - 1.00 m2	0.34	5.17	0.34	**5.51**	m2
extra large - over 1.00 m2	0.31	4.65	0.27	**4.92**	m2
037 Frames, linings and associated mouldings:					
over 300 mm girth	0.19	2.93	0.56	**3.49**	m2
not exceeding 150 mm girth	0.06	0.88	0.09	**0.97**	m
150 - 300 mm girth	0.09	1.34	0.16	**1.50**	m
038 Cornices:					
over 300 mm girth	0.23	3.45	0.56	**4.01**	m2
not exceeding 150 mm girth	0.07	1.05	0.09	**1.14**	m

Unit Rates		Man-Hours	Net Labour Price £	Net Mats Price £	Net Unit Price £	Unit
	150 - 300 mm girth	0.10	1.58	0.16	**1.74**	m
039	Skirtings, dado rails, picture rails and the like:					
	over 300 mm girth	0.21	3.22	0.56	**3.78**	m2
	not exceeding 150 mm girth	0.06	0.97	0.09	**1.06**	m
	150 - 300 mm girth	0.10	1.47	0.16	**1.63**	m
040	Staircases:					
	over 300 mm girth	0.20	3.09	0.56	**3.65**	m2
	not exceeding 150 mm girth	0.06	0.93	0.09	**1.02**	m
	150 - 300 mm girth	0.09	1.40	0.16	**1.56**	m
	Note: 041 - 064 not used					
	WOODWORK, INTUMESCENT PAINT					
065	**One coat and subsequent coats Thermoguard Timber Coat to primed**					
066	General surfaces:					
	over 300 mm girth	0.20	2.97	2.84	**5.81**	m2
	not exceeding 150 mm girth	0.06	0.94	0.42	**1.36**	m
	150 - 300 mm girth	0.09	1.41	0.85	**2.26**	m
	isolated; not exceeding 0.50 m2	0.12	1.78	1.27	**3.05**	nr
067	Fire resistant glazed doors, screens and windows:					
	small - not exceeding 0.10 m2	0.53	7.98	1.91	**9.89**	m2
	medium - 0.10 - 0.50 m2	0.39	5.95	1.58	**7.53**	m2
	large - 0.50 - 1.00 m2	0.34	5.17	1.28	**6.45**	m2
	extra large - over 1.00 m2	0.28	4.31	1.15	**5.46**	m2
	opening edge	0.07	1.10	0.30	**1.40**	m
068	Staircases:					
	over 300 mm girth	0.22	3.27	3.12	**6.39**	m2
	not exceeding 150 mm girth	0.07	1.03	0.46	**1.49**	m
	150 - 300 mm girth	0.10	1.55	0.93	**2.48**	m
	isolated; not exceeding 0.50 m2	0.13	1.96	1.39	**3.35**	nr
	balustrade (measured both sides)	0.17	2.54	17.51	**20.05**	m2
	Note: 069 - 100 not used					
	WOODWORK, STAINING					
101	**Prepare; one coat interior satin sheen wood stain**					
102	General surfaces:					
	over 300 mm girth	0.13	2.04	0.77	**2.81**	m2
	not exceeding 150 mm girth	0.03	0.47	0.15	**0.62**	m
	150 - 300 mm girth	0.06	0.94	0.22	**1.16**	m
	isolated; not exceeding 0.50 m2	0.07	1.09	0.37	**1.46**	Nr
103	Glazed doors and screens in panes:					
	small - not exceeding 0.10 m2	0.29	4.38	0.62	**5.00**	m2
	medium - 0.10 - 0.50 m2	0.22	3.28	0.47	**3.75**	m2
	large - 0.50 - 1.00 m2	0.21	3.13	0.40	**3.53**	m2
	extra large - over 1.00 m2	0.20	2.98	0.32	**3.30**	m2
104	Windows in panes:					
	small - not exceeding 0.10 m2	0.32	4.85	0.62	**5.47**	m2
	medium - 0.10 - 0.50 m2	0.24	3.60	0.47	**4.07**	m2
	large - 0.50 - 1.00 m2	0.23	3.45	0.40	**3.85**	m2
	extra large - over 1.00 m2	0.22	3.28	0.32	**3.60**	m2
105	Frames, linings and associated mouldings:					
	over 300 mm girth	0.13	2.04	0.77	**2.81**	m2
	not exceeding 150 mm girth	0.03	0.47	0.15	**0.62**	m
	150 - 300 mm girth	0.06	0.94	0.22	**1.16**	m
106	Skirtings, dado rails, picture rails and the like:					
	over 300 mm girth	0.13	2.04	0.77	**2.81**	m2
	not exceeding 150 mm girth	0.03	0.47	0.15	**0.62**	m
	150 - 300 mm girth	0.06	0.94	0.22	**1.16**	m
107	Staircases:					
	over 300 mm girth	0.13	2.04	0.77	**2.81**	m2
	not exceeding 150 mm girth	0.03	0.47	0.15	**0.62**	m
	150 - 300 mm girth	0.06	0.94	0.22	**1.16**	m
VG	**CLEAR FINISHES ON WOODWORK - INTERNALLY**					
	WOODWORK POLYURETHANE - INTERNALLY					
001	**Prepare; one coat, polyurethane varnish, first coat on unprimed wood surfaces**					
002	General surfaces:					
	over 300 mm girth	0.23	3.45	1.06	**4.51**	m2
	not exceeding 150 mm girth	0.07	1.03	0.21	**1.24**	m
	150 - 300 mm girth	0.10	1.55	0.37	**1.92**	m
	isolated; not exceeding 0.50 m2	0.17	2.51	0.56	**3.07**	Nr

	Unit Rates	Man-Hours	Net Labour Price £	Net Mats Price £	Net Unit Price £	Unit
003	Glazed doors and screens in panes:					
	small - not exceeding 0.10 m2	0.60	9.07	0.67	**9.74**	m2
	medium - 0.10 - 0.50 m2	0.37	5.68	0.58	**6.26**	m2
	large - 0.50 - 1.00 m2	0.34	5.17	0.46	**5.63**	m2
	extra large - over 1.00 m2	0.32	4.82	0.36	**5.18**	m2
004	Windows in panes:					
	small - not exceeding 0.10 m2	0.65	9.86	0.89	**10.75**	m2
	medium - 0.10 - 0.50 m2	0.40	6.03	0.77	**6.80**	m2
	large - 0.50 - 1.00 m2	0.37	5.68	0.67	**6.35**	m2
	extra large - over 1.00 m2	0.34	5.17	0.58	**5.75**	m2
005	Frames, linings and associated mouldings:					
	over 300 mm girth	0.23	3.45	1.16	**4.61**	m2
	not exceeding 150 mm girth	0.07	1.03	0.21	**1.24**	m
	150 - 300 mm girth	0.10	1.55	0.41	**1.96**	m
006	Cornices:					
	over 300 mm girth	0.27	4.13	1.16	**5.29**	m2
	not exceeding 150 mm girth	0.08	1.20	0.21	**1.41**	m
	150 - 300 mm girth	0.13	1.90	0.41	**2.31**	m
007	Skirtings, dado rails, picture rails and the like:					
	over 300 mm girth	0.25	3.78	1.16	**4.94**	m2
	not exceeding 150 mm girth	0.08	1.14	0.23	**1.37**	m
	150 - 300 mm girth	0.11	1.72	0.41	**2.13**	m
008	Staircases:					
	over 300 mm girth	0.24	3.62	1.06	**4.68**	m2
	not exceeding 150 mm girth	0.07	1.08	0.21	**1.29**	m
	150 - 300 mm girth	0.11	1.64	0.37	**2.01**	m
009	Floor surfaces	0.06	0.87	1.06	**1.93**	m2
010	**Prepare; one coat polyurethane varnish, second and subsequent coats**					
011	General surfaces:					
	over 300 mm girth	0.19	2.93	0.85	**3.78**	m2
	not exceeding 150 mm girth	0.06	0.88	0.12	**1.00**	m
	150 - 300 mm girth	0.09	1.34	0.28	**1.62**	m
	isolated; not exceeding 0.50 m2	0.17	2.51	0.40	**2.91**	Nr
012	Glazed doors and screens in panes:					
	small - not exceeding 0.10	0.57	8.62	0.51	**9.13**	m2
	medium - 0.10 - 0.50 m2	0.34	5.17	0.42	**5.59**	m2
	large - 0.50 - 1.00 m2	0.31	4.65	0.36	**5.01**	m2
	extra large - over 1.00 m2	0.28	4.30	0.27	**4.57**	m2
013	Windows in panes:					
	small - not exceeding 0.10 m2	0.61	9.24	0.67	**9.91**	m2
	medium - 0.10 - 0.50 m2	0.36	5.52	0.61	**6.13**	m2
	large - 0.50 - 1.00 m2	0.34	5.17	0.51	**5.68**	m2
	extra large - over 1.00 m2	0.31	4.65	0.42	**5.07**	m2
014	Frames, linings and associated mouldings:					
	over 300 mm girth	0.19	2.93	0.91	**3.84**	m2
	not exceeding 150 mm girth	0.06	0.88	0.15	**1.03**	m
	150 - 300 mm girth	0.09	1.34	0.28	**1.62**	m
015	Cornices:					
	over 300 mm girth	0.23	3.45	0.91	**4.36**	m2
	not exceeding 150 mm girth	0.07	1.05	0.15	**1.20**	m
	150 - 300 mm girth	0.10	1.58	0.28	**1.86**	m
016	Skirtings, dado rails, picture rails and the like:					
	over 300 mm girth	0.21	3.22	0.91	**4.13**	m2
	not exceeding 150 mm girth	0.06	0.97	0.15	**1.12**	m
	150 - 300 mm girth	0.10	1.47	0.28	**1.75**	m
017	Staircases:					
	over 300 mm girth	0.20	3.09	0.85	**3.94**	m2
	not exceeding 150 mm girth	0.06	0.93	0.12	**1.05**	m
	150 - 300 mm girth	0.09	1.40	0.28	**1.68**	m
018	Floor surfaces	0.05	0.68	0.85	**1.53**	m2
	CLEAR FINISHES ON WOODWORK - INTERNALLY					
019	**Prepare; one coat Thermoguard fire varnish, unprimed wood surfaces**					
020	General surfaces:					
	over 300 mm girth	0.23	3.44	2.58	**6.02**	m2
	not exceeding 150 mm girth	0.07	1.08	0.39	**1.47**	m
	150 - 300 mm girth	0.11	1.63	0.77	**2.40**	m
	isolated; not exceeding 0.50 m2	0.14	2.07	1.17	**3.24**	nr
021	Fire resistant glazed doors, screens and windows:					
	small - not exceeding 0.10 m2	0.56	8.45	1.74	**10.19**	m2
	medium - 0.10 - 0.50 m2	0.39	5.95	1.43	**7.38**	m2

Unit Rates	Man-Hours	Net Labour Price £	Net Mats Price £	Net Unit Price £	Unit
large - 0.50 - 1.00 m2	0.34	5.17	1.17	**6.34**	m2
extra large - over 1.00 m2	0.32	4.85	10.29	**15.14**	m2
opening edge	0.07	1.10	0.28	**1.38**	m

022 Staircases:

over 300 mm girth	0.24	3.60	2.58	**6.18**	m2
not exceeding 150 mm girth	0.07	1.10	0.39	**1.49**	m
150 - 300 mm girth	0.11	1.72	0.77	**2.49**	m
isolated; not exceeding 0.5 m2	0.14	2.19	1.16	**3.35**	m
balustrade (measured both sides)	0.20	2.97	2.20	**5.17**	m2

023 **Prepare; one coat Thermoguard fire varnish, second and subsequent coats**

024 General surfaces:

over 300 mm girth	0.20	2.97	1.56	**4.53**	m2
not exceeding 150 mm girth	0.06	0.94	0.23	**1.17**	m
150 - 300 mm girth	0.09	1.41	0.47	**1.88**	m
isolated; not exceeding 0.50 m2	0.12	1.78	0.70	**2.48**	m

025 Fire resistant glazed doors, screens and windows:

small - not exceeding 0.10 m2	0.53	7.98	1.05	**9.03**	m2
medium - 0.10 - 0.50 m2	0.39	5.95	0.87	**6.82**	m2
large - 0.50 - 1.00 m2	0.34	5.17	0.71	**5.88**	m2
extra large - over 1.00 m2	0.28	4.31	0.64	**4.95**	m2
opening edge	0.07	1.10	0.16	**1.26**	m

026 Staircases:

over 300 mm girth	0.21	3.13	0.18	**3.31**	m2
not exceeding 150 mm girth	0.07	1.02	0.23	**1.25**	m
150 - 300 mm girth	0.10	1.57	0.47	**2.04**	m
isolated; not exceeding 0.5 m2	0.13	2.04	0.70	**2.74**	m
balustrade (measured both sides)	0.18	2.66	1.33	**3.99**	m2

VH **NEW WORK EXTERNALLY**

SEE ALSO SECTION VZ FOR COMPOSITE EXAMPLES

WALLS - EXTERNALLY

MASONRY SEALER - WALLS EXTERNALLY

001 **One coat of masonry sealer to unprimed surfaces**

002 To walls:

smooth concrete	0.17	2.58	1.41	**3.99**	m2
cement rendered	0.16	2.37	1.49	**3.86**	m2
fair face brickwork	0.20	3.09	1.60	**4.69**	m2
fair face blockwork	0.24	3.62	1.94	**5.56**	m2
rough cast/pebbledash rendered	0.30	4.53	3.21	**7.74**	m2
Tyrolean rendered	0.40	6.03	6.36	**12.39**	m2

PRIMER SEALER - WALLS EXTERNALLY

003 **One coat of acrylic primer/undercoat, to unprimed surfaces**

004 To walls:

smooth concrete	0.23	3.45	1.12	**4.57**	m2
cement rendered	0.20	3.02	1.18	**4.20**	m2
fair face brickwork	0.26	4.01	1.27	**5.28**	m2
fair face blockwork	0.32	4.82	1.54	**6.36**	m2
rough cast/pebbledash rendered	0.40	6.03	2.54	**8.57**	m2
Tyrolean rendered	0.53	8.03	5.04	**13.07**	m2

ALKALI RESISTING PRIMER - WALLS EXTERNALLY

005 **One coat of alkali resisting primer to unprimed surfaces**

006 To walls:

smooth concrete	0.23	3.45	1.48	**4.93**	m2
fibre cement	0.23	3.45	1.47	**4.92**	m2
cement rendered	0.20	3.02	1.93	**4.95**	m2
fair face brickwork	0.26	4.01	1.94	**5.95**	m2
fair face blockwork	0.32	4.82	2.67	**7.49**	m2
rough cast/pebbledash rendered	0.40	6.03	4.43	**10.46**	m2
Tyrolean rendered	0.53	8.03	8.78	**16.81**	m2

EMULSION PAINT, MATT - WALLS EXTERNALLY

007 **One coat of emulsion paint, matt finish (white); first coat to unprimed surfaces**

008 To walls:

smooth concrete	0.17	2.58	0.48	**3.06**	m2
fibre cement	0.17	2.58	0.47	**3.05**	m2
cement rendered	0.16	2.37	0.56	**2.93**	m2
fair face brickwork	0.20	3.09	0.63	**3.72**	m2
fair face blockwork	0.24	3.62	0.73	**4.35**	m2
rough cast/pebbledash rendered	0.30	4.53	1.66	**6.19**	m2
Tyrolean rendered	0.40	6.03	3.36	**9.39**	m2

	Man-Hours	Net Labour Price £	Net Mats Price £	Net Unit Price £	Unit
Unit Rates					

009 One coat of emulsion paint, matt finish (white); second and subsequent coats

010 To walls:

smooth concrete	0.12	1.79	0.43	**2.22**	m2
fibre cement	0.12	1.79	0.42	**2.21**	m2
cement rendered	0.11	1.64	0.47	**2.11**	m2
fair face brickwork	0.15	2.25	0.53	**2.78**	m2
fair face blockwork	0.17	2.54	0.59	**3.13**	m2
rough cast/pebbledash rendered	0.24	3.62	1.27	**4.89**	m2
Tyrolean rendered	0.30	4.53	2.52	**7.05**	m2

MASONRY PAINT - WALLS EXTERNALLY

011 **One coat of Masonry paint on sealed surfaces**

012 To walls:

smooth concrete	0.12	1.79	0.71	**2.50**	m2
fibre cement	0.12	1.79	0.70	**2.49**	m2
cement rendered	0.11	1.64	0.84	**2.48**	m2
fair face brickwork	0.15	2.25	0.85	**3.10**	m2
fair face blockwork	0.17	2.54	1.01	**3.55**	m2
rough cast/pebbledash rendered	0.24	3.62	1.24	**4.86**	m2
Tyrolean rendered	0.30	4.53	1.99	**6.52**	m2

013 **One coat of Masonry paint; first coat to unprimed surfaces**

014 To walls:

smooth concrete	0.18	2.66	0.41	**3.07**	m2
fibre cement	0.16	2.36	0.40	**2.76**	m2
cement rendered	0.16	2.36	0.46	**2.82**	m2
fair face brickwork	0.21	3.13	0.47	**3.60**	m2
fair face blockwork	0.24	3.60	0.56	**4.16**	m2
rough cast/pebbledash rendered	0.30	4.54	0.76	**5.30**	m2
Tyrolean rendered	0.39	5.94	1.52	**7.46**	m2

Note: 015 - 022 not used

SNOWCEM PAINT - WALLS EXTERNALLY

023 **One coat of Snowcem cement paint; first coat including base coat of stabilising solution to unprimed surfaces**

024 To walls:

smooth concrete	0.29	4.39	0.54	**4.93**	m2
fibre cement	0.29	4.39	0.52	**4.91**	m2
cement rendered	0.26	3.98	0.61	**4.59**	m2
fair face brickwork	0.35	5.34	0.64	**5.98**	m2
fair face blockwork	0.41	6.16	0.79	**6.95**	m2
rough cast/pebbledash rendered	0.54	8.15	1.12	**9.27**	m2
Tyrolean rendered	0.69	10.53	2.25	**12.78**	m2

025 **One coat of Snowcem cement paint; second and subsequent coats**

026 To walls:

smooth concrete	0.12	1.79	0.27	**2.06**	m2
fibre cement	0.12	1.79	0.25	**2.04**	m2
cement rendered	0.11	1.64	0.25	**1.89**	m2
fair face brickwork	0.15	2.25	0.27	**2.52**	m2
fair face blockwork	0.17	2.54	0.33	**2.87**	m2
rough cast/pebbledash rendered	0.24	3.62	0.38	**4.00**	m2
Tyrolean rendered	0.30	4.53	0.81	**5.34**	m2

SANDTEX MATT - WALLS EXTERNALLY

027 **One coat of Sandtex Matt including base coat of stabilising solution to unprimed surfaces**

028 To walls:

smooth concrete	0.29	4.39	1.57	**5.96**	m2
fibre cement	0.29	4.39	1.54	**5.93**	m2
cement rendered	0.26	3.98	1.83	**5.81**	m2
fair face brickwork	0.35	5.34	1.85	**7.19**	m2
fair face blockwork	0.41	6.16	1.53	**7.69**	m2

029 **One coat of Sandtex Fine Build textured finish**

030 To walls:

smooth concrete	0.23	3.45	3.83	**7.28**	m2
fibre cement	0.23	3.45	3.82	**7.27**	m2
cement rendered	0.22	3.27	4.77	**8.04**	m2
fair face brickwork	0.28	4.30	5.73	**10.03**	m2
fair face blockwork	0.31	4.65	5.74	**10.39**	m2

Unit Rates	Man-Hours	Net Labour Price £	Net Mats Price £	Net Unit Price £	Unit

VK **METALWORK - EXTERNALLY**					
METALWORK PRIMERS - EXTERNALLY					
001 **Prepare; one coat etching primer, metalwork surfaces, applied to a dry film thickness of 3 microns**					
002 General surfaces:					
over 300 mm girth	0.24	3.62	0.61	**4.23**	m2
not exceeding 150 mm girth	0.07	1.08	0.11	**1.19**	m
150 - 300 mm girth	0.11	1.64	0.22	**1.86**	m
isolated; not exceeding 0.50 m2	0.17	2.51	0.32	**2.83**	Nr
003 Glazed doors and screens in panes:					
small - not exceeding 0.10 m2	0.60	9.04	0.35	**9.39**	m2
medium - 0.10 - 0.50 m2	0.42	6.34	0.29	**6.63**	m2
large - 0.50 - 1.00 m2	0.39	5.97	0.24	**6.21**	m2
extra large - over 1.00 m2	0.36	5.43	0.24	**5.67**	m2
004 Windows in panes:					
small - not exceeding 0.10 m2	0.60	9.04	0.29	**9.33**	m2
medium - 0.10 - 0.50 m2	0.42	6.34	0.24	**6.58**	m2
large - 0.50 - 1.00 m2	0.39	5.97	0.24	**6.21**	m2
extra large - over 1.00 m2	0.36	5.43	0.18	**5.61**	m2
005 Edges of opening casements	0.06	0.91	0.05	**0.96**	m
006 Structural members:					
over 300 mm girth	0.27	4.16	0.61	**4.77**	m2
not exceeding 150 mm girth	0.08	1.23	0.11	**1.34**	m
150 - 300 mm girth	0.12	1.88	0.22	**2.10**	m
007 Each side of ornamental railings, gates and the like (grouped together) measured both sides overall regardless of voids:					
over 300 mm girth	0.18	2.80	1.37	**4.17**	m2
008 Pipes, conduits, ducting, trunking and the like:					
over 300 mm girth	0.26	3.98	0.72	**4.70**	m2
not exceeding 150 mm girth	0.08	1.19	0.11	**1.30**	m
150 - 300 mm girth	0.12	1.78	0.22	**2.00**	m
009 Eaves gutters:					
over 300 mm girth	0.26	3.98	0.72	**4.70**	m2
not exceeding 150 mm girth	0.08	1.19	0.11	**1.30**	m
150 - 300 mm girth	0.12	1.78	0.22	**2.00**	m
010 Staircases:					
over 300 mm girth	0.26	3.98	0.61	**4.59**	m2
not exceeding 150 mm girth	0.08	1.19	0.11	**1.30**	m
150 - 300 mm girth	0.12	1.78	0.22	**2.00**	m
011 **Prepare; one coat zinc phosphate primer, metalwork surfaces**					
012 General surfaces:					
over 300 mm girth	0.24	3.62	1.01	**4.63**	m2
not exceeding 150 mm girth	0.07	1.08	0.17	**1.25**	m
150 - 300 mm girth	0.11	1.64	0.29	**1.93**	m
isolated; not exceeding 0.50 m2	0.17	2.51	0.50	**3.01**	Nr
013 Glazed doors and screens in panes:					
small - not exceeding 0.10 m2	0.60	9.04	0.52	**9.56**	m2
medium - 0.10 - 0.50 m2	0.42	6.34	0.39	**6.73**	m2
large - 0.50 - 1.00 m2	0.39	5.97	0.35	**6.32**	m2
extra large - over 1.00 m2	0.36	5.43	0.31	**5.74**	m2
014 Windows in panes:					
small - not exceeding 0.10 m2	0.61	9.24	0.39	**9.63**	m2
medium - 0.10 - 0.50 m2	0.42	6.34	0.35	**6.69**	m2
large - 0.50 - 1.00 m2	0.39	5.97	0.31	**6.28**	m2
extra large - over 1.00 m2	0.36	5.43	0.27	**5.70**	m2
015 Edges of opening casements	0.06	0.91	0.08	**0.99**	m
016 Structural members:					
over 300 mm girth	0.27	4.16	1.01	**5.17**	m2
not exceeding 150 mm girth	0.08	1.23	0.17	**1.40**	m
150 - 300 mm girth	0.12	1.88	0.29	**2.17**	m
017 Each side of ornamental railings, gates and the like (grouped together) measured both sides overall regardless of voids:					
over 300 mm girth	0.18	2.80	0.68	**3.48**	m2
018 Pipes and conduits, ducting, trunking and the like:					
over 300 mm girth	0.26	3.98	1.05	**5.03**	m2
not exceeding 150 mm girth	0.08	1.19	0.17	**1.36**	m
150 - 300 mm girth	0.12	1.78	0.33	**2.11**	m
019 Eaves gutters:					
over 300 mm girth	0.26	3.98	1.05	**5.03**	m2

	Unit Rates	Man-Hours	Net Labour Price £	Net Mats Price £	Net Unit Price £	Unit
	not exceeding 150 mm girth	0.08	1.19	0.17	**1.36**	m
	150 - 300 mm girth	0.12	1.78	0.33	**2.11**	m
020	Staircases:					
	over 300 mm girth	0.26	3.98	1.01	**4.99**	m2
	not exceeding 150 mm girth	0.08	1.19	0.17	**1.36**	m
	150 - 300 mm girth	0.12	1.78	0.29	**2.07**	m
021	**Prepare; one coat zinc chromate primer, metalwork surfaces**					
022	General surfaces:					
	over 300 mm girth	0.24	3.62	0.94	**4.56**	m2
	not exceeding 150 mm girth	0.07	1.08	0.15	**1.23**	m
	150 - 300 mm girth	0.11	1.64	0.27	**1.91**	m
	isolated; not exceeding 0.50 m2	0.17	2.51	0.46	**2.97**	Nr
023	Glazed doors and screens in panes:					
	small - not exceeding 0.10 m2	0.60	9.04	0.48	**9.52**	m2
	medium - 0.10 - 0.50 m2	0.42	6.34	0.37	**6.71**	m2
	large - 0.50 - 1.00 m2	0.39	5.97	0.33	**6.30**	m2
	extra large - over 1.00 m2	0.36	5.43	0.29	**5.72**	m2
024	Windows in panes:					
	small - not exceeding 0.10 m2	0.60	9.04	0.37	**9.41**	m2
	medium - 0.10 - 0.50 m2	0.42	6.34	0.33	**6.67**	m2
	large - 0.50 - 1.00 m2	0.39	5.97	0.29	**6.26**	m2
	extra large - over 1.00 m2	0.36	5.43	0.25	**5.68**	m2
025	Edges of opening casements	0.06	0.91	0.08	**0.99**	m
026	Structural members:					
	over 300 mm girth	0.27	4.16	0.94	**5.10**	m2
	not exceeding 150 mm girth	0.08	1.23	0.15	**1.38**	m
	150 - 300 mm girth	0.12	1.88	0.27	**2.15**	m
027	Each side of ornamental railings, gates and the like (grouped together) measured both sides overall regardless of voids:					
	over 300 mm girth	0.18	2.80	0.63	**3.43**	m2
028	Pipes and conduits, ducting, trunking and the like:					
	over 300 mm girth	0.26	3.98	0.98	**4.96**	m2
	not exceeding 150 mm girth	0.08	1.19	0.15	**1.34**	m
	150 - 300 mm girth	0.12	1.78	0.30	**2.08**	m
029	Eaves gutters:					
	over 300 mm girth	0.26	3.98	0.98	**4.96**	m2
	not exceeding 150 mm girth	0.08	1.19	0.15	**1.34**	m
	150 - 300 mm girth	0.12	1.78	0.30	**2.08**	m
030	Staircases:					
	over 300 mm girth	0.26	3.98	0.94	**4.92**	m2
	not exceeding 150 mm girth	0.08	1.19	0.15	**1.34**	m
	150 - 300 mm girth	0.12	1.78	0.27	**2.05**	m
031	**Prepare; one coat zinc rich primer, metalwork surfaces**					
032	General surfaces:					
	over 300 mm girth	0.24	3.62	4.87	**8.49**	m2
	not exceeding 150 mm girth	0.07	1.08	0.81	**1.89**	m
	150 - 300 mm girth	0.11	1.64	1.41	**3.05**	m
	isolated; not exceeding 0.50 m2	0.17	2.51	2.42	**4.93**	Nr
033	Glazed doors and screens in panes:					
	small - not exceeding 0.10 m2	0.60	9.04	2.44	**11.48**	m2
	medium - 0.10 - 0.50 m2	0.42	6.34	1.84	**8.18**	m2
	large - 0.50 - 1.00 m2	0.39	5.97	1.64	**7.61**	m2
	extra large - over 1.00 m2	0.36	5.43	1.43	**6.86**	m2
034	Windows in panes:					
	small - not exceeding 0.10 m2	0.60	9.04	1.84	**10.88**	m2
	medium - 0.10 - 0.50 m2	0.42	6.34	1.64	**7.98**	m2
	large - 0.50 - 1.00 m2	0.39	5.97	1.43	**7.40**	m2
	extra large - over 1.00 m2	0.36	5.43	1.23	**6.66**	m2
035	Edges of opening casements	0.06	0.91	0.40	**1.31**	m
036	Structural members:					
	over 300 mm girth	0.27	4.16	4.87	**9.03**	m2
	not exceeding 150 mm girth	0.08	1.23	0.81	**2.04**	m
	150 - 300 mm girth	0.12	1.88	1.41	**3.29**	m
037	Pipes and conduits, ducting, trunking and the like:					
	over 300 mm girth	0.26	3.98	5.07	**9.05**	m2
	not exceeding 150 mm girth	0.08	1.19	0.81	**2.00**	m
	150 - 300 mm girth	0.12	1.78	1.61	**3.39**	m
038	Each side of ornamental railings, gates and the like (grouped together) measured both sides overall regardless of voids:					
	over 300 mm girth	0.18	2.80	3.25	**6.05**	m2

	Unit Rates	Man-Hours	Net Labour Price £	Net Mats Price £	Net Unit Price £	Unit
039	Eaves gutters:					
	over 300 mm girth	0.26	3.98	5.07	**9.05**	m2
	not exceeding 150 mm girth	0.08	1.19	0.81	**2.00**	m
	150 - 300 mm girth	0.12	1.78	1.61	**3.39**	m
040	Staircases:					
	over 300 mm girth	0.26	3.98	4.87	**8.85**	m2
	not exceeding 150 mm girth	0.08	1.19	0.81	**2.00**	m
	150 - 300 mm girth	0.12	1.78	1.41	**3.19**	m
041	**Prepare; one coat red oxide primer, metalwork surfaces**					
042	General surfaces:					
	over 300 mm girth	0.24	3.62	1.01	**4.63**	m2
	not exceeding 150 mm girth	0.07	1.08	0.16	**1.24**	m
	150 - 300 mm girth	0.11	1.64	0.29	**1.93**	m
	isolated; not exceeding 0.50 m2	0.17	2.51	0.49	**3.00**	Nr
043	Glazed doors and screens in panes:					
	small - not exceeding 0.10 m2	0.60	9.04	0.52	**9.56**	m2
	medium - 0.10 - 0.50 m2	0.42	6.34	0.39	**6.73**	m2
	large - 0.50 - 1.00 m2	0.39	5.97	0.35	**6.32**	m2
	extra large - over 1.00 m2	0.36	5.43	0.31	**5.74**	m2
044	Windows in panes:					
	small - not exceeding 0.10 m2	0.60	9.04	0.39	**9.43**	m2
	medium - 0.10 - 0.50 m2	0.42	6.34	0.35	**6.69**	m2
	large - 0.50 - 1.00 m2	0.39	5.97	0.31	**6.28**	m2
	extra large - over 1.00 m2	0.36	5.43	0.27	**5.70**	m2
045	Edges of opening casements	0.06	0.91	0.08	**0.99**	m
046	Structural members:					
	over 300 mm girth	0.27	4.16	1.01	**5.17**	m2
	not exceeding 150 mm girth	0.08	1.23	0.16	**1.39**	m
	150 - 300 mm girth	0.12	1.88	0.29	**2.17**	m
047	Each side of ornamental railings, gates and the like (grouped together) measured both sides overall regardless of voids:					
	over 300 mm girth	0.18	2.80	0.68	**3.48**	m2
048	Pipes and conduits, ducting, trunking and the like:					
	over 300 mm girth	0.26	3.98	1.05	**5.03**	m2
	not exceeding 150 mm girth	0.08	1.19	0.16	**1.35**	m
	150 - 300 mm girth	0.12	1.78	0.33	**2.11**	m
049	Eaves gutters:					
	over 300 mm girth	0.26	3.98	1.05	**5.03**	m2
	not exceeding 150 mm girth	0.08	1.19	0.16	**1.35**	m
	150 - 300 mm girth	0.12	1.78	0.33	**2.11**	m
050	Staircases:					
	over 300 mm girth	0.26	3.98	1.01	**4.99**	m2
	not exceeding 150 mm girth	0.08	1.19	0.16	**1.35**	m
	150 - 300 mm girth	0.12	1.78	0.29	**2.07**	m
051	**Prepare; one coat galvanising paint, metalwork surfaces, applied to a dry film thickness of 125 microns**					
052	General surfaces:					
	over 300 mm girth	0.21	3.13	1.90	**5.03**	m2
	not exceeding 150 mm girth	0.06	0.91	0.30	**1.21**	m
	150 - 300 mm girth	0.09	1.41	0.60	**2.01**	m
	isolated; not exceeding 0.50 m2	0.17	2.51	1.35	**3.86**	Nr
053	Glazed doors and screens in panes:					
	small - not exceeding 0.10 m2	0.62	9.36	1.07	**10.43**	m2
	medium - 0.10 - 0.50 m2	0.41	6.23	0.85	**7.08**	m2
	large - 0.50 - 1.00 m2	0.38	5.82	0.77	**6.59**	m2
	extra large - over 1.00 m2	0.34	5.20	0.62	**5.82**	m2
054	Windows in panes:					
	small - not exceeding 0.10 m2	0.62	9.36	0.85	**10.21**	m2
	medium - 0.10 - 0.50 m2	0.41	6.23	0.77	**7.00**	m2
	large - 0.50 - 1.00 m2	0.38	5.82	0.62	**6.44**	m2
	extra large - over 1.00 m2	0.34	5.20	0.55	**5.75**	m2
055	Edges of opening casements	0.07	1.09	0.15	**1.24**	m
056	Structural members:					
	over 300 mm girth	0.27	4.16	1.90	**6.06**	m2
	not exceeding 150 mm girth	0.08	1.23	0.30	**1.53**	m
	150 - 300 mm girth	0.12	1.88	0.60	**2.48**	m
057	Each side of ornamental railings, gates and the like (grouped together) measured both sides overall regardless of voids:					
	over 300 mm girth	0.16	2.43	1.90	**4.33**	m2

Unit Rates	Man-Hours	Net Labour Price £	Net Mats Price £	Net Unit Price £	Unit
058 Pipes and conduits, ducting, trunking and the like:					
over 300 mm girth	0.23	3.45	2.20	**5.65**	m2
not exceeding 150 mm girth	0.07	1.05	0.38	**1.43**	m
150 - 300 mm girth	0.10	1.54	0.75	**2.29**	m
059 Eaves gutters:					
over 300 mm girth	0.23	3.45	2.20	**5.65**	m2
not exceeding 150 mm girth	0.07	1.05	0.38	**1.43**	m
150 - 300 mm girth	0.10	1.54	0.75	**2.29**	m
060 Staircases:					
over 300 mm girth	0.27	4.16	1.90	**6.06**	m2
not exceeding 150 mm girth	0.08	1.23	0.30	**1.53**	m
150 - 300 mm girth	0.12	1.88	0.60	**2.48**	m
061 One coat of galvanising paint; second and subsequent coats to previously coated metalwork surfaces; applied to a film thickness of 125 microns					
062 General surfaces:					
over 300 mm girth	0.19	2.81	1.60	**4.41**	m2
not exceeding 150 mm girth	0.05	0.81	0.23	**1.04**	m
150 - 300 mm girth	0.08	1.22	0.53	**1.75**	m
isolated; not exceeding 0.50 m2	0.14	2.19	0.75	**2.94**	Nr
063 Glazed doors and screens in panes:					
small - not exceeding 0.10 m2	0.60	9.07	0.77	**9.84**	m2
medium - 0.10 - 0.50 m2	0.44	6.67	0.62	**7.29**	m2
large - 0.50 - 1.00 m2	0.41	6.23	0.55	**6.78**	m2
extra large - over 1.00 m2	0.37	5.59	0.47	**6.06**	m2
064 Windows in panes:					
small - not exceeding 0.10 m2	0.60	9.07	0.62	**9.69**	m2
medium - 0.10 - 0.50 m2	0.44	6.67	0.55	**7.22**	m2
large - 0.50 - 1.00 m2	0.41	6.23	0.47	**6.70**	m2
extra large - over 1.00 m2	0.37	5.59	0.40	**5.99**	m2
065 Edges of opening casements	0.07	1.00	0.15	**1.15**	m
066 Structural members:					
over 300 mm girth	0.25	3.86	1.60	**5.46**	m2
not exceeding 150 mm girth	0.07	1.12	0.23	**1.35**	m
150 - 300 mm girth	0.11	1.70	0.53	**2.23**	m
067 Each side of ornamental railings, gates and the like (grouped together) measured both sides overall regardless of voids:					
over 300 mm girth	0.14	2.19	1.90	**4.09**	m2
068 Pipes, conduits, ducting, trunking and the like:					
over 300 mm girth	0.21	3.15	1.90	**5.05**	m2
not exceeding 150 mm girth	0.06	0.90	0.30	**1.20**	m
150 - 300 mm girth	0.10	1.47	0.60	**2.07**	m
069 Eaves gutters:					
over 300 mm girth	0.21	3.15	1.90	**5.05**	m2
not exceeding 150 mm girth	0.06	0.90	0.30	**1.20**	m
150 - 300 mm girth	0.09	1.32	0.60	**1.92**	m
070 Staircases:					
over 300 mm girth	0.24	3.66	1.60	**5.26**	m2
not exceeding 150 mm girth	0.05	0.71	0.23	**0.94**	m
150 - 300 mm girth	0.12	1.75	0.53	**2.28**	m
METALWORK UNDERCOATS - EXTERNALLY					
071 One undercoat alkyd based paint; primed metalwork surfaces					
072 General surfaces:					
over 300 mm girth	0.19	2.89	0.56	**3.45**	m2
not exceeding 150 mm girth	0.05	0.82	0.09	**0.91**	m
150 - 300 mm girth	0.08	1.22	0.16	**1.38**	m
isolated; not exceeding 0.50 m2	0.17	2.51	0.25	**2.76**	Nr
073 Glazed doors and screens in panes:					
small - not exceeding 0.10 m2	0.54	8.15	0.27	**8.42**	m2
medium - 0.10 - 0.50 m2	0.36	5.43	0.24	**5.67**	m2
large - 0.50 - 1.00 m2	0.33	5.06	0.21	**5.27**	m2
extra large - over 1.00 m2	0.30	4.53	0.18	**4.71**	m2
074 Windows in panes:					
small - not exceeding 0.10 m2	0.54	8.15	0.24	**8.39**	m2
medium - 0.10 - 0.50 m2	0.36	5.43	0.21	**5.64**	m2
large - 0.50 - 1.00 m2	0.33	5.06	0.18	**5.24**	m2
extra large - over 1.00 m2	0.30	4.53	0.15	**4.68**	m2
075 Edges of opening casements	0.06	0.91	0.03	**0.94**	m
076 Structural members:					
over 300 mm girth					
not exceeding 150 mm girth	0.24	3.62	0.56	**4.18**	m2
	0.07	1.08	0.09	**1.17**	m

Unit Rates

		Man-Hours	Net Labour Price £	Net Mats Price £	Net Unit Price £	Unit
	150 - 300 mm girth	0.11	1.64	0.16	**1.80**	m
077	Each side of ornamental railings, gates and the like (grouped together) measured both sides overall regardless of voids:					
	over 300 mm girth	0.14	2.19	0.44	**2.63**	m2
078	Pipes and conduits, ducting, trunking and the like:					
	over 300 mm girth	0.20	2.98	0.59	**3.57**	m2
	not exceeding 150 mm girth	0.06	0.91	0.09	**1.00**	m
	150 - 300 mm girth	0.09	1.35	0.19	**1.54**	m
079	Eaves gutters:					
	over 300 mm girth	0.20	2.98	0.59	**3.57**	m2
	not exceeding 150 mm girth	0.06	0.91	0.09	**1.00**	m
	150 - 300 mm girth	0.09	1.35	0.16	**1.51**	m
080	Staircases:					
	over 300 mm girth	0.24	3.62	0.56	**4.18**	m2
	not exceeding 150 mm girth	0.07	1.08	0.09	**1.17**	m
	150 - 300 mm girth	0.11	1.64	0.16	**1.80**	m
	METALWORK GLOSS FINISH - EXTERNALLY					
081	**One coat alkyd based paint, gloss finish; undercoated metalwork surfaces**					
082	General surfaces:					
	over 300 mm girth	0.20	3.09	0.56	**3.65**	m2
	not exceeding 150 mm girth	0.06	0.93	0.09	**1.02**	m
	150 - 300 mm girth	0.09	1.40	0.16	**1.56**	m
	isolated; not exceeding 0.50 m2	0.17	2.51	0.25	**2.76**	Nr
083	Glazed doors and screens in panes:					
	small - not exceeding 0.10 m2	0.56	8.50	0.27	**8.77**	m2
	medium - 0.10 - 0.50 m2	0.38	5.79	0.24	**6.03**	m2
	large - 0.50 - 1.00 m2	0.36	5.43	0.21	**5.64**	m2
	extra large - over 1.00 m2	0.32	4.88	0.18	**5.06**	m2
084	Windows in panes:					
	small - not exceeding 0.10 m2	0.56	8.50	0.24	**8.74**	m2
	medium - 0.10 - 0.50 m2	0.38	5.79	0.21	**6.00**	m2
	large - 0.50 - 1.00 m2	0.36	5.43	0.18	**5.61**	m2
	extra large - over 1.00 m2	0.32	4.88	0.15	**5.03**	m2
085	Edges of opening casements	0.06	0.91	0.03	**0.94**	m
086	Structural members:					
	over 300 mm girth	0.26	3.98	0.56	**4.54**	m2
	not exceeding 150 mm girth	0.08	1.19	0.09	**1.28**	m
	150 - 300 mm girth	0.12	1.78	0.16	**1.94**	m
087	Each side of ornamental railings, gates and the like (grouped together) measured both sides overall regardless of voids:					
	over 300 mm girth	0.16	2.43	0.58	**3.01**	m2
088	Pipes and conduits, ducting, trunking and the like:					
	over 300 mm girth	0.22	3.37	0.59	**3.96**	m2
	not exceeding 150 mm girth	0.07	1.02	0.09	**1.11**	m
	150 - 300 mm girth	0.10	1.52	0.19	**1.71**	m
089	Eaves gutters:					
	over 300 mm girth	0.22	3.37	0.59	**3.96**	m2
	not exceeding 150 mm girth	0.07	1.02	0.09	**1.11**	m
	150 - 300 mm girth	0.10	1.52	0.19	**1.71**	m
090	Staircases:					
	over 300 mm girth	0.25	3.80	0.56	**4.36**	m2
	not exceeding 150 mm girth	0.08	1.14	0.09	**1.23**	m
	150 - 300 mm girth	0.11	1.72	0.16	**1.88**	m
	METALWORK PRIMER FINISH - EXTERNALLY					
091	**Prepare; one coat Hammerite No. 1 primer; metalwork surfaces**					
092	General surfaces:					
	over 300 mm girth	0.20	2.98	0.99	**3.97**	m2
	not exceeding 150 mm girth	0.06	0.90	0.12	**1.02**	m
	150 - 300 mm girth	0.09	1.35	0.25	**1.60**	m
	isolated; not exceeding 0.50 m2	0.06	0.94	0.43	**1.37**	Nr
093	Glazed doors and screens in panes:					
	small - not exceeding 0.10 m2	0.56	8.45	0.45	**8.90**	m2
	medium - 0.10 - 0.50 m2	0.38	5.79	0.35	**6.14**	m2
	large - 0.50 - 1.00 m2	0.37	5.55	0.35	**5.90**	m2
	extra large - over 1.00 m2	0.33	4.97	0.28	**5.25**	m2
094	Windows in panes:					
	small - not exceeding 0.10 m2	0.56	8.45	0.35	**8.80**	m2
	medium - 0.10 - 0.50 m2	0.38	5.79	0.32	**6.11**	m2
	large - 0.50 - 1.00 m2	0.37	5.55	0.28	**5.83**	m2

			Man-Hours	Net Labour Price £	Net Mats Price £	Net Unit Price £	Unit
		Unit Rates					
		extra large - over 1.00 m2	0.33	4.97	0.26	**5.23**	m2
095		Structural members:					
		over 300 mm girth	0.26	3.97	0.75	**4.72**	m2
		not exceeding 150 mm girth	0.08	1.19	0.13	**1.32**	m
		150 - 300 mm girth	0.12	1.78	0.26	**2.04**	m
096		Members of roof trusses:					
		over 300 mm girth	0.33	5.02	1.00	**6.02**	m2
		not exceeding 150 mm girth	0.11	1.60	0.17	**1.77**	m
		150 - 300 mm girth	0.16	2.42	0.33	**2.75**	m
097		Edges of opening casements	0.06	0.94	0.10	**1.04**	m
098		Each side of ornamental railings, gates and the like (grouped together) measured both sides overall regardless of voids:					
		over 300 mm girth	0.16	2.43	0.90	**3.33**	m2
099		Pipes and conduits, ducting, trunking and the like:					
		over 300 mm girth	0.22	3.27	0.94	**4.21**	m2
		not exceeding 150 mm girth	0.07	1.00	0.17	**1.17**	m
		150 - 300 mm girth	0.10	1.47	0.33	**1.80**	m
100		Staircases:					
		over 300 mm girth	0.26	3.97	0.75	**4.72**	m2
		not exceeding 150 mm girth	0.08	1.19	0.13	**1.32**	m
		150 - 300 mm girth	0.12	1.78	0.26	**2.04**	m
VL		**WOODWORK - EXTERNALLY**					
		WOODWORK PRIMERS - EXTERNALLY					
001		**Prepare, knotting, stopping; one coat aluminium wood primer, wood surfaces**					
002		General surfaces:					
		over 300 mm girth	0.24	3.62	1.04	**4.66**	m2
		not exceeding 150 mm girth	0.07	1.08	0.17	**1.25**	m
		150 - 300 mm girth	0.11	1.64	0.28	**1.92**	m
		isolated; not exceeding 0.50 m2	0.17	2.51	0.53	**3.04**	Nr
003		Glazed doors and screens in panes:					
		small - not exceeding 0.10 m2	0.54	8.15	0.65	**8.80**	m2
		medium - 0.10 - 0.50 m2	0.39	5.97	0.55	**6.52**	m2
		large - 0.50 - 1.00 m2	0.36	5.43	0.41	**5.84**	m2
		extra large - over 1.00 m2	0.33	5.06	0.30	**5.36**	m2
004		Windows in panes:					
		small - not exceeding 0.10 m2	0.60	9.04	0.83	**9.87**	m2
		medium - 0.10 - 0.50 m2	0.42	6.34	0.76	**7.10**	m2
		large - 0.50 - 1.00 m2	0.39	5.97	0.65	**6.62**	m2
		extra large - over 1.00 m2	0.36	5.43	0.55	**5.98**	m2
005		Edges of opening casements	0.06	0.91	0.14	**1.05**	m
006		Frames, linings and associated mouldings:					
		over 300 mm girth	0.24	3.62	1.04	**4.66**	m2
		not exceeding 150 mm girth	0.07	1.08	0.17	**1.25**	m
		150 - 300 mm girth	0.11	1.64	0.28	**1.92**	m
007		**Prepare, knotting, stopping; one coat wood primer, wood surfaces**					
008		General surfaces:					
		over 300 mm girth	0.24	3.62	1.08	**4.70**	m2
		not exceeding 150 mm girth	0.07	1.08	0.18	**1.26**	m
		150 - 300 mm girth	0.11	1.64	0.29	**1.93**	m
		isolated; not exceeding 0.50 m2	0.17	2.51	0.55	**3.06**	Nr
009		Glazed doors and screens in panes:					
		small - not exceeding 0.10 m2	0.54	8.15	0.68	**8.83**	m2
		medium - 0.10 - 0.50 m2	0.39	5.97	0.57	**6.54**	m2
		large - 0.50 - 1.00 m2	0.36	5.43	0.42	**5.85**	m2
		extra large - over 1.00 m2	0.33	5.06	0.31	**5.37**	m2
010		Windows in panes:					
		small - not exceeding 0.10 m2	0.60	9.04	0.86	**9.90**	m2
		medium - 0.10 - 0.50 m2	0.42	6.34	0.78	**7.12**	m2
		large - 0.50 - 1.00 m2	0.39	5.97	0.68	**6.65**	m2
		extra large - over 1.00 m2	0.36	5.43	0.57	**6.00**	m2
011		Edges of opening casements	0.06	0.91	0.14	**1.05**	m
012		Frames, linings and associated mouldings:					
		over 300 mm girth	0.24	3.62	1.08	**4.70**	m2
		not exceeding 150 mm girth	0.07	1.08	0.18	**1.26**	m
		150 - 300 mm girth	0.11	1.64	0.29	**1.93**	m

Unit Rates	Man-Hours	Net Labour Price £	Net Mats Price £	Net Unit Price £	Unit
013 **Prepare, knotting, stopping; one coat acrylic wood primer, wood surfaces**					
014 General surfaces:					
over 300 mm girth	0.24	3.62	1.63	**5.25**	m2
not exceeding 150 mm girth	0.07	1.08	0.26	**1.34**	m
150 - 300 mm girth	0.11	1.64	0.45	**2.09**	m
isolated; not exceeding 0.50 m2	0.17	2.51	0.84	**3.35**	Nr
015 Glazed doors and screens in panes:					
small - not exceeding 0.10 m2	0.54	8.15	1.02	**9.17**	m2
medium - 0.10 - 0.50 m2	0.39	5.97	0.86	**6.83**	m2
large - 0.50 - 1.00 m2	0.36	5.43	0.63	**6.06**	m2
extra large - over 1.00 m2	0.33	5.06	0.47	**5.53**	m2
016 Windows in panes:					
small - not exceeding 0.10 m2	0.60	9.04	1.31	**10.35**	m2
medium - 0.10 - 0.50 m2	0.42	6.34	1.18	**7.52**	m2
large - 0.50 - 1.00 m2	0.39	5.97	1.02	**6.99**	m2
extra large - over 1.00 m2	0.36	5.43	0.86	**6.29**	m2
017 Edges of opening casements	0.06	0.91	0.19	**1.10**	m
018 Frames, linings and associated mouldings:					
over 300 mm girth	0.24	3.62	1.63	**5.25**	m2
not exceeding 150 mm girth	0.07	1.08	0.26	**1.34**	m
150 - 300 mm girth	0.11	1.64	0.45	**2.09**	m
WOODWORK UNDERCOAT - EXTERNALLY					
019 **One undercoat alkyd based paint, white; primed wood surfaces**					
020 General surfaces:					
over 300 mm girth	0.19	2.89	0.56	**3.45**	m2
not exceeding 150 mm girth	0.05	0.82	0.09	**0.91**	m
150 - 300 mm girth	0.08	1.22	0.16	**1.38**	m
isolated; not exceeding 0.50 m2	0.16	2.36	0.25	**2.61**	Nr
021 Glazed doors and screens in panes:					
small - not exceeding 0.10 m2	0.48	7.24	0.34	**7.58**	m2
medium - 0.10 - 0.50 m2	0.33	5.06	0.27	**5.33**	m2
large - 0.50 - 1.00 m2	0.30	4.53	0.24	**4.77**	m2
extra large - over 1.00 m2	0.27	4.16	0.18	**4.34**	m2
022 Windows in panes:					
small - not exceeding 0.10 m2	0.54	8.15	0.43	**8.58**	m2
medium - 0.10 - 0.50 m2	0.36	5.43	0.40	**5.83**	m2
large - 0.50 - 1.00 m2	0.33	5.06	0.34	**5.40**	m2
extra large - over 1.00 m2	0.30	4.53	0.27	**4.80**	m2
023 Edges of opening casements	0.06	0.91	0.03	**0.94**	m
024 Frames, linings and associated mouldings:					
over 300 mm girth	0.18	2.72	0.56	**3.28**	m2
not exceeding 150 mm girth	0.05	0.82	0.09	**0.91**	m
150 - 300 mm girth	0.08	1.22	0.16	**1.38**	m
Note: 025 not used					
WOODWORK ALKYD BASED GLOSS FINISH - EXTERNALLY					
026 **One coat alkyd based paint, gloss finish; undercoated wood surfaces**					
027 General surfaces:					
over 300 mm girth	0.20	3.09	0.56	**3.65**	m2
not exceeding 150 mm girth	0.06	0.93	0.09	**1.02**	m
150 - 300 mm girth	0.09	1.40	0.16	**1.56**	m
isolated; not exceeding 0.50 m2	0.16	2.36	0.25	**2.61**	Nr
028 Glazed doors and screens in panes:					
small - not exceeding 0.10 m2	0.50	7.60	0.34	**7.94**	m2
medium - 0.10 - 0.50 m2	0.36	5.43	0.27	**5.70**	m2
large - 0.50 - 1.00 m2	0.32	4.88	0.24	**5.12**	m2
extra large - over 1.00 m2	0.30	4.53	0.18	**4.71**	m2
029 Windows in panes:					
small - not exceeding 0.10 m2	0.56	8.50	0.43	**8.93**	m2
medium - 0.10 - 0.50 m2	0.38	5.79	0.40	**6.19**	m2
large - 0.50 - 1.00 m2	0.36	5.43	0.34	**5.77**	m2
extra large - over 1.00 m2	0.32	4.88	0.27	**5.15**	m2
030 Edges of opening casements	0.06	0.91	0.03	**0.94**	m
031 Frames, linings and associated mouldings:					
over 300 mm girth	0.20	3.09	0.56	**3.65**	m2
not exceeding 150 mm girth	0.06	0.93	0.09	**1.02**	m
150 - 300 mm girth	0.09	1.40	0.16	**1.56**	m
Note: 032 not used					

Unit Rates	Man-Hours	Net Labour Price £	Net Mats Price £	Net Unit Price £	Unit

VARNISH ON WOODWORK - EXTERNALLY

033 Prepare; one coat external grade varnish, wood surfaces; first coat to unprimed wood surfaces

034 General surfaces:					
over 300 mm girth	0.24	3.62	1.46	**5.08**	m2
not exceeding 150 mm girth	0.07	1.08	0.29	**1.37**	m
150 - 300 mm girth	0.11	1.64	0.51	**2.15**	m
isolated; not exceeding 0.50 m2	0.17	2.51	0.76	**3.27**	Nr
035 Glazed doors and screens in panes:					
small - not exceeding 0.10 m2	0.61	9.24	0.91	**10.15**	m2
medium - 0.10 - 0.50 m2	0.39	5.97	0.79	**6.76**	m2
large - 0.50 - 1.00 m2	0.36	5.43	0.62	**6.05**	m2
extra large - over 1.00 m2	0.33	5.06	0.48	**5.54**	m2
036 Windows in panes:					
small - not exceeding 0.10 m2	0.66	10.02	1.21	**11.23**	m2
medium - 0.10 - 0.50 m2	0.42	6.34	1.04	**7.38**	m2
large - 0.50 - 1.00 m2	0.39	5.97	0.91	**6.88**	m2
extra large - over 1.00 m2	0.36	5.43	0.79	**6.22**	m2
037 Edges of opening casements	0.06	0.91	0.12	**1.03**	m
038 Frames, linings and associated mouldings:					
over 300 mm girth	0.24	3.62	1.59	**5.21**	m2
not exceeding 150 mm girth	0.07	1.08	0.29	**1.37**	m
150 - 300 mm girth	0.11	1.64	0.55	**2.19**	m

039 Prepare; one coat external grade varnish, wood surfaces; second and subsequent coats

040 General surfaces:					
over 300 mm girth	0.20	3.09	1.18	**4.27**	m2
not exceeding 150 mm girth	0.06	0.93	0.17	**1.10**	m
150 - 300 mm girth	0.09	1.40	0.38	**1.78**	m
isolated; not exceeding 0.50 m2	0.16	2.36	0.56	**2.92**	Nr
041 Glazed doors and screens in panes:					
small - not exceeding 0.10 m2	0.58	8.77	0.71	**9.48**	m2
medium - 0.10 - 0.50 m2	0.36	5.43	0.58	**6.01**	m2
large - 0.50 - 1.00 m2	0.32	4.88	0.49	**5.37**	m2
extra large - over 1.00 m2	0.30	4.53	0.36	**4.89**	m2
042 Windows in panes:					
small - not exceeding 0.10 m2	0.63	9.55	0.92	**10.47**	m2
medium - 0.10 - 0.50 m2	0.38	5.79	0.83	**6.62**	m2
large - 0.50 - 1.00 m2	0.36	5.43	0.71	**6.14**	m2
extra large - over 1.00 m2	0.32	4.88	0.58	**5.46**	m2
043 Edges of opening casements	0.06	0.91	0.09	**1.00**	m
044 Frames, linings and associated mouldings:					
over 300 mm girth	0.20	3.09	1.26	**4.35**	m2
not exceeding 150 mm girth	0.06	0.93	0.21	**1.14**	m
150 - 300 mm girth	0.09	1.40	0.38	**1.78**	m

OIL ON WOODWORK - EXTERNALLY

045 Prepare; one coat raw linseed oil, general wood surfaces

046 First coat to untreated surfaces:					
Wrought softwood:					
over 300 mm girth	0.14	2.07	0.30	**2.37**	m2
not exceeding 150 mm girth	0.03	0.52	0.04	**0.56**	m
150 - 300 mm girth	0.06	0.87	0.08	**0.95**	m
isolated; not exceeding 0.50 m2	0.08	1.25	0.14	**1.39**	Nr
Sawn softwood:					
over 300 mm girth	0.17	2.58	0.39	**2.97**	m2
not exceeding 150 mm girth	0.05	0.68	0.07	**0.75**	m
150 - 300 mm girth	0.07	1.03	0.09	**1.12**	m
isolated; not exceeding 0.50 m2	0.10	1.57	0.19	**1.76**	Nr
047 Second and subsequent coats:					
Wrought softwood:					
over 300 mm girth	0.14	2.07	0.26	**2.33**	m2
not exceeding 150 mm girth	0.03	0.52	0.04	**0.56**	m
150 - 300 mm girth	0.06	0.87	0.07	**0.94**	m
isolated; not exceeding 0.50 m2	0.08	1.25	0.13	**1.38**	Nr
Sawn softwood:					
over 300 mm girth	0.17	2.58	0.34	**2.92**	m2
not exceeding 150 mm girth	0.05	0.68	0.05	**0.73**	m
150 - 300 mm girth	0.07	1.03	0.08	**1.11**	m
isolated; not exceeding 0.50 m2	0.10	1.57	0.15	**1.72**	Nr

Unit Rates	Man-Hours	Net Labour Price £	Net Mats Price £	Net Unit Price £	Unit
048	**Prepare; one coat boiled linseed oil, general wood surfaces**				
049	First coat to untreated surfaces:				
	Wrought softwood:				
	over 300 mm girth	0.14	2.07	0.33	**2.40**	m2
	not exceeding 150 mm girth	0.03	0.52	0.05	**0.57**	m
	150 - 300 mm girth	0.06	0.87	0.09	**0.96**	m
	isolated; not exceeding 0.50 m2	0.08	1.25	0.01	**1.26**	Nr
	Sawn softwood:				
	over 300 mm girth	0.17	2.58	0.44	**3.02**	m2
	not exceeding 150 mm girth	0.05	0.68	0.07	**0.75**	m
	150 - 300 mm girth	0.07	1.03	0.10	**1.13**	m
	isolated; not exceeding 0.50 m2	0.10	1.57	0.21	**1.78**	Nr
050	Second and subsequent coats:				
	Wrought softwood:				
	over 300 mm girth	0.14	2.07	0.29	**2.36**	m2
	not exceeding 150 mm girth	0.03	0.52	0.05	**0.57**	m
	150 - 300 mm girth	0.06	0.87	0.07	**0.94**	m
	isolated; not exceeding 0.50 m2	0.08	1.25	0.15	**1.40**	Nr
	Sawn softwood:				
	over 300 mm girth	0.17	2.58	0.38	**2.96**	m2
	not exceeding 150 mm girth	0.05	0.68	0.06	**0.74**	m
	150 - 300 mm girth	0.07	1.03	0.09	**1.12**	m
	isolated; not exceeding 0.50 m2	0.10	1.57	0.17	**1.74**	Nr

Note: 051 not used

CUPRINOL ON WOODWORK - EXTERNALLY

052	**Prepare; one coat Cuprinol clear wood preserver, general wood surfaces**				
053	Wrought softwood:				
	over 300 mm girth	0.14	2.07	0.97	**3.04**	m2
	not exceeding 150 mm girth	0.03	0.52	0.12	**0.64**	m
	150 - 300 mm girth	0.06	0.87	0.24	**1.11**	m
	isolated; not exceeding 0.50 m2	0.08	1.25	0.12	**1.37**	Nr
054	Sawn softwood:				
	over 300 mm girth	0.17	2.58	1.57	**4.15**	m2
	not exceeding 150 mm girth	0.05	0.68	0.24	**0.92**	m
	150 - 300 mm girth	0.07	1.03	0.47	**1.50**	m
	isolated; not exceeding 0.50 m2	0.10	1.57	0.24	**1.81**	Nr
055	**Prepare; one coat Cuprinol light oak/dark oak wood preserver general wood surfaces**				
056	Wrought softwood:				
	over 300 mm girth	0.14	2.07	0.97	**3.04**	m2
	not exceeding 150 mm girth	0.03	0.52	0.12	**0.64**	m
	150 - 300 mm girth	0.06	0.87	0.24	**1.11**	m
	isolated; not exceeding 0.50 m2	0.08	1.25	0.12	**1.37**	Nr
057	Sawn softwood:				
	over 300 mm girth	0.17	2.58	1.57	**4.15**	m2
	not exceeding 150 mm girth	0.05	0.68	0.24	**0.92**	m
	150 - 300 mm girth	0.07	1.03	0.47	**1.50**	m
	isolated; not exceeding 0.50 m2	0.10	1.57	0.24	**1.81**	Nr

Note: 058 - 060 not used

061	**Prepare; one coat Cuprinol exterior wood preserver, general wood surfaces**				
062	Wrought softwood:				
	over 300 mm girth	0.14	2.07	1.03	**3.10**	m2
	not exceeding 150 mm girth	0.03	0.52	0.13	**0.65**	m
	150 - 300 mm girth	0.06	0.87	0.25	**1.12**	m
	isolated; not exceeding 0.50 m2	0.08	1.25	0.45	**1.70**	Nr
063	Sawn softwood:				
	over 300 mm girth	0.17	2.58	1.84	**4.42**	m2
	not exceeding 150 mm girth	0.05	0.68	0.23	**0.91**	m
	150 - 300 mm girth	0.07	1.03	0.45	**1.48**	m
	isolated; not exceeding 0.50 m2	0.10	1.57	0.90	**2.47**	Nr
064	**Prepare; one coat Cuprinol red cedar wood preservative, general wood surfaces**				
065	Wrought softwood:				
	over 300 mm girth	0.14	2.07	0.54	**2.61**	m2
	not exceeding 150 mm girth	0.03	0.52	0.17	**0.69**	m
	150 - 300 mm girth	0.06	0.87	0.17	**1.04**	m
	isolated; not exceeding 0.50 m2	0.08	1.25	0.34	**1.59**	Nr
066	Sawn softwood:				
	over 300 mm girth	0.17	2.58	1.05	**3.63**	m2
	not exceeding 150 mm girth	0.05	0.68	0.17	**0.85**	m
	150 - 300 mm girth	0.07	1.03	0.34	**1.37**	m
	isolated; not exceeding 0.50 m2	0.10	1.57	0.52	**2.09**	Nr

		Man-Hours	Net Labour Price £	Net Mats Price £	Net Unit Price £	Unit
Unit Rates						
067	**Prepare; one coat Cuprinol Premier 5 wood stain, general wood surfaces**					
068	Wrought softwood:					
	over 300 mm girth	0.14	2.07	0.18	**2.25**	m2
	not exceeding 150 mm girth	0.03	0.52	0.08	**0.60**	m
	150 - 300 mm girth	0.06	0.87	0.08	**0.95**	m
	isolated; not exceeding 0.50 m2	0.08	1.25	0.08	**1.33**	Nr
069	Sawn softwood:					
	over 300 mm girth	0.17	2.58	0.35	**2.93**	m2
	not exceeding 150 mm girth	0.05	0.68	0.08	**0.76**	m
	150 - 300 mm girth	0.07	1.03	0.08	**1.11**	m
	isolated; not exceeding 0.50 m2	0.10	1.57	0.16	**1.73**	Nr
070	**Prepare; one coat Cuprinol Select woodstain, general wood surfaces**					
071	Wrought softwood:					
	over 300 mm girth	0.14	2.07	0.77	**2.84**	m2
	not exceeding 150 mm girth	0.03	0.52	0.15	**0.67**	m
	150 - 300 mm girth	0.06	0.87	0.22	**1.09**	m
	isolated; not exceeding 0.50 m2	0.08	1.25	0.37	**1.62**	Nr
072	Sawn softwood:					
	over 300 mm girth	0.17	2.58	1.31	**3.89**	m2
	not exceeding 150 mm girth	0.05	0.68	0.22	**0.90**	m
	150 - 300 mm girth	0.07	1.03	0.52	**1.55**	m
	isolated; not exceeding 0.50 m2	0.10	1.57	0.75	**2.32**	Nr
	SADOLIN ON WOODWORK - EXTERNALLY					
073	**Prepare, two coats Sadolin Base and two coats Sadolin Extra; general wood surfaces**					
074	To untreated surfaces of wrought softwood:					
	over 300 mm girth	0.54	8.27	1.85	**10.12**	m2
	not exceeding 150 mm girth	0.14	2.07	0.47	**2.54**	m
	150 - 300 mm girth	0.26	3.92	0.70	**4.62**	m
	isolated; not exceeding 0.50 m2	0.33	5.02	0.94	**5.96**	Nr
075	**Prepare, two coats Sadolin Extra; general wood surfaces**					
076	To untreated surfaces of wrought hardwood:					
	over 300 mm girth	0.27	4.07	1.57	**5.64**	m2
	not exceeding 150 mm girth	0.07	1.02	0.23	**1.25**	m
	150 - 300 mm girth	0.11	1.69	0.47	**2.16**	m
	isolated; not exceeding 0.50 m2	0.14	2.19	0.70	**2.89**	Nr
077	**Prepare, one coat Sadolin Base and two coats Sadolin Superdec; general wood surfaces**					
078	To untreated surfaces of wrought softwood:					
	over 300 mm girth	0.40	6.11	2.73	**8.84**	m2
	not exceeding 150 mm girth	0.10	1.52	0.77	**2.29**	m
	150 - 300 mm girth	0.17	2.55	1.18	**3.73**	m
	isolated; not exceeding 0.50 m2	0.21	3.13	1.58	**4.71**	Nr
079	**Prepare, one coat Sadolin Base and two coats Sadolin Classic; general wood surfaces**					
080	To untreated surfaces of wrought softwood:					
	over 300 mm girth	0.40	6.11	3.12	**9.23**	m2
	not exceeding 150 mm girth	0.10	1.52	0.70	**2.22**	m
	150 - 300 mm girth	0.17	2.55	0.94	**3.49**	m
	isolated; not exceeding 0.50 m2	0.21	3.13	1.64	**4.77**	Nr
VN	**DECORATIVE PAPER AND SHEET PLASTIC OR FABRIC LININGS - INTERNALLY**					
001	**Preparing and sizing surfaces prior to hanging paper**					
002	Walls over 300 mm wide:					
	generally	0.09	1.43	0.15	**1.58**	m2
	3.50 - 5.00 m high where ceiling is of dissimilar finish	0.10	1.52	0.15	**1.67**	m2
	staircase areas	0.10	1.52	0.15	**1.67**	m2
003	Ceilings over 300 mm wide:					
	generally	0.11	1.72	0.15	**1.87**	m2
	3.50 - 5.00 m high	0.12	1.84	0.15	**1.99**	m2
	staircase areas	0.12	1.84	0.15	**1.99**	m2
004	**Providing and hanging**					
005	Plain lining paper P.C. £2.10 per roll:					
	walls over 300 mm wide:					
	generally	0.23	3.45	0.62	**4.07**	m2
	3.50 - 5.00 m high where ceiling is of dissimilar finish	0.28	4.30	0.62	**4.92**	m2
	staircase areas	0.28	4.30	0.62	**4.92**	m2
	ceilings over 300 mm wide:					
	generally	0.29	4.47	0.62	**5.09**	m2
	3.50 - 5.00 m high	0.34	5.17	0.62	**5.79**	m2
	staircase areas	0.34	5.17	0.62	**5.79**	m2

	Unit Rates	Man-Hours	Net Labour Price £	Net Mats Price £	Net Unit Price £	Unit
006	Woodchip paper P.C. £2.10 per roll:					
	walls over 300 mm wide:					
	generally	0.25	3.78	0.60	**4.38**	m2
	3.50 - 5.00 m high where ceiling is of dissimilar finish	0.31	4.65	0.60	**5.25**	m2
	staircase areas	0.31	4.65	0.60	**5.25**	m2
	ceilings over 300 mm wide:					
	generally	0.32	4.80	0.60	**5.40**	m2
	3.50 - 5.00 m high	0.36	5.52	0.60	**6.12**	m2
	staircase areas	0.36	5.52	0.60	**6.12**	m2
007	Heavy embossed wallpaper P.C. £9.92 per roll:					
	walls over 300 mm wide:					
	generally	0.30	4.54	2.56	**7.10**	m2
	3.50 - 5.00 m high where ceiling is of dissimilar finish	0.36	5.52	2.56	**8.08**	m2
	staircase areas	0.36	5.52	2.56	**8.08**	m2
	ceilings over 300 mm wide:					
	generally	0.37	5.64	2.56	**8.20**	m2
	3.50 - 5.00 m high	0.42	6.37	2.56	**8.93**	m2
	staircase areas	0.42	6.37	2.56	**8.93**	m2
008	**Providing and hanging decorative paper**					
009	Vinyl surfaced wallpaper P.C. £12.13 per roll:					
	walls over 300 mm wide:					
	generally	0.30	4.61	3.65	**8.26**	m2
	3.50 - 5.00 m high where ceiling is of dissimilar finish	0.36	5.52	3.65	**9.17**	m2
	staircase areas	0.36	5.52	3.65	**9.17**	m2
	ceilings over 300 mm wide:					
	generally	0.37	5.67	3.65	**9.32**	m2
	3.50 - 5.00 m high	0.42	6.37	3.65	**10.02**	m2
	staircase areas	0.42	6.37	3.65	**10.02**	m2
010	Ready pasted vinyl surfaced wallpaper P.C. £15.43 per roll:					
	walls over 300 mm wide:					
	generally	0.28	4.27	4.27	**8.54**	m2
	3.50 - 5.00 m high where ceiling is of dissimilar finish	0.34	5.17	4.27	**9.44**	m2
	staircase areas	0.34	5.17	4.27	**9.44**	m2
	ceilings over 300 mm wide:					
	generally	0.35	5.32	4.27	**9.59**	m2
	3.50 - 5.00 m high	0.40	6.06	4.27	**10.33**	m2
	staircase areas	0.40	6.06	4.27	**10.33**	m2
011	Average quality wallpaper P.C. £13.23 per roll:					
	walls over 300 mm wide:					
	generally	0.30	4.54	3.95	**8.49**	m2
	3.50 - 5.00 m high where ceiling is of dissimilar finish	0.36	5.44	3.95	**9.39**	m2
	staircase areas	0.36	5.44	3.95	**9.39**	m2
	ceilings over 300 mm wide:					
	generally	0.37	5.61	3.95	**9.56**	m2
	3.50 - 5.00 m high	0.42	6.38	3.95	**10.33**	m2
	staircase areas	0.42	6.38	3.95	**10.33**	m2
012	Blown nylon surfaced paper P.C. £8.26 per roll:					
	walls over 300 mm wide:					
	generally	0.31	4.70	2.65	**7.35**	m2
	3.50 - 5.00 m high where ceiling is of dissimilar finish	0.37	5.64	2.65	**8.29**	m2
	staircase areas	0.37	5.64	2.65	**8.29**	m2
	ceilings over 300 mm wide:					
	generally	0.38	5.79	2.65	**8.44**	m2
	3.50 - 5.00 m high	0.43	6.58	2.65	**9.23**	m2
	staircase areas	0.43	6.58	2.65	**9.23**	m2
013	**Providing and hanging wide-width textile wall coverings; to walls with Grade 3 adhesive**					
014	High quality textile P.C. £29.15 per square metre:					
	walls over 300 mm wide:					
	generally	0.34	5.09	37.69	**42.78**	m2
	3.50 - 5.00 m high where ceiling is of dissimilar finish	0.39	5.93	37.69	**43.62**	m2
	staircase areas	0.39	5.93	37.69	**43.62**	m2
015	Mid range textile P.C. £21.84 per square metre:					
	walls over 300 mm wide:					
	generally	0.34	5.09	28.40	**33.49**	m2
	3.50 - 5.00 m high where ceiling is of dissimilar finish	0.39	5.93	28.40	**34.33**	m2
	staircase areas	0.39	5.93	28.40	**34.33**	m2
016	**Providing and hanging wide-width glass fibre wall coverings; to walls with Grade 2 adhesive**					
017	P.C. £5.68 per square metre:					
	walls over 300 mm wide:					
	generally	0.31	4.70	7.88	**12.58**	m2
	3.50 - 5.00 m high where ceiling is of dissimilar finish	0.37	5.64	7.88	**13.52**	m2
	staircase areas	0.37	5.64	7.88	**13.52**	m2

Unit Rates	Man-Hours	Net Labour Price £	Net Mats Price £	Net Unit Price £	Unit
018 **Providing and hanging wide-width suede effect wall coverings; to walls with 'Suedefix' adhesive**					
019 P.C. £23.11 per square metre:					
walls over 300 mm wide:					
generally	0.39	5.93	30.02	**35.95**	m2
3.50 - 5.00 m high where ceiling is of dissimilar finish	0.48	7.30	30.02	**37.32**	m2
staircase areas	0.48	7.30	30.02	**37.32**	m2
020 **Providing and hanging wide-width cotton backed vinyl wall coverings; to walls with Grade 1 adhesive**					
021 P.C. £10.60 per square metre:					
walls over 300 mm wide:					
generally	0.29	4.38	14.20	**18.58**	m2
3.50 - 5.00 m high where ceiling is of dissimilar finish	0.35	5.32	14.20	**19.52**	m2
staircase areas	0.35	5.32	14.20	**19.52**	m2
022 **Providing and hanging wide-width vinyl wall coverings; to walls with Grade 3 adhesive**					
023 P.C. £2.31 per square metre:					
walls over 300 mm wide:					
generally	0.29	4.38	3.38	**7.76**	m2
3.50 - 5.00 m high where ceiling is of dissimilar finish	0.35	5.32	3.38	**8.70**	m2
staircase areas	0.35	5.32	3.38	**8.70**	m2

VO   **REPAINTING AND REDECORATION WORK**

The following prices are for preparation of existing surfaces to a condition ready to receive the new paint system. Prices for the new paint system are the same as for painting on new surfaces and they have not been repeated. See sub-sections VA-VN and VZ for new paint prices to obtain total prices for complete redecoration of existing surfaces in accordance with the required specification.

OLD WALLS AND CEILINGS - PREPARATION

PREVIOUSLY SIZE DISTEMPERED SURFACES IN ANY CONDITION

	Man-Hours	Net Labour Price £	Net Mats Price £	Net Unit Price £	Unit
001 **Wash down to remove all traces of old distemper; stop in cracks and rub down; one coat of primer sealer**					
002 Walls over 300 mm wide:					
plastered	0.41	6.26	1.12	**7.38**	m2
smooth concrete	0.52	7.84	1.14	**8.98**	m2
fibre cement	0.45	6.89	1.12	**8.01**	m2
embossed or textured papered	0.62	9.39	1.12	**10.51**	m2
cement rendered	0.52	7.84	1.12	**8.96**	m2
fair face brickwork	0.52	7.84	1.29	**9.13**	m2
fair face blockwork	0.56	8.45	1.57	**10.02**	m2
Note: 003 not used					
004 Walls in staircase areas over 300 mm wide:					
plastered	0.42	6.41	1.12	**7.53**	m2
smooth concrete	0.53	8.04	1.14	**9.18**	m2
fibre cement	0.47	7.07	1.12	**8.19**	m2
embossed or textured papered	0.65	9.86	1.12	**10.98**	m2
cement rendered	0.53	8.04	1.12	**9.16**	m2
fair face brickwork	0.53	8.04	1.29	**9.33**	m2
fair face blockwork	0.57	8.68	1.57	**10.25**	m2
005 Ceilings over 300 mm wide:					
plastered	0.43	6.58	1.12	**7.70**	m2
smooth concrete	0.54	8.22	1.14	**9.36**	m2
fibre cement	0.48	7.24	1.12	**8.36**	m2
embossed or textured papered	0.66	10.02	1.12	**11.14**	m2
cement rendered	0.54	8.22	1.12	**9.34**	m2
Note: 006 not used					
007 Ceilings in staircase areas over 300 mm wide:					
plastered	0.44	6.72	1.12	**7.84**	m2
smooth concrete	0.55	8.41	1.14	**9.55**	m2
fibre cement	0.49	7.39	1.12	**8.51**	m2
embossed or textured papered	0.67	10.17	10.90	**21.07**	m2
cement rendered	0.55	8.41	1.12	**9.53**	m2

PREVIOUSLY WATER PAINTED, LIME WASHED OR CEMENT PAINTED SURFACES - GOOD CONDITION

	Man-Hours	Net Labour Price £	Net Mats Price £	Net Unit Price £	Unit
008 **Clean down; stop in cracks and rub down; one coat acrylic primer/undercoat**					
009 Walls over 300 mm wide:					
plastered	0.25	3.80	1.12	**4.92**	m2
smooth concrete	0.31	4.77	1.14	**5.91**	m2
fibre cement	0.27	4.16	1.12	**5.28**	m2
embossed or textured papered	0.32	4.85	1.12	**5.97**	m2
cement rendered	0.31	4.77	1.12	**5.89**	m2
fair face brickwork	0.31	4.77	1.29	**6.06**	m2
fair face blockwork	0.34	5.14	1.57	**6.71**	m2

Unit Rates	Man-Hours	Net Labour Price £	Net Mats Price £	Net Unit Price £	Unit

Note: 010 not used

011 Walls in staircase areas over 300 mm wide:

	Man-Hours	Net Labour Price £	Net Mats Price £	Net Unit Price £	Unit
plastered	0.27	4.09	1.12	**5.21**	m2
smooth concrete	0.33	5.02	1.14	**6.16**	m2
fibre cement	0.29	4.38	1.12	**5.50**	m2
embossed or textured papered	0.33	5.02	1.12	**6.14**	m2
cement rendered	0.33	5.02	1.12	**6.14**	m2
fair face brickwork	0.33	5.02	1.29	**6.31**	m2
fair face blockwork	0.35	5.26	1.57	**6.83**	m2

012 Ceilings over 300 mm wide:

plastered	0.26	4.00	1.12	**5.12**	m2
smooth concrete	0.33	5.00	1.14	**6.14**	m2
fibre cement	0.29	4.39	1.12	**5.51**	m2
embossed or textured papered	0.33	5.02	1.12	**6.14**	m2
cement rendered	0.33	5.00	1.12	**6.12**	m2

Note: 013 not used

014 Ceilings in staircase areas over 300 mm wide:

plastered	0.28	4.27	1.12	**5.39**	m2
smooth concrete	0.34	5.11	1.14	**6.25**	m2
fibre cement	0.30	4.48	1.12	**5.60**	m2
embossed or textured papered	0.34	5.17	1.12	**6.29**	m2
cement rendered	0.34	5.11	1.12	**6.23**	m2

PREVIOUSLY WATER PAINTED, LIME WASHED OR CEMENT PAINTED SURFACES - POOR CONDITION

015 **Remove poorly adhering, flaky, powdery, friable paint; cut back to a firm edge; stop in cracks and rub down; one coat acrylic primer/undercoat**

016 Walls over 300 mm wide:

plastered	0.46	7.04	1.12	**8.16**	m2
smooth concrete	0.58	8.82	1.14	**9.96**	m2
fibre cement	0.51	7.75	1.12	**8.87**	m2
embossed or textured papered	0.68	10.34	1.12	**11.46**	m2
cement rendered	0.58	8.82	1.12	**9.94**	m2
fair face brickwork	0.58	8.82	1.29	**10.11**	m2
fair face blockwork	0.63	9.50	1.57	**11.07**	m2

Note: 017 not used

018 Walls in staircase areas over 300 mm wide:

plastered	0.48	7.22	1.12	**8.34**	m2
smooth concrete	0.59	9.01	1.14	**10.15**	m2
fibre cement	0.52	7.93	1.12	**9.05**	m2
embossed or textured papered	0.70	10.64	1.12	**11.76**	m2
cement rendered	0.59	9.01	1.12	**10.13**	m2
fair face brickwork	0.59	9.01	1.29	**10.30**	m2
fair face blockwork	0.64	9.77	1.57	**11.34**	m2

019 Ceilings over 300 mm wide:

plastered	0.49	7.40	1.12	**8.52**	m2
smooth concrete	0.61	9.26	1.14	**10.40**	m2
fibre cement	0.54	8.15	1.12	**9.27**	m2
embossed or textured papered	0.71	10.81	1.12	**11.93**	m2
cement rendered	0.61	9.26	1.12	**10.38**	m2

Note: 020 not used

021 Ceilings in staircase areas over 300 mm wide:

plastered	0.50	7.55	1.12	**8.67**	m2
smooth concrete	0.62	9.45	1.14	**10.59**	m2
fibre cement	0.55	8.31	1.12	**9.43**	m2
embossed or textured papered	0.72	10.96	1.12	**12.08**	m2
cement rendered	0.62	9.45	1.12	**10.57**	m2

PREVIOUSLY EMULSION PAINTED SURFACES - GOOD CONDITION

022 **Clean down; stop in cracks and rub down; one coat acrylic primer/undercoat**

023 Walls over 300 mm wide:

plastered	0.25	3.80	1.12	**4.92**	m2
smooth concrete	0.31	4.77	1.14	**5.91**	m2
fibre cement	0.27	4.16	1.12	**5.28**	m2
embossed or textured papered	0.32	4.85	1.12	**5.97**	m2
cement rendered	0.31	4.77	1.12	**5.89**	m2
fair face brickwork	0.31	4.77	1.29	**6.06**	m2
fair face blockwork	0.34	5.14	1.57	**6.71**	m2

Note: 024 not used

025 Walls in staircase areas over 300 mm wide:

plastered	0.27	4.09	1.12	**5.21**	m2
smooth concrete	0.33	5.02	1.14	**6.16**	m2
fibre cement	0.29	4.38	1.12	**5.50**	m2
embossed or textured papered	0.33	5.02	1.12	**6.14**	m2

		Man-Hours	Net Labour Price £	Net Mats Price £	Net Unit Price £	Unit
	Unit Rates					
	cement rendered	0.33	5.02	1.12	**6.14**	m2
	fair face brickwork	0.33	5.02	1.29	**6.31**	m2
	fair face blockwork	0.35	5.26	1.57	**6.83**	m2
026	Ceilings over 300 mm wide:					
	plastered	0.26	4.00	1.12	**5.12**	m2
	smooth concrete	0.33	5.00	1.14	**6.14**	m2
	fibre cement	0.29	4.39	1.12	**5.51**	m2
	embossed or textured papered	0.33	5.02	1.12	**6.14**	m2
	cement rendered	0.33	5.00	1.12	**6.12**	m2
	Note: 027 not used					
028	Ceilings in staircase areas over 300 mm wide:					
	plastered	0.28	4.23	1.12	**5.35**	m2
	smooth concrete	0.34	5.11	1.14	**6.25**	m2
	fibre cement	0.30	4.48	1.12	**5.60**	m2
	embossed or textured papered	0.34	5.17	1.12	**6.29**	m2
	cement rendered	0.34	5.11	1.12	**6.23**	m2

PREVIOUSLY EMULSION PAINTED SURFACES - POOR CONDITION

		Man-Hours	Net Labour Price £	Net Mats Price £	Net Unit Price £	Unit
029	**Remove poorly adhering, flaky, powdery, friable paint; cut back to a firm edge; stop in cracks and rub down; one coat acrylic primer/undercoat**					
030	Walls over 300 mm wide:					
	plastered	0.38	5.73	1.12	**6.85**	m2
	smooth concrete	0.47	7.19	1.14	**8.33**	m2
	fibre cement	0.42	6.34	1.12	**7.46**	m2
	embossed or textured papered	0.58	8.77	1.12	**9.89**	m2
	cement rendered	0.47	7.19	1.12	**8.31**	m2
	fair face brickwork	0.47	7.19	1.29	**8.48**	m2
	fair face blockwork	0.51	7.75	1.57	**9.32**	m2
	Note: 031 not used					
032	Walls in staircase areas over 300 mm wide:					
	plastered	0.39	5.87	1.12	**6.99**	m2
	smooth concrete	0.49	7.51	1.14	**8.65**	m2
	fibre cement	0.44	6.73	1.12	**7.85**	m2
	embossed or textured papered	0.61	9.24	1.12	**10.36**	m2
	cement rendered	0.49	7.51	1.12	**8.63**	m2
	fair face brickwork	0.49	7.51	1.29	**8.80**	m2
	fair face blockwork	0.54	8.15	1.57	**9.72**	m2
033	Ceilings over 300 mm wide:					
	plastered	0.40	6.02	1.12	**7.14**	m2
	smooth concrete	0.50	7.54	1.14	**8.68**	m2
	fibre cement	0.44	6.66	1.12	**7.78**	m2
	embossed or textured papered	0.62	9.39	1.12	**10.51**	m2
	cement rendered	0.50	7.54	1.12	**8.66**	m2
	Note: 034 not used					
035	Ceilings in staircase areas over 300 mm wide:					
	plastered	0.41	6.19	1.12	**7.31**	m2
	smooth concrete	0.51	7.72	1.14	**8.86**	m2
	fibre cement	0.45	6.89	1.12	**8.01**	m2
	embossed or textured papered	0.63	9.55	1.12	**10.67**	m2
	cement rendered	0.51	7.72	1.12	**8.84**	m2

PREVIOUSLY ALKYD PAINTED SURFACES - GOOD CONDITION

		Man-Hours	Net Labour Price £	Net Mats Price £	Net Unit Price £	Unit
036	**Clean down; stop in and rub down; touch in primer and bring forward**					
037	Walls over 300 mm wide:					
	plastered	0.10	1.57	0.05	**1.62**	m2
	smooth concrete	0.13	1.96	0.07	**2.03**	m2
	fibre cement	0.11	1.72	0.05	**1.77**	m2
	embossed or textured papered	0.13	1.96	0.05	**2.01**	m2
	cement rendered	0.13	1.96	0.05	**2.01**	m2
	fair face brickwork	0.13	1.96	0.07	**2.03**	m2
	fair face blockwork	0.14	2.11	0.09	**2.20**	m2
	Note: 038 not used					
039	Walls in staircase areas over 300 mm wide:					
	plastered	0.11	1.72	0.05	**1.77**	m2
	smooth concrete	0.14	2.19	0.07	**2.26**	m2
	fibre cement	0.12	1.88	0.05	**1.93**	m2
	embossed or textured papered	0.14	2.19	0.05	**2.24**	m2
	cement rendered	0.14	2.19	0.05	**2.24**	m2
	fair face brickwork	0.14	2.19	0.07	**2.26**	m2
	fair face blockwork	0.16	2.36	0.09	**2.45**	m2
040	Ceilings over 300 mm wide:					
	plastered	0.11	1.72	0.05	**1.77**	m2
	smooth concrete	0.14	2.19	0.07	**2.26**	m2
	fibre cement	0.12	1.88	0.05	**1.93**	m2

Unit Rates	Man-Hours	Net Labour Price £	Net Mats Price £	Net Unit Price £	Unit
embossed or textured papered	0.14	2.19	0.05	**2.24**	m2
cement rendered	0.14	2.19	0.05	**2.24**	m2
Note: 041 not used					
042 Ceilings in staircase areas over 300 mm wide:					
plastered	0.11	1.67	0.05	**1.72**	m2
smooth concrete	0.14	2.19	0.07	**2.26**	m2
fibre cement	0.12	1.85	0.05	**1.90**	m2
embossed or textured papered	0.14	2.19	0.05	**2.24**	m2
cement rendered	0.14	2.19	0.05	**2.24**	m2
PREVIOUSLY ALKYD PAINTED SURFACES - POOR CONDITION					
043 **Remove old paint completely by burning off; stop in cracks and rub down**					
044 Walls over 300 mm wide:					
plastered	0.86	13.03	0.11	**13.14**	m2
smooth concrete	1.07	16.28	0.17	**16.45**	m2
fibre cement	0.94	14.27	0.11	**14.38**	m2
cement rendered	1.07	16.28	0.11	**16.39**	m2
fair face brickwork	1.07	16.28	0.17	**16.45**	m2
fair face blockwork	1.16	17.62	0.23	**17.85**	m2
Note: 045 not used					
046 Walls in staircase areas over 300 mm wide:					
plastered	0.88	13.35	0.11	**13.46**	m2
smooth concrete	1.10	16.67	0.17	**16.84**	m2
fibre cement	0.96	14.64	0.11	**14.75**	m2
cement rendered	1.10	16.67	0.11	**16.78**	m2
fair face brickwork	1.10	16.67	0.17	**16.84**	m2
fair face blockwork	1.19	18.04	0.23	**18.27**	m2
047 Ceilings over 300 mm wide:					
plastered	0.90	13.70	0.11	**13.81**	m2
smooth concrete	1.13	17.10	0.17	**17.27**	m2
fibre cement	0.99	15.03	0.11	**15.14**	m2
cement rendered	1.13	17.10	0.11	**17.21**	m2
Note: 048 not used					
049 Ceilings in staircase areas over 300 mm wide:					
plastered	0.92	13.94	0.11	**14.05**	m2
smooth concrete	1.15	17.45	0.17	**17.62**	m2
fibre cement	1.02	15.43	0.11	**15.54**	m2
cement rendered	1.15	17.45	0.11	**17.56**	m2
050 **Remove old paint completely by chemical means; wash down; stop in cracks and rub down**					
051 Walls over 300 mm wide:					
plastered	1.03	15.66	3.75	**19.41**	m2
smooth concrete	1.29	19.56	4.69	**24.25**	m2
fibre cement	1.13	17.22	4.12	**21.34**	m2
cement rendered	1.29	19.56	4.68	**24.24**	m2
fair face brickwork	1.29	19.56	4.69	**24.25**	m2
fair face blockwork	1.39	21.14	5.07	**26.21**	m2
Note: 052 not used					
053 Walls in staircase areas over 300 mm wide:					
plastered	1.06	16.04	3.75	**19.79**	m2
smooth concrete	1.32	20.06	4.69	**24.75**	m2
fibre cement	1.16	17.66	4.12	**21.78**	m2
cement rendered	1.32	20.06	4.68	**24.74**	m2
fair face brickwork	1.32	20.06	4.69	**24.75**	m2
fair face blockwork	1.43	21.68	5.07	**26.75**	m2
054 Ceilings over 300 mm wide:					
plastered	1.08	16.42	3.75	**20.17**	m2
smooth concrete	1.35	20.55	4.69	**25.24**	m2
fibre cement	1.19	18.09	4.12	**22.21**	m2
cement rendered	1.35	20.55	4.68	**25.23**	m2
Note: 055 not used					
056 Ceilings in staircase areas over 300 mm wide:					
plastered	1.11	16.81	3.75	**20.56**	m2
smooth concrete	1.38	20.99	4.69	**25.68**	m2
fibre cement	1.22	18.47	4.12	**22.59**	m2
cement rendered	1.38	20.99	4.68	**25.67**	m2

Unit Rates	Man-Hours	Net Labour Price £	Net Mats Price £	Net Unit Price £	Unit
OLD METALWORK - PREPARATION					
PREVIOUSLY ALKYD PAINTED METALWORK SURFACES - REASONABLY GOOD CONDITION					
057 **Wash down to remove dirt, oil, grease etc.; remove loose and flaking paint; prime bare patches with chromate primer**					
058 General surfaces:					
over 300 mm girth	0.26	3.92	0.12	**4.04**	m2
not exceeding 150 mm girth	0.08	1.25	0.05	**1.30**	m
150 - 300 mm girth	0.11	1.72	0.06	**1.78**	m
isolated; not exceeding 0.50m2	0.14	2.19	0.09	**2.28**	Nr
059 Glazed doors and screens in panes:					
small - not exceeding 0.10 m2	0.36	5.47	0.10	**5.57**	m2
medium - 0.10 - 0.50 m2	0.31	4.70	0.10	**4.80**	m2
large - 0.50 m2 - 1.00 m2	0.29	4.39	0.06	**4.45**	m2
extra large - over 1.00 m2	0.26	3.92	0.06	**3.98**	m2
060 Windows in panes:					
small - not exceeding 0.10 m2	0.36	5.47	0.10	**5.57**	m2
medium - 0.10 - 0.50 m2	0.31	4.70	0.10	**4.80**	m2
large - 0.50 m2 - 1.00 m2	0.29	4.39	0.06	**4.45**	m2
extra large - over 1.00 m2	0.26	3.92	0.06	**3.98**	m2
061 Structural members:					
over 300 mm girth	0.31	4.70	0.12	**4.82**	m2
not exceeding 150 mm girth	0.09	1.41	0.05	**1.46**	m
150 - 300 mm girth	0.14	2.19	0.06	**2.25**	m
062 Members of roof trusses:					
over 300 mm girth	0.39	5.94	0.12	**6.06**	m2
not exceeding 150 mm girth	0.11	1.72	0.05	**1.77**	m
150 - 300 mm girth	0.18	2.68	0.06	**2.74**	m
063 Radiators:					
over 300 mm girth	0.36	5.47	0.12	**5.59**	m2
064 Pipes and conduits, ducting, trunking and the like:					
over 300 mm girth	0.29	4.39	0.12	**4.51**	m2
not exceeding 150 mm girth	0.09	1.41	0.05	**1.46**	m
150 - 300 mm girth	0.12	1.88	0.06	**1.94**	m
065 Staircases:					
over 300 mm girth	0.29	4.39	0.12	**4.51**	m2
not exceeding 150 mm girth	0.09	1.41	0.05	**1.46**	m
150 - 300 mm girth	0.12	1.88	0.06	**1.94**	m
Note: 066 not used					
PREVIOUSLY ALKYD PAINTED METALWORK SURFACES - POOR CONDITION					
067 **Remove old paint completely by chemical means; remove rust by wire brushing, chipping and scraping; stop in and rub down**					
068 General surfaces:					
over 300 mm girth	1.03	15.66	3.77	**19.43**	m2
not exceeding 150 mm girth	0.31	4.70	1.13	**5.83**	m
150 - 300 mm girth	0.46	7.04	1.70	**8.74**	m
isolated; not exceeding 0.50m2	0.62	9.39	1.88	**11.27**	Nr
069 Glazed doors and screens in panes:					
small - not exceeding 0.10 m2	1.44	21.92	3.37	**25.29**	m2
medium - 0.10 - 0.50 m2	1.24	18.79	3.00	**21.79**	m2
large - 0.50 m2 - 1.00 m2	1.03	15.66	2.63	**18.29**	m2
extra large - over 1.00 m2	0.82	12.52	2.26	**14.78**	m2
070 Windows in panes:					
small - not exceeding 0.10 m2	1.44	21.92	3.37	**25.29**	m2
medium - 0.10 - 0.50 m2	1.24	18.79	3.00	**21.79**	m2
large - 0.50 m2 - 1.00 m2	1.03	15.66	2.63	**18.29**	m2
extra large - over 1.00 m2	0.82	12.52	2.26	**14.78**	m2
071 Structural members:					
over 300 mm girth	1.13	17.22	3.77	**20.99**	m2
not exceeding 150 mm girth	0.36	5.47	1.13	**6.60**	m
150 - 300 mm girth	0.52	7.84	1.70	**9.54**	m
072 Members of roof trusses:					
over 300 mm girth	1.55	23.48	3.77	**27.25**	m2
not exceeding 150 mm girth	0.46	7.04	1.13	**8.17**	m
150 - 300 mm girth	0.70	10.64	1.70	**12.34**	m
073 Radiators:					
over 300 mm girth	1.44	21.92	4.14	**26.06**	m2
074 Pipes and conduits, ducting, trunking and the like:					
over 300 mm girth	1.13	17.22	3.77	**20.99**	m2

Unit Rates	Man-Hours	Net Labour Price £	Net Mats Price £	Net Unit Price £	Unit
not exceeding 150 mm girth	0.36	5.47	1.13	**6.60**	m
150 - 300 mm girth	0.52	7.84	1.70	**9.54**	m
075 Staircases:					
over 300 mm girth	1.13	17.22	3.77	**20.99**	m2
not exceeding 150 mm girth	0.36	5.47	1.13	**6.60**	m
150 - 300 mm girth	0.52	7.84	1.70	**9.54**	m

Note: 076 not used

OLD WOODWORK - PREPARATION

PREVIOUSLY ALKYD PAINTED WOODWORK SURFACES - GOOD CONDITION

077 Wash down to remove dirt, oil, grease etc.; remove loose and flaking paint; stop in, rub down and prime bare patches

	Man-Hours	Net Labour Price £	Net Mats Price £	Net Unit Price £	Unit
078 General surfaces:					
over 300 mm girth	0.26	3.92	0.05	**3.97**	m2
not exceeding 150 mm girth	0.08	1.25	0.03	**1.28**	m
150 - 300 mm girth	0.11	1.72	0.02	**1.74**	m
isolated; not exceeding 0.50m2	0.14	2.19	0.02	**2.21**	Nr
079 Glazed doors and screens in panes:					
small - not exceeding 0.10 m2	0.52	7.84	0.02	**7.86**	m2
medium - 0.10 - 0.50 m2	0.46	7.04	0.02	**7.06**	m2
large - 0.50 m2 - 1.00 m2	0.41	6.26	0.02	**6.28**	m2
extra large - over 1.00 m2	0.36	5.47	0.02	**5.49**	m2
080 Windows in panes:					
small - not exceeding 0.10 m2	0.57	8.62	0.02	**8.64**	m2
medium - 0.10 - 0.50 m2	0.52	7.84	0.02	**7.86**	m2
large - 0.50 m2 - 1.00 m2	0.46	7.04	0.02	**7.06**	m2
extra large - over 1.00 m2	0.41	6.26	0.02	**6.28**	m2
081 Frames, linings and associated mouldings:					
over 300 mm girth	0.26	3.92	0.05	**3.97**	m2
not exceeding 150 mm girth	0.08	1.25	0.01	**1.26**	m
150 - 300 mm girth	0.11	1.72	0.02	**1.74**	m
082 Cornices:					
over 300 mm girth	0.31	4.70	0.05	**4.75**	m2
not exceeding 150 mm girth	0.09	1.41	0.01	**1.42**	m
150 - 300 mm girth	0.14	2.19	0.02	**2.21**	m
083 Skirtings, Dado rails, picture rails and the like:					
over 300 mm girth	0.29	4.39	0.05	**4.44**	m2
not exceeding 150 mm girth	0.09	1.41	0.01	**1.42**	m
150 - 300 mm girth	0.12	1.88	0.02	**1.90**	m
084 Staircases:					
over 300 mm girth	0.27	4.07	0.05	**4.12**	m2
not exceeding 150 mm girth	0.08	1.25	0.01	**1.26**	m
150 - 300 mm girth	0.12	1.88	0.02	**1.90**	m

PREVIOUSLY ALKYD PAINTED WOODWORK SURFACES - POOR CONDITION

085 Remove old paint completely by burning off; knot, stop in and rub down; one coat wood primer

	Man-Hours	Net Labour Price £	Net Mats Price £	Net Unit Price £	Unit
086 General surfaces:					
over 300 mm girth	0.90	13.70	1.17	**14.87**	m2
not exceeding 150 mm girth	0.26	3.92	0.21	**4.13**	m
150 - 300 mm girth	0.39	5.87	0.34	**6.21**	m
isolated; not exceeding 0.50m2	0.52	7.83	0.69	**8.52**	Nr
087 Glazed doors and screens in panes:					
small - not exceeding 0.10 m2	1.67	25.37	0.77	**26.14**	m2
medium - 0.10 - 0.50 m2	1.55	23.48	0.64	**24.12**	m2
large - 0.50 m2 - 1.00 m2	1.41	21.45	0.47	**21.92**	m2
extra large - over 1.00 m2	1.29	19.59	0.34	**19.93**	m2
088 Windows in panes:					
small - not exceeding 0.10 m2	1.80	27.41	0.95	**28.36**	m2
medium - 0.10 - 0.50 m2	1.67	25.44	0.85	**26.29**	m2
large - 0.50 m2 - 1.00 m2	1.55	23.48	0.72	**24.20**	m2
extra large - over 1.00 m2	1.42	21.52	0.59	**22.11**	m2
089 Frames, linings and associated mouldings:					
over 300 mm girth	0.90	13.70	1.17	**14.87**	m2
not exceeding 150 mm girth	0.26	3.92	0.21	**4.13**	m
150 - 300 mm girth	0.39	5.87	0.34	**6.21**	m
090 Cornices:					
over 300 mm girth	1.08	16.43	1.17	**17.60**	m2
not exceeding 150 mm girth	0.33	5.02	0.21	**5.23**	m
150 - 300 mm girth	0.49	7.43	0.34	**7.77**	m

Unit Rates

		Man-Hours	Net Labour Price £	Net Mats Price £	Net Unit Price £	Unit
091	Skirtings, Dado rails, picture rails and the like:					
	over 300 mm girth	1.01	15.29	1.17	**16.46**	m2
	not exceeding 150 mm girth	0.31	4.70	0.21	**4.91**	m
	150 - 300 mm girth	0.44	6.69	0.34	**7.03**	m
092	Staircases:					
	over 300 mm girth	0.95	14.49	1.17	**15.66**	m2
	not exceeding 150 mm girth	0.28	4.30	0.21	**4.51**	m
	150 - 300 mm girth	0.44	6.69	0.34	**7.03**	m
093	**Remove old paint completely by chemical means; wash down; knot, stop in and rub down; one coat wood primer**					
094	General surfaces:					
	over 300 mm girth	1.03	15.66	4.82	**20.48**	m2
	not exceeding 150 mm girth	0.31	4.70	1.31	**6.01**	m
	150 - 300 mm girth	0.46	7.04	1.99	**9.03**	m
	isolated; not exceeding 0.50m2	0.62	9.39	2.54	**11.93**	Nr
095	Glazed doors and screens in panes:					
	small - not exceeding 0.10 m2	2.06	31.31	4.03	**35.34**	m2
	medium - 0.10 - 0.50 m2	1.85	28.18	3.55	**31.73**	m2
	large - 0.50 m2 - 1.00 m2	1.65	25.03	3.03	**28.06**	m2
	extra large - over 1.00 m2	1.44	21.92	2.55	**24.47**	m2
096	Windows in panes:					
	small - not exceeding 0.10 m2	2.27	34.44	4.58	**39.02**	m2
	medium - 0.10 - 0.50 m2	2.06	31.31	4.14	**35.45**	m2
	large - 0.50 m2 - 1.00 m2	1.85	28.18	3.65	**31.83**	m2
	extra large - over 1.00 m2	1.65	25.03	2.80	**27.83**	m2
097	Frames, linings and associated mouldings:					
	over 300 mm girth	1.03	15.66	4.82	**20.48**	m2
	not exceeding 150 mm girth	0.31	4.70	1.31	**6.01**	m
	150 - 300 mm girth	0.46	7.04	1.99	**9.03**	m
098	Cornices:					
	over 300 mm girth	1.24	18.79	4.82	**23.61**	m2
	not exceeding 150 mm girth	0.37	5.64	1.31	**6.95**	m
	150 - 300 mm girth	0.56	8.45	1.99	**10.44**	m
099	Skirtings, Dado rails, picture rails and the like:					
	over 300 mm girth	1.13	17.22	4.82	**22.04**	m2
	not exceeding 150 mm girth	0.34	5.17	1.31	**6.48**	m
	150 - 300 mm girth	0.52	7.84	1.99	**9.83**	m
100	Staircases:					
	over 300 mm girth	1.08	16.42	4.82	**21.24**	m2
	not exceeding 150 mm girth	0.33	5.02	1.31	**6.33**	m
	150 - 300 mm girth	0.48	7.36	17.10	**24.46**	m
	PREVIOUSLY STAINED WOODWORK SURFACES - GOOD CONDITION					
101	**Stop in, rub down and clean off; one coat interior semi-gloss wood stain**					
102	General surfaces:					
	over 300 mm girth	0.16	2.36	0.61	**2.97**	m2
	not exceeding 150 mm girth	0.05	0.79	0.12	**0.91**	m
	150 - 300 mm girth	0.07	1.09	0.12	**1.21**	m
	isolated; not exceeding 0.50 m2	0.08	1.25	0.35	**1.60**	Nr
103	Glazed doors and screens in panes:					
	small - not exceeding 0.10 m2	0.31	4.70	0.49	**5.19**	m2
	medium - 0.10 - 0.50 m2	0.24	3.60	0.37	**3.97**	m2
	large - 0.50 - 1.00 m2	0.23	3.45	0.37	**3.82**	m2
	extra large - over 1.00 m2	0.22	3.28	0.26	**3.54**	m2
104	Windows in panes:					
	small - not exceeding 0.10 m2	0.34	5.17	0.49	**5.66**	m2
	medium - 0.10 - 0.50 m2	0.26	3.92	0.37	**4.29**	m2
	large - 0.50 - 1.00 m2	0.25	3.75	0.37	**4.12**	m2
	extra large - over 1.00 m2	0.24	3.60	0.26	**3.86**	m2
105	Frames, linings and associated mouldings:					
	over 300 mm girth	0.16	2.36	0.61	**2.97**	m2
	not exceeding 150 mm girth	0.05	0.79	0.12	**0.91**	m
	150 - 300 mm girth	0.07	1.09	0.12	**1.21**	m
106	Skirtings, dado rails, picture rails and the like:					
	over 300 mm girth	0.16	2.36	0.61	**2.97**	m2
	not exceeding 150 mm girth	0.05	0.79	0.12	**0.91**	m
	150 - 300 mm girth	0.07	1.09	0.12	**1.21**	m
107	Staircases:					
	over 300 mm girth	0.16	2.36	0.61	**2.97**	m2
	not exceeding 150 mm girth	0.05	0.79	0.12	**0.91**	m
	150 - 300 mm girth	0.07	1.09	0.12	**1.21**	m

		Man-Hours	Net Labour Price £	Net Mats Price £	Net Unit Price £	Unit
Unit Rates						
VP	**STRIPPING OFF WALLPAPER**					
001	**Strip off old decorative paper; stop in cracks and rub down**					
002	Lining paper, woodchip paper:					
	one layer from:					
	walls	0.16	2.36	0.07	**2.43**	m2
	ceilings	0.21	3.13	0.07	**3.20**	m2
	two layers from:					
	walls	0.24	3.60	0.07	**3.67**	m2
	ceilings	0.31	4.70	0.07	**4.77**	m2
003	Decorative paper:					
	one layer from:					
	walls	0.19	2.81	0.07	**2.88**	m2
	ceilings	0.25	3.75	0.07	**3.82**	m2
	two layers from:					
	walls	0.28	4.23	0.07	**4.30**	m2
	ceilings	0.37	5.64	0.07	**5.71**	m2
004	Embossed or textured paper, vinyl surfaced paper:					
	one layer from:					
	walls	0.21	3.13	0.07	**3.20**	m2
	ceilings	0.28	4.23	0.07	**4.30**	m2
	two layers from:					
	walls	0.31	4.70	0.07	**4.77**	m2
	ceilings	0.41	6.26	0.07	**6.33**	m2
005	Anaglypta paper, heavy wallpaper:					
	one layer from:					
	walls	0.31	4.70	0.07	**4.77**	m2
	ceilings	0.41	6.26	0.07	**6.33**	m2
	two layers from:					
	walls	0.41	6.26	0.07	**6.33**	m2
	ceilings	0.57	8.62	0.07	**8.69**	m2
VQ	**REDECORATION WORK EXTERNALLY**					
	PREVIOUSLY EMULSION PAINTED SURFACES - GOOD CONDITION					
001	**Wash down to remove dirt, deposits etc.; stop in cracks, depressions etc. and smooth off; one coat acrylic primer/undercoat**					
002	Walls over 300 mm girth:					
	smooth concrete	0.36	5.47	1.14	**6.61**	m2
	fibre cement	0.31	4.70	1.12	**5.82**	m2
	cement rendered	0.36	5.47	1.12	**6.59**	m2
	rough cast/pebble dash rendered	0.45	6.89	3.06	**9.95**	m2
	Tyrolean rendered	0.72	10.96	3.83	**14.79**	m2
003	Ceilings, beams, soffits etc. over 300 mm girth:					
	smooth concrete	0.39	5.94	1.14	**7.08**	m2
	fibre cement	0.33	5.02	1.12	**6.14**	m2
	cement rendered	0.40	6.11	1.12	**7.23**	m2
	PREVIOUSLY EMULSION PAINTED SURFACES - POOR CONDITION					
004	**Scrape off to remove all flaking or loose material; wash down to remove dirt, deposits etc.; stop in cracks, depressions etc. and smooth off; one coat acrylic primer/undercoat**					
005	Walls over 300 mm girth:					
	smooth concrete	0.53	7.98	1.14	**9.12**	m2
	fibre cement	0.45	6.89	1.12	**8.01**	m2
	cement rendered	0.53	7.98	1.12	**9.10**	m2
	rough cast/pebble dash rendered	0.70	10.64	3.06	**13.70**	m2
	Tyrolean rendered	1.13	17.22	3.83	**21.05**	m2
006	Ceilings, beams, soffits etc. over 300 mm girth:					
	smooth concrete	0.57	8.62	1.14	**9.76**	m2
	fibre cement	0.49	7.51	1.12	**8.63**	m2
	cement rendered	0.58	8.77	1.12	**9.89**	m2
	Note: 007 - 009 not used					
	PREVIOUSLY EMULSION PAINTED SURFACES - GOOD CONDITION					
010	**Apply one coat fungicidal solution; wash off (this treatment is in addition to other preparation as required)**					
011	Walls over 300 mm girth:					
	smooth concrete	0.08	1.25	0.22	**1.47**	m2
	fibre cement	0.08	1.25	0.21	**1.46**	m2
	cement rendered	0.09	1.41	0.30	**1.71**	m2
	rough cast/pebble dash rendered	0.10	1.57	0.41	**1.98**	m2
	Tyrolean rendered	0.12	1.88	0.60	**2.48**	m2
012	Ceilings, beams, soffits etc. over 300 mm girth:					
	smooth concrete	0.09	1.41	0.22	**1.63**	m2
	fibre cement	0.09	1.41	0.21	**1.62**	m2

Unit Rates

		Man-Hours	Net Labour Price £	Net Mats Price £	Net Unit Price £	Unit
	cement rendered	0.10	1.57	0.30	**1.87**	m2

Note: 013 - 019 not used

PREVIOUSLY ALKYD PAINTED METALWORK SURFACES - GOOD CONDITION

020	**Wash down to remove dirt, oil, grease etc.; remove loose and flaking paint; rub down any corroded areas; prime bare patches with zinc phosphate**					
021	General surfaces:					
	over 300 mm girth	0.28	4.23	0.13	**4.36**	m2
	not exceeding 150 mm girth	0.09	1.41	0.05	**1.46**	m
	150 - 300 mm girth	0.12	1.88	0.06	**1.94**	m
	isolated; not exceeding 0.50 m2	0.16	2.36	0.05	**2.41**	Nr
022	Glazed doors and screens in panes:					
	small - not exceeding 0.10 m2	0.38	5.79	0.06	**5.85**	m2
	medium - 0.10 - 0.50 m2	0.33	5.02	0.06	**5.08**	m2
	large - 0.50 - 1.00 m2	0.31	4.70	0.06	**4.76**	m2
	extra large - over 1.00 m2	0.28	4.23	0.06	**4.29**	m2
023	Windows in panes:					
	small - not exceeding 0.10 m2	0.38	5.79	0.06	**5.85**	m2
	medium - 0.10 - 0.50 m2	0.33	5.02	0.06	**5.08**	m2
	large - 0.50 - 1.00 m2	0.31	4.70	0.06	**4.76**	m2
	extra large - over 1.00 m2	0.28	4.23	0.06	**4.29**	m2
024	Eaves gutters:					
	over 300 mm girth	0.31	4.70	0.13	**4.83**	m2
	not exceeding 150 mm girth	0.10	1.57	0.05	**1.62**	m
	150 - 300 mm girth	0.13	2.04	0.06	**2.10**	m

Note: 025 - 029 not used

PREVIOUSLY ALKYD PAINTED METALWORK SURFACES - POOR CONDITION

030	**Scrape off loose paint and corrosion; wire brush and rub down back to sound or bare metal surface; wash off with white spirit; prime bare patches with zinc phosphate primer**					
031	General surfaces:					
	over 300 mm girth	0.41	6.26	0.29	**6.55**	m2
	not exceeding 150 mm girth	0.13	2.04	0.08	**2.12**	m
	150 - 300 mm girth	0.19	2.81	0.09	**2.90**	m
	isolated; not exceeding 0.50 m2	0.23	3.45	0.13	**3.58**	Nr
032	Glazed doors and screens in panes:					
	small - not exceeding 0.10 m2	0.57	8.62	0.14	**8.76**	m2
	medium - 0.10 - 0.50 m2	0.52	7.83	0.14	**7.97**	m2
	large - 0.50 - 1.00 m2	0.41	6.26	0.09	**6.35**	m2
	extra large - over 1.00 m2	0.36	5.47	0.09	**5.56**	m2
033	Windows in panes:					
	small - not exceeding 0.10 m2	0.57	8.62	0.14	**8.76**	m2
	medium - 0.10 - 0.50 m2	0.52	7.83	0.14	**7.97**	m2
	large - 0.50 - 1.00 m2	0.41	6.26	0.09	**6.35**	m2
	extra large - over 1.00 m2	0.36	5.47	0.09	**5.56**	m2
034	Eaves gutters:					
	over 300 mm girth	0.45	6.89	0.29	**7.18**	m2
	not exceeding 150 mm girth	0.15	2.23	0.08	**2.31**	m
	150 - 300 mm girth	0.20	3.10	0.14	**3.24**	m

Note: 035 - 039 not used

PREVIOUSLY ALKYD PAINTED WOODWORK SURFACES - GOOD CONDITION

040	**Wash down to remove dirt, oil, grease etc.; scrape off any loose or flaking paint; stop in, rub down and prime bare patches**					
041	General surfaces:					
	over 300 mm girth	0.28	4.23	0.12	**4.35**	m2
	not exceeding 150 mm girth	0.09	1.41	0.05	**1.46**	m
	150 - 300 mm girth	0.12	1.88	0.05	**1.93**	m
	isolated; not exceeding 0.50 m2	0.17	2.51	0.05	**2.56**	Nr
042	Glazed doors and screens in panes:					
	small - not exceeding 0.10 m2	0.56	8.45	0.06	**8.51**	m2
	medium - 0.10 - 0.50 m2	0.49	7.51	0.06	**7.57**	m2
	large - 0.50 - 1.00 m2	0.45	6.89	0.06	**6.95**	m2
	extra large - over 1.00 m2	0.40	6.11	0.06	**6.17**	m2
043	Windows in panes:					
	small - not exceeding 0.10 m2	0.61	9.24	0.06	**9.30**	m2
	medium - 0.10 - 0.50 m2	0.55	8.30	0.06	**8.36**	m2
	large - 0.50 - 1.00 m2	0.51	7.68	0.06	**7.74**	m2
	extra large - over 1.00 m2	0.45	6.89	0.06	**6.95**	m2
044	Frames, linings and associated mouldings:					
	over 300 mm girth	0.28	4.23	0.12	**4.35**	m2

Unit Rates	Man-Hours	Net Labour Price £	Net Mats Price £	Net Unit Price £	Unit
not exceeding 150 mm girth	0.09	1.41	0.05	**1.46**	m
150 - 300 mm girth	0.12	1.88	0.05	**1.93**	m

Note: 045 - 049 not used

PREVIOUSLY ALKYD PAINTED WOODWORK SURFACES - POOR CONDITION

050 **Remove old paint completely by burning off; knot, stop in and rub down; one coat wood primer**

051 General surfaces:					
over 300 mm girth	0.95	14.41	1.17	**15.58**	m2
not exceeding 150 mm girth	0.29	4.38	0.21	**4.59**	m
150 - 300 mm girth	0.43	6.58	0.34	**6.92**	m
isolated; not exceeding 0.50 m2	0.54	8.15	0.69	**8.84**	Nr
052 Glazed doors and screens in panes:					
small - not exceeding 0.10 m2	1.71	25.99	0.77	**26.76**	m2
medium - 0.10 - 0.50 m2	1.59	24.11	0.64	**24.75**	m2
large - 0.50 - 1.00 m2	1.44	21.92	0.47	**22.39**	m2
extra large - over 1.00 m2	1.32	20.03	0.34	**20.37**	m2
053 Windows in panes:					
small - not exceeding 0.10 m2	1.85	28.18	0.95	**29.13**	m2
medium - 0.10 - 0.50 m2	1.73	26.30	0.85	**27.15**	m2
large - 0.50 - 1.00 m2	1.59	24.11	0.72	**24.83**	m2
extra large - over 1.00 m2	1.46	22.24	0.59	**22.83**	m2
054 Frames, linings and associated mouldings:					
over 300 mm girth	0.95	14.41	1.17	**15.58**	m2
not exceeding 150 mm girth	0.29	4.38	0.21	**4.59**	m
150 - 300 mm girth	0.43	6.58	0.34	**6.92**	m

VZ **COMPOSITE RATES FOR PAINTING. The following is a range of prices compiled from the earlier sections.**

WALLS AND CEILINGS - INTERNALLY

EMULSION; VINYL SILK - INTERNALLY

001 **One mist and two full coats vinyl silk emulsion paint, white.** Emulsion Paint @ £5.71 per 1 ltr

002 Walls over 300 mm wide:					
plastered	0.31	4.70	1.49	**6.19**	m2
smooth concrete	0.39	5.90	1.53	**7.43**	m2
fibre cement	0.39	5.90	1.84	**7.74**	m2
embossed or textured papered	0.42	6.37	1.72	**8.09**	m2
cement rendered	0.35	5.26	1.72	**6.98**	m2
fair face brickwork	0.47	7.20	1.87	**9.07**	m2
fair face blockwork	0.54	8.27	2.10	**10.37**	m2

Note: 003 not used

004 Walls in staircase areas over 300 mm wide:					
plastered	0.35	5.37	1.49	**6.86**	m2
smooth concrete	0.40	6.07	1.53	**7.60**	m2
fibre cement	0.40	6.07	1.84	**7.91**	m2
embossed or textured papered	0.43	6.54	1.72	**8.26**	m2
cement rendered	0.35	5.37	1.72	**7.09**	m2
fair face brickwork	0.48	7.36	1.87	**9.23**	m2
fair face blockwork	0.56	8.49	2.10	**10.59**	m2
005 Ceilings over 300 mm wide:					
plastered	0.36	5.54	1.49	**7.03**	m2
smooth concrete	0.41	6.18	1.53	**7.71**	m2
fibre cement	0.41	6.18	1.84	**8.02**	m2
embossed or textured papered	0.44	6.65	1.72	**8.37**	m2
cement rendered	0.36	5.54	1.72	**7.26**	m2

Note: 006 not used

007 Ceilings in staircase areas over 300 mm wide:					
plastered	0.37	5.65	1.49	**7.14**	m2
smooth concrete	0.42	6.36	1.53	**7.89**	m2
fibre cement	0.42	6.36	1.84	**8.20**	m2
embossed or textured papered	0.45	6.83	1.72	**8.55**	m2
cement rendered	0.37	5.65	1.72	**7.37**	m2

PRIMERS - INTERNALLY

008 **ADD to the foregoing if with alkali-resisting primer in lieu of mist coat.** Primer @ £13.12 per 1 ltr

009 Walls and Ceilings:					
plastered	0.07	1.03	1.19	**2.22**	m2
smooth concrete	0.07	1.08	1.19	**2.27**	m2
fibre cement	0.07	1.08	1.19	**2.27**	m2
cement rendered	0.07	1.03	1.59	**2.62**	m2
fair face brickwork	0.08	1.28	1.59	**2.87**	m2

Unit Rates	Man-Hours	Net Labour Price £	Net Mats Price £	Net Unit Price £	Unit
fair face blockwork	0.10	1.57	2.25	**3.82**	m2

ALKYD BASED PAINT; EGGSHELL FINISH - INTERNALLY

010 **One coat of all-purpose primer; and two coats eggshell finish alkyd paint.** Primer @ £15.82 per 1 ltr; Eggshell @ £6.84 per 1 ltr

011 Walls over 300 mm wide:					
plastered	0.40	6.04	1.44	**7.48**	m2
smooth concrete	0.44	6.72	1.48	**8.20**	m2
fibre cement	0.45	6.79	2.16	**8.95**	m2
embossed or textured papered	0.47	7.19	1.89	**9.08**	m2
cement rendered	0.40	6.04	2.13	**8.17**	m2
fair face brickwork	0.49	7.51	2.27	**9.78**	m2
fair face blockwork	0.58	8.83	2.61	**11.44**	m2

Note: 012 not used

013 Walls in staircase areas over 300 mm wide:					
plastered	0.41	6.22	1.44	**7.66**	m2
smooth concrete	0.46	6.98	2.06	**9.04**	m2
fibre cement	0.46	6.98	2.16	**9.14**	m2
embossed or textured papered	0.49	7.45	1.89	**9.34**	m2
cement rendered	0.41	6.22	2.13	**8.35**	m2
fair face brickwork	0.52	7.83	2.27	**10.10**	m2
fair face blockwork	0.60	9.08	2.61	**11.69**	m2

014 Ceilings over 300 mm wide:					
plastered	0.42	6.39	1.44	**7.83**	m2
smooth concrete	0.47	7.14	2.06	**9.20**	m2
fibre cement	0.47	7.14	2.16	**9.30**	m2
embossed or textured papered	0.49	7.51	1.89	**9.40**	m2
cement rendered	0.42	6.39	2.13	**8.52**	m2

Note: 015 not used

016 Ceilings in staircase areas over 300 mm wide:					
plastered	0.43	6.53	1.44	**7.97**	m2
smooth concrete	0.48	7.33	2.06	**9.39**	m2
fibre cement	0.48	7.33	2.16	**9.49**	m2
embossed or textured papered	0.51	7.73	1.83	**9.56**	m2
cement rendered	0.43	6.53	2.13	**8.66**	m2

ALKYD BASED PAINT; GLOSS FINISH - INTERNALLY

017 **One coat of all-purpose primer; one coat alkyd based undercoat; one coat alkyd based gloss finish.** Primer @ £15.82 per 1 ltr; Undercoat @ £6.26 per 1 ltr; Gloss @ £6.26 per 1 ltr

018 Walls over 300 mm wide:					
plastered	0.40	6.11	1.36	**7.47**	m2
smooth concrete	0.45	6.81	1.70	**8.51**	m2
fibre cement	0.45	6.81	1.76	**8.57**	m2
embossed or textured papered	0.48	7.23	2.00	**9.23**	m2
cement rendered	0.40	6.11	2.00	**8.11**	m2
fair face brickwork	0.51	7.80	2.25	**10.05**	m2
fair face blockwork	0.60	9.07	2.58	**11.65**	m2

Note: 019 not used

020 Walls in staircase areas over 300 mm wide:					
plastered	0.41	6.25	1.36	**7.61**	m2
smooth concrete	0.46	7.00	1.70	**8.70**	m2
fibre cement	0.46	7.00	1.76	**8.76**	m2
embossed or textured papered	0.49	7.37	2.00	**9.37**	m2
cement rendered	0.41	6.25	2.00	**8.25**	m2
fair face brickwork	0.53	8.00	2.25	**10.25**	m2
fair face blockwork	0.62	9.39	2.58	**11.97**	m2

021 Ceilings over 300 mm wide:					
plastered	0.44	6.67	1.36	**8.03**	m2
smooth concrete	0.47	7.15	1.70	**8.85**	m2
fibre cement	0.47	7.15	1.76	**8.91**	m2
embossed or textured papered	0.52	7.83	2.00	**9.83**	m2
cement rendered	0.42	6.42	2.00	**8.42**	m2

Note: 022 not used

023 Ceilings in staircase areas over 300 mm wide:					
plastered	0.45	6.89	1.36	**8.25**	m2
smooth concrete	0.48	7.34	1.70	**9.04**	m2
fibre cement	0.48	7.34	1.76	**9.10**	m2
embossed or textured papered	0.53	7.98	2.00	**9.98**	m2
cement rendered	0.44	6.73	2.00	**8.73**	m2

Unit Rates	Man-Hours	Net Labour Price £	Net Mats Price £	Net Unit Price £	Unit

ANTI-BACTERIAL PAINT SYSTEM - INTERNALLY

024 **Prepare; apply one coat primer/adhesive, two coats water based hygiene paint, high performance two component epoxy coating to**

025 | Walls over 300 mm wide:

	Man-Hours	Net Labour Price £	Net Mats Price £	Net Unit Price £	Unit
plastered	0.32	4.94	7.38	**12.32**	m2
smooth concrete	0.36	5.43	7.38	**12.81**	m2
fibre cement	0.39	5.97	7.85	**13.82**	m2
embossed or textured papered	0.39	5.97	7.85	**13.82**	m2
cement rendered	0.43	6.57	7.85	**14.42**	m2
fair face brickwork	0.47	7.23	7.85	**15.08**	m2
fair face blockwork	0.52	7.95	8.17	**16.12**	m2

Note: 026 not used

027 | Walls in staircase areas over 300 mm wide:

	Man-Hours	Net Labour Price £	Net Mats Price £	Net Unit Price £	Unit
plastered	0.38	5.72	7.38	**13.10**	m2
smooth concrete	0.41	6.28	7.38	**13.66**	m2
fibre cement	0.46	6.92	7.85	**14.77**	m2
embossed or textured papered	0.32	4.85	7.85	**12.70**	m2
cement rendered	0.50	7.61	7.85	**15.46**	m2
fair face brickwork	0.55	8.37	7.85	**16.22**	m2
fair face blockwork	0.60	9.19	8.34	**17.53**	m2

028 | Ceilings over 300 mm wide:

	Man-Hours	Net Labour Price £	Net Mats Price £	Net Unit Price £	Unit
plastered	0.36	5.43	7.38	**12.81**	m2
smooth concrete	0.39	5.97	7.38	**13.35**	m2
fibre cement	0.43	6.57	7.85	**14.42**	m2
cement rendered	0.47	7.23	7.85	**15.08**	m2

Note: 029 not used

030 | Ceilings in staircase areas over 300 mm wide:

	Man-Hours	Net Labour Price £	Net Mats Price £	Net Unit Price £	Unit
plastered	0.40	6.08	7.38	**13.46**	m2
smooth concrete	0.44	6.68	7.38	**14.06**	m2
fibre cement	0.48	7.36	7.80	**15.16**	m2
cement rendered	0.53	8.07	7.80	**15.87**	m2

INTUMESCENT PAINT SYSTEMS - INTERNALLY

031 **Prepare; one coat Thermoguard Wallcoat and one coat Thermoguard flame retardant acrylic matt, designated class O surface spread of frame**

032 | Walls over 300 mm wide:

	Man-Hours	Net Labour Price £	Net Mats Price £	Net Unit Price £	Unit
plastered	0.25	3.76	3.79	**7.55**	m2
smooth concrete	0.27	4.13	4.07	**8.20**	m2
fibre cement	0.30	4.54	4.24	**8.78**	m2
embossed or textured papered	0.25	3.78	4.24	**8.02**	m2
cement rendered	0.33	5.00	4.24	**9.24**	m2
fair face brickwork	0.36	5.49	4.24	**9.73**	m2
fair face blockwork	0.40	6.04	4.80	**10.84**	m2

Note: 033 not used

034 | Walls in staircase areas over 300 mm wide:

	Man-Hours	Net Labour Price £	Net Mats Price £	Net Unit Price £	Unit
plastered	0.28	4.26	3.79	**8.05**	m2
smooth concrete	0.32	4.79	4.07	**8.86**	m2
fibre cement	0.35	5.26	4.24	**9.50**	m2
embossed or textured papered	0.29	4.38	4.24	**8.62**	m2
cement rendered	0.38	5.78	4.24	**10.02**	m2
fair face brickwork	0.42	6.34	4.24	**10.58**	m2
fair face blockwork	0.46	6.98	4.45	**11.43**	m2

035 | Ceilings over 300 mm wide:

	Man-Hours	Net Labour Price £	Net Mats Price £	Net Unit Price £	Unit
plastered	0.27	4.13	4.07	**8.20**	m2
smooth concrete	0.30	4.54	4.07	**8.61**	m2
fibre cement	0.33	5.00	4.24	**9.24**	m2
cement rendered	0.36	5.49	4.24	**9.73**	m2

Note: 036 not used

037 | Ceilings in staircase areas over 300 mm wide:

	Man-Hours	Net Labour Price £	Net Mats Price £	Net Unit Price £	Unit
plastered	0.30	4.55	4.07	**8.62**	m2
smooth concrete	0.33	5.01	4.07	**9.08**	m2
fibre cement	0.36	5.51	4.24	**9.75**	m2
cement rendered	0.40	6.06	4.24	**10.30**	m2

038 **Prepare; one coat Thermoguard Wallcoat and two coats Thermoguard flame retardant acrylic eggshell, designated class O surface spread of frame**

039 | Walls over 300 mm wide:

	Man-Hours	Net Labour Price £	Net Mats Price £	Net Unit Price £	Unit
plastered	0.36	5.48	5.36	**10.84**	m2
smooth concrete	0.40	6.02	5.64	**11.66**	m2
fibre cement	0.44	6.62	5.98	**12.60**	m2
embossed or textured papered	0.37	5.67	5.98	**11.65**	m2
cement rendered	0.48	7.29	5.98	**13.27**	m2
fair face brickwork	0.53	8.01	5.98	**13.99**	m2
fair face blockwork	0.58	8.81	6.75	**15.56**	m2

Unit Rates

		Man-Hours	Net Labour Price £	Net Mats Price £	Net Unit Price £	Unit
	Note: 040 not used					
041	Walls in staircase areas over 300 mm wide:					
	plastered	0.41	6.22	5.36	**11.58**	m2
	smooth concrete	0.46	6.98	5.64	**12.62**	m2
	fibre cement	0.50	7.67	5.98	**13.65**	m2
	embossed or textured papered	0.43	6.57	5.98	**12.55**	m2
	cement rendered	0.55	8.43	5.98	**14.41**	m2
	fair face brickwork	0.61	9.25	5.98	**15.23**	m2
	fair face blockwork	0.67	10.17	6.40	**16.57**	m2
042	Ceilings over 300 mm wide:					
	plastered	0.40	6.02	5.64	**11.66**	m2
	smooth concrete	0.44	6.62	5.64	**12.26**	m2
	fibre cement	0.48	7.29	5.98	**13.27**	m2
	cement rendered	0.53	8.01	5.98	**13.99**	m2
	Note: 043 not used					
044	Ceilings in staircase areas over 300 mm wide:					
	plastered	0.44	6.63	5.64	**12.27**	m2
	smooth concrete	0.48	7.31	5.64	**12.95**	m2
	fibre cement	0.53	8.03	5.98	**14.01**	m2
	cement rendered	0.58	8.83	5.98	**14.81**	m2
	METALWORK - INTERNALLY					
045	**Prepare; one coat zinc phosphate primer; one undercoat alkyd based paint; one coat alkyd based paint gloss finish.** Primer @ £8.25 ; Undercoat @ £6.26 ; Gloss @ £6.26 (All per 1 ltr)					
046	General surfaces:					
	over 300 mm girth	0.60	9.05	2.08	**11.13**	m2
	not exceeding 150 mm girth	0.18	2.71	0.29	**3.00**	m
	150 - 300 mm girth	0.27	4.09	0.60	**4.69**	m
	isolated; not exceeding 0.50 m2	0.31	4.70	1.00	**5.70**	Nr
047	Glazed doors and screens in panes:					
	small - not exceeding 0.10 m2	1.63	24.70	1.06	**25.76**	m2
	medium - 0.10 - 0.50 m2	1.11	16.88	0.88	**17.76**	m2
	large - 0.50 - 1.00 m2	1.04	15.83	0.77	**16.60**	m2
	extra large - over 1.00 m2	0.94	14.26	0.67	**14.93**	m2
048	Windows in panes:					
	small - not exceeding 0.10 m2	1.63	24.70	0.88	**25.58**	m2
	medium - 0.10 - 0.50 m2	1.11	16.88	0.77	**17.65**	m2
	large - 0.50 - 1.00 m2	1.04	15.83	0.67	**16.50**	m2
	extra large - over 1.00 m2	0.94	14.26	0.57	**14.83**	m2
049	Structural members:					
	over 300 mm girth	0.74	11.30	2.08	**13.38**	m2
	not exceeding 150 mm girth	0.22	3.40	0.29	**3.69**	m
	150 - 300 mm girth	0.34	5.10	0.60	**5.70**	m
050	Members of roof trusses:					
	over 300 mm girth	0.97	14.78	2.73	**17.51**	m2
	not exceeding 150 mm girth	0.29	4.43	0.39	**4.82**	m
	150 - 300 mm girth	0.44	6.67	0.81	**7.48**	m
051	Radiators:					
	over 300 mm girth	0.86	13.04	2.31	**15.35**	m2
052	Pipes and conduits, ducting, trunking and the like:					
	over 300 mm girth	0.66	9.96	2.23	**12.19**	m2
	not exceeding 150 mm girth	0.20	2.99	0.35	**3.34**	m
	150 - 300 mm girth	0.29	4.48	0.66	**5.14**	m
053	Staircases:					
	over 300 mm girth	0.72	10.96	2.08	**13.04**	m2
	not exceeding 150 mm girth	0.22	3.29	0.29	**3.58**	m
	150 - 300 mm girth	0.33	4.95	0.60	**5.55**	m
054	**Prepare; one coat Thermoguard high build primer, one coat 'Thermoguard Thermacoat W' intumescent paint to high build primer, protection given 30 minutes, second coat Thermoguard flame retardant acrylic matt/eggshell**					
055	Structural members:					
	over 300 mm girth	0.72	10.95	4.38	**15.33**	m2
	not exceeding 150 mm girth	0.26	3.91	0.68	**4.59**	m
	150 - 300 mm girth	0.36	5.40	1.30	**6.70**	m
056	Members of roof trusses:					
	over 300 mm girth	0.79	12.06	4.42	**16.48**	m2
	not exceeding 150 mm girth	0.28	4.18	0.68	**4.86**	m
	150 - 300 mm girth	0.38	5.77	1.33	**7.10**	m

Unit Rates	Man-Hours	Net Labour Price £	Net Mats Price £	Net Unit Price £	Unit
057 **Prepare; one coat Thermoguard high build primer, two coats 'Thermoguard Thermacoat W' intumescent paint to high build primer, protection given 60 minutes, third coat Thermoguard flame retardant acrylic matt/eggshell**					
058 Structural members:					
over 300 mm girth	0.91	13.77	6.12	**19.89**	m2
not exceeding 150 mm girth	0.34	5.16	0.95	**6.11**	m
150 - 300 mm girth	0.47	7.12	1.82	**8.94**	m
059 Members of roof trusses:					
over 300 mm girth	1.00	15.16	6.13	**21.29**	m2
not exceeding 150 mm girth	0.37	5.56	0.95	**6.51**	m
150 - 300 mm girth	0.50	7.66	1.85	**9.51**	m
060 **One coat wood primer, one coat Thermo Guard Timber, one coat flame retardant matt paint, giving class O spread of flame, to timber surface**					
061 General surfaces:					
over 300 mm girth	0.54	8.14	5.49	**13.63**	m2
not exceeding 150 mm girth	0.15	2.23	0.84	**3.07**	m
150 - 300 mm girth	0.23	3.48	1.61	**5.09**	m
isolated; not exceeding 0.50 m2	0.33	4.98	2.45	**7.43**	m
062 Fire resistant glazed doors, screens and windows:					
small - not exceeding 0.10 m2	1.35	20.55	13.73	**34.28**	m2
medium - 0.10 - 0.50 m2	1.01	15.33	10.40	**25.73**	m2
large - 0.50 - 1 m2	0.88	13.33	8.95	**22.28**	m2
extra large - over 1.00 m2	0.73	11.11	7.54	**18.65**	m2
063 Staircases:					
over 300 mm girth	0.56	8.50	7.81	**16.31**	m2
not exceeding 150 mm girth	0.16	2.35	1.16	**3.51**	m
150 - 300 mm girth	0.24	3.69	2.33	**6.02**	m
isolated; not exceeding 0.5 m2	0.31	4.70	3.41	**8.11**	nr
balustrade (measured both sides)	0.37	5.63	29.27	**34.90**	m2
WOODWORK - INTERNALLY					
064 **Prepare, knotting, stopping; one coat wood primer; one undercoat alkyd based paint; one coat alkyd based paint gloss finish.** Primer @ £7.49 ; Undercoat @ £6.26 ; Gloss @ £6.26 (All per 1 ltr)					
065 General surfaces:					
over 300 mm girth	0.60	9.05	2.19	**11.24**	m2
not exceeding 150 mm girth	0.18	2.71	0.30	**3.01**	m
150 - 300 mm girth	0.27	4.09	0.60	**4.69**	m
isolated; not exceeding 0.50 m2	0.31	4.70	1.05	**5.75**	Nr
066 Glazed doors and screens in panes:					
small - not exceeding 0.10 m2	1.56	23.66	1.35	**25.01**	m2
medium - 0.10 - 0.50 m2	1.04	15.81	1.11	**16.92**	m2
large - 0.50 - 1.00 m2	0.94	14.26	0.91	**15.17**	m2
extra large - over 1.00 m2	0.87	13.21	0.67	**13.88**	m2
067 Windows in panes:					
small - not exceeding 0.10 m2	1.63	24.70	1.72	**26.42**	m2
medium - 0.10 - 0.50 m2	1.11	16.88	1.58	**18.46**	m2
large - 0.50 - 1.00 m2	1.01	15.31	1.35	**16.66**	m2
extra large - over 1.00 m2	0.94	14.26	1.11	**15.37**	m2
068 Frames, linings and associated mouldings:					
over 300 mm girth	0.60	9.05	2.19	**11.24**	m2
not exceeding 150 mm girth	0.18	2.71	0.30	**3.01**	m
150 - 300 mm girth	0.27	4.09	0.60	**4.69**	m
069 Cornices:					
over 300 mm girth	0.71	10.79	2.19	**12.98**	m2
not exceeding 150 mm girth	0.21	3.23	0.30	**3.53**	m
150 - 300 mm girth	0.33	4.95	0.60	**5.55**	m
070 Skirtings, dado rails, picture rails and the like:					
over 300 mm girth	0.66	9.96	2.19	**12.15**	m2
not exceeding 150 mm girth	0.20	2.99	0.30	**3.29**	m
150 - 300 mm girth	0.30	4.53	0.60	**5.13**	m
071 Staircases:					
over 300 mm girth	0.63	9.52	2.19	**11.71**	m2
not exceeding 150 mm girth	0.19	2.85	0.30	**3.15**	m
150 - 300 mm girth	0.28	4.29	0.60	**4.89**	m
072 **One coat wood primer, one coat Thermo Guard Timber, two coats flame retardant eggshell paint, giving class O spread of flame, to timber surface**					
073 General surfaces:					
over 300 mm girth	0.65	9.86	7.06	**16.92**	m2
not exceeding 150 mm girth	0.16	2.49	1.07	**3.56**	m
150 - 300 mm girth	0.26	3.99	2.08	**6.07**	m

Unit Rates		Man-Hours	Net Labour Price £	Net Mats Price £	Net Unit Price £	Unit
	CLEAR FINISHES ON WOODWORK - INTERNALLY					
074	**Prepare; two coats polyurethane varnish; first coat on unprimed surfaces.** Varnish @£12.26 Thinners @ £3.75 (Both per 1 ltr)					
075	General surfaces:					
	over 300 mm girth	0.42	6.42	1.91	**8.33**	m2
	not exceeding 150 mm girth	0.13	1.93	0.34	**2.27**	m
	150 - 300 mm girth	0.19	2.91	0.64	**3.55**	m
	isolated; not exceeding 0.50 m2	0.25	3.76	0.95	**4.71**	Nr
076	Glazed doors and screens in panes:					
	small - not exceeding 0.10 m2	1.00	15.14	1.18	**16.32**	m2
	medium - 0.10 - 0.50 m2	0.72	10.96	0.99	**11.95**	m2
	large - 0.50 - 1.00 m2	0.65	9.91	0.81	**10.72**	m2
	extra large - over 1.00 m2	0.61	9.22	0.63	**9.85**	m2
077	Windows in panes:					
	small - not exceeding 0.10 m2	1.11	16.88	1.55	**18.43**	m2
	medium - 0.10 - 0.50 m2	0.77	11.65	1.36	**13.01**	m2
	large - 0.50 - 1.00 m2	0.72	10.96	1.18	**12.14**	m2
	extra large - over 1.00 m2	0.65	9.91	0.99	**10.90**	m2
078	Frames, linings and associated mouldings:					
	over 300 mm girth	0.42	6.43	2.07	**8.50**	m2
	not exceeding 150 mm girth	0.13	1.93	0.37	**2.30**	m
	150 - 300 mm girth	0.19	2.91	0.67	**3.58**	m
079	Cornices:					
	over 300 mm girth	0.50	7.66	2.07	**9.73**	m2
	not exceeding 150 mm girth	0.15	2.29	0.37	**2.66**	m
	150 - 300 mm girth	0.23	3.51	0.67	**4.18**	m
080	Skirtings, dado rails, picture rails and the like:					
	over 300 mm girth	0.47	7.08	2.07	**9.15**	m2
	not exceeding 150 mm girth	0.14	2.13	0.37	**2.50**	m
	150 - 300 mm girth	0.21	3.23	0.67	**3.90**	m
081	Staircases:					
	over 300 mm girth	0.45	6.76	1.91	**8.67**	m2
	not exceeding 150 mm girth	0.13	2.04	0.34	**2.38**	m
	150 - 300 mm girth	0.20	3.07	0.67	**3.74**	m
082	**Prepare; two coats Thermoguard fire varnish on timber, giving Class O flame spread**					
083	General surfaces:					
	over 300 mm girth	0.42	6.41	4.14	**10.55**	m2
	not exceeding 150 mm girth	0.13	2.02	0.62	**2.64**	m
	150 - 300 mm girth	0.20	3.04	1.24	**4.28**	m
	isolated; not exceeding 0.50 m2	0.25	3.85	1.87	**5.72**	nr
084	Fire resistant glazed doors, screens and windows:					
	small - not exceeding 0.10 m2	1.08	16.43	2.79	**19.22**	m2
	medium - 0.10 - 0.50 m2	0.78	11.90	2.30	**14.20**	m2
	large - 0.50 - 1 m2	0.68	10.34	1.88	**12.22**	m2
	extra large - over 1 m2	0.60	9.16	10.93	**20.09**	m2
	opening edge	0.14	2.20	0.44	**2.64**	m
085	Staircases:					
	over 300 mm girth	0.44	6.73	2.76	**9.49**	m2
	not exceeding 150 mm girth	0.14	2.12	0.62	**2.74**	m
	150 - 300 mm girth	0.22	3.29	1.24	**4.53**	m
	isolated; not exceeding 0.5 m2	0.28	4.23	1.86	**6.09**	m
	balustrade (measured both sides)	0.37	5.63	3.53	**9.16**	m2
086	**Prepare; one thin coat sealer, one full coat quick drying floor, one coat anti-slip paint to**					
087	Floor, concrete or the like:					
	over 300 mm girth	0.30	4.63	1.36	**5.99**	m2
	not exceeding 150 mm girth	0.08	1.17	0.26	**1.43**	m
	150 - 300 mm girth	0.11	1.65	0.40	**2.05**	m
	NEW WORK EXTERNALLY					
	WALLS - EXTERNALLY					
	EMULSION PAINT - WALLS EXTERNALLY					
088	**Two coats of exterior emulsion paint, matt finish, first coat to unprimed surfaces.** Exterior emulsion @ £4.93 per 1 ltr)					
089	To walls:					
	smooth concrete	0.29	4.43	0.91	**5.34**	m2
	fibre cement	0.29	4.43	0.88	**5.31**	m2
	cement rendered	0.27	4.04	1.03	**5.07**	Unit
	fair face brickwork	0.35	5.39	1.15	**6.54**	m2
	fair face blockwork	0.41	6.22	1.32	**7.54**	m2
	rough cast/pebbledash rendered	0.54	8.24	2.93	**11.17**	m2
	Tyrolean rendered	0.70	10.66	3.66	**14.32**	m2

	Unit Rates	Man-Hours	Net Labour Price £	Net Mats Price £	Net Unit Price £	Unit
	MASONRY PAINT - WALLS EXTERNALLY					
090	**One coat of masonry sealer, to unprimed surfaces and two coats masonry paint (white).** Masonry sealer @ £9.48 ; Masonry paint @ £9.66 (Both per 1 ltr)					
091	To walls:					
	smooth concrete	0.41	6.26	2.68	**8.94**	m2
	fibre cement	0.41	6.26	2.65	**8.91**	m2
	cement rendered	0.37	5.68	3.03	**8.71**	m2
	fair face brickwork	0.50	7.67	3.16	**10.83**	m2
	fair face blockwork	0.58	8.81	2.90	**11.71**	m2
	rough cast/pebbledash rendered	0.78	11.88	5.45	**17.33**	m2
	Tyrolean rendered	1.00	15.23	8.21	**23.44**	m2
	SNOWCEM PAINT - WALLS EXTERNALLY					
092	**Two coats of 'Snowcem' cement paint; including base coat of stabilising solution to unprimed surface.** Stabilising solution @ £6.98 per 1 ltr; 'Snowcem' @ £1.44 per 1 kg					
093	To walls:					
	smooth concrete	0.41	6.26	0.81	**7.07**	m2
	fibre cement	0.41	6.26	0.77	**7.03**	m2
	cement rendered	0.37	5.67	0.87	**6.54**	m2
	fair face brickwork	0.50	7.67	0.90	**8.57**	m2
	fair face blockwork	0.58	8.77	1.12	**9.89**	m2
	rough cast/pebbledash rendered	0.78	11.88	1.50	**13.38**	m2
	Tyrolean rendered	1.00	15.22	3.05	**18.27**	m2
	SANDTEX MATT - WALLS EXTERNALLY					
094	**Two coats 'Sandtex' (Fine build on Matt), including base coat of stabilising solution to unprimed surface.** Stabilising solution @ £6.98 per 1 ltr; 'Sandtex' Matt @ £3.73 per 1 ltr; 'Sandtex' Fine Build @ £3.16 per 1 kg					
095	To walls:					
	smooth concrete	0.52	7.92	5.61	**13.53**	m2
	fibre cement	0.52	7.92	5.58	**13.50**	m2
	cement rendered	0.48	7.33	5.72	**13.05**	m2
	fair face brickwork	0.64	9.74	5.76	**15.50**	m2
	fair face blockwork	0.72	10.91	5.97	**16.88**	m2
	Note: 096 - 097 not used					
	METALWORK - EXTERNALLY					
098	**Prepare; one coat zinc phosphate primer; one undercoat alkyd based paint; one coat alkyd based paint gloss finish.** Primer @ £8.25 ; Undercoat @ £6.26 ; Gloss @ £6.26 (All per 1 ltr)					
099	General surfaces:					
	over 300 mm girth	0.63	9.57	2.08	**11.65**	m2
	not exceeding 150 mm girth	0.18	2.80	0.29	**3.09**	m
	150 - 300 mm girth	0.28	4.18	0.60	**4.78**	m
	isolated; not exceeding 0.50 m2	0.37	5.64	1.00	**6.64**	Nr
100	Glazed doors and screens in panes:					
	small - not exceeding 0.10 m2	1.69	25.74	1.06	**26.80**	m2
	medium - 0.10 - 0.50 m2	1.18	17.91	0.88	**18.79**	m2
	large - 0.50 - 1.00 m2	1.10	16.70	0.77	**17.47**	m2
	extra large - over 1.00 m2	0.98	14.97	0.67	**15.64**	m2
101	Windows in panes:					
	small - not exceeding 0.10 m2	1.69	25.74	0.88	**26.62**	m2
	medium - 0.10 - 0.50 m2	1.18	17.91	0.77	**18.68**	m2
	large - 0.50 - 1.00 m2	1.10	16.70	0.67	**17.37**	m2
	extra large - over 1.00 m2	0.98	14.97	0.57	**15.54**	m2
102	Edges of opening casements	0.17	2.61	0.10	**2.71**	m
103	Structural members:					
	over 300 mm girth	0.78	11.84	2.08	**13.92**	m2
	not exceeding 150 mm girth	0.23	3.48	0.29	**3.77**	m
	150 - 300 mm girth	0.34	5.21	0.60	**5.81**	m
	Note: 104 not used					
105	Each side of ornamental railings, gates and the like (grouped together) measured both sides overall regardless of voids:					
	over 300 mm girth	0.49	7.42	1.70	**9.12**	m2
106	Pipes and conduits, ducting, trunking and the like:					
	over 300 mm girth	0.69	10.44	2.23	**12.67**	m2
	not exceeding 150 mm girth	0.21	3.13	0.35	**3.48**	m
	150 - 300 mm girth	0.31	4.70	0.66	**5.36**	m
107	Eaves gutters:					
	over 300 mm girth	0.69	10.44	2.08	**12.52**	m2
	not exceeding 150 mm girth	0.21	3.13	0.29	**3.42**	m
	150 - 300 mm girth	0.31	4.70	0.60	**5.30**	m

Unit Rates

		Man-Hours	Net Labour Price £	Net Mats Price £	Net Unit Price £	Unit
108	Staircases:					
	over 300 mm girth	0.76	11.48	2.08	**13.56**	m2
	not exceeding 150 mm girth	0.23	3.48	0.29	**3.77**	m
	150 - 300 mm girth	0.33	5.04	0.60	**5.64**	m
	Note: 109 - 110 not used					
	WOODWORK - EXTERNALLY					
111	**Prepare, knotting and stopping; one coat wood primer, one undercoat alkyd based paint, one coat alkyd based paint gloss finish.** Primer @ £7.49 ; Undercoat @ £6.26 ; Gloss @ £6.26 (All per 1 ltr)					
112	General surfaces:					
	over 300 mm girth	0.63	9.57	2.19	**11.76**	m2
	not exceeding 150 mm girth	0.18	2.79	0.30	**3.09**	m
	150 - 300 mm girth	0.28	4.18	0.60	**4.78**	m
	isolated; not exceeding 0.50 m2	0.37	5.64	1.05	**6.69**	Nr
113	Glazed doors and screens in panes:					
	small - not exceeding 0.10 m2	1.63	24.70	1.35	**26.05**	m2
	medium - 0.10 - 0.50 m2	1.10	16.70	1.11	**17.81**	m2
	large - 0.50 - 1.00 m2	0.98	14.97	0.91	**15.88**	m2
	extra large - over 1.00 m2	0.90	13.75	0.67	**14.42**	m2
114	Windows in panes:					
	small - not exceeding 0.10 m2	1.69	25.74	1.72	**27.46**	m2
	medium - 0.10 - 0.50 m2	1.18	17.91	1.58	**19.49**	m2
	large - 0.50 - 1.00 m2	1.10	16.70	1.35	**18.05**	m2
	extra large - over 1.00 m2	0.98	14.97	1.11	**16.08**	m2
115	Edges of opening casements	0.17	2.61	0.17	**2.78**	m
116	Frames, linings and associated mouldings:					
	over 300 mm girth	0.63	9.57	2.19	**11.76**	m2
	not exceeding 150 mm girth	0.18	2.79	0.30	**3.09**	m
	150 - 300 mm girth	0.28	4.18	0.60	**4.78**	m
	VARNISH ON WOODWORK - EXTERNALLY					
117	**Prepare; one coat preservative basecoat; two coats external grade varnish, wood surfaces; first coat to untreated surfaces.** Preservative basecoat @ £12.59 per 1 ltr; External grade varnish @ £17.08 per 1 ltr					
118	General surfaces:					
	over 300 mm girth	0.58	8.81	3.57	**12.38**	m2
	not exceeding 150 mm girth	0.17	2.63	0.62	**3.25**	m
	150 - 300 mm girth	0.26	3.93	1.17	**5.10**	m
	isolated; not exceeding 0.50 m2	0.34	5.17	1.79	**6.96**	Nr
119	Glazed doors and screens in panes:					
	small - not exceeding 0.10 m2	1.55	23.50	2.17	**25.67**	m2
	medium - 0.10 - 0.50 m2	1.08	16.34	1.85	**18.19**	m2
	large - 0.50 - 1.00 m2	0.94	14.36	1.47	**15.83**	m2
	extra large - over 1.00 m2	0.86	13.12	1.15	**14.27**	m2
120	Windows in panes:					
	small - not exceeding 0.10 m2	1.60	24.28	2.87	**27.15**	m2
	medium - 0.10 - 0.50 m2	1.18	17.91	2.55	**20.46**	m2
	large - 0.50 - 1.00 m2	1.00	15.14	2.17	**17.31**	m2
	extra large - over 1.00 m2	0.90	13.75	1.85	**15.60**	m2
121	Edges of opening casements	0.16	2.36	0.15	**2.51**	m
122	Frames, linings and associated mouldings:					
	over 300 mm girth	0.58	8.81	3.85	**12.66**	m2
	not exceeding 150 mm girth	0.18	2.66	0.66	**3.32**	m
	150 - 300 mm girth	0.26	3.91	1.21	**5.12**	m
123	**Prepare; two coats Breather Paint, wood surfaces** Breather paint @ £10.08 per 1 ltr					
124	General surfaces:					
	over 300 mm girth	0.29	4.38	2.57	**6.95**	m2
	not exceeding 150 mm girth	0.07	1.02	0.40	**1.42**	m
	150 - 300 mm girth	0.12	1.88	0.60	**2.48**	m
	isolated; not exceeding 0.50 m2	0.14	2.19	1.11	**3.30**	Nr
125	Windows in panes:					
	small - not exceeding 0.10 m2	0.62	9.39	1.96	**11.35**	m2
	medium - 0.10 - 0.50 m2	0.46	7.05	1.56	**8.61**	m2
	large - 0.50 - 1.00 m2	0.43	6.58	1.31	**7.89**	m2
	extra large - over 1.00 m2	0.40	6.11	1.05	**7.16**	m2
126	Frames, linings and associated mouldings:					
	over 300 mm girth	0.27	4.07	2.57	**6.64**	m2
	not exceeding 150 mm girth	0.08	1.25	0.40	**1.65**	m
	150 - 300 mm girth	0.13	2.04	0.60	**2.64**	m

Unit Rates	Man-Hours	Net Labour Price £	Net Mats Price £	Net Unit Price £	Unit
127 **Prepare; two coats semi-gloss wood stain** Sadolin 'Extra' @ £11.74 per 1 ltr					
128 General surfaces:					
over 300 mm girth	0.27	4.07	1.45	**5.52**	m2
not exceeding 150 mm girth	0.06	0.94	0.23	**1.17**	m
150 - 300 mm girth	0.11	1.72	0.47	**2.19**	m
isolated; not exceeding 0.50 m2	0.14	2.19	0.70	**2.89**	Nr
129 Glazed doors and screens in panes:					
small - not exceeding 0.10 m2	0.57	8.61	1.10	**9.71**	m2
medium - 0.10 - 0.50 m2	0.42	6.42	0.87	**7.29**	m2
large - 0.50 - 1.00 m2	0.39	5.95	0.75	**6.70**	m2
extra large - over 1.00 m2	0.37	5.64	0.63	**6.27**	m2
130 Windows in panes:					
small - not exceeding 0.10 m2	0.62	9.39	1.10	**10.49**	m2
medium - 0.10 - 0.50 m2	0.46	7.05	0.87	**7.92**	m2
large - 0.50 - 1.00 m2	0.43	6.58	0.75	**7.33**	m2
extra large - over 1.00 m2	0.40	6.11	0.63	**6.74**	m2
131 Frames, linings and associated mouldings:					
over 300 mm girth	0.27	4.07	1.57	**5.64**	m2
not exceeding 150 mm girth	0.07	1.10	0.23	**1.33**	m
150 - 300 mm girth	0.12	1.88	0.35	**2.23**	m
Note: 132 to 199 not used					
PAPERHANGING AND DECORATION					
200 **Prepare plastered surfaces, size, hang woodchip paper, P.C. £2.10 per roll; one priming coat and two full coats vinyl silk emulsion paint** @ £5.71 (white) per 1 litre					
201 Walls:					
over 300 mm wide	0.76	11.59	2.43	**14.02**	m2
3.50 - 5.00 m high where ceiling is dissimilar finish; over 300 mm wide	0.84	12.82	2.43	**15.25**	m2
in staircase areas over 300 mm wide	0.84	12.71	2.43	**15.14**	m2
202 Ceilings:					
over 300 mm wide	0.84	12.82	2.43	**15.25**	m2
3.50 - 5.00 m high over 300 mm wide	0.93	14.08	2.43	**16.51**	m2
in staircase areas over 300 mm wide	0.92	13.92	2.43	**16.35**	m2

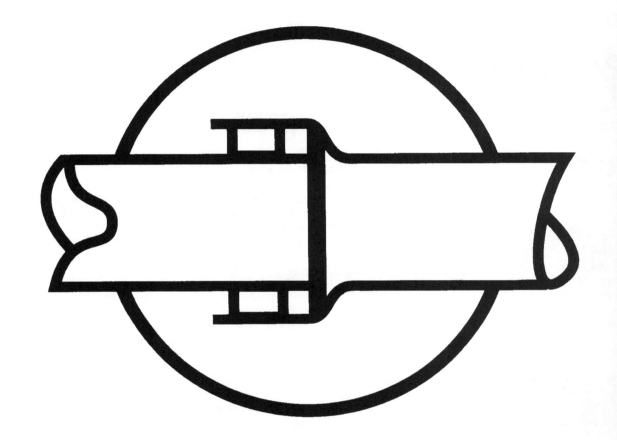

Drainage

BCIS
Independent cost information
for the built environment

CONSTRUCTION
BCIS PRICE DATA 2013

Comprehensive Building Price Book 2013
Major and Minor Works dataset

The Major Works dataset focuses predominantly on large 'new build' projects reflecting the economies of scale found in these forms of construction. The Minor Works Estimating Dataset focuses on small to medium sized 'new build' projects reflecting the increase in costs brought about the reduced output, less discounts, increased carriage and supervision, to the similar items in the Major Works dataset. The dataset is presented in trade order. Revised and reworked items in underpinning composites; flue linings and rainwater goods.

Item code: 19215 **Price: £165.99**

SMM7 Estimating Price Book 2013

The SMM7 Estimating dataset focuses predominantly on large 'new build' projects reflecting the economies of scale found in these forms of construction. The dataset is presented in SMM7 grouping and order in accordance with the Common Arrangement of Work Sections. It is compiled using the latest independent costing information from manufacturers, material and plant suppliers, legislation effects and working rule agreements. Revised and reworked items in underpinning composites; flue linings and rainwater goods.

Item code: 19216 **Price: £139.99**

Alterations and Refurbishment Price Book 2013

The Alterations & Refurbishment dataset focuses on small to medium sized projects, generally working within an existing building and reflecting the increase in costs brought about the reduction in output, smaller discounts, increased carriage, increased supervision, and less productivity brought about by smaller economies of scale, increased production costs, more difficult access and the possibility of working in occupied premises. The dataset is presented in trade order. Revised and reworked items in underpinning composites; flue linings and rainwater goods.

Item code: 19217 **Price £109.99**

BCIS Guide to Estimating for Small Works 2012

The BCIS Guide to Estimating for Small Works 2012 is a unique dataset which shows the true power of resource based estimating. A set of composite built-up measured items are used to build up priced estimates for a large number of common specification extensions. The intention is to show estimating techniques in use and allow users to build up accurate estimates for their own projects, simply and easily, with up-to-date and independent cost information.

Item code: 19064 **Price: £59.99**

BCIS Painting and Decorating Price Book 2012

The BCIS Painting and Decorating dataset is the most handy pricing tool available to the painting and decorating sector of the industry, suitable for all projects needing more than a 'guess-timate'. Using this dataset a more accurate calculation based quotation or variation can be prepared. From these calculations an assessment of labour, plant and material content can be produced. This in turn enables the contractor to negotiate discounts on known material requirements and the effect of this workload on the availability of labour.

Item code: 19065 **Price: £39.99**

For more information call **0870 333 1600** email **contact@bcis.co.uk** or visit **www.bcis.co.uk**

BCIS is the Building Cost Information Service of **RICS**
the mark of property professionalism worldwide

Labour Rates

Please note: The labour hours throughout this section are representative of the time required for one productive man to carry out the unit of work.

Gang rates are calculated as follows by obtaining the overall gang cost and then dividing this by the number of productive members in the gang. The resulting rate is the Gang Cost per **Man - hour.** By using the same principle, any size gang may be built-up and used against the standard labour hours in this section.

Excavations Generally
Labourer (BATJIC Oper. Rate) -   £11.22 per hour

Breaking rock concrete and the like with air or electric percussion drills, hammers, rammers etc.
Labourer (skill rate A) -   £11.82 per hour

Earthwork Support
Labourer (semi skill A) -   £14.02 per hour

Laying pipes up to but not including 300 mm diameter
Drainlayer (skill rate B) -   £12.12 per hour

Laying pipes 300 mm diameter and over
Drainlayer (skill rate C) -   £12.45 per hour

A0220 Drainage Gang

Drainlayer (skill rate C)	1.00	x	£	12.45	=	£	12.45
Drainlayer (skill rate B)	1.00	x	£	12.12	=	£	12.12
Total hourly cost of gang					=	£	24.57

Gang rate (divided by 2) = £12.29 per Man-hour

A0216 Brickwork in manholes and the like

Brick/Block Layer	1.00	x	£	15.20	=	£	15.20
Brick/Blockwork Labourer	1.00	x	£	11.22	=	£	11.22
Total hourly cost of gang					=	£	26.42

Gang rate (divided by 1) = £26.42 per Man-hour

A0211 Laying and jointing cast iron pipes and fittings:

Advanced PHMES Operative	1.00	x	£	19.59	=	£	19.59
Apprentice Plumber (3rd Year)	1.00	x	£	12.01	=	£	12.01
Total hourly cost of gang					=	£	31.60

Gang rate (divided by 1) = £31.60 per Man-hour

Making and fixing formwork:
Craftsman (BATJIC Craft Rate) -   £15.20 per hour

Plant Hire Charges		Daily Hire Charge £	Pro-ductive Hours Hrs	Cost Per Hour £	Operator Per Hour £	Fuel Per Hour £	Total Cost Per Hour £
The hire charges shown exclude the cost of operators and fuel but are inclusive of oil, grease and the like. Fuel costs have been added in the following table as appropriate. The operator costs are either added in the table below or, where no operator shown, have been allowed for in the rates given in the individual items of work. The cost of delivery to, or collection from site is EXCLUDED and allowance for this should be made in Preliminaries.							
A0021	JCB 3C	85.00	6.00	14.17	14.38	5.63	**34.18**
A0022	Cat D5 1CY	145.00	6.00	24.17	14.38	8.29	**46.84**
A0024	Hymac 580 with breaker hammer and 230 cfm compressor	230.00	7.00	32.86	14.38	9.15	**56.39**
A0031	Dumper 2000 kg capacity, hydraulic tip	45.00	6.00	7.50	11.82	2.52	**21.84**
A0041	16 Tonne tipper truck	224.00	8.00	28.00	-	-	**28.00**
A0051	8 Tonne roller	80.00	6.00	13.33	11.82	6.63	**31.78**
A0061	Whacker	16.50	6.00	2.75	-	0.86	**3.61**
A0023	Hymac 580	154.00	6.00	25.67	14.38	7.49	**47.54**
A0063	Compressor 100 cfm and one breaker tool	32.00	6.00	5.33	-	0.86	**6.19**
A0200	Tipping Charges per load	110.00	1.00	110.00	-	-	**110.00**
A0111	Props (per week)	2.20	1.00	2.20	-	-	**2.20**

Plant and Equipment Hours

The abbreviations under the headings on the succeeding pages have the following meanings:
    Excav = Excavating plant (JCB, Cat, etc.)
    Brkng = Breaking equipment (Hymac 580 with breaker hammer or compressor and one breaker tool)
    Cmptg = Compacting equipment (Whacker, 8 Tonne roller etc.)
    Trans = Transportation plant (Dumper, lorry etc.)

Basic Prices of Materials

		Supply Price £	Waste Factor %	Unload. Labour £	Unload. Plant £	Total Unit Cost £	Unit
Note:							
	Prices for Hepworth goods are based upon delivery to Zone 2 and are for full articulated vehicle loads with mechanical off loading						
	Prices for cast iron drainage goods are based upon delivery within a 60 mile radius from the point of supply						
	Prices for other goods are based upon delivery in full loads up to about 10 miles radius from point of supply						
	Basic Prices of Materials						
A0361	Timber for earthwork support	280.30	5%	11.22	-	306.09	m3
A0351	Hardcore	18.11	-	-	-	18.11	m3
Y0074	Granular material 19 mm down	26.01	10%	-	-	28.61	tonne
Y0073	Granular material for bedding MOT grade 1	18.11	10%	-	-	19.92	tonne
A0331	Sand for bedding, BS 1199	29.64	10%	-	-	32.60	tonne
A0301	Portland cement delivered in bags	137.81	5%	11.22	-	156.48	tonne
A0322	Sharp Sand BS 882 Zone M	25.26	10%	-	-	27.78	tonne
A0331	Concreting sand	29.64	10%	-	-	32.60	tonne
A0343	20 mm Aggregate	30.95	10%	-	-	34.05	tonne
A0346	Pea shingle 10 mm down	30.15	10%	-	-	33.16	tonne
F0507	Lean mix concrete (1:12) - ready mixed	79.51	5%	-	-	83.49	m3
	Steel fabric reinforcement to BS 4483, supplied in standard sheets reference:						
F0462	A142	2.05	2.5%	0.03	-	2.13	m2
F0464	A252	3.47	2.5%	0.08	-	3.64	m2
F0466	B196	2.90	2.5%	0.08	-	3.05	m2
F0469	B503	4.95	2.5%	0.11	-	5.19	m2
F0260	Sawn softwood for formwork	295.00	12.5%	11.22	-	344.50	m3
F0261	19 mm plywood for formwork	8.60	10%	2.81	-	12.55	m2
F0266	Formwork oil	1.54	20%	-	-	1.85	ltr
F0263	Nails	2.90	10%	-	-	3.19	kg
G0102	Common bricks	311.01	5%	-	-	326.56	1000
G0104	Class B Engineering bricks	391.75	5%	-	-	411.33	1000
G0106	Adjustment factor for price of bricks	10.00	-	-	-	10.00	1000
	"HepLine" vitrified clay perforated pipe and fittings; with integral PVCu couplings:						
	pipes:						
W0091	100 mm	4.22	5%	-	-	4.43	m
W0092	150 mm	7.66	5%	-	-	8.04	m
W0093	225 mm	16.22	5%	-	-	17.03	m
	Note: For bends and junctions see SuperSleve						
	"SuperSleve" vitrified clay drainage systems to BS EN295:1991:						
	pipes:						
W0120	100 mm	2.54	5%	-	-	2.67	m
W0121	150 mm	5.13	5%	-	-	5.39	m
W0122	225 mm	13.11	5%	-	-	13.76	m
W0871	300 mm	25.35	5%	-	-	26.62	m
	couplings (polyprop.) with standard sealing rings:						
W0123	100 mm	1.87	2.5%	-	-	1.92	nr
W0124	150 mm	3.40	2.5%	-	-	3.48	nr
W0125	225 mm	6.53	2.5%	-	-	6.69	nr
W0873	300 mm	13.40	2.5%	-	-	13.73	nr
	bends (ref. SB1, 2, 3, 4):						
W0126	100 mm	3.43	2.5%	-	-	3.51	nr
W0127	150 mm	7.06	2.5%	-	-	7.23	nr
W0128	225 mm	35.98	2.5%	-	-	36.88	nr
W0875	300 mm	68.27	2.5%	-	-	69.98	nr
	junctions (oblique or curved square: ref.SJ1 & 2):						
W0129	100 x 100 mm	7.40	2.5%	-	-	7.58	nr
W0130	150 x 150 mm	9.44	2.5%	-	-	9.68	nr
W0131	225 mm x 225 mm	63.92	2.5%	-	-	65.52	nr
W0877	300 x 300 mm	136.67	2.5%	-	-	140.08	nr
	saddle (oblique or square: ref. SJS1 & 4):						
W0132	100 mm	7.26	2.5%	-	-	7.45	nr
W0133	150 mm	10.81	2.5%	-	-	11.08	nr
W0134	225 mm	40.21	2.5%	-	-	41.22	nr
W0879	300 mm	69.92	2.5%	-	-	71.66	nr
	rest bend (ref. SBR):						
W0135	100 mm	6.06	2.5%	-	-	6.22	nr
W0136	150 mm	9.06	2.5%	-	-	9.29	nr
W0137	225 mm	39.35	2.5%	-	-	40.33	nr
W0881	300 mm	103.92	2.5%	-	-	106.52	nr
	taper pipe (ref. ST):						
W0138	100 : 150 mm	8.74	2.5%	-	-	8.96	nr
W0139	150 : 225 mm	27.26	2.5%	-	-	27.94	nr
W0883	225 - 300 mm	75.18	2.5%	-	-	77.06	nr
	socket adaptor (ref. SA):						
W0140	100 mm	3.63	2.5%	-	-	3.72	nr
W0141	150 mm	7.16	2.5%	-	-	7.33	nr
W0142	225 mm	14.75	2.5%	-	-	15.12	nr
	adaptor to HepSeal:						
W0143	100 mm	2.95	2.5%	-	-	3.03	nr
W0144	150 mm	5.08	2.5%	-	-	5.21	nr
W0145	225 mm	7.01	2.5%	-	-	7.19	nr
	low-back P-trap:						
W0146	100 mm	7.40	2.5%	-	-	7.58	nr

Basic Prices of Materials

		Supply Price £	Waste Factor %	Unload. Labour £	Unload. Plant £	Total Unit Cost £	Unit
W0147	150 mm	11.95	2.5%	-	-	12.25	nr
W0524	PRG (P) Poly road gully MGP1/1	56.58	2.5%	-	-	58.00	nr
W0525	PRG (LT) Poly trap MGPT	14.34	2.5%	-	-	14.69	nr
W0148	hopper square 100 mm	13.93	2.5%	-	-	14.28	nr
W0149	square P-trap gully 100 mm	20.94	2.5%	-	-	21.46	nr
W0150	access gully 100 mm	28.79	2.5%	-	-	29.51	nr
W0151	access gully 100 mm horiz. back inlet	29.10	2.5%	-	-	29.82	nr
W0152	hopper square 100 mm; plastic grid	13.93	2.5%	-	-	14.28	nr
W0153	grid 150 mm square	2.06	2.5%	-	-	2.11	nr
W0154	hopper square 100 mm	7.72	2.5%	-	-	7.91	nr
W0156	sealing plate 120 mm	4.65	2.5%	-	-	4.77	nr
W0157	hinged grid and frame 120 mm	4.61	2.5%	-	-	4.73	nr
	rodding point oval, aluminium:						
W0159	150 mm	24.24	2.5%	-	-	24.85	nr
W0160	100 mm - square, sealed and socketed (ref SRPS 1/1)	15.80	2.5%	-	-	16.19	nr
	access pipe:						
W0161	100 mm	24.01	2.5%	-	-	24.61	nr
W0162	150 mm	26.61	2.5%	-	-	27.28	nr
W0163	access bend (ref. SBA) 150 mm	31.14	2.5%	-	-	31.92	nr
	single oblique access junction (ref. SJA):						
W0164	100 x 100 mm	26.06	2.5%	-	-	26.71	nr
W0165	150 x 100 mm or 150 x 150 mm	38.74	2.5%	-	-	39.71	nr
W0166	access raising piece 225 mm high	9.55	2.5%	-	-	9.79	nr
W0167	alloy lid and frame (for SBA)	14.81	2.5%	-	-	15.18	nr
W0168	WC pan S-trap 1.25"/1.5" - adaptor 4" - 100 mm	5.65	2.5%	-	-	5.79	nr
W0169	soil pipe adaptor 100 mm	5.65	2.5%	-	-	5.79	nr
W0170	waste pipe adaptor (ref. SA7) 100 mm	5.47	2.5%	-	-	5.61	nr
W0810	universal rainwater adaptor, spigot 100 mm	5.65	2.5%	-	-	5.79	nr
W0811	adaptor to cast iron pipes, 100 mm	5.65	2.5%	-	-	5.79	nr
W0812	adaptor coupling to Hepsleve pipes, 100 mm	2.06	2.5%	-	-	2.11	nr
W0526	SuperSleve/Hepsleve adaptor coupling SA3/2	8.28	2.5%	-	-	8.49	nr
	"SuperSeal" vitrified clay drainage system to BS EN295:1991 pipes; (integral socket and sealing rings):						
W0171	150 mm	8.78	5%	-	-	9.22	m
W0172	225 mm	18.23	5%	-	-	19.14	m
W0173	300 mm	27.96	5%	-	-	29.36	m
	bends "SuperSeal" (ref. FB1,2,3,4):						
W0178	150 mm	16.89	2.5%	-	-	17.31	nr
W0179	225 mm	39.57	2.5%	-	-	40.56	nr
W0180	300 mm	75.15	2.5%	-	-	77.03	nr
	rest bend (ref. SBR2):						
W0185	150 mm	9.06	2.5%	-	-	9.29	nr
	junctions (ref. FJ1,2 & 3); (supersleve arm):						
W0187	150 mm	22.07	2.5%	-	-	22.62	nr
W0188	225 mm	55.23	2.5%	-	-	56.62	nr
W0189	300 mm	115.71	2.5%	-	-	118.60	nr
	low back P trap:						
W0227	100 mm trap and 100 mm outlet	7.40	2.5%	-	-	7.58	nr
	aluminium alloy gulley grid:						
W0229	150 mm diameter	3.07	2.5%	-	-	3.15	nr
	yard gulley:						
W0230	225 mm internal diameter with 100 mm outlet	54.66	2.5%	-	-	56.02	nr
	cast iron gulley grid:						
W0231	150 mm diameter	3.07	2.5%	-	-	3.15	nr
W0193	Hepworth lubricant 1 kg containers	2.67	2.5%	-	-	2.74	kg
	Hepworth vitrified clay unjointed spigot and socket pipes and fittings BS 65:						
W0200	100 mm in 1.00m pipe lengths	5.50	5%	-	-	5.78	m
W0201	150 mm in 1.5m pipe lengths	8.47	5%	-	-	8.89	m
W0202	225 mm in 1.75m pipe lengths	16.77	5%	-	-	17.61	m
	bends, (ref. RB1,2,3 & 5):						
W0203	100 mm	5.50	2.5%	-	-	5.64	nr
W0204	150 mm	8.55	2.5%	-	-	8.76	nr
W0205	225 mm	26.77	2.5%	-	-	27.44	nr
	rest bends (ref. RBR1 & 2):						
W0206	100 mm	9.04	2.5%	-	-	9.27	nr
W0207	150 mm	15.43	2.5%	-	-	15.81	nr
	junctions, single (ref. RJ1 & 2):						
W0208	100 x 100 mm	10.11	2.5%	-	-	10.36	nr
W0209	150 x 100 mm	16.88	2.5%	-	-	17.30	nr
W0210	150 x 150 mm	16.88	2.5%	-	-	17.30	nr
W0211	tarred gaskin	0.26	10%	-	-	0.28	m
	CPM Group Concrete cylindrical pipes and fittings with flexible joints to BS 5911-1:2002:						
	Class 120:						
W0236	225 mm	16.85	5%	0.24	0.72	18.70	m
W0237	300 mm	18.16	5%	0.33	0.99	20.46	m
	bends:						
W0243	225 mm	168.51	2.5%	0.08	0.24	173.05	nr
W0244	300 mm	181.63	2.5%	0.16	0.48	186.83	nr
	junctions (special order, form hole in standard size pipe and fit 150 mm diameter arm at works):						
W0249	225 mm	117.96	2.5%	0.18	0.55	121.65	nr
W0250	300 mm	127.14	2.5%	0.28	0.85	131.48	nr
W0251	375 mm	157.42	2.5%	0.50	1.54	163.45	nr
W0252	450 mm	185.76	2.5%	0.67	2.05	193.19	nr
W0253	525 mm	243.38	2.5%	0.82	2.50	252.86	nr

	Basic Prices of Materials	Supply Price £	Waste Factor %	Unload. Labour £	Unload. Plant £	Total Unit Cost £	Unit
W0254	600 mm	305.37	2.5%	1.10	3.35	**317.56**	nr
	road gulley BS 5911 with trapped outlet complete with rodding eye, stopper and chain:						
W0256	450 mm diameter x 900 mm deep with 150 mm outlet	45.44	2.5%	0.43	1.30	**48.35**	nr
W0257	hinged ductile iron gully, grate and frame, 75 mm deep, BS EN 124, class 250, 440 x 336 mm	86.91	2.5%	0.15	0.44	**89.69**	nr
	UPO Plastic underground drainage pipes, fittings and accessories, generally as BS 4660:						
	pipes:						
W0310	110 mm	3.68	5%	-	-	**3.86**	m
W0311	160 mm	8.64	5%	-	-	**9.07**	m
	bend 87.5 degrees:						
W0312	110 mm	9.14	-	-	-	**9.14**	nr
W0313	160 mm	22.33	-	-	-	**22.33**	nr
	bend 45 degrees:						
W0314	110 mm	9.14	-	-	-	**9.14**	nr
W0315	160 mm	22.33	-	-	-	**22.33**	nr
	junction:						
W0316	110 x 110mm x 87.5 degrees	14.99	-	-	-	**14.99**	nr
W0317	160 x 110mm x 45 degrees	35.24	-	-	-	**35.24**	nr
	double socket pipe couplers:						
W0318	110 mm	3.62	5%	-	-	**3.81**	nr
W0319	160 mm	8.12	5%	-	-	**8.52**	nr
	aluminium rodding eye:						
W0320	110 mm	28.52	-	-	-	**28.52**	nr
	universal trap:						
W0321	110 mm	18.59	-	-	-	**18.59**	nr
	plain square hopper:						
W0322	110 mm	7.86	-	-	-	**7.86**	nr
	universal gully:						
W0323	110 mm	28.31	-	-	-	**28.31**	nr
W0324	shallow inspection chamber 300 mm diameter x 600 mm 3 inlets for 110 mm pipes; screw down aluminium cover	75.60	-	-	-	**75.60**	nr
W0328	joint lubricant	6.84	-	-	-	**6.84**	kg
	inspection chamber 470 mm diameter; with 5 inlets for 110 mm:						
W0329	base 240 mm invert	36.14	-	-	-	**36.14**	nr
W0330	raising piece 235 mm deep	15.35	-	-	-	**15.35**	nr
W0332	grade C cast iron cover & frame	36.14	-	-	-	**36.14**	nr
	Cast iron Timesaver pipes and fittings to BS 437; flexible joints to BS 6087:						
	pipes (ref. TD00):						
W0601	100 mm nominal size in 3.00 m lengths	30.59	5%	0.13	-	**32.26**	m
W0602	150 mm nominal size in 3.00 m lengths	56.77	5%	0.19	-	**59.81**	m
	couplings (ref. TD01):						
W0603	100 mm nominal size	19.61	5%	-	-	**20.59**	nr
W0604	150 mm nominal size	23.75	5%	-	-	**24.93**	nr
	medium radius bends, 87.5 degrees (ref. TD06):						
W0605	100 mm	36.67	-	0.06	-	**36.73**	nr
W0606	150 mm	84.37	-	0.09	-	**84.46**	nr
	medium radius bends with heel rest 87.5 degrees (TD07):						
W0607	100 mm	42.06	-	0.07	-	**42.13**	nr
W0608	150 mm	103.15	-	0.16	-	**103.31**	nr
	long radius bends with heel rest 87.5 degrees (ref. TD22):						
W0609	100 mm	65.14	-	0.07	-	**65.21**	nr
	branches 87.5 degrees (ref. TD37):						
W0610	100 x 100 mm	48.65	-	0.06	-	**48.71**	nr
W0611	150 x 100 mm	105.04	-	0.10	-	**105.14**	nr
W0612	150 x 150 mm	120.04	-	0.12	-	**120.16**	nr
	transitional pipes with sockets for clayware (ref. TD42):						
W0613	100 mm	61.57	-	0.09	-	**61.66**	nr
W0614	150 mm	63.99	-	0.12	-	**64.11**	nr
	transitional pipes with sockets for WCs (ref. TD45):						
W0615	100 mm	27.54	-	0.07	-	**27.61**	nr
	transitional pipes with sockets for BS 437 pipes (ref. TD47):						
W0616	100 mm	51.53	-	0.09	-	**51.62**	nr
W0617	150 mm	65.99	-	0.12	-	**66.11**	nr
	access pipes (ref. TD56):						
W0618	100 mm	90.59	-	0.15	-	**90.74**	nr
W0619	150 mm	165.41	-	0.28	-	**165.69**	nr
W0620	pipe diminishing 150 - 100 mm (ref. TD41)	47.80	-	0.12	-	**47.92**	nr
	gully 'P' traps:						
W0621	(ref. TD60) 100 mm spigot inlet and outlet	48.65	-	0.09	-	**48.74**	nr
W0622	(ref. TD64) 225 mm socket inlet; 100 mm outlet	94.97	-	0.22	-	**95.19**	nr
W0623	(ref. TD107) 100 mm socket inlet; 100 mm outlet with access	122.49	-	0.11	-	**122.60**	nr
W0386	additional 75 mm perforation	5.17	-	-	-	**5.17**	nr
W0305	Caulking lead	2.47	-	-	-	**2.47**	kg
	Manhole step irons, BS 1247:						
	general purpose pattern:						
W0390	115 mm tail	5.61	5%	-	-	**5.90**	nr
W0391	230 mm tail	7.11	5%	-	-	**7.47**	nr
	Manhole covers and frames, to BS EN124:						
	light duty:						
W1408	600 x 450 mm, 45 mm thick, cast iron, type A15, solid top, single seal, ref MHC - 5145	53.21	2.5%	-	-	**54.54**	nr
W1409	600 x 600 mm, 45 mm thick, cast iron, type A15, solid top, single seal, ref MHC - 5155	70.95	2.5%	-	-	**72.72**	nr

Basic Prices of Materials	Supply Price £	Waste Factor %	Unload. Labour £	Unload. Plant £	Total Unit Cost £	Unit
medium duty:						
W1406 600 x 450 mm, 45 mm thick, cast iron, type B125, ref MHC - 5245	105.35	2.5%	-	-	107.98	nr
W1410 600 x 450 mm, 45 mm thick, steel, recessed top, double seal, ref MHC - 5148	79.55	2.5%	-	-	81.54	nr
W1403 600 x 600 mm, 45 mm thick, cast iron, type B125, ref MHC - 5255	106.42	2.5%	-	-	109.09	nr
W1411 600 x 600 mm, 45 mm thick, steel, recesed top, double seal, ref MHC - 5158	95.67	2.5%	-	-	98.07	nr
W1407 600 x 600 mm, 75 mm thick, cast iron, type B125, ref MHC - 5256	117.17	2.5%	-	-	120.10	nr
W1405 600 mm diameter, 45 mm thick, cast iron, type B125, ref MHC - 5251	126.85	2.5%	-	-	130.02	nr
heavy duty:						
W1402 600 x 450 mm, 110 mm thick, cast iron, type D400, ref MHC - 5445	138.68	2.5%	-	-	142.14	nr
W1404 600 x 6000 mm, 110 mm thick, cast iron, type D400, ref MHC - 5445	145.13	2.5%	-	-	148.75	nr
W1400 600 mm diameter, 110 mm thick, cast iron, type D400, ref MHC - 5450L	137.60	2.5%	-	-	141.04	nr
W1401 600 mm diameter, 150 mm thick, cast iron, type D400, ref MHC - 5451L	166.63	2.5%		-	170.79	nr
Broadstel Universal access covers and frames with rubber seal and locking devices; Drainage Systems:						
medium duty:						
W0655 600 x 450 mm (ref. X7367B)	90.47	-	0.13	-	90.61	nr
W0656 600 x 600 mm (ref. X7367C)	101.69	-	0.16	-	101.85	nr
medium heavy duty:						
W0657 600 x 450 mm (ref. X6331B)	106.00	-	0.13	-	106.13	nr
W0658 600 x 600 mm (ref. X6331C)	120.95	-	0.16	-	121.11	nr
the foregoing covers with brass tops to visible edges:						
W0659 600 x 450 mm (ref. X7369B)	284.33	-	0.13	-	284.46	nr
W0660 600 x 600 mm (ref. X7369C)	297.16	-	0.16	-	297.32	nr
W0661 600 x 450 mm (ref. X7379B)	295.35	-	0.13	-	295.48	nr
W0662 600 x 600 mm (ref. X7379C)	314.23	-	0.16	-	314.39	nr
Channels and fittings, socketed, vitrified clay, Hepworth:						
half section straight main channel:						
W0415 100 x 600 mm long	2.32	5%	-	-	2.43	nr
W0416 150 x 600 mm long	3.73	5%	-	-	3.91	nr
W0417 225 x 1000 mm long	11.76	5%	-	-	12.35	nr
W0418 300 x 1000 mm long	24.14	5%	-	-	25.35	nr
half section main channel enlarger/reducer:						
W0423 150 - 100 mm	14.89	5%	-	-	15.63	nr
W0424 225 - 150 mm	32.86	5%	-	-	34.50	nr
W0425 300 - 225 mm	64.62	5%	-	-	67.85	nr
half section main channel bends (CB1,2,3,4):						
W0419 100 mm	3.54	5%	-	-	3.71	nr
W0420 150 mm	5.84	5%	-	-	6.13	nr
W0421 225 mm	19.48	5%	-	-	20.46	nr
W0422 300 mm	39.72	5%	-	-	41.71	nr
half section tapered main channel bend:						
W0426 150 - 100 mm	22.41	5%	-	-	23.53	nr
W0427 225 - 150 mm	64.22	5%	-	-	67.43	nr
W0428 300 - 225 mm	130.33	5%	-	-	136.85	nr
half section branch channel bends:						
W0429 100 mm	7.31	5%	-	-	7.68	nr
W0430 150 mm	11.99	5%	-	-	12.59	nr
W0431 225 mm	39.86	5%	-	-	41.85	nr
W0432 300 mm	78.98	5%	-	-	82.92	nr
three-quarter section branch channel bends:						
W0433 100 mm	8.07	5%	-	-	8.47	nr
W0434 150 mm	13.55	5%	-	-	14.22	nr
W0435 225 mm	49.43	5%	-	-	51.90	nr
Cast iron inspection chambers BS 437 with bolted access covers ("Timesaver" couplings required):						
100 mm nominal bore:						
W0440 without branches (ref. TD)	85.87	-	0.34	-	86.21	nr
W0442 with two 100 mm branches one side (ref. TD14)	162.51	-	0.71	-	163.22	nr
W0443 with three 100 mm branches one side (ref. TD17)	319.90	-	0.91	-	320.81	nr
W0441 100 mm plain blanking cap (ref. TD34)	14.94	-	0.46	-	15.40	nr
150 mm nominal bore:						
W0444 without branches (ref. TD)	156.79	-	0.56	-	157.35	nr
W0446 with two 150 mm branches one side (ref. TD14)	267.18	-	1.09	-	268.27	nr
W0447 with three 150 mm branches one side (ref. TD17)	533.50	-	1.39	-	534.89	nr
W0445 150 mm plain blanking cap (ref. TD34)	28.50	-	0.73	-	29.23	nr
Hepworth Intercepting traps:						
vitrified clay reverse action with stopper:						
(ref. RI3):						
W0450 100 mm	42.00	5%	0.11	-	44.22	nr
W0451 150 mm	60.56	5%	0.17	-	63.77	nr
W0452 225 mm	189.01	5%	0.26	-	198.73	nr
Glassfibre septic tank:						
W0460 7500 litres, standard grade	1536.47	-	2.81	8.54	1547.83	nr
W0461 **Extra over** for light access cover and frame	97.38	-	-	-	97.38	nr

Basic Prices of Materials		Supply Price £	Waste Factor %	Unload. Labour £	Unload. Plant £	Total Unit Cost £	Unit
	Hepworth SuperSleve PPIC polypropylene inspection chamber 475 mm diameter:						
W0521	940 mm deep, 5 x 100 mm inlets	112.76	-	1.68	-	**114.44**	nr
W0522	595 mm deep, 5 x 100 mm inlets	84.89	-	1.68	-	**86.57**	nr
W0523	940 mm deep, 3 x 150 mm inlets	119.40	-	1.68	-	**121.08**	nr
W0527	cover and frame to chamber	36.46	-	-	-	**36.46**	nr
W0528	raising piece 175 mm deep	15.49	-	-	-	**15.49**	nr
	Hepworth Polypropylene mini chamber:						
W0885	600 mm deep, 3 x 100 mm inlets; square sealed cover (ref.SDAC1/1)	76.27	-	-	-	**76.27**	nr

Mortar & Concrete Mix Analysis

Analysis of mortar and concrete prices

The prices of 1 m3 of mortar or concrete are calculated as follows:

Note: The cost of mixers or mortar mills should be costed in preliminaries.

A0601 Cement mortar (1:2)

Cement (bagged)	0.59 tonne	x	£	156.48	=	£	92.32
Building sand	1.64 tonne	x	£	26.57	=	£	43.57
Labourer BATJIC A	2.00 hour	x	£	11.22	=	£	22.44
						£	158.33
Waste	10%				=	£	15.83
Cost per m3					=	£	**174.16**

A0612 Cement mortar (1:3)

Cement (bagged)	0.44 tonne	x	£	156.48	=	£	68.85
Sharp sand BS 882 Zone M	1.83 tonne	x	£	27.78	=	£	50.84
Labourer BATJIC A	2.00 hour	x	£	11.22	=	£	22.44
						£	142.13
Waste	10%				=	£	14.21
Cost per m3					=	£	**156.34**

A0662 Concrete mix (1:3:6) 20 mm aggregate

Cement (bagged)	0.23 tonne	x	£	156.48	=	£	35.99
Fine aggregate BS 882	0.95 tonne	x	£	32.60	=	£	30.97
20 mm Aggregate	1.37 tonne	x	£	34.05	=	£	46.65
Labourer BATJIC A	2.00 hour	x	£	11.22	=	£	22.44
						£	136.05
Waste	10%				=	£	13.61
Cost per m3					=	£	**149.66**

A0663 Concrete (25 N/mm2 x 20 mm aggregate)

Cement (bagged)	0.33 tonne	x	£	156.48	=	£	51.64
Fine aggregate BS 882	0.90 tonne	x	£	32.60	=	£	29.34
20 mm Aggregate	1.30 tonne	x	£	34.05	=	£	44.27
Labourer BATJIC A	2.00 hour	x	£	11.22	=	£	22.44
						£	147.69
Waste	10%				=	£	14.77
Cost per m3					=	£	**162.46**

Unit Rates	Man-Hours	Excav Hours	Brkng Hours	Cmptg Hours	Trans Hours	Net Labour Price £	Net Plant Price £	Net Mats Price £	Net Unit Price £	Unit
WA UNIT RATES **EXCAVATING TRENCHES TO RECEIVE PIPES; GRADING BOTTOMS; BACKFILLING COMPLETELY WITH EXCAVATED MATERIAL**										

001 Notes:

1. Removal of surplus spoil and earthwork support are priced separately - see Sections WE and WF.

2. The prices in this Section allow for backfilling completely with excavated material. To adjust prices to allow for removal of surplus spoil displaced by the volumes of pipes, use may be made of the following table:

Nominal size of pipe	Volume (m3/m)
100 mm	0.013 m3
150 mm	0.025 m3
225 mm	0.053 m3
300 mm	0.096 m3
375 mm	0.149 m3
450 mm	0.189 m3
525 mm	0.307 m3
600 mm	0.396 m3

The volumes of spoil displaced by bed and surrounds to pipes is given with the beds and surrounds - see Section WG

3. The rates for excavation in the work in this section allow for excavating in firm earth. For other types of ground the following additions should be made:

(a) To prices for machine excavation	
dry clay	15%
hard compact gravel	20%
highly weathered rock not requiring breaker tools	50%
running silt, running sand	100%
running silt, running sand, below ground water level	150%
(b) To prices for hand excavation	
dry clay	15%
wet clay	20%
hard compact gravel	50%
highly weathered rock not requiring compressor tools	75%
running silt, running sand	150%
running silt, running sand, below ground water level	200%

Unit Rates	Man-Hours	Excav Hours	Brkng Hours	Cmptg Hours	Trans Hours	Net Labour Price £	Net Plant Price £	Net Mats Price £	Net Unit Price £	Unit
002 Excavating by machine; backfilling by machine; compacting with Whacker										
003 Trenches 450 mm wide average depth (JCB):										
0.50 m	0.14	0.06	-	0.05	-	1.74	2.23	-	**3.97**	m
0.75 m	0.21	0.09	-	0.07	-	2.59	3.33	-	**5.92**	m
1.00 m	0.28	0.12	-	0.09	-	3.49	4.42	-	**7.91**	m
1.25 m	0.40	0.16	-	0.11	-	4.89	5.87	-	**10.76**	m
1.50 m	0.48	0.19	-	0.14	-	5.87	7.00	-	**12.87**	m
1.75 m	0.56	0.22	-	0.16	-	6.84	8.10	-	**14.94**	m
2.00 m	0.64	0.25	-	0.18	-	7.83	9.19	-	**17.02**	m
2.25 m	0.83	0.30	-	0.20	-	10.20	10.97	-	**21.17**	m
2.50 m	0.92	0.34	-	0.23	-	11.31	12.45	-	**23.76**	m
2.75 m	1.01	0.37	-	0.25	-	12.42	13.55	-	**25.97**	m
3.00 m	1.10	0.40	-	0.27	-	13.55	14.64	-	**28.19**	m
004 Trenches 600 mm wide average depth (JCB):										
0.50 m	0.19	0.08	-	0.06	-	2.38	2.95	-	**5.33**	m
0.75 m	0.28	0.12	-	0.09	-	3.49	4.42	-	**7.91**	m
1.00 m	0.38	0.16	-	0.12	-	4.62	5.90	-	**10.52**	m
1.25 m	0.54	0.21	-	0.15	-	6.57	7.72	-	**14.29**	m
1.50 m	0.64	0.25	-	0.18	-	7.83	9.19	-	**17.02**	m
1.75 m	0.75	0.29	-	0.21	-	9.23	10.67	-	**19.90**	m
2.00 m	0.85	0.33	-	0.24	-	10.48	12.15	-	**22.63**	m
2.25 m	1.10	0.40	-	0.27	-	13.55	14.64	-	**28.19**	m
2.50 m	1.23	0.45	-	0.30	-	15.09	16.46	-	**31.55**	m
2.75 m	1.35	0.49	-	0.33	-	16.62	17.94	-	**34.56**	m
3.00 m	1.47	0.54	-	0.36	-	18.02	19.76	-	**37.78**	m
005 Trenches 750 mm wide average depth (JCB):										
0.50 m	0.23	0.09	-	0.08	-	2.80	3.37	-	**6.17**	m
0.75 m	0.34	0.14	-	0.11	-	4.19	5.18	-	**9.37**	m
1.00 m	0.46	0.19	-	0.15	-	5.59	7.03	-	**12.62**	m
1.25 m	0.64	0.25	-	0.19	-	7.83	9.23	-	**17.06**	m
1.50 m	0.77	0.30	-	0.23	-	9.51	11.08	-	**20.59**	m

Unit Rates

		Man-Hours	Excav Hours	Brkng Hours	Cmptg Hours	Trans Hours	Net Labour Price £	Net Plant Price £	Net Mats Price £	Net Unit Price £	Unit
	1.75 m	0.90	0.36	-	0.26	-	11.04	13.24	-	**24.28**	m
	2.00 m	1.02	0.41	-	0.30	-	12.58	15.09	-	**27.67**	m
	2.25 m	1.33	0.49	-	0.34	-	16.34	17.98	-	**34.32**	m
	2.50 m	1.48	0.54	-	0.38	-	18.14	19.83	-	**37.97**	m
	2.75 m	1.62	0.60	-	0.41	-	19.84	21.99	-	**41.83**	m
	3.00 m	1.76	0.65	-	0.45	-	21.65	23.83	-	**45.48**	m
006	**Trenches 900 mm wide average depth (JCB):**										
	0.50 m	0.27	0.11	-	0.09	-	3.35	4.08	-	**7.43**	m
	0.75 m	0.41	0.17	-	0.14	-	5.02	6.32	-	**11.34**	m
	1.00 m	0.55	0.23	-	0.18	-	6.71	8.51	-	**15.22**	m
	1.25 m	0.75	0.30	-	0.23	-	9.23	11.08	-	**20.31**	m
	1.50 m	0.92	0.37	-	0.27	-	11.31	13.62	-	**24.93**	m
	1.75 m	1.08	0.43	-	0.32	-	13.27	15.86	-	**29.13**	m
	2.00 m	1.23	0.49	-	0.36	-	15.09	18.05	-	**33.14**	m
	2.25 m	1.59	0.59	-	0.41	-	19.56	21.64	-	**41.20**	m
	2.50 m	1.76	0.65	-	0.45	-	21.65	23.83	-	**45.48**	m
	2.75 m	1.95	0.72	-	0.50	-	23.89	26.42	-	**50.31**	m
	3.00 m	2.12	0.78	-	0.54	-	25.98	28.61	-	**54.59**	m
	Note: 007 - 009 not used										
010	**Excavating by hand, backfilling by hand compacting with Whacker**										
011	Trenches 450 mm wide average depth:										
	0.50 m	1.13	-	-	0.05	-	13.83	0.18	-	**14.01**	m
	0.75 m	1.69	-	-	0.07	-	20.81	0.25	-	**21.06**	m
	1.00 m	2.25	-	-	0.09	-	27.67	0.32	-	**27.99**	m
	1.25 m	3.37	-	-	0.11	-	41.35	0.40	-	**41.75**	m
	1.50 m	4.03	-	-	0.14	-	49.45	0.51	-	**49.96**	m
	1.75 m	4.71	-	-	0.16	-	57.84	0.58	-	**58.42**	m
	2.00 m	5.38	-	-	0.18	-	66.08	0.65	-	**66.73**	m
	2.25 m	7.31	-	-	0.20	-	89.83	0.72	-	**90.55**	m
	2.50 m	8.12	-	-	0.23	-	99.74	0.83	-	**100.57**	m
	2.75 m	8.94	-	-	0.25	-	109.79	0.90	-	**110.69**	m
	3.00 m	9.75	-	-	0.27	-	119.72	0.97	-	**120.69**	m
012	Trenches 600 mm wide average depth:										
	0.50 m	1.50	-	-	0.06	-	18.44	0.22	-	**18.66**	m
	0.75 m	2.25	-	-	0.09	-	27.67	0.32	-	**27.99**	m
	1.00 m	3.00	-	-	0.12	-	36.88	0.43	-	**37.31**	m
	1.25 m	4.48	-	-	0.15	-	55.04	0.54	-	**55.58**	m
	1.50 m	5.38	-	-	0.18	-	66.08	0.65	-	**66.73**	m
	1.75 m	6.27	-	-	0.21	-	76.99	0.76	-	**77.75**	m
	2.00 m	7.16	-	-	0.24	-	88.01	0.87	-	**88.88**	m
	2.25 m	9.75	-	-	0.27	-	119.72	0.97	-	**120.69**	m
	2.50 m	10.84	-	-	0.30	-	133.13	1.08	-	**134.21**	m
	2.75 m	11.92	-	-	0.33	-	146.40	1.19	-	**147.59**	m
	3.00 m	13.00	-	-	0.36	-	159.68	1.30	-	**160.98**	m
013	Trenches 750 mm wide average depth:										
	0.50 m	1.88	-	-	0.08	-	23.05	0.29	-	**23.34**	m
	0.75 m	2.82	-	-	0.11	-	34.64	0.40	-	**35.04**	m
	1.00 m	3.75	-	-	0.15	-	46.09	0.54	-	**46.63**	m
	1.25 m	5.62	-	-	0.19	-	69.02	0.69	-	**69.71**	m
	1.50 m	6.72	-	-	0.23	-	82.56	0.83	-	**83.39**	m
	1.75 m	7.83	-	-	0.26	-	96.24	0.94	-	**97.18**	m
	2.00 m	8.96	-	-	0.30	-	110.09	1.08	-	**111.17**	m
	2.25 m	12.19	-	-	0.34	-	149.75	1.23	-	**150.98**	m
	2.50 m	13.54	-	-	0.38	-	166.38	1.37	-	**167.75**	m
	2.75 m	14.90	-	-	0.41	-	183.00	1.48	-	**184.48**	m
	3.00 m	16.25	-	-	0.45	-	199.63	1.62	-	**201.25**	m
014	Trenches 900 mm wide average depth:										
	0.50 m	2.25	-	-	0.09	-	27.67	0.32	-	**27.99**	m
	0.75 m	3.38	-	-	0.14	-	41.49	0.51	-	**42.00**	m
	1.00 m	4.50	-	-	0.18	-	55.32	0.65	-	**55.97**	m
	1.25 m	6.72	-	-	0.23	-	82.56	0.83	-	**83.39**	m
	1.50 m	8.06	-	-	0.27	-	99.04	0.97	-	**100.01**	m
	1.75 m	9.41	-	-	0.32	-	115.54	1.16	-	**116.70**	m
	2.00 m	10.75	-	-	0.36	-	132.00	1.30	-	**133.30**	m
	2.25 m	14.62	-	-	0.41	-	179.64	1.48	-	**181.12**	m
	2.50 m	16.25	-	-	0.45	-	199.63	1.62	-	**201.25**	m
	2.75 m	17.88	-	-	0.50	-	219.61	1.81	-	**221.42**	m
	3.00 m	19.50	-	-	0.54	-	239.58	1.95	-	**241.53**	m

		Man-Hours	Excav Hours	Brkng Hours	Cmptg Hours	Trans Hours	Net Labour Price £	Net Plant Price £	Net Mats Price £	Net Unit Price £	Unit
WB	**EXCAVATION IN ROCK, BREAKING OUT OBSTRUCTIONS MET WITH IN EXCAVATION**										
	Note: The following prices are given 'Full value'. If items on both quantities are described as **Extra over** excavation in normal ground' the prices for items under Section WA should be DEDUCTED, pro-rata from the following prices:										
001	**Excavating by hand using hand held compressor tools; backfilling by hand; compacting with Whacker**										
002	Excavating in SOFT ROCK or BRICKWORK in trench, maximum depth not exceeding:										
	2.00 m	10.35	2.76	-	0.20	-	127.11	17.81	-	**144.92**	m3
	4.00 m	13.62	3.00	-	0.20	-	167.36	19.30	-	**186.66**	m3
003	Excavating in HARD ROCK in trench, maximum depth not exceeding:										
	2.00 m	14.16	6.10	-	0.20	-	173.91	38.50	-	**212.41**	m3
	4.00 m	17.74	6.65	-	0.20	-	217.92	41.91	-	**259.83**	m3
004	Excavating in PLAIN CONCRETE in trench, maximum depth not exceeding:										
	2.00 m	11.80	4.03	-	0.20	-	145.01	25.68	-	**170.69**	m3
	4.00 m	15.18	4.38	-	0.20	-	186.50	27.85	-	**214.35**	m3
005	Excavating in REINFORCED CONCRETE in trench, maximum depth not exceeding:										
	2.00 m	16.20	6.10	-	0.20	-	199.07	38.50	-	**237.57**	m3
	4.00 m	20.81	6.65	-	0.20	-	255.64	41.91	-	**297.55**	m3
WC	**BREAKING UP PAVINGS ON THE SURFACE OF THE GROUND**										
	Note: The following prices are given 'full value'. If items on both quantities are described as **Extra over** excavation in normal ground' the prices for items under Section WA should be DEDUCTED, pro-rata from the following prices:										
	Note: 001 - 004 not used										
005	**Excavating by hand using hand held compressor tools**										
006	Excavating in TARMACADAM paving of the following thicknesses:										
	50 mm	0.24	0.09	-	0.01	-	3.00	0.60	-	**3.60**	m2
	100 mm	0.52	0.18	-	0.02	-	6.43	1.18	-	**7.61**	m2
007	Excavating in PLAIN CONCRETE paving of the following thicknesses:										
	100 mm	0.92	0.35	-	0.02	-	11.31	2.24	-	**13.55**	m2
	150 mm	1.38	0.53	-	0.03	-	16.97	3.39	-	**20.36**	m2
	200 mm	1.84	0.70	-	0.04	-	22.63	4.48	-	**27.11**	m2
008	Excavating in REINFORCED CONCRETE paving of the following thicknesses:										
	100 mm	1.26	0.53	-	0.02	-	15.52	3.35	-	**18.87**	m2
	150 mm	1.89	0.80	-	0.03	-	23.26	5.06	-	**28.32**	m2
	200 mm	2.53	1.06	-	0.04	-	31.02	6.70	-	**37.72**	m2
WD	**EARTHWORK SUPPORT**										
001	**Timber earthwork support**										
	Note: The 'Net Material' price allows for TEN (10) uses of Timber. The 'Net Labour' price allows for fixing and striking once.										
002	Earthwork support in firm ground to opposing faces not exceeding 2.00 m apart, maximum depth not exceeding:										
	1.00 m	0.17	-	-	-	-	2.09	-	0.61	**2.70**	m2
	2.00 m	0.26	-	-	-	-	3.21	-	0.61	**3.82**	m2
	4.00 m	0.34	-	-	-	-	4.18	-	0.61	**4.79**	m2
003	Earthwork support in moderately firm ground to opposing faces not exceeding 2.00 m apart, maximum depth not exceeding:										
	1.00 m	0.57	-	-	-	-	6.97	-	1.84	**8.81**	m2
	2.00 m	0.79	-	-	-	-	9.74	-	2.14	**11.88**	m2
	4.00 m	1.02	-	-	-	-	12.53	-	2.45	**14.98**	m2

Unit Rates	Man-Hours	Excav Hours	Brkng Hours	Cmptg Hours	Trans Hours	Net Labour Price £	Net Plant Price £	Net Mats Price £	Net Unit Price £	Unit
004 Earthwork support in loose ground, running sand, and the like, to opposing faces not exceeding 2.00 m apart, maximum depth not exceeding:										
1.00 m	1.13	-	-	-	-	13.92	-	2.75	**16.67**	m2
2.00 m	1.70	-	-	-	-	20.88	-	3.06	**23.94**	m2
4.00 m	2.27	-	-	-	-	27.84	-	3.67	**31.51**	m2
005 Timber earthwork support below ground water level										
Allow an additional 10% to 'Net Labour Price' to cover the cost of working in wet ground conditions										
006 Earthwork support next roadways or existing buildings										
The advice of a structural engineer should be sought on the type and extent of support required to excavations next roadways or existing buildings, as costs will vary from site to site due to ground conditions, amount of traffic on roads and heights or conditions of adjacent buildings.										
WE　DISPOSAL OF EXCAVATED MATERIAL										
For Disposal items, see Excavation.										
WF　FILLING										
Note: The following prices **do not** allow for disposal of surplus spoil.										
001 Extra over backfilling drain trenches for filling by machine (JCB); compacting in 250 mm layers; imported materials										
002 Imported granular MOT grade 1 (compacting with Whacker)	0.08	0.01	-	-	-	0.98	0.34	37.46	**38.78**	m3
003 Lean mix concrete (1:12)	-	0.03	-	-0.20	-	-	0.31	83.49	**83.80**	m3
004 Extra over backfilling drain trenches for filling by hand, compacting in 250 mm layers; imported materials										
005 Imported granular MOT grade 1 (compacting with Whacker)	0.17	-	-	-	-	2.10	-	37.46	**39.56**	m3
006 Lean mix concrete (1:12)	0.46	-	-	-0.20	1.00	5.59	21.12	83.49	**110.20**	m3

		Man-Hours	Net Labour Price £	Net Mats Price £	Net Unit Price £	Unit
WG	**PIPE BEDS AND COVERINGS**					
	Note: The prices for drain trenches include for backfilling completely with excavated material. To assist the adjustment of prices to allow for disposal of excavated material displaced by beds and coverings, the volumes in m3/m are given in parenthesis (0.023 m3/m)					
001	**Sand**					
002	50 mm Bed:					
	450 mm wide (0.023)	0.09	1.09	1.34	**2.43**	m
	525 mm wide (0.026)	0.11	1.29	1.56	**2.85**	m
	600 mm wide (0.030)	0.10	1.27	1.79	**3.06**	m
	750 mm wide (0.038)	0.15	1.83	2.25	**4.08**	m
	900 mm wide (0.045)	0.18	2.21	2.71	**4.92**	m
003	**Granular material 10 mm pea shingle**					
004	50 mm Bed:					
	450 mm wide (0.023)	0.09	1.09	1.79	**2.88**	m
	525 mm wide (0.026)	0.11	1.29	2.12	**3.41**	m
	600 mm wide (0.030)	0.10	1.27	2.39	**3.66**	m
	750 mm wide (0.038)	0.15	1.83	3.02	**4.85**	m
	900 mm wide (0.045)	0.18	2.21	3.58	**5.79**	m
005	100 mm Bed:					
	450 mm wide (0.045)	0.18	2.21	3.58	**5.79**	m
	525 mm wide (0.053)	0.21	2.58	4.25	**6.83**	m
	600 mm wide (0.060)	0.24	2.92	4.81	**7.73**	m
	750 mm wide (0.075)	0.30	3.67	6.04	**9.71**	m
	900 mm wide (0.090)	0.36	4.40	7.26	**11.66**	m
006	150 mm Bed:					
	450 mm wide (0.068)	0.27	3.30	5.41	**8.71**	m
	525 mm wide (0.079)	0.31	3.85	6.30	**10.15**	m
	600 mm wide (0.090)	0.36	4.40	7.26	**11.66**	m

Unit Rates	Man-Hours	Net Labour Price £	Net Mats Price £	Net Unit Price £	Unit
750 mm wide (0.113)	0.45	5.50	9.05	**14.55**	m
900 mm wide (0.135)	0.54	6.60	10.88	**17.48**	m
007 100 mm Bed and filling to half height of pipe:					
450 mm wide to 100 mm pipe (0.060)	0.28	3.43	4.81	**8.24**	m
525 mm wide to 150 mm pipe (0.077)	0.36	4.36	5.87	**10.23**	m
600 mm wide to 225 mm pipe (0.096)	0.45	5.53	7.73	**13.26**	m
750 mm wide to 300 mm pipe (0.134)	0.63	7.73	10.78	**18.51**	m
900 mm wide to 375 mm pipe (0.178)	0.73	8.96	14.33	**23.29**	m
008 150 mm Bed and filling to half height of pipe:					
450 mm wide to 100 mm pipe (0.083)	0.37	4.51	6.70	**11.21**	m
525 mm wide to 150 mm pipe (0.103)	0.46	5.66	8.29	**13.95**	m
600 mm wide to 225 mm pipe (0.126)	0.57	7.00	10.15	**17.15**	m
750 mm wide to 300 mm pipe (0.172)	0.78	9.58	13.83	**23.41**	m
900 mm wide to 375 mm pipe (0.223)	0.86	10.52	17.94	**28.46**	m
009 Bed and covering (volumes include pipes):					
450 mm wide x 350 mm thick to 100 mm pipe (0.158)	0.60	7.33	12.07	**19.40**	m
450 mm wide x 450 mm thick to 100 mm pipe (0.203)	0.78	9.55	15.69	**25.24**	m
525 mm wide x 400 mm thick to 150 mm pipe (0.210)	0.76	9.39	15.42	**24.81**	m
525 mm wide x 500 mm thick to 150 mm pipe (0.263)	0.98	11.99	19.67	**31.66**	m
600 mm wide x 475 mm thick to 225 mm pipe (0.285)	0.98	11.99	19.67	**31.66**	m
600 mm wide x 575 mm thick to 225 mm pipe (0.345)	1.21	14.91	24.48	**39.39**	m
750 mm wide x 550 mm thick to 300 mm pipe (0.413)	1.36	16.73	27.49	**44.22**	m
750 mm wide x 650 mm thick to 300 mm pipe (0.488)	1.64	20.15	33.10	**53.25**	m
900 mm wide x 725 mm thick to 375 and 400 mm pipe (0.653)	2.16	26.51	43.58	**70.09**	m
900 mm wide x 825 mm thick to 450 mm pipe (0.743)	2.32	28.51	46.86	**75.37**	m
010 **Plain concrete mix (1:3:6) 19 mm aggregate**					
011 100 mm Bed:					
450 mm wide (0.045)	0.25	3.01	6.73	**9.74**	m
525 mm wide (0.053)	0.29	3.51	7.93	**11.44**	m
600 mm wide (0.060)	0.33	4.03	8.98	**13.01**	m
750 mm wide (0.075)	0.41	5.02	11.22	**16.24**	m
900 mm wide (0.090)	0.49	6.03	13.47	**19.50**	m
012 150 mm Bed:					
450 mm wide (0.068)	0.37	4.53	10.18	**14.71**	m
525 mm wide (0.079)	0.43	5.29	11.82	**17.11**	m
600 mm wide (0.090)	0.49	6.03	13.47	**19.50**	m
750 mm wide (0.113)	0.61	7.54	16.91	**24.45**	m
900 mm wide (0.135)	0.74	9.04	20.20	**29.24**	m
013 100 mm Bed and filling to half height of pipe:					
450 mm wide to 100 mm pipe (0.060)	0.38	4.69	8.98	**13.67**	m
525 mm wide to 150 mm pipe (0.077)	0.49	5.96	11.52	**17.48**	m
600 mm wide to 225 mm pipe (0.096)	0.62	7.57	14.37	**21.94**	m
750 mm wide to 300 mm pipe (0.134)	0.86	10.59	20.05	**30.64**	m
900 mm wide to 375 mm pipe (0.178)	0.99	12.21	26.64	**38.85**	m
014 150 mm Bed and filling to half height of pipe:					
450 mm wide to 100 mm pipe (0.083)	0.51	6.23	12.42	**18.65**	m
525 mm wide to 150 mm pipe (0.103)	0.63	7.78	15.41	**23.19**	m
600 mm wide to 225 mm pipe (0.126)	0.78	9.58	18.86	**28.44**	m
750 mm wide to 300 mm pipe (0.172)	1.07	13.14	25.74	**38.88**	m
900 mm wide to 375 mm pipe (0.223)	1.17	14.42	33.37	**47.79**	m
015 Bed and covering (volumes include pipes):					
450 mm wide x 350 mm thick to 100 mm pipe (0.158)	0.82	10.06	22.45	**32.51**	m
450 mm wide x 450 mm thick to 100 mm pipe (0.203)	1.06	13.07	29.18	**42.25**	m
525 mm wide x 400 mm thick to 150 mm pipe (0.210)	1.05	12.89	28.73	**41.62**	m
525 mm wide x 500 mm thick to 150 mm pipe (0.263)	1.34	16.43	36.67	**53.10**	m
600 mm wide x 475 mm thick to 225 mm pipe (0.285)	1.34	16.43	36.67	**53.10**	m
600 mm wide x 575 mm thick to 225 mm pipe (0.345)	1.67	20.47	45.64	**66.11**	m
750 mm wide x 550 mm thick to 300 mm pipe (0.413)	1.87	22.92	51.18	**74.10**	m
750 mm wide x 650 mm thick to 300 mm pipe (0.488)	2.25	27.64	61.66	**89.30**	m
900 mm wide x 725 mm thick to 375 and 400 mm pipe (0.653)	2.96	36.34	81.11	**117.45**	m
900 mm wide x 825 mm thick to 450 mm pipe (0.743)	3.18	39.09	87.25	**126.34**	m
WH **REINFORCEMENT**					
001 **Steel fabric reinforcement BS 4483, with one width mesh end lap**					
002 Fabric reinforcement reference A142, 200 mm end lap laid in beds or coverings in trenches:					
450 mm wide	0.15	1.88	0.98	**2.86**	m
525 mm wide	0.18	2.21	1.14	**3.35**	m
600 mm wide	0.21	2.52	1.31	**3.83**	m
750 mm wide	0.26	3.14	1.63	**4.77**	m
900 mm wide	0.31	3.78	1.96	**5.74**	m

	Unit Rates	Man-Hours	Net Labour Price £	Net Mats Price £	Net Unit Price £	Unit
WJ	**PIPEWORK**					
	Note: Fittings are priced **Extra over** the cost of pipes.					
	Note: 001 - 003 not used					
	HEPLINE PERFORATED/SLOTTED PIPES					
004	**Pipes and fittings, Hepline; dry push fit flexible integral polyethylene sleeve joints**					
005	100 mm nominal size pipes laid in trench:					
	in runs exceeding 3.00 m long	0.22	2.64	4.43	**7.07**	m
	in runs not exceeding 3.00 m long	0.27	3.35	4.43	**7.78**	m
	Extra over for:					
	bends (ref. SB1,2,3,4)	0.28	3.49	2.63	**6.12**	Nr
	junction 100 mm (ref. SJ1&2)	0.25	3.07	5.81	**8.88**	Nr
006	150 mm nominal size pipes laid in trench:					
	in runs exceeding 3.00 m long	0.28	3.49	8.04	**11.53**	m
	in runs not exceeding 3.00 m long	0.38	4.62	8.04	**12.66**	m
	Extra over for:					
	bends (ref. SB1,2,3,4)	0.32	3.91	3.21	**7.12**	Nr
	junction 150 mm (ref. SJ1&2)	0.28	3.49	5.66	**9.15**	Nr
007	225 mm nominal size pipes laid in trench:					
	in runs exceeding 3.00 m long	0.49	6.01	17.03	**23.04**	m
	in runs not exceeding 3.00 m long	0.55	6.71	17.03	**23.74**	m
	Extra over for:					
	bends (ref. SB1,2,3,4)	0.55	6.71	36.88	**43.59**	Nr
	junction 225 mm (ref. SJ1,2,3,4)	0.43	5.32	65.52	**70.84**	Nr
	SUPERSLEVE PIPES					
008	**Pipes and fittings, SuperSleve; polypropylene couplings with integral sealing rings**					
009	100 mm nominal size pipes laid in trench:					
	in runs exceeding 3.00 m long	0.23	2.80	3.91	**6.71**	m
	in runs not exceeding 3.00 m long	0.28	3.49	3.91	**7.40**	m
	Extra over for:					
	bends (ref. SB1,2,3,4)	0.28	3.49	4.83	**8.32**	Nr
	rest bends with plain ends (ref. SBR)	0.28	3.49	7.40	**10.89**	Nr
	junctions 100 x 100 mm (ref. SJ1&2)	0.26	3.22	9.53	**12.75**	Nr
010	150 mm nominal size pipes laid in trench:					
	in runs exceeding 3.00 m long	0.28	3.49	7.63	**11.12**	m
	in runs not exceeding 3.00 m long	0.38	4.61	7.63	**12.24**	m
	Extra over for:					
	bends (ref. SB1,2,3,4)	0.32	3.91	9.47	**13.38**	Nr
	rest bends with plain ends (ref. SBR)	0.32	3.91	11.26	**15.17**	Nr
	junctions 150 x 150 mm (ref. SJ1&2)	0.28	3.49	13.06	**16.55**	Nr
011	225 mm nominal size pipes laid in trench:					
	in runs exceeding 3.00 m long	0.31	3.83	18.04	**21.87**	m
	in runs not exceeding 3.00 m long	0.41	5.04	18.04	**23.08**	m
	Extra over for:					
	bends (ref. SB1, 2, 3, 4)	0.35	4.28	40.28	**44.56**	Nr
	rest bends with plain ends (ref. SBR)	0.35	4.28	43.05	**47.33**	Nr
	junctions 225 x 225 mm (ref. SJ)	0.31	3.83	70.36	**74.19**	Nr
013	300 mm nominal size pipes laid in trench:					
	in runs exceeding 3.00 m long	0.33	3.99	35.30	**39.29**	m
	in runs not exceeding 3.00 m long	0.43	5.29	35.30	**40.59**	m
	Extra over for:					
	bends (ref. VB1,2,3,4)	0.36	4.39	77.21	**81.60**	Nr
	rest bends with plain ends (ref. VBR4)	0.36	4.39	112.42	**116.81**	Nr
	junctions 300 x 300 mm (ref. VJ1,2,3,4)	0.34	4.13	150.26	**154.39**	Nr
	Note: 012 & 014 not used					
015	**Accessories, jointing to drains**					
016	Saddle (oblique or square. ref. SJ:VJS3&6):					
	SuperSleve:					
	100 mm	6.82	83.77	10.30	**94.07**	Nr
	150 mm	9.09	111.71	15.89	**127.60**	Nr
	225 mm	11.25	138.22	50.03	**188.25**	Nr
	300 mm	11.59	142.38	88.18	**230.56**	Nr
017	Taper pipe (ref. ST:VT3&4):					
	SuperSleve:					
	100 : 150 mm	0.28	3.49	9.72	**13.21**	Nr
	150 : 225 mm	0.42	5.12	32.73	**37.85**	Nr
	225 : 300 mm	0.45	5.53	81.90	**87.43**	Nr
018	Adaptors:					
	soil pipe SA9	0.06	0.70	5.86	**6.56**	Nr
	w.c. pan SA13	0.06	0.70	5.86	**6.56**	Nr
	waste pipe SA7	0.06	0.70	5.67	**6.37**	Nr

Unit Rates

	Man-Hours	Net Labour Price £	Net Mats Price £	Net Unit Price £	Unit
019 SA/VA Adaptor to HepSeal:					
100 mm	0.06	0.71	4.02	**4.73**	Nr
150 mm	0.09	1.12	6.72	**7.84**	Nr
225 mm	0.11	1.39	9.41	**10.80**	Nr
020 Rodding point:					
Oval; 150 mm (ref. SRP1)	0.45	5.58	28.44	**34.02**	Nr
Square; 100 mm (ref. SRPS 1/1) with airtight seal	0.34	4.19	18.18	**22.37**	Nr
Extra over for plain in situ concrete surround	0.34	4.19	4.49	**8.68**	Nr
021 Two-piece gullies:					
low back 'P' trap, 100 mm inlet and outlet, (ref. SG1); 100 mm hopper with horizontal inlet (ref. SH2); and grid (ref. IG2)	1.82	22.35	28.08	**50.43**	Nr
Extra over for plain in situ concrete surround (1:3:6), 19 mm aggregate, min. 150 mm thick	0.34	4.19	26.94	**31.13**	Nr
022 Road gullies:					
polypropylene 510 mm internal diameter x 920 mm deep, 150 mm outlet, Hepworth (ref. PRG) (P) with trap (ref. PRG) (LT)	3.18	39.12	81.38	**120.50**	Nr
ADD for; 440 x 336 mm cast iron grating and frame, BS EN 124 class c250, bedding frame in cement mortar (1:3)	1.48	18.16	91.23	**109.39**	Nr
ADD for; three courses engineering brick kerb 225 mm wide in cement mortar (1:3)	0.57	6.99	31.36	**38.35**	Nr
ADD for; completely surrounding with plain in situ concrete mix (1:3:6) 19 mm aggregate minimum 150 mm thick	0.57	6.99	59.86	**66.85**	Nr
023 Inspection chambers:					
PPIC polypropylene; 475 dia. x 930 mm deep, (ref. 100) with five 100 mm stoppered inlets, base and cover	2.05	25.15	119.57	**144.72**	Nr
PPIC polypropylene; 475 dia. x 585 mm deep (ref. 100) with five 100 mm stoppered inlets, base and cover	2.05	25.15	91.67	**116.82**	Nr
PPIC polypropylene; 475 dia. x 930 mm deep (ref. 150) with three 150 mm stoppered inlets, base and cover	2.05	25.15	126.64	**151.79**	Nr
Polypropylene mini chamber; 225 dia. x 600 mm deep (ref. SDAC1/1) with three 100 mm stoppered inlets and square sealed cover	1.59	19.53	78.45	**97.98**	Nr
SUPERSEAL PIPES					
024 **Pipes and fittings, SuperSeal, integrated plastic socket joints with sealing rings**					
025 150 mm nominal size pipes laid in trench:					
in runs exceeding 3.00 m long	0.36	4.47	9.62	**14.09**	m
in runs not exceeding 3.00 m long	0.46	5.59	9.62	**15.21**	m
Extra over for:					
bends (ref. FB1, 2, 3, 4)	0.48	5.87	15.10	**20.97**	Nr
rest bends (ref. SBR)	0.48	5.87	7.08	**12.95**	Nr
junctions 150 mm (ref. FJ1,2&3)	0.31	3.78	19.16	**22.94**	Nr
026 225 mm nominal size pipes laid in trench:					
in runs exceeding 3.00 m long	0.41	5.02	19.66	**24.68**	m
in runs not exceeding 3.00 m long	0.50	6.15	19.66	**25.81**	m
Extra over for:					
bends (ref. FB1, 2, 3, 4)	0.50	6.15	33.90	**40.05**	Nr
junctions 225 mm (ref. FJ1,2&3)	0.46	5.59	49.03	**54.62**	Nr
027 300 mm nominal size pipes laid in trench:					
in runs exceeding 3.00 m long	0.63	7.69	29.87	**37.56**	m
in runs not exceeding 3.00 m long	0.80	9.78	29.87	**39.65**	m
Extra over for:					
bends (ref. FB1, 2, 3, 4)	0.80	9.78	66.60	**76.38**	Nr
junctions 300 mm (ref. FJ1,2&3)	0.76	9.36	106.58	**115.94**	Nr
Note: 028 - 030 not used					
CLAY PIPES					
031 **Pipes and fittings vitrified clay, BS 65, spigot and socket joints in cement mortar (1:2) with tarred gaskin**					
032 100 mm nominal size pipes laid in trench:					
in runs exceeding 3.00 m long	0.40	4.89	6.79	**11.68**	m
in runs not exceeding 3.00 m long	0.44	5.44	6.79	**12.23**	m
Extra over for:					
bends, medium 90 degree	0.27	3.35	5.20	**8.55**	Nr
rest bends	0.27	3.35	8.55	**11.90**	Nr
junctions 100 x 100 mm single	0.21	2.52	10.07	**12.59**	Nr
033 150 mm nominal size pipes laid in trench:					
in runs exceeding 3.00 m long	0.43	5.32	9.96	**15.28**	m
in runs not exceeding 3.00 m long	0.50	6.15	9.96	**16.11**	m
Extra over for:					
bends, medium 90 degree	0.40	4.89	7.65	**12.54**	Nr
rest bends	0.40	4.89	13.81	**18.70**	Nr
junctions 150 x 100 mm single	0.28	3.49	16.86	**20.35**	Nr
034 225 mm nominal size pipes laid in trench:					
in runs exceeding 3.00 m long	0.51	6.29	19.31	**25.60**	m
in runs not exceeding 3.00 m long	0.57	6.99	19.31	**26.30**	m
Extra over for:					
bends, medium 90 degree	0.55	6.71	22.96	**29.67**	Nr
junctions 225 x 100 mm single	0.38	4.62	13.62	**18.24**	Nr

Unit Rates	Man-Hours	Net Labour Price £	Net Mats Price £	Net Unit Price £	Unit
Note: 035 - 038 not used					
039	**Accessories, vitrified clay BS 65; jointing to drains**					
040	Two-piece gully:					
	low back 'P' trap with 100 mm inlet and 100 mm outlet (ref.SG1); 100 mm hopper with 150 mm x 150 mm top , (ref. SH1)	1.25	15.36	17.52	**32.88**	Nr
	ADD for; 197 mm diameter aluminium alloy gulley grid, (ref. IG7)	0.06	0.71	3.15	**3.86**	Nr
	ADD for; completely surrounding with plain in situ concrete mix (1:3:6) 19 mm aggregate minimum 150 mm thick	0.34	4.19	26.94	**31.13**	Nr
041	Yard gullies:					
	trapped, 225 mm internal diameter with 100 mm outlet (ref. RGP5)	1.71	20.96	57.03	**77.99**	Nr
	ADD for; 197 mm diameter aluminium alloy gulley grid, (ref. IG7)	0.06	0.71	3.15	**3.86**	Nr
	ADD for; completely surrounding with plain in situ concrete mix (1:3:6) 19 mm aggregate minimum 150 mm thick	0.51	6.29	13.47	**19.76**	Nr
	CONCRETE PIPES					
042	**Pipes and fittings, concrete cylindrical; BS 5911-1:2002; with flexible joints**					
	Note: 043 not used					
044	225 mm nominal size pipes laid in trench:					
	in runs exceeding 3.00 m long	0.77	9.51	18.70	**28.21**	m
	in runs not exceeding 3.00 m long	1.02	12.58	18.70	**31.28**	m
	Extra over for:					
	bends, 22.5 degree	0.34	4.19	167.44	**171.63**	Nr
	Extra over pipe for 150 mm junction arm	0.21	2.52	121.65	**124.17**	Nr
045	300 mm nominal size pipes laid in trench:					
	in runs exceeding 3.00 m long	0.91	11.17	20.46	**31.63**	m
	in runs not exceeding 3.00 m long	1.14	13.97	20.46	**34.43**	m
	Extra over for:					
	bends, 22.5 degree	0.43	5.32	180.69	**186.01**	Nr
	Extra over pipe for 150 mm junction arm	0.21	2.52	131.48	**134.00**	Nr
	Note: 046 - 049 not used					
050	**Accessories, precast concrete, BS 5911; jointing to drains**					
051	Road gullies:					
	375 mm internal diameter 900 mm deep, 150 mm trapped outlet, rodding eye with stopper and galvanised chain	5.12	62.86	48.35	**111.21**	Nr
	ADD for; 336 x 308 mm cast iron grating and frame BS EN 124 class c250, bedding frame in cement mortar (1:3)	1.48	18.16	62.29	**80.45**	Nr
	ADD for; three courses engineering brick kerb 225 mm wide in cement mortar (1:3)	0.57	6.99	31.36	**38.35**	Nr
	ADD for; completely surrounding with plain in- situ concrete mix (1:3:6) 19 mm aggregate	0.34	4.19	44.90	**49.09**	Nr
	Note: 052 - 058 not used					

	Man-Hours	Plant Hours	Net Labour Price £	Net Plant Price £	Net Mats Price £	Net Unit Price £	Unit
CAST IRON PIPES							
059	**Pipes and fittings, Drainage Systems Timesaver; cast iron couplings with stainless steel bolts and nuts and synthetic rubber gaskets**							
060	100 mm nominal size pipes (ref. TD 00) laid in trench:							
	in runs exceeding 3.00 m long	0.19	0.11	5.94	5.15	17.60	**28.69**	m
	in runs not exceeding 3.00 m long	0.43	-	13.59	-	31.88	**45.47**	m
	Extra over for:							
	medium radius bends 87.5 degrees (ref. TD06)	0.24	-	7.68	-	52.17	**59.85**	Nr
	medium radius bends 87.5 degrees with heel rest (ref. TD07)	0.24	-	7.68	-	57.57	**65.25**	Nr
	long radius bends 87.5 degrees with heel rest (ref. TD15)	0.22	-	6.92	-	78.60	**85.52**	Nr
	branch 100 x 100 mm x 87.5 degrees (ref. TD37)	0.52	-	16.34	-	79.59	**95.93**	Nr
	transitional pipe with socket for clayware (ref. 42)	0.23	-	7.27	-	75.97	**83.24**	Nr
	transitional pipe with socket for WC (ref. TD43)	0.23	-	7.27	-	41.92	**49.19**	Nr
	transitional pipe with socket for BS 437 pipe (ref. TD47)	0.28	-	8.78	-	70.05	**78.83**	Nr
	access pipe (ref. TD56)	0.25	-	7.93	-	106.91	**114.84**	Nr
061	150 mm nominal size pipes (ref. TD 00) laid in trench:							
	in runs exceeding 3.00 m long	0.27	0.17	8.41	7.82	68.11	**84.34**	m
	in runs not exceeding 3.00 m long	0.51	0.08	16.02	3.93	80.58	**100.53**	m
	Extra over for:							
	medium radius bends 87.5 degrees (ref. TD06)	0.32	-	10.05	-	103.69	**113.74**	Nr
	medium radius bends 87.5 degrees with heel rest (ref. TD07)	0.32	-	10.05	-	122.53	**132.58**	Nr
	branch 150 x 100 mm x 87.5 degrees (ref. TD37)	0.58	-	18.30	-	136.40	**154.70**	Nr
	branch 150 x 150 mm x 87.5 degrees (ref. TD37)	0.66	-	20.76	-	153.62	**174.38**	Nr
	pipe diminishing 150-100 mm (ref. TD41)	0.33	-	10.55	-	68.69	**79.24**	Nr
	transitional pipe with socket for clayware (ref. TD42)	0.31	-	9.80	-	82.71	**92.51**	Nr
	transitional pipe with socket for BS 437 pipe (ref. TD43)	0.36	-	11.31	-	89.18	**100.49**	Nr
	access pipe (ref. TD56)	0.33	-	10.49	-	186.16	**196.65**	Nr

Unit Rates	Man-Hours	Net Labour Price £	Net Mats Price £	Net Unit Price £	Unit
062 **Accessories for cast iron drain pipes; Drainage Systems Timesaver, mechanical joints to drains with cast iron couplings with stainless steel bolts and nuts with synthetic rubber gaskets**					
063 Gully trap (ref.TD60); 100 mm spigot inlet and outlet:	0.59	18.58	69.33	**87.91**	Nr
Extra over for:					
transitional pipe with socket for BS 437 pipe (ref.TD43) fixed to inlet	0.32	10.21	72.21	**82.42**	Nr
064 Gully trap (ref.TD64); 225 mm socket inlet, 100 mm outlet	0.59	18.58	115.78	**134.36**	Nr
065 Gully trap (ref.TD66); 100 mm socket inlet, 100 mm outlet	0.59	18.58	143.19	**161.77**	Nr
066 **Extra over**; setting gully on and surrounding with plain in situ concrete mix (1:3:6) minimum 150 mm thick PVCu PIPES	0.47	5.23	20.50	**25.73**	Nr
067 **Pipes and fittings; PVCu underground drainage**					
068 110 mm nominal size pipes laid in trench:					
in runs exceeding 3.00 m long	0.25	3.07	4.52	**7.59**	m
in runs not exceeding 3.00 m long	0.28	3.49	4.52	**8.01**	m
Extra over for:					
short radius bends 87.5 degrees	0.25	3.07	8.51	**11.58**	Nr
long radius bends 87.5 degrees	0.25	3.07	11.93	**15.00**	Nr
junction 110 x 110mm x 87.5 degs.	0.23	2.80	14.52	**17.32**	Nr
069 160 mm nominal size pipes laid in trench:					
in runs exceeding 3.00 m long	0.30	3.64	10.53	**14.17**	m
in runs not exceeding 3.00 m long	0.34	4.19	10.53	**14.72**	m
Extra over for:					
short radius bends 87.5 degrees	0.36	4.47	19.31	**23.78**	Nr
long radius bends 87.5 degrees	0.36	4.47	26.54	**31.01**	Nr
junction 160 x 110mm x 87.5 degs.	0.34	4.19	33.65	**37.84**	Nr
070 **Accessories, PVCu, jointing to drains**					
071 Rodding eyes; 110 mm rodding point	0.73	8.94	28.55	**37.49**	Nr
072 Two piece gully:					
universal gully trap with 110 mm inlet and 110 mm outlet and plain square hopper	0.91	11.17	30.36	**41.53**	Nr
ADD for bedding 150 mm thick and haunching with plain in situ concrete mix (1:3:6) 19 mm aggregate	0.34	4.19	4.49	**8.68**	Nr
073 Universal gully:					
readable, 110 mm outlet, complete with plastic gully grid	0.80	9.78	28.38	**38.16**	Nr
ADD for bedding 150 mm thick and haunching with plain in situ concrete mix (1:3:6) 19 mm aggregate	0.34	4.19	7.48	**11.67**	Nr
074 Shallow inspection chamber 300 mm diameter x 600 mm invert with 3 inlets for 110 mm complete with screw down aluminium cover	0.91	11.13	75.60	**86.73**	Nr
WK **SUNDRIES**					
001 Gulley surrounds 215 x 215 mm internally; common brick on edge kerb in cement mortar (1:3) to three sides of gulley; rendering internally and to top and three sides externally; matching skirting to fourth side:					
one courses high	1.99	22.32	1.93	**24.25**	Nr
three courses high	2.84	31.89	5.31	**37.20**	Nr
002 **Holes in structure for pipes and the like; making good around pipes with matching construction**					
003 Holes for large pipes in:					
100 mm concrete bed	0.51	5.74	15.27	**21.01**	Nr
150 mm concrete bed	0.74	8.29	22.91	**31.20**	Nr
common brick walls; thickness:					
102.5 mm	0.41	10.81	2.27	**13.08**	Nr
215 mm	0.77	20.45	4.69	**25.14**	Nr
327.5 mm	1.14	30.04	6.96	**37.00**	Nr
engineering brick walls; thickness:					
102.5 mm	0.52	13.82	2.78	**16.60**	Nr
215 mm	0.93	24.62	5.71	**30.33**	Nr
327.5 mm	1.39	36.64	8.48	**45.12**	Nr
concrete blockwork walls; thickness:					
100 mm	0.52	13.82	2.75	**16.57**	Nr
140 mm	0.64	16.83	3.94	**20.77**	Nr
215 mm	0.84	22.19	7.96	**30.15**	Nr
004 Holes for extra large pipes in:					
100 mm concrete bed	0.64	7.14	19.17	**26.31**	Nr
150 mm concrete bed	0.92	10.33	28.76	**39.09**	Nr
common brick walls; thickness:					
102.5 mm	0.51	13.53	2.92	**16.45**	Nr
215 mm	0.96	25.23	6.14	**31.37**	Nr
327.5 mm	1.43	37.86	9.38	**47.24**	Nr
engineering brick walls; thickness:					
102.5 mm	0.61	16.22	3.60	**19.82**	Nr
215 mm	1.14	30.04	7.50	**37.54**	Nr

Unit Rates	Man-Hours	Net Labour Price £	Net Mats Price £	Net Unit Price £	Unit
327.5 mm	1.68	44.46	11.41	**55.87**	Nr
concrete blockwork walls; thickness:					
100 mm	0.66	17.41	3.56	**20.97**	Nr
140 mm	0.80	21.03	5.31	**26.34**	Nr
215 mm	1.03	27.11	10.62	**37.73**	Nr

005 Holes in structure for pipes and the like; providing and building in extra strength clayware pipe sleeves; making good around sleeves with matching construction

006 150 mm nominal size sleeve projecting 100 mm each side in:

	Man-Hours	Net Labour Price £	Net Mats Price £	Net Unit Price £	Unit
concrete wall foundation or ground beam (sleeve cast in); thickness:					
300 mm	0.57	6.38	5.07	**11.45**	Nr
600 mm	0.63	7.02	8.12	**15.14**	Nr
900 mm	0.68	7.65	9.13	**16.78**	Nr
1200 mm	0.74	8.29	12.17	**20.46**	Nr
common brick walls; thickness:					
102.5 mm	0.42	11.12	4.64	**15.76**	Nr
215 mm	0.56	14.72	6.63	**21.35**	Nr
327.5 mm	0.69	18.34	8.94	**27.28**	Nr
engineering brick walls; thickness:					
102.5 mm	0.43	11.44	4.89	**16.33**	Nr
215 mm	0.58	15.35	7.14	**22.49**	Nr
327.5 mm	0.73	19.23	9.70	**28.93**	Nr
concrete blockwork walls; thickness:					
100 mm	0.49	12.92	4.41	**17.33**	Nr
140 mm	0.52	13.82	5.52	**19.34**	Nr
215 mm	0.59	15.46	8.12	**23.58**	Nr

007 225 mm nominal size sleeve projecting 100 mm each side in:

	Man-Hours	Net Labour Price £	Net Mats Price £	Net Unit Price £	Unit
concrete wall foundation or ground beam (sleeve cast in); thickness:					
300 mm	0.63	7.02	10.53	**17.55**	Nr
600 mm	0.68	7.65	16.84	**24.49**	Nr
900 mm	0.74	8.29	18.95	**27.24**	Nr
1200 mm	0.80	8.93	25.27	**34.20**	Nr
common brick walls; thickness:					
102.5 mm	0.52	13.82	8.40	**22.22**	Nr
215 mm	0.71	18.63	11.82	**30.45**	Nr
327.5 mm	0.89	23.43	15.85	**39.28**	Nr
engineering brick walls; thickness:					
102.5 mm	0.54	14.13	8.74	**22.87**	Nr
215 mm	0.73	19.23	12.50	**31.73**	Nr
327.5 mm	0.99	26.13	16.86	**42.99**	Nr
concrete blockwork walls; thickness:					
100 mm	0.61	16.22	8.09	**24.31**	Nr
150 mm	0.66	17.41	10.10	**27.51**	Nr
200 mm	0.74	19.55	13.73	**33.28**	Nr

	Man-Hours	Plant Hours	Net Labour Price £	Net Plant Price £	Net Mats Price £	Net Unit Price £	Unit
WL INSPECTION CHAMBERS, MANHOLES, SOAKAWAYS AND THE LIKE							
EXCAVATION AND EARTHWORK							
001 Rates for excavation; refer to Section WA							
002 Excavating by machine (JCB)							
003 Pits to receive inspection chambers, manholes, soakaways and the like, maximum depth not exceeding:							
0.25 m	0.28	0.25	3.19	8.54	-	**11.73**	m3
1.00 m	0.19	0.17	2.13	5.71	-	**7.84**	m3
2.00 m	0.20	0.18	2.23	5.98	-	**8.21**	m3
4.00 m	0.23	0.20	2.56	6.84	-	**9.40**	m3
004 Pits to receive inspection chambers, manholes soakaways and the like having both plan dimensions less than 1.25 m, maximum depth not exceeding:							
0.25 m	0.30	0.26	3.35	8.99	-	**12.34**	m3
1.00 m	0.20	0.18	2.23	5.98	-	**8.21**	m3
2.00 m	0.21	0.19	2.36	6.32	-	**8.68**	m3
4.00 m	0.24	0.21	2.69	7.21	-	**9.90**	m3
005 Excavating by hand							
006 Pits to receive inspection chambers, manholes, soakaways and the like maximum depth not exceeding:							
0.25 m	3.41	-	38.26	-	-	**38.26**	m3
1.00 m	3.75	-	42.08	-	-	**42.08**	m3
2.00 m	4.72	-	52.93	-	-	**52.93**	m3
4.00 m	7.73	-	86.72	-	-	**86.72**	m3
007 Pits to receive inspection chambers, manholes soakaways and the like having both plan dimensions less than 1.25 m, maximum depth not exceeding:							
0.25 m	3.53	-	39.54	-	-	**39.54**	m3
1.00 m	3.98	-	44.64	-	-	**44.64**	m3
2.00 m	5.00	-	56.13	-	-	**56.13**	m3

Unit Rates	Man-Hours	Plant Hours	Net Labour Price £	Net Plant Price £	Net Mats Price £	Net Unit Price £	Unit
4.00 m	8.19	-	91.83	-	-	**91.83**	m3

008 **Excavating in rock, breaking out obstructions met with in excavation by hand using hand held compressor tools**

Note: The following prices are given 'full value'. If items in bills of quantities are described as '**Extra over** excavation in normal ground' the prices for items under excavating should be DEDUCTED from the following prices

009 Excavating in SOFT ROCK or BRICKWORK, maximum depth not exceeding:

	Man-Hours	Plant Hours	Net Labour Price £	Net Plant Price £	Net Mats Price £	Net Unit Price £	Unit
0.25 m	6.71	2.40	79.30	14.86	-	**94.16**	m3
1.00 m	6.82	2.64	80.65	16.35	-	**97.00**	m3
2.00 m	7.85	2.76	92.75	17.09	-	**109.84**	m3
4.00 m	11.20	3.36	132.40	20.81	-	**153.21**	m3

010 Excavating in HARD ROCK, maximum depth not exceeding:

0.25 m	10.01	5.30	118.27	32.82	-	**151.09**	m3
1.00 m	10.12	5.83	119.63	36.11	-	**155.74**	m3
2.00 m	11.14	6.10	131.73	37.78	-	**169.51**	m3
4.00 m	14.50	7.42	171.37	45.95	-	**217.32**	m3

011 Excavating in PLAIN CONCRETE, maximum depth not exceeding:

0.25 m	7.96	3.50	94.09	21.68	-	**115.77**	m3
1.00 m	8.07	3.85	95.43	23.84	-	**119.27**	m3
2.00 m	9.10	4.03	107.53	24.96	-	**132.49**	m3
4.00 m	12.45	4.90	147.19	30.35	-	**177.54**	m3

012 Excavating in REINFORCED CONCRETE, maximum depth not exceeding:

0.25 m	10.35	5.30	122.31	32.82	-	**155.13**	m3
1.00 m	10.46	5.83	123.67	36.11	-	**159.78**	m3
2.00 m	11.83	6.10	139.79	37.78	-	**177.57**	m3
4.00 m	17.28	7.42	204.30	45.95	-	**250.25**	m3

Note: 013 - 016 not used

017 **Breaking up pavings on the surface of the ground; excavating by hand using hand held compressor tools**

018 Excavating in TARMACADAM paving of the following thicknesses:

50 mm	0.18	0.09	2.15	0.56	-	**2.71**	m2
100 mm	0.40	0.18	4.70	1.11	-	**5.81**	m2

019 Excavating in PLAIN CONCRETE paving of the following thicknesses:

100 mm	0.80	0.35	9.41	2.17	-	**11.58**	m2
150 mm	1.19	0.53	14.11	3.28	-	**17.39**	m2
200 mm	1.59	0.70	18.82	4.34	-	**23.16**	m2

020 Excavating in REINFORCED CONCRETE paving of the following thicknesses:

100 mm	1.14	0.53	13.44	3.28	-	**16.72**	m2
150 mm	1.71	0.80	20.17	4.95	-	**25.12**	m2
200 mm	2.27	1.60	26.88	9.91	-	**36.79**	m2

	Man-Hours	Net Labour Price £	Net Mats Price £	Net Unit Price £	Unit
021 **Timber earthwork support**					

Note: 1 The 'Net Material' price allows for 6 uses of timber. The 'Net Labour' prices allows for fixing and striking once

Note: 2 The prices for earthwork support are for straight surfaces, the following additions should be made for curved surfaces:
Labour 10%
Material 5%

022 Earthwork support in firm ground to opposing faces not exceeding 2.00 m apart, maximum depth not exceeding:

	Man-Hours	Net Labour Price £	Net Mats Price £	Net Unit Price £	Unit
1.00 m	0.17	2.38	0.61	**2.99**	m2
2.00 m	0.26	3.66	0.61	**4.27**	m2
4.00 m	0.34	4.77	0.61	**5.38**	m2

023 Earthwork support in firm ground to opposing faces 2.00 - 4.00 m apart, maximum depth not exceeding:

1.00 m	0.19	2.61	0.61	**3.22**	m2
2.00 m	0.29	4.01	0.92	**4.93**	m2
4.00 m	0.37	5.24	0.92	**6.16**	m2

024 Earthwork support in firm ground to opposing faces exceeding 4.00 m apart, maximum depth not exceeding:

1.00 m	0.23	3.18	0.92	**4.10**	m2
2.00 m	0.35	4.92	0.92	**5.84**	m2
4.00 m	0.45	6.35	1.22	**7.57**	m2

025 Earthwork support in moderately firm ground to opposing faces not exceeding 2.00 m apart, maximum depth not exceeding:

1.00 m	0.57	7.95	1.84	**9.79**	m2
2.00 m	0.79	11.12	2.14	**13.26**	m2

	Unit Rates	Man-Hours	Net Labour Price £	Net Mats Price £	Net Unit Price £	Unit
	4.00 m	1.02	14.30	2.45	**16.75**	m2
026	Earthwork support in moderately firm ground to opposing faces not exceeding 2.00 - 4.00 m apart, maximum depth not exceeding:					
	1.00 m	0.62	8.74	2.14	**10.88**	m2
	2.00 m	0.87	12.23	2.45	**14.68**	m2
	4.00 m	1.12	15.73	2.75	**18.48**	m2
027	Earthwork support in moderately firm ground to opposing faces exceeding 4.00 m apart, maximum depth not exceeding:					
	1.00 m	0.76	10.64	2.45	**13.09**	m2
	2.00 m	1.05	14.78	2.45	**17.23**	m2
	4.00 m	1.36	19.07	3.06	**22.13**	m2
028	Earthwork support in loose ground, running sand and the like to opposing faces not exceeding 2.00 m apart, maximum depth not exceeding:					
	1.00 m	1.13	15.89	2.75	**18.64**	m2
	2.00 m	1.70	23.84	3.06	**26.90**	m2
	4.00 m	2.27	31.77	3.67	**35.44**	m2
029	Earthwork support in loose ground, running sand and the like to opposing faces 2.00 - 4.00 m apart, maximum depth not exceeding:					
	1.00 m	1.25	17.47	3.06	**20.53**	m2
	2.00 m	1.87	26.21	3.67	**29.88**	m2
	4.00 m	2.49	34.96	4.29	**39.25**	m2
030	Earthwork support in loose ground, running sand and the like to opposing faces exceeding 4.00 m apart, maximum depth not exceeding:					
	1.00 m	1.53	21.45	3.67	**25.12**	m2
	2.00 m	2.27	31.77	3.98	**35.75**	m2
	4.00 m	3.06	42.89	4.90	**47.79**	m2
031	**Timber earthwork support below ground water level**					
032	Allow an additional 10% to 'Net Labour Price' to cover the cost of working in wet ground conditions					
033	**Earthwork support next roadways or existing buildings**					
034	The advice of a structural engineer should be sought on the type and extent of support required to excavations next to roadways or existing buildings, as costs will vary from site to site due to ground conditions, amount of traffic on roads and heights or conditions of adjacent buildings					
	For Disposal, Filling and Surface Treatment items, see Excavation.					
	Note: 035 - 051 not used					
	IN SITU CONCRETE WORK					
052	**PLAIN concrete mix (1:3:6) 19 mm aggregate**					
053	Base, laid on earth:					
	100 - 150 mm thick	3.07	34.43	149.66	**184.09**	m3
	150 - 300 mm thick	2.62	29.33	149.66	**178.99**	m3
054	Surrounds to manhole, filled into formwork:					
	100 - 150 mm thick	4.89	54.84	149.66	**204.50**	m3
	150 - 300 mm thick	4.44	49.74	149.66	**199.40**	m3
055	Surrounds to manhole, poured against face of excavation:					
	100 - 150 mm thick	3.64	40.82	149.66	**190.48**	m3
	150 - 300 mm thick	3.18	35.71	149.66	**185.37**	m3
056	Benching formed to steep slopes to channels and branches and finished with 13 mm cement mortar (1:3) trowelled smooth average:					
	225 mm thick	2.27	60.08	40.01	**100.09**	m2
	300 mm thick	2.84	75.11	46.90	**122.01**	m2
	450 mm thick	3.98	105.15	67.50	**172.65**	m2
057	**REINFORCED concrete grade 25N/mm2 filled into formwork**					
058	Suspended cover slab:					
	100 - 150 mm thick	4.55	51.01	162.46	**213.47**	m3
	150 - 300 mm thick	3.64	40.82	162.46	**203.28**	m3
059	**Labours on concrete**					
060	Tamping surfaces of unset concrete, laid level	0.32	3.57	-	**3.57**	m2
061	Spade finishing surfaces of unset concrete, laid level	0.25	2.80	-	**2.80**	m2
062	**Steel fabric reinforcement BS 4483, with one width side laps and one width mesh end laps**					
063	Fabric reinforcement laid in suspended cover slabs, reference:					
	A 142, 200 mm side lap, 200 mm end lap	0.32	3.57	2.31	**5.88**	m2
	A 252	0.32	3.57	3.94	**7.51**	m2
	B 196, 100 mm side lap, 200 mm end lap	0.38	4.22	3.21	**7.43**	m2
	B 503	0.38	4.22	5.45	**9.67**	m2

Unit Rates

		Man-Hours	Net Labour Price £	Net Mats Price £	Net Unit Price £	Unit
064	Circular cutting fabric, reference:					
	A 142	0.14	1.53	0.11	1.64	m
	A 252	0.23	2.56	0.18	2.74	m
	B 196	0.21	2.30	0.15	2.45	m
	B 503	0.25	2.80	0.26	3.06	m

		Man-Hours	Plant Hours	Net Labour Price £	Net Plant Price £	Net Mats Price £	Net Unit Price £	Unit
	FORMWORK							
065	**Formwork generally**							
	Note: The prices for formwork in this section are combined making and fixing prices The 'Net Materials Prices' allow for 6 uses of timber, if more or less uses are possible adjustments should be made as required. The prices for formwork are for horizontal or vertical straight or plain surfaces, the following additions should be made for curved surfaces not exceeding 1.5 m radius: labour 200% material 100%							
066	Edges of bases:							
	not exceeding 250 mm high	0.89	-	13.47	-	2.61	16.08	m
	250 - 500 mm high	1.22	-	18.47	-	4.43	22.90	m
067	Soffit of cover slabs:							
	not exceeding 200 mm thick	1.48	4.00	22.54	8.80	6.81	38.15	m2
	200 - 300 mm thick	1.94	4.00	29.43	8.80	7.16	45.39	m2
068	Vertical edge of slabs:							
	not exceeding 250 mm deep	0.88	-	13.32	-	2.21	15.53	m
	250 - 500 mm deep	1.08	-	16.43	-	4.03	20.46	m
069	Vertical sides of surrounds to manholes:							
	one side shuttered	1.81	-	27.56	-	8.02	35.58	m2

		Man-Hours	Net Labour Price £	Net Mats Price £	Net Unit Price £	Unit
070	**Formwork Sundries**					
071	Curved cutting on formwork	0.51	7.78	0.88	8.66	m
	Note: 072 - 090 not used					
	BRICKWORK					
091	**Common bricks, BS 3921, P.C. £311.01 for 1000 in cement mortar (1:3)**					
092	Manhole walls:					
	102.5 mm	1.42	37.54	23.33	60.87	m2
	215 mm	2.75	72.71	44.27	116.98	m2
093	**Class B Engineering Bricks to BS 3921, P.C. £391.75 for 1000 in cement mortar (1:3)**					
094	Manhole walls:					
	102.5 mm	1.82	48.06	28.58	76.64	m2
	215 mm	3.47	91.65	53.77	145.42	m2
095	**ADJUSTMENT to prices for common brickwork and engineering brickwork for variations in the price of bricks delivered to site**					
096	For each £10.00 difference in price of brick ADD or DEDUCT from 'Net Materials' prices for the following:					
	102.5 mm thick walls	-	-	0.62	0.62	m2
	215 mm thick walls	-	-	1.12	1.12	m2
097	**Extra over common bricks in cement mortar (1:3) fair face**					
098	Flush pointing as the work proceeds in:					
	Stretcher bond	0.40	10.52	-	10.52	m2
	English bond	0.48	12.63	-	12.63	m2
099	Pointing to margins	0.06	1.53	-	1.53	m
100	**Extra over Class B engineering bricks in cement mortar (1:3) for fair face**					
101	Flush pointing as the work proceeds in:					
	Stretcher bond	0.40	10.52	-	10.52	m2
	English bond	0.48	12.63	-	12.63	m2
102	Pointing to margins	0.06	1.53	-	1.53	m

Unit Rates

		Man-Hours	Net Labour Price £	Net Mats Price £	Net Unit Price £	Unit
103	**Sundries**					
104	Building in end of pipe to 102.5 mm common brickwork:					
	100 mm pipe	0.15	3.91	-	**3.91**	Nr
	150 mm pipe	0.17	4.52	-	**4.52**	Nr
	225 mm pipe	0.18	4.81	-	**4.81**	Nr
	300 mm pipe	0.21	5.42	-	**5.42**	Nr
105	Building in end of pipe to 102.5 mm engineering brickwork:					
	100 mm pipe	0.17	4.52	-	**4.52**	Nr
	150 mm pipe	0.19	5.13	-	**5.13**	Nr
	225 mm pipe	0.21	5.42	-	**5.42**	Nr
	300 mm pipe	0.23	6.02	-	**6.02**	Nr
106	Building in end of pipe to 215 mm common brickwork:					
	100 mm pipe	0.25	6.61	-	**6.61**	Nr
	150 mm pipe	0.30	7.82	-	**7.82**	Nr
	225 mm pipe	0.33	8.75	-	**8.75**	Nr
	300 mm pipe	0.36	9.62	-	**9.62**	Nr
107	Building in end of pipe to 215 mm engineering brickwork:					
	100 mm pipe	0.27	7.21	-	**7.21**	Nr
	150 mm pipe	0.32	8.40	-	**8.40**	Nr
	225 mm pipe	0.36	9.62	-	**9.62**	Nr
	300 mm pipe	0.40	10.52	-	**10.52**	Nr
	IN SITU FINISHINGS					
108	**Mortar, one coat work cement and sand (1:3), steel trowelled finish**					
109	13 mm work to manhole walls; on brickwork base:					
	over 300 mm wide	0.68	18.02	2.00	**20.02**	m2
	not exceeding 300 mm wide	1.37	36.06	2.00	**38.06**	m2
	METALWORK					
110	**Manhole step irons, BS 1247, building into brickwork**					
111	General purpose pattern:					
	115 mm tails	0.09	2.40	5.90	**8.30**	Nr
	230 mm tails	0.11	2.99	7.47	**10.46**	Nr
112	**Manhole covers and frames BS EN124, tar coated; bedding frame in cement mortar (1:3), sealing cover in grease and sand**					
113	Light duty, cast iron:					
	600 x 450 mm, solid top, single seal, 45 mm thick, type A15, ref MHC - 5145	0.77	20.36	55.00	**75.36**	Nr
	600 x 600 mm, solid top, single seal, 45 mm thick, type A15, ref MHC - 5155	0.77	20.36	73.18	**93.54**	Nr
114	Medium duty, steel:					
	600 x 450 mm, recessed top, double seal, 45 mm thick, ref MHC - 5148	0.77	20.36	82.31	**102.67**	Nr
	600 x 600 mm, recessed top, double seal, 45 mm thick, ref MHC - 5158	0.77	20.36	98.84	**119.20**	Nr
115	Medium duty, cast iron:					
	600 mm diameter, 45 mm thick, type B125, ref MHC - 5251	0.98	25.83	130.48	**156.31**	Nr
	600 x 450 mm, 45 mm thick, type B125, ref MHC - 5245	1.09	28.86	108.44	**137.30**	Nr
	600 x 600 mm, 45 mm thick, type B125, ref MHC - 5255	1.09	28.86	109.55	**138.41**	Nr
	600 x 600 mm, 75 mm thick, type B125, ref MHC - 5256	1.32	34.94	120.56	**155.50**	Nr
116	Heavy duty, cast iron:					
	600 mm diameter, 110 mm thick, type D400, ref MHC - 5450L	1.38	36.46	141.50	**177.96**	Nr
	600 mm diameter, 150 mm thick, type D400, ref MHC - 5451L	1.78	47.09	171.25	**218.34**	Nr
	600 x 450 mm, 100 mm thick, type D400, ref MHC - 5445	1.67	44.06	142.60	**186.66**	Nr
	600 x 600 mm, 100 mm thick, type D400, ref MHC - 5455	1.92	50.74	149.21	**199.95**	Nr
	Note: 117 to 119 not used					
120	**Broadstel Universal access covers and frames with rubber seals and locking devices; Drainage Systems Ltd; bedding frames in cement mortar (1:3)**					
121	Medium duty access covers and frames:					
	600 x 450 mm (ref. X7367B)	0.85	22.54	92.00	**114.54**	Nr
	600 x 600 mm (ref. X7367C)	1.25	33.03	103.54	**136.57**	Nr
122	Medium heavy duty access covers and frames:					
	600 x 450 mm (ref. X6331B)	0.91	24.02	107.52	**131.54**	Nr
	600 x 600 mm (ref. X6331C)	1.31	34.56	122.80	**157.36**	Nr
123	**Extra over** for:					
	brass tops to visible edges:					
	600 x 450 mm (ref. X7369B)	-	-	193.85	**193.85**	Nr
	600 x 600 mm (ref. X7369C)	-	-	195.47	**195.47**	Nr
	600 x 450 mm (ref. X7379B)	-	-	189.35	**189.35**	Nr
	600 x 600 mm (ref. X7379C)	-	-	193.28	**193.28**	Nr
	filling with 25N/mm2 concrete trowelled smooth:					
	600 x 450 mm	0.46	12.02	4.19	**16.21**	Nr
	600 x 600 mm	0.57	15.03	5.39	**20.42**	Nr

Unit Rates

		Man-Hours	Net Labour Price £	Net Mats Price £	Net Unit Price £	Unit
	CHANNELS AND THE LIKE					
124	**Channels and fittings, vitrified clay, Hepworth; spigot and socket joints in cement mortar (1:2)**					
125	Half section straight main channel:					
	100 x 600 mm long	0.34	4.19	3.05	**7.24**	Nr
	150 x 600 mm long	0.48	5.87	5.14	**11.01**	Nr
	225 x 1000 mm long	0.74	9.08	15.12	**24.20**	Nr
	300 x 1000 mm long	0.91	11.17	30.89	**42.06**	Nr
126	Half section tapered main channel:					
	100 - 150 mm	0.51	6.29	16.25	**22.54**	Nr
	150 - 225 mm	0.77	9.51	36.19	**45.70**	Nr
	225 - 300 mm	0.97	11.88	71.85	**83.73**	Nr
127	Half section main channel bends 90 degrees medium:					
	100 mm	0.36	4.47	4.02	**8.49**	Nr
	150 mm	0.51	6.29	6.75	**13.04**	Nr
	225 mm	0.77	9.51	22.00	**31.51**	Nr
	300 mm	0.97	11.88	45.25	**57.13**	Nr
128	Half section tapered main channel bend:					
	100 - 150 mm	0.51	6.29	24.15	**30.44**	Nr
	150 - 225 mm	0.77	9.51	69.12	**78.63**	Nr
	225 - 300 mm	0.97	11.88	140.85	**152.73**	Nr
129	Half section branch channel bends:					
	100 mm	0.36	4.47	7.99	**12.46**	Nr
	150 mm	0.50	6.15	13.21	**19.36**	Nr
	225 mm	0.74	9.08	43.70	**52.78**	Nr
	300 mm	0.97	11.88	87.38	**99.26**	Nr
130	Three quarter section branch channel bends:					
	100 mm	0.36	4.47	9.09	**13.56**	Nr
	150 mm	0.50	6.15	15.30	**21.45**	Nr
	225 mm	0.74	9.08	54.67	**63.75**	Nr
131	**Inspection chambers cast iron, BS 437, Fig 65; bolted access covers; spigot and socket joints caulked in lead**					
132	100 mm nominal bore:					
	without branches (ref. TD)	1.41	44.56	92.00	**136.56**	Nr
	with two 100 mm branches one side (ref. TD14)	1.48	46.70	180.58	**227.28**	Nr
	with three 100 mm branches one side (ref. TD17)	1.48	46.70	343.96	**390.66**	Nr
	Extra over:					
	100 mm branch blanking cap (ref. TD34) and coupling	0.03	1.04	35.99	**37.03**	Nr
133	150 mm nominal bore:					
	without branches (ref. TD)	1.73	54.60	166.44	**221.04**	Nr
	with two 150 mm branches one side (ref. TD14)	1.82	57.48	295.54	**353.02**	Nr
	with three 150 mm branches one side (ref. TD17)	1.82	57.48	571.95	**629.43**	Nr
	Extra over:					
	150 mm branch blanking cap (ref. TD34) and coupling	0.03	1.04	54.16	**55.20**	Nr
134	**Intercepting traps**					
135	Vitrified clay, reverse action, stopper joints to drains in cement mortar 1:2); building into brickwork; (ref. RI3):					
	100 mm	0.57	15.03	45.23	**60.26**	Nr
	150 mm	0.91	24.02	65.32	**89.34**	Nr
	225 mm	1.37	36.06	201.29	**237.35**	Nr
	Note: 136 not used					
137	ADD for Completely surrounding intercepting traps with plain in situ concrete mix (1:3:6) 19 mm aggregate 150 mm thick	0.34	4.19	47.89	**52.08**	Nr
138	**PVC Inspection Chambers (UPO)**					
139	Universal inspection chambers 450 mm diameter and placing in excavation:					
	240 mm Base unit	0.28	3.49	36.14	**39.63**	Nr
	235 mm Raising piece	0.28	3.49	15.35	**18.84**	Nr
	Grade C cast iron cover and frame	0.57	6.99	36.14	**43.13**	Nr

		Man-Hours	Plant Hours	Net Labour Price £	Net Plant Price £	Net Mats Price £	Net Unit Price £	Unit
140	**Glassfibre prefabricated septic tanks**							
141	Septic tank 7500 litres capacity; standard grade:							
	placing in excavation	2.27	1.00	27.94	34.18	1547.83	**1609.95**	Nr
	manhole cover and frame	0.57	-	6.99	-	97.38	**104.37**	Nr

		Man-Hours	Net Labour Price £	Net Mats Price £	Net Unit Price £	Unit
Unit Rates						
WN	**ALTERATIONS TO EXISTING MANHOLES**					
001	Removing manhole cover and frame and setting aside for re-use:					
	light duty	0.85	22.54	-	**22.54**	Nr
	heavy duty	1.14	30.04	-	**30.04**	Nr
002	Preparing brick walls for raising:					
	102.5 mm	0.11	2.99	-	**2.99**	m
	215 mm	0.14	3.59	-	**3.59**	m
003	Reducing height of brick walls of manholes by one course:					
	102.5 mm	0.08	2.11	-	**2.11**	m
	215 mm	0.17	4.52	-	**4.52**	m
004	Refixing manhole cover and frame; bedding frame in cement mortar (1:3), sealing cover in grease and sand:					
	light duty	0.57	15.03	0.15	**15.18**	Nr
	heavy duty	0.97	25.55	0.15	**25.70**	Nr
WO	**CONNECTIONS TO SEWERS**					
001	Excavating by hand and searching for existing 225 mm nominal size vitrified clay live sewer, breaking into and connecting new 100 mm vitrified clay saddle junction; making good; backfilling and consolidating:					
	2000 mm deep:					
	excavation, backfilling	13.36	164.14	-	**164.14**	Nr
	connection, making good	5.12	135.19	6.31	**141.50**	Nr
	3000 mm deep:					
	excavation, backfilling	17.91	220.02	-	**220.02**	Nr
	connection, making good	5.12	135.19	6.31	**141.50**	Nr
WP	**TESTING DRAINS**					
001	Testing pipes with water:					
	100 mm	0.15	1.82	-	**1.82**	m
	150 mm	0.22	2.64	-	**2.64**	m
	225 mm	0.23	2.80	-	**2.80**	m
	300 mm	0.32	3.91	-	**3.91**	m

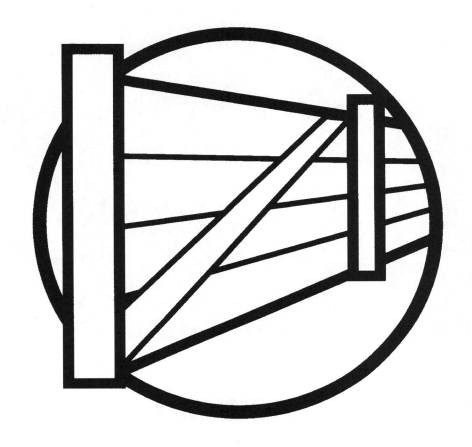

Fencing

HOW LONG? HOW MUCH?

THE FASTEST, MOST UP-TO-DATE ANSWERS ARE AVAILABLE NOW

Cost information underpins every aspect of the built environment, from construction and rebuilding to maintenance and operation publications.

BCIS, the RICS' Building Cost Information Service, is the leading provider of cost information to the construction industry and anyone else who needs comprehensive, accurate and independent data.

For the past 50 years, BCIS has been collecting, collating, analysing, modelling and interpreting cost information.Today, BCIS make that information easily accessible through online applications, data licensing and publications.

For more information call **0870 333 1600** email **contact@bcis.co.uk** or visit **www.bcis.co.uk**

BCIS is the **Building Cost Information Service** of  the mark of property professionalism worldwide

Specialist	£	Unit

FENCING
UNIT RATES
The prices for work in this section are **specialist** guide prices provided by R.M. Smith Fencing Limited, Duck Island Lane, Ringwood, Hants, BH24 3AA; (Telephone: 01425 476617, Fax: 01425 476610, E-mail: enquiries@smith-fencing.co.uk; Internet: www.smith-fencing.co.uk)

Price Guide to fencing and gates in general use with BS 1722 Parts 1 - 11 Type reference no's used: -
Supplied and fixed complete.

XA   **OPEN TYPE FENCING**

Note: The prices for fencing include all necessary post hole excavation and disposal of surplus soil where required by the specification.

		£	Unit
001	**Chain link fencing to BS 1722 Part 1 with 3 mm galvanised mesh, line and tying wire; intermediate posts at 3.00 m centres**		
002	Timber posts:		
	0.9 m high fencing (GLW 90)	15.00	m
	Extra over for:		
	end posts	55.00	Nr
	corner posts	75.00	Nr
	1.2 m high fencing (GLW 120)	17.00	m
	Extra over for:		
	end posts	58.00	Nr
	corner posts	79.00	Nr
	1.4 m high fencing (GLW 140)	19.00	m
	Extra over for:		
	end posts	63.00	Nr
	corner posts	82.00	Nr
	1.8 m high fencing (GLW 180)	22.00	m
	Extra over for:		
	end posts	75.00	Nr
	corner posts	91.00	Nr
003	Concrete Posts / GL5 Steel posts:		
	0.9 m high fencing (GLC 90)	22.40	m
	Extra over for:		
	end posts	85.00	Nr
	corner posts	115.00	Nr
	1.2 m high fencing (GLC 120)	24.00	m
	Extra over for:		
	end posts	96.00	Nr
	corner posts	125.00	Nr
	1.4 m high fencing (GLC 140)	26.50	m
	Extra over for:		
	end posts	107.00	Nr
	corner posts	134.00	Nr
	1.8 m high fencing (GLC 180)	30.00	m
	Extra over for:		
	end posts	115.00	Nr
	corner posts	145.00	Nr
004	Cranked top steel or concrete posts; 3 lines barbed wire:		
	2.1 m high fencing (GLC / GLS210)	45.00	m
	Extra over for:		
	end posts	135.00	Nr
	corner posts	160.00	Nr
005	**Extra over** for concrete to post holes	2.32	Nr
006	**Extra over** for:		
	galvanised core, plastic coated chain link 2.50 / 3.55 mm mesh	ADD	2.5%
	galvanised core, plastic coated chain link 3.00 / 4.00 mm mesh	ADD	10%
007	**Anti-intruder chain link fencing to BS 1722, part 10 with galvanised mesh, lines and tying wire; intermediate posts at 3.00 m centres with cranked tops; 3 lines barbed wire protection at top; bottom of mesh buried vertically 0.30 m deep including trenching; 2.90 m vertical height**		
008	Concrete or steel posts	65.81	m
	Extra over for:		
	end posts	155.00	Nr
	corner posts	188.00	Nr
009	**Extra over** for:		
	additional 3 lines barbed wire on cranked angles bolted to post tops	8.65	m
	Extra over on end posts	8.62	Nr
	Extra over on corner posts	11.46	Nr
010	**Extra over** for concrete to post holes	3.06	Nr
011	**Extra over** for:		
	3.55 / 4.75 plastic coated chain link	ADD	5%
012	**Chain link fencing for tennis court surrounds to BS 1722, Part 13 with 3 mm galvanised mesh, line and tying wire; galvanised mild steel intermediate angle posts at 3.00 m centres**		
013	2.75 m high	38.00	m
	Extra over for:		
	end posts	145.00	Nr

	Specialist	£	Unit
	corner posts	188.10	Nr
014	**3.00 m high**	42.00	m
	Extra over for:		
	end posts	153.00	Nr
	corner posts	192.00	Nr
015	Single gates 1 m wide x 2 m high	525.00	Nr
016	**Extra over** for Concrete to post holes	2.91	Nr
017	**Post and wire fencing to BS 1722, Part 3 with galvanised lines and tying wire; intermediate posts at 3.00 m centres**		
018	Round posts:		
	5 lines plain wire:		
	0.9m high fencing (SW 90)	5.75	m
	Extra over for:		
	end posts	35.00	Nr
	corner posts	45.00	Nr
	6 lines plain wire:		
	1.2 m high fencing (SW 120)	6.90	m
	Extra over for:		
	end posts	36.00	Nr
	corner posts	45.50	Nr
	7 lines plain wire:		
	1.35 m high fencing (SW 135)	7.50	m
	Extra over for:		
	end posts	37.00	Nr
	corner posts	48.00	Nr
019	**Extra over** for sawn posts with the above	ADD	10%
020	Concrete posts / SS 90 Steel posts:		
	5 lines of wire:		
	0.9 m high fencing (SC 90)	10.75	m
	Extra over for:		
	end posts	59.00	Nr
	corner posts	82.00	Nr
	6 lines of wire:		
	1.2 m high fencing (SC 120)	11.50	m
	Extra over for:		
	end posts	66.00	Nr
	corner posts	88.00	Nr
	7 lines of wire:		
	1.35 m high fencing (SC 135)	12.60	m
	Extra over for:		
	end posts	74.00	Nr
	corner posts	96.00	Nr
021	Each additional strand of plain wire	0.75	m
022	Each additional strand of barbed wire	0.75	m
023	Galvanised stock fence 800 mm high type C 8/80/15; fixed to above fences	2.50	m
024	**Extra over** for concrete to post holes	2.71	Nr
025	**Chestnut pale fencing to BS 1722, Part 4 with intermediate posts of round timber or cleft chestnut at maximum centres and spacings as table 1**		
026	Round timber or cleft chestnut posts:		
	1.05 m high fencing (CW 105)	7.50	m
	Extra over for:		
	end posts	35.00	Nr
	corner posts	45.00	Nr
	1.2 m high fencing (CW 120)	7.75	m
	Extra over for:		
	end posts	36.00	Nr
	corner posts	46.00	Nr
	1.5 m high fencing (CW 150)	8.15	m
	Extra over for:		
	end posts	37.00	Nr
	corner posts	47.00	Nr
	1.8 m high fencing (CW 180)	9.30	m
	Extra over for:		
	end posts	38.00	Nr
	corner posts	48.00	Nr
027	**Wooden palisade fencing to BS 1722, Part 6 with 75 x 19 mm rectangular pales and square tops spaced 75 mm apart; intermediate posts at 3.00 m centres**		
028	Timber posts:		
	1.05 m high fencing (WPW 105)	30.00	m
	1.2 m high fencing (WPW 120)	32.00	m
	1.5 m high fencing (WPW 150)	36.00	m
	1.8 m high fencing (WPW 180)	38.00	m
029	Concrete posts:		
	1.05 m high fencing (WPC 105)	34.00	m
	1.2 m high fencing (WPC 120)	36.00	m

Specialist	£	Unit
1.5 m high fencing (WPC 150)	40.00	m
1.8 m high fencing (WPC 180)	42.00	m

030   **Wooden post and rail fencing to BS 1722, Part 7; intermediate main posts at 1.80 m centres**

031   Nailed type:
    1.1 m high:

	£	Unit
SPR 11/3 - 3 rail	26.50	m
SPR 11/4 - 4 rail	27.50	m
1.3 m high:		
SPR 13/4 - 4 rail	28.50	m

032   Morticed posts:
    1.1 m high:

	£	Unit
MPR 11/3 - 3 rail	27.50	m
MPR 11/4 - 4 rail	28.50	m
1.3 m high:		
MPR 13/4 - 4 rail	29.50	m

XB   **CLOSE BOARDED FENCING**

001   **Close boarded fencing BS 1722, Part 5 with softwood pressure treated pales, horizontal rails, capping and gravel boards; intermediate posts at 3.00 m centres; centre stump in each bay**

002   Timber posts:

	£	Unit
1.05 m high fencing (BW 105)	34.00	m
1.2 m high fencing (BW 120)	36.00	m
1.5 m high fencing (BW 150)	40.00	m
1.8 m high fencing (BW 180)	42.00	m

003   Morticed concrete posts:

	£	Unit
1.05 m high fencing (BCM 105)	38.00	m
1.2 m high fencing (BCM 120)	40.00	m
1.5 m high fencing (BCM 150)	44.00	m
1.8 m high fencing (BCM 180)	46.00	m

004   Recessed concrete posts:

	£	Unit
1.05 m high fencing (BCR 105)	37.50	m
1.2 m high fencing (BCR 120)	39.50	m
1.5 m high fencing (BCR 150)	43.50	m
1.8 m high fencing (BCR 180)	45.50	m

005   **Extra over** for:

	£	Unit
concrete gravel boards all types	3.50	m
capping and counter rail	3.50	m

006   **Extra over** for concrete to post holes   3.03   Nr

007   **Woven wood fencing to BS 1722; Part 11, treated softwood panels between posts at 1.80 m centres**

008   75 mm square timber posts:

	£	Unit
0.9 m high fencing (WW 90)	26.00	m
1.2 m high fencing (WW 120)	28.00	m
1.5 m high fencing (WW 150)	32.00	m
1.8 m high fencing (WW 180)	34.00	m

009   **Extra over** for 100 mm square timber posts   ADD   6%

010   Slotted concrete posts:

	£	Unit
0.9 m high fencing (WC 90)	33.00	m
1.2 m high fencing (WC 120)	35.00	m
1.5 m high fencing (WC 150)	37.00	m
1.8 m high fencing (WC 180)	38.00	m

011   **Extra over** for concrete gravel board 150 x 150 mm   3.50   m

XC   **GATES**

001   **Timber field gates and posts to BS 3470, Table 1**

002   Gates 1.20 m high in softwood including galvanised fittings and posts:

	£	Unit
2.4 m wide	355.00	Nr
3.0 m wide	365.00	Nr
3.6 m wide	375.00	Nr

003   Gates 1.20 m high in hardwood including galvanised fittings and posts:

	£	Unit
2.4 m wide	530.00	Nr
3.0 m wide	540.00	Nr
3.6 m wide	545.00	Nr

004   **Steel field gates and posts**

005   Gates 1.20 m high in galvanised tubular steel:

	£	Unit
3.0 m wide	360.00	Nr
3.6 m wide	365.00	Nr
4.0 m wide	375.00	Nr
4.5 m wide	385.00	Nr

Specialist	£	Unit
006	**Close Boarded gates including fittings (INC posts)**		
007	Single gate, 0.9 m wide:		
	x 0.9 m high	175.00	Nr
	x 1.2 m high	180.00	Nr
	x 1.5 m high	183.00	Nr
	x 1.8 m high	185.00	Nr
008	Double gate, 2.4 m wide:		
	x 0.9 m high	405.00	Nr
	x 1.2 m high	425.00	Nr
	x 1.5 m high	455.00	Nr
	x 1.8 m high	475.00	Nr
009	Double gate, 3.0 m wide:		
	x 0.9 m high	425.00	Nr
	x 1.5 m high	475.00	Nr
	x 1.8 m high	495.00	Nr
010	**Palisade Gates including fittings (NOT posts)**		
011	Single gate, 0.9 m wide:		
	x 0.9 m high	80.00	Nr
	x 1.2 m high	85.00	Nr
	x 1.5 m high	90.00	Nr
	x 1.8 m high	95.00	Nr
012	**Gate posts, treated softwood; set in concrete**		
013	1.5 m long x 100 x 100 mm	80.00	Nr
	1.8 m long x 125 x 125 mm	88.00	Nr
	2.65 m long x 150 x 150 mm	95.00	Nr
014	**Gates; galvanised steel angle, 3 mm galvanised chain link infill**		
015	Single gate, 0.9 m wide:		
	40 x 40 mm angle (including posts):		
	x 0.9 m high	300.00	Nr
	x 1.2 m high	315.00	Nr
	x 1.4 m high	350.00	Nr
	x 1.8 m high	375.00	Nr
	50 x 50 mm angle:		
	x 2.4 m high	400.00	Nr
016	Double gate; 3.0 m wide (not including posts):		
	50 x 50 mm angle:		
	x 0.9 m high	525.00	Nr
	x 1.2 m high	560.00	Nr
	x 1.4 m high	600.00	Nr
	x 1.8 m high	650.00	Nr
017	Double gate; 3.5 m wide:		
	50 x 50 mm angle:		
	x 1.2 m high	575.00	Nr
	x 1.4 m high	615.00	Nr
	x 1.8 m high	665.00	Nr
018	Double gate; 4.0 m wide:		
	50 x 50 mm angle:		
	x 1.2 m high	600.00	Nr
	x 1.4 m high	630.00	Nr
	x 1.8 m high	690.00	Nr
019	Double gate; 4.5 m wide:		
	50 x 50 mm angle:		
	x 1.8 m high	750.00	Nr
020	Double gate; 5.0 m wide:		
	50 x 50 mm angle:		
	x 1.8 m high	825.00	Nr
021	Double gate; 6.0 m wide:		
	50 x 50 mm angle:		
	x 1.8 m high	915.00	Nr
022	Double gate; 7.0 m wide:		
	60 x 60 mm angle:		
	x 1.8 m high	1100.00	Nr
023	Double gate; 2.4 m high:		
	50 x 50 mm angle:		
	3.0 m wide	750.00	Nr
	3.5 m wide	775.00	Nr
	4.0 m wide	790.00	Nr
	4.5 m wide	850.00	Nr
	5.0 m wide	985.00	Nr
	6.0 m wide	1100.00	Nr
	7.0 m wide	1500.00	Nr

Specialist	£	Unit
8.0 m wide	1900.00	Nr
024 **Extra over** for 3 lines barbed wire to all angle steel gates:		
singles	30.00	Nr
doubles	60.00	Nr
025 **End / Gate posts, galvanised steel box section including setting in concrete**		
026 1.5 m high x 50 mm	145.00	Nr
1.8 m high x 80 mm	150.00	Nr
2.65 m high x 100 mm	165.00	Nr
3.2 m high x 150 mm	175.00	Nr
027 **Barbed wire extensions to gate posts**		
028 50 mm square section posts	12.30	Nr
80 mm square section posts	15.82	Nr
100 mm square section posts	18.28	Nr
150 mm square section posts	29.88	Nr
XF **FENCING REPAIRS**		
001 Take down and clear away:		
line wire	1.77	m
timber post and wire fence	7.07	m
concrete port and wire fence	8.25	m
chain link fencing, posts left in	1.77	m
chain link fencing with concrete posts	3.69	m
chain link fencing with steel posts	9.13	m
chestnut pale fencing, posts left in	2.21	m
chestnut pale fencing with posts	3.82	m
002 Refix to existing posts:		
plain wire	0.23	m
barbed wire	0.27	m
chain link fencing	3.33	m
003 Renew to existing posts:		
plain wire	2.12	m
barbed wire	2.20	m
004 New galvanised chain link to existing posts:		
0.9 m high	14.86	m
1.2 m high	17.44	m
1.4 m high	20.17	m
1.8 m high	21.24	m
005 New plastic coated chain link to existing posts:		
0.9 m high	13.80	m
1.2 m high	16.53	m
1.4 m high	18.95	m
1.8 m high	20.32	m
006 New chestnut pale fencing to existing posts:		
1000 mm high, 2 wires	11.83	m
1200 mm high, 3 wires	14.86	m
007 New treated softwood interwoven panel 2000 mm long to existing posts:		
1000 mm high	36.40	Nr
2000 mm high	52.03	Nr
008 New treated softwood lap panel 2000 mm long to existing posts:		
1000 mm high	36.40	Nr
2000 mm high	52.03	Nr
009 **Remove defective fence posts and replace with new**		
010 post and wire fencing:		
softwood post 925 mm high	12.14	Nr
concrete post 925 mm high	27.60	Nr
011 chain link fencing, angle iron posts:		
925 mm high	26.54	Nr
1200 mm high	28.82	Nr
1400 mm high	29.73	Nr
1800 mm high	33.67	Nr
012 chain link fencing, concrete posts:		
925 mm high	27.15	Nr
1200 mm high	29.57	Nr
1400 mm high	30.94	Nr
1800 mm high	32.00	Nr

Specialist	£	Unit
013	chestnut pale fencing:		
	softwood posts 1200 mm high	6.37	Nr
014	timber panel fencing:		
	softwood posts 2000 mm high	13.95	Nr
	concrete posts 2000 mm high	39.43	Nr

External Works

Diploma in Adjudication in the Construction Industry

Comprised of four units, this qualification is designed for those **seeking to become an adjudicator**, and provides a pathway towards potential entry onto the **RICS Panel of Adjudicators**.

With a focus on contract and tort law and how they apply to adjudication, this course is designed to prepare you to progress to practice as an adjudicator. This course is suitable for those with experience in dispute resolution procedures with an understanding of the general principles of construction adjudication. The course content will focus on the format and content of an enforceable decision.

Learning Outcomes:

- Knowledge and understanding of the nature of law and its' place in society
- How the law of contract is applied to the practice of adjudication
- How the law of tort is applied to the practice of adjudication
- The practical application in the production of an enforceable decision.

Attainment of the learning outcomes will be assessed by a case study, whereby candidates will be required to produce an enforceable reasoned decision, based on material supplied in the case study.

Labour Rates

Please note: The labour hours throughout this section are representative of the time required for one productive man to carry out the unit of work.

Gang rates are calculated as follows by obtaining the overall gang cost and then dividing this by the number of productive members in the gang. The resulting rate is the Gang Cost per **Man - hour.** By using the same principle, any size gang may be built-up and used against the standard labour hours in this section.

Demolitions, excavation, generally, in situ plain concrete works:
   Demolition Labourer - £11.22 per hour

Earthwork support
   Labourer (semi skill A) - £14.02 per hour

A0201 Reinforced concrete:

Shuttering Carpenter	1.00	x	£	15.20	= £	15.20
Concretor	4.00	x	£	11.22	= £	44.88
Poker vibrator	3.00	x	£	4.68	= £	14.04
Total hourly cost of gang					= £	74.12

   Gang rate (divided by 4) = £18.53 per Man-hour

Reinforcement, formwork:
   Shuttering Carpenter - £15.20 per hour

Precast concrete paving slabs, reconstructed stone paving slabs, precast concrete kerbs, channels, edgings and the like, hardcore, sand and other beds.
   Brick/Blockwork Labourer - £11.22 per hour

A0204 Precast concrete screen walling blocks, brick pavings, brick kerbs and the like.

Brick/Block Layer	2.00	x	£	15.20	= £	30.40
Brick/Blockwork Labourer	1.00	x	£	11.22	= £	11.22
Total hourly cost of gang					= £	41.62

   Gang rate (divided by 2) = £20.81 per Man-hour

A0211 Pipework in external services:

Advanced PHMES Operative	1.00	x	£	19.59	= £	19.59
Apprentice Plumber (3rd Year)	1.00	x	£	12.01	= £	12.01
Total hourly cost of gang					= £	31.60

   Gang rate (divided by 1) = £31.60 per Man-hour

Ductwork in external services, up to but not exceeding 300 mm diameter:
   Labourer (semi skill B) - £14.38 per hour

Painting on fencing and gates:
   Painter and Decorator - £15.20 per hour

Plant Hire Charges

		Daily Hire Charge £	Pro-ductive Hours Hrs	Cost Per Hour £	Operator Per Hour £	Fuel Per Hour £	Total Cost Per Hour £
	The hire charges shown exclude the cost of operators and fuel but are inclusive of oil, grease and the like. Fuel costs have been added in the following table as appropriate. The operator costs are either added in the table below or, where no operator shown, have been allowed for in the rates given in the individual items of work. The cost of delivery to, or collection from site is EXCLUDED and allowance for this should be made in Preliminaries.						
A0021	JCB 3C	85.00	6.00	14.17	14.38	5.63	**34.18**
A0022	Cat D5 1CY	145.00	6.00	24.17	14.38	8.29	**46.84**
A0024	Hymac 580 with breaker hammer and 230 CFM compressor	230.00	7.00	32.86	14.38	9.15	**56.39**
A0031	Dumper 2000 kg capacity, hydraulic tip	45.00	6.00	7.50	11.82	2.52	**21.84**
A0041	16 tonne tipper truck	224.00	8.00	28.00	-	-	**28.00**
A0051	8 tonne roller	80.00	6.00	13.33	11.82	6.63	**31.78**
A0061	Whacker	16.50	6.00	2.75	-	0.86	**3.61**
A0052	Vibrating roller, 400 Kg	24.00	6.00	4.00	11.82	1.66	**17.48**
A0062	Hand guided vibrating plate	17.00	6.00	2.83	-	0.86	**3.69**
A0063	Compressor 100 CFM and one breaker	32.00	6.00	5.33	-	0.86	**6.19**
A0131	Melter pourer for expansion jointing	16.50	6.00	2.75	-	3.84	**6.59**
A0181	Chain saw	38.40	5.00	7.68	-	1.46	**9.14**
A0182	Rotovator	42.00	6.00	7.00	-	13.26	**20.26**
A0191	Oxy-acetylene burning equipment and gas	19.50	4.00	4.88	-	4.6	**9.48**
A0192	Blow lamp equipment and gas	6.00	6.00	1.00	-	7.39	**8.39**
A0200	Tipping charges	110.00	1.00	110.00	-	-	**110.00**

The abbreviations under the headings on the succeeding pages have the following meanings:

Excav = Excavating plant (JCB, Cat, etc.)
Brkng = Breaking equipment (Hymac 580 with breaker hammer or compressor and three breakers)
Cmptg = Compacting equipment (Whacker, 8 tonne roller etc.)
Trans = Transportation plant (Dumper, Lorry etc.)

Basic Prices of Materials

		Supply Price £	Waste Factor %	Unload. Labour £	Unload. Plant £	Total Unit Cost £	Unit
A0361	Timber for earthwork support	280.30	5%	11.22	-	306.09	m3
A0351	Hardcore	18.11	-	-	-	18.11	m3
Y0073	Granular material MOT Grade 1	18.11	10%	-	-	19.92	tonne
Y0074	Granular material 20 mm down	26.01	10%	-	-	28.61	tonne
Y0075	Quarry scalpings	16.14	10%	-	-	17.75	tonne
A0322	Sharp sand BS 882 Zone M	25.26	10%	-	-	27.78	tonne
A0301	Portland cement delivered in bags	137.81	5%	11.22	-	156.48	tonne
A0321	Sand for mortar, BS 1200	24.16	10%	-	-	26.57	tonne
A0343	19 mm Aggregate	30.95	10%	-	-	34.05	tonne
F0507	Lean mix (1:12) concrete ready mixed	79.51	5%	-	-	83.49	m3
F0508	21 N/mm2 concrete ready mixed	86.13	5%	-	-	90.44	m3

Additives, special mixes

The following additions should be made to the prices of lightweight aggregate grade C20/25 concrete in this section, when required:

		Supply Price £	Waste Factor %	Unload. Labour £	Unload. Plant £	Total Unit Cost £	Unit
F1500	Sulphate resisting cement	11.98	-	-	-	11.98	m3
F1501	Accelerating admixture	11.98	-	-	-	11.98	m3
F1502	Retarding admixture	11.98	-	-	-	11.98	m3
F1503	Normal water-reducing admixture	5.99	-	-	-	5.99	m3
F1504	Waterproof concrete	59.92	-	-	-	59.92	m3
F1505	Pumping grade concrete	11.98	-	-	-	11.98	m3
F1506	Minimum 360 kg cement	11.98	-	-	-	11.98	m3

Steel fabric reinforcement:

		Supply Price £	Waste Factor %	Unload. Labour £	Unload. Plant £	Total Unit Cost £	Unit
F0462	A142	2.05	2.5%	0.03	-	2.13	m2
F0463	A193	2.60	2.5%	0.08	-	2.75	m2
F0464	A252	3.47	2.5%	0.08	-	3.64	m2
F0466	B196	2.90	2.5%	0.08	-	3.05	m2
F0469	B503	4.95	2.5%	0.11	-	5.19	m2
F0260	Sawn softwood for formwork	295.00	12.5%	11.22	-	344.50	m3
F0266	Formwork oil	1.54	20%	-	-	1.85	ltr
F0263	Nails	2.90	10%	-	-	3.19	kg
F0261	19 mm plywood for formwork	8.60	10%	2.81	-	12.55	m2
F0264	12 mm dowel bars 500 mm long and PVC dowel caps	0.44	5%	-	-	0.46	nr
F0265	D/Bar debonding agent	1.76	10%	0.01	-	1.95	ltr

'Aerofil' high density joint filler uncut boards:

		Supply Price £	Waste Factor %	Unload. Labour £	Unload. Plant £	Total Unit Cost £	Unit
F0215	10 mm thick	8.54	5%	-	-	8.97	m2

Bricks

Note: All bricks are 215 x 102.5 x 65 mm; where no labour unloading prices are shown the materials are supplied palletised for crane unloading (surcharge for pallets excluded).

		Supply Price £	Waste Factor %	Unload. Labour £	Unload. Plant £	Total Unit Cost £	Unit
G0105	Facing bricks	351.38	5%	-	-	368.95	1000
G0106	Adjustment factor for price of bricks	10.00	-	-	-	10.00	1000
	Special bricks:						
G0531	single cant or bullnose headers	3.40	2%	-	-	3.46	nr
G0528	single cant or bullnose stretchers	2.78	2%	-	-	2.83	nr
G0530	returned ends	38.50	2%	-	-	39.27	nr
G0534	internal angles	9.06	2%	-	-	9.24	nr
G0537	external angles	22.65	2%	-	-	23.10	nr
N1501	Proprietary plugs 'Rawlplug' plastic type; No 8 x 38	0.02	10%	-	-	0.02	nr
N1502	Steel wood screws No 8 x 38	0.02	10%	-	-	0.02	nr

The following prices were provided by CAMAS and are applicable to sites approximately 100 miles from the point of supply.
Precast concrete hydraulically pressed kerbs and channels BS 340:

		Supply Price £	Waste Factor %	Unload. Labour £	Unload. Plant £	Total Unit Cost £	Unit
Y0114	150 x 305 x 915 mm Figs 1, 4, 6, 8	8.47	2.5%	-	-	8.68	nr
Y0115	125 x 255 x 915 mm Figs 2, 5, 7, 8	4.41	2.5%	-	-	4.52	nr
Y0116	125 x 150 x 915 mm Figs 2a, 5, 7a, 8, 9	3.22	2.5%	-	-	3.30	nr
	Extra over over prices for:						
Y0117	standard dish channels	2.24	2.5%	-	-	2.30	nr
Y0118	radius and droppers	2.90	2.5%	-	-	2.97	nr
Y0119	quadrant angles	10.90	2.5%	-	-	11.18	nr
	Precast concrete hydraulically pressed edgings BS 340:						
Y0120	50 x 150 x 915 mm Figs 11, 12, 13	1.80	2.5%	-	-	1.84	nr
Y0121	50 x 200 x 915 mm Figs 11, 13	3.07	2.5%	-	-	3.14	nr
Y0122	50 x 250 x 915 mm Figs 11, 13	3.59	2.5%	-	-	3.68	nr
	Safeticurb drainage units:						
Y0124	DBA slot unit 250 x 250 x 914 mm 125 mm bore	36.78	2.5%	-	-	37.70	nr
Y0126	DBM slot unit 250 x 250 x 414 mm 125 mm bore	65.46	2.5%	-	-	67.10	nr
Y0130	DBG/PS grid insp. unit 250 x 250 x 914 mm 125 mm bore	57.54	2.5%	-	-	58.98	nr
	Safeticurb fittings:						
Y0133	Silt box top type A (cast iron)	256.53	2.5%	-	-	262.94	nr
Y0136	Kerb inspection unit DBK SP (or HB2)	133.61	2.5%	-	-	136.95	nr
Y0137	Kerb transition unit SP (or HB2)	54.06	2.5%	-	-	55.41	nr
Y0138	Kerb manhole cover SP (or HB2)	480.99	2.5%	-	-	493.01	nr
	Precast concrete paving slabs hydraulically pressed BS 368; natural grey; plain smooth face:						
Y0202	450 x 600 x 50 mm	4.10	2.5%	-	-	4.20	nr
Y0203	600 x 600 x 50 mm	4.62	2.5%	-	-	4.74	nr
Y0204	750 x 600 x 50 mm	5.71	2.5%	-	-	5.86	nr
Y0205	900 x 600 x 50 mm	6.07	2.5%	-	-	6.22	nr

Basic Prices of Materials

	Supply Price £	Waste Factor %	Unload. Labour £	Unload. Plant £	Total Unit Cost £	Unit
Bradstone 'Riven' type reconstructed stone paving delivered site in full 15 tonne loads:						
600 x 450 x 40 mm:						
Y0206 Cotswold honey-brown	12.34	5%	-	-	12.95	nr
Y0207 weathered York-grey	13.15	5%	-	-	13.81	nr
450 x 450 x 40 mm:						
Y0208 Cotswold honey-brown	9.27	5%	-	-	9.74	nr
Y0209 weathered York-grey	9.82	5%	-	-	10.31	nr
Grass Concrete Limited, Precast Landscape grass and concrete paving:						
Y0620 Grassblock GB83 units	17.87	2.5%	-	-	18.32	m2
Y0621 Grassblock GB103 units	20.33	2.5%	-	-	20.84	m2
Y0622 Grassblock GB125 units	21.49	2.5%	-	-	22.03	m2
Y0623 **Extra over** over for brown earth colour	3.36	2.5%	-	-	3.44	m2
Y0624 Grass road polypropylene paving, 635 x 330 x 42 mm, including fixing pins	13.96	2.5%	-	-	14.31	m2
Y0625 Grass kerb HDPE kerbing, 1000 x 80 x 60 mm, including fixing pins	6.36	2.5%	-	-	6.52	m
Grass Concrete Limited Betoflor dry laid interlocking retaining/acoustic walling systems:						
Y0626 Betoflor 250 mm wide units, grey	46.26	2.5%	-	-	47.42	m2
Y0627 **Extra over** over for colour	6.66	2.5%	-	-	6.82	m2
Y0628 Betoatlas 500 mm wide units, grey	85.43	2.5%	-	-	87.56	m2
Y0629 **Extra over** over for colour	12.82	2.5%	-	-	13.14	m2
Y0630 Leromur split stone units, 500 mm split width	145.81	2.5%	-	-	149.46	m2
Y0631 **Extra over** over for colour	24.54	2.5%	-	-	25.15	m2
Y0632 Betojard 250 mm wide units, grey	85.29	2.5%	-	-	87.42	m2
Y0633 **Extra over** over for colour	11.92	2.5%	-	-	12.22	m2
The following prices were provided by Marshalls Mono Ltd and are applicable to sites approximately 100 miles from the point of supply.						
Marshalls Mono 'Keyblok' concrete block paving in blocks size 200 x 100 mm:						
Y0110 natural, 60 mm thick	8.99	2.5%	-	-	9.21	m2
Y0111 natural, 80 mm thick	10.00	2.5%	-	-	10.25	m2
Y0112 coloured, 60 mm thick	10.00	2.5%	-	-	10.25	m2
Y0113 coloured, 80 mm thick	11.55	2.5%	-	-	11.84	m2
Y0161 Marshalls Beany block combined kerb and drainage system	58.39	2.5%	-	-	59.85	m
MEADRAIN® surface drainage channels from MEA UK Ltd:						
MEADRAIN Z1000 series and accessories:						
Y0261 channel unit 1000 mm long x av. 225 mm deep to fall with sloping bottom (155441)	42.43	2.5%	-	-	43.49	nr
Y0262 end cap (151471)	8.98	2.5%	-	-	9.20	nr
Y0263 end cap with PVC 110 mm connector (151473)	14.41	2.5%	-	-	14.77	nr
Y0264 channel unit 500 mm long x 225 mm deep with "knock-out" opening both sides (155445)	42.45	2.5%	-	-	43.51	nr
Y0265 silt box unit without trap (151085)	97.63	-	-	-	97.63	nr
Y0266 silt box unit with roddable in-line foul air trap 100 mm diameter (155485)	119.63	-	-	-	119.63	nr
Y0267 silt box unit with roddable side foul air trap 100 mm diameter (155487)	119.63	-	-	-	119.63	nr
Y0268 gully upper section (154707)	233.33	-	-	-	233.33	nr
Y0269 gully lower section (154711)	86.30	-	-	-	86.30	nr
Y0271 middle section (154709)	56.24	-	-	-	56.24	nr
Y0272 PVC connector 100 mm diameter (154501)	2.63	5%	-	-	2.76	nr
Y0273 PVC connector 160 mm diameter (154503)	7.59	5%	-	-	7.97	nr
Y0275 Galv. Mild Steel Grating 1000 mm long (152101)	9.86	-	-	-	9.86	nr
Y0276 Galv. Mild Steel Grating 1000 mm long (152301)	19.88	-	-	-	19.88	nr
Y0277 Galv. Mild Steel Grating 1000 mm long (152303)	27.34	-	-	-	27.34	nr
Y0279 CI Grating 500 mm long, loading class C 250 (152411)	15.60	-	-	-	15.60	nr
Y0281 CI Grating 500 mm long, loading class C 250 (152541)	19.20	-	-	-	19.20	nr
Y0283 Galv steel grating locking mechanism (152116)	2.94	2.5%	-	-	3.01	nr
Y0284 Galv steel grating locking mechanism (152311)	2.94	2.5%	-	-	3.01	nr
Y0285 galvanised sediment bucket for shallow gully (154713)	52.75	-	-	-	52.75	nr
Y0286 galvanised sediment bucket for deep gully (154715)	62.61	-	-	-	62.61	nr
Y0175 8 mm diameter high yield round steel reinforcing bars	0.36	2.5%	-	-	0.37	m
Y0172 12 mm diameter high yield round steel reinforcing bars	0.77	2.5%	-	-	0.79	m
Marshalls Mono precast concrete bollards:						
White finish:						
Y0176 Bridgeford	97.69	2.5%	-	-	100.13	nr
Y0177 Woodhouse	81.36	2.5%	-	-	83.40	nr
Y0178 Richmond	131.36	2.5%	-	-	134.64	nr
Y0179 Truro	176.40	2.5%	-	-	180.81	nr
Exposed aggregate finish bollards:						
Y0180 Truro	263.73	2.5%	-	-	270.32	nr
Y0181 Worcester	136.11	2.5%	-	-	139.51	nr
Y0182 Wexham	152.24	2.5%	-	-	156.05	nr
'Beadalite' finish:						
Y0183 Richmond	185.18	2.5%	-	-	189.81	nr
Y0184 Wexham	217.72	2.5%	-	-	223.16	nr
Y0185 Bridgford	185.18	2.5%	-	-	189.81	nr
Marshalls Mono boulevard range of street furniture in precast concrete:						
Y0186 1400 rectangular planter, complete unit, 1 ring high	751.80	-	-	-	751.80	nr
Y0187 1200 circular planter, complete unit, 1 ring high	634.33	-	-	-	634.33	nr
Y0188 1400 rectangular seat, complete unit	762.22	-	-	-	762.22	nr
Y0189 700 planter, complete unit, 1 ring high	549.99	-	-	-	549.99	nr
Y0190 700 circular litter bin with cover	321.21	-	-	-	321.21	nr
'Kelvin' seat:						
Y0192 free standing	607.88	-	-	-	607.88	nr
Y0193 ground fixed	536.15	-	-	-	536.15	nr

Mortar Mix Analysis

The cost of mixers or mortar mills should be costed in Preliminaries.
The prices of 1 m3 of mortar are calculated as follows:

A0611 Cement mortar (1:3)

Cement (bagged)	0.44 tonne	x	£	156.48	=	£	68.85
Building sand	1.83 tonne	x	£	26.57	=	£	48.62
Labourer BATJIC A	2.00 hour	x	£	11.22	=	£	22.44
						£	139.91
Waste	10%				=	£	13.99
Cost per m3					**=**	**£**	**153.90**

A0641 Cement lime mortar (1:1:6)

Cement (bagged)	0.23 tonne	x	£	156.48	=	£	35.99
Hydrated lime (del. in bags)	0.12 tonne	x	£	238.58	=	£	28.63
Building sand	1.93 tonne	x	£	26.57	=	£	51.28
Labourer BATJIC A	2.00 hour	x	£	11.22	=	£	22.44
						£	138.34
Waste	10%				=	£	13.83
Cost per m3					**=**	**£**	**152.17**

A0643 Coloured cement lime mortar (1:1:6)

Cement (bagged)	0.23 tonne	x	£	156.48	=	£	35.99
Hydrated lime (del. in bags)	0.12 tonne	x	£	238.58	=	£	28.63
Building sand	1.93 tonne	x	£	26.57	=	£	51.28
Febtone colour pigment (red)	8.00 kg	x	£	7.82	=	£	62.56
Labourer BATJIC A	2.00 hour	x	£	11.22	=	£	22.44
						£	200.90
Waste	10%				=	£	20.09
Cost per m3					**=**	**£**	**220.99**

Unit Rates	Man-Hours	Excav Hours	Brkng Hours	Cmptg Hours	Trans Hours	Net Labour Price £	Net Plant Price £	Net Mats Price £	Net Unit Price £	Unit
YA UNIT RATES **EXTERNAL WORKS**										
SITE PREPARATION LANDSCAPING AND PLANTING										
DEMOLITION										
Prices for removing debris and excavated material allow for payments of tipping charges and transporting to tip 15 km from site. No allowance has been made for Credit value of demolished materials.										
001 **Demolition; clearing site of all structures down to the underside of the lowest floor slabs together with all slabs on the ground, wall foundations, column bases etc.; removing all debris from site to tip 15 km from site and paying tipping charges**										
002 Timber framed and timber clad sheds, garages etc.; 150 mm concrete floor slab; overall:										
3.00 x 2.00 x 2.00 m high	6.08	0.83	-	-	0.69	68.25	94.28	-	**162.53**	item
6.00 x 3.00 x 2.50 m high	15.92	2.92	-	-	1.45	178.62	86.89	-	**265.51**	item
003 Steel framed and fibre cement clad single storey buildings; 150 mm reinforced concrete floor slabs; overall:										
10.00 x 6.00 x 4.00 m high	48.90	10.75	1.50	-	2.75	548.61	695.11	-	**1243.72**	item
30.00 x 10.00 x 5.00 m high	181.93	56.50	8.00	-	12.50	2041.25	3587.52	-	**5628.77**	item
004 Brick built buildings, pitched tiled or slated roof; 150 mm reinforced concrete floor slabs; overall:										
5.00 x 3.00 x 4.00 m high	55.72	15.50	1.00	-	5.50	625.17	1220.59	-	**1845.76**	item
10.00 x 5.00 x 4.00 m high	67.09	38.00	4.00	-	12.00	752.75	2972.98	-	**3725.73**	item
005 Brick built buildings, 150 mm reinforced concrete flat roof; 200 mm reinforced concrete floor slab; overall:										
5.00 x 3.00 x 4.00 m high	44.35	31.00	2.50	-	6.00	497.58	1548.36	-	**2045.94**	item
10.00 x 5.00 x 4.00 m high	134.18	81.50	5.00	-	13.00	1505.50	3401.20	-	**4906.70**	item
YB **PAVINGS AND KERBS**										
EXCAVATION										
Basis of prices										
The rates for excavation in the work in this section allow for excavation in firm earth. For other types of ground refer to the percentage additions listed in section D. For excavation to reduce levels refer to section YC.										
For any further excavation items, excavation in rock, breaking up pavings in the surface of the ground etc. refer to Section D.										
001 **Excavating by machine**										
002 Excavating (JCB) trenches to receive kerb foundations:										
300 x 100 mm	0.01	0.01	-	-	-	0.09	0.24	-	**0.33**	m
450 x 150 mm	0.02	0.02	-	-	-	0.18	0.51	-	**0.69**	m
600 x 200 mm	0.03	0.03	-	-	-	0.35	0.92	-	**1.27**	m
003 Excavating (JCB) curved trenches to receive kerb foundations:										
300 x 100 mm	0.01	0.01	-	-	-	0.10	0.24	-	**0.34**	m
450 x 150 mm	0.02	0.02	-	-	-	0.21	0.58	-	**0.79**	m
600 x 200 mm	0.03	0.03	-	-	-	0.38	0.99	-	**1.37**	m
004 **Excavating by hand**										
005 Excavating trenches to receive kerb foundations:										
150 x 75 mm	0.04	-	-	-	-	0.41	-	-	**0.41**	m
250 x 100 mm	0.08	-	-	-	-	0.92	-	-	**0.92**	m
300 x 100 mm	0.10	-	-	-	-	1.11	-	-	**1.11**	m
006 Excavating curved trenches to receive kerb foundations:										
150 x 75 mm	0.04	-	-	-	-	0.45	-	-	**0.45**	m
250 x 100 mm	0.09	-	-	-	-	1.02	-	-	**1.02**	m
300 x 100 mm	0.11	-	-	-	-	1.22	-	-	**1.22**	m

Unit Rates	Man-Hours	Excav Hours	Brkng Hours	Cmptg Hours	Trans Hours	Net Labour Price £	Net Plant Price £	Net Mats Price £	Net Unit Price £	Unit
007 Surface treatments										
008 Levelling and compacting with a vibrating roller:										
surfaces of open excavation and filling	0.15	-	-	0.05	-	1.66	0.87		**2.53**	m2
surfaces of open excavation and filling; including grading to falls	0.18	-	-	0.05	-	2.04	0.87		**2.91**	m2
surfaces of open excavation and filling; including grading to falls and crossfalls	0.21	-	-	0.05	-	2.30	0.87		**3.17**	m2

HARDCORE AND OTHER BEDS

Filling materials in this section apply specifically to road and pavement construction; for other filling materials refer to section D.

	Man-Hours	Excav Hours	Brkng Hours	Cmptg Hours	Trans Hours	Net Labour Price £	Net Plant Price £	Net Mats Price £	Net Unit Price £	Unit
009 Imported quarry scalpings filling; level or to falls, crossfalls or slopes; levelling and compacting with a vibrating roller										
010 Filling to make up levels, by hand, wheeling average 25 m; average thickness:										
75 mm	0.21	-	-	0.05	-	2.30	0.87	3.20	**6.37**	m2
100 mm	0.26	-	-	0.05	-	2.94	0.87	4.26	**8.07**	m2
150 mm	0.35	-	-	0.05	-	3.96	0.87	6.39	**11.22**	m2
011 Filling to make up levels, by machine (Cat), transporting average 25 m; average thickness:										
75 mm	0.11	0.02	-	0.05	-	1.22	1.95	3.20	**6.37**	m2
100 mm	0.13	0.03	-	0.05	-	1.40	2.04	4.26	**7.70**	m2
150 mm	0.13	0.03	-	0.05	-	1.44	2.32	6.39	**10.15**	m2
012 Imported hardcore filling, including 25 mm sand blinding; level or to falls, crossfalls and slopes; levelling and compacting with a vibrating roller										
013 Filling to make up levels, by hand, wheeling average 25 m; average thickness:										
75 mm	0.34	-	-	0.07	-	3.82	1.22	1.70	**6.74**	m2
100 mm	0.38	-	-	0.07	-	4.22	1.22	2.26	**7.70**	m2
150 mm	0.52	-	-	0.07	-	5.87	1.22	3.40	**10.49**	m2
014 Filling to make up levels, by machine (Cat), transporting average 25 m; average thickness:										
75 mm	0.09	0.04	-	0.07	-	0.98	3.00	1.70	**5.68**	m2
100 mm	0.09	0.04	-	0.07	-	1.02	3.09	2.26	**6.37**	m2
150 mm	0.11	0.05	-	0.07	-	1.27	3.56	3.40	**8.23**	m2
015 Imported granular fill material, M.O.T. grade 1; level or to falls, crossfalls and slopes; levelling and compacting with a 6.00 - 8.00 TONNE roller										
016 Filling to make up levels, by machine (Cat), transporting average 25 m; average thickness:										
150 mm	0.08	0.03	-	0.01	-	0.84	1.93	10.16	**12.93**	m2
200 mm	0.09	0.04	-	0.01	-	0.98	2.16	13.55	**16.69**	m2
300 mm; two layers	0.15	0.07	-	0.02	-	1.68	3.85	20.32	**25.85**	m2

	Man-Hours	Net Labour Price £	Net Mats Price £	Net Unit Price £	Unit
IN SITU CONCRETE PAVING					
Basis of prices					
The prices of in situ concrete in this section are based upon ready mixed concrete grade 21 N/mm2 supplied to site at a price of £90.44 per m3					
For every £1.00 per m3 difference in the supply price of the required grade of concrete ADD or DEDUCT £1.05 per m3 to, or from the 'Net Materials' prices and the 'NET UNIT' prices in this section.					
017 Additives, special mixes					
018 The following additions should be made to the prices of grade 21 N/mm2 concrete in this section, when required:					
sulphate resisting cement	-	-	11.98	**11.98**	m3
accelerating	-	-	11.98	**11.98**	m3
retarding admixture	-	-	11.98	**11.98**	m3
normal water - reducing admixture (setcrete RMW)	-	-	5.99	**5.99**	m3
waterproof concrete (setcrete RMW)	-	-	59.92	**59.92**	m3
pumping concrete	-	-	11.98	**11.98**	m3
minimum 360 kg cement	-	-	11.98	**11.98**	m3

Unit Rates

		Man-Hours	Net Labour Price £	Net Mats Price £	Net Unit Price £	Unit
019	**PLAIN concrete grade 21 N/mm2, poured against face of excavation**					
020	Foundations in trenches; kerbs:					
	150 x 75 mm	0.04	0.39	1.45	**1.84**	m
	250 x 100 mm	0.08	0.90	2.71	**3.61**	m
	300 x 100 mm	0.09	1.02	3.35	**4.37**	m
	450 x 150 mm	0.19	2.18	6.78	**8.96**	m
	600 x 200 mm	0.26	2.94	11.76	**14.70**	m
021	**PLAIN concrete, grade 21 N/mm2, filled into formwork; laid on hardcore to slopes not exceeding 15 degrees from horizontal**					
022	Beds forming roads; poured in bays:					
	not exceeding 100 mm thick	2.84	31.90	90.44	**122.34**	m3
	100 - 150 mm thick	2.14	23.99	90.44	**114.43**	m3
	150 - 300 mm thick	1.42	15.94	90.44	**106.38**	m3
	exceeding 300 mm thick	1.00	11.23	90.44	**101.67**	m3
023	Beds forming footpaths; poured in bays:					
	not exceeding 100 mm thick	3.41	38.27	90.44	**128.71**	m3
	100 - 150 mm thick	2.56	28.71	90.44	**119.15**	m3
	150 - 300 mm thick	1.71	19.14	90.44	**109.58**	m3
	exceeding 300 mm thick	1.19	13.40	90.44	**103.84**	m3
024	Beds forming pavings; poured in bays:					
	not exceeding 100 mm thick	2.27	25.51	90.44	**115.95**	m3
	100 - 150 mm thick	1.71	19.14	90.44	**109.58**	m3
	150 - 300 mm thick	1.14	12.76	90.44	**103.20**	m3
	exceeding 300 mm thick	0.80	8.93	90.44	**99.37**	m3
025	**REINFORCED concrete, grade 21 N/mm2, filled into formwork; laid on hardcore to slopes not exceeding 15 degrees from horizontal**					
026	Beds forming roads; poured in bays:					
	not exceeding 100 mm thick	3.70	68.49	90.44	**158.93**	m3
	100 - 150 mm thick	2.84	52.68	90.44	**143.12**	m3
	150 - 300 mm thick	1.99	36.87	90.44	**127.31**	m3
	exceeding 300 mm thick	1.42	26.33	90.44	**116.77**	m3
027	Beds forming footpaths; poured in bays:					
	not exceeding 100 mm thick	4.44	82.18	90.44	**172.62**	m3
	100 - 150 mm thick	3.41	63.21	90.44	**153.65**	m3
	150 - 300 mm thick	2.39	44.25	90.44	**134.69**	m3
	exceeding 300 mm thick	1.71	31.61	90.44	**122.05**	m3
028	Beds forming pavings; poured in bays:					
	not exceeding 100 mm thick	2.96	54.77	90.44	**145.21**	m3
	100 - 150 mm thick	2.27	42.14	90.44	**132.58**	m3
	150 - 300 mm thick	1.59	29.50	90.44	**119.94**	m3
	exceeding 300 mm thick	1.14	21.07	90.44	**111.51**	m3
029	**Labours on concrete**					
030	Tamping surfaces of unset concrete, laid:					
	level	0.05	0.83	-	**0.83**	m2
	to falls	0.06	1.07	-	**1.07**	m2
	to crossfalls	0.07	1.26	-	**1.26**	m2
	to cambers	0.09	1.69	-	**1.69**	m2
	to slopes not exceeding 15 degrees from horizontal	0.06	1.07	-	**1.07**	m2
031	Spade finishing surfaces of unset concrete, laid:					
	level	0.13	2.32	-	**2.32**	m2
	to falls	0.17	3.17	-	**3.17**	m2
	to crossfalls	0.22	3.98	-	**3.98**	m2
	to cambers	0.26	4.85	-	**4.85**	m2
	to slopes not exceeding 15 degrees from horizontal	0.17	3.17	-	**3.17**	m2
032	Trowelling surfaces of unset concrete, laid:					
	level	0.22	3.98	-	**3.98**	m2
	to falls	0.28	5.26	-	**5.26**	m2
	to crossfalls	0.38	6.97	-	**6.97**	m2
	to cambers	0.44	8.21	-	**8.21**	m2
	to slopes not exceeding 15 degrees from horizontal	0.28	5.26	-	**5.26**	m2
033	**Plain joints in concrete including formwork**					

The prices for **making** allow ONE use of timber formwork. Where multiple uses are possible 'Net Labour Materials and NET UNIT' prices should be divided by the number of uses and allowance made for waste in use of both labour and materials as follows:

Nr of uses	Waste in use
up to 4	nil
5 to 6	10%
7 to 8	15%
9 to 10	17.5%
11 to 12	20%

No adjustment should be made for 'fixing' prices as these apply irrespective of the number of uses.

Unit Rates	Man-Hours	Net Labour Price £	Net Mats Price £	Net Unit Price £	Unit
034	Horizontal joints in beds:					
	75 mm deep:					
	making	0.23	3.47	4.82	8.29	m
	fixing in pavings	0.17	2.60	0.85	3.45	m
	fixing in footpaths	0.23	3.47	0.85	4.32	m
	100 mm deep:					
	making	0.28	4.32	6.28	10.60	m
	fixing in pavings	0.23	3.47	0.86	4.33	m
	fixing in footpaths	0.28	4.32	0.86	5.18	m
	200 mm deep:					
	making	0.57	8.65	5.72	14.37	m
	fixing in pavings	0.51	7.78	1.73	9.51	m
	fixing in footpaths	0.46	6.92	1.73	8.65	m
	300 mm deep:					
	making	0.85	12.97	19.52	32.49	m
	fixing in pavings	0.51	7.78	2.59	10.37	m
	fixing in footpaths	0.57	8.65	2.59	11.24	m
035	**ADD to prices of joints for**					
036	Notching formwork around reinforcing bars up to and including 25 mm diameter passing through joint at:					
	150 mm centres:					
	making	0.40	6.05	-	6.05	m
	fixing	-	-	-	0.00	m
	200 mm centres:					
	making	0.31	4.68	-	4.68	m
	fixing	-	-	-	0.00	m
	250 mm centres:					
	making	0.25	3.80	-	3.80	m
	fixing	-	-	-	0.00	m
	300 mm centres:					
	making	0.21	3.12	-	3.12	m
	fixing	-	-	-	0.00	m
037	12 mm diameter steel dowel bars 500 mm long cast into one side of joint and de-bonded for a length of 250 mm and capped with PVC dowel caps; notching formwork at:					
	150 mm centres:					
	making	0.40	6.05	-	6.05	m
	fixing	0.68	10.37	3.58	13.95	m
	200 mm centres:					
	making	0.31	4.68	-	4.68	m
	fixing	0.51	7.78	2.36	10.14	m
	250 mm centres:					
	making	0.25	3.80	-	3.80	m
	fixing	0.41	6.22	1.90	8.12	m
	300 mm centres:					
	making	0.21	3.12	-	3.12	m
	fixing	0.35	5.37	1.59	6.96	m
038	**'Aerofil' high density fibreboard joint filler and fixing in place in joint formwork**					
039	10 mm Thick cut to required widths on site:					
	64 mm wide	0.08	1.26	0.57	1.83	m
	78 mm wide	0.08	1.26	0.70	1.96	m
040	25 mm Thick cut to required widths on site:					
	152 mm wide	0.11	1.67	3.26	4.93	m
	279 mm wide	0.19	2.93	5.99	8.92	m
041	**ADD to prices for 'Aerofil' for**					
042	Notching any thickness around reinforcing bars up to and including 25 mm diameter passing through joint at:					
	150 mm centres	0.46	6.92	-	6.92	m
	200 mm centres	0.36	5.53	-	5.53	m
	250 mm centres	0.31	4.68	-	4.68	m
	300 mm centres	0.26	3.98	-	3.98	m
043	**Joint sealants**					
044	'Vertiseal' polysulphide rubber joint sealing compound applied by gun to joint:					
	10 x 10 mm	0.04	0.67	0.87	1.54	m
	13 x 15 mm	0.09	1.31	1.61	2.92	m
	19 x 20 mm	0.17	2.54	3.78	6.32	m
	25 x 25 mm	0.28	4.18	5.07	9.25	m
045	**Formwork**					
046	Formwork to edges of concrete bed:					
	not exceeding 250 mm high:					
	making (one use allowed)	1.14	17.28	18.27	35.55	m
	fixing	0.91	13.82	2.27	16.09	m
	250 mm to 500 mm high:					
	making (one use allowed)	1.71	25.93	36.55	62.48	m
	fixing	1.06	16.08	4.41	20.49	m

Unit Rates	Man-Hours	Net Labour Price £	Net Mats Price £	Net Unit Price £	Unit
047	**Steel fabric reinforcement BS 4483 with one width mesh side laps and one width mesh end laps**				
048	Fabric reinforcement laid in pavings, footpaths and roads:				
	200 mm side laps, 200 mm end laps:				
	A142	0.05	0.68	2.31	**2.99**	m2
	A252	0.06	0.88	3.94	**4.82**	m2
	100 mm side laps, 200 mm end laps:				
	B196	0.06	0.88	3.21	**4.09**	m2
	B503	0.07	1.03	5.45	**6.48**	m2
	PAVING SLABS AND BLOCKS				
049	**Precast concrete flags BS 368 natural finish; 50 mm thick; spot bedding in cement lime mortar (1:1:6) to symmetrical layout; on concrete; to pavings; to falls crossfalls and slopes not exceeding 15 degrees from horizontal; over 300 mm wide; laid with**				
050	10 mm joints, straight both ways, pointing joints with cement, lime mortar (1:1:6):				
	600 x 450 mm	0.68	7.65	16.79	**24.44**	m2
	600 x 600 mm	0.51	5.74	14.11	**19.85**	m2
	600 x 750 mm	0.41	4.59	13.62	**18.21**	m2
	600 x 900 mm	0.34	3.82	11.96	**15.78**	m2
051	Close butt joints, straight both ways:				
	600 x 450 mm	0.57	6.38	16.30	**22.68**	m2
	600 x 600 mm	0.42	4.72	13.78	**18.50**	m2
	600 x 750 mm	0.34	3.82	13.46	**17.28**	m2
	600 x 900 mm	0.28	3.19	11.82	**15.01**	m2
052	Raking cutting	0.08	0.90	0.17	**1.07**	m
053	Curved cutting	0.09	1.02	0.17	**1.19**	m
054	Cutting and making good around steel joists, angles, pipes, tubes, manhole covers, gully gratings, bollards and the like:				
	over 2.00 mm girth	0.08	0.90	1.12	**2.02**	m
	not exceeding 0.30 m girth	0.04	0.39	0.50	**0.89**	Nr
	0.30 - 1.00 m girth	0.06	0.65	0.80	**1.45**	Nr
	1.00 - 2.00 m girth	0.13	1.40	1.68	**3.08**	Nr
055	**Reconstructed stone paving slabs, riven finish, 40 mm thick; spot bedding in cement lime mortar (1:1:6); 10 mm open joints, straight both ways, to symmetrical layout; pointing with coloured cement lime mortar (1:1:6); on concrete base; to pavings; to falls, crossfalls and slopes not exceeding 15 degrees from horizontal; over 300 mm wide**				
056	600 x 450 mm, colour:				
	Cotswold honey-brown	0.80	8.93	48.42	**57.35**	m2
	weathered York grey	0.80	8.93	51.48	**60.41**	m2
057	450 x 450 mm, colour:				
	Cotswold honey-brown	1.08	12.11	49.18	**61.29**	m2
	weathered York grey	1.08	12.11	51.93	**64.04**	m2
058	Raking cutting:				
	Cotswold honey-brown	0.07	0.76	1.94	**2.70**	m
	weathered York grey	0.07	0.76	2.07	**2.83**	m
059	Curved cutting:				
	Cotswold honey-brown	0.08	0.90	1.94	**2.84**	m
	weathered York grey	0.08	0.90	2.07	**2.97**	m
060	Cutting and making good around steel columns, angles, pipes, tubes, manhole covers, gully gratings, bollards and the like:				
	over 2.00 mm girth:				
	Cotswold honey-brown	0.07	0.76	6.74	**7.50**	m
	weathered York grey	0.07	0.76	7.18	**7.94**	m
	not exceeding 0.30 m girth:				
	Cotswold honey-brown	0.04	0.39	2.98	**3.37**	Nr
	weathered York grey	0.04	0.39	3.18	**3.57**	Nr
	0.30 - 1.00 m girth:				
	Cotswold honey-brown	0.05	0.58	4.92	**5.50**	Nr
	weathered York grey	0.05	0.58	5.25	**5.83**	Nr
	1.00 - 2.00 m girth:				
	Cotswold honey-brown	0.10	1.16	10.10	**11.26**	Nr
	weathered York grey	0.10	1.16	10.77	**11.93**	Nr
	Note: 061 - 064 not used				

Unit Rates	Man-Hours	Excav Hours	Brkng Hours	Cmptg Hours	Trans Hours	Net Labour Price £	Net Plant Price £	Net Mats Price £	Net Unit Price £	Unit
065 **Marshalls Mono 'Keyblok' concrete block paviors 200 x 100 mm natural colour laid on screeded bed of sand 50 mm thick, including compacting and vibrating with hand guided vibrating plate; to pavings over 300 mm wide**										
066 Laid to falls, cross falls and slopes not exceeding 15 degrees from horizontal, blocks laid flat in:										
half bond:										
60 mm thick	1.22	-	-	0.05	-	13.65	0.18	13.93	**27.76**	m2
80 mm thick	1.39	-	-	0.05	-	15.56	0.18	14.97	**30.71**	m2
parquet:										
60 mm thick	1.34	-	-	0.05	-	15.05	0.18	13.93	**29.16**	m2
80 mm thick	1.52	-	-	0.05	-	17.08	0.18	14.97	**32.23**	m2
90 degrees herringbone:										
60 mm thick	1.27	-	-	0.05	-	14.28	0.18	13.93	**28.39**	m2
80 mm thick	1.46	-	-	0.05	-	16.32	0.18	14.97	**31.47**	m2
45 degrees herringbone:										
60 mm thick	1.34	-	-	0.05	-	15.05	0.18	13.93	**29.16**	m2
80 mm thick	1.52	-	-	0.05	-	17.08	0.18	14.97	**32.23**	m2
067 Laid to slopes exceeding 15 degrees from the horizontal, laid flat:										
half bond:										
60 mm thick	1.34	-	-	0.05	-	15.05	0.18	13.93	**29.16**	m2
80 mm thick	1.52	-	-	0.05	-	17.08	0.18	14.97	**32.23**	m2
parquet:										
60 mm thick	1.48	-	-	0.05	-	16.58	0.18	13.93	**30.69**	m2
80 mm thick	1.67	-	-	0.05	-	18.75	0.18	14.97	**33.90**	m2
90 degrees herringbone:										
60 mm thick	1.41	-	-	0.05	-	15.81	0.18	13.93	**29.92**	m2
80 mm thick	1.60	-	-	0.05	-	17.98	0.18	14.97	**33.13**	m2
45 degrees herringbone:										
60 mm thick	1.48	-	-	0.05	-	16.58	0.18	13.93	**30.69**	m2
80 mm thick	1.67	-	-	0.05	-	18.75	0.18	14.97	**33.90**	m2

	Man-Hours	Net Labour Price £	Net Mats Price £	Net Unit Price £	Unit
068 **Extra over** for coloured blocks:					
60 mm thick	-	-	1.04	**1.04**	m2
80 mm thick	-	-	1.59	**1.59**	m2
069 Raking cutting:					
60 mm thick	0.08	0.90	1.38	**2.28**	m
80 mm thick	0.09	1.02	1.54	**2.56**	m
070 Cutting at perimeter of 45 degrees herringbone pattern paving:					
60 mm thick	0.08	0.90	1.38	**2.28**	m
80 mm thick	0.09	1.02	1.54	**2.56**	m
071 Curved cutting:					
60 mm thick	0.11	1.27	1.38	**2.65**	m
80 mm thick	0.15	1.66	1.54	**3.20**	m
072 Cutting and making good around steel columns, angles, pipes, tubes, manhole covers, gully gratings, bollards and the like:					
over 2.00 m girth:					
60 mm thick	0.08	0.90	0.69	**1.59**	m
80 mm thick	0.09	1.02	0.77	**1.79**	m
not exceeding 0.30 m girth:					
60 mm thick	0.04	0.39	0.31	**0.70**	Nr
80 mm thick	0.05	0.50	0.35	**0.85**	Nr
0.30 - 1.00 m girth:					
60 mm thick	0.06	0.65	0.51	**1.16**	Nr
80 mm thick	0.07	0.76	0.56	**1.32**	Nr
1.00 - 2.00 m girth:					
60 mm thick	0.13	1.40	1.04	**2.44**	Nr
80 mm thick	0.14	1.53	1.16	**2.69**	Nr

	£	Unit
YB The following **specialist** guide prices were provided by Grass Concrete Limited, Walker House, 22 Bond Street, Wakefield, West Yorkshire, WF1 2QP (Telephone: 01924 379443, E-mail: info@grasscrete.com; Internet: www.grasscrete.com)		
GRASS CONCRETE PAVING		
073 **Grasscrete paving complete comprising 600 x 600 mm polystyrene formers supplied and laid by Grass Concrete Limited. Laid on 20 mm sand blinding (m.s); including C28 concrete placed around formers, steel reinforcement, burning out tops of formers, filling voids with selected topsoil, sowing grass seed at a rate of 0.05 kg/m2 (based upon 1000 m2 +)**		
100 mm thick type GC1 paving reinforced with Ref A193 mesh	33.75	m2
150 mm thick type GC2 paving reinforced with Ref A252 mesh	43.46	m2
150 mm thick type GC2 paving reinforced with Ref A393 mesh	46.22	m2
76 mm thick type GC3 paving reinforced with Ref A193 mesh	29.86	m2

Unit Rates	Man-Hours	Net Labour Price £	Net Mats Price £	Net Unit Price £	Unit
Note: **074 - 077 not used**					
078 **'Grassblock' paving complete, comprising precast concrete perforated slabs supplied by Landscape Grass (Concrete) Ltd, laid on and including 20 mm sand blinding bed; filling voids with selected imported vegetable soil; sowing grass seed at the rate of 0.05 kg/m2; maintaining and cutting**					
079 Grassblock units 406 x 406 mm:					
83 mm thick paving ref. GB83	0.59	6.66	22.53	**29.19**	m2
103 mm thick paving ref. GB103	0.65	7.27	25.42	**32.69**	m2
125 mm thick paving ref. GB125	0.70	7.87	27.19	**35.06**	m2
Extra over; brown earth colour	-	-	3.44	**3.44**	m2
080 Grassroad units:					
635 x 330 x 42 mm	0.46	5.15	17.72	**30.89**	m2
Kerbing 80 x 60 mm high	0.19	2.12	6.78	**8.90**	m
081 Raking cutting on:					
42 mm HDPE paving	0.15	1.70	2.15	**3.85**	m
83 mm concrete paving	0.17	1.93	2.75	**4.68**	m
103 mm concrete paving	0.22	2.42	3.13	**5.55**	m
125 mm concrete paving	0.24	2.69	3.30	**5.99**	m

	Laid Area:					
	21 - 50 m2 £	51 - 100 m2 £	101 - 200 m2 £	201 - 500 m2 £	501 - 2000 m2 £	Unit
YB RESIN BOUND PAVING						
The following specialist guide prices were provided SureSet UK Limited, Unit 32, Deverill Road Trading Estate.Sutton Veny, Warminster, BA12 7BZ (Telephone: 01985 841180, Fax: 01985 841260; E-mail: mail@sureset.co.uk; Internet: www.sureset.co.uk)						
082 **Resin bound surface paving course 16 mm thick. Aggregate particles fully coated with two-part, UV stabilized, clear resin. Laid on prepared base of hardcore and asphalt (measured elsewhere). Compacted by roller and trowelled surface finish.**						
083 Aggregate type:						
natural gravel	78.80	63.04	54.63	50.43	45.18	m2
crushed rock & marble	84.05	68.29	59.88	55.68	48.33	m2
recycled glass	89.30	73.54	70.39	66.19	55.68	m2
Note: 084 - 093 not used						

	Man-Hours	Net Labour Price £	Net Mats Price £	Net Unit Price £	Unit
BRICK PAVING AND KERBS					
094 **Facing bricks, BS 3921, P.C. £351.38 per 1000; bedding and grouting joints in cement mortar (1:3); to pavings; over 300 mm wide**					
095 Laid to falls, crossfalls and slopes not exceeding 15 degrees from the horizontal; bricks laid:					
flat; 75 mm thick:					
stretcher bond	1.42	29.57	17.90	**47.47**	m2
herringbone pattern	1.54	31.96	17.90	**49.86**	m2
on edge; 112.5 mm thick:					
stretcher bond	1.82	37.85	26.36	**64.21**	m2
herringbone pattern	1.93	40.23	26.36	**66.59**	m2
096 Laid to slopes exceeding 15 degrees from the horizontal; bricks laid:					
flat; 75 mm thick:					
stretcher bond	1.48	30.76	17.90	**48.66**	m2
herringbone pattern	1.59	33.13	17.90	**51.03**	m2
on edge; 112.5 mm thick:					
stretcher bond	1.91	39.77	26.36	**66.13**	m2
herringbone pattern	2.02	42.12	26.36	**68.48**	m2
097 ADD TO OR DEDUCT FROM the above prices for each £10.00 per 1000 difference in the price of bricks paving:					
75 mm thick	-	-	0.41	**0.41**	m2
112.5 mm thick	-	-	0.61	**0.61**	m2
098 Raking cutting:					
flat; 65 mm thick	0.08	1.66	2.21	**3.87**	m
on edge; 112.5 mm thick	0.11	2.35	3.32	**5.67**	m
099 Curved cutting:					
flat; 65 mm thick	0.11	2.35	2.21	**4.56**	m
on edge; 112.5 mm thick	0.17	3.56	3.32	**6.88**	m
100 Cutting and making good around steel joists, angles, pipes, tubes, manhole covers, gully gratings, bollards and the like:					
over 2.00 mm girth:					
flat; 65 mm thick	0.08	1.66	1.11	**2.77**	m

	Unit Rates	Man-Hours	Net Labour Price £	Net Mats Price £	Net Unit Price £	Unit
	on edge; 112.5 mm thick	0.11	2.35	1.84	**4.19**	m
	not exceeding 0.30 m girth:					
	flat; 65 mm thick	0.04	0.73	0.37	**1.10**	Nr
	on edge; 112.5 mm thick	0.06	1.21	1.11	**2.32**	Nr
	0.30 - 1.00 m girth:					
	flat; 65 mm thick	0.06	1.21	0.74	**1.95**	Nr
	on edge; 112.5 mm thick	0.09	1.89	1.11	**3.00**	Nr
	1.00 - 2.00 mm girth:					
	flat; 65 mm thick	0.13	2.60	1.84	**4.44**	Nr
	on edge; 112.5 mm thick	0.17	3.56	2.58	**6.14**	Nr

YB 101 — **Kerbs and the like in facing bricks, BS 3921, P.C. £351.38 per 1000; bedding, jointing and flush pointing in cement mortar (1:3)**

		Man-Hours	Net Labour Price £	Net Mats Price £	Net Unit Price £	Unit
102	Brick-on-flat, 102.5 mm wide x 75 mm high:					
	square edge:					
	straight	0.15	3.08	2.15	**5.23**	m
	curved; radius:					
	not exceeding 3.00 m	0.23	4.74	2.15	**6.89**	m
	3.00 - 6.00 m	0.21	4.27	2.15	**6.42**	m
	6.00 - 9.00 m	0.19	4.04	2.15	**6.19**	m
	exceeding 9.00 m	0.18	3.79	2.15	**5.94**	m
	ends	0.05	0.94	0.37	**1.31**	Nr
	angles	0.09	1.89	0.74	**2.63**	Nr
	bullnosed or single cant stretchers:					
	straight	0.15	3.08	14.48	**17.56**	m
	curved; radius:					
	not exceeding 3.00 m	0.23	4.74	14.48	**19.22**	m
	3.00 - 6.00 m	0.21	4.27	14.48	**18.75**	m
	6.00 - 9.00 m	0.19	4.04	14.48	**18.52**	m
	exceeding 9.00 m	0.18	3.79	14.48	**18.27**	m
	ends	0.05	0.94	39.27	**40.21**	Nr
	internal angles	0.09	1.89	9.24	**11.13**	Nr
	external angles	0.09	1.89	23.10	**24.99**	Nr
103	Brick-on-flat, 215 mm wide x 75 mm high:					
	square edge:					
	straight	0.26	5.45	3.94	**9.39**	m
	curved; radius:					
	not exceeding 3.00 m	0.40	8.28	3.94	**12.22**	m
	3.00 - 6.00 m	0.36	7.57	3.94	**11.51**	m
	6.00 - 9.00 m	0.34	7.10	3.94	**11.04**	m
	exceeding 9.00 m	0.32	6.62	3.94	**10.56**	m
	ends	0.05	0.94	0.37	**1.31**	Nr
	angles	0.09	1.89	0.74	**2.63**	Nr
104	Brick-on-edge, 215 mm wide x 112.5 mm high:					
	square edge:					
	straight	0.40	8.28	6.09	**14.37**	m
	curved; radius:					
	not exceeding 3.00 m	0.60	12.55	6.09	**18.64**	m
	3.00 - 6.00 m	0.56	11.59	6.09	**17.68**	m
	6.00 - 9.00 m	0.52	10.88	6.09	**16.97**	m
	exceeding 9.00 m	0.48	9.95	6.09	**16.04**	m
	ends	0.05	0.94	0.37	**1.31**	Nr
	angles	0.09	1.89	6.93	**8.82**	Nr
	bullnosed or single cant headers:					
	straight	0.40	8.28	49.43	**57.71**	m
	curved; radius:					
	not exceeding 3.00 m	0.60	12.55	49.43	**61.98**	m
	3.00 - 6.00 m	0.56	11.59	49.43	**61.02**	m
	6.00 - 9.00 m	0.52	10.88	49.43	**60.31**	m
	exceeding 9.00 m	0.48	9.95	49.43	**59.38**	m
	ends	0.05	0.94	39.27	**40.21**	Nr
	internal angles	0.09	1.89	9.24	**11.13**	Nr
	external angles	0.09	1.89	23.10	**24.99**	Nr
105	Brick-on-end; 102.5 mm wide x 225 mm high:					
	square edge:					
	straight	0.40	8.28	5.94	**14.22**	m
	curved; radius:					
	not exceeding 3.00 m	0.60	12.55	5.94	**18.49**	m
	3.00 - 6.00 m	0.56	11.59	5.94	**17.53**	m
	6.00 - 9.00 m	0.52	10.88	5.94	**16.82**	m
	exceeding 9.00 m	0.48	9.95	5.94	**15.89**	m
	ends	0.05	0.94	0.37	**1.31**	Nr
	angles	0.09	1.89	0.74	**2.63**	Nr
	bullnosed or single cant headers:					
	straight	0.40	8.28	49.28	**57.56**	m
	curved; radius:					
	not exceeding 3.00 m	0.60	12.55	49.28	**61.83**	m
	3.00 - 6.00 m	0.56	11.59	49.28	**60.87**	m
	6.00 - 9.00 m	0.52	10.88	49.28	**60.16**	m
	exceeding 9.00 m	0.48	9.95	49.28	**59.23**	m
	ends	0.05	0.94	39.27	**40.21**	Unit
	internal angles	0.09	1.89	9.24	**11.13**	Nr
	external angles	0.09	1.89	23.10	**24.99**	Nr

	Unit Rates	Man-Hours	Net Labour Price £	Net Mats Price £	Net Unit Price £	Unit
106	Brick-on-end; two courses wide, 225 x 225 mm high overall:					
	square edge:					
	straight	0.74	15.38	11.74	**27.12**	m
	curved; radius:					
	not exceeding 3.00 m	1.11	23.18	11.74	**34.92**	m
	3.00 - 6.00 m	1.04	21.54	11.74	**33.28**	m
	6.00 - 9.00 m	0.97	20.12	11.74	**31.86**	m
	exceeding 9.00 m	0.89	18.46	11.74	**30.20**	m
	ends	0.09	1.89	0.74	**2.63**	Nr
	angles	0.19	4.04	1.48	**5.52**	Nr
	bullnosed or single cant headers:					
	straight	0.74	15.38	96.74	**112.12**	m
	curved; radius:					
	not exceeding 3.00 m	1.11	23.18	96.74	**119.92**	m
	3.00 - 6.00 m	1.04	21.54	96.74	**118.28**	m
	6.00 - 9.00 m	0.97	20.12	96.74	**116.86**	m
	exceeding 9.00 m	0.89	18.46	96.74	**115.20**	m
	ends	0.09	1.89	78.55	**80.44**	Nr
	internal angles	0.19	4.04	32.34	**36.38**	Nr
	external angles	0.19	4.04	32.34	**36.38**	Nr
107	Kerb two courses high, 215 x 187.5 mm high overall; top course brick-on-edge:					
	square edge:					
	straight	0.66	13.71	10.03	**23.74**	m
	curved; radius:					
	not exceeding 3.00 m	0.99	20.58	10.03	**30.61**	m
	3.00 - 6.00 m	0.92	19.17	10.03	**29.20**	m
	6.00 - 9.00 m	0.85	17.75	10.03	**27.78**	m
	exceeding 9.00 m	0.80	16.56	10.03	**26.59**	m
	ends	0.09	1.89	0.74	**2.63**	Nr
	angles	0.19	4.04	1.48	**5.52**	Nr
	bullnosed or single cant headers:					
	straight	0.66	13.71	53.37	**67.08**	m
	curved; radius:					
	not exceeding 3.00 m	0.99	20.58	53.37	**73.95**	m
	3.00 - 6.00 m	0.92	19.17	53.37	**72.54**	m
	6.00 - 9.00 m	0.85	17.75	53.37	**71.12**	m
	exceeding 9.00 m	0.80	16.56	53.37	**69.93**	m
	ends	0.09	1.89	39.64	**41.53**	Nr
	internal angles	0.19	4.04	9.61	**13.65**	Nr
	external angles	0.19	4.04	23.47	**27.51**	Nr
YC	**PRECAST CONCRETE KERBS, CHANNELS ETC.**					
001	**Precast concrete kerbs, channels, edgings and quadrants to BS 340; ordinary; bedding and jointing in cement mortar (1:3); haunching both sides with concrete, grade C12/15**					
002	Kerb; 150 x 305 mm overall, figures 1, 4, 6, 8:					
	straight	0.57	6.38	14.20	**20.58**	m
	curved; radius:					
	not exceeding 3.00 m	0.80	8.93	17.18	**26.11**	m
	3.00 - 6.00 m	0.74	8.29	17.18	**25.47**	m
	6.00 - 9.00 m	0.68	7.65	17.18	**24.83**	m
	over 9.00 m	0.63	7.02	17.18	**24.20**	m
	Extra over for:					
	angles	0.11	1.27	11.18	**12.45**	Nr
	ends	0.11	1.27	1.30	**2.57**	Nr
	dropper kerb 152 x 305 to 203 mm, figure 16	-	-	2.97	**2.97**	Nr
003	Kerb; 125 x 255 mm overall, figures 2, 5, 7, 8:					
	straight	0.57	6.38	9.67	**16.05**	m
	curved; radius:					
	not exceeding 3.00 m	0.80	8.93	10.12	**19.05**	m
	3.00 - 6.00 m	0.74	8.29	10.12	**18.41**	m
	6.00 - 9.00 m	0.68	7.65	10.12	**17.77**	m
	over 9.00 m	0.63	7.02	10.12	**17.14**	m
	Extra over for:					
	angles	0.11	1.27	11.18	**12.45**	Nr
	ends	0.11	1.27	0.68	**1.95**	Nr
	dropper kerb 127 x 254 to 152 mm, figure 16	-	-	2.97	**2.97**	Nr
004	Kerb; 125 x 150 mm overall, figures 9, 2a, 7a, 8:					
	straight	0.46	5.10	4.81	**9.91**	m
	curved; radius:					
	not exceeding 3.00 m	0.68	7.65	7.78	**15.43**	m
	3.00 - 6.00 m	0.63	7.02	7.78	**14.80**	m
	6.00 - 9.00 m	0.57	6.38	7.78	**14.16**	m
	over 9.00 m	0.51	5.74	7.78	**13.52**	m
	Extra over for:					
	angles	0.11	1.27	11.18	**12.45**	Nr
	ends	0.11	1.27	0.49	**1.76**	Nr
005	Channel 150 x 305 mm overall, figures 1, 8:					
	straight	0.51	5.74	14.20	**19.94**	m
	curved; radius:					
	not exceeding 3.00 m	0.74	8.29	17.18	**25.47**	m
	3.00 - 6.00 m	0.68	7.65	17.18	**24.83**	m
	6.00 - 9.00 m	0.63	7.02	17.18	**24.20**	m
	over 9.00 m	0.57	6.38	17.18	**23.56**	m

Unit Rates	Man-Hours	Net Labour Price £	Net Mats Price £	Net Unit Price £	Unit
Extra over for:					
angles	0.11	1.27	8.68	**9.95**	Nr
ends	0.11	1.27	1.30	**2.57**	Nr
standard dish channels	-	-	2.51	**2.51**	m
006 Channel 125 x 255 mm overall, figures 2, 8:					
straight	0.51	5.74	9.67	**15.41**	m
curved; radius:					
not exceeding 3.00 m	0.74	8.29	12.65	**20.94**	m
3.00 - 6.00 m	0.68	7.65	12.65	**20.30**	m
6.00 - 9.00 m	0.63	7.02	12.65	**19.67**	m
over 9.00 m	0.57	6.38	12.65	**19.03**	m
Extra over for:					
angles	0.11	1.27	4.52	**5.79**	Nr
ends	0.11	1.27	0.68	**1.95**	Nr
standard dish channels	-	-	2.51	**2.51**	m
007 Channel 125 x 150 mm overall, figures 2a, 8:					
straight	0.46	5.10	4.81	**9.91**	m
curved; radius:					
not exceeding 3.00 m	0.68	7.65	7.78	**15.43**	m
3.00 - 6.00 m	0.63	7.02	7.78	**14.80**	m
6.00 - 9.00 m	0.57	6.38	7.78	**14.16**	m
over 9.00 m	0.51	5.74	7.78	**13.52**	m
Extra over for:					
angles	0.11	1.27	3.30	**4.57**	Nr
ends	0.11	1.27	0.49	**1.76**	Nr
standard dish channels	-	-	2.30	**2.30**	m
008 Edgings 50 x 150 mm overall, figures 11, 12, 13:					
straight	0.34	3.82	3.96	**7.78**	m
laid in large radius bends	0.40	4.46	3.96	**8.42**	m
Extra over for:					
ends	0.06	0.65	0.28	**0.93**	Nr
angles	0.06	0.65	0.28	**0.93**	Nr
009 Edgings 50 x 200 mm overall, figures 11, 13:					
straight	0.34	3.82	6.29	**10.11**	m
laid in large radius bends	0.40	4.46	6.29	**10.75**	m
Extra over for:					
ends	0.06	0.65	0.47	**1.12**	Nr
angles	0.06	0.65	0.47	**1.12**	Nr
010 Edgings 50 x 250 mm overall, figures 11, 13:					
straight	0.38	4.22	7.78	**12.00**	m
laid in large radius bends	0.43	4.86	7.78	**12.64**	m
Extra over for:					
ends	0.06	0.65	0.55	**1.20**	Nr
angles	0.06	0.65	0.55	**1.20**	Nr
011 Quadrants 457 x 457 x 254 mm, figures 14	0.28	3.19	11.64	**14.83**	Nr
012 Safeticurb drainage unit type DBA 250 x 250 mm 125 mm bore:					
straight	0.75	8.41	54.61	**63.02**	m
laid in large radius bends	0.85	9.53	54.61	**64.14**	m
Extra over for:					
ends	0.25	2.80	5.65	**8.45**	Nr
Extra over for fittings:					
inspection grid unit DBG/PS	0.15	1.68	21.28	**22.96**	Nr
silt box top type A	0.50	5.61	243.22	**248.83**	Nr
013 Safeticurb drainage unit type DBM 250 x 250 mm 125 mm bore:					
straight	0.75	8.41	86.78	**95.19**	m
laid in large radius bends	0.85	9.53	86.78	**96.31**	m
Extra over for:					
ends	0.25	2.80	10.06	**12.86**	Nr
Extra over for fittings:					
inspection grid unit DBG/CI	0.15	1.68	32.41	**34.09**	Nr
silt box top type A	0.50	5.61	227.14	**232.75**	Nr
014 Safeticurb drainage unit type DBJ 305 x 305 mm 150 mm bore:					
straight	0.80	8.97	85.10	**94.07**	m
laid in large radius bends	0.90	10.09	85.10	**95.19**	m
Extra over for:					
ends	0.25	2.80	9.55	**12.35**	Nr
Extra over for fittings:					
inspection unit DBGJ/PS	0.26	2.92	19.62	**22.54**	Nr
silt box top type J	0.60	6.73	392.92	**399.65**	Nr
015 Safeticurb unit type DBK/SP (or HB2) 250 x 320 (or 350) mm 125 mm bore:					
straight	0.80	8.97	68.82	**77.79**	m
laid in large radius bends	0.90	10.09	68.82	**78.91**	m
Extra over for:					
ends	0.25	2.80	7.31	**10.11**	Nr
Extra over for fittings:					
inspection unit SP or HB2	0.15	1.68	88.19	**89.87**	Nr
manhole cover SP or HB2	0.75	8.41	469.69	**478.10**	Nr
transition unit SP or HB2	0.15	1.68	6.66	**8.34**	Nr

Unit Rates	Man-Hours	Net Labour Price £	Net Mats Price £	Net Unit Price £	Unit
Note: 016 - 019 not used					
020 Marshall's 'Beany block' combined kerb and drainage system; units 430 x 560 mm overall:					
Base and top blocks:					
straight	1.71	19.13	65.86	**84.99**	m
021 **Polymer concrete channel surface area drainage system; dry spigot and socket joints; setting on and surrounding with in situ concrete 21N/mm2 minimum 100 mm thick (excavating trenches priced elsewhere); MEADRAIN Type Z 1000 Drainage System.**					
022 Drainage channel 130 mm wide overall with built-in fall (tops laid level) in 1000 mm lengths:					
minimum depth 150 mm, maximum depth 300 mm, average depth 225 mm:	0.74	8.96	50.64	**59.60**	m
Extra over for:					
forming T-junction with channel unit 500 mm long x 225 mm deep with "knock-out" opening	0.27	3.29	21.76	**25.05**	Nr
end cap (ref 151471)	0.10	1.16	9.20	**10.36**	Nr
end cap with PVC 100 mm connector (ref 151473)	0.10	1.16	14.77	**15.93**	Nr
silt box unit with galvanised steel sediment bucket (ref 151085), 500 mm long x 580 mm deep; additional excavation and disposal	1.02	12.41	105.31	**117.72**	Nr
silt box unit with roddable in-line foul air trap 100 mm diameter (ref 155485), 500 mm long x 580 mm deep; additional excavation and disposal	1.10	13.37	128.68	**142.05**	Nr
silt box unit with roddable side foul air trap 100 mm diameter (ref 155487), 500 mm long x 580 mm deep; additional excavation and disposal	1.00	12.13	126.96	**139.09**	Nr
outlet to channel; 100 mm PVC connector fixed into "knock-out" opening (ref 154501)	0.19	2.30	2.76	**5.06**	Nr
outlet to channel; 150 mm PVC connector fixed into "knock-out" opening (ref 154503)	0.19	2.30	7.97	**10.27**	Nr
023 Gully assembly 520 x 360 mm overall with locking gratings and frames, galvanised sediment buckets and PVC spigot outlets; setting on and surrounding with in situ concrete 21N/mm2 minimum 100 mm thick; additional excavation and disposal:					
two element unit (upper and lower sections) total 700 mm deep	2.10	25.51	407.50	**433.01**	Nr
three element unit (upper, middle and lower sections) total 1050 mm deep	2.90	35.16	481.19	**516.35**	Nr
Extra over for raising element 350 mm deep (may be used with all assemblies)	0.80	9.65	63.93	**73.58**	Nr
Gully assembly 520 x 360 mm overall with locking gratings and frames, galvanised sediment buckets and PVC spigot outlets; setting on and surrounding with in situ concrete 21N/mm2 minimum 100 mm thick; additional excavation and disposal:					
024 Galvanised mild steel gratings in 1000 mm lengths to suit MEADRAIN Z 1000 channel; securing with locking straps and bolts:					
loading class A 15 (ref 152101)	0.32	3.85	15.88	**19.73**	m
loading class B 150 (ref 152301)	0.40	4.82	25.91	**30.73**	m
loading class C 250 (ref 152503)	0.51	6.21	33.37	**39.58**	m
025 Cast iron gratings in 500 mm lengths to suit MEADRAIN Z 1000 channel; securing with locking straps and bolts:					
loading class C 250 (ref 152411)	0.45	5.46	37.23	**42.69**	m
loading class C 250 (ref 152541)	0.65	7.88	44.43	**52.31**	m

	Method of application						
	Hand laid; in areas:			Machine laid; in areas:			
	Up to 100 m2 £	100 to 500 m2 £	Over 500 m2 £	Up to 500 m2 £	500 to 1500 m2 £	Over 1500 m2 £	Unit
YD **MACADAM PAVINGS AND ROADS**							
The following **Specialist** guide prices were provided by Tarmac National Contracting South West, Stancombe Quarry, Stancombe Lane, Flax Bourton, BS48 3QD (Telephone: 01275 464441 E-mail: info@tarmac-contracting.co.uk; Internet: www.tarmac.co.uk)							
001 **Coated macadam, BS 4987; to pavings and roads; to falls, crossfalls and slopes not exceeding 15 degrees from the horizontal; rolled with a 6.00 tonne roller; over 300 mm wide**							
002 Group One; roadbase materials:							
40 mm nominal size macadam:							
dense; average thickness:							
65 mm	23.63	18.12	16.26	17.91	15.46	14.42	m2
80 mm	26.62	21.12	19.22	21.05	18.51	17.41	m2
100 mm	31.11	25.57	23.71	25.57	23.06	22.00	m2
003 Group Two; basecourse materials:							
40 mm nominal size macadam:							
open textured; average thickness:							
60 mm	20.77	15.26	13.40	15.05	12.54	11.44	m2
80 mm	23.78	18.27	16.41	18.09	15.61	14.52	m2
single course; average thickness:							
60 mm	21.81	16.31	14.45	16.13	13.65	12.54	m2
80 mm	25.29	19.79	17.94	19.64	17.14	16.06	m2
dense; average thickness:							
60 mm	23.28	17.69	15.83	17.94	15.05	13.97	m2
80 mm	27.20	21.70	19.84	21.65	19.14	18.02	m2
28 mm nominal size macadam:							
dense; average thickness:							
50 mm	21.45	15.96	14.07	15.70	13.22	12.15	m2
60 mm	23.51	17.97	16.11	17.82	15.38	14.30	m2

Specialist	Method of application						
	Hand laid; in areas:			Machine laid; in areas:			
	Up to 100 m2 £	100 to 500 m2 £	Over 500 m2 £	Up to 500 m2 £	500 to 1500 m2 £	Over 1500 m2 £	Unit
20 mm nominal size macadam:							
open textured; average thickness:							
35 mm	17.19	11.66	10.87	11.37	8.86	7.80	m2
50 mm	19.52	14.02	12.15	12.00	11.26	10.18	m2
dense; average thickness:							
35 mm	18.62	13.09	11.22	12.84	10.29	9.19	m2
50 mm	21.45	15.96	14.07	15.70	13.22	12.15	m2
004 Group Three; wearing course materials:							
14 mm nominal size macadam:							
open textured; average thickness:							
25 mm	16.23	10.69	9.21	10.39	7.88	6.75	m2
30 mm	17.08	11.54	9.68	11.22	8.75	7.62	m2
40 mm	18.85	13.35	11.47	13.07	10.54	9.46	m2
dense; average thickness:							
30 mm	18.06	12.55	10.69	12.27	9.79	8.66	m2
40 mm	20.17	14.63	12.77	14.42	11.85	10.77	m2
45 mm	21.18	15.68	13.82	15.46	12.92	11.85	m2
10 mm nominal size macadam:							
open textured; average thickness:							
20 mm	15.36	9.88	7.98	9.49	7.02	5.94	m2
25 mm	16.38	10.81	8.95	10.51	7.96	6.90	m2
dense; average thickness:							
25 mm	17.51	12.04	10.11	11.71	9.16	8.10	m2
30 mm	18.32	12.79	10.92	12.54	9.98	8.90	m2
35 mm	19.40	13.87	12.04	13.65	11.14	10.03	m2
6 mm nominal size macadam:							
medium textured; average thickness:							
15 mm	15.03	9.53	7.66	9.13	6.63	5.64	m2
20 mm	15.60	10.03	8.18	9.64	7.17	6.09	m2
coarse cold asphalt; average thickness:							
25 mm	17.51	11.97	10.11	11.71	9.16	8.10	m2
30 mm	18.32	12.79	10.92	12.54	9.98	8.90	m2
35 mm	19.40	13.87	12.04	13.67	11.14	10.03	m2
fine cold asphalt; average thickness:							
15 mm	15.48	9.96	8.10	9.58	7.10	6.00	m2
20 mm	16.96	11.47	9.56	11.14	8.63	7.55	m2
25 mm	18.29	12.77	10.89	12.49	9.94	8.86	m2
005 Cationic bitumen emulsion tack coat; applied to:							
new surfaces	0.42	0.35	0.32	0.33	0.33	0.33	m2
old surfaces	0.42	0.35	0.32	0.33	0.33	0.33	m2
006 Coated chippings evenly applied to fine cold asphalt surfaces; rolled or otherwise pressed into surface; nominal size:							
10 mm, at the rate of:							
4 kg per m2	3.76	1.90	1.25	7.50	2.99	1.95	m2
6 kg per m2	3.76	2.05	1.48	7.50	3.64	2.56	m2
8 kg per m2	3.76	2.29	1.66	7.50	4.27	3.23	m2
14 mm, at the rate of:							
4 kg per m2	3.76	2.05	1.48	7.50	3.64	2.56	m2
6 kg per m2	3.76	2.29	1.66	7.50	4.27	3.23	m2
8 kg per m2	3.76	2.51	1.90	7.50	4.92	3.86	m2
007 Uncoated chippings evenly applied to macadam surface rolled or otherwise pressed into surface; nominal size:							
10 mm, at the rate of:							
4 kg per m2	2.36	1.40	0.81	6.33	2.69	1.61	m2
6 kg per m2	2.36	1.58	1.00	6.33	3.04	1.88	m2
8 kg per m2	2.36	1.83	1.20	6.33	3.49	2.03	m2
14 mm, at the rate of:							
4 kg per m2	2.36	1.58	1.00	6.33	3.04	1.88	m2
6 kg per m2	2.36	1.83	1.23	6.33	5.10	2.03	m2
8 kg per m2	2.36	1.98	1.40	6.33	3.87	2.26	m2
008 Making good around manhole covers, gully gratings and the like:							
over 2.00 m girth	2.05	2.05	2.05	2.10	2.10	2.10	Nr
not exceeding 0.30 m girth	2.05	2.05	2.05	2.10	2.10	2.10	Nr
0.30 - 1.00 m girth	2.05	2.05	2.05	2.10	2.10	2.10	Nr
1.00 - 2.00 m girth	2.05	2.05	2.05	2.10	2.10	2.10	Nr

Approximate
Estimating

ZA	APPROXIMATE ESTIMATING **GUIDANCE NOTES**

THIS SECTION CONTAINS GUIDANCE NOTES AND COMPOSITE PRICES FOR PREPARING APPROXIMATE ESTIMATES BASED UPON APPROXIMATE QUANTITIES.

The guidance notes and composite prices are listed under elemental sections as recommended by the Cost Information Service of the Royal Institution of Chartered Surveyors. These elemental sections are:-

SUBSTRUCTURE	*
FRAME	
UPPER FLOORS	*
ROOFS	*
STAIRS	
EXTERNAL WALLS	*
WINDOWS AND EXTERNAL DOORS	*
INTERNAL WALLS AND PARTITIONS	
INTERNAL DOORS	*
WALL FINISHES	
FLOOR FINISHES	
CEILING FINISHES	
FITTINGS AND FURNISHINGS	
SERVICES	
SITE WORKS	
DRAINAGE	*
EXTERNAL SERVICES	
PRELIMINARIES	

* indicates that composite prices may be found in the following pages

001 | Unmeasured sundries

The cost of sundry minor items, which may amount to 2.5% - 5% of the total cost of measured items should be covered by percentage additions at the end of each elemental sub-section. The appropriate percentage should be selected bearing in mind such factors as building type and the amount of detailing required. Experience will dictate which end of the percentage range will apply for the likely degree of detailing on a particular project.

002 | Design contingency

A further allowance which should be considered is that of 'design contingency'. The decision whether to apply this and the scale of the percentage will depend upon the stage in the design process at which the estimate is prepared and the degree of detail and specification available. The addition may be progressively reduced with successive estimates for the same project as the design advances and is 'firmed up'.

003 | Prices

The prices for approximate estimating based upon approximate quantities should always be based upon 'Net Unit' prices i.e., those prices which are exclusive of overheads and profit.

Additions for overheads and profit should be made separately at the end of the estimate, usually in the form of a percentage calculation. If this method is adopted then market conditions may be taken into account and simply adjusted at whatever date the estimate is prepared.

It is a simple calculating procedure to incorporate the percentage additions into the various prices which will appear on elemental estimate forms. This procedure is particularly helpful when estimating for projects with negotiated tenders, when the overheads and profits are agreed separately.

Composite prices included in Composite Prices for Approximate Estimating have been calculated from the 'Net Unit Prices' in the price book to cover those items which are too time consuming to measure in detail e.g., timber framed roof construction.

It is recommended that the 'Net Unit Prices' in the price book and in the composite prices in this section are applied to the measured rates without additions for unmeasured sundry items or for unknown factors which may eventuate during the design process. Allowances for unmeasured sundries and 'Design Contingency' should always be made by means of percentage additions at the end of each elemental section.

Composites

	Depth of wall:				
	600 mm £	900 mm £	1200 mm £	1500 mm £	Unit

ZB | **COMPOSITE PRICES FOR APPROXIMATE ESTIMATING**

The composite prices in this Section are based upon the prices contained in the various work sections of the price book. The prices are net, without allowance for Builder's off-site overheads and profit and are exclusive of 'Preliminary' costs, which should be separately calculated.

The Composite prices are based on the assumption that, with the exception of site works, all of the work is carried out within the confines of an existing building.

The 'P.C.' prices quoted in this Section are the identical P.C. prices quoted in previous Sections but are <u>inclusive</u> of waste and handling charges to facilitate pricing/substitution.

The Composite prices are subject to the addition of the Sundries Percentages applicable to each Elemental Section of the approximate estimate, detailed in Section ZA - Measurement check-list.

SUBSTRUCTURE

All excavation work in this section is executed by hand.

Note: 001 - 015 not used

016 | **Strip footings; excavate trench in firm earth; earthwork support; level and compact bottoms; backfill and remove surplus spoil from site; foundation in grade 25N/mm2 concrete; walls built up to and including horizontal damp proof course, 150 mm above original natural ground level. (N.B. Excavation commencing at 150 mm below natural ground level, i.e. after stripping vegetable soil, priced elsewhere)**

Note: 017 - 018 not used

019 | Half brick thick wall in 300 mm wide trench on 150 mm thick concrete foundation, built in:

	600 mm £	900 mm £	1200 mm £	1500 mm £	Unit
Common bricks, P.C. £326.56 per 1000, stretcher bond, in cement mortar (1:3)	57.41	84.10	115.56	143.64	m
Class A Engineering bricks, P.C. £518.09 per 1000, stretcher bond, in cement mortar (1:3)	67.92	91.24	114.56	137.88	m
Class B Engineering bricks, P.C. £411.33 per 1000, stretcher bond, in cement mortar (1:3)	67.92	91.24	114.56	137.88	m
Extra over for excavating in hard rock	12.32	20.52	25.54	32.85	m

020 | One brick thick wall in 415 mm wide trench on 150 mm thick concrete foundation, built in:

	600 mm £	900 mm £	1200 mm £	1500 mm £	Unit
Common bricks, P.C. £326.56 per 1000, English bond, in cement mortar (1:3)	86.39	126.40	193.23	237.10	m
Class A Engineering bricks, P.C. £518.09 per 1000, English bond, in cement mortar (1:3)	116.29	158.90	201.49	244.08	m
Class B Engineering bricks, P.C. £411.33 per 1000, English bond, in cement mortar (1:3)	116.29	158.90	201.49	244.08	m
Extra over for excavating in hard rock	17.24	28.72	35.76	45.99	m

Note: 021 - 022 not used

023 | 100 mm thick dense concrete block wall, in cement mortar (1:3); in 350 mm wide trench on 150 mm thick concrete foundation

	600 mm £	900 mm £	1200 mm £	1500 mm £	Unit
	50.97	73.97	102.25	126.76	m
Extra over for excavating in hard rock	14.40	23.99	29.85	38.35	m

024 | 140 mm thick dense concrete block wall, in cement mortar (1:3); in 350 mm wide trench on 150 mm thick concrete foundation

	600 mm £	900 mm £	1200 mm £	1500 mm £	Unit
	64.44	90.26	129.12	160.36	m
Extra over for excavating in hard rock	14.40	23.99	29.85	38.35	m

Note: 025 - 026 not used

027 | 275 mm thick cavity wall having a 75 mm wide cavity, 5 No wall ties per m2; filling cavity to ground level with concrete grade C20/25; in a 575 mm wide trench on a 150 mm thick concrete foundation; walls comprising:

	600 mm £	900 mm £	1200 mm £	1500 mm £	Unit
two skins of common bricks P.C. £326.56 per 1000, stretcher bond cement mortar (1:3)	118.51	174.83	238.58	297.29	m
outer skin of common P.C. £326.56 per 1000, stretcher bond; inner skin of 100 mm thick dense concrete blocks, cement mortar (1:3)	109.38	161.13	220.30	274.45	m
two skins of Class A Engineering bricks P.C. £518.09 per 1000, stretcher bond, cement mortar (1:3)	139.93	206.33	280.57	349.79	m
outer skin of Class A Engineering bricks P.C. £518.09 per 1000, stretcher bond; inner skin of 100 mm thick dense concrete blocks, cement mortar (1:3)	119.87	176.88	241.31	300.71	m
two skins of Class B Engineering bricks P.C. £411.33 per 1000, stretcher bond, cement mortar (1:3)	139.51	206.33	280.57	349.79	m
outer skin of Class B Engineering bricks P.C. £411.33 per 1000, stretcher bond; inner skin of 100 mm thick dense concrete blocks, cement mortar (1:3)	119.87	176.88	241.31	300.71	m
two skins of 100 mm thick dense concrete blocks, cement mortar (1:3)	83.29	121.99	168.14	209.24	m
275 mm thick dense concrete blocks to within 225 mm of damp proof course; remaining 225 mm comprising outer skin of facing bricks P.C. £351.38 per 1000, stretcher bond, 75 mm wide cavity and inner skin of 100 mm thick dense concrete blocks, cement mortar (1:3)	107.91	154.83	209.93	260.03	m
Extra over for excavating in hard rock	23.80	39.66	49.38	63.49	m

Note: 028 - 029 not used

Composites

	Depth of wall:				
	600 mm £	900 mm £	1200 mm £	1500 mm £	Unit
030	300 mm thick cavity wall having a 50 mm wide cavity, 5 No wall ties per m2; filling cavity to ground level with concrete grade C20/25; in a 600 mm wide trench on a 150 mm thick concrete foundation; comprising inner skin of 140 mm thick dense concrete blocks, outer skin of:				
	Common bricks, P.C. £326.56 per 1000, stretcher bond, cement mortar (1:3) — 121.59	178.68	244.94	297.45	m
	Class A Engineering bricks, P.C. £518.09 per 1000, stretcher bond, cement mortar (1:3) — 132.09	194.45	265.94	323.68	m
	Class B Engineering bricks, P.C. £411.33 per 1000, stretcher bond, cement mortar (1:3) — 132.09	194.45	265.94	323.68	m
	100 mm thick dense concrete blocks, cement mortar (1:3) — 112.46	165.00	225.29	274.60	m
	Extra over for excavating in hard rock for full depth of trench — 24.61	41.04	58.38	65.68	m

	Extra over each of the following: £	Unit
031	**Extra over** for three courses of facing bricks P.C. £351.38 per 1000, 225 mm high; weather struck pointing one side as the work proceeds, instead of:	
	external skin of cavity wall in:	
	Common bricks — 5.97	m
	Class A Engineering bricks — 2.04	m
	Class B Engineering bricks — 2.04	m
	100 mm thick dense concrete blocks — 9.41	m
032	**Extra over** one brick thick wall for three courses of facing bricks P.C. £351.38 per 1000, one side; 225 mm high; weather struck pointing as the work proceeds:	
	Common bricks built in:	
	Flemish bond — 5.03	m
	English bond — 5.67	m
	Class A Engineering bricks built in:	
	Flemish bond — 1.86	m
	English bond — 2.03	m
	Class B Engineering bricks built in:	
	Flemish bond — 7.32	m
	English bond — 8.07	m

	Excavation commencing at:				
	Ground Level £	1.00 m Basement Level £	2.00 m Basement Level £	3.00 m Basement Level £	Unit
033	**Underpinning; carried out from one side in lengths not exceeding 1200 mm; hand excavating preliminary trench down to the level of the base of the existing foundation, in firm earth; earthwork support; cutting away two courses of projecting brick footing; cutting away 200 x 200 mm projecting concrete foundation; preparing underside of existing foundation to receive new pinning up; hand excavating below the level of the base of the existing foundation; level and compact bottoms; remove spoil from site; reinforced foundation in grade C20/25 concrete; pinning up with Class B engineering bricks P.C. £411.33 per 1000, in cement mortar (1:3)**				
034	Excavating 500 mm deep to underside of existing footing:				
	500 mm depth of underpinning in:				
	one brick thick brickwork; 625 mm wide foundation — 282.20	302.73	331.30	427.58	m
	Extra over for excavating using compressed air gear (soft rock, brickwork or the like) — 142.09	166.44	193.35	232.74	m
	two brick thick brickwork, 850 mm wide foundation — 349.72	372.14	403.44	451.95	m
	Extra over for excavating using compressed air gear (soft rock, brickwork or the like) — 153.40	179.70	208.76	251.28	m
035	1500 mm depth of underpinning in:				
	one brick thick brickwork; 625 mm wide foundation — 732.21	819.17	923.99	1355.13	m
	Extra over for excavating using compressed air gear (soft rock, brickwork or the like) — 475.74	552.69	665.26	857.02	m
	two brick thick brickwork, 850 mm wide foundation — 874.16	969.29	1083.89	1284.27	m
	Extra over for excavating using compressed air gear (soft rock, brickwork or the like) — 515.50	598.90	720.87	857.02	m
036	Excavating 1200 mm deep to underside of existing footing:				
	900 mm depth of underpinning in:				
	one brick thick brickwork; 625 mm wide foundation — 610.52	656.86	784.96	885.98	m
	Extra over for excavating using compressed air gear (soft rock, brickwork or the like) — 397.58	465.72	541.06	651.26	m
	two brick thick brickwork, 850 mm wide foundation — 714.46	795.91	864.55	899.66	m
	Extra over for excavating using compressed air gear (soft rock, brickwork or the like) — 417.95	489.58	568.78	684.62	m
037	1500 mm depth of underpinning in:				
	one brick thick brickwork; 625 mm wide foundation — 930.35	1022.59	1228.33	1426.78	m
	Extra over for excavating using compressed air gear (soft rock, brickwork or the like) — 615.95	715.59	861.34	1024.02	m
	two brick thick brickwork, 850 mm wide foundation — 1082.98	1215.20	1404.81	1669.22	m
	Extra over for excavating using compressed air gear (soft rock, brickwork or the like) — 655.72	761.79	916.95	1090.13	m

Composites	£	Unit

038	Solid ground floors; level and compact surfaces of the ground; 150 mm thick hard-core filling, including levelling, blinding and compacting; grade C20/25 concrete bed; 1200 gauge polythene sheet		
039	100 mm thick plain concrete	32.06	m2
040	150 mm thick reinforced concrete, including fabric reinforcement, reference A193	54.51	m2
041	200 mm thick reinforced concrete, including 2 layers fabric reinforcement, reference A193	65.90	m2
042	Hollow ground floor; levelling and compacting bottom of excavation; 100 mm thick concrete bed 15 N/mm2; 100 mm hard-core filling including levelling and compacting, half brick wall in common bricks P.C. £326.56 per 1000 built honeycomb bond 300 mm high, cement mortar (1:3) at 2 m centres, horizontal damp proof course, 100 x 50 mm softwood wallplate, bedding in cement mortar (1:3); 150 x 50 mm softwood joists at 400 mm centres		
043	Floor construction boarded with:		
	19 mm tongued and grooved softwood 125 mm wide	92.02	m2
	18 mm tongued and grooved chipboard BS 5669	59.26	m2
	Note: 044 - 058 not used		

		Joist size:				
		50 x 150 mm span 2400 mm £	50 x 200 mm span 3600 mm £	75 x 250 mm span 4800 mm £	75 x 300 mm span 6000 mm £	Unit
	UPPER FLOORS					
059	**Suspended timber floors; boarding; sawn softwood joists; 50 x 50 mm herringbone strutting at mid span; joist hangers fixed to wall; all timber treated**					
060	25 mm tongued and grooved wrought softwood; joist centres:					
	450 mm	70.34	69.62	88.61	101.16	m2
	600 mm	64.91	64.17	76.58	84.70	m2
061	22 mm tongued and grooved chipboard; joist centres:					
	450 mm	46.02	45.30	64.29	76.84	m2
	600 mm	40.59	39.85	52.26	60.38	m2
062	18 mm tongued and grooved plywood; joist centres:					
	450 mm	59.81	59.09	78.08	90.63	m2
	600 mm	54.38	53.64	66.05	74.17	m2

		£	Unit
063	Form new opening size 600 x 800 mm in existing ceiling for access hatch, trim opening with 50 x 200 mm sawn softwood joists, cut out redundant ceiling joists, construct lining around opening of 12 mm plywood with 25 x 25 m stop fillet, 25 x 75 mm moulded architrave including decoration and making good		
064	Hatch comprising:		
	18 mm chipboard	105.66	Nr
	25 mm blockboard	114.79	Nr
	9 mm plywood	104.62	Nr
	12 mm plywood	105.64	Nr
	Note: 065 - 091 not used		

		Length of dormer front wall:				
		2.00 m £	2.40 m £	2.80 m £	3.20 m £	Unit
	ROOFS					
092	**Forming opening in plain tiled roof for dormer with flat roof; size 1.5 m high x 1.5 m wide**					
093	Strip existing roof coverings	22.59	27.10	31.62	36.14	Nr
094	Form new dormer structure in existing roof; 50 x 200 mm treated roof joists at 400 mm centres; 50 x 150 mm treated studs to front and sides; 1200 mm high stained softwood casement window(s) P.C. £143.87 each, double glazed, 50 x 200 mm additional rafters at sides including cutting out existing roof timbers	685.96	702.75	903.57	941.07	Nr
095	Flat dormer roof comprising three layer mineral finish felt on 25 mm external grade plywood on 50 mm firrings, 200 mm fibreglass insulation; vapour barrier; 12.7 mm plasterboard and skim ceiling, mist and two coats emulsion	545.76	619.99	757.77	832.01	Nr
096	Dormer floor comprising 22 mm tongued and grooved flooring grade chipboard on new 50 x 200 mm softwood joists at 400 mm centres between existing ceiling joists	296.36	349.51	402.68	455.82	Nr
097	Dormer fascia and soffit; 12 mm Supalux soffit 200 mm wide; 25 mm exterior grade plywood fascia 250 mm high, sawn softwood bearers; painted finish; 112 mm diameter half round PVCu gutter fixed with standard brackets; 68 mm diameter PVCu pipe fixed with standard brackets	330.97	350.90	370.83	390.74	Nr
098	Dormer sides and front with 265 x 165 mm plain concrete tiles; 114 mm gauge, 38 mm lap to vertical faces on 38 x 50 mm battens; underfelt; 150 mm fibreglass insulation; 12 mm Supalux board to inside face; Code 4 lead flashings	1386.15	1557.62	1391.08	1562.56	Nr

Note: 099 not used

NB: For Windows see WINDOWS AND EXTERNAL DOORS

omposites	£	Unit

Remove coverings, battens and felt; form opening for Velux roof light including standard flashing with sawn softwood joists 50 x 150 mm; insert roof light, flashings; reinstate roof coverings; make good

		£	Unit
101	Window type:		
	GGL 304	412.21	Nr
	GGL 308	478.66	Nr
	GGL 410	537.15	Nr
	GGL 606	483.73	Nr

Note: 102 to 119 not used

EXTERNAL WALLS

120	**Cavity walling comprising outer skin in facing bricks P.C. £351.38 per 1000, in gauged mortar (1:2:9); flush pointing as the work proceeds; inner skin in natural aggregate concrete blocks in gauged mortar; wall ties, five per m2**		
121	250 mm cavity wall; half brick outer skin, 100 mm solid block inner skin prepared for plastering	113.76	m2
	300 mm cavity wall; half brick outer skin, 140 mm solid block inner skin prepared for plastering	123.91	m2
	Extra over for fair face and flush pointing to inner skin	3.86	m2
122	**Making good jambs and sills of openings cut in cavity walling comprising facing brick outer skins and concrete block inner skins, with new facing bricks, blocks and mortar to match existing**		
123	Facing bricks P.C. £351.38 per 1000, and natural aggregate concrete blocks in gauged mortar (1:2:9); returning inner skin to close cavity; building in vertical damp proof course:		
	pointing with a flush joint externally and prepared for plastering internally:		
	250 mm thick (100 mm inner skin)	30.71	m2
	300 mm thick (150 mm inner skin)	38.24	m2
	pointing with a flush joint internally and externally:		
	250 mm thick (100 mm inner skin)	30.71	m2
	300 mm thick (150 mm inner skin)	38.24	m2

Note: 124 to 151 not used

WINDOWS AND EXTERNAL DOORS

		Single: £	Double: £	Unit
152	**External doors, inserted in newly prepared openings (openings measured separately)**			
153	Softwood external doors, including frame, ironmongery and finishings:			
	framed, ledged and braced	468.32	752.59	Nr
	flush	438.77	693.50	Nr
	half hour fire resisting	597.26	969.85	Nr
	casement and panel door (type 2XGG	546.24	932.89	Nr

Note: 154 not used

		Single glazed: £	Double glazed: £	Unit
155	**Windows, inserted in newly prepared openings (openings measured separately)**			
156	Standard softwood windows, including glazing, windowboard and decoration; casement type, non-bar reference:			
	2N09CV 915 mm x 900 mm	302.67	326.90	Nr
	313CVC 1769 mm x 1350 mm	622.46	744.27	Nr
157	Standard hardwood windows, including glazing, windowboard and decoration:			
	630 mm x 900 mm	580.52	591.78	Nr
	1200 mm x 1050 mm	979.15	1003.43	Nr
	1800 mm x 1050 mm	1465.44	1500.99	Nr

Note: 158 to 167 not used

INTERNAL DOORS

		Single: £	Double: £	Unit
168	**Doors, inserted into newly prepared openings (openings measured separately) including frames, ironmongery and decoration**			
169	Internal doors, including frame, ironmongery and finishings:			
	flush door	201.11	370.12	Nr
	flush, half hour fire resisting door	318.17	492.92	Nr
	casement and panel door (glazed)	261.61	491.11	Nr
170	Hardwood internal doors, including frame, ironmongery and finishings:			
	flush door	358.04	574.32	Nr
	flush, half hour fire resisting door	489.71	684.06	Nr
	Traditional hardwood door	431.32	717.32	Nr

Note: 171 to 194 not used

Composites

	Pavi comple. £

SITE WORKS

The work in this section is assumed to be outside the confines of an existing building.

195 **Pavings, stripping vegetable soil 150 mm thick; excavating to reduce levels average 300 mm deep and removing from site; hard-core bed 150 mm thick to falls; surface paving**

196 Plain in situ concrete laid in bays; trowel smooth finish; expansion joints between bays; formwork to edges; thickness:

	£	Unit
75 mm	43.61	m2
100 mm	47.78	m2
150 mm	54.36	m2
200 mm	50.96	m2

197 Reinforced in situ grass-concrete paving including soil filling and grass seeding; thickness:

	£	Unit
100 mm	55.84	m2
150 mm	65.55	m2

198 Precast grass-concrete paving including soil filling and grass seeding; thickness:

	£	Unit
83 mm	51.28	m2
103 mm	54.78	m2

199 Precast paving; 10 mm open joints; pointing joints with cement, lime, mortar (1:1:6):

	£	Unit
600 x 900 x 50 mm precast concrete flags	37.87	m2
600 x 450 x 40 mm reconstructed stone; weathered York grey finish; coloured mortar pointing	82.50	m2

200 Charcon Europa 200 x 100 mm concrete blocks laid on screeded bed of sand and compacted with vibrating plate:

	£	Unit
65 mm thick	49.85	m2
80 mm thick	52.80	m2

201 Facing bricks P.C. £351.38 per 1000 bedding and grouting joints with cement mortar (1:3); herringbone pattern:

	£	Unit
75 mm thick, bricks laid flat	71.95	m2
112.5 mm thick, bricks laid on edge	88.68	m2

202 Bitumen macadam paving 75 mm thick in two coats laid by machine, comprising 28 mm nominal size bitumen base course and various wearing courses:

	£	Unit
paving of 50 mm thick base course and 25 mm thick wearing course of 14 mm nominal size open textured bitumen macadam	48.18	m2
paving of 50 mm thick base course and 25 mm thick wearing course of 10 mm nominal size dense bitumen macadam	49.50	m2
paving of 60 mm thick base course and 15 mm thick wearing course of fine cold asphalt	49.49	m2

203 **Edgings, Kerbs and Channels**

204 Precast concrete edgings, kerbs and channels including excavating trenches and concrete foundations:

	£	Unit
51 x 152 mm edging on 150 x 75 mm foundation:		
straight	10.03	m
127 x 254 mm half battered kerb on 450 x 150 mm foundation:		
straight	25.70	m
curved	28.80	m
127 x 254 mm half battered kerb and 254 x 127 mm channel on 600 x 200 mm foundation:		
straight	47.53	m
curved	56.06	m

	Road width between kerbs:				
	3.00 m £	4.50 m £	6.00 m £	7.50 m £	Unit
205 **Roads and footpaths comprising roads of bitumen macadam surfacing on Type 1 granular road base material with 12 x 25 mm half battered kerbs both sides and pavements 2000 mm wide**					
Note: Prices allow for 500 mm reduced level excavation in addition to excavation for construction					
206 Road construction 500 mm thick overall comprising 300 mm granular sub-base, 105 mm dense bitumen macadam road base, 60 mm dense bitumen macadam base course and 35 mm wearing course with:					
pavement comprising 60 mm dense bitumen macadam base course and 15 mm cold asphalt wearing course on 100 mm hard-core:					
one side of road	590.12	770.49	926.48	1066.06	m
both sides of road	735.44	911.00	1142.72	1207.20	m
pavement comprising 100 mm in situ concrete paving on 100 mm hard-core:					
one side of road	582.86	759.37	934.93	1111.12	m
both sides of road	727.46	888.76	1064.95	1240.49	m
pavement comprising 50 mm precast concrete paving flags on 100 mm hard-core:					
one side of road	569.25	745.76	921.32	1097.51	m
both sides of road	685.98	861.54	1037.73	1213.27	m
207 **Extra over** for road construction being 650 mm thick overall with 450 mm granular sub-base	18.83	26.56	33.95	41.69	m

	All Road Widths £	Unit
208 **Extra over** for 254 x 127 mm precast concrete channel:		
one side of road	8.66	m
both sides of road	17.32	m

Composites

DRAINAGE

Drain pipes with allowance for bends, junctions, saddles, tapers and the like; excavating trenches by machine; removing surplus spoil to tip within 10 km of site

Note: 210 - 215 not used

Drainpipes laid on 150 mm granular bed with granular filling to half height of pipe; backfilling of excavated material:

	1000 mm £	1500 mm £	2000 mm £	2500 mm £	3000 mm £	Unit
			Trenches average depth:			
vitrified clay pipes and fittings; BS 565 normal quality; nominal size:						
100 mm	61.35	89.38	109.97	152.48	177.39	m
150 mm	69.55	97.58	118.17	160.68	185.59	m
225 mm	95.99	131.47	157.44	211.44	119.33	m
217 concrete pipes and fittings; BS 5911 part 1; nominal size:						
225 mm	118.34	153.82	179.79	233.79	265.35	m
300 mm	142.08	184.90	216.50	281.75	320.04	m
218 cast iron pipes and fittings; all spigot; mechanical joints; nominal size:						
100 mm	89.31	117.34	137.93	180.44	205.35	m
150 mm	160.66	188.69	209.28	251.79	276.70	m
219 PVCu pipes and fittings; nominal size:						
110 mm	57.57	82.24	106.19	148.70	173.61	m
160 mm	70.37	98.40	118.99	161.50	186.41	m

Note: 220 - 221 not used

222 Drain pipes laid on 150 mm granular bed and completely surrounded with granular filling to 150 mm above top of pipe; backfilling with imported granular material:

	1000 mm £	1500 mm £	2000 mm £	2500 mm £	3000 mm £	Unit
vitrified clay pipes and fittings; BS 565 normal quality; nominal size:						
100 mm	95.64	139.18	175.37	233.39	273.91	m
150 mm	109.38	155.79	194.66	255.55	298.73	m
225 mm	140.95	197.18	243.90	318.64	370.95	m
223 concrete pipes and fittings; BS 5911 part 1; nominal size:						
225 mm	163.30	219.53	266.25	340.99	393.30	m
300 mm	196.42	265.51	322.70	414.24	461.35	m
224 cast iron pipes and fittings BS 437; caulked lead joints; nominal size:						
100 mm	109.05	152.59	188.78	246.80	287.32	m
150 mm	182.78	229.19	268.06	328.95	372.13	m
225 cast iron pipes and fittings; all spigot; mechanical joints; nominal size:						
100 mm	109.57	153.11	189.30	247.32	287.84	m
150 mm	182.78	229.19	268.06	328.95	372.13	m
226 PVCu pipes and fittings; nominal size:						
110 mm	77.83	118.01	157.56	215.58	256.10	m
160 mm	92.49	138.90	177.77	238.66	281.84	m

Note: 227 not used

228 Drain pipes laid on 150 mm plain in situ concrete and completely surrounded with plain in situ concrete to 150 mm above top of pipe; backfilling with imported granular material:

	1000 mm £	1500 mm £	2000 mm £	2500 mm £	3000 mm £	Unit
vitrified clay pipes and fittings; BS 565 normal quality; nominal size:						
100 mm	112.65	156.19	192.38	250.40	290.92	m
150 mm	128.46	177.23	216.10	276.99	320.17	m
225 mm	167.67	223.90	270.62	345.36	397.67	m

BRICK MANHOLES

229 **The following prices allow for excavation, backfilling 150 mm working space with excavated material, removing surplus spoil from site; in situ concrete base; one brick wall in Class B engineering bricks, struck pointed internally; 200 mm in situ reinforced concrete cover slabs (where required); cast in light duty inspection cover and frames; step irons at 300 mm vertical centres; curved main channel and 2 Nr branch channel bends and benching finished with cement and sand (1:3)**

NB: manholes over 2000 mm deep have shaft 600 x 450 mm in Class B engineering bricks

230 Manholes depth from cover to invert:

Internal size; mm :	600 x 450 £	900 x 600 £	1200 x 750 £	1500 x 900 £	Unit
500 mm	526.11	743.04	-	-	Nr
750 mm	680.05	-	-	-	Nr
1000 mm	834.09	1146.40	1472.63	1893.03	Nr
1250 mm	1025.33	-	-	-	Nr
1500 mm	1168.29	1593.80	2031.67	2573.80	Nr
2000 mm	-	2020.88	-	-	Nr
231 2500 mm	-	2600.06	3227.78	4001.05	Nr
3000 mm	-	-	3654.30	4472.78	Nr
4000 mm	-	-	4596.07	5403.73	Nr

Note: 232 - 234 not used

ZB BCIS   APPROXIMATE ES

Composites

	Wall thickness:			Random ru...	
	Half brick £	One brick £	One and a half bricks £	300 mm £	600 £

ALTERATIONS TO EXISTING BUILDINGS

CUTTING OPENINGS IN WALLS

		Half brick £	One brick £	One and a half bricks £	300 mm £	600 £
235	**Cutting openings in old walls to the finished sizes given and for lintels or beams over, including needling, propping and supports; inserting lintels, wedging up to work over; making good jambs, removing needles and making good needle holes**					
236	Openings in internal walls; making good plasterwork both sides and extending to jambs; openings with: concrete lintels; opening size:					
	900 x 600 mm	152.83	207.82	261.64	429.44	576.43
	600 x 900 mm	147.71	205.10	262.58	357.63	487.08
	1200 x 900 mm	209.83	290.24	371.85	576.06	784.43
	1500 x 1200 mm	243.76	336.71	431.68	554.60	806.10
237	900 x 2000 mm	214.34	302.09	391.90	493.42	611.72
	1800 x 2000 mm	336.29	469.73	612.40	840.21	1160.77
	2400 x 2000 mm	358.65	521.75	678.41	1003.72	1378.52
238	steel beams encased in plasterboard; opening size:					
	3000 x 2000 mm	602.84	875.81	1184.07	824.39	1510.29	Nr
	4000 x 2000 mm	770.55	1128.77	1535.79	1109.43	1892.93	Nr
	5000 x 2000 mm	1009.81	1436.87	2023.66	1527.94	2518.02	Nr

		External skins:				
		Facing bricks £	Bradstone walling £	Random rubble £	Portland stone £	Unit
239	Openings in 250 mm external cavity walls with 100 mm concrete block inner skins; lintels, cavity gutters, closing cavities, vertical d.p.c.'s; external arches; facing to reveals; making good plasterwork internally and extending to reveals: door openings size:					
	900 x 2000 mm	447.35	424.13	325.24	595.12	Nr
	1800 x 2000 mm	722.88	639.82	543.94	1083.86	Nr
	2400 x 2000 mm	820.19	697.25	603.38	1323.31	Nr
240	window openings with sills; size:					
	600 x 900 mm	304.31	285.72	497.80	679.21	Nr
	1200 x 900 mm	450.67	397.42	867.39	1230.38	Nr
	1500 x 1200 mm	525.41	456.82	1064.30	1493.85	Nr
	1800 x 1500 mm	672.05	586.83	1285.70	1827.75	Nr

		Wall thickness:			Random rubble:		
		Half brick £	One brick £	One and a half bricks £	300 mm £	600 mm £	Unit
	FILLING IN OPENINGS IN WALLS						
241	**Filling in openings in old walls in matching construction; preparing for raising, including cutting out sills where required; cutting, toothing and bonding to old work both sides; wedging and filling up to work over**						
242	Openings in internal walls; making good plasterwork both sides: door opening size:						
	900 x 2000 mm	280.96	401.47	503.64	154.56	158.81	Nr
	1800 x 2000 mm	474.32	691.53	863.81	262.12	270.62	Nr
	4000 x 2000 mm	832.13	1283.93	1624.95	360.16	379.05	Nr
243	window opening size:						
	600 x 600 mm	86.76	115.70	145.02	57.76	62.42	Nr
	600 x 900 mm	116.11	157.48	197.88	72.64	77.30	Nr
	900 x 900 mm	151.47	208.19	261.09	94.53	100.75	Nr
	1200 x 900 mm	186.84	258.88	324.28	116.39	124.16	Nr
	1500 x 1200 mm	276.99	390.07	488.49	166.31	175.63	Nr

		External skins:				
		Facing bricks £	Bradstone walling £	Random rubble £	Portland stone £	Unit
244	Openings in 250 mm external cavity walls with 100 mm concrete block inner skins; making good plasterwork internally: door opening size:					
	900 x 2000 mm	369.26	168.70	143.26	2320.34	Nr
	1800 x 2000 mm	639.30	275.70	250.26	4604.41	Nr
	4000 x 2000 mm	1243.72	481.56	456.12	10132.01	Nr
	window opening size:					
	600 x 600 mm	106.24	65.63	48.29	486.83	Nr
	900 x 900 mm	192.23	93.03	95.09	1067.49	Nr
	1500 x 1200 mm	361.46	166.29	169.37	2337.43	Nr